THE

WAR OF THE REBELLION:

A COMPILATION OF THE

OFFICIAL RECORDS

OF THE

UNION AND CONFEDERATE ARMIES.

PREPARED BY

The late Lieut. Col. **ROBERT N. SCOTT**, Third U. S. Artillery.

PUBLISHED UNDER THE DIRECTION OF

The Hon. **REDFIELD PROCTOR**, Secretary of War,

BY

MAJ. GEORGE B. DAVIS, U. S. A.,
MR. LESLIE J. PERRY,
MR. JOSEPH W. KIRKLEY,
Board of Publication.

SERIES I—VOLUME XXX—IN FOUR PARTS.

PART I—REPORTS.

WASHINGTON:
GOVERNMENT PRINTING OFFICE.
1890.

PREFACE.

By an act approved June 23, 1874, Congress made an appropriation "to enable the Secretary of War to begin the publication of the Official Records of the War of the Rebellion, both of the Union and Confederate Armies," and directed him "to have copied for the Public Printer all reports, letters, telegrams, and general orders not heretofore copied or printed, and properly arranged in chronological order."

Appropriations for continuing such preparation have been made from time to time, and the act approved June 16, 1880, has provided "for the printing and binding, under direction of the Secretary of War, of 10,000 copies of a compilation of the Official Records (Union and Confederate) of the War of the Rebellion, so far as the same may be ready for publication, during the fiscal year"; and that "of said number 7,000 copies shall be for the use of the House of Representatives, 2,000 copies for the use of the Senate, and 1,000 copies for the use of the Executive Departments."*

---

* Volumes I to V distributed under act approved June 16, 1880. The act approved August 7, 1882, provides that—

"The volumes of the Official Records of the War of the Rebellion shall be distributed as follows : One thousand copies to the Executive Departments, as now provided by law. One thousand copies for distribution by the Secretary of War among officers of the Army and contributors to the work. Eight thousand three hundred copies shall be sent by the Secretary of War to such libraries, organizations, and individuals as may be designated by the Senators, Representatives, and Delegates of the Forty-seventh Congress. Each Senator shall designate not exceeding twenty-six, and each Representative and Delegate not exceeding twenty-one of such addresses, and the volumes shall be sent thereto from time to time as they are published, until the publication is completed. Senators, Representatives, and Delegates shall inform the Secretary of War in each case how many volumes of those heretofore published they have forwarded to such addresses. The remaining copies of the eleven thousand to be published, and all sets that may not be ordered to be distributed as provided herein, shall be sold by the Secretary of War for cost of publication with ten per cent. added thereto, and the proceeds of such sale shall be covered into the Treasury. If two or more sets of said volumes are ordered to the same address the Secretary of War shall inform the Senators, Representatives, or Delegates, who have designated the same, who thereupon may designate other libraries, organizations, or individuals. The Secretary of War shall report to the first session of the Forty-eighth Congress what volumes of the series heretofore published have not been furnished to such libraries, organizations, and individuals. He shall also inform distributees at whose instance the volumes are sent."

This compilation will be the first general publication of the military records of the war, and will embrace all official documents that can be obtained by the compiler, and that appear to be of any historical value.

The publication will present the records in the following order of arrangement:

The **1st Series** will embrace the formal reports, both Union and Confederate, of the first seizures of United States property in the Southern States, and of all military operations in the field, with the correspondence, orders, and returns relating specially thereto, and, as proposed, is to be accompanied by an Atlas.

In this series the reports will be arranged according to the campaigns and several theaters of operations (in the chronological order of the events), and the Union reports of any event will, as a rule, be immediately followed by the Confederate accounts. The correspondence, &c., not embraced in the " reports " proper will follow (first Union and next Confederate) in chronological order.

The **2d Series** will contain the correspondence, orders, reports, and returns, Union and Confederate, relating to prisoners of war, and (so far as the military authorities were concerned) to State or political prisoners.

The **3d Series** will contain the correspondence, orders, reports, and returns of the Union authorities (embracing their correspondence with the Confederate officials) not relating specially to the subjects of the *first* and *second* series. It will set forth the annual and special reports of the Secretary of War, of the General-in-Chief, and of the chiefs of the several staff corps and departments; the calls for troops, and the correspondence between the national and the several State authorities.

The **4th Series** will exhibit the correspondence, orders, reports, and returns of the Confederate authorities, similar to that indicated for the Union officials, as of the *third* series, but excluding the correspondence between the Union and Confederate authorities given in that series.

ROBERT N. SCOTT,
Major Third Art., and Bvt. Lieut. Col.

WAR DEPARTMENT, *August 23,* 1880.

Approved:

ALEX. RAMSEY,
Secretary of War.

CONTENTS.

CHAPTER XLII.

Page.

(v)

CONTENTS OF PRECEDING VOLUMES.

VOLUME I.

VOLUME II.

VOLUME III.

VOLUME IV.

VOLUME V.

VOLUME VI.

VOLUME VII.

1863.

	Sunday.	Monday.	Tuesday.	Wednesday.	Thursday.	Friday.	Saturday.		Sunday.	Monday.	Tuesday.	Wednesday.	Thursday.	Friday.	Saturday.
Jan...	....	....	....	....	1	2	3	**July**...	....	....	....	1	2	3	4
	4	5	6	7	8	9	10		5	6	7	8	9	10	11
	11	12	13	14	15	16	17		12	13	14	15	16	17	18
	18	19	20	21	22	23	24		19	20	21	22	23	24	25
	25	26	27	28	29	30	31		26	27	28	29	30	31	....
	....	....	....	....	....	....	....	**Aug**...	....	....	....	....	....	....	1
Feb...	1	2	3	4	5	6	7		2	3	4	5	6	7	8
	8	9	10	11	12	13	14		9	10	11	12	13	14	15
	15	16	17	18	19	20	21		16	17	18	19	20	21	22
	22	23	24	25	26	27	28		23	24	25	26	27	28	29
	....	....	....	....	....	....	....		30	31	....	....	....	....	....
Mar..	1	2	3	4	5	6	7	**Sept**...	....	....	1	2	3	4	5
	8	9	10	11	12	13	14		6	7	8	9	10	11	12
	15	16	17	18	19	20	21		13	14	15	16	17	18	19
	22	23	24	25	26	27	28		20	21	22	23	24	25	26
	29	30	31	....	....	....	....		27	28	29	30	....	....	....
Apr..	....	....	....	1	2	3	4	**Oct**...	....	....	....	....	1	2	3
	5	6	7	8	9	10	11		4	5	6	7	8	9	10
	12	13	14	15	16	17	18		11	12	13	14	15	16	17
	19	20	21	22	23	24	25		18	19	20	21	22	23	24
	26	27	28	29	30	....	....		25	26	27	28	29	30	31
May..	....	....	....	....	....	1	2		....	....	....	....	....	....	....
	3	4	5	6	7	8	9	**Nov**..	1	2	3	4	5	6	7
	10	11	12	13	14	15	16		8	9	10	11	12	13	14
	17	18	19	20	21	22	23		15	16	17	18	19	20	21
	24	25	26	27	28	29	30		22	23	24	25	26	27	28
	31	....	....	....	....	....	....		29	30	....	....	....	....	....
June..	....	1	2	3	4	5	6	**Dec**...	....	....	1	2	3	4	5
	7	8	9	10	11	12	13		6	7	8	9	10	11	12
	14	15	16	17	18	19	20		13	14	15	16	17	18	19
	21	22	23	24	25	26	27		20	21	22	23	24	25	26
	28	29	30	....	....	....	....		27	28	29	30	31	....	....

OPERATIONS IN KENTUCKY, SOUTHWEST VIRGINIA, TENNESSEE, MISSISSIPPI, NORTH ALABAMA, AND NORTH GEORGIA.

August 11–October 19, 1863.

PART I.*

REPORTS—August 11–September 22, 1863.

SUMMARY OF THE PRINCIPAL EVENTS.†

Aug. 10–22, 1863.—Raid on the Mississippi Central Railroad from the Big Black River, Miss., to Memphis, Tenn., with skirmishes at Payne's Plantation, near Grénada, Miss. (18th); at Panola, Miss. (20th), and at the Coldwater, Miss. (21st).

10–26, 1863.—The Thirteenth Army Corps transferred from Vicksburg, Miss., to Carrollton, La.

12, 1863.—The First Division, Ninth Army Corps, arrives from Vicksburg, at Covington, Ky.

Skirmish at Big Black River Bridge, Miss.

12–23, 1863.—Expedition from Memphis, Tenn., to Grenada, Miss., with skirmishes at Craven's Plantation, Miss. (14th), and Grenada, Miss. (17th).

13, 1863.—Skirmish at Jacinto, Miss.

16, 1863.—Skirmish near Corinth, Miss.

16–20, 1863.—Expedition from Memphis, Tenn., to Hernando, Miss., with skirmish (17th) near Panola, Miss.

16–Sept. 22, 1863.—The Chickamauga Campaign.

---

* Contains the Union and Confederate reports of miscellaneous operations August 11–16, and Union reports of the Chickamauga Campaign August 16–September 22. Part II embraces the Confederate reports of the Chickamauga Campaign and the Union and Confederate reports of the East Tennessee Campaign, and of all other miscellaneous events, within the territory covered by the volume, from August 16–October 19.

† Of some of the minor conflicts noted in this Summary, no circumstantial reports are on file. All such are designated in the Index.

(3)

Aug.   16–Oct. 19, 1863.—The East Tennessee Campaign.
           19, 1863.—Skirmish at Weems' Springs, Tenn.
           20–Sept. 2, 1863.—Expedition from Vicksburg, Miss., to Monroe, La.*
           27, 1863.—Skirmish at Mount Pleasant, Miss.
               Skirmish near Vicksburg, Miss.
Sept.   1– 7, 1863.—Expedition from Natchez, Miss., to Harrisonburg, La.†
           1–10, 1863.—Expeditions from Paducah, Ky., and Union City, Tenn., to Con-
               yersville, Tenn., and skirmish September 5.
           7, 1863.—Skirmish at Holly Springs, Miss.
               Skirmish near Jacinto (or Glendale), Miss.
           11, 1863.—Skirmish at Baldwin's Ferry, Big Black River, Miss.
        11–16, 1863.—Expedition from Corinth, Miss., to Henderson, Tenn., with skir-
               mishes at Clark's Creek Church (13th) and near Henderson
               (14th).
               Expedition from La Grange to Toone's Station, Tenn., with skir-
               mish (16th) at Montezuma.
           13, 1863.—Maj. Gen. U. S. Grant, commanding Army of the Tennessee,
               ordered to send all his available forces to Corinth and Tus-
               cumbia to support Major-General Rosecrans on the Tennes-
               see River.
               Skirmish at Paris, Tenn.
           18, 1863.—Affair near Fort Donelson, Tenn.
           19, 1863.—Skirmish at Como, Tenn.
        19–25, 1863.—Expedition from Fort Pillow to Jackson, Tenn.
        20–30, 1863.—Expedition from Paducah, Ky., to McLemoresville, Tenn.
        22–30, 1863.—The First, Second, and Fourth Divisions of the Fifteenth Army
               Corps start *en route* from Vicksburg, Miss., to Chattanooga,
               Tenn.
           23, 1863.—Skirmishes at Summertown and Lookout Mountain, Tenn.
        23–26, 1863.—Skirmishes in front of Chattanooga, Tenn.
        24–Oct. 3, 1863.—The Eleventh and Twelfth Army Corps transferred from
               the Army of the Potomac to the Army of the Cumberland.‡
           26, 1863.—Skirmish near Winchester, Tenn.
               Skirmish at Hunt's Mill, near Larkinsville, Ala.
           27, 1863.—Skirmish at Locke's Mill, near Moscow, Tenn.
        27–Oct. 1, 1863.—Expedition from Messinger's Ford, Big Black River, to
               Yazoo City, Miss., with skirmishes at Brownsville
               (September 28) and Moore's Ford, near Benton (Sep-
               tember 29).
               Expedition from Corinth, Miss., into West Tennessee,
               with skirmish at Swallow Bluffs, Tenn. (September 30).
           28, 1863.—Skirmish at Buell's Ford, Tenn.
           29, 1863.—Skirmish at Friendship Church, Tenn.
        30–Oct. 17, 1863.—Wheeler and Roddey's raid on Rosecrans' communica-
               tions.
Oct.   2, 1863.—Skirmish near Chattanooga, Tenn.
           3, 1863.—Skirmish at Forked Deer Creek, Miss.
               Skirmish at Bear Creek, Tenn.

---

* See Series I, Vol. XXVI, Part I, p. 248.
† See Series I, Vol. XXVI, Part I, p. 273.
‡ For orders, correspondence, and reports relating to this movement, see Series I,
Vol. XXIX, Part I, p. 146.

Oct.   4–17, 1863.—Chalmers' raid in West Tennessee and North Mississippi.
   5, 1863.—The Second Division, Seventeenth Army Corps, starts *en route*
       from Memphis to Chattanooga, Tenn.
   8, 1863.—Skirmish near Chattanooga, Tenn.
   9, 1863.—Skirmish at Elk River, Tenn.
   10, 1863.—Maj. Gen. Gordon Granger, U. S. Army, assumes command of
       the Fourth Army Corps, formed by the consolidation of the
       Twentieth and Twenty-first Army Corps.
       Skirmish at Ingraham's Plantation, near Port Gibson, Miss.
   10–11, 1863.—Expedition from Memphis, Tenn., to Hernando, Miss., with skir-
       mish (11th) near Hernando.
   10–14, 1863.—Expedition from Gallatin to Carthage, Tenn., with skirmish (10th)
       near Hartsville.
   14–20, 1863.—Expedition from Messinger's Ferry, on the Big Black River,
       toward Canton, Miss.
       Expeditions from Natchez and Fort Adams, Miss., to Red River,
       La., with skirmish at Red River (14th).
   16, 1863.—The Military Division of the Mississippi (consisting of the De-
       partments of the Cumberland, Ohio, and Tennessee) created,
       and Maj. Gen. U. S. Grant assigned to the command.   Maj.
       Gen. George H. Thomas ordered to command the Department
       of the Cumberland, *vice* Maj. Gen. W. S. Rosecrans, relieved.
       Skirmish near Island No. 10, Tenn.
   17, 1863.—Skirmish near Satartia, Miss.
   18, 1863.—Maj. Gen. U. S. Grant, U. S. Army, assumes command of the
       Military Division of the Mississippi.
   19, 1863.—Skirmish at Smith's Bridge, Miss.

**AUGUST 10–22, 1863.—Raid on the Mississippi Central Railroad from the
Big Black River, Miss., to Memphis, Tenn., with Skirmishes at Payne's
Plantation, near Grenada, Miss. (18th); at Panola, Miss. (20th), and at
the Coldwater, Miss. (21st).***

REPORTS.

No. 1.—Maj. Gen. William T. Sherman, U. S. Army, with instructions to Col. Edwin F. Winslow.
No. 2.—Col. Edward F. Winslow, Fourth Iowa Cavalry, commanding expedition.

No. 1.

*Report of Maj. Gen. William T. Sherman, U. S. Army, with
instructions to Col. Edwin F. Winslow.*

HEADQUARTERS FIFTEENTH ARMY CORPS,
   Camp on Big Black, September 5, 1863.

   SIR: Inclosed please find report of Col. E. F. Winslow, Fourth
Iowa, of the results of his expedition to Grenada, Memphis, and
back to camp.
   His movement was skillful and eminently successful.   It would
have been better that he should have destroyed the locomotives and

---

* See also expedition from Memphis, Tenn., to Grenada, Miss., August 12–23, 1863.
p. 11.

cars left at Winona, but my instructions to him, based on those of General Grant to me, were to run the cars beyond Grenada and into Memphis. The destruction of the bridges of the Yalabusha at Grenada made that impossible, and then it was too late to bring up the cars from Winona. These can be of little use to the enemy, as they cannot come below Durant, the road being useless thence to Jackson.

I am, &c.,

W. T. SHERMAN,
Major-General, Commanding.

Brig. Gen. JOHN A. RAWLINS,
  Assistant Adjutant-General, Vicksburg, Miss.

· [Instructions.]

HEADQUARTERS FIFTEENTH ARMY CORPS,
Camp on Black River, August 8, 1863.

Col. E. F. WINSLOW,
  Fourth Iowa Cavalry:

SIR: In pursuance of Special Orders, No. 156, of the 6th instant, you will take command of the cavalry forces designated in these orders, and start on the 10th instant for the north.

You will strike for the lower Benton road, and follow it to Mechanicsburg, and thence to Yazoo City. There you will find a gunboat and a supply of provisions, with which you can replenish.

After a short rest, keeping well quiet as to your destination, proceed to Lexington, and thence strike the Great Central Railroad and ascertain if possible if the locomotives and cars belonging to the road are still above Grenada. At our last accounts there were between Grenada and Water Valley an immense number of locomotives (70) and near 500 cars.

If you find any locomotives below Grenada, you will endeavor to have them and all cars sent up to and above Grenada, and you will proceed to that place with your cavalry. General Grant has ordered a force from Memphis to meet you at or near Grenada. Communicate with them as soon as possible, and with your joint force use all possible efforts to get these cars and locomotives into Memphis.

I take it for granted that parties are now employed in repairing the track out from Memphis, and that you will find everything done on that end of the road.

You know that we have so crippled the road from Canton south that no railroad stock can be carried off by the enemy ; and therefore we have no interest in destroying it, and therefore you will confine your labors and efforts to save it, by moving it toward and into Memphis.

You will find plenty of engineers and conductors whom you can employ, or, if necessary, use force to compel them to work their engines and trains.

I am satisfied all of Jackson's cavalry is at or near Brandon, east of the Pearl. If any detachments have been made they are toward Natchez. The Memphis forces will, of course, drive out of that neighborhood all of Chalmers' men and other detachments of guerrillas, more intent on collecting conscripts than on fighting.

No matter which force you meet, attack promptly and resolutely, and so handle your forces that they cannot count your numbers. Do not stay in Grenada, but occupy the bank of the Yalabusha, the other side of Grenada, till you are in connection with the Memphis forces, after which act according to your judgment.

You carry money with you, and it is now to the interest of our Government that all plundering and pillaging should cease. Impress this on your men from the start, and let your chief quartermaster and commissary provide liberally and fairly for the wants of your command by paying.

Union people and the poorer farmers, without being too critical as to politics, should be paid for their corn, bacon, beef, and vegetables, but where the larger planters and farmers have an abundance to spare you can take of the surplus, giving in all such cases a simple receipt, signed by your chief quartermaster and commissary. Also, when your horses break down, you can take a remount, exchanging the broken-down animal and giving a certificate of the transaction, fixing the cash difference in value—the boot.

Deal firmly but fairly with the inhabitants. I am satisfied a change of feeling is now going on in this State, and we should encourage it. Much importance is attached to this branch of the subject, and you will see that every officer and man is informed of it.

Punish on the spot and with rigor any wanton burning of houses or property without your specific orders. If at Grenada you find the Memphis force fully competent to the task of saving the railroad stock enumerated you can return via Yazoo City; but if there be any doubt remain with them and go on into Memphis and return to my command by the river. On your application the quartermaster, Captain Eddy, will furnish boats. Report to me by letter as often as possible, either by the route you go or around by way of Memphis. I inclose you the best map* we are able to compile. Add to it as you progress, and on your return I shall expect it to be filled with roads and names of localities not now on it.

With great respect,

W. T. SHERMAN,
Major-General, Commanding.

No. 2.

Reports of Col. Edward F. Winslow, Fourth Iowa Cavalry, commanding expedition.

MEMPHIS, TENN., *August* 22, 1863.

DEAR SIR: I have the honor to report that with my command I arrived here this evening, having been thirteen days from camp.

I captured a down train at Durant, 14 miles east of Lexington; burned a piece of trestle 5 miles below that place, and moved directly on Grenada with all engines, cars, &c., arriving there at 7 p. m., 17th instant. I was obliged to leave all rolling stock collected (17 engines and about 100 cars) at Winona, 20 miles below Grenada, as the enemy had destroyed a bridge just above Winona.

Found Lieutenant-Colonel Phillips, with 1,500 cavalry, had reached G[renada] about four hours in advance of my coming, having driven out Slemons (with, say, 600 men), but not before the railroad bridges had both been destroyed by fire.

---

* Not found.

Lieutenant-Colonel Phillips, fearing an attack from Jackson, had set fire to all the engines and cars in Grenada, about 30 and 200, respectively.

I remained in Grenada one day, and with the whole command moved northward via Panola and Coldwater, separating from Colonel Phillips at a point 10 miles north of Panola.

Found the crossing at the Coldwater in possession of a force of the enemy under Colonel Blythe, but he was speedily driven out.

I had not a day's rations when we left Yazoo City, yet we made a very favorable impression south of Grenada.

Lieutenant-Colonel Phillips had instructions directly antagonistic to those in my possession.

I shall have the honor to make an official report at once, and send or carry it to you.

Very truly, I have the pleasure of being your obedient servant to command,

E. F. WINSLOW,
Colonel, Commanding Cavalry Forces.

Major-General SHERMAN,
Commanding Fifteenth Army Corps.

HDQRS. CAVALRY FORCES, FIFTEENTH ARMY CORPS,
Memphis, Tenn., August 23, 1863.

CAPTAIN: In accordance with instructions, the forces under my command, consisting of the Third Iowa, Fourth Iowa, and Fifth Illinois Cavalry Regiments, 800 men, left camp on Big Black River, at 5 a. m., 10th instant, and halted at 1 p. m. 8 miles below Mechanicsburg, 18 miles from camp, until 5 o'clock next morning, when we moved through Mechanicsburg to the plantation of Mr. Roach, and halted at noon, being then 9 miles from Yazoo City, which place was reached at 8 o'clock on the morning of the 12th instant.

The gunboat, transports, and troops had left this place early on the 11th instant, and after waiting in bivouac until the morning of the 14th I decided, in opposition to the voices of officers commanding the regiments, to push forward without further delay, and accordingly moved at 4.30 for Lexington via Rankin.

We bivouacked at 10 p. m. on Harlan's Creek, 30 miles from Yazoo City, 8 miles from Lexington, and entered Lexington at 8 a. m., where the Third Iowa, Major Noble, with Lieutenant Jones, acting assistant commissary of subsistence, was left to procure rations, while the main force pushed forward to Durant, 14 miles, and captured at noon a train of cars just from Grenada.

Captain Peters was immediately placed in charge of the engine, and proceeded 5 miles below Durant and burned a bridge on the track.

I learned that there was one engine and about ten cars below Durant, also that the railroad bridge over Big Black had just been repaired, the captured train being the first one ordered over it.

Resting till 6 p. m., when the Third Iowa came up, the column was moved to West's Station, going into bivouac at 11 p. m. on Jordan's Creek, 24 miles via Durant and 20 miles direct from Lexington. At this point some engines and cars were found, and with the train from Durant, forwarded to Vaiden, 12 miles, arriving at 11 o'clock, the 16th, where the cavalry was delayed until 5 p. m. to make up trains.

Reaching Winona, 12 miles, at daybreak, the 17th, it was found that the enemy, who now appeared in front, had destroyed a small bridge above town; therefore I decided to leave the trains, now composing 13 engines and 60 cars, and push forward into Grenada, where I heard of some force of the enemy being posted.

I had caused to be burned a bridge below West's Station, one below Vaiden, and two below and near Winona, that the trains could not be carried off if we should be forced to abandon them temporarily.

Under my instructions I expected to return to Winona, and run the trains to Grenada. Leaving Winona at 7.30 a. m., the column reached Duck Hill Station, 12 miles, at 11 o'clock, and was halted to feed and rest at Jackson's Creek, 11½ miles from Grenada, till 3 p. m., then moved to that place, arriving at 7.

From Winona to Grenada, 25 miles, the advance, Third Iowa, was briskly skirmishing, and at Payne's plantation, 5 miles from Grenada, we came upon quite a force posted behind Berry Creek, which, however, was speedily forced to abandon the position, retreating eastward.

Upon arriving at Grenada, I found Lieutenant-Colonel Phillips, Ninth Illinois Mounted Infantry, with two brigades, 1,500 men. The railroad bridge over the Yalabusha having been burned by the enemy, Colonel Phillips, hearing nothing of our advance, and fearing an immediate attack from Jackson's cavalry, set fire to the long trains of cars and engines which he found there.

His arrival about noon had been followed by the burning of the bridges and the retiring of the enemy (at 4 o'clock), after several hours' skirmishing, with little or no loss on either side.

Colonel Phillips had retired most of his troops north of the river, intending to move northward at once, believing General Ruggles would intercept him at or near Panola.

The whole command being without rations, I decided to remain one day and procure them, and placing the Third Iowa in charge of the town, with Major Noble as provost-marshal, I caused the fires on the bridges to be extinguished and prevented the extension of a conflagration which threatened to destroy the town, two large blocks having already been burned. Keeping the entire command, except provost guard, picket, and commissary details, on the north side of the river, I had the condition of the trains examined into, and herewith I submit a statement showing the number, condition, &c., of all rolling stock on the Mississippi Central and Mississippi and Tennessee Railroads.

At 4.30 a. m. the 19th instant, the entire force moved northward, via Oakland, to Panola, where the Tallahatchie was crossed during the evening of the 20th instant after a slight skirmish with some guerrillas.

On the 21st the command of Lieutenant-Colonel Phillips moved east toward Tchulahoma, while my proper command marched to the crossing of the Coldwater.

At this point the enemy was found in some force, posted on the opposite bank of the river. Directing Major Noble, with 75 men of the Third Iowa, to occupy their attention in front, I sent Major Farnan, Fifth Illinois, with three companies of his own and two companies of the Third Iowa Regiment (supported by four companies of the Fifth Illinois), all dismounted, with instructions to cross the river lower down half a mile, and get in the rear of the enemy, if possible. Through the indiscretion of some of his command the alarm was given ere this was done, and the enemy in front retreated with some loss, just as the flanking party came in sight. During this time there was continued skirmishing in our rear and on both flanks, several hundred men being in that direction.

Repairing the boat we crossed and encamped at dark 4 miles from the river, and arrived at Cane Creek, 4 miles from Memphis, at noon the 22d instant, having marched 265 miles, with loss as follows :

Third Iowa, 4 privates wounded, not dangerously ; Fourth Iowa, 4 privates and 1 sergeant missing ; Fifth Illinois, 1 private killed and 1 wounded seriously.

There were captured and paroled 55 prisoners of war, and I brought to this point 25 railroad engineers and mechanics, thus damaging the enemy much, as this latter class of persons are not numerous in Mississippi.

The regiments which I have the honor to command did not commit any excesses ; did not enter one house from camp to Grenada, except on duty, and the property was respected, while the inhabitants were kindly, firmly, and fairly treated by the entire command.

Very few able-bodied citizens were in the country, and there was little hope, apparently, of success of the Confederate cause.

A large amount of growing corn was everywhere seen and some beef cattle, but bacon is quite scarce. In the central portions of the State considerable wheat has been harvested.

I could not have returned via Yazoo City without undoing the good conduct and feeling created, because of the scarcity of provisions, and on account of condition of my command as regards rations, health, and ammunition, and with consideration for the horses, many of whom became temporarily unserviceable from sore backs, &c., I deemed it best to return via this city. I had every reason to believe that a portion of Jackson's cavalry would endeavor to prevent my return southward.

Nothing could be done toward running the railroad stock toward Memphis because of lack of means of repairing bridges over the Yalabusha, Tallahatchie, and Coldwater Rivers.

At Grenada there had been burned by Colonel Phillips a large mill with a quantity of flour sufficient for our entire force, though his division was out of food.

I take pleasure in stating that the cavalry as a whole did everything which could be asked, and would mention particularly the valuable services of Captain Peters, Fourth Iowa Cavalry ; Lieut. D. E. Jones, acting assistant quartermaster of the expedition, and the gallant conduct of Major Noble and Major Farnan.

Trusting my conduct and operations will meet your approval, I have the honor to be, your obedient servant to command,

E. F. WINSLOW,
Colonel, Commanding Cavalry Forces.

Capt. R. M. SAWYER,
Assistant Adjutant-General, 15th Army Corps.

[Inclosure.]

ON MISS. CENTRAL AND MISS. AND TENN. RAILROADS,
August 20, 1863.

No.	Character.	Condition.	Where left.
2	Engines	Good	Grenada.
28	....do	Partially burned	Do.
3	....do	Good	Winona.
10	....do	Need repairs	Do.
4	....do	Good	Duck Hill.
6	....do	Partially burned	Above Grenada on Miss. Central Railroad.
82	Cars, box and platform	Burned	Grenada.
59	....do	Running order	Winona.
10	....do	....do	Big Black River.
20	....do	....do	Duck Hill.
4	....do	Burned	Above Grenada.
5	Passenger	Good	Do.
86	....do	Burned	Grenada.
2	....do	Good	Do.
11	....do	....do	Below Grenada and Duck Hill and Winona.
2	Baggage	....do	Grenada.
21	Box and platform	....do	Do.
2	Hand cars	....do	Do.

Summary.—Engines, 53 ; cars, passenger, 99; baggage, 2; box, &c., 196; hand, 2. Total, 299.
E. F. WINSLOW,
Colonel, &c.

AUGUST 12–23, 1863.—Expedition from Memphis, Tenn., to Grenada, Miss., with Skirmishes at Craven's Plantation, Miss. (14th), and Grenada, Miss. (17th).

REPORTS.

No. 1.—Maj. Gen. Stephen A. Hurlbut, U. S. Army, commanding Sixteenth Army Corps.

No. 2.—Col. John K. Mizner, Third Michigan Cavalry, chief of cavalry, Sixteenth Army Corps.

No. 3.—Col. August Mersy, Ninth Illinois (Mounted) Infantry, commanding post of Corinth.

No. 4.—Lieut. Col. Jesse J. Phillips, Ninth Illinois (Mounted) Infantry, commanding expedition.

No. 5.—Maj. Datus E. Coon, Second Iowa Cavalry.

No. 6.—Lieut. Col. Martin R. M. Wallace, Fourth Illinois Cavalry.

No. 1.

Reports of Maj. Gen. Stephen A. Hurlbut, U. S. Army, commanding Sixteenth Army Corps.

HEADQUARTERS SIXTEENTH ARMY CORPS,
MEMPHIS, TENN., *August 20, 1863.*

SIR : I have honor to transmit copy of report of expedition ordered from these headquarters.

Cavalry force from La Grange on 13th, under command of Lieutenant-Colonel Phillips, Ninth Illinois Infantry (mounted), reached Grenada 17th, drove Slemons, with 2,000 men and three pieces artillery, from the place, destroyed 57 engines, 400 cars, the depot buildings, machine-shops, several blacksmith-shops, and a quantity of ordnance and commissary stores, and captured 50 railroad men and a number of prisoners.

After Colonel Phillips had accomplished his work Colonel Winslow, ordered up by Major-General Grant, appeared with a force. Detailed report will be forwarded.

> S. A. HURLBUT,
> *Major-General.*

Maj. Gen. H. W. HALLECK,
    General-in-Chief, Washington, D. C.

—

HEADQUARTERS SIXTEENTH ARMY CORPS,
Memphis, Tenn., September 13, 1863.

GENERAL: I have the honor to forward you report of Lieutenant-Colonel Phillips, and documents. Major-General Sherman's orders, as I am informed, left no discretion to Colonel Winslow on the subject of the rolling stock on this railroad.

It was, as I well knew, impossible to bring it in and its thorough destruction I considered imperative. The cavalry detachments which composed this expedition were very handsomely handled, and I take occasion here to say that the cavalry of this command, almost without exception, have been steadily and energetically at work through the entire summer.

I am informed by citizens that the enemy have completed the demolition of the engines and are removing part of the machinery in wagons.

If they can save the driving wheels of the locomotives it will be a great thing for them, as they cannot be replaced in the Confederacy. Breaking the flanges renders them entirely useless, and if another party should move up in that direction it should be done.

I am, general, very respectfully, your obedient servant,

> S. A. HURLBUT,
> *Major-General.*

Brig. Gen. JOHN A. RAWLINS,
    Asst. Adjt. Gen., Dept. of the Tenn., Vicksburg, Miss.

———

No. 2.

Reports of Col. John K. Mizner, Third Michigan Cavalry, Chief of Cavalry, Sixteenth Army Corps.

LA GRANGE, *August* 17, 1863.
(Received Headquarters Memphis, August 17, 1863.)

Our cavalry, 1,500 strong, have been out five days. Their return is looked for to-morrow. From information received here I judge the enemy were too much scattered to harm them, and that they fell back before us in consequence of the move made from below. I have no apprehensions. The cavalry at Corinth is available.

> J. K. MIZNER,
> *Colonel, and Chief of Cavalry.*

Major-General HURLBUT.

LA GRANGE, *August* 19, 1863.
(Received Headquarters Memphis, August 19, 1863.)

The cavalry force sent from here on the 13th instant, under command of Lieutenant-Colonel Phillips, reached Grenada on the 17th instant, drove Slemons, with 2,000 men and three pieces of artillery, from the place, destroying 57 engines, upwards of 400 cars, the depot buildings, machine-shops, several blacksmith-shops, and a quantity of ordnance and commissary stores, capturing about 50 railroad men and a number of prisoners. After Colonel Phillips, with his command, had accomplished his work, Colonel Winslow appeared with a force from below. His brief report will be sent by to-day's train.

J. K. MIZNER,
Colonel, and Chief of Cavalry.

Major-General HURLBUT.

No. 3.

Report of Col. August Mersy, Ninth Illinois (Mounted) Infantry, commanding post of Corinth.

CORINTH, *August* 20, 1863.
(Received Headquarters Memphis, August 20, 1863.)

Colonel Mizner reports the cavalry sent out from La Grange on 13th ultimo, under Lieutenant-Colonel Phillips, reached Grenada on 17th, drove Slemons, with 2,000 men and three pieces of artillery, from the place, destroying 57 engines, upward of 400 cars, depot buildings, machine-shops, and quantity of ordnance, and command captured 50 railroad men and number of prisoners. After Colonel Phillips had accomplished his work, Colonel Winslow appeared with a force from below. Detailed report will follow immediately.

Very respectfully,

AUG. MERSY,
Colonel, Commanding.

Maj. Gen. STEPHEN A. HURLBUT,
Commanding.

No. 4.

Reports of Lieut. Col. Jesse J. Phillips, Ninth Illinois (Mounted) Infantry, commanding expedition.

HEADQUARTERS CAVALRY DIVISION,
Grenada, Miss., August 17, 1863—5 p. m.

SIR : I have to report that in obedience to your order I joined the column from La Grange, at Oxford, and found that brigade under command of Major Coon, Second Iowa Cavalry. I moved, without instructions, to Water Valley, being joined 5 miles south of Oxford by the First Brigade of Cavalry, Lieutenant-Colonel Wallace commanding. The command not having been designed for me, I had no instructions whatever, either as to the object or destination of the expedition, though I was the ranking officer; but gathering the object of the expedition from Major Coon's and Lieutenant-Colonel Wallace's instructions, I moved to Water Valley, where I found that all the rolling stock of the railroad had been moved toward Grenada. I moved very rapidly on Grenada, Major Coon's brigade in advance. Brisk skirmishing commenced and was kept up from a point 8 miles north of Grenada, until I arrived at the Yalabusha River at Grenada. When within 4 miles of Grenada a dense smoke was seen rising from the town, which we afterward found to be the railroad bridges burning. At the river, Chalmers' forces contended the crossing with artillery, and a severe skirmish ensued. The regiments fighting us were Slemons' regiment, McCulloch's regiment, McGuirk's regiment, and Stocks' regiment, with three pieces of artillery. We found both bridges burned. I captured north of the Yalabusha River 6 engines and 20 cars. At Grenada, I captured 51 engines and about 500 cars. Owing to the destruction of the bridges, and I not being able to learn of any force from below, as was anticipated, I destroyed these engines and cars, together with a quantity of ordnance stores and commissary stores in the depot, as the destruction of the bridges by the enemy would prevent my running them up the road. I captured a train of 6 wagons with teams belonging to the Confederate Government; also about 50 prisoners, among them Maj. P. M. Leath, chief quartermaster of Chalmers' division; and with him I captured $5,700 Government (Confederate) funds. My loss is 2 men wounded; the enemy had several killed and wounded.

I am, sir, very respectfully, your obedient servant,

JESSE J. PHILLIPS,
Lieutenant-Colonel, Commanding.

Brig. Gen. GRENVILLE M. DODGE,
Commanding Left Wing, Sixteenth Army Corps.

—

HEADQUARTERS NINTH ILLINOIS INFANTRY,
Pocahontas, Tenn., September 3, 1863.

SIR: I have to report that in pursuance of orders from the commanding officer of the Second Brigade, Second Division, Left Wing, Sixteenth Army Corps, I left my camp on the night of the 12th ultimo in command of 330 men of the Ninth Illinois Infantry Regiment, mounted, with orders, copies of which are herewith sent, marked A and B, but when ready to march a telegram was sent to me from brigade headquarters directing my march, a copy of which telegram is herewith sent, marked C, and in accordance with that dispatch I moved toward Salem ; thence crossing the Tippah River at Buck's Springs; thence through Hickory Flats to Rocky Ford, crossing the Tallahatchie River at that place on the night of the 13th ultimo, moving at 4 a. m. of the 14th ultimo toward Oxford, where I arrived at 2 o'clock.

At Oxford I found detachments of the Second Iowa Cavalry, Third Michigan Cavalry, and Eleventh Illinois Cavalry, the aggregate of which was 520 men, all under the command of Maj. D. E. Coon, Second Iowa Cavalry.

I was without orders or instructions in regard to the object of the expedition, but Major Coon furnished me with those supplied him, a copy of which is herewith sent, marked E, and from those instructions I believed the success of the expedition would depend on the rapidity of movement, and at once moved toward Water Valley.

About 6 miles south of Oxford I was joined by the First Brigade of cavalry under Lieutenant-Colonel Wallace, with an aggregate of about 750 men with four 12-pounder mountain howitzers, who I also found my junior in rank, which placed me in command of the expedition, and that without further instructions than those kindly furnished by Maj. D. E. Coon already referred to.

I arrived with my advance at Water Valley at 11 a. m. on the 15th ultimo. At this place my advance captured a train of 6 wagons, 6 mule teams, four of which wagons I burned ; the other two I directed Major Coon to use for transportation for his command. The crossing of the Yoh-na-pata-fa River, 6 miles north of Water Valley, being very difficult, the boat being very small and the river quite high and very rapid, I did not get all my command across until near 5 p. m. I moved from Water Valley to Coffeeville, thence toward Grenada. We met 8 miles north of Grenada a force of the enemy estimated at about 600. Constant skirmishing was kept up from this point until we arrived at the Yalabusha river at Grenada, though we advanced rapidly. Six miles north of Grenada I captured a train of 20 cars and 6 locomotives. With these I left a guard and ordered them to be run to Grenada when I arrived at that place.

When I arrived at a point about 4 miles north of Grenada I saw a dense smoke rising from the direction of the city, which afterward I found to be occasioned by the burning of the two railroad bridges over the Yalabusha River at that place. When within a half mile of the river the enemy contested my advance vigorously, but were driven across the river. At 2 p. m., the Second Brigade, Major Coon commanding, was ordered to attack the enemy at the upper ferry, and two guns of the four attached to Lieutenant-Colonel Wallace's brigade I ordered forward, and also three companies of the Ninth Illinois Cavalry, of Colonel Wallace's brigade, as a support to co-operate with Major Coon's brigade. The greatest part of the enemy's forces were in position on the south side of the river at the upper ferry, and had in position in field fortifications three pieces of artillery, one a rifled gun, while the supports were protected by rifle-pits. I ordered Lieutenant-Colonel Wallace to move to the right 2 miles below, and, if possible, effect a crossing and attack the enemy on their left flank and rear, whilst at the same time I ordered Major Coon to attack as vigorously as possible, to insure the success of the First Brigade, under Lieutenant-Colonel Wallace, in effecting a crossing below, by keeping the forces of the enemy engaged at the upper ferry. Having no guides, and not aware of the direction of the roads, I had a regiment from Major Coon's brigade left at the forks of the road at Statem's [?] Station, 2 miles north of the river.

Lieutenant-Colonel Wallace having gained the ferry without opposition, I found the enemy giving way very rapidly and moving toward their right, when I ordered a prompt advance, and sending several dismounted companies over on the boat, I also ordered that a regiment of cavalry should be sent across, swimming the river if it could not be forded. The enemy retreated from the city in a south-east direction. Having gained the city, I sent an order to Major Coon to burn all cars, car or railroad shops and buildings, and also destroy all engines. I ordered Lieutenant Cardy, of the Third Michigan, to count the cars and locomotives, and report the number to me. This he did, reporting the number of engines at 51, and the cars at about 500 (including box, platform, and passenger) ; much the greater number of these were destroyed by fire.

I had also burned several buildings in which was stored large quantities of commissary stores, and in the cars a considerable quantity of ordnance stores. I had ordered all my force, except the picket, the provost-marshal's guard, and the detail ordered for the purpose of destroying the cars, engines, and shops, to recross the river and encamp for the night, which recrossing was effected by 8 p. m. This was done that in case of an attack I would have the advantage of position, and I could follow the next day in pursuit of the enemy and a large train of wagons sent out on my approach to the city, and could follow without much loss of time.

After I had commenced the destruction of property, and had partially succeeded, I could learn nothing positive in regard to a force of ours being near us from below, and did not learn anything positive or reliable until the arrival of the advance of Colonel Winslow's column, at about 9.30 p. m. The order for the destruction of cars and engines was countermanded by Colonel Winslow on his arrival. Colonel Winslow assumed command and ordered my command to remain at Grenada during the 17th [18th] ultimo.

At 4.30 a. m. of the 18th [19th] ultimo the column left Grenada, proceeding to Oakland, thence to Panola, thence toward Senatobia 12 miles, where my command turned to the right, and I marched through Luxahoma and Bucksnort to Wall Hill, where I sent the First Brigade, under Lieutenant-Colonel Wallace, toward Collierville. With the Second Brigade I moved to Holly Springs, thence to Lamar, where I ordered the detachments of the Second Iowa Cavalry, Third Michigan Cavalry, and Eleventh Illinois Cavalry, under Major Coon, to move toward La Grange whilst I moved via Spring Hill and Saulsbury to Pocahontas, where I arrived at 9 a. m. of the 23d ultimo.

During this expedition nearly 60 locomotives were captured and partially destroyed, and over 500 cars were captured and destroyed. I also burned two large steam-mills, in which was stored several thousand sacks of meal and flour ; several machine-shops, the depot buildings and warerooms, as also a considerable quantity of commissary stores stored therein. Up to 8 p. m. I could learn nothing of a Federal force from below which was reliable, but was informed by one or two citizens that a force of ours had captured a train at Durant Station and another at Vaiden Station, but could learn nothing further. Other citizens stated that after the capture of the train at Vaiden, Jackson overtook our forces and retook the train. I had learned that a wagon-train of near 100 wagons had left Grenada, the rear of the train leaving the city about 2 p. m. of the same day on which I arrived. This train was loaded with commissary and ordnance stores, and moved toward West Point, Miss. It was my intention to follow after and capture the train the next day, but at 9 p. m., the brigade from Yazoo City having arrived, and the commanding officer assuming command, I was ordered to remain at Grenada during the next day and succeeding night.

I have to express my regret that, for the good of the service, the instructions from Major-General Hurlbut were not carried out completely, but before this could be done another officer assumed command who acted under different instructions. My reason for this regret is that the railroad is in running order from Panola to Grenada, 42 miles; on this portion of the road is an engine and three or four cars in running order. The Mississippi Central Railroad from the Yoh-na-pata-fa River to Grenada, a distance of 36 miles, is in good condition, and one engine and six or seven cars thereon are also in running order. These Colonel Winslow forbade the destruction of, although I had almost effected the destruction before he arrived. From Grenada to Canton, with slight repairs, the Mississippi Central Railroad could be put in running order, and all the engines and cars captured by the brigade from Yazoo City, under Colonel Winslow, with a very few of those which I captured, were left in running order; and for shipments of corn and wheat, of which there is an immense quantity in that portion of Mississippi, these engines and cars will be of immense benefit to our enemies.

During the expedition I captured 58 prisoners, 18 of whom were paroled; the others were brought in. A list of those paroled is herewith sent, marked Exhibit E ;* a list of those brought in, marked F.* Several hundred horses and mules were also brought in, of which no full report has been made to me by brigade commanders, but which I ordered them to have regimental commanders turn over to the quartermasters of their respective posts.

In accordance with the instructions I brought in several hundred negroes. From the quartermaster of General Chalmers' staff I took $5,630, Government (Confederate) funds. From other parties captured several thousand dollars were taken, all of which was turned over to the provost-marshal at Pocahontas; receipts marked H. I send herewith the reports of brigade commanders, marked G,† to which I would refer as to statements of captured property. A list of the wounded and prisoners lost by my command not having been furnished me by brigade commanders, I am unable to make any report in regard thereto.

I am under great obligations to the officers of my command for their compliance with all orders and their prompt discharge of duties. To Major Coon I must award great praise for the energy with which he moved his command and his management of them on the field. The enlisted men of the command exhibited a true and soldierly bearing and conduct, undergoing great fatigue and hardship, the last few days of the expedition subsisting on green corn instead of bread, without murmur or complaint.

I am, sir, very respectfully, your obedient servant,

JESSE J. PHILLIPS,
Lieutenant-Colonel, Commanding.

Lieut. R. K. RANDOLPH,
Actg. Asst. Adjt. Gen., Second Brigade.

[Inclosure A.]

HDQRS. SECOND BRIGADE, SECOND DIVISION,
Pocahontas, August 12, 1863.

Lieut. Col. J. J. PHILLIPS,
Commanding Ninth Illinois Infantry:

Have your regiment in readiness to move at noon with six days' rations.

AUG. MERSY,
Colonel, Commanding.

---

* Omitted.
† See Nos. 5 and 6, following.

[Inclosure B.]

HDQRS. SECOND BRIGADE, SECOND DIVISION,
Pocahontas, August 12, 1863.

Lieut. Col. J. J. PHILLIPS,
Commanding Ninth Illinois Infantry:

You will move immediately via Ripley and Oxford, where you will form a junction with the column from La Grange.

AUG. MERSY,
Colonel, Commanding.

[Inclosure C.]

LA GRANGE, August 12, 1863.

Colonel MERSY:

The cavalry leave here at daylight. Send word to the Ninth Illinois to bear well west, to join cavalry from here, southwest of Salem or near Hickory Flats.

J. K. MIZNER,
Colonel, and Chief of Cavalry.

[Inclosure D.]

HEADQUARTERS SIXTEENTH ARMY CORPS,
Memphis, Tenn., August 11, 1863.

Col. J. K. MIZNER,
Chief of Cavalry, Left Wing:

You will dispatch as soon as practicable a force of cavalry and mounted infantry, not less than 1,000 men, with six days' rations, to proceed as rapidly as possible to the neighborhood of Water Valley. The object of the expedition is to secure and, if practicable, bring in the engines and rolling stock on the railroad. You will take 50 men of the Engineer Regiment with you, selected by Major Flad. If the enemy commence the destruction, or you find you cannot bring them in, you will cause them to be thoroughly destroyed, especially the iron-works. Wheels and axles are difficult to get in the South. And even if the woodwork has been destroyed by fire, complete it by breaking the wheels and axles. I expect you will meet a column, of about the same number, from General Grant's force below. These were to have left on the 8th. As far as possible let no damage be done the country; we may need the crops. In returning it will be expected that the expedition bring in as many able-bodied negroes as can readily be obtained for troops. Unless the expedition is able to secure the stock, it will take a different route on its return, striking toward such points as the commanding officer deems best for the service.

Your obedient servant,

S. A. HURLBUT,
Major-General.

[Inclosure H.]

POCAHONTAS, TENN.,
August 24, 1863.

Received of Lieut. Col. Jesse J. Phillips, commanding Ninth Illinois Volunteer Infantry, $8,641.50, Confederate funds, and $3.38 specie, captured during expedition to Grenada, Miss.

W. F. ARMSTRONG,
Captain, Provost-Marshal.

No. 5.

Report of Maj. Datus E. Coon, Second Iowa Cavalry.

CAMP SECOND IOWA CAVALRY,
Germantown, August 25, 1863.

SIR: I have to make the following report in regard to the recent scout and raid on Grenada, Miss.:

In compliance with orders from Col. E. Hatch, commanding Second Cavalry Brigade, La Grange, Tenn., I started at 5 a. m. of the 13th of this month, with 200 men of the Second Iowa Cavalry, and on arriving at Wolf River was joined by a detachment of 200 men of the Third Michigan Cavalry, and 100 men of the Eleventh Illinois Cavalry, making in all 500 well-mounted men. Leaving the Wolf, we passed through Salem, thence to the Tippah River, which we forded, though the water was very high, by emptying all the contents of the wagons and ambulances into an old scow, which we found near by, and ferrying them across by means of a rope which we had taken along.

This difficult fording place was passed just before dark, when we moved on some 2 miles and camped for the night.

At daylight of the 14th we moved on the road toward Hickory Flats, at which place we arrived at 9 a. m. Not finding the Ninth Illinois Mounted Infantry, as instructions stated, moved on to Rocky Ford, at which place we arrived at 3 p. m.

At 5 p. m. all were over the Tallahatchie, and after two hours' march we made Pegee's plantation, a distance of 5 miles, and camped for the night.

At daylight moved on the Oxford road, and at 10 a. m. arrived in that place. The excessive heat rendering it necessary for a long halt, we gathered corn about the town and fed and rested the animals until 2 p. m., when you arrived and I reported to you for orders.

At 2 p. m. we moved on Water Valley road and camped 6 miles below for the night, hoping that before morning we might hear from the First Brigade, which was to meet us at Oxford. During the night, however, the First Brigade reported, Lieutenant-Colonel Wallace commanding.

At sunrise of the 16th we moved on the Water Valley road, reaching the Yoh-na-pata-fa River at 10 a. m., found a good ferry-boat in good order, and immediately commenced crossing. Some 5 prisoners were caught by the advance at this place, who gave information of a wagon train of some six wagons that had passed the ferry but an hour before us.

When some four companies of cavalry and infantry were over they were sent in pursuit; they overtook them at Water Valley. The result of the capture was six heavy wagons and six six-mule teams fully equipped and in running order. By your order I turned one full team over to the Third Michigan Cavalry, one to the Ninth Infantry, and one to the Second Iowa Cavalry. There being no use for the remaining three wagons they were ordered to be burned and the mules turned in to the regiments to supply the place of worn-out animals.

At 6 p. m., after a delay of near six hours, in consequence of the First Brigade having failed to close up, we moved out on the Coffeeville road. After a march of two hours a most terrific rain-storm set in, accompanied by one continual flash of lightning. It was with the utmost difficulty that we continued the march; the rain fell in torrents, making the road nearly impassable in the blackness of the night.

It would have been impossible for man or beast to have marched but for the continual flash of lightning which kept us in the road a part of the time.

It was so difficult to keep the road that many a horse, rider and all, tumbled into the ditch, where they would struggle for some time before they could extricate themselves.

At 12 o'clock midnight we reached the old battle-ground of Coffeeville, when we became tired of the slow progress making, and concluded to halt awhile for the clouds to move off that there might be a little more light. After an hour's halt we moved on, and after a mile's travel were overtaken by yourself, who directed that we halt until morning.

Soon after sunrise of the 17th we moved on toward Coffeeville, where we arrived in an hour afterward. Here we captured some 3 prisoners, and after a few minutes' halt moved out on the Grenada road. The advance struck the enemy's pickets about 2 miles below the town, where they captured a soldier belonging to McCulloch's command.

When 6 miles below Coffeeville I saw a locomotive moving up the road slowly and ordered the advance to send some men in its rear, hoping that they might reach the track in time to prevent its return by throwing obstructions upon the track. But, unfortunately, the movement was discovered in time for the engine to escape, not, however, without receiving some fifty shots from our carbines, which was the only means left for halting it. One car was found here loaded with car equipments which were left by the company.

The locomotive was undoubtedly after this car, as no other business was apparent.

From this on skirmishing was continuous all the way to Grenada. When within 8 miles of Grenada we discovered a large number of cars and locomotives, which we afterward learned amounted to 6 locomotives and 25 cars, all in good order.

When within 4 miles of Grenada we discovered a heavy column of smoke which we took to mean destruction of some kind, and immediately took a gallop that we might get to the place as soon as possible.

At three-fourths of a mile of town our advance came upon a heavy force, as they thought, and called for assistance, when I dismounted one battalion of the Third Michigan Rifles [Cavalry] and one battalion of the Ninth [Illinois] Infantry, deploying them on either side of the road as skirmishers, and pushed forward.

To make the command entirely safe from any show of ambuscade, I sent a company of sabers on each flank to feel the timber all through, and see the enemy driven out.

We had not advanced more than one-half a mile when they opened upon us with 6 and 10 pounder artillery.

This did not check our movements, however, until we had driven them all over the river. Here they exhibited a strong determination to resist us.

In an hour we succeeded in bringing two of our 12-pounder howitzers to bear upon them, when nothing more was to be heard from them.

As soon as it was practicable to cross I took some 200 men and went into town at about 3.30 p. m., and immediately commenced the destruction of the cars and locomotives.

They were so closely packed together as to make a small town of themselves. The amount of rolling stock here was immense. I immediately detailed parties to count the cars and locomotives while other squads were setting the fires.

Soon after the fires were set an engineer came to me and reported a Federal force below, and that they were trying to save the property, while citizens reported that there could be no truth in the statement, as they were informed that the Federals had captured a train at Durant, some ways below, but that Jackson's cavalry had recaptured the train and driven the Federals away.

Having much doubt as to which was true, I reported to you for further instructions, when you decided that it was impossible to get the rolling stock off with the force we had were the bridges perfect, and that the bridges having been so perfectly destroyed, and there being certainty of assistance from below, we had better complete the destruction and return home.

The destruction resulted, as near as I could estimate, as follows:

Sixty locomotives (40 in good running order), and some 500 cars of all kinds, coaches, sleeping cars, freight cars, flats, &c. Some few of these were not completely destroyed, but very few were left that were not disabled.

There were two depots, one a very fine one, destroyed; also two large machine-shops, containing a large amount of machinery; also two large steam flouring mills, containing each not less than 1,000 sacks of flour and meal. There were some ten flats loaded with army wagons—the number I did not learn—which were all burned.

At sundown the destruction was thorough and complete, and in obedience to your orders, I moved my brigade across to the north side, after having procured forage out of different cribs in town. In obedience to your instruction, I remained in bivouac during the 18th.

At daylight of the 19th, we started on our return north, passing through Oakland, Panola, Bucksnort, Wall Hill, Holly Springs, Lamar, and La Grange, which latter place I reached on Sunday, the 23d, after an absence of eleven days.

Very respectfully, your obedient servant,

DATUS E. COON,
Major, Second Iowa Cavalry, Comdg. Second Brigade.

Colonel PHILLIPS.

No. 6.

Report of Lieut. Col. Martin R. M. Wallace, Fourth Illinois Cavalry.

HEADQUARTERS FOURTH ILLINOIS CAVALRY,
Collierville, Tenn., August 23, 1863.

SIR: In pursuance of duty, I have the honor to report that in obedience to orders from Col. L. F. McCrillis, commanding First Brigade, Cavalry Division, Sixteenth Army Corps, I assumed command of said brigade on the 13th day of August, and on that day, in obedience to instructions from Colonel Mizner, chief of cavalry, Left Wing, Sixteenth Army Corps, I proceeded, with a force of 720 enlisted men from the Third, Fourth, and Ninth Illinois Cavalry, by the most direct route from this place to the crossing of the Talla-hatchie River, at Abbeville, Miss., passing through on my way Byhalia, Tallaloosa, Cox's Corners, and Waterford.

At Byhalia we met a squad of the enemy and gave chase. One of my men, belonging to the Ninth Illinois Cavalry, being dressed in citizen's dress, having arms, was wounded by one of his comrades in the chase. Too much care cannot be given to the matter of dress of soldiers by commanding officers of companies and regiments.

I camped the night of the 13th at the plantation of Mr. Withers.

On the 14th instant, when about 10 miles southeast of Byhalia, near the house of Mrs. Craven, my advance guard (Company M, Fourth Illinois Cavalry, Captain Hitt commanding) ran on to the enemy and opened fire, which was returned, and Roderick Justin, private of that company, was slightly wounded in the upper arm.

About 1 mile north of Cox's Corners the same advance captured Private Dickson, Captain Middleton's company, Major Chalmers' battalion, bearing a dispatch from Captain Middleton to Major Chalmers, informing him of our approach.

The crossing of the Tallahatchie was very difficult and slow, oc-cupying all the night of the 14th instant and until 11 a. m. of the 15th instant, at which time I moved forward, passing through Ox-ford, Miss., at about 4 p. m. of that day, camping that night at the plantation of Mr. Buckner, $2\frac{1}{2}$ miles south of Oxford.

August 16.—I started at daylight, overtaking the rear of the Second Brigade about 9 a. m., where Lieutenant-Colonel Phillips, Ninth Illinois Mounted Infantry, assumed command of both brigades.

Near the crossing of the Yoh-na-pata-fa River, at the mouth of Taylor's Creek, I captured 2 of the enemy, privates, belonging to Major Chalmers' battalion.

As the pioneer corps of the First Brigade (Lieutenant Hyde, Fourth Illinois Cavalry, commanding) was crossing the Yoh-na-pata-fa the boat sunk, drowning 1 negro. This delayed my crossing for about two hours. After crossing, I proceeded to Water Valley, pursuant to orders from Lieutenant-Colonel Phillips. A halt was ordered at this place for one hour to feed the stock, and then to move on that night to Coffeeville, but a most terrible rain-storm and the pitchy darkness of the night rendered a forward march utterly out of the question.

At daylight of the 17th we left Water Valley, and proceeded with-out incident or casualty through Coffeeville to within 5 or 6 miles of Grenada, when, by order of the lieutenant-colonel commanding, I sent forward one section of the battery attached to the Ninth Illi-nois Cavalry, under Lieutenant Butler, of that regiment, with Com-pany A, Ninth Illinois Cavalry, and Companies M, E, and K, Fourth Illinois Cavalry. Here I also sent the Third Illinois Cavalry, under Major O'Connor, to a station on the Mississippi Central Railroad where there were some rolling stock. I pushed forward my column and soon received orders to send forward the other section of the battery, all under the command of Captain Perkins, Ninth Illinois Cavalry, and by order of the lieutenant-colonel commanding I proceeded with the balance of my command to the lower ferry across the Yalabusha ; just before I reached the bank of the river I re-ceived orders to push into town to destroy rolling stock. I pushed on through the river into town ; but before we reached the scene of destruction I received orders to push my command across the river again without delay, which I did, and moved out to Stateam [?] Station, Mississippi Central Railroad, and went into camp for the night. During the night Major O'Connor rejoined me with his command.

August 18.—We remained all day in camp without incident.

August 19.—We moved in advance of the forces on the road to Panola, Miss., passing through Oakland, crossing the Yocona on that road, camping for the night about 1 mile north of the river.

August 20.—By order of the colonel commanding, my command moved in the rear of the column; arrived in Panola without casualty worthy of note about 12 m., the troops in advance of me getting across the Tallahatchie about 4.30 p. m. I proceeded to cross my command, finishing about 6.30 p. m., and moved out about 6 miles on the Memphis road to camp.

August 21.—This morning I was ordered to take the advance. I moved north to a point about a mile north of Dr. Wallace's plantation, where I turned to the right, taking the road leading to Tuxahoma. After feeding I took the road for Bucksnort, where I camped for the night. During this day, after I had left the Memphis road, I ordered details from each company as forage parties, all from each regiment to be placed under the command of a commissioned officer, six days' rations having been ordered, and this being the ninth day out, and we still two days' march from home. This a. m. Captain Lee, Company F, Third Illinois Cavalry, was accidentally shot by one of his men; wound probably mortal.

August 22.—I again took the advance this a. m., and moved on the road from Bucksnort to Wall Hill, at which place I took the road to Byhalia, under orders to proceed to camp, which I did without incident. The Ninth Illinois Cavalry proceeded to Germantown that night.

The Fourth Illinois Cavalry went into their camp at this place, and the Third, after resting here over night, proceeded to their camp at La Fayette.

I learned in the afternoon of the 22d that the forage party of the Ninth Illinois Cavalry, sent out under Lieutenant Shattuck on the morning of the 21st, had not returned to the column, and since coming into camp I learn that they got behind the column, missed the road, and attempting to cross the Coldwater, were attacked by the enemy from both sides, and 14 of the party and 15 stand of arms are missing.

Casualties.—Capt. W. S. Lee, Company F, Third Illinois Cavalry, dangerously wounded by accidental shot by one of his company.

Jasper Bonds, private, Company C, Third Illinois Cavalry, slightly wounded in heel.

First Lieut. and Adjt. William McEvoy, Third Illinois Cavalry, captured while straggling.

Peter F. Summers, private, Company M; James Mooney, John R. Stephens, and Albert Gilbert, Company C, Third Illinois Cavalry, captured by the enemy while straggling.

Roderick Justin, private, Company M, Fourth Illinois Cavalry, wounded in the arm while on duty as extreme advance guard.

Charles W. Jones, corporal, Company G, severely wounded by kick of mule on back of his head.

Fourteen soldiers, with horses, arms, and equipments, from the Ninth Illinois Cavalry, are missing, supposed to have been captured.

Prisoners taken by First Brigade, cavalry division :

By the Ninth Illinois Cavalry 14
By the Fourth Illinois Cavalry 2

Total... 16

These were all turned over to the Second Brigade by order of the colonel commanding expedition.

Captured stock.—Third Illinois Cavalry, Major O'Connor commanding :

Horses 8
Mules 9

Total... 17

One two-horse carriage, 1 single buggy.

Fourth Illinois Cavalry, Major Wemple commanding :

Mules... 34
Horses.. 27

Total... 61

Ninth Illinois Cavalry, Captain Buell commanding :

Mules... 64
Horses.. 35

Total.. 99
Total captured, 177.

Respectfully submitted.

M. R. M. WALLACE,
Lieut. Col., Comdg. First Brigade, Cavalry Division.

H. H. BLACK,
Captain, and Acting Assistant Adjutant General.

AUGUST 16–20, 1863.—Expedition from Memphis, Tenn., to Hernando, Miss., with Skirmish (17th) near Panola, Miss.

REPORTS.

No. 1.—Report of Brig. Gen. James C. Veatch, U. S. Army, commanding District of Memphis.

No. 2.—Report of Lieut. Col. Hervey Craven, Eighty-ninth Indiana Infantry, commanding expedition.

No. 1.

Report of Brig. Gen. James C. Veatch, U. S. Army, commanding District of Memphis.

HEADQUARTERS DISTRICT OF MEMPHIS,
Memphis, August 23, 1863.

COLONEL : I have the honor to forward herewith a copy of the report of Lieut. Col. Hervey Craven, Eighty-ninth Indiana Infantry Volunteers, of the recent scout made to Hernando and vicinity by a party under his command.

I am, colonel, your obedient servant,

JAMES C. VEATCH,
Brigadier-General.

Lieut. Col. HENRY BINMORE, *A. A. G. Sixteenth Army Corps.*

No. 2.

Report of Lieut. Col. Hervey Craven, Eighty-ninth Indiana Infantry, commanding expedition.

FORT PICKERING, TENN.,
August 21, 1863.

SIR : On the morning of the 16th, in obedience to the order of Brig. Gen. J. C. Veatch, the scouts under my command, composed of the Eighty-ninth Indiana Volunteer Infantry and one company of the Sixth Illinois Cavalry, under command of Lieutenant Guiteau, moved for Hernando, going out on the Horn Lake road, and were joined on the next day by another company of the Sixth Cavalry, under command of Captain Grimes.

The command arrived and camped on the banks of Horn Lake Creek on the evening of the 16th, when I was informed that at the Widow May's, about 1 mile south of the creek, there had been some ten or a dozen of the cotton-burning guerrillas on that day, who, having learned of the advance of our forces, fled. No pursuit was made after them, as they had fled some hours before I received the information that they had been there. The next morning we encountered much difficulty in crossing the creek, as the bridge had been burned and the channel is deep, and the banks very steep, in consequence of which we had to unload and pack the forage across, it being with difficulty that we crossed with empty wagons. During the day the cavalry in advance, under command of Lieutenant Guiteau, pursued 2 men on horseback, said to be cotton burners, one of them a lieutenant in the rebel army ; and in the afternoon, while the command were resting during the heat of the day, 4 men on horseback, coming along the road, discovered our pickets, when they immediately wheeled and rode off at speed, the pickets having fired on them after they had refused to halt. From a negro I learned their names to be Cyrus Smith, Henry Douglass, Robert Scales, and Horace Polk, the latter living within 3 miles of Hernando, and the others in the same neighborhood, but farther this way, Cyrus Smith living some 5 or 6 miles this side of Hernando, and all between the Horn Lake and Hernando roads. They seem to be well understood in the neighborhood as active rebels, and doing considerable in the way of cotton burning. On the next evening the command arrived at Hernando, the advance, under command of Captain Grimes, having found on their arrival in the place some 6 or 8 cavalry there, among whom was Captain Perry, a citizen of that neighborhood, and now at home recruiting for the rebel army. The captain and his squad, having notice of our approach by the rising of the dust, succeeded in making their escape, but were pursued and fired upon, and one of the fugitives, who was riding a mule not remarkable for its speed, was captured, he and his mule held until the next morning, when, from information which I deemed reliable that he did not belong to the squad of cavalry that had fled, and that he was a citizen of the neighborhood, and had indiscreetly fled simply because he supposed we would take his mule from him if it was found there, and also being informed that he was violently opposing the Southern conscription, I deemed it advisable to release him and did so, handing him over his mule also. The citizens seemed rather well disposed toward us, many of them meeting us very cordially.

The next day (Tuesday, the 18th) the command was moved for Memphis by the Hernando road, and in the afternoon a detachment of infantry, under command of Adjutant Dent, of the Eighty-ninth, and a squad of cavalry, under command of Lieutenant Fulton, were sent to reconnoiter, and, if possible, to arrest the said Cyrus Smith and others, taking with them a negro who professed to be well posted with the paths, and well acquainted with the men and their respective places of residence. Smith and Scales were found at the residence of Smith, but discovered their approach in time to make their escape, but were fired on and pursued some distance. The negro then informed the detachment of the place where the guer illas were in the habit of concealing their horses, and on examination of the premises, in a very dense undergrowth of timber, they found a mare, saddle and bridle, new, and probably manufactured in Memphis. The negro professed to know the mare, and represented her as belonging to Captain Foster or Forrest; I am not positive as to the name. The mare and equipments are here subject to your order, as she was brought in by the cavalry and remains in their possession. The men were tired and short of rations; otherwise, they might have arrested some of the parties they went out after.

The next day we marched as far as Nonconnah Creek without interruption, and without making the discovery of any rebels; but a detachment that I sent back and across to the Horn Lake road, on their return to the command, reported that they were informed by a lady that some 50 rebel cavalry had been seen by her, and that they were lying in ambush as we passed along the road. Whether this statement is correct or not I cannot say.

From all the circumstances I concluded that there are in the neighborhood below and in the vicinity of the Hernando and Horn Lake roads some resident cavalrymen and some recruiting officers, and that they probably have a small camp some 2 or 3 miles, but am inclined to think that their number, all told, would not exceed 25 or 30 men, unless they were brought in from other neighborhoods. The command all arrived safely at their respective camps on yesterday, about 8 a. m., the officers and men of the Eighty-ninth Regiment Indiana Infantry much improved in spirits, and in health also, as I have reason to believe.

All of which is most respectfully submitted.

HERVEY CRAVEN,
Lieut. Col., Comdg. 89th Ind. Inf. and Cav. Scouts.

Maj. JAMES O. PIERCE,
Assistant Adjutant-General, District of Memphis.

P. S.—I almost forgot to say that during the night of the 17th, while at Hernando, the pickets on the road leading to Coldwater were attacked by about 30 men on foot, but supposed to be dismounted cavalry. One of the pickets was struck with a buckshot, but was not seriously injured. The attacking party being sharply resisted by the pickets fled and did not return.

AUGUST 16-SEPTEMBER 22, 1863.—The Chickamauga Campaign.

SUMMARY OF THE PRINCIPAL EVENTS.

Aug. 16–17, 1863.—General advance of the Army of the Cumberland.
17, 1863.—Skirmish at Calfkiller Creek, near Sparta, Tenn.
21, 1863.—Skirmish at Maysville, Ala.
Action at Shellmound, Tenn.
Bombardment of Chattanooga, Tenn.
22–24, 1863.—Expedition from Tracy City, Tenn., to the Tennessee River.
24, 1863.—Skirmish at Gunter's Landing, near Port Deposit, Ala.
26–27, 1863.—Skirmishes at Harrison's Landing, Tenn.
27–28, 1863.—Skirmish at the Narrows, near Shellmound, Tenn.
28–31, 1863.—Reconnaissance from Stevenson, Ala., to Trenton, Ga.
29, 1863.—Skirmish at Caperton's Ferry, Ala.
30–31, 1863.—Reconnaissance from Shellmound toward Chattanooga, Tenn.
31, 1863.—Skirmish in Will's Valley, Ala.
Sept.   1, 1863.—Skirmishes at Will's Creek and at Davis', Tap's, and Neal's Gaps, Ala.
3, 1863.—Skirmish near Alpine, Ga.
5, 1863.—Reconnaissance from Winston's Gap into Broomtown Valley, Ala.
Skirmish at Lebanon, Ala.
Skirmish near Alpine, Ga.
Destruction of salt-works at Rawlingsville, Ala.
6, 1863.—Skirmish at Stevens' Gap, Ga.
6– 7, 1863.—Skirmishes at Summerville, Ga.
7, 1863.—Skirmish at Stevenson, Ala.
Reconnaissance toward Chattanooga and skirmish in Lookout Valley, Tenn.
8, 1863.—Skirmish at Winston's Gap, Ala.
Skirmish at Alpine, Ga.
9, 1863.—Chattanooga, Tenn., occupied by the Union forces.
Skirmish at Friar's Island, Tenn.
Skirmish at Lookout Mountain, Ga.
10, 1863.—Reconnaissance from Alpine toward Rome, La Fayette, and Summerville, Ga., and skirmish at Summerville.
Skirmishes at Pea Vine Creek and near Graysville, Ga.
11, 1863.—Reconnaissance toward Rome, Ga.
Skirmish near Blue Bird Gap, Ga.
Skirmish at Davis' Cross-Roads (or Davis' House), near Dug Gap, Ga.
Skirmish near Rossville, Ga.
Skirmish near Ringgold, Ga.
11–13, 1863.—Skirmishes near Lee and Gordon's Mills, Ga.
12, 1863.—Skirmish at Alpine, Ga.
Skirmish at Dirt Town, Ga.
Skirmish near Leet's Tan-yard, or Rock Spring, Ga.
Skirmish on the La Fayette road, near Chattooga River, Ga.
13, 1863.—Reconnaissance from Lee and Gordon's Mills toward La Fayette, Ga., and skirmish.
Reconnaissance from Henderson's Gap, Ala., to La Fayette, Ga., and skirmish.
Skirmish near Summerville, Ga.
14, 1863.—Skirmish near La Fayette, Ga.

Sept.   15, 1863.—Skirmish at Trion Factory, Ga.
               Skirmish at Summerville, Ga.
        15–18, 1863.—Skirmishes at Catlett's Gap, Pigeon Mountain, Ga.
        16–18, 1863.—Skirmishes near Lee and Gordon's Mills, Ga.
           17, 1863.—Reconnaissance from Rossville and skirmish at Ringgold, Ga.
               Skirmish at Neal's Gap, Ala.
               Skirmish at Owens' Ford, West Chickamauga Creek, Ga.
           18, 1863.—Skirmishes at Pea Vine Ridge, Alexander's and Reed's Bridges,
               Dyer's Ford, Spring Creek, and near Stevens' Gap, Ga.
        19–20, 1863.—Battle of Chickamauga, Ga.
           21, 1863.—Skirmishes at Rossville, Lookout Church, and Dry Valley, Ga.
        21–22, 1863.—Army of the Cumberland retreats to Chattanooga, Tenn.
           22, 1863.—Skirmishes at Missionary Ridge and Shallow Ford Gap, near
               Chattanooga, Tenn.

REPORTS, ETC.

THE UNION ARMY.

No.   1.—Maj. Gen. Henry W. Halleck, U. S. Army, General-in-Chief.
No.   2.—Organization of the Army of the Cumberland, September 19 and 20.
No.   3.—Maj. Gen. William S. Rosecrans, U. S. Army, commanding Army of the
          Cumberland.
No.   4.—Abstract from returns of the Army of the Cumberland, September 10
          and 20.
No.   5.—Return of Casualties in the Army of the Cumberland.
No.   6.—Dispatches of Charles A. Dana, Assistant Secretary of War.
No.   7.—Surg. Glover Perin, U. S. Army, Medical Director, Department of the
          Cumberland.
No.   8.—Lieut. Col. William M. Wiles, Twenty-second Indiana Infantry, Provost-
          Marshal-General.
No.   9.—Capt. Horace Porter, U. S. Ordnance Corps, Chief of Ordnance.
No. 10.—Col. James Barnett, First Ohio Light Artillery, Chief of Artillery.
No. 11.—Capt. Jesse Merrill, U. S. Signal Corps, Chief Signal Officer.
No. 12.—Surg. Israel Moses, U. S. Army, Medical Director, post of Chattanooga.
No. 13.—Maj. Gen. George H. Thomas, U. S. Army, commanding Fourteenth Army
          Corps.
No. 14.—Surg. Ferdinand H. Gross, U. S. Army, Medical Director.
No. 15.—Col. John G. Parkhurst, Ninth Michigan Infantry, Provost-Marshal.
No. 16.—Capt. John D. Barker, First Ohio Cavalry, Acting Assistant Inspector-
          General.
No. 17.—Lieut. Col. Andrew J. Mackay, U. S. Army, Chief Quartermaster.
No. 18.—Brig. Gen. Absalom Baird, U. S. Army, commanding First Division, with
          complimentary orders of General Rosecrans.
No. 19.—Capt. George A. Kensel, Fifth U. S. Artillery, Chief of Artillery.
No. 20.—Col. Benjamin F. Scribner, Thirty-eighth Indiana Infantry, commanding
          First Brigade.
No. 21.—Lieut. Col. Daniel F. Griffin, Thirty-eighth Indiana Infantry.
No. 22.—Capt. James Warnock, Second Ohio Infantry.
No. 23.—Col. Oscar F. Moore, Thirty-third Ohio Infantry.
No. 24.—Maj. Rue P. Hutchins, Ninety-fourth Ohio Infantry.
No. 25.—Capt. Jacob W. Robey, Tenth Wisconsin Infantry.
No. 26.—Brig. Gen. John C. Starkweather, U. S. Army, commanding Second
          Brigade.

No. 27.—Brig. Gen. John H. King, U. S. Army, commanding Third Brigade.
No. 28.—Capt. Albert B. Dod, Fifteenth U. S. Infantry.
No. 29.—Capt. Robert E. A. Crofton, Sixteenth U. S. Infantry.
No. 30.—Capt. George W. Smith, Eighteenth U. S. Infantry.
No. 31.—Capt. Henry Haymond, Eighteenth U. S. Infantry.
No. 32.—Lieut. Robert Ayres, Nineteenth U. S. Infantry.
No. 33.—Lieut. Joshua A. Fessenden, Battery H, Fifth U. S. Artillery.
No. 34.—Maj. Gen. James S. Negley, U. S. Army, commanding Second Division.
No. 35.—Capt. Frederick Schultz, First Ohio Light Artillery, Chief of Artillery.
No. 36.—Brig. Gen. John Beatty, U. S. Army, commanding First Brigade.
No. 37.—Lieut. Col. Douglas Hapeman, One hundred and fourth Illinois Infantry.
No. 38.—Capt. Lyman Bridges, Bridges' Battery, Illinois Light Artillery.
No. 39.—Col. Timothy R. Stanley, Eighteenth Ohio Infantry, commanding Second
           Brigade.
No. 40.—Col. William L. Stoughton, Eleventh Michigan Infantry, commanding
           Second Brigade.
No. 41.—Capt. Frederick Schultz, Battery M, First Ohio Light Artillery.
No. 42.—Col. William Sirwell, Seventy-eighth Pennsylvania Infantry, commanding
           Third Brigade.
No. 43.—Lieut. Col. William D. Ward, Thirty-seventh Indiana Infantry.
No. 44.—Maj. Arnold McMahan and Capt. Charles H. Vantine, Twenty-first Ohio
           Infantry.
No. 45.—Capt. Joseph Fisher, Seventy-fourth Ohio Infantry.
No. 46.—Capt. Alexander Marshall, Battery G, First Ohio Light Artillery.
No. 47.—Brig. Gen. John M. Brannan, U. S. Army, commanding Third Division.
No. 48.—Capt. Josiah W. Church, First Michigan Light Artillery, Chief of Artillery.
No. 49.—Col. John M. Connell, Seventeenth Ohio Infantry, commanding First Bri-
           gade.
No. 50.—Capt. Josiah W. Church, Battery D, First Michigan Light Artillery.
No. 51.—Col. Charles W. Chapman, Seventy-fourth Indiana Infantry, command-
           ing Second Brigade.
No. 52.—Lieut. Col. Myron Baker, Seventy-fourth Indiana Infantry.
No. 53.—Col. William H. Hays, Tenth Kentucky Infantry.
No. 54.—Lieut. Col. Gabriel C. Wharton, Tenth Kentucky Infantry.
No. 55.—Lieut. Col. Henry D. Kingsbury, Fourteenth Ohio Infantry.
No. 56.—Lieut. Marco B. Gary, Battery C, First Ohio Light Artillery.
No. 57.—Col. Ferdinand Van Derveer, Thirty-fifth Ohio Infantry, commanding
           Third Brigade.
No. 58.—Col. James George, Second Minnesota Infantry.
No. 59.—Lieut. Col. Henry V. N. Boynton, Thirty-fifth Ohio Infantry.
No. 60.—Lieut. Frank G. Smith, Battery I, Fourth U. S. Artillery.
No. 61.—Maj. Gen. Joseph J. Reynolds, U. S. Army, commanding Fourth Division.
No. 62.—Capt. Samuel J. Harris, Nineteenth Indiana Battery, Acting Chief of Ar-
           tillery.
No. 63.—Col. John T. Wilder, Seventeenth Indiana Infantry, commanding First
           Brigade (Mounted Infantry).
No. 64.—Col. Abram O. Miller, Seventy-second Indiana Infantry, commanding
           First Brigade (Mounted Infantry).
No. 65.—Col. Smith D. Atkins, Ninety-second Illinois (Mounted) Infantry.
No. 66.—Lieut. Col. Edward Kitchell, Ninety-eighth Illinois (Mounted) Infantry.
No. 67.—Col. James Monroe, One hundred and twenty-third Illinois (Mounted)
           Infantry.
No. 68.—Maj. William T. Jones, Seventeenth Indiana (Mounted) Infantry.
No. 69.—Col. Abram O. Miller, Seventy-second Indiana (Mounted) Infantry.

No. 70.—Capt. Eli Lilly, Eighteenth Indiana Battery.
No. 71.—Col. Edward A. King, Sixty-eighth Indiana Infantry, commanding Second Brigade.
No. 72.—Itinerary of the Second Brigade.
No. 73.—Capt. Samuel J. Harris, Nineteenth Indiana Battery.
No. 74.—Lieut. Robert S. Lackey, Nineteenth Indiana Battery.
No. 75.—Brig. Gen. John B. Turchin, U. S. Army, commanding Third Brigade.
No. 76.—Lieut. Col. Hubbard K. Milward, Eighteenth Kentucky Infantry.
No. 77.—Capt. John B. Heltemes, Eighteenth Kentucky Infantry.
No. 78.—Col. Philander P. Lane, Eleventh Ohio Infantry.
No. 79.—Lieut. Col. Hiram F. Devol, Thirty-sixth Ohio Infantry.
No. 80.—Lieut. Col. Douglas Putnam, jr., Ninety-second Ohio Infantry.
No. 81.—Lieut. William E. Chess, Twenty-first Indiana Battery.
No. 82.—Maj. Gen. Alexander McD. McCook, U. S. Army, commanding Twentieth Army Corps.
No. 83.—Surg. Jabez Perkins, Tenth Kentucky Infantry, Acting Medical Director.
No. 84.—Brig. Gen. Jefferson C. Davis, U. S. Army, commanding First Division.
No. 85.—Capt. William A. Hotchkiss, Second Minnesota Battery, Chief of Artillery.
No. 86.—Col. P. Sidney Post, Fifty-ninth Illinois Infantry, commanding First Brigade.
No. 87.—Lieut. Col. Joshua C. Winters, Fifty-ninth Illinois Infantry.
No. 88.—Col. John E. Bennett, Seventy-fifth Illinois Infantry.
No. 89.—Lieut. Col. William M. Kilgour, Seventy-fifth Illinois Infantry.
No. 90.—Col. Michael Gooding, Twenty-second Indiana Infantry.
No. 91.—Capt. George Q. Gardner, Fifth Wisconsin Battery.
No. 92.—Brig. Gen. William P. Carlin, U. S. Army, commanding Second Brigade.
No. 93.—Capt. Chester K. Knight, Twenty-first Illinois Infantry.
No. 94.—Capt. William C. Harris, Thirty-eighth Illinois Infantry.
No. 95.—Maj. James E. Calloway, Twenty-first Illinois Infantry, commanding Eighty-first Indiana Infantry.
No. 96.—Capt. Leonard D. Smith, One hundred and first Ohio Infantry.
No. 97.—Col. John A. Martin, Eighth Kansas Infantry, commanding Third Brigade.
No. 98.—Lieut. Col. James L. Abernathy, Eighth Kansas Infantry.
No. 99.—Capt. Mons Grinager, Fifteenth Wisconsin Infantry.
No. 100.—Brig. Gen. Richard W. Johnson, U. S. Army, commanding Second Division.
No. 101.—Capt. Peter Simonson, Fifth Indiana Battery, Chief of Artillery.
No. 102.—Brig. Gen. August Willich, U. S. Army, commanding First Brigade.
No. 103.—Maj. William D. Williams, Eighty-ninth Illinois Infantry.
No. 104.—Lieut. Col. Frank Erdelmeyer, Thirty-second Indiana Infantry.
No. 105.—Col. Thomas J. Harrison, Thirty-ninth Indiana (Mounted) Infantry.
No. 106.—Lieut. Col. Frank Askew, Fifteenth Ohio Infantry.
No. 107.—Maj. Samuel F. Gray, Forty-ninth Ohio Infantry.
No. 108.—Capt. Wilbur F. Goodspeed, Battery A, First Ohio Light Artillery.
No. 109.—Col. Joseph B. Dodge, Thirtieth Indiana Infantry, commanding Second Brigade.
No. 110.—Col. Allen Buckner, Seventy-ninth Illinois Infantry.
No. 111.—Lieut. Col. David M. Dunn, Twenty-ninth Indiana Infantry.
No. 112.—Lieut. Col. Orrin D. Hurd, Thirtieth Indiana Infantry.
No. 113.—Capt. Edward Grosskopff, Twentieth Ohio Battery.
No. 114.—Col. William W. Berry, Fifth Kentucky Infantry, commanding Third Brigade.
No. 115.—Maj. Calvin D. Campbell, Sixth Indiana Infantry.

No. 116.—Col. William W. Berry, Fifth Kentucky Infantry.
No. 117.—Capt. John M. Huston, Fifth Kentucky Infantry.
No. 118.—Lieut. Col. Bassett Langdon, First Ohio Infantry.
No. 119.—Lieut. Col. William H. Martin, Ninety-third Ohio Infantry.
No. 120.—Capt. Peter Simonson, Fifth Indiana Battery.
No. 121.—Maj. Gen. Philip H. Sheridan, U. S. Army, commanding Third Division.
No. 122.—Col. Silas Miller, Thirty-sixth Illinois Infantry, commanding First Brigade.
No. 123.—Maj. Seymour Chase, Twenty-first Michigan Infantry.
No. 124.—Maj. Carl von Baumbach, Twenty-fourth Wisconsin Infantry.
No. 125.—Capt. Arnold Sutermeister, Eleventh Indiana Battery.
No. 126.—Col. Bernard Laiboldt, Second Missouri Infantry, commanding Second Brigade.
No. 127.—Maj. Arnold Beck, Second Missouri Infantry.
No. 128.—Col. Joseph Conrad, Fifteenth Missouri Infantry.
No. 129.—Lieut. Gustavus Schueler, Battery G, First Missouri Light Artillery.
No. 130.—Col. Nathan H. Walworth, Forty-second Illinois Infantry, commanding Third Brigade.
No. 131.—Col. Jonathan R. Miles, Twenty-seventh Illinois Infantry.
No. 132.—Capt. Mark H. Prescott, Battery C, First Illinois Light Artillery.
No. 133.—Maj. Gen. Thomas L. Crittenden, U. S. Army, commanding Twenty-first Army Corps.
No. 134.—Surg. Alonzo J. Phelps, U. S. Army, Medical Director.
No. 135.—Maj. John Mendenhall, U. S. Army, Chief of Artillery.
No. 136.—Brig. Gen. Thomas J. Wood, U. S. Army, commanding First Division.
No. 137.—Capt. Cullen Bradley, Sixth Ohio Battery, Chief of Artillery.
No. 138.—Col. George P. Buell, Fifty-eighth Indiana Infantry, commanding First Brigade.
No. 139.—Maj. Charles M. Hammond, One hundredth Illinois Infantry.
No. 140.—Lieut. Col. James T. Embree, Fifty-eighth Indiana Infantry.
No. 141.—Col. Joshua B. Culver and Maj. Willard G. Eaton, Thirteenth Michigan Infantry.
No. 142.—Lieut. Col. William H. Young, Twenty-sixth Ohio Infantry.
No. 143.—Capt. George Estep, Eighth Indiana Battery.
No. 144.—Brig. Gen. George D. Wagner, U. S. Army, commanding Second Brigade.
No. 145.—Col. Charles G. Harker, Sixty-fifth Ohio Infantry, commanding Third Brigade.
No. 146.—Col. Henry C. Dunlap, Third Kentucky Infantry.
No. 147.—Col. Alexander McIlvain, Sixty-fourth Ohio Infantry.
No. 148.—Capt. Thomas Powell, Sixty-fifth Ohio Infantry.
No. 149.—Col. Emerson Opdycke, One hundred and twenty-fifth Ohio Infantry.
No. 150.—Maj. Gen. John M. Palmer, U. S. Army, commanding Second Division.
No. 151.—Capt. William E. Standart, First Ohio Light Artillery, Chief of Artillery.
No. 152.—Brig. Gen. Charles Cruft, U. S. Army, commanding First Brigade.
No. 153.—Lieut. John A. Wright, Aide-de-Camp.
No. 154.—Col. John T. Smith, Thirty-first Indiana Infantry.
No. 155.—Lieut. Col. Alva R. Hadlock, First Kentucky Infantry.
No. 156.—Maj. James W. Mitchell, First Kentucky Infantry.
No. 157.—Capt. David J. Jones, First Kentucky Infantry.
No. 158.—Lieut. George Hornung, First Kentucky Infantry.
No. 159.—Lieut. Patrick J. Brown, First Kentucky Infantry.
No. 160.—Lieut. David Hammond, First Kentucky Infantry.
No. 161.—Col. Thomas D. Sedgewick, Second Kentucky Infantry.
No. 162.—Col. Charles H. Rippey, Ninetieth Ohio Infantry.

No. 163.—Lieut. Norman A. Baldwin, Battery B, First Ohio Light Artillery.

No. 164.—Brig. Gen. William B. Hazen, U. S. Army, commanding Second Brigade.

No. 165.—Col. Isaac C. B. Suman, Ninth Indiana Infantry.

No. 166.—Maj. Richard T. Whitaker, Sixth Kentucky Infantry.

No. 167.—Col. Aquila Wiley, Forty-first Ohio Infantry.

No. 168.—Maj. James B. Hampson, One hundred and twenty-fourth Ohio Infantry.

No. 169.—Lieut. Giles J. Cockerill, Battery F, First Ohio Light Artillery.

No. 170.—Col. William Grose, Thirty-sixth Indiana Infantry, commanding Third Brigade.

No. 171.—Col. Louis H. Waters, Eighty-fourth Illinois Infantry.

No. 172.—Maj. Gilbert Trusler, Thirty-sixth Indiana Infantry.

No. 173.—Lieut. Col. James C. Foy, Twenty-third Kentucky Infantry.

No. 174.—Maj. Samuel C. Erwin, Sixth Ohio Infantry.

No. 175.—Col. David J. Higgins, Twenty-fourth Ohio Infantry.

No. 176.—Lieut. Harry C. Cushing, Battery H, Fourth U. S. Artillery.

No. 177.—Lieut. Francis L. D. Russell, Battery M, Fourth U. S. Artillery.

No. 178.—Brig. Gen. Horatio P. Van Cleve, U. S. Army, commanding Third Division.

No. 179.—Capt. George R. Swallow, Seventh Indiana Battery, Chief of Artillery.

No. 180.—Brig. Gen. Samuel Beatty, U. S. Army, commanding First Brigade.

No. 181.—Col. Frederick Knefler, Seventy-ninth Indiana Infantry.

No. 182.—Col. George H. Cram, Ninth Kentucky Infantry.

No. 183.—Col. Alexander M. Stout, Seventeenth Kentucky Infantry.

No. 184.—Lieut. Col. Henry G. Stratton, Ninteenth Ohio Infantry.

No. 185.—Lieut. Samuel M. McDowell, Twenty-sixth Pennsylvania Battery.

No. 186.—Col. George F. Dick, Eighty-sixth Indiana Infantry, commanding Second Brigade.

No. 187.—Lieut. Col. Simeon C. Aldrich, Forty-fourth Indiana Infantry.

No. 188.—Maj. Jacob C. Dick, Eighty-sixth Indiana Infantry.

No. 189.—Capt. Horatio G. Cosgrove, Thirteenth Ohio Infantry.

No. 190.—Lieut. Col. Granville A. Frambes, Fifty-ninth Ohio Infantry.

No. 191.—Capt. George R. Swallow, Seventh Indiana Battery.

No. 192.—Col. Sidney M. Barnes, Eighth Kentucky Infantry, commanding Third Brigade.

No. 193.—Maj. John P. Dufficy, Thirty-fifth Indiana Infantry.

No. 194.—Maj. John S. Clark, Eighth Kentucky Infantry.

No. 195.—Lieut. Col. Charles H. Wood, Fifty-first Ohio Infantry.

No. 196.—Col. Peter T. Swaine, Ninety-ninth Ohio Infantry.

No. 197.—Lieut. Cortland Livingston, Third Wisconsin Battery.

No. 198.—Maj. Gen. Gordon Granger, U. S. Army, commanding Reserve Corps.

No. 199.—Brig. Gen. James B. Steedman, U. S. Army, commanding First Division.

No. 200.—Brig. Gen. Walter C. Whitaker, U. S. Army, commanding First Brigade.

No. 201.—Col. Thomas E. Champion, Ninety-sixth Illinois Infantry.

No. 202.—Capt. Isaac C. Nelson, Eighty-ninth Ohio Infantry.

No. 203.—Col. John G. Mitchell, One hundred and thirteenth Ohio Infantry, commanding Second Brigade.

No. 204.—Lieut. Col. Carter Van Vleck, Seventy-eighth Illinois Infantry.

No. 205.—Lieut. George Green, Seventy-eighth Illinois Infantry.

No. 206.—Col. Daniel McCook, Fifty-second Ohio Infantry, commanding Second Brigade, Second Division.

No. 207.—Col. Caleb J. Dilworth, Eighty-fifth Illinois Infantry.

No. 208.—Lieut. Col. David W. Magee, Eighty-sixth Illinois Infantry.

No. 209.—Col. Oscar F. Harmon, One hundred and twenty-fifth Illinois Infantry.

No. 210.—Maj. James T. Holmes, Fifty-second Ohio Infantry.

No. 211.—Capt. Charles M. Barnett, Battery I, Second Illinois Light Artillery.
No. 212.—Brig. Gen. James G. Spears, U. S. Army, commanding Third Brigade, Third Division.
No. 213.—Maj. Gen. David S. Stanley, U. S. Army, Chief of Cavalry, Army of the Cumberland.
No. 214.—Brig. Gen. Robert B. Mitchell, U. S. Army, Chief of Cavalry.
No. 215.—Col. Edward M. McCook, Second Indiana Cavalry, commanding First Division, Cavalry Corps.
No. 216.—Col. Archibald P. Campbell, Fourth Michigan Cavalry, commanding First Brigade.
No. 217.—Maj. Leonidas S. Scranton, Second Michigan Cavalry.
No. 218.—Lieut. Col. Roswell M. Russell, Ninth Pennsylvania Cavalry.
No. 219.—Lieut. Col. James P. Brownlow, First Tennessee Cavalry.
No. 220.—Col. Daniel M. Ray, Second Tennessee Cavalry, commanding Second Brigade.
No. 221.—Maj. David A. Briggs, Second Indiana Cavalry.
No. 222.—Maj. George H. Purdy, Fourth Indiana Cavalry.
No. 223.—Lieut. William G. Anderson, Adjutant, Fourth Indiana Cavalry.
No. 224.—Col. Daniel M. Ray, Second Tennessee Cavalry.
No. 225.—Col. Oscar H. La Grange, First Wisconsin Cavalry.
No. 226.—Col. Louis D. Watkins, Sixth Kentucky Cavalry, commanding Third Brigade.
No. 227.—Brig. Gen. George Crook, U. S. Army, commanding Second Division.
No. 228.—Col. Robert H. G. Minty, Fourth Michigan Cavalry, commanding First Brigade.
No. 229.—Col. Eli Long, Fourth Ohio Cavalry, commanding Second Brigade.
No. 230.—Lieut. Col. Valentine Cupp, First Ohio Cavalry.
No. 231.—Itinerary of the Pioneer Brigade.
No. 232.—Record of the McCook Court of Inquiry.
No. 233.—Record of the Crittenden Court of Inquiry.
No. 234.—Record of the Negley Court of Inquiry.
[The Confederate reports appear in Part II.]

No. 1.

Report of Maj. Gen. Henry W. Halleck, U. S. Army, General-in-Chief.

HEADQUARTERS OF THE ARMY,
Washington, D. C., November 15, 1863.

SIR: In compliance with your orders, I submit the following summary of military operations since my last annual report:*

* * * * * * *

Having put the railroad in condition to forward supplies, Rosecrans, on the 16th of August, commenced his advance across the Cumberland Mountains, Chattanooga and its covering ridges on the southeast being his objective point. In order to command and avail himself of the most important passes, the front of his movement extended from the head of Sequatchie Valley, in East Tennessee, to Athens, Ala., thus threatening the line of the Tennessee River from Whitesburg to Blythe's Ferry, a distance of over 150 miles.

The Tennessee River was reached on the 20th of August, and Chattanooga shelled from the north bank on the 21st. Pontoon, boat, raft,

---

* Portion here omitted (relating to the Middle Tennessee Campaign) is printed in Series I, Vol. XXIII, Part I, p. 6.

and trestle bridges were rapidly prepared at Caperton's Ferry, Bridgeport, mouth of Battle Creek, and Shellmound, and the army, except cavalry, safely crossed the Tennessee in face of the enemy. By the 8th of September Thomas had moved on Trenton, seizing Frick's and Stevens' Gaps on the Lookout Mountain; McCook had advanced to Valley Head and taken Winston's Gap; while Crittenden had crossed to Wauhatchie, communicating on the right with Thomas, and threatening Chattanooga by the pass over the point of Lookout Mountain.

The first mountain barrier south of the Tennessee being successfully passed, General Rosecrans decided to threaten the enemy's communication with his right, while his center and left seized the gaps and commanding points of the mountains in front. General Crittenden's reconnaissance on the 9th developed the fact that the enemy had evacuated Chattanooga on the day and night previous.

While General Crittenden's corps took peaceable possession of Chattanooga, the objective point of the campaign, General Rosecrans, with the remainder of his army, pressed forward through the difficult passes of the Lookout and Missionary Mountains, apparently directing his march upon La Fayette and Rome.

On ascertaining these facts, and that General Burnside was in possession of all East Tennessee above Chattanooga, and hearing that Lee was being rapidly re-enforced on the Rapidan, it seemed probable that the enemy had determined to concentrate his forces for the defense of Richmond, or a new invasion of the North. The slight resistance made by him in East Tennessee, and his abandonment, without defense, of so important a position as Chattanooga, gave plausibility to the reports of spies and deserters from Lee's army of re-enforcements arriving there from Bragg.

Fearing that General Rosecrans' army might be drawn too far into the mountains of Georgia, where it could not be supplied, and might be attacked before re-enforcements could reach it from Burnside, I sent him, on the 11th, the following telegram:

HEADQUARTERS OF THE ARMY,
Washington, D. C., September 11, 1863—1.35 p. m.
Major-General ROSECRANS,
Chattanooga :

General Burnside telegraphs from Cumberland Gap that he holds all East Tennessee above Loudon, and also the gaps of the North Carolina mountains. A cavalry force is moving toward Athens to connect with you.

After holding the mountain passes on the west, and Dalton, or some other point on the railroad, to prevent the return of Bragg's army, it will be decided whether your army shall move farther south into Georgia and Alabama.

It is reported here by deserters that a part of Bragg's army is re-enforcing Lee. It is important that the truth of this should be ascertained as early as possible.
H. W. HALLECK,
General-in-Chief.

On the same day the following telegram was sent to General Burnside:

HEADQUARTERS OF THE ARMY,
Washington, D. C., September 11, 1863—2 p. m.
Major-General BURNSIDE,
Cumberland Gap :

I congratulate you on your successes.

Hold the gaps of the North Carolina mountains, the line of the Holston River, or some point, if there be one, to prevent access from Virginia, and connect with General Rosecrans, at least with your cavalry.*

---

* For paragraph, here omitted, see p. 149.

General Rosecrans will occupy Dalton or some point on the railroad to close all access from Atlanta, and also the mountain passes on the west.   This being done, it will be determined whether the movable forces shall advance into Georgia and Alabama, or into the Valley of Virginia and North Carolina.

H. W. HALLECK,
General-in-Chief.

On the 12th, General Rosecrans telegraphed that although he was "sufficiently strong for the enemy then in his front," there were indications that the rebels intended to turn his flanks and cut his communications.   He therefore desired that Burnside should move down his infantry toward Chattanooga on his left, and that Grant should cover the Tennessee River toward Whitesburg to prevent any raid on Nashville.   He was of opinion that no troops had been sent east from Bragg's army, but that Bragg was being re-enforced by Loring from Mississippi.

On the night of the 13th, General Foster telegraphed from Fort Monroe that "trains of cars had been heard running all the time, day and night, for the last thirty-six hours, on the Petersburg and Richmond road, evidently indicating a movement of troops in some direction;" and on the morning of the 14th, that Longstreet's corps was reported to be going south through North Carolina.   General Meade had been directed to ascertain, by giving battle if necessary, whether any of Lee's troops had left.   It was not till the 14th that he could give me any information on this point, and then he telegraphed:

My judgment, formed of the variety of meager and conflicting testimony, is, that Lee's army has been reduced by Longstreet's corps, and perhaps by some regiments from Ewell's and Hill's.

As soon as I received General Rosecrans' and General Foster's telegrams of the 12th and 13th, I sent the following telegrams to Generals Burnside, Rosecrans, Hurlbut, Grant, and Sherman :

HEADQUARTERS OF THE ARMY,
Washington, D. C., September 13, 1863—1 p. m.

Major-General BURNSIDE,
   Knoxville :

It is important that all the available forces of your command be pushed forward into East Tennessee.   All your scattered forces should be concentrated there.   So long as we hold Tennessee, Kentucky is perfectly safe.   Move down your infantry as rapidly as possible toward Chattanooga to connect with Rosecrans.   Bragg may merely hold the passes of the mountains to cover Atlanta, and move his main army through Northern Alabama to reach the Tennessee River and turn Rosecrans' right and cut off his supplies.   In this case he will turn Chattanooga over to you and move to intercept Bragg.

H. W. HALLECK,
General-in-Chief.

HEADQUARTERS OF THE ARMY,
Washington, D. C., September 13, 1863—1 p. m.

Major-General ROSECRANS,
  Chattanooga :

There is no intention of sending General Burnside into North Carolina.   He is ordered to move down and connect with you.   Should the enemy attempt to turn your right flank through Alabama, Chattanooga should be turned over to Burnside, and your army, or such part of it as may not be required there, should move to prevent Bragg from re-entering Middle Tennessee.   Hurlbut will aid you all he can, but most of Grant's available force is west of the Mississippi.

H. W. HALLECK,
General-in-Chief.

HEADQUARTERS OF THE ARMY,
Washington, D. C.. September 13, 1863—1.30 p. m.
(Received 22d.)
Major-General HURLBUT,* *Memphis:*

I think from all accounts that Steele is sufficiently strong. All your available forces should be sent to Corinth and Tuscumbia to operate against Bragg should he attempt to turn Rosecrans' right and recross the river into Tennessee. Send to General Sherman at Vicksburg for re-enforcements for this purpose. General Grant, it is understood, is sick in New Orleans.

H. W. HALLECK,
General-in-Chief.

HEADQUARTERS OF THE ARMY,
Washington, D. C., September 13, 1863—1.30 p. m.
(Received Memphis, 22d.)
Major-General GRANT* or
Major-General SHERMAN,
Vicksburg:

It is quite possible that Bragg and Johnston will move through Northern Alabama to the Tennessee River to turn General Rosecrans' right, and cut off his communications. All of General Grant's available forces should be sent to Memphis, thence to Corinth and Tuscumbia, to co-operate with Rosecrans should the rebels attempt that movement.†

H. W. HALLECK,
General-in-Chief.

On the 14th the following telegrams were sent to Generals Foster, Burnside, and Hurlbut :

HEADQUARTERS OF THE ARMY,
Washington, D. C., September 14, 1863—1 p. m.
Major-General FOSTER, *Fort Monroe:*

Information received here indicates that part of Lee's forces have gone to Petersburg. There are various suppositions for this. Some think it is intended to put down the Union feeling in North Carolina ; others, to make an attempt to capture Norfolk ; others, again, to threaten Norfolk, so as to compel us to send re-enforcements there from the Army of the Potomac, and then to move rapidly against Meade. Such was the plan last spring when Longstreet invested Suffolk. It will be well to strengthen Norfolk as much as possible and to closely watch the enemy's movements. I think he will soon strike a blow somewhere.

H. W. HALLECK,
General-in-Chief.

HEADQUARTERS OF THE ARMY,
Washington, D. C., September 14, 1863—3 p. m.
(Received 22d.)
Major-General HURLBUT,* *Memphis:*

There are good reasons why troops should be sent to assist General Rosecrans' right with all possible dispatch. Communicate with Sherman to assist you, and hurry forward re-enforcements as previously directed.

H. W. HALLECK,
General-in-Chief.

HEADQUARTERS OF THE ARMY,
Washington, D. C., September 14, 1863—3 p. m.
Major-General BURNSIDE, *Knoxville:*

There are reasons why you should re-enforce General Rosecrans with all possible dispatch. It is believed that the enemy will concentrate to give him battle You must be there to help him.

H. W. HALLECK,
General-in-Chief.

---

*This dispatch was delayed on the river between Cairo and Memphis, having left Cairo September 14, on the steamer Minnehaha, marked, "Important Government dispatches, to be delivered immediately." She failed to deliver the package.
†See answer, Grant to Halleck, September 25, 1863, 12 noon, Part III.

In addition to General Burnside's general instructions, a number of dispatches of the same purport as the above were sent to him. Generals Schofield and Pope were directed to send forward to the Tennessee line every available man in their departments; and the commanding officers in Indiana, Ohio, and Kentucky were ordered to make every possible exertion to secure General Rosecrans' line of communication. General Meade was urged to attack General Lee's army while in its present reduced condition, or at least to prevent him from sending off any more detachments.

It seemed useless to send any more troops into East Tennessee and Georgia, on account of the impossibility of supplying them in a country which the enemy had nearly exhausted. General Burnside's army was on short rations, and that of the Cumberland inadequately supplied. General Rosecrans had complained of his inadequate cavalry force, but the stables of his depots were overcrowded with animals, and the horses of his artillery, cavalry, and trains were dying in large numbers for want of forage.

As three separate armies were now to operate in the same field, it seemed necessary to have a single commander, in order to secure a more perfect co-operation than had been obtained with the separate commands of Burnside and Rosecrans. General Grant, by his distinguished services, and his superior rank to all the other generals in the West, seemed entitled to this general command; but, unfortunately, he was at this time in New Orleans, unable to take the field. Moreover, there was no telegraphic communication with him, and the dispatches of the 13th, directed to him and General Sherman, did not reach them until some days after their dates, thus delaying the movement of General Grant's forces from Vicksburg. General Hurlbut, however, had moved the troops of his own corps, then in West Tennessee, with commendable promptness. These were to be replaced by re-enforcements from Steele's corps in Arkansas, which also formed part of Grant's army.

Hearing nothing from General Grant, or from General Sherman's corps at Vicksburg, it was determined, on the 23d, to detach the Eleventh and Twelfth Corps from the Army of the Potomac, and to send them by rail, under the command of General Hooker, to protect General Rosecrans' line of communication from Bridgeport to Nashville. It was known that these troops could not go immediately to the front. To send more men to Chattanooga, when those already there could not be fully supplied, would only increase the embarrassment, and probably cause the evacuation of that place. In other words, Hooker's command was to temporarily perform the duties previously assigned to the re-enforcements ordered from Grant's army.

We will now return to General Rosecrans' army, the main body of which we left, on the 14th, in the passes of Pigeon Mountain, with the enemy concentrating his forces near La Fayette to dispute his further advance. Bragg's threatened movements to the right and left were merely cavalry raids to cut Rosecrans' line of supplies, and threaten his communications with Burnside. His main army was probably only awaiting the arrival of Longstreet's corps to give battle in the mountains of Georgia.

Of the movements of this corps, so well known to the enemy, we could get no reliable information. All we knew positively was, that one of Longstreet's divisions had arrived in Charleston to re-enforce that place. It was said that other divisions had gone to Mobile to protect it from an attack by Banks' army. But as there was no real danger of such an attack at that moment, it was more probably on its way to re-enforce Bragg's army. But the time of its arrival was uncertain, as we had no reliable information of its departure from Richmond. We knew that Bragg had been re-enforced by troops sent by Johnston from Mississippi, and it was afterward ascertained that the rebel authorities had falsely declared as exchanged and released from parole the prisoners of war captured by Grant and Banks at Vicksburg and Port Hudson. This shameless violation of the cartel, and of the well-established usages of civilized warfare, was resorted to by the enemy in order to swell the numbers of Bragg's army in the approaching conflict.

General Rosecrans' troops were at this time scattered along an extended line from Gordon's Mills to Alpine, a distance of some 40 miles. By the 17th they were brought more within supporting distance, and on the morning of the 18th a concentration was begun toward Crawfish Spring, but slowly executed.

The battle of Chickamauga commenced on the morning of the 19th, McCook's corps forming the right of our line of battle, Crittenden's the center, and Thomas' the left. The enemy first attacked our left with heavy masses, endeavoring to turn it, so as to occupy the road to Chattanooga; but all their efforts proved abortive. The center was next assailed, and temporarily driven back; but being promptly re-enforced, maintained its ground. As night approached, the battle ceased, and the combatants rested on their arms.

The attack was furiously renewed on the morning of the 20th, against our left and center. Division after division was pushed forward to resist the attacking masses of the enemy, when, according to General Rosecrans' report, General Wood, overlooking the direction—

To "close up" on Reynolds, supposed he was to support him by withdrawing from the line and passing in the rear of General Brannan.

By this unfortunate mistake a gap was opened in the line of battle, of which the enemy took instant advantage, and, striking Davis in flank and rear, threw his whole division into confusion.

General Wood claims that the orders he received were of such a character as to leave him no option but to obey them in the manner he did. Pouring in through this break in our line, the enemy cut off our right and right center, and attacked Sheridan's division, which was advancing to the support of our left. After gallant but fruitless efforts against this rebel torrent, he was compelled to give way, but afterward rallied a considerable portion of his force, and, by a circuitous route, joined General Thomas, who now had to breast the tide of battle against the whole rebel army. Our right and part of the center had been completely broken and fled in confusion from the field, carrying with them toward Chattanooga their commanders, Generals McCook and Crittenden, and also General Rosecrans, who was on that part of the line. His chief of staff, General Garfield, however, made his way to the left and joined General Thomas, who still remained immovable in his position. His line had assumed a crescent form, with its flanks supported by the lower spurs of the mountain, and here, like a lion at bay, he repulsed the terrible onsets of the enemy. About half past 3 p. m. the enemy discovered a gap in the hills in the rear of his right flank, and Longstreet commenced pouring his massive column through the opening. At this critical moment Maj. Gen. Gordon Granger, who had been posted with his reserves to cover our left and rear, arrived upon the field. He knew nothing of the condition of the battle, but, with the true instincts of a soldier, he had marched to the sound of the cannon. General Thomas merely pointed out to him the gap through which the enemy was debouching, when, quick as thought, he threw upon it Steedman's brigade of cavalry. In the words of General Rosecrans' official report—

Swift was the charge and terrible the conflict, but the enemy was broken. A thousand of our brave men, killed and wounded, paid for its possession, but we held the gap. Two divisions of Longstreet's corps confronted the position. Determined to take it, they successively came to the assault. A battery of six guns placed in the gorge poured death and slaughter into them. They charged to within a few yards of the pieces, but our grape and canister, and the leaden hail of our musketry, delivered in sparing but terrible volleys from cartridges taken, in many instances, from the boxes of their fallen companions, was too much even for Longstreet's men. About sunset they made their last charge, when our men, being out of ammunition, rushed on them with bayonet, and they gave way to return no more.

In the meantime the enemy made repeated attempts to carry General Thomas' position on the left and front, but were as often driven back with great loss. At nightfall the enemy fell back beyond the range of our artillery, leaving Thomas victorious on his hard-fought field.

As most of the corps of McCook and Crittenden had retreated to Chattanooga, it was deemed advisable also to withdraw the left wing to that place. Thomas consequently fell back during the night to Rossville, leaving the dead and most of the wounded in the hands of the enemy. He here received a supply of ammunition, and during all the 21st offered battle to the enemy; but the attack was not seriously renewed. On the night of the 21st he withdrew the remainder of the army within the defenses of Chattanooga.

The enemy suffered severely in these battles, and on the night of the 20th was virtually defeated; but being permitted to gather the trophies of the field on the 21st, he is entitled to claim a victory, however barren in its results. His loss in killed, wounded, and missing, as reported in rebel papers, was 18,000.

Our loss in these battles was 1,644 killed, 9,262 wounded, and 4,945 missing. If we add the loss of the cavalry, in its several engagements, at about 500, we have a total of 16,351. We lost in *matériel*, 36 guns, 20 caissons, 8,450 small-arms, and 5,834 infantry accouterments. We captured 2,003 prisoners.

After General Rosecrans' retreat to Chattanooga, he withdrew his forces from the passes of Lookout Mountain, which covered his line of supplies from Bridgeport. These were immediately occupied by the enemy, who also sent a cavalry force across the Tennessee above Chattanooga, which destroyed a large wagon train in the Sequatchie Valley, captured McMinnville and other points on the railroad, thus almost completely cutting off the supplies of General Rosecrans' army. Fortunately for us the line of railroad was well defended; and the enemy's cavalry being successfully attacked by Colonel McCook at Anderson's Cross-Roads on the 2d of October, by General Mitchell at Shelbyville on the 6th, and by General Crook at Farmington on the 8th, were mostly captured or destroyed.

Major-General Grant arrived at Louisville, and on the 19th, in obedience to the orders of the President, assumed general command of the Departments of the Tennessee, Cumberland, and Ohio. In accordance with his recommendation, Maj. Gen. G. H. Thomas was placed in the immediate command of the Department of the Cumberland, and Maj. Gen. W. T. Sherman of that of the Tennessee.

*   *   *   *   *   *   *

All of which is respectfully submitted.

H. W. HALLECK,
General-in-Chief.

Hon. E. M. STANTON, *Secretary of War.*

No. 2.

Organization of the Army of the Cumberland, commanded by Maj. Gen. William S. Rosecrans, at the battle of Chickamauga, Ga., September 19 *and* 20, 1863.

GENERAL HEADQUARTERS.

1st Battalion Ohio Sharpshooters, Capt. Gershom M. Barber.
10th Ohio Infantry, Lieut. Col. William M. Ward.
15th Pennsylvania Cavalry, Col. William J. Palmer.

FOURTEENTH ARMY CORPS.

Maj. Gen. GEORGE H. THOMAS.

GENERAL HEADQUARTERS.

Provost guard—9th Michigan Infantry,* Col. John G. Parkhurst.
Escort—1st Ohio Cavalry, Company L, Capt. John D. Barker.

FIRST DIVISION.

Brig. Gen. ABSALOM BAIRD.

First Brigade.

Col. BENJAMIN F. SCRIBNER.

38th Indiana, Lieut. Col. Daniel F. Griffin.
2d Ohio, Lieut. Col. Obadiah C. Maxwell, Maj. William T. Beatty, Capt. James Warnock.
33d Ohio, Col. Oscar F. Moore.
94th Ohio, Maj. Rue P. Hutchins.
10th Wisconsin, Lieut. Col. John H. Ely, Capt. Jacob W. Roby.

Second Brigade.

Brig. Gen. JOHN C. STARKWEATHER.

24th Illinois, Col. Geza Mihalotzy, Capt. August Mauff.
79th Pennsylvania, Col. Henry A. Hambright.
1st Wisconsin, Lieut. Col. George B. Bingham.
21st Wisconsin, Lieut. Col. Harrison C. Hobart, Capt. Charles H. Walker.

Third Brigade.†

Brig. Gen. JOHN H. KING.

15th United States, 1st Battalion, Capt. Albert B. Dod.
16th United States, 1st Battalion, Maj. Sidney Coolidge, Capt. R. E. A. Crofton.
18th United States, 1st Battalion, Capt. George W. Smith.
18th United States, 2d Battalion, Capt. Henry Haymond.
19th United States, 1st Battalion, Maj. Samuel K. Dawson, Capt. Edmund L. Smith.

Artillery.

Indiana Light, 4th Battery (2d Brigade), Lieut. David Flansburg, Lieut. Henry J. Willits.
1st Michigan Light, Battery A (1st Brigade), Lieut. George W. Van Pelt, Lieut. Almerick W. Wilbur.
5th United States, Battery H (3d Brigade), Lieut. Howard M. Burnham, Lieut. Joshua A. Fessenden.

---

* Not engaged ; guarding trains and performing provost duty.
† For composition of the battalions, see return of casualties, p. 171.

SECOND DIVISION.

Maj. Gen. JAMES S. NEGLEY.

First Brigade.

Brig. Gen. JOHN BEATTY.

104th Illinois, Lieut. Col. Douglas Hapeman.
42d Indiana, Lieut. Col. William T. B.
McIntire.
88th Indiana, Col. George Humphrey.
15th Kentucky, Col. Marion C. Taylor.

Second Brigade.

Col. TIMOTHY R. STANLEY.
Col. WILLIAM L. STOUGHTON.

19th Illinois, Lieut. Col. Alexander W.
Raffen.
11th Michigan, Col. William L. Stoughton, Lieut. Col. Melvin Mudge.
18th Ohio, Lieut. Col. Charles H. Grosvenor.

Third Brigade.

Col. WILLIAM SIRWELL.

37th Indiana, Lieut. Col. William D. Ward.
21st Ohio, Lieut. Col. Dwella M. Stoughton, Maj. Arnold McMahan, Capt. Charles
H. Vantine.
74th Ohio, Capt. Joseph Fisher.
78th Pennsylvania, Lieut. Col. Archibald Blakeley.

Artillery.

Illinois Light, Bridges' Battery (1st Brigade), Capt. Lyman Bridges.
1st Ohio Light, Battery G (3d Brigade), Capt. Alexander Marshall.
1st Ohio Light, Battery M (2d Brigade), Capt. Frederick Schultz.

THIRD DIVISION.

Brig. Gen. JOHN M. BRANNAN.

First Brigade.

Col. JOHN M. CONNELL.

82d Indiana, Col. Morton C. Hunter.
17th Ohio, Lieut. Col. Durbin Ward.
31st Ohio, Lieut. Col. Frederick W. Lister.
38th Ohio,* Col. Edward H. Phelps.

Second Brigade.

Col. JOHN T. CROXTON.
Col. WILLIAM H. HAYS.

10th Indiana, Col. William B. Carroll,
Lieut. Col. Marsh B. Taylor.
74th Indiana, Col. Charles W. Chapman,
Lieut. Col. Myron Baker.
4th Kentucky, Lieut. Col. P. Burgess
Hunt, Maj. Robert M. Kelly.
10th Kentucky, Col. William H. Hays,
Lieut. Col. Gabriel C. Wharton.
14th Ohio, Lieut. Col. Henry D. Kingsbury.

Third Brigade.

Col. FERDINAND VAN DERVEER.

87th Indiana, Col. Newell Gleason.
2d Minnesota, Col. James George.
9th Ohio, Col. Gustave Kammerling.
35th Ohio, Lieut. Col. Henry V. N. Boynton.

Artillery.

1st Michigan Light, Battery D (1st Brigade), Capt. Josiah W. Church.
1st Ohio Light, Battery C (2d Brigade), Lieut. Marco B. Gary.
4th United States, Battery I (3d Brigade), Lieut. Frank G. Smith.

*Not engaged ; train guard.

FOURTH DIVISION.

Maj. Gen. JOSEPH J. REYNOLDS.

First Brigade. *	*Second Brigade.*
Col. JOHN T. WILDER.	Col. EDWARD A. KING.
	Col. MILTON S. ROBINSON.
92d Illinois, Col. Smith D. Atkins.	68th Indiana, Capt. Harvey J. Espy.
98th Illinois, Col. John J. Funkhouser,	75th Indiana, Col. Milton S. Robinson,
Lieut. Col. Edward Kitchell.	Lieut. Col. William O'Brien.
123d Illinois, Col. James Monroe.	101st Indiana, Lieut. Col. Thomas Doan.
17th Indiana, Maj. William T. Jones.	105th Ohio, Maj. George T. Perkins.
72d Indiana, Col. Abram O. Miller.	

Third Brigade.

Brig. Gen. JOHN B. TURCHIN.

18th Kentucky, Lieut. Col. Hubbard K. Milward, Capt. John B. Heltemes.
11th Ohio, Col. Philander P. Lane.
36th Ohio, Col. William G. Jones, Lieut. Col. Hiram F. Devol.
92d Ohio, Col. Benjamin D. Fearing, Lieut. Col. Douglas Putnam, jr.

Artillery.

Indiana Light, 18th Battery (1st Brigade), Capt. Eli Lilly.
Indiana Light, 19th Battery (2d Brigade), Capt. Samuel J. Harris, Lieut. Robert S.
   Lackey.
Indiana Light, 21st Battery (3d Brigade), Capt. William W. Andrew.

TWENTIETH ARMY CORPS.

Maj. Gen. ALEXANDER McD. McCOOK.

GENERAL HEADQUARTERS.

Provost guard—81st Indiana Infantry, Company H, Capt. William J. Richards.
Escort—2d Kentucky Cavalry. Company I, Lieut. George W. L. Batman.

FIRST DIVISION.

Brig. Gen. JEFFERSON C. DAVIS.

First Brigade.†	*Second Brigade.*
Col. P. SIDNEY POST.	Brig. Gen. WILLIAM P. CARLIN.
59th Illinois, Lieut. Col. Joshua C. Win-	21st Illinois, Col. John W. S. Alexan-
ters.	der, Capt. Chester K. Knight.
74th Illinois, Col. Jason Marsh.	38th Illinois, Lieut. Col. Daniel H. Gil-
75th Illinois, Col. John E. Bennett.	mer, Capt. Willis G. Whitehurst.
22d Indiana, Col. Michael Gooding.	81st Indiana, Capt. Nevil B. Boone,
Wisconsin Light Artillery, 5th Battery,	Maj. James E. Calloway.
Capt. George Q. Gardner.	101st Ohio, Lieut. Col. John Messer, Maj.
	Bedan B. McDanald, Capt. Leon-
	ard D. Smith.
	Minnesota Light Artillery, 2d Battery,‡
	Lieut. Albert Woodbury, Lieut.
	Richard L. Dawley.

---

* Detached from its division and serving as mounted infantry.
† Not engaged ; guarding supply train.
‡ Capt. William A. Hotchkiss, chief of division artillery.

Third Brigade.

Col. HANS C. HEG.
Col. JOHN A. MARTIN.

25th Illinois, Maj. Samuel D. Wall, Capt. Wesford Taggart.
35th Illinois, Lieut. Col. William P. Chandler.
8th Kansas, Col. John A. Martin, Lieut. Col. James L. Abernathy.
15th Wisconsin, Lieut. Col. Ole C. Johnson.
Wisconsin Light Artillery, 8th Battery, Lieut. John D. McLean.

SECOND DIVISION.

Brig. Gen. RICHARD W. JOHNSON.

First Brigade.	*Second Brigade.*
Brig. Gen. AUGUST WILLICH.	Col. JOSEPH B. DODGE.
89th Illinois, Lieut. Col. Duncan J. Hall, Maj. William D. Williams.	79th Illinois, Col. Allen Buckner.
32d Indiana, Lieut. Col. Frank Erdelmeyer.	29th Indiana, Lieut. Col. David M. Dunn.
39th Indiana,* Col. Thomas J. Harrison.	30th Indiana, Lieut. Col. Orrin D. Hurd.
15th Ohio, Lieut. Col. Frank Askew.	77th Pennsylvania, Col. Thomas E. Rose, Capt. Joseph J. Lawson.
49th Ohio, Maj. Samuel F. Gray, Capt. Luther M. Strong.	Ohio Light Artillery, 20th Battery, Capt. Edward Grosskopff.
1st Ohio Light Artillery, Battery A, Capt. Wilbur F. Goodspeed.	

Third Brigade.

Col. PHILEMON P. BALDWIN.
Col. WILLIAM W. BERRY.

6th Indiana, Lieut. Col. Hagerman Tripp, Maj. Calvin D. Campbell.
5th Kentucky, Col. William W. Berry, Capt. John M. Huston.
1st Ohio, Lieut. Col. Bassett Langdon.
93d Ohio, Col. Hiram Strong, Lieut. Col. William H. Martin.
Indiana Light Artillery, 5th Battery, Capt. Peter Simonson.

THIRD DIVISION.

Maj. Gen. PHILIP H. SHERIDAN.

First Brigade.	*Second Brigade.*
Brig. Gen. WILLIAM H. LYTLE. Col. SILAS MILLER.	Col. BERNARD LAIBOLDT.
36th Illinois, Col. Silas Miller, Lieut. Col. Porter C. Olson.	44th Illinois, Col. Wallace W. Barrett.
88th Illinois, Lieut. Col. Alexander S. Chadbourne.	73d Illinois, Col. James F. Jaquess.
21st Michigan, Col. William B. McCreery, Maj. Seymour Chase.	2d Missouri, Maj. Arnold Beck.
24th Wisconsin, Lieut. Col. Theodore S. West, Maj. Carl von Baumbach.	15th Missouri, Col. Joseph Conrad.
Indiana Light Artillery, 11th Battery, Capt. Arnold Sutermeister.	1st Missouri Light Artillery, Battery G,† Lieut. Gustavus Schueler.

* Detached from its brigade and serving as mounted infantry.
† Capt. Henry Hescock, chief of division artillery.

Third Brigade.

Col. LUTHER P. BRADLEY.
Col. NATHAN H. WALWORTH.

22d Illinois, Lieut. Col. Francis Swanwick.
27th Illinois, Col. Jonathan R. Miles.
42d Illinois, Col. Nathan H. Walworth, Lieut. Col. John A. Hottenstein.
51st Illinois, Lieut. Col. Samuel B. Raymond.
1st Illinois Light Artillery, Battery C, Capt. Mark H. Prescott.

TWENTY-FIRST ARMY CORPS.

Maj. Gen. THOMAS L. CRITTENDEN.

GENERAL HEADQUARTERS.

Escort—15th Illinois Cavalry, Company K, Capt. Samuel B. Sherer.

FIRST DIVISION.

Brig. Gen. THOMAS J. WOOD.

First Brigade.

Col. GEORGE P. BUELL.

100th Illinois, Col. Frederick A. Bartleson, Maj. Charles M. Hammond.
58th Indiana, Lieut. Col. James T. Embree.
13th Michigan, Col. Joshua B. Culver,
Maj. Willard G. Eaton.
26th Ohio, Lieut. Col. William H.
Young.

*Second Brigade.**

Brig. Gen. GEORGE D. WAGNER.

15th Indiana, Col. Gustavus A. Wood.
40th Indiana, Col. John W. Blake.
57th Indiana, Lieut. Col. George W. Lennard.
97th Ohio, Lieut. Col. Milton Barnes.

Third Brigade.

Col. CHARLES G. HARKER.

3d Kentucky, Col. Henry C. Dunlap.
64th Ohio, Col. Alexander McIlvain.
65th Ohio, Lieut. Col. Horatio N. Whitbeck, Maj. Samuel C. Brown, Capt. Thomas Powell.
125th Ohio, Col. Emerson Opdycke.

Artillery.

Indiana Light, 8th Battery (1st Brigade), Capt. George Estep.
Indiana Light, 10th Battery* (2d Brigade), Lieut. William A. Naylor.
Ohio Light, 6th Battery (3d Brigade), Capt. Cullen Bradley.

SECOND DIVISION.

Maj. Gen. JOHN M. PALMER.

First Brigade.

Brig. Gen. CHARLES CRUFT.

31st Indiana, Col. John T. Smith.
1st Kentucky,† Lieut. Col. Alva R. Hadlock.
2d Kentucky, Col. Thomas D. Sedgewick.
90th Ohio, Col. Charles H. Rippey.

Second Brigade.

Brig. Gen. WILLIAM B. HAZEN.

9th Indiana, Col. Isaac C. B. Suman.
6th Kentucky, Col. George T. Shackelford, Lieut. Col. Richard Rockingham, Maj. Richard T. Whitaker.
41st Ohio, Col. Aquila Wiley.
124th Ohio, Col. Oliver H. Payne, Maj.
James B. Hampson.

---

* Stationed at Chattanooga, and not engaged.
† Five companies detached as wagon guard.

Third Brigade.

Col. WILLIAM GROSE.

84th Illinois, Col. Louis H. Waters.
36th Indiana, Lieut. Col. Oliver H. P. Carey, Maj. Gilbert Trusler.
23d Kentucky, Lieut. Col. James C. Foy.
6th Ohio, Col. Nicholas L. Anderson, Maj. Samuel C. Erwin.
24th Ohio, Col. David J. Higgins.

Artillery.

Capt. WILLIAM E. STANDART.

1st Ohio Light, Battery B (1st Brigade), Lieut. Norman A. Baldwin.
1st Ohio Light, Battery F (2d Brigade), Lieut. Giles J. Cockerill.
4th United States, Battery H (3d Brigade), Lieut. Harry C. Cushing.
4th United States, Battery M (3d Brigade), Lieut. Francis L. D. Russell.

Unattached.

110th Illinois (battalion),* Capt. E. Hibbard Topping.

THIRD DIVISION.

Brig. Gen. HORATIO P. VAN CLEVE.

First Brigade.

Brig. Gen. SAMUEL BEATTY.

79th Indiana, Col. Frederick Knefler.
9th Kentucky, Col. George H. Cram.
17th Kentucky, Col. Alexander M. Stout.
19th Ohio, Lieut. Col. Henry G. Stratton.

Second Brigade.

Col. GEORGE F. DICK.

44th Indiana, Lieut. Col. Simeon C. Aldrich.
86th Indiana, Maj. Jacob C. Dick.
13th Ohio, Lieut. Col. Elhannon M. Mast, Capt. Horatio G. Cosgrove.
59th Ohio, Lieut. Col. Granville A. Frambes.

Third Brigade.

Col. SIDNEY M. BARNES.

35th Indiana, Maj. John P. Dufficy.
 8th Kentucky, Lieut. Col. James D. Mayhew, Maj. John S. Clark.
21st Kentucky,† Col. S. Woodson Price.
51st Ohio, Col. Richard W. McClain, Lieut. Col. Charles H. Wood.
99th Ohio, Col. Peter T. Swaine.

Artillery.

Indiana Light, 7th Battery, Capt. George R. Swallow.
Pennsylvania Light, 26th Battery, Capt. Alanson J. Stevens, Lieut. Samuel M. Mc-
Dowell.
Wisconsin Light, 3d Battery, Lieut. Cortland Livingston.

---

* Not engaged.
† Stationed at Whiteside's, and not engaged.

RESERVE CORPS.

Maj. Gen. GORDON GRANGER.

FIRST DIVISION.

Brig. Gen. JAMES B. STEEDMAN.

First Brigade.	*Second Brigade.*
Brig. Gen. WALTER C. WHITAKER.	Col. JOHN G. MITCHELL.

First Brigade.

Brig. Gen. WALTER C. WHITAKER.

96th Illinois, Col. Thomas E. Champion.
115th Illinois, Col. Jesse H. Moore.
84th Indiana, Col. Nelson Trusler.
22d Michigan,* Col. Heber Le Favour, Lieut. Col. William Sanborn, Capt. Alonzo M. Keeler.
40th Ohio, Lieut. Col. William Jones.
89th Ohio,* Col. Caleb H. Carlton, Capt. Isaac C. Nelson.
Ohio Light Artillery, 18th Battery, Capt. Charles C. Aleshire.

Second Brigade.

Col. JOHN G. MITCHELL.

78th Illinois, Lieut. Col. Carter Van Vleck, Lieut. George Green.
98th Ohio, Capt. Moses J. Urquhart, Capt. Armstrong J. Thomas.
113th Ohio, Lieut. Col. Darius B. Warner.
121st Ohio, Lieut. Col. Henry B. Banning.
1st Illinois Light Artillery, Battery M, Lieut. Thomas Burton.

SECOND DIVISION.

Second Brigade.

Col. DANIEL McCOOK.

85th Illinois, Col. Caleb J. Dilworth.
86th Illinois, Lieut. Col. David W. Magee.
125th Illinois, Col. Oscar F. Harmon.
52d Ohio, Maj. James T. Holmes.
69th Ohio,* Lieut. Col. Joseph H. Brigham.
2d Illinois Light Artillery, Battery I, Capt. Charles M. Barnett.

CAVALRY CORPS.

Brig. Gen. ROBERT B. MITCHELL.

FIRST DIVISION.

Col. EDWARD M. McCOOK.

First Brigade.

Col. ARCHIBALD P. CAMPBELL.

2d Michigan, Maj. Leonidas S. Scranton.
9th Pennsylvania, Lieut. Col. Roswell M. Russell.
1st Tennessee, Lieut. Col. James P. Brownlow.

Second Brigade.

Col. DANIEL M. RAY.

2d Indiana, Maj. Joseph B. Presdee.
4th Indiana, Lieut. Col. John T. Deweese.
2d Tennessee, Lieut. Col. William R. Cook.
1st Wisconsin, Col. Oscar H. La Grange.
1st Ohio Light Artillery, Battery D (section), Lieut. Nathaniel M. Newell.

Third Brigade.

Col. LOUIS D. WATKINS.

4th Kentucky, Col. Wickliffe Cooper.
5th Kentucky, Lieut. Col. William T. Hoblitzell.
6th Kentucky, Maj. Louis A. Gratz.

---

*Temporarily attached.

SECOND DIVISION.

Brig. Gen. GEORGE CROOK.

First Brigade.

Col. ROBERT H. G. MINTY.

3d Indiana (battalion), Lieut. Col. Robert Klein.
4th Michigan, Maj. Horace Gray.
7th Pennsylvania, Lieut. Col. James J. Seibert.
4th United States, Capt. James B. McIntyre.

Second Brigade.

Col. ELI LONG.

2d Kentucky, Col. Thomas P. Nicholas.
1st Ohio, Lieut. Col. Valentine Cupp, Maj. Thomas J. Patten.
3d Ohio, Lieut. Col. Charles B. Seidel.
4th Ohio, Lieut. Col. Oliver P. Robie.

Artillery.

Chicago (Illinois) Board of Trade Battery, Capt. James H. Stokes.

No. 3.

*Report of Maj. Gen. William S. Rosecrans, U. S. Army, command-
ing the Army of the Cumberland.*

[OCTOBER —, 1863.]

THE OCCUPATION OF MIDDLE TENNESSEE AND PASSAGE OVER THE
CUMBERLAND MOUNTAINS.

The rebel army, after its expulsion from Middle Tennessee, crossed the Cumberland Mountains by way of the Tantallon and University roads, then moved down Battle Creek, and crossed the Tennessee River on bridges, it is said, near the mouth of Battle Creek and at Kelley's Ferry, and on the railroad bridge at Bridgeport. They destroyed a part of the latter after having passed over it, and re-tired to Chattanooga and Tyner's Station, leaving guards along the river. On their arrival at Chattanooga, they commenced imme-diately to throw up some defensive fieldworks at that place and also at each of the crossings of the Tennessee as far up as Blythe's Ferry.

Our troops, having pursued the rebels as far as supplies and the state of the roads rendered it practicable, took position from Mc-Minnville to Winchester, with advances at Pelham and Stevenson. The latter soon after moved to Bridgeport in time to save from total destruction a saw-mill there, but not to prevent the destruction of the railroad bridge.

After the expulsion of Bragg's forces from Middle Tennessee, the next objective point of this army was Chattanooga. It commands the southern entrance into East Tennessee, the most valuable if not the chief sources of supplies of coal for the manufactories and ma-chine-shops of the Southern States, and is one of the great gateways through the mountains to the champaign counties of Georgia and Alabama.

For the better understanding of the campaign, I submit a brief outline of the topography of the country from the barrens of the northwestern base of the Cumberland range to Chattanooga and its vicinity.

The Cumberland range is a lofty mass of rocks, separating the waters which flow into the Cumberland from those which flow into the Tennessee, and extending from beyond the Kentucky line, in a southwesterly direction, nearly to Athens, Ala. Its northwestern slopes are steep and rocky, and scalloped into coves, in which are the heads of numerous streams that water Middle Tennessee. Its top is undulating or rough, covered with timber, soil comparatively barren, and in dry seasons scantily supplied with water. Its southeastern slope, above Chattanooga, for many miles, is precipitous, rough, and difficult all the way up to Kingston. The valley between the foot of this slope and the river seldom exceeds 4 or 5 miles in width, and with the exception of a narrow border along the banks is undulating or hilly.

The Sequatchie Valley is along the river of that name, and is a cañon or deep cut, splitting the Cumberland range parallel to its length. It is only 3 or 4 miles in breadth and 50 miles in length. The sides of this valley are even more precipitous than the great eastern and western slopes of the Cumberland which have just been described. To reach Chattanooga from McMinnville or north of the Tennessee it is necessary to turn the head of this valley by Pikeville and pass down the Valley of the Tennessee, or to cross it by Dunlap or Therman.

That part of the Cumberland range between Sequatchie and the Tennessee, called Walden's Ridge, abuts on the Tennessee in high, rocky bluffs, leaving no practicable space sufficient for a good wagon road along the river. The Nashville and Chattanooga Railroad crosses that branch of the Cumberland range west of the Sequatchie, through a low gap, by a tunnel, 2 miles east of Cowan, down the gorge of Big Crow Creek to Stevenson at the foot of the mountain, on the Memphis and Charleston Railroad, 3 miles from the Tennessee and 10 miles from Bridgeport.

Between Stevenson and Chattanooga, on the south of the Tennessee, are two ranges of mountains, the Tennessee River separating them from the Cumberland, its channel a great chasm cut through the mountain masses, which in those places abut directly on the river. These two ranges are separated by a narrow valley, through which runs Lookout Creek.

The Sand Mountain is next the Tennessee and its northern extremity is called Raccoon Mountain. Its sides are precipitous and its top barren oak ridges, nearly destitute of water. There are but few, and these very difficult, wagon roads, by which to ascend and descend the slopes of this mountain.

East of Lookout Valley is Lookout Mountain a vast palisade of rocks rising 2,400 feet above the level of the sea, in abrupt, rocky cliffs, from a steep wooded base. Its eastern sides are no less precipitous. Its top varies from 1 to 6 or 7 miles in breadth, is heavily timbered, sparsely settled, and poorly watered. It terminates abruptly upon the Tennessee, 2 miles below Chattanooga, and the only practicable wagon roads across it are one over the nose of the mountain, at this point, one at Johnson's Crook, 26 miles distant, and one at Winston's Gap, 42 miles distant from Chattanooga.

Between the eastern base of this range and the line of the Chattanooga and Atlanta or Georgia State Railroad are a series of narrow valleys separated by smaller ranges of hills or low mountains, over which there are quite a number of practicable wagon roads running eastward toward the railroad.

The first of these ranges is Missionary Ridge, separating the waters of Chickamauga from Chattanooga Creek.

A higher range with fewer gaps, on the southeast side of the Chickamauga, is Pigeon Mountain, branching from Lookout, near Dougherty's Gap, some 40 miles south from Chattanooga. It extends in a northerly direction, bearing eastward until it is lost in the general level of the country, near the line of the Chattanooga and La Fayette road.

East of these two ranges and of the Chickamauga, starting from Ooltewah and passing by Ringgold to the west of Dalton, is Taylor's Ridge, a rough, rocky range, traversable by wagon roads only through gaps, generally several miles apart.

Missionary Ridge passes about 3 miles east of Chattanooga, ending near the Tennessee at the mouth of the Chickamauga. Taylor's Ridge separates the East Tennessee and Georgia Railroad from the Chattanooga and Atlanta Railroad.

The junction of these roads is at Dalton, in a valley east of Taylor's Ridge and west of the rough mountain region, in which are the sources of the Coosa River. This valley, only about 9 or 10 miles wide, is the natural southern gateway into East Tennessee, while the other valleys just mentioned terminate northwardly on the Tennessee to the west of it, and extend in a southwesterly direction toward the line of the Coosa, the general direction of which, from the crossing of the Atlanta road to Rome and thence to Gadsden, is southwest.

From the position of our army at McMinnville, Tullahoma, Decherd, and Winchester, to reach Chattanooga, crossing the Tennessee above it, it was necessary either to pass north of the Sequatchie Valley, by Pikeville or Kingston, or to cross the main Cumberland and the Sequatchie Valley, by Dunlap or Therman and Walden's Ridge, by the routes passing through these places, a distance from 65 to 70 miles, over a country destitute of forage, poorly supplied with water, by narrow and difficult wagon roads.

The main Cumberland range could also have been passed, on an inferior road, by Pelham and Tracy City to Therman.

The most southerly route on which to move troops and transportation to the Tennessee, above Chattanooga, was by Cowan, University, Battle Creek, and Jasper or by Tantallon, Anderson, Stevenson, Bridgeport, and the mouth of Battle Creek, to same point, and thence by Therman or Dunlap and Poe's Tavern, across Walden's Ridge. The University road, though difficult, was the best of these two, that by Cowan, Tantalon, and Stevenson being very rough between Cowan and Anderson and much longer.

There were also three roads across the mountains to the Tennessee River below Stevenson, the best but much the longest by Fayetteville and Athens, a distance of 70 miles.

The next, a very rough wagon road from Winchester, by Salem, to Larkinsville, and an exceedingly rough road by the way of Mount Top, one branch leading thence to Bellefonte and the other to Stevenson.

On these latter routes little or no forage was to be found except at the extremities of the lines, and they were also scarce of water. The one by Athens has both forage and water in abundance.

It is evident from this description of the topography that to reach Chattanooga, or penetrate the country south of it, on the railroad, by crossing the Tennessee below Chattanooga was a difficult task. It was necessary to cross the Cumberland Mountains, with subsistence, ammunition, at least a limited supply of forage, and a bridge train; to cross Sand or Raccoon Mountains into Lookout Valley, then Lookout Mountain, and finally the lesser ranges, Missionary Ridge, if we went directly to Chattanooga, or Missionary Ridge, Pigeon Mountain, and Taylor's Ridge, if we struck the railroad at Dalton or south of it. The Valley of the Tennessee River, though several miles in breadth between the bases of the mountains, below Bridgeport, is not a broad, alluvial farming country, but full of barren oak ridges, sparsely settled, and but a small part of it under cultivation.

OPERATIONS OF THE ARMY UNTIL IT REACHED THE TENNESSEE RIVER.

The first step was to repair the Nashville and Chattanooga Railroad, to bring forward to Tullahoma, McMinnville, Decherd, and Winchester needful forage and subsistence, which it was impossible to transport from Murfreesborough to those points over the horrible roads which we encountered on our advance to Tullahoma. The next was to extend the repairs of the main stem to Stevenson and Bridgeport, and the Tracy City branch, so that we could place supplies in depot at those points, from which to draw after we had crossed the mountains.

Through the zeal and energy of Colonel Innes and his regiment of Michigan Engineers, the main road was open to the Elk River Bridge by the 13th of July, and Elk River Bridge and the main stem to Bridgeport by the 25th, and the branch to Tracy City by the 13th of August.

As soon as the main stem was finished to Stevenson, Sheridan's division was advanced, two brigades to Bridgeport and one to Stevenson, and commissary and quartermaster stores pushed forward to the latter place with all practicable speed. These supplies began to be accumulated at this point in sufficient quantities by the 8th of August, and corps commanders were that day directed to supply their troops, as soon as possible, with rations and forage sufficient for a general movement.

The Tracy City branch, built for bringing coal down the mountains, has such high grades and sharp curves as to require a peculiar engine. The only one we had answering the purpose, having been broken on its way from Nashville, was not repaired until about the 12th of August. It was deemed best, therefore, to delay the movement of the troops until that road was completely available for transporting stores to Tracy City.

THE MOVEMENT OVER THE CUMBERLAND MOUNTAINS

began on the morning of the 16th of August, as follows:

General Crittenden's corps in three columns, General Wood, from Hillsborough, by Pelham, to Therman, in Sequatchie Valley.

General Palmer, from Manchester by the most practicable route to Dunlap.

General Van Cleve, with two brigades from McMinnville—the third being left in garrison there—by the most practicable route to Pikeville, the head of the Sequatchie Valley.

Colonel Minty's cavalry to move on the left by Sparta, to drive back Dibrell's cavalry toward Kingston, where the enemy's mounted troops, under Forrest, were concentrated, and then, covering the left flank of Van Cleve's column, to proceed to Pikeville.

The Fourteenth Army Corps, Maj. Gen. George H. Thomas commanding. moved as follows :

General Reynolds, from University, by way of Battle Creek, to take post concealed near its mouth.

General Brannan to follow him.

General Negley to go by Tantallon and halt on Crow Creek, between Anderson and Stevenson.

General Baird to follow him and camp near Anderson.

The Twentieth Corps, Maj. Gen. A. McD. McCook commanding, moved as follows:

General Johnson by Salem and Larkin's Fork to Bellefonte.

General Davis by Mount Top and Crow Creek, to near Stevenson.

The three brigades of cavalry by Fayetteville and Athens, to cover the line of the Tennessee from Whitesburg up.

On his arrival in the Sequatchie Valley, General Crittenden was to send a brigade of infantry to reconnoiter the Tennessee near Harrison's Landing, and take post at Poe's Cross-Roads. Minty was to reconnoiter from Washington down, and take post at Smith's Cross-Roads, and Wilder's brigade of mounted infantry was to reconnoiter from Harrison's Landing to Chattanooga and be supported by a brigade of infantry, which General Crittenden was to send from Therman to the foot of the eastern slope of Walden's Ridge, in front of Chattanooga.

These movements were completed by the evening of the 20th of August. Hazen's brigade made the reconnoissance on Harrison's Landing, and reported the enemy throwing up works there, and took post at Poe's Cross-Roads on the 21st. Wagner, with his brigade, supported Wilder in his reconnaissance on Chattanooga, which they surprised and shelled from across the river, creating no little agitation.

Thus the army passed the first great barrier between it and the objective point, and arrived opposite the enemy on the banks of the Tennessee.

THE CROSSING OF THE RIVER

required that the best points should be chosen, and means provided for the crossing. The river was reconnoitered, the pontoons and trains ordered forward as rapidly as possible, hidden from view in rear of Stevenson and prepared for use. By the time they were ready the places of crossing had been selected and dispositions made to begin the operation.

It was very desirable to conceal to the last moment the points of crossing, but as the mountains on the south side of the Tennessee rise in precipitous rocky bluffs to the height of 800 or 1,000 feet, completely overlooking the whole valley and its coves, this was next to impossible.

Not having pontoons for two bridges across the river, General Sheridan began trestlework for parts of one at Bridgeport, while

General Reynolds' division, seizing Shellmound, captured some boats, and from these and material picked up prepared the means of crossing at that point, and General Brannan prepared rafts for crossing his troops at the mouth of Battle Creek.

The laying of the pontoon bridge at Caperton's Ferry was very handsomely done by the troops of General Davis, under the directions of General McCook, who crossed his advance in pontoons at daylight, driving the enemy's cavalry from the opposite side. The bridge was ready for crossing by 11 a. m. the same day, but in plain view from the rebel signal stations opposite Bridgeport.

The bridge at Bridgeport was finished on the 29th of August, but an accident occurred which delayed its final completion till September 2.

THE MOVEMENT ACROSS THE RIVER

was commenced on the 29th and completed on the 4th of September, leaving the regular brigade in charge of the railroad and depot at Stevenson until relieved by Major-General Granger, who was directed, as soon as practicable, to relieve it and take charge of the rear.

General Thomas' corps was to cross as follows: One division at Caperton's and one at Bridgeport, Reynolds at Shellmound in boats, and one division at Battle Creek on rafts. All were to use the bridge at Bridgeport for such portions of their trains as they might find necessary, and to concentrate near Trenton, and send an advance to seize Frick's or Cooper's and Stevens' Gaps on the Lookout Mountain, the only practicable routes leading down the mountains into the valley called McLemore's Cove, which lies at its eastern base and stretches northeastwardly toward Chattanooga.

General McCook's corps was to cross two divisions at Caperton's Ferry, move to Valley Head, and seize Winston's Gap, while Sheridan was to cross at Bridgeport as soon as the bridge was laid and join the rest of his corps near Winston's, by way of Trenton.

General Crittenden's corps was ordered down the Sequatchie, leaving the two advanced brigades, under Hazen and Wagner, with Minty's cavalry and Wilder's mounted infantry to watch and annoy the enemy. It was to cross the river, following Thomas' corps at all three crossings, and to take post on the Murphy's Hollow road, push an advance brigade to reconnoiter the enemy at the foot of Lookout, and take post at Wauhatchie, communicating from his main body with Thomas on the right up the Trenton Valley and threatening Chattanooga by the pass over the point of Lookout.

The cavalry, crossed at Caperton's and a ford near Island Creek, were to unite in Lookout Valley, take post at Rawlingsville, and reconnoiter boldly toward Rome and Alpine.

These movements were completed by McCook's and Crittenden's corps on the 6th, and by Thomas' corps on the 8th of September. The cavalry for some reason was not pushed with the vigor nor to the extent which orders and the necessities of the campaign required. Its continual movement since that period and the absence of Major-General Stanley, the chief of cavalry, have prevented a report which may throw some light on the subject.

The first barrier south of the Tennessee being crossed, the enemy was found firmly holding the point of Lookout Mountain with infantry and artillery, while our force on the north side of the river reported the movement of the rebel forces from East Tennessee and their concentration at Chattanooga. To dislodge him from that place it was necessary to carry Lookout Mountain, or so to move as to compel him to quit his position by endangering his line of communication. The latter plan was chosen.

The cavalry was ordered to advance on our extreme right to Summerville, in Broomtown Valley, and General McCook was ordered to support the movement by a division of infantry thrown forward to the vicinity of Alpine, which was executed on the 8th and 9th of September.

General Thomas was ordered to cross his corps by Frick's or Cooper's and Stevens' Gaps and occupy the head of McLemore's Cove.

General Crittenden was ordered to reconnoiter the front of Lookout Mountain, sending a brigade up an almost impracticable path called the Nickajack trace to Summertown, a hamlet on the summit of the mountain overlooking Chattanooga, and holding the main body of his corps either to support these reconnaissances to prevent a sortie of the enemy over the nose of Lookout, or to enter Chattanooga in case the enemy should evacuate it or make but feeble resistance. Simultaneously with this movement, the cavalry was ordered to push by way of Alpine and Broomtown Valley and strike the enemy's railroad communication between Resaca bridge and Dalton.

These movements were promptly begun on the 8th and 9th of September. The reconnaissance of General Crittenden on the 9th developed the fact that the enemy had evacuated Chattanooga the day and night previous and his advance took peaceable possession at 1 p. m.

His whole corps, with its trains, passed around the point of Lookout Mountain on the 10th and encamped for the night at Rossville, 5 miles south of Chattanooga.

During these operations, General Thomas pushed his corps over the mountains at the designated points, each division consuming two days in the passage.

The weight of evidence, gathered from all sources, was that Bragg was moving on Rome, and that his movement began on the 6th of September. General Crittenden was therefore directed to hold Chattanooga, with one brigade, calling all the forces on the north side of the Tennessee across, and to follow the enemy's retreat vigorously, anticipating that the main body had retired by Ringgold and Dalton.

Additional information, obtained during the afternoon and the evening of the 10th of September, rendered it certain that his main body had retired by the La Fayette road, but uncertain whether he had gone far. General Crittenden was ordered, at 1 a. m. on the 11th, to proceed to the front and report, directing his command to advance only as far as Ringgold, and order a reconnaissance to Gordon's Mills. His report, and further evidence, satisfied me that the main body of the rebel army was in the vicinity of La Fayette.

General Crittenden was therefore ordered to move his corps, with all possible dispatch, from Ringgold to Gordon's Mills, and communicate with General Thomas, who had by that time reached the eastern foot of Lookout Mountain. General Crittenden occupied Ringgold during the 11th, pushing Wilder's mounted infantry as far as Tunnel Hill, skirmishing heavily with the enemy's cavalry. Hazen joined him near Ringgold on the 11th, and the whole corps moved rapidly and successfully across to Gordon's Mills on the 12th. Wilder following, and covering the movement, had a severe fight with the enemy at Leet's Tan-yard.

During the same day the Fourth U. S. Cavalry was ordered to move up the Dry Valley road, to discover if the enemy was in the proximity of that road on Crittenden's right, and open communication with Thomas' command, which, passing over the mountain, was debouching from Stevens' and Cooper's Gaps, and moving on La Fayette through Dug Gap of the Pigeon Mountain.

On the 10th, Negley's division advanced to within a mile of Dug Gap, which he found heavily obstructed, and Baird's division came up to his support on the morning of the 11th. Negley became satisfied that the enemy was advancing upon him, in heavy force, and perceiving that if he accepted battle in that position he would probably be cut off, he fell back after a sharp skirmish, in which General Baird's division participated, skillfully covering and securing their trains, to a strong position in front of Stevens' Gap. On the 12th, Reynolds and Brannan, under orders to move promptly, closed up to the support of these two advanced divisions.

During the same day General McCook had reached the vicinity of Alpine, and, with infantry and cavalry, had reconnoitered the Broomtown Valley to Summerville, and ascertained that the enemy had not retreated on Rome, but was concentrating at La Fayette.

Thus it was ascertained that the enemy was concentrating all his forces, both infantry and cavalry, behind the Pigeon Mountain, in the vicinity of La Fayette, while the corps of this army were at Gordon's Mills, Bailey's Cross-Roads, at the foot of Stevens' Gap, and at Alpine, a distance of 40 miles, from flank to flank, by the nearest practicable roads, and 57 miles by the route subsequently taken by the Twentieth Army Corps. It had already been ascertained that the main body of Johnston's army had joined Bragg, and an accumulation of evidence showed that the troops from Virginia had reached Atlanta on the 1st of the month, and that re-enforcements were expected soon to arrive from that quarter. It was therefore a matter of life and death to effect the

CONCENTRATION OF THE ARMY.

General McCook had already been directed to support General Thomas, but was now ordered to send two brigades to hold Dougherty's Gap, and to join General Thomas with the remainder of his command with the utmost celerity, directing his march over the road on the top of the mountain. He had, with great prudence, already moved his trains back to the rear of Little River, on the mountain, but, unfortunately being ignorant of the mountain road, moved down the mountain at Winston's Gap, down Lookout Valley to Cooper's Gap, up the mountain and down again, closing up with General Thomas on the 17th, and having posted Davis at Brooks', in front of Dug Gap, Johnson at Pond Spring, in front of Catlett's Gap, and Sheridan at the foot of Stevens' Gap.

As soon as General McCook's corps arrived General Thomas moved down the Chickamauga toward Gordon's Mills. Meanwhile, to bring General Crittenden within reach of General Thomas and beyond the danger of separation, he was withdrawn from Gordon's Mills, on the 14th, and ordered to take post on the southern spur of Missionary

Ridge, his right communicating with General Thomas, where he remained until General McCook had effected a junction with General Thomas.

Minty, with his cavalry, reconnoitered the enemy on the 15th and reported him in force at Dalton, Ringgold, and Leet's, and Rock Springs Church. The head of General McCook's column being reported near the same day, General Crittenden was ordered to return to his old position at Gordon's Mills, his line resting along the Chickamauga via Crawfish Spring.

Thus, on the evening of the 17th, the troops were substantially within supporting distance. Orders were given at once to move the whole line northeastwardly down the Chickamauga, with a view to covering the La Fayette road toward Chattanooga, and facing the most practicable route to the enemy's front.

The position of our troops and the narrowness of the roads retarded our movements. During the day while they were in progress, our cavalry, under Colonel Minty, was attacked on the left in the vicinity of Reed's Bridge, and Wilder's mounted infantry were attacked by infantry and driven into the La Fayette road.

It became apparent that the enemy was massing heavily on our left, crossing Reed's and Alexander's Bridges in force while he had threatened Gordon's Mills.

Orders were therefore promptly given to General Thomas to relieve General Crittenden's corps, posting one division near Crawfish Spring, and to move with the remainder of his corps by the Widow Glenn's house to the Rossville and La Fayette road, his left extending obliquely across it near Kelly's house.

General Crittenden was ordered to proceed with Van Cleve's and Palmer's divisions, to drive the enemy from the Rossville road and form on the left of General Wood, then at Gordon's Mills.

General McCook's corps was to close up on General Thomas, occupy the position at Crawfish Spring, and protect General Crittenden's right, while holding his corps mainly in reserve.

The main cavalry force was ordered to close in on General McCook's right, watch the crossing of the Chickamauga, and act under his orders.

The movement for the concentration of the corps more compactly toward Crawfish Spring was begun on the morning of the 18th, under orders to conduct it very secretly, and was executed so slowly that McCook's corps only reached Pond Spring at dark, and bivouacked, resting on their arms during the night. Crittenden's corps reached its position on the Rossville road near midnight.

Evidence accumulated during the day of the 18th that the enemy was moving to our left. Minty's cavalry and Wilder's mounted brigade encountered the enemy's cavalry at Reed's and Alexander's Bridges, and toward evening were driven into the Rossville road. At the same time the enemy had been demonstrating for 3 miles up the Chickamauga. Heavy clouds of dust had been observed 3 or 4 miles beyond the Chickamauga, sweeping to the northeast.

In view of all these facts, the necessity became apparent that General Thomas must use all possible dispatch in moving his corps to the position assigned it. He was therefore directed to proceed with all dispatch, and General McCook to close up to Crawfish Spring as soon as Thomas' column was out of the way. Thomas pushed forward uninterruptedly during the night, and at daylight the head of his column had reached Kelly's house on the La Fayette road, where

Baird's division was posted. Brannan followed, and was posted on Baird's left, covering the roads leading to Reed's and Alexander's Bridges.

At this point Colonel McCook, of General Granger's command, who had made a reconnaissance to the Chickamauga the evening before and had burned Reed's Bridge, met General Thomas, and reported that an isolated brigade of the enemy was this side of the Chickamauga, and, the bridge being destroyed, a rapid movement in that direction might result in the capture of the force thus isolated.

General Thomas ordered Brannan with two brigades to reconnoiter in that direction and attack any small force he should meet. The advance brigade, supported by the rest of the division, soon encountered a strong body of the enemy, attacked it vigorously, and drove it back more than half a mile, where a very strong column of the enemy was found, with the evident intention of turning our left and gaining possession of the La Fayette road between us and Chattanooga.

This vigorous movement disconcerted the plans of the enemy to move on our left, and opened the

BATTLE OF THE 19TH SEPTEMBER.

The leading brigade became engaged about 10 a. m. on the 19th, on our extreme left, and extending to the right, where the enemy combined to move in heavy masses. Apprehending this movement, I had ordered General McCook to send Johnson's division to Thomas' assistance. He arrived opportunely.

General Crittenden, with great good sense, had already dispatched Palmer's, reporting the fact to me, and received my approval. The enemy returned our attack, and was driving back Baird's right in disorder, when Johnson struck the attacking column in flank and drove it back more than a half a mile till his own right was overlapped, and in imminent danger of being turned, when Palmer, coming in on Johnson's right, threw his division against the enemy and drove back his advance columns.

Palmer's right was soon overlapped, when Van Cleve's division came to his support, but was beaten back, when Reynolds' division came in and was in turn overpowered. Davis' division came into the fight then, most opportunely, and drove the enemy, who soon, however, developed a superior force against his line and pressed him so heavily that he was giving ground, when Wood's division came and turned the tide of battle the other way.

About 3 p. m. General McCook was ordered to send Sheridan's division to support our line near Wood and Davis, directing Lytle's brigade to hold Gordon's Mills, our extreme right. Sheridan also arrived opportunely to save Wood from disaster, and the rebel tide was thoroughly staid in that quarter.

Meanwhile, the roar of musketry in our center grew louder, and evidently approached headquarters at Widow Glenn's house, until musket balls came near and shells burst about it. Our center was being driven.

Orders were sent to General Negley to move his division from Crawfish Spring and above, where he had been holding the line of the Chickamauga, to Widow Glenn's, to be held in reserve to give succor wherever it might be required. At 4.30 p. m. he reported with his division, and as the indications that our center was being driven became clearer, he was dispatched in that direction, and soon found the enemy had dislodged Van Cleve from the line, and was forming there even while Thomas was driving their right. Orders were promptly given Negley to attack him, which he soon did, and drove him steadily until night closed the combat.

General Brannan, having repulsed the enemy in our extreme left, was sent by General Thomas to support the center, and at night took a position on the right of Reynolds.

Colonel Wilder's brigade of mounted infantry occupied during the day a position on the La Fayette road, 1 mile north of Gordon's Mills, where he had taken position on the afternoon previous when, contesting the ground step by step, he had been driven by the enemy's advance from Alexander's Bridge.

Minty's cavalry had been ordered from the same position about noon of the 19th, to report to Major-General Granger, at Rossville, which he did at daylight on the 20th, and was posted near Mission Mills, to hold in check the enemy's cavalry on their right, from the direction of Ringgold and Graysville.

The Reserve Corps covered the approaches from the Chickamauga toward Rossville and the extension of our left.

The roar of battle hushed in the darkness of night, and our troops, weary with a night of marching and a day of fighting, rested on their arms, having everywhere maintained their positions, developed the enemy, and gained thorough command of the Rossville and Dry Valley roads to Chattanooga, the great object of the battle of the 19th of September.

The battle had secured us these objects. Our flanks covered the Dry Valley and Rossville roads, while our cavalry covered the Missionary Ridge and the Valley of Chattanooga Creek, into which latter place our spare trains had been sent on Friday, the 18th.

We also had indubitable evidence of the presence of Longstreet's corps and Johnston's forces, by the capture of prisoners from each, and the fact that at the close of the day we had present but two brigades which had not been opportunely and squarely in action, opposed to superior numbers of the enemy, assured us that we were greatly outnumbered, and that the battle the next day must be for the safety of the army and the possession of Chattanooga.

THE BATTLE OF THE 20TH.

During the evening of the 19th the corps commanders were assembled at headquarters at Widow Glenn's house, the reports of the positions and condition of their commands heard, and orders given for the disposition of the troops for the following day.

Thomas' corps, with the troops which had re-enforced him, was to maintain substantially his present line, with Brannan in reserve.

McCook, maintaining his picket line till it was driven in, was to close on Thomas, his right refused, and covering the position at Widow Glenn's, and Crittenden to have two divisions in reserve near the junction of McCook's and Thomas' lines to be able to succor either.

Plans having been explained, written orders given to each and read in the presence of all, the wearied corps commanders returned about midnight to their commands.

No firing took place during the night. The troops had assumed position when day dawned. The sky was red and sultry, the atmosphere and all the woods enveloped in fog and smoke. As soon as it was sufficiently light I proceeded, accompanied by General Garfield and some aides, to inspect the lines.

I found General McCook's right too far up on the crest, and General Davis in reserve on a wooded hill-side west of and parallel to the Dry Valley road. I mentioned these defects to the general, desiring Davis' division to be brought down at once, moved more to the left and placed in close column by division, doubled on the center, in a sheltered position.

I found General Crittenden's two divisions massed at the foot of the same hill in the valley and called his attention to it, desiring them to be moved farther to the left.

General Thomas' troops were in the position indicated, except Palmer's line was to be closed more compactly.

Satisfied that the enemy's first attempt would be on our left, orders were dispatched to General Negley to join General Thomas and to General McCook to relieve Negley. Returning to the right, I found Negley had not moved, nor were McCook's troops coming in to relieve him. Negley was preparing to withdraw his two brigades from the line. He was ordered to send his reserve brigade immediately and follow it with the others only when relieved on the line of battle. General Crittenden, whose troops were nearest, was ordered to fill General Negley's place at once, and General McCook was notified of this order growing out of the necessity of promptly sending Negley to Thomas.

Proceeding to the extreme right I felt the disadvantages of its positions, mentioned them to General McCook, and when I left him enjoined on him that it was an indispensable necessity that we should keep closed to the left, and that we must do so at all hazards.

On my return to the position of General Negley, I found to my astonishment that General Crittenden had not relieved him, Wood's division having reached the position of Negley's reserve. Peremptory orders were given to repair this, and Wood's troops moved into position, but this delay subsequently proved of serious consequence. The battle began on the extreme left at 8.30 a. m., and it was 9.30 o'clock when Negley was relieved.

An aide arriving from General Thomas, requesting that Negley's remaining brigades be sent forward as speedily as possible to succor the left, General Crittenden was ordered to move Van Cleve, with all possible dispatch, to a position in the rear of Wood, who closed in on Brannan's right. General McCook was ordered to move Davis up to close in on Wood, and fill an opening in the line.

On my return from an examination of the ground in the rear of our left center, I found to my surprise that General Van Cleve was posted in line of battle on a high ridge much too far to the rear to give immediate support to the main line of battle, and General Davis in line of battle in rear of the ridge occupied by Negley's reserve in the morning. General Crittenden was ordered to move Van Cleve at once down the hill to a better position, and General Davis was also ordered to close up the support of the line near Wood's right.

The battle, in the meanwhile, roared with increasing fury, and approached from the left to the center. Two aides arrived successively within a few minutes, from General Thomas, asking for re-enforcements. The first was directed to say that General Negley had already gone and should be near at hand at that time, and that Brannan's reserve brigade was available. The other was directed to say that General Van Cleve would at once be sent to his assistance, which was accordingly done.

A message from General Thomas soon followed, that he was heavily pressed, Captain Kellogg, aide-de-camp, the bearer, informing me at the same time that General Brannan was out of line, and General Reynolds' right was exposed. Orders were dispatched to General Wood to close up on Reynolds, and word was sent to General Thomas that he should be supported, even if it took away the whole corps of Crittenden and McCook.

General Davis was ordered to close on General Wood, and General McCook was advised of the state of affairs and ordered to close his whole command to the left with all dispatch.

General Wood, overlooking the direction to " close up " on General Reynolds, supposed he was to support him, by withdrawing from the line and passing to the rear of General Brannan, who, it appears, was not out of line, but was *en échelon*, and slightly in rear of Reynolds' right. By this unfortunate mistake a gap was opened in the line of battle, of which the enemy took instant advantage, and striking Davis in flank and rear, as well as in front, threw his whole division in confusion.

The same attack shattered the right brigade of Wood before it had cleared the space. The right of Brannan was thrown back, and two of his batteries, then in movement to a new position, were taken in flank and thrown back through two brigades of Van Cleve, then on the march to the left, throwing his division into confusion from which it never recovered until it reached Rossville.

While the enemy poured in through this breach, a long line stretching beyond Sheridan's right was advancing. Laiboldt's brigade shared in the rout of Davis. Sheridan's other two brigades, in movement toward the left, under orders to support Thomas, made a gallant charge against the enemy's advancing column, but were thrown into disorder by the enemy's line advancing on their flank, and were likewise compelled to fall back, rallying on the Dry Valley road, and repulsing the enemy, but they were again compelled to yield to superior numbers and retired westward of the Dry Valley road, and by a circuitous route reached Rossville, from which they advanced by the La Fayette road to support our left.

Thus Davis' two brigades, one of Van Cleve's, and Sheridan's entire division were driven from the field, and the remainder, consisting of the divisions of Baird, Johnson, Palmer, Reynolds, Brannan, and Wood, two of Negley's brigades and one of Van Cleve's, were left to sustain the conflict against the whole power of the rebel army, which, desisting from pursuit on the right, concentrated their whole efforts to destroy them.

At the moment of the repulse of Davis' division, I was standing in rear of his right, waiting the completion of the closing of McCook's corps to the left. Seeing confusion among Van Cleve's troops, and the distance Davis' men were falling back, and the tide of battle surging toward us, the urgency for Sheridan's troops to intervene became imminent, and I hastened in person to the extreme right, to direct Sheridan's movement on the flank of the advancing rebels. It was too late. The crowd of returning troops rolled back, and the enemy advanced. Giving the troops directions to rally behind the ridge west of the Dry Valley road, I passed down it accompanied by General Garfield, Major McMichael, Major Bond, and Captain Young, of my staff, and a few of the escort, under a shower of grape, canister, and musketry, for 200 or 300 yards, and attempted to rejoin General Thomas and the troops sent to his support, by passing to the rear of the broken portion of our lines, but found the routed troops far toward the left, and hearing the enemy's advancing musketry and cheers, I became doubtful whether the left had held its ground, and started for Rossville. On consultation and further reflection, however, I determined to send General Garfield there, while I went to Chattanooga, to give orders for the security of the pontoon bridges at Battle Creek and Bridgeport, and to make pre. liminary dispositions either to forward ammunition and supplies, should we hold our ground, or to withdraw the troops into good position.

General Garfield dispatched me, from Rossville, that the left and center still held its ground. General Granger had gone to its support. General Sheridan had rallied his division, and was advancing toward the same point, and General Davis was going up the Dry Valley road to our right. General Garfield proceeded to the front, remained there until the close of the fight, and dispatched me the triumphant defense our troops there made against the assaults of the enemy.

THE FIGHT ON THE LEFT,

after 2 p. m., was that of the army. Never, in the history of this war at least, have troops fought with greater energy and determination. Bayonet charges, often heard of but seldom seen, were repeatedly made by brigades and regiments in several of our divisions.

After the yielding and severance of the divisions of the right, the enemy bent all efforts to break the solid portions of our line. Under the pressure of the rebel onset, the flanks of the line were gradually retired until they occupied strong advantageous ground, giving to the whole a flattened crescent shape.

From 1 to half past 3 o'clock, the unequal contest was sustained throughout our line. Then the enemy in overpowering numbers flowed around our right, held by General Brannan, and occupied a low gap in the ridge of our defensive position, which commanded our rear. The moment was critical. Twenty minutes more and our right would have been turned, our position taken in reverse, and probably the army routed.

Fortunately, Major-General Granger, whose troops had been posted to cover our left and rear, with the instinct of a true soldier and a general, hearing the roar of battle on our left, and being beyond the reach of orders from the general commanding, determined to move to its assistance. He advanced and soon encountered the enemy's skirmishers, whom he disregarded, well knowing that, at that stage of the conflict, the battle was not there. Posting Col. Daniel McCook's brigade to take care of anything in the vicinity and beyond the left of our line, he moved the remainder to the scene of action, reporting to General Thomas, who directed him to our suffering right.

Arrived in sight, General Granger discovered at once the peril and the point of danger—the gap. Quick as thought he directed his advance brigade upon the enemy. General Steedman, taking a regimental color, led the column. Swift was the charge and terrible the conflict, but the enemy was broken. A thousand of our brave men, killed and wounded, paid for its possession, but we held the gap.

Two divisions of Longstreet's corps confronted the position. Determined to take it, they successively came to the assault. A battery of six guns, placed in the gorge, poured death and slaughter into them. They charged to within a few yards of the pieces, but our grape and canister, and the leaden hail of our musketry, delivered in sparing but terrible volleys from cartridges taken in many instances from the boxes of their fallen companions, was too much even for Longstreet's men. About sunset they made their last charge, when our men, being out of ammunition, rushed on them with bayonet, and they gave way to return no more.

The fury of the conflict was nearly as great on the fronts of Brannan and Wood, being less furious toward the left. But a column of the enemy had made its way to near our left and to the right of Colonel McCook's position. Apprised of this, General Thomas directed Reynolds to move his division from its position, and pointing out the rebels told him to go in there.

To save time, the troops of Reynolds were faced by the rear rank and moved with the bayonet at a double-quick, with a shout walked over the rebels, capturing some 500. This closed the battle of the 20th. At nightfall the enemy had been repulsed along the whole line, and sunk into quietude without attempting to renew the combat.

General Thomas, considering the excessive labors of the troops, the scarcity of ammunition, food, and water, and having orders from the general commanding to use his discretion, determined to retire on Rossville, where they arrived in good order, took post before morning, receiving supplies from Chattanooga, and offering the enemy battle during all the next day and repulsing his reconnaissance. On the night of the 21st we withdrew from Rossville, took firm possession of the objective point of our campaign—Chattanooga—and prepared to hold it.

The operations of the cavalry during the battle on the 19th were very important. General Mitchell, with three brigades, covered our right flank along the line of the Chickamauga, above Crawfish Spring, against the combined efforts of the great body of the rebel cavalry, whose attempts to cross the stream they several times repulsed.

Wilder fought, dismounted, near the center, intervening two or three times with mountain howitzers and Spencer rifles very opportunely.

On the 20th Minty covered our left and rear at Missionary Mills, and later in the day on the Ringgold road.

General Mitchell, with his three brigades, covered our extreme right, and with Wilder, after its repulse, extended over Missionary Ridge, held the whole country to the base of Lookout Mountain, and all our trains, artillery, caissons, and spare wagons sent there for greater safety retiring from the field. He was joined by Post's brigade of Davis' division, which had not closed on the army and was not in action.

On the 21st the cavalry still covered our right as securely as before, fighting and holding at bay very superior numbers. The number of cavalry combats during the whole campaign have been numerous, tho successes as numerous, but the army could not have dispensed with those of the 19th, 20th, and 21st.

OUR ARTILLERY

fired fewer shots than at Stone's River, but with even greater effect. I cannot but congratulate the country on the rapid improvement evidenced in this arm of the service. Our loss of pieces is, in part, attributable to the rough, wooded ground in which we fought, and the want of experience in posting artillery, and partly to the unequal nature of the contest, our infantry being heavily outnumbered.

For the details of these actions, the innumerable instances of distinguished bravery, skill, and gallantry displayed by officers of every rank, and, above all, for self-reliant, cool, and steady courage displayed by the soldiers of the army, in all arms, in many instances even shining above that of their officers, I must refer to the accompanying reports of the corps, division, brigade, regimental, and battery commanders. The reports of the cavalry command are not in, for the best of all reasons, that they have been out nearly ever since, writing with their sabers on the heads and backs of the enemy.

The signal corps has been growing into usefulness and favor daily for the last four months, and now bids fair to become one of the most esteemed of the staff services. It rendered very important service from the time we reached the Valley of the Tennessee. For its operations, I refer to the report of Capt. Jesse Merrill, chief signal officer.

Our medical corps proved very efficient during the whole campaign, and especially during and subsequent to the battle. A full share of praise is due to Dr. Glover Perin, the medical director of the department, ably assisted by Dr. Gross, medical director of the Fourteenth, Dr. Perkins, Twentieth, and Dr. Phelps, Twenty-first Army Corps.

A very great meed of praise is due Capt. Horace Porter, of the Ordnance, for the wise system of arming each regiment with arms of the same caliber, and having the ammunition wagons properly marked, by which most of the difficulties in supplying ammunition where troops had exhausted it in battle were obviated. From his report will be seen that we expended 2,650,000 rounds of musket cartridges, 7,325 rounds of cannon ammunition; we lost 36 pieces of artillery, 20 caissons, 8,450 stand of small-arms, 5,834 infantry accouterments; being 12,675 rounds less of artillery and 650,000 rounds more of musketry than at Stone's River.

From the report of Lieutenant-Colonel Wiles, provost-marshal-general, it will be seen that we took 2,005 prisoners. We have missing [4,945], of which some 600 have escaped and come in, and probably 700 or 800 are among the killed and wounded; of our wounded about 2,500 fell into the hands of the enemy, swelling the balance of prisoners against us to about 5,500.

It is proper to observe the battle of Chickamauga was absolutely necessary to secure our concentration and cover Chattanooga. It was fought in a country covered with woods and undergrowth, and wholly unknown to us. Every division came into action opportunely and fought squarely on the 19th. We were largely outnumbered, yet we foiled the enemy's flank movement on our left, and secured our own position on the road to Chattanooga. The battle of the 20th was fought with all the troops we had, and but for the extension and delay in closing in our right, we should probably have driven the enemy, whom we really beat on the field. I am fully satisfied that the enemy's loss largely exceeds ours.

It is my duty to notice the services of those faithful officers who have none but myself to mention them.

To Major-General Thomas, the true soldier, the prudent and undaunted commander, the modest and incorruptible patriot, the thanks and gratitude of the country are due for his conduct at the battle of Chickamauga.

Major-General Granger, by his promptitude, arrived and carried his troops into action in time to save the day. He deserves the highest praise.

Major-General McCook, for the care of his command, prompt and willing execution of orders, to the best of his ability, deserves this testimonial of my approbation.

I bear testimony likewise to the high-hearted, noble Major-General Crittenden. Prompt in the moving and reporting the position of his troops, always fearless on the field of battle, I return my thanks for the promptness and military good sense with which he sent his divisions toward the noise of battle on the 19th.

To Brig. Gen. James A. Garfield, chief of staff, I am especially indebted for the clear and ready manner in which he seized the points of action and movement, and expressed in orders the ideas of the general commanding.

Col. J. C. McKibbin, aide-de-camp, always efficient, gallant, and untiring, and fearless in battle.

Lieut. Col. A. C. Ducat, brave, prompt, and energetic in action.

Maj. Frank S. Bond, senior aide-de-camp; Capt. J. P. Drouillard, aide-de-camp; and Capt. R. S. Thoms, aide-de-camp, deserve very honorable mention for the faithful and efficient discharge of their appropriate duties always, and especially during the battle.

Col. James Barnett, chief of artillery; Lieut. Col. S. Simmons, chief commissary; Lieut. Col. H. C. Hodges, chief quartermaster; Dr. G. Perin, medical director; Capt. Horace Porter, chief of ordnance; Capt. William E. Merrill, chief topographical engineer, and Brig. Gen. J. St. Clair Morton, were all in the battle and discharged their duties with ability and to my entire satisfaction.

Col. William J. Palmer, Fifteenth Pennsylvania Cavalry, and his command, have rendered very valuable services in keeping open communications and watching the movements of the enemy, which deserve my warmest thanks.

Lieut. Col. W. M. Ward, with the Tenth Ohio, provost and headquarters guard, rendered efficient and valuable services, especially on the 20th, in covering the movement of retiring trains on the Dry Valley road, and stopping the stragglers from the fight. Captain Garner and the escort deserve mention for untiring energy in carrying orders.

Lieut. Col. C. Goddard, assistant adjutant-general; Lieut. Col. William M. Wiles, provost-marshal-general; Maj. William McMichael, assistant adjutant-general; Surg. H. H. Seys, medical inspector; Capt. D. G. Swaim, assistant adjutant-general, chief of the secret service; Capt. William Farrar, aide-de-camp; Capt. J. H. Young, chief commissary of musters; Capt. A. S. Burt, acting assistant inspector-general; Capt. Hunter Brooke, acting judge-advocate; Capt. W. C. Margedant, acting topographical engineer; Lieut. George Burroughs, topographical engineer; Lieut. William L. Porter, acting aide-de-camp; Lieut. James K. Reynolds, acting aide-de-camp; Lieut. M. J. Kelly, chief of couriers, and Asst. Surg. D. Bache were on the field of battle, and there and elsewhere discharged their duties with zeal and ability.

I must not omit Col. J. P. Sanderson, of the regular infantry, who, having lately joined us, on those two days of battle acted as aide-de-camp and carried orders to the hottest portions of the field.

Of those division and brigade commanders whose gallantry, skill, and services were prominent, individual special mentions accompany this report. A list of names of these and others of every grade whose, conduct according to the reports of their commanders, deserves special praise, is also herewith sent.

W. S. ROSECRANS,
Major-General.

[The ADJUTANT-GENERAL U. S. ARMY.]

[Inclosures.]

Report of Casualties in the Army of the Cumberland at the battle of the Chickamauga, Ga.

Command.	Killed.			Wounded.			Missing.			Aggregate.		
	Commissioned.	Enlisted.	Total.	Commissioned.	Enlisted.	Total.	Commissioned.	Enlisted.	Total.	Commissioned.	Enlisted.	Total.
Headquarters							2		2	2		2
Fourteenth Army Corps:												
First Division	14	161	175	43	672	715	75	1,179	1,254	132	2,012	2,144
Second Division	3	66	69	28	388	416	19	293	312	50	747	797
Third Division	15	310	325	91	1,542	1,633	7	194	201	113	2,046	2,159
Fourth Division	4	98	102	44	695	739	24	334	358	72	1,127	1,199
Total	36	635	671	206	3,297	3,503	127	2,000	2,127	369	5,932	6,301
Twentieth Army Corps:												
First Division	12	104	116	57	765	822	18	416	434	87	1,285	1,372
Second Division	15	120	135	56	945	1,001	31	462	493	102	1,527	1,629
Third Division	13	139	152	55	657	712	28	625	653	96	1,421	1,517
Total	40	363	403	168	2,367	2,535	77	1,503	1,580	285	4,233	4,518
Twenty-first Army Corps:												
First Division	14	116	130	41	672	713	7	184	191	62	972	1,034
Second Division	18	132	150	56	944	1,000	4	195	199	78	1,271	1,349
Third Division	7	48	55	34	541	575	11	276	287	52	865	917
Total	39	296	335	131	2,157	2,288	22	655	677	192	3,108	3,300
Reserve Corps:												
First Division	16	219	235	59	877	936	34	527	561	109	1,623	1,732
Total	16	219	235	59	877	936	34	527	561	109	1,623	1,732
RECAPITULATION.												
Fourteenth Army Corps	36	635	671	206	3,297	3,503	127	2,000	2,127	369	5,932	6,301
Twentieth Army Corps	40	363	403	168	2,367	2,535	77	1,503	1,580	285	4,233	4,518
Twenty-first Army Corps	39	296	335	131	2,157	2,288	22	655	677	192	3,108	3,300
Reserve Corps	16	219	235	59	877	936	34	527	561	109	1,623	1,732
Grand total*	131	1,513	1,644	564	8,698	9,262	260	4,685	4,945	955	14,896	15,851
Cavalry, estimated at												500
Total Department*												16,351

*See revised statement, p. 171.

HEADQUARTERS DEPARTMENT OF THE CUMBERLAND,
Crawfish Spring, September 18, 1863—12.40 p. m.

Major-General THOMAS,
Commanding Fourteenth Army Corps:

GENERAL : The enemy is advancing on General Wood at Gordon's Mills with cavalry and infantry. He opened on the rebel column a few minutes ago with artillery and they fell back. Colonel Minty's pickets have been driven in, and he is now skirmishing heavily with what appears to be both cavalry and infantry. He is at Reed's Mill, between Gordon's Mills and Ringgold. It is probable that the enemy is attempting to turn our left. The general commanding directs you to hold your command in readiness to come over to Crittenden's support, if it shall be necessary. In that case McCook will close up and occupy your newly assigned position.

Very respectfully, your obedient servant,
J. A. GARFIELD,
Brigadier-General, Chief of Staff.

—

HEADQUARTERS DEPARTMENT OF THE CUMBERLAND,
Crawfish Spring, September 18, 1863—1 p. m.

Major-General McCOOK :

GENERAL : The enemy is making a heavy demonstration on our left. It is not yet clear whether he means to strike us here, or is merely making a feint preparatory to striking a blow elsewhere. The general commanding thinks it prudent in you to stop Lytle in his march at the top or foot of Stevens' Gap, or in case he has passed too far to be returned with ease, that you see in some other way to the support of the cavalry which is guarding that pass until the plans of the enemy are more fully developed. He must not get the mountain road.

Very respectfully, your obedient servant,
J. A. GARFIELD,
Brigadier-General, Chief of Staff.

—

HEADQUARTERS DEPARTMENT OF THE CUMBERLAND,
Crawfish Spring, September 18, 1863—1.20 p. m.

Major-General THOMAS,
Commanding Fourteenth Army Corps:

GENERAL : The general commanding desires that the movement indicated in the orders of this morning should be executed with utmost promptness. General Negley should be in position very soon.

Very respectfully, your obedient servant,
J. A. GARFIELD,
Brigadier-General, Chief of Staff.

HEADQUARTERS DEPARTMENT OF THE CUMBERLAND,
Crawfish Spring, September 18, 1863—3.45 p. m.

Major-General GRANGER :*

The general commanding directs that you send another brigade out toward Minty in direction of Reed's Bridge, to assist him in falling back if necessary.

Very respectfully, your obedient servant,
J. A. GARFIELD,
Brigadier-General, Chief of Staff.

—

HEADQUARTERS DEPARTMENT OF THE CUMBERLAND,
Crawfish Spring, September 19, 1863—10 a. m.

Major-General McCOOK:

From present indications the general commanding thinks you had better make your dispositions to relieve General Negley and hold the right.   He sends you this that you need not get too far from water.

Very respectfully, your obedient servant,
J. A. GARFIELD,
Brigadier-General, Chief of Staff.

—

HEADQUARTERS DEPARTMENT OF THE CUMBERLAND,
Widow Glenn's House, September 19, 1863—11.30 a. m.

Major-General THOMAS,
Commanding Fourteenth Army Corps:

General Johnson's division is here moving to your support.   Send back an officer to conduct it to the position you desire.

J. A. G[ARFIELD].

—

HEADQUARTERS DEPARTMENT OF THE CUMBERLAND,
Widow Glenn's, September 19, 1863—noon

Major-General THOMAS,
Commanding Fourteenth Army Corps:

The general commanding desires you to inform him of the general direction of your line of battle.   He suggests that it should be *en échelon* in the general direction of northwest and southeast, with your left hugging the mountain and keeping your right refused. This is based on the supposition that Bragg has formed a line facing westward, and is attempting to turn your left by the Ringgold road. Of course circumstances should modify your position.

J. A. G[ARFIELD].

—

HEADQUARTERS DEPARTMENT OF THE CUMBERLAND,
Widow Glenn's, September 19, 1863—1 p. m.

Major-General McCOOK,
Commanding Twentieth Army Corps:

General Thomas is heavily engaged, and Palmer and Johnson have been ordered up to support him.   All goes well thus far.   A con

* For reply see Russell to Garfield, September 18, and Granger to Garfield, 4.30 p. m., September 18, p. 116.

siderable cavalry force of the enemy has got in behind us, and are threatening some of our trains. The general commanding directs you to hurry Mitchell's cavalry in upon our right, and send a detachment to look out for our rear.

J. A. G[ARFIELD].

—

HEADQUARTERS DEPARTMENT OF THE CUMBERLAND,
Widow Glenn's, September 19, 1863—1.45 p. m.
Major-General McCOOK,
Commanding Twentieth Army Corps:
Your dispatch of 1.30 p. m. is received. The general commanding directs you to move Generals Negley and Sheridan this way. Send a brigade to relieve Crittenden and hold Gordon's Mills. Perhaps Sheridan may be spared to move up that way and be ready for emergencies. Send the forces that you are to spare to General Thomas at once.

J. A. G[ARFIELD].

—

HEADQUARTERS DEPARTMENT OF THE CUMBERLAND,
Widow Glenn's, September 19, 1863—2.42 p. m.
Major-General McCOOK,
Commanding Twentieth Army Corps:
The tide of battle sweeps to the right. The general commanding thinks you can now move the two brigades of Sheridan's up to this place. Leave the one brigade posted at Gordon's Mills, to be used there or this way, as circumstances may require. If the right is secure, come forward and direct your forces now fighting.

J. A. G[ARFIELD].

—

HEADQUARTERS DEPARTMENT OF THE CUMBERLAND,
Widow Glenn's, September 19, 1863—3.10 p. m.
Major-General THOMAS,
Commanding Fourteenth Army Corps:
The tide of battle sweeps to the right, and the center is heavily engaged. Crittenden is doing finely on the right. Your dispatch of 3 p. m. is just received when the above was written. All goes well. Save every available man for reserves who is not needed for work now. If your left is not likely to be threatened soon throw some forces in rear of your center as reserves. Communicate with Granger. Push the enemy.

J. A. G[ARFIELD].

—

HEADQUARTERS DEPARTMENT OF THE CUMBERLAND,
Widow Glenn's, September 19, 1863—3.45 p. m.
Major-General CRITTENDEN,
Commanding Twenty-first Army Corps:
General Davis is being heavily pressed, or was when the messenger left. Assist him if you can by a movement of some of your command.

J. A. G[ARFIELD].

HEADQUARTERS DEPARTMENT OF THE CUMBERLAND,
Widow Glenn's, September 19, 1863—4 p. m.
Brigadier-General MITCHELL,
Commanding Cavalry:

The general commanding directs you to bring up every available cavalryman, except one battalion, to be left at Stevens' Gap. Do this without a moment's delay. We need all your help to guard our right and rear.

J. A. G[ARFIELD],
Brigadier-General, Chief of Staff.

—

HEADQUARTERS DEPARTMENT OF THE CUMBERLAND,
Widow Glenn's, September 19, 1863—4.25 p. m.
Major-General THOMAS,
Commanding Fourteenth Army Corps:

General Negley has arrived and is just going in to the left of this place. There seems to be a gap in our line. Van Cleve has been driven in, but is now rallying. We have not heard from you for some time. Is the left clear of rebels? Do you know anything of the gap in the line referred to above?

J. A. G[ARFIELD].

—

HEADQUARTERS DEPARTMENT OF THE CUMBERLAND,
Via Widow Glenn's, September 19, 1863—5 p. m.
Major-General THOMAS,
Commanding Fourteenth Army Corps:

The general commanding is very anxious to hear from you. There is a break in the line between you and this place, and we do not yet know how it occurred. Where is Palmer, and how is he posted? Let us know from you at once.

J. A. G[ARFIELD].

—

HEADQUARTERS DEPARTMENT OF THE CUMBERLAND,
September 19, 1863—6.30 p. m.
Brigadier-General MITCHELL,
Commanding Cavalry:

The general commanding directs you to protect the hospital at Crawfish Spring, and give the surgeons any assistance they may need.

J. A. G[ARFIELD].

—

HEADQUARTERS DEPARTMENT OF THE CUMBERLAND,
September 19, 1863—7.30 p. m.
Colonel MINTY,
Commanding Cavalry Brigade:

Two orders have been sent you to-day to report to General Granger at Rossville. Why have you not done so? Since you are now at General Thomas', as stated in your dispatch of 7 p. m., you may take orders from General Thomas for the present.

J. A. G[ARFIELD].

HEADQUARTERS DEPARTMENT OF THE CUMBERLAND,
Widow Glenn's House, September 19, 1863—10.20 p. m.
[General GORDON GRANGER]:

GENERAL : The general commanding directs me to inform you that General McCook has been ordered to hold this gap to-morrow, crossing the Dry Valley road, his right resting near this place, his left connecting with General Thomas' right. The general places your corps in reserve to-morrow, and directs you to post it on the eastern slope of Missionary Ridge to support McCook or Thomas. Leave the grand guards from your command out, with instructions to hold their ground until driven in, and then to return slowly, contesting the ground stubbornly.

Very respectfully, your obedient servant,
J. A. GARFIELD,
Brigadier-General, Chief of Staff.

(Same to Major-General Crittenden, 10.20 p. m.)

—

HEADQUARTERS DEPARTMENT OF THE CUMBERLAND,
Widow Glenn's, September 19, 1863—11.45 p. m.
Major-General THOMAS:

The line of battle for to-morrow is your present line, and a line which General McCook will form from your right to this place. General Crittenden will be held in reserve on the eastern slope of Missionary Ridge, in rear of your right. You will defend your position with the utmost stubbornness. In case our army should be overwhelmed it will retire on Rossville and Chattanooga. Send your trains back to the latter place.

Respectfully,

J. A. GARFIELD,
Brigadier-General, Chief of Staff.

—

HEADQUARTERS DEPARTMENT OF THE CUMBERLAND,
Widow Glenn's, September 19, 1863.
Brigadier-General MITCHELL, *Comdg. Cavalry:*

The general commanding directs you to bring up to your present position every available cavalryman, except one battalion, to be left at Stevens' Gap. Do this without a moment's delay. We need all your help to guard our right and rear.

J. A. GARFIELD.

—

HEADQUARTERS DEPARTMENT OF THE CUMBERLAND,
McDonald's House, September 20, 1863—6.30 a. m.
Major-General NEGLEY,
Comdg. Second Division, Fourteenth Army Corps:

The general commanding directs you to report with your command to General Thomas at once. You are to be posted on his extreme left. Send a staff officer to show General McCook your present position, who is directed to occupy it. Move with dispatch, gathering up all your stragglers.

Very respectfully, your obedient servant,
J. A. GARFIELD,
Brigadier-General, Chief of Staff.

HEADQUARTERS DEPARTMENT OF THE CUMBERLAND,
McDonald's House, September 20, 1863—6.35 a. m.

General McCook,
Commanding Twentieth Army Corps:

General Negley's division has been ordered to General Thomas' left. The general commanding directs you to fill the space left vacant by his removal, if practicable. The enemy appears to be moving toward our left.

Very respectfully, your obedient servant.

J. A. GARFIELD,
Brigadier-General, Chief of Staff.

—

HEADQUARTERS DEPARTMENT OF THE CUMBERLAND,
September 21 [20], 1863—10.10 a. m.

Major-General McCook,
Commanding Twentieth Army Corps:

General Thomas is being heavily pressed on the left. The general commanding directs you to make immediate disposition to withdraw the right, so as to spare as much force as possible to re-enforce Thomas. The left must be held at all hazards—even if the right is drawn wholly back to the present left. Select a good position back this way, and be ready to start re-enforcements to Thomas at a moment's warning.

J. A. G[ARFIELD].

—

HEADQUARTERS DEPARTMENT OF THE CUMBERLAND,
In the Field, September 20, 1863—10.30 a. m.

Major-General McCook,
Commanding Twentieth Army Corps:

The general commanding directs you to send two brigades, General Sheridan's division, at once and with all dispatch to support General Thomas, and send the third brigade as soon as the line can be drawn up sufficiently. March them as rapidly as you can without exhausting the men. Report to these headquarters as soon as your orders are given in regard to Sheridan's movement. Have you any news from Colonel Post ?

J. A. G[ARFIELD].

—

HEADQUARTERS DEPARTMENT OF THE CUMBERLAND,
September 20, 1863—10.35 a. m.

Major-General THOMAS,*
Commanding Fourteenth Army Corps:

The general commanding directs me to say, if possible, refuse your left, sending in your reserves to the northward, as he would prefer having Crittenden and McCook on your right.

Very respectfully, your obedient servant,

FRANK S. BOND,
Major, and Aide-de-Camp.

---

* See duplicate, with indorsement, p. 139.

HEADQUARTERS DEPARTMENT OF THE CUMBERLAND,
In the Field, September 20, 1863—10.45 a. m.

Major-General CRITTENDEN,
Commanding Twenty-first Army Corps:

The general commanding directs you to send General Van Cleve's command to General Thomas' support with all dispatch. General Van Cleve will put his force in on General Thomas' left as quickly as he can do so without exhausting the men too much.

J. A. G[ARFIELD].

—

HEADQUARTERS DEPARTMENT OF THE CUMBERLAND,
Chattanooga, September 20, 1863.

Brigadier-General GARFIELD,
Chief of Staff, Rossville:

Your dispatch of 3.45 received. What you propose is correct. I have seen Farch, who left at 5 p. m. I trust General Thomas has been able to hold his position. Ammunition will be sent up.

W. S. R[OSECRANS].

—

HEADQUARTERS DEPARTMENT OF THE CUMBERLAND,
Chattanooga, September 20, 1863.

Colonel WILDER,
Commanding Brigade:

The general commanding directs that you order one of your regiments to report to Brigadier-General Wagner, commanding this post, to conduct prisoners.

Very respectfully,

J. P. DROUILLARD,
Captain, and Aide-de-Camp.

—

HEADQUARTERS DEPARTMENT OF THE CUMBERLAND,
Chattanooga, Tenn., September 20, 1863—7.15 p. m.

Brigadier-General MITCHELL,
Commanding Cavalry:

You must watch the movements of Wheeler, lest he goes over the mountains and seize our bridges. If you can spare a cavalry force, pitch into the enemy's left flank. Crook ought to be sufficient to watch Wheeler. I leave to your good judgment what should be done. You will be able to accomplish these two. Hang on the flank of the enemy's infantry, reporting his movements. Let me hear from you often. Had you been on our right to-day you could have charged the enemy's flank and done much incalculable mischief.

W. S. R[OSECRANS],
Major-General.

—

HEADQUARTERS DEPARTMENT OF THE CUMBERLAND,
Chattanooga, September 21, 1863.

General R. B. MITCHELL:

The general commanding directs you to move your command, except one brigade, back immediately and without the least noise

and cross the bridge over Chattanooga Creek at the tan-yard.
Leave one brigade and your grand guards to cover your movement
and fight their way in if necessary.   Your infantry support must halt
at the forks of the roads at the foot of the mountain and take a good
position to repel all cavalry.   This is in consequence of the retiring
of our troops from Rossville, except a strong rear guard, and a line
of pickets to retire as skirmishers and see that the road may not be
blocked so as to prevent the crossing of the creek should the enemy
push rapidly through the gap at Rossville.   Send staff officers in
advance to look out the fords of Chattanooga Creek above the bridge
and blaze the trees.

By order of General Rosecrans:

C. GODDARD,
Assistant Adjutant-General.

—

HEADQUARTERS DEPARTMENT OF THE CUMBERLAND,
Chattanooga, September 22, 1863.
[General THOMAS:]

GENERAL: The general commanding directs that the two regiments on Missionary Ridge be left there by all means.   General
Garfield directed them to be recalled this morning through mistake.
It is our picket line there, and it is to be contested inch by inch.
The general commanding wants a good officer with the grand guards
at that point.   Please countermand the order to relieve them, and
have a good line selected for defense and a clear way to retreat
should it be necessary.

Very respectfully,

J. P. DROUILLARD,
Captain, and Aide-de-Camp.

———

HEADQUARTERS DEPARTMENT OF THE CUMBERLAND,
Chattanooga, Tenn., October 16, 1863.

SIR: I transmit inclosed copies of dispatches which are to accompany my last official report, in addition to those already sent
with it.

W. S. ROSECRANS,
Major-General, Commanding.

ADJUTANT-GENERAL U. S. ARMY.

[Inclosures.]

HDQRS. DEPARTMENT OF THE CUMBERLAND,
Crawfish Spring, September 18, 1863—12.15 p. m.
(Received 12.30.)

Major-General McCOOK:

The general commanding directs me to say that there are some
appearances that the enemy are endeavoring to turn our left, in
which case you will hold your corps in readiness to move up and
take Thomas' place, or possibly to this point, as may be thought
best.

Very respectfully, your obedient servant,

FRANK S. BOND,
Major.

HEADQUARTERS DEPARTMENT OF THE CUMBERLAND,
Crawfish Spring, September 18, 1863—12.15 a. m.

Major-General McCOOK:

The general commanding directs me to acknowledge the receipt of your 8 p. m. dispatch, and to say so soon as General Thomas' command is out of the way you will close up to this place.

Very respectfully, your obedient servant,

FRANK S. BOND,
Major, and Aide-de-Camp.

—

HEADQUARTERS DEPARTMENT OF THE CUMBERLAND,
Crawfish Spring, September 19, 1863—9.50 a. m.

Maj. Gen. GEORGE H. THOMAS:

Your note of 9.30 is received. The general commanding does not think you should commit yourself to any considerable movement before we hear from our extreme left. The rumor that the enemy is between Alexander's and Reed's bridges can hardly be true. McCook was at the former place last night, and Colonel Grose's brigade started in that direction nearly two hours ago. The general commanding directs you to reconnoiter thoroughly before moving out in force. Meantime get a good position.

Very respectfully, your obedient servant,

J. A. GARFIELD,
Brigadier-General, Chief of Staff.

—

HEADQUARTERS DEPARTMENT OF THE CUMBERLAND,
Widow Glenn's, September 19, 1863—1.25 p. m.

Maj. Gen. GEORGE H. THOMAS:

Davis' division and two brigades of Van Cleve's division have been sent to you. Spare your reserves as much as possible for the decisive movement. A considerable force of rebel cavalry have got into Chattanooga Valley, in our rear. Two brigades of Minty's have been sent after them. How are you progressing?

Very respectfully, your obedient servant,

J. A. GARFIELD,
Brigadier-General, Chief of Staff.

—

HEADQUARTERS DEPARTMENT OF THE CUMBERLAND,
Widow Glenn's, September 19, 1863—1.45 p. m.

Colonel WILDER,
Commanding Mounted Brigade:

The general commanding directs you to put your command in position in the right flank of the fighting line, so as to observe the movements of the enemy in that direction and also cover the left flank.

Very respectfully, your obedient servant,

J. A. GARFIELD.

HEADQUARTERS DEPARTMENT OF THE CUMBERLAND,
Widow Glenn's, September 19, 1863—3 p. m.

Major-General McCook:

The general commanding directs me to say that he thinks you had better send one brigade from Sheridan to support Davis, who is hardly pressed.*

Very respectfully, your obedient servant,

FRANK S. BOND,
Major, and Aide-de-Camp.

HEADQUARTERS DEPARTMENT OF THE CUMBERLAND,
Chattanooga, October 23, 1863.

Brigadier-General THOMAS:

I have the honor to transmit herewith some copies of orders issued previous to and during the battles of Chickamauga, which it was the intention of General Rosecrans to forward with his official report, but they were mislaid by him, and not discovered until subsequent to his departure.

I have to request that they be placed on file with those previously forwarded.

I am, sir, very respectfully, your obedient servant,

C. GODDARD,
Lieutenant-Colonel, and Assistant Adjutant-General.

[Inclosures.]

HEADQUARTERS DEPARTMENT OF THE CUMBERLAND,
Crawfish Spring, September 18, 1863.

Maj. Gen. GORDON GRANGER,
Commanding Reserve Corps:

GENERAL: It is probable that the enemy intends to give us battle on the line of the Chickamauga. To provide against possible contingencies the general commanding directs that in case the enemy should get possession of Stevens' Gap and Lookout Valley, your force lately at Jasper, now at Wauhatchie Junction, shall take possession of the route to Bridgeport and dispute the enemy's advance stubbornly, and if compelled to cross the river take up the bridge and resist the passage to the utmost. The river should be thoroughly patrolled and the force at Bridgeport held well in hand.

Very respectfully, your obedient servant,

J. A. GARFIELD,
Brigadier-General, Chief of Staff.

—

HEADQUARTERS DEPARTMENT OF THE CUMBERLAND,
Crawfish Spring, September 18, 1863—4.10 p. m.

Brigadier-General MITCHELL,
Comdg. Cavalry, Department of the Cumberland:

GENERAL: The enemy seems to be attempting to turn our left flank. Should this supposition prove correct, it will necessitate the removal of Generals Thomas' and McCook's corps to our left and

---

*See Bond to McCook, 3.40 p. m., p. 77.

thus leave Stevens' Gap without a very strong support. In this case the general commanding directs that the brigade of General McCook's corps which he has been ordered to detach for the defense of the gap shall hold that pass at all hazards till General G. Crook and the cavalry at Dougherty's Gap and Valley Head can close up and join the brigade at Stevens' Gap. Should these forces be compelled to fall back, they will retire along the mountain road to Chattanooga, contesting the ground inch by inch, and giving due notice of their retreat.

You will direct General Crook to hold his command well in hand and keep his trains ready for ready [rapid] march to Stevens' Gap. General Crook must watch the movements of the two armies closely, and use his discretion as to the time when he should retire.

Very respectfully, your obedient servant,

J. A. GARFIELD,
Brigadier-General, Chief of Staff.

—

HEADQUARTERS DEPARTMENT OF THE CUMBERLAND,
Crawfish Spring, September 18, 1863—4.25 p. m.

Major-General McCook,
Commanding Twentieth Army Corps:

GENERAL: The general commanding directs that you leave Post's brigade at Stevens' Gap to hold that position and cover the retreat of General Crook and the cavalry at Valley Head, should it be necessary. He must hold the gap at all hazards till the cavalry can join him, and in case he should be compelled to abandon the gap he must retire along the mountain road to Chattanooga, contesting the ground inch by inch. Make such dispositions and give such instructions as may be necessary to effect the desired end.

Very respectfully, your obedient servant,

J. A. GARFIELD,
Brigadier-General, Chief of Staff.

—

HEADQUARTERS DEPARTMENT OF THE CUMBERLAND,
Crawfish Spring, September 18, 1863—8.30 p. m.

Brigadier-General MITCHELL,
Commanding Cavalry:

GENERAL: The general commanding directs you, immediately on the receipt of this order, to order General Crook's command and all the cavalry force both at Dougherty's Gap and Valley Head to move with all dispatch and close down upon the right flank of the army. Detail what you may deem a sufficient force to operate in conjunction with Post's brigade to hold Stevens' Gap and the crest of the mountain. The courier line from Stevens' Gap to Chattanooga along the crest of the mountain must be established, and frequent reports forwarded to these headquarters of all that occurs and can be observed by the force left at Stevens' Gap. There is not a moment to be lost in moving the cavalry this way.

Very respectfully, your obedient servant,

J. A. GARFIELD,
Brigadier-General, Chief of Staff.

HEADQUARTERS DEPARTMENT OF THE CUMBERLAND,
Crawfish Spring, September 19, 1863—8.45 a. m.

Major-General SHERIDAN,
Comdg. Third Division, Twentieth Army Corps:

Explanatory of orders to General McCook, the general commanding directs you to put your command in position to support General Negley in watching and holding the fords of the Chickamauga Creek. Consult with General Negley and select the best position that the ground offers. Allow the enemy to cross in small force and attempt to cut him off. Resist the crossing of any large force. Report when you have taken your position how your forces are situated.

J. A. GARFIELD.

—

HEADQUARTERS DEPARTMENT OF THE CUMBERLAND,
Crawfish Spring, September 19, 1863—10.15 a. m.

Major-General McCOOK,
Commanding Twentieth Army Corps:

The enemy are still attempting to turn our left and secure the Kingsville [?] and Ringgold road. The demonstrations on the right are a feint. The general commanding directs you to send one division of your corps to Widow Eliza Glenn's, and send forward to report its march to General Thomas, with orders to close up to General Thomas if he shall so direct. The division will receive orders from General Thomas. General McCook will take command of the right and cavalry, and hold yourself in readiness to support either flank.

J. A. G[ARFIELD].

—

HEADQUARTERS DEPARTMENT OF THE CUMBERLAND,
Widow Glenn's, September 19, 1863—11.10 a. m.

Major-General CRITTENDEN,
Twenty-first Army Corps:

The general commanding directs you to order Minty to go to Chattanooga with all practicable speed. Let him come by Widow Glenn's and report for orders.

C. GODDARD,
Assistant Adjutant-General.

—

HEADQUARTERS DEPARTMENT OF THE CUMBERLAND,
Widow Glenn's, September 19, 1863—11.45 a. m.

Major-General PALMER,
Commanding Division, Twentieth Army Corps:

The general commanding received [sees] your movement and suggests that it will be well for you to move *en échelon*, keeping your right refused and closing your left well up on Reynolds.

J. A. G[ARFIELD].

HEADQUARTERS DEPARTMENT OF THE CUMBERLAND,
Widow Glenn's, September 19, 1863—3.40 p. m.

Major-General McCOOK :

The general commanding directs me to say that he thinks you had better send one brigade from Sheridan to support Davis, who is hard pressed.*

Very respectfully, your obedient servant,

FRANK S. BOND,
Major, and Aide-de-Camp.

—

HEADQUARTERS DEPARTMENT OF THE CUMBERLAND,
Chattanooga, September 20, 1863.

Major-General NEGLEY,
Commanding at Rossville :

The general commanding directs that all the spare artillery which cannot be used to advantage be sent to this place at once.

J. P. DROUILLARD,
Captain, and Aide-de-Camp.

—

[HEADQUARTERS DEPARTMENT OF THE CUMBERLAND,
Chattanooga,] *September* 21, 1863—4.40 p. m.

Major-General THOMAS,
Commanding Forces at Rossville :

The general commanding directs you to withdraw all your forces to a new line of battle in front of this place during the night. To-night directions will be given you as to the order and route for the movement. If the events of the day do not preclude it, you must hold your position till night. We have moved Spears' force up Chattanooga Creek to protect your right flank. As far as possible withdraw the divisions *en masse,* so that our troops will be organized when they encamp on the new line. The general commanding is now arranging the positions you are to take up, which will be, in general terms, on the left, east of Chattanooga, yourself in the center and McCook on the right. Crittenden might move back by his present left by the most practicable route. You might come in on the right-hand road coming this way from Rossville, and McCook on the left. These are the views of the general commanding. Of course, being on the ground, you will make such modifications as the circumstances may require. The gap ought to be held to-night, if practicable, by a small force, which should be withdrawn before dawn. Each corps should leave a division as rear guard to fall back slowly, covering the retreat and contesting the ground inch by inch.

Very respectfully, your obedient servant,

J. A. GARFIELD,
Brigadier-General, Chief of Staff.

(Same to Major-General McCook.)

---

*See Bond to McCook, 3 p. m., p. 74.

COMPLIMENTARY ORDERS.

Orders.]   Hdqrs. Department of the Cumberland,
                        Chattanooga, October 2, 1863.
Army of the Cumberland :

You have made a grand and successful campaign. You have driven the rebels from Middle Tennessee.

You crossed a great mountain range, placed yourselves on the banks of a broad river, crossed it in the face of a powerful opposing army, and crossed two other great mountain ranges at the only practicable passes some 40 miles between extremes. You concentrated in the face of superior numbers, fought the combined armies of Bragg, which you drove from Shelbyville and Tullahoma ; of Johnston's army from Mississippi, and the tried veterans of Longstreet's corps, and for two days held them at bay, giving them blow for blow with heavy interest. When the day closed you held the field, from which you withdrew in the face of overpowering numbers, to occupy the point for which you set out—Chattanooga.

You have accomplished the great work of the campaign. You hold the key of East Tennessee, of North Georgia, and of the enemy's mines of coal and niter.

Let these achievements console you for the regret you experience that arrivals of fresh hostile troops forbade your remaining on the field to renew the battle for the right of burying your gallant dead, and caring for your brave companions who lay wounded on the field. The losses you have sustained, though heavy, are slight considering the odds against you and the stake you have won. You hold in your hands the substantial fruits of a victory, and deserve and will receive the honor and plaudits of a grateful nation which asks nothing of even those who have been fighting us but obedience to the constitution and laws established for our common benefit.

The general commanding earnestly begs every officer and soldier of this army to unite with him in thanking Almighty God for his favor to us. He presents his hearty thanks and congratulations to all the officers and soldiers of this command for their energy, patience, and perseverance, and the undaunted courage displayed by those who fought with such unflinching resolution.

Neither the history of this war nor probably the annals of any battle furnish a loftier example of obstinate bravery and enduring resistance to superior numbers, when troops, having exhausted their ammunition, resorted to the bayonet so many times to hold their position against such odds as did our left and center on the afternoon of the 20th of September, at the battle of Chickamauga.

                        W. S. ROSECRANS,
                        Major-General Commanding.

        Headquarters Department of the Cumberland,
                        Chattanooga, October 16, 1863.
Brig. Gen. Lorenzo Thomas,
        Adjutant-General, U. S. Army:

I desire to make the following change in my last official report of the operations of the Army of the Cumberland. In the chapter headed " The battle of the 20th," and the paragraph commencing "At the moment of the repulse of Davis' division, I was standing in the rear of his right," I wish to add the words " and Captain Young " after the words "Major Bond "and before the words "of my staff," and omit the word "and" before the words "Major Bond," so that the passage when corrected will read, "Giving the troops directions to rally behind the ridge west of the Dry Valley road. I passed down it accompanied by General Garfield, Major McMichael, Major Bond, and Captain Young, of my staff."

Very respectfully, your obedient servant,

W. S. ROSECRANS,
Major-General, Commanding.

CINCINNATI, OHIO, *January* 4, 1864.

GENERAL: Accompanying this are the reports of Brig. Gen. R. B. Mitchell,* acting chief of cavalry, of the operations of the cavalry in Chattanooga Campaign, and of Colonel Wilder,† who details the work performed by his mounted infantry during the same period.

It will be remembered that these reports did not accompany my official account of the campaign, in consequence of the absence of these commanders and their troops in pursuit of Wheeler's rebel cavalry.

Having, in my general report, given an outline of the brilliant part taken by Wilder's brigade in the great demonstration on the enemy's front above Chattanooga, I respectfully call attention to the facts that he was able to attract almost two divisions of rebels to that part of the river, and that for thirty days some of his command were daily skirmishing with the enemy, while our troops crossed below.

His bold and successful advance on Dalton and reconnaissance thence by Leet's Tan-yard to Gordon's Mills, unquestionably checked a very serious movement on Crittenden's corps, at a time when it would have been very dangerous to us. His command also merits the thanks of the country for its noble stand at the crossing of the Chickamauga, where his and Minty's cavalry brigade resisted the enemy so obstinately on the afternoon of the 18th as to give us that night to anticipate him on the Rossville road.

I trust Colonel Wilder will be promoted for his many gallant services.

As to the cavalry, the accompanying reports are so full that I need only add that as an arm of the service it has been equal to its duty on all occasions, and on the 18th, 19th, and 20th of September it behaved with conspicuous gallantry, covering our shattered right and protected our trains in the valley of Chattanooga Creek on the 20th.

It was to provide for the security of these trains, which had been sent to that valley on the 18th, and that they should be moved into Chattanooga after our right was driven back on the 20th, that I directed special attention, and it is greatly due to the behavior of the cavalry on that day that we lost none of our wagons, and that many of our ambulances and some of our artillery and caissons came safely into the place.

The losses of the cavalry appear in the accompanying report, 43 killed, 132 wounded, and 283 missing, making a total of 439, instead of 500, as conjecturally stated in my official report.

I cannot forbear calling the special attention of the General-in-Chief and the War Department to the conspicuous gallantry and laborious services of this arm. Exposed in all weather, almost always

---

* See p. 890.   † See p. 444.

moving, even in winter, without tents or wagons, operating in a country poorly supplied with forage, combating for the most part very superior numbers, from the feeble beginnings of one year ago, when its operations were mostly within the infantry lines, it has become master of the field, and hesitates not to attack the enemy wherever it finds him. This great change, due chiefly to the joint efforts of both officers and men, has been greatly promoted by giving them arms in which they had confidence, and by the adoption of the determined use of the saber.

To Maj. Gen. D. S. Stanley is justly due great credit for his agency in bringing about these results, and giving firmness and vigor to the discipline of the cavalry.

It requires both nature and experience to make cavalry officers, and by judicious selections and promotions this arm may become still more useful and distinguished.

W. S. ROSECRANS,
Major-General.

Brig. Gen. LORENZO THOMAS,
Adjutant-General, U. S. Army.

LIST OF SPECIAL MENTIONS.

CINCINNATI, OHIO,
January 7, 1864.

Respectfully forwarded.

List of all persons specially mentioned by regimental, brigade, division, and corps commanders in their reports of the battle of Chickamauga, with the remark made in each case. I would particularly recommend for promotion to the rank of brigadier-general, in the order in which they are named, the following colonels, who have commanded brigades so long and so well that they have fully earned the additional grade, viz:

Col. Charles G. Harker, Sixty-fifth Ohio Volunteer Infantry; Col. Ferd. Van Derveer, Thirty-fifth Ohio Volunteer Infantry; Col. B. F. Scribner, Thirty-eighth Indiana Infantry; Col. William Grose, Thirth-sixth Indiana Infantry; Col. John T. Croxton, Fourth Kentucky Volunteer Infantry; Col. Dan. McCook, Fifty-second Ohio Volunteer Infantry; and Col. T. R. Stanley, Eighteenth Ohio Volunteer Infantry.

W. S. ROSECRANS,
Major-General.

[Inclosure.]

Name, rank, and command.	Remarks.
Maj. Gen. George H. Thomas, Fourteenth Army Corps.	Major-General Rosecrans, commanding, names him "the true soldier, the prudent and undaunted commander, the modest and incorruptible patriot. To him the thanks and gratitude of the country are due for his conduct at the battle of Chickamauga."
Maj. Gen. Gordon Granger, Reserve Corps.....	"He," says Major-General Rosecrans, commanding, "by his promptitude, arrived and carried his troops into action in time to save the day. He deserves the highest praise."
Maj. Gen. Alexander McD. McCook, Twentieth Army Corps.	"For the care of his command, prompt and willing execution of orders to the best of his ability, deserves this testimonial of my approbation," says Major-General Rosecrans, commanding.

Name, rank, and command.	Remarks.
Maj. Gen. Thomas L. Crittenden, Twenty-first Army Corps.	Major-General Rosecrans, commanding, says, "I bear testimony to the high-hearted, noble Major-General Crittenden. Prompt in the moving and reporting the position of his troops, always fearless on the field of battle, I return my thanks for the promptness and military good sense with which he sent his divisions toward the noise of battle on the 19th."
Maj. Gen. John M. Palmer, Second Division, Twenty-first Army Corps.	Commended for the ability with which he handled his command by both Major-Generals Crittenden and Thomas.
Maj. Gen. J. J. Reynolds, Fourth Division, Fourteenth Army Corps.	Commended for the ability with which he conducted his command by Major-General Thomas.
Maj. Gen. Philip H. Sheridan, Third Division, Twentieth Army Corps.	Major-General McCook thanks him for his earnest co-operation and attention to duty, and says, "I commend him to his country."
Brig. Gen. John M. Brannan, Third Division, Fourteenth Army Corps.	Is commended for the ability with which he commanded by Major-General Thomas.
Brig. Gen. Thomas J. Wood, First Division, Twenty-first Army Corps.	Major-General Crittenden says, "With pride I point to the service of Brigadier-General Wood," and Major-General Thomas names him as having "with two brigades of his division nobly sustained Richard W. Johnson." Is commended for the ability with which he handled his command; and Major-General McCook says his "thanks are due to him for his earnest co-operation and devotion to duty," commends him to his country, and recommends his promotion.
Brig. Gen. James A. Garfield, chief of staff......	Major-General Rosecrans, commanding, acknowledges himself "especially indebted for the clear and ready manner with which he seized the points of action and movements, and expressed in orders the ideas of the general commanding."
Brig. Gen. J. St. Clair Morton, chief engineer.....	"Was in the battle and discharged his duties with ability and to my entire satisfaction," says Major-General Rosecrans, commanding.
Brig. Gen. Richard W. Johnson, Second Division, Twentieth Army Corps.	Major-General McCook thanks him for his earnest co-operation and devotion to duty, commends him to the country, and recommends him to his superiors for promotion. Major-General Thomas names him as having fought most ga'lantly on both days, and ably handled his troops.
Brig. Gen. Jefferson C. Davis, First Division, Twentieth Army Corps.	Is commended to his country and recommended for promotion by Major-General McCook.
Brig. Gen. Absalom Baird, First Division, Fourteenth Army Corps.	Is commended for the ability with which he handled his command by Major-General Thomas.
Brig. Gen. James B. Steedman, First Division, Reserve Corps.	Major-General Thomas speaks of him as having "valiantly maintained Brannan's right," and Major-General Granger calls attention "to the bravery and gallantry displayed during the battle" by him, and says "ne fearlessly rushed into the midst of danger and was ever present with his troops, handling them with ease, rallying them, and encouraging them, and established order and confidence."
Brig. Gen. August Willich, First Brigade, Second Division, Twentieth Army Corps.	Brigadier-General Johnson says "he was always in the right place, and by his individual daring rendered the country great service." "This gallant old veteran deserves promotion, and I hope may receive it." Major-General Thomas speaks of him as having nobly sustained his reputation as a soldier. Major-General McCook joins General Johnson in recommending his promotion.
Brig. Gen. John Beatty, First Brigade, Second Division, Fourteenth Army Corps.	Major-General Thomas says he "bravely supported Baird's left in the morning of Sunday," and Major-General Negley says he "gallantly remained upon the field of battle in command of scattered troops after most of his brigade had been driven from it and separated from him by the charge of the enemy." Brigadier-General Brannan says he "gave great assistance in rallying the troops and keeping them in position."
Brig. Gen. J. B. Turchin, Third Brigade, Fourth Division, Fourteenth Army Corps.	Major-General Reynolds speaks of him as having handled his brigade with skill and judgment, and no instance of confusion or disorder occurred.
Brig. Gen. W. C. Whitaker, First Brigade, First Division, Reserve Corps.	Major-General Granger speaks of him as conspicuous for his bravery and activity, managing his troops well, and contributing much to our success.
Brig. Gen. John H. King, Third Brigade, First Division, Fourteenth Army Corps.	Brigadier-General Baird speaks of him as deserving a debt of great gratitude for the courage displayed in the fight and good judgment with which he handled his troops, and that the performance of his command on Saturday morning was particularly brilliant.

Name, rank, and command.	Remarks.
Brig. Gen. John C. Starkweather, Second Brigade, First Division, Fourteenth Army Corps.	Brigadier-General Baird says that "he, holding the key points at one of our positions, rendered distinguished service by his own coolness, inspiring his men with confidence."
Brig. Gen. Samuel Beatty, First Brigade, Third Division, Twenty-first Army Corps.	Commended to especial notice for his good conduct as brigade commander by Brigadier-General Van Cleve and Major-General Crittenden.
Brig. Gen. William B. Hazen, Second Brigade, Second Division, Twenty-first Army Corps. Brig. Gen. Charles Cruft, First Brigade, Second Division, Twenty-first Army Corps.	Commended for their good conduct by Major-General Palmer and Major-General Crittenden.
Brig. Gen. H. P. Van Cleve, Third Division, Twenty-first Army Corps.	Noticed with commendation by Major-General Crittenden.

HEADQUARTERS,
Cincinnati, Ohio, January 8, 1864.

As Brig. Gen. William H. Lytle fell leading a gallant charge against the foe, advancing on our retreating troops, I may be excused from departing from the strict rule of mentioning those officers whose good conduct could be properly officially noticed by the general commanding only. This brave and generous young officer, whose first wounds were received while fighting under my command at Carnifix Ferry, where he fell desperately wounded at the head of his regiment, was also badly wounded and taken prisoner at the battle of Perryville, where he repelled a desperate onslaughter of the enemy.

On rejoining the Army of the Cumberland with his well-earned rank of brigadier, he was assigned second in command to General Sheridan. When he fell gloriously on the field of Chickamauga, Ohio lost one of her jewels and the service one of its most patriotic and promising general officers.

W. S. ROSECRANS,
Major-General.

[Inclosure in report of January 7—Continued.]

Name, rank, and command.	Remarks.
Col. J. B. Dodge, Second Brigade, Second Division, Twentieth Army Corps.	Brigadier-General Johnson speaks of him as a "brave and gallant soldier," handled his brigade well, and is worthy and deserving of promotion.
Col. B. F. Scribner, Thirty-eighth Indiana, First Brigade, First Division, Fourteenth Army Corps.	Brigadier-General Baird speaks of him, thus: "Commanding one of the best brigades in the army, he has been recommended for promotion after previous battles, and has again distinguished himself. I renew the recommendation for his promotion." General Thomas, says, "Colonel Scribner, commanding First Brigade, Baird's division, on Saturday morning when it was attacked in flank by an overwhelming force of the enemy and driven back, yet Colonel Scribner was enabled to rally and reorganize without the least difficulty."
Col. John T. Croxton, Fourth Kentucky, Second Brigade, Third Division, Fourteenth Army Corps.	Brigadier-General Brannan speaks of him as the "gallant and dashing Croxton, commanding Second Brigade, who, though severely and painfully wounded early the second day, remained on the field, rallying and encouraging his men, until utterly exhausted." Major-General Thomas confirms the report given of him by his division commander.
Col. F. Van Derveer, Third Brigade, Third Division, Fourteenth Army Corps.	Brigadier-General Brannan brings to the especial notice of the commanding general the gallant and meritorious conduct of the colonel commanding Third Brigade, "whose fearlessness and calm judgment in the most trying situations," he says, "added materially to the efficiency of his command, which he handled both days in the most skillful way, punishing the enemy severely." Major-General Thomas confirms this report of General Brannan.

Name, rank, and command.	Remarks.
Col. Charles G. Harker, Third Brigade, First Division, Twenty-first Army Corps.	Brigadier-General Wood says, "In my report of the battle of Stone's River I especially signalized the service of Colonel Harker, commanding Third Brigade of my division, and earnestly recommend him for promotion both as a reward for merit and an act of simple justice. In the late campaign he has particularly distinguished himself ; I earnestly recommend him for immediate promotion to the rank of brigadier-general." Major-General Crittenden calls "attention to the brilliant conduct" of Colonel Harker and compliments him highly for "the skill with which he managed his command, and more than all, the gallantry with which he fought." Major-General Thomas speaks of him as "the brave" Colonel Harker who "most nobly sustained" Brannan's left.
Col. George P. Buell, Fifty-eighth Indiana, Third Brigade, First Division, Twenty-first Army Corps.	Brigadier-General Wood speaks of him as commander of the First Brigade of his division and says that "he bore himself with great gallantry, and with a little more experience would make an excellent brigadier and should receive promotion." Major-General Thomas calls him "the brave Buell," who most nobly sustained Brannan's left.
Col. W. W. Berry, Fifth Kentucky, Third Brigade, Second Division, Twentieth Army Corps.	Brigadier-General Johnson says, "He behaved with so much coolness and displayed so much skill and ability in the management of his brigade that I hope he may be promoted at once. He first joined the troops under Rousseau after the first outbreak of the rebellion, and has participated in all the battles and skirmishes of his regiment with distinguished gallantry." Major-General McCook joins earnestly and strongly in the recommendation of Brigadier-General Johnson.
Col. J. C. McKibbin, aide-de-camp	"Always efficient, gallant, and untiring, and fearless in battle," says Major-General Rosecrans, commanding, and Major-General McCook also notices him for "valuable assistance in rallying the troops."
Col. James Barnett, chief of artillery...........	Major-General Rosecrans, commanding, says, "Colonel Barnett was in the battle and discharged his duties with ability and entire satisfaction."
Col. William J. Palmer, Fifteenth Pennsylvania Cavalry.	Major-General Rosecrans, speaking of him and his command, says. "They have rendered very valuable service in keeping open communications and watching the movements of the enemy, which deserves my warmest thanks."
Col. John P. Sanderson, acting aide-de-camp ...	Major-General Rosecrans, commanding, says, "I must not omit Col. J. P. Sanderson, of the regular infantry, who, having lately joined us, on those two days of battle acted as aide-in-camp and carried orders to the hottest portions of the field."
Col. Dan McCook, Second Brigade, Second Division Reserve Corps.	Major-General Granger says "that although commanding a brigade not in the battle it had a very important position protecting the rear of those who were fighting," and that he "properly and promptly carried out all orders and instructions." Major-General Thomas speaks of him as having "kept a large force of the enemy's cavalry, and with his battery materially aided Turchin's handsome charge on the enemy, who had closed on our left."
Col. L. P. Bradley, Fifty-first Illinois, Third Brigade, Third Division, Twentieth Army Corps.	Major-General Sheridan speaks of him as having been twice severely wounded in the action of the 19th, and greatly distinguished himself as commander of the Third Brigade of his division, and recommends him for promotion, in which Major-General McCook joins him.
Col. William Grose, Thirty-sixth Indiana, Third Brigade, Second Division, Twenty-first Army Corps.	Major-General Palmer commends his conduct as entirely satisfactory, and Major-General Crittenden calls attention to his distinguished services.
Col. Bernard Laiboldt, Second Missouri, Second Brigade, Third Division, Twentieth Army Corps.	Major-General Sheridan says that "Colonel Laiboldt, commanding my Second Brigade, behaved with conspicuous gallantry in the action of the 20th," and recommends him for promotion, in which Major-General McCook fully unites.
Col. T. R. Stanley, Second Brigade, Second Division, Fourteenth Army Corps.	Major-General Negley speaks of his conduct as highly creditable. Major-General Thomas says that he, with one of Negley's brigades, bravely supported Baird's left the morning of Sunday, and was "struck by the fragment of a shell and disabled in the afternoon."
Col. S. M. Barnes, Eighth Kentucky, Third Brigade, Third Division, Twenty-first Army Corps.	Brigadier-General Van Cleve speaks of him as "cool, intrepid, and judicious," who has proven himself on all occasions an able commander, and has well earned promotion. Major-General Crittenden also commends him highly.

Name, rank, and command.	Remarks.
Col. J. F. Jaquess, Seventy-third Illinois, Third Division, Twentieth Army Corps.	Major-General Sheridan mentions him as "especially distinguished for skill and great personal courage," and that "he is almost the only regimental officer left with his regiment, 17 of them having been killed or wounded."
Col. N. L. Anderson, Sixth Ohio, Second Division, Twenty-first Army Corps.	Major-General Palmer says he received a painful wound on Saturday, but remained with his regiment until night, and that "his courage and prudence deserve high praise."
Colonel Champion, Ninety-sixth Illinois, Reserve Corps. Colonel Moore, One hundred and fifteenth Illinois, Reserve Corps. Colonel Le Favour, Twenty-second Michigan, Reserve Corps. Colonel Carlton, Eighty-ninth Ohio, Reserve Corps.	Major-General Granger gives the names of these officers of his command as most conspicuous for efficiency and deserving special mention.
Col. T. D. Sedgewick, Second Kentucky, Second Division, Twenty-first Army Corps.	Major-General Palmer recommends his promotion for capacity to command and good conduct.
Col. W. W. Barrett, Forty-fourth Illinois, Third Division, Twentieth Army Corps.	Major-General Sheridan mentions him as wounded and having especially distinguished himself.
Col. Allen Buckner, Seventy-ninth Illinois, Second Division, Twentieth Army Corps. Colonel Rose, Seventy-seventh Pennsylvania, Second Division, Twentieth Army Corps. Colonel Strong, Ninety-third Ohio, Second Division, Twentieth Army Corps.	Brigadier-General Johnson mentions these officers as distinguished for coolness and gallantry.
Col. J. M. Connell, Seventeenth Ohio, First Brigade, Third Division, Fourteenth Army Corps.	Brigadier-General Brannan mentions him as having acted with coolness and judgment, and fighting most gallantly.
Col. P. T. Swaine, Ninety-ninth Ohio, Third Division, Twenty-first Army Corps.	Brigadier-General Van Cleve says he displayed much judgment and skill in his conduct on the field, and recommends him to the notice of the commanding general. Colonel Barnes, commanding brigade, says he gave evidence of undoubted courage and ability to command.
Col. J. R. Miles, Twenty-seventh Illinois, Third Division, Twentieth Army Corps. Col. Joseph Conrad, Fifteenth Missouri, Third Division, Twentieth Army Corps.	Are named by Major-General Sheridan as having especially distinguished themselves.
Colonel Rippey, Ninetieth Ohio, First Brigade, Second Division, Twenty-first Army Corps. Col. J. T. Smith, Thirty-first Indiana, First Brigade, Second Division, Twenty-first Army Corps. Col. Aquila Wiley, Forty-first Ohio, Second Division, Twenty-first Army Corps. Col. L. H. Waters, Eighty-fourth Illinois, Second Division, Twenty-first Army Corps.	Are named by Major-General Palmer for courage and coolness, and good conduct in the field.
Col. N. H. Walworth, Forty-second Illinois, Third Division, Twentieth Army Corps. Col. Silas Miller, Thirty-sixth Illinois, Third Division, Twentieth Army Corps.	Are named by Major-General Sheridan for skill and bravery.
Col. J. G. Mitchell, Reserve Corps..............	Major-General Granger speaks of him as conspicuous for his bravery and activity, having managed his troops well and contributed much to our success.
Col. George F. Dick, Third Division, Twenty-first Army Corps.	Commended by Brigadier-General Van Cleve to special notice for good conduct.
Col. H. C. Dunlap, Third Kentucky, First Division, Twenty-first Army Corps. Col. Alexander McIlvain, Sixty-fourth Ohio, First Division, Twenty-first Army Corps.	Are commended to notice by Brigadier-General Wood as having rendered distinguished service.
Col. W. L. Stoughton, Eleventh Michigan, Second Division, Fourteenth Army Corps.	Colonel Stanley, commanding brigade, commends him for coolness and fearlessness. Major-General Negley also notices him favorably.
Col. M. B. Walker, Thirty-first Ohio, Third Division, Fourteenth Army Corps.	Brigadier-General Brannan, being short of staff officers, accepted Colonel Walker's services, and says, "Well he served me and his country, rallying and collecting the men, and encouraging them to stand, by his energy and personal courage."
Col. E. Opdycke, One hundred and twenty-fifth Ohio, First Division, Twenty-first Army Corps.	Brigadier-General Wood commends Colonel Opdycke "especially to the favorable consideration" of the commanding general as "an officer capable and worthy of commanding a brigade." Colonel Harker, commanding brigade, speaks highly of his ability and bravery, and recommends him for the command of a brigade.
Col. J. F. Harrison, volunteer aide-de-camp to General Lytle, First Brigade, Third Division, Twentieth Army Corps.	Colonel Miller, commanding brigade, says, "In the rally for the formation of the second line, he seized a stand of colors, and under the influence of his example the men rapidly went forward, again forming, under terrible fire. Major-General Sheridan says, "After General Lytle's death Colonel Harrison reported to him and behaved very handsomely."

Name, rank, and command.	Remarks.
Col. J. B. Culver, Thirteenth Michigan, First Brigade, First Division, Twenty-first Army Corps.	Mentioned for good conduct by Colonel Buell, commanding brigade.
Lieut. Col. H. N. Whitbeck, Third Brigade, First Division, Twenty-First Army Corps.	Colonel Harker, commanding brigade, says the country is indebted to him for gallant and distinguished services.
Col. D. J. Higgins, Twenty-fourth Ohio, Third Brigade, Second Division, Twenty-first Army Corps.	Colonel Grose, commanding brigade, makes special mention of him for good conduct.
Col. M. Gooding, Colonel Marsh, Col. John E. Bennett, Colonel Winters, First Brigade, First Division, Twentieth Army Corps.	Commended by Colonel Post, commanding brigade, for good conduct.
Col. I. C. B. Suman, Ninth Indiana, Second Brigade, Second Division, Twenty-first Army Corps.	Brigadier-General Hazen says the country cannot too highly cherish his services.
Col O. F. Moore, Thirty-third Ohio, First Brigade, First Division, Fourteenth Army Corps.	Colonel Scribner, commanding brigade, speaks of him as worthy of special mention.
Col. G. Mihalotzy, Col. H. A. Hambright, Second Brigade, First Division, Fourteenth Army Corps.	Brigadier-General Starkweather says, "These officers are entitled to the greatest praise for their coolness and bravery."
Col. James George, Second Minnesota, Third Brigade, Third Division, Fourteenth Army Corps. Col. G. Kammerling, Ninth Ohio, Third Brigade, Third Division, Fourteenth Army Corps. Col. N. Gleason, Eighty-seventh Indiana, Third Brigade, Third Division, Fourteenth Army Corps.	Colonel Van Derveer calls particular attention to the conduct of these officers, and speaks of their conduct with great commendation.
Col. P. P. Lane, Eleventh Ohio, Third Brigade, Fourth Division, Fourteenth Army Corps. Col. B. D. Fearing, Ninety-second Ohio, Third Brigade, Fourth Division, Fourteenth Army Corps.	Brigadier-General Turchin commends them for their gallantry.
Col. M. C. Hunter, Eighty-second Indiana, First Brigade, Third Division, Fourteenth Army Corps.	Colonel Connell mentions him for heroic conduct, under his own personal observation, in making a charge upon the enemy.
Col. A. Beck, Second Missouri, Second Brigade, Third Division, Twentieth Army Corps.	Specially mentioned as deserving by Colonel Laiboldt, commanding brigade.
Col. J. G. Parkhurst, Ninth Michigan, Fourteenth Army Corps.	Major-General Thomas says that as provost-marshal, at the head of his regiment, he did most valuable service in reorganizing the troops that had been driven from the field.
Col. T. J. Harrison, Thirty-ninth Indiana (mounted), Twentieth Army Corps.	Major-General McCook highly compliments him and his regiment, for arduous and important service.
Lieut. Col. A. C. Ducat, chief assistant inspector-general.	"Brave, prompt, and energetic in action," says Major-General Rosecrans, commanding.
Lieut. Col. S. Simmons, chief commissary of subsistence.	"Were in the battle, and discharged their duties with ability and to my entire satisfaction," says Major-General Rosecrans, commanding.
Lieut. Col. H. C. Hodges, chief quartermaster. Lieut. Col. C. Goddard, assistant adjutant-general. Lieut. Col. W. M. Wiles, provost-marshal.....	"Were on the field of battle, and there, as elsewhere, discharged their duties with zeal and ability," says Major-General Rosecrans, commanding.
Lieut. Col. W. M. Ward, Tenth Ohio, headquarters provost guard.	Rendered efficient and valuable services, especially on the 20th, in covering the movements of the retiring trains on the Dry Valley road, and stopping the stragglers from the fight.
Lieut. Col. Francis L. Neff, Thirty-first Indiana, Second Division, Twenty-first Army Corps.	Commended for good conduct by Major-General Palmer, who says he received a painful wound in the arm on the 19th, but refused to quit his command, and fought through both days.
Lieut. Col. John Weber, Fifteenth Missouri, Third Division, Twentieth Army Corps. Lieut. Col. John Russell, Forty-fourth Illinois, Third Division, Twentieth Army Corps. Lieut. Col. J. I. Davidson, Seventy-third Illinois, Third Division, Twentieth Army Corps. Lieut. Col. T. S. West, Twenty-fourth Wisconsin, Third Division, Twentieth Army Corps.	These were wounded and are reported by Major-General Sheridan as having especially distinguished themselves, the last-named as being captured.
Lieut. Col. O. H. P. Carey, Thirty-sixth Indiana, Second Division, Twenty-first Army Corps.	Was wounded on Saturday, but remained with his command during the day, and is mentioned by Major-General Palmer as having "behaved with great courage."
Lieut. Col. S. B. Raymond, Fifty-first Illinois, Third Division, Twentieth Army Corps. Lieut. Col. J. A. Hottenstein, Forty-second Illinois, Third Division, Twentieth Army Corps. Lieut. Col. F. Swanwick, Twenty-second Illinois, Third Division, Twentieth Army Corps. Lieut. Col. W. A. Schmitt, Twenty-seventh Illinois, Third Division, Twentieth Army Corps. Lieut. Col. A. S. Chadbourne, Eighty-eighth Illinois, Third Division, Twentieth Army Corps. Lieut. Col. P. C. Olson, Thirty-sixth Illinois, Third Division, Twentieth Army Corps.	Are named by Major-General Sheridan as having especially distinguished themselves.

Name, rank, and command.	Remarks.
Lieut. Col. B. Langdon, First Ohio, Second Division, Twentieth Army Corps. Lieut. Col. Frank Askew, Fifteenth Ohio, Second Division, Twentieth Army Corps. Lieut. Col. D. J. Hall, Eighty-ninth Illinois, Second Division, Twentieth Army Corps. Lieut. Col. H. E. Rives, Seventy-ninth Illinois, Second Division, Twentieth Army Corps. Lieut. Col. O. D. Hurd, Thirtieth Indiana, Second Division, Twentieth Army Corps. Lieut. Col. F. S. Pyfer, Seventy-seventh Pennsylvania, Second Division, Twentieth Army Corps. Lieut. Col. William H. Martin, Ninety-third Ohio, Second Division, Twentieth Army Corps.	Are named by Brigadier-General Johnson for " distinguished gallantry."
Lieut. Col. Carter Van Vleck, Seventy eighth Illinois, Reserve Corps. Lieutenant-Colonel Banning, One hundred and twenty-first Ohio, Reserve Corps. Lieut. Col. D. B. Warner, One hundred and thirteenth Ohio, Reserve Corps. Lieut. Col. William Sanborn, Twenty-second Michigan, Reserve Corps.	Are named by Major-General Granger as conspicuous for efficiency and deserving of especial mention.
Lieut. Col. D. Ward, Seventeenth Ohio, First Brigade, Third Division, Fourteenth Army Corps. Lieutenant-Colonel Lister, Thirty-first Ohio, First Brigade, Third Division, Fourteenth Army Corps.	Colonel Connell speaks in terms of commendation of their heroic conduct, under his own personal observation, in making a charge upon the enemy.
Lieut. Col. H. V. N. Boynton. Thirty-fifth Ohio, Third Brigade, Third Division, Fourteenth Army Corps.	[Colonel Van Derveer, brigade commander,] calls particular attention to the conduct of this officer, and speaks of it as highly creditable.
Lieutenant-Colonel Devol, Thirty-sixth Ohio, Third Brigade, Fourth Division, Fourteenth Army Corps. Lieutenant-Colonel Putnam, Ninety-second Ohio, Third Brigade, Fourth Division, Fourteenth Army Corps.	Brigadier-General Turchin commends the good conduct of these officers.
Lieutenant-Colonel Milward, Third Brigade, Fourth Division, Fourteenth Army Corps.	Brigadier-General Turchin says, though severely bruised by being overrun by a horse, remained until Sunday afternoon, and behaved gallantly.
Lieutenant-Colonel Griffin, Thirty-eighth Indiana, First Brigade, First Division, Fourteenth Army Corps.	Colonel Scribner, commanding brigade, speaks of him as worthy of special praise.
Lieut. Col. G. B. Bingham, Second Brigade. First Division, Fourteenth Army Corps. Lieut. Col. H. C. Hobart, Second Brigade, First Division, Fourteenth Army Corps.	Brigadier-General Starkweather speaks of these as entitled to great praise for coolness and bravery.
Lieutenant-Colonel Raffen, Second Brigade, Second Division, Fourteenth Army Corps. Lieutenant-Colonel Grosvenor, Eighteenth Ohio, Second Brigade, Second Division, Fourteenth Army Corps.	Colonel Stanley, commanding brigade, makes special mention of these for gallant conduct.
Lieutenant-Colonel Bullitt, Third Kentucky, Third Brigade, First Division, Twenty-first Army Corps. Lieutenant-Colonel Brown, Sixty-fourth Ohio, Third Brigade, First Division, Twenty-first Army Corps.	Colonel Harker says the highest praise is due for their excellent conduct.
Lieutenant-Colonel Foy, Twenty-third Kentucky, Third Brigade, Second Division, Twenty-first Army Corps.	Colonel Grose, commanding brigade, makes special mention of the good conduct of this officer.
Lieut. Col. S. C. Aldrich, Forty-fourth Indiana, Second Brigade, Third Division, Twenty-first Army Corps. Lieut. Col. G. A. Frambes, Fifty-ninth Ohio, Second Brigade, Third Division, Twenty-first Army Corps.	Mentioned by Colonel Dick, commanding brigade, for good conduct.
Lieutenant-Colonel Kimberly, Second Brigade, Second Division, Twenty-first Army Corps. Lieutenant-Colonel Lasselle, Ninth Indiana, Second Brigade, Second Division, Twenty-first Army Corps.	Spoken of by Brigadier-General Hazen as having rendered valuable services, Lieut. Col. Kimberly having two horses shot from under him.
Lieut. Col. J. Messer, One hundred and first Ohio, Second Brigade, First Division, Twentieth Army Corps.	Brigadier-General Carlin recommends his promotion to the command of a regiment, and says he was brave and efficient under a most terrible fire.
Lieut. Col. Frank Erdelmeyer, First Brigade, Second Division, Twentieth Army Corps. Lieut. Col. Frank Askew, First Brigade, Second Division, Twentieth Army Corps.	Commended for their judgment, skill, and bravery by Brigadier-General Willich.
Lieut. Col. Charles H. Wood, Fifty-first Ohio, Third Brigade, Third Division, Twenty-first Army Corps.	Colonel Barnes, commanding brigade, says he behaved well and deserves well of his country.

Name, rank, and command.	Remarks.
Lieutenant-Colonel Cummins, Ninety-ninth Ohio, First Brigade, First Division, Twenty-first Army Corps. Lieut. Col. W. H. Young, Twenty-sixth Ohio, First Brigade, First Division, Twenty-first Army Corps. Lieut. Col. James T. Embree, Fifty-eighth Indiana, First Brigade, First Division, Twenty-first Army Corps.	Colonel Buell, commanding brigade, speaks of these as deserving of mention for good conduct.
Lieutenant-Colonel Waterman, First Brigade, First Division, Twenty-first Army Corps.	
Lieut. Col. A. R. Hadlock, First Brigade, Second Division, Twenty-first Army Corps.	Mentioned for good conduct by Brigadier-General Cruft.
Lieutenant-Colonel Tripp, Third Brigade, Second Division, Twentieth Army Corps.	Highly complimented for good conduct by Colonel Berry.
Lieut. Col. A. von Schrader, assistant inspector-general, Fourteenth Army Corps.	Major-General Thomas says, "Rendered most efficient service as aide-de-camp during first days of fight, and was taken prisoner on the afternoon of the 19th while in discharge of his duty."
Lieut. Col. G. E. Flynt, assistant adjutant-general. Lieut. Col. A. J. Mackay, chief quartermaster. Lieut. Col. J. R. Paul, chief commissary of subsistence.	Major-General Thomas says they "rendered good service, and, although not on the field of battle, discharged their respective duties to his entire satisfaction."
Lieut. Col. G. P. Thruston, assistant adjutant-general, Twentieth Army Corps. Lieut. Col. G. W. Burton, commissary of subsistence. Lieut. Col. J. F. Boyd, quartermaster......... Lieut. Col. H. N. Fisher, assistant inspector-general.	Noticed by Major-General McCook for their devotion to duty, gallantry in action, and intelligence upon the field.
Lieut. Col. Lyne Starling, chief of staff, Twenty-first Army Corps.	Major-General Crittenden says, "Was courageous and active as always upon the field of battle."
Lieut. Col. Richard Lodor, assistant inspector-general, Twenty-first Army Corps.	Major-General Crittenden says of him, "I can say no more than that he was as brave and active as at Stone's River."
Lieut. Col. Alexander Sympson, quartermaster, Twenty-first Army Corps. Lieut. Col. G. C. Kniffin, commissary of subsistence.	Major-General Crittenden commends them for efficient service.
Lieut. Col. T. R. Palmer, assistant inspector-general, First Division, Twenty-first Army Corps.	Specially named by Brigadier-General Wood for efficient service.
Maj. S. C. Erwin, Sixth Ohio, Second Division, Twenty-first Army Corps.	Commended for good conduct by Major-General Palmer.
Maj. H. A. Rust, Twenty-seventh Illinois, Twentieth Army Corps. Maj. Arnold Beck, Second Missouri, Twentieth Army Corps. Maj. George D. Sherman, Thirty-sixth Illinois, Twentieth Army Corps. Major Chandler, Eighty-eighth Illinois, Twentieth Army Corps.	Are mentioned by Major-General Sheridan as having especially distinguished themselves.
Major Stafford, First Ohio, Third Brigade, Second Division, Twentieth Army Corps. Major Gray, Forty-ninth Ohio, Twentieth Army Corps. Major McClenahan, Fifteenth Ohio, Twentieth Army Corps. Maj. W. D. Williams, Eighty-ninth Illinois, Twentieth Army Corps. Major Van Deren, Seventy-ninth Illinois, Twentieth Army Corps. Major Collins, Twenty-ninth Indiana, Twentieth Army Corps. Major Fitzsimmons, Thirtieth Indiana, Twentieth Army Corps. Major Phillips, Seventy-seventh Pennsylvania, Twentieth Army Corps. Major Birch, Ninety-third Ohio, Twentieth Army Corps. Major Thomasson, Fifth Kentucky, Twentieth Army Corps.	Are remembered by Brigadier-General Johnson for coolness and distinguished gallantry.
Major Yager, One hundred and twenty-first Ohio, Reserve Corps.	Mentioned by Major-General Granger as conspicuous for efficiency and deserving of especial mention.
Major Chase, Twenty-first Michigan, First Brigade, Third Division, Twentieth Army Corps.	Colonel Miller, commanding brigade, says that "the colonel and lieutenant-colonel being killed, the command of the regiment devolved upon Major Chase, who performed his duties with signal gallantry and bravery."
Maj. Ben. F. Le Fever, Third Brigade, Third Division, Twenty-first Army Corps. Maj. John P. Dufficy, Third Brigade, Third Division, Twenty-first Army Corps. Maj. John S. Clark, Eighth Kentucky, Third Brigade, Third Division, Twenty-first Army Corps.	Colonel Barnes, commanding brigade, speaks of these as having behaved well, and deserve well of their country.

Name, rank, and command.	Remarks.
Major Moore, [Fifty-eighth Indiana, First Brigade, First Division, Twenty-first Army Corps]. Major Eaton, Thirteenth Michigan, First Brigade, First Division, Twenty-First Army Corps. Maj. C. M. Hammond, One hundredth Illinois, First Brigade, First Division, Twenty-first Army Corps.	Commended for good conduct by Colonel Buell, commanding brigade.
Major Brennan, Third Kentucky, Third Brigade. First Division, Twenty-first Army Corps.	Colonel Harker, commanding brigade, bestows the highest praise upon his conduct.
Maj. G. Trusler, Thirty-sixth Indiana, Third Brigade, Second Division, Twenty-first Army Corps.	Named for good conduct by Colonel Grose, commanding brigade.
Major Snider, Thirteenth Ohio, Second Brigade, Third Division, Twenty-first Army Corps.	Commended for good conduct by Colonel Dick, commanding brigade.
Maj. J. B. Hampson, One hundred and twenty-fourth Ohio, Second Brigade, Second Division, Twenty-first Army Corps.	Brigadier-General Hazen commends him for ability and success.
Major McDanald, One hundred and first Ohio, Second Brigade, First Division, Twentieth Army Corps. Major Calloway, Twenty-first Illinois, Second Brigade, First Division, Twentieth Army Corps. Maj. Henry N. Alden, Thirty-eighth Illinois, Second Brigade, First Division, Twentieth Army Corps.	Brigadier-General Carlin names these among the most conspicuous of those who proved themselves brave and efficient under the most terrible fire, and recommends them to commands of regiments.
Maj. S. K. Dawson, Nineteenth Infantry, Third Brigade, First Division, Fourteenth Army Corps. Maj. Sidney Coolidge, Sixteenth Infantry, Third Brigade, First Division, Fourteenth Army Corps.	Brigadier-General King speaks in the highest terms of their conduct.
Maj. A. McMahan, Twenty-first Ohio, Third Brigade, Second Division, Fourteenth Army Corps.	Colonel Sirwell, commanding brigade, specially mentions him as having fought until disabled by a wound.
Major Higgins, Eleventh Ohio, Third Brigade, Fourth Division, Fourteenth Army Corps. Major Adney, Thirty-sixth Ohio, Third Brigade, Fourth Division, Fourteenth Army Corps. Major Golden, Ninety-second Ohio, Third Brigade, Fourth Division, Fourteenth Army Corps.	Specially mentioned for their skill and bravery by Brigadier-General Turchin.
Maj. James Leighton, Forty-second Illinois, Third Brigade, Third Division, Twentieth Army Corps. Maj. Samuel Johnson, Twenty-second Illinois, Third Brigade, Third Division, Twentieth Army Corps.	Colonel Walworth, commanding brigade, says, "They deserve the thanks of the country for their gallantry."
Maj. Calvin D. Campbell, Sixth Indiana, Third Brigade, Second Division, Twentieth Army Corps.	Mentioned by Colonel Berry, commanding brigade, as always ready to set an example of daring.
Major von Baumbach, First Brigade, Third Division, Twentieth Army Corps.	Coming in command of his regiment when the lieutenant-colonel fell into the hands of the enemy, acquitted himself, says Colonel Miller, commanding brigade, with great honor.
Maj. Walker E. Lawrence, First Ohio Artillery, Fourteenth Army Corps.	Major-General Thomas commends him for the assistance he rendered him as chief of artillery, Fourteenth Army Corps.
Maj. J. D. Evans, Thirty-ninth Indiana, Second Division, Twentieth Army Corps.	Colonel Harrison, commanding regiment, mentions him for gallant conduct.
Maj. G. W. Northup, Twenty-third Kentucky, Second Division, Twenty-first Army Corps.	Mentioned for good conduct by Lieutenant-Colonel Foy, commanding regiment.
Maj. J. H. Williston, Forty-first Ohio, Second Division, Twenty-first Army Corps.	Specially mentioned for his gallantry in action by Colonel Wiley.
Maj. W. G. Eaton, Thirteenth Michigan, First Division, Twenty-first Army Corps.	Col. J. B. Culver, commanding regiment, calls special attention to his gallant and soldierly conduct.
Major Nash, Nineteenth Ohio, First Brigade, Third Division, Twenty-first Army Corps.	Lieutenant-Colonel Stratton, commanding regiment, specially mentions him for efficient service.
Major Dufficy, Ninety-ninth Ohio, Third Brigade, Third Division, Twenty-first Army Corps.	Colonel Swaine, commanding regiment, specially mentions him for good conduct.
Maj. Frank S. Bond, senior aide-de-camp	Says Major-General Rosecrans, commanding, "Deserves very honorable mention for the very efficient discharge of his duties always. and especially during the battle."
Maj. William McMichael, assistant adjutant-general.	Was on the field of battle, and there as elsewhere discharged his duties with zeal and ability, says Major-General Rosecrans, commanding.
Dr. G. Perin, medical director..... .... Dr. H. H. Seys, medical inspector	Were in the battle and discharged their duties with zeal and ability, says Major-General Rosecrans, commanding.

Name, rank, and command.	Remarks.
Medical Director S. D. Turney, Twenty-first Army Corps.	Brigadier-General Van Cleve says, "By his skill, prudence, and industry, he had so arranged the division field hospital that the wounded were readily attended to without loss of time.
Medical Director W. W. Blair, First Division, Twenty-first Army Corps.	Brigadier-General Wood mentions him for efficient services.
Medical Director E. J. Darken, Third Brigade, First Division, Fourteenth Army Corps.	Named by Brigadier-General King for good conduct.
Medical Director M. G. Sherman [Second Brigade, Second Division, Twenty-first Army Corps.]	Mentioned by Brigadier-General Hazen for good conduct.
Medical Director A. J. Phelps, Twenty-first Army Corps.	Major-General Crittenden says by his judicious arrangements nothing that could be done for our wounded was neglected.
Medical Purveyor B. H. Cheney, Twenty-first Army Corps.	Managed his department creditably, says Major-General Crittenden.
Medical Director Menzies, Second Division, Twenty-first Army Corps.	Major-General Palmer says did all that was possible.
Assistant Medical Director Sherman, Second Division, Twenty-first Army Corps.	
Medical Director D. J. Griffiths, Third Division, Twentieth Army Corps.	Major-General Sheridan commends to special notice his good conduct.
Medical Director L. D. Waterman, First Division, Twentieth Army Corps.	Brigadier-General Davis names him for good conduct.
Medical Director Charles Schussler [Second Division], Twentieth Army Corps.	Brigadier-General Johnson says he was untiring in exertions to alleviate the pain of the suffering.
Dr. Gray, Thirty-ninth Indiana, Second Brigade, Second Division, Twentieth Army Corps.	Colonel Harrison, commanding, specially mentions his good conduct.
Dr. J. H. Rerick, Forty-fourth Indiana, Third Division, Twenty-first Army Corps.	"The ever-faithful surgeon," says Lieutenant-Colonel Aldrich, "followed us from point to point, assisted by Dr. Carr, and I am pleased to say that no regiment had better care of the wounded. He succeeded in getting all our wounded from the hospital which was captured by the enemy."
Dr. Gross, Fourteenth Army Corps.	Major-General Thomas says he (Dr. Gross) was wounded early in the engagement on Sunday, but continued untiring in his efforts to relieve the wants of the wounded.
Medical Purveyor H. C. Barrell	
Maj. Caleb Bates, aide-de-camp, Twentieth Army Corps.	Major-General McCook compliments them for devotion to duty, gallantry, and attention upon the field.
Maj. George A. Kensel, chief of artillery	
Maj. J. Perkins, medical director	
Maj. John Mendenhall, chief of artillery, Twenty-first Army Corps.	Major-General Crittenden says he, "Has fairly earned and I hope may receive promotion."
Major Sabin, staff, Second Brigade, Third Division, Twentieth Army Corps.	Noticed by Colonel Laiboldt, commanding brigade, for gallant conduct.
Maj. J. S. Fullerton, staff, Reserve Corps.	Major-General Granger says he rendered most efficient aid and service.
Major Smith, staff, First Division, Reserve Corps.	Major-General Granger says he deserves special mention.
Maj. John Levering, assistant adjutant-general	Specially mentioned by Major-General Reynolds for the prompt discharge of their duties.
Maj. O. Q. Herrick, medical director	
Maj. S. L. Coulter, acting assistant adjutant-general, Third Brigade, First Division, Twenty-first Army Corps.	Colonel Harker says the highest praise is due for excellent conduct.
Major Kersey, medical director, Third Brigade, Second Division, Twenty-first Army Corps.	Mentioned for good conduct by Colonel Grose, commanding brigade.
Major Spinzig, medical director, Second Brigade, Third Division, Twentieth Army Corps.	Mentioned by Colonel Laiboldt, commanding brigade, for good conduct.
Major Wagner, surgeon, Second Brigade, First Division, Fourteenth Army Corps.	Commended by Brigadier-General Starkweather for good conduct.
Major Buford, aide-de-camp, Twenty-first Army Corps.	Specially mentioned for good conduct by Major-General Crittenden.
Capt. J. P. Drouillard, aide-de-camp	"Deserve very honorable mention for the faithful and efficient discharge of their duties always, and especially during the battle," says Major-General Rosecrans, commanding. Major-General McCook also notices Captain Thoms for valuable assistance in rallying the troops.
Capt. R. S. Thoms, aide-de-camp	
Capt. Horace Porter, chief of ordnance.	"Were in the battle and discharged their duties with ability and to my entire satisfaction," says Major-General Rosecrans, commanding.
Capt. William E. Merrill, chief of topographical engineers.	
Capt. D. G. Swaim, assistant adjutant-general and chief of secret service.	"Were on the field of battle, and there as elsewhere discharged their duties with zeal and ability," says Major-General Rosecrans, commanding. Major-General McCook also notices Capt. A. S. Burt for valuable assistance in rallying the troops.
Capt. William Farrar, aide-de-camp.	
Capt. J. H. Young, chief commissary of musters.	
Capt. A. S. Burt, acting assistant inspector-general.	
Capt. Hunter Brooke, acting judge-advocate.	
Capt. W. C. Margedant, acting topographical engineer.	
Captain Garner, commanding escort	"He and the escort," says Major-General Rosecrans, commanding, "deserve mention for untiring energy."

Name, rank, and command.	Remarks.
Captain Prather, Sixth Indiana	Colonel Berry, commanding brigade, says, "He displayed the highest qualities of an officer in the night fight of the 19th."
Captain Hicks, Ninety-sixth Illinois, Reserve Corps. Captain Urquhart, Ninety-eighth Ohio, Reserve Corps.	Named by Major-General Granger as conspicuous for efficiency and deserving especial mention.
Captain Bishop, Twenty-first Michigan, First Brigade, Third Division, Twentieth Army Corps.	Colonel Miller, commanding brigade, speaks of him as having particularly distinguished himself.
Capt. H. G. Cosgrove, Thirteenth Ohio, Second Brigade, Third Division, Twenty-first Army Corps.	Named by Colonel Dick, commanding regiment, as deserving of special notice.
Capt. Robert Hale, Seventy-fifth Illinois, First Brigade, First Division, Twentieth Army Corps.	Colonel Post, commanding brigade, says he twice succeeded in communicating with the division commander when none of the cavalry were able to do so.
Capt. E. P. Edsall, Thirtieth Indiana, Second Brigade, Second Division, Twentieth Army Corps.	Especially mentioned by Colonel Dodge, commanding brigade, for good conduct.
Captain Strong, Forty-ninth Ohio, First Brigade, Second Division, Twentieth Army Corps.	Major Gray, commanding regiment, says, "He distinguished himself for gallantry and capacity to command."
Capt. John M. Huston, Fifth Kentucky, Third Brigade, Second Division, Twentieth Army Corps.	Commended by Colonel Berry, commanding brigade, as conspicuous for good conduct, and also by Brigadier-General Johnson.
Capt. G. W. Smith, Eighteenth Infantry, Third Brigade, First Division, Fourteenth Army Corps. Capt. Henry Haymond, Eighteenth Infantry, Third Brigade, First Division, Fourteenth Army Corps. Capt. A. B. Dod, Fifteenth Infantry, Third Brigade, First Division, Fourteenth Army Corps.	Commended for good conduct by Brigadier-General King.
Captain Mauff, Twenty-fourth Illinois, Second Brigade, First Division, Fourteenth Army Corps. Captain Walker, Twenty-first Wisconsin, Second Brigade, First Division, Fourteenth Army Corps.	Commended for good conduct by Brigadier-General Starkweather.
Captain Kendrick, Seventy-ninth Pennsylvania Second Brigade, Second Division, Fourteenth Army Corps.	Colonel Stanley, commanding brigade, says, "For his courage, unflinching bravery, and thorough acquaintance with all his duties, he deserves that promotion which has too long been withheld."
Capt. Cullen Bradley, Third Brigade, First Division, Twenty-first Army Corps.	Specially mentioned by Colonel Harker, commanding brigade, who says, "This experienced soldier has served his country most faithfully for seventeen years. He greatly distinguished himself in the battle of Stone's River and maneuvered his own battery with matchless skill in the late battle on the Chickamauga, saving his guns and nearly all his caissons when deserted by the infantry, and when almost any other officer would have lost his entire battery " and recommends that he be rewarded with a commission in the Regular U. S. Artillery. Major-General Crittenden also speaks of him as having "acted with great energy and effect in repelling the advance of the enemy on Saturday."
Capt. Leonard D. Smith, One hundred and first Ohio, Second Brigade, First Division, Twentieth Army Corps.	Is commended by Brigadier-General Carlin as conspicuous for bravery and efficiency.
Capt. Peter Simonson, chief of artillery, Second Division, Twentieth Army Corps.	Brigadier-General Johnson commends him highly for his skill and bravery.
Captain Heltemes, Eighteenth Kentucky, Third Brigade, Fourth Division, Fourteenth Army Corps.	Brigadier-General Turchin says, "Conducting his regiment in the last charge, distinguished himself by taking two guns."
Capt. W. E. Standart, chief of artillery, Second Division, Twenty-first Army Corps.	Major-General Palmer speaks in terms of praise of his skill and behavior.
Capt. J. W. Church, Fourth Michigan Battery, Third Division, Fourteenth Army Corps.	Brigadier-General Brannan and also Brigadier-General Turchin highly commend him for skillful conduct.
Captain Swallow, Seventh Indiana Battery, Third Division, Twenty-first Army Corps.	"Is deserving of particular notice for good conduct," says Brigadier-General Van Cleve.
Captain Aleshire, Eighteenth Ohio Battery, First Brigade, First Division, Reserve Corps.	Commended by Brigadier-General Whitaker for great gallantry and courage.
Capt. Thomas Powell, Sixty-fifth Ohio, Third Brigade, First Division, Twenty-first Army Corps.	Colonel Harker, commanding brigade, says, "The country is indebted to him for gallant and distinguished services."
Captain Gardner, Fifth Wisconsin Battery, First Brigade, First Division, Twentieth Army Corps.	Mentioned for good conduct by Colonel Post, commanding brigade.
Capt. W. F. Goodspeed, Battery A, First Ohio Light Artillery, Second Division, Twentieth Army Corps.	Commended highly by Brigadier-General Willich.

Name, rank, and command.	Remarks.
Capt. John M. Farquhar, Eighty-ninth Illinois, First Brigade, Second Division, Twentieth Army Corps. Capt. H. L. Rowell, Eighty-ninth Illinois, First Brigade, Second Division, Twentieth Army Corps.	Major Williams, commanding Eighty-ninth Illinois, says, "A nation's gratitude is due them for their conduct."
Capt. J. H. M. Jenkins, Twenty-ninth Indiana, Second Division, Twentieth Army Corps.	Deserving of special notice for praiseworthy conduct.
Captain Ervin, Eighty-fourth Illinois, Third Brigade, Second Division, Twenty-first Army Corps.	Colonel Waters, commanding regiment, mentions him for good conduct.
Captain Wadsworth, Twenty-fourth Ohio, Third Brigade, Second Division, Twenty-first Army Corps.	Colonel Higgins, commanding regiment, mentions him for his bravery. He was pierced with two balls and captured by the enemy.
Captain Dryden, Twenty-fourth Ohio, Third Brigade, Second Division, Twenty-first Army Corps.	Colonel Higgins, commanding regiment, mentions him for conspicuous bravery, and was borne from the field severely wounded.
Captain Tifft, Twenty-third Kentucky, Second Division, Twenty-first Army Corps.	Lieutenant-Colonel Foy, commanding regiment, mentions him for undaunted courage.
Capt. T. J. Williams, Twenty-third Kentucky, Second Division, Twenty-first Army Corps. Captain Hardiman, Twenty-third Kentucky, Second Division, Twenty-first Army Corps.	Mentioned for good conduct by Lieutenant-Colonel Foy, commanding regiment.
Captain Bense, Captain Thatcher, Captain Russell, Sixth Ohio, Second Division, Twenty-first Army Corps.	Specially mentioned for conspicuous gallantry by Major Erwin, commanding.
Capt. Anson Mills, Eighteenth Infantry, Fourteenth Army Corps.	Captain Smith, commanding regiment, specially mentions him for gallant and meritorious conduct on both days.
Capt. Green McDonald, Captain George Whitman, Captain William E. Chappell, Fifty-eighth Indiana, First Division, Twenty-first Army Corps.	Named for good conduct by Lieutenant-Colonel Embree.
Capt. E. P. Bates, One hundred and twenty-fifth Ohio, First Division, Twenty-first Army Corps.	Commended by Colonel Opdycke, commanding regiment, for his coolness and efficiency.
Captain Yeomans, One hundred and twenty-fifth Ohio, First Division, Twenty-first Army Corps.	Colonel Opdycke, commanding regiment, says, "He received a ball in his upper leg, but remained with his company during the battle under severe pain."
Captain Trapp, First Ohio, Third Brigade, Second Division, Twentieth Army Corps.	Specially mentioned as an experienced soldier of tried courage and ability by Lieutenant-Colonel Langdon, commanding regiment.
Captain Bope, Captain Barnd, Ninety-ninth Ohio, Third Division, Twenty-first Army Corps.	Colonel Swaine, commanding regiment, specially mentions them for valuable services.
Captain Gunsenhouser, Forty-fourth Indiana, Third Division, Twenty-first Army Corps.	Lieutenant-Colonel Aldrich, commanding regiment, speaks of him as a brave man, who, at the head of his company, was dangerously if not fatally wounded.
Captain Curtis, Forty-fourth Indiana, Third Division, Twenty-first Army Corps.	Mentioned by Lieutenant-Colonel Aldrich, commanding regiment, as especially deserving, and having fought like a hero.
Captain Wilson, Forty-fourth Indiana, Third Division, Twenty-first Army Corps.	Mentioned by Lieutenant-Colonel Aldrich, commanding regiment, for good conduct.
Captain Hurley, Fifth Kentucky, Second Division, Twentieth Army Corps. Captain Lindenfelser, Second Division, Twentieth Army Corps. Captain Wilson, Second Division, Twentieth Army Corps.	Mentioned for gallantry by Captain Huston, commanding regiment.
Capt. John E. Ray, Thirteenth Ohio, Second Brigade, Third Division, Twenty-first Army Corps.	Captain Cosgrove, commanding regiment, specially mentions him for gallant and untiring efforts in rallying the men and encouraging them ; this, too, at a time when he was excused from field duty.
Capt. R. E. A. Crofton, Sixteenth Infantry, Third Brigade, First Division, Fourteenth Army Corps.	Brigadier-General King says after the first day's fight he acted as aide-de-camp and was of great assistance.
Captain Knappen, Forty-fourth Illinois, Second Brigade, Third Division, Twentieth Army Corps.	Colonel Laiboldt specially names him for brave behaviour.
Capt. George Estep, Eighth Indiana Battery, First Brigade, First Division, Twenty-first Army Corps.	Specially mentioned by Colonel Buell, commanding brigade, for good conduct.
Capt. J. P. Willard, aide-de-camp, Fourteenth Army Corps. Capt. S. C. Kellogg, aide-de camp, Fourteenth Army Corps. Capt. J. D. Barker, First Ohio Cavalry, commanding escort, Fourteenth Army Corps. Capt. W. B. Gaw, chief topographical engineer, Fourteenth Army Corps. Capt. G. C. Moody, Nineteenth Infantry, commissary of musters, Fourteenth Army Corps.	Major-General Thomas says were of great assistance in conducting the operations of his command, the last-named rendering efficient service as aide-de-camp.

Name, rank, and command.	Remarks.
Capt. G. M. L. Johnson, Second Indiana Cavalry, Baird's staff. Capt. Thomas C. Williams, Nineteenth U. S. Infantry, Baird's staff.	Major-General Thomas says that having been cut off from their respective commanders, reported to him and were of great assistance as aides.
Capt. B. D. Williams, aide-de-camp, Twentieth Army Corps. Capt. F. J. Jones, aide-de-camp, Twentieth Army Corps. Capt. J. H. Fisher, volunteer aide-de-camp, Twentieth Army Corps. Capt. A. C. McClurg, ordnance, Twentieth Army Corps. Capt. A. T. Snodgrass, provost-marshal, Twentieth Army Corps. Capt. I. C. McElfatrick, topographical engineer, Twentieth Army Corps.	Major-General McCook says his thanks are due for their devotion to duty, gallantry in action, and intelligence upon the field.
Captain Kaldenbaugh, provost-marshal, Twenty-first Army Corps.	"I have rarely seen an officer of his department so thoroughly efficient as he has proven himself to be, both in camp and on the field," says Major-General Crittenden.
Captain Sherer, commanding escort, Twenty-first Army Corps.	To habitual good conduct in camp he has added good conduct on the field, says Major-General Crittenden.
Captain Bartlett, commanding escort, Second Division, Twenty-first Army Corps.	Exhibited commendable courage, says Major-General Palmer.
Captain Steele, topographical engineer, Second Division, Twenty-first Army Corps.	Major-General Palmer says he rendered most efficient services, and on both days of the battle was on all occasions where duty called, exhibiting the highest courage.
Capt. H. Hescock, chief of artillery, Third Division, Twentieth Army Corps. Capt. George Lee, assistant adjutant-general, Third Division, Twentieth Army Corps. Capt. A. F. Stevenson, assistant inspector-general, Third Division, Twentieth Army Corps. Capt. W. L. Mallory, chief commissary of subsistence, Third Division, Twentieth Army Corps. Capt. P. U. Schmitt, chief quartermaster, Third Division, Twentieth Army Corps. Capt. J. S. Ransom, provost-marshal, Third Division, Twentieth Army Corps.	Major-General Sheridan commends these officers to the notice of the commanding general, "all of whom rendered valuable services."
Capt. F. T. Starkweather, chief quartermaster, Fourth Division, Fourteenth Army Corps. Captain Leech, chief commissary of subsistence, Fourth Division, Fourteenth Army Corps. Capt. C. O. Howard, assistant commissary of musters, Fourth Division, Fourteenth Army Corps. Captain Floyd, aide-de-camp, Fourth Division, Fourteenth Army Corps. Captain Hanna, provost-marshal, Fourth Division, Fourteenth Army Corps.	Major-General Reynolds says these officers were at their posts, discharged their duties promptly and faithfully.
Capt. J. Gordon Taylor, Capt. W. L. Avery, staff, Reserve Corps. Capt. Seth B. Moe, staff, First Division, Reserve Corps.	"Were with me and rendered me efficient service," says Major-General Granger. Of General Steedman's staff and deserve special mention, says Major-General Granger.
Capt. T. W. Morrison, aide-de-camp, First Division, Twentieth Army Corps. Capt. T. H. Daily, aide-de-camp, First Division, Twentieth Army Corps. Capt. F. E. Reynolds, aide-de-camp, First Division, Twentieth Army Corps. Capt. W. A. Hotchkiss, chief of artillery, First Division, Twentieth Army Corps. Capt. H. N. Snyder, assistant commissary of musters, First Division, Twentieth Army Corps. Capt. H. W. Hall, assistant inspector-general, First Division, Twentieth Army Corps. Capt. J. P. Pope, commissary of subsistence, First Division, Twentieth Army Corps.	Brigadier-General Davis says their efficiency was well tested, and expresses many obligations to them.
Capt. M. P. Bestow, assistant adjutant-general, First Division, Twenty-first Army Corps. Capt. L. D. Myers, assistant quartermaster, First Division, Twenty-first Army Corps. Capt. James McDonald, commissary of subsistence, First Division, Twenty-first Army Corps. Capt. J. E. George, assistant commissary of musters, First Division, Twenty-first Army Corps. Capt. W. McLoughlin, topographical engineer, First Division, Twenty-first Army Corps.	Brigadier-General Wood says these officers performed their duties well, both in camp and on the battle-field.

Name, rank, and command.	Remarks.
Capt. J. S. Wilson, assistant adjutant-general, First Brigade, Second Division, Fourteenth Army Corps.	Brig. Gen. John Beatty expresses himself most particularly indebted for most valuable assistance.
Capt. J. W. Forsyth, acting assistant inspector-general, Third Brigade, First Division, Fourteenth Army Corps.	Rendered prompt and efficient service, says Brigadier-General King.
Capt. J. B. Mulligan, Nineteenth U. S. Infantry, provost marshal, Third Brigade, First Division, Fourteenth Army Corps.	
Capt. R. M. Dysart, Capt. W. Wall, Second Brigade, First Division, Fourteenth Army Corps.	Commended for general good conduct by Brigadier-General Starkweather.
Captain Curtis, assistant adjutant-general, Third Brigade, Fourth Division, Fourteenth Army Corps.	
Captain Price, acting assistant inspector general, Third Brigade, Fourth Division, Fourteenth Army Corps.	Commended for good conduct by Brigadier-General Turchin.
Captain Robbins, provost-marshal, Third Brigade, Fourth Division, Fourteenth Army Corps.	
Capt. A. J. Davis, assistant adjutant-general, First Brigade, Third Division, Fourteenth Army Corps.	Commended by Colonel Connell for good conduct.
Captain Bartlett, Captain Wells, Captain Metzner, Captain Taft, staff, Second Division, Twentieth Army Corps.	Brigadier-General Johnson commends them for gallantry on the battle-field, and says "Captains Bartlett and Wells were with me all the time."
Capt. Louis J. Lambert, assistant adjutant-general, Third Division, Fourteenth Army Corps.	Brigadier-General Brannan says they performed their duties with fearlessness and great gallantry, carrying orders under the severest fire, and using every effort to rally and encourage the troops.
Capt. George S. Roper, commissary of subsistence, Third Division, Fourteenth Army Corps.	
Capt. Lewis Johnson, provost-marshal, Third Division, Fourteenth Army Corps.	
Capt. E. A. Otis, assistant adjutant-general, Third Division, Twenty-first Army Corps.	
Capt. Carter B. Harrison, acting assistant inspector-general, Third Division, Twenty-first Army Corps.	
Capt. J. O. Stanage, commissary of subsistence, Third Division, Twenty-first Army Corps.	Brigadier-General Van Cleve applauds them for the readiness with which they performed every duty.
Capt. A. K. Robinson, topographical engineer, Third Division, Twenty-first Army Corps.	
Captain Sheafe, provost-marshal, Third Division, Twenty-first Army Corps.	
Capt. A. L. Hough, assistant commissary of musters, Second Division, Fourteenth Army Corps.	Performed important services, exhibiting gallantry and efficiency, and worthy of special mention, says Major-General Negley.
Captain Johnson, acting assistant inspector-general, Fourteenth Army Corps.	
Capt. Charles B. Mann, provost-marshal, Second Brigade, Third Division, Fourteenth Army Corps.	Mentioned for good conduct by Colonel Chapman, commanding brigade.
Capt. J. W. Riley, topographical engineer, Second Brigade, Third Division, Fourteenth Army Corps.	
Capt. R. M. Black, staff, Reserve Corps.	Mentioned for good conduct by Colonel Mitchell, commanding.
Captain Anderson, Fifty-second Ohio, staff, Second Brigade, Second Division, Reserve Corps.	Mentioned for good conduct by Col. Daniel McCook.
Captain Swift, Fifty-second Ohio, staff	
Captain Deane, Eighty-sixth Illinois, staff	
Dr. Hooton, Eighty-sixth Illinois, staff	
Capt. Joseph M. Randall, acting assistant quartermaster, Third Brigade, First Division, Twenty-first Army Corps	Commended for good conduct by Colonel Harker, commanding.
Capt. G. W. Roberts, acting commissary of subsistence, Third Brigade, First Division, Twenty-first Army Corps.	
Captain Peden, provost-marshal, Third Brigade, Second Division, Twenty-first Army Corps.	Commended for good conduct by Colonel Grose, commanding.
Captain Brooks, acting assistant inspector-general, Third Brigade, Second Division, Twenty-first Army Corps.	
Capt. C. F. King, assistant adjutant-general, Second Brigade, Third Division, Twenty-first Army Corps.	Mentioned for good conduct by Colonel Dick, commanding.
Capt. S. West, acting assistant adjutant-general, First Brigade, First Division, Twentieth Army Corps.	Colonel Post, commanding, says deserve the highest praise.
Captain Hatch, acting assistant inspector-general, First Brigade, First Division, Twentieth Army Corps.	

Name, rank, and command.	Remarks.
Capt. John Crowell, jr., assistant adjutant-general, Second Brigade, Second Division, Twenty-first Army Corps.	
Capt. H. W. Johnson, assistant quartermaster.	Mentioned for good conduct by Brigadier-General Hazen.
Capt. James McCleery, acting assistant inspector-general.	
Capt. L. A. Cole, provost-marshal............	
Capt. W. C. Harris, Thirty-eighth Illinois, Second Brigade, First Division, Twentieth Army Corps.	Brigadier-General Carlin says, "Acted as aide-de-camp on the field, and frequently volunteered to perform the most perilous duties."
Capt. S. P. Voris, Thirty-eighth Illinois, Second Brigade, First Division, Twentieth Army Corps.	"Was constantly under fire, and deserves credit for gallantry and efficiency," says Brigadier-General Hazen.
Captain Strader, staff, Sixth Indiana, Third Brigade, Second Division, Twentieth Army Corps.	Colonel Berry, commanding, says, "Although he received a painful wound in the knee, like a true soldier refused to leave the field."
Capt. J. E. Jones, staff, First Ohio, Third Brigade, Second Division, Twentieth Army Corps.	Colonel Berry, commanding, calls him a brave and earnest officer.
Captain Warner, Twenty-sixth Ohio, staff, First Brigade, First Division, Twenty-first Army Corps.	Noticed for good conduct by Colonel Buell, commanding.
Lieut. S. Sterne, First Brigade, First Division, Twenty-first Army Corps.	
Capt. W. H. Fairbanks, acting assistant adjutant-general, First Brigade, Second Division, Twenty-first Army Corps.	Mentioned by Brigadier General Cruft for good conduct.
Capt. James A. Grover, assistant adjutant-general, First Brigade, Third Division, Twentieth Army Corps.	Colonel Miller, commanding, says, "He was continually found in the thickest fire, and where his presence was most required."
Capt. Carl Schmitt, assistant adjutant-general, First Brigade, Second Division, Twentieth Army Corps.	Mentioned by Brigadier-General Willich for especial good conduct.
Capt. W. H. Catching, assistant adjutant-general, Third Brigade, Third Division, Twenty-first Army Corps.	Mentioned by Colonel Barnes, commanding, as deserving of promotion for good conduct in aiding to rally the command when forced back.
Capt. John North, assistant inspector-general.	
Capt. James G. Elwood, acting assistant adjutant-general, First Brigade, First Division, Twenty-first Army Corps.	Mentioned by Colonel Buell, commanding, for good conduct in the hottest of the fight.
Capt. William Baldwin, assistant inspector-general.	
Capt. H. Gardner, provost-marshal............	
Capt. B. A. Carroll, Second Brigade, Third Division, Twentieth Army Corps.	
Captain Fuelle, acting assistant adjutant-general.	Mentioned for good conduct by Colonel Laiboldt, commanding brigade.
Captain Morgan, assistant inspector-general..	
Captain Gale, assistant quartermaster and commissary of subsistence.	
Capt. G. Freysleben, staff, Second Brigade, Third Division, Twentieth Army Corps.	Colonel Laiboldt, commanding brigade, mentions him for gallant conduct.
Captain Mohrhardt, topographical engineer, Third Division, Twentieth Army Corps.	Mentioned by Major-General Sheridan as having rendered valuable services.
Captain Knox, aide-de-camp, Twenty-first Army Corps.	Specially mentioned for good conduct by Major-General Crittenden.
Captain McCook, aide-de-camp, Twenty-first Army Corps.	
Capt. J. R. Beatty, assistant adjutant-general, Third Brigade, Third Division, Fourteenth Army Corps.	
Capt. E. B. Thoenssen, aide-de-camp, Third Brigade, Third Division, Fourteenth Army Corps.	Colonel Van Derveer commends them for their efficiency, personal courage, and energy, whose conduct, he says, deserve more than praise.
Capt. C. A. Cilley, topographical engineer, Third Brigade, Third Division, Fourteenth Army Corps.	
Lieutenant Burroughs, assistant engineer.	Mentioned by Major-General Rosecrans, commanding, for the zeal and ability with which he discharged his duties. Major-General McCook also mentions him for valuable assistance in rallying the troops.
Lieut. William L. Porter, acting aide-de-camp.	
Lieut. James K. Reynolds, acting aide-de-camp.	Were on the field of battle. There, as elsewhere, discharged their duties with zeal and energy.
Lieut. M. J. Kelly, chief of couriers	
Asst. Surg. D. Bache........................	
Lieut. Jacob C. Donaldson, Thirty-eighth Ohio, First Brigade, Third Division, Fourteenth Army Corps.	Mentioned by Colonel Connell for great gallantry.
Lieut. Friedrich Lipps, Second Brigade, Third Division, Twentieth Army Corps.	Specially mentioned for true courage and valor by Colonel Laiboldt, commanding brigade.
Lieut. J. M. Ruffner, Seventeenth Ohio, First Brigade, Third Division, Fourteenth Army Corps.	Colonel Connell specially mentions his "daring and coolness," and says, "After our lines fell back he remained at the breastworks, standing with the colors of the Eighty-second Indiana in his hands, firing with his revolver upon the enemy."

Name, rank, and command.	Remarks.
Lieut. T. R. Thatcher, Seventeenth Ohio, First Brigade, Third Division, Fourteenth Army Corps.	Colonel Connell, says of him that while rallying men he was struck from his horse, one already having been shot under him, and lay on the field until the enemy's lines had passed over him, when he succeeded in escaping.
Lieut. J. J. Donohoe, Thirty-first Ohio, First Brigade, Third Division, Fourteenth Army Corps.	Colonel Connell says that while making his way through the enemy's lines was severely wounded, but still remained on duty.
Lieut. David Flansburg, Fourth Indiana Battery, Second Brigade, First Division, Fourteenth Army Corps.	Was wounded, and specially named by Brigadier-General Starkweather for his coolness and bravery.
Lieut. S. T. Davis, Seventy-seventh Pennsylvania, Second Brigade, Second Division, Twentieth Army Corps.	Mentioned by Colonel Dodge, commanding brigade, for good conduct.
Lieutenant and Adjutant Morse, Twenty first Michigan, First Brigade, Third Division, Twentieth Army Corps.	Mentioned, as having particularly distinguished himself, by Colonel Miller, commanding brigade.
Adjutant Miller, Eighty-eighth Illinois, First Brigade, Third Division, Twentieth Army Corps. Adjutant Clark, Thirty-sixth Illinois, First Brigade, Third Division, Twentieth Army Corps. Adjutant Baldwin, Twenty-fourth Wisconsin, First Brigade, Third Division, Twentieth Army Corps.	Mentioned, as having particularly distinguished themselves, by Colonel Miller, commanding brigade.
Adjutant Turner, Ninety-second Ohio, Third Brigade, Fourth Division, Fourteenth Army Corps.	Lieutenant-Colonel Putnam, commanding regiment, commends him for distinguished bravery.
Adjutant Hamilton [One hundred and thirteenth Ohio], Reserve Corps.	Major-General Granger names him as conspicuous for efficiency and deserving of especial notice.
First Lieut. M. B. Gary, First Ohio Artillery, Second Brigade, Third Division, Fourteenth Army Corps.	Named by Brigadier-General Brannan for good conduct.
Lieut. C. Livingston, Third Wisconsin Battery, First Brigade, Third Division, Twenty-first Army Corps.	"Deserves particular notice for good conduct," says Brigadier-General Van Cleve.
First Lieut. F. G. Smith, Company I, Fourth U. S. Artillery, Third Division, Fourteenth Army Corps. First Lieut. George B. Rodney, Company I, Fourth U. S. Artillery, Third Division, Fourteenth Army Corps.	Commended for ability and good conduct by Brigadier-General Brannan and Colonel Van Derveer.
Second Lieut. Israel Ludlow, Company H, Fifth U. S. Artillery, Third Brigade, First Division, Fourteenth Army Corps. Second Lieut. J. A. Fessenden, Company H, Fifth U. S. Artillery, Third Brigade, First Division, Fourteenth Army Corps.	Commended highly by Brigadier-General King for their bravery, the first being shot down and taken prisoner, and the last named, though wounded several times, remained on duty till the close of the fight.
Second Lieutenant Miller, Company G, First Missouri Artillery, Second Brigade, Third Division, Twentieth Army Corps. First Lieut. G. Schueler, Second Brigade, Third Division, Twentieth Army Corps.	Highly commended for bravery by Colonel Laiboldt, commanding brigade.
Lieut. D. H. Throup, First Brigade, Second Division, Twenty-first Army Corps.	Commended by Brigadier-General Cruft for good conduct.
Lieut. G. J. Cockerill, Second Division, Twenty-first Army Corps. Lieut. N. A. Baldwin, Second Division, Twenty-first Army Corps.	Major-General Palmer commends them for their skill and gallantry and says they deserve well of their country.
Lieutenant Willits, Second Brigade, First Division, Fourteenth Army Corps.	Mentioned for good conduct by Brigadier-General Starkweather.
Lieut. H. C. Cushing, Company H, Fourth U. S. Artillery, Second Division, Twenty-first Army Corps. Lieut. F. L. D Russell, Company M, Fourth U. S. Artillery, Second Division, Twenty first Army Corps.	Colonel Grose, commanding brigade, says, "Although they look like mere boys, yet for bravery and effective service they are not excelled, if equaled, by any artillerist in the army; they have the credit of being in the last of the fighting, and then retiring all but the loss of one piece, disabled." Major-Generals Crittenden and Palmer also commend them as especially conspicuous for their skill and gallantry.
Adjt. E. F. Bishop, Eighty-ninth Illinois, First Brigade, Second Division, Twentieth Army Corps. Lieutenant Warren, Eighty-ninth Illinois, First Brigade, Second Division, Twentieth Army Corps. Lieutenant Ellis, Eighty-ninth Illinois, First Brigade, Second Division, Twentieth Army Corps.	Major Williams, commanding regiment, says they distinguished themselves.
Lieutenant Norvell, Thirty-ninth Indiana, Second Division, Twentieth Army Corps. Adjutant Fortner, Thirty-ninth Indiana, Second Division, Twentieth Army Corps.	Colonel Harrison, commanding regiment, calls attention to the gallant conduct of these officers.

Name, rank, and command.	Remarks.
Adjt. H. H. Clark, Sixteenth U. S. Infantry, Third Brigade, First Division, Fourteenth Army Corps.	Captain Crofton, commanding regiment, mentions him for efficient services.
Adjt. C. D. Hammer, One hundred and twenty-fourth Ohio, Second Brigade, Second Division, Twenty-first Army Corps.	Major Hampson, commanding regiment, mentions him for efficient services.
Adjutant Mundy, Twenty-third Kentucky, Second Division, Twenty-first Army Corps. Lieutenant Duke, Twenty-third Kentucky..... Lieut. H. G. Shiner, Twenty-third Kentucky..	Mentioned specially for good conduct.
Lieutenant Choate, Sixth Ohio, Second Division, Twenty-first Army Corps.	
Lieutenant Irwin, Sixth Ohio.................. Lieutenant Lewis, Sixth Ohio... .... Lieutenant Meline, Sixth Ohio .... Lieutenant Glisan, Sixth Ohio..........	Mentioned by Major Erwin, commanding regiment, for gallant conduct.
Lieutenant Hills, Sixth Ohio, Second Division, Twenty-first Army Corps.	Colonel Wiley says, "Deserves special mention for deliberation and coolness and the obstinacy with which he held his ground."
Lieut. J. N. Clark, Forty-first Ohio, Second Division, Twenty-first Army Corps. Lieutenant Fisher, Forty-first Ohio, Second Division, Twenty-first Army Corps.	For zeal and gallantry and general good conduct, specially mentioned by Colonel Wiley, commanding regiment.
Lieut. A. Townsend, Eighteenth U. S. Infantry, Fourteenth Army Corps. Lieut. J. Powell .... Lieut. F. T. Bennett .... Lieut. E. D. Harding .... Lieut. M. N. Hutchinson .... Lieut. O. E. Davis...........................	Specially mentioned by Captain Smith, commanding regiment, for gallant and meritorious conduct on both days.
Adjt. Charles C. Whiting, Fifty-eighth Indiana, First Division, Twenty-first Army Corps. Lieutenant Davis, Fifty-eighth Indiana.	Specially named for good conduct by Lieutenant-Colonel Embree, commanding regiment.
Adjt. E. G. Whitesides, One hundred and twenty-fifth Ohio, First Division, Twenty-first Army Corps.	Specially named by Colonel Opdycke, commanding regiment, as conspicuous for gallant daring.
Adjt. A. B. Case, Thirteenth Michigan, First Division, Twenty-first Army Corps.	Col. J. B. Culver, commanding, calls special attention to his gallant and soldierly conduct.
Acting Adjt. Emery Malin, Thirteenth Ohio, Second Brigade, Third Division, Twenty-first Army Corps.	Captain Cosgrove specially mentions him for valuable services on the field, and for rallying the men.
Lieutenant Sieg, Thirteenth Ohio, Second Brigade, Third Division, Twenty-first Army Corps. Lieutenant Henderson, Thirteenth Ohio, Second Brigade, Third Division, Twenty-first Army Corps.	Captain Cosgrove, commanding regiment, specially mentions them for gallant conduct.
First Lieutenant Grove, First Ohio, Third Brigade, Second Division, Twentieth Army Corps. Second Lieutenant Hallenberg, First Ohio, Third Brigade, Second Division, Twentieth Army Corps.	Colonel Langdon, commanding, says both were seriously wounded and afterward rejoined, but were compelled to leave, being unable to continue with the regiment.
Lieutenant Davison, Ninety-ninth Ohio, Third Division, Twenty-first Army Corps. Lieutenant McConnell, Ninety-ninth Ohio, Third Division, Twenty-first Army Corps. Lieutenant Harper, Ninety-ninth Ohio, Third Division, Twenty-first Army Corps.	Colonel Swaine, commanding regiment, specially mentions them for valuable services.
Lieutenant Zoller, Fifth Kentucky.............	Captain Huston, commanding regiment, specially mentions him and says, "He kept his position most manfully."
Lieutenant McCorkhill, Fifth Kentucky, Second Division, Twentieth Army Corps. Lieutenant Miller, Fifth Kentucky............ Lieutenant Powell, Fifth Kentucky........... Lieutenant Thomas, Fifth Kentucky.......... Lieutenant Jones, Fifth Kentucky............	Mentioned for good conduct by Captain Huston, commanding regiment.
Adjutant Johnstone, Fifth Kentucky, Second Division, Twentieth Army Corps.	Mentioned by Captain Huston, commanding regiment, as conspicuous for courage.
First Lieut. Alfred Morrison, Fifth Indiana Battery, Third Brigade, Second Division, Twentieth Army Corps.	Captain Simonson, commanding, says he was wounded, and behaved gallantly.
Lieutenant Briggs, Fifth Indiana Battery, Third Brigade, Second Division, Twentieth Army Corps.	Captain Simonson, commanding, says he saved the battery on Sunday by his coolness.
Lieut. William Zay, Ninety-ninth Ohio, Third Brigade, Third Division, Twenty-first Army Corps.	Colonel Swaine, commanding regiment, says he held his position on the picket lines and captured a pistol from one of General Bragg's escort.
Adjutant Hodges, Forty-fourth Indiana, Second Brigade, Third Division, Twenty-first Army Corps.	Colonel Aldrich, commanding regiment, mentions him for good conduct.
Lieut. Harrison M. Shuey, Ninety-ninth Ohio, Third Brigade, Third Division, Twenty-first Army Corps.	Mentioned by Colonel Swaine as having volunteered his services to march skirmishers upon the enemy that was marching to a certain point, and performed efficient service.

Name, rank, and command.	Remarks.
Lieut. W. Eilanch, Second Brigade, Third Division, Twentieth Army Corps.	Colonel Laiboldt, commanding brigade, names him for good behavior.
Lieut. B. R. Wood, jr., Signal Corps, Twentieth Army Corps.	Favorably noticed by Major-General McCook.
Lieutenant Neudorff, Second Brigade, Third Division, Twentieth Army Corps. Lieutenant Heydtman, topographical engineer.	Mentioned for good conduct by Colonel Laiboldt, commanding brigade.
Lieut. C. M. Harvey, escort, Twenty-first Army Corps.	Major-General Crittenden says, "To habitual good conduct in camp he has added good conduct in the field."
Lieutenant Shaw, escort, Second Division, Twenty-first Army Corps.	Major-General Palmer says he exhibited commendable courage.
Lieutenant Scarritt, aide-de-camp, Second Division, Twenty-first Army Corps. Lieutenant Thomas, aide-de-camp.	Major-General Palmer says, "Behaved with great gallantry."
Lieutenant Chilton, Second Division, Twenty-first Army Corps. Lieutenant Peck, chief of transportation. Lieutenant Croxton, ordnance.	Major-General Palmer commends them for faithful performance of duties.
Lieut. Robert W. Williams, aide-de-camp, Third Brigade, Fourth Division, Fourteenth Army Corps.	Mentioned by Brigadier-General Turchin for good conduct.
Lieut. A. O. Johnson, staff, Third Brigade, Third Division, Twentieth Army Corps. Lieutenant Hanback, staff. Lieut. C. Montague, staff.	Mentioned by Colonel Walworth for good conduct.
Lieut. A. J. Douglass, ordnance, Third Division, Twentieth Army Corps. Lieut. F. H. Allen, aide-de-camp, Third Division, Twentieth Army Corps. Lieut. M. V. Sheridan, aide-de-camp. Lieut. T. W. C. Moore, aide-de-camp.	Commended to the notice of the commanding general as having rendered valuable services by Major-General Sheridan.
Lieut. Alfred Pirtle, aide-de-camp, Third Division, Twentieth Army Corps.	After the death of Brigadier-General Lytle this officer reported to Major-General Sheridan, who says, "He behaved very handsomely."
Lieut. J. E. Remington, acting assistant quartermaster, First Division, Twentieth Army Corps. Lieut. J. P. Kuntze, topographical engineer. Lieut. J. M. Butler, ordnance.	Mentioned by Brigadier-General Davis for good conduct.
Lieut. A. S. Smith, staff, Second Division, Twentieth Army Corps. Lieut. J. J. Kessler, staff. Lieut. Edward Davis, staff.	Brigadier-General Johnson expresses his thanks for their gallantry on the battle-field.
Lieut. Ira V. Germain, aide-de-camp, Third Division, Fourteenth Army Corps. Lieut. T. V. Webb, aide-de-camp. Lieutenant Dunn, topographical engineer.	Brigadier-General Brannan compliments them for gallant conduct under the severest fire.
Lieut. J. W. White, ordnance, Third Division, Fourteenth Army Corps.	Specially mentioned for efficient services by Brigadier-General Brannan.
Lieut. W. H. H. Sheets, ordnance, Third Division, Twenty-first Army Corps.	Mentioned for good conduct by Brigadier-General Van Cleve.
Lieutenant Moody, aide-de-camp, Second Division, Fourteenth Army Corps.	Major-General Negley names him for gallantry and efficient services.
Lieut. A. E. Alden, acting assistant inspector-general, Third Brigade, Third Division, Fourteenth Army Corps.	Colonel Van Derveer, commanding brigade, praises him highly for his courage and efficiency.
Lieut. Charles V. Ray, acting assistant adjutant-general, Second Brigade, Third Division, Fourteenth Army Corps. Lieut. W. F. Spofford, acting assistant inspector-general. Lieut. J. E. Simpson, aide-de-camp.	Colonel Chapman mentions these for good conduct.
Lieut. J. L. Yaryan, First Division, Twenty-first Army Corps. Lieut. George Shaffer, aide-de-camp. Lieut. P. Haldeman, ordnance.	Brigadier-General Wood mentions these for good conduct.
Lieut. T. G. Beaham, staff, Reserve Corps.	Major-General Granger says that he rendered efficient aid and service.
Lieutenant Blandin, staff, First Division Reserve Corps.	Major-General Granger names him as deserving special mention.
Lieut. J. W. Armstrong, ordnance, Fourth Division, Fourteenth Army Corps. Lieut. W. P. Bainbridge, aide-de-camp, Fourth Division, Fourteenth Army Corps. Lieut. W. J. Lyster, Nineteenth U. S. Infantry, aide-de-camp, Third Brigade, First Division, Fourteenth Army Corps.	Major-General Reynolds mentions these for the prompt and faithful manner they discharged their duties.
Lieut. H. G. Litchfield, Eighteenth U. S. Infantry, acting assistant inspector-general. Lieut. J. J. Wagoner, acting assistant quartermaster. Lieut. S. S. Culbertson, acting commissary of subsistence.	Mentioned by Brigadier-General King for prompt and effective service.

Name, rank, and command.	Remarks.
Lieutenant Reichardt, staff, Second Brigade, First Division, Fourteenth Army Corps. Lieutenant Hazzard..	Mentioned for good conduct by Brigadier-General Starkweather.
Lieutenant Collins, staff, Second Brigade, First Division, Reserve Corps. Lieutenant Hamilton.........................	Named by Colonel Mitchell, commanding, for good conduct.
Lieutenant Rogers, staff, Reserve Corps	Mentioned by Col. Dan McCook for good conduct.
Lieut. W. E. Carlin, aide-de-camp, Second Brigade, First Division, Twentieth Army Corps. Lieut. J. W. Vance, acting assistant inspector general.	Brigadier-General Carlin says they were constantly under fire, gallant and efficient, the two last named being both captured while in the discharge of their duties.
Lieutenant McGowan, acting aide-de-camp .. Lieutenant Culbertson, acting aide-de-camp...	
Lieutenant Scott, topographical engineer, Third Brigade, Second Division, Twenty-first Army Corps.	Colonel Grose, commanding brigade, mentions him for good conduct.
Lieutenant Lindsay,* staff, Second Brigade, Third Division, Twenty-first Army Corps. Lieut. F. F. Kibler, topographical engineer....	Noticed by Colonel Dick, commanding brigade, for good conduct.
Lieutenant Mason, aide-de-camp, First Brigade, First Division, Twentieth Army Corps.	Mentioned by Colonel Post, commanding brigade, as deserving the highest praise.
Lieut. W. N. Williams, staff, Third Brigade, Second Division, Twentieth Army Corps. Lieut. J. J. Siddall, staff	Mentioned by Colonel Berry, commanding brigade, as earnest and efficient officers.
Lieut. W. M. Beebe, jr., aide-de-camp, Second Brigade, Second Division, Twenty-first Army Corps.	
Lieutenant Atwood, aide-de-camp, Second Brigade, Second Division, Twenty-first Army Corps.	
Lieutenant Cobb, acting commissary of subsistence, Second Brigade, Second Division, Twenty-first Army Corps.	Mentioned for good conduct by Brigadier-General Hazen.
Lieut. A. G. Bierce, topographical engineer, Second Brigade, Second Division, Twenty-first Army Corps.	
Lieutenant Sterne, staff, First Brigade, First Division, Twenty-first Army Corps.	
Lieut J. C. Williams, staff .... Lieut. Zach. Jones, staff . ... Lieutenant Ludden, staff.....................	Mentioned by Colonel Buell, commanding, for good conduct.
Lieut. John A. Wright, aide-de-camp, First Brigade, Second Division, Twenty-first Army Corps.	
Lieut. H. Weincdel, acting assistant inspector-general, First Brigade, Second Division, Twenty-first Army Corps.	Mentioned by Brigadier-General Cruft for good conduct.
Lieut. J. B. Socwell, acting commissary of subsistence, First Brigade, Second Division, Twenty-first Army Corps.	
Lieut. George R. Crow, topographical engineer, First Brigade, Second Division, Twenty-first Army Corps.	
Lieut. J. P. Phipps, aide-de-camp, Third Brigade, Third Division, Twenty-first Army Corps.	
Lieut. Jerry R. Dean, aide-de-camp, Third Brigade, Third Division, Twenty-first Army Corps.	Colonel Barnes, commanding brigade, recommends these for promotion for good conduct in aiding to rally the command when forced back on the 19th.
Lieut. T. M. Gunn, topographical engineer, Third Brigade, Third Division, Twenty-first Army Corps.	
Lieutenant Turnbull, acting assistant inspector-general, First Brigade, Third Division, Twentieth Army Corps.	
Lieutenant Boal, topographical engineer ..... Lieutenant Jackson, provost-marshal. .... Lieutenant Pirtle, aide-de-camp.............. Lieutenant Eaton, aide-de-camp	Colonel Miller, commanding brigade, names these for good conduct.
Lieutenant Butler, aide-de-camp, First Brigade, Second Division, Twentieth Army Corps.	
Lieutenant McGrath, aide-de-camp .... Lieutenant Green, acting assistant inspector-general.	Specially commended for good conduct by Brigadier-General Willich.
Lieutenant Blume, topographical engineer....	
Lieut. George Devol, acting assistant adjutant-general, First Brigade, First Division, Fourteenth Army Corps.	
Lieutenant Kelso, acting commissary of subsistence.	Mentioned by Colonel Scribner, commanding brigade, as worthy of especial praise.
Lieutenant Bird, acting assistant quartermaster.	
Lieutenant Hollister, aide-de-camp..........	

---

*Probably intended for Lieut. John C. Livezey, of Colonel Grose's staff.

Name, rank, and command.	Remarks.
Sergt. William C. Miles, Company H, Third Kentucky Cavalry, Second Division, Twentieth Army Corps.	Specially named for good conduct by Brigadier-General Johnson.
Sergt. Samuel Goodwin, One hundredth Illinois, First Division, Twenty-first Army Corps.	Brigadier-General Wood speaks of him as having taken the division colors when the bearer of them was shot down, and bore them aloft during the day, remaining with him all the time.
Sergt. Charles A. Allen, Company E, Seventy-fourth Illinois, First Brigade, First Division, Twentieth Army Corps.	Colonel Post says that in the performance of delicate and important duty he displayed much tact and gallantry.
Corp. Dorsey A. Leimin, Company I, Twenty-fourth Ohio Regiment, Third Brigade, Second Division, Twenty-first Army Corps.	Colonel Grose, commanding brigade, says of him, "Seeing the bearer of the brigade flag fall, he rushed to it and bore it off the field, as he did his own regimental colors on two occasions the day before. He is highly deserving the notice of the appointing power."
Sergeant S. Jennings, First Missouri Artillery, Second Brigade, Third Division, Twentieth Army Corps.	Mentioned for brave behavior by Colonel Laiboldt.
Corp. Jesse R. Dodd, Thirty-first Indiana, First Brigade, Second Division, Twenty-first Army Corps.	
Corp. James J. Holliday, Ninetieth Ohio	Both complimented by Brigadier-General Cruft for gallant conduct in seizing the colors of their regiments upon the fall of their color-bearers and bravely bearing them during the rest of the fight.
Sergt. Maj. E. J. Stivers, Eighty-ninth Illinois, First Brigade, Second Division, Twentieth Army Corps.	Major Williams, commanding regiment, says he deserves special mention for his bravery.
Sergt. J. Holmes, Company B, Ninety-third Ohio, Third Brigade, Second Division, Twentieth Army Corps.	
Corp. George Rosscoe, Company C, Ninety-third Ohio.	Colonel Martin, commanding regiment, says of these, "Their coolness, bravery, and determination, who were wounded slightly, but remained with their companies and performed duty, deserve special mention."
Corp. G. W. Gifford, Company C, Ninety-third Ohio.	
Sergt. Maj. Stanley G. Pope, Sixty-fifth Ohio, Third Brigade, First Division, Twenty-first Army Corps.	
First Sergt. Samuel P. Snider, Company D, Sixty-fifth Ohio.	Captain Powell, commanding regiment, makes special mention of these for general good conduct—the first deserving special credit for his efforts to keep the men together; the second, commanding a company, for his bravery in leading his men; and the third, color-bearer, for bravely facing the storm of bullets, and on being severely wounded continuing at his post until ordered to the rear.
Sergt. G. W. Harlam, Company B, Sixty-fifth Ohio.	
Corporal Strock, Company E, Forty-first Ohio, Second Division, Twenty-first Army Corps.	Colonel Wiley, commanding regiment, says, "For pursuing two prisoners, who took refuge in a house when the regiment repelled the last charge on Saturday afternoon, he deserves special mention."
Sergt. Maj. Isaac D'Isay, Eighteenth U. S. Infantry, Third Brigade, First Division, Fourteenth Army Corps.	
Sergt. R. W. Evans, Eighteenth U. S. Infantry, Third Brigade, First Division, Fourteenth Army Corps.	Captain Smith, commanding regiment, specially mentions them for gallant and meritorious conduct.
Sergeant-Major Fowler, Fifty-eighth Indiana, First Division, Twenty-first Army Corps.	Lieutenant-Colonel Embree, commanding regiment, says he proved himself worthy of promotion.
Sergeant Miller, Company K, Fifty-eighth Indiana, First Division, Twenty-first Army Corps.	Lieutenant-Colonel Embree, commanding regiment, says that though sick and almost unable to move about the field, he stood bravely to his post.
Sergeant Miller, Company C, First Ohio, Third Brigade, Second Division, Twentieth Army Corps.	Lieutenant-Colonel Langdon, commanding regiment, specially mentions him for gallant conduct.
Sergt. William Duncan, Company C, Ninety-ninth Ohio, Third Division, Twenty-first Army Corps.	Colonel Swaine, commanding regiment, says he deserves the warmest praise for his gallantry and coolness, holding the colors aloft during retreat, that the men might rally.
Sergt. Maj. D. R. Cook, Forty-ninth Ohio, First Brigade, Second Division, Twentieth Army Corps.	Major Gray, commanding regiment, mentions him for gallantry.
Corp. William Murphy, Company I, Fifth Kentucky, Third Brigade, Second Division, Twentieth Army Corps.	Captain Huston, commanding, says when the color-bearer was shot he seized the flag and thenceforth bore it.
Sergt. L. Schile, Third Brigade, Second Division, Twentieth Army Corps.	
Sergt. Thomas Dunn	Colonel Berry, commanding, mentions them for good conduct.
Sergt. J. H. Parks, Company D, Ninety-third Ohio, Third Brigade, Second Division, Twentieth Army Corps.	Colonel Martin, commanding, specially mentions him for good conduct.
Sergt. Maj. O. M. Gottschall, Ninety-third Ohio, Third Brigade, Second Division, Twentieth Army Corps.	Colonel Martin, commanding, mentions him as having remained upon the field after being wounded.
Sergt. Thomas J. Myers, Battery I, Fourth U. S. Artillery, Third Division, Fourteenth Army Corps.	
Sergt. Charles Ellis, Battery I, Fourth U. S. Artillery, Third Division, Fourteenth Army Corps.	Lieutenant Smith, commanding battery, specially mentions them for gallantry.

Name, rank, and command.	Remarks.
Sergt. S. E. Lawrence, Fourth Michigan Battery, Third Division, Fourteenth Army Corps.	Captain Church, commanding battery, mentions him for gallantry.
Sergt. A. C. Dilley, Company C, One hundred and twenty-fifth Ohio, First Division, Twenty-first Army Corps.	
Sergt. R. D. Barnes, Company B, One hundred and twenty-fifth Ohio, First Division, Twenty-first Army Corps.	Colonel Opdycke, commanding regiment, specially mentions them for good conduct.
Sergt. H. N. Steadman, Company B, One hundred and twenty-fifth Ohio, First Division, Twenty-first Army Corps.	
Private John Adkins, Company D, Second Kentucky, Twenty-first Army Corps.	Major-General Crittenden says they remained on the field with his staff both days and aided as much as any one in rallying the men ; that they are competent to command and deserving of it.
Private George C. James, Company A, Sixth Ohio, Twenty-first Army Corps.	
Private H. H. Eby, Company C, Seventh Illinois Cavalry, Twenty-first Army Corps.	Major-General Palmer says, "He remained with me all day as orderly, but at the close of the battle, on Sunday, was wounded and fell into the hands of the enemy."
Private Robert Hays, Company C, Thirtieth Indiana, Twentieth Army Corps.	Is specially mentioned for good conduct by Brigadier-General Johnson.
Private Robert Lemon, Company I, Fifty-eighth Indiana, Twenty-first Army Corps.	Being one of Brigadier-General Wood's escort, he says, "When I called, this brave and devoted boy, a youth of not more than sixteen or seventeen years of age, responded."
Orderly T. Marr, Company C, Twenty-ninth Indiana, Second Brigade, Second Division, Twentieth Army Corps.	Colonel Dodge, commanding brigade, says, "By their coolness and courage showed that they were worthy of holding commissions."
Orderly J. McCarty, Company E, Thirty-fourth Illinois, Second Brigade, Second Division, Twentieth Army Corps.	
Orderly G. Hirshheurser, First Brigade, Second Division, Twentieth Army Corps.	Brigadier-General Willich says he distinguished himself greatly and fell wounded in the enemy's hands.
Orderly Black, Seventy-seventh Pennsylvania, Twentieth Army Corps.	Colonel Dodge, commanding brigade, says he was severely wounded, if not killed, while with Lieutenant Davis, of his staff, collecting men that were separated from their commands.
Private Samuel Morris, Company B, First Ohio Cavalry, Third Brigade, First Division, Twenty-first Army Corps.	Colonel Harker, commanding brigade, says, "Throughout the fight this brave youth was ever at my side ready for the performance of his duty."
Orderly Isaac Bigelow, Third Brigade, Second Division, Twenty-first Army Corps.	Colonel Grose, commanding brigade, mentions these for good conduct, both being wounded on the 20th, Shirk seriously while carrying the brigade flag.
Orderly George Shirk, Thirty-sixth Indiana, Third Brigade, Second Division, Twenty-first Army Corps.	
Orderly Waffle, Company K, Ninth Indiana Infantry, Second Brigade, Second Division, Twenty-first Army Corps.	
Orderly Bierce, Second Brigade, Second Division, Twenty-first Army Corps.	Brigadier-General Hazen speaks of these as deserving of special notice for their good conduct.
Orderly Morrison, Second Brigade, Second Division, Twenty-first Army Corps.	
Orderly Sweeney, Company K, Ninth Indiana, Second Brigade, Second Division, Twenty-first Army Corps.	
Orderly Shepherd Scott, Company I, Forty-first Ohio Infantry, Second Brigade, Second Division, Twenty-first Army Corps.	Brigadier-General Hazen speaks of him as particularly distinguished for bravery and good service on two occasions ; that he brought on two occasions brigades to his assistance when needed, and was shot and killed or captured. If restored he recommends his promotion as second lieutenant.
Private Richard Sloane, Company G, Thirtieth Indiana, Second Brigade, Second Division, Twentieth Army Corps.	Colonel Dodge mentions him as conspicuous for good conduct; was severely wounded in the hand and head on Saturday while carrying an order and taken to the rear, but returned again for duty on the morning of the 20th.
Orderly Horace A. Hall, Company K, Fifty-eighth Indiana, First Brigade, First Division, Twenty-first Army Corps.	Colonel Buell, commanding brigade, specially mentions these for good conduct in the hottest of the fight.
Orderly John Scheck, First Brigade, First Division, Twenty-first Army Corps.	
Private Albia C. Zearing, Company B, Ninety-third Ohio, Third Brigade, Second Division, Twentieth Army Corps.	
Private John Sloan, Company B, Ninety-third Ohio, Third Brigade, Second Division, Twentieth Army Corps.	Colonel Martin, commanding regiment, says of these, their coolness, bravery, and determination, who were wounded slightly but remained with their companies and performed duty, "deserve special mention."
Private John Drewry, Company B, Ninety-third Ohio, Third Brigade, Second Division, Twentieth Army Corps.	
Private Henry Linn, Company B, Ninety-third Ohio, Third Brigade, Second Division, Twentieth Army Corps.	

Name, rank, and command.	Remarks.
Private Isaac C. Snavely, Company B, Ninety-third Ohio, Third Brigade, Second Division, Twentieth Army Corps. Private Samuel Rohrer, Company B, Ninety-third Ohio, Third Brigade, Second Division, Twentieth Army Corps. Private Allen Dodge, Company C, Ninety-third Ohio, Third Brigade, Second Division, Twentieth Army Corps. Private John McClay, Company D, Ninety-third Ohio, Third Brigade, Second Division, Twentieth Army Corps. Private William Armstrong, Company D, Ninety-third Ohio, Third Brigade, Second Division, Twentieth Army Corps. Private James M. Logan, Company D, Ninety-third Ohio, Third Brigade, Second Division, Twentieth Army Corps.	Colonel Martin, commanding regiment, says of these, their coolness, bravery, and determination, who were wounded slightly but remained with their companies and performed duty, " deserve special mention."
Private Charles C. Chapman, Company G, One hundred and twenty-fifth Ohio, First Division, Twenty-first Army Corps.	Colonel Opdycke specially mentions him as having distinguished himself for cool courage and capacity to command.
Private Samuel A. Hayes, Company F, Sixty-fourth Ohio, Third Brigade, First Division, Twenty-first Army Corps.	Colonel McIlvain, commanding regiment, mentions this incident in connection with his bravery: " He had lost his speech and had not spoken a word for nearly six months; on seeing a rebel fall he had shot at, exclaimed, in a clear voice, ' I have hit him !' and after that t·lked quite freely, being greatly rejoiced at his fortune. The brave fellow later in the day was wounded and left on the field."
Private J. H. Springher, Company I, First Ohio, Third Brigade, Second Division, Twentieth Army Corps. Private Caleb Copeland, Company A, First Ohio Private John McCarthy, Company A, First Ohio	Lieutenant-Colonel Langdon, commanding regiment, specially mentions them for gallant conduct.
Private Alexander Beecher, Company B, Eighty-ninth Illinois, First Brigade, Second Division, Twentieth Army Corps.	Major Williams, commanding, says that his company commissioned and non-commissioned officers being killed or disabled, he took command and was respected and obeyed.
Private David Kinsey, Company K, Ninety-third Ohio, Third Brigade, Second Division, Twentieth Army Corps.	Colonel Martin, commanding, specially mentions him for good conduct and capturing maps and papers while skirmishing.
Private John T. Steele, Company B, Fifth Kentucky, Third Brigade, Second Division, Twentieth Army Corps.	Captain Huston, commanding, says, " Struck four times; he stuck to his guns. When he was with the Ninety-third Ohio, when the cannons were captured, he captured the battle flag."

CINCINNATI, OHIO,
January 8, 1864.

GENERAL : I have the honor to transmit inclosed, through the proper military channels, a communication addressed to the President of the United States.

W. S. ROSECRANS,
Major-General.

Brig. Gen. LORENZO THOMAS,
Adjutant-General, U. S. Army, Washington, D. C.

[Indorsement.]

Inclosure not marked. Shown to Secretary of War and General-in-Chief. and sent to the President, January 14, 1864.

[Inclosure.]

CINCINNATI, OHIO, *January* 8, 1864.

TO THE PRESIDENT OF THE UNITED STATES :

I beg leave to respectfully invite the attention of Your Excellency to a violation of military usage and courtesy which, while it does me personal injustice, strikes a blow at discipline throughout the entire service.

A communication from Brig. Gen. Thomas J. Wood, one of my subordinate commanders, dated October 23, 1863,* based upon an extract from my official report, which he had no right to know anything about at that time, has been submitted to the War Department, and been received, publicly commented on by the General-in-Chief, and its publication authorized by the Secretary of War, without passing through me or being submitted to me, according to military custom and usage, for my remarks thereon.

It must be obvious to Your Excellency that if this practice is to be allowed in one case, all other subordinates are entitled to the same privileges concerning the reports of their superiors touching them, the admission of which would be destructive to all discipline, as it must also be obvious that, should this act go unrebuked, it will tend to impair the confidence of all officers in the justice of the Government and thereby weaken the military arm of the nation.

Very respectfully, your obedient servant,

W. S. ROSECRANS,
Major-General.

CINCINNATI, OHIO,
January 13, 1864.

GENERAL : The report of the General-in-Chief shows that a letter from one of my division commanders at the battle of Chickamauga, commenting on the report of his commanding general, has been received at the War Department, and subsequently published by its authority.   The General-in-Chief refers to that letter as a rival authority to my own and as raising doubt upon the accuracy of a point in my report.

The letter, dated October 23 [21] ultimo, four days after I left the command, is based on a quotation from my official report to which, evidently, the writer was not at that time entitled, and which, therefore, *prima facie,* was surreptitiously obtained.   It has been received and publicly used as a document disparaging my report, without having been referred to me or passing through my hands, as required by military courtesy and Army Regulations.

The War Department is therefore respectfully requested, as an act of justice, to cause the above and following observations to be filed and published as an appendix to my official report of the battle of Chickamauga.

Note in reference to General Wood's letter.—Brig. Gen. T. J. Wood writes and sends to the War Department a clandestine letter to show—contrary to the inference drawn in my report—that he did right, under an order to "close up on General Reynolds and support him," in taking his division out of the line of battle and in rear of Brannan's division to a reserve position in rear of Reynolds.

My report, dealing with facts and avoiding personal censure, shows that General Reynolds sent me word by Captain Kellogg, aide-de-camp to General Thomas, that there were no troops on his immediate right, and that he wanted support there; that supposing Bran-

---

* See p. 645.

nan's division had been called away, I told an aide to write General
Wood an order to close up on Reynolds and support him, who wrote
as follows:

HEADQUARTERS,
September 20—10.45 a. m.

Brigadier-General WOOD,
    Commanding Division:

The general commanding directs that you close up on Reynolds as fast as possible
and support him.
    Respectfully,

FRANK S. BOND,
Major, and Aide-de-Camp.

Now, with this order in his hand—
First. When General Wood found there was no interval to close,
because Brannan's troops had not left, his plain duty as a division
commander was to have reported that fact to the general commanding, who was not more than 600 yards from him, and asked further
orders. His failure to do so was a grave mistake, showing want of
military discretion.

Second. When about to move, notwithstanding this, his duty, on
being informed, as he was by one of his brigade commanders, that
his skirmishers were engaged and the enemy in line of battle opposite his position, General Wood was renewedly bound to have reported
these facts and taken orders before leaving his position at such a
critical time. But, instead of doing so, he precipitately withdrew his
troops from the line and let the enemy in, in the face of an order the
wording of which shows that no such operation as the opening but,
on the contrary, the closing of a gap was intended by it.

Third. This conduct of General Wood, treated in the report with
all the reserve consistent with the truth of history, contrasts most
unfavorably with that of General Brannan, commanding the division next on his left, who, a little earlier in the day, when he received an order to leave his position and support the left, finding
his skirmishers engaged, reported the fact to General Thomas, desiring to know if, under such circumstances, he should execute the
order, he was told, "No; stay where you are."

Fourth. It also contrasts with General Wood's own conduct and correspondence only a few days previously, when he protested against
a reprimand of his corps commander for not occupying a position at
Wauhatchie, lecturing his senior on the impropriety of what he
termed " blind obedience to orders," and in upward of fifty pages of
manuscript trying to prove his conduct consistent with that sound
discretion which a division commander ought to exercise in removing his troops from the danger threatened by the too literal execution of orders. The material difference of circumstances in the two
cases, as appears from his own writings, being that the discretion
he exercises at Wauhatchie and the " blind obedience " he pleads
at Chickamauga both have the effect of getting his troops out of
danger.

As the best of generals are liable to mistakes, I should have been
content to leave those of General Wood to the simple historical
statement of them, presuming he regretted them far more deeply
than even myself ; and so feeling I called attention to his military
virtues, vigilance, discipline, providence of his commissariat, and

care of his transportation, but his mean and unsoldierly defense of error shows him wrong both in head and heart.*

Respectfully, your obedient servant,

W. S. ROSECRANS,
Major-General.

Brig. Gen. Lorenzo Thomas,
Adjutant-General, U. S. Army.

[Indorsement.]

HEADQUARTERS OF THE ARMY,
Washington, D. C., January 25, 1864.

This communication is forwarded to the Secretary of War, with the following remarks :

According to the within statement, General Wood's letter is dated after General Rosecrans had been relieved from the command, and he then had no claim whatever that any report or other communication from officers not under his orders should pass through him. On the contrary, General Wood would have violated the Army Regulations and the usage of the service had he sent his report through General Rosecrans after the latter had been removed from command.

If the charge be true that General Wood surreptitiously obtained a copy of General Rosecrans' official report, it must have been so obtained at General Rosecrans' headquarters, or from some one of his staff, as his original report, sent through his chief of staff, was not received at the office of the Adjutant-General of the Army till October 28. Moreover, no publication of that or of General Wood's report has been authorized or permitted by the War Department, while it is known that portions of the former were published in the newspapers even before it reached the Adjutant-General's Office.

As General Rosecrans charges General Wood in this communication with obtaining an official document " surreptitiously," and with a "mean and unsoldierlike defense of error," I respectfully recommend that it be withheld from publication till the charges be investigated. I think a copy of General Rosecrans' letter should be sent to General Wood, in order that he may apply for such investigation, for if guilty as charged he is unfit for command.

H. W. HALLECK,
General-in-Chief.

___

HEADQUARTERS DEPARTMENT OF THE MISSOURI,
Saint Louis, Mo., March 3, 1864.

Colonel : About the 12th of January I addressed a letter to the President, calling his attention to the breach of military regulations and etiquette in publishing Brig. Gen. Thomas J. Wood's letter commenting on my official report of the battle of Chickamauga. I respectfully ask what indorsements have been made and what action taken thereon.

I also addressed a letter to Brig. Gen. L. Thomas, Adjutant-General U. S. Army, desiring it to be appended to my official report of the battle of Chickamauga, in reference to that letter of General Wood's, which was publicly alluded to by the General-in-Chief in his official report.

___

* See Wood to L. Thomas, p. 647, and Wood to Hardie, p. 648.

Please inform me whether that letter was received, what, if any, are the reasons why my request that it should be published as a part of my report has not been acceded to ?

The publication of General Wood's letter, by permission of the War Department, as an addenda to my report, was unjust, and the publication of my letter referring thereto was the least that should have been done to correct the injustice.

Very respectfully, your obedient servant,
W. S. ROSECRANS,
Major-General.

Col. E. D. TOWNSEND,
Assistant Adjutant-General, Washington, D. C.

WAR DEPARTMENT, ADJUTANT-GENERAL'S OFFICE,
March 23, 1864.

Maj. Gen. W. S. ROSECRANS, U. S. Vols.,
St. Louis, Mo.:

SIR: I have respectfully to acknowledge the receipt of your letter of the 3d instant, and to inform you that, in compliance with orders from the Secretary of War, a copy of your communication of January 13, 1864, in relation to the letter of Brig. Gen. T. J. Wood, dated October 21, 1863, has been sent to be printed as an appendix to your official report of the battle of Chickamauga.

I am, sir, very respectfully, your obedient servant,
E. D. TOWNSEND,
Assistant Adjutant-General.

WAR DEPARTMENT, ADJUTANT-GENERAL'S OFFICE,
March 23, 1864.

JOHN D. DEFREES, Esq.,
Superintendent of Public Printing:

SIR : By direction of the Secretary of War, I send herewith a copy of a communication* which Major-General Rosecrans desires to have published as an appendix to his report of the battle of Chickamauga, dated January 13, 1864.

I am, &c.,
E. D. TOWNSEND,
Assistant Adjutant-General.

ADDENDA.†

CRAWFISH SPRING, GA., *September* 18, 1863.
(Received September 19—12 m.)

Maj. Gen. H. W. HALLECK,
General-in-Chief:

Everything indicates that the enemy is determined to make every effort to overthrow this army. What we most need is to have our flanks well covered. You do not say how soon Hurlbut is to move. Please advise me what orders he has received, and from whence he is to draw subsistence. Even a movement in Tuscumbia Valley would

---

*See page 102.

† Comprising field dispatches, &c. (September 18–23), not forwarded as inclosures to Rosecrans' report. See pp. 65–77.

be of great importance at this time. Enemy demonstrating on our front now. We occupy line of West Chickamauga. Our cavalry on right covers Stevens' Gap.

W. S. ROSECRANS,
Major-General.

—

HDQRS. DEPARTMENT OF THE CUMBERLAND,
Crawfish Spring, Chickamauga Valley, September 18, 1863.

Major-General BURNSIDE:

I dispatched you on my arrival at Chattanooga, again on the 13th, and twice since then. It was very important you should close in on our left as soon as possible. Our cavalry has been worked so hard that it has decreased 2,100 from sickness and dismounted men since the commencement of campaign. Byrd should come down to Cleveland at once. If he is in any danger there he can come down to Tyner's Station, on our left. The remainder of your force should close down as soon as possible. The enemy are in our front in large force, occupying Pea Vine Valley and covering the roads to Dalton and Rome, headquarters at La Fayette. Johnston is with Bragg, with a large portion of his force, and re-enforcements have arrived from Virginia. We need all we can concentrate to oppose them. Let me hear from you.

W. S. ROSECRANS,
Major-General.

—

HEADQUARTERS FIRST CAVALRY BRIGADE,
Reed's Bridge, September 18, 1863—12.15 a. m.

Brigadier-General WOOD,
Commanding Gordon's Mills:

GENERAL: I sent report to General Rosecrans at 7 p. m. last evening. My report was delayed waiting for return of patrols, &c. A force of infantry passed through or near Graysville late yesterday a. m., which the citizens there state was General Spears'. Cannonading was heard yesterday afternoon north of Ringgold. Pegram's pickets are 9 miles up the Pea Vine Valley. Colonel Wilder encamped within 2 miles of me late last night. He states that he remarked a column of dust moving in the direction of La Fayette.

I am, respectfully, your obedient servant,
ROBT. H. G. MINTY,
Colonel, Cavalry Brigade.

—

HEADQUARTERS TWENTY-FIRST ARMY CORPS,
September 18, 1863—3 a. m.

E. A. OTIS,
Assistant Adjutant-General:

We have had indications of the enemy in our front. Some shots have been fired by men on foot at our pickets. A column of dust appears rather to the right of our front. Enemy have been seen both to the right and left of the road in front. I think they are advancing.

SIDNEY M. BARNES,
Colonel, Commanding Brigade.

HEADQUARTERS TWENTIETH ARMY CORPS,
Pond Spring, Ga., September 18, 1863—6.30 a. m.
Brig. Gen. JAMES A. GARFIELD,
Chief of Staff:
GENERAL : I have the honor to state for the information of the
general commanding that all is perfectly quiet on the right this morn-
ing.   I am just starting to ride my lines and make the changes in the
disposition of my forces prescribed in the latest orders.   General
Mitchell and I go to the right together.
　　Respectfully,
A. McD. McCOOK,
Major-General, Commanding.

—

ROSSVILLE,
September 18, 1863—8. a. m.
Captain MERRILL :
Nothing new.   All quiet here.

J. L. JONES.

—

SIGNAL STATION,
September 18, 1863—9 a. m.
Colonel FLYNT,
Chief of Staff:
A squad of the enemy can be seen in the field at the same point at
which they were observed last evening.
　　Respectfully,
W. A. SEITER,
Captain, Acting Signal Officer.
By H. C. JONES,
Acting Signal Officer.

—

HEADQUARTERS DEPARTMENT OF THE CUMBERLAND,
Crawfish Spring, September 18, 1863—9 a. m.
Maj. Gen. GEORGE H. THOMAS :
GENERAL : Clouds of dust and smoke indicate the enemy's cavalry
is moving in heavy force from Worthen's to Knaper's [Napier's],
and are sweeping around to our left.   Have you any news from your
front ?
　　Very respectfully, your obedient servant,
J. A. GARFIELD,
Brigadier-General, and Chief of Staff.

—

HEADQUARTERS DEPARTMENT OF THE CUMBERLAND,
September 18, 1863.   (Received 10 a. m.)
Major-General THOMAS :
The general commanding directs that I inform you that cavalry is
seen advancing toward our lines 10 degrees southeast from here.
Considerable dust seen among the timber.
JESSE MERRILL,
Captain, and Acting Signal Officer.

HIGH POINT,
September 18, 1863—9.50 a. m.
Captain MERRILL :

The cavalry spoken of as advancing has turned back. I counted seven wagons or ambulances.

MEEKER.

—

HEADQUARTERS FOURTEENTH ARMY CORPS,
Alley's Spring, September 18, 1863.
Brigadier-General GARFIELD,
Chief of Staff:

Your dispatch of 9 a. m. just received, also dispatch from Captain Merrill. General Thomas is looking after the troops and regulating their positions. All quiet in front of our line. Two reports from the signal station on the mountain have been received. Can see no movements worthy of note.

Very respectfully, your obedient servant,
[GEO. E. FLYNT,]
Assistant Adjutant-General, and Chief of Staff.

—

HEADQUARTERS DEPARTMENT OF THE CUMBERLAND,
Crawfish Spring, September 18, 1863—10.15 a. m.
Major-General THOMAS :

The general commanding desires you to report immediately the position of your pickets, and also to hold your command in readiness for any movement. There seems to be great activity on the part of the enemy in our front.

Very respectfully, your obedient servant,
J. A. GARFIELD,
Brigadier-General, and Chief of Staff.

—

HEADQUARTERS DEPARTMENT OF THE CUMBERLAND,
Crawfish Spring, September 18, 1863—10.45 a. m.
Major-General McCOOK :

The general commanding directs you to move your command down the Chickamauga and close it up compactly on General Thomas' right. The Fourteenth Army Corps is being drawn this way, and you will close in upon it in its new position. General Mitchell has been ordered to hold Stevens' Gap and watch the enemy's movements in the direction of the gaps of Pigeon Mountain. Hold your command in readiness for any movement. The enemy appear to be making a demonstration on Crittenden's left. Reconnoiter well your front.

Very respectfully, your obedient servant,
J. A. GARFIELD,
Brigadier-General, and Chief of Staff.

HIGH POINT,
September 18, 1863—10.30 a. m.
Captain MERRILL:

Three regiments of infantry passing due northeast by 15 degrees south from here. Eight wagons to the rear of each regiment; 12 miles off.

BRENT.

Presumed to be a reconnaissance on La Fayette road toward Gordon's Mills.

J. S. FEE.

Since the above the supposition is corroborated by reports from Gordon's Mills.

J. S. FEE.

—

HDQRS. FIRST BRIGADE, SECOND CAVALRY DIVISION,
September 18, 1863—11 a. m.
Brigadier-General WOOD,
Commanding, Gordon's Mills:

SIR: The enemy has driven in my scout from toward Ringgold and are following up apparently in force. Cavalry and infantry are reported. I am now skirmishing heavily. I have had 1 man killed and several wounded. Please report by signal to Generals Rosecrans and Crittenden.

Respectfully,

ROBT. H. G. MINTY,
Colonel, Commanding.

—

HEADQUARTERS DEPARTMENT OF THE CUMBERLAND,
Crawfish Spring, September 18, 1863—11 a. m.
Brig. Gen. R. B. MITCHELL :

The Fourteenth and Twentieth Army Corps have been ordered farther down the Chickamauga to close up on General Crittenden. The general commanding directs you to make immediate arrangements to hold Stevens' Gap and watch any movements of the enemy in the direction of the gaps of Pigeon Mountain. Keep communication with General McCook and cover his right flank. Report frequently.

Very respectfully, your obedient servant,

J. A. GARFIELD,
Brigadier-General, and Chief of Staff.

—

HIGH POINT,
September 18, 1863—11.30 a. m.
Captain MERRILL :

See heavy dust 70 degrees east of north.

MEEKER.

This bearing is toward Reed's and Alexander's Bridges, the vicinity of Steedman's and Minty's commands.

J. S. FEE.

HEADQUARTERS DEPARTMENT OF THE CUMBERLAND,
Crawfish Spring, September 18, 1863—11.45 a. m.

Maj. Gen. THOMAS L. CRITTENDEN:

The general commanding directs you to move General Van Cleve's division in the vicinity of Gordon's Mills and close it up on General Wood's division. Post General Palmer's division in General Van Cleve's present position, and hold your whole command in readiness for any movement. The enemy appears to be making demonstrations on your left.

Very respectfully, your obedient servant,

J. A. GARFIELD,
Brigadier-General, and Chief of Staff.

—

GENERAL PALMER'S HEADQUARTERS,
September 18, 1863—12.30 p. m.

[General ROSECRANS ?]:

GENERAL: General Palmer has notified General Negley that he will leave his present position at 2 p. m. General Palmer's grand guards will not be removed until properly relieved. No demonstration on General Palmer's front so far. As I came out I think I heard brisk firing on Colonel Barnes' front. I did not like the position of this brigade on yesterday. General Palmer will make it right as he can.

Very respectfully,

ARTHUR C. DUCAT,
Lieutenant-Colonel, and Inspector-General.

—

HIGH POINT,
September 18, 1863—12.30 p. m.

Captain MERRILL:

Large bodies of cavalry and, I think, infantry at a point 12 degrees south of east, filed, I think, on the State road, and then marched north. Dust and smoke are increasing in the east. Do not know whether friends or enemies.

MEEKER.

Conjectured to be our own troops.

J. S. FEE.

—

HIGH POINT,
September 18, 1863.

Brigadier-General GARFIELD,
Chief of Staff:

Lieutenant Meeker says, in answer to inquiry as to dispatch of 12.30 p. m., that the troops mentioned were in front of our lines as he understood them this morning.

Respectfully, yours,

JESSE MERRILL,
Captain, and Chief Signal Officer.

HEADQUARTERS FOURTEENTH ARMY CORPS,
Alley's Spring, September 18, 1863—12.45 [p. m.]

Major-General REYNOLDS,
Commanding Fourth Division:

You are directed by Major-General Thomas to move with your division and take post at or near Cook's Mill, with your left connecting with General Palmer's division. Take three days' rations in haversacks and sixty rounds of ammunition on the persons of the men. Move your trains in the rear of our camp, if there is any road to be found, so as to cover your trains while making the move. Notify General McCook of your movement, and move with as much celerity as possible without overtasking your command.

Very respectfully, your obedient servant,

[GEO. E. FLYNT,]
Assistant Adjutant-General, and Chief of Staff.

—

HEADQUARTERS FOURTEENTH ARMY CORPS,
Alley's Spring, September 18, 1863.

Brigadier-General BRANNAN,
Commanding Third Division:

You are directed by Maj. Gen. George H. Thomas to hold your command in readiness to move at any time. The enemy, it seems, are making demonstrations on our extreme left, and orders have been received for the corps to move if necessary. General Reynolds has been ordered to move to Cook's Mill, his left connecting with Palmer's command. Should it be necessary you will receive orders to connect with Reynolds' right.

Very respectfully, your obedient servant,

[GEO. E. FLYNT,]
Assistant Adjutant-General, and Chief of Staff.

—

HEADQUARTERS FOURTEENTH ARMY CORPS,
Alley's Spring, September 18, 1863.

General BRANNAN,
Commanding Third Division:

You are directed to move your division and follow General Baird as soon as he gets out of your way or the road is clear, keeping your line of skirmishers connected with General Baird's. Follow previous instructions as to ammunition and rations, and move your train on rear road if possible, so as to be out of the way and be covered by your movement. If you have time the general would like to see you.

By command of Major-General Thomas:

[GEO. E. FLYNT,]
Assistant Adjutant-General, and Chief of Staff.

—

HEADQUARTERS FOURTEENTH ARMY CORPS,
Alley's Spring, September 18, 1863.

Major-General McCOOK,
Commanding Twentieth Army Corps:

GENERAL : I am instructed by Major-General Thomas to say that he is directed to move his corps farther to the left, the left connecting with Palmer's division at Cook's Mill, and to notify you of this movement. Reynolds has been ordered to move at once. Firing at intervals has been heard on the extreme left. Please acknowledge receipt immediately.

Very respectfully, your obedient servant,
[GEO. E. FLYNT,]
Assistant Adjutant-General, and Chief of Staff.

—

HEADQUARTERS FOURTEENTH ARMY CORPS,
Alley's Spring, September 18, 1863.

General McCook,
Commanding Twentieth Army Corps:

GENERAL: The general instructs me to say that he has received orders to move, and will send you word where his right rests as soon as he gets in position.

Very respectfully, your obedient servant,
[GEO. E. FLYNT,]
Assistant Adjutant-General, and Chief of Staff.

—

ROSSVILLE, *September* 18, 1863—1 p. m.

General GARFIELD:
Have ordered Spears to Wauhatchie.

G. GRANGER,
Major-General.

—

STEVENS' GAP, *September* 18, 1863.
(Received 12.50 p. m.)

Captain MERRILL:
Have heard a dozen heavy reports of artillery in the direction of Gordon's Mills, on State road.

FULLER.

—

HEADQUARTERS,
September 18, 1863—2 p. m.

Maj. Gen. THOMAS L. CRITTENDEN,
Commanding:

GENERAL: My right rests at the point we selected on Sunday last and the left extends to about one-quarter of a mile east of the Rossville and La Fayette roads. A brigade and a half of Van Cleve's hold the left of the line and the remainder is held by my two brigades. I have a small part of my two brigades in reserve and two regiments of Van Cleve's. General Palmer should be forced up against my right. The enemy appears to have a heavy force of infantry opposite my right and center, and the lookouts from trees report another column or force moving toward our left. He has just opened on me with artillery for the first time.

Respectfully,
TH. J. WOOD,
Brigadier-General of Volunteers, Commanding.

SEPTEMBER 18, 1863—2.30 p. m.

General ROSECRANS :

Steedman has just returned to camp. Report is now on the way to your headquarters. Went to Graysville and Ringgold. Scott's brigade of rebel cavalry moved in two columns toward La Fayette and Dalton upon his approaching. Minty is at Reed's Bridge.

G. GRANGER,
—   *Major-General.*

HEADQUARTERS RESERVE CORPS,
Rossville, Ga., September 18, 1863.

Brig. Gen. JAMES A. GARFIELD, *Chief of Staff:*

GENERAL : General Steedman has just returned. He moved by the way of Graysville to Ringgold, reaching the latter-named place at 5 p. m. He saw what, from the best information he could gather, was supposed to be Scott's brigade of rebel cavalry, which made but little resistance, but moved off in two columns—one to the south-west toward La Fayette, the other to the southeast toward Dalton, the transportation moving toward La Fayette. He encamped at Battle Springs. Six shells were thrown into his camp about 10 p. m., but no one hurt. Moving from the north upon them led them to believe that the troops were the advance of Burnside's column. Inclosed please find notes from Colonel Minty. The brigade he speaks of as Spears' having passed through Graysville to Ringgold was undoubtedly Steedman.

Very respectfully, your obedient servant,

G. GRANGER,
Major-General.

[Inclosure No. 1.]

HDQRS. FIRST BRIGADE, SECOND CAVALRY DIVISION,
Reed's Bridge, September 18, 1863—9 a. m.

Captain RUSSELL, *Asst. Adjt. Gen., Reserve Corps:*

SIR : I have to acknowledge receipt of your dispatch of this a. m. Pegram's pickets were about 9 miles up the Pea Vine Valley yesterday evening. A brigade of infantry, reported by the citizens to be Spears', passed Graysville toward Ringgold yesterday forenoon, and cannonading was heard a little north of Ringgold yesterday p. m. I have sent strong scouts up the valley and toward Ringgold. If anything of importance is learned from them I will advise General Granger by special courier.

I am, respectfully, your obedient servant,

R. H. G. MINTY,
Colonel, Commanding.

[Inclosure No. 2.]

HDQRS. FIRST BRIGADE, SECOND CAVALRY DIVISION,
Reed's Bridge, September 18, 1863—11 a. m.

Captain RUSSELL, *Asst. Adjt. Gen., Reserve Corps:*

SIR: The scout which I sent to Ringgold this a. m. has been driven back, and is followed by the enemy apparently in force. They appear to be pushing toward left and rear.

Yours, respectfully,

R. H. G. MINTY,
Colonel, Commanding.

SIGNAL STATION,
Lookout Point, Stevens' Gap, September 18, 1863—2 p. m.
Captain SEITER:
Heavy and continuous firing in direction of Gordon's Mills. Large clouds of dust near there and moving north on State road.
FULLER,
Lieutenant, Acting Signal Officer.

⁂

SUMMERTOWN,
September 18, 1863—2.25 p. m.
Captain MERRILL:
I see a cloud of dust moving toward our left, on a road 15 miles distant east of here.
AYERS.

—

HIGH POINT,
September 18, 1863—2.30 p. m.
Captain MERRILL:
Fuller (at Stevens' Gap) reports large clouds of dust moving north on State road near Lee's Mill.
MEEKER.

—

HEADQUARTERS TWENTIETH ARMY CORPS,
Pond Spring, September 18, 1863—2.05 p. m.
Brigadier-General GARFIELD,
Chief of Staff:
GENERAL : During my absence an order came for me to move, and Colonel Thruston carried it in person to Davis and Sheridan. This moment a telegram came for me to hold myself in readiness to move. Which order will I obey? All is quiet on the right, and no indications of a movement. Two deserters who came in last night state that Bragg's infantry was at La Fayette night before last. Bragg driving all the beef and stock south. The demonstration yesterday was made by Wheeler's cavalry.
Respectfully,
A. McD. McCOOK,
Major-General, Commanding.

—

SEPTEMBER 18, 1863—2.40 p. m.
General GARFIELD :
An order came in my absence for me to close up on Thomas. This moment a telegram comes to hold myself in readiness. Shall I move or be ready to move? All quiet on my front and right. General Reynolds wishes to know where Cook's Mill is.
McCOOK,
Major-General, Commanding.

September 18, 1863.   (Received 4.15 p. m. ?)

General McCook :
  Move up.

W. S. ROSECRANS.

—

September 18, 1863—4 p. m.

General McCook :
  Your dispatch of 3 p. m. received.   The general commanding intends in the two dispatches that you should move to Thomas' position and then hold yourself in readiness to move farther if necessary.
Do so as soon as practicable.

GARFIELD,
Brigadier-General, and Chief of Staff.

—

September 18, 1863.

Colonel GODDARD, *Assistant Adjutant-General:*
  Officer on mountain at Stevens' Gap reports small camp fires and
large columns of dust.   Thinks troops were moving north on State
road toward Ringgold.
  Respectfully,

JESSE MERRILL,
Captain, and Signal Officer.

—

SUMMERTOWN,
September 18, 1863—2.40 p. m.

Captain MERRILL :
  Twenty-five degrees east of south is where the troops camped all
morning.   Infantry, artillery, and cavalry; much dust about and
beyond the gap, several miles from Gordon's Mills.   Two columns
of cavalry east, east of south, some 12 miles distant.   Some artillery and musketry firing during the last hour in these directions.
The rebel force lies toward the gap.

BACHTELL.

—

HIGH POINT,
September 18. 1863—3.15 p. m.

Captain MERRILL :
  I think Wilder has found the enemy, from the sound of his guns.
Sound comes from his direction, 70 degrees east of north.   The firing
is desultory cannonading.

MEEKER.

—

HEADQUARTERS POST,
Chattanooga, September 18, 1863.

Major-General GRANGER :
  A soldier and citizen just in reports a portion of a forage train
captured, which I sent up the river to-day.   I am just sending out
cavalry to look the matter up.   The enemy reported 150 strong.
  Yours, respectfully,

G. D. WAGNER,
Brigadier-General. Commanding.

ROSSVILLE, *September* 18, 1863.

General GARFIELD :

General Steedman sent the Second Brigade toward Reed's Bridge immediately upon receipt of your order,

WILLIAM C. RUSSELL,
Captain, and Assistant Adjutant-General.

—

CHATTANOOGA AND GORDON'S MILLS ROAD,
ONE AND A HALF MILES FROM GORDON'S MILLS,
September 18, 1863—4 p. m.

Colonel GODDARD,
Assistant Adjutant-General, and Chief of Staff:

The enemy are crossing (infantry and cavalry) Chickamauga Creek at Alexander's and Byram's Ford below. Colonel Minty has fallen back toward Rossville; has two of my regiments. Colonel Minty reports cannonading toward Cleveland last night. This forenoon a column of dust arose in Napier's Gap; three hours in passing. A large camp fire is now seen at Napier's. The column that attacked me came through Napier's Gap; another column came from the direction of Peeler's. Colonel Minty reports infantry flanking him on both flanks.

I am, sir, very respectfully, &c.,

J. T. WILDER,
Colonel, Commanding Brigade.

—

SEPTEMBER 18, 1863—4.30 p. m.

Brigadier-General GARFIELD,
Chief of Staff:

Brigade left an hour ago to support Minty. Have ordered Spears to Wauhatchie, 4.30 p. m.

GRANGER.

—

HEADQUARTERS TWENTIETH ARMY CORPS,
Pond Spring, September 18, 1863—5 p. m.

Brig. Gen. JEFFERSON C. DAVIS,
Commanding First Division:

General McCook directs that you move your command immediately on the main road leading in this direction. Further orders designating your new position will reach you on the way. Orders from department headquarters just received order this movement. Respectfully,

G. P. THRUSTON,
Assistant Adjutant-General, and Chief of Staff.

—

SUMMERTOWN,
September 18, 1863—6.40 p. m.

Captain MERRILL :

Southeast 25 miles I see a heavy wagon train moving east to a gap. By the dust, I think it goes southeast through the gap. Has been passing one hour or two, and still continues.

[SAMUEL BACHTELL.]

HDQRS. 1ST BRIG., 3D DIV., TWENTY-FIRST ARMY CORPS,
Camp in the Field, September 18, 1863—7 p. m.

Brigadier-General GARFIELD, Chief of Staff:

SIR : I have the honor to make the following report :

I am assistant inspector of General Beatty's staff, and as such was in charge of the picket line of the brigade. I had an officer of the day (a captain), 3 commissioned officers, 18 non-commissioned officers, and 150 men. My line extended from the creek, which has its source at Crawfish Spring, to Colonel Barnes' pickets, on my right, a distance of about 1½ miles. Very little skirmishing occurred on my own line, but there were indications of the enemy in the immediate front of my line.

About 10 o'clock they moved a column of cavalry and infantry down the road leading toward General Wood. The first column was not more than a half hour passing. A second column was afterward reported to me as passing the same way. Of this I know very little, and have reason to believe but few troops passed at this time.

About 1 o'clock troops of the enemy moved down and apparently established themselves in the vicinity of the creek. Of the number I could not attempt to form an estimate. They soon afterward opened a section of artillery (I think not more) on General Wood's position. This battery was about the center of my picket line, and but a very short distance beyond the creek, and not more than a mile and a quarter from General Rosecrans' headquarters. I was relieved about dusk by pickets of General Palmer's division, and when I left the enemy were trying to establish pickets in the timber this side of the creek. The line now is a distance of over a mile from any support, and consists of six companies of about 200 men from General Cruft's brigade. The country this side of the creek, with the exception of a skirt of timber along the creek bank, is clear for a distance of three-quarters of a mile toward us, and a front of a mile; then comes a road crossing the creek and leading into the one the enemy moved on this morning ; then succeeds dense woods, in which the enemy were establishing themselves at dark this evening. This open ground has many commanding knolls, which, if once occupied by them in force, will trouble us much.

About 2 p. m. 2 of the men from my central station went to the creek for water, were fired on, and 1 taken prisoner.

This report is made in accordance with an order from Major-General Rosecrans.

All of which is respectfully submitted.

W. A. SUTHERLAND,
Lieut., 19th Ohio, and Insp. 1st Brig., 3d Div., 21st A. C.

—

HEADQUARTERS TWENTIETH ARMY CORPS,
Pond Spring, September 18, 1863.

[General R. B. MITCHELL :]

GENERAL : I am directed by General McCook to inform you that Generals Sheridan's and Davis' divisions have just been ordered from the positions they occupied to-day to a position nearer these headquarters, where they will remain to-night unless a change of location is ordered by the general commanding. General Johnson remains in General Reynolds' position of yesterday. Colonel Harrison, Thirty-ninth Indiana, has been ordered to withdraw to a position nearer his infantry supports, somewhere near where General Davis had his headquarters to-day. Instructions were sent you from the general commanding directing that you close in to our right, and this communication will inform you particularly as to the position of our forces. Our headquarters will be at this place to-night, but we will probably strike tents at a very early hour in the morning.

I am, general, very respectfully, your obedient servant,

G. P. THRUSTON,
Assistant Adjutant-General, and Chief of Staff.

7 p. m.

P. S.—Colonel Post's brigade has orders to hold Stevens' Gap at all hazards, as stated within. This dispatch has been delayed by our ignorance of your whereabouts. Colonel Harrison has been given peremptory orders to open communication with you. General McCook is anxious to hear from you as frequently as practicable.

[Indorsement.]

9.45 p. m.

General R. B. MITCHELL :

The within communication was sent you to-day (or ordered sent you) through Colonel Harrison. A copy is now forwarded. In case the others are lost or do not reach you, these will instruct you. General McCook has been anxious to open communication with you all day, and is now much relieved at receiving your courier. General Rosecrans is very particular that complete and speedy communication should be maintained. Several of your staff are here, not having been able to find you to-day. The firing on the left to-day was caused by the enemy making a reconnaissance with a large cavalry force. Sheridan and Davis are here. Their troops encamp to-night between here and Gower's. Colonel Post has had full instructions about holding the gap (Stevens').

Respectfully,

G. P. THRUSTON,
Assistant Adjutant-General, and Chief of Staff.

—

HEADQUARTERS FOURTEENTH ARMY CORPS,
Crawfish Spring, September 18, 1863—8 p. m.

Maj. Gen. JAMES S. NEGLEY,
Commanding Second Division :

GENERAL: As soon as possible push down strong pickets along your whole front from the Crawfish Creek, on your left, to your right beyond Matthews' house, or till you connect with the pickets on your right. You will push them well down to the Chickamauga River, as the enemy are reported as lodging their pickets in the woods on our side. Much of the defensible ground is between the road you are on and the river. All the range there is for artillery consists of the clearings which run from the river to the ridge tops. They must be held.

GEO. H. THOMAS,
Major-General, U. S. Volunteers, Commanding.

HEADQUARTERS TWENTIETH ARMY CORPS,
POND SPRING, NEAR FOOT OF COOPER'S GAP,
September 18, 1863—8 p. m.

Col. P. SIDNEY POST,
    Comdg. First Brig., First Div., near Stevens' Gap:

COLONEL: I send you inclosed for your instruction a copy of a dispatch received from General Rosecrans.* We have had no communication with you since your dispatch of yesterday from Valley Head, 3 p. m. Our infantry has been withdrawn from near Stevens' Gap several miles toward Chattanooga, and General Mitchell has been ordered to cover our right and extend his line of cavalry so as to cover Stevens' Gap. The inclosed order indicates that he may be drawn from there entirely and your brigade have no further support from the cavalry. The order explains itself. We are in some doubt as to your position and as to your trains, rations, &c. All the trains of the corps except your share of your ammunition train (First Division) and about six days' to ten days' rations for your command are ordered to be brought down into this valley to Chattanooga Creek. Keep these wagons (with ammunition and supplies) with you if they are still on the mountain. If you get out of supplies provide yourself as far as you can on the mountain. Your communications in regard to the sick at Valley Head received due attention, but the difficulty at that time could not be remedied, as we had no empty wagons. We have wagons to send now, and they will start in the morning, via Cooper's Gap and Lookout Valley for Valley Head, with suitable guard. Orders will be given to immediately remove the sick in them on the Lookout Valley or Trenton road to Chattanooga, where hospitals are stationed now and supplies drawn. We are in ignorance as to your position on the mountain and as to the condition of affairs at Valley Head, and also as to the exact position of some of the corps trains. Please inform us as fully and speedily as possible, and we will communicate with you again if necessary in the morning.

Very respectfully, your obedient servant,

G. P. THRUSTON,
Assistant Adjutant-General, and Chief of Staff.

P. S.—Send to us at Pond Spring or Gower's. If you notify us in time that you want rations—have got six days' on the mountain that you can get from General Davis' train there—we will send you some. Let us hear from you.

—

CRAWFISH SPRING, *September* 18, 1863—8 p. m.

Captain RUSSELL,
    Rossville:

Send full reports of Whitaker's and McCook's movements, and where they are and what is in their front.

G. GRANGER,
Major-General, Commanding.

[Indorsement.]

ROSSVILLE, GA., *September* 18, 1863.

General STEEDMAN:

Will you please make an immediate report based upon latest information received and send to me to be forwarded by courier? I

---

*Not identified.

sent as explicit a statement of how affairs stood as it was possible to do by signal.

Very respectfully,

WILLIAM C. RUSSELL,
Assistant Adjutant-General.

—

ROSSVILLE, SIGNAL STATION, *September* 18, 1863.
(Received 11 p. m.)

General GORDON GRANGER,
(Care of Major-General Rosecrans):

McCook has just reported his arrival at Reed's Bridge, but could not find Minty. He captured 5 prisoners, who said they belonged to Johnson's brigade. They represent Texas, Louisiana, and Arkansas. Firing has been heard by McCook in the direction of Whitaker. The citizens report that Minty moved off to the north, which is not believed. Mitchell's brigade was sent to re-enforce McCook, but General Steedman thinks that he should direct Mitchell to re-enforce Whitaker, but will await your orders, as Mitchell's brigade was sent on General Rosecrans' orders. A wagon train crossed Reed's Bridge just in advance of McCook's vanguard. Reed's Bridge and Peeler's Mills are certainly separate and distinct. Please give necessary instructions.

Very respectfully, your obedient servant,

WILLIAM C. RUSSELL,
Assistant Adjutant-General.

—

HDQRS. 1ST BRIGADE. 1ST DIVISION, RESERVE CORPS,
September 18, 1863—8.30 p. m.

[Capt. S. B. MOE,]
Assistant Adjutant-General, First Division:

My command has advanced as far as the first creek out. The ford is a little difficult. Found the enemy at this ford at 5.45 o'clock. Drove him one-half mile. We are now resting part of the command on one side of the creek, part on the side next Chattanooga. He has more than one brigade and a battery that I know of. How far shall I feel him in the morning? Have had 1 killed and 4 wounded. We have killed several of them. No forces with me but my brigade. Do not know where McCook is.

W. C. WHITAKER,
Brigadier-General, Commanding.

[Indorsement.]

Capt. WILLIAM C. RUSSELL,
Assistant Adjutant-General:

CAPTAIN: I have just received this note from Whitaker, and the dispatch to Garfield for you to forward.*

JAMES B. STEEDMAN,
Brigadier-General.

---

*See Steedman to Garfield, 11 p. m., p. 121.

HIGH POINT,
September 18, 1863—9 p. m.

Captain MERRILL :
No rebel camp-fires can be seen.

MEEKER.

—

HEADQUARTERS DEPARTMENT OF THE CUMBERLAND,
Crawfish Spring, September 18, 1863—10.45 a. m.

Maj. Gen. GEORGE H. THOMAS :

The general commanding directs you to move your corps down the Chickamauga, so that your left will join General Palmer's division at Cook's Mill. Close the line up compactly and report to General McCook as soon as possible where your right will rest. Reconnoiter your front thoroughly.

Very respectfully, your obedient servant,
J. A. GARFIELD,
Brigadier-General, and Chief of Staff.

—

HEADQUARTERS FIRST DIVISION, RESERVE CORPS,
Rossville, Ga., September 18, 1863—11 p. m.

General GARFIELD :

General Whitaker met resistance 3 miles from this point on the Rossville road. He drove the enemy half a mile, lost 1 killed and 4 wounded, and is now on a creek that crosses the road this side of the Chickamauga. I have ordered him to hold his position until daylight, and then, if able to do so with safety, to advance to the Chickamauga. I have but two regiments to take care of the property here and re-enforce Whitaker.

JAMES B. STEEDMAN,
Brigadier-General.

—

ROSSVILLE, GA.,
September 19, 1863—2.25 a. m.

Maj. Gen. GORDON GRANGER,
Crawfish Spring :

GENERAL : I signaled you last evening, giving a short account of McCook's movement and asking for orders to General Steedman relative to changing the order relative to Mitchell's brigade, he (General Steedman) being of opinion that Whitaker should be supported by Mitchell. As yet no orders have been received. I inclose herewith note* sent me by General Steedman a few hours since—the only one received from Whitaker since leaving camp. Thinking it probable that General Steedman had received later information from McCook and Whitaker than that reported to you, I sent your note to General Steedman with the request that he make the reports as required, but he directed me by verbal message to the orderly to make the reports. McCook's advance captured 5 prisoners near Reed's Bridge. They were straggling behind the train and reported themselves as belonging to regiments in Johnson's brigade, which was moving off toward the east as McCook advanced. The men represented regiments from

*See Whitaker to Moe, 8.30 p. m., p. 120.

ArKansas, Texas, and Louisiana, and McCook reports himself unable to gather the least information from them. He did not find Minty, who it is supposed had formed a junction with Wilder. General Steedman has directed Whitaker to drive the enemy across the Chickamauga in the morning, if possible. In the mean time he awaits orders relative to Mitchell's brigade. I inclose herewith a communication from General Wagner concerning the capture of a forage train by rebels.* Please send General Steedman orders about Mitchell's brigade.

Very respectfully, your obedient servant,
WILLIAM C. RUSSELL,
Captain, and Assistant Adjutant-General.

—

DEPARTMENT HEADQUARTERS, *September* 19, 1863.
(Received 3 a. m.)
General JAMES B. STEEDMAN :

The general commanding directs that you send for McCook and the other brigade with all possible speed for orders to you. Orders to Whitaker are right.

R. S. THOMS,
Captain, and Aide-de-Camp.

—

HEADQUARTERS CHIEF OF CAVALRY,
DEPARTMENT OF THE CUMBERLAND,
RODGERS' HOUSE, NEAR BLUE BIRD GAP,
September 19, 1863—3.30 a. m.

Brigadier-General CROOK,
Commanding Second Cavalry Division:

GENERAL : The general commanding directs that immediately on receipt of the inclosed order you † move with your command to Stevens' Gap. If you can get your artillery through Dougherty's Gap, come the Valley road and send your train via mountain route ; if not, come the mountain route. Before coming down the mountain at Stevens' Gap supply your command with three days' rations. Move with all possible dispatch. Colonel Watkins is ordered up from Valley Head, and his column will protect your train.

I am, your obedient servant,
WILLIAM H. SINCLAIR,
Assistant Adjutant-General.

—

CRAWFISH SPRING, *September* 19, 1863.
Maj. Gen. GEORGE H. THOMAS :

Wagner reports the capture of a man who saw heavy forces of the enemy moving on the Ringgold road toward Chattanooga. Steedman reports that Whitaker drove the force in front of him about one-half a mile.

Very respectfully, your obedient servant,
J. A. GARFIELD,
Brigadier-General, and Chief of Staff.

_____

* See p. 115.
† See Garfield to Mitchell, 8.30 p. m., September 18, p. 75.

HEADQUARTERS TWENTIETH ARMY CORPS,
Pond Spring, September 19, 1863—3.30 a. m.

Brig. Gen. JEFFERSON C. DAVIS,
    Comdg. First Division, Twentieth Army Corps:

General Johnson has orders to move at early dawn this morning on the road from here to Crawfish Spring and close up on General Thomas, who is now 4 miles in advance. General McCook directs that you move your division upon the same road immediately in the rear of General Johnson, keeping well closed up to him. He directs that you have the officer in charge of your train report in person here to Colonel Boyd, who will inform him of the direction your train will take and the position it will occupy. When on the road you will receive proper directions where to encamp. General McCook directs that if you have any information from your front you do not fail to communicate it.

I am, general, very respectfully, your obedient servant, &c.,
                            A. C. McCLURG,
        Captain, and Acting Assistant Adjutant-General.

ROSSVILLE, *September* 19, 1863—7.30 a. m.

[Brig. Gen. G. D. WAGNER :]

• There is every indication of an early attack on our left flank. The enemy is massing his troops on his right. General Rosecrans is closing up this way. You should send your cavalry well out to the northeast, east, and southeast, and keep me advised of every movement. It is probable that the first shock will fall on your command and mine. Keep your troops well in hand. I have this moment returned from General Rosecrans' headquarters.
                            G. GRANGER,
                                Major-General.

HDQRS. TWENTY-FIRST ARMY CORPS,
ON GORDON'S MILLS AND ROSSVILLE ROAD,
ONE AND A HALF MILES NORTH OF MILLS,
September 19, 1863—7.40 a. m. (Received 8 a. m.)

Brig. Gen. JAMES A. GARFIELD :

SIR : I have the honor to report that four or five cannon have just fired in the direction of Reed's Mill from this point. General Palmer in position on the left of my corps, and Grose's brigade just under orders to make a reconnaissance in direction of Reed's Bridge. Will report again as soon as I learn anything. I can hear General Thomas' artillery passing up on my rear, and it has been so passing since 2 a. m.

Respectfully, your obedient servant,
                            T. L. CRITTENDEN,
                                Major-General, Commanding.

HDQRS. DEPARTMENT OF THE CUMBERLAND,
Crawfish Spring, Ga., September 19, 1863—8.10 a. m.

Major-General CRITTENDEN,
    Commanding Twenty-first Army Corps:

Your dispatch of 7.40 this a. m. is received. Col. Dan. McCook's brigade was at Reed's Bridge early this morning and captured a few prisoners from the rear of a retreating column. The general commanding is anxious to know what are the developments on the left. We hear artillery at Gordon's Mills and a few dropped shots in Negley's front.

Very respectfully, your obedient servant,
                                        J. A. GARFIELD,
                        Brigadier-General, Chief of Staff.

—

                                        ROSSVILLE,
                        September 19, 1863—8.15 a. m.
General GARFIELD :

McCook took Reed's Bridge and burned it this morning. Whitaker was unable to reach Red House. Is now in position at McAfee's Spring. Whitaker reports the enemy moving on his front and left this morning. No other indications of the enemy. Have ordered McCook's and Mitchell's brigades to fall back from Reed's Bridge to this place. I have requested Wagner to keep the cavalry [out] and to keep me well advised.

                                        G. GRANGER,
                                        Major-General.

—

            HEADQUARTERS FOURTEENTH ARMY CORPS,
        Near McDonald's House, September 19, 1863—9 a. m.
Major-General PALMER :

The rebels are reported in quite heavy force between you and Alexander's Mill. If you will advance on them in front while I attack them in flank, I think we can use them up.

Respectfully, your obedient servant,
                                        GEO. H. THOMAS,
                        Major-General, U. S. Volunteers, Commanding.

—

            HEADQUARTERS FOURTEENTH ARMY CORPS,
        Near McDonald's House, September 19, 1863—9.30 a. m.
General ROSECRANS :

The enemy are reported this side of the Chickamauga, between Alexander's Bridge and Reed's Bridge. I am advancing in the direction of Reed's Bridge, holding a front in the direction of Alexander's Bridge. If General Crittenden will advance from Gordon's Mills on them at Alexander's Bridge we can, I think, use them up. I have two divisions ready to advance ; the other will be up soon. Some prisoners taken by Colonel McCook last night say they belong to Hood's division.

Very respectfully, your obedient servant,
                                        GEO. H. THOMAS,
                        Major-General, U. S. Volunteers.

HEADQUARTERS TWENTY-FIRST ARMY CORPS,
Gordon's Mills, September 19, 1863—10 a. m.

Major-General THOMAS,
    Commanding Fourteenth Army Corps:

GENERAL : Your note of 9 a. m. received. Colonel Grose is out
on a reconnaissance on our flank. As soon as he returns will advance as you propose.

Very respectfully, &c.,

                                        J. M. PALMER.

—

WIDOW GLENN'S, *September* 19, 1863.

General WAGNER :

Have you any news? Do you know whether the enemy is making
any demonstrations in the direction of Turner's? Heavy engagement progressing between Rossville and Gordon's Mills. All goes
well thus far.

                            J. A. GARFIELD,
                Brigadier-General, Chief of Staff.

—

CHATTANOOGA, *September* 19, 1863—10.15 a. m.

Brigadier-General GARFIELD :

We have but little. Part of Forrest's cavalry are about Tyner's
Station. I have party watching them. Indications are they intend
to cross river. I have force at the fords. Signal lights seen in
three different places on Mission Ridge last night. Messengers to
Burnside with your dispatch could not proceed on this side of river.
Came back and started at midnight on opposite side of river. Think
they will get through. Boat is running. Bridge done to-day.

                            G. D. WAGNER,
                            Brigadier-General.

—

WIDOW GLENN'S HOUSE,
September 19, 1863—a. m.

Major-General McCOOK,
    Commanding Twentieth Army Corps:

GENERAL : The general commanding desires to know how affairs
progress on your front. General Thomas has been engaged, and
reports everything favorable. Preserve your signal station, communicate with Summerville [Summertown], and let anything be reported
which occurs. Re-enforcements have gone to General Thomas, and
he is again engaged.

Very respectfully, your obedient servant,

                        WILLIAM McMICHAEL,
                Major, and Assistant Adjutant-General.

—

McAFEE'S SPRING,
September [20], 1863—10.30 a. m.*

General ROSECRANS, *Widow Glenn's:*

I am moving two brigades, under Steedman, to assist General
Thomas' left, although it does not seem to be engaged. Very heavy

---

* In its proper sequence should appear on p. 139.

firing on his center and right. Shall try and strike the enemy in flank and rear. McCook will hold the north Ringgold road. Minty reports nothing at Chickamauga Depot.

G. GRANGER,
Major-General.

HEADQUARTERS FOURTEENTH ARMY CORPS,
NEAR McDANIEL'S [McDONALD'S] HOUSE,
September 19, 1863—10.30 a. m.

Major-General REYNOLDS,
Commanding Fourth Division:

The general commanding directs that you press forward with dispatch, and advise him by the orderly where this meets you.

By command of Major-General Thomas :

[J. P. WILLARD,]
Captain, and Aide-de-Camp.

HEADQUARTERS FOURTEENTH ARMY CORPS,
NEAR McDANIEL'S [McDONALD'S] HOUSE,
September 19, 1863—10.45.

Major-General CRITTENDEN,
Commanding Twenty-first Army Corps:

If another division can be spared, it would be well to send it up without any delay.

Very respectfully, your obedient servant,

GEO. H. THOMAS,
Major-General, U. S. Volunteers, Commanding.

HEADQUARTERS DEPARTMENT OF THE CUMBERLAND,
Crawfish Spring, September 19, 1863—10.45 a. m.

Maj. Gen. JAMES S. NEGLEY :

The general commanding directs you to take orders from Major-General McCook.

Respectfully,

C. GODDARD,
Lieutenant-Colonel, and Assistant Adjutant-General.

HEADQUARTERS FOURTEENTH ARMY CORPS,
NEAR McDANIEL'S [McDONALD'S] HOUSE,
September 19, 1863—11.30 a. m.

Lieutenant-Colonel FLYNT :

The general commanding directs that you have everything packed up and be ready to move toward Chattanooga at a moment's notice.

By command of Major-General Thomas :

J. P. WILLARD,
Captain, and Aide-de-Camp.

GENERAL NEGLEY'S HEADQUARTERS,
ONE AND A HALF MILES FROM CRAWFISH SPRING,
RIGHT SIDE OF ROAD GOING SOUTH,
September 19, 1863—12 m.

Major-General ROSECRANS :

GENERAL : General Sheridan is up, and General McCook is closing his left up. Am of opinion that firing on General Negley's front is a demonstration to attract your attention from another point, although General Beatty has twice asked for re-enforcements. I think he is all right while he has nothing hurt and no musketry firing yet. " I can't see it." As soon as General McCook is in position he intends drawing off Negley's right and letting them come if they want to. All will be in shape very soon. As soon as General McCook has established headquarters, I will send you word or join you with the information.

Very respectfully,

ARTHUR C. DUCAT,
Lieutenant-Colonel, Assistant Inspector-General.

P. S.—General McCook and self have examined the ground beyond where his right will rest, and will now select the ground for position here. Firing on General Negley's front has ceased.

—

NEAR MCDANIEL'S [MCDONALD'S] HOUSE,
[*September* 19,] 1863—12 m.

[General ROSECRANS :]

GENERAL : General Thomas, whom I have met on his second line, wishes me to say that one of his brigades was this morning attacked by overwhelming force and driven back, and two others have since been driven. General Thomas says that he is now holding his position, and has ordered up General Reynolds. He thought General Palmer was on his right, but found he was not. Thinks he is moving in now. General Brannan has driven the enemy across the creek and turned their right. Enemy opposite from Joe Johnston's army. All on Thomas' left appears quiet. General Thomas expects to drive the rebels as soon as Reynolds and Palmer get up.

Respectfully,

G. BURROUGHS,
Lieutenant of Engineers.

—

HEADQUARTERS FOURTEENTH ARMY CORPS,
NEAR MCDANIEL'S [MCDONALD'S] HOUSE,
September 19, 1863—1 p. m.

General GORDON GRANGER,
Rossville :

Please give me the state of affairs with you. The enemy are fighting me with very heavy forces. We have taken many prisoners from Virginia regiments and Johnston's army, showing Bragg has been re-enforced from both.

Very respectfully, your obedient servant,

GEO. H. THOMAS,
Major-General, U. S. Volunteers, Commanding.

HEADQUARTERS DEPARTMENT OF THE CUMBERLAND,
Widow Glenn's, September 19, 1863—1 p. m.

Major-General McCOOK,
Commanding Twentieth Army Corps:

General Thomas is heavily engaged, and Palmer and Johnson have been ordered up to support him. All goes well thus far. A considerable cavalry force have got in behind us, and are threatening some of our trains. The general commanding directs you to hurry Mitchell's cavalry in upon our right, and send a detachment to look out for our rear.

J. A. G[ARFIELD],
Brigadier-General, Chief of Staff.

[Indorsement.]

HEADQUARTERS TWENTIETH ARMY CORPS,
September 19, 1863—1.50 p. m.
(Received Cavalry Headquarters 2.25 p. m.)

General Mitchell will comply with this order at once.

By command of Major-General McCook:

FRANK J. JONES,
Captain, and Aide-de-Camp.

—

HEADQUARTERS TWENTIETH ARMY CORPS,
Near Crawfish Spring, September 19, 1863—1 p. m.
(Received 1.20 p. m.)

Brig. Gen. JAMES A. GARFIELD, *Chief of Staff:*

All the enemy apparently have left Negley's front. Johnson's and Davis' divisions are marching rapidly to Mrs. Glenn's. Sheridan's division is watering here at Crawfish Spring. I am posting it in line, so as to effectively cover Wood's right. Negley, as soon as Sheridan's line is formed, will be withdrawn from his position in front and thrown to the right and rear. I have heard nothing of the cavalry, but I am expecting it up every moment. If you want Sheridan at once I think he can move up with safety. Nothing appears to be going on in our front. I suppose the cavalry will take good care of our right rear and teams.

Very respectfully,

A. McD. McCOOK,
Major-General.

—

HEADQUARTERS TWENTIETH ARMY CORPS,
Near Crawfish Spring, September 19, 1863—1.30 p. m.)
(Received 1.45 p. m.)

Brig. Gen. JAMES A. GARFIELD, *Chief of Staff:*

Your dispatch reporting everything favorable is just received. Everything quiet on the right. I have taken a strong position, protecting Wood's right flank. I will withdraw Negley from his position and place him on my right and rear, a little retired. I am ready here for any emergency.

Very respectfully,

A. McD. McCOOK,
Major-General.

HEADQUARTERS TWENTIETH ARMY CORPS,
Near Crawfish Spring, September 19, 1863—1.40 p. m.

Brigadier-General GARFIELD,
Chief of Staff:

I am sending Sheridan's division to Gordon's Mills to occupy the ground just vacated without my knowledge by General Wood. I will retain Negley here until further orders, as I think this point needs great attention, and I do not know how far I am without support on my left. General Wood has gone to my left; how far I do not know. All quiet here thus far. Lieutenant Yaryan reports Bushrod R. Johnson in front of Gordon's Mills.

A. McD. McCOOK,
Major-General, Commanding.

—

HDQRS. SECOND DIVISION, FOURTEENTH ARMY CORPS,
In the Field, September 19, 1863—p. m.

Major-General ROSECRANS:

GENERAL: It is getting very warm in our front. Musketry very heavy. I cannot use my artillery in the dense woods. General Palmer is engaged hotly on my left and driving the enemy.

I have the honor to remain, yours, very truly,

JAS. S. NEGLEY,
Major-General.

—

HEADQUARTERS DEPARTMENT OF THE CUMBERLAND,
Widow Glenn's, September 19, 1863—1.45 p. m.

Maj. Gen. THOMAS L. CRITTENDEN:

Colonel Starling was here just now. I have ordered McCook to relieve you. You will proceed at once to take command of your corps. Make your dispositions as best you can. Cheer them up; see that their ammunition is right. Sheridan will come in if necessary on your right, leaving a nominal force to cover your rear. Take care of your right.

By command Major-General Rosecrans:

C. GODDARD,
Assistant Adjutant-General.

—

HEADQUARTERS TWENTIETH ARMY CORPS,
Near Crawfish Spring, September 19, 1863—2 p. m.

Brigadier-General MITCHELL,
Commanding Cavalry:

General McCook directs me to state that it is absolutely necessary for you to dispatch a portion of your force down Chattanooga Valley to dispose of some rebel cavalry reported there, and to close down this way to our right with the remainder of your force. General Negley, on our right, is ordered to be withdrawn immediately, and your force will have to closely cover the right. All goes favorably thus far on the left.

Respectfully,

G. P. THRUSTON,
Assistant Adjutant-General, Chief of Staff.

HEADQUARTERS DEPARTMENT OF THE CUMBERLAND,
Widow Glenn's, September 19, 1863—2 p. m.

Major-General THOMAS,
Commanding Fourteenth Army Corps:

The general commanding is anxious to know how you are progressing. It is necessary that we should hear from you frequently in order to put in the reserves properly. Is your ammunition up where you can replenish it?

Very respectfully,

J. A. GARFIELD,
Brigadier-General, and Chief of Staff.

—

CHATTANOOGA, *September* 19, 1863.

Brigadier-General GARFIELD:

SIR: I have from 40 to 50 water barrels which I can send you at any time. I am making more.

G. D. WAGNER,
Brigadier-General, Commanding.

—

CHATTANOOGA, *September* 19, 1863—2 p. m.

Brigadier-General GARFIELD:

I have cavalry out in the direction of Tyner's. Have heard nothing from there yet. There can be nothing wrong there, or should have heard. Will keep all my cavalry in that direction. Have advised you by courier more particularly. A citizen just in reported Burnside's cavalry was driven out of Cleveland last evening by Forrest, with loss of 25.

G. D. WAGNER,
Brigadier-General, Commanding.

—

HEADQUARTERS,
Chattanooga, September 19, 1863.

Brigadier-General GARFIELD:

GENERAL: A citizen just in from near Cleveland says Forrest's command yesterday morning drove Burnside's advance (140 men) out of Cleveland, capturing 30. The citizen says the rebels claim they will capture all of them. He says Forrest is there in force.

Your obedient servant,

G. D. WAGNER,
Brigadier-General, Commanding.

—

WAR DEPARTMENT,
Washington, September 19, 1863—2 p. m.

Major-General ROSECRANS,
Chattanooga, Tenn.:

I have no direct communication with General Burnside or General Hurlbut. On the 15th Hurlbut says he is moving forces toward Decatur. I hear nothing of Sherman's troops ordered from Vicksburg.   A telegram from Burnside, dated the 17th, just received, says my orders to move down to re-enforce you will be obeyed as soon as possible.   The chief quartermaster and commissary at Saint Louis were directed to arrange for the transportation and supply of the troops sent up the Tennessee River to support your right.   Burnside's cavalry ought to be near or with you by this time.   I expect more definite information to-day or to-morrow.

H. W. HALLECK,
General-in-Chief.

—

GENERAL McCOOK'S HEADQUARTERS,
September 19, [1863]—2.15 p. m.
Major-General ROSECRANS,
Commanding:

GENERAL : General McCook had heard from a staff officer of the movement of Wood to the left.   Anticipating your order, he ordered Sheridan forward to hold the position occupied by Wood.   General Negley has been ordered up from his position by General McCook and a staff officer sent to conduct him.   General McCook will retain General Negley here until further orders, as this position is of vital importance and is the key to our right, as the fight is now.

Very respectfully,

ARTHUR C. DUCAT,
Lieutenant-Colonel, Assistant Inspector-General.

—

WAR DEPARTMENT,
Washington, September 19, 1863—2.30 p. m.
Major-General BURNSIDE,
Knoxville, Tenn.:

General Rosecrans is on the Chickamauga River 20 miles south of Chattanooga.   He is expecting a battle and wants you to sustain his left.   Every possible effort must be made to assist him.

H. W. HALLECK,
General-in-Chief

—

GREENVILLE, TENN., *September* 19, 1863.
(Received 1.25 p. m.,
Maj. Gen. H. W. HALLECK,
General-in-Chief:

Will obey your directions in reference to Rosecrans.   Our troops occupy Jonesborough.   Enemy retreating to Abingdon ; our cavalry in pursuit.

A. E. BURNSIDE,
Major-General.

—

GREENVILLE, EAST TENNESSEE, *September* 19, 1863.
(Received 10.40 a. m., 21st.)
Maj. Gen. H. W. HALLECK,
General-in-Chief:

Am now sending every man that can be spared to aid Rosecrans. I shall go on to-day to Jonesborough.   As soon as I learn the result of our movements to the east, will go down by railroad and direct the movements of re-enforcements for Rosecrans. I have directed every available man in Kentucky to be sent down.

> A. E. BURNSIDE,
> *Major-General.*

ROSSVILLE, *September* 19, 1863—3 p. m.

Brig. Gen. JAMES A. GARFIELD, *Chief of Staff:*

Your dispatch received. From station on Missionary Ridge the officer sends the following :

2.30 p. m.

Heavy firing has developed on the line of the Chickamauga near the bridge of northern road leading to Ringgold. Troops are apparently moving to that point.

The general commanding directs me to say he will keep you informed as far as it is possible to discover their intention.

Respectfully,

> J. G. TAYLOR,
> *Captain, and Aide-de-Camp.*

ROSSVILLE, *September* 19, 1863—3.10 p. m.

General JAMES A. GARFIELD :

Whitaker has just reported that the enemy is attacking him in force and asks for re-enforcements. He is on the Red House road about 2½ miles from here. There can be no doubt about there being a large force in and about Ringgold, although it has kept very quiet until this movement against Whitaker.

> G. GRANGER,
> *Major-General.*

HEADQUARTERS DEPARTMENT OF THE CUMBERLAND,
Widow Glenn's, September 19, 1863.

Maj. Gen. THOMAS L. CRITTENDEN :

Dispatch from General Thomas of 3 p. m., just received, says :

We are driving the rebels in the center handsomely, so General Johnson's aide reports to me. Says First Division was considerably cut up, but we have taken many prisoners.

I am in hopes we will drive them across the Chickamauga to-night.

By order of Major-General Rosecrans :

> FRANK S. BOND,
> *Major, and Aide-de-Camp.*

HEADQUARTERS TWENTIETH ARMY CORPS,
September 19, [1863]—3.15 p. m.

Major-General SHERIDAN, *Commanding:*

General McCook directs that you move two brigades up the road in the direction of Mrs. Glenn's, and leave one brigade to hold the position at Gordon's Mills. He wishes this order carried out immediately.

Very respectfully, your obedient servant,

> G. P. THRUSTON,
> *Assistant Adjutant-General, and Chief of Staff.*

HEADQUARTERS,
Battle-field, September 19, 1863—3.30 p. m.
[Major-General ROSECRANS:]

Inclosed dispatch* received. It is just reported to me that the enemy are pressing General Palmer across the road from Gordon's Mills to Rossville; but we have driven on our left. It has been very hard fighting. I would respectfully suggest that Van Cleve go to the assistance of Palmer.

Respectfully,

GEO. H. THOMAS.

—

HEADQUARTERS DEPARTMENT OF THE CUMBERLAND,
Widow Glenn's, September 19, 1863
Major-General THOMAS,
Commanding Fourteenth Army Corps:

The general commanding directs you to press the enemy with all vigor. Do not give him time to form. Dispatch often, giving position and prospect.

Respectfully,

R. S. THOMS,
Captain, and Aide-de-Camp.

—

HEADQUARTERS TWENTIETH ARMY CORPS,
Alley's, September 19, 1863—4 p. m.†
General SHERIDAN:

Take a position near the one occupied by General Negley last night. Keep your transportation well back, and keep a good watch to the front. Harrison will picket in front of the gaps. I await orders here and will join you this evening.

A. McD. McCOOK,
Major-General.

—

EN ROUTE, *September* 19, [1863]—4 [p. m.]
Major-General SHERIDAN,
Commanding Third Division:

General McCook directs that instead of moving those two brigades up toward the center, you keep them there well in hand, and re-enforce Wood, on your left, as he needs them. Communicate with General Wood. Do not give up the position at Gordon's Mills. All goes well on the left. Send General Wood re-enforcements, brigade at a time, as he needs them.

Very respectfully,

G. P. THRUSTON,
Assistant Adjutant-General, and Chief of Staff.

—

GENERAL ROSECRANS' HEADQUARTERS,
September 19, [1863]—4.50 p. m.
Col. P. SIDNEY POST,
Commanding First Brigade, First Division:

General McCook directs that you move with all possible dispatch to the battle-field of to-day, 2 miles from Crawfish Spring toward Chat-

---

* Not found.   † September 18 is probably the correct date.

tanooga, on Chickamauga Creek.   Send all your trains, except your
ammunition, to Chattanooga by the Lookout Mountain route.   Send
word to all the cavalry in your vicinity to move up here immediately;
their services are needed here.   March to-night.   Get a good guide
to bring you straight here via Pond Spring, Alley's, and Crawfish
Spring, and report to me at General Rosecrans' headquarters.   All
seems to have progressed favorably to-day.
　　　Very respectfully, your obedient servant,
　　　　　　　　　　　　　　　　G. P. THRUSTON,
　　　　　　Assistant Adjutant-General, and Chief of Staff.

P. S.—The enemy have fallen back.

———

　　　　　　　　　　　　　　　　　　　　　ROSSVILLE,
　　　　　　　　　　　　　September 19, 1863—4.50 p. m.
General JAMES A. GARFIELD:
　　The enemy are engaging General Whitaker's brigade about 2½
miles from here.   The enemy are now receiving re-enforcements.
I am just sending re-enforcements to General Whitaker.
　　　　　　　　　　　　　　　　G. GRANGER,
　　　　　　　　　　　　　　　　　　Major-General.

———

HEADQUARTERS DEPARTMENT OF THE CUMBERLAND,
　　　　In the Field, September 19, 1863—5.35 p. m.
Maj. Gen. JAMES S. NEGLEY:
　　The general commanding wishes to know the result of your ad-
vance ; how far you have gone and where you will be found, and
what you know of General Palmer.   He thinks if you are not sup-
ported, you had better halt and take a good position for the night.
　　　Very respectfully, your obedient servant,
　　　　　　　　　　　　・　　　　J. A. GARFIELD,
　　　　　　　　　　　　Brigadier-General, Chief of Staff.

———

HDQRS. SECOND DIVISION, FOURTEENTH ARMY CORPS,
　　　　In the Field, September 19, 1863—6 p. m.
Major-General ROSECRANS,
　　　Commanding Department of the Cumberland:
GENERAL : We are driving the enemy handsomely.
　　I have the honor to remain, yours, very truly,
　　　　　　　　　　　　　　　JAS. S. NEGLEY,
　　　　　　　　　　　　　　　　　　Major-General.

———

HEADQUARTERS FOURTEENTH ARMY CORPS,
　　Near McDonald's House, September 19, 1863—7.10 p. m.
Major-General ROSECRANS,
　　　　　　　Widow Glenn's:
　　Your dispatch of 5 p. m. is just received.   We drove the enemy
in front of us steadily to-day, but, our lines being very much atten-
uated, I have drawn them in to-night, and they now reach from the
road leading through Mission Ridge from Crawfish Spring to Ross-

ville, across the direct road from Rossville to Gordon's Mills to a road leading from Rossville to Reed's Bridge. Just at dark they made a terrific attack on Johnson's division and threw them into considerable confusion, and for that reason I should very much like to have [re-enforcements sent] up to support my left. The positions of the divisions are as follows : Brannan's right occupying the slopes of Mission Ridge, Reynolds next, Palmer next, Johnson next, and Baird on the left.

Very respectfully, your obedient servant,

GEO. H. THOMAS,
Major-General, U. S. Volunteers, Commanding.

—

HEADQUARTERS FOURTEENTH ARMY CORPS,
Battle-field, September 19, 1863.
Maj. Gen. GORDON GRANGER :

We had a severe engagement with the enemy to-day, driving the rebels on the left and holding our own on the right.

Very respectfully, your obedient servant,

GEO. H. THOMAS,
Major-General, U. S. Volunteers, Commanding.

—

HEADQUARTERS FIRST DIVISION, RESERVE CORPS,
McAfee's Chapel or Spring, September 19, 1863—9 p. m.
COMMANDING OFFICER FORCES ON THE LEFT,
Fourteenth Army Corps, Dept. of the Cumberland :

GENERAL : I have the honor to report that my command is now occupying a line extending across the old Federal or Upper Ringgold road, extending to the Cleveland road on the left, and in the supposed direction of the left of the Fourteenth Army Corps, on the right, some half mile. I am some 3 miles from Rossville, on a small stream designated on our map as the West Chickamauga. I send an orderly to find your left. The enemy are in considerable force in my front this side of the Chickamauga River. I intend to attack them in the morning. Please give me such information as will be of interest in regard to the position of your left. A portion of my command was engaged this evening with a superior force of the enemy, much to the credit of my troops engaged.

I have the honor, &c., respectfully, your obedient servant,

JAMES B. STEEDMAN,
Brigadier-General, Commanding Division.

—

HEADQUARTERS DEPARTMENT OF THE CUMBERLAND,
September 19, 1863.
Major-General THOMAS,
Commanding Fourteenth Army Corps :

The general commanding desires you to call on him at headquarters immediately. The other corps commanders are here. He regrets to ask you to come so far, but it is necessary.

Yours, truly,

J. A. GARFIELD,
Brigadier-General, and Chief of Staff.

ROSSVILLE,
September 19, 1863—10 p. m.

General GARFIELD :

Wagner reports heavy columns of cavalry at Missionary Mills. I have sent to General Thomas' headquarters for Minty to push his whole command, except one battalion, to Missionary Mills and secure our train from destruction. Spears crossed at Battle Creek this morning. I suppose you received my message transmitted at 8 p. m.

G. GRANGER,
Major-General.

—

HEADQUARTERS DEPARTMENT OF THE CUMBERLAND,
Widow Glenn's, September 19, 1863.

Col. R. H. G. MINTY :

Your dispatch received. All right. Watch our left and keep us well advised.

Respectfully,

W. S. ROSECRANS.

—

HDQRS. DEPARTMENT OF THE CUMBERLAND,
September 19, 1863—8 p. m.
(Received 12.30 a. m., 21st.)

Maj. Gen. H. W. HALLECK,
General-in-Chief:

We have just concluded a terrific day's fighting, and have another in prospect for to-morrow. The enemy attempted to turn our left, but his design was anticipated, and a sufficient force placed there to render his attempt abortive. The battle-ground was densely wooded and its surface irregular and difficult. We could make but little use of our artillery. The number of our killed is inconsiderable ; that of our wounded very heavy. The enemy was greatly our superior in numbers. Among our prisoners are men from some thirty regiments. We have taken 10 cannon and lost 7. The army is in excellent condition and spirits, and, by the blessing of Providence, the defeat of the enemy will be total to-morrow.

W. S. ROSECRANS,
Major-General.

—

[VIA] CHATTANOOGA, *September* 19, 1863.

The PRESIDENT :

Have captured 10 pieces of artillery. Took prisoners from thirty different regiments, and with the blessing of God will do more to-morrow

W. S. ROSECRANS.

—

LA FAYETTE [ROAD], *September* 19, 1863.

General BURNSIDE :

Joe Johnston is with Bragg with large portion of his force, and re-enforcements have arrived from Virginia. We need all we can concentrate to oppose them. Let me hear from you.

ROSECRANS,
Major-General.

HEADQUARTERS ARMY OF THE CUMBERLAND,
September 19, 1863.
Major-General BURNSIDE:

The enemy, re-enforced by Joe Johnston, and Longstreet from Virginia, doubtless intended us all the mischief in their power. It is of the utmost importance that you close down this way to cover our left flank. Your cavalry ought to be in the vicinity of Tyner's now. We have not the force to cover our flank against forces [Forrest] now. He could cross the river above us before we could discover it, having to mass the three brigades to cover the gaps and Will's Valley, on our right and rear, and are massed in Chattooga Valley, from 15 to 20 miles south of Chattanooga. The enemy's main force at La Fayette, and thence toward Dalton and Ringgold. We may want all the help we can get promptly.

W. S. ROSECRANS,
Major-General.

—

HEADQUARTERS DEPARTMENT OF THE CUMBERLAND,
September 20, 1863.
Brig. Gen. R. B. MITCHELL,
Commanding Cavalry:

GENERAL: With your entire cavalry force adhere close to General McCook's right, sending patrols with all the wagon trains to the rear. You will defend the hospitals at all hazards. Cover also the closing up of Post's brigade, now on its march to join the main army. The general is dissatisfied that you do not report oftener.

Very respectfully, your obedient servant,
J. A. GARFIELD,
Brigadier-General, Chief of Staff.

—

HEADQUARTERS CHIEF OF CAVALRY,
DEPARTMENT OF THE CUMBERLAND,
Crawfish Spring, September 20, 1863—2 a. m.
General GARFIELD,
Chief of Staff:

GENERAL: A company has been sent back to hurry up General Crook and Colonel Watkins. I will send another at once and report the position of General Crook as soon as heard from. The Second East Tennessee was also ordered up from Stevens' Gap, and has joined me at this place. I have had no intelligence of Watkins' arrival at Stevens' Gap. All of my command is on duty in positions ordered by yourself or on picket duty. I am endeavoring to observe McCook's right closely.

ROBT. B. MITCHELL,
Brigadier-General.

—

HEADQUARTERS FOURTEENTH ARMY CORPS,
Near McDonald's House, September 20, 1863—6 a. m.
Major-General ROSECRANS:

Since my return this morning I have found it necessary to concentrate my lines more. My left does not now extend to the road that branches off at McDonald's house to Reed's Bridge. I earnestly request that Negley's division be placed on my left immediately. The enemy's skirmishers have been discovered about three-quarters of a mile from our left picket-line, facing toward the Rossville road. A division on my left would be exactly in their front.

Very respectfully, your obedient servant,

GEO. H. THOMAS,
Major-General, U. S. Volunteers, Commanding.

P. S.—General Baird has just reported to me that the enemy are moving toward our left.

—

HEADQUARTERS DEPARTMENT OF THE CUMBERLAND,
McDonald's House, September 20, 1863—6.30 a. m.

Brig. Gen. JAMES B. STEEDMAN:

The general commanding directs me to say that General Thomas reports the enemy in force on his left, and he wishes you to be on the lookout.

Very respectfully, your obedient servant,

FRANK S. BOND,
Major, and Aide-de-Camp.

—

KNOXVILLE,
September 20, [1863]—7 a. m.

For ROSECRANS:

Your dispatches received, and were answered at the time. I had a large portion of my force in the eastern part of the State so situated in reference to the enemy that I could not withdraw them. I have now ordered down every available man, and will order more as soon as possible. Byrd was in possession of Cleveland, but with a force so light it was driven out. I will order him to push on as fast as possible, but I hope you will not exaggerate his force, and will remember that he is confronted with a cavalry force that is trying to cross the Hiwassee above him. I am re-enforcing him all I can, and if possible will connect with you. From dispatches received when you took Chattanooga I supposed the enemy were running; otherwise might have probably made different moves. Depend upon it, I will help you all I can. You will hear from me again to-morrow. God bless you.

A. E. BURNSIDE.

—

HEADQUARTERS CHIEF OF CAVALRY,
Crawfish Spring, September 20, 1863—7.45 a. m.

General GARFIELD,
Chief of Staff:

GENERAL: The enemy attempted to cross at the first ford below the spring. We have repulsed them, and I think they have sustained considerable loss. Our loss nothing. Nothing heard from General Crook yet.

ROBT. B. MITCHELL,
Brigadier-General, Commanding.

HEADQUARTERS FOURTEENTH ARMY CORPS,
In the Field, September 20, 1863—8 o'clock [a. m.]

[General GORDON GRANGER] :

Your note of this morning just received. I am moving my forces near the road leading from McDonald's to Reed's Bridge, ready for any attack that the enemy may make on myself or on General Steedman's front, who I understand is posted near the Little Chickamauga, on the Red House road. Are we in supporting distance of each other? If not, you had better report to General Rosecrans at once.

Very respectfully,

GEO. H. THOMAS,
Major-General, Commanding.

—

HEADQUARTERS DEPARTMENT OF THE CUMBERLAND,
September 20, 1863—10.35 a. m.

Major-General THOMAS,
Commanding Fourteenth Army Corps:

The general commanding directs me to say, if possible refuse your left, sending in your reserves to the northward, as he would prefer having Crittenden and McCook on your right.

Very respectfully, your obedient servant,

FRANK S. BOND,
Major, and Aide-de-Camp.

[Indorsement.]

Dispatch received. The enemy are pushing me so hard that I cannot make any changes. The troops are posted behind temporary breastworks.

GEO. H. THOMAS.

—

HEADQUARTERS FOURTEENTH ARMY CORPS,
Battle-field, September 20, 1863—11 a. m.

Major-General ROSECRANS,
Commanding Department of the Cumberland:

The enemy penetrated a short time since to the road leading to McDaniel's [McDonald's] house, and I fear they are trying to cut off our communication with Rossville through the hills behind the center of our army. I think, therefore, it is of the utmost importance that Negley's division be ordered to that point—the left of my line.

Very respectfully, your obedient servant,

GEO. H. THOMAS,
Major-General, U. S. Volunteers, Commanding.

—

HEADQUARTERS DEPARTMENT OF THE CUMBERLAND,
Widow Glenn's, September 20, 1863.

General GRANGER,
Rossville :

Is Missionary Ridge available, supposing we should fall back ?

W. S. ROSECRANS,
Major-General.

HEADQUARTERS DEPARTMENT OF THE CUMBERLAND,
September 20, 1863.
General GORDON GRANGER, *Rossville:*

Do the ridges in front and left of Rossville admit of placing artillery in position with any possibility of commanding the valley and road?

W. S. ROSECRANS,
Major-General.

—

HEADQUARTERS DEPARTMENT OF THE CUMBERLAND,
In the Field, September 20, 1863—11.45 a. m.
Brig. Gen. R. B. MITCHELL, *Commanding Cavalry:*

The general commanding directs me to say that more frequent reports from you is a matter of duty. Send at once an intelligent officer with a squad of men to meet Crook, and report his position without delay.

I am, general, very respectfully, your obedient servant,
J. P. DROUILLARD,
Captain, and Aide-de-Camp.

—

HEADQUARTERS DEPARTMENT OF THE CUMBERLAND,
Chattanooga, September 20, 1863—12.15 p. m.[?]*
Major-General THOMAS:

Assume command of all the forces, and with Crittenden and McCook take a strong position and assume a threatening attitude at Rossville. Send all the unorganized force to this place for re-organization. I will examine the ground here and make such dispositions for defense as the case may require and join you. Have sent out ammunition and rations.

W. S. ROSECRANS,
Major-General.

—

CHATTANOOGA, *September* 20, 1863.
Brigadier-General GARFIELD:

See General McCook and other general officers. Ascertain extent of disaster as nearly as you can and report. Tell General Granger to contest the enemy's advance stubbornly, making them advance with caution. Should General Thomas be retiring in order, tell him to resist the enemy's advance, retiring on Rossville to-night.

By command of Major-General Rosecrans:
WILLIAM McMICHAEL,
Major, and Assistant Adjutant-General.

—

HDQRS. CHIEF OF CAV., DEPT. OF THE CUMBERLAND,
Crawfish Spring, Ga., September 20, 1863.
Brig. Gen. JAMES A. GARFIELD,
Chief of Staff, Department of the Cumberland:

General Crook has arrived and we are warmly engaged at the fords. They are trying to force a passage. We have repulsed them

---

* See Rosecrans to Thomas, p. 256; also Thomas to Rosecrans, p. 257.

once since I wrote you last in regard to the fight this morning. General Crook says when he left Stevens' Gap Colonel Post had no orders to leave the gap. I have sent through to Post all dispatches sent me yesterday. I learn from signal officer that Watkins' brigade is coming down the gap. I sent a letter addressed to Colonel P. at the same time I sent Colonel Watkins an order to come up. Did not know the contents ; suppose it was an order to come here, however.

  I am, your obedient servant,

          ROBT. B. MITCHELL.

GENERAL THOMAS' HEADQUARTERS,
Battle-field, Five Miles South of Rossville,
September 20, 1863—3.45 p. m.

General ROSECRANS :

  I arrived here ten minutes ago, via Rossville. General Thomas has Brannan's, Baird's, Reynolds', Wood's, Palmer's, and Johnson's divisions still intact after terrible fighting. Granger is here, closed up with Thomas, and is fighting terribly on the right. Sheridan is in with the bulk of his division, but in ragged shape, though plucky and fighting. General Thomas holds nearly his old ground of this morning. Negley was coming down on Rossville from the road leading from where we saw the trains in our route, and I sent word to him to cover the retreat of trains through Rossville. I also met the Fourth U. S. Battery at that place, and posted it as a reserve in case of need. As I turned in from the Rossville road to General Thomas' line I was opened upon by a rebel battalion. One orderly killed ; Captain Gaw's horse killed and my own wounded.

  The hardest fighting I have seen to-day is now going on here. I hope General Thomas will be able to hold on here till night, and will not need to fall back farther than Rossville ; perhaps not any. All fighting men should be stopped there, and the Dry Valley and Lookout roads held by them. I think we may in the main retrieve our morning disaster. I never saw better fighting than our men are now doing. The rebel ammunition must be nearly exhausted. Ours is fast failing. If we can hold out an hour more it will be all right. Granger thinks we can defeat them badly to-morrow if all our forces come in. I think you had better come to Rossville to-night and bring ammunition.

  Very truly, yours.

         J. A. GARFIELD,
          Brigadier-General.

HDQRS. FIRST BRIGADE, SECOND CAVALRY DIVISION,
On Ringgold Road, September 20, 1863—3.50 p. m.

General GARFIELD :

  SIR : Forrest (said to be about 1,500 strong) is immediately in my front skirmishing. I will endeavor to drive him.

  Respectfully, &c.,

        R. H. G. MINTY,
         Colonel, Commanding.

WAR DEPARTMENT,
Washington, September 20, 1863.

Major-General ROSECRANS,
Chattanooga, Tenn.:

General Burnside's instructions before he left Kentucky were to connect with your left. These instructions have been repeated five or six times, and he has answered that he was moving with that object. I think his advance cannot be far from you.

H. W. HALLECK,
General-in-Chief.

—

HEADQUARTERS DEPARTMENT OF THE CUMBERLAND,
Chattanooga, September 20, 1863—5 p. m.

OFFICER COMMANDING ADVANCE,
General Burnside's Army, Cleveland:

SIR: Hasten forward with your command to this place as rapidly as possible. We need you as soon as you can get here. The route by Tyner's will probably be the best. I send you a dispatch for General Burnside, which please forward to him with all possible speed.

By order of Major-General Rosecrans:

C. GODDARD,
Assistant Adjutant-General.

—

CHATTANOOGA,
September 20. 1863—5 p. m.

Major-General BURNSIDE:

We have met with a severe disaster. The extent of it is not yet known. If you are near enough to join us, do so at once. If you are |still too far away to form a junction, let me know your exact position, and I will advise you what you had better do.

W. S. ROSECRANS,
Major-General.

—

CHATTANOOGA, *September* 20, 1863—5 o'clock.

General SHERIDAN,
Rossville:

Verbal message by Captain Hill received. Support General Thomas by all means. If he is obliged to fall back he must secure the Dug [Dry] Valley. Right falling back slowly, contesting the ground inch by inch.

By order of Major-General Rosecrans:

C. GODDARD,
Assistant Adjutant-General.

—

CHATTANOOGA, TENN., *September* 20, 1863—5 p. m.
(Received 8.40 p. m.)

Maj. Gen. H. W. HALLECK,
General-in-Chief:

We have met with a serious disaster; extent not yet ascertained. Enemy overwhelmed us, drove our right, pierced our center, and scattered troops there.   Thomas, wno had seven divisions, remained intact at last news.   Granger, with two brigades, had gone to support Thomas on the left.   Every available reserve was used when the men stampeded.   Burnside will be notified of the state of things at once, and you will be informed.   Troops from Charleston, Florida, Virginia, and all along the seaboard are found among the prisoners. It seems that every available man was thrown against us.

W. S. ROSECRANS,
Major-General, Commanding.

—

ROSSVILLE, *September* 20, 1863—6.30 p. m.

Major-General ROSECRANS :

Would it not be well to send a flag of truce to make arrangements to recover our wounded ?   Otherwise their suffering will be very great.   They have only provisions enough for to-night.

G. PERIN,
Medical Director.

—

HEADQUARTERS DEPARTMENT ,OF THE CUMBERLAND,
Chattanooga, September 20, 1863—6.40 p. m.

Col. J. T. WILDER :

The general commanding directs me to say that you should have reported to General Mitchell at Crawfish Spring, so that he might cover that point and also threaten the enemy's flank.   Our latest advices from General Thomas were that he was holding his ground with six, and probably seven, divisions.   Instead of falling back this way the general commanding directs that you push on Missionary Ridge and try to open communication with General Mitchell, and, if successful, take orders from him.   You should pick up all stragglers, sending them by detachments to this place.   Report fully and often by the safest route. either down the valley or on Lookout Mountain.

Very respectfully, your obedient servant,

FRANK S. BOND,
Major, and Aide-de-Camp.

—

ROSSVILLE,
September 20, 1863—7 p. m.

Major-General ROSECRANS:

Just returned from up the Crawfish Spring road with the command that General Davis and I organize some 1,500 men, five companies Tenth Ohio [*sic*].   Did not find any of the enemy, having gone to within 1½ miles of the Widow Glenn's, our old headquarters. We are turned back by an order from Colonel Thruston to take position at Rossville.   The troops here are utterly exhausted and without rations.   I have sent to Chattanooga for supplies.   Could you not send ten or fifteen wagon-loads of meat and crackers immediately?

I have the honor to remain, yours, very truly,

JAS. S. NEGLEY,
Major-General.

ROSSVILLE,
September 20, 1863—7.05 p. m.

Major-General ROSECRANS:

After inexpressible labor we have succeeded in getting the troops organized at this place, with some six or seven batteries, intact, excepting the troops of General Crittenden's corps, which went forward to Chattanooga by his order, and General Sheridan's, who went to the support of General Thomas. By a mutual arrangement via La Fayette or Eastern road, cavalry could make a powerful demonstration in the rear of the enemy down Crawfish road.

BURT,
Captain.

HDQRS. FIRST BRIGADE, SECOND CAVALRY DIVISION,
Ringgold Road. September 20. 1863—7.35 p. m.

General GARFIELD,
Chief of Staff:

GENERAL: My brigade was so much scattered by details that it was almost dark before I got sufficient force together to enable me to attack Scott (not Forrest), and then it being so dark I had to move cautiously, but succeeded in driving him over the creek. I took but 1 prisoner. He states that Scott had 1,500 men and four pieces of artillery. I had 2 men wounded. I have heard nothing whatever from General Granger or Colonel McCook since they moved from here. I have fallen back to within about half a mile of the cross-roads, so as to enable me to cover both roads.

I am, respectfully,

R. H. G. MINTY,
Colonel, Commanding.

ROSSVILLE,
September 20, 1863—8.40 p. m.

Major-General ROSECRANS:

One of my staff officers has just returned from General Sheridan's command. He reached the meeting house 3 miles from this point. He reports communication with General Thomas cut off by the presence of a considerable force of the enemy. Forrest's cavalry harassed Sheridan all the way. There is evidently a column moving on our left from the direction of Ringgold. Just heard from General Mitchell's cavalry command. He left Crawfish Spring at 5 o'clock. He reports our trains safe with him. General King's brigade is just arriving. General Johnson's division is about 2 miles back.

JAS. S. NEGLEY,
Major-General.

[ROSSVILLE,] *September* 20, 1863—8.40 p. m.

Major-General ROSECRANS:

I have this moment returned from the front. I wrote you a long dispatch as I arrived on the field and while the battle was in progress, but it was so difficult to get communication to the rear that I fear you have not yet received it. Thomas has kept Baird's, Brannan's, Reynolds', Wood's, and Palmer's divisions in good order, and has maintained almost the exact position he occupied this morning, except that his right has swung back nearly at right angles with the Gordon's Mills and Rossville road. Negley has stopped about 6,000 men at this place. Sheridan gathered 1,500 of his division, and reached a point 3 miles south of here at sunset. Davis is here with two brigades. General Thomas has fought a most terrific battle and has damaged the enemy badly. General Granger's troops moved up just in time and fought magnificently. From the time I reached the battle-field (3.45 p. m.) till sunset the fighting was by far the fiercest I have ever seen. Our men not only held their ground, but at many points drove the enemy splendidly. Longstreet's Virginians have got their bellies full. Nearly every division in the field exhausted its ammunition, got supplies, and exhausted it again. Turchin charged the rebel lines and took 500 prisoners; became enveloped, swept around behind their lines and cut his way out in another place, but abandoned his prisoners. Another brigade was attacked just at the close of the fight, and its ammunition being exhausted, it went in with the bayonet and drove the rebels, taking over 200 prisoners, and have got them yet. On the whole, Generals Thomas and Granger have done the enemy fully as much injury to-day as they have suffered from him, and they have successfully repelled the repeated combined attacks, most fiercely made, of the whole rebel army, frequently pressing the front and both flanks at the same time. The disaster on the right cannot, of course, be estimated now. It must be very considerable in men and *matériel*, especially the latter. The rebels have, however, done their best to-day, and I believe we can whip them to-morrow. I believe we can now crown the whole battle with victory. Granger regards them as thoroughly whipped to-night, and thinks they would not renew the fight were we to remain on the field. Clouds of dust to the eastward and northward seem to indicate some movement to our left. Sheridan thinks they may be projecting to come in directly on Chattanooga. I do not think so. Your order to retire on this place was received a little after sunset and communicated to Generals Thomas and Granger. The troops are now moving back, and will be here in good shape and strong position before morning. I hope you will not budge an inch from this place, but come up early in the morning, and if the rebs try it on, accommodate them. General Mitchell left Crawfish Spring at 5 p. m. Our trains are reported safe with him. We have not heard from General McCook. General Crittenden reported with you. General Lytle killed; also Colonel King and many officers. If I am not needed at headquarters to-night I will stay here. I am half dead with fatigue. Answer if I can do anything here.

J. A. GARFIELD,
Brigadier-General, Chief of Staff.

—

HEADQUARTERS DEPARTMENT OF THE CUMBERLAND,
September 20, 1863—9.30 p. m.
Brigadier-General GARFIELD,
Chief of Staff:

You may stay all night. If the enemy are drifting toward our left (Rossville position), have men ordered up. I like your suggestions.

W. S. ROSECRANS,
Major-General.

HEADQUARTERS DEPARTMENT OF THE CUMBERLAND,
Chattanooga, September 20, 1863—9.45 p. m.
Col. J. T. WILDER:
Your dispatch of 6 p. m. received. The general commanding
directs me to say that he is highly pleased with your report, and
directs that you send the guns on as soon as possible.
Very respectfully, your obedient servant,
J. A. GARFIELD,
Brigadier-General, Chief of Staff.

—

WASHINGTON,
September 21, 1863—12.35 a. m.
Major-General ROSECRANS,
Chattanooga:
Be of good cheer. We have unabated confidence in you and in
your soldiers and officers. In the main you must be the judge as to
what is to be done. If I was to suggest, I would say save your army
by taking strong positions until Burnside joins you, when I hope you
can turn the tide. I think you had better send a courier to Burnside
to hurry him up. We cannot reach him by telegraph. We suppose some force is going to you from Corinth, but for want of communication we do not know how they are getting along. We shall
do our utmost to assist you. Send us your present posting.
A. LINCOLN.

—

ROSSVILLE, *September 21, 1863—1.30 p. m. [a. m.]*
Major-General ROSECRANS,
Chattanooga:
Minty reports at 9 p. m. last night that he drove Scott's brigade
across the river on the Ringgold road, and now holds the cross-roads
at that place. This seems to dispose of the story of the enemy attempting to get round our left into Chattanooga. I have been to
General Thomas to inquire what disposition he has made for fight in
the morning. We do not seem to be in the best trim for an early
fight.
I hope you will get here as soon as possible to organize the army
and victory before the storm sets in. General Thomas bid me say
he will make the best dispositions for the morrow he can. He
came here (General Granger's headquarters) with me, and is now
consulting on the lines to be held. The officers in charge of supply
and ammunition trains should come forward and report to General
Thomas at McFarland's house, at the fork of the road, now used as
a hospital. I hope there will be no failure in the bringing up of
these supplies.
J. A. GARFIELD,
Brigadier-General.

—

WAR DEPARTMENT,
September 21, 1863—2 a. m.
General BURNSIDE,
Knoxville, Tenn.:
Go to Rosecrans with your force without a moment's delay.
A. LINCOLN.

HEADQUARTERS FOURTEENTH ARMY CORPS,
Rossville, September 21, *1863*—6.45 a. m.

Capt. J. P. [DROUILLARD],
    Aide-de-Camp:

CAPTAIN: I have posted Negley's division in the pass at Rossville;
General McCook's corps on the right, across Dry Creek Valley, his
left resting on Negley's right; General Crittenden's two divisions on
the top of the ridge and to the left of the pass; the remainder of my
corps and General Granger's massed in reserve behind the center.
These are the best dispositions I can make for the present. Colonel
Minty is on the Ringgold road, 2 or 3 miles in front of the pass. He
reported at 5 a. m. to-day all quiet on his front.

Very respectfully, your obedient servant,
                        GEO. H. THOMAS,
            Major-General, U. S. Volunteers.

—

[SEPTEMBER [21], 1863.]
(Received Hdqrs. Dept. of the Cumberland, 21st.)

Position of the troops: General McCook on our extreme right; General Reynolds' division, Fourteenth Army Corps, on the left of Mc-
Cook; Negley on left of Reynolds; Baird supporting one brigade of
Negley's in the pass, and the right of Crittenden's corps, which is
posted on the hills to the left of the pass; Steedman supporting Crittenden's left. Minty has been driven in from the front and is now
posted on the hills on the extreme left. E. M. McCook up Dry
Creek Valley observing our right and front. There is a hill beyond
the pass from which they can shell us if they can get possession.

                        GEO. H. THOMAS,
                            Major-General.

—

HDQRS. SECOND DIVISION, FOURTEENTH ARMY CORPS,
            Rossville, September 21, 1863—7.30 a. m.

Major-General ROSECRANS,
    Comdg. Department of the Cumberland:

GENERAL: I have the pleasure to assure you that everything is
progressing most favorably. I have my division properly organized,
armed, fed, and in position. Will have the other troops here in preliminary organization in less than an hour. Affairs present a very
satisfactory appearance.

Yours, very truly,

                        JAS. S. NEGLEY,
                            Major-General.

—

ROSSVILLE,
September 21, 1863—7.45 a. m.

General ROSECRANS:

I do not feel sure of this line as a good one for a general battle, and
I do not know how much reliance can be placed on the stampeded
troops. I understand from General Crittenden that you expect me
in town this morning. I will start in a few minutes, after seeing

General Thomas. On the whole, I do not feel sure but that you ought to remain at Chattanooga till we see the developments and organize the rear.

Very truly, yours,

J. A. GARFIELD,
Brigadier-General.

—

EXECUTIVE MANSION,
Washington, D. C., September 21, 1863.

Major-General HALLECK:

I think it very important for General Rosecrans to hold his position at or about Chattanooga, because if held from that place to Cleveland, both inclusive, it keeps all Tennessee clear of the enemy, and also breaks one of his most important railroad lines. To prevent these consequences is so vital to his cause that he cannot give up the effort to dislodge us from the position, thus bringing him to us, and saving us the labor, expense, and hazard of going farther to find him and also giving us the advantage of choosing our own ground and preparing it to fight him upon. The details must, of course, be left to General Rosecrans, while we must furnish him the means to the utmost of our ability. If you concur, I think he should better be informed that we are not pushing him beyond this position, and that, in fact, our judgment is rather against his going beyond it. If he can only maintain this position without more, the rebellion can only eke out a short and feeble existence, as an animal sometimes may with a thorn in its vitals.

Yours, truly,

A. LINCOLN.

—

HEADQUARTERS OF THE ARMY,
September 21, 1863.

It is respectfully submitted that the within instructions, given ten days ago, conform to those suggested in the President's letter of this morning.

H. W. HALLECK,
General-in-Chief.

[Inclosure No. 1.]

HEADQUARTERS OF THE ARMY,
Washington, D. C. September 11, 1863—1.35 p. m.

Major-General ROSECRANS,
Chattanooga:

General Burnside telegraphs from Cumberland Gap that he holds all East Tennessee above Loudon, and also the gaps of the North Carolina mountains. A cavalry force is moving toward Athens to connect with you. After holding the mountain passes on the west, and Dalton, or some other point on the railroad, to prevent the return of Bragg's army, it will be decided whether your army shall move farther south into Georgia and Alabama. It is reported here by deserters that a part of Bragg's army is re-enforcing Lee. It is important that the truth of this should be ascertained as early as possible.

H. W. HALLECK,
General-in-Chief.

[Inclosure No. 2.]

HEADQUARTERS OF THE ARMY,
Washington, D. C., September 11, 1863—2 p. m.

Major-General BURNSIDE,
Cumberland Gap:

I congratulate you on your successes. Hold the gaps of the North Carolina mountains, the line of the Holston River, or some point, if there be one, to prevent access from Virginia and connect with General Rosecrans, at least with your cavalry. The Secretary of War directs that you raise all the volunteers you can in East Tennessee. Select the officers, and if not commissioned by Governor Johnson they will be by the President. If you have not arms and equipments at your disposal telegraph for them. How is the supply of forage and provisions in East Tennessee? General Rosecrans will occupy Dalton, or some point on the railroad, to close all access from Atlanta, and also the mountain passes on the west. This being done it will be determined whether the movable forces shall advance into Georgia and Alabama, or into the Valley of Virginia and North Carolina.

H. W. HALLECK,
General-in-Chief.

—

WAR DEPARTMENT, *September* 21, 1863—11 a. m.

General BURNSIDE, *Greeneville, Tenn.:*

If you are to do any good to Rosecrans it will not do to waste time with Jonesborough. It is already too late to do the most good that might have been done, but I hope it will still do some good. Please do not lose a moment.

A. LINCOLN.

—

CHATTANOOGA, *September* 21, 1863.
(Received Knoxville, 22d.)

Major-General BURNSIDE :

Your courier, Hicks, arrived. I dispatched you yesterday in cipher by courier. After a sanguinary battle of two days, in which all our troops were engaged repeatedly, our right and center were forced. Our left maintained its position till night, when it fell back to Rossville, where we are now in position. Unless your troops can join us at once, it will not be practicable for them to come down on east side of river; the enemy will occupy that country. Come down on west side Tennessee as rapidly as possible. We shall probably have to hold Chattanooga as a *tête-de-pont* until re-enforcements come up.

W. S. ROSECRANS,
Major-General.

—

CHATTANOOGA, TENN., *September* 21, 1863—9 a.m.
(Received War Department 12.45 p. m.)

His Excellency ABRAHAM LINCOLN,
President of the United States:

After two days of the severest fighting I ever witnessed our right and center were beaten. The left held its position until sunset.

Our loss is heavy and our troops worn down. The enemy received heavy re-enforcements Saturday night. Every man of ours was in action Sunday and all but one brigade on Saturday. Our wounded large compared with the killed. We took prisoners from two divisions of Longstreet. We have no certainty of holding our position here. If Burnside could come immediately it would be well ; otherwise he may not be able to join us unless he comes on west side of river.

W. S. ROSECRANS,
Major-General, Commanding.

—

GREENEVILLE, TENN.,
September 21, 1863—9.20 a. m.

General ROSECRANS :

I will send you all the men I can spare you. I have much work to do, as my line is long, but you shall have all the help I can give you. Will telegraph you to-night more in detail.

A. E. BURNSIDE,
Major-General.

—

HEADQUARTERS DEPARTMENT OF THE CUMBERLAND,
Chattanooga, September 20 [21], 1863—9.25 a. m. [?]

Brigadier-General GARFIELD,
Chief of Staff, Rossville :

Mitchell has been ordered to occupy the Dry Valley road and Missionary Ridge, Post's brigade to support and protect Chattanooga Valley. If the enemy does not attack vigorously this a. m., the probabilities are that he will, while collecting property and burying the dead, send a strong force to the ferries at Harrison's and above. Wilder has been ordered up the river, preceded by the Second Michigan Cavalry, to protect the crossings. This will probably secure our communications for a day or two. Meanwhile all the spare transportation has been ordered over the river and across the mountain via Therman. Have dispatched you to call for a report of the corps, to find out their strength, &c., the great point now being to hold Chattanooga and secure our communications. I write this by the direction of the general commanding.

Very respectfully, &c.,

FRANK S. BOND,
Major, and Aide-de-Camp.

—

HEADQUARTERS CHIEF OF CAVALRY,
DEPARTMENT OF THE CUMBERLAND,
Near Rock Creek Ford, Ga., September 21, 1863—10.15 a. m.

Brig. Gen. JAMES A. GARFIELD,
Chief of Staff, Department of the Cumberland :

I have sent out a force as directed by you last evening into Dry Valley and another well down to Chattanooga. They have both pushed well out and discover nothing of the enemy. Colonel McCook had gone into Dry Valley with two brigades. I have ordered him to open communication with the commanding officers of the right wing of the army. When he left I directed him to feel well out, and a messenger from him reports no enemy found so far. From prisoners captured yesterday near Crawfish Spring, I find that I was fighting Withers' old division, now commanded by Hindman; also a part of Breckinridge's division. Colonel Wilder is very sick, and I have permitted him to go into town. I am lying here quietly watching the corners. Wilder's command has reported to me, but I have not put it into position yet. I am holding it here waiting developments. So far I have not heard a shot in front. I have not been able to open communication with Colonel Watkins, and am at a loss to know what has become of him.

I am, very respectfully, your obedient servant,

ROBT. B. MITCHELL,
Brigadier-General, and Chief of Cavalry.

—

ROSSVILLE,
September 21, 1863—11 o'clock.

Major-General Rosecrans,
Commanding Department of the Cumberland:

GENERAL: A Kentucky prisoner, belonging to Helm's brigade, Breckinridge's divison, reports the enemy 100,000 strong yesterday; that General Ewell was expected last night with re-enforcements to the number of 20,000; that Bragg says this is the first time he has had a respectable army, and he is sure of victory.

I remain, &c.,

J. G. PARKHURST,
Colonel and Provost-Marshal, Fourteenth Army Corps.

—

CHATTANOOGA,
September 21, 1863.

Brigadier-General SPEARS:

The general commanding directs you to report to Major-General Granger for duty with your command.

Very respectfully, your obedient servant,

C. GODDARD,
Lieutenant-Colonel, and Assistant Adjutant-General.

—

LOOKOUT, MISSIONARY RANGE,
(September 21, 1863—11.30 a. m.)

General THOMAS:

A column of men is advancing on the northern or lower Ringgold road. It moves slowly. It heads this side of Chickamauga River.

S. D. CONOVER,
Captain.

—

SEPTEMBER 21, 1863—12.15 p. m.

Major-General THOMAS:

My pickets on front and right are attacked.

Respectfully,

ROBT. H. G. MINTY,
Colonel.

HDQRS. FIRST BRIGADE, SECOND CAVALRY DIVISION,
September 21, [1863]—12.50 p. m.
[Major-General THOMAS :]

I have fallen back to the ridge directly in front of your line of
battle.

ROBT. H. G. MINTY,
Colonel.

—

HEADQUARTERS FOURTEENTH ARMY CORPS,
Rossville, September 21, 1863—1.25 p. m.
Major-General ROSECRANS,
Comdg. Department of the Cumberland :

Your dispatch just received. Colonel Minty reports the enemy
advancing on both our flanks in strong force. I am making the best
possible dispositions of the troops to meet them. Skirmishing quite
brisk.

Very respectfully, your obedient servant,
GEO. H. THOMAS,
Major-General, U. S. Volunteers. Commanding.

—

HEADQUARTERS DEPARTMENT OF THE CUMBERLAND,
Chattanooga, September 21, 1863.
Major-General THOMAS, *Rossville :*

The general commanding directs me to inform you that Sherman
and McPherson are ordered to this department. Three cheers! He
says, "Tell the boys."

R. S. THOMS,
Aide-de-Camp.

—

HEADQUARTERS DEPARTMENT OF THE ,CUMBERLAND,
Chattanooga, September 21, 1863—1 p. m.
Major-General THOMAS,
Comdg. Fourteenth Army Corps, Rossville:

General Mitchell has reconnoitered up Dry Valley road to near
Rock Creek, and reports that so far he has found nothing.

W. S. ROSECRANS,
Major-General.

—

HEADQUARTERS DEPARTMENT OF THE CUMBERLAND,
Chattanooga, Tenn., September 21, 1863.
Brig. Gen. H. P. VAN CLEVE :

The general commanding directs you to place your division for the
present to the right and rear of the works on the Knoxville Railroad,
throwing forward a regiment to the bridge over the Chickamauga,
one at the gap in Missionary Ridge on the Ooltewah or Shallow Ford
road, and one at the gap on the Missionary Mills or Chickamauga
Station road. General Wagner's cavalry is scouting in front of
these positions.

Very respectfully, your obedient servant,
C. GODDARD,
Lieutenant-Colonel, and Assistant Adjutant-General.

HEADQUARTERS DEPARTMENT OF THE CUMBERLAND,
Chattanooga, September 21, 1863.

Brig. Gen. H. P. VAN CLEVE:

The general commanding directs you to detail 500 men to report at 6 a. m. to-morrow to General Morton to work on rifle-pits. General Morton will be at your headquarters at that hour. He further directs you to have 500 men ready to relieve the first 500 at 1.30 to-morrow.

Very respectfully, your obedient servant,

C. GODDARD,
Lieutenant-Colonel, and Assistant Adjutant-General.

—

CHATTANOOGA, TENN., *September 21, 1863—2 p. m.*
(Received 9.20 p. m.)

Maj. Gen. H. W. HALLECK,
General-in-Chief:

A man of Company C, Tennessee Artillery, deserted from Mobile September 1. When he left, the garrison was but two Alabama regiments and three batteries—one of six and two of four guns—and 200 cavalry. Johnston's army all came here except one division. Nineteen forts around city, mounting three siege guns, each 32-pounders and larger, besides three field guns. Two miles down the bay from the city three batteries heavy guns. Two rams in bay, six heavy guns each. On Pensacola side three batteries heavy guns. Forts are all man saw. Colonel and lieutenant-colonel from Little Rock said Arkansas army was very much demoralized. They said Bragg would not hold Chattanooga, but would draw Rosecrans across the river and overwhelm him with numbers. Said if rebels were successful at Chattanooga their cause would be greatly encouraged. If whipped there and at Charleston Confederacy was gone. Three thousand home guards were at Mobile. Officers said they feared they would turn against them if the place was attacked. Home guards and Tennessee battery said they would not fire a shot if they could help it. Force at Mobile fear advance by General Banks. One division of Johnston's army between Meridian and Selma ready to go to Mobile or Chattanooga as required. Five thousand cavalry at Pollard, Ala., to guard against raids. No other force beyond there between Atlanta and Montgomery. There are three floating batteries in harbor of Mobile well manned. If necessary they intend to sink them to obstruct navigation. New breech-loading Whitworth gun on point near Fort Morgan.

W. S. ROSECRANS,
Major-General.

—

ROSSVILLE, *September 21, 1863—2 p. m.*

General GARFIELD:

Dispatch received. General Thomas sent you Colonel Minty's report of advance on both our flanks. All quiet at present. General Thomas is making dispositions in accordance with information. My time is by General Rosecrans' watch.

ARTHUR C. DUCAT,
Lieutenant-Colonel, and Inspector-General.

ROSSVILLE, *September* 21, 1863.

General ROSECRANS:

The enemy have made an attack with musketry on here directly in front of the forks. Some artillery firing to the left.

ARTHUR C. DUCAT,
Lieutenant-Colonel, Inspector-General.

—

HEADQUARTERS CHIEF OF CAVALRY,
Rock Creek Ford, September 21, 1863—2.15 p. m.

General GARFIELD:

GENERAL: We have a hell of a front here. We will do the best we can. Their skirmishers are along my whole front. A soldier who left Crawfish Spring this morning and stole past them says two divisions of Longstreet's corps left there early this morning on this road.

ROBT. B. MITCHELL,
Brigadier-General, Chief of Cavalry.

—

HEADQUARTERS DEPARTMENT OF THE CUMBERLAND,
Chattanooga, September 21, 1863.

Brig. Gen. R. B. MITCHELL:

Is Watkins watching the gaps in the Lookout Valley? If not, send him up the Nickajack Trace and along the top of the mountain as far as Cooper's Gap to observe what, if anything, is going on in the valley or vicinity. Have him report often and fully all he sees, and reply yourself to this communication by return courier.

By order of Major-General Rosecrans:

FRANK S. BOND,
Major, and Aide-de-Camp.

—

CHATTANOOGA, *September* 21, 1863—2.20 p. m.

General BURNSIDE:

Dispatched you this morning by Hicks, stating that the enemy after two days' hard fighting, in which all our available troops had been repeatedly engaged, our center and the right was routed. Our left maintained its position till night and retired to Rossville, where we are now in position, and at this time heavy skirmishing is reported. You had better join me at once by the west side Tennessee River. Should we have to fall back you will have to vacate East Tennessee. Enemy outnumbered us greatly. The battle was one of the hardest of the war.

W. S. ROSECRANS,
Major-General.

—

WAR DEPARTMENT,
Washington, September 21, 1863—3 p. m.

Major-General ROSECRANS,
Chattanooga, Tenn.:

Nothing heard from General Burnside since the 19th. He was then sending to your aid all his available force. It is hoped that you will hold out till he can re-enforce you. He was directed to connect with you ten days ago, and the order has been repeated several times since. I can get no reply from Hurlbut or Sherman.

H. W. HALLECK,
General-in-Chief.

HEADQUARTERS CHIEF OF CAVALRY,
DEPARTMENT OF THE CUMBERLAND,
Rock Creek Ford, Ga., September 21, 1863—3.30 p. m.

Brig. Gen. JAMES A. GARFIELD,
Chief of Staff:

Everything quiet in front except occasional skirmishing. Colonel Campbell just reports a column moving up apparently between him and General Thomas ; thinks it is cavalry. I have sent him an additional company. As I said in my previous communication, I have no knowledge of the whereabouts of Colonel Watkins' brigade, nor have I had since I ordered it up from Valley Head. There have been two companies with orders, besides one courier sent to him. I will send another company over the mountain to try and find him.

I am, very respectfully, your obedient servant,

ROBT. B. MITCHELL,
Brigadier-General, and Chief of Cavalry.

ROSSVILLE, *September* 21, 1863—3.35 p. m.

Brigadier-General GARFIELD :

Fight appearing briskly on the left. General Thomas informs me that the enemy are advancing very strong on both flanks.

ARTHUR C. DUCAT,
Lieutenant-Colonel, and Inspector-General.

CHATTANOOGA, *September* 21, 1863.

General THOMAS :

Make your preparations to retire to the front of this place to-night. Orders have been sent you by courier, and a brief of them will soon be sent by telegraph.

J. A. GARFIELD,
Brigadier-General, and Chief of Staff.

ROSSVILLE, *September* 21, 1863—4.45 p. m.

Brigadier-General GARFIELD :

The firing has ceased in the gap. Very little musketry to-day. Do not know what is coming, but from the heavy clouds of dust on the ridge in front I think they are getting in position in force in front this afternoon. I notice a heavy cloud of dust over Mission Ridge to the left. Should the enemy go on the ridge in front with artillery, the position in this valley will be a very open one.

ARTHUR C. DUCAT,
Lieutenant-Colonel, and Inspector-General.

HEADQUARTERS DEPARTMENT OF THE CUMBERLAND,
Chattanooga, September 21, 1863—5.30 p. m.
Maj. Gen. GEORGE H. THOMAS, *Comdg. Forces at Rossville:*

GENERAL: Supposing you are assaulted in your present position, you will maintain it if possible till close of day ; then quietly withdraw your command, Crittenden on the left, by the most practicable road or the fields, you by middle or right-hand road, both looking this way, and McCook by Chattanooga Valley road. Troops should use the fields, and everything should be done as quietly as possible. Fires should be built along the present lines—not excessive, and not on the roads. Each corps to leave grand guards and outposts, to be withdrawn only by order, and certainly not till late in the morning, retiring as skirmishers. Each corps will detail not less than one brigade, more if necessary, to contest every inch of the road. These brigades to be of picked men, with section of artillery, at least, to be used in commanding positions as you retire. Fuller details have been sent by courier.

J. A. GARFIELD,
Brigadier-General, Chief of Staff.

—

HEADQUARTERS FOURTEENTH ARMY CORPS,
DEPARTMENT OF THE CUMBERLAND,
Rossville, September 21, 1863—5.40 p. m.
Major-General ROSECRANS, *Commanding Department:*

Your dispatch just received. I will make all the dispositions I can before dark. Please have places assigned for the troops as they arrive, with officers to direct them to their respective places.

Very respectfully, your obedient servant,
GEO. H. THOMAS,
Major-General, U. S. Volunteers, Commanding.

—

HEADQUARTERS DEPARTMENT OF THE CUMBERLAND,
Chattanooga, September 21, 1863.
Brig. Gen. H. P. VAN CLEVE:

The general commanding directs you to station sentinels and build a line of fires to guide General Crittenden's command in on the Missionary Mills road; also along the cut and embankment of the railroad nearest the river. A few small fires will answer the purpose. Lieutenant Burroughs, of the Engineers, will be sent with this to point out the line.

Very respectfully, your obedient servant,
C. GODDARD,
Lieutenant-Colonel, and Assistant Adjutant-General.

—

HEADQUARTERS DEPARTMENT OF THE CUMBERLAND,
Chattanooga, Tenn., September 21, 1863.
Col. J. T. WILDER:

The general commanding directs you to demolish the rebel batteries on the south side of the river at the ford near Friar's Island. Dig down the works, so that the rebels cannot use them.

Very respectfully, your obedient servant,
C. GODDARD,
Lieutenant-Colonel, and Assistant Adjutant-General.

HEADQUARTERS DEPARTMENT OF THE CUMBERLAND,
Chattanooga, September 21, 1863.

Col. J. T. WILDER,
Commanding Mounted Brigade:

COLONEL: Your dispatch of 7 p. m. just received. If you find that the report of Pegram's crossing is correct, you mu.. arrange to protect our wagon train on the north side of the river, leaving a regiment to watch and with the rest of your available force pursue Pegram's force.

By order of Major-General Rosecrans:

C. GODDARD,
Lieutenant-Colonel, and Assistant Adjutant-General.

—

HEADQUARTERS DEPARTMENT OF THE CUMBERLAND,
Chattanooga, September 21, 1863—8.15 p. m.

Brigadier-General MITCHELL,
Commanding Cavalry:

General Spears has been sent forward to Rock Creek Ford to support you in case you should be pressed. The general commanding directs you to assume temporary command of Spears' and Post's brigades, and use them as support. Cover the right of General McCook, and, if compelled to fall back, do so slowly, contesting the ground inch by inch. In falling back, post Spears at the forks of the road near the point of Lookout Mountain. Report frequently.

J. A. GARFIELD,
Brigadier-General, Chief of Staff.

—

HEADQUARTERS DEPARTMENT OF THE CUMBERLAND,
Chattanooga, September 21, 1863—8.35 p. m.

Brigadier-General MITCHELL,
Commanding Cavalry:

The general commanding directs you to send General Spears' command back to the forks of the road at the point of the mountain, and order him to send one regiment immediately to Summertown, on the top of Lookout Mountain, and throw up log breastworks, so as to defend themselves. We have a small cavalry force in front of the position indicated. The bearer of this dispatch will conduct the regiment to Summertown.

Send Post's brigade back immediately to hold the forks of the road 1 mile this side of Blowing Spring.

The movements of your cavalry will be as directed in my dispatch of 8.15 p. m.

J. A. GARFIELD,
Brigadier-General, Chief of Staff.

—

CHATTANOOGA, *September 21, 1863—8.40 p. m.*

Major-General THOMAS,
Commanding Fourteenth Army Corps:

There will be an officer to direct the heads of columns to their proper places. Water can be had in some of the places, but at others a detail must be made to furnish it. The troops will not encamp on the line of battle exactly, on account of the lack of water. The fighting ground in front being good, it will not be necessary that they should be on it.

W. S. ROSECRANS,
Major-General.

—

HEADQUARTERS DEPARTMENT OF THE CUMBERLAND,
Chattanooga, September 21, 1863—10 p. m.
Major-General THOMAS,
Commanding, &c., Rossville:
The general commanding directs me to say, if the opinion is well founded that the enemy only made to-day a reconnaissance in force, and that they did not advance their infantry and are still encamped where there is water, it would be well to hold our ground with the rear guard, using the picket line as skirmishers, directing them to retire under cover, taking new positions and keeping the artillery well in the distance. He also directs that a staff officer be sent well in advance of your columns to meet the officer sent from these head-quarters to indicate the position to be taken by the command.
Very respectfully, your obedient servant,

FRANK S. BOND,
Major, and Aide-de-Camp.

—

HEADQUARTERS FOURTEENTH ARMY CORPS,
DEPARTMENT OF THE CUMBERLAND,
Rossville, September 21, 1863—10.20 p. m.
Major-General ROSECRANS,
Commanding Department:
The movement of the troops has commenced; the men moving very orderly and quietly.
Very respectfully, your obedient servant,

GEO. H. THOMAS,
Major-General, U. S. Volunteers, Commanding.

—

HEADQUARTERS DEPARTMENT OF THE CUMBERLAND,
Chattanooga, Tenn., September 21, 1863.
Maj. Gen. GEORGE H. THOMAS,
Commanding Fourteenth Army Corps:
GENERAL: The general commanding directs you to make details to be ready to commence work at 6 a. m. to-morrow on rifle-pits which will be laid out by engineer officers to connect the work. Rude breastworks must be constructed with all possible speed. Each corps will picket its own front, throwing out grand guards at least a mile to the front, and farther if practicable. The picket line must be a strong skirmish line. Abatis must be constructed in front of the breastworks whenever possible.
Very respectfully, your obedient servant,

C. GODDARD,
Lieutenant-Colonel, and Assistant Adjutant-General.

(Same to Major-Generals Crittenden, McCook,* and Stanley.)

---

* Seems to have been duplicated on the 22d, 1.15 a. m.

HEADQUARTERS DEPARTMENT OF THE CUMBERLAND,
Chattanooga, September 22, 1863.
Commanding Officer, Bridgeport, Ala.:

Report at once situation of bridges at Bridgeport. Have you heard of any enemy in vicinity? After everything has crossed at that point take up the pontoon part of the bridge and float it around, and defend the island to the last. Have your patrols down the river. Do you hear of any enemy in that direction? Make every disposition to prevent enemy from crossing. Be sure that all transportation is across before taking up bridge between island and this side.

W. S. ROSECRANS,
Major-General.

—

STEVENSON, *September* 22, 1863.
General GARFIELD, *Chief of Staff:*

Just received copy of your dispatch to Colonel Smith at Bridgeport. Have two companies of cavalry patroling the river from Bridgeport to 10 or 15 miles below Stevenson. One ferry-boat destroyed yesterday and another ordered to be destroyed to-day. Hear of no enemy crossing or attempting to cross the river. Edgarton's battery just arrived from Nashville. A section has been ordered to move immediately to Battle Creek; two regiments of infantry are there.

JAMES D. MORGAN,
Brigadier-General.

—

HDQRS. FIRST BRIGADE, SECOND CAVALRY DIVISION,
September 22, 1863—7.30 a. m.
Colonel FLYNT:

At 5.30 a. m. Captain McIntyre reported to me that the enemy had discovered the evacuation and were advancing on him, and that he must fall back. I immediately moved out on the main road. and am there now.

Respectfully,

ROBT. H. G. MINTY,
Colonel.

—

HDQRS. FIRST BRIGADE, SECOND CAVALRY DIVISION,
September 22, 1863—8.30 a. m.

COLONEL: The enemy (mounted infantry) is following up cautiously but steadily. I am falling back.

Respectfully, &c.,

ROBT. H. G. MINTY,
Colonel.

—

HEADQUARTERS DEPARTMENT OF THE CUMBERLAND,
Chattanooga, September 22, 1863—9 a. m.
Brigadier-General WAGNER, *Commanding Post:*

The general commanding directs you to draw in all your pickets and outposts whose positions are now occupied by other portions of the army.   Encamp your command as compactly as practicable where it can be used as a reserve to the Twenty-first Army Corps. You will continue to perform the duties of post commandant, and furnish as many men from your command for fatigue and other duty as possible.

Very respectfully, your obedient servant,

J. A. GARFIELD,
Brigadier-General, and Chief of Staff.

—

HEADQUARTERS FOURTEENTH ARMY CORPS,
Chattanooga, September 22, 1863—9.05 a. m.

Brig. Gen. JAMES A. GARFIELD,
Chief of Staff:

Colonel Minty reports that the enemy discovered the evacuation at 5.30 this morning. They are advancing. General Brannan reports skirmishing heard in front. Colonel Minty also reports, at 8.30, enemy's massed [mounted] infantry certainly advancing, but steadily. Cavalry seen in front.

Very respectfully, your obedient servant,

GEO. H. THOMAS,
Major-General, U. S. Volunteers, Commanding.

—

CHATTANOOGA, TENN., *September 22, 1863—9.30 a. m.*
(Received 2.30 p. m.)

Maj. Gen. H. W. HALLECK,
General-in-Chief:

We have fought a most sanguinary battle against vastly superior numbers. Longstreet is here, and probably Ewell, and a force is coming from Charleston. We have suffered terribly, but have inflicted equal injury upon the enemy. The mass of this army is intact and in good spirits. Disaster not as great as I anticipated. We held our position in the main up to Sunday night. Retired on Rossville, which we held yesterday; then retired on Chattanooga. Our position is a strong one. Think we can hold out several days, and if re-enforcements come up soon everything will come out right. Our transportation is mostly across the river. Have one bridge. Another will be done to-day. Our cavalry will be concentrated on the west side of the river, to guard it on our left. Telegraph communication will probably be cut off for several days, as we will be compelled to abandon south side of the Tennessee River below this point.

W. S. ROSECRANS,
Major-General.

—

CHATTANOOGA, *September 22, 1863.*

General BURNSIDE:

Dispatch received from your advance saying it was in Athens. My previous dispatches have advised you of the position of affairs here. The demonstration down this side to Byrd Point, as proposed, would be dangerous in present state of affairs and unproductive of good to us; hence I would advise massing your troops and sending them down the west side of the river. If your mounted force is as strong as I suppose, I would suggest uniting it with mine and wiping out the rebel cavalry.

> W. S. ROSECRANS,
> *Major-General.*

—

> WAR DEPARTMENT,
> *September* 22, 1863—8.30 a. m.

Major-General ROSECRANS,
    Chattanooga, Tenn.:

We have not a word here as to the whereabouts or condition of your army up to a later hour than sunset Sunday, the 20th. Your dispatches to me of 9 a. m. and to General Halleck of 2 p. m., yesterday, tell us nothing later on those points. Please relieve my anxiety as to the position and condition of your army up to the latest moment.

> A. LINCOLN.

—

> CHATTANOOGA, TENN., *September* 22, 1863—5.40 p. m.
> (Received 9.50 p. m.)

His Excellency ABRAHAM LINCOLN,
    President of the United States:

Have dispatched daily (Mr. Dana oftener) to the War Department. I trust you will receive those dispatches. We are now in Chattanooga in line of battle, the enemy threatening our whole front; have pushed to our picket line. Whether they will attack to-day uncertain. General Burnside will be too late to help us. We are about 30,000 brave and determined men; but our fate is in the hands of God, in whom I hope.

> W. S. ROSECRANS,
> *Major-General.*

—

> VICKSBURG,
> *September* 22, 1863.

Maj. Gen. WILLIAM T. SHERMAN,
    Commanding Fifteenth Army Corps:

GENERAL: The following dispatch is just received:

> WASHINGTON CITY, *September* 15. [1863]—5 p. m.
> (Received 4 p. m., 18th.)

Maj. Gen. STEPHEN A. HURLBUT,
    Memphis:

All the troops that can possibly be spared in Western Tennessee and on the Mississippi River should be sent without delay to assist General Rosecrans on the Tennessee River. Urge Sherman to act with all possible promptness. If you have boats, send them down to bring up his troops. Information just received indicates that a part of Lee's army has been sent to re-enforce Bragg.

> H. W. HALLECK,
> *General-in-Chief.*

Please order at once one division of your army corps to proceed to re-enforce Rosecrans, moving from here by brigades as fast as transportation can be had. Orders have been given to detain all steamers available for such purpose. McPherson will send one division.

By order of Major-General Grant:

JNO. A. RAWLINS,
Brigadier-General, and Acting Assistant Adjutant-General.

—

VICKSBURG, MISS., VIA MEMPHIS,
September 22, 1863—10.30 a. m.
(Received, 12.40 a. m, 29th.)

Maj. Gen. H. W. HALLECK,
General-in-Chief:

Your dispatch to Major-General Hurlbut of the 15th instant, directing re-enforcements to be sent Major-General Rosecrans, is just received. I have ordered two divisions from here, one from each the Fifteenth and Seventeenth Army Corps. The one from the Seventeenth Army Corps is already on steamboats between Vicksburg and Helena, having been previously ordered to Steele. Hurlbut should be able to send one full division, if not two, besides the troops that may return from the expedition against Little Rock, and I have so directed. General Banks has asked for another division. This, of course, I cannot send him, in view of what you require for Rosecrans. Should more troops be required from here for Rosecrans, there is sufficient time for orders to reach before transportation can be had. An army corps commander will be sent in command of all troops from here.

U. S. GRANT,
Major-General, Commanding.

—

HEADQUARTERS FOURTEENTH ARMY CORPS,
Chattanooga, September 22, 1863.

Brigadier-General GARFIELD,
Chief of Staff, Department of the Cumberland:

I have the honor to state that my corps occupies the center, General Reynolds the right front, General Negley the reserve, and General Brannan the left front, with General Rousseau in reserve.

Very respectfully,

GEO. H. THOMAS,
Major-General, U. S. Volunteers, Commanding.

—

HEADQUARTERS DEPARTMENT OF THE CUMBERLAND,
Chattanooga, September 22, 1863.

Major-General THOMAS,
Commanding Fourteenth Army Corps:

The general commanding directs that, in addition to the instructions already given you for arranging and adjusting your line, you form a strong line of skirmishers well in front, your right connecting with General McCook and resting near the springs in the vicinity of the hospital buildings, and extending to Chattanooga Creek, if practicable, and connecting with those of General Crittenden on your left, with heavy reserves in center at some suitable point, say near Warner's house.

Very respectfully, your obedient servant,

J. A. GARFIELD,
Brigadier-General, Chief of Staff.

—

HEADQUARTERS DEPARTMENT OF THE CUMRERLAND,
September 22, 1863.

General GARFIELD,
Chief of Staff:

General Wagner has messenger just in from Harrison's position on Shallow Ford road. Reports enemy advancing in two lines (infantry and cavalry). It is about 4 miles from here.

R. S. THOMS,
Aide-de-Camp.

—

HEADQUARTERS DEPARTMENT OF THE CUMBERLAND,
Chattanooga, Tenn., September 22, 1863.

Maj. Gen. THOMAS L. CRITTENDEN:

The general commanding directs you to send one regiment of infantry out on the Shallow Ford road to support Colonel Harrison's cavalry.

Very respectfully, your obedient servant,

J. P. DROUILLARD,
Captain, and Aide-de-Camp.

—

SEPTEMBER 22, 1863—10.30 a. m.

Captain MERRILL:

From hill west of town a column of dust is visible to the northeast about 8 miles distant, approaching quite rapidly, and very heavy north of river. Valley north of Lookout Point is full of dust near by the summit of it. Good view in arc of circle from that point to north and round to east, not toward south. What may be a column of smoke appears on side of Lookout about region of road, suggesting possibility of burning train.

[J. R.] PUTNAM.

—

HEADQUARTERS DEPARTMENT OF THE CUMBERLAND,
Chattanooga, September 22, 1863.

Maj. Gen. GORDON GRANGER:

The general commanding directs that you order General Whitaker's brigade at once across the river to occupy the heights opposite the point of Lookout Mountain.

Very respectfully, your obedient servant,

D. G. SWAIM,
Captain, and Assistant Adjutant-General.

GENERAL McCOOK'S HEADQUARTERS,
September 22, 1863—11 a. m.

Colonel POST:

General McCook directs me to say to you, hold the enemy in front of you in check if you can, but do not permit them to get in your rear or press you too hard. Retire on the main road, and your crossing the bridge will be covered by his troops and artillery. I think there are now some stragglers (cavalry, perhaps) in your rear. As soon as you retire and cross the bridge you will rejoin your division, which is on the right of my line.

Respectfully, yours,

WILLIAM H. SINCLAIR,
Assistant Adjutant-General.

—

RIGHT OF 21ST ARMY CORPS,
Signal Station near Railroad, September 22, 1863—1 p. m.

Capt. JESSE MERRILL:

Heavy column of dust is seen extending from Chattanooga Valley road, 1½ miles east of Rossville. Seems to be in the valley near range of hills.

W. LEONARD,
Signal Officer.

—

SIGNAL CORPS ACROSS THE RIVER,
September 22, 1863.

Captain MERRILL:

The rebels have advanced and formed at the foot of the ridge.

FORAKER,
Lieutenant, and Acting Signal Officer.

—

HDQRS. THIRD BRIG., THIRD DIV., RESERVE CORPS,
On First Bench of Lookout Mountain Point, September 22, 1863.

Major-General ROSECRANS:

GENERAL: The enemy attacked us to-day at 12.30 with four regiments (infantry and artillery). My forces fought well and never yielded the ground until they were overpowered and compelled to fall back, which was done in good order, and we now have our position on the first bench of the mountain. The enemy seems to be reluctant in advancing. I have several men killed and many wounded.

I will contest it, according to your order this day, inch by inch and foot by foot.

Respectfully, your obedient servant,

JAMES G. SPEARS,
Brigadier-General, Commanding.

P. S.—I am informed the enemy is endeavoring to flank me across the mountain below; whether true or not I am unable to state. The enemy holds the position I occupied this morning.

HEADQUARTERS DEPARTMENT OF THE CUMBERLAND,
Chattanooga, September 22, 1863—1.30 p. m.

Col. J. T. WILDER:

The general commanding directs you to establish a courier line from your headquarters to these, and report at least twice a day, and oftener if anything of importance occurs. I inclose a dispatch for Colonel Byrd, commanding Burnside's advance at Cleveland, which the general directs you to read and forward at all possible speed.

Very respectfully, your obedient servant,

C. GODDARD,
Lieutenant-Colonel, and Assistant Adjutant-General.

[Inclosure.]

HDQRS. DEPARTMENT OF THE CUMBERLAND,
Chattanooga, September 22, 1863.

Colonel BYRD:

If you are beyond reach of orders from General Burnside, cross the river at the most practicable point and join Colonel Wilder's force. Wilder's headquarters are at Friar's Island, 7 miles above Chattanooga, and he pickets the river up to Harrison's Landing.

By order of Major-General Rosecrans:

C. GODDARD,
Lieutenant-Colonel, and Assistant Adjutant-General.

—

ON THE RIGHT OF 21ST ARMY CORPS, FRONT LINE,
September 22, 1863—2 p. m.

Captain MERRILL:

I see rebel infantry south 80 degrees east. One regiment is in line of battle. They are on top of the ridge. Were deployed as skirmishers, but assembled where the road leads down the hill.

W. LEONARD,
Acting Signal Officer.

—

SIGNAL CORPS ACROSS RIVER,
September 22, 1863—3.25 p. m.

Captain MERRILL:

The rebels on the ridge are in line as if to receive our attack.

FORAKER,
Lieutenant, and Acting Signal Officer.

—

GENERAL CRITTENDEN'S HEADQUARTERS,
September 22, 1863—3.30 p. m.

Captain MERRILL:

The ridge in our front is covered with rebel troops in column of company moving northward.

[A. F.] BERRY,
Lieutenant, and Acting Signal Officer.

SEPTEMBER 22, 1863—3.30 p. m.

General THOMAS:

Heavy columns of the enemy on ridge in front of Crittenden, and moving to our left slowly and deploying in line of battle.

H. C. JONES,
Captain, and Acting Signal Officer

—

HEADQUARTERS DEPARTMENT OF THE CUMBERLAND,
Chattanooga, September 22, 1863—3.50 p. m.

Colonel MINTY:

Place your cavalry in position as ordered, and send pack mules across the river at the ford to pack forage across.

By order of Major-General Rosecrans:

C. GODDARD,
Assistant Adjutant-General.

—

LOOKOUT MOUNTAIN, *September* 22, 1863—4 p. m.

Captain MERRILL:

Principal force on our right is cavalry, on Rossville road about 3 miles from Chattanooga.

H. W. HOWGATE,
Lieutenant, and Acting Signal Officer.

—

RIGHT OF TWENTY-FIRST ARMY CORPS,
September 22, 1863—4.10 p. m.

Captain MERRILL:

I have just counted four rebel regiments of infantry and one battery coming down Mission Ridge at a gap south 80 degrees east of this point. There are also other forces on the ridge that have been standing in the road for two hours.

I am, captain, very respectfully,

W. LEONARD.

—

HEADQUARTERS DEPARTMENT OF THE CUMBERLAND,
Chattanooga, September 22, 1863—5 p. m.

General MITCHELL, *Commanding Cavalry:*

The general commanding directs you to pass to the north side of the river with all your force except Minty's brigade. You will carefully watch all the fords and ferries above as far as Harrison's, and down as near Bridgeport as you may deem necessary. Mass your force at some convenient point, so that you can defend any point at which the rebels may attempt to cross. Use your artillery to assist you in holding any threatened point. Look out for corn and let us know where it is. Patrol the road from here to Bridgeport, on north side of the river, frequently. Send scouting parties above Harrison's daily—and oftener at irregular intervals, if you deem it expedient—to watch for any attempt of the enemy to cross. Colonel Wilder's command is now over the river on duty similar to that you are ordered to perform. Until further orders it will report to you. Report frequently.

Very respectfully, your obedient servant,

C. GODDARD,
Assistant Adjutant-General.

HEADQUARTERS DEPARTMENT OF THE CUMBERLAND,
Chattanooga, Tenn., September 22, 1863—5 p. m.
Col. J. T. WILDER,
   Comdg. First Brig., Fourth Div., 14th Army Corps:
   General Mitchell has been ordered across the river to protect the
crossing with his cavalry. Until further orders you will report to
him and act under his instructions.
   By order of Major-General Rosecrans :
                                 C. GODDARD,
                           Assistant Adjutant-General.

—

SIGNAL STATION 2231, NEAR DEPT. HDQRS.,
                            September 22, 1863—5.05 p. m.
Captain MERRILL :
   A rebel battery is seen on brow of Mission Ridge, on road running nearly east from this point in a pass about a mile north of the
pass at Moore's house. It is supported by infantry, apparently a
continuation of the line, which can be seen in General Crittenden's
front at Moore's house.
                             H. C. JONES,
                   Captain, and Acting Signal Officer.

5.10 p. m.
   A body of cavalry moving by flank are passing the pass to our left.
                                     JONES.

—

SIGNAL CORPS OVER THE RIVER,
                 September 22, 1863—5.30 p. m.
Captain MERRILL :
   The rebels have stacked arms and are getting supper.
                                 FORAKER,
                   Lieutenant, and Acting Signal Officer.

—

LOOKOUT POINT, *September 22, 1863*—6 p. m.
Captain MERRILL :
   The rebel cavalry are massing on both sides of the Rossville pike
near Mr. Hopkins' house. I think General Wheeler's headquarters
are at the house this side. They have established a picket line up to
the foot of the mountain, and will, no doubt, try us to-night, but
we have made all preparations to receive them. If you will send an
officer to the bridge on our right, near our batteries, we can give them
all the directions they want for firing. Had there been one there
to-day, we could have been of much service.
                                 [A. S.] COLE.

—

SEPTEMBER 22, 1863—7 p. m.
Captain MERRILL :
   A number of camp fires can be seen on top of mountain directly in
front of General Crittenden, in gap near Moore's house. Faint lights
can be seen along the mountain-top to right and left.
                             H. C. JONES,
                   Captain, and Acting Signal Officer.

SEPTEMBER 22, 1863—7.40 p. m.
Captain MERRILL :
Enemy's fires 2 miles long front and east-northeast on the ridge, but not many.

SAMUEL BACHTELL,
Lieutenant, and Acting Signal Officer.

—

OVER THE RIVER, *September 22, 1863.*
Captain MERRILL :
I can see camp fires north of the tunnel, also on the ridge east of town.

FORAKER.

—

SIGNAL STATION 2231, NEAR DEPT. HDQRS.,
September 22, 1863—11 p. m.
Captain MERRILL:
The enemy keep up fires along the crest of the mountain in front of General Crittenden's command, and as they burn low they are relit, being much brighter now than an hour since. No lights are seen from this point in front of our center or right.
Respectfully,

H. C. JONES,
Captain, and Acting Signal Officer.

—

HEADQUARTERS DEPARTMENT OF THE CUMBERLAND,
Chattanooga, September 22, 1863—11 p. m.
Major-General CRITTENDEN, *Comdg. Twenty-first Army Corps:*
GENERAL: The general commanding directs that all troops occupying rifle-pits be instructed to reserve their fire until the enemy are within close range, and then to deliver their fire by volley and by ranks. Caution your troops not to waste ammunition. This caution is especially necessary to the artillery. From the reports of signal officers, it is possible that the large camp fires on the left and the total absence of them in the center and right is intended as a ruse to cover an attack upon the center or right to-morrow. The general directs that the pickets be directed to listen carefully for any sounds which would indicate the movement of troops, and to notify the commanding officers of troops toward which such sounds are moving, and sending reports to these headquarters also.
Very respectfully, your obedient servant,

C. GODDARD,
Assistant Adjutant-General.
(Same to Generals Thomas and Sheridan.)

—

CHATTANOOGA, TENN., *September 23, 1863*—11.40 a. m.
(Received 10.35 p. m.)
His Excellency ABRAHAM LINCOLN, *President:*
We hold this point, and I cannot be dislodged except by very superior numbers and after a great battle. Immediate disposition should be made for covering our communications by ordering down every available man from Kentucky to Bridgeport and Stevenson, and having all re-enforcements you can send hurried up.

W. S. ROSECRANS,
Major-General.

No. 4.

Abstract from tri-monthly returns of the Army of the Cumberland, September 10 and 20, 1863.

SEPTEMBER 10, 1863.

Command.	Present for duty.		Aggregate present.	Aggregate present and absent.	Serviceable horses.	Pieces of field artillery.
	Officers.	Men.				
General headquarters a	75	929	1,230	1,593	....	....
Fourteenth Army Corps b	1,333	21,448	26,952	35,654	....	68
Twentieth Army Corps	831	12,325	15,314	24,551	....	54
Twenty-first Army Corps c	1,025	13,635	16,834	24,828	....	58
Reserve Corps d	385	6,987	8,781	11,496	....	24
Cavalry Corps e	561	9,517	12,106	16,714	9,913	9
Pioneer Brigade, First, Second, and Third Battalions. f	57	857	1,255	2,646	....	....
Artillery Reserve g	8	198	215	250	....	18
Unattached artillery h	2	95	105	120	....	6
Signal corps i	34	119	154	169	....	....
1st Michigan Engineers and Mechanics and 2d Kentucky Battery. k	23	785	885	1,000	....	4
Total	4,243	65,919	93,062	115,375	9,913	241

Command.	Present for duty, equipped.							
	Infantry.		Cavalry.		Artillery.		Total.	
	Officers.	Men.	Officers.	Men.	Officers.	Men.	Officers.	Men.
General headquarters a	34	496	25	450	.....	.....	59	946
Fourteenth Army Corps b	1,150	20,434	.....	.....	42	1,132	1,192	21,566
Twentieth Army Corps	801	11,524	.....	.....	32	1,015	833	12,539
Twenty-first Army Corps c	910	12,164	.....	.....	35	1,081	945	13,245
Reserve Corps d	262	4,909	.....	.....	9	299	271	5,208
Cavalry Corps e	.....	.....	532	9,144	6	160	538	9,304
Pioneer Brigade, First, Second, and Third Battalions. f	47	857	.....	.....	.....	.....	47	857
Artillery Reserve g	.....	.....	.....	.....	8	198	8	198
Unattached artillery h	.....	.....	.....	.....	3	95	3	95
Signal corps i	.....	.....	.....	.....	.....	.....	.....	.....
1st Michigan Engineers and Mechanics and 2d Kentucky Battery. k	23	652	.....	.....	4	73	27	725
Total	3,180	50,179	557	9,594	139	4,053	3,876	63,816

a Including department staff, 10th Ohio Infantry, 1st Battalion Ohio Sharpshooters, and 15th Pennsylvania Cavalry.

b 3d Ohio, 69th Ohio, and 89th Ohio detached.

c See also report of effective strength in battle of Chickamauga, p. 617.

d Including corps headquarters, the First Division, and the Second (McCook's) Brigade of the Second Division. Coburn's brigade of the First Division (four regiments and a battery) is also included ; it was stationed at Murfreesborough, and had, on August 31, 92 officers and 1,895 men for duty. Between August 31 and September 12 the 22d Michigan (numbering on August 31, 26 officers and 576 men for duty) and the 89th Ohio (numbering on August 31, 20 officers and 420 men for duty) were added to the First Brigade of the First Division, and the 69th Ohio (numbering on August 31, 15 officers and 334 men) was added to the Second Brigade of the Second Division. The strength given under the heading "Present for duty, equipped " includes the First Division only.

e 3d Tennessee Cavalry and 7th Kentucky Cavalry detached. The returns include Lowe's brigade, which had at Murfreesborough, on August 31, 33 officers and 541 men for duty.

f Not added in total ; accounted for elsewhere.

g At Nashville, Tenn.

h At Gallatin, Tenn.

i Not added in total ; accounted for elsewhere.

k At Elk River Bridge, Tenn.

SEPTEMBER 20, 1863.

Command.	Present for duty. Officers.	Present for duty. Men.	Aggregate present.	Aggregate present and absent.	Serviceable horses.	Pieces of field artillery.
General headquarters a................	75	929	1,211	1,593	....	....
Fourteenth Army Corps b	987	15,898	19,687	31,650	....	54
Twentieth Army Corps c...............	700	9,869	12,518	22,287	....	53
Twenty-first Army Corps d	976	12,926	16,181	24,635	....	58
Reserve Corps, headquarters First and Second Divisions. e	629	10,966	13,283	17,962	....	34
Cavalry Corps f.......................	560	9,517	12,105	16,713	9,913	9
Wilder's Brigade Mounted Infantry g ..	137	2,282	2,878	3,450	....	10
Pioneer Brigade, First, Second, and Third Battalions. h	54	742	1,088	2,644	....	....
Signal corps h......................	34	119	154	169	....	....
Artillery Reserve i	8	198	215	250	....	18
Unattached artillery k	2	95	105	120	....	6
1st Michigan Engineers and Mechanics and 2d Kentucky Battery. l	23	785	885	1,000	....	4
1st U. S. Colored Troops l	14	301	390	949	....	....
Total	4,111	63,766	79,458	130,609	9,913	246

Present for duty, equipped.

Command.	Infantry. Officers.	Infantry. Men.	Cavalry. Officers.	Cavalry. Men.	Artillery. Officers.	Artillery. Men.	Total. Officers.	Total. Men.
General headquarters a	34	496	27	411	....	....	61	907
Fourteenth Army Corps b.......	840	11,598	....	....	30	860	870	12,458
Twentieth Army Corps c	667	8,909	....	....	32	1,042	699	9,951
Twenty-first Army Corps d...........	871	11,555	....	....	33	1,083	904	12,638
Reserve Corps, headquarters First and Second Divisions. e	578	10,336	....	....	15	550	593	10,886
Cavalry corps f.......................	....	....	532	9,144	6	160	538	9,304
Wilder's Brigade Mounted Infantry g..	....	....	....	....	....	....	....	....
Pioneer Brigade, First, Second, and Third Battalions. h	45	742	....	....	....	....	45	742
Signal corps h.........	....	....	....	....	....	....	....	....
Artillery Reserve i.............. ..	....	....	....	....	8	198	8	198
Unattached artillery k.............	....	....	....	....	3	95	3	95
1st Michigan Engineers and Mechanics and 2d Kentucky Battery. l	25	652	....	....	4	73	29	725
1st U. S. Colored Troops l.............	....	....	....	....	....	....	....	....
Total	3,015	43,546	559	9,555	131	4,061	3,705	57,162

a Including department staff, 10th Ohio Infantry, 1st Battalion Ohio Sharpshooters, and 15th Pennsylvania Cavalry.

b Reports losses in action of 30 officers and 412 men killed and 47 officers and 720 men missing.

c Reports losses in action of 25 officers and 225 men killed and 38 officers and 697 men missing.

d Reports losses in action (in Second Division) of 5 officers and 53 men killed and 40 officers and 114 men missing.

e The First Division and the Second Brigade, Second Division, took part in the battle of Chickamauga. The First and Third Brigades of the Second Division were at Stevenson, Ala., and elsewhere. The Third Division was at Nashville.

f Lowe's brigade and the 3d Tennessee and 7th Kentucky Cavalry detached.

g From brigade return of September 30.

h Not added in total; accounted for elsewhere.

i At Nashville, Tenn.

k At Gallatin, Tenn.

l At Elk River Bridge, Tenn.

No. 5.

Return of Casualties in the Army of the Cumberland, commanded by Maj. Gen. William S. Rosecrans, at the battle of Chickamauga, Ga., September 19 and 20, 1863.*

Command.	Killed.		Wounded.		Captured or missing.		Aggregate.
	Officers.	Enlisted men.	Officers.	Enlisted men.	Officers.	Enlisted men.	
GENERAL HEADQUARTERS.							
10th Ohio Infantry.........................	... ..				......	1	1
15th Pennsylvania Cavalry	......	......		2	......	3	5
Total general headquarters	......	....		2	......	4	6
FOURTEENTH ARMY CORPS.							
Maj. Gen. GEORGE H. THOMAS.							
Staff..................................	......				1	....	1
FIRST DIVISION.							
Brig. Gen. ABSALOM BAIRD.							
First Brigade.							
Col. BENJAMIN F. SCRIBNER.							
38th Indiana...............................	1	12	3	54	......	39	109
2d Ohio...........................	1	8	3	47	6	116	181
33d Ohio...........................	2	12	4	59	4	79	160
94th Ohio...........................	.....	2	1	21	1	21	46
10th Wisconsin	2	9	3	52	13	132	211
1st Michigan Light Artillery, Battery A	1	5	......	7	......	12	25
Total First Brigade........................	7	48	14	240	24	399	732
Second Brigade.							
Brig. Gen. JOHN C. STARKWEATHER.							
Staff...	......		1		....	....	1
24th Illinois...........................	1	18	9	67	3	53	151
79th Pennsylvania.......................	1	15	5	62	1	41	125
1st Wisconsin..........................	4	23	5	79	4	73	188
21st Wisconsin.........................	......	2	4	39	9	67	121
Indiana Light Artillery, 4th Battery		1	......	14	1	4	20
Total Second Brigade.....................	6	59	24	261	18	238	606
Third Brigade.							
Brig. Gen. JOHN H. KING.							
15th United States, A, C, E, F, G, and H, 1st Battalion, and E, 2d Battalion.	......	9	2	47	6	96	160
16th United States, A, B, D, F, and H, 1st Battalion, and B, C, and D, 2d Battalion.	1	2	3	16	10	104	190
18th United States, B, D, E, F, G, and H, 1st Battalion, and G and H, 3d Battalion.	......	19	4	67	2	66	158
18th United States, 2d Battalion...................	1	13	3	78	2	48	145
19th United States, A, B, C, E, F, G, and H, 1st Battalion, and A, 2d Battalion.	1	2	4	13	6	110	136
5th U. S. Artillery, Battery H....................	1	12	2	16	......	13	44
Total Third Brigade...............	4	57	18	237	26	497	839
Total First Division......................	17	164	56	738	68	1,134	2,177

* Losses sustained by the troops engaged at Chickamauga, in the skirmishes at Rossville, Lookout Church, and Dry Valley, Ga., September 21, and at Missionary Ridge and Shallow Ford Gap, September 22, are also included.

Return of Casualties in the Army of the Cumberland, &c.—Continued.

Command.	Killed.		Wounded.		Captured or missing.		Aggregate.
	Officers.	Enlisted men.	Officers.	Enlisted men.	Officers.	Enlisted men.	
SECOND DIVISION.							
Maj. Gen. JAMES S. NEGLEY.							
First Brigade.							
Brig. Gen. JOHN BEATTY.							
104th Illinois....	......	2	6	40	......	16	64
42d Indiana.........................	......	1	3	49	3	50	106
88th Indiana.........................	......	3	4	29	2	14	52
15th Kentucky.......................	......	5	....	42	1	14	62
Bridges' (Illinois) Battery.........	1	5	....	16	......	4	26
Total First Brigade..............	1	16	13	176	6	98	310
Second Brigade.							
Col. TIMOTHY R. STANLEY.a Col. WILLIAM L. STOUGHTON.							
19th Illinois.......	......	10	4	41	1	15	71
11th Michigan.....................	1	4	4	38	.. ....	19	66
18th Ohio.........................	......	5	6	49	......	14	74
1st Ohio Light Artillery, Battery M.	......	......	......	4	......	......	4
Total Second Brigade.......	1	19	14	132	1	48	215
Third Brigade.							
Col. WILLIAM SIRWELL.							
37th Indiana......................	......	......	....	7	......	2	9
21st Ohio.........................	......	28	4	80	11	120	243
74th Ohio.........................	......	1	....	2	......	6	9
78th Pennsylvania.................	......	......	....	2	......	3	5
Total Third Brigade............	......	29	4	91	11	131	266
Total Second Division...........	2	64	31	399	18	277	791
THIRD DIVISION.							
Brig. Gen. JOHN M. BRANNAN.							
Staff...........................	......	......	......	1	......	......	1
First Brigade.							
Col. JOHN M. CONNELL.							
82d Indiana......................	1	19	1	67	2	21	111
17th Ohio.........................	1	15	11	103	3	18	151
31st Ohio.........................	......	13	7	127	......	22	169
1st Michigan Light Artillery, Battery D	......	......	1	6	......	4	11
Total First Brigade.............	2	47	20	303	5	65	442
Second Brigade.							
Col. JOHN T. CROXTON.a Col. WILLIAM H. HAYS.							
10th Indiana......................	2	22	6	130	1	5	166
74th Indiana......................	2	20	11	114	......	10	157
4th Kentucky.....................	......	25	13	144	......	9	191
10th Kentucky....................	1	20	9	125	1	10	166
14th Ohio.........................	......	35	8	159	......	43	245
1st Ohio Light Artillery, Battery C.	......	4	....	9	......	......	13
Total Second Brigade............	5	126	47	681	2	77	938

a Wounded September 20.

Return of Casualties in the Army of the Cumberland, &c.—Continued.

Command.	Killed.		Wounded.		Captured. or missing.		Aggregate.
	Officers.	Enlisted men.	Officers.	Enlisted men.	Officers.	Enlisted men.	
Third Brigade.							
Col. FERDINAND VAN DERVEER.							
87th Indiana	7	33	4	138	......	8	190
2d Minnesota	......	35	6	107	1	13	162
9th Ohio	2	46	9	176	1	15	249
35th Ohio	2	19	7	132	1	26	187
4th U. S. Artillery, Battery I	......	1	1	20	......	......	22
Total Third Brigade	11	134	27	573	3	62	810
Total Third Division	18	307	94	1,558	10	204	2,191
FOURTH DIVISION.							
Maj. Gen. JOSEPH J. REYNOLDS.							
Staff	......	......	1	......	1	......	2
First Brigade.							
Col. JOHN T. WILDER.							
92d Illinois	......	2	2	20	......	2	26
98th Illinois	......	2	2	29	......	2	35
123d Illinois	......	1	2	11	1	9	24
17th Indiana	......	4	2	8	......	2	16
72d Indiana	......	3	1	15	......	2	21
Indiana Light Artillery, 18th Battery	......	1	......	2	......	......	3
Total First Brigade	......	13	9	85	1	17	125
Second Brigade.							
Col. EDWARD A. KING.*a*							
Col. MILTON S. ROBINSON.							
68th Indiana	2	15	5	103	1	11	137
75th Indiana	......	17	4	104	2	11	138
101st Indiana	......	11	5	85	1	17	119
105th Ohio	......	3	4	37	2	24	70
Indiana Light Artillery, 19th Battery	......	2	1	15	......	2	20
Total Second Brigade	2	48	19	344	6	65	484
Third Brigade.							
Brig. Gen. JOHN B. TURCHIN.							
18th Kentucky	......	7	8	38	4	29	86
11th Ohio	......	5	1	35	2	20	63
36th Ohio	1	11	3	62	......	14	91
92d Ohio	......	6	6	62	......	17	91
Indiana Light Artillery, 21st Battery	......	......	......	12	......	......	12
Total Third Brigade	1	29	18	209	6	80	343
Total Fourth Division	3	90	47	638	14	162	954
Total Fourteenth Army Corps	40	625	228	3,333	111	1,777	6,114
TWENTIETH ARMY CORPS.							
Maj. Gen. ALEXANDER McD. McCOOK.							
FIRST DIVISION.							
Brig. Gen. JEFFERSON C. DAVIS.							
Second Brigade.b							
Brig. Gen. WILLIAM P. CARLIN.							
21st Illinois	2	20	6	64	8	138	238
38th Illinois	2	13	8	79	2	76	180
81st Indiana	......	4	4	56	2	21	87
101st Ohio	3	10	6	76	....	51	146
Total Second Brigade	7	47	24	275	12	286	651

a Killed September 20.   *b* First Brigade, Col. P. Sidney Post commanding, not engaged

Return of Casualties in the Army of the Cumberland, &c.—Continued.

Command.	Killed.		Wounded.		Captured or missing.		Aggregate.
	Officers.	Enlisted men.	Officers.	Enlisted men.	Officers.	Enlisted men.	
Third Brigade.							
Col. Hans C. Heg.*a*							
Col. John A. Martin.							
25th Illinois	.....	10	11	160	1	23	205
35th Illinois	3	14	5	125	.....	13	160
8th Kansas	2	28	9	156	.....	25	220
15th Wisconsin	4	9	6	47	2	43	111
Total Third Brigade	9	61	31	488	3	104	696
Artillery.							
Capt. William A. Hotchkiss.							
Minnesota Light, 2d Battery	.....	....	1	1	.....	......	2
Total First Division	16	108	56	764	15	390	1,349
SECOND DIVISION.							
Brig. Gen. Richard W. Johnson.							
Staff	1	....	.....	......	......	2	3
First Brigade.							
Brig. Gen. August Willich.							
Staff	1	....	.....	1	......	....	2
89th Illinois	4	10	5	83	2	28	132
32d Indiana	1	20	4	77	......	20	122
39th Indiana *b*	.....	5	3	32	......	....	40
15th Ohio	1	9	2	75	......	33	120
49th Ohio	.....	10	2	57	2	28	99
1st Ohio Light Artillery, Battery A	.....	2	1	13	.....	4	20
Total First Brigade	7	56	17	338	4	113	535
Second Brigade.							
Col. Joseph B. Dodge.							
Staff	.....	......	1	1	2	5	9
79th Illinois	.....	3	1	20	6	91	121
29th Indiana	2	9	5	87	7	62	172
30th Indiana	2	8	5	50	4	57	126
77th Pennsylvania	.....	3	4	24	9	64	104
Ohio Light Artillery, 20th Battery	.....	......	.....	2	......	2	4
Total Second Brigade	4	23	16	184	28	281	536
Third Brigade.							
Col. Philemon P. Baldwin.*a*							
Col. William W. Berry.							
Staff	.....	1	1	....	......	......	2
6th Indiana	2	11	6	110	.....	31	160
5th Kentucky	2	12	6	73	2	30	125
1st Ohio	1	12	3	93	......	33	142
93d Ohio	.....	15	3	83	2	27	130
Indiana Light Artillery, 5th Battery	.....	1	1	6	......	1	0
Total Third Brigade	5	52	20	365	4	122	568
Total Second Division	17	131	53	887	36	518	1,642

a Killed September 19.
b Detached from brigade and serving as mounted infantry.

Return of Casualties in the Army of the Cumberland, &c.—Continued.

Command.	Killed.		Wounded.		Captured or missing.		Aggregate.
	Officers.	Enlisted men.	Officers.	Enlisted men.	Officers.	Enlisted men.	
THIRD DIVISION.							
Maj. Gen. PHILIP H. SHERIDAN.							
First Brigade.							
Brig. Gen. WILLIAM H. LYTLE.*a* Col. SILAS MILLER.							
Staff	1						1
36th Illinois	3	17	6	95		20	141
88th Illinois		12	7	55		14	88
21st Michigan	1	15	4	69	2	15	106
24th Wisconsin		3	4	69		29	105
Indiana Light Artillery, 11th Battery		3	1	11		4	19
Total First Brigade	5	50	22	299	2	82	460
Second Brigade.							
Col. BERNARD LAIBOLDT.							
44th Illinois		6	5	55	1	33	100
73d Illinois	2	11	4	53	3	19	92
2d Missouri	1	6	2	54	1	28	92
15th Missouri	2	9	5	62		22	100
1st Missouri Light Artillery, Battery G		1		3	1		5
Total Second Brigade	5	33	16	227	6	102	389
Third Brigade.							
Col. LUTHER P. BRADLEY.*b* Col. NATHAN H. WALWORTH.							
22d Illinois		23	5	71	2	29	130
27th Illinois	1	1	4	75		10	91
42d Illinois	3	12	4	119	1	4	143
51st Illinois	2	16	4	89	1	87	149
1st Illinois Light Artillery, Battery C				4			4
Total Third Brigade	6	52	17	358	4	80	517
Total Third Division	16	135	55	884	12	264	1,366
Total Twentieth Army Corps	49	374	164	2,535	63	1,172	4,357
TWENTY-FIRST ARMY CORPS.							
Maj. Gen. THOMAS L. CRITTENDEN.							
Escort				3			3
FIRST DIVISION.							
Brig. Gen. THOMAS J. WOOD.							
Staff				1			1
First Brigade.							
Col. GEORGE P. BUELL.							
100th Illinois		23	6	111	2	22	164
58th Indiana	2	14	5	114	3	31	169
26th Ohio	4	23	6	134	2	43	212
13th Michigan	2	11	6	61	2	24	106
Total First Brigade	8	71	23	420	9	120	651

a Killed September 20.
b Wounded September 19.

Return of Casualties in the Army of the Cumberland, &c.—Continued.

Command.	Killed.		Wounded.		Captured or missing.		Aggregate.
	Officers.	Enlisted men.	Officers.	Enlisted men.	Officers.	Enlisted men.	
Third Brigade.a							
Col. CHARLES G. HARKER.							
3d Kentucky	1	12	8	70	......	22	113
64th Ohio	1	7	2	48	......	13	71
65th Ohio	2	12	6	65	......	18	103
125th Ohio	......	16	3	81	......	5	105
Total Third Brigade	4	47	19	264	......	58	392
Artillery.							
Indiana Light, 8th Battery b	......	1	......	9	......	7	17
Ohio Light, 6th Battery c	......	1	1	7	......	......	9
Total Artillery	......	2	1	16	......	7	26
Total First Division	12	120	44	700	9	185	1,070
SECOND DIVISION.							
Maj. Gen. JOHN M. PALMER.							
Staff	......	1	2	......	2	1	6
First Brigade.							
Brig. Gen. CHARLES CRUFT.							
31st Indiana	1	4	2	59	......	17	83
1st Kentucky (battalion)	......	2	1	25	......	3	31
2d Kentucky	1	9	5	59	......	18	92
90th Ohio	2	5	2	60	1	14	84
Total First Brigade	4	20	10	203	1	52	290
Second Brigade.							
Brig. Gen. WILLIAM B. HAZEN.							
9th Indiana	2	11	8	83	1	21	126
6th Kentucky	3	9	7	88	1	10	118
41st Ohio	......	6	5	95	......	9	115
124th Ohio	......	15	5	87	......	34	141
Total Second Brigade	5	41	25	353	2	74	500
Third Brigade.							
Col. WILLIAM GROSE.							
Staff	......	......	......	3	......	......	3
84th Illinois	1	12	2	81	......	9	105
36th Indiana	......	13	10	89	......	17	129
23d Kentucky	1	10	3	49	......	6	69
6th Ohio	......	13	8	94	1	16	132
24th Ohio	......	3	3	57	......	16	79
Total Third Brigade	2	51	26	373	1	64	517
Artillery.							
Capt. WILLIAM E. STANDART.							
1st Ohio Light, Battery B b	......	1	......	8	......	4	13
1st Ohio Light, Battery F d	1	1	......	8	......	2	12
4th United States, Battery H c	......	5	1	16	......	......	22
4th United States, Battery M c	......	2	......	6	......	......	8
Total Artillery	1	9	1	38	......	6	55
Total Second Division	12	122	64	967	6	197	1,368

a The Second Brigade was stationed at Chattanooga and not engaged.
b Attached to First Brigade.

c Attached to Third Brigade.
d Attached to Second Brigade.

Return of Casualties in the Army of the Cumberland, &c.—Continued.

Command.	Killed.		Wounded.		Captured or missing.		Aggregate.
	Officers.	Enlisted men.	Officers.	Enlisted men.	Officers.	Enlisted men.	
THIRD DIVISION.							
Brig. Gen. HORATIO P. VAN CLEVE.							
Staff ...					1		1
First Brigade.							
Brig. Gen. SAMUEL BEATTY.							
79th Indiana		1	2	42	1	9	55
9th Kentucky		2	4	41	1	12	60
17th Kentucky	1	5	2	103	......	15	126
19th Ohio		7	2	58	....	23	90
Total First Brigade	1	15	10	244	2	59	331
Second Brigade.							
Col. GEORGE F. DICK.							
44th Indiana	1	2	9	52	......	10	74
86th Indiana		1	3	28	......	21	53
13th Ohio	2	3	4	43	......	22	74
59th Ohio	2	5	1	40	2	28	78
Total Second Brigade	5	11	17	163	2	81	279
Third Brigade.							
Col. SIDNEY M. BARNES.							
35th Indiana		5	3	20	2	35	65
8th Kentucky		4	2	45	1	27	79
51st Ohio		8	1	34	4	51	98
99th Ohio		3	2	28	......	24	57
Total Third Brigade		20	8	127	7	137	299
Artillery.							
Indiana Light, 7th Battery				8	1		9
Pennsylvania Light, 26th Battery	1	1	1	13	......	1	17
Wisconsin Light, 3d Battery		2		13	....	11	26
Total Artillery	1	3	1	34	1	12	52
Total Third Division	7	49	36	568	13	289	962
Total Twenty-first Army Corps	31	291	144	2,238	28	671	3,403
RESERVE CORPS.							
Maj. Gen. GORDON GRANGER.							
Staff	1						1
FIRST DIVISION.							
Brig. Gen. JAMES D. STEEDMAN.							
First Brigade.							
Brig. Gen. WALTER C. WHITAKER.							
Staff			1				1
96th Illinois		39	9	125	2	50	225
115th Illinois	2	20	9	142	1	9	183
84th Indiana	3	20	6	91	......	13	133
22d Michigan a		32	3	93	14	247	389
40th Ohio	2	17	8	94	......	11	132
89th Ohio a	2	17	2	61	13	158	253
Ohio Light Artillery, 18th Battery			2	8			10
Total First Brigade	9	145	40	614	30	488	1,326

a Temporarily attached.

Return of Casualties in the Army of the Cumberland, &c.—Continued.

Command.	Killed.		Wounded.		Captured or missing.		Aggregate.
	Officers.	Enlisted men.	Officers.	Enlisted men.	Officers.	Enlisted men.	
Second Brigade.							
Col. JOHN G. MITCHELL.							
78th Illinois.............................	1	16	8	69	4	58	156
98th Ohio..............................	2	7	3	38	1	12	63
113th Ohio....	1	20	8	90	......	12	131
121st Ohio	2	7	7	76	......	7	99
1st Illinois Light Artillery, Battery M..........	......	2	......	9	......	1	12
Total Second Brigade	6	52	26	282	5	90	461
Total First Division.....	15	197	66	896	35	578	1,787
SECOND DIVISION.							
Second Brigade.							
Col. DANIEL McCOOK.							
85th Illinois.........................							
86th Illinois.........................							
125th Illinois.........................							
52d Ohio							
69th Ohio							
2d Illinois Light Artillery, Battery I							
Total Second Brigade *a*......................	......	2	......	14	......	18	34
Total Reserve Corps..	16	199	66	910	35	596	1,822
CAVALRY CORPS.							
Brig. Gen. ROBERT B. MITCHELL.							
FIRST DIVISION.							
Col. EDWARD M. McCOOK.							
First Brigade.							
Col. ARCHIBALD P. CAMPBELL.							
2d Michigan........................	1	1	......	6	1	2	11
9th Pennsylvania						3	3
1st Tennessee........................						1	1
Total First Brigade......................	1	1	......	6	1	6	15
Second Brigade.							
Col. DANIEL M. RAY.							
2d Indiana........................		1	......	4	......		5
4th Indiana........................				2	......	7	9
2d Tennessee........................		1	......	2	......		3
1st Wisconsin				2	......	4	6
Total Second Brigade	......	2	......	10	......	11	23
Third Brigade.							
Col. LOUIS D. WATKINS.							
4th Kentucky...				1	4	90	95
5th Kentucky........................					2	18	20
6th Kentucky........................	......	2	1	6	2	120	131
Total Third Brigade ......,........	......	2	1	7	8	228	246
Total First Division........................	1	5	1	23	9	245	284

a Nominal lists showing losses in detail are not on file.

Return of Casualties in the Army of the Cumberland, &c.—Continued.

Command.	Killed.		Wounded.		Captured or missing.		Aggregate.
	Officers.	Enlisted men.	Officers.	Enlisted men.	Officers.	Enlisted men.	
SECOND DIVISION.							
Brig. Gen. George Crook.							
First Brigade.							
Col. Robert H. G. Minty.							
3d Indiana (battalion)				3			3
4th Michigan		1	1	11		6	19
7th Pennsylvania	1	4		13		1	19
4th United States		1		5		1	7
Total First Brigade	1	6	1	32		8	48
Second Brigade.							
Col. Eli Long.							
2d Kentucky		11	5	45		2	63
1st Ohio	1	1		13		7	22
3d Ohio		2		7		8	17
4th Ohio	1	3		9	2	19	34
Total Second Brigade	2	17	5	74	2	36	136
Total Second Division	3	23	6	106	2	44	184
Total Cavalry Corps	4	28	7	129	11	289	468

RECAPITULATION.

General headquarters				2		4	6
Fourteenth Army Corps	40	625	228	3,333	111	1,777	6,114
Twentieth Army Corps	49	374	164	2,535	63	1,172	4,357
Twenty-first Army Corps	31	291	144	2,238	28	671	3,403
Reserve Corps	16	199	66	910	35	596	1,822
Cavalry Corps	4	28	7	129	11	289	468
Total Army of the Cumberland	140	1,517	609	9,147	248	4,509	16,170

OFFICERS KILLED OR MORTALLY WOUNDED.

GENERAL AND GENERAL STAFF OFFICERS.

Brig. Gen. William H. Lytle.
Capt. William C. Russell, Assistant Adjutant-General.

ILLINOIS.

Lieut. William Bishop, Bridges' Battery.
Col. John W. S. Alexander, 21st Infantry.
Capt. Andrew George, 21st Infantry.
Capt. Benjamin F. Reed, 21st Infantry.
Lieut. John F. Weitzel, 21st Infantry.
Capt. Milton A. French, 22d Infantry.
Capt. George Heinricks, 24th Infantry.
Capt. William S. Bryan, 27th Infantry.
Lieut. Joseph Voellinger, 27th Infantry.
Capt. Collins P. Jones, 35th Infantry.

Lieut. John W. Snyder, 35th Infantry.
Lieut. James P. Butler, 35th Infantry.
Capt. Sanford H. Wakeman, 36th Infantry.
Lieut. Myron A. Smith, 36th Infantry.
Lieut. Orison Smith, 36th Infantry.
Lieut. Col. Daniel H. Gilmer, 38th Infantry.
Capt. Thomas Cole, 38th Infantry.
Maj. James Leighton, 42d Infantry.
Lieut. Edward H. Brown, 42d Infantry.

ILLINOIS—Continued.

Lieut. Ezra A. Montgomery, 42d Infantry.
Lieut. Otis Moody, 51st Infantry.
Lieut. Albert G. Simons, 51st Infantry.
Maj. William E. Smith, 73d Infantry.
Lieut. Calvin R. Winget, 73d Infantry.
Maj. William L. Broaddus, 78th Infantry.
Capt. Thomas D. Adams, 84th Infantry.
Lieut. Col. Duncan J. Hall, 89th Infantry.

Capt. William H. Rice, 89th Infantry.
Capt. John W. Spink, 89th Infantry.
Capt. Thomas Whiting, 89th Infantry.
Lieut. Amory P. Ellis, 89th Infantry.
Lieut. Col. Isaac L. Clarke, 96th Infantry.
Lieut. George F. Barnes, 96th Infantry.
Lieut. Nelson R. Sims, 96th Infantry.
Lieut. Col. William Kinman, 115th Infantry.
Capt. S. Barlow Espy, 115th Infantry.

INDIANA.

Col. Philemon P. Baldwin, 6th Infantry.
Capt. Samuel Russell, 6th Infantry.
Lieut. William H. Criswell, 9th Infantry.
Lieut. Benjamin Franklin, 9th Infantry.
Lieut. Lewis S. Nickerson, 9th Infantry.
Lieut. Seth B. Parks, 9th Infantry.
Lieut. Leander C. Shipherd, 9th Infantry.
Col. William B. Carroll, 10th Infantry.
Capt. Jehu W. Perkins, 10th Infantry.
Lieut. Martin T. Jones, 10th Infantry.
Capt. N. Palmer Dunn, 29th Infantry.
Lieut. John Cutler, 29th Infantry.
Lieut. Joshua Eberly, 30th Infantry.
Lieut. Douglas L. Phelps, 30th Infantry.
Capt. William I. Leas, 31st Infantry.
Capt. John D. Ritter, 32d Infantry.
Capt. George M. Graves, 36th Infantry.
Lieut. William Butler, 36th Infantry.
Lieut. Salathial D. Colvin, 36th Infantry.
Lieut. James Patterson, 36th Infantry.
Lieut. Rufus H. Peck, 38th Infantry.
Lieut. John B. Southern, 38th Infantry.
Capt. Joseph C. Potts, 39th Infantry.
Lieut. Stephen D. Butler, 39th Infantry.
Lieut. William H. Garboden, 39th Infantry.

Capt. John Gunsenhouser, 44th Infantry.
Capt. Charles H. Bruce, 58th Infantry.
Lieut. Hugh J. Barnett, 58th Infantry.
Lieut. James D. Foster, 58th Infantry.
Col. Edward A. King, 68th Infantry.
Lieut. Robert J. Price, 68th Infantry.
Lieut. Thomas Bodley, 74th Infantry.
Lieut. Ananias Davis, 74th Infantry.
Lieut. Richard H. Hall, 74th Infantry.
Capt. Elijah R. Mitchell, 81st Infantry.
Capt. Harrison McAllister, 82d Infantry.
Capt. John H. Ellis, 84th Infantry.
Lieut. George C. Hatfield, 84th Infantry.
Lieut. Jerome B. Mason, 84th Infantry.
Capt. George W. Baker, 87th Infantry.
Capt. James M. Holliday, 87th Infantry.
Capt. Lewis Hughs, 87th Infantry.
Lieut. Abram C. Andrew, 87th Infantry.
Lieut. Franklin H. Bennett, 87th Infantry.
Lieut. Elisha Brown, 87th Infantry.
Lieut. Sloan D. Martin, 87th Infantry.
Lieut. Fredus Ryland, 87th Infantry.
Maj. George W. Stough, 88th Infantry.
Capt. Isaac H. Le Fevre, 88th Infantry.
Lieut. Richard H. Busick, 101st Infantry.

KANSAS.

Capt. Edgar P. Trego, 8th Infantry.
Lieut. Zacharias Burckhardt, 8th Infantry.

Lieut. John L. Graham, 8th Infantry.

KENTUCKY.

Lieut. Frank N. Sheets, 4th Cavalry.
Capt. James M. Bodine, 2d Infantry.
Capt. Henry S. Taylor, 3d Infantry.
Lieut. Alban D. Bradshaw, 3d Infantry.
Maj. Charles L. Thomasson, 5th Infantry.
Lieut. John W. Huston, 5th Infantry.
Lieut. John Ryan, 5th Infantry.
Lieut. Col. Richard Rockingham, 6th Infantry.
Capt. Peter Marker, 6th Infantry.

Capt. John McGraw, 6th Infantry.
Lieut. Thomas Eubanks, 6th Infantry.
Lieut. Frederick V. Lockman, 6th Infantry.
Capt. Seth P. Bevill, 10th Infantry.
Lieut. John H. Myers, 10th Infantry.
Capt. James W. Anthony, 17th Infantry.
Lieut. John D. Millman, 17th Infantry.
Lieut. Joseph C. Hoffman, 23d Infantry.

MICHIGAN.

Capt. James Hawley, 2d Cavalry.
Lieut. George W. Van Pelt, 1st Battery.
Capt. Charles W. Newbury, 11th Infantry.
Capt. Clark D. Fox, 13th Infantry.
Capt. Daniel B. Hosmer, 13th Infantry.

Lieut. Col. Morris B. Wells, 21st Infantry.
Capt. Edgar W. Smith, 21st Infantry.
Capt. William A. Smith, 22d Infantry.
Capt. Elijah Snell, 22d Infantry.

MINNESOTA.

Lieut. Albert Woodbury, 2d Battery.

MISSOURI.

Capt. Charles Deyhle, 2d Infantry.
Capt. John V. Krebs, 15th Infantry.

Lieut. Hermann C. Koerner, 15th Infantry.

OHIO.

Lieut. Col. Valentine Cupp, 1st Cavalry.
Lieut. Richard W. Neff, 4th Cavalry.
Lieut. John Lynch, Battery F, 1st Light Artillery.
Lieut. John W. Jackson, 1st Infantry.
Lieut. George W. Landrum, 2d Infantry.
Capt. Ferdinand Mueller, 9th Infantry.
Capt. Gustav Richter, 9th Infantry.
Lieut. Raymond Hermann, 9th Infantry.
Lieut. Theodore Lammers, 9th Infantry.
Lieut. Henry Liedke, 9th Infantry.
Lieut. Col. Elhannon M. Mast, 13th Infantry.
Capt. Thomas F. Murdock, 13th Infantry.
Lieut. Nicholas M. Fowler, 15th Infantry.
Capt. Ezra Ricketts, 17th Infantry.
Capt. Uriah W. Irwin, 19th Infantry.
Lieut. Col. Dwella M. Stoughton, 21st Infantry.
Capt. Isaac N. Dryden, 24th Infantry.
Capt. Dewitt C. Wadsworth, 24th Infantry.
Capt. William H. Ross, 26th Infantry.
Lieut. James W. Burbridge, 26th Infantry.
Lieut. John W. Ruley, 26th Infantry.
Lieut. Francis M. Williams, 26th Infantry.
Maj. Ephraim J. Ellis, 33d Infantry.
Lieut. Joseph H. Cole, 33d Infantry.
Capt. Joel K. Deardorff, 35th Infantry.
Capt. Oliver H. Parshall, 35th Infantry.
Lieut. Thomas M. Harlan, 35th Infantry.
Col. William G. Jones, 36th Infantry.
Lieut. William A. Rhodes, 36th Infantry.
Lieut. Benjamin F. Snodgrass, 40th Infantry.

Lieut. Cyrenius Van Mater, 40th Infantry.
Lieut. Frank H. Woods, 59th Infantry.
Lieut. Jesse Ellis, 59th Infantry.
Capt. John K. Ziegler, 64th Infantry.
Maj. Samuel C. Brown, 65th Infantry.
Lieut. Samuel C. Henwood, 65th Infantry.
Lieut. Nelson Smith, 65th Infantry.
Lieut. Granville Jackson, 89th Infantry.
Lieut. Stephen V. Walker, 89th Infantry.
Capt. Robert D. Caddy, 90th Infantry.
Lieut. Daniel N. Kingery, 90th Infantry.
Lieut. Nelson A. Patterson, 90th Infantry.
Capt. John Brown, 92d Infantry.
Col. Hiram Strong, 93d Infantry.
Capt. William C. Lochary, 98th Infantry.
Capt. Armstrong J. Thomas, 98th Infantry.
Lieut. Richard B. McGuire, 98th Infantry.
Capt. William H. Kilmer, 101st Infantry.
Lieut. Charles McGraw, 101st Infantry.
Lieut. Isaac P. Rule, 101st Infantry.
Capt. E. Abbott Spaulding, 105th Infantry.
Capt. Joshua M. Wells, 113th Infantry.
Lieut. William R. Hanawalt, 113th Infantry.
Lieut. George W. Holmes, 113th Infantry.
Lieut. James L. Wheelock, 113th Infantry.
Lieut. Robert F. Fleming, 121st Infantry.
Lieut. James A. Porter, 121st Infantry.
Lieut. Albert Barnes, 125th Infantry.

PENNSYLVANIA.

Capt. David G. May, 7th Cavalry.
Capt. Alanson J. Stevens, Battery B, Light Artillery.

Capt. Lewis Heidegger, 79th Infantry.
Lieut. Frederick Strasbaugh, 79th Infantry.

UNITED STATES ARMY.

Lieut. Robert Floyd, Battery H, 4th Artillery.
Lieut. Howard M. Burnham, Battery H, 5th Artillery.
Maj. Sidney Coolidge, 16th Infantry.
Lieut. Homer H. Clark, 16th Infantry.

Lieut. Lucius F. Brown, 18th Infantry.
Lieut. John Lane, 18th Infantry.
Lieut. Charles L. Truman, 18th Infantry.
Lieut. Michael B. Fogarty, 19th Infantry.
Lieut. Charles F. Miller, 19th Infantry.

Capt. Abner O. Heald, 1st Infantry.
Capt. William S. Mitchell, 1st Infantry.
Lieut. Robert J. Nickles, 1st Infantry.
Lieut. Jairus S. Richardson, 1st Infantry.
Lieut. Charles A. Searles, 1st Infantry.
Lieut. Col. John H. Ely, 10th Infantry.
Capt. George M. West, 10th Infantry.

Lieut. Robert Rennie, 10th Infantry.
Col. Hans C. Heg, 15th Infantry.
Capt. Hans Hansen, 15th Infantry.
Capt. Henry Hauff, 15th Infantry.
Capt. John M. Johnson, 15th Infantry.
Lieut. Oliver Thompson, 15th Infantry.
Capt. Gustavus Goldsmith, 24th Infantry.

No. 6.

Dispatches of Charles A. Dana, Assistant Secretary of War.

LOUISVILLE, *September* 6, 1863.

I arrived here this forenoon, having been much delayed on railroads and steamboats. Finding at Cincinnati that it was impossible to join Burnside by his line of march, I determined to go to Nashville, and thence to Rosecrans. Shall be at Nashville to-morrow. Burnside abandoned his base nearly a fortnight ago, and has since been living on the country. His animals have suffered severely for want of forage; nevertheless, he occupied Knoxville on the 4th instant. Of this event no particulars are known here. He has ordered the Ninth Corps to that place, and it will march at once, though, as it is considerably scattered, some time will be required for its concentration. Its present effective force is under 5,000 men. The effective force with which Burnside set out was under 18,000. Rosecrans has telegraphed to the clergy all over the country that he expected to fight a great battle to-day and desired their prayers.

General Boyle complains that he is unable to get new troops mustered in, although the need for their services is pressing. The ordnance officer here, Boyle says, also throws obstacles in the way of arming even those who have been mustered. Orders for arms, issued even by Burnside, have been subjected to the delay of first sending to Washington for General Ripley's consideration and approval.

[C. A. DANA.]

[Hon. E. M. STANTON,
        Secretary of War.]

—

NASHVILLE, *September* 8, 1863.

I have had this morning a prolonged conversation with Governor Johnson. With regard to the general condition of Tennessee he expresses himself in cheering terms. The occupation of Knoxville he regards as completing the expulsion of rebel power, and he proposes to order a general election for the first week in October. A Governor and other State officers, Legislature, and members of Congress will then be elected. The judiciary, now entirely lacking, he intends to fill by appointment, previous to this election. Judges of the election will also be appointed by him throughout the State. Sufficient means will be taken to prevent all except loyal citizens from voting or being voted for. Slavery he says is destroyed in fact, but must be abolished legally. He is thoroughly in favor of immediate emancipation, both as a matter of moral right and as the indispensable condition of that large immigration of industrious freemen which is necessary to repeople and regenerate the State. He has already declared himself publicly in behalf of unconditional abolition, and will recommend it emphatically to the Legislature when it assembles. He says the great majority of the people of Tennessee are to-day in favor of freedom, their only doubt being about the subsequent status of the negro. He is confident that the Legislature will provide for emancipation, either immediately or at an early day. The time of its meeting will be the first week in December, probably. Respecting military movements, Johnson complains of the tardiness of Rosecrans, and of these long months of precious time wasted in the construction of useless fortifications. Rosecrans he regards as a patriot at heart and not a damned traitor like his predecessor ; but he has fallen under bad influence and especially under that of his chief of detective police, a man named Truesdail. This man is deep in all kinds of plunder, and has kept the army inactive to enable his accomplices and himself to become rich by jobs and contracts. These statements, it is hardly necessary to say, were made to me confidentially, and were not attended by the allegation of any special facts. Of Gordon Granger, here, Johnson speaks in high terms. I should add that he says he will not himself be a candidate for any office at the coming election.

From North Carolina, he tells me, he has some communications, especially from Holden, of the Raleigh Register. The people of the whole State, and particularly of the western portion, are true to the Union and will seize the first opportunity to free themselves from the Confederate Government. In this respect the occupation of East Tennessee is of the highest importance. There is the center of the whole mountain region with its population of a million and a half, all naturally haters of slavery and of the rebellion. Gordon Granger and Johnson are going to the front to-morrow or next day. I shall go with them. It is but a day's distance by rail. Before leaving Louisville impressive testimony was presented to me of various frauds in the quartermaster's department, there and here. There is an extensive swindle now being consummated at Louisville by the furnishing of two-year old mules on a contract requiring three-year olds.

[C. A. DANA.]

[Hon. E. M. STANTON,
     Secretary of War.]

—

NASHVILLE, *September* 8, [1863]—7 p. m.

I have spent the afternoon in examining the fortifications for the defense of this place. The principal works are three in number, all on the southern side of the town. One of these, the easternmost, named Fort Negley, is finished, or nearly so, and armed. It is a work of very intricate design, and requires about a thousand men for its garrison. The central work, known as Fort Morton, is scarcely yet commenced. Simpler in design and more powerful when done than Negley. It is situated on a hill of hard limestone, and the very extensive excavations required must all be done by blasting. At the present rate of progress it will take two years to finish it. A part of it, namely, the demilune in its front, is partly done, so far in fact that its parapet might be used as a rifle-pit and might afford some protection to field guns. This work will require a garrison of from 1,500 to 2,000 men. The two redoubts and barracks connecting them, of which its main body consists, will be altogether 700 feet long. The third and westernmost fort is precisely the same in plan as Morton, but is on land that can be easily dug. This fort is about one-quarter done, and can be completed with comparative rapidity and cheapness. The cost of Morton must be heavy.

Nothing new from the front. Judicious men here think there will be no battle, and that Bragg has only the shadow of a force at Chattanooga to delay Rosecrans' advance.

[C. A. DANA.]

[Hon. E. M. STANTON,
   Secretary of War.]

—

BRIDGEPORT, *September* 10—5 p. m.

We have no particulars of the occupation of C[hattanooga], except that it took place at 10 a. m. yesterday, and that Rosecrans arrived there to-day. The place is held by Crittenden's corps. Thomas is at Trenton, Rosecrans 7 miles farther up the Lookout Valley, and McCook has the extreme right, some 8 miles farther. Of the Reserve Corps the division of Steedman has arrived here, and other troops, making in all 10,000 men, are rapidly approaching. Gordon Granger is here in command of all the forces north of the [river]. To strengthen this part of the army the garrisons between here and Nashville have been reduced to the last degree. Fears of incursions upon the railroad are entertained, especially as it is not known here whether Bragg has taken his cavalry with him. The stock of commissary supplies is running short. There are but insufficient stores at [Nashville] instead of those amply filled deposits which have been reported. The railroad between Louisville and [Nashville] is not transporting these necessaries as rapidly as is requisite, but 16 car-loads being sent over daily, while 65 are but enough. The reserve ammunition train of 800 wagons will be closed up to-night at Stevenson. No further advance of the army can take place until this gets up to Trenton or Chattanooga. There will also be delay in getting the troops closed up ready to move again, I presume. Indeed, it will be ten days before any new step is taken. Probably the depot of commissary and quartermaster's supplies will be brought forward from Stevenson to this place. It will require a month at least to replace the railroad bridge here, of which three-quarters is destroyed. I shall reach headquarters to-morrow.

[C. A. DANA.]

[Hon. E. M. STANTON,
   Secretary of War.]

—

CHATTANOOGA, *September* 12—11 a. m.

Arriving here last evening I at once found that my report from Bridgeport, that the advance would be stopped and the army concentrated before moving farther forward, was incorrect. McCook and Thomas had both been moved from the Valley of Lookout Creek through the gaps of Lookout Mountain, the former toward Summerville and the latter toward La Fayette, while Crittenden had marched to Ringgold. The enemy have, however, unexpectedly appeared in force on the south bank of the Chickamauga, on the road hence to La Fayette, while a force of from 10,000 to 20,000, debouching westward through Catlett's Gap, attacked Negley in front of Stevens' Gap yesterday afternoon and compelled him to fall back to the gap. Last night it seemed probable that Bragg had abandoned his retreat on Rome and returned with the purpose of falling upon the different corps and divisions of our army, now widely separated by the necessity of crossing the mountains at gaps far apart, and destroying them in detail. The indications of this morning are that he was merely making a stand to check pursuit, the attack on Negley appearing to have been stopped as soon as he fell back. Crittenden is now ordered to move from Ringgold to his own right flank, and should have had his main body at the Chickamauga crossing on the La Fayette road by 10 a. m. to-day. This is the place where his right wing found the enemy in force yesterday. Thomas has sent Brannan to help Negley, who will thus renew this advance from Stevens' Gap toward Dug Gap in Pigeon Mountain, while Thomas himself, with the remainder of his corps, putting himself into communication with Crittenden, will advance toward Catlett's Gap. McCook at the same time is to rest his left flank on the southern base of Mission Ridge and, extending his line toward Summerville, fall on the flank of the enemy should he follow the valley that way.

It is probable, however, that before these dispositions are completed he will have got east of Pigeon Mountain and made good his escape to Rome. This region is composed of long mountains with few practicable passes. It is above 30 miles from the head of Lookout Mountain to the first gap, for instance. The roads are worse than those over any other mountains in the country; not impassable, but very destructive to wagons. The valleys are narrow, irregular, and bare of corn and cattle. R[osecrans] thinks, however, that he will be able to find forage a short distance ahead. Two million rations now remain to be drawn from Stevenson depot.

[C. A. DANA.]

[Hon. E. M. STANTON,
     Secretary of War.]

—

CHATTANOOGA, *September* 13—7 a. m.

General disposition of troops remains as yesterday. Crittenden has concentrated his corps at Gordon's Mills, where the road hence to La Fayette crosses the West Chickamauga, and is near enough to Thomas for either to open when the other is attacked, though they have not yet opened communication with each other, the enemy's cavalry being in possession of the intervening part of the valley.

At the latest reports received last night the enemy was still in force in front of Crittenden, though he did not seem to have a distinct idea in what force. Crittenden had some unimportant skirmishes during yesterday. Thomas reported last night that he had moved from Stevens' Gap toward Dug and Catlett's Gaps, finding no enemy, his scouts and citizens all stating the rebels had withdrawn to La Fayette to make a stand there. This being true, Crittenden will find his roads clear before him to-day, and will easily get through Pigeon Mountain.

At the latest advices from McCook he was taking up position from southern extremity of Mission Ridge toward Summerville. There is a possibility that the corps attacking Negley on Friday, now reported as D. H. Hill's, may have attacked McCook, but the latter is strong enough to fight successfully. Rosecrans leaves here immediately for Thomas' headquarters.

As the telegraph ends here my dispatches will be delayed accordingly.

[C. A. DANA.]

[Hon. E. M. STANTON,
    Secretary of War.]

—

HEADQUARTERS FOURTEENTH ARMY CORPS,
    Before Stevens' Gap, September 14—11 a. m.

Everything progresses favorably ; concentration of the three corps already substantially effected. Enemy has withdrawn from this basin, and the reports of scouts show that he is evacuating La Fayette and moving toward Rome. Our forces will to-day occupy gaps leading toward La Fayette, and that place will probably be occupied to-morrow. Army now has provisions for ten days, by the end of which time depot will be established at Chattanooga. Forage abounds everywhere.

[C. A. DANA.]

[Hon. E. M. STANTON,
    Secretary of War.]

—

BEFORE STEVENS' GAP,
    September 14—12.30 p. m.

Johnston is here in command of enemy, having arrived just before evacuation of Chattanooga. His Mississippi army is mainly here also. There is no evidence that any troops have come from Lee's army, but deserters all report that heavy re-enforcements are on road from there. Deserters continue to be picked up. Provost-marshal of Rosecrans reports he has taken 2,500 since leaving Tullahoma, mainly men of Kentucky and East Tennessee.

No news here from Burnside.

One steamboat taken at Chattanooga will be repaired and ready for work within ten days. Supplies can then be towed in flat-boats from Bridgeport to Chattanooga, saving wagoning over mountains. Thermometer now at 75.

[C. A. DANA.]

[Hon. E. M. STANTON,
    Secretary of War.]

—

BEFORE STEVENS' GAP, *September* 14.

This army has now gained a position from which it can effectually advance upon Rome and Atlanta, and deliver there the finishing blow of the war. The difficulties of gaining this position, of crossing the

Cumberland Mountains, passing the Tennessee, turning and occupying Chattanooga, traversing the mountain ridges of Northern Georgia, and seizing the passes which lead southward have been enormous, and can only be fully appreciated by one who has personally examined the region. These difficulties are now all substantially overcome. The army is in the best possible condition, and is advancing with all the rapidity which the nature of the country allows. Burnside will secure its left flank, but a sudden movement of the enemy to its right would endanger its long and precarious line of communications and compel a retreat to the Tennessee.

To avoid this danger a column as strong as possible should be pushed eastward from Corinth. The advantages already gained are so great, and the possibilities of further triumphs so important, that I take the liberty of especially urging the subject upon your attention. Would it not be better even to recall Steele from Arkansas than to risk a check here, where heart of rebellion is within reach and the final blow already prepared?

[C. A. DANA.]

[Hon. E. M. STANTON,
    Secretary of War.]

—

CRAWFISH SPRING, *September* 16—12.30 p. m.

Your dispatches concerning an obscure passage in mine of 12th, have just come to hand. The words not understood are:

It is probable, however, that before these dispositions are completed he will have got east of Pigeon Mountain and made good his escape to Rome. This region is composed of long mountains with few practicable passes. For instance, it is about 30 miles from the head of Lookout Mountain to the first gap. The roads are worse than those over any other mountains in the Union; not impassable, but very destructive to wagons.

This place is 13 miles south-southwest from Chattanooga. Weather pleasant.

[C. A. DANA.]

Major ECKERT.

—

CRAWFISH SPRING, *September* 16—1 p. m.

McCook mistook the order of march prescribed for him to concentrate upon Thomas; marched from Alpine around the southwestern flank of Lookout Mountain, coming down into this valley by way of Stevens' Gap, instead of moving directly northward and coming in by Dougherty's Gap. This mistake has caused two days' delay. Sheridan's division got down into the valley yesterday, and the others will get down to-day. The concentration of the army will then be perfect, McCook holding the right, as before, Thomas the center, and Crittenden the left, while Granger, with Steedman's division and Col. Daniel McCook's brigade of the Reserve Corps, is posted at Rossville on the extreme left to guard the approach to Chattanooga from the direction of Cleveland and Ringgold. The concurrent testimony of spies and deserters shows that the enemy are concentrated at La Fayette. No re-enforcements from Virginia have yet arrived there, nor does it seem that any considerable body has reached Dalton. The present plan of Rosecrans is to hold gaps in Lookout Mountain in his rear, and to seem to threaten the gaps of

Catlett, Dug, and Blue Bird in Pigeon Mountain, and then, taking great care to show camp fires and every other evidence that his forces remain in their camps in this valley, to march by night from Pigeon Mountain by taking the road which leads around its northern extremity and surprise the rebels at La Fayette. This road you will find laid down on the maps as Shields' Gap, but really it is no gap, but a complete cessation of the mountain. Everything will be completely ready for this movement by to-morrow night, and, should no new development prevent, it will then be executed.

Nothing heard from Burnside. It is exceedingly necessary that his cavalry should appear on that flank to prevent cavalry attacking trains.

[C. A. DANA.]

[Hon. E. M. STANTON,
Secretary of War.]

—

CRAWFISH SPRING, September 16—3 p. m.

Though the Louisville and Nashville Railroad is paid by the Government for transportation at its own rates of charge, those rates being some 25 per cent. higher than are charged by other roads, it persists in preferring private freight over that of Government. It will be impossible to maintain this army without a complete change in the management of that road. The Government is its great customer, and should control its movements.

The excuse now made by the company is that some 50 of its cars have been taken for the Chattanooga road, but that is no reason why it should carry private freight rather than our supplies.

[C. A. DANA.]

[Hon. E. M. STANTON,
Secretary of War.]

—

CRAWFISH SPRING, September 17—9 a. m.

The character of the roads here and the severity of the service, owing to the numerical superiority of the enemy's cavalry, use up horses very rapidly. Two thousand are now necessary to remount men whose animals are unserviceable. They can be procured in Nashville and in the region between here and there as cheaply and more promptly than elsewhere. It would be greatly for advantage of service if Lieutenant-Colonel Hodges, chief quartermaster of this department, could be authorized by General Stoneman to purchase. He can be relied on perfectly.

[C. A. DANA.]

[Hon. E. M. STANTON,
Secretary of War.]

—

CRAWFISH SPRING, September 17—10 a. m.

McCook's divisions not yet all over the mountain, but must be in position before night. Column of enemy moving yesterday on road between Ringgold and Shields' Gap, and his pickets were posted last

night in front of Wood, on Crittenden's left. He is apparently disposed to dispute passage of Shields' Gap. We are still without
information of Longstreet's arrival.

[C. A. DANA.]

[Hon. E. M. STANTON,
   Secretary of War.]

—

CRAWFISH SPRING, *September* 17—5 p. m.

There are pretty clear indications that the rebels are massing their
forces about Rock Spring Church, east of Pigeon Mountain, between
Shields' and Catlett's Gaps. A body of rebel infantry and cavalry
has just come into this valley by way of Dug Gap, and the rebel
column reported in my dispatch of this morning continues to raise a
cloud of dust on the road between Shields' Gap and Ringgold.

Reports that Longstreet has reached Atlanta begin to come in from
various sources. A rebel deserter reported this morning at Chattanooga that some of Burnside's cavalry were at Cleveland on 15th,
but nothing positive reaches us from Burnside. His forces needed
here.

[C. A. DANA.]

[Hon. E. M. STANTON,
   Secretary of War.]

—

CRAWFISH SPRING, *September* 18—12 m.

Rebel cavalry and infantry are appearing along front of Wood,
whose division holds Crittenden's left, and on right of Van Cleve,
who holds Crittenden's center. Apparently it is a reconnaissance in
force, but everything is ready for serious attack. Our position is
excellent, with West Chickamauga River in front of greater part of
our lines. Minty's cavalry and Wilder's mounted infantry on left
flank, and on right two divisions cavalry under Mitchell, who succeeds Stanley, the latter being very sick. Thomas with the central
corps is moving down the Chickamauga in this direction, and Mc-
Cook, whose troops have all got over into this valley, except one brigade yet on Lookout Mountain, is closing up on Thomas' right. Sky
cloudy, thermometer 62; perfect day for fighting. Nothing from
Burnside; his cavalry at Cleveland, reported yesterday, were only
scouts sent out from Byrd's brigade, which has been at Athens some
time.

[C. A. DANA.]

[Hon. E. M. STANTON,
   Secretary of War.]

—

CRAWFISH SPRING, *September* 18—5 p. m.

Rebel demonstration to-day proves to have been reconnaissance
in force. Some 10,000 men of all arms were engaged. They felt
our line along Wood's position on Crittenden's left, exchanging a
few shots, and attacked Minty and Wilder with vigor, compelling
them to retire west of Chickamauga. Casualties not yet reported.

Enemy are reported by our watchmen on Lookout Mountain as having lighted extensive camp-fires on hither side of Shields' Gap, as well as beyond. Our troops are now being drawn toward our left, and concentrated as much as possible. Rosecrans has not yet determined whether to make a night march and fall on them at daylight or to await their onset.

[C. A. DANA.]

[Hon. E. M. STANTON,
    Secretary of War.]

—

CRAWFISH SPRING, *September* 19—10.30 a. m.

Battle opened at 9 this morning on our right. Bragg in command of rebels. His force not yet ascertained. Engagement not yet general. His effort is to push into Chattanooga. In anticipation of this movement Thomas marched last night to our left. Crittenden pushed up behind him and McCook brought here as reserve.

As I write enemy are making diversion on our right, where Negley was left to hold fords. Negley is supported by Sheridan. An orderly of Bragg's just captured says there are reports in rebel army of Longstreet's arrival, but he does not know that they are true. Rosecrans has everything ready to grind up Bragg's flank.

[C. A. DANA.]

[Hon. E. M. STANTON,
    Secretary of War.]

—

NEAR CRAWFISH SPRING, *September* 19, 1863—1 p. m.

In my dispatch of this morning where it is said battle has begun on our right it should have been left. There is the fighting. Everything is going well, but the full proportions of the conflict are not yet developed. The engagement is now between here and Rossville, where Thomas has his headquarters.

[C. A. DANA.]

[Hon. E. M. STANTON,
    Secretary of War.]

—

WIDOW GLENN'S, *September* 19, 1863—2.30 p. m.

Fight continues to rage. Enemy, repulsed on left by Thomas, has suddenly fallen on right of our line of battle, held by Van Cleve ; musketry and artillery there fierce and obstinate. Crittenden with remainder of his corps is just going in. Negley's and Sheridan's divisions and cavalry alone remain unengaged and Sheridan is ordered here, leaving Negley to hold the fords beyond Crawfish Spring. The mass of cavalry guards the gaps beyond it. Thomas loses pretty heavily in men ; also lost one battery of Brannan. Decisive victory seems assured to us.

[C. A. DANA.]

[Hon. E. M. STANTON,
    Secretary of War.]

WIDOW GLENN'S, *September* 19—3 p. m.
Enemy, forced back by Crittenden on right, has just massed his artillery against Davis on center. His attack there is the most furious of the day. He seems giving way.

[C. A. DANA.]

[Hon. E. M. STANTON,
          Secretary of War.]

—

WIDOW GLENN'S, *September* 19—3.20 p. m.
Thomas reports that he is driving rebels, and will force them into Chickamauga to-night. It is evident here their line is falling back. The battle is fought altogether in a thick forest, and is invisible to outsiders. Line is 2 miles long.

4 p. m.
Negley being nearer than Sheridan has come up in his stead. Negley's first brigade is just going in. Everything is prosperous. Sheridan is coming up. Cavalry has been brought to Crawfish Spring ready for use.

4.30 p. m.
I do not yet dare to say our victory is complete, but it seems certain. Enemy silenced on nearly whole line. Longstreet is here. Governor Brown has taken part in battle.

[C. A. DANA.]

[Hon. E. M. STANTON,
          Secretary of War.]

—

WIDOW GLENN'S, *September* 19—5.20 p. m.
Firing has ceased. Reports are coming in. Enemy holds his ground in many places. We have suffered severely. Reynolds reported killed. Now appears to be undecided contest, but later reports will enable us to understand more clearly.

[C. A. DANA.]

[Hon. E. M. STANTON,
          Secretary of War.]

—

WIDOW GLENN'S, *September* 19—7.30 p. m.
Immediately after my last dispatch Negley opened on enemy with two fresh brigades and drove him back half a mile. The firing did not cease till an hour after dark, the feeble light of the moon favoring the combatants. This gives us decidedly the advantage in respect of ground. The result of the battle is that enemy is defeated in attempt to turn and crush our left flank and regain possession of Chattanooga. His attempt was furious and obstinate, his repulse was bloody, and maintained till the end. If he does not retreat Rosecrans will renew the fight at daylight. His dispositions are now being made. There are here two brigades and one regiment which have not been engaged at all, and two brigades which have been en-

gaged but little. At Rossville are 8,000 men of Reserve Corps not engaged at all. We have lost no prominent officer. Reynolds safe. Weather cool; favorable to wounded.

[C. A. DANA.]

[Hon. E. M. Stanton,
        Secretary of War.]

—

[September 19]—8 p. m.

We have taken about 250 prisoners, including men from thirty different regiments. We have captured 10 guns and lost 7. I cannot learn that we have lost any considerable number of prisoners. Battle-field is 3 miles north from Crawfish Spring, and about 8 south of Rossville. It is mainly in a forest 4 miles square.

[C. A. DANA.]

[Hon. E. M. Stanton,
        Secretary of War.]

—

[September 19]—11 p. m.

Dr. Perin, medical director of this department, estimates the number of our wounded as not exceeding 2,000.

[C. A. DANA.]

[Hon. E. M. Stanton,
        Secretary of War.]

—

Chattanooga, *September* 20—4 p. m.

My report to-day is of deplorable importance. Chickamauga is as fatal a name in our history as Bull Run. The battle began late this morning. The first cannon was fired at 9, but no considerable firing till 10. Previous to 10 Rosecrans rode the whole length of lines. All seemed promising, except columns of dust within rebel lines moving north, and report from our right that enemy had been felling timber there during night. Soon after the battle commenced Thomas, who held the left, began to call for re-enforcements. Then about 12 came word that he had been forced to retire to his second line. Re-enforcements were sent him, and McCook's whole corps, which was on right and as reserve in the center, was ordered to his assistance. Wood, of Crittenden's corps, and Van Cleve, who held the front in center, were also ordered to left, where the fury of cannonade showed that enormous rebel force was massed. Their places were filled by Davis and Sheridan, of McCook's corps. But hardly had these divisions taken their places in the line when the rebel fire, which had slackened on our left ever since it was turned and driven back about three-quarters of an hour previously, suddenly burst over in enormous volume upon our center.

Never in any battle I have witnessed was there such a mass of cannon and musketry. This lasted some twenty minutes, and then Van Cleve, on Thomas' right, was seen to give way, but in tolerable order, soon after which the lines of Sheridan and Davis broke in disorder, borne down by immense columns of enemy. These columns

are said to have consisted of Polk's entire corps.   They came through
with resistless impulse, composed of brigades formed in divisions.
Before them our soldiers turned and fled.   It was wholesale panic.
Vain were all attempts to rally them.   They retreated directly across
two lines of considerable ridges running parallel to our line of battle,
and then most of them made their way over Missionary Ridge, and
are coming here by Chattanooga Valley road.   Our wagon trains
have mostly got here already, and the road is full of a disordered
throng of fugitives.   McCook, with the right of his corps and Wilder's
mounted infantry, attempted to recover the day, but it was useless.
Davis and Sheridan are said to be coming off at the head of a couple
of regiments in order, and Wilder's brigade marches out unbroken.
Thomas, too, is coming down the Rossville road with an organized
command, but all the rest is confusion.   Our wounded are all left
behind, some 6,000 in number.   We have lost heavily in killed to-
day.   The total of our killed, wounded, and prisoners can hardly be
less than 20,000, and may be much more.

How much artillery we lose I cannot guess, nor do I yet know what
officers have been lost.   Lytle said to be killed.   Rosecrans escaped
by Rossville road.   Enemy not yet arrived before Chattanooga.
Preparations making to resist his entrance for a time.

                                                [C. A. DANA.]
[Hon. E. M. STANTON,
        Secretary of War.]

—

            CHATTANOOGA, September 20, 1863—8 p. m.

I am happy to report that my dispatch of 4 p. m. to-day proves
to have given too dark a view of our disaster.   Having been myself
swept bodily off the battle-field by the panic-struck rabble into
which the divisions of Davis and Sheridan were temporarily converted, my own impressions were naturally colored by the aspect of
that part of the field.   It appears, however, that only those two
divisions were actually routed, and that Thomas, with the remainder
of the army, still holds his part of the field.   Beside the two divisions of Davis and Sheridan, those of Negley and Van Cleve were
thrown into confusion, but were soon rallied and hold their places, the
first on the left, the second on the right of Thomas' fighting column.
In addition to this Davis and Sheridan have succeeded in rallying
some 8,000 or 10,000 of the fugitives, and have also joined Thomas.
This corps, consisting, after all losses, of at least 30,000 men, has still
further been strengthened by the addition of that portion of the reserve lately stationed at Rossville under Granger.   It has changed
its front from the nearly north-and-south line of this morning, and
faces the enemy in an east-and-west line.   It will at once fall back
to the strongest line of defense, for the purpose of defeating enemy's
design of regaining Chattanooga and the Tennessee.

The latest report from Thomas is that he was driving back the
advance of the rebels.   In addition to these forces we have the cavalry and mounted infantry, not less than 10,000 in number, who are
perfectly intact, and with this army it is not difficult to make good
our lines until re-enforcements can arrive.   The cavalry at our last
advices had their headquarters at Crawfish Spring, where they will
perhaps be able to protect our main hospital until the wounded can

be brought here by the Chattanooga Valley road, which still is free from rebels.

The number of the enemy yesterday and to-day I estimate at not less than 70,000. He was able to touch and threaten our lines at all points, and still form the tremendous columns whose onset drove Thomas back and dissolved Sheridan and Davis in panic. I learn from General Rosecrans, who himself took part in the effort previously to the final stampede of Sheridan's division, that that general charged the advancing columns of the enemy in flank. The charge was too spasmodic to be effectual; our men became involved in the rushing mass and did not break it. Rosecrans has telegraphed Burnside to hurry forward his re-enforcements. The advance of his cavalry is reported as having reached Cleveland yesterday morning.

Some gentlemen of Rosecrans' staff say Chickamauga is not very much worse than was Murfreesborough. I can testify to the conspicuous and steady gallantry of Rosecrans on the field. He made all possible efforts to rally the broken columns; nor do I see that there was any fault in the disposition of his forces.

The disaster might perhaps have been avoided but for the blunder of McCook in marching back from his previous advanced position. That blunder cost us four days of precious time.

[C. A. DANA.]

[Hon E. M. STANTON,
        Secretary of War.]

—

CHATTANOOGA, September 21—1 p. m.

Deserters and captives both report that Ewell's corps is on its way to join Bragg. One of the latter, taken this morning by Thomas, says the corps has arrived, though not in season to fight yesterday. Is now moving on the Tennessee River above this. Longstreet, as we know, is here.

[C. A. DANA.]

[Hon. E. M. STANTON,
        Secretary of War.]

—

CHATTANOOGA, September 21—2 p. m.

Garfield, chief of staff, becoming separated from Rosecrans in the route of our right wing yesterday, made his way to the left, and spent the afternoon and night with General Thomas. He arrived here before noon to-day, having witnessed the sequel of the battle in that part of the field. Thomas, finding himself cut off from Rosecrans and the right, at once brought his seven divisions into position for independent fighting. Refusing both his right and left, his line assumed the form of a horse-shoe posted along the slope and crest of a partly wooded ridge. He was soon joined by Granger from Rossville, with the brigade of McCook and division of Steedman, and with these forces firmly maintained the fight till after dark. Our troops were as immovable as the rocks they stood on. The enemy hurled against them repeatedly the dense columns which had routed Davis and Sheridan in the morning, but every onset was repulsed with dreadful slaughter. Falling first on one and then another point of our lines, for hours the rebels vainly sought to break them-

Thomas seemed to have filled every soldier with his own unconquerable firmness, and Granger, his hat torn by bullets, raged like a lion wherever the combat was hottest with the electrical courage of a Ney.

Every division commander bore himself gloriously, and among brigade commanders, Turchin, Hazen, and Harker especially distinguished themselves. Turchin charged through the rebel lines with the bayonet, and becoming surrounded, forced his way back again. Harker, who had two horses shot under him on the 19th, forming his men in four lines, made them lie down till the enemy were close upon him when they suddenly rose and delivered their fire with such effect that the assaulting columns fell back in confusion, leaving the ground covered with the fallen. When night fell this body of heroes stood on the same ground they had occupied in the morning, their spirit unbroken, but their numbers greatly diminished. Their losses are not yet ascertained. Van Cleve had this morning 1,200 men in the ranks, but this number will probably be doubled by evening in stragglers. Neither he, Sheridan, nor Davis fought with Thomas. The divisions of Wood, Johnson, Brannan, Palmer, Reynolds, and Baird, which never broke at all, have lost very severely. We hear unofficially from Brannan that but about 2,000 effective men remain in his division. Steedman lost one-third of his men. Thomas retired to Rossville after battle. Dispositions have been made to resist the enemy's approach on that line, but if Ewell be really there, Rosecrans will have to retreat beyond the Tennessee.

Thomas telegraphs this morning that the troops are in high spirits. He brought off all his wounded. Of those at Crawfish Spring, our main field hospital, nearly all have been brought away. It now seems probable that not more than 1,000 of our wounded are in the enemy's hands, and Rosecrans has sent flag to recover them. The number of prisoners taken by enemy is still uncertain. It will hardly surpass 3,000, besides wounded.

In artillery our loss is probably forty pieces. Many were left because all of their horses had been killed. Of rebel prisoners we have already sent 1,300 to Nashville.

[C. A. DANA.]

[Hon. E. M. STANTON,
          Secretary of War.]

—

CHATTANOOGA, September 21—4.30 p. m.

An intelligent deserter from Bragg's army who came in this morning says he belonged to Johnston's Mississippi army, that it is all here, and that Mobile has been stripped of soldiers. Granger tells me they took prisoners in the battle yesterday afternoon who said they had just come from Charleston.

Confederacy seems concentrated here.

[C. A. DANA.]

[Hon. E. M. STANTON,
          Secretary of War.]

—

CHATTANOOGA, September 21.

Rosecrans has issued orders for all our troops to be concentrated here to-night. Thomas, with the forces at Rossville, will get in about

11 [p. m.] unless prevented by enemy who have been fighting him this afternoon. Mitchell also reports from our right flank, where he is watching with his cavalry, that two divisions of Longstreet are advancing on him. There is no time to wait for re-enforcements, and R[osecrans] is determined not to abandon Chattanooga and [Bridgeport] without another effort. Battle here will probably be fought to-morrow or next day. Granger, who is here, says that in yesterday's battle rebels were finally defeated, and if Thomas had not withdrawn during night enemy would not have dared attack further. In last two assaults our troops fought with bayonet, their ammunition being quite exhausted.

[C. A. DANA.]

[Hon. E. M. STANTON,
        Secretary of War.]

—

CHATTANOOGA, *September 22—3* p. m.

Whole army withdrew into this place last night without difficulty, leaving only necessary outposts and parties of observation.

The troops arrived here about midnight in wonderful spirits, considering their excessive fatigues and heavy losses. They have been working all day improvising rifle-pits. Line of defense is about 3 miles long, crossing the peninsula some 2 miles from its extremity. It includes two redoubts erected by rebels, and is pretty strong, though much weakened by a blunder made by somebody in pushing McCook's wing half mile forward of line designed by Chief Engineer Morton. This cannot be remedied to-day, but if possible mistake repaired to-night. McCook holds the right, that noble old hero Thomas the center, the weakest part of the line, and Crittenden the left. The enemy have been approaching all morning in three columns, resisted by our advance parties, but the artillery firing has now drawn very near and battle may be fought before dark. Rosecrans estimates our effectives at 30,000 besides cavalry, but I fear our numbers are hardly so great as that. There are provisions here for fifteen days. Mass of cavalry under Mitchell has been sent across river to guard the road to Bridgeport via Jasper, and to strengthen Wilder, who is watching fords above here. Mitchell will there find forage for horses, of which none is here. Only cavalry remaining on this side are Minty's brigade, in front toward Rossville and Missionary Ridge, and Watkins' brigade, left behind by Mitchell, and now making its way over Lookout Mountain.

How large force enemy brings here, you know as well as we.

He was awfully slaughtered on Sunday, but certainly outnumbers this army even if he has received no re-enforcements. Our losses on that awful day are still uncertain. Four thousand wounded have already been sent hence to Bridgeport. General King, commanding brigade of regulars, went into action with 1,600, brought out only 450. He lost two battalions, taken prisoners. General Baird, who commanded Rousseau's division, estimates his loss in prisoners at 2,000, though his line never flinched. This army looks anxiously for re-enforcements. No signs of approach of Burnside.

[C. A. DANA.]

[Hon. E. M. STANTON,
        Secretary of War.]

CHATTANOOGA, *Septemver* 22—6 p. m.

Rosecrans is considering question of retreat from here. I judge that he thinks that unless he can have assurance of ample re-enforcements within one week, the attempt to hold this place will be much more disastrous than retreat. That part of the army which was routed on Sunday is much demoralized.

If you have any advice to give, it should come to-night.

[C. A. DANA.]

[Hon. E. M. STANTON,
          Secretary of War.]

—

CHATTANOOGA, *September* 22—9.30 p. m.

Rosecrans has determined to fight it out here at all hazards. The official returns show the army to consist of 35,000 effectives. There are here ten days' full rations, sufficient for twenty days in case of need. Besides it will be difficult for enemy to interfere with our hauling from Bridgeport via Jasper. Of ammunition there is enough here for two days' hard fighting in field, and this will last much longer behind rifle-pits.

The enemy will most probably attack in morning.

[C. A. DANA.]

[Hon. E. M. STANTON,
          Secretary of War.]

—

CHATTANOOGA, *September* 23—7 a. m.

Your dispatch to me yesterday was lost before reaching me, while I was absent in the field. Please repeat.

[C. A. DANA.]

[Hon. E. M. STANTON,
          Secretary of War.]

—

CHATTANOOGA, *September* 23—10 a. m.

All quiet yet. Enemy is in front along our whole line. The troops rested well last night, and are greatly refreshed. Everything ready.

[C. A. DANA.]

[Hon. E. M. STANTON,
          Secretary of War.]

—

CHATTANOOGA, *September* 23—11.30 a. m.

The net result of the campaign thus far is that we hold Chattanooga and the line of Tennessee River. It is true this result has been attended by a great battle with heavy losses, but it is certain that the enemy has suffered quite as severely as we have.

The first great object of the campaign, the possession of Chattanooga and the Tennessee line, still remains in our hands, and can be held by this army for from fifteen to twenty days against all efforts of the enemy, unless he should receive re-enforcements of overwhelming strength. But to render our hold here perfectly safe no time should be lost in pushing 20,000 to 25,000 efficient troops to Bridgeport. If such re-enforcements can be got there in season, everything is safe, and this place—indispensable alike to the defense of Tennessee and as the base of future operations in Georgia—will remain ours.

[C. A. DANA.]
[Hon. E. M. STANTON,
    Secretary of War.]

—

CHATTANOOGA, September 23—1.30 p. m.
Enemy still slowly advancing three columns, but no attack yet. Our rifle-pits are now strong and every preparation complete as possible considering shortness of time. Ammunition train of 50 wagons from Bridgeport has arrived, increasing our supply materially.

Orders have been given to construct an interior line of defenses, so that 5,000 to 10,000 troops can hold the place and rest of army move wherever needed. This will probably be accomplished to-night.

Official report received from Burnside's advance, which was at Athens night before last. Mass of his forces far behind that place. R[osecrans] advises B[urnside] to come here by road on the north side Tennessee River.

[C. A. DANA.]
[Hon. E. M. STANTON,
    Secretary of War.]

—

CHATTANOOGA, September 23—2 p. m.
After careful study of the disaster to our right wing on Sunday, I am of opinion that it arose from the following causes:

First, great numerical superiority of the enemy.

Second, the too great extent and consequent thinness of our line.

Third, and in its results the most fatal of all, the disobedience of orders of General McCook in placing his corps from one-third to one-half mile farther to the right than he had been directed, thus elongating the line still farther.

Fourth, the attempt of Rosecrans to re-enforce the left wing when Thomas reported it had been forced to fall back. In this attempt he necessarily had to move troops from the right, the whole reserve being already engaged. While this movement was taking place the enemy suddenly fell upon Davis as he was marching by the left flank. The attack was tremendous, and resulted in our rout. Sheridan, who joined Davis on the latter's right, and formed the right extremity of our line, was also engaged in moving by the flank at double-quick time and in line of battle, when Davis broke. Sheridan had not time to halt, and attempted to convert his movement into a charge, but it failed, of course, and his men became routed also. Had McCook taken the right place in the morning his movement to the left, passing over a shorter distance, would sooner have been completed and Davis and Sheridan would not have been taken in flank and routed. These two generals, however, remained and rallied their men, as did Van Cleve, who was almost as badly dissolved as they; but McCook and Crittenden, two corps commanders, made their way here and slept here all night, and did not look after their troops till Monday. True they were tired, but so were those who remained and fought the glorious battle of Sunday afternoon, in which Granger would seem to have been right when he pronounced the enemy defeated and urged Thomas to disregard Rosecrans' order to retire on the ground that latter was at Chattanooga ignorant of the facts.

[C. A. DANA.]

[Hon. E. M. STANTON,
    Secretary of War.]

—

CHATTANOOGA, *September* 24—8 a. m.

Your telegrams of last night and this morning received. Have no further doubt about this place ; it will hold out. Indeed, it has now been made so strong that it can only be taken by regular siege. The labors of this army for last forty-eight hours have been herculean. As soon as Hooker arrives and Sherman and Hurlbut make their appearance in Tuscumbia Valley, it will be able to resume the offensive irresistibly.

[C. A. DANA.]

[Hon. E. M. STANTON,
    Secretary of War.]

—

CHATTANOOGA, *September* 24—11 a. m.

No attack yet. Division rebel cavalry advanced from Stevens' Gap on Lookout Mountain yesterday and compelled a regiment R[osecrans] had left at Summertown, on the head of mountain, to guard signal station to retire. Another rebel column on Missionary Ridge on east side Chattanooga Valley, and no doubt mass of their infantry is in that valley in front of us. R[osecrans] will make reconnaissance in force to-day.

With our present defenses it is very desirable they should attack us.

[C. A. DANA.]

[Hon. E. M. STANTON,
    Secretary of War.]

—

CHATTANOOGA, *September* 24—12 m.

Words telegram 21st you desire repeated are :

With the electrical courage of a Ney.

My cipher clerk, myself, shall be more careful.

[C. A. DANA.]

[Hon. E. M. STANTON,
    Secretary of War.]

—

CHATTANOOGA, *September* 24.

In my report yesterday upon causes of Sunday's disaster to our right wing I omitted to mention, under my second head, that, before the battle began, Rosecrans evidently saw that his line was too long, and then attempted to shorten it. To this end he withdrew Negley's division from the place assigned to it, between Reynolds and Brannan, and placed Negley as a support, behind Baird, on the extreme left. The gap thus made in the line he filled by moving Brannan, Johnson, and Wood to the left, leaving a gap which he intended to fill by crowding Davis and Sheridan likewise to the left, which would have made the whole line shorter by the extent of one division. But before this operation could be completed the battle became so hot that, instead of filling this gap in the manner he had intended, he had to precipitate Van Cleve's division into it, thus leaving himself no reserves and no means of re-enforcing the left wing, except by withdrawing forces from his right, and in the very act of this withdrawal the enemy fell upon him.

It is plain that having committed an error in too much extending his line originally, he committed another and a more pregnant error in the mode of contracting it which he adopted.

The fatal consequences of these errors might have been escaped but for the act of that dangerous blunderhead McCook, who always imperils everything.

[C. A. DANA.]

[Hon. E. M. Stanton,
        Secretary of War.]

—

Chattanooga, *September* 24—8.30 p. m.

Reconnaissance in force to-day shows enemy encamped on Chattanooga Creek along base Lookout Mountain. Probably other camps east of Missionary Ridge on Chickamauga. No other places near here where an army can find water. No distinct evidence rebels intend attack Chattanooga, nor is it certain all Bragg's army is here, nor are there any signs he is moving elsewhere.

[C. A. DANA.]

[Hon. E. M. Stanton,
        Secretary of War.]

—

Chattanooga, *September* 25—10.30 a. m.

No demonstration from enemy. A captain of our cavalry out on scouting expedition with 35 men came in last night, making his way through Bragg's camps on Chickamauga east of Missionary Ridge. Led by a shrewd guide he came through by-ways in the woods, and was not seen till he reached infantry pickets at west base of ridge, and there he dashed through, losing 4 men. He reports the Chickamauga Valley full of rebels. Evidently gross of rebel army is there. McCook reports this morning from our right that noise of wagons and artillery moving was heard during the night. He thinks rebel force discovered on Chattanooga Creek by reconnaissance yesterday has been withdrawn from fear of being cut off, a thing Rosecrans had determined to try.

A negro brought in from Forrest's cavalry last night reports that since Monday 10,000 men have left Bragg for Mobile. Among our wounded prisoners are 10 or 12 who say they belong to General Ewell's corps. Rebel General Adams, wounded, in hospital here, says slaughter in their army was awful, and he has enough of war.

[C. A. DANA.]

[Hon. E. M. Stanton,
        Secretary of War.]

CHATTANOOGA, *September* 25—11.30 a. m.

Advices from Burnside received this morning. He was at Carter's Depot 23d ; had defeated rebels there and burned bridge. Was about to move hitherward with whole available force. Will probably get here about Wednesday next week.

[C. A. DANA.]

[Hon. E. M. STANTON,
 Secretary of War.]

—

CHATTANOOGA, *September* 25—9 p. m.

No change of importance. Rebels still remain in Chattanooga Valley ; report they had withdrawn erroneous. Telegraph cut to-day between here and Bridgeport. New line ordered on north side Tennessee.

[C. A. DANA].

[Hon. E. M. STANTON,
 Secretary of War.]

—

CHATTANOOGA, *September* 26—10 a. m.

Enemy pushed forward his pickets on our left at 5 a. m. to-day, driving in ours. Sharp skirmish ensued, rebels being driven at 6.30. General Palmer received severe flesh wound while standing in embrasure of one of our forts. Our loss otherwise inconsiderable. We took several prisoners from Breckinridge's division, who report the main rebel force encamped along Missionary Ridge. We have reports that rebel cavalry have appeared in Lookout Valley, threatening Bridgeport, but other evidence contradict them. R[osecrans] is about to lay a bridge across Tennessee at mouth of Lookout Creek, so that he can operate from here in that valley without crossing the mountain. Weather bright, cool, pleasant.

[C. A. DANA].

[Hon. E. M. STANTON,
 Secretary of War.]

—

CHATTANOOGA, *September* 27.

A very serious fermentation reigns in the Twentieth and Twenty-first Army Corps, and, indeed, throughout this whole army, growing out of events connected with the battle on Sunday last.

I have already reported that the generals of those two corps left the field of battle amid the rout of the right wing, made their way here with the crowd of fugitives, and went to sleep, while one division of each corps remained fighting with the left wing to the end. The generals of division and of brigade feel deeply this desertion of their commanders, and say, as I am informed on good evidence, for only two or three have spoken to me on the subject, that they can no longer serve under such superiors, and that if it is required of them they must resign. This feeling is universal among them, including men like Major-Generals Palmer and Sheridan and Brigadier-Generals Wood, Johnson, and Hazen. What is the sentiment of Davis I do not know, but I judge from his expressions on a kindred subject that he must agree with the others.

Of course this is a matter which I cannot directly inquire into, and cannot be so fully informed about as if it were an ordinary affair. The feeling in the case of McCook is deepened by the recollection of his faults at Perryville and Murfreesborough, and of the great waste of life which they caused ; while toward Crittenden it is relieved somewhat by consideration for his excellent heart, general good sense, and charming social qualities. Against these, however, is balanced the fact, which I can testify to from my own observation, that he is constantly wanting in attention to the duties of his command, never rides his lines, or exercises any special care for the well-being and safety of his troops, and, in fact, discharges no other function than that of a medium for the transmission of orders.

The feeling of the officers I have mentioned above does not seem in the least to partake of a mutinous or disorderly character; it is rather conscientious unwillingness to risk their men and the country's cause in hands proved to be so uncertain and unsafe. No formal representation of this unwillingness has been made to Rosecrans, but he has been made aware of the state of things by private conversations with several of the parties. The defects of his character complicate the difficulty. He abounds in friendliness and approbativeness, and is greatly lacking in firmness and steadiness of will. He is a temporizing man, dreads so heavy an alternative as is now presented, and hates to break with McCook and Crittenden. Besides, there is a more serious obstacle to his acting decisively in the fact that if Crittenden and McCook fled to Chattanooga, with the sound of artillery in their ears, from that glorious field where Thomas and Granger were saving their army and their country's honor, he fled also ; and although it may be said in his excuse that, under the circumstances, it was proper for the commanding general to go to his base of operations, while the corps commanders ought to remain with their troops, still he feels that that excuse cannot entirely clear him either in his own eyes or in those of the army. In fact, it is perfectly plain that while the subordinate commanders will not resign if he is retained in the chief command, as I believe they certainly will if McCook and Crittenden are not relieved, their respect for him as a general has received an irreparable blow. And that not from his abandonment of the army alone but from his faulty management on the field, especially in leaving a gap of a whole brigade distance between the divisions of Wood and Davis, and not providing for it till after the battle had become furious, when he attempted to fill it with Van Cleve's forces as I have explained in former reports. But for this gap General Davis thinks the enemy could not have broken his lines and routed the right wing. Thus you will see that here in the face of the enemy this army is in a dangerous condition. The officers who have taken this grave resolution are among the bravest and most discreet in our service. In my judgment the removal of Crittenden and McCook is imperatively required, not merely as a matter of discipline, but to preserve the efficacy, not to say the organization, of this army.

If it be decided to change the chief commander also, I would take the liberty of suggesting that some Western general of high rank and great prestige, like Grant, for instance, would be preferable as his successor to any one who has hitherto commanded in East alone.

I should add that Rosecrans himself intends to punish Negley for having withdrawn his division from the battle on Sunday without orders and with his ranks undisturbed, he having been directed to post himself behind Baird on the extreme left ; and all parties feel that Van Cleve ought to be relieved on account of his age, and the utter confusion of mind and incapacity which he manifested on Saturday and Sunday both.

C. A. DANA.

[Hon. E. M. STANTON,
      Secretary of War.]

—

CHATTANOOGA, *September* 28—4 a. m.

All quiet along the lines.   Enemy apparently lying still, except occasional picket skirmishing.   We are fortifying.   We know that rebels have force at all points in Chattanooga Valley in our front, but their principal camps are on the Chickamauga, just over Missionary Ridge.   Our signal officers have deciphered signals from their signal stations showing that Longstreet is still here.   We learn from prisoners and from a flag of truce Rosecrans sent out yesterday that two brigades of Longstreet's corps have come up since the battle. Bragg yesterday agreed to surrender our wounded after paroling them, and to allow supplies to be sent to those who cannot be moved. I go to Nashville to-day ; will be here again Thursday.

[C. A. DANA.]

[Hon. E. M. STANTON,
      Secretary of War.]

—

NASHVILLE, *September* 29—8 a. m.

Arrived here at 6 a. m.   All quiet at Bridgeport, except that pickets occasionally fire across the Tennessee.   No considerable rebel force in that vicinity.   Railroad bridge there will soon be done, and that over Running Water also ready to put up.   Hooker will first be stationed at Wauhatchie in Lookout Valley, at the junction of the Chattanooga and Trenton and Memphis and Charleston Railroads.   Weather warm, pleasant.

[C. A. DANA.]

[Hon. E. M. STANTON,
      Secretary of War.]

—

NASHVILLE, *September* 29.

An intelligent refugee from Georgia arrived here yesterday.   His name is Upsham and he has a brother who is post quartermaster at Dalton, which place he left two days after Chickamauga battle.   He says that the facts he states were learned by him in his brother's office.

According to his report when Bragg retreated from Chattanooga he had but 25,000 men.   He was re-enforced by Longstreet, with the divisions of Hood and McLaws, 21,000 men ; together with Buckner, from East Tennessee, with 10,000; by Joe Johnston, from Mississippi, with the division of Breckinridge, 8,000 strong, and one brigade from McCown's division, about 3,000 strong, while Governor Brown furnished 15,000 Georgia militia armed with shot-guns and squirrel rifles, who were not to remain after the battle.

Upsham says Bragg had no intention to flank or outwit Rosecrans, but simply to crush his army, and that the result is felt to be failure. General Gillem tells me he will have the Northwestern Railroad to Reynoldsburg finished two months hence.

[C. A. DANA.]

[Hon. E. M. STANTON,
                Secretary of War.]

—

NASHVILLE, September 30.

Six thousand one hundred wounded are suddenly accumulated here from the battle-field of the Chickamauga, and, on representation of the medical officers that it is indispensable for the proper care of these wounded that Surgeon Clendenin, who has been or-- dered to West Virginia, should remain here for the present, I have taken the liberty to authorize it until you can be heard from. Please confirm or withdraw the permission thus given.

[C. A. DANA.]

[Hon. E. M. STANTON,
                Secretary of War.]

—

NASHVILLE, September 30.

Since my dispatch of the 27th, several officers of prominence and worth—such as General Garfield, General Wood, and Colonel Opdycke—have spontaneously waited upon me to represent the state of feeling in the army upon the subject of that dispatch.

They all confirm in the strongest manner the tenor of that report, and tell me in addition that the same conviction pervades all ranks; in fact, I was myself aware that the soldiers believed victory to be impossible so long as McCook and Crittenden command army corps. The other day, as General Rosecrans was making one of those little speeches to a group of men which it is his constant practice to deliver as he passes among them, a soldier asked him if General McCook still commanded the Twentieth Army Corps. "Yes," was the answer. "Then the right will be licked again," said the man ; and all the others agreed with him. This Colonel Opdycke represents as the unanimous sentiment respecting both the generals in question, and I have no doubt he is right.

I learn also, confidentially, from these officers and others, that the soldiers have lost their attachment for General Rosecrans since he failed them in the battle, and that they now do not cheer him until they are ordered to do so by officers.

On the other hand, General Thomas has risen to the highest point in their esteem, as he has in that of every one who witnessed his conduct on that unfortunate and glorious day ; and should there be a change in the chief command, there is no other man whose appointment would be so welcome to this army. I would earnestly recommend that in such an event his merits be considered. He is certainly an officer of the very highest qualities, soldierly and personal. He refused before because a battle was imminent and he unacquainted with the combinations. No such reason now exists, and I presume that he would accept.

[C. A. DANA.]

[Hon. E. M. STANTON,
        Secretary of War.]

—

NASHVILLE, *September* 30.

Nothing important occurred at Chattanooga yesterday. Four regiments, Steinwehr's division, passed through here to Bridgeport last night. One division of Sherman's corps arrived at Louisville yesterday. I return to Chattanooga this afternoon.

[C. A. DANA.]

[Hon. E. M. STANTON,
        Secretary of War.]

—

CHATTANOOGA, *October* 3—12 m.

Yours of 30th arrived here at midnight last night. Wheeler, with a force of cavalry, forded the Tennessee Wednesday night [30th] at various places above and below Washington. The highest statement concerning this force is that it consisted of two divisions ; the lowest, two brigades. Crook, with two small brigades, was lying along the river watching the fords, but was unable to prevent the rebels from crossing.

Immediately on receiving this news, Rosecrans ordered General Edward M. McCook with a division of cavalry about Bridgeport to hasten to the Sequatchie Valley to protect our wagon trains. McCook marched Thursday, but the violent storm that day prevented his reaching Anderson, the distance being 39 miles, in season, and Wheeler fell upon a train yesterday morning at the foot of the mountain where the road rises out of the Sequatchie Valley. The Twenty-first Kentucky Infantry, which was there to guard the wagons, made a gallant fight, but was driven back, and the wagons were destroyed. How many were lost is unknown, but probably from 250 to 300, all belonging to Fourteenth Corps. One-third of them contained ammunition. McCook being not far off soon attacked the rebels and drove them up the valley, but we have no particulars. When McCook was ordered up from Bridgeport, Burnside was also requested to send his cavalry down the west bank of the Tennessee to cut off Wheeler's retreat, and if he has done so it is hardly possible Wheeler should escape. Under Bragg's agreement, 1,742 Union wounded have been brought from Crawfish Spring within our lines, and about 750 remain in his hands, of whom one-third can be moved, leaving 500 severe cases which must remain. In return for those already delivered to us he demands an equal number of well men from among rebel prisoners taken at Chickamauga. This Rosecrans has decisively refused.

Of our surgeons, 52 were left behind with our wounded, and 4 rebel surgeons came into our hands. The latter Rosecrans released, and Bragg thereupon released 4 of ours, but refuses to release any more on the ground that we have detained rebel surgeons at the East contrary to the cartel, and Dr. Flewellen, Bragg's medical director, has notified our surgeons that they will not only be removed to Atlanta, but be confined in prison.

Dr. Perin, medical director, Department of the Cumberland, informs me that he has ample medical supplies, but is temporarily prevented from moving them here from Nashville by the monopoly of the road transporting soldiers. Of medical officers he has already received 8 from Saint Louis, but owing to Bragg's sequestration will need 30 more.

[C. A. DANA.]

[Hon. E. M. STANTON,
      Secretary of War.]

—

CHATTANOOGA, *October* 4—11 a. m.

No direct advices from McCook's cavalry since Rosecrans' dispatch to Halleck yesterday, but Colonel Palmer, of Anderson Cavalry, on western slope Walden's Ridge, reports last evening that enemy was hotly engaged by McCook, and was retreating toward McMinnville. That place was attacked yesterday morning by another detachment of Wheeler's which had moved by way of Pikeville. The telegraph to McMinnville being cut, no particulars have reached us. Stores at McMinnville moderate in amount. Hooker has been ordered to post strong detachments of Twelfth Corps along railroad till this raid is over.

No news of Burnside's cavalry, nor of Crook's cavalry brigade belonging to this army, which was concentrated after enemy had forced the passage of the Tennessee and started in pursuit. Affairs here unchanged; enemy apparently still in force from Lookout Mountain on west to Missionary Ridge on east.

Approximate returns from Chickamauga battle make our total loss 1,536 killed, 8,747 wounded, 4,998 missing.* Of cannon we lost 36 and captured 2. Of rebel prisoners we took 2,005. Assistant Surgeon Walton, Eighty-sixth Indiana, captured by rebels and since released, reports that he was on battle-field during Monday and Tuesday after contest, and carefully endeavored to ascertain enemy's comparative loss. He concludes it was double ours, and many Confederate officers thought so too. Even on Wednesday they had not yet finished burying their dead or begun to bury ours. The Atlanta Appeal of Wednesday last states that the rebel wounded had all been moved there from the field, except 2,500 cases which could not bear removal. Same paper says Bragg has two hundred guns, including some siege guns, bearing on Chattanooga.

I ask your attention to the case of General Negley. Being ordered to post himself behind Baird's division in the battle of Chickamauga, he seems to have sent one of his brigades somewhere to the left, but General Baird tells me it did not come to him. With the remainder of his force Negley took up a position out of fire in the rear, and a little to the left of the place from which he had been ordered to move, and there remained doing nothing till about noon, when the conflict had grown hot, when he marched his troops to Rossville without firing a shot, leaving the rest of Thomas' corps to fight the desperate battle without help from him. These facts were stated to me by

*See revised statement, p. 171.

R[osecrans], who, when I said Negley ought to be shot, answered, "That is my opinion." He added that he should have him punished, yet now he has determined to do nothing more than apply to have him relieved and ordered elsewhere.

Engineers are now engaged upon the pontoon bridge to cross the Tennessee at mouth of Lookout Creek. Nothing done yet on interior fortifications here, without which a very large garrison is necessary.

General Thomas desires me to say to you that he is deeply obliged to you for good opinion.

[C. A. DANA.]

[Hon. E. M. STANTON,
           Secretary of War.]

—

CHATTANOOGA, *October* 4—1 p. m.

Sheridan reports rebels very active building works on Lookout Mountain, and thinks they are massing cannon there.

[C. A. DANA.]

[Hon. E. M. STANTON,
           Secretary of War.]

—

CHATTANOOGA, *October* 5—9 a. m.

All quiet in front. Rebels seem to be intrenching themselves, but this cannot be positively known, as their lines are covered by woods. One of our trestle bridges over the Tennessee here gave way last night, owing to a rise in the river, and the other bridge threatens to fail. A new pontoon bridge will take their place to-day. Two 30-pounder Parrotts have arrived and are placed in Fort Wood, on our left. The largest rifle guns in this army previously were 3-inch.

At McMinnville the rebels captured a Tennessee infantry regiment, about 250 strong, also one locomotive and eleven cars, which they burned. Notice of their approach and full instructions had been sent there in season. Burnside telegraphed last night inquiring if it was true rebel cavalry had crossed Tennessee. As he was not only notified of the fact four days ago, but promised to send his cavalry in pursuit, this inquiry is astonishing. It proves that he has done nothing. Had he taken the proper measures to protect the left flank of this army this disaster could not have happened, and unless he acts now he will probably be responsible for worse calamities.

[C. A. DANA.]

[Hon. E. M. STANTON,
           Secretary of War.]

—

CHATTANOOGA, *October* 5, 1863.

I learn that part or all of my first report of the second day of the great battle was translated and shown about at Nashville on the evening of that day. Horace Maynard even repeated at Cincinnati, a few days ago, a whole sentence of it. General R. S. Granger is said to have had it. I have inquired of him respecting the facts, and suggest to you that I ought to have a new cipher with many more arbitrary words and combinations less easy to discover. You ought also to deal with your faithless subordinates who betrayed me.

[C. A. DANA.]

[Hon. E. M. STANTON,
    Secretary of War.]

CHATTANOOGA, *October 5.*

General R. S. GRANGER,
    Nashville:

GENERAL: I am informed that on the evening of the 20th ultimo, or soon afterward, you were in possession of part or all of a dispatch of mine to the Secretary of War. Will you kindly oblige me by telling me if my information be correct, and, if so, by whom this dispatch was communicated to you?

Yours, very respectfully,

C. A. DANA.

—

CHATTANOOGA, *October 5—4 p. m.*

About 1 o'clock rebels opened from batteries planted on eastern slope of Lookout Mountain, and also from 2 guns on the west base of Missionary Ridge, and have been firing steadily but not rapidly since. On Lookout and low spur thereof, which stretches eastwardly toward Chattanooga Creek, they fire 7 guns in all. They are apparently shooting to get the range. No damage done. Knoxville Register, now issued at Atlanta, says, in its impression of 3d instant, that Polk and Hindman have come to Atlanta under arrest, by order of General Bragg, for disobedience in second day's battle.

[C. A. DANA.]

[Hon. E. M. STANTON,
    Secretary of War.]

—

CHATTANOOGA, *October 6—4 p. m.*

Result of rebel bombardment yesterday was that 1 private artilleryman, Stanley's brigade, Negley's division, Fourteenth Corps, had foot shattered and leg amputated. No other casualty. Firing not yet resumed to-day. Chattanooga Rebel, 4th instant, published at Atlanta, says re-enforcements are constantly going forward to Bragg. Stevenson's division went up last Saturday. This is a Vicksburg division. Tennessee here fell 4 inches last night, and the remaining trestle bridge is safe for the present. New pontoon bridge nearly completed. A boom of heavy logs is being stretched across above the bridges to guard them against objects that may be sent down the river by the rebels. Baldy Smith, appointed chief engineer of the department, infuses much energy and judgment into that branch of the operations. The news of consolidation of the two corps reached here last night in a Nashville newspaper; not having been previously promulgated it caused sensation. Crittenden was much excited; said as the Government no longer required his services he would resign to-day. At any rate, he would not hibernate like others, drawing pay and doing no work. He has admirable qualities of character. McCook takes it easily.

Reports of corps, division, and brigade commanders in recent battle now nearly all in. Careful examination of them seems to prove that the gap in the lines through which the enemy poured, flanking and routing all of three divisions and a part of a fourth, was caused by an order of the commanding general. They prove also that there was much confusion and uncertainty in the general movements of the day, though the probability still remains very strong that but for this unfortunate order we should have gained a decisive victory.

To make the case clear to you, let me state the position of the various divisions. On the extreme left was Baird, supported by one brigade of Negley, which had moved there, leaving the remainder of division under Negley halting in rear of Brannan, though he had been ordered to move his whole force to support Baird. Next to Baird was Palmer; next to Palmer, Johnson; next to Johnson, Reynolds. At least such was the original order, but after the line was formed, a gap appearing between Johnson and Reynolds, and the latter having no reserve, inasmuch as his third brigade, Wilder's, being mounted, was detached and posted on the extreme right, under McCook, Brannan's reserve brigade was marched into this gap and fought there. Next to Reynolds, on his right, stood Brannan, and next to Brannan, in the original line, Negley. When that line was formed Wood and Van Cleve, of Crittenden's corps, were both held in reserve, while McCook with the two divisions remaining under his command, Davis' and Sheridan's, flanked on the right by Wilder's mounted infantry, was to hold the right, and also to be ready to re-enforce the left when necessary. On taking Negley out to support Baird, Wood, of Crittenden's corps, was ordered to fill Negley's place and did so, having Davis closed in upon his right, as McCook maintains, though Davis tells me that there was always a space between him and Wood. However that may be, it is now certain that the fatal gap was caused by an order of Rosecrans issued at fifteen minutes before 11 a. m. R[osecrans] had been informed by a staff officer of Thomas' that Brannan had been ordered out of the line to support the extreme left, and supposing him to have left the line accordingly, R[osecrans] sent a written order to Wood "to close up on Reynolds and support him." When Wood received this order he was, as he says, in some doubt about obeying it, as Brannan was between him and Reynolds, and thus he could not close up on Reynolds, but supposing from the additional words, " and support him," that Reynolds must be hard pressed and in danger, he at once took his command out of the line and marched past the rear of Brannan to the rear of Reynolds' right, where he found that Reynolds needed no support. McCook endeavored to close the vacancy thus left by Wood by moving Davis to the left, but before this could be accomplished, the enemy had broken through and all was over in that part of the field.

Had Wood remained in the line, there is little reason to doubt that the partial repulse which the enemy suffered from our diminished forces later in the day would have been changed into a complete and final victory for us.

General Rosecrans says that in obeying this order Wood was guilty of an error of judgment; that he should have seen in the fact that it required him to close up on Reynolds evidence that it was based on mistaken information, and should therefore have remained where he was. To this Wood replies that he was partially of that opinion, but that he consulted General McCook, who was with him at the moment, and the latter advised him not to take the responsibility of disobeying a written order, especially as he could not know what was passing on the part of the field where he was ordered to go.

I judge from intimations that have reached me that in writing his own report General Rosecrans will elaborately show that the blame of his failure in this great battle rests on the Administration; that is, on the Secretary of War and General-in-Chief, who did not foresee Bragg would be re-enforced, and who compelled him to move forward without cavalry enough, and very inadequately prepared in many other respects.

[C. A. DANA.]

[Hon. E. M. STANTON,
   Secretary of War.]

—

CHATTANOOGA, *October* 8—8 a. m.

We have heard nothing of Burnside since the 4th, nor anything positive from his troops. But some things have occurred in the rebel lines which give ground for the surmise that he is executing the third of the plans he proposed ten days since. That plan was to throw out a flanking force toward the enemy's army before Chattanooga, and with his main body to move rapidly, without baggage, against Dalton, Rome, and Atlanta, destroying railroad and bridges as he went along, and after burning depots and shops in the three places above mentioned, strike for the Atlantic coast.

Now, on the 5th instant, cannonade was heard in the direction of Ringgold, and on the 6th, forenoon, the sounds of a battle were distinguished east of Missionary Ridge, in that direction.

More than this, the combat was actually witnessed on that day by one of the signal stations from Walden's Ridge, by two civilians, and Col. Daniel McCook, from his post at the mouth of Chickamauga. It lasted for some hours, and from the descriptions of the witnesses, none of whom, however, saw it near enough to distinguish who the combatants actually were, it was the attempt of a weak party to resist the advance of a strong one. In addition to this evidence, on the night of the 6th the whole rebel camps were in motion as if they were about to retreat, and their guns on Lookout Mountain were all brought down. Now, this was either a conflict with Burnside's flanking column or a mutiny, more probably the former. An intelligent deserter who came in last night, and who arrived in Chattanooga Valley on the 5th, knows nothing of any such engagement. This deserter, a paroled man from Vicksburg, reports that all the troops captured there are being brought back into service.

[C. A. DANA.]

[Hon. E. M. STANTON,
   Secretary of War.]

—

CHATTANOOGA, *October* 8—10 a. m.

All our reports show that Wheeler broke up railroad, destroyed bridges between Wartrace and Murfreesborough. At M[urfreesborough] sacked the town but did nothing to fortifications. Wheeler sent detachment, about 2,000, to Wartrace, where Colonel Lowe overtook them, afternoon of 6th, just as they were about to fire the town, and after they had burned railroad bridge, fought them an hour, drove them toward Shelbyville, and pursued 3 miles till stopped by darkness.   On 7th, Mitchell, with main cavalry force, Crook having joined him, overtook them at Shelbyville [Farmington] and put them to flight, killing 100 and capturing 200.   Butterfield, who came up during this action with Lowe's cavalry and a regiment of Granger's infantry from Wartrace, reports that Mitchell will probably capture and destroy all of Wheeler's force.

[C. A. DANA.]

[Hon. E. M. Stanton,
          Secretary of War.]

—

CHATTANOOGA, *October* 8—11 a. m.

A sergeant of Fifth (rebel) Kentucky Regiment, who deserted to us this morning, says it was understood in the rebel camps in Chattanooga Valley that the firing beyond Missionary Ridge on the 6th was occasioned by the refusal of a brigade of Georgia militia, 5,000 strong, to cross the State line.   The result of fight deserter does not know.

[C. A. DANA.]

[Hon. E. M. Stanton,
          Secretary of War.]

—

CHATTANOOGA, *October* 8.

General Rousseau, who seems to be regarded throughout this army as an ass of eminent gifts, having reported to General Thomas that you had inquired how the army would like to have him in the chief command, that officer has sent a confidential friend to me to say that while he would gladly accept any command out of this department to which you might see fit to assign him, he could not consent to become the successor of General Rosecrans, because he would not do anything to give countenance to the suspicion that he had intrigued against his commander.   Besides he has as perfect confidence in capacity and fidelity of Rosecrans as he had in those of General Buell.

[C. A. DANA.]

[Hon. E. M. Stanton,
          Secretary of War.]

—

CHATTANOOGA, *October* 8—1 p. m.

The consolidation of the two corps is universally well received, and being followed by a general reorganization of the army, with consolidation of reduced regiments and new and more equal combinations of brigades and divisions, must produce the most happy consequences.   The men, however, of the consolidated corps are somewhat troubled by letters from home, showing that their friends regard the consolidation as a token of disgrace and punishment.   It is very desirable to obviate any such feeling, especially as of the six divisions composing the consolidated corps, three fought with heroism and success throughout the battle. Will it not then be practicable to publish an order at Washington, complimenting the steadiness and gallantry of the two corps, and putting the consolidation on the ground of the great reduction in their numbers, and especially on necessity of rendering our brigades numerically more equal to those of the enemy against which they are sent to fight?

[C. A. DANA.]

[Hon. E. M. STANTON,
        Secretary of War.]

—

CHATTANOOGA, *October* 9—11 a. m.

Deserters yesterday reported Bragg making hard bread and constructing pontoons at La Fayette. Last evening our pickets reported his troops to be felling trees in front as if to obstruct roads. Pickets this morning, however, seem to have noticed nothing of the sort during the night, nor is any special symptom reported. Bragg's force is now said by some deserters to be 80,000, by others 125,000.

Chattanooga Rebel of 6th, published at Marietta, contains Polk's farewell to his soldiers on being relieved. He says he retires from the army. Cheatham succeeds to the command of corps. Same paper says these are reports. Jeff. Davis on his way to the seat of war in Tennessee. It also publishes a letter from Davis to Confederate Society, of Enterprise, Miss., formed to keep currency at par with gold. He says:

The passion for speculation has seduced citizens of all classes from a determined prosecution of the war to a sordid effort to amass money.

And also—

I am burdened by the complaining and despondent letters of many who have stood all the day idle, and now blame anybody but themselves for reverses which have come and dangers which threaten.

[C. A. DANA.]

[Hon. E. M. STANTON,
        Secretary of War.]

—

[OCTOBER 9]—12.30 p. m.

An intelligent Union citizen who has just got in from beyond rebel lines reports Bragg's main body retreating to Dalton. Forage very scarce with rebels as with us. We are now losing some twenty animals daily of starvation, in addition to the usual mortality.

Work on interior fortifications actively begun. When finished, with garrison of 10,000 men, Chattanooga will be absolutely impregnable.

I desire to call your attention to the fact that there are too few telegraph operators between Chattanooga and Nashville, and that many of those we have are drunken, worthless fellows, who should be dismissed immediately.

[C. A. DANA.]

[Hon. E. M. STANTON,
        Secretary of War.]

Chattanooga, *October* 10—2 p. m.

No demonstration from enemy. Union people from Cleveland report Bragg's main body retiring to Dalton. General Pillow has taken command of conscript bureau at Marietta. Buckner has taken command of Polk's corps. Lieutenant-Colonel Napier, commanding Eighth Georgia Battalion, advertises $2,800 reward for 96 deserters from seven companies.

President Davis is positively announced as on his way to visit Bragg's army.

The reorganization of our forces here, consequent on consolidation of the two corps, is nearly complete. The combination of divisions and brigades is as follows:

Fourth Corps.—First Division, Major-General Palmer: First Brigade, Cruft, nine regiments, 2,044 men; Second Brigade, Brigadier-General Whitaker, eight regiments, 2,035 men; Third Brigade, Colonel Grose, eight regiments, 1,968 men. Second Division, Sheridan: First Brigade, Brigadier-General Steedman, ten regiments, 2,385 men; Second Brigade, Brigadier-General Wagner, eight regiments, 2,188 men; Third Brigade, Colonel Harker, 2,026 men. Third Division, Wood: First Brigade, Willich, nine regiments, 2,069 men; Second Brigade, Brigadier-General Hazen, nine regiments, 2,195 men; Third Brigade, Brig. Gen. Samuel Beatty, eight regiments, 2,222 men.

Fourteenth Corps.—First Division, Rousseau: First Brigade, Brigadier-General Carlin, nine regiments, 2,072 men; Second Brigade, Brigadier-General King, four regiments regulars and four regiments volunteers, 2,070 men; Third Brigade, Brigadier-General Starkweather, eight regiments, 2,214 men. Second Division, J. C. Davis: First Brigade, Morgan, five regiments, 2,285 men; Second Brigade, Brig. Gen. John Beatty, seven regiments, 2,460 men; Third Brigade, Col. Daniel McCook, six regiments, 2,099 men. Third Division, Brigadier-General Baird: First Brigade, Turchin, seven regiments, 2,175 men; Second Brigade, Colonel Van Derveer, seven regiments, 2,116 men; Third Brigade, Colonel Croxton, seven regiments, 2,165 men.

This does not include those portions of the late Reserve Corps which still remain as garrisons along the railroad and elsewhere in Tennessee. It does, however, include the troops under General Morgan who have occupied Stevenson, Bridgeport, and Battle Creek until relieved by Hooker. It is intended to divide Tennessee into two districts, the northern commanded by General R. S. Granger, having his headquarters at Nashville, and the southern under General Johnson, having his headquarters at Stevenson.

The department staff is also reorganized by the appointment of Major-General Reynolds chief of staff, General Smith chief engineer, and General Brannan chief of artillery. The artillery, heretofore serving one battery with each brigade, will now be attached to divisions only, three batteries to each division, the remainder being organized as a reserve.

These changes, and especially the remarkable strength of the new staff, cannot fail to add much to the discipline and efficiency of the army.

McCook and Crittenden have just left.

[C. A. DANA.]

[Hon. E. M. Stanton,
      Secretary of War.]

CHATTANOOGA, *October* 10—5 p. m.

Rebels are holding reviews to-day, and troops hitherto posted near Lookout Mountain have been moved east to Missionary Ridge for this purpose. Possibly Jefferson Davis is with them.

[C. A. DANA.]

[Hon. E. M. STANTON,
    Secretary of War.]

—

CHATTANOOGA, *October* 11—9 a. m.

The dispatch disclosed was the first one of September 20. General R. S. Granger explains that, being very anxious for news, he went with General Gillem to the telegraph office as my dispatch was passing through, some portions of which were guessed at by the operator. The person who guessed out the dispatch was Mr. Smith, who informed us at the time "it was mere surmise, as he had no key to the cipher." It is rather curious, however, that the agent of the Associated Press at Louisville, in a private printed circular, quoted me as authority for reporting the battle as a total defeat, while Horace Maynard repeated in Cincinnati the entire second sentence of the dispatch. If practicable, send me a cipher whose meaning no operator can guess out.

[C. A. DANA.]

Major ECKERT.

—

CHATTANOOGA, *October* 12—8 a. m.

Reports arrived last night from up the river to the effect that the rebels are concentrating a force on the Hiwassee at a point about 12 miles from its mouth. These reports lack confirmation, but they are very probable, and agree with the apparent disappearance of Longstreet from our front.

If a serious attempt should be made by Bragg to march into Kentucky, this army will find itself in a very helpless and dangerous position. Owing to the destruction of our wagon train by Wheeler, on the 2d instant, with all the forage on board which had been brought to Stevenson, and the subsequent occupation of the railroad transporting Hooker's troops, with its interruption by Wheeler and by guerrillas, our animals have had no regular supply of forage for ten days. Corn enough has been hauled from the Sequatchie Valley, from the Tennessee bottoms below Bridgeport, and from places up the river 30 and 40 miles distant, to furnish the mass of the animals with about quarter rations, while all that could be sent away have been taken to Stevenson to be fed as best they might. The result is that a large number, say 250, have died of starvation, in addition to the usual mortality, and those which remain are already so debilitated as to render impracticable any efficient attack or pursuit of the enemy marching through East Tennessee toward Kentucky.

Nor is this all. We have now on hand here but two days' rations for the troops, with bad mountain roads from hence to the west base of Walden's Ridge, while from thence to Bridgeport the roads pass through the bottoms of the Sequatchie and the Tennessee, which a little rain will render impracticable.

In addition to all this the road used for empty trains from here to Walden's Ridge was yesterday rendered impassable by a few rebel sharpshooters posted on the south bank of the river at a place some 5 miles from here, where this road runs for a mile or so along the bank. It is true that we have here at Chattanooga one steamboat in good running order which can navigate the river with 27 inches water, and that another is nearly completed at Bridgeport which will run with 12 inches, and that flat-boats for towage have been prepared there. Could the river be used, 400 tons freight might daily be delivered here. But the same military error which gave the enemy control of the south shore between here and Bridgeport, and which is illustrated by the stoppage of our trains by sharpshooters, deprives us of the power of using our steamboats, and also prevents our rebuilding and using the railroad between here and Bridgeport. That error is the abandonment of Lookout Mountain to the rebels. Immediately after the retreat to Chattanooga, Rosecrans ordered the withdrawal of Spears' brigade, which held the head of the mountain, and the destruction of the wagon road which winds along its side at about one-third of its height and connects the valleys of Chattanooga and Lookout. Both Granger and Garfield earnestly protested against this order and contended that the mountain and the road could be held by not more than seven regiments against the whole power of the enemy, whether he should attack from below or, passing up Stevens' Gap, make his approach by the road extending longitudinally upon the crest. There can, I think, be no question that they were right, but Rosecrans, who is sometimes as obstinate and inaccessible to reason as at others he is irresolute, vacillating, and inconclusive, pettishly rejected all their arguments, and the mountain was given up. It is difficult to say which was the greater error, this order or that which on the day of battle created the gap in our lines. At any rate, such is our present situation ; our animals starved and the men with starvation before them, and the enemy bound to make desperate efforts to dislodge us. In the midst of this the commanding general devotes that part of the time which is not employed in pleasant gossip to the composition of a long report to prove that the Government is to blame for his failure. It is my duty to declare that while few persons exhibit more estimable social qualities, I have never seen a public man possessing talent with less administrative power, less clearness and steadiness in difficulty, and greater practical incapacity than General Rosecrans. He has inventive fertility and knowledge, but he has no strength of will and no concentration of purpose. His mind scatters; there is no system in the use of his busy days and restless nights, no courage against individuals in his composition, and, with great love of command, he is a feeble commander. He is conscientious and honest, just as he is imperious and disputatious; always with a stray vein of caprice and an overweening passion for the approbation of his personal friends and the public outside.

Under the present circumstances I consider this army to be very unsafe in his hands ; but do know of no man except Thomas who could now be safely put in his place. Weather pleasant but cloudy.

[C. A. DANA.]

Hon. E. M. Stanton,
    Secretary of War.

—

Chattanooga, *October* 12—1 p. m.

A rebel deserter, who came in this morning, reports Jeff. Davis reviewed Bragg's army Saturday, riding through lines, but not addressing troops. Bragg, he says, has one hundred and thirty pontoons already finished in Chickamauga Valley, and is building more to cross the Tennessee.

[C. A. DANA.]

Hon. E. M. STANTON,
    [*Secretary of War.*]

—

CHATTANOOGA, *October* 12—9 p. m.

Would it not be possible for General Halleck to come here? What is needed to extricate this army is the highest administrative talent, and that without delay. Weather cloudy ; rain threatened.

[C. A. DANA.]

Hon. E. M. STANTON,
    [*Secretary of War.*]

—

CHATTANOOGA, *October* 13—10.30 a. m.

No demonstrations from the enemy. Granger, who rode the picket lines yesterday afternoon, is convinced that Bragg's main body is still here. We have, however, pretty good reason for believing that Ector's, McNair's, and Ormes' [?] brigades have gone to Mobile. We had heavy rain all night ; still raining.

[C. A. DANA.]

Hon. E. M. STANTON,
    [*Secretary of War.*]

—

CHATTANOOGA, *October* 14—12 m.

After thirty-six hours heavy rain there is now a prospect of clearing up. The river has risen 8 or 10 inches, and General Smith has ordered the trestle bridge to be taken up, leaving only the new pontoon bridge to connect us with the north side. The roads have been greatly injured by the storm, one of them, the Anderson road, used by the loaded wagons, having been rendered impracticable on the eastern side of the mountain.

In the Sequatchie and Tennessee bottoms all the roads must be nearly spoiled, but no reports from them have yet arrived. Some forage got in here yesterday, and we hear from Bridgeport that a train load of forage has got there from Nashville, but it is clearly impossible to haul, from Bridgeport here, both food for men and forage for animals. All the forage in the country near here is exhausted and the chief quartermaster reports that there is none left in the Sequatchie Valley, the only region within convenient reach where it could be procured. A wagon train loaded with rations got here yesterday, and last night we had here 300,000 full rations. The troops now receive but three-quarter rations.

The necessity of opening the river being thus imperative, General Rosecrans has ordered Hooker to concentrate his troops preparatory to seizing the passes of Raccoon Mountain and occupying Shell-mound, and, if possible, Lookout Valley. If this can be done we shall greatly shorten our lines of wagon transportation ; if we could regain Lookout Mountain we could use water all the way. Deserters from the enemy report Jeff. Davis as still in Bragg's camp. Pemberton is there also, and some say Lee. Davis made a speech on

Sunday, the 11th instant, in which he said that they would have East Tennessee again, even if they had to withdraw every man from Richmond and Charleston. A captain of Arkansas cavalry, who deserted to us this morning, and of whose honesty we have proofs, says that only one brigade has gone from Bragg to Mobile, and that another has taken its place. He says an additional force of 30,000 men is promised to Bragg's soldiers, and that the conviction everywhere prevails among both people and army that unless they can recover East Tennessee the Confederacy is ruined. Having lost Texas they have no other place to procure cattle. The official report of rebel killed and wounded at Chickamauga makes the number 17,000. Efforts are anxiously made here to complete our inner fortifications. Were they finished 10,000 men could hold this place against the world, leaving the rest of the army to operate against the enemy, or to retire to points where it could be more easily subsisted while covering the approaches to Chattanooga. But by some strange improvidence the needful tools are not here, and instead of working 10,000 men per day, General Smith is only able to work 1,000.

Before General McCook left, General Rosecrans gave him a letter stating that McCook had never disobeyed an order.

The Ohio soldiers voted yesterday almost unanimously for Brough. So far I hear 249 for Vallandigham.

[C. A. DANA.]

Hon. E. M. STANTON,
　　　[*Secretary of War.*]

—

CHATTANOOGA, October 14—1.30 p. m.

Atlanta Intelligencer of yesterday has report of Jeff. Davis' visit to Bragg's army. He arrived at the camp on the evening of the 10th, reviewed the troops on the 11th, and was to return to Atlanta on the 13th. Intelligencer says he was received with great enthusiasm by troops, which is false. Raining here again.

[C. A. DANA.]

Hon. E. M. STANTON,
　　　[*Secretary of War.*]

—

CHATTANOOGA, October 14—8 p. m.

The Ohio regiments in this army, so far as heard from, have cast for Brough 9,234 votes, for Vallandigham 252. Eleven regiments infantry, four cavalry, and eight batteries still to be heard from. This does not include regiments under Hooker.

[C. A. DANA.]

Hon. E. M. STANTON,
　　　[*Secretary of War.*]

—

CHATTANOOGA, October 15—10 a. m.

Rain continued through the night with great violence and still falling. Barometer indicates no change. Sequatchie River has risen so that it can no longer be forded near Jasper, and all wagons are now compelled to make the circuit to Therman, while the mud in the roads constantly grows deeper. Work on the fortifications and movements of troops are alike stopped by the rain. Troops here receiving half rations. It will soon become necessary for all persons except soldiers to leave here. Shall I then return to Washington or endeavor to make my way to Burnside?

[C. A. DANA.]

Hon. E. M. STANTON,
[*Secretary of War.*]

—

CHATTANOOGA, *October* 16—12 m.

For fifteen hours little rain has fallen, but the skies remain threatening and the barometer still points to rain. The river has risen some 4 feet, and old boatmen predict a rise of 6 feet more. Our bridge was broken by drift-wood at 10 p. m. yesterday, but all the pontoons and chess planks were saved. The rebels sent down two or three rafts to break it, but they came after it was broken. The steamer Paint Rock and a flat-boat were employed during the night in gathering these masses of floating timber, much of which may prove useful. The bridge is not yet replaced, it being thought more prudent to wait till to-morrow when the rise will be complete and the drift will have mainly passed down.

Our couriers report that from Bridgeport to the foot of the mountain the mud is up to their horses' bellies. The mortality among animals here rapidly increases, and those remaining must soon perish. Day before yesterday the mules attached to the empty train returning to Bridgeport were too weak to haul the wagons up the mountain without doubling the teams, though they went on the easiest of all our roads, which had just been put in thorough order. General Brannan tells me he could not possibly haul away the artillery with the horses that are left.

I think I reported some time ago that all the artillery horses, except four per gun, had been sent to Stevenson to be fed, but those that are there are so far reduced that it will require a month's feeding to make them effective.

Nothing can prevent the retreat of the army from this place within a fortnight, and with a vast loss of public property and possibly of life, except the opening of the river. General Hooker has been ordered to prepare for this, but Rosecrans thinks he cannot move till his transportation arrives from Nashville, from which place it marched on the 8th. It should have been in Bridgeport on the 14th, but is not yet reported. The telegraph between there and here is broken, however, and it now requires ten to twelve hours for couriers to make the distance.

In the midst of all these difficulties General Rosecrans seems to be insensible to the impending danger, and dawdles with trifles in a manner which can scarcely be imagined. Having completed his report, which he sent off for Washington by General Garfield yesterday, he is now much occupied with the map of the battle-field and with the topography of the country between here and Burnside's lower posts. Most probably the enemy contemplates crossing in that region, but we are no longer able to pursue him, hardly to strike a sudden blow at his flank before he shall have crushed Burnside. Meanwhile, with plenty of zealous and energetic officers ready to do whatever can be done, all this precious time is lost because our dazed and mazy commander cannot perceive the catastrophe that is close upon us, nor fix his mind upon the means of preventing it.   I never saw anything which seemed so lamentable and hopeless.

A rebel officer last evening shouted to one of our pickets that Bragg had been relieved and either Johnston or Longstreet put in his place.

Reports from our cavalry, which Rosecrans will forward to-day, make the rebel loss in the recent raid 2,000 men and five guns. Thirty-eight men captured in our uniform were summarily executed. Nothing heard from forces of Sherman.

[C. A. DANA.]

Hon. E. M. Stanton,
  [Secretary of War.]

—

CHATTANOOGA, October 16—4 p. m.

I have just had a full conversation with General Rosecrans upon the situation.   He says the possession of the river as far up as the head of Williams' Island, at least, is a sine qua non to the holding of Chattanooga, but that it is impossible for him to make any movement toward gaining such possession until General Hooker's troops are concentrated and his transportation gets up.   Hooker's troops are now scattered along the line of the railroad, and cannot be got together before next Wednesday.   The wagons must all have arrived by that time, and if the enemy does not interfere sooner the movement upon Raccoon Mountain and Lookout Valley may then be attempted.   Rosecrans, however, expects that as soon as the weather will allow the enemy will cross the river in force on our left, and then it will be necessary for us to fight a battle, or else to retreat from here and attempt to hold the line of the Cumberland Mountains.   Such movement against this army he thinks will be made only in the event that they accumulate here a force enormously superior to ours, so that we should fight, if at all, at a great disadvantage.   It is his opinion that they are collecting such a force, because, first, it is a military probability ; secondly, we hear of their gathering men here from every place whence troops can be scraped ; thirdly, most of the deserters represent their numbers as greatly increased, and a smart negro boy, who came in this morning, said that two train loads arrived at Chickamauga Station yesterday, and they are coming all the time.   But General Rosecrans says he inclines to the opinion that they will rather attempt to crush Burnside first. The same negro boy reports that he heard Jefferson Davis say in a speech at Chickamauga Station last Saturday that they would have East Tennessee if it took every soldier in the South.

When I suggested that his animals were too weak to move the army with any promptness and efficacy, Rosecrans answered that the case was by no means so bad as I supposed.   It was true, he said, that the mules were a great deal worn down, but both they and the artillery horses were still capable of use.   But even if he could get along without being obliged to evacuate Chattanooga, he said it was certain that even with Hooker he is too weak for any offensive movement.   It is his opinion that 100,000 to 125,000 men is the smallest army with which a movement can be made upon Atlanta, with reasonable certainty of success.

[C. A. DANA.]

Hon. E. M. Stanton,
  [Secretary of War.]

CHATTANOOGA, *October* 17—10 a. m.

Skies clear; barometer indicates fair weather. Courier from Burnside reports rains much heavier in East Tennessee than here, and streams more swollen. Tennessee here still rising, but Sequatchie falling. Wagons will probably be able to ford near Jasper to-day. Colonel Atkins, commanding at Dallas [Harrison's Landing?], reports some small indications of rebel purpose to cross in that vicinity.

Atlanta papers of 13th report that previous to Jeff. Davis' visit here he sent an aide, who reported that the dissensions in Bragg's army could only be composed by Davis himself. Deserters report rebel bridge across Chickamauga carried away, and army on short rations in consequence.

No news from Sherman. Weather warm.

[C. A. DANA.]

Hon. E. M. STANTON,
    [*Secretary of War.*]

—

CHATTANOOGA, *October* 17—11 a. m.

The general organization of this army is inefficient and its discipline defective. The former proceeds from the fact that General R[osecrans] insists on personally directing every department, and keeps every one waiting and uncertain till he himself can directly supervise every operation. The latter proceeds from his utter lack of firmness, his passion for universal applause, and his incapacity to hurt any man's feelings by just severity. It is certain that if it had been left to him, McCook and Crittenden might have lost other battles and fled from other fields without a word of censure. As I have already reported, McCook got from him a whitewashing letter, and Crittenden might have got one had he not been too proud to ask for it. In the same way he gave Negley a similar letter, although he had repeatedly declared that he ought to be shot, and although the official reports of General Brannan, General Wood, and Colonel Harker leave no doubt of his guilt. I learn, on the best evidence, that a few months ago General Stanley defeated an important operation by being drunk at the critical moment, and that he has repeatedly been guilty of that offense while in the discharge of most important duties in the field, yet General Rosecrans has never taken any notice of the fact. He cannot bear to hurt Stanley's feelings, and prefers, instead, to jeopardize the cause of the country. Another illustration is found in the case of General Rousseau, who is discontented because he only commands a division. General Rosecrans told me on Thursday that he was thinking of giving him the command of all Tennessee lately held by Granger, and requiring all his extraordinary talent, quickness, and energy.

There is thus practically no discipline for superior officers, and of course the evil, though less pernicious in the lower grades, is everywhere perceptible.

[C. A. DANA.]

Hon. E. M. STANTON,
    [*Secretary of War.*]

—

CHATTANOOGA, *October* 18—11 a. m.

Rain began again about midnight and still continues, but the barometer is rising and the wind has shifted, so that we hope for the final cessation of the storm.   Meanwhile, our condition and prospects grow worse and worse.   The roads are in such a state that wagons are eight days making the journey from Stevenson to Chattanooga, and some which left on the 10th have not yet arrived. Though subsistence stores are so nearly exhausted here, the wagons are compelled to throw overboard portions of their precious cargo in order to get through at all.   The returning trains have now for some days been stopped on this side of the Sequatchie, and a civilian who reached here last night states that he saw fully five hundred teams halted between the mountain and the river, without forage for the animals and unable to move in any direction.

I rode through the camps here yesterday, and can testify that my previous reports respecting the starvation of the battery horses were not exaggerated.   A few days more and most of them will be dead. If the effort which Rosecrans intends to make to open the river should be futile, the immediate retreat of this army will follow.   It does not seem possible to hold out here another week without a new avenue of supplies.   General Smith says that as he passed among the men working on the fortifications yesterday several shouted "crackers" at him.

Amid all this, the practical incapacity of the general commanding is astonishing, and it often seems difficult to believe him of sound mind.   His imbecility appears to be contagious, and it is difficult for any one to get anything done.

The pontoon bridge broken three days ago is not yet replaced, though every part is ready to be laid.   The telegraph is broken by our pioneers as fast as it is re-established, and the steamboat is rendered useless by the carelessness or wantonness of her crew, while the work on the fortifications is carried on so slowly that they might as well be abandoned ; and if the army is finally obliged to retreat, the probability is that it will fall back like a rabble, leaving its artillery, and protected only by the river behind it.   If, on the other hand, we regain control of the river and keep it, subsistence and forage can be got here, and we may escape with no worse misfortune than the loss of 12,000 animals.

[C. A. DANA.]

Hon. E. M. STANTON,
        [*Secretary of War.*]

No. 7.

*Report of Surg. Glover Perin, U. S. Army, Medical Director,
Department of the Cumberland.*

HDQRS. DEPARTMENT OF THE CUMBERLAND,
            MEDICAL DIRECTOR'S OFFICE,
                Chattanooga, February —, 1864.

SIR : I have the honor to transmit herewith a nominal list* of the wounded at the battle of Chickamauga, together with report from the medical directors of the corps, giving brief accounts of such points as relate to the operations of the medical department.

In this place I would beg leave to review briefly the medical history of the movement which led to the great battle of Chickamauga,

---

* Embodied in revised statement, p. 171.

as well as to add some further details of what occurred during and subsequent to that event.

Soon after joining this army, in February, 1863, my attention was directed, first, to the diet of the men, the method of cooking, &c., which resulted in the publication of Department General Orders, No. 76. The medical officers generally took a great interest in the matter, and I may safely say the health of the command was much improved in consequence. While this subject was receiving the attention it deserved, a large tent hospital was established near the railroad, on the banks of Stone's River, of capacity sufficient to accommodate 1,500 patients. This hospital was provided, as far as practicable, with movable furniture, such as light cots of the Chicago pattern, bed sacks, camp kettles, &c. As soon as the tents were erected, patients were sent to that point instead of to the hospitals in the town of Murfreesborough. A large garden was planted near the field hospital, which soon afforded an abundant harvest of vegetables.

Ambulance trains were organized in accordance with the provisions of Department General Orders, No. 41, and subsequently modified by Paragraph I, Department General Orders, No. 62, series 1863. I will remark, in this connection, that the ambulance trains were generally well served in this organization, but there were grave defects, among which I may mention that the ambulance master was not a commissioned officer and could not, consequently, exercise the authority necessary to secure efficiency; next, there were no men detailed to assist in placing the wounded in or in taking them out of the ambulance. The ambulances were receipted for and held under the control of the quartermaster's department.

The regimental ambulances were found to be almost useless for general service in transporting wounded, because they were used as carriages and for transporting personal baggage and other freights, so that, when required for legitimate use, they were either out of order or the animals were broken down.

So seriously were these defects experienced that I recommended for adoption the plan of an ambulance corps and train arranged upon the same basis as that in use in the Army of the Potomac. (See Department General Orders, No. 2, current series.)

In the month of May and early in June the regiments drew supplies for three months; reserve supplies were also provided for each army corps, consisting mostly of those articles required for the treatment of wounded men, and a reserve supply of hospital tents. Each regiment was allowed a hospital tent.

During the month of May the sick were sent to Nashville as fast as a due regard for their welfare would permit, so that by the time the army was ready to make the advance, there was enough room in the various hospitals of Murfreesborough to accommodate all that could not march.

The buildings used as hospitals in the town were vacated first, that they might be thoroughly aired and purified by whitewashing. These buildings were not re-occupied until the wounded brought from the battle-field of the gaps were placed in them.

The medical officers, after the experience of Shiloh, Perryville, and Stone's River, were alive to the necessity of thorough organization, and cheerfully acquiesced in the adoption of the plan proposed in Circular No. 4, from the Surgeon-General's Office.

The command prior to setting out on the campaign was in fair health, the sickness being but 5.6 per cent. This rate remained about the same until the men were able to procure blackberries, which were very abundant, and green corn, when it diminished to 4 per cent., and continued at that rate until after the battle of Chickamauga.

When the army marched from Murfreesborough, on the 24th of June, everything that related to preparation—in the medical department—for a vigorous campaign was in readiness and as complete in appointments as could be desired.

Skirmishing with the enemy was quite brisk at Hoover's and Liberty Gaps, on the 25th and 26th of June. As the result of these encounters, together with the subsequent pursuit of the enemy as far as the foot of the Cumberland chain of mountains, about 400 wounded had to be provided for. These were mostly sent to Murfreesborough. At Tullahoma a number of tents abandoned by the enemy were erected for men broken down on the march, and a building constructed for a hotel, of capacity sufficient for one hundred beds, was opened as a hospital. Four hospital tents were erected in the hospital yard for wounded men.

A few days after the occupancy of Tullahoma, the railroad was repaired and such of the sick and wounded as would bear removal were sent to the rear.

As the Twenty-first Army Corps occupied the line of the railway to McMinnville, I directed Surgeon Phelps, U. S. Volunteers, medical director, to open temporary hospitals at Manchester and McMinnville, making use of his reserve supplies for this purpose. The Fourteenth Army Corps established itself at Decherd, at the same time occupying the town of Winchester. A few hospital tents were erected at Winchester, and a church and school-house were occupied as temporary hospitals. A division of the Twentieth Army Corps was pushed forward on the line of the railroad, the advance occupying Stevenson about the 25th of July.

In order to secure ample hospital accommodations, as well as to be prepared for a general advance, I directed that half of the field hospital at Murfreesborough be brought to Cowan, a small town at the foot of the Cumberland Mountains. This was accomplished, and the hospital made ready for the reception of patients several days before the army crossed the mountain.

As soon as the army took up its march for the Valley of the Tennessee River, I directed the remainder of the Murfreesborough field hospital to be transferred to Stevenson, and, upon the occupancy of Bridgeport, I directed that a small tent hospital be established at that point also.

During these movements, the hospital train was running regularly to Nashville, where all proper cases for hospital treatment that could bear removal were sent. The tent hospitals were thus kept comparatively empty until the order was given to march. The supplies for these hospitals were brought from Nashville and Murfreesborough, leaving the reserve supplies for the corps almost untouched.

There was nothing of special interest transpired while the army lay on the north side of the river. A slight increase of the malarial diseases was observed, but not enough to excite apprehension.

By the 25th of August, every preparation had been made for an advance upon Chattanooga; the field hospitals at Stevenson and Bridgeport were in readiness for reception of patients, though not as complete in appointments as was desirable.

During the 1st day of September the army crossed the river and passed over Sand Mountain into Lookout Valley; this movement was attended with but few casualties.

After the passage of the Tennessee River a collision with the enemy was to be looked for any day, and I made every effort to familiarize myself with the topography and resources of the country. As a great struggle was anticipated, food for the wounded and an easy way to the rear were the main points to be kept in view.

During the few days the army lay in Lookout Valley there was comparatively no sickness; it was not considered necessary to make any depot; the few cases of sickness that occurred were sent to Stevenson by the returning supply train. When the heads of our columns penetrated the gaps in Lookout Mountain the enemy hastily evacuated Chattanooga, and on the 9th of September the Twenty-first Army Corps occupied it. As soon as I learned this fact I made immediate disposition to have supplies forwarded and such buildings as were suitable for hospitals prepared for reception of patients. Surg. Israel Moses, U. S. Volunteers, was relieved from duty at Murfreesborough to superintend this work. By reference to his accompanying report a more detailed account of the preparations made will be found.

By the 13th the army had crossed Lookout Mountain, and the advance had felt the enemy in several skirmishes. As the presence of the enemy in force was well established, dispositions to concentrate our army were made; it was soon discovered that the main body of the enemy was moving down the Valley of the Chickamauga toward Rossville.

The ridge that divides the Valley of Chickamauga from that of Chattanooga was traversed in several places by wagon roads; it was by these roads that our wounded must be conveyed to the rear. The wagon road down the Chickamauga Valley was near the base of this ridge, on the south side, where there are but few springs. As every indication pointed to a conflict on the north side of the creek, our wounded were to be provided for at these springs or taken over Mission Ridge into Chattanooga Valley.

After consultation with the general commanding, I selected Crawfish Spring as the main depot for the wounded. Division hospitals for the Twentieth and Twenty-first Corps, together with two divisions of the Fourteenth Corps, were accordingly established at that point.

On the 19th, as the battle progressed, the army moved down the Valley of the Chickamauga, so that when night closed it was about 4 miles distant from the hospitals, and the only road to the latter was the one spoken of at the south base of Mission Ridge. This movement made the removal of the wounded a task of considerable magnitude, as our loss in wounded on Saturday afternoon was very severe, being, as nearly as I could estimate, about 4,500.

The ambulance trains were worked very steadily until midnight, when almost all of the wounded accessible had been removed and placed in the hospitals or in groups around, adjacent.

Every effort was made to place the men under shelter, but particularly to provide them with covering, as the night was cold. When this could not be done the men were arranged in rows near each other and lines of camp fires built at their feet.

The medical officers continued their attentions to the relief of the immediate wants of the wounded, and to the performance of such operations as admitted of no delay, until exhaustion and the lateness of the hour warned them that a little rest was necessary to prepare them for the next day's work.

On the morning of the 20th the movement of the army to the left continued. Our hospitals on the right becoming more distant, and communication with them precarious, it was deemed best to establish small depots immediately in rear of the left wing.

As soon as the right gave way communication with Crawfish Spring, the main hospital depot, was cut off. The position, too, was becoming quite unsafe, when Surgeon Phelps, U. S. Volunteers, medical director of the Twenty-first Army Corps, and Surgeons Waterman and Griffiths, medical directors of the First and Third Divisions, of the Twentieth Army Corps, appreciating the danger, availed themselves of the empty supply trains parked at that point to send the wounded across Mission Ridge and by the Chattanooga, Valley road to Chattanooga. In this place I take pleasure in acknowledging the valuable assistance of Lieutenant-Colonel Boyd, chief quartermaster of the Twentieth Army Corps, and Captain Leech, commissary of subsistence.

Although these officers labored faithfully to remove all the wounded from Crawfish Spring, it was found impracticable. Medical officers were therefore detailed to remain, and provisions distributed in such manner as to insure them for the benefit of the patients during the confusion that must result immediately after a battle.

The wounded at the hospitals on the left were detained only long enough to perform such operations as admitted of no delay, and then sent to the rear by the Rossville road. About 1,500 of the graver cases were left on this part of the field.

From the best information I can procure, I should estimate the total number of wounded left upon the field to be about 2,500. Great care was taken by medical directors of divisions to detail medical officers with the necessary dressings, medicines, &c., to remain; and provisions were usually divided out among the men to prevent any possible suffering from hunger.

In the retreat every vehicle, baggage wagons, and supply trains, as well as the ambulances, were filled with wounded. Great numbers that were able to walk found their way on foot to the north side of the Tennessee River and continued their journey toward Bridgeport. The graver cases were removed from the ambulances and wagons and placed in hospitals at Chattanooga, while the others were taken to Bridgeport and Stevenson. A tent hospital, sufficiently large for 1,500 patients, was established on the 21st and 22d instant, at Stringer's Spring, on the north side of the river and about 2 miles distant.

Ambulances were sent out on the Bridgeport road to take up and bring back the wounded who had undertaken the journey to Bridgeport on foot and had fallen by the wayside. By the evening of the 23d the wounded not sent to the rear were provided for and received professional attention.

It has been a cause of great regret that in the confusion of the retreat primary operations could not be performed to the extent desired; thus, many cases of injuries of the knee and ankle joints subsequently proved fatal that might have been saved by timely amputation.

As soon as the army had taken up its position in front of Chattanooga, and order restored, the commanding general sent a flag of truce with propositions for the recovery of our wounded left upon the field; 1,740 were thus restored to our care. They were, of course, the graver cases, and, as timely preparations had been made for their reception, they were soon as comfortable as circumstances would admit.

It may be mentioned here that, upon the occupancy of the town, over 200 bales of cotton were found secreted in various places, which were seized, carefully guarded, and reserved for mattresses. Had it not been for this fortunate circumstance the sufferings of our wounded would have been much greater, as it was impossible to have procured straw, and the supply of blankets was limited.

About 150 upholsterers, tailors, and saddlers were detailed to make mattresses, so that by the tenth day every severely wounded man was provided with a comfortable bed.

The ambulance trains were busily employed transporting such cases as could bear transportation to Bridgeport, until the autumnal rains rendered the roads impassable.

The policy of transporting patients to the rear when they could only be transported over a rough, circuitous, and mountainous road, necessarily subjecting them to more or less pain, was dictated by necessity; for, if the army maintained its position, it was evident that the wounded must suffer from want of proper diet, while, on the other hand, if the town was abandoned, they must fall into the hands of the enemy. This view was unfortunately too well verified, for as the roads became more and more difficult by reason of the rains, only those subsistence stores that were absolutely essential could be brought, and even these were soon reduced in quantity far below the standard ration. The country on the north side of the river was gleaned of everything in the way of vegetables.

Every effort was made to secure to the wounded enough food from the regular ration, including soft bread, but in the absence of vegetables and other delicacies, they exhibited but too plainly the sad evidences of deficient nutrition. Superadded to the deficiency of proper food, a want of fuel was also felt during the latter part of October and all of November.

It was very discouraging to the medical attendants to witness the gradual but certain decline of patients who should have recovered, while they felt themselves powerless to apply the proper remedy. Partial relief from this condition of affairs was afforded after the battle of Wauhatchie, which opened a new and shorter route to the base of supply. A few days after this battle, the small steamer Paint Rock passed the enemy's batteries successfully and we were enabled to resume the transfer of patients to the rear. At Kelley's Ferry, a point 10 miles distant, where the boats discharged their freights, a few hospital tents were erected and other preparations made for the care of the wounded in transit. Patients were sent in ambulances from the hospitals in town, as well as Stringer's Spring, to this point as rapidly as circumstances would admit, the roads being bad and the weather rainy and cold. The patients were also exposed, while going from Kelley's Ferry to Bridgeport, for the boats were small, with open decks, having been hastily constructed for carrying freight only. Yet, painful as it was, it appeared necessary to send men exposed in this manner in order to make room for the care of others.

It was evident that a struggle for the possession of Lookout Mountain and the recovery of our line of railroad communication with the rear was at hand ; with our limited means for the care of many wounded, the approaching conflict was viewed with much anxiety, and every preparation must be made that circumstances would admit.

By the 20th of November the number in the various hospitals was reduced to about 450.

When it is remembered that the battle of Chickamauga, fought at a long distance from the base of supply, in a region already gleaned of resources and difficult of access, was lost, and the army subsequently cooped up in a basin, with but one outlet by a circuitous and difficult route of 50 miles in length, it may be safely asserted that the obstacles to be overcome in the successful care and treatment of wounded were more formidable in this than any other of the great battles of the war. An indulgent criticism may therefore be fairly claimed when reviewing the results of treatment.

The wounds received were inflicted by a variety of missiles, but those from the rifled-musket ball were perhaps more numerous in proportion than usual for so great a battle. The ground on which the battle was fought, being undulating and thickly timbered, was therefore unfavorable for the use of artillery.

I can bear testimony to the zeal and efficiency of the medical staff during this trying battle. While it is a difficult task to take care of the wounded of a victorious army, it is doubly so of one obliged to retreat.

To Surgs. F. H. Gross, U. S. Volunteers, medical director, Fourteenth Army Corps; A. J. Phelps, U. S. Volunteers, medical director of the Twenty-first Army Corps, and J. Perkins, Tenth Regiment Kentucky Volunteer Infantry, medical director of the Twentieth Army Corps, great credit is due for their efficiency and untiring devotion to their duties during the whole campaign. I would respectfully invite your attention to their reports,* herewith transmitted.

I will here mention that the wounded sent to the rear were provided for in a proper manner under the direction of Surg. A. H. Thurston, U. S. Volunteers, assistant medical director at Nashville.

I have to acknowledge my indebtedness to Asst. Surg. Dallas Bache, U. S. Army, assistant medical director, for most valuable assistance upon the field and in the duties of this office.

Surg. H. H. Seys, Fifteenth Regiment Ohio Volunteer Infantry, medical inspector, was attentive and faithful in his duties.

The purveying department has been conducted in a most able and satisfactory manner by Surg. Robert Fletcher, First Regiment Ohio Volunteer Infantry, now surgeon of volunteers.

This report has been unavoidably delayed, because the wounded were sent to the rear in such a rapid and irregular manner as to preclude the possibility of taking lists until the men arrived at the hospitals on the route.

The reports taken in hospitals have been diligently compared with regimental returns, and the inclosed list is believed to be nearly, if not quite, correct.

No little embarrassment has been experienced, also, from the destruction of all the records of this office by the Confederate General Wheeler during his attack on our train in the Sequatchie Valley in the early part of October.

Very respectfully, your obedient servant,

G. PERIN,
Surgeon, U. S. Army, Medical Director.

Brig. Gen. WILLIAM D. WHIPPLE, U. S. Volunteers,
Assistant Adjutant-General.

---

* Inserted with their respective army corps.

No. 8.

Report of Lieut. Col. William M. Wiles, Twenty-second Indiana Infantry, Provost-Marshal-General.

HDQRS. DEPARTMENT OF THE CUMBERLAND,
OFFICE PROVOST-MARSHAL-GENERAL,
Chattanooga, Tenn., October 7, 1863.

GENERAL : I have the honor to submit the following report for the information of the general commanding, in regard to prisoners captured and deserters from the enemy, since the Army of the Cumberland crossed the Tennessee River, the results of the battle of Chickamauga, with other information relating to their present organization and strength.

Prisoners captured at the battle of Chickamauga :

Captured by Fourteenth Army Corps	1,068
Captured by Twentieth Army Corps	728
Captured by Twenty-first Army Corps	98
Captured by Reserve Corps	111
Total	2,005

Among which are one brigadier-general, D. W. Adams, commanding brigade of Breckinridge's division, of Hill's corps; 1 colonel, J. I. Scales, Thirtieth Mississippi, commanding brigade of Walker's division, Hill's corps; 2 majors, W. D. C. Lloyd, of Brig. Gen. J. K. Jackson's staff, and J. C. Davis, of the Seventeenth Tennessee ; 8 captains, 1, E. B. Sayers, chief engineer Polk's corps, and 7 representing seven different regiments of their army ; 20 lieutenants, representing fourteen regiments.

Regiments represented by prisoners :

Tennessee	36
Alabama	22
Georgia	23
Arkansas	14
Texas	12
Kentucky	7
Mississippi	13
North Carolina	4
South Carolina	7
Louisiana	7
Florida	3
C. S. Regulars	5
Total number of regiments represented by prisoners	153

Total number of batteries represented by prisoners, 7.

Number of brigades, with division and corps, represented : Deas' brigade, Hindman's division, Polk's corps; Manigault's brigade, Hindman's division, Polk's corps; P. Anderson's brigade, Hindman's division, Polk's corps ; Jackson's brigade, Hindman's [Cheatham's] division, Polk's corps ; P. Smith's brigade, Cheatham's division, Polk's corps ; Wright's brigade, Cheatham's division, Polk's corps ; Maney's brigade, Cheatham's division, Polk's corps ; Strahl's brigade, Cheatham's division, Polk's corps ; Colonel Govan's brigade, Liddell's division, Reserve Corps ; Walthall's brigade, Liddell's Division, Reserve Corps ; Law's brigade, Hood's division, Longstreet's corps ; Benning's brigade, Hood's division, Longstreet's corps ; Robertson's brigade, Hood's division, Longstreet's corps ; Anderson's brigade, Hood's division, Longstreet's corps ; Brown's brigade, Stewart's division, Buckner's corps ; Bate's brigade, Stewart's division, Buckner's corps ; Johnson's brigade, Stewart's division, Buckner's corps ; D. W. Adams' brigade, Breckinridge's division, Hill's corps ; Helm's brigade, Breckinridge's division, Hill's corps; Stovall's brigade, Breckinridge's division, Hill's corps; Wood's brigade, Cleburne's division, Hill's corps ; Deshler's brigade, Cleburne's division, Hill's corps ; L. E. Polk's brigade, Cleburne's division, Hill's corps ; Wilson's brigade, Walker's division, Hill's corps ; Ector's brigade, Walker's division, Hill's corps ; Gist's brigade, Walker's division, Hill's corps ; Gregg's brigade, Walker's division, Hill's corps ; Humphreys' brigade, McLaws' division, Longstreet's corps ; Kershaw's brigade, McLaws' division, Longstreet's corps ; Gracie's brigade, Preston's division, Buckner's corps ; Colonel Kelly's brigade, Preston's division, Buckner's corps ; McNair's brigade, French's [old] division, Johnson's corps.

Total number of infantry brigades represented by prisoners, 32.

Number of cavalry brigades, with division and corps, represented: Crews' brigade, Wharton's division, Wheeler's corps; Colonel Hagan's brigade, Wharton's division, Wheeler's corps; Harrison's brigade, Wharton's division, Wheeler' corps; Scott's brigade, Forrest's division, Wheeler's corps; Dibrell's brigade, Forrest's division, Wheeler's corps; Armstrong's brigade and Martin's brigade, Wheeler's corps.

Total number of cavalry brigades represented by prisoners, 7.

From information received of prisoners, we have the following as their present organization. Although not entirely complete, it is believed to be perfect as far as it goes:

POLK'S CORPS.

CHEATHAM'S DIVISION.

Strahl's Brigade.

4th Tennessee Infantry.
5th Tennessee Infantry.
19th Tennessee Infantry.
24th Tennessee Infantry.
31st Tennessee Infantry.
33d Tennessee Infantry.
Stanford's Battery.

Preston Smith's Brigade.

11th Tennessee Infantry.
12th and 47th Tennessee Infantry (consolidated).
13th and 154th Tennessee Infantry (consolidated).
29th Tennessee Infantry.
Scott's Battery.

Maney's Brigade.

1st and 27th Tennessee Infantry (consolidated).
4th Tennessee Infantry [Provisional Army].
6th Tennessee Infantry.
9th Tennessee Infantry.
Turner's [Smith's] Battery.

Wright's Brigade.

8th Tennessee Infantry.
16th Tennessee Infantry.
28th Tennessee Infantry.
51st and 52d Tennessee Infantry (consolidated).
38th Tennessee Infantry.
Carnes' Battery.

HINDMAN'S DIVISION.

Deas' Brigade.

50th Alabama Infantry.
39th Alabama Infantry.
25th Alabama Infantry.
22d Alabama Infantry.
26th Alabama Infantry.*
19th Alabama Infantry.
Robertson's Battery.

Patton Anderson's Brigade.

7th Mississippi Infantry.
9th Mississippi Infantry.
10th Mississippi Infantry.
41st Mississippi Infantry.
44th Mississippi Infantry.
1st [9th Mississippi] Battalion Sharpshooters.
Ketchum's [Garrity's] Battery.

* In Army of Northern Virginia.

Manigault's Brigade.

34th Alabama Infantry.
28th Alabama Infantry.
24th Alabama Infantry.
19th and 10th South Carolina Infantry
  (consolidated).
Waters' Battery.

Jackson's Brigade.*

1st Georgia [Confederate] Infantry.
5th Mississippi Infantry.
8th Mississippi Infantry.
5th Georgia Infantry.
Cox's [Whiteley's] Battalion [Sharp-
  shooters].

HILL'S CORPS.

BRECKINRIDGE'S DIVISION.

D. W. Adams' Brigade.

19th Louisiana Infantry.
11th,† 13th, and 20th Louisiana Infantry
  (consolidated).
16th and 25th Louisiana Infantry (consolidated).
32d Alabama Infantry.
Austin's Battalion Sharpshooters.
Slocomb's Battery.

Stovall's Brigade.

47th Georgia Infantry.
60th North Carolina Infantry.
1st and 3d Florida Infantry (consolidated).
4th Florida Infantry.

Helm's Brigade.

4th Kentucky Infantry.
2d Kentucky Infantry.
6th Kentucky Infantry.

9th Kentucky Infantry.
41st Alabama Infantry.
Cobb's Battery.

CLEBURNE'S DIVISION.

Wood's Brigade.

45th and 32d Mississippi Infantry (consolidated).
45th Alabama Infantry.
33d Alabama Infantry.
16th Alabama Infantry.
[Semple's] Battery.

Deshler's Brigade.

19th Arkansas Infantry.
17th, 18th, 24th, and 25th Texas dismounted Cavalry, now called 1st
  Consolidated.
6th, 10th, and [15th] Texas Infantry.
[Douglas'] Battery of four pieces.

L. E. Polk's Brigade.

35th Tennessee Infantry.
2d Tennessee Infantry.
48th Tennessee Infantry.
1st Arkansas Infantry.

3d Confederate Infantry.
5th Confederate Infantry.
Calvert's battery of four pieces.

WALKER'S DIVISION. a

Wilson's Brigade.

30th Georgia Infantry.
29th Georgia Infantry.
25th Georgia Infantry.
4th Louisiana Battalion Infantry.
1st Louisiana Battalion Sharpshooters.
1st Georgia Battalion Sharpshooters.
Martin's Battery (four pieces).

Gregg's Brigade.

41st Tennessee Infantry.
50th Tennessee Infantry.
10th and 30th Tennessee Infantry (consolidated).
3d Tennessee Infantry.
7th Texas Infantry.
1st Tennessee Battalion.

Ector's Brigade.

46th Mississippi Infantry.‡
9th Texas Infantry.
29th North Carolina Infantry.
15th and 32d Texas Dismounted Cavalry
  (consolidated).
10th and 14th Texas Dismounted Cavalry
  (consolidated).

Gist's Brigade.

46th Georgia Infantry.
8th Georgia Battalion Infantry.
16th South Carolina Infantry.
24th South Carolina Infantry.
Preston's [Ferguson's] Battery.

a Walker's and Liddell's divisions, by some called Reserve Corps, used to be in Johnson's corps.

*Of Cheatham's division.
†Was disbanded August 25, 1862.
‡Was in the State of Mississippi.

LIDDELL'S DIVISION.*

Walthall's Brigade.

27th Mississippi Infantry.
29th Mississippi Infantry.
24th Mississippi Infantry.
30th Mississippi Infantry.
34th Mississippi Infantry.
Fowler's Battery.

Liddell's (old) Brigade.

Commanded by Colonel GOVAN.

1st Louisiana [Regulars] Infantry.
8th Arkansas Infantry.
5th and 13th Arkansas Infantry (consolidated).
2d and 15th Arkansas Infantry (consolidated).
6th and 7th Arkansas Infantry (consolidated).
Swett's Battery.

LONGSTREET'S CORPS.

HOOD'S DIVISION.

Law's Brigade.

4th Alabama Infantry.
15th Alabama Infantry.
44th Alabama Infantry.
47th Alabama Infantry.
48th Alabama Infantry.

Benning's Brigade.

2d Georgia Infantry.
15th Georgia Infantry.
17th Georgia Infantry.
20th Georgia Infantry.

Robertson's Brigade.

1st Texas Infantry.
4th Texas Infantry.
5th Texas Infantry.
3d Arkansas Infantry.

Anderson's Brigade.

7th Georgia Infantry.
8th Georgia Infantry.
9th Georgia Infantry.
11th Georgia Infantry.
59th Georgia Infantry.

M'LAWS' DIVISION.

Humphreys' Brigade.

13th Mississippi Infantry.
17th Mississippi Infantry.
18th Mississippi Infantry.
21st Mississippi Infantry.

Kershaw's Brigade.

2d South Carolina Infantry.
3d South Carolina Infantry.
7th South Carolina Infantry.
8th South Carolina Infantry.
15th South Carolina Infantry.
3d South Carolina Battalion.

JOHNSON'S CORPS.

FRENCH'S [OLD] DIVISION.

McNair's Brigade.

39th North Carolina Infantry.
31st Arkansas Infantry.
4th Arkansas Battalion Infantry.

1st Arkansas Mounted Rifles [dismounted].
2d Arkansas Mounted Rifles [dismounted].

BUCKNER'S CORPS.

STEWART'S DIVISION.

Brown's Brigade.

18th Tennessee Infantry.
26th Tennessee Infantry.
32d Tennessee Infantry.
45th Tennessee Infantry.
Newman's Tennessee Battalion.

Bate's Brigade.

37th Georgia Infantry.
4th Georgia Battalion Sharpshooters.
37th and 15th Tennessee Infantry (consolidated).
9th [Tennessee †] and 58th Tennessee [Alabama] Infantry.
20th Tennessee Infantry.
Eufaula Battery.

---

*See note *a*, p. 230.
†Was in Maney's brigade, Cheatham's division.

Johnson's Brigade, commanded by Colonel Fulton.

17th Tennessee.
23d Tennessee.
25th Tennessee.

[44th] Tennessee.
Jackson's [York's Georgia] Battery.

PRESTON'S DIVISION.

Gracie's Brigade.

1st Battalion [Hilliard's] Alabama Legion.
2d Battalion [Hilliard's] Alabama Legion.
3d Battalion [Hilliard's] Alabama Legion.
4th Battalion [Hilliard's] Alabama Legion.
43d Alabama Infantry.
63d Tennessee Infantry.

Colonel Kelly, commanding Brigade.

58th North Carolina Infantry.
63d Virginia Infantry.
65th Georgia Infantry.
56th Florida Infantry.*
5th Kentucky Infantry.

WHEELER'S [CAVALRY] CORPS.

WHARTON'S DIVISION.

Crews' Brigade.

3d Georgia Cavalry.
4th Georgia Cavalry.
7th Georgia Cavalry.†
2d Georgia Cavalry.
White's Battery, 6 pieces.

Harrison's Brigade.

11th Texas Cavalry.
1st [3d] Kentucky Cavalry.
3d Confederate Cavalry.
8th Texas Cavalry.
Battery six small guns.

Colonel Hagan, commanding Brigade.

1st Alabama Cavalry.
4th Alabama Cavalry.
51st Alabama Mounted Rifles.

Armstrong's Brigade.a

1st [6th] Tennessee Cavalry.
4th [18th] Tennessee Battalion Cavalry.

Martin's Brigade. a

FORREST'S DIVISION.

Scott's Brigade.

2d Tennessee Cavalry.
4th Tennessee Cavalry.
5th Tennessee Cavalry.
1st Louisiana Cavalry.
2d and 4th Kentucky Cavalry (remnants of Morgan's command).

Dibrell's Brigade.

8th Tennessee Cavalry.
Hamilton's [Tennessee] Battalion.

a No definite information to which division Martin's and Armstrong's brigades are attached.

The number of deserters from the enemy since the crossing of the Tennessee River up to the present time is 750, who have been disposed of in compliance with War Department Orders and Department General Orders, No. 175.

Great pains have been taken to ascertain as near as possible the strength of their army at the battle of Chickamauga, but no information has been elicited upon which to form anything like a definite conclusion, their regiments, many of them, being consolidated and transferred from one command to another upon the eve of battle,

---

*Reference probably to 6th Florida Infantry, which belonged to Trigg's brigade of Preston's division.
†Not organized.

and being variously estimated from 80,000 to 100,000 infantry and 15,000 to 20,000 cavalry, with an unusual quantity of artillery. By some, including 10,000 Georgia militia, it is thought their infantry force numbered 120,000.

I am, general, very respectfully, your obedient servant,

WM. M. WILES,
Lieutenant-Colonel, and Provost-Marshal-General.

Brig. Gen. JAMES A. GARFIELD,
Chief of Staff.

No. 9.

Report of Capt. Horace Porter, U. S. Ordnance Corps, Chief of Ordnance.

ORDNANCE OFFICE, HDQRS. DEPT. OF THE CUMBERLAND,
October 1, 1863.

SIR : I have the honor to submit the following report of ordnance and ordnance stores expended, captured, and lost in the battle of Chickamauga, September 19 and 20, 1863 :

Pieces of artillery captured..	36
Artillery carriages captured..	36
Caissons captured	22
Limbers captured..	20
Rifled muskets lost and captured	8,008
Spencer rifles lost and captured	70
Carbines lost and captured	350
Colt's revolving rifles lost and captured...............................	22
Colt's revolving pistols lost and captured..............................	410
Cavalry sabers lost and captured	305
Sets of infantry accouterments lost and captured	5,834
Rounds of artillery ammunition expended in firing......................	7,325
Rounds of artillery ammunition lost and captured......................	2,550
Rounds of infantry ammunition expended in firing......................	2,529,952
Rounds of infantry ammunition lost and captured......................	150,280
Rounds of cavalry ammunition expended in firing.......................	121,000

Very respectfully, your obedient servant,

HORACE PORTER,
Captain of Ordnance, U. S. Army.

Brig. Gen. JAMES A. GARFIELD,
Chief of Staff.

No. 10.

Report of Col. James Barnett, First Ohio Light Artillery, Chief of Artillery.

OFFICE OF CHIEF OF ARTY., DEPT. OF THE CUMBERLAND,
Chattanooga, October 10, 1863.

COLONEL : I have the honor to present, for the information of the general commanding, the following report, showing the batteries engaged in the recent battle of Chickamauga :

FOURTEENTH ARMY CORPS.

First Division.—Battery H, Fifth U. S. Artillery, Lieutenant Burnham commanding: Four 12-pounder Napoleons, two 10-pounder

Parrotts. Fourth Indiana Battery, Lieutenant Flansburg command-ing: Two 12-pounder Napoleons, two 6-pounder James rifles, two 12-pounder howitzers. Battery A, First Michigan, Lieut. G. W. Van Pelt commanding : Six 10-pounder Parrotts.

These batteries were charged upon by overpowering numbers of the enemy, and the loss of guns is to be attributed to the want of supports.

Second Division.—Company M, First Ohio Artillery, Capt. F. Schultz commanding: Four James rifles, two 3-inch rifled guns. Company G, First Ohio Artillery, Capt. A. Marshall commanding : Four 12-pounder Napoleons, two 3-inch rifled guns. Bridges' (Illi-nois) Battery, Capt. L. Bridges commanding : Two 12-pounder Napo-leons, four 3-inch rifled guns.

The loss in Bridges' Battery is attributed to want of support.

Third Division.—Fourth Michigan Battery, Capt. J. W. Church commanding : Two 10-pounder Parrotts, two 6-pounder James rifles, two 12-pounder howitzers. Company I, Fourth U. S. Artillery, Lieut. F. G. Smith commanding : Four 12-pounder Napoleons. Company C, First Ohio Artillery, Lieut. M. B. Gary commanding : Four James rifles, two 12-pounder Napoleons.

The loss of guns in this division, as will be seen by the reports, was owing to the giving way of light supports. It would seem that all that could be done by both battery officers and men to save them was done.

Fourth Division.—Eighteenth Indiana Battery, Capt. Eli Lilly commanding : Six 3-inch rifled guns, four mountain howitzers. Nineteenth Indiana Battery, Capt. S. J. Harris commanding : Four 12-pounder Napoleons, two 3-inch guns. Twenty-first Indiana Battery, Lieutenant Chess commanding : Six 12-pounder Napoleons.

The batteries of this division held important positions and did good service. No report has been received at my office, up to this time, of the Eighteenth Indiana Battery, serving with Colonel Wilder.

TWENTIETH ARMY CORPS.

First Division.—Second Minnesota Battery, Lieut. A. Woodbury commanding: Two 10-pounder Parrotts, four 12-pounder Napoleons. Eighth Wisconsin, Lieut. J. D. McLean commanding: Two 12-pounder Napoleons, four 3-inch guns.

The Fifth Wisconsin Battery, being on duty with Colonel Post's brigade, was not engaged. The batteries of this division met with but slight loss in men or *matériel*.

Second Division.—Fifth Indiana Battery, Capt. P. Simonson, commanding : Four 6-pounder James rifles, two light 12-pounder guns. Company A, First Ohio Artillery, Capt. W. F. Goodspeed commanding : Four 6-pounder James rifles, two light 12-pounder guns. Twentieth Ohio Battery, Capt. E. Grosskopff commanding: Four 3-inch rifled guns, two light 12-pounder guns.

The batteries of this division acted with their respective brigades, and held well the positions to which they were assigned. The part taken by Captain Goodspeed's battery is much commended. Their loss shows that they were handled with good judgment.

Third Division.—Company G, First Missouri Artillery, Capt. H. Hescock commanding : Four light 12-pounder guns, two 10-pounder Parrotts. Company C, First Illinois Artillery, Captain Prescott commanding : Four 3-inch rifled guns, two 12-pounder howitzers. Eleventh Indiana Battery, Capt. A. Sutermeister commanding: Four 12-pounder light guns, two 3-inch rifled guns.

These batteries were not seriously engaged on the 19th, and the losses sustained occurred after our troops gave way on the 20th.

TWENTY-FIRST ARMY CORPS.

First Division.—Sixth Ohio Battery, Capt. Cullen Bradley commanding : Four 10-pounder Parrotts, two light 12-pounder guns. Eighth Indiana Battery, Capt. George Estep commanding: Four 6-pounder smooth-bore guns, two 12-pounder howitzers.

The Tenth Indiana Battery, belonging to this division, was not engaged, being with General Wagner's brigade at Chattanooga. The two batteries engaged acted under the orders of their brigade commanders. These batteries were well handled, but the loss of the the Eighth Indiana was owing to no supports being at hand (as reported by Captain Estep).

Second Division.—Company B, First Ohio Artillery, Lieut. N. A. Baldwin commanding: Four James rifles, two 6-pounder smoothbore guns. Company M, Fourth U. S. Artillery, Lieut. F. L. D. Russell commanding : Four 12-pounder Napoleons, two 24-pounder howitzers. Company H, Fourth U. S. Artillery, Lieut. H. C. Cushing commanding: Four 12-pounder howitzers. Company F, First Ohio Artillery, Lieut. G. J. Cockerill commanding: Four 6-pounder James rifles, two 12-pounder howitzers.

The batteries of this division were all well handled, and held during the entire fighting their position, punishing the enemy severely, and repulsing him at several points.

Third Division.—Third Wisconsin Battery, Lieut. C. Livingston: Four 10-pounder Parrotts, two 12-pounder howitzers. Seventh Indiana Battery, Capt. George R. Swallow: Four 10-pounder Parrotts, two 12-pounder Napoleons. Twenty-sixth Pennsylvania Battery, Capt. A. J. Stevens: Four 6-pounder smooth-bore guns, two 6-pounder James rifles.

The batteries of this division had, for the most part, very unfavorable ground, and their loss in men and *matériel* may be attributed to the fact that the heavy masses of the enemy could get within very short range before the batteries could open upon them. Captain Drury, chief of artillery of the division, was severely wounded in a skirmish several days before the battle. Captain Stevens, commanding Twenty-sixth Pennsylvania Battery, was killed early in the engagement of the 20th, the command of the battery devolving upon Lieut. S M. McDowell.

RESERVE CORPS.

Eighteenth Ohio Battery, Capt. C. C. Aleshire commanding : Six 3-inch rifled guns. Company M, First Illinois Artillery, Capt. George W. Spencer commanding : Four 12-pounder Napoleons, two 3-inch rifled guns. Company I, Second Illinois Artillery, Capt. C. M. Barnett commanding : Two 12-pounder Napoleons, two 6-pounder James rifles, two 10-pounder Parrotts.

I regret that I have no official report of the part taken by these batteries, or of their losses. They, however, held important positions on our left, and did good service, without serious loss.

From personal observation and investigation, I am fully convinced that all or nearly all the batteries engaged were as well posted as the nature of the country would permit, and although our loss of guns was large, it would have been much larger but for the great efficiency of the officers in charge of batteries and the good conduct of the men; but four cases of cowardice have been reported to me.

As important changes in the artillery arm are now being made in the department, it is unnecessary for me to make suggestions which the experience of the last battle would dictate. The accomplished soldier now at the head of the artillery department will, I am sure, much improve the efficiency of this arm.

We have to deplore the loss of Capt. A. J. Stevens, Twenty-sixth Pennsylvania Battery, who died like a hero defending his guns; a more gallant soldier or a purer patriot is seldom found. Lieutenant Burnham, Company H, Fifth Artillery, nobly lost his life in defense of his guns; he was a young man of promise, and in his death the army sustains a loss.

Lieutenant Van Pelt, commanding First Michigan Battery, well known and appreciated in this army, fell like a hero at his post.

Lieutenant Bishop, Bridges' Battery, brave and efficient, an honor to his profession, fell, gallantly doing his duty.

Lieutenant Lynch, First Ohio, died a true soldier, while advancing on the enemy.

I beg leave to call to the favorable notice of the general commanding the following officers and non-commissioned officers, for meritorious service, coolness, and bravery in battle, and for efficiency in their duties:

Lieutenant McElroy, Sixth Ohio Battery; Lieutenant Smetts, Sixth Ohio Battery; Lieutenant Woodbury, Second Minnesota Battery; Lieutenant Williams, Eleventh Indiana Battery; Lieutenant Belding, Company A, First Ohio Artillery; Lieutenant Scovill, Company A, First Ohio Artillery; Lieutenant Flansburg, Fourth Michigan Battery; Lieutenant Temple, Bridges' Battery; Lieutenant Rodney, Company I, Fourth Artillery; Lieutenant Butler, Company M, Fourth Artillery; Lieutenant Floyd, Company H, Fourth Artillery; Lieutenant Lackey, Nineteenth Indiana Battery; Lieutenant Stackhouse, Nineteenth Indiana Battery; Sergt. Edward Downey, Third Wisconsin Battery; Sergt. T. J. Myers, Company I, Fourth Artillery; Sergt. Charles Ellis, Company I, Fourth Artillery; Sergt. S. H. Jennings, Company G, First Missouri; Corpl. J. W. Fletcher, Third Wisconsin Battery.

I inclose herewith the reports of the battery commanders and chiefs of artillery, to which I would call the attention of the general commanding; I also inclose statement of losses in men and *matériel* all of which is respectfully submitted.

I am, colonel, very respectfully, your obedient servant,

JAMES BARNETT,
Colonel, and Chief of Arty., Dept. of the Cumberland.

Lieut. Col. C. GODDARD,
Assistant Adjutant-General.

[Inclosure.]

Statement of losses sustained by the batteries serving with the Army of the Cumberland in the actions at Chickamauga Creek, September 19 and 20, 1863.

Designation of battery.	Killed.		Wounded.		Missing.		Guns.						
	Officers.	Enlisted men.	Officers.	Enlisted men.	Officers.	Enlisted men.	3-pdr. smooth-bores.	12-pdr. light.	2-pdr. howitzers.	Mountain howitzers.	8-inch rifled.	10-pdr. Parrotts.	6-pdr. James rifled.
FOURTEENTH ARMY CORPS.													
First Division:													
Battery H, 5th U. S. Artillery	1	12	1	11	1	13							
Battery A, 1st Michigan Artillery	1	5		6		13							
4th Indiana Battery		1		16	1	4							1
Total	2	18	1	33	2	30							1
Second Division:													
Battery G, 1st Ohio Artillery													
Battery M, 1st Ohio Artillery				4									
Bridges' (Illinois) Battery	1	5		16		4		1			1		
Total	1	5		20		4		1			1		
Third Division:													
Battery I, 4th U. S. Artillery		1	1	19									
Battery C, 1st Ohio Artillery		4		9									1
4th Michigan Battery				7		4			1			2	2
Total		5	1	35		4			1			2	3
Fourth Division:													
18th Indiana Battery a										1			
19th Indiana Battery		2		16		2		1			1		
21st Indiana Battery				10				1					
Total		2		26		2		2		1	1		
Total Fourteenth Army Corps	3	30	2	114	2	40		3	1	1	2	2	4
TWENTIETH ARMY CORPS.													
First Division:													
2d Minnesota Battery			1	1									
5th Wisconsin Battery													
8th Wisconsin Battery													
Total			1	1									
Second Division:													
Battery A, 1st Ohio Artillery		2	1	13		4							
5th Indiana Battery		1	1	7		1		1					1
20th Ohio Battery				2		2							
Total		3	2	22		7		1					1
Third Division:													
Battery G, 1st Missouri Artillery		1		3	1								
Battery C, 1st Illinois Artillery				4					1			2	
11th Indiana Battery		3	1	11		4						2	
Total		4	1	18	1	4			1			4	
Total Twentieth Corps		7	4	41	1	11		1	1			4	1
TWENTY-FIRST ARMY CORPS.													
First Division:													
6th Ohio Battery		1	1	5									
8th Indiana Battery		1	1	7		9	4		2				
10th Indiana Battery b													
Total		2	2	12		9	4		2				

a No report received from this battery.　　　　b This battery was not engaged.

Statement of losses sustained by the batteries, &c.—Continued.

Designation of battery.	Killed.		Wounded.		Missing.		Guns.						
	Officers.	Enlisted men.	Officers.	Enlisted men.	Officers.	Enlisted men.	6-pdr. smooth-bores.	12-pdr. light.	12-pdr. howitzers.	Mountain howitzers.	3-inch rifled.	10-pdr. Parrotts.	6-pdr. James rifled.
Second Division:													
Battery B, 1st Ohio Artillery		1		4		4							2
Battery F, 1st Ohio Artillery	1	1		8									
Battery H, 4th U. S. Artillery		4	1	14		2				1			
Battery M, 4th U. S. Artillery		2		6									
Total	1	8	1	32		6				1			2
Third Division:													
3d Wisconsin Battery		2		13		11				1		4	
7th Indiana Battery			1			8						1	
26th Pennsylvania Battery	1	1	1	13		1	2						2
Total	1	3	2	26		20	2			1		5	2
Total Twenty-first Army Corps.	2	13	5	70		35	6			4		5	4
Grand total	5	50	9	225	1	86	6	4	6	1	6	7	9

Designation of battery.	Pistols.	Sabers.	Gun carriages.	Limbers, extra.	Caissons.	Battery wagons.	Harness, wheel. sets.	Harness, lead, sets.	Saddles.	Paulins.	Horses killed.	Horses disabled.	Rounds of ammunition expended.
FOURTEENTH ARMY CORPS.													
First Division:													
Battery H, 5th U. S. Artillery	8	21		1	6		7	14			65		728
Battery A, 1st Michigan Artillery	2	1		3	2		5½	12½			46		380
4th Indiana Battery	3	6	2		3		2	12			34		(a)
Total	13	28	2	4	11		14½	38½			145		
Second Division:													
Battery G, 1st Ohio Artillery											5		294
Battery M, 1st Ohio Artillery	1	2						1	2	1	8		415
Bridges' (Illinois) Battery		5	2		1		2	6	2	3	46		(a)
Total	1	7	2		1		2	7	4	4	59		
Third Division:													
Battery I, 4th U. S. Artillery				1			2	6	1	3	19		(a)
Battery C, 1st Ohio Artillery		1	1		4		5	5	1		26		498
4th Michigan Battery	4	5	5	4			6	12	5	4	35		(a)
Total	4	6	6	5	4		8	23	11	8	80		
Fourth Division:													
18th Indiana Battery b													(a)
19th Indiana Battery	4	3	2				10	4			15	6	1,100
21st Indiana Battery			1	1			1	1			12		442
Total	4	3	3	1			11	5			27	6	
Total Fourteenth Army Corps.	22	44	13	10	16		24½	79½	20	12	311	6	

a Ammunition expended not reported.   *b* No report received from this battery.

Statement of losses sustained by the batteries, &c.—Continued.

Designation of battery.	Pistols.	Sabers.	Gun carriages.	Limbers, extra.	Caissons.	Battery wagons.	Harness, wheel, sets.	Harness, lead, sets.	Saddles.	Paulins.	Horses killed.	Horses disabled.	Rounds of ammunition expended.
TWENTIETH ARMY CORPS.													
First Division:													
2d Minnesota Battery													(a)
5th Wisconsin Battery													
8th Wisconsin Battery													
Total													
Second Division:													
Battery A, 1st Ohio Artillery								1				15	(a)
5th Indiana Battery			2		2		1	2			30		1,247
20th Ohio Battery					1						9	2	85
Total			2		3		1	3			39	17	1,332
Third Division:													
Battery G, 1st Missouri Artillery				1			1	2					277
Battery C, 1st Illinois Artillery			3		1						12		194
11th Indiana Battery	3	2	2				2	4	2	2	19		120
Total	3	2	5	1	1		3	6	2	2	31		591
Total Twentieth Army Corps	3	2	7	1	4		4	9	2	2	70	17	
TWENTY-FIRST ARMY CORPS.													
First Division:													
6th Ohio Battery					2	1						2	336
8th Indiana Battery			6		5						56		750
10th Indiana Battery b													
Total			6		7	1					56	2	1,086
Second Division:													
Battery B, 1st Ohio Artillery			2						6		13		(a)
Battery F, 1st Ohio Artillery													(a)
Battery H, 4th U. S. Artillery			1				3½	3			19	5	760
Battery M, 4th U. S. Artillery				1	3				1		7	6	(a)
Total			3	1	3		3½	3	7		39	11	
Third Division:													
3d Wisconsin Battery			5				5	10			32		(a)
7th Indiana Battery			1				1	2			14		250
26th Pennsylvania Battery			4	1			5	10			37		(a)
Total			10	1			11	22			83		
Total Twenty-first Army Corps			19	2	10	1	14½	25	7		178	13	
Grand total	25	46	39	13	30	1	43	113½	29	14	559	36	

a Ammunition expended not reported.   b This battery was not engaged.

No. 11.

Reports of Capt. Jesse Merrill, U. S. Signal Corps, Chief Signal Officer.

HEADQUARTERS DEPARTMENT OF THE CUMBERLAND,
Chattanooga, September 27, 1863.

COLONEL: I have the honor to state that our official report of the working of this detachment before, during, and immediately after the battles of 19th, 20th, and 21st instant is being prepared, and a copy will be forwarded to you soon.

Stations of observation communicating directly with department headquarters were occupied on Lookout Mountain, and much valuable information obtained. They were valuable also for communication, as the map* I will send you with my report shows. Brigadier-General Morton, chief engineer, informed me that every movement indicated by the reports of observations made had been by the result proved correct. It was impossible to communicate on the battle-field, owing to the dense timber, but communication was kept up with our flanks, and observations continued until the army had safely retired to Chattanooga. Four officers were left on the point of Lookout Mountain, and a regiment of infantry sent there to guard them. Their horses and wagons were sent to camp, they retaining three days' rations. The road to the top of the mountain was destroyed. They remained there until the enemy, having ascended some 10 miles farther down the mountain, demonstrated on them so strongly that General Rosecrans ordered them to withdraw under cover of night. They got off safely after having climbed down the side of a mountain more than 2,000 feet high. Lieut. George W. Landrum, a valuable and efficient officer, is missing, and nothing of his whereabouts can be learned. Private William L. Vorhis was slightly wounded, and is missing.

I have to report the loss of almost 3 miles of insulated wire, which, by direction of General Rosecrans, was used in completing his telegraphic communication with Chattanooga.

Very respectfully, colonel, your obedient servant,

JESSE MERRILL,
Capt., and Chief Sig. Officer, Dept. of the Cumberland.

Col. ALBERT J. MYER,
Signal Officer of the Army.

—

HDQRS. SIGNAL CORPS, DEPT. OF THE CUMBERLAND,
Chattanooga, Tenn., October 1, 1863.

COLONEL: I have the honor to submit the following report of the operations of the detachment of the signal corps with this army, under my command during this campaign, commencing with our arrival at Stevenson:

Immediately after the occupation of Sequatchie Valley by the Twenty-first Army Corps, communication by signals was established from Pikeville to Dunlap (corps headquarters), and from there to Therman. This was afterward connected with line from Stevenson (department headquarters) to Jasper, via Bridgeport, and subsequently with that part of the Twentieth Army Corps which crossed the Tennessee River at Caperton's Ferry. This formed a continuous line of signals from the right to the left of the army.

On the 4th of September, a line branching from the main line at Crown Point, on Walden's Ridge, running across that ridge to the front of Chattanooga, the position occupied by Wagner's and Wilder's brigades, was established.

After the crossing of the river by the troops, our line was changed so as to connect with the telegraph at Shellmound. The telegraph

*Not found.

having then been extended to Whiteside's, from which point, after department headquarters were established near Trenton, the signal telegraph line connected with it and extended to the mouth of Murphy's Cove, signal communication was attempted to be established from this point to headquarters, but it was found impossible, as the enemy held Lookout Mountain. When, however, General Beatty's brigade advanced to the top of the mountain, this was established, and from the same point constant communication kept with this brigade as it advanced toward Chattanooga.

After reaching Chattanooga, officers were immediately sent to the point of Lookout Mountain for observation, and soon after a station communicating with department headquarters, through this station on Lookout Mountain, was established at Rossville.

Communication from department headquarters to headquarters Fourteenth Army Corps was established up Lookout Valley as rapidly as possible.

The delay and length of time consumed in getting this line in working order to corps headquarters at Stevens' Gap, on south side of Lookout Mountain, was occasioned by the length of time necessarily consumed by the officers in coming from the stations held by them on the opposite side of the river to the stations assigned them on this line.

It was opened to Deer-head Cove on the 13th of September, and on the following day, by using the signal telegraph to connect stations across the mountain, the line was completed.

On the 12th instant a station for observation was established on top of mountain, communicating with a station at headquarters Twentieth Army Corps, then near Alpine; valuable information regarding the movements of the enemy was thus obtained and sent to Major-General McCook.

Stations communicating with our advance in Chattanooga Valley were established at Ringgold, Gordon's Mills, and Alley's house, headquarters Twenty-first Army Corps, at different times. When department headquarters were established at Crawfish Spring on the 16th instant, communication with Major-General Crittenden at Alley's house was opened via High Point, on Lookout Mountain. On the 17th, from the same point, communication was opened with Major-Generals Thomas and McCook, the former near Alley's house and the latter at Pond Spring. The signal telegraph connected General Thomas with General McCook, and from the headquarters of the former a communicating station with station of observation at Stevens' Gap. During the night of the 17th three more officers were sent to High Point, so that the movements of the enemy could be more closely watched and these observations and the official messages passing over our lines be more easily transmitted. Communication was at the same time opened with Summertown, the communicating station with Rossville. These lines were all worked during the 18th and 19th. On the night of the 19th a station communicating with High Point was opened near the battle-field, and kept open on the 20th. The station at Crawfish Spring was also kept open as long as the cavalry on our right were there.

The observation of the movements of the enemy on the battle-field or communication by signal between different parts of the army on the field was totally impossible on account of the dense timber. The same reason, together with smoke and dust, prevented our officers on

Lookout Mountain at High Point and Summertown from seeing and reporting their movements.

On the night of the 20th the officers were ordered in from High Point and those on the point of Lookout Mountain ordered to send their wagons and horses to camp, to retain three days' rations, and remain there as long as possible.

On the evening of the 23d, the regiment sent there as a guard was attacked by what was supposed to be a largely superior force. It was deemed imprudent to keep the position any longer, and that night, in accordance with orders from the commanding general, they were withdrawn.

On the 21st, at Rossville, a short line was established from that front to a point near General Thomas' headquarters.

It is not easy to distinguish between officers who do and officers who do not do their duty, when they are scattered along lines of such length and over so large an extent of country that they cannot be under the personal observation of the person reporting them. The reports of the transmission of messages, and the time occupied, gives this more truly than anything else. These reports have not all been made, and I can only say that so far as my own observation goes, the officers and men of this detachment have all labored hard and zealously to accomplish the end for which the corps was formed. At times we have failed as much through my own error as any other cause. I would ask that it be remembered in excuse for this that the system is almost a new one, and now only being fully developed. Without any books of instruction or precedents to guide us, the signal corps has been made what it is, and with the experience which our work gives us, and the advice and direction of those over us, we hope to bring it to the full standard of usefulness.

I have to report Lieut. George W. Landrum, a valuable and efficient officer, as missing. He was dispatched by General Thomas with a message for General Rosecrans, on the afternoon of the 21st instant, since which time nothing is known of him. Private William L. Vorhis was wounded same day, and is also missing.

Very respectfully, your obedient servant,

JESSE MERRILL,
Capt., and Chief Sig. Officer, Dept. of the Cumberland.

Lieut. Col. C. GODDARD,
Asst. Adjt. Gen., Department of the Cumberland.

—

HDQRS. SIGNAL CORPS, DEPT. OF THE CUMBERLAND,
Chattanooga, October 31, 1863.

COLONEL: I have the honor to make the following report of the operations of this detachment for the month ending to-day. In order to do it I will have to begin with last few days in September, during which some of the lines and stations were established that have been worked during this month.

On the 24th of September a high hill on the west side of the town known as Cameron's Hill was occupied, timber cut away, a lookout built on top of a tree, and communication opened with these headquarters. Officers were stationed at every available point along our front, and every point at all valuable for observation was occupied. Several of these stations were connected by signal, but owing to wood and other obstructions it was found easier and more rapid to use couriers.

On the 25th of September a station was established on Stringer's Ridge, 4 miles up the river, communicating with Cameron's Hill station. It was established as a station of observation. A better point having been found, Crane's Hill, this station was moved to that point on the 27th, and communication opened.

On the 27th, officers were ordered to different stations on the line to Jasper, and the line was reported open on the 29th. This line was kept open until October 12, when the telegraph line having been completed, all the stations beyond Bob White's, in accordance with orders from General Rosecrans, were taken up. The stations on Walden's Ridge and at Bob White's were left for observing the movements of the enemy on the opposite side of the river along the base of Raccoon Mountain. They were made very useful afterward (when the telegraph was cut and every courier who ventured along the road was shot by a concealed rebel on the opposite side of the river from the road) as a means of reaching the courier line at a point from which they could reach telegraphic communication with safety. On the 20th communication was established between Fort Whitaker, a point on the opposite side of the river directly opposite the point of Lookout Mountain, and Cameron's Hill.

On the night of the 26th an expedition under General Smith crossed the river at Brown's Ferry. Four officers were sent out with it, and on the morning of the 27th after our troops had taken position communication was established with Cameron's Hill. Three stations are now being worked, connecting General Smith with his brigade commanders. During the night of the 28th General Hooker connected his left with the troops of General Smith, having marched down Lookout Valley from Wauhatchie Junction. On the morning of the 29th, 2 officers were sent to him, and communication was opened in the afternoon of that day. I will be able to report more fully with reference to these expeditions when I receive the reports of the officers who are with them. Much valuable information has been collected by the officers on stations of observation with reference to the movements, number, and position of the enemy.

The field telegraph was used to connect the stations at Bob White's and Crown Point, department headquarters was connected with each of the corps headquarters, and the Morse instrument used for some days. Our own instruments were then put in, connecting Generals Rosecrans' and Thomas' headquarters, and the line taken up to the headquarters Twentieth and Twenty-first Corps, as there was no further use for them. On the 27th a line connecting these headquarters with Cameron's Hill was established.

What we have accomplished during the month has been done under great difficulties. Forage could only be obtained by hauling it for 20 or 30 miles. For awhile we were able to supply ourselves, but the distance it had to be hauled grew greater as the roads grew worse, until the rains made them totally impassable except for wagons double teamed.

General Rosecrans directed that all the animals that could be spared be sent to where forage could be obtained. We sent all but a very few of our horses, and since then have been compelled to send all to keep them from starvation. Officers have done duty on foot, and been exposed at night because we could not transport their tents to their stations, and am glad to say they have done so without a murmur. We have been as efficient as possible under the circumstances, and I know have rendered good service.

I am, sir, very respectfully, your obedient servant,

JESSE MERRILL,
Captain, and Chief Signal Officer.

Col. ALBERT J. MYER,
Signal Officer of the Army.

No. 12.

Report of Surg. Israel Moses, U. S. Army, Medical Director, Post of Chattanooga.

OFFICE OF MEDICAL DIRECTOR OF POST,
Chattanooga, Tenn., October 1, 1863.

SIR: In obedience to orders, I repaired to this post, and, arriving September 18, reported to the commanding officer as medical director. Receiving orders from you to prepare beds for 5,000 wounded, I found scant supplies for not more than 500, and buildings capable of holding that number built by the Confederates and occupied as a hospital, with about 150 sick already in. Also a large building, two stories high, built by the Confederates as a receiving hospital, capable of holding 150. These buildings were without doors or windows and destitute of every convenience.

A partial supply of medicines, blankets, furniture, and dressings was on hand, estimated for 1,000 men, but deficient in many articles.

I selected several buildings which might be converted into hospitals.

On September 19, Saturday, an engagement took place about 7 or 8 miles distant, and was renewed with great fierceness during the forenoon of the 20th (Sunday), during which our wounded numbered over 6,000. On this and the following day (Monday), as nearly as I can estimate, 4,000 wounded officers and men were received and assigned to various buildings and private houses, hotels, and churches.

The following general hospitals were established during Sunday and Monday:

No. 1. Buildings (13) on the hill, which received nearly 1,000.

No. 2. Receiving hospital at base of hill, which received about 300.

No. 3. Crutchfield Hotel, which was taken possession of, and accommodated, on beds and floors, about 500.

No. 4. Three churches, which held about 200.

No. 5. Lofts over buildings occupied as the commissary storehouses, which received about 300.

No. 6. Buildings opposite the above, which accommodated 400.

No. 7. Officers' Hospital No. 1, a large brick building on a hill, which received 100 officers.

No. 8. Officers' Hospital No. 2, a large private mansion, which received 35.

No. 9. Private houses were taken late at night, and about 150 to 200 obtained shelter.

All the severe cases were dressed the same night they arrived, and others the next day, and all received food, of which many had been deprived for two days.

This work was performed by a corps of 43 surgeons who reported to me either by your order or as volunteers (of whom 4 were Confederate medical officers).

About three-fourths of the wounds were flesh, or of a lighter character, the other fourth being of the gravest character inflicted by musketry.

Few shell wounds or by round shot were seen, owing to the fact that little artillery was employed by the enemy.

On Monday the lighter cases were sent across the pontoon bridge, and on Tuesday others to the number of nearly 3,000. The officers who could bear transportation were sent in ambulances toward Stevenson.

On Wednesday not more than 800 of the gravest cases remained in town, and many of them have since been removed to the camp hospital.

Owing to the establishment of division hospitals there remains under my charge only Hospital No. 1, the Crutchfield Hospital, and Officers' Hospital.

Into these hospitals were received, on the evening of September 29, about 250 wounded, who were brought in from the Confederate lines.

Our hospitals are at the present time crowded beyond their capacity, and should they thus continue it would render a serious fear in my mind that our operations would be unsuccessful.

I have performed a large number of amputations and resections in the several hospitals, all of which thus far promise well.

Operations have been performed by various surgeons, in charge of hospitals and on the field, with a fair amount of success thus far. The amputations have been mostly circular mode. To this date five cases of tetanus have come to my notice, but none of hospital gangrene or erysipelas.

The general condition of the patients is good, but our hospitals are greatly in need of bunks and mattresses, at least one-third of the grave cases being still on the floor, with only a folded blanket to lie on.

In view of the increasing risk of so many patients with suppurating wounds being crowded together, I would respectfully suggest an early provision for increased accommodations by tents with flooring, and that new temporary pavilions be constructed out of some incomplete buildings south of the railroad depot.

I am, sir, very respectfully, your obedient servant,

I. MOSES,
Surgeon, U. S. Volunteers, Medical Director of Post.

Surg. G. PERIN, U. S. Army,
Medical Director, &c.

No. 13.

Report of Maj. Gen. George H. Thomas, U. S. Army, commanding Fourteenth Army Corps.

HEADQUARTERS FOURTEENTH ARMY CORPS,
Chattanooga, Tenn., September 30, 1863.

GENERAL: I have the honor to report the operations of my corps from the 1st September up to date, as follows, viz:

General Brannan's division crossed the Tennessee River at Battle

Creek; General Baird ordered to cross his division at Bridgeport, and to move to Taylor's Store; General Negley's division to cross the river at Caperton's Ferry, and to report at Taylor's Store also.

September 2.—General Baird's division moved to Widow's Creek. General Negley reports having arrived at Moore's Spring, 1¼ miles from Taylor's Store, and 2 miles from Bridgeport; he was ordered to cross the mountain at that point, it being the most direct route to Trenton, in the vicinity of which place the corps was ordered to concentrate.

September 3.—Headquarters Fourteenth Army Corps moved from Bolivar Springs at 6 a. m. via Caperton's Ferry to Moore's Spring, on the road from Bridgeport to Trenton. Baird's division reached Bridgeport, but could not cross in consequence of damage to the bridge; Negley's division marched to Warren's Mill, on the top of Sand Mountain, on the road to Trenton; Brannan's division reached Graham's Store, on the road from Shellmound to Trenton; Reynolds' division marched 6 miles on the Trenton road from Shellmound.

September 4.—Negley's division camped at Brown's Spring, at the foot of Sand Mountain, in Lookout Valley; Brannan's division at Gordon's Mill, on Sand Mountain; Reynolds' division at foot of Sand Mountain, 2 miles from Trenton; Baird's division crossed the river at Bridgeport, and camped at that point; corps headquarters at Moore's Spring.

September 5.—Baird's division arrived at Moore's Spring; Negley's division still in camp at Brown's Spring. He reports having sent forward a reconnaissance of two regiments of infantry and a section of artillery to scour the country toward Chattanooga, and secure some captured stores near Macon Iron-Works. They captured some Confederate army supplies. No report from Brannan's division; Reynolds' division in camp at Trenton; Brannan somewhere in the neighborhood; corps headquarters at Warren's Mill.

September 6.—Baird's division encamped at Warren's Mill ; Negley's division reached Johnson's Crook ; Beatty's brigade was sent up the road to seize Stevens' Gap ; met the enemy's pickets, and, it being dark, did not proceed farther. The Eighteenth Ohio, of Negley's division, went to the top of Lookout Mountain, beyond Payne's Mill ; met the enemy's pickets and dispersed them. The head of Brannan's column reached Lookout Valley, 2 miles below Trenton. Reynolds' division in camp at Trenton. Rumors of the enemy's design to evacuate Chattanooga. Corps headquarters at Brown's Spring.

September 7.—Baird's division closed up with Negley's in the mouth of Johnson's Crook. Negley's gained possession of the top of the mountain, and secured the forks of the road. Brannan's division reached Trenton ; Reynolds' remained in camp at that place. Corps headquarters still at Brown's Spring.

September 8.—Baird's division remained in its camp of yesterday, at the junction of Hurricane and Lookout Creeks. Negley's division moved up to the top of Lookout Mountain, at the head of Johnson's Crook, one brigade occupying the pass ; another brigade was sent forward and seized Cooper's Gap, sending one regiment to the foot of the gap to occupy and hold it ; one regiment was also sent forward to seize Stevens' Gap, which was heavily obstructed with fallen trees. Brannan's division occupied the same position as last night. Reynolds' division headquarters at Trenton, with one brigade at Payne's Mill, 3 miles south of Trenton. Headquarters of the corps still at Brown's Spring.

September 9.—Baird's division moved across Lookout Mountain to the support of Negley. Negley's division moved across the mountain and took up a position in McLemore's Cove, near Rodgers' farm, throwing out his skirmishers as far as Bailey's Cross-Roads ; saw the enemy's cavalry in front, drawn up in line ; citizens reported a heavy force concentrated in his front at Dug Gap, consisting of infantry, cavalry, and artillery. Brannan's division in camp same as yesterday ; Reynolds' division also. The Ninety-second Illinois (mounted infantry) sent on a reconnaissance toward Chattanooga, along the ridge of Lookout Mountain. Colonel Atkins, commanding Ninety-second Illinois, reports September 9, 11 a. m., entered Chattanooga as the rear of the enemy's column was evacuating the place ; corps headquarters moved from Brown's Spring to Easley's farm, on Trenton and Lebanon road.

September 10.—General Negley's in front of or 1 mile west of Dug Gap, which has been heavily obstructed by the enemy and occupied by a strong picket line. General Baird ordered to move up to-night to Negley's support. General Reynolds to move at daylight to support Baird's left, and General Brannan to move at 8 a. m. to-morrow morning to support Reynolds. Headquarters and General Reynolds' division camped at foot of the mountain ; Brannan's division at Easley's.

September 11.—Baird's division closed up on Negley's at Widow Davis' house about 8 a. m. Soon afterward, Negley being satisfied, from his own observations and from the reports of officers sent out to reconnoiter, and also from loyal citizens, that the enemy was advancing on him in very superior force, and that his train was in imminent danger of being cut off if he accepted battle at Davis' Cross-Roads, determined to fall back to a strong position in front of Stevens' Gap. This movement he immediately proceeded to put into execution, and by his untiring energy and skill, and with the prompt co-operation of Baird, succeeded in gaining possession of the hills in front of Stevens' Gap and securing his trains, without losing a single wagon. For a detailed account of this movement, see reports* of Generals Negley and Baird, annexed, marked A and B. General Turchin, commanding Third Brigade, Reynolds' division, was pushed forward, by way of Cooper's Gap, to Negley's support, on the left, reaching his position about 10 a. m. Orders were sent to General Brannan to close up as rapidly as possible. Corps headquarters at top of Cooper's Gap.

September 12.—Brannan's division reached Negley's position by 8 a. m., and took post next on the left of Baird. Reynolds' division was posted on the left of Brannan, one brigade covering Cooper's Gap. Reports from citizens go to confirm the impression that a large force of the enemy is concentrated at La Fayette. A report from General McCook confirms that fact. A later dispatch from the same source says it is reported that Bragg's whole army, with Johnston's, is at La Fayette. Generals Brannan and Baird, with parts of their commands, went out on a reconnaissance toward Dug Gap at 1 p. m. to-day. General Brannan reports they advanced 2 miles beyond Davis' Cross-Roads without finding any enemy with the exception of a few mounted men. Corps headquarters encamped at top of Stevens' Gap.

* See pp. 270, 327.

September 13.—Negley's, Baird's, and Brannan's divisions remained in their camps of yesterday awaiting the arrival of McCook's corps, which had been ordered to close up to the left. Reynolds concentrated his division on the road from Cooper's Gap to Catlett's Gap. Two deserters from Eighteenth Tennessee state that they belong to Buckner's corps. Buckner's corps consists of eight brigades and two batteries of six guns each; were in the fight with Negley. Saw a brigade of Forrest's cavalry, commanded by Forrest in person, pass toward the fight on the 11th. Hill's and Buckner's corps were both engaged. Bragg's army is concentrated at La Fayette. Headquarters moved by way of Cooper's Gap to the foot of the mountain.

September 14.—General Reynolds took up a position at Pond Spring with his two infantry brigades, and was joined by Wilder at that place. Turchin's brigade, of Reynolds' division, made a reconnaissance to the mouth of Catlett's Gap with the Ninety-second Illinois (mounted infantry). Was opposed by rebel mounted pickets from Chickamauga Creek to mouth of Catlett's Gap, at which place he found their reserve drawn up, also a strong line of skirmishers to the right of the road; but having received instructions to avoid bringing on an engagement, he returned to camp with the brigade, leaving two regiments on Chattanooga Valley road, strongly posted on outposts. General Brannan advanced one brigade of his division to Chickamauga Creek, east of Lee's Mill, 1 mile to the right and south of Reynolds' position at Pond Spring. A mounted reconnaissance was also pushed forward to within a mile of Blue Bird Gap without encountering any of the enemy. A negro who had been taken before General Buckner yesterday and released again reports that Buckner and his corps are in Catlett's Gap preparing to defend that place. A negro woman, lately from the neighborhood of Dug Gap, reports a large force of rebels between Dug Gap and La Fayette.

September 16.—Corps headquarters and First and Second Divisions remained camped, as last reported, at foot of Stevens' Gap. Turchin's brigade, of Reynolds' division, made a reconnaissance toward Catlett's Gap. The enemy fell back as he advanced, until he came upon a force strongly posted, with two pieces of artillery, in the road. He made a second reconnaissance at 2 p: m. that day with but little further result, as he could advance but a short distance farther, the enemy being in force in his front.

September 17.—First, Second, and Third Divisions changed their positions from their camps of yesterday: Baird's (First) division, with its right resting at Gower's Ford and extending along Chickamauga Creek to Bird's Mill; Negley's (Second) division, with its right at Bird's Mill and its left connecting with Van Cleve's division at Owens' Ford; Brannan's (Third) division on the right of the First, covering four fords between Gower's Ford and Pond Spring. One brigade of the Fourth Division (Reynolds') thrown out in front of Pond Spring, on the Catlett's Gap road, covering the pass through the mountains. Wilder's brigade detached and ordered to report to department headquarters. The left of McCook's corps closed in; connected with our right near Pond Spring.

September 18.—At 4 p. m. the whole corps moved to the left along Chickamauga Creek to Crawfish Spring. On arriving at that place received orders to march on the cross-road leading by Widow Glenn's house to the Chattanooga and La Fayette road, and take up a position near Kelly's farm, on the La Fayette road, connecting with Crittenden on my right at Gordon's Mills. The head of the column reached Kelly's farm about daylight on the 19th, Baird's division in front, and took up a position at the forks of the road, facing toward Reed's and Alexander's Bridges over the Chickamauga. Colonel Wilder, commanding the mounted brigade of Reynolds' division, informed me that the enemy had crossed the Chickamauga in force at those two bridges the evening before and drove his brigade across the State road, or Chattanooga and La Fayette road, to the heights east of Widow Glenn's house.

Kelly's house is situated in an opening about three-fourths of a mile long and one-fourth of a mile wide, on the east side of the State road, and stretches along that road in a northerly direction, with a small field of perhaps 20 acres on the west side of the road, directly opposite to the house. From thence to the Chickamauga the surface of the country is undulating and covered with original forest timber, interspersed with undergrowth, in many places so dense that it is difficult to see 50 paces ahead. There is a cleared field near Jay's Mill, and cleared land in the vicinity of Reed's and Alexander's Bridges. A narrow field commences at a point about a fourth of a mile south of Kelly's house, on the east side of the State road, and extends, perhaps, for half a mile along the road toward Gordon's Mills. Between the State road and the foot of Missionary Ridge there is a skirt of timber stretching from the vicinity of Widow Glenn's house, south of the forks of the road to McDonald's house, three-fourths of a mile north of Kelly's. The eastern slope of the Missionary Ridge, between Glenn's and McDonald's, is cleared and mostly under cultivation. This position of Baird's threw my right in close proximity to Wilder's brigade ; the interval I intended to fill up with the two remaining brigades of Reynolds' division on their arrival. General Brannan, closely following Baird's division, was placed in position on his left, on the two roads leading from the State road to Reed's and Alexander's Bridges.

Col. Dan. McCook, commanding a brigade of the Reserve Corps, met me at General Baird's headquarters, and reported to me that he had been stationed the previous night on the road leading to Reed's Bridge, and that he could discover no force of the enemy except one brigade, which had crossed to the west side of the Chickamauga at Reed's Bridge the day before; and he believed it could be cut off, because, after it had crossed, he had destroyed the bridge, the enemy having retired toward Alexander's Bridge. Upon this information I directed General Brannan to post a brigade, within supporting distance of Baird, on the road to Alexander's Bridge, and with his other two brigades to reconnoiter the road leading to Reed's Bridge to see if he could locate the brigade reported by Colonel McCook, and, if a favorable opportunity occurred, to capture it. His dispositions were made according to instructions by 9 a. m.

General Baird was directed to throw forward his right wing, so as to get more nearly in line with Brannan, but to watch well on his right flank. Soon after this disposition of those two divisions, a portion of Palmer's division, of Crittenden's corps, took position to the right of General Baird's division. About 10 o'clock Croxton's brigade of Brannan's division, posted on the road leading to Alexander's Bridge, became engaged with the enemy, and I rode forward to his position to ascertain the character of the attack. Colonel Croxton reported to me that he had driven the enemy nearly half a mile, but that he was then meeting with obstinate resistance. I then rode back to Baird's position, and directed him to advance to

Croxton's support, which he did with his whole division, Stark-weather's brigade in reserve, and drove the enemy steadily before him for some distance, taking many prisoners. Croxton's brigade, which had been heavily engaged for over an hour with greatly superior numbers of the enemy, and being nearly exhausted of ammunition, was then moved to the rear to enable the men to fill up their boxes; and Baird and Brannan, having united their forces, drove the enemy from their immediate front. General Baird then halted for the purpose of readjusting his line; and hearing from prisoners that the enemy were in heavy force on his immediate right, he threw back his right wing in order to be ready for an attack from that quarter.

Before his dispositions could be completed, the enemy, in over-whelming numbers, furiously assaulted Scribner's and King's bri-gades, and drove them in disorder. Fortunately, at this time John-son's division, of McCook's corps, and Reynolds' division, of my corps, arrived, and were immediately placed in position. Johnson preceded Reynolds, his left connecting with Baird's right, and Palmer being immediately on Johnson's right, Reynolds was placed on the right of Palmer, with one brigade of his division in reserve. As soon as formed they advanced upon the enemy, attacking him in flank and driving him in great disorder for a mile and a half, while Bran-nan's troops met him in front as he was pursuing Baird's retiring brigades, driving the head of his column back and retaking the artillery, which had been temporarily lost by Baird's brigades, the Ninth Ohio recovering Battery H, Fifth U. S. Artillery, at the point of the bayonet. The enemy, at this time being hardly pressed by Johnson, Palmer, and Reynolds in flank, fell back in confusion upon his reserves, posted in a strong position on the west side of Chickamauga Creek between Reed's and Alexander's Bridges.

Brannan and Baird were then ordered to reorganize their commands and take position on commanding ground on the road from Mc-Donald's to Reed's Bridge, and hold it to the last extremity, as I ex-pected the next effort of the enemy would be to gain that road and our rear. This was about 2 p. m. After a lull of about one hour, a furious attack was made upon Reynolds' right, and he having called upon me for re-enforcements, I directed Brannan's division to move to his support, leaving King's brigade, of Baird's division, to hold the position at which Baird and Brannan had been posted, the balance of Baird's division closing up to the right on Johnson's division. It will be seen by General Reynolds' report, Croxton's brigade, of Brannan's division, reached his right just in time to de-feat the enemy's efforts to turn Reynolds' right and rear.

About 5 p. m., my lines being at that time very much extended in pursuing the enemy, I determined to concentrate them on more com-manding ground, as I felt confident that we should have a renewal of the battle in the morning. I rode forward to General Johnson's position and designated to him where to place his division; also to General Baird, who was present with Johnson. I then rode back to the cross-roads to locate Palmer and Reynolds on Johnson's right and on the crest of the ridge about 500 yards east of the State road. Soon after Palmer and Reynolds got their positions, and while Brannan was getting his on the ridge to the west of the State road, near Dyer's house, and to the rear and right of Reynolds, where I had ordered him as a reserve, the enemy assaulted first Johnson and then Baird in a most furious manner, producing some confusion, but order was soon restored, and the enemy repulsed in fine style ; after which these two divisions took up the positions assigned them for the night.

Before adjusting the line satisfactorily, I received an order to report to department headquarters immediately, and was absent from my command until near midnight. After my return from department headquarters, about 2 a. m. on the 20th, I received a report from General Baird that the left of his division did not rest on the Reed's Bridge road, as I had intended, and that he could not reach it without weakening his line too much. I immediately addressed a note to the general commanding requesting that General Negley be sent me to take position on Baird's left and rear, and thus secure our left from assault. During the night the troops threw up temporary breastworks of logs, and prepared for the encounter which all anticipated would come off the next day.

Although informed by note, from General Rosecrans' headquarters, that Negley's division would be sent immediately to take post on my left, it had not arrived at 7 a. m. on the 20th, and I sent Captain Willard, of my staff, to General Negley to urge him forward as rapidly as possible, and to point out his position to him. General Negley, in his official report, mentions that he received this order through Captain Willard at 8 a. m. on the 20th, and that he immediately commenced withdrawing his division for that purpose, when the enemy was reported to be massing a heavy force in his front, sharply engaging his skirmishers, and that he was directed by General Rosecrans to hold his position until relieved by some other command. General Beatty's brigade, however, was sent under the guidance of Captain Willard, who took it to its position, and it went into action immediately. The enemy at that time commenced a furious assault on Baird's left, and partially succeeded in gaining his rear. Beatty, meeting with superior numbers, was compelled to fall back until relieved by the fire of several regiments of Palmer's reserve, which I had ordered to the support of the left, being placed in position by General Baird, and which regiments, with the co-operation of Van Derveer's brigade of Brannan's division and a portion of Stanley's brigade of Negley's division, drove the enemy entirely from Baird's left and rear. General Baird being still hardly pressed in front, I ordered General Wood, who had just reported to me in person, to send one of the brigades of his division to General Baird. He replied that his division had been ordered by General Rosecrans to support Reynolds' right, but that if I would take the responsibility of changing his orders, he would cheerfully obey them, and sent Barnes' brigade, the head of which had just reached my position. General Wood then left me to rejoin the remainder of his division, which was still coming up.

To prevent a repetition of this attack of the enemy on our left I directed Captain Gaw, chief topographical officer on my staff, to go to the commanding officer of the troops on the left and rear of Baird, and direct him to mass as much artillery on the slopes of Missionary Ridge, west of the State road, as he could conveniently spare from his lines, supported strongly by infantry, so as to sweep the ground to the left and rear of Baird's position. This order General Negley, in his official report, mentions having received through Captain Gaw, but from his description of the position he assumed he must have misunderstood my order, and instead of massing the artillery near Baird's left, it was posted on the right of Brannan's division, nearly in rear of Reynolds' right.   At the time that the assault just described was made on Baird, the enemy attacked Johnson, Palmer, and Reynolds, with equal fierceness, which was continued at least two hours, making assault after assault with fresh troops, which were met by my troops with a most determined coolness and deliberation.   The enemy having exhausted his utmost energies to dislodge us, apparently fell back entirely from our front, and we were not disturbed again until near night, after the withdrawal of the troops to Rossville had commenced.   Just before the repulse of the enemy on our left, General Beatty came to me for fresh troops, in person, stating that most of those I had sent to him had gone back to the rear and right, and he was anxious to get at least another brigade before they attacked him again.   I immediately sent Captain Kellogg to hurry up General Sheridan, whose division I had been informed would be sent to me.

About 2 p. m., very soon after Captain Kellogg left me, hearing heavy firing to my right and rear through the woods, I turned in that direction and was riding to the slope of the hill in my rear to ascertain the cause.   Just as I passed out of the woods bordering the State road, I met Captain Kellogg returning, who reported to me that in attempting to reach General Sheridan he had met a large force in an open corn-field to the rear of Reynolds' position, advancing cautiously, with a strong line of skirmishers thrown out to their front, and that they had fired on him and forced him to return.   He had reported this to Colonel Harker, commanding a brigade of Wood's division, posted on a ridge a short distance to the rear of Reynolds' position, who also saw this force advancing, but, with Captain Kellogg, was of the opinion that they might be Sheridan's troops coming to our assistance.   I rode forward to Colonel Harker's position, and told him that, although I was expecting Sheridan from that direction, if those troops fired on him, seeing his flag, he must return their fire and resist their farther advance.   He immediately ordered his skirmishers to commence firing, and took up a position with his brigade on the crest of a hill a short distance to his right and rear, placing his right in connection with Brannan's division and portions of Beatty's and Stanley's brigades of Negley's division, which had been retired to that point from the left, as circumstantially narrated in the reports of General John Beatty and Colonel Stanley. I then rode to the crest of the hill referred to above.   On my way I met General Wood, who confirmed me in the opinion that the troops advancing upon us were the enemy, although we were not then aware of the disaster to the right and center of our army.   I then directed him to place his division on the prolongation of Brannan's, who, I had ascertained from Wood, was on the top of the hill above referred to, and to resist the farther advance of the enemy as long as possible. I sent my aide, Captain Kellogg, to notify General Reynolds that our right had been turned, and that the enemy was in his rear in force.

General Wood barely had time to dispose his troops on the left of Brannan before another of those fierce assaults, similar to those made in the morning on my lines, was made on him and Brannan combined, and kept up by the enemy throwing in fresh troops as fast as those in their front were driven back, until near nightfall.   About the time that Wood took up his position, General Gordon Granger appeared on my left flank at the head of Steedman's division of his corps. I immediately dispatched a staff officer, Captain Johnson, Second

Indiana Cavalry, of Negley's division, to him with orders to push forward and take position on Brannan's right, which order was complied with with the greatest promptness and alacrity. Steedman, moving his division into position with almost as much precision as if on drill, and fighting his way to the crest of the hill on Brannan's right, moved forward his artillery and drove the enemy down the southern slope, inflicting on him a most terrible loss in killed and wounded. This opportune arrival of fresh troops revived the flagging spirits of our men on the right, and inspired them with new ard r for the contest. Every assault of the enemy from that time until nightfall was repulsed in the most gallant style by the whole line.

By this time the ammunition in the boxes of the men was reduced, on an average, to 2 or 3 rounds per man, and my ammunition trains having been unfortunately ordered to the rear by some unauthorized person, we should have been entirely without ammunition in a very short time had not a small supply come up with General Steedman's command. This, being distributed among the troops, gave them about 10 rounds per man.

General Garfield, chief of staff of General Rosecrans, reached this position about 4 p. m., in company with Lieutenant-Colonel Thruston, of McCook's staff, and Captains Gaw and Barker, of my staff, who had been sent to the rear to bring back the ammunition, if possible. General Garfield gave me the first reliable information that the right and center of our army had been driven, and of its condition at that time. I soon after received a dispatch from General Rosecrans, directing me to assume command of all the forces, and, with Crittenden and McCook, take a strong position and assume a threatening attitude at Rossville, sending the unorganized forces to Chattanooga for reorganization, stating that he would examine the ground at Chattanooga, and then join me; also that he had sent out rations and ammunition to meet me at Rossville.

I determined to hold the position until nightfall, if possible, in the meantime sending Captains Barker and Kellogg to distribute the ammunition, Major Lawrence, my chief of artillery, having been previously sent to notify the different commanders that ammunition would be supplied them shortly. As soon as they reported the distribution of the ammunition, I directed Captain Willard to inform the division commanders to prepare to withdraw their commands as soon as they received orders. At 5.30 p. m. Captain Barker, commanding my escort, was sent to notify General Reynolds to commence the movement, and I left the position behind General Wood's command to meet Reynolds and point out to him the position where I wished him to form line to cover the retirement of the other troops on the left.

In passing through an open woods bordering the State road, and between my last and Reynolds' position, I was cautioned by a couple of soldiers, who had been to hunt water, that there was a large force of the rebels in these woods, drawn up in line and advancing toward me. Just at this time I saw the head of Reynolds' column approaching, and calling to the general himself, directed him to form line perpendicular to the State road, changing the head of his column to the left, with his right resting on that road, and to charge the enemy, who were then in his immediate front. This movement was made with the utmost promptitude, and facing to the right while on the march, Turchin threw his brigade upon the rebel force, routing them and driving them in utter confusion entirely beyond Baird's left. In this splendid advance more than 200 prisoners were captured and sent to the rear.

Colonel Robinson, commanding the Second Brigade, Reynolds' division, followed closely upon Turchin, and I posted him on the road leading through the ridge to hold the ground while the troops on our right and left passed by. In a few moments General Willich, commanding a brigade of Johnson's division, reported to me that his brigade was in position on a commanding piece of ground to the right of the Ridge road. I directed him to report to General Reynolds, and assist in covering the retirement of the troops. Turchin's brigade, after driving the enemy a mile and a half, was reassembled, and took its position on the Ridge road, with Robinson and Willich.

These dispositions being made, I sent orders to Generals Wood, Brannan, and Granger to withdraw from their positions. Johnson's and Baird's divisions were attacked at the moment of retiring, but, by being prepared, retired without confusion or any serious losses. General Palmer was also attacked while retiring. Grose's brigade was thrown into some confusion, but Cruft's brigade came off in good style, both, however, with little loss. I then proceeded to Rossville, accompanied by Generals Garfield and Gordon Granger, and immediately prepared to place the troops in position at that point. One brigade of Negley's division was posted in the gap, on the Ringgold road, and two brigades on the top of the ridge to the right of the road, adjoining the brigade in the road; Reynolds' division on the right of Negley's and reaching to the Dry Valley road; Brannan's division in the rear of Reynolds' right, as a reserve; McCook's corps on the right of the Dry Valley road, and stretching toward the west, his right reaching nearly to Chattanooga Creek; Crittenden's entire corps was posted on the heights to the left of the Ringgold road, with Steedman's division of Granger's corps in reserve behind his left; Baird's division in reserve, and in supporting distance of the brigade in the gap; McCook's brigade of Granger's corps was also posted as a reserve to the brigade of Negley on the top of the ridge, to the right of the road; Minty's brigade of cavalry was on the Ringgold road, about a mile and a half in advance of the gap.

About 10 a. m. of the 21st, receiving a message from Minty that the enemy were advancing on him with a strong force of cavalry and infantry, I directed him to retire through the gap and post his command on our left flank, and throw out strong reconnoitering parties across the ridge to observe and report any movements of the enemy on our left front. From information received from citizens, I was convinced that the position was untenable in the face of the odds we had opposed to us, as the enemy could easily concentrate upon our right flank, which, if driven, would expose our center and left to be entirely cut off from our communications. I therefore advised the commanding general to concentrate the troops at Chattanooga. About the time I made the suggestion to withdraw, the enemy made a demonstration on the direct road, but were soon repulsed. In anticipation of this order to concentrate at Chattanooga, I sent for the corps commanders, and gave such general instructions as would enable them to prepare their commands for making the movement without confusion. All wagons, ambulances, and surplus artillery carriages were sent to the rear before night.

The order for the withdrawal being received about 6 p. m. the movement commenced at 9 p. m., in the following order: Strong skirmish lines, under the direction of judicious officers, were thrown out to the front of each division to cover this movement, with directions to retire at daylight, deployed and in supporting distance, the whole to be supported by the First Division, Fourteenth Army Corps, under the superintendence of Major-General Rousseau, assisted by Minty's brigade of cavalry, which was to follow after the skirmishers. Crittenden's corps was to move from the hill to the left of the road at 9 p. m., followed by Steedman's division. Next Negley's division was to withdraw at 10 p. m. ; then Reynolds, McCook's corps, by divisions from left to right, moving within supporting distance one after the other ; Brannan's division was posted at 6 p. m. on the road about half way between Rossville and Chattanooga to cover the movement. The troops were withdrawn in a quiet, orderly manner, without the loss of a single man, and by 7 a. m. on the 22d were in their positions in front of Chattanooga, which had been assigned to them previous to their arrival, and which they now occupy, covered by strong intrenchments thrown up on the day of our arrival, and strengthened from day to day until they were considered sufficiently strong for all defensive purposes.

I respectfully refer you to the reports of division, brigade, and regimental commanders for the names of those of their respective commands who distinguished themselves. Among them I am much gratified to find the names of Col. F. Van Derveer, Thirty-fifth Ohio, commanding Third Brigade, and Col. John T. Croxton, Fourth Kentucky, commanding Second Brigade, Brannan's division, both of whom I saw on Saturday, and I can confirm the reports given of them by their division commander. Col. B. F. Scribner, Thirty-eighth Indiana, commanding First Brigade, Baird's division, was on the right of that division on Saturday morning, when it was attacked in flank by an overwhelming force of the enemy and driven back ; yet Colonel Scribner was enabled to rally and reorganize it without the least difficulty, as soon as supported by Johnson's division.

All the troops under my immediate command fought most gallantly on both days, and were ably handled by their respective commanders, viz : Major-Generals Palmer and Reynolds, and Brigadier-Generals Brannan, Johnson, and Baird, on Saturday, and on Sunday, in the afternoon, in addition to the above, Maj. Gen. Gordon Granger, commanding Reserve Corps, and Brigadier-General Wood, commanding First Division, Twenty-first Army Corps, who, with two brigades of his division, under their brave commanders, Colonels Harker and Buell, most nobly sustained Brannan's left, while Brigadier-General Steedman, commanding a division of the Reserve Corps, as valiantly maintained his right. Col. Dan. McCook, commanding a brigade of the Reserve Corps, and left by General Granger near McDonald's house, in a commanding position, kept a large force of the enemy's cavalry at bay while hovering on Baird's left, and with his battery materially aided Turchin's handsome charge on the enemy, who had closed in on our left. Brigadier-General Willich, commanding a brigade of Johnson's division, on Saturday, in the attack, and especially on Sunday, nobly sustained his reputation as a soldier. Brig. Gen. John Beatty and Col. T. R. Stanley, commanding brigades of Negley's division, bravely supported Baird's left in the morning of Sunday. Colonel Stanley being struck by the fragments of a shell and disabled in the afternoon, the brigade fought with Brannan's division, under the command of Col. W. L. Stoughton, Eleventh Michigan.   Col. J. G. Parkhurst, commanding Ninth Michigan Volunteers, and provost-marshal Fourteenth Army Corps, at the head of his regiment, did most valuable service on the 20th, in arresting stragglers and reorganizing the troops which had been driven from the field.   His report is herewith inclosed, and special reference made thereto for particulars.

I also tender my thanks to the members of my staff for the services they rendered me.   To Lieut. Col. G. E. Flynt, my assistant adjutant-general; Lieut. Col. A. J. Mackay, chief quartermaster; Lieut. Col. J. R. Paul, chief commissary of subsistence, who, although not present on the field of battle, were discharging their duties in their respective departments entirely to my satisfaction. Lieut. Col. A. von Schrader, Seventy-fourth Ohio, assistant inspector-general, who rendered most efficient service as aide-de-camp during the first day's fight, and who was taken prisoner on the afternoon of the 19th while in the discharge of his duty; Maj. W. E. Lawrence, First Ohio Artillery, my chief of artillery; Capts. J. P. Willard and S. C. Kellogg, aides-de-camp; Capt. J. D. Barker, First Ohio Cavalry, commanding my escort; Capt. W. B. Gaw, chief topographical officer Fourteenth Army Corps, as also the signal officers of the corps, who did duty on the field as aides, and were of great assistance in conducting the operations of my command.   Surgs. F. H. Gross, medical director, and H. C. Barrell, medical purveyor, were untiring in their efforts to relieve the wants of the wounded. Dr. Gross was wounded early in the engagement Sunday, but continued in the discharge of his duties.   Capt. G. C. Moody, Nineteenth U. S. Infantry, commissary of musters, also rendered efficient service as aide-de-camp.   Captain Johnson, Second Indiana Cavalry, of General Negley's staff, and Capt. T. C. Williams, Nineteenth U. S. Infantry, of General Baird's staff, having been cut off from their respective commanders, reported to me for duty, and were of great assistance as aides.

I submit herewith annexed a consolidated report of the casualties. of the Fourteenth Army Corps.*

Very respectfully, your obedient servant,

GEO. H. THOMAS,
Major-General U. S. Volunteers, Commanding.

Brig. Gen. JAMES A. GARFIELD,
Chief of Staff, Department of the Cumberland.

ADDENDA.

[CHATTANOOGA, TENN.,
September 30, 1863.]

General THOMAS:

Your report says you received my dispatch of 12.15 p. m., directing you to retire on Rossville.   This is an error in the hour of the dispatch.   I did not leave the battle-field until after that hour, nor reach Chattanooga before 3.40 p. m.

Please have the error corrected.   The first dispatch to you must have been written as late as 4.15.

W. S. ROSECRANS.

---

* Embodied in revised statement, p. 171.

HEADQUARTERS FOURTEENTH ARMY CORPS,
Chattanooga, October 3, 1863.

Major-General ROSECRANS,
        Commanding Department:

GENERAL: Your dispatch just received. I made mention of the time of receiving your dispatch on the battle-field to call attention to the fact, believing it to have been an error. I will make the correction in my forthcoming report, or in my fair copy.*
        Very respectfully, your obedient servant,
                        GEO. H. THOMAS,
                Major-General U. S. Volunteers, Commanding.

—

CHATTANOOGA, TENN.,
January 11, 1864—9.30 p. m.
(Received 10.50 a. m., 12th.)

Maj. Gen. H. W. HALLECK,
        General-in-Chief:

The papers are publishing what purports to be my official report of the operations of the Fourteenth Army Corps at the battle of Chickamauga. It is not a full copy of the report which I sent in, to be forwarded to Washington, and, in addition, contains many inaccuracies.
                        GEO. H. THOMAS,
                                Major-General.

—

HEADQUARTERS OF THE ARMY,
Washington, January 12, 1864.

Maj. Gen. GEORGE H. THOMAS,
        Chattanooga:

GENERAL: Your telegram in regard to the newspapers publishing an incorrect version of your official report of the battle of Chickamauga is received, and I have telegraphed a brief reply. I deem it my duty to write you some additional facts in relation to the publication complained of.

Before the reports on that battle were received here the Secretary of War, from some suspicion or intimation that copies or extracts would be given clandestinely to the newspapers, directed Colonel Townsend to lock them up as soon as they arrived, and to keep the keys in his own possession till they were called for by Congress.

As no copies or extracts from your report could possibly have been obtained from these headquarters, you will form your own conclusions in regard to how and where they were obtained. It is stated that portions of these reports were telegraphed to the New York newspapers even before the originals were received at the Adjutant-General's Office here.

I will only add that I have never read or seen your report.
        Truly, yours,

                        H. W. HALLECK.

_____

*See p. 253.

WAR DEPARTMENT, *Washington City, March* 9, 1864.

Maj. Gen. GEORGE H. THOMAS, *Chattanooga, Tenn.* :

GENERAL : It is stated by a newspaper correspondent that on the 19th of January you were serenaded by the Ninth Ohio Regiment, and on that occasion declared to some of the officers of the regiment that you had praised them in your official report of the battle of Chickamauga, and then added:

I wanted to do justice to the regiment, and I cannot understand why—I feel sorry—that the War Department saw fit to curtail my report so as to leave this out.

I presume that you are aware that the only copy of your report which has yet been published was the rough draft furnished by you to Major-General Rosecrans, that officer being in great haste to make out his own report. General Rosecrans gave this rough draft which you had sent him to Mr. Villard, the correspondent of the Tribune, and it was published in that paper. The final report which you sent to Washington was, so far as I am aware, never seen by Mr. Villard. I am confident that you have not imputed to the War Department the mutilation of any official documents, but it seems proper that you should be aware of a statement which pretends to be made on the authority of your own language.

I am, general, with great regard, yours, faithfully,

C. A. DANA.

—

ITINERARY OF THE FOURTEENTH ARMY CORPS.*

August 1.—Corps headquarters and Second and Third Divisions at Decherd, First Division at Cowan, and Fourth Division at University Place.

August 10.—First Division left Cowan for a point on the railroad between Anderson and Stevenson, Stanley's brigade of Second Division relieving them at Cowan.

August 16.—Second Division entire moved from Decherd to a point a little north of Stevenson.

August 17.—Third and Fourth Divisions were moved to the Sequatchie and Battle Creek Valleys.

Corps headquarters moved on the 18th from Decherd.

The positions of the divisions on the 21st stood as follows, viz: Corps headquarters at Bolivar, Ala., First Division at Anderson Station, Second Division 2 miles north of Stevenson, Third Division at Battle Creek, and Fourth Division at Jasper, operating at and near Shellmound, also in front of Chattanooga and Harrison's, which places were shelled by Colonel Wilder on the 21st.

Preparations made by the whole command to cross the Tennessee River on or about the 1st of September.

No. 14.

Report of Surg. Ferdinand H. Gross, U. S. Army, Medical Director.

HEADQUARTERS FOURTEENTH ARMY CORPS,
MEDICAL DIRECTOR'S OFFICE,
Chattanooga, Tenn., October 11, 1863.

GENERAL: I have the honor to submit the following report as regards the medical and hospital supplies, the means of transporta-

---

*From return for August.

tion of the sick and wounded, and the general transactions of the medical department of the Fourteenth Army Corps, since its passage of the Tennessee River up to the time of reaching Chattanooga.

The regiments and batteries were all abundantly supplied with medicines and surgical instruments, the latter having, previous to our march, been thoroughly inspected and repaired by an expert.

Aside from the usual regimental supplies, which are transported in the hospital wagons and accompany the regiments, we were provided with a reserve supply, consisting of hospital tents, blankets, sheets, hair pillows, shirts, drawers, bed-sacks, surgical instruments, bandages, lint, mess-chests (including cooking utensils), concentrated milk and beef, liquor, chloroform, and such other medicines, surgical apparatus, and hospital stores as experience has taught to be most needed and useful in emergencies in the field.

These supplies were in possession of the medical purveyor of the corps, subject to my order. They were transported in a train of 15 army wagons. Although these reserve supplies had been drawn upon since our advance from Murfreesborough in June last, they were still deemed ample in quantity.

The four divisions of the corps were each provided with a train of 30 light two-horse ambulances, under the general control of the corps and division medical directors. In addition to these, each regiment and each battery had permanently attached to it 1 ambulance, which is usually driven in the rear of these commands. This arrangement of our ambulances has operated more satisfactorily than any other that has yet been tried in this army.

Before the command entered upon the march it was directed that all men who were sick and who, in the judgment of the medical officers, would not be able to endure the fatigues of the campaign should be sent to the General Field Hospital at Stevenson.

The First Division crossed the river at Bridgeport on the 4th of September, and on the 7th reached the valley between Raccoon and Lookout Mountains, where it remained in camp for two days. The march was continued on the 10th, crossing Lookout Mountain and encamping in McLemore's Cove. On the 11th it was ordered to close up on the Second Division, which had crossed the river at Caperton's Ferry on or about the 1st of September, and had continued its march in advance of the First Division, without interruptions, until it reached a point near Dug Gap, in Pigeon Ridge, where the enemy was encountered. About 7 a. m. on the 11th, the First Division closed up on the Second, and shortly before noon skirmishing began. Surgs. S. Marks and R. G. Bogue, the respective directors of the First and Second Divisions, established the hospital at Mrs. Davis' house, in the rear of the line of battle. Eight or 10 wounded had been brought in, when it was noticed that our forces began to retire. The wounded were promptly removed by ambulances; first to Bailey's Cross-Roads, and finally to Stevens' house, at the foot of Lookout Mountain, near Stevens' Gap. No wounded were left upon the field.

The casualties of the affair were as follows:

Command.	Killed.	Wounded.
First Division	2	5
Second Division	9	22
Total	11	27

The wounded were well cared for at this temporary hospital, and on the 16th, after consulting the general commanding the corps, I directed the wounded and those of the sick who were hospital cases to be sent to Chattanooga by the Chattanooga Valley road. A medical officer and a number of nurses were detailed to accompany this train. I regret to say that, up to this time, 2 of the wounded had died. Three were so seriously injured as not to be transportable, and, by the direction of the medical director of the Second Division, a medical officer was detailed to remain and take care of them.

The Third Division moved from the mouth of Battle Creek and effected the passage of the Tennessee River by the evening of the 3d of September, with the loss of 3 men by drowning. This command also crossed Raccoon and Lookout Mountains, reaching the southeast side of the latter on the forenoon of the 13th without any casualties.

The Fourth Division, having crossed the river at Shellmound, marched over the above-mentioned mountains, and arrived in McLemore's Cove about the same time with the division last referred to. I regret to say that the medical director, Surg. O. Q. Herrick, and the brigade surgeons of the command, who were subsequently captured at the battle of Chickamauga, still remain in the hands of the enemy, preventing me in a great measure from furnishing an account of those incidents of the march that might be of interest to our branch of the service without having been furnished with the particulars.

I respectfully refer to an encounter with the enemy which took place on the 11th and 12th of September, in which the Seventeenth and Seventy-second Indiana and Ninety-second Regiment Illinois Volunteers were engaged, and sustained the loss of 8 killed and 19 wounded.

Our forces were heavily pressed by the rebels, and as soon as the wounded were removed from the field they were sent to Chattanooga for treatment.

The manner in which both officers and men accomplished the laborious and fatiguing marches over the rough mountains, with a frequent scarcity of water, and through the dusty valley roads of this sandy region, where the atmosphere about the moving columns was at times almost suffocating, has demonstrated in a marvelous degree the power of endurance of our troops.

On the 17th of September the command commenced moving toward the left, and continued marching in that direction, when early on the morning of the 19th it was discovered that the enemy confronted us. Our troops were rapidly placed in line of battle on the grounds now known as the "Chickamauga battle-field." The Second Division, however, had been left at a point near Crawfish Spring, about 4½ miles distant to the right.

On the morning of the 19th one brigade of this division became engaged with the enemy at that point. The wounded of this affair were conveyed to hospitals which were about being established in that vicinity.

Upon information received from Asst. Surg. D. Bache, assistant medical director, Department of the Cumberland, that Crawfish Spring was intended for the principal depot for the reception of the wounded, the directors of the Second and Fourth Divisions of this corps at once commenced establishing their division hospitals at that place, making use of the regimental hospital supplies for that purpose.

Along the line of battle previously referred to the engagement had commenced, and the wounded were being rapidly removed from the field and conveyed to the hospitals.

When it was discovered at Crawfish Spring that the fighting bore toward the left, an attempt was made to move the Fourth Division hospital nearer to the line of battle. The troops on the right, however, began to fall back, planting a battery in the vicinity of the new site for this hospital, and consequently compelling the surgeons to remove again to Crawfish Spring.

The hospital of the First Division was established on the morning of the 19th at Dyer's house, which at that time was located in the rear of the right of this corps. A fine spring, a number of outbuildings, and plenty of straw near by rendered this a desirable locality for hospital purposes. Shortly before noon it was found necessary, on account of the large number of wounded at this place, to pitch the hospital tents. Everything went on quite well until about 5 p. m., when our troops began to retire in that direction, and soon the "enemy's grape and canister were being thrown in and around the hospital, making the locality entirely unsafe for the wounded." Orders were received from Surg. G. Perin, medical director of the department, to send the wounded to Crawfish. Our forces having repulsed the enemy from Dyer's house the surgeons were enabled to return to their duty.

On the morning of the 20th about 40 wounded were still at this house, which it now became necessary to abandon. Surgeon Reeve, who had been placed in charge of this hospital, succeeded, with the medical officers under him, in removing all the wounded and property, except the hospital tent of the Seventy-ninth Pennsylvania. By 10 o'clock they were on the road to Chattanooga.

The Third Division became engaged with the enemy early on the 19th. The hospital was located on the grounds at Cloud's house, in the rear, and between 1 and 2 miles to the left of the point where the fighting first commenced, and on the direct road to Rossville.

The wounded from various divisions, including a large number of those of the enemy, were accumulating at this hospital, and before night the number reached near 1,000. Straw was brought for bedding, hot coffee and soup served, and fires built as near as practicable to the wounded, for their protection from the cold of the night air. I remained here until the next morning, and continued operating with the medical officers present on such cases as imperatively demanded it, until the lowness of the temperature caused us to discontinue for the night. During the next morning I returned to headquarters in the field, and while there this hospital became cut off by the enemy. I was unable either to reach it myself or to get a messenger through.

Surgeon Tollman, the division director, reports that while on that forenoon the medical officers were engaged with wounded, a furious cannonade opened upon them, slightly injuring several men and killing a wounded officer. Those who were able to walk were started on foot, and all available ambulances and wagons were loaded with wounded and started for Rossville, distant about 4 miles to the left and toward Chattanooga. About 60 non-transportable cases were left, and as in all probability more of our wounded would subsequently reach this point, 3 medical officers were detailed to remain. The regimental hospital tents and tents of the medical officers of this division, together with a portion of the regimental supplies, fell into the hands of the enemy.

During the forenoon of the 20th, I endeavored, in company with the medical director of General McCook's corps, to reach the hospitals at Crawfish Spring. We were soon met, however, by the enemy's skirmishers and compelled to return. About noon we noticed numerous wagons and ambulances moving on the roads to the rear, and subsequently large numbers of troops from the right and center were also moving in that direction. The ambulances were mostly loaded with wounded. We directed them to move to Chattanooga, via Rossville.

I had directed the medical purveyor of the corps, Asst. Surg. H. C. Barrell, on the evening of the 19th, to bring up the reserve supplies on the road leading from Rossville to the Third Division hospital at Cloud's house, believing this to be the most suitable locality (from the knowledge I possessed of the country) at which to collect the larger number of wounded, on account of the direct communication, by good roads, with Chattanooga. On the morning of the 20th I sent a messenger to Dr. Barrell, informing him that the Third Division hospital had fallen into the hands of the enemy, and directing him to take the Dry Valley road, which it appears he had already done. Being met by retreating troops and wagons, it was deemed prudent to halt this train of supplies, which was thus saved and subsequently taken to Chattanooga, where, by order of the medical director of the department, they were issued to the hospitals at this place and served a good purpose.

During the latter part of the afternoon the wounded from the left, where the battle was still raging, crowded the road leading from McDonald's house to the Dry Valley road. Many were conveyed in ambulances, and hundreds of the slightly injured who were able to walk or be led by their comrades moved along on foot.

After nightfall the command retired upon Rossville. The wounded continued to move to the rear nearly all night. On Monday morning, the 21st, ambulances were driven as far front as it was safe for them to go, and gathered up such wounded as had not been recovered in that vicinity during the night; a large number still at Rossville that morning were also sent to the rear.

A new line of battle was formed at the latter place. We suffered but little here, and the very small number of injured were all brought away.

Aside from the hospital arrangements, which had been made by the medical director of the department previous to our reaching this point, a general field hospital was about being established on the opposite side of the river. At my request I was permitted to appropriate a part of this for a corps field hospital. It remained under my general superintendence, with Surgeon Marks in charge, until the 10th instant, when all hospitals of this character were consolidated into one general field hospital.

It is the opinion generally of our surgeons that the wounded are doing remarkably well.

I regret to say that 19 of our medical officers, who remained at the captured hospitals, are still in the hands of the enemy, notwithstanding that our wounded have been paroled and brought within our lines. The following is a list of the names of these officers:

Surg. O. Q. Herrick, Surg. C. S. Arthur, Surg. C. N. Fowler, Surg. Joseph Fithian, Surg. J. L. Worden, Surg. John McCurdy, Surg. J. R. Brelsford, Surg. James P. Reeve, Surg. L. J. Dixon, Asst. Surg. W. B. Graham, Asst. Surg. J. C. Elliott, Asst. Surg. A. H. Shaffer, Asst. Surg. E. F. Purdum, Asst. Surg. N. H. Sidwell, Asst. Surg.

Frederick Corfe, Asst. Surg. William P. Hornbrook, Asst. Surg. D. D. Benedict, Asst. Surg. C. O. Wright, Asst. Surg. A. H. Landis.

I have been informed by Surg. O. Q. Herrick, from the enemy's lines, that all the medical officers with him have been paroled to report to the commandant of the post at Atlanta as soon as relieved from taking care of the United States sick and wounded prisoners.

The conduct of the medical officers of this corps has, with few exceptions, been highly commendable. Special mentions have been made in division reports, which will be forwarded to Surg. G. Perin, medical director, Department of the Cumberland. I refer especially to the services of the following:

Surg. S. Marks, medical director, First Division; Surg. R. G. Bogue, medical director, Second Division; Surg. M. C. Tollman, medical director, Third Division; O. Q. Herrick, medical director, Fourth Division, and the efficient medical purveyor of the corps, Asst. Surg. H. C. Barrell.

Arrangements have been made to get an accurate list of the names of the wounded, including those sent to the hospitals in the rear. When this has been accomplished in a satisfactory manner a copy will be forwarded. At present I add only the following estimates of numbers: *

Fourteenth Army Corps.	Killed.	Wounded.	Total.
First Division	200	650	850
Second Division	71	491	562
Third Division	325	1,642	1,967
Fourth Division	109	725	834
Total	705	3,508	4,213

It is believed by the director of the First Division that future information from those marked as missing on other reports will swell this estimate of wounded in that command.

While attempting to reach the Third Division hospital, on the morning of the 20th, in company with the topographical engineer, Captain Gaw, I received a slight wound in the neck, by a musket ball, not disabling me, however, for duty.

I am, general, very respectfully, your obedient servant.

F. H. GROSS,
Surg., U. S. Vols., Medical Director, 14*th Army Corps.*

Maj. Gen. GEORGE H. THOMAS,
Commanding Fourteenth Army Corps.

No. 15.

Report of Col. John G. Parkhurst, Ninth Michigan Infantry, Provost-Marshal.

HEADQUARTERS FOURTEENTH ARMY CORPS,
DEPARTMENT OF THE CUMBERLAND,
PROVOST-MARSHAL'S OFFICE,
Chattanooga, September 27, 1863.

COLONEL: I have the honor to submit the following report of the part taken by the Ninth Regiment Michigan Infantry, provost

* See revised statement p. 171.

guard to the Fourteenth Army Corps, in the advance upon the enemy, from Stevenson, Ala.

Agreeably to orders received from corps headquarters, the regiment marched from Bolivar at 6 o'clock on the morning of the 3d of September, in charge of headquarters train, and continued to move with the general commanding, from day to day, up to the morning of the 17th, performing the usual provost duties of the corps.

On the 15th one company of the regiment was detailed as a guard to the supply train and sent to Stevenson.

On the 17th I was ordered to take the train to Dickey's Post-Office, on the Valley road.

On the evening of the 17th the regiment and train was again moved to the headquarters of the general commanding.

On the evening of the 18th, by direction of the general commanding, the regiment in charge of the train moved on to the Valley road in rear of Crawfish Spring and camped for the night.

On the 19th, by direction of the general commanding, I moved the train into Chattanooga and parked it on the bank of the Tennessee River.

About 9 o'clock in the evening of the 19th, Dr. Gross, medical director, ordered the medical supply train to the hospital established for the Third Division on Missionary Ridge. Deeming it unsafe to send the medical supply train without a guard, I left one company in camp to guard the balance of headquarters train, and on the morning of the 20th I left Chattanooga with eight companies of my regiment in charge of the medical train, intending to take it to the battle-field. I reached Rossville without any difficulty and proceeded up the Dry Valley road to a point on the ridge to the right and rear of the field hospital, and about 1½ miles from it, where Dr. Barrell, medical purveyor, reported to me that the hospital to which I was going had fallen into the hands of the enemy.

I immediately sent Adjutant Duffield forward to ascertain the position of the troops, and as to the truth of the report of Dr. Barrell, and meantime halted the train and regiment and stacked arms. Before my adjutant returned, and about half past 12 o'clock, many stragglers from the front began to make their appearance. I deployed two companies of the regiment on the right and left of the road and arrested the stragglers as they came up and organized them into companies.

About 1 o'clock a large body of troops, several batteries, and transportation wagons came rushing through the woods and over the road in the utmost confusion. I formed a line of battle across the road with fixed bayonets, and with much difficulty succeeded in checking the stampede. I at once put the troops thus stopped in position to resist a pursuing force, the artillery under command of Captain Hitchcock [Hotchkiss] and the stragglers under command of Major Jenney, of the Ninth Michigan. The troops from the front continued to rush on toward my line in great confusion, and at this moment I discovered Major-General Crittenden, of the Twenty-first Army Corps, with some of his staff. I immediately rode up to him and respectfully asked him to stop and take command of the forces I was collecting and had then collected, and place them in a position to resist an attack or take them back to the battle-field, which I then supposed and now believe could have been successfully accomplished. Major-General Crittenden declined to take command, saying, "This," meaning the forces there collected, "is no command for me." I remarked to the general that the force I then had collected and should succeed in collecting was too much of a command for me. General Crittenden replied, "You have done marvelously well and you had better keep command." Just at that moment a sergeant reported to General Crittenden that a large force of the enemy was advancing upon the left flank of my line. General Crittenden suggested that I had better change the position of my force to meet the attack, which I at once commenced doing, and General Crittenden proceeded to the rear. Before I had taken a new position General Crittenden's aide came to me, and said that the general requested that I should take the force I had and move it with the trains on the road in as much order as possible to Chattanooga, which would be our next point for making a stand. Agreeably to this request I ordered the wagon trains into the road, headed toward Chattanooga, and put my regiment and the force in command of Major Jenney in the rear and moved quietly down the road some 3 miles to a large open field, where I found a captain of the Anderson Cavalry collecting stragglers in our advance. Soon after reaching this point General J. C. Davis arrived and assumed command and took the management of reorganizing the straggling troops. I soon afterward saw Lieutenant-Colonel Ducat assisting in the reorganization, and soon thereafter Major-General Negley arrived and took command. Major-General Sheridan also came up with a small force.

I directed Lieutenant Dobbelaere, of the Ninth Michigan, to take the medical train into Chattanooga, which he did, and I reported to Major-General Negley with my regiment and a regiment of stragglers for duty. That portion of the army which retreated and left the field was at this point reorganized under the direction of Major-General Negley, and moved on to Rossville and placed in position, the Ninth Michigan Infantry forming a part of a brigade.

I remained under command of Major-General Negley until about 2 o'clock on the morning of the 21st, when, by direction of the general commanding, I put my regiment in a position to enable me to arrest stragglers from the field in the anticipated battle of the 21st. During the engagement on the 21st I arrested a large number of stragglers, and sent them to their commands in the field, and by direction of the general commanding, forwarded 167 to the provost-marshal-general at Chattanooga, with directions to have them sent to Nashville for trial as cowards and skulkers from the battle-field. Many of these last-named were arrested leaving the field with their arms, which I took from them. The most of the arms thus taken have since been put into the hands of returned convalescents who have been forwarded to their commands.

On the night of the 21st I retired with my regiment to Chattanooga, since which time it has been on provost and fatigue duty at corps headquarters and at the corps hospitals.

I append hereto a statement of casualties in the corps since crossing the Tennessee River. Also a statement of the number of prisoners captured by this corps from the enemy.

I remain, colonel, your obedient servant,

J. G. PARKHURST,
Col., Comdg. 9th Mich. Infty., and Prov. Mar., 14th A. C.

Lieut. Col. George E. Flynt,
　Assistant Adjutant-General, and Chief of Staff.

[Inclosures.]

Statement of Casualties in the Fourteenth Army Corps since crossing the Tennessee River.

Command.	Commissioned officers.				Enlisted men.				Aggregate.
	Killed.	Wounded.	Captured.	Total.	Killed.	Wounded.	Captured.	Total.	
First Division............................	13	44	82	139	182	738	1,333	2,253	2,392
Second Division	5	32	13	50	81	420	334	725	875
Third Division a...........................	......	......	......	......	317	1,629	407	2,353	2,353
Fourth Division	5	39	21	65	121	719	359	1,199	1,264
Headquarters Fourteenth Army Corps ...	......	......	1	1	......	......	1	1	2
Total...............................	23	115	117	255	701	3,506	2,434	6,531	6,886

a This division does not discriminate in its report between officers and men captured.

—

Statement of prisoners captured by the Fourteenth Army Corps since crossing the Tennessee River, number of deserters from the enemy, and number paroled.

Command.	Number.	Number of deserters.	Sent to provost-marshal, Fourteenth Army Corps.	Sent to provost-marshal-general.	Paroled.
First Division................................	477	8	7	478	....
Second Division	62	23	12	63	10
Third Division................................	95	4	....	99	....
Fourth Division	445	26	34	437	....
Total...................................	1,079	61	53	1,077	10

No. 16.

Report of Capt. John D. Barker, First Ohio Cavalry, Acting Assistant Inspector-General.

Report of small-arms and accouterments lost in Fourteenth Army Corps in the engagements of September 19 and 20, 1863, at Chickamauga, Ga.

Material.	Commands.				
	First Division, Maj. Gen. L. H. Rousseau.	Second Division, Maj. Gen. James S. Negley.	Third Division, Brig. Gen. John M. Brannan.	Fourth Division, Maj. Gen. J. J. Reynolds.	Total.
Arms:					
Enfield rifles	581	482	714	....	1,777
Springfield rifles	1,013	70	1,814	802	3,199
Colt's revolving rifles	....	167	....	....	167
English Enfield rifles........................	....	....	....	239	239
Austrian rifles..........................	537	....	....	....	537
Navy revolvers...........................	....	....	....	1	1
Total.......................................	2,131	719	2,028	1,042	5,920

Report of small-arms and accouterments lost, &c.—Continued.

Material.	Commands.				
	First Division, Maj. Gen. L. H. Rousseau.	Second Division, Maj. Gen. James S. Negley.	Third Division, Brig. Gen. John M. Braman.	Fourth Division, Maj. Gen. J. J. Reynolds.	Total.
Accouterments:					
Enfield bayonets	....	160	....	....	· 160
Springfield bayonets	....	1	2,035	1,053	3,089
Cartridge boxes	2,093	408	2,003	1,000	5,504
Bayonet scabbards	2,113	333	2,004	1,036	5,486
Cap boxes	2,084	404	1,998	1,001	5,487
Cartridge-box belts	2,062	259	1,996	1,000	5,317
Cartridge-box belt plates	737	....	....	....	737
Waist belts	2,085	419	1,991	1,002	5,497
Cartridge-box plates	2,062	....	....	1,001	3,063
Waist-belt plates	2,095	....	2,002	1,000	5,097
Cone picks	....	28	....	....	28
Screw drivers	1,803	31	....	250	2,084
Gun-slings	....	181	1,927	594	2,702
Sets accouterments complete	....	302	....	....	302
Non-commissioned swords	....	2	....	1	3
Sword belts and plates	....	2	....	....	2
Nippers	....	....	22	....	22
Ball-screws	192	4	....	91	287
Wipers	1,789	....	1,896	242	3,927
Spring vises	· 190	....	....	87	277

J. D. BARKER,
Captain, and A. A. I. G., Fourteenth Army Corps.

No. 17.

Reports of Lieut. Col. Andrew J. Mackay, Chief Quartermaster.

Report of clothing, camp and garrison equipage captured and destroyed by the enemy at the battle of Chickamauga, September 19 and 20, 1863.

Class.	First Division.	Second Division.	Third Division.	Fourth Division.	Total.
Clothing:					
Knapsacks	....	....	726	....	726
Haversacks	....	....	375	....	375
Canteens	....	....	44	....	44
Wool blankets	....	....	133	....	133
Rubber blankets	....	....	137	....	137
Stockings	....	....	45	....	45
Shirts	....	....	62	....	62
Trowsers	....	....	8	....	8
Blouses	....	....	11	....	11
Drawers	....	....	22	....	22
Overcoats	....	....	5	....	5
Equipage:					
Regimental flag	....	....	....	1	1
Axes	....	....	62	6	68
Ax handles	....	....	02	80	142
Hatchets	....	....	16	4	20
Spades	....	....	50	5	55

Report of clothing, camp and garrison equipage captured, &c.—Continued.

Class.	First Division.	Second Division.	Third Division.	Fourth Division.	Total.
Equipage—Continued.					
Picks and handles...............................			11	3	14
Camp kettles....................................			56	40	96
Mess pans			50	30	80
Wall tents......................................			6	3	9
Bell tents......................................				4	4
Shelter tents			481	170	651
Hospital tents				1	1
Bugle...			1		1
Drums...			2		2
Ruling pen			1		1

A. J. MACKAY,
Lieut. Col., and Quartermaster, Fourteenth Army Corps.

—

Report of quartermaster's stores captured and destroyed by the enemy at the battle of Chickamauga, September 19 and 20, 1863.

	Commands.				
Class.	First Division.	Second Division.	Third Division.	Fourth Division.	Total.
Means of transportation:					
Horses...	61		8	7	76
Mules...	2	3	62		67
Wagons	4	1	17	1	23
Wagon bows	36			6	42
Wagon covers......................................			14	1	15
Fifth chains......................................			14	1	15
Bearing chains			14	1	15
Spreaders			7	2	9
Halter chains.....................................			55	5	60
Saddles...			14	3	17
Water buckets	8		14		22
Halter straps.....................................	46				46
Sets of harness...................................	4	3	90		97
Riding saddles....................................			14	2	16
Riding bridles				2	2
Single trees			28		28
Double trees			14		14
Jockey sticks.....................................			14		14
King bolts..			19		19
Feed boxes..			14		14
Lead lines..			14		14
Lanterns				4	4
Pounds wagon grease			100		100
Wagon whips.......................................			28		28
Currycombs			14		14
Horse brushes.....................................			14		14
Tar pots..			14		14
Linchpins			7		7
Hame strings......................................			84		84
Ridge poles.......................................			14		14
Stores:					
Chest horse medicine..............................				1	1
Pounds wrought nails			15		15
Pounds assorted iron..............................			14		14
Pounds rope.......................................			140		140
Pounds cut nails..................................			195		195
Pounds mule shoes			175		175
Washer.			1		1

Report of quartermaster's stores captured, &c.—Continued.

Class.	First Division.	Second Division.	Third Division.	Fourth Division.	Total.
Artificers' tools:					
Forge..				1	1
Sets smiths' tools...			3	1	4
Anvil...				1	1
Vise..				1	1
Sets carpenters' tools...			3		3
Sets saddlers' tools...			3		3
Set shoeing tools..			1		1
Hand-saw files...			8		8
Horse rasps..			5		5
Draw knife...			1		1
Hand ax..			1		1
Brace and bits...			2		2
Gimlet bits..			2		2
Scribe awl...			1		1
Clawhammer...			1		1
Try-squares..			2		2
Rule...			1		1
Mallet...			1		1
Buck saw...			1		1
Flat files...			2		2
Auger and handle...			1		1
Braces...			2		2
Framing chisels..			3		3
Spoke-shave..			1		1
Fore-plane...			1		1
Smooth plane...		1			1
Oil-stone..			1		1
Blacksmith tools...			3		3

A. J. MACKAY,
Lieut. Col. and Quartermaster, Fourteenth Army Corps.

No. 18.

Reports of Brig. Gen. Absalom Baird, U. S. Army, commanding First Division, with complimentary orders of General Rosecrans.

HDQRS. FIRST DIVISION, FOURTEENTH ARMY CORPS,
Chattanooga, Tenn., September [25], 1863.

COLONEL: I have the honor to submit the following report of the operations of this division from the 2d of September, when we moved from our camp on Crow Creek to cross the Tennessee River, to the 22d, when we reached this place. The reports of battles are made separate and in detail.

I marched from the point above named on the 2d instant, and concentrated my force near Bridgeport, but was unable, from the great accumulation of *matériel*, troops, and trains, as well as the frequent breaking of the bridge, to pass the river until the 4th. I then crossed without an accident or moment of delay, occupying the day in so doing, and encamped at night near the south end of the bridge.

Upon the 5th I moved up to Moore's Spring, at the foot of Sand

Mountain, but was delayed there until night by trains of other divisions in advance of me.

On the 6th, after a day of hard labor, I got my troops, artillery, and wagons upon the mountain, and late at night went into camp at Warren's Mill, 4 miles from the summit.

On the 7th I moved on, descended the mountain, again detained by troops and trains in our front; and leaving the Seventy-ninth Pennsylvania Volunteers to work the road down the mountain, encamped at a late hour of the night in Lookout Valley at the junction of Lookout and Hurricane Creeks.

On the 8th and 9th I remained in camp, waiting for General Negley in front to get over Lookout Mountain.

On the 10th, in obedience to orders to unite with General Negley in McLemore's Cove, I labored hard during the whole day, and at 10 o'clock at night had only got my troops, artillery, and portion of my train to the foot of the mountain in Stevens' Gap, and was compelled to leave the rest of my train on the summit with a regiment to guard it.

On the 11th I moved forward with the portion of my force present, and joined General Negley near the entrance to Dug Gap in Pigeon Mountain. We here had an encounter with the enemy, which forms the subject of a separate report, hereto attached, and at night fell back to Stevens' Gap.

During the 12th, my men having been under arms all night, and having had no sleep for two nights, were still kept in position, awaiting an attack from the enemy. General Brannan came up during the day, and taking Colonel Scribner's brigade I united with him in a reconnaissance to Dug Gap, and returned at night.

During the 13th, 14th, 15th, and 16th we remained in camp at Stevens' Gap, awaiting the arrival of Major-General McCook, the first of whose divisions arrived on the 16th.

On the 17th we marched to Bird's Mill, on the Chickamauga, and encamped between there and Owens' Ford.

On the 18th received orders in the afternoon to march to the left by way of Crawfish Spring, which place we reached about midnight, and there received orders for our dispositions next day.

On the 19th and 20th were engaged with the enemy, the events being reported separately; the reports herewith annexed.

On the 21st, after collecting our forces at Rossville, we fell back to this place, bringing in the pickets and covering the retreat. We reached here on Monday, the 22d instant.

Most respectfully, your obedient servant,

A. BAIRD,
Brigadier-General, Commanding.

Lieut. Col. GEORGE E. FLYNT,
Asst. Adjt. Gen., Hdqrs. Fourteenth Army Corps.

———

HDQRS. FIRST DIVISION, FOURTEENTH ARMY CORPS,
Stevens' Gap, Ga., September 11, 1863.

COLONEL: In obedience to orders from the major-general commanding, I moved on the 10th instant with the First and Second Brigades of my division from Johnson's Crook, Lookout Valley, to cross Lookout Mountain and unite with Major-General Negley's command, then at or slightly in advance of this place. With much difficulty and great labor, I succeeded by 9 p. m. in getting to the foot of the mountain, with three regiments of General Stark-weather's brigade, the First and Twenty-first Wisconsin and Twenty-fourth Illinois, and his battery; also a portion of my transportation train and four regiments of Colonel Scribner's brigade, the Thirty-third and Ninety-fourth Ohio, the Thirty-eighth Indiana, and the Tenth Wisconsin, together with the First Michigan Battery. The remainder of the division was in rear, employed either in guarding trains and depots or other important duty, so that I had with me only about 2,800 men.

On my arrival here I received intelligence from General Negley, who had moved forward in the morning, to the effect that he had driven the enemy before him during the day, and had got up quite close to Dug Gap, on the road to La Fayette; that he had here met with a stout resistance, perhaps too great for his force to overcome, and at the same time that he had learned of a large rebel force with twelve pieces of artillery, on his left flank, lower down the valley. The communication expressed anxiety for the safety of his own party, and a wish that I should move forward as rapidly as possible. The fact of a rebel force, both of artillery and infantry, being near us down the valley was likewise reported to me by citizens of credibility.

In the condition in which I was, with a portion of my train at the foot and the rest on the mountain, requiring a guard to protect it from approach by way of Cooper's Gap, I felt somewhat embarrassed.

I sent word, however, to General Negley, suggesting that if he believed in the reports regarding the forces opposed to us, that it might be better for him to fall back upon me at this place, where we could defend ourselves and trains until other forces could arrive, nevertheless, that if he thought otherwise, I would march at 3 o'clock in the morning with the force at hand and join him. This, he replied, would be satisfactory.

As soon as possible after 3 a. m. on the 11th instant I moved forward, taking everything with me, as I was not able to leave a guard for it here. At about 8 o'clock I reached General Negley's headquarters at the Widow Davis' house. All then appeared to be quiet, and I soon after started with him to ride around his lines, so as to acquire some knowledge of the country. General Negley upon this ride explained to me that his left flank and rear were in danger, and that he intended drawing back some portion of his force from the front beyond the creek, to prolong our line to the left and rear, and that he wished me to occupy with my troops the position from which he would withdraw his.

Returning from this ride, we were informed that firing had commenced in the front, and we at once rode to the spot.

About half a mile beyond (eastward) the Widow Davis' house, beyond the woods and with open fields in front, our line of infantry and artillery was formed, the right resting upon the Dug Gap road, supported by skirmishers in a wood upon the other side of the road, extending one-fourth mile farther, as far as Shaw's house.

Our main line curved over the ridge to the Chattanooga road, and thence fell back to the left and rear, being, for the greater part of its extent, in the woods.

In front of our right our line of skirmishers occupied some woods beyond the open ground, about 800 yards from our line of battle.

Just as we arrived upon the ground our skirmishers were driven back some 200 yards from the wood and took shelter behind a fence. The enemy then had the advantage and his fire was quite sharp, but indicated nothing serious. Attracted by the appearance of mounted officers on the line, many shots were directed toward them, with much accuracy, notwithstanding the distance, and one passing quite near inflicted a serious, if not fatal, wound upon my orderly just in rear.

We then returned to General Negley's headquarters, and I [proceeded] to get my men under arms and to remove my wagons, which I found to be too much exposed, to a more secure locality. I was about the same time told by General Negley that a large force was coming toward us from Blue Bird Gap, and his informant said within three-quarters of a mile ; also that the enemy was working around our left, and that he must make his new dispositions at once. I then, as speedily as possible, posted my several regiments on the line extending from the Dug Gap road to the Chattanooga road, relieving those of General Negley.

The line was so extended that it left me nothing with which to guard or support my right flank had it been heavily attacked. This was the portion of our line then immediately under the fire of the enemy's skirmishers, and the replacement of General Negley's men by my own, and throwing out a new line of skirmishers, was an operation of some delicacy ; but, thanks to the skill of my commanders and the good instruction of the men, was performed without a mishap. Hardly had I got my men in position when General Negley informed me that his information became more threatening, and that he would fall back and take up a new position on the Missionary Ridge. He asked what I thought of this, and I replied that I concurred with him, and mentioned my suggestion of the night before that he should fall back to me at Stevens' Gap.

The plan he adopted was to form a second line with a portion of his troops, on the first rise west of the creek, and then to pass his train to the rear, to be followed by mine. Then I was to withdraw and form again a third line upon Missionary Ridge.

It was immediately put in operation and rapidly executed.

The enemy saw, without doubt, the movement of our trains to the rear, and hastened the collection of troops in the woods to assail both of my flanks. The sequel showed that it was their intention to throw a strong force upon Widow Davis' house, where it would have been one-half mile in rear of my right flank. I was not aware of this at the time, but had made preparations to draw troops from the other flank to meet such a contingency. The trains having all passed, I prepared to bring back my troops, the line first and then the skirmishers, each 500 yards at a time, pivoting on my left already on the Chattanooga road, and swinging around to reform our line at the cross-roads.

To do this successfully required a complete understanding between the commanders, and as my regiments were all in a dense wood where one could not see the length of a regiment, it required a little time to put it in operation. It had barely commenced when General Negley sent me word that I could not get my men over the creek too soon, and I hastened accordingly.

Our line was reformed with regularity by columns of battalions, and I then sent all my artillery to the rear ; afterward the remaining troops of General Negley, and then directed Colonel Scribner to retire by regiments from his left.   They thus passed through a wood by which the movement was concealed.

This completed, General Starkweather was left at the cross-roads with three regiments, and at the same time the plans of the enemy developed themselves, but a little too late to do us much damage. A battery planted on our left, out of sight, on the prolongation of the Chattanooga road, attempted to shell these regiments, but not seeing them the shells passed over ; simultaneously a heavy line of skirmishers pushed out into the field on the right of Dug Gap road and beyond Bird Gap road, under cover of which a double line of battle was formed and advanced.

Our men fell back, covered by their skirmishers, to the creek, and here a brief but sharp contest took place.   The enemy pressed on vigorously, but being repulsed by the fire of our men, many of whom had taken position behind a stone fence, we had time to retire behind the second line.   In passing, Colonel Scribner had been ordered by General Negley to move on with the train to Bailey's Cross-Roads and there take position, while General Starkweather was to be posted in line south of the road upon Missionary Ridge.   A brigade of General Negley was upon the north, thus forming the third and last line we established.

The only portion of my command in the second line was the Fourth Indiana Battery, which was supported by regiments from General Negley's division, and contributed in no small degree to the repulse of the enemy, who, supported by a heavy fire from his batteries, charged boldly upon the second line.

The third line having been established, the second retired behind it, and was no longer molested.   The third fell back gradually, and night coming on I drew the regiment of Colonel Mihalotzy (Twenty-fourth Illinois) into the road, and remained with it in rear until we reached this place.   General Negley, in advance, had selected positions for the troops, anticipating a renewal of the attack in the morning, and thus closed the events of the day.

These operations, while of too unimportant a character to be dignified by the name of a battle, and really not sufficient to test the mettle of my troops, who would have been glad to have pushed further, still presented occasions of as severe trial to the parties involved as a general engagement.

I claim for my command the credit of having handsomely performed the difficult military operation of retiring step by step in good order, while constantly engaged with the enemy.   It is an evidence of what may be expected from these men in the future.   They have my highest commendation, and I trust their conduct will meet with the approval of the major-general commanding.

It would be wrong for me to name those whose good conduct attracted my attention, lest I might do injustice to others whom I did not see.   I leave this to the brigade commanders, more constantly upon the spot, and their reports I inclose herewith.   Not an instance of bad conduct has been brought to my notice.

The brigade commanders themselves, Brigadier-General Starkweather and Colonel Scribner, I desire to name to the general for their coolness and bravery, as well as the skill and good judgment with which they managed their commands.   The officers of my staff

I must likewise mention for the zeal, energy, and efficiency with which they discharged their duties. It is the best method I have of thanking these officers.

My losses, considering the amount of powder expended by the enemy and the circumstances in which we were placed, are remarkably small. We fired but little, yet I am satisfied inflicted far greater loss on him.

My list of casualties is as follows:

Private Benjamin Singer, Company E, Second Kentucky Cavalry, orderly at these headquarters, severely wounded.

First Brigade.—Killed, Corpl. Daniel M. Pope, Company B, Thirty-eighth Indiana Volunteer Infantry. Wounded severely, Private Frank M. Kelly, Company B, Thirty-eighth Indiana Volunteer Infantry. Wounded mortally, Private William Nofrey, Company C, Thirty-eighth Indiana Volunteer Infantry. Prisoners, Sergt. W. H. Hutsler, Company E, Thirty-eighth Indiana Volunteer Infantry ; Private Isaiah Carter, Company E, Thirty-eighth Indiana Volunteer Infantry.

Second Brigade.—Killed, First Lieut. Robert J. Nickles, First Wisconsin Volunteers, aide-de-camp ; Private F. J. Stearns, 4th Indiana Battery. Wounded, Sergt. H. A. Youngs, Fourth Indiana Battery.

Recapitulation.—Total killed, 3 ; wounded, 4 ; prisoners, 2.

I am, very respectfully, your obedient servant,

A. BAIRD,
Brigadier-General, Commanding.

Lieut. Col. GEORGE E. FLYNT,
Assistant Adjutant-General.

—

REPORT OF THE OPERATIONS OF THE FIRST DIVISION, FOURTEENTH ARMY CORPS, IN THE BATTLE OF CHICKAMAUGA CREEK, SEPTEMBER 19–21, 1863.

Being encamped upon Chickamauga Creek, between Bird's Mill and Owens' Ford, with the divisions of General Brannan on my right and General Negley on my left, I received orders on the 18th instant from the major-general commanding to move immediately to the left, lower down the creek, for the support of General Crittenden's corps, as the enemy appeared to be gathering in that direction.

The road being encumbered by troops in advance, I did not reach Crawfish Spring, the headquarters of the army, until near midnight, when we halted a short time until the way was clear, and then I received my final orders from the general commanding.

Under the direction of a guide, I was to take a road which, leaving the Chattanooga road near Widow Glenn's, came into the State road from Chattanooga to La Fayette at Kelly's, about 3 miles north of Lee's Mills. I would thus pass around the rear of General Crittenden's corps, located about that mill, and come into position on his left. I was to post one brigade on the west of the State road, facing toward the south, and my other two brigades on the east of it. General Brannan, following me, was to post his division on the prolongation of my left. I reached the point indicated about daybreak, and posted General Starkweather on my right, Colonel Scribner in the center, the right of his brigade upon the road, and the regular brigade, General King, upon the left. General Thomas arrived upon the ground almost immediately after these dispositions were made, and General Brannan soon followed.　While the latter was getting into position, Colonel McCook, who commanded a brigade of the Reserve Corps, came in and reported a brigade of the enemy not far distant upon our left, with which he had been skirmishing.　General Brannan was then formed facing to the eastward, and I was directed to change my front to the left, conforming my line to his, and at the same time to watch well upon my right flank against an approach from that direction.　We were then in a thick wood interspersed with thickets and openings, which extended in front, I believe, as far as the Chickamauga.

I formed General King's brigade upon the left, with orders to dress and close upon General Brannan, and a portion of Colonel Scribner's force upon the same line to be guarded by King's right, and the rest of his force I had bent to the rear so as to march by flank in rear of his right, and be ready to front in that direction or toward the south should it be required.　To General Starkweather I gave orders to move in column in rear, holding his brigade as a reserve.　I had particularly in view the support of our right flank.

The artillery could not advance in line with the infantry, nor, indeed, could it have been used except at rare intervals.　It could not, at the same time, be left behind for want of protection, and it was directed to follow closely the brigades, making its way through the trees.

I had scarcely got my line formed when General Brannan's men, a little in advance, began to skirmish hotly.　My men were soon after engaged.　We drove the enemy before us, and covered the ground quite thickly with his dead and wounded, besides sending 200 prisoners to the rear, some just from the Army of Virginia.　During this forward movement, I received orders from the general commanding to push rapidly toward the left to support Colonel Croxton's brigade of Brannan's division, then hard pressed by the enemy and almost out of ammunition.

About the same time, General Starkweather, as will be seen by his report, received an order of similar effect, and at once acted upon it.　I was not, until subsequently, aware of this, and thus lost my knowledge of his position.　Before I had closed up with General Brannan's left, word was brought me that General Palmer had arrived upon my right, and that his skirmishers were then passing across my front.　I sent a caution, in consequence, to my men not to fire into them.　The evidence seems clear that men of our forces were in the position indicated ; but to whom they could have belonged, or how they came there, I cannot now conjecture.　Arrived close up to General Brannan, and the enemy having disappeared from our front, I halted to readjust my line.　We had now advanced about three-fourths of a mile from where we first became engaged, and the troops had behaved admirably.　While arranging my line, I learned from prisoners that there had been but one division in our front, while the main body of the rebel force, which they exaggerated at 90,000, had crossed the river at Alexander's Bridge, above us, and was then upon my right flank.　I immediately ordered General King to change his front so as to face the south; his left being supported by General Brannan's troops, in order to face the new danger. I also dispatched staff officers to General Starkweather to bring him to the same point, but having moved toward the left, as before stated, they failed for some time to find him.　I went myself toward Colonel Scribner to see his command properly posted, but before I could reach him, the attack had been made in such force that he was unable to withstand it, and I met his men coming back in disorder, driven by the enemy across the rear of what had been our previous position. For the particulars of this attack, and the manner in which it was met, I refer to the lucid report of Colonel Scribner. Our troops behaved with gallantry and yielded only to overwhelming force. Assisted by my staff officers, Major Fitch, Captain Cary, and Captain Williams, I strove to restore confidence to these men, and induce them to make another stand, but it was only after they had passed far to the rear that I could do so. Complete destruction seemed inevitable. Four pieces of Colonel Scribner's battery were captured after firing sixty-four rounds, and the enemy, sweeping like a torrent, fell upon the regular brigade before it had got into position, took its battery, and after a struggle in which whole battalions were wiped out of existence, drove it back upon the line of General Brannan. We are indebted to the Ninth Ohio Regiment, of Brannan's division, for recapturing this battery.

In this onslaught of the enemy General Starkweather was brought into action a little after Scribner, and more to his rear and right. His brigade suffered severely, and his battery was almost entirely disabled by the loss of horses and men; the guns, however, were saved. The appearance of other forces upon the left of the enemy caused further pressure upon us to cease, and probably saved us from destruction.

Having collected my forces, they were united to those of General Brannan, in a strong position on the road leading from McDonald's house to Reed's Bridge, and this post we were ordered by General Thomas to hold to the last extremity. A period of quiet to us then ensued, during which a fierce conflict was going on upon the ground we had fought over in the morning, and, as we learned later, with the division of General Johnson.

I would here testify to the high qualities for a commander exhibited by General Brannan, for the moment (a trying one) the commander of our united divisions.

Toward evening I received orders to support General Johnson, while General Brannan was withdrawn for the assistance of General Reynolds, to the right of the cross-roads, near Kelly's. Leaving the small brigade of King to hold the road where we were, I moved with those of General Starkweather and Colonel Scribner to the right, and caused them to be posted under the direction of a staff officer of General Johnson, nearly in prolongation of his left. We were then upon the very ground from which we had driven the enemy in the morning, and from which we had subsequently to fall back. We found a number of our dead there stretched upon the ground. With the exception of an occasional shot from rebel sharpshooters, entire quiet prevailed along the line, and I remained with General Johnson until toward dark, when the general commanding arrived, and directed us to retire some half mile to a better position for the night. Orders were given accordingly to have the troops withdraw after nightfall, and General Johnson and myself rode back with the general to ascertain the position we would occupy. I was returning, when, just as the light of day began to disappear, I heard the sounds of a fierce battle in front. The enemy attacked with both artillery and infantry, in apparently large force, and with greater determination than previously, shelling at the same time the entire woods which we occupied, as far back even as the road where my ammunition was parked. This attack came first upon General Johnson's division, and then extended to the left on to mine. It was quite dark before it was repulsed, when we remained in possession of the ground. Quiet being again restored, we fell back as had been designed. Thus ended the first day.

At 3 o'clock on the morning of the 20th, I put my men in position, ready to meet the enemy. We were posted upon a wooded ridge running parallel to the State road, and about one-fourth of a mile to the east of it. An open field extending along the east side of the road, from near one-fourth of a mile south of McDonald's to a point beyond Kelly's, lay a short distance in our rear. The rest of the country as far as the Chickamauga, in all directions, was thickly wooded. My division was posted around the northeast corner of the field, but about 150 yards in advance of it, in the woods. General Johnson's division was on my right, and beyond him, I think, General Palmer's. My Second Brigade, Brigadier-General Starkweather, was placed next to Johnson, facing to the east, with four guns in position, so as to enfilade our front, besides having a direct fire. The First Brigade, Colonel Scribner, was upon the turn, a portion of his force facing in the same direction as Starkweather, and the rest sloping to the rear, so as to face partially to the north. The Third Brigade, Brigadier-General King, was upon the left of Scribner. When the line was established there was no force whatever upon King's left, and no natural obstruction, and I was compelled thus to refuse or en échelon that flank in order to cover it.

I formed my men generally in two lines ; King's brigade was even more concentrated, and I used only the four pieces of artillery of General Starkweather ; the rest, much of it disabled, indeed, was held in reserve in rear.

About 7 o'clock General Beatty's brigade, four regiments, of Negley's division, came up and formed line on the north side of the field, and then passed into the woods, when I had his right joined on to King's left ; but subsequent orders caused him to move farther to the left, and, as he informs me, he posted one of his regiments on the west of the State road, looking toward McDonald's, and the other three on the east in line with it, and all looking toward the north. This arrangement gave General Beatty a long, thin line, easily brushed away, and at the same time left an important gap between him and King. To fill this gap I had no troops, but finally I induced a regiment—perhaps the Seventy-ninth Indiana—coming to this quarter with only general instructions, to move into it. I am sorry to have lost the name of the colonel of this regiment.

During the interval between daylight and the first attack our men worked vigorously and covered themselves with a hastily constructed breastwork of logs and rails, which proved of vast service to them during the day.

I believe that the battle began upon my front at about 8.30 a. m. Previous to this there had been some sharp skirmishing along the front, and our skirmishers were at times compelled to fall back, but as often returned to their original position, and continued throughout the day to reform their first line whenever the assaults of the enemy were repulsed. It was also reported to me that distinct words of command were heard by our advanced pickets, as in the formation of bodies of rebel troops, both upon our front and flank, and we awaited their attack, quietly working upon our defenses.

At about 9 o'clock the enemy, in force, advanced upon us through the woods, and attempted, by throwing strong bodies of infantry upon King and Scribner on the left, while they likewise assailed Starkweather furiously in front, to crush that portion of our line. I judge the general direction of all the attacks made upon us to have been from the northeast. This attack continued about an hour, during which repeated efforts were made to dislodge us from our position, but in vain. The battle-flags of the rebel generals, borne with the lines of troops, approached quite close to our position, but each time those lines exposed themselves they were broken and driven back. When they withdrew, our skirmishers were thrown to the front and took many prisoners, by whom we were informed that it was the division of Breckinridge which we had been fighting, together with troops from Virginia.

An interval of about an hour now elapsed, during which there was but little fighting upon our portion of the line. Warned, however, by the previous attack, of the vulnerability of my left, I strove to obtain forces to secure it. There were regiments lying in reserve in rear of General Johnson's division, I know not what, which I thought might be of more service on the left. I went to their commanders, and explaining to them the danger of an attack from that quarter, and that it might certainly be looked for, I asked them to keep a lookout in that direction, and, should the regiments on the left seem to waver, to rush to their assistance. As all had different orders, I received no satisfactory reply. I then went to General Johnson and got him to visit with me the left of his own line, where I pointed out the condition of things, and asked him to take his left regiment of the second line and place it in column in rear, so as to be ready to move to whatever point should require it the most.

While speaking of this matter the attack came, as I had anticipated, and was made with large force and great impetuosity. General Beatty's line was cut in two in the middle, two regiments being driven beyond the road to the west; the other two were forced back into the open field toward my rear. My own left was also forced back, and our line seemed ready to crumble away on this flank. The rebels were already in the field behind us, and the column which had forced Beatty's center was pushing down the road toward Kelly's house. I immediately caused the second line to rise and face about, and then to wheel forward toward the right, so as to support our men and meet the advancing enemy. This line was composed of regiments from various commands, a part only my own. The unexpected direction of the attack, the facing to the rear, and the crowd of our retiring troops coming upon them caused some disorder in their line, but, riding to their front with a cheer, two regiments took it up, formed a good line, and advanced gallantly. The rest followed, and the rebels were driven back into the woods. The column upon the road was at the same time driven back by troops, I believe, of General Brannan's division, and at this juncture Colonel Barnes, commanding a brigade of General Wood's division, came up and pushed his brigade in line into the woods on the north side of the field.

I saw at once that this attack was at an end, and requested Colonel Barnes to withdraw two of his regiments, to be held in reserve in the northeast corner of the field, near my own position, to be used upon the next point assailed. He complied, and brought the two regiments commanded by Colonel Swaine, which remained near me until the close of the fight.

My line was re-established as it had been in the morning, and was not for some four hours again attacked in force. Immediately that this assault upon my left ceased, the sound of a tremendous conflict reached us from the southwest, beyond Kelly's house. I could not tell how it was progressing, but, knowing it must be a desperate struggle, I sent word to General Thomas that I held the two regiments under Colonel Swaine in reserve, and that if he required them there more than we did that they were disposable. The fighting in the direction I have named was continued throughout the afternoon, with only intervals, when it was partially suspended. During this period re-enforcements seemed to arrive from the direction of Chattanooga, and about 4 o'clock the firing seemed more vigorous than before. At 5 o'clock it had almost ceased, but I was still ignorant of the course of events upon the right, and had no idea that any portion of the troops had given way. An officer then arrived, with orders for myself and General Johnson to withdraw our troops and fall back in the direction of the hills and of Rossville.

Just as this order reached me the heavy firing on the right ceased, and it seemed to be the signal for another attack, the most violent of all, upon my portion of the line. This time the enemy used artillery, and concentrated the fire of three batteries upon us, while his infantry pressed on with the utmost vigor. Still we held our position, yielding not an inch, and I am confident could have continued to do so; to fall back was more difficult than to remain, and I should have taken the responsibility of holding on for a time had I not seen the troops on my right, first those of General Palmer and then those of General Johnson, passing off to the rear. I saw then that no time was to be lost and transmitted the order to my brigade commanders. I am indebted to Captain Forsyth, of General King's staff, for assisting Captain Cary, of my own staff, in bearing this order. The remainder of my staff officers I had sent away upon other missions.

As my men fell back the enemy pressed after them, and in crossing the open field very many were struck down. They reached the woods, west of the road, in as good order as could be expected, but then, uncertain which direction to take, and having no landmark to guide them, many became separated from their regiments, and in groups joined other commands, with which they fell back to Rossville, where all were united during the night. A number, doubtless, became confused at this time and marched into the lines of the rebels. We had, during the day, been fired into from every point of the compass, and when we fell back, no other portions of our troops being in sight, it was impossible to tell where they could be found or when we would encounter the enemy. My loss, up to the time of falling back, was small compared with the punishment inflicted on the rebels. In retiring, it was great. A list of those lost is appended. Brave men, their names will live, the pride of their children and a monument of glory for their country.

On the 21st, at Rossville, my division was again put upon duty to defend one of the main approaches to that position, and I believe it was the only one that was attacked. The gorge which we occupied was shelled during the afternoon, and I lost 5 men in killed and wounded from the brigade of regulars.

During the same afternoon Major-General Rousseau arrived and resumed command of this, his old division, inspiring it with new life after the arduous duties it had performed. By his courtesy I have since remained with it, co-operating with him.

On the night of the 21st our army was withdrawn from Rossville to this place, and the First Division was selected to bring up the rear. Under its protection the pickets of all commands were withdrawn and marched here, Colonel Scribner's brigade, the last, arriving about sunrise.

The campaign thus terminated, although brilliant, has been one of unusual hardship upon the soldier. The labor in marching and transporting our trains over the mountain ridges has been enormous, and from Saturday morning until late Sunday night, throughout two days' of battle, my horses and most of my men were without water. The First Division, thus sorely tried, has not murmured, but with its thinned ranks stands proudly ready to meet any foe. Its record is as bright as any, and all may be proud to have belonged to it. Its losses are heavy, but they were incurred in gallant resistance to overwhelming force. We report 1,034 killed and wounded, and 1,319 missing. Many of the latter we know were left dead or wounded on the field, and in exchange for our prisoners lost we have captured and brought back over 400 of the enemy.

Some of our artillery was lost, but it has all been recovered, a part of it, it is true, temporarily disabled. In the battery of Starkweather's brigade, one limber box was blown up and two axles broken by the recoil of guns during the fight of Sunday. And I must here thank the officer in command, Lieutenant Willits, for the service it rendered.

To my brigade commanders, Brig. Gen. John H. King, Brigadier-General Starkweather, and Colonel Scribner, the country owes a debt of gratitude for the courage with which they maintained the fight, and the good judgment with which their troops were handled. The performance of General King's command upon Saturday morning was particularly brilliant. In the fight upon Sunday, General Starkweather, holding one of the key points of our position, rendered distinguished service by his own coolness, inspiring his men with confidence. He received a slight wound in the leg, but I am happy to say not such as to make him quit the field. Colonel Scribner, who has long commanded one of the best brigades in the army, and has been recommended for promotion after previous battles, has again distinguished himself. Two missiles from the enemy passed through his clothes, one inflicting a slight wound in the face, and another a bruise on the shoulder. I renew the recommendation for his promotion as a reward for the good conduct of his brigade.

I would be glad to name to the general commanding the officers in command of troops belonging to other divisions, who were brought into action in the neighborhood of my own, but I do not know them all. Colonel Barnes, commanding a brigade of General Wood's division, and Colonel Swaine, who reported to me with two regiments of the same brigade, were among the number.

To the officers of my staff I tender my thanks for the efficient service they rendered, and commend them to the notice of the general commanding for their gallant bearing on the field.

A tabular statement* of the killed, wounded, and missing is annexed, and the reports of brigade commanders are likewise inclosed.

Respectfully submitted.

A. BAIRD,
Brigadier-General, Commanding.

Lieut. Col. George E. Flynt,
    Assistant Adjutant-General.

---

* Embodied in revised statement, p. 171.

Special Field Orders, } Hdqrs. Dept. of the Cumberland,
       No. 257.   }   Chattanooga, Tenn., Sept. 27, 1863.

＊   ＊   ＊   ＊   ＊   ＊   ＊

VI. On the return of Major-General Rousseau from an important mission for the benefit of this army, he resumed the command of his division. Brig. Gen. A. Baird being thus relieved of this division, the general commanding tenders to him his thanks for the prudence and ability which he displayed while in command, for the unflinching courage and ability with which he carried his troops into action on the 19th and maintained his position during the terrific fight of the 20th in the glorious battle of the Chickamauga.

＊   ＊   ＊   ＊   ＊   ＊   ＊

By command of Major-General Rosecrans:

H. M. CIST,
Lieutenant, and Acting Assistant Adjutant-General.

No. 19.

*Reports of Capt. George A. Kensel, Fifth U. S. Artillery, Chief of
Artillery.*

Headquarters Battery H, Fifth U. S. Artillery,
                Chattanooga, Tenn., October 2, 1863.

Major: I have the honor to make the following report of the part taken by the batteries in the First Division, Fourteenth Army Corps, in the battle of Chickamauga :

As regards Battery H, Fifth Artillery, I will have recourse to the brief report of Lieutenant Fessenden and the remarks obtained from him in conversation on the subject. The battery went into action on the 19th of September, under command of First Lieut. H. M. Burnham, full and complete, four Napoleon guns and two 10-pounder Parrotts. Shortly after noon, being placed in position in a dense wood, it fired 16 rounds of canister, was overpowered by an overwhelming force of the enemy, and, left without support, fell into the hands of the enemy. The success of the enemy was only momentary, as very soon our forces charged on them and regained the battery. Lieutenant Burnham was killed, Lieutenant Ludlow made prisoner, and Lieutenant Fessenden, slightly wounded, made his escape. Four non-commissioned officers and 8 men killed ; 3 non-commissioned officers and 11 men missing, and 2 non-commissioned officers and 13 men wounded.

Lieutenant Fessenden, with the assistance of Captain Dod, of the Fifteenth Infantry, removed the guns to the rear. He was forced to abandon his caissons to use the limbers on the pieces. There are now in the battery four Napoleon guns, complete ; two 10-pounder Parrott guns, one without a limber, and battery wagon and forge, complete.

The Fourth Indiana Battery entered the field with six guns and six caissons, under command of Lieutenant Flansburg. At the first advance made by the enemy the battery lost 1 officer missing, 1 man killed, and 9 men wounded. The enemy captured five of the guns, which were soon retaken.   The loss of men, horses, and harness prevented Lieutenant Willits from sustaining his position ; he consequently moved to the rear, but soon re-entered the field with four guns.   At dark he was ordered by General Starkweather to retire, which he did, and again took the field on the 20th and retired with the brigade at evening.

Loss on the 20th, 8 men wounded and 4 missing.   The axle-trees of his two James rifles were broken, one was abandoned, the other brought off the field.   Privates Bailey and Perdoil brought off the field a rebel 6-pounder gun, smooth-bore, which the lieutenant yet has.

His battery now consists of two 12-pounder light guns, two 12-pounder howitzers, one 6-pounder smooth-bore (rebel), unservicable, and one 6-pounder James gun (dismounted); four gun carriages, three caissons, one forge, and one battery wagon.

The First Michigan Battery entered the field complete, under command of First Lieut. George W. Van Pelt.   The battery took several positions before opening fire on the enemy.   On forming in its fourth position the battery fired sixty-four rounds of canister and percussion shell.   The enemy rushed upon the battery in overwhelming numbers, compelling the infantry support to fall back.   The men remained with the battery until the enemy's bayonets were at their breasts.

Five guns fell into the enemy's hands ; one was got safely off the field.   One gun was subsequently recaptured.   Lieutenant Van Pelt and 5 men were killed, 6 seriously wounded, and 13 made prisoners.

Lieutenant Wilbur speaks highly of the gallant bearing of Lieutenant Van Pelt on the field of battle.   Before being killed he cheered on his men to victory, and his death has left a blank in the army of the Union.

Not having myself been present in person with the batteries of the division, I can give no opinion myself regarding the action on their part.   I am convinced, however, from what I have since learned, that everything was done by them which bravery and a devotion to the cause could accomplish.

The army, in the death of Lieut. H. M. Burnham, has experienced a sad loss; although a young man he had the bearing of a true soldier, and had he been spared, would have earned a fame which many would have envied.

It is to be hoped that Lieutenant Ludlow, now a prisoner in the hands of the enemy, will at an early date be restored to the battery, with which he has fought ever since its organization and of which he was a bright ornament.

I am, sir, very respectfully, your obedient servant,
GEO. A. KENSEL,
Captain Fifth Artillery.

Maj. W. E. Lawrence,
Chief of Artillery, Fourteenth Army Corps.

CHATTANOOGA, TENN.,
October 4, 1863.

Report of Casualties in batteries of First Division, Fourteenth Army Corps, in battle of Chickamauga, Ga.

[Command.]	Officers and men.								Matériel.					
	Killed.		Wounded.		Missing.		Since paroled.		Guns.				Caissons (comp).	
	Officers.	Enlisted men.	Officers.	Enlisted men.	Officers.	Enlisted men.	Officers.	Enlisted men.	12-pounder, light.	10-pounder Parrott.	6-pounder James rifle.	Gun carriages.	12-pounders, light.	10-pounder Parrott.
Battery H, 5th Artillery	1	12	1	11	1	13	....	4					4	2
1st Michigan Battery	1	5	......	6	....	13								2
4th Indiana Battery	....	1	......	16	1	4					1	2	3	....
Total*	2	18	1	33	2	30	....	4			1	2	7	4

[Command.]	Matériel.													
	Limbers, 12-pounder light.	Limbers, 10-pounder Parrott.	Limbers.	Pistols.	Sabers.	Ammunition, rounds.	Blank cartridges, 12-pounder, rounds.	Blank cartridges, 10-pounder, rounds.	Blank cartridges, 6-pounder, rounds.	Saddle blankets.	Harness (sets), 2 wheel horses.	Harness, 2 lead horses (sets).	Halters.	Horses.
Battery H, 5th Artillery	......	1	....	8	21	728	......	245	......	66	7	14	...	65
1st Michigan Battery	......	3	....	2	1	380				40	5½	12½	40	46
4th Indiana Battery	......	......	3	6	(a)					36	2	12	....	34
Total*	......	4	....	13	28	1,108	......	245	......	142	14½	38½	40	145

a No report made.

Of the part taken by Battery H, Fifth Artillery, on the 20th and 21st, I have to state that Lieutenant Fessenden fitted up two Napoleon guns on the morning of the 20th and took position near the Third Brigade, remaining until near noon, when he was ordered to Chattanooga; again on Monday, the 21st, he went back to near Rossville and remained until nightfall with two guns; when he was ordered by Major Mendenhall to proceed with Battery M, Fourth Artillery, to the rear, which he did, and on Tuesday morning his four Napoleon guns were placed in position, while his two Parrott guns were placed in the fort near the river, where they yet remain.

GEO. A. KENSEL,
Captain Fifth Artillery, Chief of Artillery, First Division.

* See revised statement, p. 171.

No. 20.

Reports of Col. Benjamin F. Scribner, Thirty-eighth Indiana Infantry, commanding First Brigade.

HDQRS. FIRST BRIG., FIRST DIV., 14TH ARMY CORPS,
Camp near Cassandra, Ga., September 13, 1863.

CAPTAIN: Pursuant to orders I moved forward from the foot of Lookout Mountain with my command, consisting of the Thirty-third Ohio Volunteer Infantry, Col. O. F. Moore ; Thirty-eighth Indiana Volunteer Infantry, Lieut. Col. D. F. Griffin; Tenth Wisconsin Volunteer Infantry, Lieut. Col. J. H. Ely ; Ninety-fourth Ohio Volunteer Infantry, Maj. R. P. Hutchins, and the First Michigan Battery, First Lieut. G. W. Van Pelt (the Second Ohio Volunteer Infantry, Lieut. Col. O. C. Maxwell, having been left on the mountain to guard the train), on the morning of the 11th instant, on the Dug Gap road, and at 10 a. m. arrived at the crossing of the Chattanooga and Bird's Gap road at Widow Davis' place.   Upon arrival, after several changes of position, I finally took up a position with my right resting in the woods about 500 yards east of the Chattanooga road and my left on the road, forming a junction with the Second Brigade, Brigadier-General Starkweather commanding, the two brigades, forming the hypotenuse of the angle made by the Dug Gap and Chattanooga roads, in a dense wood filled with undergrowth.   My line was thus disposed : The Thirty-eighth Indiana Volunteer Infantry with their left resting on the road, and Tenth Wisconsin Volunteer Infantry on the right of the Thirty-eighth Indiana, formed the first line.   The Ninety-fourth Ohio Volunteer Infantry and Thirty-third Ohio Volunteer Infantry formed the second line ; the battery in position at the crossing of the roads ; the skirmishers covering my front, thrown forward through the woods to a field ; the enemy's skirmishers opposite in a wood beyond.

Sharp skirmishing was kept up along the entire line for the space of two hours.   Being heavier on the left, it soon became manifest that the enemy designed turning our left.   Lieutenant-Colonel Griffin reported that they were enfilading him on the left, upon which I immediately ordered him to extend his line of skirmishers farther to the left, which order was promptly obeyed.

Upon being notified by the general commanding that he had received information of a heavy column of the enemy moving around our left to our rear, and of his orders to retire my line to a point in the woods parallel to the road, I immediately did so, thus placing my right near the Dug Gap road, forming our line of retreat, from which position we retired down the road on which we came. Great praise is due the men and officers of my command for their skill and coolness in the execution of this hazardous movement, the skirmishers on our left boldly holding their position from the enemy, whose skirmish-line was pressing on with a strong force of artillery, infantry, and cavalry behind them.   Five men of the skirmishers on the left were captured by the enemy's cavalry, and were carried along with them in their charge until opened upon by Colonel Mihalotzy's command, which was in ambush behind the stone wall near Chickamauga Creek, when they were dispersed and the prisoners retaken.

Near this place I was ordered by Major-General Negley to move on with two regiments on the right of the wagon train, leaving two regiments and the battery to follow in the train, and take position with my command at Bailey's Cross-Roads, which point was then held by Brigadier-General Beatty, commanding First Brigade, Second Division. Upon my arrival General Beatty took another position farther to the rear, and I immediately placed myself in position to protect the passage of the train and troops from an attack of the enemy, said to have been in large force designing an attack on that point. Upon learning from the rear guard that they were closely pursued by the enemy's cavalry, I sent a company of 40 men to picket the road, who were suddenly charged upon by the enemy's cavalry in the darkness and 2 of our men were taken prisoners. Upon the arrival of another company, sent as a support, they disappeared.

I maintained this position until next morning, and after assuming several intermediate positions was ordered to occupy the ground I now hold.

My casualties were as follows : Thirty-eighth Indiana Volunteer Infantry—Killed, Corp. Daniel M. Pope, Company B; wounded severely, Private Frank M. Kelly, Company B ; wounded mortally, Private William Nofrey, Company C; prisoners, Private Isaiah Carter, Company E, and Sergt. W. H. Hutsler, Company E.

Very respectfully, your obedient servant,

B. F. SCRIBNER,
Colonel, Commanding Brigade.

Capt. B. H. Polk,
Assistant Adjutant-General.

—

Hdqrs. First Brig., First Div., 14th Army Corps,
In the Field, near Chattanooga, Tenn., September 25, 1863.

Captain : I have the honor to submit the following report of the part my command took in the battles of the 19th and 20th instant :

On the evening of the 18th instant we marched from Bird's Mill, on the Cove road, and passing headquarters at Crawfish Spring we arrived at daylight at the intersection of the La Fayette and Chattanooga roads, about 10 miles from the latter place. We took position in the center of the division, on the left and at right angles with the road, the Second Brigade on the other side with its right thrown forward, the First Michigan Battery, Lieutenant Van Pelt, near the road between the two brigades.

I formed in two lines ; the Thirty-third Ohio, Colonel Moore, Second Ohio, Lieutenant-Colonel Maxwell, in the first line ; the Tenth Wisconsin, Lieutenant-Colonel Ely, and the Ninety-fourth Ohio, Maj. R. P. Hutchins, the second line. The Thirty-eighth Indiana, Lieutenant-Colonel Griffin, was sent farther up the road to protect our rear from surprise. Skirmishers from the whole division were thrown forward, and Major Beatty, Second Ohio, was placed in charge. While thus disposed General Brannan's division arrived and passed up the road and into the woods on our left. It was rumored that a part of General Granger's forces on our left had cut off a brigade of the enemy and that General Brannan was going in to capture them. Sharp firing was soon heard in that direction, and soon after I was ordered to change the direction of my lines, with my rear on the road, and advance, conforming as much as possible with the direction of the regular brigade on my left. I left the second brigade in its position on the road; also my battery, supported by Lieutenant-Colonel Griffin, Thirty-eighth Indiana. When the nature of the movement became more developed, and a position for the battery discovered, I sent for instructions as to the disposition of the battery, and was ordered to let it follow in my rear ; also that General Palmer was on my right, and was cautioned not to fire into his skirmishers. About this time my line became sharply engaged, and the enemy receding, we closely pressed them. The woods impeding the progress of the battery, Lieutenant-Colonel Griffin hurried forward and took position on the right of the Thirty-third Ohio, having left two companies with the battery. Success appeared to have followed the movement of our left, who were pressing forward with cheers. This state of things extended along my line also. Passing over the enemy's killed and wounded, overtaking and capturing prisoners attended our progress until we arrived at a corn-field in our front, over which we had driven the enemy. Here their battery essayed to get into position, but their horses and men were shot down as often as attempted. Here I was cautioned not to fire into Palmer on my right ; that we had passed over a part of his skirmishers, and the exact spot was pointed out on an elevation on my right where they were lying down.

The advance on my left having ceased, I halted in front of the field and placed the battery in position, bearing to my left and the point where the enemy attempted to place a battery. About this time I was informed by my skirmishers that the enemy was passing to our right. I immediately sent a staff officer to notify General Palmer, who, after proceeding a short distance in the supposed direction of General Palmer's line, found himself within 20 paces and confronting a strong skirmish line of the enemy. After adroitly making his escape, and being unable to find my intermediate commander, [he] reported in person the presence of the enemy on the right to Major-General Thomas, who immediately directed him to order any forces that could be found in the woods to meet the enemy in his new position. Three separate commands were thus notified. I was immediately after informed that my right was being turned. Dr. Miller, my brigade surgeon, coming up, reported the enemy in my rear; that he had been in their hands. As information like this came in I dispatched the same to the general commanding division, and threw a company of skirmishers to my right and rear. Scarcely had their deployment been completed when the enemy opened upon them a destructive fire. To form a front to the right by causing the Thirty-eighth Indiana to change their front to the rear and to change the Tenth Wisconsin to the right of the Thirty-eighth Indiana and limber the battery to the rear, between the two regiments, employed but a few moments; this, too, under a heavy fire. The enemy charged down upon me along my whole line, pouring in canister and shell. I had now dispatched every staff officer and orderly with information of my position, asking for support, expressing my intention to hold my place with desperation until assistance arrived; for I felt that the safety of the forces on my left depended upon holding this position. I had observed a line of our forces in my rear passing to the left. I sent to the officer for assistance, but he had other orders. Thus, contending with an overwhelming force in my front and on my flank, was [fought] one of the most stubborn and heroic fights that ever fell to my lot to witness. The gallant Lieutenant Van Pelt was shot down at his guns, having fired 64 rounds into the midst of the enemy as they came charging down the hill, the two regiments on the right and left of the battery at the same time pouring in a well-directed fire. The enemy would hesitate but a moment, when they continued to press on. Their augmenting forces at length broke my lines, and forced me to fall back. The nature of my line, being in a right angle, the intricacies of the woods, overwhelming numbers, and the impetuosity of the charge rendered it impossible to withdraw in order, and not until they had reached a point near the road could order be restored. To show the impossibility of my brigade, unsupported, to hold the place, I would respectfully refer the general commanding to the fact that a force more than four times as strong as mine was only able, after many hours' hard fighting, to regain my position.

About 4 o'clock in the afternoon, together with the Second and Third Brigades of this division, we took another position on the left of General Brannan, and at about sundown advanced into the woods toward the left of the position I had occupied in the morning to the support of General Johnson. Here we got possession of many of our wounded, who had been left upon the field in the morning. General Johnson, on our right, was vigorously attacked, which soon passed over to our position, the enemy's shells bursting among us. My extreme left was also fiercely assaulted by the enemy, who, by accident or design, fell upon my flank, when, it being so dark that nothing but the flash of the guns could be seen, I ordered my left to fall back into the edge of a clear space in the woods. From this position we passed a short distance to the rear and right, where we remained during the night.

Before daylight on the morning of the 20th we took up a position on the left of General Johnson, the Second Brigade of our division on my right and the regular brigade on my left. I formed in two lines on the crest of a wooded slope. Between my front and the woods was a clear space, averaging 75 yards. This space was enfiladed by two guns of the Fourth Indiana Battery. Here we built temporary breastworks in front of both lines, and got all things arranged, when the enemy advanced upon us in strong force, driving in our skirmishers and approaching to the edge of the clearing with their battle-flag (a large white ball in a blue field). My men were cautioned to hold their fire. The second line closed up to the first, and at the opportune moment the first line fired; then the second, which caused the enemy to fall back in haste and disorder, leaving the ground strewn with their dead and wounded. Three times in succession the enemy made similar attempts to drive us from our position, but were as often repulsed. Sometimes they would swing to the right in front of the Second Brigade, then to the left on the regulars, but without success. In the afternoon several bodies of troops passed into the woods beyond and in rear of our left, who soon became hotly engaged, and after some hours were forced to fall back. They were seen coming out of the woods on our left and rear. This having been observed by General Baird, commanding division, he promptly ordered me to form my second line, faced to the rear in an acute angle, and successively formed the troops as they emerged from the woods upon the prolongation of this line. Wherever a regiment or party of men could be found, they were persuaded to extend or support this line, so that when the enemy, flushed with success, came charging from the woods into the corn-field in our rear, they met with a deadly fire from this line, which soon compelled them to fall back, being closely pressed by the troops who had just been driven out. General Baird then apprehending that they would swing round upon us, our first line was put upon its guard, while the Second Ohio and Tenth Wisconsin, of my second line, and the regulars, together with some other detached forces, proceeded to strengthen our left, hastily throwing up barricades of logs.

These preparations had scarcely been made before the enemy came upon our left flank. Having been repulsed, they stubbornly persisted, and only after being repelled several times did they abandon their design. Thus the day was spent. During the intervals of the heavy attacks, constant skirmishing was kept up by the sharpshooters. About 5 o'clock in the afternoon the enemy, with great zeal and force, seemed to attack simultaneously our whole line. They had got a battery in position, and rained upon us shot and shell. Everything assumed a discouraging aspect. Our ammunition was almost gone; staff officers and details who had been sent for it returned without it. About this time I observed a column of our forces from our right passing to our left and rear. Then not knowing that the army was falling back, I encouraged my men to believe that re-enforcements were going around our left to turn the enemy's right, and urged them to economize the few rounds of ammunition they had left, and hold out until this maneuver could be accomplished. About this time an officer of the regular brigade notified me that the general ordered my command to retire. He not having been announced on the general's staff, I was unwilling to obey, and called his attention to the supposed re-enforcements and the fact that hitherto we had driven them off. Soon after this I observed the troops who were passing to my left were not in such good order, and that the two guns on my right were retiring, and that the Second Brigade was falling back. At this juncture, Captain Cary, of the general's staff, came up and delivered General Baird's order to fall back, firing. This order I promptly gave. We moved to the rear into the woods, across the Chattanooga road, my design being to join the forces who had been fighting there all the afternoon. Here we halted and re-formed our lines as best we could in the dark, when I was ordered to move to Rossville.

At noon on the 21st we took position in the gaps on the left of General Negley, forming breastworks, but met with no enemy save their skirmishers and sharpshooters, and a few shots from the enemy's shells. In this position I only had one man wounded.

In the night the army fell back upon Chattanooga. My command was designated as rear guard, and, according to instructions, at 4 o'clock in the morning followed the army to this place.

Before closing this report, already made too long, I would respectfully call the attention of the general commanding to the good conduct of the officers and men of my command. I have had but few stragglers ; my missing are mostly in the hands of the enemy or cut off. The service and the country lost heavily when Major Ellis, Thirty-third Ohio Volunteer Infantry, and Lieutenant Van Pelt, commanding battery, were killed. Lieutenant-Colonel Maxwell, commanding Second Ohio Volunteer Infantry, in the absence of Colonel McCook, who is absent on special duty, was dangerously wounded by two shots on the first day, after [performing] many praiseworthy acts. He was succeeded by Major Beatty, who filled his place with credit; he, also, was wounded late on the second day, and is supposed to be a prisoner. Lieutenant-Colonel Ely and Major McKercher, of the Tenth Wisconsin, are prisoners, with all of the command they took into the fight, with the exception of 2 officers and 32 men. The noble conduct of these officers and regiments greatly augments the loss. I feel greatly indebted to all of my regimental commanders for their gallant bearing, and the hearty support they have rendered me during these days of trial. Colonel Moore, commanding Thirty-third Ohio Volunteer Infantry, and Lieutenant-Colonel Griffin, commanding Thirty-eighth Indiana, are worthy of especial praise. I would also commend the gentlemen of my staff for the faithful performance of their arduous duties. Lieut. George Devol, acting assistant adjutant-general; Lieutenant Kelso, acting commissary of subsistence; and Lieutenant Bird, acting assistant quartermaster, are worthy of especial praise. Lieutenant Hollister, aide-de-camp, was thrown from his horse and seriously disabled early in action in the faithful performance of his duties.

I went into action on the morning of the 19th instant with 120 officers and 1,759 men, and came out with 70 officers and 872 men ; a loss of 50 officers and 887 men in killed, wounded, and prisoners.* For their names and for further particulars I would respectfully refer to the accompanying papers.†

> B. F. SCRIBNER,
> *Colonel Thirty-eighth Indiana, Commanding First Brigade.*
Capt. B. H. POLK,
> *Assistant Adjutant-General, First Division.*

ADDENDA.

Weekly report of effective force of the First Brigade, First Division, Fourteenth Army Corps, Col. Benjamin F. Scribner, commanding.

Command.	Headquarters.			Infantry.			Artillery.			Total.			Number of horses.	Number of guns.
	Commissioned officers.	Enlisted men.	Total.	Commissioned officers.	Enlisted men.	Total.	Commissioned officers.	Enlisted men.	Total.	Commissioned officers.	Enlisted men.	Aggregate.		
Headquarters, Col. B. F. Scribner.	7	45	52	.....	.....	.....	.....	.....	.....	7	45	52	.....	.....
38th Indiana, Lieut. Col. D. F. Griffin.	.....	.....	.....	28	382	410	.....	.....	.....	28	382	410	.....	.....
33d Ohio, Col. O. F. Moore.				24	391	415				24	391	415	.....	.....
2d Ohio, Lieut. Col. O. C. Maxwell.				23	391	414				23	391	414	.....	.....
94th Ohio, Lieut. Col. D. King.				22	287	309				22	287	309	.....	.....
10th Wisconsin, Lieut. Col. J. H. Ely.				26	297	323				26	297	323	.....	.....
Total infantry.	7	45	52	123	1,748	1,871	.....	.....	.....	130	1,793	1,923	.....	.....
1st Michigan Battery, First Lieut. G. W. Van Pelt.	.....	.....	.....	.....	.....	.....	3	115	118	3	115	118	130	6
Grand total infantry and artillery.	7	45	52	123	1,748	1,871	3	115	118	133	1,908	2,041	130	a6

a 10-pounders.

> B. F. SCRIBNER,
> *Colonel, Commanding Brigade.*
SEPTEMBER 15, 1863,

---

* See revised statement, p. 171.   † Nominal lists of casualties omitted.

No. 21.

Report of Lieut. Col. Daniel F. Griffin, Thirty-eighth Indiana Infantry.

HDQRS. THIRTY-EIGHTH INDIANA VOLUNTEERS,
Chattanooga, Tenn., September 23, 1863.

LIEUTENANT: I have the honor to report the following as the part taken by this command in the engagements and movements of the 19th, 20th, and 21st days of September, 1863:

The regiment, with the brigade, after marching about 10 miles, moved into position at daylight on the 19th instant, near the forks of Chattanooga and La Fayette roads and road running to the Crawfish Spring, occupying the right of the second line, with three companies thrown to the rear and left as pickets. About 9 a. m. brisk skirmishing commenced on our left by General Brannan's division, which soon assumed the magnitude of an engagement. About 10 a. m. our brigade moved in a southeasterly direction to their support on the right of regular brigade, my command of eight companies occupying extreme right of first line (Companies B and H moving in our rear as support to First Michigan Battery, also advancing with us). I was notified that General Palmer's troops were moving on our right as supports, and cautioned not to fire on their skirmishers.

The enemy now being driven by the troops on our left and center, a very rapid movement to the front for three-fourths of a mile was made, my command, with the brigade, moving to and swinging to the left, capturing many prisoners, who were sent to the rear. The command was now halted on the crest of a hill, with a corn-field on our left and front, and on our right a wooded hill with heavy undergrowth. In coming to this position I had passed within sight of the left of General Palmer's troops moving to the front, and passed through the left of their skirmish line, but for the last quarter of a mile had not seen any of them, which fact was promptly reported; the firing had now ceased on the left, and only occasional skirmish shots [were] exchanged on our front.

Company F, Captain Jenkins commanding, my line of skirmishers, now reported the enemy advancing and moving to our right, as though intending to flank the position and gain our rear. These facts being reported, I was ordered to change my line perpendicularly to the rear, forming almost a right angle with the line of the Thirty-third Ohio, next on my left. The Tenth Wisconsin now moved on our right, and First Michigan Battery, with companies B and H of my command, also on our right. This position was hardly taken when the enemy charged down on our front, driving in skirmishers and advancing in heavy column. Fire was immediately opened by whole line and battery, momentarily checking the advance. But they again pressed forward with such vigor, while raking both fronts of the brigade with an enfilading fire of musketry, that the left was compelled to fall back, which was soon followed by the whole line, the enemy meantime having charged in heavy force up the hill and into the right and center of my command, which gave way under the pressure, not, however, without suffering much loss in killed, wounded, and prisoners. In passing to the rear I found no troops to rally with, and did not get my command together until nearing the Chattanooga road. Here the brigade was reformed, and about 4 p. m. moved with the division into position again south of road. From this point an advance was made about sundown, going to within a few hundred yards of the former position, and relieving many of the wounded that had been left on the field in the afternoon.

The lines of General Johnson's command on our right were attacked vigorously at this time, driving in their left and advancing on our position. Our left, in consequence of not being joined by Third Brigade, was exposed to a flank movement, and very soon the enemy came in at this point, advancing in the darkness and pouring in a volley of musketry on our flank that caused the line to retire a few hundred yards to prevent their gaining our rear in the darkness. Here the brigade was formed, and about 9 p. m. we marched to position near Chattanooga road, remaining until 4 a. m. of the 20th, when the brigade again moved into position south of Chattanooga road, my command occupying the right of first line, connecting with left of Second Brigade, supported by a section of artillery. Here temporary breastworks of logs, rails, and stones were quickly thrown up, and about 8 a. m. the enemy in force moved on our position, and after three attempts to advance, each of which was handsomely repulsed with heavy loss to the enemy, they retired in some confusion, and did not again renew it on our immediate front in force until about 4.30 p. m., when, after their desperate attack on the right, they again pressed their forces against our position (this time supported by a battery that hurled the grape around us in showers), and were again handsomely checked with heavy loss.

About this time, near 5 p. m., an order reached me through Captain Cary, acting assistant adjutant-general, division staff, that the army was ordered to retire. I directed the captain to your headquarters, continued my fire with renewed vigor on the enemy, and awaited your orders, until seeing regiment after regiment of Second Brigade and the section of artillery on my right move rapidly to the rear, nothing was left me but to follow or suffer total capture, as the enemy pressed up the hill at once on the departure of the Second Brigade, and immediately on my flank. At this point I ordered the command to retire, and moved on the double-quick through the corn-field, crossing Chattanooga road, and again reforming my command on the wooded hill beyond about sundown. Here, having become temporarily separated from the brigade, I reported to Brigadier-General Cruft, and asked that I might move with, and as part of, his command. This was granted, and soon after moved with it on the road to Rossville. Hearing of your being on the road with balance of brigade, and General Cruft having to wait the arrival of part of his command, permission was given me to advance, which was done, joining you at Rossville, and going into bivouac about 9 p. m.

About 11 p. m. marched for Chattanooga, but ere it was reached about-faced and returned to vicinity of Rossville, bivouacking on side of road, and remaining in this position until 1 p. m. of the 21st, receiving and issuing ammunition and rations. At this hour, skirmishing having commenced on the front, we moved rapidly forward, gaining position on range of hills, throwing up temporary breastworks, and there awaiting the enemy's advance. At 4 a. m. of the 22d, received your order to retire, acting as rear guard to the command, and did so successfully, arriving at Chattanooga and going into our present position about 8 a. m.

I cannot close this report without commending to your consideration both officers and men for their coolness, courage, and perseverance under the trying scenes through which they have passed. Cheerfulness and readiness to act has marked their conduct on every occasion. To Capt. William L. Carter, Company E, acting major, I am indebted for much valuable assistance throughout the whole affair. My command went into action with an aggregate strength of 354 officers and men, and lost as follows:

Casualties.	Officers.	Enlisted men.	Total.
Killed..	......	10	10
Wounded..	3	45	48
Wounded and missing (in hands of enemy)...........................	1	11	12
Missing (in hands of enemy)...	......	39	39
Grand total *..	4	105	109

Accompanying I transmit list of casualties.†
Very respectfully, your most obedient servant,
D. F. GRIFFIN,
Lieut. Col., Comdg. 38th Indiana Vol. Infantry.
Lieut. GEORGE H. DEVOL,
A. A. A. G., 1st Brig., 1st Div., 14th A. C.

No. 22.

Report of Capt. James Warnock, Second Ohio Infantry.

BIVOUAC SECOND OHIO VOLUNTEER INFANTRY,
In the Field, Chattanooga, September 25, 1863.

SIR: The Second Ohio Regiment, under the command of Lieut. Col. O. C. Maxwell, Col. A. G. McCook being absent on detached duty, marched with the brigade of Colonel Scribner on Friday evening, September 18, from Bird's Mill; passed Crawfish Spring, and soon after daybreak arrived at the crossing of the La Fayette and Chattanooga road. The command was halted there and formed into line of battle. About 8 a. m. two brigades passed our regiment toward the left of the field, and soon afterward heavy firing of musketry was heard in that direction. The First Brigade was put in motion, the Second Ohio being in the front line of battle, and marched in the direction of the firing, but keeping somewhat to the right. In half an hour the regiment came within sight of the enemy and opened a rapid and steady fire, advancing all the time, firing, loading, and cheering loudly. The enemy in a few minutes gave way and fled, leaving about a dozen killed and wounded in our immediate front, also about 15 or 20 prisoners, who were sent to the rear. A section of Martin's (Georgia) battery was in our front. The regiment killed all the horses belonging to one of the guns, and it was left on the field by us because we had no means to bring it off. The firing here ceased in front, and our line was halted about

---

* See revised statement, p. 171.   † Omitted.

an hour. Skirmishing was then heard on our right flank; the regiment changed front forward, facing a corn-field through which the enemy was coming massed in heavy force. Immediately the engagement was renewed with great fury, the enemy pressing forward heavily on the right. So overwhelming was his force that the right of the brigade gave way by regiments, successively, until the Second Ohio, being on the left, retired, after all the regiments on the right had been driven from their position. In falling back from this position we expected to find a line of our troops supporting us, behind which the regiment would halt. In this we were disappointed, and the result was that the line retired thereafter in considerable confusion, but the regiment was rallied about half a mile to the rear. During this engagement Lieutenant-Colonel Maxwell was wounded, and the command devolved on Major Beatty. Here also the regiment lost heavily, particularly in missing, most of whom fell into the hands of the enemy. In the afternoon the regiment remained in line of battle, and was in the rear of General Johnson's division when the latter was attacked by the enemy, at nightfall. After that engagement ceased, the brigade was moved to an open field, where it bivouacked for the night.

On the morning of Sunday, the 20th, at daybreak, the regiment marched back, and with the brigade and division was formed in order of battle on the crest of a hill; the enemy approached in front, feeling our position, but retired after a few shots were fired. We could see his flags. He then moved over on our left, and very soon heavy firing commenced there and in our front. The Second Ohio advanced to the front line, on the left of the Thirty-third Ohio, in fine spirits, and opened a steady and deadly fire, shouting and cheering the meanwhile with the greatest enthusiasm. Just as we advanced to this position a portion of the regular brigade gave way on our left, leaving for a time the Second Ohio alone on that part of the field, supported, however, by the Thirty-third Ohio. Our regiment took no notice of the vacancy, but rather redoubled their firing and cheering. The regulars were rallied and returned to their position. The firing on this part of the field was steady and unceasing for two hours and a half. Our line was held steadfastly; not an inch of ground was yielded. On the left of us our troops, after alternately advancing and retiring, finally drove the enemy from the field in front and the firing nearly ceased about 1 p. m. We threw up a slight breastwork meanwhile in our front, and threw skirmishers forward. About 4.30 or 5 p. m. our skirmishers were driven in, and the battle was immediately renewed with great fury. Heavy columns of the enemy with artillery opened a tremendous fire all along the line, but their attack was steadfastly resisted; no impression whatever was made on our line, which remained unbroken some time after the troops on the right of our division gave way and retired. The falling back of the right forced us to retire to prevent capture. Here again the regiment, in retiring, became confused, and lost many men.

Major Beatty, who commanded during the day, was wounded and taken prisoner. The army during that night retired toward Chattanooga, halted about midnight, and the regiment was again collected as far as possible. On the morning of the 22d we entered Chattanooga.

Inclosed herewith is a statement of the loss of the regiment, as accurate as it can be now prepared.*

---

*See revised statement, p. 171.

The loss of our field officers, Lieutenant-Colonel Maxwell and Major Beatty, which is greatly deplored, and the temporary illness of Captain Mitchell, left the regiment under my command. Of our commissioned officers, Lieutenant-Colonel Maxwell, Major Beatty, and Lieutenant Purlier are wounded ; Major Beatty, Adjutant Thomas, Captain Randall, Captain Gallaher, Lieutenants Purlier, McCune, Teeter, and Assistant Surgeon Carmichael are missing.

Our effective force on the evening of the 18th was 18 officers and 394 men. Our loss known is: Killed, 8; wounded, 49; missing, 124, including the above officers.*

The regiment fired about eighty rounds of cartridges in the battle.

Respectfully,

JAMES WARNOCK,
Captain Second Ohio Vol. Infty., Comdg. Regiment.

Lieutenant DEVOL,
Acting Assistant Adjutant-General.

No. 23.

Report of Col. Oscar F. Moore, Thirty-third Ohio Infantry.

HDQRS. THIRTY-THIRD REGIMENT OHIO VOL. INFTY.,
Chattanooga, Tenn., September 24, 1863.

SIR : I have the honor to submit the following statement of the part taken by the Thirty-third Ohio Volunteer Infantry in the engagement near Crawfish Spring, on the 19th and 20th instant :

Having moved during the night of the 18th from Bird's Mill to a point about 3 miles east of the spring, at daylight on the morning of the 19th the brigade was formed in line of battle, with the right of the Thirty-third Ohio Volunteer Infantry resting on the east side of the State road, and the line extending east parallel with a fence in front, and connecting with the Second Ohio on the left. Immediately across the road on our right, on more elevated ground, was posted a section of the First Michigan Battery. On the right of that again was the Second Brigade in line, and on the left of the Second Ohio was the Third Brigade. Our line was nearly at right angles with the State road.

Shortly after our line was formed the Third Division of the Fourteenth Corps began to arrive, and upon being informed by Col. Dan. McCook that a brigade of rebels had been cut off and was only a short distance in front, one of the brigades of that division was sent by General Brannan to engage them. In a short time heavy firing was heard on the left and front of us and immediately our entire division was ordered to advance. The Second Ohio marched by the left flank, filing left until the right reached where the left had rested, when it moved by the right flank in line of battle, bearing off in an easterly course ; the Thirty-third also marching by the left flank until its right reached where its left had rested, when by order of the brigade commander it marched by the right flank in line of battle, wheeling to the left so as to form quite an obtuse angle with the Second Ohio, and thus continued its march, obliquing, however, to the left and occasionally marching by the left flank so as to keep up

---

* See revised statement, p. 171.

close connection with the right of the Second. The enemy was soon encountered, but was driven before us steadily, and with considerable loss to them in killed, wounded, and prisoners.

While thus advancing, information, which at the time was deemed reliable, reached us that Palmer's division was in our front, and in order that we might be unmasked and hold a postion on their left, the brigade obliqued rapidly to the left, and in the meantime the Second Brigade fell to the rear, thus leaving our right entirely unprotected, unless, as was reported, Palmer was really there. The enemy having disappeared from our front, the brigade was halted near a corn-field and the lines readjusted. The Thirty-third was wheeled to the left and advanced so as to form a continuous line with the Second, while the Thirty-eighth Indiana and Tenth Wisconsin, then forming the second line, were wheeled to the right and advanced so as to form a line at right angles with us and connect with and cover the right. The First Michigan Battery in the meantime was brought into position on the right, between the Thirty-eighth Indiana and Tenth Wisconsin. Immediately after this the enemy made a most furious attack in front and simultaneously threw an overwhelming column on our flank. The assault on the flank was so irresistible and the column so heavy as to force, in a few moments, the Thirty-eighth Indiana and Tenth Wisconsin from their position and endanger the battery. Our right flank being thus exposed, and the regiment subjected to a most murderous enfilading fire, without being able to confer with the brigade commander, in order to avoid annihilation or capture, the regiment was ordered to fall back, which it did; but on account of the heavy fire of artillery and musketry upon its flank and rear, its retreat was confused and disorderly, amounting almost to a rout, so that it was impossible to rally it until it had reached the State road. Our loss in this engagement was heavy.

About 3 p. m. the brigade was brought together, reformed, and marched to the front to support Johnson's division, where we remained, without being actively engaged, until after dark, when we were withdrawn to an adjoining field to bivouac during the night.

About 4 o'clock on the morning of the 20th the regiment moved from its bivouac with the brigade to the east, about 400 yards, and formed in line of battle, our right resting on the left of the Ninety-fourth Ohio, and our line forming with its line an obtuse angle. Temporary works of stones and logs were thrown up in the edge of the woods, on a gentle slope, in front of which to the east for a distance of 60 yards was an open plain, and in front of that again the ground descended, covered with a light growth of timber. Behind these works the regiment was posted and fought during the day. About 8 a. m. our entire line, formed by Johnson's division on the right, our division in the center, and a portion of Negley's division on the left, was fiercely assaulted by a large force, said by prisoners to be under the command of Breckinridge. The fighting was very severe with both artillery and musketry, and for awhile the result was doubtful, but finally the enemy was repulsed and driven back with great slaughter.

With the exception of occasional skirmishing and the annoyance of sharpshooters, resulting in a few casualties, among which I regret to note the death of our gallant Maj. E. J. Ellis and the severe wounding of Capt. George P. Singer, no more serious fighting occurred on our front until near 4 p. m., although for several hours evident preparation had been going on for a heavy attack. About 4

p. m., while the battle was raging on the right, the assault was renewed with the utmost vehemence and ferocity and with apparently an overwhelming force, but, availing themselves of the temporary works thrown up in our front, the men with great coolness and bravery held the enemy at bay and repulsed with great gallantry every assault until near sundown, when the order was given to fall back. Owing, however, to the roar of artillery and musketry, the order to retire was not understood by me or those commanding battalions on our left. Perceiving, however, that the artillery on the right of our line had been withdrawn and that the infantry also was retiring somewhat in haste and disorder, a partial stampede was caused on our left, the effect of which was to expose our center to an attack on either flank. In order, therefore, to save my command I directed it to fall back. This order, however, in the din of battle was not heard by a portion of the regiment, nor was any such communicated to a portion of the Second Ohio and Tenth Wisconsin. The result was that these obstinately held their ground and continued to fight until completely surrounded and either killed, wounded, or captured. The fate of these, embracing from my command 3 officers and about 75 enlisted men, is shrouded in uncertainty. With the exception of some six or eight casualties arising from causes already noticed, nearly the entire loss of the regiment on that day thus occurred from an unwillingness to fall back without receiving an order to do so.

Having gathered together nearly all of my command that had escaped, we fell in with the retreating column and joined the brigade that night near Rossville. Our loss has been heavy, a detailed statement of which accompanies this; but nearly one-half of it occurred on account of not understanding the order to retire and in the obstinacy with which a portion maintained their ground and continued to fight, even after nearly everybody else had retired from the field. The regiment was thrown somewhat in confusion in retiring under orders when so fiercely attacked on the flank in the first day's fight, but aside from that it maintained its position and fought in perfect order throughout the entire engagement. If at any time the regiment failed to do its duty, ceased to hold its position, or fight when it ought to have fought, the fault is with its commander, and not with its valiant officers and men. All my officers, all my men, with the exception of a very few cowards, who ingloriously fled early in the fight, and upon whom the severest penalty should be inflicted, acted with marked bravery and coolness, and obeyed promptly every order communicated during the trying ordeal. Many of the bravest and best of my command have fallen, and a monument should be erected to their memory. Of those who have survived, when all have behaved so well, it may be invidious to discriminate, but, without disparagement or offense to others, I may be permitted to note with hearty commendation and praise the gallant bearing and heroism of Corpl. Sylvester Keller, of Company A.

Respectfully,

O. F. MOORE,
Colonel Thirty-third Ohio Volunteer Infantry.

Lieut. GEORGE H. DEVOL,
Acting Assistant Adjutant-General, First Brigade.

No. 24.

Report of Maj. Rue P. Hutchins, Ninety-fourth Ohio Infantry.

HDQRS. NINETY-FOURTH OHIO VOL. INFANTRY,
September 26, 1863.

SIR: I have the honor to make the following report of the part borne by the Ninety-fourth Ohio Volunteer Infantry in the engagements of Saturday and Sunday, September 19 and 20:

On Saturday morning, when the firing began on our left, the brigade was swung around in such a position as to face nearly northeast; the Ninety-fourth was in the second line on the left and immediately behind the Second Ohio, our right joining on the left of the Tenth Wisconsin. We moved forward with the brigade, maintaining our relative position for a distance of perhaps 40 rods, when General Baird rode along the line and told us that we were bearing too much to the right. In reply to the answer that I had been ordered to follow the Second Ohio, he stated that the whole brigade was bearing too far to the right, and ordered us to the left. We obliqued to the left until we moved in a direction forming an angle of about 20 degrees with the direction taken by the brigade, when we were ordered to move forward on the double-quick. We moved in this manner for a distance of nearly or quite half a mile, a considerable number of the enemy passing our lines to the rear as prisoners. I then halted. Nothing could be seen of the brigade on the right, but on the left and about 25 rods to the rear a column of troops was bearing leisurely down, which I ascertained by inquiry to be the regular brigade. General Baird coming up, I reported to him for orders, and was told to move on. I did so for a considerable distance, moving over part of the space at double-quick. On looking back, I found the regulars moving by the rear rank, and heard considerable firing on that part of the field over which I supposed our troops had passed. I immediately sent an officer to learn the meaning of it. He returned and reported that the enemy were in our rear, and that we were to fall back to the support of the regulars. I immediately moved back and formed on the (now) left of the regular brigade.

By the time my lines were dressed the enemy opened a most terrific fire on us, and charged on a section of the regular battery. The troops fell back and I ordered my command back with them. We soon again rallied and moved off to the left. Here we were ordered by some general officer to the support of a battery. We were almost immediately ordered still farther to the left and formed again on a line with the regulars. We were then fronting very nearly to the north, on a hill, as nearly as I can judge, to the rear of where we had stacked arms in the morning. The troops to our right were the regulars, and to the right of them all or a part of Brannan's division; we appeared to be on the extreme left. Here the enemy again charged the lines, their right covering the right wing of the regiment, but were speedily repulsed with considerable loss. We remained here with but little change until about 3 o'clock, when I was ordered to move back until I struck the road, then to proceed down it. I did so, and after moving a short distance fell in with the brigade and formed on the left of the Second Ohio. We moved forward with the brigade from this point in the same position until the second order of battle was formed, when we were again thrown on the left of the second line and immediately behind the Thirty-eighth Indiana. When the brigade was moved forward to the support of the troops engaged on our front, I threw out two companies (B and G) as skirmishers. They had been deployed but a few moments when a volley was discharged into the left of the regiment. So close were the enemy that we could plainly see into the barrels of their muskets at each discharge. The regiment fell back to an open field at the foot of the hill, and from there we moved to our place of bivouac for the night.

On Sunday my regiment was placed in the front line on the left of the Thirty-eighth Indiana and right of the Thirty-third Ohio. During the day we maintained the same position. A few were here wounded, among them Lieutenant Cushman, Company A. When the enemy made their last charge in the evening we felt confident of holding our position, and after the right gave way I gave the command to fall back twice before the regiment started. As was generally the case the regiment was considerably scattered, and it was some time before the command was all got together, the officers who rallied squads having considerable difficulty in finding the remaining portions. There are but few absent from the regiment now unaccounted for. Those that are missing are, I have but little reason to doubt, prisoners in the hands of the enemy.

During the two days' fight the regiment showed decided courage and coolness. Notwithstanding the heavy losses of Saturday the men went forward on Sunday cheerfully and willingly. Many instances of bravery among the men came under my notice which I shall take occasion to reward. I cannot, in justice, close this report without bearing testimony to the gallantry of my officers. They all did their duty. Captain Edmonds deserves special mention for his conduct in assisting in rallying the command on two different occasions. Lieut. James Mitchell showed great personal bravery when skirmishing, and when the regiment was engaged. Adjutant Sherlock proved himself an efficient officer, and to him, in the absence of the colonel and lieutenant-colonel, I am indebted for much valuable assistance.

I am, very respectfully, your obedient servant,

RUE P. HUTCHINS,
Major, Comdg. Ninety-fourth Ohio Vol. Infantry.

Lieut. GEORGE H. DEVOL,
Acting Assistant Adjutant-General.

No. 25.

Report of Capt. Jacob W. Roby, Tenth Wisconsin Infantry.

HEADQUARTERS TENTH WISCONSIN INFANTRY,
Chattanooga, September 23, 1863.

SIR: I have the honor to make the following report of the Tenth Regiment Wisconsin Volunteer Infantry during the late engagement:

The regiment marched from near Stevens' Gap on the night of the 18th instant to within 10 miles of Chattanooga. Saturday morning, September 19, we were ordered to advance on the enemy in the second line of battle with the brigade. After advancing a short distance we received a fire from the enemy, but they were driven some distance through the woods. At this time we were ordered up in the front line on the right of the brigade. We threw out skirmishers and soon engaged the enemy; our skirmishers were soon driven in and the enemy advanced on us in heavy force. We held our position a few moments, but the enemy turning our right flank, we were forced to fall back and did so with the brigade. We lost at this time 1 officer and 9 men killed and several wounded. In the afternoon we again advanced to the front with the brigade and in the evening fell back.

Sunday morning, 20th instant, our regiment was again moved to the front and formed behind the Thirty-eighth Indiana. We remained here till about 10 o'clock, when we were ordered forward to support the Thirty-eighth Indiana, where we remained but a short time when the enemy turned the left of our division and were advancing through the woods on our left flank. Our right was now thrown to the left of the brigade and engaged the enemy. They were soon forced to fall back. They made another attempt to break through on our left about noon, but were repulsed as before and we held our own till nearly dark, when we received a flank and rear fire from the enemy and were forced to fall back. Our regiment, being on the left and not knowing the position of the enemy on that side, fell back in that direction and therefore ran into the lines of the enemy. Colonel Ely, Major McKercher, and nearly all of the officers we had on the field, together with most of the men, were supposed to have been captured at this time. All we could find were brought off with the balance of the brigade. Monday morning, September 21, we numbered 3 officers and 26 men. We were moved to the front about 1 p. m. and formed in rear of the brigade, where we remained until about 4 a. m., September 22, when we were ordered to retire and moved with the brigade to Chattanooga, where we have remained since.

Very respectfully, your obedient servant,

J. W. ROBY,
Captain, Commanding Tenth Wisconsin Infantry.

Lieut. GEORGE H. DEVOL,
Acting Assistant Adjutant-General.

No. 26.

Report of Brig. Gen. John C. Starkweather, U. S. Army, commanding Second Brigade.

HDQRS. SECOND BRIG., FIRST DIV., 14TH ARMY CORPS,
Chattanooga, Tenn., September 23, 1863.

SIR: I have the honor to report that on the 17th instant my command moved from Stevens' Gap, Ga., to Owens' Ford, Ga., 9 miles. On the 18th moved to Crawfish Spring, Ga., a distance of 4 miles. On the morning of the 19th moved and took up position on left of Colonel Wilder's brigade, at cross-roads. At 10 a. m. received orders from general commanding to move command in support of First and Third Brigades, troops being engaged on extreme left when order was received; came up with a portion of Third Brigade, then received orders from Major-General Thomas to move to the left and relieve Colonel Croxton, commanding Second Brigade, of Brannan's division, who was out of ammunition; found and relieved his brigade by moving to the front and taking position, reporting such change of the disposition of my command to the general commanding through

Captain Cary, one of his staff. Heavy firing to my front and on my right. On investigation found the enemy advancing in heavy columns on my right flank. Wheeled directly to the right and took position ; no sooner done than found that the enemy were moving in heavy columns on my then right, late my rear. Immediately changed direction by moving to the right, faced to the front and retired on my right and left so as to form a half semicircle, covering, as was supposed, the advance of the enemy; I immediately ordered my battery in position and ordered Lieutenant Searles, my acting assistant adjutant-general, to the rear, to report the disposition of my own command and the position of the enemy's advance. The order had only been issued when the enemy struck me with heavy columns on my then right and front. At this moment my adjutant-general, Lieutenant Searles, was killed.

Finding the enemy so strong on my front and to my right, in order to save my command from destruction a slow retirement was ordered to the ridge directly to the rear, by obliquing in direction to the left from my front, or to the right when faced to the rear. This movement was accomplished as well as could have been expected under the circumstances, three or four discharges only having been made by my battery and about the same number by my troops. Formed my command on the retired ridge, and reported my position and the condition of affairs in person to General Thomas. The enemy was then struck by some of our troops in his rear and on his flank, throwing him into confusion, thus leaving my guns not withdrawn untouched. All these movements were covered by my skirmishers, who changed direction as I changed direction. I immediately set to work to place my battery again in fighting condition ; received orders from general commanding to close on First and Third Brigades, taking position in support of General Johnson's division. Was then ordered to move forward so that my right regiments might lap the left regiments of General Johnson's division (at his request). First Brigade was in position on my left, swung around by a left half wheel in support of General Johnson's lines, by his (General Johnson's) request and by order of general commanding. The troops upon my right and front being hard pressed by the enemy, and their ammunition being reported as failing, the whole line was ordered to move forward to the support of the first line ; my battery, two guns, being thrown into position in center of brigade.

By this time it was dark, and the positions could only be known by the flashing of the musketry and artillery of the first line. Supposing that the First Brigade was moving parallel with the Second by a left half wheel, no caution was taken on my part to prevent any accident arising from the First Brigade being in a wrong position. The regiments on the right lapping the left regiments of General Johnson's division were instructed not to fire unless their position was changed so as to put them in fighting position, which, of course, was done by the movement of left half wheel, unmasking Johnson's troops, and the command was then moved forward and immediately brought under the heavy and murderous fire of the enemy. The troops of the First Brigade also opened fire, but having swung or obliqued to the right instead of moving parallel to the Second Brigade by a left half wheel, opened with their fire upon the left regiments of my brigade and the left of Johnson's division, thus destroying my men by a rear and right-oblique fire, as well as by the front fire of the enemy.

The left of Johnson's troops, supposing that they were attacked in the rear from the effect of this rear and right-oblique fire, and not being aware, as I suppose, of the position of my brigade and the First Brigade, faced about and fired into my right with a right-oblique fire, they believing my command, as I think, to be the enemy. This fire from the front, right, and rear left no alternative save that of retirement in confusion and disorder. No blame can be attached to any of the troops for these mistakes, as they were unavoidable.

Line was immediately reformed at the foot of the ridge east, where it remained until all the troops had retired, when it moved back in good condition, going into bivouac in an open field on the left of General Johnson's ammunition train, from which point the command was moved by order of the general commanding, at 3 a. m. on the 20th, taking position on a ridge; formed in two lines, with two guns in the center of the two lines and two guns upon the left, my right resting upon General Johnson's division and my left upon the right of the First Brigade. I immediately commenced felling trees, and formed two barricades, one to the front of my first line and one to the front of my second line. This first line so formed was supported by a second line, and to my right and rear was the Fifth Indiana Battery, covering with their fire to the front the point where my right rested on General Johnson's left. Skirmishers from my lines were kept continually to the front, retaking again and again their positions when driven to the breastworks, holding their positions faithfully and well until the whole line retired at night. This position was held and retained during the whole day under repeated attacks from the enemy in heavy columns supported with batteries, repulsing and driving the enemy back from time to time; driving the enemy also back from the extreme left with my artillery, thus supporting the left with my battery and portions of my command thrown into position for that purpose, until peremptory orders were received through Captain Cary, one of the general's staff, that I should fall back as well as possible from my position.

While holding this position the ammunition of my first line was expended, and most of that of the second line, together with all the ammunition of the battery except 3 rounds of canister. While working the battery at this point my guns, caissons, and limbers from time to time were made unserviceable from the shot and shell of the enemy's batteries, and from the fire of his infantry; so that I retired guns, limbers, and caissons when necessary, refitting and replacing those portions thereof damaged from the two guns left unused, so keeping four guns in continuous operation. When ordered to retire, I instructed the two rear regiments to fall back upon the second line together with the battery; and when such was accomplished, for the first line to retire upon the second, which had been retired, not knowing that the Fifth Indiana Battery, together with the second line, was also being retired. When the movement was made, the enemy opened upon my position three batteries with grape and canister. On reaching the second line, and finding the troops retiring and retired, with the battery gone, the enemy charging my front line with the bayonet, supported by their batteries, the troops gave way and a portion only rallied at the point where General Willich's command rested near sunset. Was then moved and ordered to proceed to Chattanooga. On arriving within a mile and a half the order was countermanded and a position reassigned me to the front, where we remained during the 21st until 3 a. m. on the 22d, when we were ordered with the balance of the division to cover the retirement of the army on Chattanooga, going into bivouac at that point at 9 a. m., where we now are. My loss in officers and men is terrible indeed, and shows how well they maintained the several positions assigned them during the different days that they were under fire and engaged with the enemy.

All have shown great patience, bravery, and endurance; no complaining, no murmuring, but all seeming to strive, one with the other, to perform to the utmost of their ability in support of our glorious stars and stripes.

Commanding officers, Cols. H. A. Hambright and G. Mihalotzy, Lieut. Cols. G. B. Bingham and H. C. Hobart, and Lieut. David Flansburg, with their staff officers, are entitled to great praise for their coolness and bravery exhibited during these protracted engagements.

Captains Mauff and Walker, who were obliged to take command of their respective regiments after the wounding of the colonels thereof, so conducted their commands as to meet with my entire approbation.

Considering the peculiarity of the country and condition of ground over which my brigade was maneuvered from day to day, points and positions advantageous to me unknown, obligating me thereby to feel my way along in darkness, I cannot express in terms too strong my satisfaction and gratification at the manner in which my officers and men conducted themselves; and although I would have desired that no falling back should have occurred, yet I believe the circumstances connected therewith are sufficient in themselves to release the troops from all blame or censure in the premises.

My battery was handled most splendidly; and although a large portion of it was destroyed by the fire of the enemy, nothing belonging thereto was left upon the field save the portions destroyed and made useless by such fire. It went into the engagement with six guns, and came out with seven. Lieutenant Flansburg was wounded and taken prisoner on the 19th, and the battery has since been handled by Lieutenant Willits, who has shown himself to be a good officer in every respect.

To my staff officers, Major Wagner, Captains Samuel, Dysart, and Wall, Lieutenants Reichardt and Hazzard, and to my orderlies, too much praise cannot be accorded for the part taken by them in the several engagements. Their personal attention was given to the delivering of orders, and to having them carried into execution. The utmost coolness and bravery was exhibited by them all; and while we mourn the death of one of our companions, the bravest of the brave, Lieutenant Searles, acting assistant adjutant-general, we know he died in a great cause, and while in the performance of his duty. All honor and glory to the dead! All sympathy and compassion for the wounded! All praise to the living!

Inclosed please find list of casualties and map of positions.*

I am, captain, very respectfully, your obedient servant,

JOHN C. STARKWEATHER,
Brigadier-General, Commanding.

Capt. B. H. Polk,
   Assistant Adjutant-General, First Division.

---

* See pp. 303–307.

1ST POSITION OF THE 2ND BRIGADE 1ST DIV. 14. A.C. BRIG. GEN'L J. C. STARKWEATHER COMMANDING SEPT. 19 1863 9. A.M.

1ST WISCONSIN VOLS.

21,ST WISCONSIN VOLS.

4TH INDIANA BATTERY

79 PENN'A. VOLS

24. ILL. VOLS.

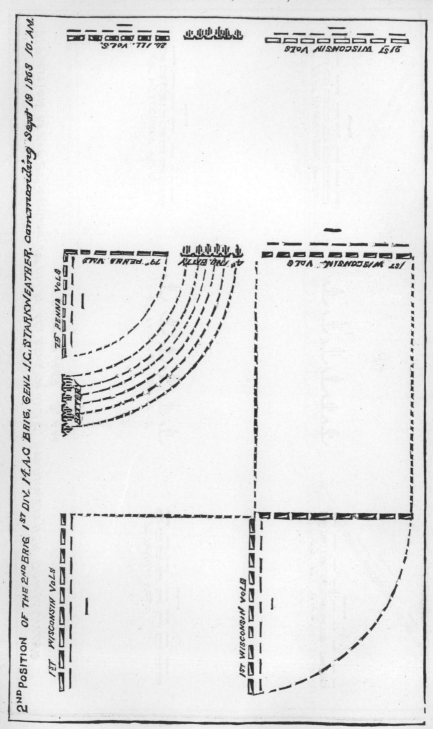

2ND POSITION OF THE 2ND BRIG. 1ST DIV. 14.A.C. BRIG. GENL J.C. STARKWEATHER. Commanding. Sept 19 1863. 10. A.M.

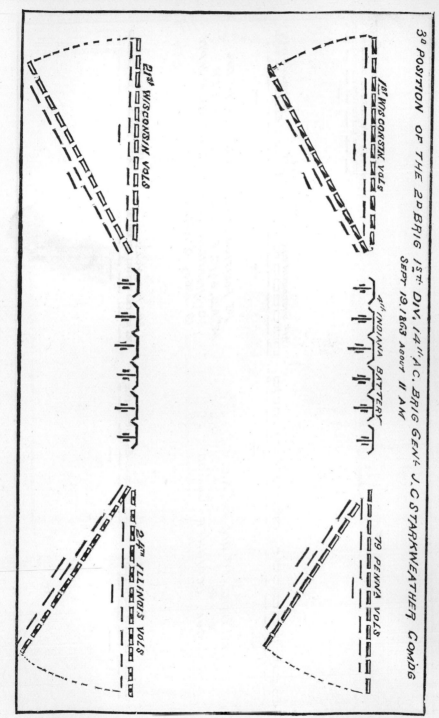

1ST. POSITION OF THE 2D BRIGADE, 1ST DIV.
14TH A.C. BRIG. GENL J.C. STARKWEATHER
COMMANDING ON THE EVENING OF SEPT.
19TH 1863, 5 P.M.

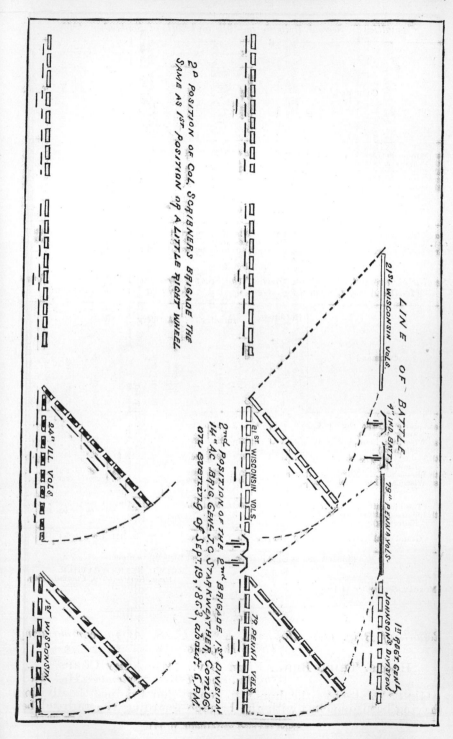

[Inclosure.]

Casualties in Second Brigade on 19th and 20th of September, 1863.

Command.	Killed.		Wounded.		Missing.		Aggregate.		Total.
	Commissioned officers.	Enlisted men.	Commissioned officers.	Enlisted men.	Commissioned officers.	Enlisted men.	Commissioned officers.	Enlisted men.	
1st Wisconsin (Lieut. Col. G. B. Bingham) ..	a4	22	3	88	4	80	11	190	201
79th Pennsylvania (Col. H. A. Hambright)....	1	14	4	63	1	54	6	131	137
24th Illinois (Col. G. Mihalotzy)...............	1	18	9	67	3	53	13	138	151
21st Wisconsin (Lieut. Col. H. C. Hobart).....	... ..	2	4	32	9	67	13	101	114
4th Indiana Battery (Lieut. David Flansburg.	......	1	.. ....	17	1	5	1	23	24
Total*......................	6	57	20	267	18	259	44	583	627

a Of the 4 commissioned officers of the First Wisconsin reported killed, 2 were members of my staff, as follows: First Lieut. Robert J. Nickles, aide-de-camp, killed on the 11th, and previously reported ; First Lieut. Charles A. Searles, acting assistant adjutant-general, killed on the 19th.

ADDENDA.

Semi-weekly report of effective force of the Second Brigade, First Division, Fourteenth Army Corps, Brig. Gen. John C. Starkweather commanding.

Command.	Headquarters.			Infantry.			Artillery.			Total.			Number of horses.	Number of guns.
	Commissioned officers.	Enlisted men.	Total.	Commissioned officers.	Enlisted men.	Total.	Commissioned officers.	Enlisted men.	Total.	Commissioned officers.	Enlisted men.	Aggregate.		
Headquarters (Brig. Gen. J. C. Starkweather).	9	a81	9							9	a81	9	...	...
1st Wisconsin (Lieut. Col. G. B. Bingham).				23	368	391				23	368	391	...	...
79th Pennsylvania (Col. H. A. Hambright).				21	424	445				21	424	445	...	...
24th Illinois (Col. G. Mihalotzy)..				25	337	362				25	337	362	...	...
21st Wisconsin (Lieut. Col. H. C. Hobart).				30	339	369				30	339	369	...	...
Total infantry	9	81	9	99	1,468	1,567				108	1,468	1,576	...	...
4th Indiana Battery (Lieut. D. Flansburg).							3	92	95	3	92	95	116	6
Grand total..............	9	81	9	99	1,468	1,567	3	92	95	111	1,560	1,671	116	6

a Enlisted men at headquarters accounted for with regiments.

JOHN C. STARKWEATHER,
Brigadier-General, Commanding.

Monday, *September* 14, 1863.

No. 27.

Reports of Brig. Gen. John H. King, U. S. Army, commanding Third Brigade.

Hdqrs. Third Brig., First Div., 14th Army Corps,
Chattanooga, Tenn., September 24, 1863.

General: I have the honor to report that I joined the division (having been detached with the brigade guarding the railroad be-

*See revised statement, p. 171.

tween Tantallon and Bridgeport) at Cooper's Gap, on the 15th day of September, 1863. My brigade marched with the rest of the division toward the left and Chattanooga on the 17th of September; went into camp same afternoon at Cave Spring.

On the 18th September I broke up my camp at about 6 p. m., and took up my line of march, my brigade having been detailed as rear guard, the division still moving to the left. I arrived on the ground and placed my brigade in its position in line of battle on the left of the division, and at that time on the left of the corps, at about 6 a. m. on the 19th of September, the command having marched all night with a rest of about two hours at Crawfish Spring. About 9 o'clock on the same morning my command was ordered to engage the enemy.

My first line was composed of First Battalion Eighteenth Infantry, Capt. G. W. Smith commanding ; First Battalion Sixteenth Infantry, Maj. Sidney Coolidge commanding; First Battalion Nineteenth Infantry, Maj. S. K. Dawson commanding; leaving on the second line First Battalion Fifteenth Infantry, Capt. Albert B. Dod commanding; Second Battalion Eighteenth Infantry, Capt. Henry Haymond commanding; Battery H, Fifth Artillery, First Lieut. H. M. Burnham commanding.

I pushed everything to the front, my first line driving the enemy before them for a mile, and meeting General A. Baird, division commander, at about 10 a. m., was ordered to make a new front at right angles with the other. I only had time, however, to get the Sixteenth Infantry and battery in position before being assailed by an overwhelming force; at this time the troops on my right were giving ground to the enemy in confusion. I immediately gave orders for the battery to limber up, but it could not be done as the horses as they were brought up to the guns were shot down.

The officers and men, finding it impossible to retire, remained with their pieces (firing) until they were forcibly taken from them by the enemy. It was at this time that I lost the First Battalion Sixteenth Infantry (made prisoners), with the exception of 5 commissioned officers and 62 men. The losses of the battery will be attached to this report.

I reformed my command some 400 yards in the rear of the battery and a short distance in the rear of the Ninth Ohio Volunteers. I then changed my position and formed on the left of General Brannan's division, where I again met General Baird, attaching the Ninety-fourth Ohio to my command, numbering some 200 men. I had been informed by General Brannan that my battery was recaptured at the point of the bayonet by the Ninth Regiment Ohio Volunteers (Col. G. Kammerling), of the Third Brigade, Third Division, Fourteenth Army Corps, commanded by Colonel Van Derveer. The Fifteenth Infantry of my command was detailed to go forward and bring the battery to the rear. On the arrival of the Fifteenth Infantry on the ground where Battery H was left, they found no men of the Ninth Ohio Volunteers, or any other regiment, present with said battery or in charge of the same. The pieces were much scattered; four were pointing toward our front and two in the direction of the enemy. The Fifteenth Infantry also brought off a piece of artillery belonging to a Mississippi battery, which was afterward abandoned by Lieutenant Fessonden, commanding Battery H, as it was impossible to take it with him to Rossville.

I am happy to say that my battery is now complete, with the

exception of caissons, four of them having been abandoned for the want of horses.

Late in the afternoon General Baird, with the other two brigades of his division, moved forward to assist General Johnson's division of McCook's corps, leaving me to guard ground immediately in my front. At dark, finding no troops in my vicinity, I changed the position of my command and remained in the woods without fires until 2 o'clock in the morning, when I fell back to General Thomas' headquarters, where I found General Baird, division commander.

At daylight on the 20th my brigade went into position on the left of the First Brigade, First Division, Colonel Scribner commanding. I formed my command in four lines, the First Battalion Eighteenth Infantry, Capt. G. W. Smith commanding, in front, and behind a breastwork of logs 2 feet in height, connecting with Colonel Scribner's. My brigade was thus again on the extreme left. Between 7 and 8 a. m. I moved Captain Smith's command forward about 50 paces across an open piece of ground to a ridge skirted by timber; he took the logs forming the breastwork in his front forward, and placed them in front of his new position. The Second Battalion Eighteenth Infantry, commanded by Capt. Henry Haymond, moved to the ground vacated by the First Battalion. The Fifteenth Infantry, Captain Dod commanding, Nineteenth Infantry, Capt. E. L. Smith commanding, were ordered to support the front line, or to wheel to the left in case of an attack on the flank.

About 9 a. m. the enemy drove in my line of skirmishers, and advancing in force, attacked my front and flank. Captain Haymond was sent forward to support Captain Smith, and the Fifteenth and Nineteenth Infantry wheeled to the left; after a contest of about an hour the enemy withdrew. I then relieved the First Battalion Eighteen Infantry by the Fifteenth Infantry; the Nineteenth Infantry was relieved by a regiment belonging to Colonel Dodge's brigade, this regiment connecting with the left of the Fifteenth Infantry, the remnants of the Eighteenth and Nineteenth Infantry constituting a reserve. These dispositions were scarcely completed when the enemy again renewed his attack, pouring in a destructive direct and enfilade fire. This attack lasted an hour; the enemy was again repulsed, my command still retaining its original position. Heavy skirmishing continued along my entire front during the afternoon until half past 4 o'clock, at which time the enemy again made an attack upon my front and flank, using both artillery and infantry, my command being exposed to a terrific fire of musketry and canister. Notwithstanding all this, they held the enemy at bay and retained their position until about 5 p. m., at which time I was ordered by the division commander to fall back to the Rossville road.

About 7 a. m. on the 20th instant a brigade of General Negley's, commanded by General Beatty, took up a position on my left and perpendicular to my front, but was forced to return early, thus exposing my left and causing me to wheel my reserve to the left and form two fronts at right angles to each other.

I take this occasion to speak in the highest terms of my battalion commanders, and the officers of Battery H, Fifth Artillery: Maj. S. K. Dawson, Nineteenth U. S. Infantry; Maj. Sidney Coolidge, Sixteenth U. S. Infantry; Capt. G. W. Smith, Eighteenth U. S. Infantry; Capt. Henry Haymond, Eighteenth U. S. Infantry; Capt. A. B. Dod, Fifteenth U. S. Infantry; First Lieut. H. M. Burnham, Battery H, Fifth U. S. Artillery; Second Lieut. Israel Ludlow, Battery H,

Fifth U. S. Artillery; Second Lieut. J. A. Fessenden, Battery H, Fifth U. S. Artillery.

Capt. E. L. Smith took command of the Nineteenth Infantry after Major Dawson was wounded on the 19th instant. Lieutenants Burnham and Ludlow were shot down while gallantly fighting their guns. Lieutenant Fessenden was wounded, but continued in the field during the remainder of the day.

I also take pleasure in mentioning the members of my staff, viz: Capt. J. W. Forsyth, Eighteenth Infantry, acting assistant adjutant-general; Capt. J. B. Mulligan, Nineteenth Infantry, provost-marshal; Lieut. W. J. Lyster, Nineteenth Infantry, aide-de-camp; Lieut. H. G. Litchfield, Eighteenth Infantry, inspector.

These officers were present with me during the entire engagement (19th and 20th September), and rendered prompt and effective aid during the two days' battle.

Capt. R. E. A. Crofton, Sixteenth Infantry, after the first day's fight reported to me and acted as aide-de-camp on my staff, rendering great assistance during the 20th instant.

I have the honor to inclose reports of my battalion and battery commanders of the conduct of the officers and men of the same. I respectfully call your attention to their reports. I also forward special report showing the number of fighting men on the 18th instant, casualties during the two days' battle, and the number of men brought out of action; also a list of commissioned officers killed, wounded, and missing, and letter of Brigadier-General Brannan, concerning the recapture of Battery H.

In conclusion I have to state that my brigade captured 126 prisoners on the first day's fight.

Very respectfully, your obedient servant,

JOHN H. KING,
Brigadier-General.

Brig. Gen. A. BAIRD,
U. S. Army.

—

HDQRS. THIRD BRIG., FIRST DIV., 14TH ARMY CORPS,
Chattanooga, Tenn., September 29, 1863.

GENERAL: I have the honor to request that the following be included in my report of the part taken by my brigade in the battle of Chickamauga Creek, Ga., viz:

Between 12 and 1 p. m. on the 20th instant, the First Battalion Eighteenth Infantry, Capt. G. W. Smith commanding, Second Battalion Eighteenth Infantry, Capt. Henry Haymond commanding, charged the enemy's lines, driving them through an open field on the left of my position for 600 yards, to their second line of battle, but being unsupported they were obliged to retire to their original position, where they were relieved by the Fifteenth Infantry, Captain Dod commanding. This charge was the most gallant act of that day's engagement.

My medical director, Asst. Surg. E. J. Darken, U. S. Army, devoted his whole time and attention to the wounded from the beginning to the end of the battle, reporting to me on the morning of the 20th instant.

Lieut. J. J. Wagoner, brigade quartermaster, managed the brigade train with much care, arriving safely at Chattanooga without accident.

My brigade commissary of subsistence, Lieut. S. S. Culbertson, Nineteenth Infantry, by his activity succeeded in meeting me early in the morning at Rossville with a train of provisions, and not only supplied my brigade with rations but also General Sheridan's division and Battery I, Fourth Artillery, General Brannan's division, both of whom were entirely out.

I have the honor to be, general, very respectfully, your obedient servant,

JOHN H. KING,
Brigadier-General.

Brig. Gen. A. BAIRD.

[Inclosure No. 1.]

Special report of effective force of the Third Brigade, First Division, Fourteenth Army Corps, commanded by Brig. Gen. John H. King, September 18, 1863.

Command.	Headquarters.			Infantry.		
	Commissioned officers.	Enlisted men.	Total.	Commissioned officers.	Enlisted men.	Total.
Brigade headquarters, Brig. Gen. J. H. King	8	5	13			
1st Battalion, 15th Infantry, Capt. A. B. Dod				14	262	276
1st Battalion, 16th Infantry, Maj. S. Coolidge				10	289	308
1st Battalion, 18th Infantry, Capt. G. W. Smith				13	278	300
2d Battalion, 18th Infantry, Capt. Henry Haymond				13	274	287
1st Battalion, 19th Infantry, Maj. S. K. Dawson				14	185	199
Battery H, 5th Artillery, First Lieut. H. M. Burnham						
Total	8	5	13	73	1,297	1,370

Command.	Artillery.			Total.				
	Commissioned officers.	Enlisted men.	Total.	Commissioned officers.	Enlisted men.	Aggregate.	Horses.	Guns.
Brigade headquarters, Brig. Gen. J. H. King				8	5	13		
1st Battalion, 15th Infantry, Capt. A. B. Dod				14	262	276		
1st Battalion, 16th Infantry, Maj. S. Coolidge				19	289	308		
1st Battalion, 18th Infantry, Capt. G. W. Smith				13	287	300		
2d Battalion, 18th Infantry, Capt. Henry Haymond				13	274	287		
1st Battalion, 19th Infantry, Maj. S. K. Dawson				14	185	199		
Battery H, 5th Artillery, First Lieut. H. M. Burnham	3	127	130	3	127	130	117	6
Total	3	127	130	84	1,429	1,513	117	6

[Inclosure No. 2.]

Report of Casualties, Third Brigade, First Division, Fourteenth Army Corps, commanded by Brig. Gen. John H. King, in the battle of Chickamauga Creek, of two days' duration, September 19 and 20, 1863.

Command.	Commissioned officers.					Enlisted men.					Aggregate.		
	Killed.	Wounded.	Wounded and missing.	Missing.	Total.	Killed.	Wounded.	Wounded and missing.	Missing.	Total.	Officers.	Men.	Total.
Brigade headquarters, Brig. Gen. J. H. King.	....	....	....	....	....	....	....	....	....	....	....	....	....
1st Battalion, 15th Infantry, Capt. A. B. Dod.	....	2	......	6	8	9	31	16	88	144	....	....	....
1st Battalion, 16th Infantry, Capt. R. E. A. Crofton.	....	3	10	1	14	10	13	......	204	227	....	....	....
1st Battalion, 18th Infantry, Capt. G. W. Smith.	1	3	......	2	6	29	73	......	39	141	....	....	....
2d Battalion, 18th Infantry, Capt. H. Haymond.	....	1	3	2	6	15	79	......	48	142	....	....	....
1st Battalion, 19th Infantry, Capt. R. E. A. Crofton.	1	2	2	6	11	5	36	......	120	161	....	....	....
Battery H, 5th Artillery, Second Lieut. J. A. Fessenden.	1	1	1	....	3	12	15	14	....	41	....	....	....
Total......................	3	12	16	17	48	80	247	30	319	856	48	856	904
Total brought from action.........											36	573	609

[Inclosure No. 3.]

LIST OF COMMISSIONED OFFICERS KILLED, WOUNDED, AND MISSING.

FIRST BATTALION, FIFTEENTH U. S. INFANTRY.

Wounded.—Capt. D. M. Meredith, Second Lieut. John Williams.
Missing.—First Lieut. E. M. Timony, First Lieut. Samuel S. Holbrook, First Lieut. William G. Galloway, First Lieut. Roman H. Gray, Second Lieut. Theodore Kendall, Second Lieut. James P. Brown.

FIRST BATTALION, SIXTEENTH U. S. INFANTRY.

Wounded.—First Lieut. W. F. Goodwin, First Lieut. H. H. Clark, First Lieut. William Mills.
Wounded and missing.—Maj. Sidney Coolidge, Capt. Alexander H. Stanton, Capt. John Christopher, Capt. M. A. Cochran, First Lieut. William J. Stewart, First Lieut. P. W. Houlihan, First Lieut. Thomas J. Durnin, First Lieut. William H. Smyth, Second Lieut. M. Mahan, Second Lieut. W. Clifford.
Missing.—Second Lieut. John T. Mackey.

FIRST BATTALION, EIGHTEENTH U. S. INFANTRY.

Killed.—Second Lieut. John Lane.
Wounded.—First Lieut. J. P. W. Neill, First Lieut. T. T. Brand, First Lieut. John T. Adair.
Missing.—First Lieut. H. B. Freeman, Second Lieut. F. T. Bennett.

SECOND BATTALION, EIGHTEENTH U. S. INFANTRY.

Wounded.—First Lieut. M. N. Hutchinson.
Wounded and missing.—Capt. T. Ten Eyck, First Lieut. C. L. Truman, First Lieut. L. F. Brown.
Missing.—Second Lieut. R. C. Gates, Second Lieut. H. C. Pohlman.

FIRST BATTALION, NINETEENTH U. S. INFANTRY.

Killed.—First Lieut. M. B. Fogarty.
Wounded.—Maj. S. K. Dawson, Second Lieut. Robert Ayres, battalion adjutant.
Wounded and missing.—Capt. Thomas Cummings, Second Lieut. C. F. Miller.
Missing.—Capt. V. K. Hart, Capt. G. S. Peirce, Capt. E. L. Smith, First Lieut. T. H. Y. Bickham, First Lieut. M. C. Causten, Second Lieut. J. H. Gageby.

BATTERY H, FIFTH U. S. ARTILLERY.

Killed.—First Lieut. H. M. Burnham.
Wounded.—Second Lieut. J. A. Fessenden.
Wounded and missing.—Second Lieut. Israel Ludlow.
Very respectfully, your obedient servant,

JOHN H. KING,
Brigadier-General, Commanding.

Brig. Gen. A. BAIRD,
Commanding First Division, Fourteenth Army Corps.

[Inclosure No. 4.]

HDQRS. THIRD DIVISION, FOURTEENTH ARMY CORPS,
DEPARTMENT OF THE CUMBERLAND,
Chattanooga, September 26, 1863.

GENERAL : Immediately after retaking the battery of your brigade, the Ninth Ohio Volunteers were ordered to the left of their brigade, which the rebels had attacked in considerable force, leaving the battery in charge of the Seventeenth Ohio Volunteers.

This regiment remained in charge of the battery until it was known you had sent a regiment to receive it, when, there being no rebels in the vicinity, the Seventeenth Ohio Volunteers hurried to the left, where their services were much needed.

Very respectfully,

J. M. BRANNAN,
Brigadier-General, Commanding Division.

General KING,
First Division.

ADDENDA.

*Semi-weekly report of effective force of the Third Brigade, First Divsiion, Four-
teenth Army Corps, Brig. Gen. John H. King commanding.*

Command.	Headquarters.			Infantry.			Artillery.			Total.			Number of horses.	Number of guns.
	Commissioned officers.	Enlisted men.	Total.	Commissioned officers.	Enlisted men.	Total.	Commissioned officers.	Enlisted men.	Total.	Commissioned officers.	Enlisted men.	Aggregate.		
Brigade headquarters, Brig. Gen. John H. King.	8	53	61	.....	.....	.....	.....	.....	.....	8	53	61	.....	.....
1st Battalion, 15th Infantry, Capt. A. B. Dod.	.....	.....	.....	14	310	324	.....	.....	.....	14	310	324	.....	.....
1st Battalion, 16th Infantry, Maj. S. Coolidge.	.....	.....	.....	20	312	332	.....	.....	.....	20	312	332	.....	.....
1st Battalion, 18th Infantry, Capt. G. W. Smith.	.....	.....	.....	14	354	368	.....	.....	.....	14	354	368	.....	.....
2d Battalion, 18th Infantry, Capt. Henry Haymond.	.....	.....	.....	14	361	375	.....	.....	.....	14	361	375	.....	.....
1st Battalion, 19th Infantry, Maj. S. K. Dawson.	.....	.....	.....	12	223	235	.....	.....	.....	12	223	235	.....	.....
Battery H, 5th Artillery, First Lieut. H. M. Burnham.	.....	.....	.....	.....	.....	.....	3	131	134	3	131	134	117	6
Total.................	8	53	61	74	1,560	1,634	3	131	134	85	1,744	1,829	117	6

SEPTEMBER 13, 1863.

JOHN H. KING,
Brigadier-General, Commanding.

No. 28.

Reports of Capt. Albert B. Dod, Fifteenth U. S. Infantry.

HDQRS. FIRST BATTALION, FIFTEENTH U. S. INFANTRY,
Chattanooga, Tenn., September 25, 1863.

SIR : I have the honor to report that on Saturday morning, September 19, this battalion, consisting of Companies A, C, E, F, G, and
H, First Battalion, Fifteenth U. S. Infantry, and Company E, Second
Battalion, was ordered to remain immediately in the rear of Battery
H, Fifth U. S. Artillery. In accordance with these instructions I
was following close on the battery, moving to the front in line of
battle, when I was informed that the skirmishers of the enemy were
about 80 rods on our right. I immediately deployed Lieutenant
Galloway's company as skirmishers, and took up position to the
right and a little in rear of the battery. These dispositions had
hardly been made when I received information from one of General
Baird's staff that General Reynolds' division had gone in that direction, and cautioning me not to fire. My skirmishers were at once
recalled, and I followed the battery, marching by the left flank.
We had proceeded about 100 yards, when the battery again unlimbered, and I took position immediately in rear of it. The enemy,
vastly our superior in numbers, opened upon us a most terrific fire
of musketry from in front and on our right flank. I marched to
the right of the battery, but was compelled to fall back about 400
yards, where the battalion was reformed under a ridge, and again

advanced, taking position on the left of General Brannan's division. Captain Meredith was wounded while gallantly endeavoring to reform the battalion.

At about half past 8 o'clock on Sunday morning, as my battalion was in line of battle, I received orders from Brigadier-General King to change front forward on the left company, and move forward to the support of the Eighteenth U. S. Infantry, who were sorely pressed. This was done while under fire, but before we could engage the enemy they were repulsed. We were left in this position (the extreme left of the division) for about an hour, the Eighteenth having moved to our right and occupied the outermost breastworks. I was then ordered to relieve the Eighteenth in these breastworks, which were only a few logs raised about a foot and a half above the ground, and which were about 100 yards beyond the woods, and while occupying it my left flank was entirely exposed. I had only occupied this position a few moments when I perceived two regiments of the enemy marching in double-quick time to my left. I waited until they commenced fire and were pouring an enfilading fire down my ranks—which it was impossible for me to return—when I gave the order to rise up, and the battalion marched across the open field to the woods under a terrific fire as steadily and in as good order as if on drill or parade.

Upon arriving in the woods I was met by Captain Forsyth, who informed me that General Baird ordered those works held at all hazards, and promising that my left should be protected. Again I marched across that field, my left this time supported by a regiment sent out for that purpose by Colonel Dodge. The enemy made four efforts to take these works, but were each time repulsed with terrible slaughter, the ground in front being literally strewn with their dead and wounded.

At about 11 o'clock we were ordered back into the position we had occupied during the morning, where we remained until all our ammunition was exhausted and we were ordered to fall back on Rossville.

Nothing could exceed the coolness and steadiness manifested by both officers and men throughout the whole of Sunday.

At about 4 o'clock the enemy took the breastworks we had occupied in the morning, and were pouring an enfilading fire of canister down our lines, while a tremendous fire of musketry was being poured into us from in front and on our left. The obstinacy with which the men fought may be inferred from the fact that this battalion, numbering less than 200 men, held a whole division in check for over an hour, until their ammunition was exhausted and they were ordered to retire. We were the last to leave the breastworks.

Annexed I attach a list of casualties as nearly as they can be ascertained.

I have the honor to be, captain, very respectfully, your obedient servant,

ALBERT B. DOD,
Captain Fifteenth Infantry, Comdg. First Battalion.

Capt. JAMES W. FORSYTH,
    Acting Assistant Adjutant-General, Third Brigade.

[Inclosure.]

*Report of Casualties in commissioned officers and enlisted men of the First Battalion, Fifteenth U. S. Infantry, at the battle of Chickamauga Creek, September 19, 20, and 21, 1863.**

COMMISSIONED OFFICERS.

Wounded.—Capt. D. M. Meredith, Second Lieut. John Williams.
Missing.—First Lieuts. E. M. Timony, Samuel S. Holbrook, William G. Galloway, and Roman H. Gray; Second Lieuts. Theodore Kendall and James P. Brown.

ENLISTED MEN.

Command.	Killed.	Wounded.	Wounded and missing.	Missing.	Total.
Company A	....	6	2	14	22
Company C...	1	4	2	10	17
Company E...	4	2	2	9	17
Company F...	1	3	......	16	20
Company G...	3	4	7	8	22
Company H	....	9	3	14	26
Company E, Second Battalion...............................	....	3	......	17	20
Total	9	31	16	88	144

ALBERT B. DOD,
Captain Fifteenth Infantry, Comdg. First Battalion.

ADDENDA.

Office Commissary of Musters, Fourth Army Corps,
Chattanooga, Tenn., October 19, 1863.

Colonel: At the request of Major-General Rosecrans, I have the honor to make the following report of Private William J. Carson, bugler in the First Battalion, Fifteenth U. S. Infantry:

On Saturday, September 19, when the regular brigade was falling back, he behaved with most conspicuous gallantry; with a sword in one hand and his bugle in the other, he sounded constantly the "Halt," the "Rally," and the "Forward;" espying a stand of colors belonging to the Eighteenth U. S. Infantry, he rushed up to them and sounded "To the color." His conduct attracted the notice and elicited the admiration of the whole brigade. On Sunday, September 20, before our battalion was engaged, the Eighteenth, being pressed by vastly superior numbers, was falling back; Carson by some means became the possessor of a musket and constituted himself a "provost guard." One of the officers attempted to pass him, but he positively refused to allow it, stating that it was against his orders. All this time he continued to sound the various calls on his bugle. I regret to state that his fate remains a mystery; he was last seen by me late on Sunday afternoon behind the breastworks. I can only hope that he is a prisoner.

Where all behaved as well as they did on Sunday, it would seem invidious to make distinctions, but I beg leave also to mention First Sergt. John Marrs, afterward killed. His company, which had never been under fire before, fell back. Sergeant Marrs was marching to the rear trying to steady the men; his gun was on his right shoulder.

* See revised statement, p. 171.

I ordered them back, when Marrs faced to the front, brought his gun down, saluted, and said, "Does the commanding officer know we are out of ammunition?" I told him to go back and fix bayonets, and every man returned, Marrs to fall almost immediately. The cool, soldierly bearing of this man under the terrific fire of Sunday evening was most commendable.

I have the honor to be, very respectfully, your obedient servant,

ALBERT B. DOD,
Captain 15th U. S. Infty., Comdg. Batt. at Chickamauga.

Col. C. Goddard,
Assistant Adjutant-General.

No. 29.

Report of Capt. Robert E. A. Crofton, Sixteenth U. S. Infantry.

HEADQUARTERS SIXTEENTH U. S. INFANTRY,
Bivouac at Chattanooga, Tenn., September 26, 1863.

SIR: I have the honor to report that on the evening of the 18th instant the Sixteenth Infantry, then commanded by Maj. Sidney Coolidge, was ordered, together with the rest of the brigade, to move farther to the left of our then position (Bird's Mill), as the enemy were reported to be massing their force to attack General Crittenden. During the night we marched some 7 miles, when we rested about two hours, and then resumed the march for some 3 miles farther, arriving near Chickamauga Creek about daylight. Here we moved into line of battle, the First Battalion, Eighteenth, being on our right, and the First Battalion, Nineteenth, being on our left; our front was covered by a strong line of skirmishers. Very soon the skirmishers on our left opened fire, and almost immediately it extended along the entire line. After a pretty sharp skirmish fire the enemy broke, and we drove him about three-quarters of a mile, taking several prisoners and killing and wounding several. From this point we moved changing our front to the right, and were ordered to support Battery H, Fifth Artillery, on a ridge about a quarter of a mile from our last position. We were formed directly in front of the guns, and the men ordered to lie down. Here, without any warning whatever, the rebels came up on our right flank and got right on us before any disposition could be made to meet them. Consequently nearly the entire battalion was killed, wounded, or captured, and at the same time the battery was also taken. Of the men engaged in this action, about 62 escaped, some of them slightly wounded. This remnant was, by order of General King, attached to the Nineteenth Infantry, and remained with the battalion during the two succeeding days' fight.

The following is a tabular statement of casualties* during the battle. I also append a list of officers wounded and missing:†

Taken into action : Commissioned officers, 19 ; enlisted men, 289.
Killed : Enlisted men, 10.
Wounded : Commissioned officers, 3 ; enlisted men, 13.
Wounded and missing : Commissioned officers, 10.

---

* See revised statement, p. 171.
† Not found ; but see p. 313.

Missing : Commissioned officers, 1 ; enlisted men, 204.

Taken out of action : Commissioned officers, 5; enlisted men, 62.

I have great pleasure in stating that both officers and men of the battalion behaved with the utmost gallantry. I take the greatest pleasure in mentioning my adjutant, First Lieut. H. H. Clark, who rendered most efficient service, but was most unfortunately seriously wounded.

Very respectfully, your obedient servant,

R. E. A. CROFTON,
Captain Sixteenth Infantry, Commanding.

Capt. JAMES W. FORSYTH,
Acting Assistant Adjutant-General, Third Brigade.

No. 30.

Report of Capt. George W. Smith, Eighteenth U. S. Infantry.

HDQRS. DETACHMENT EIGHTEENTH U. S. INFANTRY,
Bivouac at Chattanooga, September 24, 1863.

SIR: In compliance with your order of this date, I have the honor to submit the following report of the part taken by my command in the battles of the 19th and 20th instant:

My command consisted of the First and Second Battalions, Eighteenth U. S. Infantry, the Second under the immediate command of Capt. Henry Haymond, who will report concerning it. The First Battalion was composed of eight companies, B, D, E, F, G, and H, First Battalion, and companies H and G, Third Battalion, with a total of 287 men and 12 commissioned officers. My battalion advanced at half past 10 a. m. in the first line on the right of the Third Brigade, First Division, Fourteenth Army Corps, under fire, and after driving the enemy nearly 2 miles, changed direction of its front by the right flank and by file right.

Believing myself supported on the left, I moved rapidly forward, firing briskly, and found myself in dense woods and hilly ground, detached from the brigade. Assailed by a vastly superior force in front and on the left flank, and suffering severely, I ordered the command to retire, and did so, firing steadily. I soon rejoined the brigade and bivouacked in front of its headquarters. On the morning of the 20th the line was formed at daybreak; the First Battalion in front of the brigade, the Second Battalion forming in its rear, and being the second line. After heavy skirmishing I discovered the enemy massing in dense columns on my left flank, and ordered the Second Battalion to support my left. This (with the sanction of General King, commanding brigade) was done at once, under fire, my battalions opening their fire at twenty minutes before 9 a. m. The command obstinately held its ground under a fire from the right oblique, the front, and finally—a brigade of volunteers giving way on my left—a galling enfilade from the left flank, causing a frightful mortality in men and officers, under which I ordered my battalions to retire to the second line. This was done, and upon being ordered to halt, the command faced about, formed on its color, and sustained itself against the advance of the enemy. About 1 p. m. I charged the enemy's line, advancing about 600 yards, and upon returning the battalions were replaced by the Fifteenth U. S. Infantry, I taking the position lately held by it in the second line. Here my command remained, after changing front slightly to the right, until after sunset, after every brigade on my right had retired, when I was ordered to do so.

Over a wide corn-field, under a terrific fire of musketry, canister, and spherical case shot, my men steadily and slowly followed their color, when, gaining the woods, they faced about, fired, and moved to the rear, where, as ordered, I reported to the general of brigade.

I desire to recommend for brevet, for gallant and meritorious conduct, under my own eye on both days, the following officers : Capts. Henry Haymond and Anson Mills, with Lieutenants Townsend, Powell, Bennett, and Harding, with Lieutenants Hutchinson and Davis, Second Battalion. I recommend for promotion for gallantry Sergt. Maj. Isaac D'Isay, and for mention Color Sergt. Rowland W. Evans. I append a list of casualties in the First Battalion.

I am, sir, very respectfully, your obedient servant,

G. W. SMITH,
Captain, Comdg. Detachment Eighteenth Infantry.

Capt. JAMES W. FORSYTH,
Acting Assistant Adjutant-General, Third Brigade.

[Inclosure.]

Report of Casualties in the First Battalion, Eighteenth U. S. Infantry, commanded by Capt. George W. Smith, Eighteenth U. S. Infantry, in the battle of September 19 and 20, 1863.

Commissioned officers :
Killed 1
Wounded... 3
Missing... 2
                                                                     ———
Total 6
                                                                     ═══
Enlisted men :
Killed.. 29
Wounded... 73
Missing... 39
                                                                     ———
Total*.. 141

CASUALTIES AMONG COMMISSIONED OFFICERS.

First Lieut. J. P. W. Neill, regimental adjutant, wounded, leg.
First Lieut. H. B. Freeman, missing.
First Lieut. T. T. Brand, commanding company, wounded, arm.
First Lieut. J. I. Adair, commanding company, wounded, arm.
Second Lieut. F. T. Bennett, missing.
Second Lieut. John Lane, commanding company, killed.

No. 31.

Report of Capt. Henry Haymond, Eighteenth U. S. Infantry.

HDQRS. SECOND BATT., EIGHTEENTH U. S. INFANTRY,
Chattanooga, Tenn., September 26, 1863.

CAPTAIN : I have the honor to submit the following report of the part taken by the battalion under my command in the engagement

---
*See revised statement, p. 171.

with the enemy on the 19th and 20th instant, on Chickamauga Creek, Ga., a few miles south of this place:

On the morning of the 19th instant, after marching all of the night before. the battalion took position on the right of Battery H, Fifth U. S. Artillery. At 10 a. m., by the order of the brigade commander, I marched to the front and joined the First Battalion of the Eighteenth U. S. Infantry, then already engaged. Shortly after doing so, the command was attacked in rear by an overwhelming force of the enemy and compelled to retire to the crest of an adjoining hill, from which position the enemy were repulsed.

The battalion bivouacked with the brigade, 1 mile from the field.

Early on the morning of the 20th instant, line was formed on the east side of the Chattanooga road. At 9 a. m. a severe attack was made upon this position. My command was ordered to the support of the First Battalion, Eighteenth U. S. Infantry, and at once became warmly engaged. The troops on my left soon gave way, and, my position being flanked and the command being exposed to an enfilading fire, I fell back to the timber in the rear, and there continued engaged until the enemy was repulsed. I afterward, in connection with Captain Smith, commanding the First Battalion, Eighteenth U. S. Infantry, assisted in driving the enemy from the open fields on the left.

The command being much reduced in numbers, I took position in the breastworks, near the place of our formation in the morning.

About 5 p. m. a severe attack was again made upon this part of the line. I remained until ordered to fall back, suffering considerable loss in the movement. I then, by order of the general commanding brigade, marched to Rossville, and remained in position near that place until the morning of the 22d instant, when the command marched to this place.

The following is a tabular statement of the loss sustained by the battalion:

Second Battalion Eighteenth U. S. Infantry.

Commissioned officers :
Taken into action 13
Loss :*
    Wounded... 1
    Wounded and missing 3
    Missing... 2
                                      6

Brought out of action 7

Enlisted men :
Taken into action 274
Loss :*
    Killed 15
    Wounded.. 79
    Missing... 48
                                       142

Brought out of action... 133

All the officers present with the battalion acted well and performed their duty; but I am especially indebted to Adjutant Lind,

---

*See revised statement, p. 171.

Lieutenants Hutchinson and Gates, for assistance during the battle. Lieut. Lucius F. Brown, after acting with the greatest gallantry, was severely wounded and left upon the field.

I am, captain, very respectfully, your obedient servant,

HENRY HAYMOND,
Captain Eighteenth U. S. Infantry, Commanding.

Capt. JAMES W. FORSYTH,
Acting Assistant Adjutant-General, Third Brigade.

[Inclosure.]

A LIST OF CASUALTIES OCCURRING AMONG THE COMMISSIONED OFFICERS OF THE SECOND BATTALION, EIGHTEENTH U. S. INFANTRY, DURING THE BATTLE OF CHICKAMAUGA, ON THE 19TH AND 20TH DAYS OF SEPTEMBER, 1863.

Capt. T. Ten Eyck, wounded and prisoner.
First Lieut. C. L. Truman, wounded and prisoner.
First Lieut. L. F. Brown, wounded and prisoner.
First Lieut. M. N. Hutchinson, wounded.
Second Lieut. R. C. Gates, missing.
Second Lieut. H. C. Pohlman, missing.

HENRY HAYMOND,
Captain Eighteenth U. S. Infantry, Commanding.

No. 32.

Report of Lieut. Robert Ayres, Nineteenth U. S. Infantry.

CHATTANOOGA, TENN.,
September 26, 1863.

SIR : I have the honor to submit the following report of the operations of the First Battalion of the Nineteenth U. S. Infantry in the battle of Chickamauga Creek, September 19 and 20, 1863 :

The battalion went into action (14 officers and 190 men strong, under command of Maj. S. K. Dawson) about 10 a. m. on the 19th. The line of battle of the Third Brigade was composed of the First and Second Battalions Eighteenth Infantry, Sixteenth Infantry, and Nineteenth Infantry, the Nineteenth forming the left of the line, Capt. E. L. Smith and Lieutenant Fogarty, with Company G, in front as skirmishers. The Fifteenth Kentucky Volunteers being engaged in our front, retired for want of ammunition, and occupying their lines, we engaged the enemy and repulsed him, pursuing direct to the front some three-fourths of a mile and halted. Here the Ninth Texas (rebel) Regiment, passing along our front from left to right, received our fire, which caused them to break and run, and many came into our lines as prisoners. Moved from this position by the flank to the right, filing right, and taking up a new position, faced to the rear, and in rear of Battery H, Fifth Artillery, on the right of the Eighteenth Infantry, and forming the third line. Here we were attacked by a greatly superior force, but after a vigorous resistance under a most galling fire of artillery and musketry, the command retired. Major Dawson being wounded, Capt. E. L. Smith assumed command. The regiment formed again on an elevation some 1,000 yards in rear of the ground where we had fought, the Nineteenth on the right of the Eighteenth, still faced to the rear toward the enemy. Moved by the right flank to the support of Battery H, Fourth Artillery, when some slight musketery and sharp artillery firing took place. After occupying this ground an hour (the enemy being driven off), moved to the rear half a mile and occupied a new line faced to the front, Nineteenth and Fifteenth forming second line—Nineteenth on the right of Fifteenth. Captain Crofton, 4 lieutenants, and 30 men of the Sixteenth Infantry joined the Nineteenth, and formed on the right as the first company. Remained in this position about an hour, and moved about one-quarter of a mile to the rear and bivouacked in line. About 9 o'clock left bivouac and moved to the right and rear about one-half or three-quarters of a mile and bivouacked. Remained in second bivouac about an hour, and moved to the front and took position in front of road some 500 yards. Reynolds' [?] brigade, of Van Cleve's division, on the right, and Beatty's brigade on the left. During the operations of the 19th the battalion lost* 1 major wounded and 66 non-commissioned officers and privates killed, wounded, and missing.

On the 20th, action commenced on skirmish line about 7 a. m. Nineteenth Infantry, Capt. E. L. Smith commanding, formed second line, Lieutenants Curtis and Carpenter, with Company H, as skirmishers one-quarter of a mile to the left. The action continued, with slight pauses, until about noon, from which time until 5 p. m. the attacks on the position occupied were almost continuous. The Nineteenth, with occasional variations, composed the second line during the action. At no time during any attack was the battalion unengaged. The attacks in the afternoon coming from front, flank, and rear, the positions of the command forming the brigade were necessarily constantly changing, and to give a precise detailed account is impossible. Of 124 non-commissioned officers and men who went into action on the 20th, there remain 51 non-commissioned officers and men, and of 12 officers who went into action 3 lieutenants are for duty.

The following is a list of casualties among the officers:

Capt. Thomas Cummings, commanding Company A, Second Battalion, wounded and prisoner.

Capt. E. L. Smith, commanding Company G, missing.

Capt. V. K. Hart, commanding Company A, First Battalion, missing.

Capt. G. S. Peirce, commanding Company B, missing.

First Lieut. M. B. Fogarty, commanding Company A, Second Battalion, killed.

First Lieut. M. C. Causten, commanding Company E, missing.

First Lieut. T. H. Y. Bickham, commanding Company F, missing.

Second Lieut. C. F. Miller, Company E, wounded and prisoner.

Second Lieut. J. H. Gageby, Company A, First Battalion, missing.

Second Lieut. Robert Ayres, adjutant First Battalion, slightly wounded and present for duty.

First Lieut. W. O. Lattimore, First Lieut. Alfred Curtis (Company H), Second Lieut. A. B. Carpenter, and Second Lieut. Robert Ayres, present for duty.

I have the honor to be, very respectfully, your most obedient servant,

ROBERT AYRES,
Second Lieut., Adjt. First Batt., 19th *U. S. Infantry.*

Capt. JAMES W. FORSYTH,
    Acting Assistant Adjutant-General, Third Brigade.

---

* See revised statement, p. 171.

No. 33.

Report of Lieut. Joshua A. Fessenden, Battery H, Fifth U. S. Artillery.

HEADQUARTERS BATTERY H, FIFTH U. S. ARTILLERY,
Chattanooga, Tenn., September 26, 1863.

SIR: I have the honor to submit the following report of the part taken by Battery H, Fifth U. S. Artillery, in the battle of Chickamauga:

The battery, under command of First Lieut. Howard M. Burnham, left camp Friday evening, September 18, and marching all night took position in line of battle with the brigade shortly after daybreak on the 19th of September. During the morning the battery was ordered forward by Brigadier-General King, and came upon the enemy about 12 m. in a dense wood. The battery was hardly in position before, the troops on the right giving way, it was exposed to a most terrific fire of musketry from the front and flank. General King ordered the battery to limber to the rear, but it was impossible to execute the order, since many of the cannoneers were killed and wounded and the horses shot at the limbers. At the first fire Lieutenant Burnham fell mortally wounded; Lieutenant Ludlow was also wounded, and myself slightly struck on the right side. The battery was taken by the enemy, but was quickly recaptured by our troops. With the assistance of the Fifteenth Infantry, Captain Dod commanding, I succeeded in bringing off the field all the guns and four caissons, but was subsequently obliged to abandon the caissons in order to take the guns to the rear. On the morning of the 20th of September I was ordered by Major-General Thomas and Brigadier-General King to take the battery to Rossville. I started for that place about noon, but came on to Chattanooga, where I reported to Brigadier-General Wagner, commanding the post, and by his order my guns were placed in the several forts.

The losses* of the battery are as follows:

*   *   *   *   *   *   *

Horses killed, 45; wounded, 20.

The battery fired four rounds of canister before receiving the order to retire. The men of the battery, without a single exception, behaved well, working until the last moment to remove the guns.

I have the honor to be, sir, most respectfully, your obedient servant,

JOSHUA A. FESSENDEN,
Second Lieut., Fifth Artillery, Commanding Battery H.

Capt. JAMES W. FORSYTH, *A. A. A. G., Third Brigade.*

No. 34.

Reports of Maj. Gen. James S. Negley, U. S. Army, commanding Second Division.

HDQRS. SECOND DIVISION, FOURTEENTH ARMY CORPS,
Owens' Ford, Ga., September 17, 1863.

COLONEL: I have the honor to submit the following report of the operations of my command since leaving Cave Spring, near Stevenson, Ala.:

In compliance with verbal instructions received from the major-

---

*Nominal list omitted. See revised statement, p. 171.

general commanding the department, I marched my command on the 1st instant across the Tennessee River at Caperton's Ferry, starting from Cave Spring at 6.30 p. m. After crossing the river my command proceeded up the east bank to Norwood's, where I arrived at 10 p. m. and bivouacked for the night.

September 2, 8 a. m., marched in the direction of Taylor's Store, where I was ordered to halt my command for further instructions.

Arriving at Moore's Spring, 2 miles south of Taylor's Store, I learned that there was an insufficiency of water at that point for my command. I therefore halted the command and bivouacked in the vicinity of the spring.

1 p. m. General Sheridan's division arrived here and encamped near the spring.

September 3, 8 a. m., marched in the direction of Trenton. Found the mountain road very rough, rocky, and steep. I at once discovered that it would be impossible to cross my transportation in safety until the road could be repaired. I therefore set the entire division at work repairing the road and assisting the trains over; at dark all my regimental trains, together with ambulances and ammunition trains, had reached the summit without the loss of a wheel.

Camped 1 mile from Warren's Mill; sent Sirwell's brigade forward to repair crossing at mill.

By 11.30 p. m. a bridge 121 feet long and 20 feet high had been constructed.

September 4, 7.30 a. m., marched the command forward; Third Brigade crossed bridge at 7 a. m.; trains commenced crossing at 8 o'clock.

Deeming the bridge unsafe for the crossing of entire train, I halted it and commenced repairs, which delayed us until 12 m., when the passage of transportation was resumed.

3 p. m. arrived at Brown's Spring, foot of mountain. Found a small spring at this point, which, after being excavated and dammed up, afforded sufficient water for my command. By 8 p. m. my entire train was parked at foot of mountain, except 8 wagons of supplies, which were left at Moore's Spring.

September 5, sent a party of two regiments of infantry and one section of artillery, under command of Colonel Sirwell, commanding Third Brigade, to reconnoiter toward Johnson's Crook, and gain an accurate description of the road and country in that direction.

Colonel Sirwell discovered a large amount of property at the works of the Empire State Iron and Coal Mining Company, consisting of machinery, tools, stationery, &c., which was brought into camp by Captain Wing, assistant quartermaster, and placed to proper use.

At Payne's Mill a quantity of wheat (some bushels) was found, which the Seventy-eighth Pennsylvania Volunteers, under the command of Lieutenant-Colonel Blakeley, was directed to convert into flour for the use of the command.

September 6, 10 a. m., marched forward on right-hand road, leading from Brown's Spring to Johnson's Crook and Stevens' Gap.

3.30 p. m. arrived at junction Hurricane and Lookout Creeks, where I parked my trains and established headquarters for the night.

General Beatty arrived at McKaig's (foot of mountain) at 5 p. m., and sent one regiment (Forty-second Indiana) half way up the mountain, where the enemy's pickets were met. About half a dozen shots were exchanged; 1 man severely wounded in leg. The object of the expedition being fully accomplished, the regiment returned at dark to the foot of the mountain.

September 7, 7 a. m., leaving all trains in rear, except ambulances and hospital wagons, with one regiment as guard, moved forward with Sirwell's and Stanley's brigades, arriving at McKaig's, foot of mountain, at 10 a. m.

12 m. arrived at top of mountain, which had been gained by General Beatty at 11 a. m., without any resistance from the enemy.

4 p. m. First and Second Brigades were on top of mountain; trains ascending slowly. Road very rough and dangerous to transportation.

September 8, 4 a. m., sent General Beatty, with two regiments, to seize and hold Cooper's Gap.

8 a. m. sent Colonel Stoughton, with the Eleventh Michigan Infantry, to take possession of and clear Stevens' Gap, which was heavily blockaded with fallen trees.

11.30 a. m. arrived at junction of State road and Cooper's Gap road, where the troops were ordered to bivouac for the night.

September 9, 8 a. m., marched the Second and Third Brigades forward via Stevens' Gap, First Brigade moving through Cooper's Gap.

4 p. m. arrived at foot of mountain (Stevens').

5 p. m. moved Stanley's brigade to the front, on a reconnaissance; drove the rebel cavalry 3½ miles. My escort, under command of Lieutenant Cooke, made a gallant charge upon a superior force of the enemy, capturing 2.

September 10, 10 a. m., pursuant to your order, marched my command from Stevens' in the direction of La Fayette.

After passing Bailey's Cross-Roads, my skirmishers were more or less engaged, until we arrived at the gorge leading to Dug Gap, where I halted the command for the purpose of ascertaining the position of the enemy in the gap.

1.30 p. m. I learned from a Union citizen that a large force of the enemy (Buckner's corps), with cavalry and artillery (then only 3 miles distant), was approaching toward my left, from the direction of Catlett's Gap. I immediately sent one regiment in the direction of this force, for the double purpose of a reconnaissance and to compel the enemy to halt, under the impression that I would attack him.

At sundown I made a strong demonstration in the direction of Dug Gap, driving the enemy's skirmishers back to his main force and holding the position until I could establish my picket lines unobserved.

Before dark the strongest positions of defense the locality afforded were selected with the intention of bivouacking the troops for the night, with my trains parked close to my rear.

From the movements of the enemy, and from information obtained from scouts, I felt confident the enemy proposed to attack me in the morning with a superior force.

I also learned from a prisoner, and from Union civilians, that I was confronted by Hill's corps of three divisions (twelve brigades); that Buckner's corps of two divisions (eight brigades), also Forrest's division of cavalry, were 3 miles to my left, and that Polk's and Breckinridge's commands were in supporting distance. From the concurrence of testimony on this point, there seemed no doubt of the fact. I therefore adopted immediate precautionary measures to guard against surprise.

At 9 o'clock on the evening of the 10th Colonels Stanley and

Sirwell were ordered to withdraw quietly, at 3 the next morning, their entire line of pickets to the west side of the road running along the foot of the ridge occupied by the enemy, and to remain under arms until morning.

It was subsequently learned that the enemy intended to surprise my picket line at daylight, if their position had not been changed. September 11, 8.30 a. m., Brigadier-General Baird, with two brigades of his division (Starkweather's and Scribner's), arrived, and General Baird courteously reported to me as his senior for instructions.

His troops were placed in position at once, near Widow Davis' Cross-Roads, and held in reserve.

I now learned positively that the enemy had removed the obstructions from Dug and Blue Bird Gaps, and was moving a heavy force through each of them; also that Buckner's corps was moving forward rapidly on the Chattanooga road, and that his advance was only 2 miles distant.

A careful examination of the ground we occupied, which was a long, low ridge, covered with a heavy growth of young timber, descending abruptly on the north end to the Chickamauga, while the east, south, and west sides were skirted by corn-fields and commanded by higher ridges, demonstrated the fact that it would be impossible to hold this or any other position south of Bailey's Cross-Roads and fight a battle without involving the certain destruction of the trains, which, from the contour of these ridges and uneven nature of the ground, we would be obliged to park in close proximity to our position.

The preservation of the trains, perhaps the safety of the entire command, demanded that I should retire to Bailey's Cross-Roads, 2 miles northwest of our position, where we could get our trains under cover and fight the enemy to a better advantage. I therefore directed that the trains should commence moving back slowly and in good order, and that General Baird should hold Widow Davis' Cross-Roads until I could withdraw a portion of the Second Division and take position on the north side of Chickamauga Creek, to cover the withdrawal of his brigades and prevent the enemy from flanking us on our left.

1 p. m. a heavy column of cavalry was seen moving steadily on our left, with the evident intention of gaining my rear.

I immediately had four pieces of artillery placed in position on the ridge at John Davis' house, which commanded the valley on my left, also sent General Beatty, with one regiment and a section of artillery, to seize and guard Bailey's Cross-Roads, which was reported to be in possession of the enemy's cavalry.

2 p. m. the trains were all in motion falling back to Bailey's Cross-Roads.

General Beatty and Colonel Scribner, of General Baird's division, were directed to proceed to that point without delay and protect the trains from the attack of a large force of cavalry approaching with that view.

3 p. m. the skirmishers of General Baird's division were directed to fall back across the creek, where they were placed in position to hold the enemy in check until I could get my artillery in position on the ridge this side.

Two companies of the Nineteenth Illinois Infantry, concealed behind a stone fence, poured into the ranks of the enemy a destructive volley, killing, as I have since learned, 30 on the spot; this partially checked the enemy, who was advancing in three heavy lines.

Meantime I had 10 pieces of artillery planted on the ridge to the rear of John Davis' house, which commanded that position, until another new line could be formed on the ridge to the rear.

The enemy now occupied the south side of the creek with a heavy force. He opened two batteries of artillery upon us, at a distance of 400 yards; two of his brigades were parallel to our position on the right.

Buckner's corps was deployed and moving up steadily on our left, within short range. Colonel Stanley's and a portion of General Starkweather's brigades sustained here a well-directed and terrific fire, which our troops returned with spirit and marked effect. The firing increased and indicated an immediate general engagement along our entire front, and would have terminated in an assault from the enemy in a few moments, which would unquestionably have been disastrous to us, considering the overwhelming force of the enemy and our very unfavorable position.

By direction, General Baird deployed General Starkweather's brigade to our right, which checked the enemy's advance in that direction and enabled Colonel Stanley to withdraw his brigade, which being done, we retired slowly and in good order to Bailey's Cross-Roads, where a strong position of defense was assumed and the troops bivouacked for the night.

During the night the enemy withdrew his force to Dug Gap.

September 13, as strong positions of defense were selected as the locality afforded, where the troops were posted and remained until this morning.

I have the honor to remain, very respectfully, your obedient servant,

JAS. S. NEGLEY,
Major-General.

Lieut. Col. GEO. E. FLYNT,
Chief of Staff, Fourteenth Army Corps.

—

HDQRS. SECOND DIVISION, FOURTEENTH ARMY CORPS,
Chattanooga, Tenn., September 26, 1863.

COLONEL: I have the honor to submit the following report of the operations of my command since September 17, 1863:

September 17, 8 a. m., marched to Owens' Ford, encamping there for the night.

September 18, 3.30 p. m., received orders to march to the left and relieve General Palmer's division; reached his First Brigade (General Hazen's) at 5 p. m. General Hazen informed me and General Beatty that he had no orders to move from his position.

I reported in person to General Rosecrans for instructions; was directed by him, through Colonel Ducat, to send one brigade to Crawfish Spring; was afterward ordered by General Thomas, through Captain Willard, to move up and encamp my division *en masse.*

Subsequently this order was changed, directing me to relieve General Palmer, which attenuated my com mand from Crawfish Spring, along the Chickamauga, a distance of 3½ miles.

My troops did not get into position until near daylight. They were greatly exhausted by fatigue and want of sleep.

September 19, at daylight I sent all my transportation, except ammunition and ambulance trains, to Chattanooga for safety.

Very early in the morning the enemy advanced a heavy line of skirmishers upon Beatty's front, which was a very exposed position, engaging his pickets sharply for some hours.

11.30 the enemy appeared in force, planting two batteries within 400 yards of Beatty's position, which was followed by a fierce cannonading, during which Bridges' Battery, of Beatty's brigade, sustained a loss in men and horses. A part of Beatty's line being gradually driven back (but soon re-established), I sent one regiment (Eighteenth Ohio Volunteers) and a section of Schultz's Battery, of Stanley's brigade, to his support.

12.30 p. m. Beatty repulsed the enemy.

2.30 General McCook's corps had passed to the left of my position, leaving me on the extreme right, General McCook assuming command.

Shortly afterward I received written orders to report to General McCook.

3.30 p. m. received orders from Generals McCook and Rosecrans to withdraw my command and push forward as rapidly as possible to the support of Major-General Thomas, who was about 3 miles distant.

Moved forward at once, and reported to Major-General Rosecrans, who directed me to take position and support General Thomas.

Moved to the left of his (General Rosecrans') headquarters, at the farm-house, one-half mile, when I discovered a gap in our line, through which the enemy was moving upon the right flank and rear of General Thomas' line.

Stanley's brigade was immediately dispatched to meet and check the advance of the enemy, Sirwell supporting him on his right.

After a brisk skirmish the enemy was driven back into the woods.

6 p. m. Stanley and Sirwell were ordered to push the enemy back vigorously, so as to connect our line with the troops on the left.

A sharp engagement with the enemy immediately followed, lasting until 7.30 p. m., during which time our line was pushed forward from one-half to three-fourths of a mile, but I was unable to connect with any of our forces on my right or left. Held this position during the night.

September 20 military operations were suspended until 8 a. m. in consequence of a dense fog.

8 a. m. received a pressing order from General Thomas, through Captain Willard, to move at once to his support. I immediately commenced withdrawing my division for that purpose, when the enemy was reported to be massing a heavy force in my front, sharply engaging my line of skirmishers. I was directed by Major-General Rosecrans to hold my position until relieved by some other command.

General Beatty, however, with his brigade was sent at 8 a. m., under guidance of Captain Willard, to report to General Thomas, going into action immediately.

Although the most strenuous efforts were made to hasten into position the troops that were to relieve me, the remaining two brigades of my command were not relieved until 9.30, when one brigade was sent from General Wood's division for that purpose.

In withdrawing these two brigades, the enemy availed himself of the change and pressed so hard upon the relieving force that I was compelled to halt and send one of the brigades back to assist in re-establishing my former line, also to protect my ammunition train, which was passing at the time.

These serious detentions had the effect of separating my division and destroying the unity of action in my command, which I was unable to restore during the day.

I deeply regret the circumstances which rendered this subdivision necessary, actually placing two of my brigades entirely beyond my personal supervision. Although I am satisfied that the causes which interfered with the unity and concerted movements of my command are properly appreciated by my corps and department commanders, and will not be allowed to detract from the credit due the division, yet I feel that it would have been more advantageous and satisfactory had it been otherwise.

10 a. m., on being informed that General Thomas' left was being turned, I left Sirwell's brigade to follow with the artillery, and pushed Stanley's brigade forward under heavy fire to the left of General Thomas' line, where Stanley met the enemy in heavy force.

Here I received orders, through Captain Gaw, to take charge of and mass all the artillery at hand on a high ridge facing the south.

I now learned with surprise that Sirwell's brigade was not yet relieved, and that Captain Johnson, of my staff, was compelled to withdraw his brigade, leaving only a weak line of skirmishers.

I immediately took charge of all batteries at this point and massed them on the ridge, placing them in position supported by Sirwell's brigade when it arrived.

1 p. m. a heavy force of the enemy was discovered to be moving to our left and rear; also, that Beatty's brigade was being overwhelmed.

Sirwell's brigade was at once sent forward to check his advance, while Bridges' Battery, of Beatty's brigade, and Smith's (Fourth Regular) battery were placed in position and immediately opened a very destructive fire upon him from the ridge facing eastward, causing him to fall back, thus temporarily relieving the left wing.

The character of the ground prevented the effective use of all the batteries; they were placed on a ridge to the rear, and the Seventy-eighth Pennsylvania Volunteers sent to protect them; the remainder of Sirwell's brigade was deployed at the most exposed points.

2 p. m., finding that our right wing and center had given way before the overwhelming numbers of the enemy, and being hard pressed on my front and right, I sent Lieutenant Moody, of my staff, to General Rosecrans for a brigade.

Upon being applied to, General Rosecrans replied that it was too late, that he could give me no help.

At this juncture, General Brannan applied to me for support, and I ordered the Twenty-first Ohio Volunteers, of Sirwell's brigade, to his assistance.

I then rode forward to the crest of the ridge over which the right wing and center were retiring, to get a position for artillery, when I was met by a strong column of the enemy, who pressed forward rapidly between me and the troops on my left, leaving me but one whole regiment (Seventy-eighth Pennsylvania Volunteers) and a part of another organized, with the artillery in my charge with its ammunition nearly exhausted; at the same time my ammunition train had been driven off the field.

At this moment reliable information reached me that a force of the enemy's cavalry was moving from our right to our rear, and a column of infantry on our front and left.

Finding it impossible to organize any of the passing troops, and unable to communicate with General Thomas, and being informed by a staff officer that Generals Rosecrans, McCook, and Crittenden had left the field, I deemed it vitally important to secure the safety of the artillery, which appeared to be threatened with immediate capture by a large force of the enemy which was pressing forward on my front and right.

I immediately took the Seventy-eighth Pennsylvania Volunteers and marched to the mouth of the gap, 2 miles from Rossville, the first open ground where the troops could be collected and reorganized.

I found Colonel Parkhurst here, with the Ninth Michigan Volunteers, energetically checking the stragglers. He informed me that General Crittenden had passed some hours before, and had ordered him, with all the troops, to fall back to Chattanooga. This I stated to him was inexpedient; that the troops must be immediately reorganized and prepared to march to the front.

In this purpose I was ably assisted by Colonel Ducat, Colonel McKibbin, and Capt. Joe Hill, of General Rosecrans' staff; Colonel Parkhurst, of General Thomas' staff; Lieutenant Elkin and Lieutenant Morris, of General Baird's staff, and Lieutenant Wilson, of General Sheridan's staff, members of my own staff, with other officers whose names I cannot now recall.

As soon as I had cleared the gap of the artillery and transportation, which extended back some distance and in great confusion, and formed the scattered troops into battalions, I learned that General Sheridan was close at hand with some 1,500 men.

I rode forward and respectfully suggested to General Sheridan to move to the support of General Thomas, stating that I would join him with all the troops I had collected. He stated his object was to march to Rossville.

I then rode forward to communicate with General Thomas. Found the enemy's cavalry in possession of the road between us, preventing my farther passage.

I then returned and held a consultation with Generals Davis, Sheridan, and Colonel Ducat.

It was determined as advisable to proceed to Rossville, to prevent the enemy from obtaining possession of the cross-roads, and from there General Sheridan would move to the support of General Thomas, via La Fayette road.

The column reached Rossville at dark, and the scattered troops were organized as rapidly as possible. Provisions and ammunition, of which the troops were destitute, were telegraphed for and received from Chattanooga.

At this moment I learned that General Granger had gone to the assistance of General Thomas, that he was safe, and that the troops were retiring to Rossville; also that General Sheridan had halted 3 miles from Rossville.

I therefore continued the organization and preparation of the troops, to hold our position against a force of the enemy who were reported to be advancing from the direction of Ringgold.

Before the disposition of the force was completed General Thomas, with a portion of his command, arrived.

September 21, early in the morning, my division was disposed so as to hold the gap and mountain crest east of Rossville.

2 p. m. the enemy advanced a heavy force, with artillery, on the La Fayette road, and on the crest of the mountain.

After a brisk engagement, with artillery and musketry, he was checked in the gap by Stanley's brigade and driven from the mountain crest by a gallant charge of the Fifteenth Kentucky, General Beatty's brigade.

5 p. m. the enemy was seen moving in heavy columns to our right, and massing a considerable force in our front.

He was able to shell our position, which was greatly exposed to his artillery and which would become immediately untenable should he plant artillery on the crest of the mountain beyond our line; at the same time communication with Chattanooga could be easily cut off.

The troops were without supplies and the animals had had no food for twenty-four hours. The troops were accordingly ordered to fall back to Chattanooga.

6 p. m. the Sixty-ninth Ohio Volunteers, of Stanley's brigade, which had been left at Cowan, arrived and took position in the gap.

My division was directed to quietly withdraw to Chattanooga at midnight, leaving three regiments to hold the picket line until daylight. This important duty was intrusted to Colonel Stoughton, Eleventh Michigan Volunteers, who performed it in a most judicious manner. My command reached Chattanooga at 2.30 a. m., and took the position designated by Major Bond, of General Rosecrans' staff.

At daylight we occupied the unfinished rebel fort on the west side of Chattanooga and La Fayette road, and immediately commenced its completion for defense.

I beg leave to refer to the reports of General Beatty and Colonel Stanley for the details of the brilliant operations of their brigades while temporarily separated by order, and the tide of battle on Sunday. The conduct of these two officers was highly creditable, and that of their troops brave and efficient.

General Beatty gallantly remained upon the field of battle, in command of scattered troops, after most of his brigade had been driven from it and separated from him by the charge of the enemy upon his left.

Colonel Stanley continued to command his brigade until he received a severe contusion from a fragment of a shell, when Colonel Stoughton, Eleventh Michigan Volunteers, assumed command and ably handled the brigade.

In Sirwell's brigade, the Twenty-first Ohio Volunteers, which assisted General Brannan, suffered severely, holding their position at the base of the ridge until they had exhausted nearly all their ammunition and were compelled to supply themselves from their dead comrades.

When General Brannan retired with his division, the remaining portion of the Twenty-first Ohio Volunteers was left to hold their position, during which time they lost heavily.

The balance of Colonel Sirwell's brigade, although deployed at several points, and compelled to change position frequently during the day, rendered valuable services not only in battle but, with the assistance of the Ninth Michigan Volunteers, in rallying and organizing a number of the scattered troops, and in saving the artillery and transportation, which occupied the road and choked up the gap, endangering the immediate capture of the whole by the enemy.

The highest compliment I am able to bestow upon both officers and men of the entire division is to simply refer to their endurance, fortitude, cheerful obedience, and heroic conduct during the entire campaign and battle.

I respectfully direct attention to the reports of brigade and regimental commanders for the lists of those deserving honorable mention, which I cordially approve.

All members of my staff performed their duties with coolness and ability and entirely satisfactory.

Captain Johnson, division inspector; Captain Hough, Nineteenth U. S. Infantry, assistant commissary of musters; Lieutenant Moody, aide-de-camp, rendered important services. Their gallantry and efficiency are worthy of special mention.

I have the honor to remain, very respectfully, your obedient servant,

JAS. S. NEGLEY,
Major-General.

Lieut. Col. GEORGE E. FLYNT,
Chief of Staff, Fourteenth Army Corps.

—

HEADQUARTERS DEPARTMENT OF THE CUMBERLAND,
Chattanooga, Tenn., October 14, 1863.

Brig. Gen. LORENZO THOMAS,
Adjutant-General, U. S. Army, Washington, D. C.:

GENERAL: Herewith I transmit a special report by Major-General Negley, with accompanying documents, explanatory of the reasons why he left his position on the field of Chickamauga, on the 20th, so early in the day, without orders and without being driven off, while the troops in front and to the left of the position held their ground.

The general has always been an active, energetic, and efficient commander, and displayed very good judgment in an affair at Widow Davis' house in front of Stevens' Gap, where he was attacked by a superior force of the enemy, and successfully extricated his train and command from a perilous position.

But an impression that he left the field on Sunday without orders or necessity having made its way through this army, and statements having appeared in the official reports of general officers appearing to support the impression, I gave General Negley leave to submit this special report on the subject. From a careful perusal of that and the accompanying papers, it seems that he acted according to his best judgment under the circumstances of the case.

But satisfied that his usefulness in this army is lost, at least until these facts can be developed by a Court of Inquiry, I have given him a leave of absence for thirty days, and advised him after this report goes in to ask for a court of inquiry.*

Very respectfully, your obedient servant,

W. S. ROSECRANS,
Major-General, Commanding.

* See record of Court of Inquiry, p. 1004.

[Inclosure.]

HDQRS. SECOND DIVISION, FOURTEENTH ARMY CORPS,
Chattanooga, October 9, 1863.

Brig. Gen. JAMES A. GARFIELD,
Chief of Staff, Department of the Cumberland:

GENERAL: In accordance with your request, I have the honor to submit to your official attention written statements from Major Lowrie, Major Welch,* Captain Barker, Captain Johnson, Captain Hough, Captain Bridges, Captain Hayden, Captain Willard, Lieutenant Moody, Lieutenant Temple, Lieutenant Cooke, Surgeon Bogue, and Captain Gaw,* giving their personal recollections of the orders conveyed to me and of the operations of my command on Friday afternoon, Saturday, and Sunday; also a valuable reference to the movements of the enemy during critical periods of the battle.

The statements were written while I was sick in bed, without any dictation or supervision from me; consequently some of them may be unnecessarily voluminous. I have not included the written statements of regimental commanders, or any others who might be reasonably biased by the interests of their own commands, and who could not be truthfully conversant with the action of other troops.

These statements illuminate several obscure points in my official report now before you; they forcibly explain certain delays which I could not refer to fully in my report without casting reflections upon other general officers. This I purposely avoided, preferring to suffer all the consequences of my silence than gain any advantage by hasty accusations.

In conclusion, general, allow me to earnestly request your official consideration of the following facts, which are elicited by the testimony placed before you:

1. The delay which occurred in placing my troops in position on Friday afternoon and night, also on Saturday night, in connection with the sleepless and severe duty the men performed, seriously affected their physical condition and unfitted them for the field on Sunday.

2. The delay on Sunday morning caused the separation of my division, placing the brigades in action successively in portions of the field previously unknown to the brigade commanders or myself, thus preventing all concert of action between the First and Second Brigades and myself.

3. My taking charge of the scattered artillery, in obedience to orders from Major-General Thomas, per Captain Gaw, occupying the position assigned to me, distinct from the line occupied by my other two brigades, and widely separated from them, with only one brigade of infantry, shifting my lines and the position of the artillery frequently so as to render some assistance to the exposed points near my position, during the constantly drifting tide of battle in that direction, rendered it utterly impossible to leave that portion of my command to acquaint myself with the general direction of our lines or the results of the battle at various points, or hold any personal communication with corps or department commanders.

4. When I comprehended the movement of the enemy, which eventually compelled me to retire the artillery, I communicated the information to General Rosecrans, sending two staff officers to insure

---

* Not found.

his receiving the message, receiving as his reply that it was too late, he could not help me.

At this critical period I learned from my staff officer, who had just arrived from the right, and from other reliable sources, that the right wing of the army and all the troops to my right and front had fallen back, vigorously pursued by strong columns of the enemy; that the enemy was passing rapidly to my right, and already held the mouth of the Rossville road, and were also occupying the ridge in front of my artillery reserve; also, that the enemy had placed artillery on the ridge and was pushing infantry up the ravine.

These facts being in my possession, I immediately turned Schultz's battery to the front, and rode forward alone to the crest of the hill to get a position for the battery where I had seen several pieces of our artillery in action a short time before. The smoke was so dense and the firing so heavy that I failed to see the enemy on the crest until I confronted his line within 100 feet of him.

Before they could seize my horse or take direct aim, I turned and rode back amidst a shower of balls. On reaching the artillery, which was not more than 300 yards back, I found several pieces (which I afterward learned belonged to Bridges' Battery) firing upon the enemy, who was coming up the ravine.

I found but two regiments of infantry in the rear of the artillery, which was rapidly falling back and becoming scattered at the same time. Artillery farther to my right was dashing past at full speed. Infantry from my front and right was also in full retreat. I attempted to halt the fugitive infantry, but found it impossible.

I now received positive information that the enemy was turning my position on both flanks, that it was impossible to hold him in check with the small force I had, and that he was pushing after the trains on the Rossville road. I immediately ordered Colonel Blakeley, Seventy-eighth Pennsylvania Volunteers, to move off in advance of the artillery, marching in double column, and sent staff officers to bring up the other two regiments of Colonel Sirwell's brigade, together with every detachment of troops that could be found to guard the rear, until the artillery could get off. We were in a dense wood, crossed by numerous ridges and ravines.

I was totally ignorant of my locality or the direction of any of the roads. I took out my pocket compass and formed an opinion as to the direction of the Rossville road, which I struck about 1 mile north of the battle-ground. I found transportation, artillery, and troops, on this road in confusion; the soldiers pressing forward under the belief that the enemy was in close pursuit, although not yet in a panic.

I moved the troops to the first open ground and gave directions for their organization and return to the front. I just then learned that General Thomas was still in position, and rode back to communicate with him if possible, but found the road in possession of the enemy. My operations, after my return, are fully understood by you, as I communicated with you from Rossville on my arrival there.

I have the honor to remain, very respectfully, your obedient servant,

JAS. S. NEGLEY,
Major-General.

[Sub-Inclosure No. 1.]

CHATTANOOGA, TENN., *October* 8, 1863.

[Maj. Gen. J. S. NEGLEY :]

GENERAL: I would respectfully make the following statement of the proceedings of yourself and command during the battle of Chickamauga Creek. I mention only those occurrences which came within my own observation, and relate only what I know.

On Friday, September 18, 1863, about 4 p. m., the division of Major-General Palmer having moved to the left, passing the Second Division, Fourteenth Army Corps, early in the evening of September 17, General Negley marched with this command, under orders to relieve General Palmer's division. Having arrived at the position occupied by General Hazen's brigade of General Palmer's division, General Negley rode up to General Hazen, who was lying on the ground, and dismounting, entered into conversation with him, but I was too far off to hear them. General Negley then rode forward to get further orders from corps or department headquarters, and soon sent back an order that General Beatty's brigade should occupy General Hazen's ground as soon as his brigade should march out.

General Beatty immediately sent staff officers to General Hazen to ascertain where his troops and pickets were placed, in order to execute this command. Colonel Stanley was ordered to move down the Culp's Mill road with his brigade to relieve Colonel Grose's brigade, and was immediately conducted there by Captain Hough and an officer of General Palmer's staff. After about half an hour's delay General Beatty reported to me that General Hazen said he had no order to be relieved and refused to move. I rode forward to find General Negley for instructions, and learned that he had gone down to Colonel Grose's position. I immediately followed. It was then quite dark, and being unacquainted with the road I was much delayed in finding the place. When I did so, I found Colonel Stanley's brigade standing in the road, and finding Colonel Grose he told me he had not received any order relieving him, and that until he did so could not move.

While I was talking to him Colonel Stanley moved back toward Crawfish Spring, under orders from General Negley, as I afterward learned. I immediately rode back and passed the head of the column searching for General Negley. I found him at Spears' house, half a mile southwest from Crawfish Spring. I reported to him the difficulties I had met with. He directed me to find General Thomas and report to him that General Palmer's brigades refused to be relieved, saying they had no orders to that effect ; that the troops (General Negley's) had been brought to Spears' house and were in bivouac there all together ; that they had been marched back and forth until they were almost exhausted, and to ask for instructions. I found General Thomas at General Rosecrans' headquarters. General Palmer was also there. General Thomas said he was very sorry, but that General Negley would have to occupy General Palmer's position. General Palmer said that he had sent the proper order to his command before dark, but would send it again, and he started to do so. I returned to General Negley with the order.

He directed that Colonel Sirwell should relieve General Hazen, and that General Beatty should relieve Colonel Grose. Colonel Stanley being already in position near Crawfish Spring, and being very much reduced by furnishing pickets on the line in front of General Rosecrans' headquarters, it was impossible to move any of these troops to their positions at that time, for the road was blocked up with troops and trains moving toward Crawfish Spring. I was again sent to General Thomas to report these difficulties, and that General Negley was very much dissatisfied with the disposition of his troops, so widely separated that he could have no control over them, and so much delayed that they could not get into position much before daylight.

It was about 10.30 p. m. when I reached General Rosecrans' headquarters, where I found General Thomas. General Rosecrans and General Thomas were very much annoyed at the delay. The troops (General Negley's) moved to the position assigned to them as soon as they could get the road, but it was about daylight before they all got into position. I get this fact from the staff officers who conducted them to their places.

Saturday, September 19, early in the morning, there was very brisk musketry firing on General Beatty's front, and he reported the enemy advancing on him in pretty strong force. The skirmishing continued with but little cessation until about 11 a. m., when artillery was used, the enemy having opened fire from two batteries. After a warm engagement they were repulsed by General Beatty's brigade with Bridges' Battery, assisted by the Eighteenth Regiment Ohio Volunteer Infantry and one section of Schultz's Battery, which had been sent from Colonel Stanley's brigade. About 8 a. m. the head of General McCook's column passed Spears' house.

In the afternoon, General McCook's corps having all passed to Crawfish Spring, General Negley was ordered to join him there with his division. He did so as soon as possible. General Beatty was much delayed by the difficulty of bringing in his long line of skirmishers. While waiting for the rest of General Beatty's command to come up, General McCook's corps moved toward the left, and General Negley was ordered to do so too. He started at once with the brigades of Colonels Stanley and Sirwell, leaving me with orders to conduct General Beatty's forward as soon as possible. After waiting for a small portion of his command, until after his artillery had supplied their deficiencies in ammunition, General Beatty, urged by me to move as quickly as possible, marched without them and moved forward in the direction taken by General Negley.

Failing to overtake or to find General Negley, I reported to General Rosecrans that General Beatty's brigade was just coming up and asked for instructions. This was before 6 p. m.; General Rosecrans directed that General Beatty should form in the woods close by his headquarters, but before he had placed his troops as directed, General Negley came up and, after a short conversation with General Rosecrans, he ordered General Beatty into position in reserve in rear of the brigades of Colonels Stanley and Sirwell. This was on the left of the road from Crawfish Spring, about a quarter of a mile from General Rosecrans' headquarters.

General Beatty had hardly got into position when an attack was made on Colonel Stanley's front, which continued until after dark. The enemy was handsomely repulsed; our front was quiet the remainder of the night.

General Negley remained on the hill where his batteries were placed until about 10 p. m., when, after having eaten a light supper, he went to General Rosecrans' headquarters, where he remained until midnight. He then returned and lay down to get some rest, which was absolutely necessary, as he had endured much fatigue and was very unwell. He had no opportunity up to that time, either himself or by his staff officers, for going over the ground to learn its character and the relative positions of troops of other commands. Had it not been for the important duties to be performed and the responsibility which rested on him, and had he not been sustained in some measure by the excitement engendered thereby, he would have been confined to his bed. He was considered so ill that when he left Bailey's Cross-Roads on the 17th of September he was advised by his medical director and other staff officers to ride in an ambulance.

Sunday, September 20, early in the morning, I was sent to examine the ground occupied by Colonels Stanley and Sirwell and to ascertain the practicability of moving artillery over it. When I returned orders were sent to brigade commanders to be in readiness to move to the left on the shortest notice. About 8 o'clock General Beatty's brigade was sent to the left to report to General Thomas. At the same time Colonels Stanley and Sirwell were ordered out into the road to follow General Beatty. I carried the order to Colonel Stanley, and as soon as he got his command into the road I reported the fact to General Negley. General Rosecrans, who was there at the time, immediately ordered that both brigades be sent back to their positions to remain there until relieved by other troops. I took the order to Colonel Stanley and Captain Hough went to Colonel Sirwell. Both brigades went back to their former positions with all possible speed.

After much delay two brigades of General Wood's division came to relieve General Negley. I met them at the top of the low ridge, about one-half mile in rear of General Negley's line. At that time they had skirmishers thrown well forward and they advanced in this way to their position. I guided Colonel Harker, commanding the left brigade, to the rear of Colonel Stanley's line, where I found an officer of Colonel Stanley's staff waiting to show him the line, but as Colonel Harker said he was ordered to move to the left to fill a gap caused by General Brannan moving away, I then conducted the staff officer (Lieutenant Keith, engineer) to Colonel Buell, commanding the right brigade, and instructed him to show Colonel Buell where Colonel Stanley's troops and pickets were. About 9 a. m. Colonel Stanley's brigade was relieved and led to the left by General Negley in person.

Just before this the roar of artillery and the rattle of volleys of musketry indicated that a warm engagement was going on on the left. General Negley marched Colonel Stanley's brigade at double-quick across the field to our left, in which some ammunition wagons had been parked. As they gained the woods, in rear of what we supposed and afterward learned to be General Reynolds' line, General Negley was met by Captain Gaw, of General Thomas' staff, who gave him some order, which I did not hear. General Negley then left Colonel Stanley's brigade and directed me to collect all the batteries I could find near the road and to order them up on the ridge, facing south. I delivered this order to Captain Schultz, Captain Marshall, and a lieutenant commanding a regular battery. These batteries were placed on the ridge as directed and changed about from one position to another as the exigencies of the battle required until about 2 p. m. For some time after they were first placed on the ridge they had no infantry supports until Colonel Sirwell, who had been very tardily relieved, came up with his brigade. Shortly after he came I was informed that the Twenty-first Ohio had been sent to assist General Brannan. The other three regiments were shifted about with the artillery.

While General Negley, with the assistance of some of his staff officers, was attending to this duty, it became evident that some disaster had happened to portions of General McCook's and General Crittenden's corps. A large number of fugitives came up through the ravines and over the ridge. Batteries were dragged up with all the haste that horses and men could exert. Some of these did not stop on the ridge, others sought positions and prepared again for action. One corps battle-flag went past without an officer or any escort. Division and brigade battle flags and regimental colors were hastily carried to the rear.

Every effort was made by General Negley's and Colonel Sirwell's staff officers, assisted by many of the officers who had come out with the fugitives, to rally and organize the scattered troops, but without avail. As soon as a detachment brought to the front to support the batteries heard the sound of the enemy's muskets in their front, they disappeared like smoke. They were soon all gone. This was before 2 p. m.

After this I went to the right of our position on the ridge to get further orders from General Negley. He directed me to go back and order all the batteries to move back on a sort of a road which went over the ridge, to collect all the organized infantry I could, to form a rear guard, and, if I could find any general officer there, to get him to take command. I executed this order as far as I could, sending back seven or eight batteries which were without support, but before I reached that portion of the ridge immediately in rear of General Thomas, I discovered that there was a battery on the ridge between me and that point, which was firing on General Thomas' troops. I feared it was a rebel battery, and my fears were soon confirmed by an officer who was trying to ascertain whether it was not one of our own batteries that was firing there by mistake. I then returned, finding portions of General Beatty's brigade, which had been shattered in the morning.

I directed Lieutenant-Colonel McIntire (who had the highest rank of any officer I could then find) to take command of the whole detachment, and move after the batteries as a rear guard, and to collect all stragglers as he moved on. I then started forward to report progress to General Negley. When I reached the Rossville road it was filled with wagons, artillery, infantry, and some cavalry, all moving toward Rossville, somewhat confusedly, but without panic. It was very difficult to pass them at all. My progress was very slow, and I did not overtake General Negley until I reached the open fields at the end of the gap through which the road runs. Here I found him and General Davis endeavoring to stop all the troops, and to organize them for service. In this they seemed to be very successful.

Very shortly after I arrived there, General Negley told me he would leave these troops in command of General Davis, and he would go back and attempt to reach General Thomas. He started for this purpose with his escort. He failed in this, and came back. Then he, General Davis, and General Sheridan (who had just come up with about 1,500 organized troops of his own division), and Lieutenant-Colonel Ducat, of General Rosecrans' staff, held a short consultation, after which the whole command moved on to Rossville,

General Sheridan immediately taking the La Fayette road toward the battle-field. General Negley disposed of his conglomerate command so as to be able to move to General Thomas' assistance immediately, if necessary. He also notified Major-General Rosecrans of what had been done, and asked for instructions. The sun had set before their arrangements were completed. Everything that was possible was done for the comfort and welfare of the troops.

When I saw Generals Negley and Davis at the mouth of the gap where the troops were first halted, I saw no evidence of undue excitement or of any trepidation on the part of either. They were cool, though energetic, using every effort to get the troops organized as quickly and as well as possible.

With much respect, I remain, general, your obedient servant,

J. A. LOWRIE,
Major, and Assistant Adjutant-General.

[Sub-Inclosure No. 2.]

HDQRS. 2D DIV., 14TH ARMY CORPS, INSPECTOR'S OFFICE,
Chattanooga, October 8, 1863.

Major-General NEGLEY,
    Comdg. Second Division, Fourteenth Army Corps:

SIR: Your note requesting me to give a brief statement of the operations of the Second Division, as they came under my notice, during the period embraced from Friday afternoon, September 8, to Sunday, September 20, has been received.

In my reply I would first embrace the following copy of a communication:

HDQRS. SECOND DIVISION, TWENTY-FIRST ARMY CORPS,
At Abercrombie's, below Owens' Ford, Chickamauga, Ga., Sept. 18, 1863.

Major-General NEGLEY,
    Commanding Second Division, Fourteenth Army Corps:

GENERAL: I am directed by Major-General Palmer to inform you that his division is under marching orders, and will move out at 2 o'clock this p. m.

The picket line of this division which connects with your left will consequently be withdrawn.

Very respectfully, your obedient servant,

C. H. MORTON,
Lieutenant-Colonel, and Aide-de-Camp.

On this note being referred to me by you, about 1 p. m. Friday, I, in company with the inspectors of the First and Third Brigades, proceeded to ascertain the position of General Palmer's line; made all arrangements to take it up when vacated by him. About 2 p. m. (General Palmer still in position) I called at General Starkweather's headquarters, where I met Captain Willard, of General Thomas' staff, inquiring for your headquarters. I attended him thither; when arriving there I ascertained he brought the order to march. I immediately countermanded the detail for picket. The division marched at about 4 p. m. I, in company with Lieutenant Moody, was sent forward to gain information relative to the route leading to Gordon's Mills; soon came up to General Hazen's brigade, Palmer's division, in camp.

It being my understanding that our division was to take position on the right of Palmer's, we there awaited your arrival. On joining us, you ordered me to take two companies of the Second

Brigade and throw out a line of skirmishers to protect the right flank, which I did, pushing them well down to the Chickamauga; I then relieved the picket line of Colonel Grose's brigade, Palmer's division, the brigade having moved during the day, and leaving the line to be relieved. I was acting under the impression that it was intended that the division should encamp there, but on my return to the road I found that Colonel Stanley had given orders for the withdrawal of the skirmishers preparatory to moving forward. I returned to the line to see the order executed, when I rejoined the command, which was now moving past General Hazen's camp. It was now dark. I followed the Second Brigade, which had the advance. It turned off to the right on what was called Culp's Mill road. I followed until it intersected a road leading to Crawfish Spring; there I met you. You expressed yourself as having not received proper directions as to the road, and ordered me back to direct the Third Brigade, Colonel Sirwell, to move on the main road to the spring, not to follow the balance of the command. I did so. On my return, after passing over about 1 mile, I came to Mr. Spears' house, occupied as your headquarters. The Third Brigade was then ordered to the place of bivouac.

About 11 p. m. you received an order requiring that one brigade be sent back to relieve General Hazen's brigade and to throw out a strong picket on the Chickamauga as far back as Matthews' house. You directed me to notify Colonel Sirwell to get his command in readiness to move; leaving one regiment and one section of artillery to guard train, the balance of the brigade was got out on the road and ordered to relieve General Hazen, when I reported to you again, Colonel Ducat being present, to ascertain if you had any further orders. You ordered me to accompany Colonel Sirwell and to assist him in the disposition of his line; the road was blockaded with troops moving to the left, and it was with great difficulty and much delay that the command reached its destination. I reported to General Hazen, and ascertained that he had withdrawn his picket. With the assistance of Captain Lord, inspector Third Brigade, added to the knowledge I had obtained of the locality before dark, I succeeded in getting out a line covering three fords, the right resting opposite Matthews' house and connecting on the left with that of the First Brigade. The line picketed by the division that night could not have been short of 3 miles. On completing the line (about 3.30 a. m., Saturday, September 19), I reported to your headquarters. Saturday morning heavy skirmishing on Beatty's front (artillery and small-arms). I accompanied you to the right of the line, when you made suggestions relative to some rude works that should be thrown up, which were immediately commenced by the Thirty-seventh Indiana Volunteers.

I then went down to the line to carry out some of your directions, you returning toward the left. In a short time I started toward headquarters, when I met you in company with Lieutenant-Colonel Ducat; returning toward the right, you directed me to accompany you; afterward by your direction I remained at the Third Brigade to await the appearance of General Sheridan, to deliver him your suggestions relative to the disposition of his troops, and to direct him to your headquarters. General McCook having appeared in the meantime and assumed command, your division retained its position till the rear of McCook's corps passed. Your division then moved up, two brigades halting at Crawfish Spring, in rear of General Sheridan.

The Third Brigade was just taking position when Colonel Fisher, of McCook's staff, rode up and delivered an order for you to move to the assistance of General Thomas. You immediately dispatched officers to the brigades directing them to move up with all possible haste, myself going to the Third Brigade, Colonel Sirwell. The division moved uninterruptedly, the order of march being, respectively, Second, Third, and First Brigades, the Second Brigade being moved to occupy a ridge to the left and front of General Rosecrans' headquarters, I being ordered to station the Third Brigade near said headquarters, then return to the road and await the arrival of the First Brigade and direct it accordingly. On arriving at said headquarters with First Brigade, I found the Third had moved to the ridge; rejoining the Second Brigade, I directed the First to follow. On arriving at the summit of the ridge, I saw the Second and Third Brigades being deployed in the valley beyond, preparatory to taking possession of the woods in their front, which was reported to be held by the rebels. On their being pushed forward, they found the enemy in some force; succeeded in driving them about one-half mile, when the firing ceased, they retaining their position during the night.

About 8 a. m., Sunday, I understood you to receive orders from General Thomas, per Captain Willard, to join him on the left with your division. You sent orders to Colonels Stanley and Sirwell to withdraw their skirmishers, preparatory to a move, while I was sent to report to General McCook that you were ordered to move your command; consequently there would be a gap in the lines that should be looked to. I inquired for him of General Sheridan, stating the nature of my mission; also of General Lytle; neither of them could direct me to his whereabouts. I shortly after met Colonel Goddard, making the same statement to him. He suggested that I had better see General Rosecrans; that he had gone out on the line, at the same time pointing toward our front. On regaining the ridge I discovered you and him (General Rosecrans) in conversation. As soon as he retired I reported that I had not been able to find General McCook. You replied, "All right; I have seen General Rosecrans." Almost immediately after the First Brigade, that had been lying in reserve, was ordered to proceed to the left and report to General Thomas. I was then ordered to take charge of the ordnance train and move it in rear of First Brigade. I proceeded to follow the brigade about three-quarters of a mile, when you sent me an order to turn the train into a field to the left of the road, where it would be less exposed to the shells of the enemy, which was immediately executed. I then reported to you on the ridge previously occupied by the First Brigade.

A short time thereafter a portion of Wood's division formed on the ridge, threw out skirmishers, and proceeded, after apparently much delay, toward our front, three-quarters of a mile distant, ostensibly for the purpose of relieving our line. I then accompanied you toward the front, when we met the Second Brigade moving on the road in column toward the left. You sent me back to hurry up Sirwell's brigade, with orders for it to follow the Second. After delivering the orders, and on my return, I met Lieutenant Moody, who stated that the general wanted Sirwell's brigade on the ridge, at the same time pointing to the ridge north of the road facing south. The brigade reported as directed. I then found you placing the artillery in position—Batteries G and M, First Ohio Volunteer Artillery, a portion of Bridges' Battery, and one section of the Fourth (regular)

Battery. There appeared small squads of the First Brigade falling back on the ridge in confusion. An officer in command of one of the parties reported to you "that the enemy were moving around on your left; that they had counted 7 stand of colors across the road in that direction." You immediately made disposition of the Third Brigade so as to cover the left, and opened an effective fire on the enemy from Bridges' Battery and a part of the Fourth (regular) Battery. You then ordered me to assist in placing a line of skirmishers to the left and rear, for the double purpose of checking the stragglers (who were then coming back in large numbers) and to prevent the enemy making a movement in that direction unperceived; also, to collect all the mounted orderlies I could find, and place them well out in the same direction as vedettes.

Some three-quarters of an hour afterward, having executed the order, I returned to the ridge and you had gone. I was told you had gone to the right. I started in pursuit; had not proceeded far when some of our men warned me that the rebels were in the direction I was going. I soon satisfied myself that such was the case, and returned again to the ridge. I there met General Beatty, who related similar experience in his endeavors to reach you.

I then reported to Major-General Thomas, with whom I served the balance of the day.

I have the honor to be, sir, very respectfully, your obedient servant,

G. M. L. JOHNSON,
Captain 2d Ind. Cav., and Insp. 2d Div., 14th A. C.

[Sub-Inclosure No. 3.]

CHATTANOOGA, TENN., *October 9, 1863.*

Maj. Gen. J. S. NEGLEY,
Comdg. Second Division, Fourteenth Army Corps:

GENERAL : Your ability to endure labor and exposure during the time of the late battle having been brought to question, you will please accept the following statement regarding the condition of your health from the 12th to the 22d of September, 1863:

On the evening of the 12th I prescribed for Maj. Gen. James S. Negley; also on the two days following, which days he was on duty; the 15th and 16th he was confined to his bed, having a severe attack of diarrhea. On the 17th the command moved, he riding his horse, with the precaution to have an ambulance near to use if necessary. He arrived at camp very much exhausted. The evening of the 18th the command moved; he was up and on duty most of the night. The 19th he was busy with the command all the day, it being engaged in battle at morning and evening. This night he was much worn down from exposure, want of sleep, rest, and sickness, and was obliged to get what rest he could that night to enable him to be on duty the day following; he slept in bivouac this night with the command. I think he had labored during the day and evening all that he was physically able to endure. He arose on the morning of the 20th feeling very unwell, but was on duty all the day until late at night. On the 21st and 22d he was on duty with the command, but not really able to be so. During the whole time he was really unable to be on duty, being a fitter case for a bed patient than one being under treatment and yet laboring.

I am, very respectfully, your obedient servant,

R. G. BOGUE,
Surg. 19th Ill. Inf., and Med. Director 2d Div., 14th A. C.

[Sub-Inclosure No. 4.]

HDQRS. SECOND DIVISION, FOURTEENTH ARMY CORPS,
Chattanooga, Tenn., October 9, 1863.

Major-General NEGLEY :

SIR : In compliance with your request, I have the honor to submit the following statement of facts relative to the movement of the ammunition train belonging to the Second Division, Fourteenth Army Corps:

On the 18th day of September my train was parked directly in rear of the division, which was in line near Owens' Ford. At 4 p. m. I received orders to move my train immediately to the rear of the division ambulance train; moved toward Crawfish Spring; was very much delayed by General Palmer's division; arrived at Spear's house and parked my train directly to the left of the house in rear of the Third Brigade of our division at about 10 p. m. Received orders from General Negley to see that all the regiments were supplied with 20 rounds of ammunition extra. I immediately did so, while the brigades were moving forward to a new position, which took the Third Brigade far to the right guarding a ford, First Brigade in the center, Second Brigade on the left, our whole line extending near 2 miles. General Brannan's division passed about the time the Third Brigade moved to the right.

General Reynolds' division passed shortly after, and at 7 a. m. the Third Brigade of Reynolds' division passed. General McCook's corps commenced passing about 9 a. m., Saturday, September 19, and had not all passed until after 2 p. m. My train was moved to the left one-half mile at 11 a. m., in rear of Crawfish Spring, at which place it remained until after 3 p. m., when I ordered it again on to the La Fayette and Chattanooga road.

Our division having been relieved by General Mitchell's corps of cavalry, I rode forward with the general (having left my train behind until all the division had passed) until he arrived at General McCook's headquarters. The division was then marching rapidly across the fields toward the left, when a staff officer ordered General Negley forward to General Thomas' assistance. General Negley then ordered me to bring the train forward as rapidly as possible. I did so, and parked my train near the headquarters of General McCook; reported to General Negley, who was then in position near Nethers' [Withers'] house.

He ordered me to send forward the section of Marshall's battery and one wing of the Seventy-fourth Ohio Volunteer Infantry, who were acting as rear or train guard, letting the train remain where it was until further orders. I did so, and soon received orders to move up and take position in rear of the division. Parked my train in rear of the division on either side of the La Fayette and Rossville road at 1 a. m., September 20. At 7 a. m. General Negley sent Lieutenant Ingraham, topographical engineer, with instructions to proceed with him to find a road in our rear across the ridge, so as to be able to move over the Valley road if we were hard pressed and the road we were then on should happen to be blocked up by the great number of trains. I went with Lieutenant Ingraham and found a pretty good road, but when I returned my train had been moved to a position in an open field, about 1 mile to the left and front of its former position. One of our brigades (the First) was far to the left fighting, the Second was moving under the direction of

General Negley toward the left, while the Third was still in position near Nethers' [Withers'] house. I received orders then from General Negley, through Captain Hough, to move forward with the division, which was moving toward the left.

I commenced the movement, when Captain Hough again brought orders for me to move the train into the woods to our left and rear; but owing to the unevenness of the ground I could not do so, but moved down the hill on to the road, as all the rest of the trains had done so and the enemy's shells were then falling near my train. After the last wagon had got into the woods the Third Brigade passed at the quick time. This was about quarter past 11 a. m. I parked my train then on the La Fayette and Rossville road, about a quarter of a mile from the gap, where the road takes a turn to the left going toward Chattanooga, and there waited orders. About half past 2 Lieutenant Cooke, aide-de-camp, brought orders to me from General Negley to move cautiously, as the enemy were marching toward our rear. I had seen this myself, and had already commenced to move the train toward the gap, so as to be able to place the ridge between my train and the enemy. But seeing the terror that seemed to prevail among the different trains, I sent part of the train through the gap in charge of my sergeant, with instructions to park it as soon as he had got to a convenient place on the left-hand side of the road, while I remained with the rest of the train (20 wagons) as near the troops as I could with safety to the train. I then turned the train around and went back toward the right, while the gap I had just left was choked up by vehicles of all descriptions, including wagons, ambulances, caissons, guns, besides couriers and stragglers. The enemy had moved to the ridge on which I had my train parked in the forenoon and in rear of the position our division had moved toward in the morning, and had planted a battery and were shelling the gap in which all the trains but mine were jammed up together. Heavy columns of the rebels then moved toward the right from our left (which led me to believe that they had broken through our left center) and in rear of our division. A section of a battery was in position on the ridge in rear of my train, supported by what I supposed to be organized troops.

Finding myself between our lines and the enemy's I concluded it was time to move. But how to do it ? The road toward Chattanooga was choked up, and no other way to move unless I could get over the ridge in our rear. I chose the latter, and commenced the movement. Thousands of stragglers passed us, but I could not prevail upon any of them to help my train up to the top of the ridge. I succeeded in getting them all up, however, excepting one wagon, although the enemy were shelling us all the time, and their skirmishers, commencing to advance across the fields, compelled me to abandon the wagon that stuck fast. The mules were taken off so the rebels would not remove the wagon, and if we were fortunate enough to regain the ground the wagon and its contents might be recovered. But I am sorry to say that the line of battle I spoke of as ours were not organized troops, and all ran away at the first fire of the enemy. I tried to rally some of the stragglers to support the two pieces that I supposed were still in position, but found that they had either been captured by the enemy or were far in the rear.

At this time I met some of General McCook's staff, and they informed me that the whole line was gone; i. e., that the right wing had been destroyed, and that there were no troops between my train and the enemy. I therefore deemed it advisable to fall back, and did so, toward Crawfish Spring and Chattanooga Valley road. I here met Lieutenant Ingraham, topographical engineer, who had explored all the roads around that vicinity, and under his guidance struck a cross-road leading to Cooper's Store on the La Fayette and Rossville road. I started on this road toward the La Fayette and Rossville road, but had not proceeded a mile ere I met a number of officers, who informed me that the enemy had possession of the road, and that I had better turn back before it was too late.

I sent forward an orderly to ascertain the truth of the assertion. He did not return, which led me to believe he was captured. I turned the train back and halted at Dyer's, about three-quarters of a mile from the Crawfish Spring and Chattanooga Valley road. I remained here until nearly all trains had passed me, hoping to receive some intelligence of the division, but none of a reliable character came. About 4.30 p. m. I was informed by Lieutenant Ingraham that Dr. Bogue, medical director, Second Division, brought an order from General McCook for all the trains, caissons, battery wagons, &c., to fall in and proceed to Chattanooga by the Crawfish Spring and Chattanooga Valley road, guarded by a brigade of cavalry, commanded by Colonel ——. My train arrived at Chattanooga Creek Bridge at 12 p. m., at which place I parked my train for the night, leaving early next morning, September 21. I learned that the division was at Rossville, and ordered the other part of my train that went by the La Fayette and Chattanooga road to join with the 19 wagons I had with me, and then, with the whole train, reported to Major-General Negley, at Rossville. Supplied the regiments and batteries with ammunition, and parked one-half mile in rear of the division, in accordance with instructions received from Major Lawrence, chief of artillery, Fourteenth Army Corps. At 2 p. m. moved about half a mile farther to the rear.

As the enemy's shells were occasionally dropping among the trains remained in this position only until dark, at which time I received orders from General Negley to fall back to Chattanooga and there park, which I did, between Market and Main streets, near the river, and at which place the train now is.

I have the honor, general, to be, yours, very truly,

J. R. HAYDEN,
Captain, and Ordnance Officer.

[Sub-Inclosure No. 5.]

HDQRS. SECOND DIVISION, FOURTEENTH ARMY CORPS,
Chattanooga, October 7, 1863.

Major-General NEGLEY:

GENERAL: In compliance with your request, I have the honor to make the following report of my duties as volunteer aide on your staff during the battles of Chickamauga:

I will preface by remarking that not expecting to make a report, I kept no account of time, and cannot definitely give you the hour of different occurrences.

Toward evening on Friday, the 18th of September, your command moved from Owens' Ford toward Crawfish Spring. When the head of the column reached General Hazen's headquarters, about one and a half miles from Crawfish Spring, it was halted, and you sent me forward to General Rosecrans' headquarters at Crawfish Spring to report and ascertain the position you were to take. General Rose-crans told me you were to relieve General Palmer, who was then present. He sent a staff officer with me to find the position of the different brigades.

They were so widely separated it was quite dark before I could report to you, Colonel Grose's brigade, which was to be relieved by your Second Brigade, being 1¼ miles directly to the front. You directed me to remain at Crawfish Spring and place the Third Brigade in the position occupied by General Cruft when it (the Third Brigade) came up, while the Second Brigade marched across to Colonel Grose, and the First Brigade would relieve General Hazen. After my waiting some hours you marched into Crawfish Spring with the whole division, and you informed me that General Hazen and Colonel Grose refused to be relieved, as they had no orders to that effect. After the command was fairly bivouacked you informed me you had again been ordered to relieve General Palmer, as they now had orders to be relieved. You sent me to conduct the First Brigade to Colonel Grose's position. The whole night was occupied with these movements, and the entire command was much fatigued and exhausted. Early the next morning, Saturday, the First Brigade was attacked fiercely by the enemy, and re-enforcements were sent to the assistance of the First from the Second. The enemy were repulsed, but the whole division was kept actively employed during the morning.

Early in the afternoon you were ordered by General McCook, under whose command you then were, to move to his support at once. The division was hastily withdrawn and moved at double-quick past Crawfish Spring to the position occupied by General McCook. At the moment of joining him a staff officer delivered to General McCook an order for you to move on to the support of General Thomas, on the left, as rapidly as possible. General McCook gave you the order and the column was moved on without halting. Upon arriving at General Rosecrans' headquarters, he personally pointed out the direction for you to find General Thomas, saying, "You will find the enemy right in there." You pushed on through the woods in the direction indicated, when, coming upon the brow of a hill with a cleared field on the front, to the right and rear of Nethers' [Withers'] house, you saw the enemy in force moving toward the hill from the woods in front. Nethers' [Withers'] house was occupied by them. You immediately took position on the hill to meet them and the enemy held back; you then directed me to report to General Rosecrans that you had not found General Thomas, but had met the enemy, and wished to know whether you should hold that position and move on them. He replied, "That is right; fight there, right there; push them hard." I delivered to you the message, when you ordered the Second and Third Brigades to move on the enemy, while the First was held in reserve on the hill and the artillery placed in battery near it. You directed me to go with the advancing columns and report if we found the enemy in force; we found only a heavy line of skirmishers in the woods, but, on pushing them rapidly back, found them in force in a cleared field beyond. After a sharp fight for half an hour we pushed them across the field, but having no support on either flank, halted, and I reported to you. It being then dark, you directed they should fall back into the woods and take position for the night. The movement was accomplished; the left resting on Brannan's division, and nothing joining us exactly on the right, but some mounted infantry—I think Wilder's—were moving around there.

The command retired for the night much wearied. Early in the morning you sent me with a message to Colonel Sirwell, commanding Third Brigade. Upon my return you informed me you had an order from General Thomas to move to the left to his support, and directed me to order the brigades to be in readiness to move at a moment's notice, as they would march as soon as relieved. I did so. Soon after you informed me you had orders to move immediately, and directed me to conduct the Third Brigade to the road in the rear of the position, leaving the skirmishers out as flankers, you sending Major Lowrie to the Second Brigade with the same orders, and an order to the reserve (First Brigade) to move at once across the fields, which latter was done. The Second and Third Brigades were very soon in column *en masse* on the road ready to march, when General Rosecrans and staff rode down the hill toward the column and asked what troops these were. I replied, "General Negley's division." He asked what they were doing there. I replied, "Going to join General Thomas." He asked if they had been relieved. I answered, "No." He then directed they resume the former position until relieved. I referred him to you and rode with him to you. He gave you the same order, adding that General Wood had been ordered to relieve you. After some time—near an hour, I should think—Captain Willard, of General Thomas' staff, rode up in haste and asked why the division had not joined General Thomas. I replied that the First Brigade had been gone some time, but that General Rosecrans had ordered that the other two brigades should not move until relieved. After getting the same answer from you, with the addition that you were anxious to get off, as you wished to keep your division together, Captain Willard then rode off to find General Rosecrans.

Immediately after this I saw troops moving on to the top of the hill where the reserve brigade had been posted. I rode up and ascertained it was Colonel Buell's brigade of General Wood's division. I asked Colonel Buell if he was ordered to relieve General Negley; he answered he was ordered to take this position. I referred him to you; he repeated that he was to take this position, and proceeded to occupy it, his line being fully one-quarter of a mile to the rear of yours. Some time having elapsed, Colonel Buell reported that he had orders to relieve you and proceeded to do so, moving down the hill slowly with skirmishers deployed. By the time you were relieved and on the march, the firing along the whole line was quite heavy, and shells were thrown into your column and over it, near to your ammunition train, which was moving along near the top of the ridge parallel to your column. You then directed me to order the train into the woods on the top of the ridge. On my return I found you had been moving the troops at double-quick, and I joined you near the wooded hill to the left of the open fields and to the right and rear of General Thomas. At this moment stragglers and wounded men were rushing to the rear across and through your column in great numbers. You moved on with the Second Brigade to place it in position, directing me to hurry up the Third Brigade, which had been stopped by an ammunition train crossing its route on the way to the rear. As quickly as possible it got up, when you informed me you had orders to take a position on the wooded hill and support the artillery there. Several batteries and parts of batteries having falling back to that point, you placed them in position (some six batteries) and supported them with the Third Brigade. They were not fairly in position when the enemy in large force appeared upon your left, making a fierce attack; the whole right of our army at this time appeared to be giving way, and the enemy were in the open fields you had just marched over. You held your position against the attack, but soon after you directed Lieutenant Moody and myself to go to General Rosecrans by different routes, describe your condition, and state that you could not hold your position unless re-enforced. We started, Lieutenant Moody taking the right of the ridge through the woods, and myself the left on the top of the ridge.

On my route I found our whole line on the right evidently giving way, but a number of guns were still in position on top of the ridge, near the left of your former position. On the top of the ridge I found General Rosecrans, with a few staff officers. I delivered your message, and he replied he had just sent you word that he could not help it. I hurried to rejoin you by the same route I had gone [come], but found myself cut off and the enemy in possession of the top of the ridge at a point a little to the right of the ravine at the foot of the wooded hill I left you upon. I was compelled to make a *détour* to the rear and pass through a fire from the enemy, aimed from the top of the ridge toward the trains, caissons, and stragglers that were rushing into the Dry Valley road. The firing produced a panic, and some of the wagons and a brass piece were abandoned there. Upon getting near the hill I met Lieutenant Moody, who informed me he had received the same message from General Rosecrans, and his horse being fresher than mine, he hastened to deliver it to you.

I here met hundreds of stragglers from the center rushing to the rear. I stopped a few moments to assist some officers in attempting to rally them, but without avail, and then hastened to join you, and found you had changed your position somewhat more to the right, and that a large column of the enemy were pushing up to the right of the hill, harassing the stragglers and threatening your artillery, which had but a slight support, and was being weakened by the constant stream of stragglers from the front passing through them. I found you had received the message from Lieutenant Moody. You immediately directed me to see what kind of ground there was in the rear for placing artillery. I did so, and upon my return I found your column in motion to the rear, all the artillery you had in charge, and three regiments of the Third Brigade (one, the Twenty-first Ohio, having been loaned to General Brannan), and what stragglers you had collected. You moved in order through the woods across to the Dry Valley road, which was found to be filled with the retreating troops from the right in great disorder. The only organized body I saw there was the Ninth Michigan, Colonel Parkhurst. You directed me to remain behind and push on the artillery, and you hastened on to find a point to rally the retreating column.

I joined you at a clearing in the road, and found you had placed your three regiments and the Ninth Michigan in line, stopping all persons except the wounded. You then directed me to report to General Jeff. C. Davis, who was organizing the straggling troops into battalions, while you made the attempt to join General Thomas. I remained on this duty until your return. Soon after, the whole column moved in good order to Rossville, and were placed in position there to resist an attack from the enemy if made. You immediately sent Lieutenant Moody to Chattanooga to bring out subsistence for them, and directed me to remain on duty, stopping other troops as they came in and putting them in position.

I remained on that duty until late in the evening, when I reported to you that the number of stragglers and disorganized bodies coming in was so great, and that they were throwing themselves among the troops in such masses, that I feared the command could not act with efficiency if attacked. Upon a personal examination, you directed me to report to General Rosecrans at Chattanooga, giving him a statement of affairs in detail, and ask for advice. I did so, and returned with orders from him that you send in to Chattanooga all disorganized troops and wounded; that you keep your organized troops well in position, and hold the gap with your command at all hazards; that General Thomas would soon be with you, if not already there; that he had ordered Generals McCook and Crittenden out there, and that he would fight them at the gaps. You then dismissed me for the night, it being about 2.30 a. m.

Early next morning General Rousseau arrived at your headquarters and asked you for my services during the day. I remained with him until evening, when I rejoined you and was upon duty on the march to Chattanooga that night.

I am, general, very truly, your obedient servant,

ALFRED L. HOUGH,
Captain 19th U. S. Infantry, A. C. M., Second Division,
14th Army Corps, and Vol. Aide-de-Camp.

[Sub-Inclosure No. 6.]

HDQRS. SECOND DIVISION, FOURTEENTH ARMY CORPS,
Chattanooga, Tenn., October 7, 1863.

Major-General NEGLEY:

SIR: I respectfully make the following statement of facts which occurred during the battle of Chickamauga Creek, which you are at liberty to use as you see proper:

About half-past 9 a. m. I carried an order to General Negley from General Thomas urging him to move to the left immediately. I met Major Lowrie, and told him what was wanted. He replied that one brigade had been sent and that the other two had not been relieved. I went back and reported this to General Thomas. I was then sent to General Rosecrans with information that the enemy were pressing the left of General Thomas very hard, and asked for more troops. General Rosecrans said that General Negley had been sent and ought to be there by this time. I told him I had just seen Major Lowrie, who told me that General Negley's troops were not relieved yet. General Rosecrans was surprised at this, and said that General Wood had been ordered to relieve them, and seemed sure that they must have been relieved.

I reported this to General Thomas and was again sent to General Rosecrans with a message. On my way I met General Negley in the rear of one or two brigades which were marching in double-quick time toward General Thomas. This was near 10 a. m. I told him what General Thomas wished. He replied those were his troops going as quickly as possible. He seemed to be doing something with artillery at that time.

About half hour later I was again sent to General Rosecrans, but failed to find him. As I was looking for him I crossed the field to the left of the road leading from Crawfish Spring, in which a large number of ammunition wagons had been parked. When I was nearly across the field I discovered a line of rebel skirmishers between me and the rear of General Reynolds' division, who opened a brisk fire on me.

I retreated toward the high ground in rear of this field to a battery which was in position there, which immediately afterward limbered up and retreated to the road leading toward Rossville.

When I saw these skirmishers they were moving up the ravine between the place where I had last seen General Negley and the ground occupied by General Thomas' forces, and in a few minutes after the rebels had possession of that position with some artillery, with which they fired on the retreating wagons and artillery. As I passed over the top of the ridge my horse received a musket shot in the neck.

I am, general, very respectfully, your obedient servant,

J. D. BARKER,
Captain First Ohio Cav., Comdg. Escort to Maj. Gen. Thomas.

[Sub-Inclosure No. 7.]

HDQRS. BRIDGES' BATTERY, ILLINOIS LIGHT ARTILLERY,
Camp at Chattanooga, Tenn., October 8, 1863.

Maj. JAMES A. LOWRIE,
Chief of Staff, Major-General Negley:

MAJOR: In accordance with the request of Major-General Negley to furnish any information of the position of our division and that of the enemy which came under my own observation, on Sunday, September 20, I have the honor to report:

That about 7 a. m. of that date General Beatty ordered me to move my battery with his brigade, which moved some 2 miles to the left and front of the position occupied during the night.

Arriving upon the line of battle my battery was posted upon either side of the road leading to Rossville and Ringgold. Soon afterward, by General Beatty's order, I moved forward some 200 yards, leaving a half battery in position at that place, which overlooked a small open field.

I took a half battery and moved it forward to a small house some 300 yards to the front and left, by order of Brigadier-General Beatty. Our brigade (Brigadier-General Beatty's), being ordered to hold the hill to the left of General Baird's division, was necessarily extended, and consequently when General Beatty saw a heavy force of the enemy massed and advancing upon him, he ordered me to retire the half battery, then in an open field without infantry support, to the edge of the woods upon my right, he expecting that his infantry would fall back over the ground they advanced over to the support of my guns.

But the force of the enemy being so much larger than ours, and there being no support, our infantry did not retire to my battery.

As soon as General Beatty saw the battle-flags of the enemy he ordered me to fire. I opened fire first with case shot, then with canister. General Beatty seeing a column of the enemy advancing through a dense woods upon my right flank, as well as the one in our immediate front, rode up and ordered me to retire the battery at once.

The enemy, seeing an order given and an attempt to retire, charged and captured two of my guns.

During this engagement and during this charge the enemy killed my senior first lieutenant, William Bishop, and 3 men, wounded 7, and disabled 34 of my horses.

Upon retiring to the first available position, Lieutenant Temple reported to General Negley, who was then present, and by General Negley's order the battery was placed in position upon the east side of a thinly wooded ridge.

After retiring my battery from the position where the enemy charged upon my guns, I went to General Beatty, who had rallied the Fifteenth Kentucky and One hundred and fourth Illinois Infantry of his brigade, and asked him to allow these regiments to charge and recover my guns.

He ordered the skirmishers forward, who, after advancing 100 yards, met the enemy advancing in force. General Beatty informed me that it was impossible to recover my guns at that time. I then asked him for a detail of infantry to remove four guns which had been abandoned by the batteries upon our right. He ordered 30 men, in charge of Captain Allen, from the Fifteenth Kentucky Infantry, with which detail they were removed from the field.

By General Negley's order I moved the battery to the left of the same ridge, taking position upon either side of two small buildings, opening fire upon the enemy, who were then entering a corn-field from the Ringgold road.

After remaining in this position some half an hour, by your order I moved to the right and rear, occupying a small hill directly in front of the corn-field, which extended from the front of the hill half a mile to the right. The musketry firing was continuous. When I moved into position our lines were steadily giving back. While I was ascertaining the exact position of our lines, so as not to fire upon our own men, a colonel of a Kansas regiment of the Twentieth Army Corps came dashing up to me and asked me who commanded that battery. I informed him that I did. He ordered me for "God's sake" to fire into the crest of the hill in our front, informing me that his men had been driven off the hill, and that there was none but rebels there then, stating that they would be up to me in five minutes. I opened with canister upon them; they ceased fire in a few moments.

During this time all the infantry and artillery had fallen back to a long ridge, some 400 yards in our right and rear. Being notified that there was no infantry support in that vicinity, and ordered by an aide of General Negley's that, if I had no support, to fall back, I retired to the ridge, then occupied by two batteries and some 200 infantry.

Before arriving there the enemy had gained the hill I had just removed from and opened fire with artillery and musketry. The infantry did not have a field-officer, and seemed to be the remnants of many regiments. As soon as the enemy's shell fell near them, they limbered to the rear; when I arrived upon their line I gave the order "Action rear;" at the same time, their infantry support having left them, the officers in command of the other batteries there gave the command "Retire."

Immediately afterward I received orders from General Negley to move to the Rossville or Chattanooga road without delay.

Upon arriving at the Rossville road, I met General Negley returning to the field, and received orders from him to report my battery to Brigadier-General Davis, who was in command of the forces then forming upon the right of the road.

At 5 p. m. I received orders from General Negley to march to Rossville, Ga.

I am, major, very respectfully, your obedient servant,

LYMAN BRIDGES,
Captain, Commanding.

[Sub-Inclosure No. 8.]

HDQRS. SECOND DIVISION, FOURTEENTH ARMY CORPS,
Chattanooga, Tenn., October 9, 1863.

Maj. Gen. J. S. NEGLEY,
Comdg. Second Division, Fourteenth Army Corps:

GENERAL: In compliance with your request, I herewith respectfully submit the following statement of what I know concerning the operations of the artillery of the Second Division, and of other divisions, on the 20th ultimo:

When the action of that day commenced, Captain Bridges' battery, of General Beatty's brigade, of which I am an officer, was in battery on the Rossville and Chattanooga road at the extreme left of the Fourteenth Army Corps. General Beatty's line had a short time previously been advanced from the position first occupied and very much extended to the left.

About 9 a. m. the enemy in strong force pressed through the center of our brigade line, cutting off two (possibly three) regiments from the rest, with the evident intention of capturing them. As soon as the enemy appeared in sight Bridges' Battery, with case shot and afterward with canister, opened a galling fire upon them, diverting their attention from the regiments which had been separated from us, and drawing their fire upon the battery and the infantry upon our right. The conflict here was short but sanguinary. The enemy had massed his forces upon this point, and the thin line of the First Brigade, covering a front that a division could hardly have held, was rent and soon overwhelmed. The infantry which had been posted upon the left of the battery could give it no support and that upon its right had fallen back, contesting the ground inch by inch.

The enemy, observing this, made a desperate effort to capture the battery, but before he could accomplish his purpose General Beatty ordered the battery to fall back. At this moment our senior first lieutenant and 4 or 5 of the men were killed, and many others placed *hors du combat.* The horses of one of the pieces were all killed and it was therefore abandoned. Of another, but 2 cannoneers were left uninjured, and before they could limber it up, the piece was in the hands of the enemy. After the remaining guns and caissons had fallen back through the woods and brush 200 or 300 yards, finding myself the senior officer present, I retired with the four guns and went into battery upon a high, wooded hill to the rear of our position in the morning.

While retiring, the woods through which I passed and the open fields to the right were filled with terror-stricken fugitives, whom no commands or appeals could halt, much less reform, as the fruitless efforts of mounted officers, with sword in hand, ordering, entreating, begging, too plainly proved. A few guns and caissons of other batteries, which I think at the beginning of the fight were on our right, preceded me up the hill. While going into battery as stated above, I met Captain Johnson, of your staff, who told me that General Negley was forming a new line upon the hill and that I had better report to him. After learning from the captain where the general was, I proceeded as rapidly as possible and reported. The general ordered me into position upon commanding ground (the crest of the hill) to the left of the position which I had selected. Here I found Captain Schultz's battery, which I had not seen since daylight. Captain Marshall's battery was in position upon high ground to our right. I understand that these last-named batteries, with their respective brigades, the Second and Third, of the Second Division, had been engaged at the commencement of the action about 3 miles to the right of ours (the First Brigade), and that afterward they were ordered to support the left.

While in position upon the hill referred to, and also when afterward I was, by your order, in position on the hillside farther to the right and front, the musketry firing in our immediate front was at intervals desperate. While in the position last mentioned, Captain Bridges came up the hillside from the front with a detail of infantry hauling four pieces of artillery, which had been abandoned by other batteries, by hand from the field. He immediately resumed command of the battery, and under orders from General Negley moved to the left, taking position at a log house on the hillside used as a hospital.

Large columns of dust being discovered in the woods and fields to our left and front, General Negley ordered Captain Bridges to open, and at the same time Captain Schultz opened from the crest of the hill, firing over our heads. All this time there was heavy musketry firing in the woods to our front, which were so dense that it was impossible to see the enemy, and to have fired from our position would have been hazardous, imperiling the lives of our own men. After checking the columns of the enemy which appeared to be moving upon our left, the batteries were ordered to fall back a short distance and take position for firing to the right, as the enemy was making an effort to get in rear of the artillery in position on the hill by means of a ravine or gully which separated the point which we held from another to the south of us. At this moment Colonel ———, of the Twentieth Army Corps, rode up and in a very excited manner urged Captain Bridges to fire, saying that the ravine was full of rebels, and that our men were all falling back, or words of like import. The captain accordingly opened with canister.

We soon found that the infantry was retiring upon both our right and left, leaving the battery without support, while the musketry fire of the enemy was increasing and one of his batteries opened with shell. One of General Negley's staff rode up and told Captain Bridges to fall back with the infantry. He accordingly retired about 300 yards, and remained there until ordered to fall back to the Chattanooga road. I have been informed by different persons that the enemy occupied the hill a few moments after we retired therefrom. During the time we were on the hill I saw but little infantry. Stragglers from the front were almost constantly coming back. Many of these were reformed by General Negley and staff and other officers. Nearly all divisions of the army seemed to be represented in the lines thus formed.

In my humble opinion the hill, which was very rugged and thickly wooded, was very inconvenient for artillery maneuvers. While changing position I saw a line of caisson bodies which had been un-limbered and apparently abandoned. Lieutenant Seeborn, of Bridges' Battery, informs me that he saw them while being unlimbered, and states that the battery to which they belonged immediately after fell back to the Chattanooga road, thereby unnecessarily abandoning them. This occurred nearly an hour previous to our retiring to the Chattanooga road. We followed this road to within 2 miles of Ross-ville, where the first open fields were discovered. General Negley here ordered the captain to immediately prepare his battery to return to the front. Afterward the general ordered the captain to report to General Davis, who would superintend the reorganization of the troops, while he (General Negley) returned to the front. About 5 p. m. Captain Bridges was ordered by General Negley to move out to the road. All supposed that we were about to return to the field, but upon reaching the road the column turned in the direction of Rossville, at which place we arrived about 6 p. m.

I have the honor to be, very respectfully, your obedient servant,

MORRIS D. TEMPLE,
Lieutenant Bridges' Battery, I. V. A., and A. A. D. C.

[Sub-Inclosure No. 9.]

HDQRS. 14TH ARMY CORPS, DEPT. OF THE CUMBERLAND,
Chattanooga, October 9, 1863.

Major-General NEGLEY,
   Comdg. Second Divison, Fourteenth Army Corps:

GENERAL : The following is a correct statement of facts which occurred within my own knowledge in connection with the move-ments of your division at the battle of Chickamauga on Sunday, September 20, 1863:

About 7 a. m. I carried a verbal order from Major-General Thomas to Major-General Negley directing him to move his division to his (General Thomas') left without delay.

The order was sent by General N[egley] to his brigade commanders to prepare to move at once, which fact I reported to General Thomas, who ordered me to return and conduct General Negley with his di-vision.

Just as I was starting General Rosecrans rode up to General Thomas' headquarters. In returning I rode along the line. When I arrived at General Negley's headquarters I found General Rosecrans there, who ordered General N[egley] not to withdraw his division until he was relieved by a division of General Crittenden's corps. General R[osecrans] directed me to conduct General Beatty's brigade (then in reserve) to General Thomas and report that the other bri-gades would be sent as soon as relieved. This I did, when General Thomas ordered [me] to return and conduct the balance of the division.

When I reached the ridge on which the headquarters of General Negley had been, I found General Wood (commanding First Divis-ion, Twenty-first Army Corps) with his division. I asked him if "he had been ordered to relieve the division of General Negley?" His reply was, "I am ordered to post my troops on this ridge." "Sir," I answered, "General Rosecrans promised to send one of the divisions of General Crittenden's corps to relieve General Negley that he might go to the relief of General Thomas' left." His reply was the same as before. I went directly to General Rosecrans and reported the facts as above stated. He sent his aide, Captain Thoms, to order General Wood to relieve General Negley at once. In returning I met Captain Thoms, who told me he had delivered the order, and that General Negley would be relieved at once (by taking the wrong road I was delayed half an hour). On my return to General Negley, he informed me General Wood's troops had just gone to the front, but the brigades were not large enough to fill the space. I requested General Negley to send the brigade that had been relieved and follow with the other as soon as possible, and told him I would go to General Crittenden to get more troops. On my reporting the facts as above stated to General C[rittenden] his reply was, "I have no more troops there, and shall be obliged to send troops back if I fill the space." My reply was, "General Thomas needs General Negley's troops very much." I started to report the facts to General Rosecrans (Colonel Starling, General Crittenden's chief of staff, reached him first); when I did so, he said it had been arranged, and General Negley would be relieved at once, which fact I reported to General Thomas. The time occupied in accomplishing what I had [done] was nearly three hours.

I next met General Negley while carrying an order from General Thomas. He was coming up to the left with artillery, which he said he should post on the ridge.

On my return the artillery was in position and operation.

I am, very respectfully, your obedient servant,

J. P. WILLARD,
Captain, and Aide-de-Camp.

[Sub-Inclosure No. 10.]

HDQRS. SECOND DIVISION, FOURTEENTH ARMY CORPS,
Chattanooga, October 8, 1863.

[General J. S. NEGLEY :]

GENERAL : In compliance to your request to make a statement as to what I know in relation to the battle of Chickamauga, I respectfully say that on Thursday, September 17, at 8 a. m., we marched to Owens' Ford (having been relieved, as I understood at the time, by General Sheridan's division), arriving there after dark of same day.

Friday, September 18, you were ordered to move to the left to relieve General Palmer's division, which you did, arriving at General Hazen's headquarters at 5 p. m., General Hazen refusing to be relieved (as I afterward understood), stating that he had received no orders to move. After considerable trouble, and working all night, you managed to get your men into position by daylight next morning, Colonel Sirwell on the right, General Beatty in the center, and Colonel Stanley on the left, the left resting at Crawfish Spring.

The division remained in this position until about 3 p. m., Saturday, 19th, when we were the right of the whole army (the cavalry excepted), General McCook's corps having passed to the left of Crawfish Spring at about 3 p. m. You ordered the division to march to the left and rear of McCook's corps, you reporting to General McCook as we passed along the road (General McCook's headquarters being about half way between Crawfish Spring and General Rosecrans' headquarters). I heard General McCook tell you to move rapidly, as he supposed you were badly needed to support the left. You answered, "General, my First Brigade is here, and the remainder is coming forward as rapidly as possible," or words to that effect. You then moved forward to General Rosecrans' headquarters, and formed your division about one-half mile to the left of it, closing up a space that had been left open, getting there in time to repulse the enemy, who had discovered the gap and was trying to press through it in heavy columns to attack General Thomas on the right and rear. We fought them until after dark, driving them nearly one-half mile, and held that position during the night. About 8 a. m. on Sunday I was ordered by you to find out where General Thomas' headquarters were, and form a courier line from you to General Thomas.

I found General Thomas nearly 2 miles to our left, on La Fayette road; reported to him, and received a verbal order from him to you telling you to move immediately to the left and support of General Baird. On my return to you I reported and found that you had received the same order through some one else, and had made preparations to withdraw your men as soon as General Wood would relieve you. You, however, sent General Beatty's brigade at once, they having been in reserve; the enemy during this time were pressing on our front.

At about 9 a. m. General Wood, with one brigade, came up and deployed his men as skirmishers in our rear, then moved forward and relieved one brigade (Colonel Stanley's), Colonel Sirwell remaining to keep the gap closed up.

You then moved to the left as fast as possible with Colonel Stanley's brigade, it being the only one left you, thus separating the whole command. At about half past 1 p. m. the enemy were found to be pressing in on our left, and seemed as though they were between us and General Thomas.

You immediately sent Colonel Sirwell's brigade (they having come up from the right) to stop their farther progress, at the same time getting several batteries in position on the ridge and opening a fire that soon drove the enemy back. At this juncture I learned that the enemy were on our right, pressing our front with overwhelming numbers, and that nothing could be found of the right wing, it having retired from the field.

You then held your position until all the artillery and trains had passed through the gap, being careful to avoid any confusion; then gradually retired to end of gap next Rossville, where you halted and rallied all the infantry, getting them in position for the night; also parked all the artillery together, so that the infantry and artillery could be run out to any line that might be formed.

During the night and next morning you had provisions and ammunition brought forward from Chattanooga to supply the deficiencies of the army, and did everything in your power to reassure the men and make them comfortable.

On the morning of the 21st our division occupied the gap and mountain to the left of the gap, while the other troops were formed into line to the right and left of our position, you sending the different batteries and regiments to their respective divisions, getting all *matériel* of war in proper position before noon.

With this statement, general, I remain, truly, your obedient servant,

CHAS. C. COOKE,
Lieutenant, and Aide-de-Camp.

[Sub-Inclosure No. 11.]

HDQRS. SECOND DIVISION, FOURTEENTH ARMY CORPS,
Camp at Chattanooga, Tenn., October —, 1863.

Major-General NEGLEY,
Comdg. Second Division, Fourteenth Army Corps:

SIR: In compliance with your request, I submit the following statement of facts relative to the position and movements of the Second Division, Fourteenth Army Corps, from September 18, 1863, to September 21, 1863:

Friday, September 18, 3 p. m., division encamped along Chickamauga Creek, the right resting at Owens' Ford, the left retired.

At 3 p. m. I carried an order from you to the brigade commanders to march immediately in the following order: Second, Third, and First Brigades.

Captain Johnson and I were sent ahead of the column to make inquiries relative to Gordon's Mills and the fords of Chickamauga Creek.

I learned that our division was ordered to relieve General Palmer's division, and about 5 p. m. our Second Brigade halted at or near the headquarters of General Hazen, commanding a brigade in Palmer's division. After a consultation with General Hazen, you gave Major Welch and myself orders to examine the configuration of the country in front and rear of Hazen's brigade, our proposed position, you immediately starting for department headquarters.

Our division now lay upon the road, our right resting at Hazen's headquarters. While examining the country in front I met Captain Johnson, inspector Second Division, Fourteenth Army Corps, engaged in stationing a line of skirmishers to protect our troops until Palmer's division should give place to us. At 7 p. m. I went forward (to the left) to report that our division train had joined the division and were awaiting orders. I passed our First (Beatty's) Brigade moving down the Culp's Mill road to relieve Colonel Grose's brigade, of Palmer's division. This was about 7.30 p. m.

Having occasion to report to you, and learning that you were on the Culp's Mill road, Major Lowrie and I started in search. We found our First Brigade lying upon the road waiting to relieve Colonel Grose, who stated he had received no orders relative to our relieving his brigade. This was about 9 p. m.

By this time the remainder of the division (Second, Fourteenth Army Corps) had been brought forward pursuant to an order to encamp the division *en masse*, the Second Brigade (Stanley) on the left near Crawfish Spring; the First Brigade (Beatty) on the right on Culp's Mill road, and the Third Brigade (Sirwell) in reserve near Spears' house.

Midnight you ordered the Third Brigade to move back and comply with the original order, "Relieve Hazen's brigade, Palmer's division." This was almost impossible, since the road was at the time occupied by Sheridan's and Palmer's divisions moving to the left, so that the way was blocked up with men and wagons. I came on duty at 3 a. m., September 19. I carried an order to Colonel Sirwell (Third Brigade) about daylight on Saturday, September 19, 1863, and found that he had just gotten a portion of his command into position, and still had some dispositions to make. So obstructed was the road that I could scarcely get along at all on account of men lying asleep in the road, and wagons blocking up the way almost effectually. I learned from an officer of Sirwell's brigade that a gap existed between the picket line of the Third and First Brigades. You sent me to communicate the fact to General Beatty, also to Colonel Sirwell. General Beatty remarked that "our line was so long that he had not a sufficient number of men to make the line continuous." You ordered me to tell Colonel Sirwell to close up the gap immediately, which he did, although his line was already attenuated.

September 19, 3 p. m., you discovered a very heavy column of dust moving toward your front and at no great distance. You sent me immediately to General McCook (then in command), to inform him of the fact. McCook said he had observed the dust, and had just sent written instructions to General Negley. He (McCook) asked me how many rounds of cartridges the men of our division had. I replied that you ordered an extra issue of 20 rounds to the men last night.

By this time Colonel Stanley had been put in position at the large brick house near Crawfish Spring. Major Lowrie had ordered General Beatty to withdraw to Crawfish Spring, and, a portion of the command having arrived, you ordered them into position near the spring to support Bridges' Battery.

You now sent me to repeat the order just carried by Major Lowrie to General Beatty, viz, "To withdraw his troops and fall back to Crawfish Spring with all possible haste." We were now upon the extreme right, in fact, almost isolated, no other troops nearer than those upon the hill (to the left), under command of General McCook.

Orders having been received to move to the left, I was sent to report your Second Brigade to McCook, he assigning the brigade a position upon Wood's left. He, McCook, told me that our Third Brigade would take position upon the hill near his, McC[ook]'s, headquarters, and the First Brigade would be held in reserve. I met you going to McCook's headquarters, I being stationed at a point where I could direct the brigades as they came forward into their several positions. Beatty's (First) brigade was compelled to halt at the spring for a short time to obtain ammunition for the battery, which had been engaged all morning with the enemy.

Major Lowrie and I came forward with Beatty's brigade, but found that the lines had advanced. The brigade moved forward, and we were soon after met by Lieutenant Kennedy bearing an order from you to push forward the brigade as quickly as possibly. Captain Johnson met us near General Rosecrans' headquarters and guided us to the division.

5 p. m. found the division formed near and to the left of department headquarters.

You reported to General Rosecrans a gap in the lines through which the enemy were moving, endangering General Thomas' right flank. General Rosecrans ordered you to close the gap.

I was sent to guide Colonel Sirwell's brigade to an eminence to the left of the La Fayette and Rossville road, from which point our movements emanated. After placing Marshall's and Schultz's batteries in position upon the ridge, the Second Brigade was thrown forward about a quarter of a mile, when the Third Brigade was placed upon the right and the two brigades advanced in two lines. They soon engaged the enemy, and for a while the firing was quite heavy.

You then sent by me an order for the two brigades to push the enemy vigorously. You at the same time ordered Captain Schultz to push forward three of his pieces to the edge of the woods in case they should be needed.

Our lines advanced, although it was now dark. The firing continued, and the enemy, after a strong resistance, were compelled to fall back across an open field, by which we were enabled to advance our line about three-quarters of a mile. After reporting to you the nature of the country in front, I carried an order to Colonels Sirwell and Stanley to halt their line and open communication with the right and left, informing them also that Schultz's three pieces were subject to their orders, if they could use artillery to any purpose.

September 20, 3 a. m., I went on duty at this time. I was sent to the front to caution the brigade commanders about having their men on the alert. I learned from the skirmish line that a movement of troops and artillery to the right could be heard between 1 and 2 a. m., also the cutting of roads (seemingly) could be heard. Upon communicating this to you I was sent to report it at department headquarters, and from there I was sent to General Thomas, in order to give him the information. I received no special instructions in return.

At 7.45 a. m. information received that the enemy are massing heavily in our front. You sent me to state to General McCook that "our line being very long and large bodies of troops being removed from our left, we were left with a very weak line, while the enemy was massing in our front." General Rosecrans, standing near to General McCook when I reported, asked me to repeat my message. General Rosecrans said, "Go to General Crittenden and tell him I say to make that line strong and good," at the same time inquiring "if Wood had not gone to our assistance." I answered that "I knew nothing of General Wood." I found General Crittenden and gave him the message from General R[osecrans]. I asked General Crittenden if he understood my directions. He answered he did.

Upon reporting to you I learned that Wood's division was to relieve us.

At 9 a. m. a brigade of Wood's division now made its appearance over the top of the ridge. They advanced very leisurely across the open field, having skirmishers deployed. I was sent to the Third Brigade to instruct Colonel Sirwell "to hold his troops in readiness to move to the left (on a road running parallel to his line of battle) as soon as relieved by Wood's troops." I remained at headquarters for an hour, during which time you were directing the movement of the troops in person.

At 10 a. m. the staff received an order to report to you near the Brannan Hospital. Here we found the Second Brigade in position, together with the artillery of the Second and Third Brigades. By this time the battle had commenced, and soon raged fearfully to our left and front. I now received an order to move all the artillery to the left across the road into the large open field.

I was now sent to order Colonel Sirwell to move to the left at a "double quick," and to march to the ridge to the left of the field. Colonel Sirwell had been but partially relieved. By the time the brigade came up it was ordered to support Schultz's, Marshall's, and one section of the Fourth (regular) Battery.

I was sent to place Marshall's battery in position upon the outer crest of the ridge, the Fourth Regular to the left of Marshall's, and

Bridges' still more to the left and in the yard of the house used as a hospital.

I was sent to bring forward Sirwell's brigade, which was placed in position to support the batteries. Schultz's battery was placed to the rear of Marshall's, upon a commanding point.

The enemy having pressed the first line of troops back some distance, and the enemy being reported advancing from the extreme left, you sent me to withdraw Sirwell's brigade and post it on the top of the ridge. You now discovered the enemy moving upon our left through a corn-field in heavy columns. It was evident to all that they were throwing a heavy force in this direction.

1.30 p. m. Captain Hough and I were now sent to communicate with General Rosecrans and ask for re-enforcements. Captain Hough took the left of the ridge and I the right. On my way I met hundreds of men going to the rear, and the farther I went to the right the more stragglers I met. The woods were literally filled with disorganized bodies of troops. The enemy's shot and shell were coming thick and fast, their infantry rushing forward with yell after yell. Across the open field I could see General Rosecrans, alone, his staff and escort, with drawn sabers, endeavoring to check the avalanche of panic-stricken men that were fleeing before the desperate onset of the enemy. It was plainly to be seen that the right had given way. I reported to General Rosecrans your situation, the appearance of the enemy on your left in heavy force. He replied, "I can't help him; it is too late." I now attempted to return, but the close proximity of the enemy compelled me to make a *détour*, striking the road and coming around behind the ridges, the right and center being driven back; the enemy were now in possession of the route by which I had come. Everywhere I saw officers endeavoring to stop the continual flow of men to the rear. I at last met Captain Hough, and inquired for you, and asked whether you were still in the same position. He replied that you were. I found you to the right of the ridge, where you had gone to give directions to a battery that was at the time playing upon the enemy. I was perfectly surprised to find the command in the same position, for the enemy were pressing upon the right and training their batteries up the gorges. You now withdrew all the batteries except Schultz's, and put them in position farther back upon the ridge. Schultz's remained on the brow of the ridge, firing continually, and supported by the Thirty-seventh Indiana.

Here you formed your troops, joined upon the left by a regiment of stragglers that had been collected from the miscellaneous mass; but the stragglers coming back panic-stricken, and by this time a battery brought to bear upon the ridge, the regiment of stragglers vanished. You then, after strenuous efforts to collect a sufficient number of troops to protect the artillery, remarked that to save the army from rout there must be a new line formed. A staff officer that had reported to you for duty informed you that the provost guard of the corps was stopping all stragglers, and forming a new line near the Chattanooga road. The enemy were now pressing forward upon the right and front of the ridge. Schultz was ordered back, and with great difficulty brought his battery back. The command, composed of the Seventy-eighth Pennsylvania, Thirty-seventh Indiana, and a portion of the Seventy-fourth Ohio, moved back toward the Chattanooga road. I was left behind to direct the movements of some caissons that had started down the Dug Valley road.

At 4 p. m., when I reached the Chattanooga road, I found Davis' division moving on the road toward Chattanooga. I joined you at the large field where you were engaged in organizing the troops and placing them in a defensible position. When you left to report to General Thomas, I reported for duty to General Davis, who carried out your plan of halting every man and placing him where he could be of service. General Sheridan and his division now made their appearance. After a consultation you ordered me to have the batteries ready to move to Rossville. The troops were soon on the march, arriving at Rossville about 5 p. m. Here the troops were put into position. I was assigned the duty of forming companies from the masses of detached men. About dark you ordered me to go to Chattanooga to procure provisions for the troops at all hazards, to stop the first train I met and get provisions. I was compelled to go to Chattanooga and there procure five wagons of provisions, which with our division train arrived at Rossville about 1 a. m.

Monday, September 21, 1863, the provisions were issued to all the troops at Rossville, which embraced some from every corps of the army.

I am, general, very respectfully, your obedient servant,

WM. H. H. MOODY,
Lieutenant, and Aide-de-Camp.

ADDENDA.

WASHINGTON CITY, *October* 29, 1863.
Hon. E. M. STANTON, *Secretary of War:*

DEAR SIR: The official action of General Rosecrans toward me in breaking up my division, assigning it to others, and even detaching a portion of my regular staff, when I was not relieved of command, or conscious of having merited this unusual procedure, is so painfully humiliating to my feelings that I shall esteem it a favor if you permit me to inform General Thomas that it is your desire that I should return to his command for duty, or a note from you to that effect.

Yours, very truly,

JAS. S. NEGLEY,
Major-General.

—

CINCINNATI, OHIO, *January* 11, 1864.
Maj. Gen. GEORGE H. THOMAS:

SIR: I have the honor to submit to your kind attention this communication, respectfully requesting such official action as the interests of the service and my rank and services entitle me to.

I visited Washington in October; had a personal interview with the Secretary of War relative to the causes which induced General Rosecrans to deprive me of a command.

I requested a Court of Inquiry, both personally and by letter (see copy annexed, marked A). Hon. J. K. Morehead also applied in my behalf.

The Secretary of War gave my request very kind consideration, informing me that he had not examined the official reports to determine from them whether a Court of Inquiry was necessary in my case.

Mr. Stanton directed me (verbally) to return to your command upon the expiration of my leave. I requested a written order to do so. This he stated was not required, as I was then absent with leave.

I reported to you by telegraph from Pittsburgh, and received in reply your order (see copy, B) "to return upon the expiration of my leave."

When I arrived at Nashville I received your telegram (see copy, C). I replied, stating that I had applied for a court of inquiry to the Secretary of War. On December 1 I addressed another letter to Mr. Stanton renewing my request. I have received no reply to either of [these] communications.

December 22 I received Special Orders, No. 26 (see copy marked D), which I returned with the information that I had applied for a Court of Inquiry. The language of the order was changed in that particular.

In reply to my letter from Cincinnati I received the communication (marked E) from the Adjutant-General's Office. The information that I belong to your command will, I hope, explain the occasion of this letter and appeal to your sense of justice.

The inference to be drawn from General Grant's Order, No. 26, and the semi-official reports which have reached my ears, intimate a reflection upon my self-respect and a want of proper regard for my military reputation. In view of the truth, this reflection does me great injustice.

Having presented my request to the Secretary of War with a clear understanding, it would certainly have been indelicate for me to exhibit any impatience respecting his decision until a reasonable time had elapsed.

The proceedings in this matter from the commencement have been painfully embarrassing to me.

I have not been furnished with a copy of the reflections made in the official reports referred to by General Rosecrans, to me, only verbally. I do not even know the precise language used.

These reflections appear to be gratuitous productions from officers my inferiors in rank (forming no portion of my command), with reference to circumstances which strongly indicate a desire to thus apologize for the conduct of themselves and their own troops.

At the same time the written statements of a greater number of equally reliable officers, who were personally observant and conversant with the facts, do not attach any blame to my official conduct.

Contemplating these facts, I feel at liberty to respectfully insist upon an early opportunity to vindicate my military reputation by a Court of Inquiry, an examination, and decision from the official reports now on file, or by assigning me to active duty.

I sincerely trust you may concur in my opinion, and if it is beyond your jurisdiction to grant my request, that you will immediately forward this paper to the President, with such indorsement as you may see proper to make upon it.

Soliciting a reply, at your convenience, informing me of the result of your conclusions, with considerations of personal respect, yours, very truly,

JAS. S. NEGLEY.

[Inclosure A.]

WASHINGTON, D. C., *October* 30, 1863.

Hon. E. M. STANTON, *Secretary of War:*

DEAR SIR: I am unofficially* informed that reflections have been expressed in certain official reports of the battle of Chickamauga

---

*Original in War Department does not contain the word "unofficially."

which may affect my reputation and impair my usefulness in the service if the facts remain unpublished.

I therefore very respectfully request a Court of Inquiry to be convened to investigate the truth and object of these reflections.

I would further request that I should be honorably relieved from duty in the Army of the Cumberland [pending this investigation],* and that my assistant adjutant-general, James A. Lowrie, be granted leave of absence to aid me in preparing the necessary papers.

I have but one aide, who is totally† ignorant of my official records.

Hoping that my past services and an attentive performance of duty may entitle my request to your official consideration and respect,‡ I have the honor to remain, yours, very truly,

JAS. S. NEGLEY,
Major-General U. S. Volunteers.

[Inclosure B.]

CHATTANOOGA, TENN., *November* 3, 1863.

Maj. Gen. J. S. NEGLEY, *Pittsburgh, Pa.:*

Dispatch received.   Return at expiration of your leave.
By order of Major-General Thomas:

C. GODDARD,
Assistant Adjutant-General.

[Inclosure C.]

CHATTANOOGA, TENN., *November* 10, 1863.

Maj. Gen. J. S. NEGLEY, *Nashville, Tenn.:*

The general commanding directs that you remain in Nashville until further orders.   It is proper that you should ask for a Court of Inquiry.   It would not be proper to assign you to a command until an investigation has been had.

J. J. REYNOLDS,
Major-General, Chief of Staff.

[Inclosure D.]

SPECIAL ORDERS, }   HDQRS. MILITARY DIVISION OF THE MISS.,
No. 26.   }   *December* 22, 1863.

*   *   *   *   *   *   *

II. Maj. Gen. James S. Negley, U. S. Volunteers, having failed to demand a Court of Inquiry for the purpose of freeing himself from charges affecting his usefulness in this command, is hereby directed to proceed to Cincinnati or to any point outside this military division, and report by letter to the Adjutant-General of the Army for orders.

By order of Maj. Gen. U. S. Grant:

T. S. BOWERS,
Assistant Adjutant-General.

---

* As it reads in the War Department original.
† The word "totally" not in War Department original.
‡ In original this sentence reads: "I sincerely trust that my past services and attentive performance of duty may entitle me to your official consideration and command respect for my request."

[Inclosure E.]
WAR DEPARTMENT, ADJUTANT-GENERAL'S OFFICE,
Washington, D. C., January 5, 1864.

Maj. Gen. J. S. NEGLEY, U. S. Vols., *Cincinnati, Ohio:*

SIR : Your communication of December 27, 1863, stating that General Grant directed you to report to this office by letter for orders, has been received.

The General-in-Chief directs me to say in reply that he has no other orders for you, as you belong to General Thomas' command.

I am, sir, very respectfully, your obedient servant,

E. D. TOWNSEND,
Assistant Adjutant-General.

LOUISVILLE, KY., *February 24, 1864.*

Brigadier-General WHIPPLE,
Chief of Staff, Army of the Cumberland:

SIR : I have the honor to inform the commanding general that the Court of Inquiry, convened to investigate my official conduct at the battle of Chickamauga, has concluded its labors.

From the highly favorable tone of the testimony, I am permitted to presume that my military reputation has been fully vindicated.

In view of the announcement by the Commander-in-Chief that I "belong to your command," I respectfully await orders, dependent, of course, upon the favorable conclusions of the Court of Inquiry and the order issued thereon by the President.

With considerations of personal esteem, yours, very truly,

JAS. S. NEGLEY,
Major-General.

No. 35.

Report of Capt. Frederick Schultz, First Ohio Light Artillery, Chief of Artillery.

Report of Losses in batteries of the Second Division, Fourteenth Army Corps, during the actions of the 19th and 20th of September, 1863.

Losses.	Company M, First Ohio Volunteer Artillery.	Company G, First Ohio Volunteer Artillery.	Bridges' Battery.	Total.
Killed :				
Officer.............				
Enlisted men.............			1	1
Wounded :			5	5
Officers.........				
Enlisted men.............	4		16	20
Missing :				
Officers........				
Enlisted men.....				
Guns and carriages.....			4	4
Caissons and limber............			2	2
Limbers........			1	1
Tube pouches , ...			3	3
Thumb-stalls........			3	3
Tow-hooks			8	8

Report of Losses in batteries of the Second Division, &c.—Continued.

Losses.	Company M, First Ohio Volunteer Artillery.	Company G, First Ohio Volunteer Artillery.	Bridges' Battery.	Total.
Pendulum hausse			1	1
Vent punches			2	2
Screwdriver			1	1
Lanyards			4	4
Gunners' gimlets			2	2
Gunners' pinchers			2	2
Priming wires			4	4
Fuse gouge			1	1
Traces	1		1	2
Artillery whips	5		18	23
Spurs and straps	3		4	7
Horses	8	5	46	59
Gunners' haversacks	1		1	2
Sponges and staffs			5	5
Sponges and rammers	6		3	9
Rubber buckets	8		5	13
Sponge buckets			2	2
Tar buckets	5		2	7
Caisson shovels	2		2	4
Pick-axes	2		1	3
Felling axes	7		8	15
Prolonges	1		4	5
Spare poles	2		1	3
Trail			1	1
Paulins	1		3	4
Wheels	1		4	5
Sets wheel harness			2	2
Sets lead harness	1		6	7
Halters	7		40	47
Nose bags	18		45	63
Currycombs			16	16
Horse brushes			17	17
Sabers and belts	2		5	7
Pistol	1			1
Handspikes	3		4	7
Saddle blankets	23		30	53
Non-commissioned officers' saddles	2		2	4

F. SCHULTZ,
Chief of Artillery, Second Div., Fourteenth Army Corps.

No. 36.

Report of Brig. Gen. John Beatty, U. S. Army, commanding First Brigade.

HDQRS. 1ST BRIGADE., 2D DIVISION, 14TH ARMY CORPS,
Chattanooga, Tenn., September 28, 1863.

MAJOR : I have the honor to submit the following report of the operations of my brigade from 30th day of August, 1863, to 21st day of September, 1863:

On Sunday night, August 30, the brigade left Cave Spring, near Stevenson, Ala., marched across Sand Mountain, by way of Moore's Spring and Brown's Spring, and on the evening of the 6th of September, without the occurrence of any incident of importance, encamped at McKaig's Spring, in Johnson's Crook, on north side of Lookout

Mountain. Here my advance regiment, the Forty-second Indiana (Lieutenant-Colonel McIntire), had a slight skirmish with the enemy.

Monday, September 7, the Fifteenth Kentucky (Colonel Taylor) in advance, marched to the summit of Lookout Mountain, the enemy's cavalry retiring before us.

Tuesday, September 8, moved to Cooper's Gap; my advance surprised the enemy's picket station at foot of the mountain, capturing 2 men, 5 sabers, 1 army pistol, 1 carbine, and wounding severely 1 man.

Wednesday, September 9, marched from Cooper's Gap through the valley to Stevens' Gap and rejoined the division.

Thursday, September 10, guarded wagon train from Stevens' Gap to Chickamauga Creek, on the road leading to Dug Gap.

Friday, September 11, about 2 p. m., it being evident that a large force of the enemy's infantry was on our right, left, and front, and that a cavalry force was moving to our rear, I was ordered to move back to Bailey's Cross-Roads and remain until the wagon train had passed on its return to Stevens' Gap. In less than an hour I had taken the position directed. The enemy's cavalry soon after made its appearance in the vicinity, but returned without firing.

Saturday, September 12, until Wednesday, September 16, remained in the vicinity of Stevens' Gap.

Thursday, September 17, marched from Bailey's Cross-Roads in a northeasterly direction to Owens' Ford on Chickamauga.

Friday, September 18, marched to Crawfish Spring. About midnight was ordered to move in a southeasterly direction to a ford on Chickamauga Creek and relieve Colonel Grose, commanding brigade in Palmer's division. Relieved him about 2 a. m.

Saturday, September 19, at an early hour in the morning, the enemy's pickets made their appearance on the west side of the Chickamauga, and engaged my skirmishers. About 11 a. m. the enemy opened with artillery; he subsequently got two batteries in position, when a sharp artillery fight ensued of nearly three hours' duration. My artillery being re-enforced by three pieces from Schultz's First Ohio Battery, [M, First Ohio Artillery,] at length succeeded in driving the enemy from his position.

Captain Bridges lost in his battery in this engagement, 2 men killed, 9 wounded, and 12 horses killed and disabled. Of the infantry, there were 8 men wounded. About 5 p. m. I was ordered to move to Crawfish Spring, and slowly withdraw my picket line, which had been greatly extended during the day in order to connect with troops on right and left. Arriving at Crawfish Spring, the men were allowed to fill their canteens with water, and the brigade was then moved northward on the Chattanooga road to a ridge near Osburn's, where it remained in reserve during the night.

Sunday, September 20, at an early hour in the morning, I was ordered to move northward on the Chattanooga road and report to Major-General Thomas, who, when I reached him, directed me to move to the extreme left of our line, form perpendicularly to the rear of General Baird's division, connecting with his left, and be in readiness to meet any force of the enemy attempting to turn General Baird's left. I disposed my brigade as ordered. General Baird's line appeared to run parallel with the road; mine, running to the rear, crossed the road.

On this road and near it I posted my artillery, and advanced my skirmishers to the open fields in front of the left and center of my line.   This was a good position, and my brigade and the one on General Baird's left could have co-operated and assisted each other in maintaining it.   Fifteen minutes after this line was formed Captain Gaw, of General Thomas' staff, brought an order to advance my line to a ridge or low hill (McDonald's house) fully one-quarter of a mile distant.   I represented to him that my line was long; that in advancing it I would necessarily leave a long interval between my right and General Baird's left, and also that I was already in the position indicated to me by General Thomas.   He replied that the order to advance was imperative; that I would be supported by General Negley.   I could not urge objections further, and advanced my line as rapidly as possible toward the point indicated.

The Eighty-eighth Indiana (Colonel Humphrey), on the left, moved into position without difficulty.   The Forty-second Indiana (Lieutenant-Colonel McIntire), on its right, met with considerable opposition in advancing through the woods, but finally reached the ridge.   The One hundred and fourth Illinois (Lieutenant-Colonel Hapeman) and the Fifteenth Kentucky (Colonel Taylor), on the right, became engaged almost immediately, and, being obstinately opposed, advanced slowly.   The enemy, in strong force, pressed them heavily in front and on the right flank, preventing them from connecting with the regiments on their left.

At this time I sent an aide to request General Baird or General King to throw in a force to cover the interval between their left and my right, and dispatched Captain Wilson, my assistant adjutant-general, to the rear to hasten forward General Negley to my support.   The two regiments forming the right of my brigade were confronted by so large a force that they were compelled to halt, and ultimately to fall back, which they did in good order, contesting the ground stoutly as they retired.

About this time a column of the enemy pressed into the interval between the One hundred and fourth Illinois and Forty-second Indiana and turned, with the evident design of capturing the latter, which was at the time busily engaged with the enemy in front. Immediately on discovering the object of this movement, I got my artillery in position and opened on them with grape and canister. The column referred to broke and fell back under shelter of the woods, in the direction from whence it came.   Colonel McIntire, but a moment before almost surrounded, was thus enabled to fight his way to the left, which he did, uniting at the same time with Colonel Humphrey, Eighty-eighth Indiana.

Soon after the enemy, pressing back the One hundred and fourth Illinois and Fifteenth Kentucky, advanced through the woods to within 100 yards of my battery and poured into it a heavy fire, killing Lieutenant Bishop, and killing or wounding all the men and horses belonging to his section, which, consequently, fell into the hands of the enemy.   Captain Bridges and his officers, by the exercise of great coolness and courage under a terrible fire, succeeded in saving the remainder of the battery.   The enemy having gained the woods south of the open fields and west of the road, I opposed his farther advance as well as I could with the Fifteenth Kentucky and One hundred and fourth Illinois, and soon after checked him entirely by directing a battery stationed on the road some distance in the rear to change front and open fire on him.

The Eighty-eighth Indiana and Forty-second Indiana, compelled to make a *détour* round the hills on the left and rear, became separated from me, but subsequently finding General Negley they reported to him and under his orders supported a battery or batteries which he had placed in position on some elevated ground on the left. Later in the day they were ordered by his assistant adjutant-general, Major Lowrie, to retire in the direction of Rossville.

Firing having ceased in my front, and being the only mounted officer present, I left the Fifteenth Kentucky and One hundred and fourth Illinois temporarily in charge of Colonel Taylor, of the former regiment, and hurried back to see General Thomas or General Negley and report the necessity for more troops; on the way I met the Second Brigade of our division, Col. T. R. Stanley commanding, advancing to my support. Had it reached me an hour earlier I would have been enabled to maintain the position which I had just been compelled to abandon, but its detention was doubtless unavoidable. I directed Colonel Stanley to form immediately at right angles with and on the left of the road, facing north, and returning to Colonel Taylor ordered him to fall back with the Fifteenth Kentucky and One hundred and fourth Illinois, and form in rear of the left of Colonel Stanley's line. Soon after the enemy pressed back the skirmishers of the Fifteenth Kentucky and One hundred and fourth Illinois, who had not been withdrawn with their regiments, and following them up drove in also the skirmish line of Colonel Stanley's brigade, upon which the Eleventh Michigan (Colonel Stoughton) and Eighteenth Ohio (Lieutenant-Colonel Grosvenor) gave him a well-directed volley, which brought him to a halt; the whole line then opened fire at short range; his line wavered. Colonel Stanley and myself, stationed at different points on the line, simultaneously gave the order to advance, then to charge, and the troops rushing forward with a shout drove the enemy on a run nearly half a mile, strewing the ground with his dead and wounded and capturing many prisoners. Among the latter was General Adams, commanding a Louisiana brigade.

Colonel Stanley, by his courage, skill, and coolness in the management of his command at this time, gave fresh proof of his ability as a brave and gallant officer, and I sincerely trust that his eminent services will speedily receive substantial recognition on the part of the Government.

Seeing the necessity for some support for a single line of such length so far advanced, I hastened to the rear and brought up three or four regiments which I found idle in the woods and formed a second line. At this time Captain Wilson, my assistant adjutant-general, whom I had sent to General Negley some time before the Second Brigade joined me, to inform him of my position, returned and brought me a verbal order to retire to the hill on the left and join General Negley. Convinced that the withdrawal of the troops at this time from the position occupied would endanger the whole left wing of the army, I thought best to defer the execution of this order until I could see General Negley and explain to him the necessity of maintaining the line and re-enforcing it. I endeavored to find him, but was unable to do so.

The enemy about this time made a fierce attack on Colonel Stanley's brigade and forced it back. The three regiments which I had posted in its rear to support it retired hastily without firing a shot. In the meantime the right wing of the army had been thrown back, and frightened soldiers and occasional shots were coming from the rear and right. Colonel Taylor, Fifteenth Kentucky, to whom an order had been given to haul off by hand two pieces of artillery which had been abandoned, enlarged somewhat upon his instructions and gathered up five pieces; attaching them to limbers found on the field, he succeeded in saving them all. In this he was assisted by the One hundred and fourth Illinois. Subsequently he placed a battery in position some distance to the left of Colonel Stanley's line, and remained with it until ordered by Major Lowrie, assistant adjutant-general, Second Division, to withdraw in the direction of Chattanooga.

Colonel Stanley's brigade, considerably scattered by the last furious attack of the enemy, was gathered up by its officers, and retired to the ridge on the right and in rear of the original line of battle. The regiments of my brigade had been previously ordered off the field, a fact which I did not learn until some six hours afterward. Supposing them to be still near I made every possible effort to find them and to find my division commander. Failing in this, I stationed myself near the Second Brigade of our division, then commanded by Colonel Stoughton, of Eleventh Michigan, and gave such general directions to him and the troops about me as under the circumstances I felt warranted in doing.

The obstinate maintenance of the ridge on the right until after sunset by detachments from nearly every division of the army, none of which, if I except Brannan's and Steedman's divisions, were more strongly represented than our own, saved the army, in my opinion, from total rout. Once during the afternoon the enemy succeeded in planting his colors almost on the crest of the ridge on our immediate front, and for a moment drove our men from the summit. An extraordinary effort of the officers present was successful in again rallying them to the crest, and the timely arrival of a detachment of the Eighteenth Ohio, led by Lieutenant-Colonel Grosvenor, drove back the enemy, who only saved his colors by throwing them down the hill. I never witnessed a higher order of heroism than that displayed on this portion of the field, and though not perhaps strictly within the province of this report, I cannot refrain from specially mentioning Colonel Stoughton, Eleventh Michigan (at that time commanding Second Brigade); Lieutenant-Colonel Raffen, Nineteenth Illinois; Lieutenant-Colonel Grosvenor, Eighteenth Ohio; Colonel Hunter, Eighty-second Indiana; Colonel Hays and Lieutenant-Colonel Wharton, Tenth Kentucky; Captain Stinchcomb, Seventeenth Ohio; Captain Kendrick, Seventy-ninth Pennsylvania, as men who deserve the gratitude of the nation for an exhibition on this occasion of determined courage which I believe unsurpassed in the history of the rebellion.

Near 8 o'clock in the evening I ascertained from General Wood that the army had been ordered to fall back toward Chattanooga. I immediately started to inform Colonel Stoughton to join the retiring column, but found he had been apprised of the movement and was then in the road.

At 10 p. m. I reached Rossville and found one of my regiments, the Forty-second Indiana (Lieutenant-Colonel McIntire), on picket 1 mile south of that place. The other regiments were encamped near the town.

Monday, September 21, my brigade was formed in line of battle in rear of the Third Brigade, on east side of Chattanooga road, fronting south. Afterward it was withdrawn from this position and placed on a high ridge east of and near Rossville.

About 10 a. m. it was attacked by a brigade of mounted infantry, a part of Forrest's command, under Colonel Dibrell, and after a sharp fight of half an hour, in which the Fifteenth Kentucky (Colonel Taylor) and Forty-second Indiana (Lieutenant-Colonel McIntire) were principally engaged, the enemy was repulsed, and retired, leaving his dead and a portion of his wounded on the field. Of his dead, 1 officer and 8 men were left within a few rods of our line. At 12 o'clock on this night the Fifteenth Kentucky was deployed on the skirmish line, and the remaining regiments of the brigade withdrawn from the ridge and marched to Chattanooga.

I regret to record the loss of Capt. Isaac H. Le Fevre, my topographical engineer, who fell mortally wounded early in the action of Sunday. He was most faithful and efficient as an officer, an educated and estimable gentleman, and his loss must be severely felt in this division. Lieut. W. W. Calkins, aide-de-camp, was slightly wounded on the morning of Sunday, and afterward taken prisoner.

I transmit herewith the reports of my regimental commanders, and of Captain Bridges, commanding battery, which, with the foregoing record of their movements, show how well their services entitle them to the thanks of the country.

To Capt. James S. Wilson, my assistant adjutant-general, I am particularly indebted for most valuable assistance, as also to the other members of my staff.

I append recapitulation of casualties in my brigade.

And in conclusion, I have the honor to subscribe myself, major, your most obedient servant,

JOHN BEATTY,
Brigadier-General.

Maj. James A. Lowrie,
　　Asst. Adjt. Gen., Second Division 14th Army Corps.

[Inclosure.]

Report of Casualties, First Brigade, Second Division, Fourteenth Army Corps.

Command.	Went into action.				Lost in action.									
					Killed.		Wounded.		Missing.		Horses.			
	Commissioned officers.	Enlisted men.	Horses.	Guns, artillery.	Commissioned officers.	Enlisted men.	Commissioned officers.	Enlisted men.	Commissioned officers.	Enlisted men.	Killed.	Wounded.	Missing.	Guns lost.
Brigade staff	7		7				2				1		1	
42d Indiana Volunteers	21	307			5	4	42	2	48					
15th Kentucky Volunteers	25	280			5		43	1	14					
88th Indiana Volunteers	34	235			2	3	30	2	15					
104th Illinois Volunteers	23	276			2	5	32	1	23					
Total	100	1,098	7		14	14	157	6	100	1		1		
Bridges' Battery	5	121		6	1	5			16		4	42	2	3	2
Total infantry and artillery.	105	1,219	7	6	1	19	14	173	6	104	43	2	4	2

JOHN BEATTY,
Brigadier-General.

No. 37.

Report of Lieut. Col. Douglas Hapeman, One hundred and fourth Illinois Infantry.

HDQRS. ONE HUNDRED AND FOURTH ILLINOIS INFANTRY,
Chattanooga, Tenn., September 26, 1863.

SIR : I have the honor to make the following report of the operations of the One hundred and fourth Illinois Infantry since they left Cave Spring, Ala., on the 30th day of August, 1863 :

The regiment had, when we left Cave Spring, an aggregate of 330 men for the line of battle. We marched to Stevenson on the night of the 30th ultimo, when we bivouacked and remained until the 1st of September, when we marched across the Tennessee River and arrived at Brown's Spring, near Trenton, Ga., on the 5th.

On the 6th we marched to Brown's Spring, and on the 9th bivouacked in the valley near Stevens' Gap.

A detachment (Company H) had a skirmish at the foot of the mountain on the 8th, and captured 2 prisoners without loss on our side.

On the 10th we moved to Davis' Cross-Roads.

On the 11th were skirmishing nearly all day, and moved back to Stevens' Gap. Our loss was 1 man wounded and 1 man missing.

Remained at Stevens' Gap until the 14th, when we moved to Bailey's Cross-Roads; marched from there to Owens' Ford on the 17th.

On the evening of the 18th we moved to within 2 miles of Crawfish Spring, and took position on a hill at the right of Bridges' Battery.

About 11 o'clock on the 19th the rebels opened a furious fire on us with their artillery, which lasted over one hour and a half. Seven of our men were wounded, 2 mortally. One company assisted the battery in working their guns during the action. The men behaved themselves well during the entire engagement. At 3 o'clock we moved back from the position, and marched up the road 3 miles from Crawfish Spring.

On the morning of the 20th we moved out with the brigade, and formed in line and commenced skirmishing with the enemy. The Fifteenth Kentucky and One hundred and fourth Illinois were formed on the same line, and advanced slowly, when we were halted and the One hundred and fourth sent forward to connect their skirmishers to the line of the Forty-second Indiana, some distance in advance and to the left. We moved forward about 250 yards, the enemy's skirmishers falling back, but failed to find the line of the Forty-second Indiana, when I discovered that the enemy was in large force in my front and on both flanks, and I ordered the regiment to fall back on the original line with the Fifteenth Kentucky on my right. When I reached that point the Fifteenth was pressed by a heavy force and was falling back, and we continued to retreat to the road about 300 yards to the rear, where we again halted. Five of my companies were deployed as skirmishers, and the regiment was thrown into some confusion, when they fell back on the line.

About 30 men, mostly from the skirmish line, became detached from the regiment and did not again join it until night. This was the only engagement we were in during the day. We remained with the Fifteenth Kentucky, in command of Colonel Taylor, on the hills between the road and mountain until 3 o'clock, when we marched back and bivouacked with the Second Division.

Our loss was 2 killed, 37 wounded, and 24 missing. Among the wounded were Captain Ludington, Company H; Lieutenant Porter, commanding Company B; Lieutenant Southwell, Company H, and Lieutenant Sapp, Company K. Lieutenant Calkins, Company E, aide to General Beatty, was also slightly wounded and probably taken prisoner.

The officers and men behaved very well and, with the exception of about 30, who were separated from the regiment when they first fell back, there was no straggling.

On the 21st we were in line with the brigade and had some skirmishing, in which Captain Leighton, Company A, was wounded in the shoulder. At night we marched to Chattanooga. The regiment was on picket on the 24th. During the skirmish in the night the batteries at the fort raked the open field in front of our line. A force was advancing in line to attack us, but were driven back by the fire from these batteries. Two of our men were struck by pieces of shell, but the injury was slight.

I append a list of the killed, wounded, and missing.*

I am, sir, very respectfully, your obedient servant,

DOUGLAS HAPEMAN,
Lieutenant-Colonel, Comdg. 104th Illinois Infantry.

Capt. J. S. WILSON,
　Assistant Adjutant-General, First Brigade.

No. 38.

Report of Capt. Lyman Bridges, Bridges' Battery, Illinois Light Artillery.

HDQRS. BRIDGES' BATTERY, ILLINOIS LIGHT ARTILLERY,
　Camp at Chattanooga, September 29, 1863.

CAPTAIN: In compliance with your order, requiring a report of the part taken by this battery in the battles of September 19 and 20, I have the honor to report that:

By order of Brig. Gen. John Beatty I moved from camp on Chickamauga Creek at 4 p. m. on the 18th instant toward Chattanooga, Tenn., halting at Crawfish Spring until 8 p. m., when, by order of Brigadier-General Beatty, I moved 1½ miles to the front, relieving two batteries of the Fifth U. S. Artillery, placing four guns in position held by a 6-gun battery and two guns in the position occupied by a 4-gun battery.

On the morning of the 19th the skirmishers in our front engaged the skirmishers of the enemy soon after daybreak.

At 8 a. m. a rebel battery opened upon the reserve of our line of skirmishers at our right.

Having received orders to commence firing whenever the enemy showed himself in force, I played upon him from the position upon the left with four guns, when he was compelled to retire.

At 11 a. m. a dense smoke arose in the edge of a wooded ridge, 1,500 yards in our front and right. Soon afterward the smoke cleared

---

*Nominal list omitted; see revised statement, p. 172.

away, when a battery was discovered in position there, which opened fire upon me.

Having learned his position and range, I opened fire upon him with the four guns having a range upon him. His fire was constant for half an hour, when he placed another battery in position, some 700 yards in my front and left, which also opened upon me, the right battery now throwing solid shot and the left battery throwing case-shot and shell.

The left section being posted upon the right of the road and not having a range from the position where it was then posted, I sent to General Beatty, asking that it might be ordered to join the two sections which had held the position upon the left of the road. General Beatty sent it at once and I placed it upon the right of the two sections then engaged.

The enemy, after contesting the ground some two hours, were driven from the field with a heavy loss.

Lieutenant Sturges, of Battery M, First Ohio Artillery, arrived upon the ground with a half battery during the engagement, doing signal service in driving the enemy from the field.

My loss during this day was 2 men killed, 9 men wounded, 12 horses killed.

Receiving orders from General Beatty, I moved to Crawfish Spring at 4 p. m., where I replenished my ammunition chests and moved 5 miles to the left, remaining in park during the night 1 mile to the left of General Rosecrans' headquarters.

At daybreak, by order of General Beatty, I changed front to the right, and at 7 a. m., by order of General Beatty, I moved 3 miles to the front and left, taking position upon either side of the Chattanooga road.

Receiving orders from General Beatty, I moved forward to the edge of a field, some 500 yards to the front.

At 8 a. m., by order of General Beatty, I moved one-half of battery to a house in the field to the left of the road, leaving the remaining half battery at the edge of the woods in position in charge of Lieut. William Bishop.

I remained in this position until ordered by General Beatty to place the half battery then in the field at the house in front upon the left of the half battery at the edge of the field.

The enemy were now pouring out of the woods into the field 400 yards in our front and right, being the ground over which our line had advanced but half an hour previously.

As soon as the battle-flags of the enemy emerged from the woods and there was no doubt about its being the enemy, I opened fire with my full battery, the first rounds with case-shot, afterward with canister.

His advance was checked for an instant, when, having formed his line again, he steadily advanced upon me.

While my guns were being worked under the fire of the enemy in our front, some of my men and horses were disabled by a musketry fire from the woods upon my right. While under this fire General Beatty ordered me to retire. I gave the order and found all of the horses of two pieces were either killed or disabled; 5 cannoneers of one of these detachments and 3 cannoneers of the other were disabled.

The enemy was each moment closing his infantry in upon my front and right, firing as they advanced, and there being no possible chance of getting these pieces off through the woods and brush, I ordered the remnant of my men still at the guns to fall back.

At this moment my senior first lieutenant, William Bishop, was killed while endeavoring to remove his section from the field, and my horse was killed under me.

I deem it my duty to state that during this action I had no infantry support whatever. I wish further to state that it was not from any fault of Brigadier-General Beatty, however.

Having fallen back to the advance line of infantry, where the Fifteenth Kentucky and One hundred and fourth Illinois Infantry had rallied, Lieut. L. A. White remained with me, both endeavoring to advance with the Fifteenth Kentucky and One hundred and fourth Illinois Infantry to recapture the two guns lost. In the meantime Lieutenants Temple and Seeborn got the remaining guns and caissons into column and retired in good order to the first available position. This done, Lieutenant Temple reported to Major-General Negley that he had four guns under command and awaited his orders.

By General Negley's order he took position on the crest of a wooded hill on the left of Captain Schultz's battery. Afterward, by General Negley's order, he moved to another position to the right and front, being in this position when I came up.

General Beatty, finding a strong force of the enemy advancing, informed me that it was impossible to recover my guns, and directed me to haul from the front four guns which had been abandoned by the different batteries upon the right.

Lieutenant Atherton, of General Beatty's staff, obtained a detail from the Fifteenth Kentucky, who reported in charge of Captain Allen, to whom much credit is due for the service rendered in saving these guns from the enemy.

Receiving orders from General Negley, I moved to the left of a ridge, taking position upon either side of two buildings used as hospitals, when by his order I opened fire upon a force of the enemy then approaching upon the Rossville road through a corn-field.

By General Negley's order I moved to a hill to the right and rear, to await the approach of the enemy, when, by General Negley's order, I moved to the Rossville road; bivouacked for the night at Rossville.

September 21, by General Beatty's order, I remained in reserve until 5 p. m., when, by General Negley's order, I moved to Chattanooga.

I desire to make honorable mention of the subaltern officers of this battery. Senior First Lieut. William Bishop, having been sent from Stevenson, Ala., to Nashville, upon business for the command, learning that an engagement was about to take place, rejoined his battery at Lookout Mountain, moving in command of his section to Dug Gap, Crawfish Spring, and the battle of Chickamauga, where, at his guns, in the discharge of his duty, he lost his life.

I wish to bear testimony to the able and self-sacrificing manner which governed all his motives and actions; ever ardent and enthusiastic in his chosen vocation, he inspired his comrades with his undaunted courage and heroism. No nobler patriot ever lost his life in freedom's priceless cause.

To Lieuts. M. D. Temple, L. A. White, and F. Seeborn much credit is due, for the promptness with which every order was carried out; to M. D. Temple, junior first lieutenant, for the promptness and ability displayed in retiring and taking a new position for the battery, immediately after Lieutenant Bishop was killed and my horse was killed under me.

Below is the list* of the killed, wounded, and missing of my command.

I am, captain, very respectfully, your obedient servant,

LYMAN BRIDGES,
Captain, Commanding.

Capt. F. SCHULTZ,
Chief of Artillery, Second Division.

No. 39.

Reports of Col. Timothy R. Stanley, Eighteenth Ohio Infantry, commanding Second Brigade.

HDQRS. 2D BRIGADE, 2D DIVISION, 14TH ARMY CORPS,
In the Field, September 12, 1863.

MAJOR : In compliance with your order of this date, I have the honor to report the following list of casualties in my command in the engagement of yesterday.†

In submitting the above report I deem it proper to add an account of the operations of my command in the engagement above alluded to.

In the skirmishing during the early part of the day nearly every company of my command was more or less engaged and acquitted themselves with credit and honor.

On taking my position on the ridge at Davis', as ordered by Major-General Negley, I placed the Nineteenth Illinois Volunteer Infantry and Eleventh Michigan Volunteer Infantry in line on the slope in front of the Fourth Indiana Battery and in rear of a fence, directing them to build breastworks of rails and stones to protect them from musketry, which they did promptly and effectually. The Eighteenth Ohio I placed in double column as a reserve.

Captain Schultz, commanding Battery M, First Ohio Volunteer Artillery, was ordered to take position on the side of the hill in my rear. He then opened on the enemy, firing over us with one section, and worked with good effect until ordered to retire.

I sent four companies of the Nineteenth Illinois forward, one in a barn, two on the bank of the creek on the right, and one (Captain Guthrie commanding) behind the stone wall on the left and near the creek. This last was the only one engaged, and with one company of the Twenty-fourth Illinois, which was temporarily there, fired one volley on a mounted party of the enemy as they were fiercely and rapidly pursuing two of the Twenty-fourth Illinois, who had fallen to the rear, which unseated all of the pursuing party who were in sight, killing 13, as reported, and wounding a large number. It is believed the pursuing party was a general officer and his staff at the head of the column of mounted men.

The enemy placed a battery in position, which was well handled and did terrible execution, especially upon the Eighteenth Ohio, which had been placed on the right flank to guard against the enemy, who appeared there in strong force.

---

* Nominal list omitted; see revised statement, p. 172.
† Nominal list (omitted) shows 5 killed, 29 wounded, and 4 missing.

Finding that it would be necessary for me to remain on or near the left in order to observe the enemy in that quarter, I gave Colonel Stoughton, who was on the right, direction to act at discretion with his regiment and the section of artillery on his right, all of which he did (sending out one of his companies as skirmishers) with proper judgment.

I have already said the enemy appeared in heavy force on my right; this force consisted of a heavy column of infantry and several pieces of artillery. Seeing the emergency, Captain Waggener, my assistant adjutant-general (I being on the left), ordered the Eighteenth Ohio into position there and immediately reported the fact to me, which I approved. The artillery soon opened, and I was then exposed to a galling cross-fire.

The Eighteenth Ohio, however, with the company of the Eleventh Michigan skirmishing and the aid of the section of artillery, directed by Colonel Stoughton, held the enemy at bay in that quarter. In the meantime the enemy in front, taught a severe lesson by Captain Guthrie's company behind the stone wall, kept at a respectful distance. His battery, however, did fearful execution, throwing shell and grape with remarkable precision.

While this was being done, and I was momentarily on the right, the four pieces on the left were withdrawn without my order, this leaving me at that point at the mercy of the well-directed fire of the enemy's artillery.

Soon after this, however, the train having arrived at the point designated by Major-General Negley, he ordered me to retire, which I did in good order, bringing with me the section on my right, which remained until ordered by me to leave.

A portion of the Eighteenth Ohio, which had been so badly cut up, was thrown temporarily in confusion, and I retired them first, bringing up with the Nineteenth Illinois and Eleventh Michigan in rear of the section, and skirmishers to their rear. I soon, however, had the Eighteenth Ohio also in line and retired with the brigade in line of battle, faced by the rear rank, ready at any time to face about to the enemy.

I know of but one officer who did not do his duty, and I am not yet sufficiently informed of his conduct to give his name.

The enemy suffered much more severely than we did, and they did not follow us closely as we fell back.

The members of my staff without exception were prompt and active in the performance of their duties, delivering my orders intelligently and readily, no matter what the danger.

Captain Waggener, assistant adjutant-general, assisted with good result in rallying and keeping together the Eighteenth Ohio when temporarily scattered, and was at all times in the right place.

Captain Kendrick, also, my inspector, was present where wanted to direct and encourage.

Captain Bissell, Lieutenants Tucker, Keith, and Stivers were at all times ready for orders and executed them promptly.

The young men composing my escort and clerks were active and ready, and deserve credit for their alacrity and courage.

I am, very respectfully, your obedient servant,

T. R. STANLEY,
Colonel, Commanding.

Maj. JAMES A. LOWRIE,
Assistant Adjutant-General, Second Division.

HDQRS. 2D BRIGADE, 2D DIVISION, 14TH ARMY CORPS,
Chattanooga, Tenn., September 28, 1863.

MAJOR : In compliance with your order, requiring a report of the operations of my brigade from the time of leaving Cave Spring, Ala., up to our arrival at this point, I have the honor to submit the following :

My command, consisting of the Eighteenth Ohio Volunteer Infantry, Nineteenth Illinois Volunteer Infantry, Eleventh Michigan Volunteer Infantry, and Battery M, First Ohio Volunteer Artillery, (the Sixty-ninth Ohio Volunteer Infantry having been left* at Cowan, Tenn.), left Cave Spring and crossed the Tennessee River at Caperton's Ferry on the evening of the 1st of September. We continued the march from day to day, crossing Raccoon Mountain, and encamped on Lookout Mountain September 8.

The Eleventh Michigan Infantry, under Colonel Stoughton, was thrown forward on the same day and moved down the mountain, clearing out the heavy timber with which the road had been blockaded, and, skirmishing briskly, drove the enemy for 1½ miles, and occupied Stevens' Gap.

September 9 my brigade made a reconnaissance to the front and drove the enemy's outposts some 3 miles, with light firing.

The next day we moved forward to Davis' Cross-Roads, and, after some maneuvering in that vicinity, the engagement took place on the 11th of September, an official report of which you have already received.

Falling back to Bailey's Cross-Roads, we remained there until the 17th September, when we moved off on the Chattanooga road and encamped at Crawfish Spring on the night of the 18th.

On the morning of the 19th I moved under orders toward the left and took position on an elevated point designated by Major-General Negley, with the Eleventh Michigan thrown considerably forward. In the afternoon I advanced my three regiments in line of battle, and, in connection with the Third Brigade deployed on my right, drove the enemy out of the woods in our front and regained the ground which had been held and lost during the day by the troops of some other command.

Later in the day we advanced still farther and drove the enemy, with heavy firing, from an open field in our front.

We subsequently withdrew to the edge of the woods, and constructing light breastworks of rails, remained during the night.

At an early hour the next morning, Sunday, September 20, I received orders from Major-General Negley to withdraw from my position, and move off up the road toward the left. I had moved but a short distance, in compliance with this command, when I was ordered to return to the former position, which I did, driving the enemy, who had in the mean time advanced and occupied it.

I was shortly afterward relieved by a brigade from General Wood's division, and again ordered toward the left, where the battle was raging loudly and heavily. Having moved my command, including the battery which had remained all night in position on the hill in my rear, some distance on and to the left, on line with the Rossville road, I was ordered by Major-General Negley to push my regiments quickly into the woods to my right, to support the forces then engaged there. This I did, moving rapidly forward and leaving my

---

* But see report of Col. Daniel McCook, p. 871.

battery in immediate charge of Major-General Negley, under whose orders Captain Schultz, commanding, having at that time become separated from the brigade, acted during the principal part of the day. I pushed my regiments quickly through the woods and reported to the officer in command, who ordered me farther to the left, to report to whomsoever I found in command there. Upon reaching a point farther to the left, I was ordered into line at right angles with the front, but finding nothing to do there, I pushed forward again until I found Major-General Thomas, from whom I received definite and positive orders to advance to the support of Brig. Gen. John Beatty, commanding First Brigade, who was then being hard pressed. Having reported to General Beatty, I, under his direction, formed my line of battle at right angles with the road.

The line was hardly formed before the enemy advanced upon us in heavy force. The Eighteenth Ohio and the Eleventh Michigan, forming the first line, opened a rapid and effective fire, which checked the enemy. Observing this, I ordered the Nineteenth Illinois forward, and upon their closing up I ordered the line forward, which all responded to with cheers of triumph, and the enemy fled in dismay, though several times our number. We thus drove them for a half mile or more, strewing the ground with killed and wounded, and taking a large number of prisoners. Among the latter were Brigadier-General Adams and one or two of his staff, who surrendered to officers of this brigade, and were sent to the rear under guard by the assistant adjutant-general, Capt. R. J. Waggener.

I myself talked with General Adams (who told me his name) and know that he was captured by my brigade. He was wounded and asked me to send him a stretcher, which I was unable to do. Quite a number of other officers were near him, dead and wounded, and one of my officers who observed closely thinks there was another brigadier-general among the number.

Our volleys were destructive to them, and I attribute their utter rout to the skillful fire and impetuosity of my brigade.

Having followed up the enemy a considerable distance, and finding myself wholly unsupported, I slowly fell back a few paces under heavy fire from the Washington Battery (which had opened on my line), for the purpose of closing up my ranks and securing some support.

General Beatty had in the mean time brought up a brigade to my rear, which he had "borrowed," and I halted my command in their front, informing them that I would check the enemy and, if the fire became too hot, would fall back on them and fight with them, but was only allowed a few minutes' rest before the enemy in strong force again attacked me. Being hard pressed I gave the order, after firing a number of rounds, to fall back fighting to the support. Upon looking around, however, I found the support had disappeared and we were left to our own resources.

I would be glad to state what brigade this was that so shamefully deserted us without firing a gun, but, although I think I am correctly informed, I am not sufficiently certain to express my opinion.

My brigade continued to fall back slowly, halting and firing at intervals, presenting a good front to the enemy, until I withdrew my command and took position next to some log buildings on the brow of the hill, near the Rossville road. The enemy soon began a fierce and determined attack on this position, defended as it was by part of a battery of the Fourth U. S. Artillery, which did its duty well, supported by my brigade and some scattered fragments of other regiments. While conducting the defense of this point and earnestly striving to employ the forces under my command to the best advantage for that purpose I was struck by a ball or piece of shell on the right shoulder, and finding myself unable to continue longer on the field, I turned over the command to Colonel Stoughton, of the Eleventh Michigan, who conducted the brigade through the rest of the engagement of that day and until we marched, on the night of Monday, 21st, from Rossville to this place.

I was, however, with the brigade on the morning and throughout the day on Monday, assisting so far as able. During the charge heretofore spoken of, Brigadier-General Beatty was with me and by his cool and gallant bearing added to the enthusiasm of my officers and men, and will be long remembered by them.

I cannot state the number of prisoners taken, for the reason that they were sent to the rear to other commands. The several commanding officers discharged their duties faithfully and well. Colonel Stoughton, of Eleventh Michigan, displayed the same coolness and fearlessness as at Stone's River. I cautioned him that he exposed himself too much, but saw no change in that respect afterward. The same may be said of Lieutenant-Colonel Raffen, of the Nineteenth Illinois, who was always ready, prompt, and courageous ; as also of Lieutenant-Colonel Grosvenor, of the Eighteenth Ohio, who, with his regiment, was in the hottest of the fight.

The members of my staff, without exception, acquitted themselves with honor. Captain Kendrick, for his cool determination, unflinching courage, and thorough acquaintance with all his duties, deserves that promotion which has too long been withheld. Captain Waggener, assistant adjutant-general, well posted in his duties in the office and mostly confined there, has on this occasion, as well as at Davis' Cross-Roads, shown his readiness to wield the sword as well as the pen.

Accompanying this is the report of Colonel Stoughton for the time he was in command. He sustained himself well and, with the brigade, made such a fight as is seldom made by so small a number of men.

After I resumed command I marched to this point with the division, leaving the Sixty-ninth Ohio, which joined us at Rossville Monday, 21st, with other regiments from the other brigades, in charge of Colonel Stoughton, who brought up the rear in good order in the morning.

Since our arrival here I have been engaged more or less, day and night, on the earth-works, and my men have displayed the same willingness to labor as to fight.

The loss of valuable officers and men of my command has been heavy both in killed and wounded. A report* of casualties has already been forwarded.

Very respectfully, your obedient servant,

T. R. STANLEY,
Colonel, Commanding.

Maj. James A. Lowrie,
    Assistant Adjutant-General.

---

*Embodied in revised statement, p. 172.

No. 40.

*Report of Col. William L. Stoughton, Eleventh Michigan Infantry,
commanding Second Brigade.*

HDQRS. 2D BRIGADE, 2D DIVISION, 14TH ARMY CORPS,
Chattanooga, September 27, 1863.

SIR: I have the honor to submit the following report of the operations of the Second Brigade while under my command in the recent
engagement:

I assumed command about 12 m. of the 20th instant, Colonel
Stanley having been wounded and left the field. About 1 o'clock
I advanced the command about 50 yards and drove the enemy,
who had opened a scattering fire upon us, from our immediate
front. I then placed the Eleventh Michigan and Nineteenth Illinois Regiments in line of battle, in a strong position, under cover
of the hill, leaving the Eighteenth Ohio to support a section of the
Fourth U. S. Artillery and watch the motions of the enemy. Soon
after the brigade had taken this position the enemy made a spirited
attack on a hill to my right, occupied by the left of General Brannan's division, apparently driving our troops back. I at once
ordered the Eleventh Michigan and Nineteenth Illinois to their support. These regiments advanced at a double-quick and charged
upon the enemy, driving him from the hill. Immediately after this
charge I was informed by General John Beatty that our position
upon this hill must be maintained, and was directed to use the forces
under my command for that purpose. I at once placed my forces
along the crest of the hill, the Nineteenth Illinois on the right, and
the Eleventh Michigan on the left, and constructed rude breastworks.

My brigade was by far the largest, if not the only, organized force
on the hill, and I accordingly assumed command. The fragments
of the regiments on the hill and all men found in the rear were
placed in the most available positions. About 4 o'clock the enemy
made a vigorous attack upon our position, and a contest ensued,
which in its fierceness and duration has few parallels. Our troops,
without exception, maintained their ground with unfaltering courage, and the few who recoiled from the storm of bullets were speedily
rallied, and returned with renewed ardor. The enemy was in heavy
force, and fought with the most determined obstinacy. As fast as
their ranks were thinned by our fire they were filled up by fresh
troops. They pressed forward and charged up to our lines, firing
across our breastworks, and planted their colors within 100 feet of
our own. A dense cloud of smoke enveloped our lines, and in some
places the position of the foe could only be known by the flash of
his guns.

At 6 p. m. the enemy still held his position, and as a last resort,
I ordered up the Eighteenth Ohio, and rallying every man that could
be got, charged forward with a cheer upon his colors. His flag
went down. His lines broke and fell back from the hill. During
the fight Brig. Gen. John Beatty rode up on the hill and assisted
materially in sustaining and inspiring the men. His assistance
there, and also in sending men forward, was timely and very valuable.

Our ammunition became exhausted during the fight and every cartridge that could be found on the persons of the killed and wounded,

as well as in the boxes of the prisoners which we took, was distributed to the men.

Lieutenant-Colonel Raffen, of the Nineteenth Illinois, Lieutenant-Colonel Grosvenor, of the Eighteenth Ohio, and Lieutenant-Colonel Mudge, of the Eleventh Michigan, behaved with great coolness and gallantry, and managed the respective regiments with skill and ability; the latter was severely wounded.

Captain Newbury of the Eleventh Michigan was killed. Captain Waggener, assistant adjutant-general, and Captain Kendrick, of the staff, discharged their duties in the most prompt and efficient manner. Colonel Hunter, of the Eighty-second Indiana, and Colonel Hays, of the Tenth Kentucky, also rendered efficient service.

About 8 o'clock orders came from General Brannan to retire, and the brigade was quietly formed and marched in good order to Rossville. About half an hour before we left a raking fire was poured into our ranks by the enemy from a hill to our right, which had been occupied and as we supposed was still held by General Granger's Reserve Corps.

On the morning of the 21st, by your orders, I took a position with my brigade on a road leading in a southeasterly direction from Rossville. The enemy appeared in force in our front and an artillery fight was kept up most of the day. At night the Sixty-ninth Ohio was posted as pickets in our front, and according to your orders I withdrew the rest of the brigade at 12 o'clock, moving the artillery by hand, and formed the column on the Chattanooga road, where Colonel Stanley again assumed command.

I was charged with the duty of remaining till morning and calling in the pickets of this division. Early in the evening I issued orders to the Sixty-ninth Ohio, Fifteenth Kentucky, Thirty-seventh Indiana, and two companies of the Eleventh Ohio to silently withdraw the picket line at ten minutes past 4 the next morning and assemble near your headquarters. These orders were executed without confusion and with little delay, and the whole picket force was marched to Chattanooga and reported at your headquarters.

I am, very respectfully, your obedient servant.

WILLIAM L. STOUGHTON,
Colonel 11th Michigan Infantry, Comdg. Second Brigade.

Maj. JAMES A. LOWRIE,
Assistant Adjutant-General, Second Division.

No. 41.

Report of Capt. Frederick Schultz, Battery M, First Ohio Light Artillery.

HDQRS. BATTERY M, FIRST OHIO VOLUNTEER ARTILLERY,
Chattanooga, Tenn., September 29, 1863.

SIR: I occupied, September 19, a. m., a place near Crawfish Spring when one-half of the battery under Lieutenant Sturges and Lieutenant Ziegler was ordered to re-enforce Captain Bridges, who was hard pressed by the rebel artillery, and had already sustained considerable loss, but the enemy's guns were soon silenced and the half battery was ordered to rejoin the other half at about 2 p. m. The whole battery and two regiments of infantry of the Second Brigade were ordered to the battle-field in a northeasterly direction, where, in the evening, again one-half of the battery under Lieutenant Sturges and Lieutenant Ziegler were ordered to assist Second and Third Brigades. After firing ten rounds canister, at about 8 p. m. they were ordered back to the other half on a hill, where the whole battery remained all night.

At about 9 a. m., September 20, 1863, I was ordered to the front and took position on the left of the brigade on a hill, but did not fire; changed position several times by order of Major-General Negley. About 12 m. I was attacked by the enemy, whereupon I opened fire with the whole battery, thereby holding the enemy in check, and sustained a loss of 4 men wounded and 8 horses killed and wounded, and some other damage, and expended 240 rounds of ammunition, 75 rounds canister and balance shell. I was ordered from there to Rossville, where I found the greatest part of the division, and camped there all night. About 9 a. m., September 21, 1863, I took position about 1 mile in front of Rossville. Two sections under my direction [were posted?] in a road leading to Rossville, supported by the Eleventh Michigan and Eighteenth Ohio Infantry, and one section under Lieutenant Sturges, supported by the Nineteenth Illinois, on a hill on the left, where we held the enemy in check all day without any serious loss on our side, and fired about 175 rounds.

At about 11 p. m. we were ordered to this place, and on the 22d was ordered in the fort partly completed, where I still remain.

I herewith send you a list of equipments and implements which were lost during the late engagements.*

F. SCHULTZ,
Capt. Comdg. Battery M, First Ohio Volunteer Artillery.

Maj. W. E. LAWRENCE,
Chief of Arty., 14th A. C., Dept. of the Cumberland.

No. 42.

Report of Col. William Sirwell, Seventy-eighth Pennsylvania Infantry, commanding Third Brigade.

HDQRS. THIRD BRIG., SECOND DIV., 14TH ARMY CORPS,
Chattanooga, September 27, 1863.

SIR: I have the honor to submit the following report of the proceedings of the Third Brigade since leaving Cave Spring, Ala.:

At 6 p. m., September 1, we left our encampment at Cave Spring, crossing the Tennessee River the same night, and bivouacked in the river bottom about 3 miles above.

The next day we moved to Moore's Spring near Bridgeport. During the whole of the 3d my brigade was engaged on the mountain side repairing the road and helping the wagons and artillery up to the summit of the Raccoon Mountain; this being safely accomplished, after incredible labor, we reached Warren's Mill the same evening.

According to the wish of the general commanding, I organized a working party from the Seventy-eighth Pennsylvania, who, under my direction, cut down the saw-mill, which is in a deep valley or ravine, and succeeded in changing it into a bridge, over which the

* See p. 305.

whole of General Thomas' corps safely crossed with all its artillery and transportation.

On the 4th we descended into Lookout Valley and bivouacked at Brown's Spring. The next morning I took out the Seventy-eighth Pennsylvania and Twenty-first Ohio on a reconnaissance, leaving one regiment for the night at Payne's Mill, the other at Cureton's Mill. Left on the morning of the 6th and bivouacked at the crossing of Lookout Creek, leaving the Seventy-eighth behind at Payne's Mill. The next day, the 7th, moved to the foot of Lookout Mountain; my command was deployed in groups up the steep mountain side to repair the road, and assist the artillery and wagons in the difficult and tedious ascent. The whole of the 8th and forenoon of the 9th were consumed in this laborious and toilsome duty. The men worked cheerfully, and with such care that no accident of any kind occurred.

On the morning of the 9th saw all our transportation on the mountain and on its way down into the famous Chattanooga Valley. The Seventy-eighth Pennsylvania rejoined my command while descending the mountains.

On the 10th, according to orders previously received, my brigade had the advance on our reconnaissance toward the Pigeon Mountain. Skirmishing with the enemy began early in the day, but we moved slowly and steadily onward, with no loss on our side, though the fire of the enemy was at times very vindictive.

When I reached the mouth of the ravine that finally forms Dug Gap, I halted my command and reported to the general commanding the presence of the enemy strongly posted in our front. At night I threw out a strong line of pickets with lookouts on the eminences, and had my men lie on their arms. At 3 o'clock at night I silently and carefully withdrew my command one-half mile to the rear, leaving the picket in its original line.

Early the next morning the fire of the rebel sharpshooters began on my right and gradually swept round to my left until the whole of my pickets in front and on either side were hotly engaged. In this fierce engagement my men nobly stood their ground, and repelled their assailants at every point. I had 3 men killed and several severely wounded. It was evident that the enemy were in great force and endeavoring to pass round on our left.

Being relieved by General Starkweather's brigade, under the direction of the general commanding, my brigade was withdrawn and again placed in position at the cross-roads, near the general's headquarters, from which it was again removed and placed in position near the Widow Davis'. During this eventful day I cannot too highly recommend the behavior of the officers and men under me, taking up new positions and abandoning others in the face of an overwhelming enemy, and all done without the least confusion or accident of any kind.

We reached the cove near Stevens' Gap late at night, where we remained, changing our position once, until the morning of the 17th, when, according to orders received from the general, my brigade was moved to Alley's Spring, and the next day to Crawfish Spring. The same night, according to orders received, I took the Seventy-eighth, Thirty-seventh Indiana, and Twenty-first Ohio back about 2 miles and took a strong position near Chickamauga Creek, in order to protect our right flank until General McCook, who was then on the march from Stevens' Gap, could join us.

General McCook's corps passed us early in the morning of the 19th. Heavy fighting to our front and left. About 2 p. m. we were ordered to the center and took a position on the edge of a field near the springs. Received an order from General Negley to take two regiments to the woods in the bottom at the foot of the hill. This was about sunset. We had some heavy fighting, the rebels being in the woods and in a corn-field in front. I had 3 men wounded and 2 killed in this engagement, which was short but fierce. Placing two pieces of artillery in position, I had them throw canister into the woods and across the field in my front, which effectually silenced the enemy's fire, and during the balance of the night they were quiet.

The Thirty-seventh Indiana took up a supporting position in my rear. During the night and on the morning of the 20th my men had thrown up breastworks, which were really quite formidable and from which it would have been no easy task to dislodge them. Receiving news early in the morning from my adjutant that the rebels were massing a heavy force in my front, I brought down a section of Marshall's battery, together with the Seventy-fourth Ohio, and put it into excellent position. These arrangements had hardly been completed when I was ordered away to the left of our division to the support of General Beatty, who had been for some time exposed to a terrible fire from an overwhelming force of the enemy. As soon as we were relieved we went at a double-quick, and at the distance of a mile, according to the general's instructions, had my men deployed in an open wood, so as to cover any flank attack from the left. In half an hour I received orders to change position, moving my command by the right flank some 400 yards. My line was now immediately in the rear of where the fiercest of the fight was going on. Marshall's battery was posted on a hill beside a log house used for a hospital, and in a few rounds completely silenced a rebel battery that was beginning to prove very mischievous. While in this position, which was a good one, with open fields in front, my men rapidly threw up fine breastworks of logs and rails; but we had no chance to try their defensive qualities, for the sharp, quick firing of skirmishers in our rear made us face about and hasten up the hill immediately behind us. Here I was solicited by General Brannan to leave a regiment to support one of his batteries. I detached the Twenty-first Ohio for that purpose, taking the Seventy-fourth Ohio to another point to protect another battery. When I returned I could not find my other two regiments where I had left them, but soon ascertained that by order of General Negley they had been taken to the Rossville road to take up a new line and gather up all the stragglers. The battery the Seventy-fourth Ohio was supporting having left, the regiment was brought back and joined to the others on the Rossville road, and did good service in assisting the general to reorganize and return into some kind of shape the confused mass of troops who were rapidly streaming back from the hard-fought battle-field. The Twenty-first Ohio faithfully remained at its post the whole of that dreadful afternoon. The men fought as heroes; almost unsupported and without hope they fought gallantly on; their ammunition giving out, they gathered the cartridges of the dead and wounded, and then finally, without a load in their guns, charged twice upon the rebel horde which was howling furiously around them. Their loss is terrible, losing 272 men* out of a regiment of 500.

---

*See revised statement, p. 172.

On the 21st my brigade was moved out on the Rossville and La Fayette road about three-quarters of a mile. After remaining in position a short time, I was ordered to move back and take position on the face of a high hill on the left of the road, where we remained all day. At 12 o'clock at night, according to previous arrangements, my command was withdrawn silently from its position on the hill, leaving the Thirty-seventh Indiana, two companies of the Seventy-eighth Pennsylvania, and two companies of the Seventy-fourth Ohio on picket, to be withdrawn at daylight, and, along with the pickets of other commands, to form a rear guard to our retreating column.

Early at daybreak on the 22d we entered Chattanooga; since which time my command has been kept constantly at work, night and day, on the fortifications.

During all these long and fatiguing marches and the many skirmishes and the heavy battles but just now over, no troops could have behaved better. I cannot commend them too highly.

The officers and men of the Twenty-first Ohio deserve great praise for their conduct upon this occasion. I respectfully mention, in terms of praise, the names of Lieutenant-Colonel Stoughton and Major McMahan, who gallantly fought and stood by their men until wounded and not able to do anything more.

The officers and men of my brigade behaved bravely, without a single exception. I cannot particularize the officers and men of my command who deserve especial mention; if I did so, my report would be so voluminous that it would scarcely be read.

I am, major, very respectfully, your obedient servant,

WILLIAM SIRWELL,
Colonel, Commanding Third Brigade.

Maj. JAMES A. LOWRIE,
Assistant Adjutant-General, Second Division.

No. 43.

Report of Lieut. Col. William D. Ward, Thirty-seventh Indiana Infantry.

HDQRS. THIRTY-SEVENTH INDIANA VOLUNTEERS,
Chattanooga, September 27, 1863.

CAPTAIN: I have the honor to submit the following report:

The regiment left Cave Spring, Ala., on the 1st day of September and marched about 7 miles, crossing the Tennessee River at Caperton's Ferry.

September 2 marched about 15 miles and camped near Bridgeport.

September 3 marched about 5 miles upon Sand Mountain and camped.

September 4 marched about 7 miles and camped at Brown's Spring.

September 5 lay in camp.

September 6 marched about 7 miles to Johnson's Crook, in Lookout Mountain.

September 7 marched 2½ miles to Stevens' Gap, in same range.

September 8 marched about 5 miles and camped on Lookout range of mountains.

September 9 marched about 5 miles off of mountain and bivouacked in orchard.

September 10 drove the enemy to within about 1 mile of Pigeon or Dug Gap, skirmishing almost constantly. Held our position until after dark, when we by order fell back to new position.

September 11 attacked by the enemy about 8 a. m. and skirmished with them almost constantly until dark, continually changing position to avoid a general engagement, when we fell back to a strong position at the foot of Lookout Mountain to await re-enforcements. The regiment formed part of the rear guard.

September 12 lay in camp.

September 13, 14, 15, 16, worked on the road leading over Lookout Mountain.

September 17 marched about 7 miles and camped.

September 18 formed line of battle. Held for a short time and changed position.

September 19 formed for battle, Thirty-seventh Regiment on the right of the division. Held our position until late in the evening, when we were moved to the left and participated as supports in a charge upon the enemy.

September 20. This was a series of maneuvers through which I am unable to follow the regiment. The regiment had some little skirmishing. About 3 p. m. the regiment received an order to fall back. It moved back to within about 5 miles of Chattanooga and bivouacked.

September 21 formed in new position, which we held during the day. At night fell back to Chattanooga, the regiment covering the rear. The regiment engaged in a slight skirmish.

September 22, 23, 24, 25, worked on fortifications.

September 26 and 27, lay quietly in camp.

I am, captain, very respectfully, your obedient servant,

WILLIAM D. WARD,
Lieut. Col., Comdg. Thirty-seventh Indiana.

Capt. CHAS. B. GILLESPIE,
Actg. Asst. Adjt. Gen., Third Brigade.

No. 44.

Reports of Maj. Arnold McMahan and Capt. Charles H. Vantine, Twenty-first Ohio Infantry.

HDQRS. 21ST REGIMENT OHIO INFANTRY VOLUNTEERS,
Near Atlanta, Ga., July 14, 1864.

SIR: Herewith is transmitted a statement of the part taken by the Twenty-first Regiment Ohio Infantry Volunteers, under my command, at the battle of Chickamauga.

The letters of Generals Negley and Brannan in reply to my letters to them, copies of all which are herewith transmitted, are made a part of this report and referred for the information of all concerned.

Special attention is called to the letter of General Brannan, in which my command is charged with "surrendering so quietly as to escape the notice of all but the regiment on my immediate left, the colonel of which promptly reported to him the facts," &c.

He will be surprised to know that Colonel Carlton, of the Eighty-ninth Regiment Ohio Volunteer Infantry, and Colonel Le Favour, of the Twenty-second Michigan, were the colonels commanding regiments on my left, both of whom were captured a short time before I was captured myself.

General Brannan may have been misinformed in regard to the position of his troops.

Very respectfully,

A. McMAHAN,
Lieut. Col., Comdg. Twenty-first Ohio Volunteers.

Brig. Gen. WILLIAM D. WHIPPLE,
Asst. Adjt. Gen., Department of the Cumberland.

[Inclosure No. 1.]

CAMP CHASE, COLUMBUS, OHIO,
April 6, 1864.

SIR: Having been a prisoner of war in the hands of the enemy, I was unable sooner to report the part taken by the Twenty-first Regiment Ohio Volunteer Infantry, Third Brigade, Second Division, Fourteenth Army Corps, in the battle of Chickamauga, fought on Saturday and Sunday, September 19 and 20, 1863.

The regiment moved into action Saturday evening, an hour before sundown, under command of Lieut. Col. D. M. Stoughton. We had position on the left of our own brigade and joined Colonel Stanley's (Second) brigade on its right.

We engaged the enemy's skirmishers until dark, when the firing ceased, after which breastworks of logs were constructed, facing east-southeast, in front of an open field. This position was held by us until Sunday morning (20th), at which time our skirmishers became engaged with the skirmishers of the enemy at daylight.

Late Sunday morning (20th) we were withdrawn from this position, and moved with our brigade to a new position. Skirmishers from the Twenty-sixth Ohio Volunteers (General Wood's division) relieved our own skirmishers, and that regiment moved to the position from which we had just withdrawn. This position is also particularly marked by two large vats, used for the manufacture of niter, about 200 yards to the rear.

At 12 o'clock Sunday (20th) our regiment was assigned a position upon a curved ridge, our front being south. A deep ravine was in front of this ridge, and on our right heavy timber; on our left an open field with timber beyond. There was an old house about 200 yards to our rear which was subsequently occupied by our wounded.

Our effective support in this position consisted of the Twenty-second Michigan Volunteers and Eighty-ninth Ohio Volunteers on our right, troops under command of Colonel Walker (of the Thirty-first Ohio Volunteers), and Ninth Ohio on our left, and the Second Minnesota Volunteers in reserve. I have not learned any name by which this position may be designated, therefore have substituted a description of it.

Immediately after taking position (12 m.) the enemy's skirmishers engaged us, and in a short time a strong force moved against us. A severe engagement resulted in the repulse of the enemy.

This demonstration of the enemy for the occupation of this important position was made before the arrival of the support heretofore stated, and though superior in numbers he was unable to endure the repeated volleys of our superior arms (Colt's revolving rifles).

Heavy skirmishing continued until 2 o'clock, when the enemy again made an attempt to carry this position, in which he failed. Our position was maintained, however, with severe loss in killed and wounded.

At 2.30 o'clock Lieutenant-Colonel Stoughton, who was commanding the regiment until this time, was severely wounded, and the command devolved upon myself. By 3 o'clock every effort had failed to procure a further supply of ammunition. Orderlies sent to report our condition and position to Colonel Sirwell, commanding our brigade, and to General Negley, commanding our division, and to obtain ammunition, returned without being able to accomplish the object for which they were sent. Our brigade had retired in the direction of Chattanooga.

I was unable to communicate with General Negley, and no general officer was designated to whom I might report. But we continued to hold our position. The cartridge-boxes of our killed and wounded were carefully searched, also the hospitals for any ammunition that might be carried there in the cartridge-boxes of our wounded, and by this means obtained sufficient ammunition to meet the enemy in a third assault upon our position about 5 o'clock.

In this assault the enemy crossed the ravine in our front and carried his banners up the hill to within 20 yards of our line. He was repulsed, and did not retire in good order. During the afternoon a battery had range upon our position, inflicting some damage upon us, also setting fire to the leaves and brush in our front, and the enemy advanced under cover of the smoke. The wounded, under cover of our fire, were removed.

A heavy line of skirmishers continued to annoy us, and a sharp fire upon this line exhausted our ammunition a short time before sundown, at which time the Second Regiment Minnesota Volunteers relieved us. A further search for ammunition resulted in finding one round each for the men composing my command, which had now become very much reduced in numbers.

At this time Colonel Van Derveer (who assumed command) ordered me to occupy a position on the extreme right, from which a part of our line had just been driven by the enemy. In obedience to the order we occupied the position and captured 9 prisoners. A sharp fire from the enemy forced us back, but we regained our position and held it until dark, at which time a brigade of four regiments, under Colonel Trigg, moved upon us and overwhelmed us.

Simultaneous with this movement of the enemy, which was upon our right flank and rear, we received a fire from the enemy, who had also opened upon our left, which took effect both upon the enemy on our right and ourselves. During the misunderstanding thus occasioned, a part of my men escaped under cover of the night. Colonel Van Derveer having withdrawn the troops under his command, my command was unsupported, and both flanks were exposed. Thus we lost our stand of colors, which were made sacred to us by the blood of many comrades who fell in their defense and for their honor on other fields as well as on the unfortunate field of Chickamauga.

Great credit is due the gallant officers and brave men of my command for their soldier-like bearing and good discipline, who stood by their colors and contested the fortunes of the day to the bitter end.

I have the honor to report that my regiment did the last firing upon and offered the latest resistance to the advance of the enemy which he received, and which checked his progress and ended the battle of Chickamauga.

Having been separated from my brigade and division commanders without orders, and not being in communication with any other general officer, I was not informed of the movements of the army, and held my regiment too closely engaged for the nature of the contest at dark.

The reference made to other officers and troops than those under my command is not intended as a report of any part of their conduct on the field, but to describe the position of my own command, yet I would be pleased to note the gallant conduct of the troops I have mentioned.

Our losses were as follows:

Casualties.	Officers.	Enlisted men.	Total.
Killed and died of wounds	1	47	48
Wounded	3	98	101
Prisoners	12	104	116
Total *	16	249	265

Rounds of ammunition expended, 43,550.

We moved into action with 22 officers, and 517 men with rifles.

Very respectfully,

A. McMAHAN,
Major Twenty-first Regiment Ohio Volunteer Infantry.

[Inclosure No. 2.]

CAMP CHASE, OHIO, *April* 12, 1864.

Maj. Gen. J. S. NEGLEY :

GENERAL : As soon as I can obtain the necessary information I will submit a report, as complete as practicable, of the part taken by the Twenty-first Regiment Ohio Volunteer Infantry in the battle of Chickamauga, fought September 19 and 20, 1863.

To obtain this information I must, under present circumstances (being a paroled prisoner), inquire by letters for several facts which I wish to embody in it.

I will state here, however, that my report of the conduct of my regiment on the field during its participation in the battle referred to is now written, and so soon as the facts above alluded to are obtained will be submitted.

I would be pleased to have my report accompanied by a letter from you, showing why I received no orders from you before night, or in time to prevent so severe a loss of my command on the 20th of September, above referred to. Be assured, general, that the unfortunate officers [and men] of my command now suffering the miseries of imprisonment in the hands of the enemy, as well as myself, will

* See statement, p. 172.

be slow to believe that our old commander, who defended Nashville with such signal ability and who acquitted himself with honor in the battle of Stone's River and Dug Gap, came short in the discharge of his high duty and the expectations of the army and country at the battle of Chickamauga.

It would be useless to call attention to the brave men of my command who fell in the line of their duty, though fighting against hope, but I would be pleased to communicate to the surviving officers and soldiers of my regiment who fought with me on that memorable occasion that their general appreciates their services and conduct on the field.

As before stated I will submit a report at the earliest possible moment, and would be glad to annex to it a copy of your letter and this.

Be assured of my kindest personal regards.

Very respectfully,

A. McMAHAN,
Major Twenty-first Ohio Volunteer Infantry.

P. S.—Address me at Perrysburg, Wood County, Ohio.

[Inclosure No. 3.]

HEADQUARTERS,
Louisville, Ky., April 18, 1864.

Maj. A. McMAHAN,
Twenty-first Ohio Volunteers, Camp Chase:

DEAR SIR: Your letter of 12th instant has my attention.

The intelligence of your safe return is highly gratifying. Please accept my grateful appreciation of the sentiments of personal respect and confidence you have so kindly expressed.

You are doubtless aware that Generals Brannan and Wood indulged in severe and unauthorized reflections upon the division and myself. These reflections received my prompt notice, and were investigated before a court of inquiry, which I requested (as you have or will read), with the most satisfactory results.

During the battle on Sunday, and after my First and Second Brigades were detached from my command, General Brannan applied earnestly for a regiment to support his position. The Twenty-first Ohio Volunteers was sent him for the purpose. Shortly afterward the tide of battle, and the assault of a largely superior force from the enemy, separated my command—which then consisted of the remainder of the Third Brigade and some 50 pieces of artillery— from the troops on my left, and compelled the withdrawal of the artillery to McFarland's for safety.

The Twenty-first Ohio Volunteers remained under the immediate command of General Brannan, and, as I have been informed, covered his retreat after dark.

I have received no official report of the operations of the Twenty-first Ohio Volunteers after it was placed under the command of General Brannan; therefore I am ignorant of the facts, and you know best what orders he gave, if any, and how far he is responsible for the circumstances which occasioned the fearful loss of so many heroic men.

I shall take pleasure in reading your statement of the facts.

Yours, very truly,

JAS. S. NEGLEY,
Major-General.

[Inclosure No. 4.]

PERRYSBURG, OHIO, *April* 22, 1864.

Brigadier-General BRANNAN,
    Comdg. Third Div., 14*th A. C.*, *September* 20, 1863 :

SIR: On the 12th instant I wrote General James S. Negley in regard to the dispositions made of the Twenty-first Regiment Ohio Volunteer Infantry, at the battle of Chickamauga, Sunday afternoon, September 20, 1863.

In reply I received his letter, dated Louisville, Ky., April 18, 1864, from which the following is an extract, viz :

> During the battle on Sunday, and after my First and Second Brigades were detached from my command, General Brannan applied earnestly for a regiment to support his position. The Twenty-first Ohio Volunteers was sent to him for the purpose.
>
>   *   *   *   *   *   *   *
>
> The Twenty-first Ohio Volunteers remained under the immediate command of General Brannan, and, as I have been informed, covered his retreat after dark.

I have lately returned from an imprisonment in the hands of the enemy, having been captured at the battle and on the day above referred to, and intend to submit a statement of the conduct of my regiment in said battle as soon as practicable.

My object in writing to you is to learn why I was not informed of the withdrawal of the troops on the Horseshoe Ridge at dark, and why I received no orders from you in regard to the retreat of my own command. Having no ammunition and the troops having been stealthily withdrawn from my flanks I was forced to meet the enemy under serious disadvantages. The interposition of my regiment between the enemy and our retiring forces made their retreat an easy matter after dark, as they were not disturbed in the even tenor of their way toward Chattanooga.

I will be glad to accompany my report—which is now written—by a letter containing such information as may seem proper to you.

    Very respectfully,

                    A. McMAHAN,
    Major Twenty-first Regiment Ohio Volunteer Infantry.

P. S.—Post-office: Perrysburg, Wood County, Ohio.

[Inclosure No. 5.]

HEADQUARTERS DEPARTMENT OF THE CUMBERLAND,
                  Chattanooga, Tenn., *May* 3, 1864.

Maj. A. McMAHAN,
    Twenty-first Ohio Volunteers :

MAJOR : I have the honor to acknowledge the receipt of your communication of April 22, 1864, inquiring wherefore you were not informed of the withdrawal of troops from your flanks, nor ordered to withdraw your command of Twenty-first Ohio Volunteers from the Horseshoe Ridge on Sunday night, September 20, at Chickamauga, and would state in reply that at the time of your command being captured no portion of my troops had been withdrawn from the field, nor had orders been issued to that effect.

The surrender of your command was accomplished so quietly as to escape the notice of all but the regiment on your immediate left, the colonel of which promptly reported the fact to me, whereupon I sent the Thirty-fifth Ohio Volunteers to hold the position, which it did successfully against a subsequent attack of the rebels.

The extract quoted from Major-General Negley's letter of April 18, 1864, to the effect that the Twenty-first Ohio Volunteers covered my retreat after dark is incorrect, as that duty was performed by the Sixty-eighth and One hundred and first Indiana Volunteer Regiments, being the only troops who had any ammunition whatever.

Very respectfully, your obedient servant,

J. M. BRANNAN,
Brig. Gen., Chief of Artillery, 14th Army Corps,
Late Comdg. Third Division, 14th Army Corps.

P. S.—The troops on your right belonged to Major-General Granger's corps and were withdrawn before you were captured without my being notified of the fact. My command was not withdrawn for a considerable time after.

—

HDQRS. TWENTY-FIRST REGIMENT OHIO VOL. INFTY.,
Chattanooga, Tenn., September 27, 1863.

SIR : In obedience to orders just received, I have the honor to submit the following as a report of the proceedings of my command since leaving Cave Spring, Ala.:

On September 1, 1863, the regiment left Cave Spring, Ala., taking up the line of march at about 7 p. m., Lieut. Col. D. M. Stoughton being in command. Passing through Stevenson we crossed the Tennessee River the same evening, bivouacked on south side of the river until morning, going into bivouac at 1 a. m. of 2d instant. Took up line of march on morning of 2d instant at 7 o'clock ; went into bivouac evening of 2d at 4 o'clock, near Bridgeport, Ala., and near foot of Big Raccoon Mountain.

On 3d we crossed Big Raccoon, the companies being scattered along the mountain to help the teams up. At about 3 p. m., the teams being over, took up line of march and marched 6 miles, going into bivouac at about sundown.

On the 4th instant we marched to foot of the mountain and went into bivouac about 4 p. m.

On the 5th a reconnaissance was made some 2 or 3 miles into the valley to the iron-works, capturing some salt and some tobacco. The troops composing the reconnoitering force were Seventy-eighth Pennsylvania Volunteers, Twenty-first Ohio Volunteer Infantry, and one section of Battery G, First Ohio Volunteer Artillery. No enemy was discovered during the day. The regiment went into bivouac at 5 p. m. Company D being detached on picket, did not rejoin the command until next day.

At daylight on the 6th the command was marched back to foot of Big Raccoon for knapsacks. After getting knapsacks started back and marched until about 6 p. m., when we went into bivouac.

On 7th we marched about 4 miles and reached the foot of Lookout Mountain.

On 8th we crossed Lookout; the companies were scattered along the mountain to assist the train up. The train was got over at 10 p. m., when we marched to the top and went into bivouac.

On the 9th we marched to the foot of the mountain and went into bivouac about 4 p. m.

On the 10th we moved from our position at the foot of Lookout and advanced slowly toward Pigeon Gap, Twenty-first being in advance, Companies F and C being deployed as skirmishers, light skirmishing being the order of the day. We reached a hill that evening within a mile or mile and one-half of the Gap. At 3 a. m. we changed position going about three-quarters of a mile to the rear of the hill occupied the evening before, the regiment being formed in the edge of a dense wood, completely concealing it from the enemy.

At 6 a. m. of the 11th we changed position a short distance to the left. We lay there until 10 a. m., when we were moved to the rear to protect the wagon train from some rebel cavalry who were reported about to attack it. While lying here we threw up a slight breastwork of rails, logs, &c. At 3 p. m. we were ordered back still farther, the corps being compelled to fall back. We marched about 2 miles to the rear and took up position in a wood on the left as support to Battery G, in double column on the center closed *en masse*. The artillery were firing quite rapidly, and in about half an hour we were moved still farther to the rear, marching by the left flank. Shortly after we were deployed in line of battle. After a short time we again commenced the retrograde movement, marching by the right of companies about 4 miles. At 9 p. m. we took position on the brow of a hill and went into bivouac.

Moved our position slightly on morning of 12th and formed line of battle; stacked arms.

On 12th and 13th we lay in the same position taken up the morning of the 12th.

On 14th changed position to the right about three-quarters of a mile. We lay in that position until the 17th, when we took up the line of march at 7 a. m. We marched to Chickamauga Creek and went into bivouac on its banks that night about dark.

On 18th took up line of march at 3 p. m., marched 5 miles to the front and got into bivouac after dark. We lay there about three hours, when we were ordered back to the Chickamauga again. We reached the creek, threw out pickets, and went into bivouac by 4 a. m. of 19th. At daylight we threw out pickets and marched back a mile, where we took position as support for Battery G; threw up breastworks of logs and stones. Lay there until 3 p. m., when we were again marched up to the front about 5 miles. Heavy fighting had been going on all day on our left. About 6 p. m. reached the battlefield, formed line of battle, and marched forward in a strip of woods about a mile. Just after entering the woods we were saluted by a volley of about ten or twelve guns. We returned the fire, when the enemy threw down their arms and fled. Lay in line of battle all night, every man on the alert. We lost 3 men wounded and 2 killed on 19th.

Next morning (20th) we were moved from our position about 9 a. m. over to the left, the enemy having made a spirited attack on that point. After changing position several times we were finally put in position on the brow of a hill as support to a battery belonging to General Brannan's division. At about 11.30 a. m. the enemy advanced on us in heavy force. We, however, held our ground until 3 p. m., when some of the Reserve Corps came up and relieved us, charging down the hill and driving the enemy in gallant style. They kept the enemy at bay for about one hour, when they fell back and we were again engaged with the enemy. In the meantime we had thrown up a slight breastwork of logs and stone, behind which we fought until about 5 p. m., when we were relieved by some of General Brannan's division. Our ammunition was exhausted, and we could not procure any more. At about half past 5 p. m. the enemy sent up messengers to Brannan's men stating that some of them were waiting for them (our men) to cease firing in order to give themselves (i. e., the enemy) up. The firing ceased and the enemy came up, but instead of giving themselves up they fired a volley and charged up the hill, gaining possession of it entirely. The commanding officer of Brannan's troops asked that the Twenty-first should charge up and retake the hill. After some delay one round of ammunition was procured per man from the dead and wounded. With this one round in our guns, we charged up the hill. We delivered our volley, but the enemy was in too large force, and we were forced back. Twice again, with no ammunition, we charged, with the vain hope of retaking the hill. But we were repulsed. In the meantime Brannan's men were reforming and we lay down to wait until they reorganized, intending to make one grand charge, and if possible retake the hill. While we were waiting a column was observed filing in a small ravine on our right flank. Supposing they were our men (they being dressed in blue jeans) we took no notice of them until they formed line of battle facing toward us. They formed and commenced advancing on us; when asked who they were, said they were "Jeff. Davis' men;" supposed they were some of J. C. Davis' division. When they were within a few rods of us they called upon us to "surrender," "lay down," &c. A portion of the men jumped up to retreat toward General Brannan's division, when they poured in a heavy volley, wounding and killing a great many. A few of the men of the Twenty-first who escaped formed, and were led to Rossville by Colonel Walker, of the Thirty-first Ohio Volunteer Infantry.

On the morning of the 21st we collected all that could be found, reported to Colonel Sirwell, our brigade commander, and took position on the left of the Seventy-eighth Regiment Pennsylvania Volunteers.

On the 21st, together with the rest of the brigade, we took up position on a hill near Rossville, where we lay until about 12 m., when we were withdrawn and marched to Chattanooga, reaching our present camp on the 22d. Since then we have done nothing but work on the fort, &c.

Of the officers and men of this command I have only to say that they have done their duty. We ask no higher praise than that. Every man fought as if the fate of the nation rested on his individual efforts. Lieut. Col. D. M. Stoughton was wounded about 3.30 p. m. on the 20th. A cooler, braver, or more patriotic officer than he never drew sword.

You will see by the official report of killed, wounded, and missing that we lost some 272 officers and men.*

I am, sir, very respectfully, your obedient servant,

CHARLES H. VANTINE,
Captain Co. I, Comdg. 21st Ohio Vol. Infantry.

Capt. Chas. B. Gillespie,
Acting Assistant Adjutant-General, Third Brigade.

* See revised statement, p. 172.

No. 45.

Report of Capt. Joseph Fisher, Seventy-fourth Ohio Infantry.

HDQRS. SEVENTY-FOURTH REGT. OHIO VOL. INFANTRY,
Chattanooga, Tenn., September 27, 1863.

SIR: In compliance with order received, I have the honor to make the following report of the proceedings of this command since leaving Cave Spring, Ala.:

September 1, 1863, left Cave Spring, Ala., at 6 p. m. Marched until 2 a. m., September 2, and halted for the night.

September 2 was ordered to march as train guards.

September 3 marched in the right center of brigade and assisted the artillery up Raccoon Mountain.

September 4 were advance guard; one company (Company C) thrown out as skirmishers, and Companies F and D, as pioneers, were ordered to encamp about 1 mile in advance of brigade.

September 5 and 6 remained in camp.

September 7, 1863, took up the line of march in left center of brigade.

Tuesday, 8th, assisted wagon train up Lookout Mountain; marched about 2 miles and encamped.

Wednesday, 9th, detailed 30 men to dig potatoes. By order of Colonel Sirwell, marched as rear guard to the foot of the mountain.

September 10 started at 7 a. m., went on reconnaissance on the left. Skirmished, and drove the enemy 1 mile. Encamped in a neck of woods to support Battery G, First Ohio Artillery.

September 11 changed position silently at 2 a. m., 40 men and 2 commissioned officers being detailed as skirmishers. Skirmished all day, in which privates Patrick McCain, Company F, was killed,* and William H. Griffith, Company A, severely wounded; Daniel Kimmel, Company G, slightly. The regiment, supporting Battery G, fell back to the foot of the mountain.

September 12 formed line of battle. Remained in camp the 13th, 14th, 15th, and 16th.

September 17, 1863, marched all day.

Friday, September 18, marched, at 3 p. m., about 5 miles, and encamped.

September 19 detailed as train guard; moved on still farther to the front, and at night took up our position.

Sunday, September 20, supported Battery G, First Ohio Artillery, in various parts of the field. Fell back within the gap, and encamped for the night.

September 21 threw up breastworks of logs, and lay in line of battle, with two companies detailed as skirmishers. Retreated in silence to Chattanooga at 11 p. m. John F. Boals, corporal, Company G, wounded in leg.

September 22 regiment detailed on picket duty at 6 a. m.; threw up breastworks of rails; in afternoon had brisk skirmishing with the enemy.

Wednesday, September 23, regiment remained on picket until 11 a. m., being relieved by the Nineteenth Regiment, Illinois Volunteers.

September 24 lay in camp all day; worked on fortifications at night.

---

* McCain was taken prisoner and subsequently died at Charleston, S. C.

September 25 still in camp; worked on fortifications at night. September 26 and 27 still in camp.

Very respectfully, your obedient servant,

JOSEPH FISHER,
Captain Co. E, Comdg. 74th Ohio Volunteer Infantry.

Capt. CHAS. B. GILLESPIE,
Actg. Asst. Adjt. Gen., Third Brigade.

No. 46.

Report of Capt. Alexander Marshall, Battery G, First Ohio Light Artillery.

HDQRS. BATTERY G, FIRST OHIO VOL. ARTILLERY,
Chattanooga, September 29, 1863.

SIR : In compliance with your order, I herewith report proceedings of Battery G, First Ohio Volunteer Artillery, during the action of 19th and 20th instant:

Broke camp near Chickamauga Creek on the 19th instant, 12 m., when we moved as ordered to a position to the left, with the brigade near General Rosecrans' headquarters. At about half past 4 p. m. moved about 80 rods to the left, taking position on an elevation in the corner of an open field. Here remained harnessed and hitched in during the night.

At about 8 a. m., the 20th instant, one section in command of Lieutenant Bills moved down to the front about one-half a mile, and joined the brigade. About 9 a. m. moved as ordered, following Captain Schultz's battery to the left and rear ; took several positions upon the hills in the woods as ordered by General Negley without firing. Opened the battery but once, firing not over 50 rounds, silencing a battery in our front which I think was one of our captured batteries that was turned by the enemy upon us.

About 3 p. m. moved to rear as ordered by General Negley, halting in an open field on low ground near the road where troops of the different divisions and corps were being reformed. At 5.30 moved to the rear with brigade, as ordered, halting for the night in an open field at cross-roads about 5 miles from Chattanooga, at camp formerly occupied by the enemy.

Ammunition expended, number of rounds, 294. Number of horses abandoned, 5.

ALEX. MARSHALL,
Captain, Comdg. Battery G, First Ohio Vol. Artillery.

Capt. F. SCHULTZ,
Chief of Artillery, Second Division, 14th Army Corps.

No. 47.

Reports of Brig. Gen. John M. Brannan, U. S. Army, commanding Third Division.

HDQRS. THIRD DIVISION, FOURTEENTH ARMY CORPS,
Camp near Trenton, Ga., September 8, 1863.

COLONEL : I have the honor to forward the following summary of the operations of my division during the advance from Winchester, Tenn., to this point :

On the 16th of August, being ordered to report to Major-General

Reynolds, commanding Fourth Division, Fourteenth Army Corps, I advanced, by his directions, from Winchester, on the Pelham road, via Decherd, and encamped that night at about 4 miles from Decherd.

On the following morning, August 17, I struck camp, but was unable to proceed, owing to the delay of the Fourth Division in ascending the mountains.

On the 18th of August I ascended the mountain, and encamped, with my entire division, near University Place, two brigades being at that point and one 2 miles in advance.

On the 19th I commenced the descent of the mountain toward Sweeden's Cove, and succeeded in bringing the division, with the entire train, into camp at the head of that cove, late the same night.

I lay at Sweeden's Cove till the 22d, when, in accordance with orders from General Reynolds, I advanced to Battle Creek, having thrown forward the Third Brigade (Colonel Van Derveer commanding) of my division the night previous to the mouth of Battle Creek.

This brigade met with no resistance in taking up a position, which it did in the earth-works erected by General McCook in 1862. The enemy's pickets were on the farther bank of the Tennessee River, but disappeared about the 24th instant.

In this position I remained until the 29th, during which stay I constructed a permanent bridge over Battle Creek, connecting the fords on the Tennessee River.

Having received permission to throw a brigade across the river, I ordered the Third Brigade (Colonel Van Derveer's) to cross the river, which he succeeded in doing without any opposition, completing the movement on the 31st, having previously sent two companies over before daylight on the 29th.

On the following day I commenced to cross with the entire division and completed the crossing on the 2d of September, with the ammunition and baggage trains, having previously sent the supply train by way of Bridgeport.

The crossing was rendered most tedious and protracted from having no transportation further than the rafts hastily constructed from such lumber as we could pick up, rendering it necessary in many instances to partially unload the wagons before placing them on the rafts.

On the night of the 3d I encamped at Graham's Station, and remained there the following day, waiting for the supply train to come up from Bridgeport, without which it was impossible for me to advance.

On the 4th (the train having come up) I proceeded through Hog Jaw Valley to Raccoon Mountain, ascending by Gordon's Mines, and succeeded in getting one brigade with its train up the mountain that day, encamping with my two remaining brigades at the foot of the mountain.

On the 5th I sent two brigades to this point, where they arrived, one at 10 a. m. and the other at 2 p. m. that day.

I succeeded in getting up the mountain with the remaining portion of my command, with the ammunition and supply trains, at 10 p. m. same day. The ascent at that point is exceedingly steep and dangerous for artillery and wagons, but by great care and exertion on part of the infantry, who acted admirably on the occasion, the artillery and wagons were brought up with but little damage, and the loss of two wagons only.

On the 7th I advanced to this point with the remaining portion of my command, and encamped at about 1 p. m.

I found a plentiful supply of excellent water along the route up the Tennessee River, sufficient for a much larger command.

At Graham's Station, 4 miles from the river, there is a good supply of water for a division, but not sufficient for the stock, within 2 miles. At the base of Raccoon Mountain I found a large spring, capable of supplying a large body of troops. On the summit, however, the water is difficult of access and not of the best quality, being far back in Gordon's coal mines, and requiring some skill and much labor in procuring it. There is, however, a sufficiency for a division with its stock.

The water at this point (Squirrel Spring) is plentiful enough for a large army.

I am, colonel, very respectfully, your obedient servant,

J. M. BRANNAN,
Brigadier-General, Commanding Division.

Lieut. Col. GEORGE E. FLYNT,
Asst. Adjt. Gen., and Chief of Staff, 14th *Army Corps.*

———

HDQRS. THIRD DIVISION, 14TH ARMY CORPS,
Camp Rodgers, McLemore's Cove, Ga., September 12, 1863

COLONEL: I have the honor to report that I left my camp at Easley's at daylight yesterday, September 11, without baggage, in accordance with an order to that effect directing me to cross Lookout Mountain without delay. On arriving at the base of the mountain I found that it would be impossible to proceed farther that night, as General Reynolds' baggage train and troops obstructed the ascent. I accordingly went into camp at that point with one brigade, leaving the other brigades at Stewart's.

Having received further orders at 6 p. m. that day, September 11, to get my division in position in McLemore's Cove by daylight on the following day, September 12, I immediately struck camp and again endeavored to ascend the mountain, but found it impossible to commence the ascent until after 12 o'clock that night, owing to the delay on part of Colonel King in moving his brigade, the troops, in the meantime, bivouacking at the foot of the mountain.

About 12.30 a. m. of the 12th I commenced the ascent and succeeded in getting up an entire brigade by daylight, with the exception of a portion of its battery, which, however, came up soon after. At daylight I followed with the remainder of my command, and, pushing forward with all speed, arrived at my present camp at 11 a. m. with the entire infantry and one battery of the division, a second battery arriving at 12.30 p. m.

At 2 p. m., in accordance with verbal orders received from the major-general commanding corps, I proceeded on a reconnaissance with my entire division (except one battery) and one brigade of the First Division, and advanced 2 miles beyond Davis' Cross-Roads without seeing anything of the rebels with the exception of a few mounted men. My entire division, with the exception of a regiment guarding the trains, is encamped at this point. The train is parked at the foot of Lookout Mountain and will move up at daylight to-morrow.

I should have joined General Negley at 7 a. m. had Colonel King moved with more promptness.

I am, colonel, very respectfully, your obedient servant,

J. M. BRANNAN,
Brigadier-General, Commanding.

Lieut. Col. GEORGE E. FLYNT,
Assistant Adjutant-General, and Chief of Staff.

—

HDQRS. THIRD DIVISION, 14TH ARMY CORPS,
Near Chattanooga, Tenn., September 29, 1863.

COLONEL : I have the honor to forward, for the information of the major-general commanding, the following report of the part taken by my division (Third, Fourteenth Army Corps) during the engagement of the 19th and 20th September, 1863, on Chickamauga Creek. In accordance with orders I struck the camp of my division at Gower's Ford, Chickamauga Creek, at about 5 p. m. on the 18th instant, and advanced by the Chattanooga road to the junction of the La Fayette road about 3 miles above Crawfish Spring, whence, taking the latter road, I arrived by daylight at a point about 2½ miles distant from its junction with the Chattanooga road. I was much retarded in this march, which continued during the entire night, by the delay of the Twenty-first Corps in getting into position, having frequently to halt for a considerable time to enable portions of that command to come up from the rear of my column.

On arriving at a point on the La Fayette road known as Kelly's house, I received orders from Major-General Thomas to capture, if possible, a rebel force represented by Col. Dan. McCook to be a brigade cut off on the west side of the Chickamauga Creek ; failing in this, to drive it across the creek. In obedience to these instructions, I advanced the Second Brigade of my division (Col. John T. Croxton, Fourth Regiment, Kentucky Volunteer Infantry, commanding) by the Reed's Bridge road toward the rebel left, while the remaining brigades of my command advanced by the Daffron's Ford road to strike the supposed right of the enemy's position.

Shortly after 7 a. m. on the 19th instant the Second Brigade, having advanced about three-quarters of a mile toward the Chickamauga, came upon a strong force of the enemy, consisting of two divisions instead of the supposed brigade, who made a furious attack, repulsing Colonel Croxton's first advance. The rebels following this up with a much superior force, a desperate conflict ensued, Colonel Croxton maintaining his ground with great determination, and though suffering considerable loss, refusing to yield his position to the most furious efforts of the rebels. At this point Colonel Carroll, Tenth Regiment Indiana Volunteer Infantry, fell mortally wounded, while gallantly leading his regiment, and Lieut. Col. P. B. Hunt, commanding Fourth Kentucky Volunteer Infantry, was carried from the field in a scarcely less precarious condition. On Colonel Hunt being wounded, I sent Maj. R. M. Kelly, division inspector, at his own request, to command the Fourth Kentucky, which he did that day and the following in the most gallant manner.

I here re-enforced Colonel Croxton with the Thirty-first Ohio Volunteer Infantry (Lieutenant-Colonel Lister commanding) from the left, being the only force available.

In the meantime the Third Brigade (Col. F. Van Derveer, Thirty-fifth Ohio Volunteer Infantry, commanding), supported by the First Brigade with two regiments (Col. J. M. Connell, Seventeenth Ohio Volunteer Infantry, commanding), having advanced about 1½ miles on the Daffron's Ford road, came into collision with the rebels strongly posted, who opened with a tremendous fire of musketry and cannon at short range. This, however, could not deter the Third Brigade which bore down upon the rebels with irresistible determination driving them back to within one-quarter of a mile of the creek, when the rebels, making a feint on the left rapidly threw a heavy force on my right, and succeeded in partially piercing the center, where the communication with the extreme right was unavoidably weak and disconnected.

About this period, at my repeated and earnest request for re-enforcements, General Thomas sent the First Division to my support, and the greater portion of that command advanced to my center to arrest the movements of the enemy in that quarter. In this, how-ever, the First Division failed, the troops retiring with some pre-cipitancy, leaving the battery of the regular brigade in the hands of the rebels, and communication entirely cut off between my extreme flanks. I however succeeded in preventing the rebels from following up their advantage at this point by a charge of portions of the First and Third Brigades, during which the battery of the regular brigade was retaken at the point of the bayonet by the Ninth Ohio Infantry (Col. Gustave Kammerling commanding). The enemy, however, continued to press heavily on the center, and finding it impossible to re-establish and hold communication between my flanks, I withdrew to a ridge about half a mile from the La Fayette road, removing my dead and wounded, and formed line there, without molestation, at about 2 p. m.

About 3 p. m., by direction of Major-General Thomas, I moved the First and Third Brigades to the right in rear of the Second Bri-gade, and subsequently, in accordance with orders to that effect, withdrew my entire division to the right, on the La Fayette road, resigning my first position to Baird's, Palmer's, and Johnson's di-visions.

During this day the Second Brigade maintained a severe conflict, without intermission, for a period of six hours, repulsing with great slaughter the repeated attacks of a much superior force, and cap-turing 5 guns, which they brought off the field.

The other brigades of the division cannot have had less severe work, owing to the number of points from which they were at dif-ferent times attacked, and the vastly superior force of the enemy immediately opposed to them.

It was only by the most unflinching courage and determination that these points could be held before the overwhelming masses of troops hurled against them by the rebels, whose every effort ap-peared to be directed toward breaking this line, and securing the line of communication in its rear.

I bivouacked on the night of the 19th on a line perpendicular to the La Fayette road, my left brigade nearly joining it at Dyer's house, and my two right brigades thrown back at right angles on the heights of the Missionary Ridge. During the night I was ordered to put two brigades into line, connecting Reynolds' and Negley's divisions, which I accordingly did, completing the move-ment before daylight on the 20th. I moved the Third Brigade of my division, shortly after daylight of the 20th, as support in rear of the First and Second Brigades. I had now two brigades in line, with one in support, Negley being on my right and Reynolds on my left.

After a continuous flank movement of some duration by the entire line to the left, the engagement began at about 9 a. m. by a furious attack on Baird's division, which, proving of a determined nature, my supporting brigade was ordered to support that division, Negley having previously been removed to the extreme left of the corps, and Van Cleve, who had replaced him, having shortly afterward been ordered in the same direction. Wood was now on my immediate right. Wood being almost immediately afterward ordered to the left, moved out of the line, while Davis took ground to his left to fill the vacancy caused by Wood. In this movement a slight interval occurred in the line, which the rebels took advantage of with great rapidity, intercepting and breaking the line of battle of the army at that point.

Wood being taken while marching by the flank, broke and fled in confusion, and my line, actually attacked from the rear, was obliged to swing back on the right, which it accomplished with wonderful regularity under such circumstances (with, however, the exception of a portion of the First Brigade, which, being much exposed, broke with considerable disorder).

The line being now broken, and severely pressed at this point, and great confusion prevailing in the supports, composed of Wood's and Van Cleve's divisions, I formed the remnant of my command (and such stragglers from other commands as I could rally and bring into position) in line to resist, if possible, the pressure of the now advancing rebels.

In this manner I succeeded in holding the enemy in check for a considerable time, until, finding that the rebels were moving on my right to gain command of the valley by which the right (McCook) was retreating, I swung back my right flank, and, moving about half a mile to the rear, took up a good position on a commanding ridge, General Negley (who had a portion of his command intact) having pledged himself to hold my right and rear.

Finding that this latter point was the key to the position so desired by the enemy, I made every preparation to defend it to the last, my command being somewhat increased by the arrival of portions of Palmer's [Van Cleve's?] and Negley's divisions, and most opportunely re-enforced by Colonel Van Derveer's brigade (Third), which having successfully, though with great loss, held its precarious position in the general line, until all in its vicinity had retreated, retired in good order, actually cutting its way through the rebels to rejoin my division. This gallant brigade was one of the few who maintained their organization perfect through the hard-fought passes of that portion of the field.

Nothing can exceed the desperate determination with which the rebels endeavored to gain possession of this point, hurling entire divisions on my small force in their fierce eagerness to obtain a position which would undoubtedly have given them the grand advantage of the day. My troops maintained their ground with obstinacy, evincing great gallantry and devotion in the most trying circumstances, until re-enforced about 3.30 p. m. by a portion of Granger's Reserve Corps, who took up the position that should have been occupied during the day by Negley's division.

General Negley, so far from holding my right as he had promised, retired, with extraordinary deliberation, to Rossville at an early period of the day, taking with him a portion of my division, as will be seen by the report of Colonel Connell, commanding First Brigade, and leaving me open to attack from the right as well as from the left and front (from which points the rebels attacked me simultaneously on four several occasions), and my rear so far exposed that my staff officers sent back for ammunition were successively cut off, and the ammunition, of such vital importance at that time, prevented from reaching me, thus necessitating the use of the bayonet as my only means of defense.

I remained in this position, heavily engaged, until sunset, re-enforced at intervals by the Ninth Regiment Indiana Volunteers, sent me at my request by General Hazen, and the Sixty-eighth and One hundred and first Regiments Indiana Volunteers, sent by order of General Thomas, also the Twenty-first Ohio Volunteer Infantry, all of whom remained in position and behaved with steadiness while their ammunition lasted. Colonel Stoughton, with a portion of a brigade, also rallied at this point and did good service.

Finding my ammunition almost entirely exhausted, some of the troops having none at all, and the remainder but one or two rounds, I ordered it to be reserved until the last final effort, and resort to be had to the bayonet as a means of defense. Several charges were made by the entire command during the last attack of the enemy, by which they were gallantly driven from the ridge, where they had obtained a momentary lodgment. My entire force during the day and afternoon on this ridge could not have been over 2,500 men, including the stragglers of various regiments and divisions, besides my own immediate command.

Shortly after sunset I withdrew without molestation to Rossville, where I bivouacked for the night, my retreat being covered by the Sixty-eighth and One hundred and first Indiana Volunteer Infantry, the only troops who had a supply of ammunition.

This duty was satisfactorily performed by these regiments under the direction of Capt. C. A. Cilley, of Colonel Van Derveer's staff.

I cannot speak too highly of the gallant conduct of my command during these engagements. The accompanying report * of killed and wounded is a sad but glorious record of the stern devotion with which the officers and men of the Third Division maintained their stand in the desperate position assigned them during the battle of the 19th and 20th.

To the commanding officers of brigades, regiments, and batteries the highest praise is due for the able and fearless manner in which they managed their commands in circumstances of more than ordinary trial.

I herewith forward their several reports, to which I respectfully refer you for an account of the individual action of the different portions of my division, and I cheerfully indorse such special mention as is made of deserving members of the command. Where the conduct of all is so commendable it is hardly possible for me to select any for particular mention, yet I cannot conclude this report without bringing to the special notice of the commanding general the gallant and meritorious conduct of Colonel Van Derveer, Thirty-fifth Regiment Ohio Volunteer Infantry, commanding Third Bri-

---

* Nominal list (omitted) embodied in revised statement, p. 172.

gade, whose fearlessness and calm judgment in the most trying situations added materially to the efficiency of his command, which he handled both days in the most skillful manner, punishing the enemy severely. As also the gallant and dashing Croxton, Fourth Kentucky Infantry, commanding Second Brigade, who, though severely and painfully wounded early the second day, remained on the field rallying and encouraging his men until utterly exhausted.

Colonel Connell, Seventeenth Ohio Infantry, commanding First Brigade, acted with coolness and judgment, and with his brigade rendered efficient service, fighting most gallantly.

Captain Church, commanding Fourth Michigan Battery, First Lieut. F. G. Smith, commanding, and First Lieutenant Rodney, Battery I, Fourth U. S. Artillery, as also First Lieutenant Gary, commanding Company C, First Ohio Volunteer Artillery, are worthy of mention for their gallantry and the skill and judgment with which they worked their guns.

The opportune arrival of Major-General Granger's command, I consider, saved the army from total rout. Being left to my own resources by General Negley, whom I supposed to be on my right, I could not have held my position against another attack had not General Granger's troops got into position to prevent my being flanked on the right. I am indebted to General Steedman for a small supply of ammunition when I was depending solely on the bayonet for repulsing the next assault.

The staff of my division, Capt. Louis J. Lambert, assistant adjutant-general; Capt. George S. Roper, commissary of subsistence; Capt. Lewis Johnson, Tenth Indiana Volunteers, provost-marshal; Lieut. Ira V. Germain, aide-de-camp; Lieut. T. V. Webb, aide-de-camp, and Lieutenant Dunn, Tenth Kentucky Infantry, topographical engineer (missing), performed their duties with fearlessness and great gallantry, carrying my orders under the severest fire, and using every effort to rally and encourage the troops to return to their flag when a panic had evidently seized many, particularly of other divisions.

The medical director, Surgeon Tollman, Second Minnesota Volunteer Infantry, made successfully all the arrangements for the care of the wounded that could be expected considering their great number.

First Lieut. J. W. White, ordnance officer, did his duty well, supplying the ammunition promptly under heavy fire until his communication with the line was cut off.

Brig. Gen. John Beatty joined me on the hill where our last stand was made and gave great assistance in rallying the troops and keeping them in position.

Col. M. B. Walker, Thirty-first Ohio Volunteer Infantry, joined me shortly after we fell back to the ridge, and offered his services to me, as being in arrest he had no command. Being short of staff officers I accepted Colonel Walker's services, and well he served me and his country, rallying and collecting the men and encouraging them to stand by his energy and personal courage. I am much indebted to him.

The Thirty-eighth Ohio Volunteer Infantry (Colonel Phelps commanding), of the First Brigade, was detailed on the 18th as guard to the supply and general train of the division, and being subsequently ordered across the river by General Rosecrans, was unable to participate in the engagements of either day.

The unavoidable absence of this splendid regiment is much to be regretted.

Total number engaged, 5,998.

Loss during 19th and 20th : Killed, 325 ; wounded, 1,639 ; missing, 210.   Total, 2,174.*

I am, colonel, very respectfully, your obedient servant,

J. M. BRANNAN,
Brigadier-General, Commanding Division.

Lieut. Col. GEORGE E. FLYNT,
Asst. Adjt. Gen., and Chief of Staff, 14th Army Corps.

—

HDQRS. THIRD DIVISION, 14TH ARMY CORPS,
Chattanooga, Tenn., October 8, 1863.

CAPTAIN : Owing to the short period allowed me in which to make the official report of the part taken by my command in the battle of Chickamauga, I have the honor to submit the following addition and correction of the list of casualties to my report of the 30th September :

In the position where the last stand was made I omitted to mention the Twenty-first Ohio Volunteer Infantry, of General Negley's division, having fought bravely up to 5 p. m. when their ammunition entirely gave out, were surrendered at about 7 o'clock by Major McMahan (some 40 strong).   It was then occupying a position on my right, which the rebels again attacked after nightfall with a furious discharge of musketry.   The rebels were immediately afterward repulsed in the most gallant manner by the Thirty-fifth Regiment Ohio Volunteer Infantry, Lieutenant-Colonel Boynton commanding.   Colonel Harker, commanding a brigade in Wood's division, held a position on my left, after retiring to the ridge, and acted with great courage and determination, pouring into the rebels an incessant roll of musketry for several hours, causing them to recoil with immense slaughter.

Colonel Hays, Tenth Regiment Kentucky Volunteer Infantry, commanded such portions of the Second Brigade of my division as were mustered on the ridge (after Colonel Croxton had been forced to leave the field by a severe wound), and behaved most gallantly during the entire action, keeping his command to the crest of the hill when he had not a cartridge left.

I desire particularly to mention First Lieut. G. B. Rodney, of Smith's battery (I, Fourth U. S. Artillery), for distinguished gallantry on both days.   He deserves promotion.

In recording the deserving conduct of my staff, I omitted to mention First Lieut. Samuel J. Dick, Eighteenth U. S. Infantry, assistant commissary of musters of this division, who was with me during the greater part of the engagement, and acted with conspicuous gallantry.   Two of my orderlies, Private L. Ballinger, Company C, Seventeenth Ohio Volunteer Infantry, and Private J. Weimer, Company F, Thirty-eighth Ohio Volunteer Infantry (wounded), who remained with me during the engagement of the 20th, are deserving the commanding general's special notice for remarkable bravery and assistance rendered in obtaining cartridges from the boxes of the killed and wounded for the fighting portion of the command.

---

* See revised statement, p. 173.

The following is the loss of my division in *matériel* and horses:

Command.	Guns.	Limbers.	Caissons.	Horses	Remarks.
Company I, 4th U. S. Artillery		1		19	
Company C, 1st Ohio Artillery	1	1	1	26	6-pounder James rifle.
4th Michigan Battery	5	4		35	{2 10-pounder Parrott. 2 6-pounder James rifles. 1 12-pounder howitzer.
Total	6	6	1	80	

Hospital wagons, 1; wagons, 14 (loaded with ammunition, chiefly infantry, caliber .58); ambulances, 1.

I am, captain, very respectfully, your obedient servant,

J. M. BRANNAN,
Brigadier-General, Commanding Division.

Capt. B. H. POLK,
Assistant Adjutant-General, Fourteenth Army Corps.

No. 48.

Report of Capt. Josiah W. Church, First Michigan Light Artillery, Chief of Artillery.

Report of Losses in batteries of the Third Division, Fourteenth Army Corps, during the actions of the 19th and 20th of September, 1863.

Losses.	Fourth Michigan.	Company C, First Ohio Volunteer Artillery.	Company I, Fourth U. S. Artillery.	Total.
		Batteries.		
[PERSONNEL.]				
Commissioned officer:				
Wounded			1	1
Enlisted men:				
Killed		4	1	5
Wounded	7	9	19	35
Missing	4			4
[MATÉRIEL.]				
10-pounder Parrott guns	2			2
10-pounder Parrott limber	1			1
12-pounder howitzer gun	1			1
12-pounder howitzer limber	1			1
12-pounder limber			1	1
12-pounder caisson body		1		1
6-pounder James rifle guns	2	1		3
6-pounder James rifle limbers	2			2
6-pounder James rifle caisson bodies		2		2
Sets wheel harness	6		2	8
Sets lead harness	12	5	6	23
Sponges and rammers	10	4		14
Wormers and staves	3			3
Paulins	4	1	3	8
Revolvers	4			4

Report of Losses in batteries of the Third Division, &c.—Continued.

Losses.	Fourth Michigan.	Company C, First Ohio Volunteer Artillery.	Company I, Fourth U. S. Artillery.	Total.
[MATÉRIEL—continued.]				
Sabers	5	1		6
Saber belts	5			5
Gunners' haversacks	5	2		7
Tube pouches	3	2		5
Handspikes	10	6	1	17
Prolonges	5	1	1	7
Thumb stalls	4	2	3	9
Lanyards	2			2
Sponge buckets	5	2		7
Tar buckets	4	1	1	6
Rubber buckets	25	4		29
Nose bags	32	20		52
Cavalry saddles	5	5	1	11
Cavalry bridles	5	5	1	11
Saddle blankets	21	25		46
Artillery bridles	18	20		38
Currycombs	33			33
Horse brushes	30			30
Baggage wagon			1	1
Mules	1		1	2
Sets mule harness			2	2
Artillery horses	35	26	19	80

J. W. CHURCH,
Captain 4th Mich. Batt., Chf. of Arty., 3d Div., 14th. A. C.

No. 49.

Report of Col. John M. Connell, Seventeenth Ohio Infantry, commanding First Brigade.

HDQRS. 1ST BRIG., 3D DIV., 14TH ARMY CORPS,
Chattanooga, Tenn., September 26, 1863.

CAPTAIN: I have the honor to submit the following report of the part taken by my command in the engagements of the 19th and 20th instant:

After marching all night of Friday and halting about 6 a. m. on the 19th for breakfast, my command—weakened by the detaching of the Thirty-eighth Ohio to guard the general supply train—was ordered forward toward one of the fords of the Chickamauga Creek, forming in line of battle on the left of the Second Brigade of this division. When in position for advance, I was ordered to take my command to a point near the house afterward used as a hospital on the Chattanooga road, and hold it in reserve, to support either the Second or Third Brigade which then moved forward to engage the enemy. In a few minutes the Second Brigade was heavily engaged on my right and skirmishing commenced in front of the Third Brigade. I was then ordered forward, and under personal directions of the general commanding the division, moved with the Fourth Michigan Battery, and the Seventeenth Ohio, and the Eighty-second Indiana, to the support of the Third Brigade, leaving the Thirty-first Ohio to be ordered, if necessary, to the support of the Second Brigade, both of which brigades were now engaged. When forming my command in line to support the Third Brigade, I received orders to move with my whole command to the right to support the Second Brigade, the Thirty-first Ohio having been ordered there also. I moved rapidly to the right, but was halted and ordered to send the Seventeenth Ohio to report to Colonel Van Derveer, Third Brigade; returning to support of Colonel Van Derveer with my whole command, except the Thirty-first Ohio, I ordered Lieutenant-Colonel Ward, Seventeenth Ohio, to report to Colonel Van Derveer, who posted him on the right of the Ninth Ohio, and I placed the Fourth Michigan Battery on the left of Colonel Van Derveer's line, supported by the Eighty-second Indiana. Here the Seventeenth Ohio supported the Ninth Ohio in a charge, resulting in the retaking of the Fifth (regular) battery, which had just fallen into the hands of the enemy.

The enemy, having broken the regular brigade into confusion, charged Colonel Van Derveer's line, but was quickly repulsed under a rapid fire of Church's Fourth Michigan and Smith's Fourth (regular) battery, and by the obstinate resistance of the Third Brigade. The casualties in my brigade during this attack and repulse of the enemy were, 1 killed and 3 wounded in the Eighty-second Indiana.

The confused flight of the regular brigade over our left had no effect upon the lines of the Eighty-second Indiana, who maintained their position, Smith and Church both working their batteries with great energy, regardless of the flight of the stragglers. I assisted in rallying a number of the fleeing regulars and formed a nucleus for a successful rally.

The heavy fighting being now over, the Seventeenth Ohio returned to my command, and I received orders to occupy a position on a hill to the right of the road, to resist an expected attack, which was done. No attack having been made I was ordered to retire to a point about 1 mile from the hospital, where with the Third Brigade I remained in position until ordered to move to the right to the assistance of General Palmer, following the Third Brigade. I arrived there just before sundown, there being joined by Lieutenant-Colonel Lister, Thirty-first Ohio, who had in supporting the Second Brigade been obstinately engaged the whole day, and moving to the neighborhood of the spring, where a hospital had been established, bivouacked with my whole command.

Lieutenant-Colonel Lister fought his regiment gallantly and well, with heavy loss, but as he at the time was detached from my command, I beg leave to refer to his report* herewith of the part taken in the engagement of that day by his command.

At 11 o'clock that night I was ordered to take up a position on the left of General Negley's line, about a quarter of a mile in front of where I was bivouacked, which was done, and the brigade rested till morning.

Second day.—Early in the morning of the 20th the Second Brigade, Colonel Croxton, having come into line on my left, my right joining Colonel Stanley's brigade, of Negley's division, slight skir-

---

* Not found.

mishing commenced on our front, but all was quiet on our front for some time. Our line about 8 o'clock commenced moving to the left. My orders were to move to the left, keeping my formation of two lines, and closing on the Second Brigade.

Heavy fighting was going on for hours on my left during the continued movement by the flank to the left, but nothing but slight skirmishing occurred for some time on my front. About 9 o'clock Stanley's brigade left our right flank, which was wholly exposed. I at once dispatched an aide to inform the commander of the division that the enemy were forming on our right and front about 300 yards distant, and received answer that my right would be supported, and in a short time a division moved down on to my right—I believe Van Cleve's.

About this time Captain Church got effective range upon the enemy then engaged to my left, and opened a continuous, rapid, and deadly fire, which was kept up, notwithstanding our continued movement to the left, for more than an hour.

The battle now steadily approached us from the left. At this time I received orders to move to the left, following Croxton's brigade and passing to the rear of Reynolds' division, but before the movement was executed the order was countermanded, and we remained in the same position, but the division on my right moved away, passing in my rear rapidly, and again uncovering and exposing my right flank. I was at this time left without support either in my rear or upon my right flank. I dispatched Lieutenant Davis, acting assistant adjutant-general, at once to inform the commander of the division of my critical position; threw out flankers to my right under command of Major Slocum, of the Eighty-second Indiana, to watch the enemy's approach there, where I knew it would be sure to come, and gave orders to the commanders of regiments to change front by the right flank as soon as the enemy appeared on that flank. These orders had scarcely been delivered before the enemy, making an oblique advance, following almost the retiring division on my right, most furiously and in tremendous force, attacked my front and flank. The Seventeenth Ohio, forming the right of my front, attempted to change front, but could not, and after vigorously resisting for a few moments, and when the enemy had approached on its front and flank to within 75 yards of its line, was completely broken on its right wing, which retired in confusion, soon followed in confusion by its left wing. The Eighty-second Indiana, forming the right of the rear line, very gallantly moved forward through the flying ranks of the Seventeenth Ohio and attacked the advancing enemy, then nearly inside of our breastworks, but was unable to stay, and fell back in confusion, at which time the whole brigade, together with the Second Brigade, broke in confusion and fled to the rear. In the meantime a portion of the Seventeenth Ohio had rallied and again moved forward upon the enemy, only, however, at great sacrifice, to be driven quickly back.

Before my brigade gave way, a large portion of the division which had passed to my rear, without firing a gun or making an effort to assist me, and without being under direct fire, fled panic stricken from the field, hurrying away over, and running down the fleeing men of my command, whom I was vainly endeavoring to rally in the road and in the corn-field in rear of our position.

All efforts after this to rally my command seemed fruitless, but pushing after the fleeing men, and with scores of other officers engaged in the same apparently vain and painful task, we succeeded in occasionally collecting squads of men from different commands, and finally halted on the second range of hills to the rear of the road. Here I found of my command, Lieutenant-Colonel Lister, of Thirty-first Ohio, with a number of men he had rallied, and Major Butterfield, of the Seventeenth Ohio, who had also a squad of his command, and several officers of the two regiments, who had been laboring hard to rally their men.

At one time it looked as if we would be able to collect enough stragglers to make a successful stand, but at this time General Negley appeared with an unbroken force, and, assuming general command, it was announced that he would conduct the retreat in an orderly manner and cover and protect the artillery and trains, then in apparently inextricable confusion on the hills. By his orders all stragglers were to be collected and marched with his command, in retreat, in as orderly manner as possible, until a point of safety could be gained, where a rally and reorganization could be effected.

Without any information that the commander of this division was making a brave and determined stand in the rear about a half a mile to the right of this point, with a handful of stragglers and broken divisions there rallied chiefly by his efforts, I accepted the announcement that General Negley was conducting the retreat and commanding the rear guard, and joined his command with all of the rallied men under my orders, and thus moved to a point about 2 miles from Rossville, and at least 3 from the battle-field, where proper precautions were taken and arrangements made for reorganizing straggling regiments and brigades.

Here I succeeded in collecting about 350 men and organizing them in their proper commands, Lieutenant-Colonel Lister being present and in command of the remnant of the Thirty-first Ohio, Major Butterfield in command of the rallied men of the Seventeenth Ohio, and Adjutant Hunter in command of a large squad of the Eighty-second Indiana. At the same time a large number of men of the Second Brigade were rallied and reorganized.

Riding back to gather up the stragglers who were still coming up the road, I saw Lieutenant Germain, of the division staff, who first informed me that General Brannan was making, with his rallied forces, a desperate but successful stand in the rear. I started back immediately to take my rallied men back to General Brannan's assistance. Reaching the point where I had left my command, I found that it had been ordered by General Negley to Chattanooga. I pressed after my men and succeeded in overtaking them about 2 miles from Chattanooga, and at once ordered them back. Before reaching the former rallying point, however, information reached me that the battle was ended, and that General Brannan was moving his forces to the rear without further molestation from the enemy.

Many of my command had joined General Brannan, and, under Colonel Hunter, Eighty-second Indiana, and Lieutenant-Colonel Ward, Seventeenth Ohio, had fought most nobly. Their conduct not having come under my personal observation, I can only refer to the reports* of Colonel Hunter and Lieutenant-Colonel Ward for the full details of that brave, determined stand by, at first, but a few unorganized rallied men, which truly and most fortunately changed the fortunes of that disastrous day, and saved the army from worse than defeat.

---

*Not found.

I refer to the regimental reports for incidents of individual heroism and gallantry, unparalleled in the history of hard-fought battles.

Under my personal observation came the truly heroic conduct of Colonel Hunter, Eighty-second Indiana; Lieutenant-Colonel Ward, Seventeenth Ohio, and Lieutenant-Colonel Lister, Thirty-first Ohio. The former charged with his brave command through our fleeing troops and retook, and, for a moment, held our breastworks, when wholly unsupported on right flank or rear.

Lieutenant-Colonel Ward, with the enemy all around him, our supports right and left fleeing, and in a storm of shells, bullets, and canister, rallied one-half of his command and charged forward to the breastworks. Lieutenant-Colonel Lister held his command in position after the line broke to the right of him, stayed with it as long as the battery could be worked, and himself left last of all, carrying off his regimental colors.

The staff officers of my brigade behaved well. Lieut. Jacob M. Ruffner, Seventeenth Ohio Volunteers, acting provost-marshal, drew upon himself the attention of all by his daring and coolness. After our lines fell back he remained at the breastworks, standing with the colors of the Eighty-second Indiana in his hand, and firing with his revolvers upon the enemy. He was wounded, in the neck, painfully but not seriously.

Lieut. Frank Spencer, Seventeenth Ohio Volunteers, acting topographical engineer, is missing, and is supposed to have been killed* on the road in rear of the breastworks, where he was most gallantly engaged in rallying our fleeing men.

Lieut. T. R. Thatcher, Seventeenth Ohio Volunteers, brigade inspector, while rallying men, was struck from his horse (one already having been shot under him), and lay on the field until the enemy's lines had passed over him, when he succeeded in escaping.

Lieut. James J. Donohoe, Thirty-first Ohio Volunteers, acting commissary, while making his way through the enemy's lines on business in his department, was severely wounded, but still remained on duty.

Lieut. Jacob C. Donaldson, Thirty-eighth Ohio, aide-de-camp, bravely and efficiently acted throughout the day; was in the thickest of the danger and received a shot through his clothes, which fortunately missed his body.

Capt. A. J. Davis, assistant adjutant-general, and Lieut. Robert H. Mullins, Twelfth Kentucky Regiment, aide-de-camp, bore themselves well on the field, and rendered most efficient service in the transmission of orders and rallying men.

I am happy to say that, notwithstanding the disasters of the 20th, on the 21st my command was all present, or accounted for in the sad list of casualties; was in perfect order and condition, in good spirits, and ready to meet the enemy with confidence.

The Thirty-eighth Ohio Volunteers, Col. E. H. Phelps commanding, much to my regret, had been detached, on the 18th instant, to guard the general supply train. The duty assigned Colonel Phelps was well done, and by his efforts and supervision the train was all safely taken to the rear; but I shall ever regret that his very fine regiment, under his efficient command, could not have been with the brigade in its hour of trial.

In the confused retreat of the brigade, when forced from its posi-

---

* Spencer was not killed.

tion, it was possible only to bring out three of the pieces of Church's battery. Two of them were subsequently lost. Thus were lost five pieces, but all of the caissons were saved; and but 5 men of the battery wounded. And here I desire to bear testimony, not only to the extraordinary efficiency of and great service done by this battery, but to call attention to the heroic conduct of Captain Church, his officers and men, who continued to work their pieces when almost surrounded, and their support on the right gone.

I send herewith the reports* of Colonel Hunter, Eighty-second Indiana, and Lieutenant-Colonel Lister, Thirty-first Ohio. No report has been received from Lieutenant-Colonel Ward, Seventeenth Ohio, on account of his inability to prepare the same, from a dangerous wound received by him on the afternoon of the 20th. The casualties† of the brigade were as follows :

*   *   *   *   *   *   *

The three regiments which went into the fight had effective strength as follows, as per last morning report before the engagement : Seventeenth Ohio, 505 ; Thirty-first Ohio, 517 ; Eighty-second Indiana, 316.

At least 10 per cent. of this force were not in the engagements.

I have the honor to be, very respectfully, your obedient servant,

J. M. CONNELL,
Colonel, Commanding Brigade.

Capt. Louis J. Lambert,
Assistant Adjutant-General.

No. 50.

Report of Capt. Josiah W. Church, Battery D, First Michigan Light Artillery.

HEADQUARTERS FOURTH MICHIGAN BATTERY,
Chattanooga, Tenn., September 26, 1863.

CAPTAIN : On the morning of the 19th instant I was ordered by Colonel Connell, commanding First Brigade, Third Division, Fourteenth Army Corps, to take a position on the left of the Chattanooga road and about 50 yards in rear of the line of battle formed by the First Brigade at this point. I remained about half an hour, when I was ordered to follow the Seventeenth Ohio Volunteer Regiment, which order I immediately obeyed. We moved into the woods about 1 mile, where we found the Third Brigade, of the Third Division ; they were in line of battle, Company I, Fourth Regular Artillery, being in position with them. Soon after the First Brigade joined the Third, Colonel Van Derveer, commanding the Third Brigade, retired his line some 50 yards and formed on the right of the First Brigade. Lieutenant Smith, commanding Company I, Fourth Regular Artillery, placed his battery on my right, the Eighty-second Indiana Volunteer Infantry, commanded by Colonel Hunter, being on my right as support. In this position we were engaged by the enemy for a short time, when they were driven back by the fire of artillery and infantry. I then changed my front a little to the left.

---

* Not found.
†Embodied in revised statement, p. 172.

Lieutenant Smith placed one section of his battery on my left, commanding an open field in his front. In this position the Fifteenth Regiment Infantry acted as support on my left. Here we were soon hotly engaged by the enemy, they advancing on our front and left. As they advanced I fired shell until they were within about 200 yards, when, seeing the support on the left break, I ordered my men to double-shot their guns with canister, and firing low and rapidly, with the help of the Fourth Regular Battery and the infantry support on my right, the enemy were soon driven from our entire front so far as could be seen by me. During this engagement I had 2 men painfully but not seriously wounded. My officers and men without exception behaved like veterans, every man doing his duty faithfully.

From this position I was ordered farther to the right, after which, in accordance with orders from General Brannan, I changed position five times, but fired no more during the day, and at eve I retired with the First Brigade about 2½ miles to the right and rear into an open field near a hospital and spring, where I bivouacked for the night.

Sunday, September 20, 1863, about 12 o'clock at night I received orders to move to the front about one-quarter of a mile, where I formed my battery in the front line on the right of the Seventeenth Regiment Ohio Volunteer Infantry, and on the left of the Eleventh Michigan Regiment, belonging to Colonel Stanley's brigade of General Negley's division. In this position I remained until daylight. I then made several moves with the First Brigade, gaining ground to the left, on the same line as before, each time getting into position for action, doing, however, but little firing until we arrived at our last position. In this last position I was supported by the Seventeenth Ohio Volunteer Infantry on a line with my pieces and the Eighty-second Indiana Volunteer Infantry on a line with my limbers on the right; on the left, by the Thirty-first Ohio Volunteer Infantry on a line with my pieces and the Fourteenth Ohio Volunteer Infantry on a line with the limbers. I had been in this position about one hour, when I received orders to limber up, the fighting being at this time very heavy on our left and was gradually coming toward our front. I had just obeyed the order to limber up when we were attacked. I then gave the order, "Action rear," and engaged the enemy as they advanced. I had an enfilading fire on a portion of their advance, and by hard firing for about fifteen minutes I succeeded in checking the enemy and silencing their battery, which had been playing on our lines. I then ceased firing until the enemy again engaged our front, when, as soon as I ascertained their position, I commenced firing. We held our front in good order some twenty minutes, when the enemy advanced obliquely on our right and in such overwhelming numbers that my support on the right was obliged to give way while endeavoring to change their front.

The enemy were then so near I ordered the pieces to be double-shotted with canister and kept the enemy back for a short time. As soon as the Seventeenth Ohio Volunteer Infantry had passed to the rear, the Eighty-second Indiana Volunteer Infantry arose and advanced to the line of rail breastworks raised and just left by the Seventeenth Ohio Volunteer Infantry, but the fire was too heavy for a small body of men to contend with, and they were forced back. I should have changed my front to the right if I could have fired, but my support was in that direction, rendering it impossible to do so. I then (after the Eighty-second Indiana Regiment had fallen back) ordered my men to run the pieces off by hand. We succeeded in getting off four pieces through some small bushes about 50 yards in rear of our fighting position. Here three pieces were limbered up with much difficulty, under the most galling fire, and got away. The horses had been shot belonging to the other limbers, so that it was impossible to get them off the ground. My caissons had already been taken away by Sergt. S. E. Lawrence, who had been in charge of them during the 19th and 20th. I ordered the three pieces I had saved moved to the ridge in our rear, where the reserve artillery was planted at this time. The Seventeenth Ohio Volunteer Infantry had rallied and went in again only to be slaughtered and driven back. Lieutenants Corbin and Wheat and myself remained with a few men hoping to recover the pieces during the charge of the Seventeenth Regiment, but it was impossible. We then went to the rear on foot, my horse having been captured and Lieutenant Corbin having given his horse to Lieutenant-Colonel Ward, of the Seventeenth Ohio Volunteer Infantry (his having been shot), to rally his command. When I reached the hill occupied by the reserve artillery, the enemy were pouring a deadly enfilading fire on our right and pressing hard on our front. Here I fired a few rounds from the 12-pounder howitzer, commanded by Sergeant Hazzard. By this time nearly all my horses had been shot down and 3 cannoneers wounded, and we were obliged to leave two of the pieces on this ridge, getting away only one 12-pounder howitzer. I then moved what I had left of my battery to the rear on the Chattanooga road.

My officers and men behaved, without a single exception, as veteran soldiers, obeying orders and attending to their duties. Lieutenants Corbin, Sawyer, and Fuller did their duty nobly during the two days' fight, and Lieutenant Wheat, although sick with a fever, could not be kept off the field on the 20th; although feeble in health, he was strong in heart and rendered me valuable service during my last engagement. Sergt. S. E. Lawrence deserves the utmost credit for his conduct while in charge of the line of caissons, and by obeying orders promptly and watching our movements, saved all the caissons and brought them off the field in good order. Sergt. S. W. Allen also deserves great praise for his coolness and courage; he remained with his gun, defending it with his revolver until he had discharged the last round and came near being run through with a rebel bayonet, when he made his escape. His piece was left on the ground for want of help to get it off. As my number of cannoneers were short the day previous, I was obliged to take a portion of his detachment to assist in getting off another piece. Sergeants Seymour, Hazzard, Haymaker, and Durfey deserve credit for their determination and courage. All my corporals discharged their duties faithfully and deserve all credit. My saddler, H. J. Bartlett, deserves much praise for his services in getting my battery wagon, forge, and headquarters wagons off the field in good condition, they being nearly surrounded by the enemy before he was aware of his condition. During the two days' fight I had 1 sergeant and 6 men wounded, and 4 men missing. I received a slight wound on my left arm from a spent musket ball.

It here becomes my duty as well as a great pleasure to tender my thanks, as well as those of my officers and men, to Col. J. M. Connell and staff for their efficiency and noble deeds on the battle-field during the two days' battle.

I also tender the thanks of myself, officers, and men to the Seventeenth Ohio Volunteer Infantry, the Thirty-first Ohio Volunteer Infantry, and Eighty-second Indiana Volunteer Infantry and their gallant commanders for the handsome manner in which they fought in support of my battery during the fight.

With respect, I remain, &c.,

J. W. CHURCH,
Captain, Comdg. Fourth Michigan Battery.

Capt. A. J. DAVIS,
Assistant Adjutant-General, First Brigade.

No. 51.

Report of Col. Charles W. Chapman, Seventy-fourth Indiana Infantry, commanding Second Brigade.

HEADQUARTERS SECOND BRIGADE, THIRD DIVISION,
Chattanooga, Tenn., September 27, 1863.

CAPTAIN : I submit the following report of the part taken by the Second Brigade, Third Division, Fourteenth Army Corps, on the 19th and 20th days of September, 1863 :

On the night of the 18th instant this brigade, with the balance of the division, Col. John T. Croxton, of the Fourth Regiment Kentucky Infantry, commanding, marched from Morgan's Ford on the Chickamauga Creek, in Walker County, Ga., along the Chattanooga road, obliquing to the right where this road intersects with the road leading to Ringgold.

The brigade was on the march all night of the 18th instant ; arrived in the vicinity of the enemy about 6 o'clock in the morning of the 19th. After halting and taking a hasty cup of coffee, firing was heard in front ; the column was immediately on the march forward, on the Ringgold road. The colonel commanding was here informed that a brigade of the enemy had been cut off, and was immediately in our front, supposed to be in the vicinity of the Chickamauga Creek. We advanced about 1 mile on this road (Ringgold) and formed line of battle in the woods, facing nearly east, the Seventy-fourth Indiana on the right, Col. C. W. Chapman commanding ; the Fourth Kentucky, Lieut. Col. P. B. Hunt commanding, on the left; the Tenth Indiana, Col. W. B. Carroll commanding, in the center, these three regiments forming the front line ; Fourteenth Ohio, Lieut. Col. H. D. Kingsbury commanding ; Tenth Kentucky, Col. William H. Hays commanding, forming the reserve. Skirmishers were thrown out in front, under command of Major Van Natta, of the Tenth Indiana. They advanced but a short distance when they were charged upon by the rebel cavalry, supposed to be those under the command of Forrest. The skirmishers immediately returned to the line. The advance line gave them one volley, fixed bayonets, and charged, which caused them to "skedaddle" in haste, with considerable loss.

The line of battle was immediately reformed, and skirmishers advanced again under command of the same officer, who soon after was wounded and taken from the field. The skirmishers advanced about 500 yards, when they came in contact with the enemy's skirmishers. After considerable firing on both sides, a flank movement was discovered. The reserve regiments were at once brought forward, the Fourteenth Ohio on the right and the Tenth Kentucky on the left.

I was here ordered by Colonel Croxton, commanding the brigade, to take command of the right wing, leaving Lieutenant-Colonel Baker in command of the Seventy-fourth Indiana.

An advance being ordered, the troops moved forward steadily, and with a determination to drive the enemy from the field, but, instead of finding one brigade to contend with, we had the combined forces of Longstreet and Breckinridge.

We succeeded in checking them, but they soon recovered, and being in force they soon commenced flanking us on the right. We were compelled to fall back, which was done in good order.

A new line of battle was now formed on the right, and nearly at right angles with the first, for the purpose of meeting the flank movement being made by the enemy, and again advanced this line, driving the enemy before us a short distance. At this time, our ammunition being nearly exhausted, we fell back to a ridge and there held our position until we were relieved by King's brigade of General Baird's division. The brigade then returned to the rear of the battery (which had been ordered back about 300 yards, to take position on a ridge commanding an open field in our rear, so that if the enemy forced us back beyond it the battery could rake them with grape and canister), forming line of battle on the right and left of it, and replenished the men with 60 rounds of ammunition. It was in this last charge (before we were relieved by King's brigade) that we lost very heavily in officers and men. Colonel Carroll, Tenth Indiana, fell mortally wounded, and Lieut. Col. P. B. Hunt was severely wounded in the leg. Both were, however, brought from the field.

It soon became apparent that the enemy was driving King's brigade. This brigade being again ordered to advance, moved by the flank to the right (in order that it might be unmasked by King's command) about 400 yards. The positions of the regiments were, viz: Fourteenth Ohio on the right, Fourth Kentucky on its left, Seventy-fourth Indiana on left of Fourth Kentucky, the Tenth Indiana on left of Seventy-fourth, the Tenth Kentucky on left of Tenth Indiana, and the Thirty-first Ohio, Lieutenant-Colonel Lister commanding, which had been ordered at the beginning of the action to our support, on the extreme left. I was directed by Colonel Croxton to take command of the right wing, he remaining on the left.

The enemy was now approaching us *en masse* of not less than three columns, and was giving us a heavy fire of grape and canister. The order was given to charge, which was done in fine style, and with the determination to drive the enemy, which they did, some 300 yards, capturing their battery of five guns and bringing them from the field. In this charge the left of the brigade retook seven pieces of artillery, five guns belonging to the Indiana cavalry,* and two Parrotts of First Michigan, and brought them off the field. There was a desperate struggle for the ground, but, they being in such overpowering force, and flanking us again on the right, we were compelled to fall back, which we did in good order, and disputing every foot of ground until we came to a good position, which we held until relieved by Johnson's division.

In the last charge we again lost heavily, as the list of killed and

---

*See report of Capt. E. Lilly, Eighteenth Indiana Battery, p. 466.

wounded will show.   It was in this charge that my horse was shot from under me, and fell heavily upon me, breaking my arm and injuring me seriously otherwise, but I continued on the field during the balance of the day.

The brigade again retired to the crest of the hill and took position by the battery, where we rested until about 4 o'clock, when we were again ordered to march by the right flank, through the woods, into a field across the Chattanooga road, then marched into line of battle south about 1 mile, to the hospital tent of the Seventy-ninth Ohio. We remained there in line until dark, when we marched by the flank into an open field on our right and bivouacked for the night.

During this day's engagement Company C, First Regiment Ohio Artillery, under command of First Lieut. M. B. Gary, had no opportunity of taking any part in the action, on account of the nature of the ground, but was always ready and willing to do so.   During the day he had 2 men wounded.

On the morning of the 20th, about 4 o'clock, we again marched out by the flank across the Chattanooga road at Kelly's house, leaving it to our left, and took position holding the front line.   Skirmishers were thrown forward, but the enemy did not appear to confront us closely.   We remained in this position about one hour.   The brigade then moved to the left, by the flank, about 300 yards and formed on the left of Reynolds' division, the Seventy-fourth and Tenth Indiana in the front line, and the Fourteenth Ohio, Fourth Kentucky, and Tenth Kentucky in the rear.   The front regiments threw up some rude fortifications, which protected them from the fire of the enemy, who often came within 40 yards of them, but was each time driven back with great slaughter, when by a flank movement on our right the brigade was compelled to change front, and in so doing the brigade became separated and at the same time Colonel Croxton was seriously wounded in the leg, and was compelled to abandon the field.

What remained of the brigade was under the command of Col. William H. Hays, Tenth Kentucky, to whom I refer you for further report of second day's proceedings.   The Seventy-fourth and Tenth Indiana, having reported to General Reynolds, fought with him during the day.

The brigade lost very heavily in killed and wounded.   See reports of regimental commanders, copies of which I herewith submit.

I cannot close this report without mentioning the manner in which the staff of the colonel commanding the brigade acquitted themselves. Lieut. Charles V. Ray, acting assistant adjutant-general ; Charles B. Mann, provost-marshal, who was seriously wounded while carrying dispatches on the field ; Capt. J. W. Riley, topographical engineer ; Wilbur F. Spofford, assistant inspector-general, and John E. Simpson, aide-de-camp (who, I regret to say, is among the missing, and is supposed to have been captured), all did their duty, always found upon the field in the thickest of the battle, and for the assistance [they gave] me while in command of the brigade the first day, I return them my thanks.

The total number of casualties in the two days' fighting is : Officers killed, 5 ; officers wounded, 48.   Enlisted men killed, 120 ; enlisted men wounded, 665.   Officer missing, 1 ; enlisted men missing, 88. Total killed, wounded, and missing, 926.*

---

*See revised statement, p. 173.

The effective force of the brigade was on the day of battle: Officers, 115; enlisted men, 2,164.   Battery officers, 4; enlisted men, 118. Aggregate, 2,401.

Before closing this report I must testify to the manner in which the officers of the brigade conducted themselves on the trying occasion of each day, and I refrain from particularizing individual instances of heroic daring and gallantry, for where all do their duty bravely and well, as the officers of this brigade did on this occasion, it would be unjust and improper to make distinctions and institute comparisons by which others equally deserving and meritorious might be injured.

I have the honor to be, captain, very respectfully, your obedient servant,

C. W. CHAPMAN,
Colonel, Commanding Second Brigade.

[Capt. LOUIS J. LAMBERT,
Assistant Adjutant-General, Third Division.]

No. 52.

Report of Lieut. Col. Myron Baker, Seventy-fourth Indiana Infantry.

HDQRS. 74TH REGT. IND. INF., 2D BRIG., 3D DIV., 14TH A. C.,
Chattanooga, September 25, 1863.

SIR : On the night of the 18th instant the Seventy-fourth Indiana Infantry, Col. Charles W. Chapman commanding, together with the brigade to which it belongs, Col. John T. Croxton commanding, marched left in front from Morgan's Ford, on the Chickamauga Creek, Walker County, Ga., along the Chattanooga road, obliquing to the right where this road intersects with the road leading to Ringgold.   The regiment was on the march all night.

At about 9 a. m. of the 19th instant the brigade, having moved up the Ringgold road about 1 mile, was halted and line of battle formed in the woods facing nearly east.   The Seventy-fourth Indiana held the right of the front line, the Tenth Indiana being on its immediate left.   At about 10 a. m. the line was advanced, changing direction slightly toward the right.   When the line had advanced about one-half a mile in the direction above indicated, the skirmishers thrown forward in our front became engaged and in a short time were driven in by the rebel cavalry, which in turn was repulsed by a volley from the Fourth Kentucky, Tenth Indiana, and Seventy-fourth Indiana.   The skirmishers again being thrown forward the men were ordered to lie down to screen themselves from shells which were being thrown into the line by a rebel battery.   In a few minutes after the attack by the rebel cavalry in front, it was discovered that the enemy was attempting to turn our right, and the line was immediately changed fronting in that direction at almost right angles with the original line of battle.   The Seventy-fourth Indiana executed the movement under a sharp fire from the rebels.   The skirmishers in front having changed direction parallel with the line were soon driven back and the whole line became engaged with the line of the enemy.   In a short time it became apparent that the right wing of the Seventy-fourth Indiana was thrown too far forward, being exposed in its new position to a terrible fire on the right flank, in consequence of which Colonel Chapman ordered that flank to be thrown farther back.

Up to this time, although exposed to a severe fire under which the loss in killed and wounded had been considerable, the regiment held its position unwaveringly and returned the enemy's fire with commendable coolness and alacrity. When the order to retire the right flank was given it was misunderstood for a command to retire the whole line, and the regiment was momentarily thrown into confusion, but immediately rallied and took position on the right of the Tenth Kentucky, where it fought unflinchingly until its 60 rounds of cartridges had been expended, when it was relieved and went to the rear for ammunition. Being replenished with 60 additional rounds of cartridges, the regiment was moved to the right along the Ringgold road about 500 yards, when it was formed again in line of battle, the Fourteenth Ohio on the right, the Fourth Kentucky in the center, and the Seventy-fourth Indiana on the left, the command of the three regiments being assigned to Colonel Chapman, devolving the command of this regiment on me. This line was advanced about 2 p. m., steadily driving the enemy before it for over half a mile, when our advance was checked by the overwhelming numbers of the enemy, who concentrated a destructive artillery and infantry fire upon our single line, which was at the time wholly unsupported. Up to this time no artillery had been employed to assist us, owing to the nature of the ground and the density of the thick woods through which the battle raged. It was in this contest that Lieut. Thomas Bodley fell mortally wounded as Lieut. Richard H. Hall had fallen in the first encounter. Both of these officers died the same day, having discharged their duties faithfully and well. It was here also that 8 other of the line officers of the regiment were wounded and the loss of enlisted men very heavy. It was at this time also that Colonel Chapman was seriously injured and disabled for command by the fall of his horse, which had been killed under him. It was here that we charged the rebel lines, but being overpowered after a desperate struggle for the mastery of the ground, I ordered the regiment to fall back, and took position on a ridge about 300 yards in rear of where our advance was checked. This was the last struggle in which the Seventy-fourth Indiana was engaged on that day.

The following are the names of the officers who were wounded on the 19th instant: Col. Charles W. Chapman, Capt. Andrew S. Milice, Capt. Samson J. North, Capt. Everett F. Abbott, Capt. Joel F. Kinney, First Lieut. George W. Harter, First Lieut. Thomas Bodley, First Lieut. Ananias Davis, First Lieut. David P. Deardoff, Second Lieut. Richard H. Hall, Second Lieut. John Snider, a total of 11 out of 24 officers who went into the engagement. I have attached hereto a list with the name and rank of each officer and enlisted man killed and wounded in the engagement.*

Recapitulation of first day's engagement: On the morning of the 19th instant the regiment numbered for active field duty—

Officers	24
Enlisted men	376
Aggregate	400

---

* Nominal list omitted.

Loss during the first day:

Officers mortally wounded, since dead.. 2
Officers wounded 9
Enlisted men killed 20
Enlisted men wounded.. 110
Missing.. 7
                                                                         ———
  Aggregate killed, wounded, and missing................................. 148

On the morning of the 20th instant, having supplied the men under my command with 60 additional rounds of ammunition, I was
ordered to relieve the Fourth Kentucky to enable that regiment to
get breakfast. I executed the order, deploying Companies H and C
(they having no commissioned officers present), under command of
Lieut. C. C. Beane as skirmishers. Before the deployment was
finished 1 man from Company C was wounded.

About 8 a. m. the Seventy-fourth Indiana, with the Tenth Indiana
on its immediate right, moved to the left and joined on the Seventy-
fifth Indiana, the right regiment of Reynolds' division. The skirmishers moved to the left at the same time covering our front. The
Seventy-fourth Indiana occupied a low ridge of ground with an open
field in front (in which were some scattered trees) on the extreme left
of the Second Brigade. On the brow of this ridge I caused the men
to construct a rude breastwork of logs and rails behind which they
could take shelter from the enemy's musketry, and which proved to
be of very great advantage in the subsequent fight. At about 10.30
a. m. the firing, which had been very heavy to my left and along the
line of Reynolds' division, struck my line of battle. I ordered the
men to kneel down behind their works and hold their fire until the
enemy were within 60 or 70 yards of our line. The companies of skirmishers were soon driven in, but not a shot was fired by us until the
rebels who were charging on us with a yell had come within 70 yards
of us, when I ordered the men to rise up and commence firing. The
men mostly aimed deliberately and fought with a spirit and determination which could not well be surpassed, for the comparative
security and strength of their position gave them increased confidence. The Seventy-fourth Indiana and Tenth Indiana held their
position, keeping up an incessant and untiring fire, until their ammunition was nearly exhausted, when they were ordered to cease
firing, fix bayonets, and await the nearer approach of the foe. Twice
during this engagement the enemy was thrown into confusion and
driven back from before our position. About this time the line to
the right of the Tenth Indiana gave way, and the rebels made their
appearance in an open field on the right flank of the Tenth Indiana.
Lieutenant-Colonel Taylor, commanding that veteran regiment,
changed his front almost perpendicularly to the rear, and the Seventy-fourth Indiana protected the original line until he had completed
that movement, when I faced the regiment by the rear rank and
formed line of battle on his right at an acute angle with the original
line and in rear of a fence and some old log buildings. Here the
regiment fought until its ammunition was completely exhausted, and
the rebels were driven back from the open field over which they were
advancing.

At this time the Tenth and Seventy-fourth Indiana were separated
from the rest of the brigade, which had been sent to the right to fill
a breach in the line, and Lieutenant-Colonel Taylor, being the ranking officer, took command of both regiments. The regiment now

moved through the woods toward the left, and awaited the arrival of ammunition in an open ground where Hazen's brigade was lying behind some log fortifications.

About 4 p. m. we got a supply of ammunition and occupied a position behind the breastworks, from which Hazen's brigade had been withdrawn.   When the retreat commenced in the evening we were the last to leave that part of the field, and brought away with us one section of artillery, which was in rear of all the infantry, except the Tenth and Seventy-fourth Indiana.   These regiments both left that part of the field in good order under a severe artillery fire from the enemy, and halted and formed line of battle facing the enemy on a hill where General Steedman's division had been fighting.   The Seventy-fourth and Tenth Indiana were the last organized bodies of infantry that left that ground.   About 8.30 p. m. the two regiments moved from that point toward Rossville by the right flank, the Seventy-fourth Indiana in front, followed by the Tenth Indiana.

On the 20th the loss of this regiment was light, and is attributable to the fact that the men in the heat of the engagement were most of the time protected by the rude fortifications they had constructed in the morning.   Adjt. George C. Smith and Capt. W. N. Rogers were the only commissioned officers injured on this day, and no enlisted man was killed.

Recapitulation of second day's engagement :

Officers wounded	2
Enlisted men wounded	6
Missing	4
Aggregate killed, wounded, and missing	12
Killed, wounded, and missing, 19th instant	148
Aggregate loss, September 19 and 20, 1863	160

I will only add that I am fully satisfied with the behavior of both officers and men on the trying occasions of each day, and I refrain from particularizing individual instances of heroic daring and gallantry, for where all do their duty bravely and well it would be unjust and improper to make distinctions which might seem invidious and institute comparisons by which others equally deserving and meritorious might be injured.

MYRON BAKER,
Lieut. Col., Comdg. Seventy-fourth Regt. Indiana Infty.

Lieut. CHARLES V. RAY,
Acting Assistant Adjutant-General, Second Brigade.

No. 53.

Report of Col. William H. Hays, Tenth Kentucky Infantry.

HDQRS. 10TH KY. VOL. INFTY., 2d BRIG., 3d DIV., 14TH A. C.,
Chattanooga, Tenn., September 27, 1863.

SIR : I have the honor to submit the following report of the part taken by the Tenth Kentucky Volunteer Infantry in the battle fought on Saturday and Sunday, September 19 and 20 :

After marching the whole of Friday night I was notified at 7 a. m.

Saturday that a brigade of the enemy were in our front, and that my regiment would proceed with the brigade to immediately attack the enemy. My regiment was formed in the second line of battle in rear of the Fourth Kentucky, and on the extreme left of the line, and marched forward in line of battle. In a very few minutes sharp skirmishing commenced in the front, when I received an order to move my regiment to the left of the Fourth Kentucky in double-quick time, thus occupying the extreme left of the line. Our skirmishers were driven in by a body of the enemy's cavalry, but a volley put them to flight. I now received an order to march by the right flank, to take a new position at almost right angles to the first. Here we met the enemy in force and had a most hotly contested fight, Company B alone, of my regiment, losing in one hour 20 men killed and wounded.

Seeing the enemy about to turn my left flank, I ordered a charge and drove them in confusion some 200 yards, when I in turn was compelled to fall back to the crest of the hill originally occupied by me. Here again, in connection with the rest of the brigade, my regiment made a desperate and successful resistance to a largely superior force, driving them completely back from the field. My ammunition being exhausted, I received an order from Col. John T. Croxton, commanding brigade, to fall back to the rear for a new supply. I immediately retired across the Ringgold road to an open space, filling the cartridge-boxes of the men, when I was again ordered to the front. The men, although wearied from the loss of sleep and two hours' hard fighting, responded to the summons with the greatest alacrity. I marched forward in line of battle on the left of the Ringgold road and took a position on the top of a long descending slope in an open woods, the Tenth Indiana on my right, the Thirty-first Ohio on my left. Here again we met the enemy in large force. I afterward ascertained from prisoners that it was the rebel General Walker's division.

Finding the enemy very stubborn, my men being shot down in large numbers, and seeing what I supposed to be a battery of artillery in position ahead of me, I ordered a bayonet charge, which was received with loud cheers by my men; the Tenth Indiana and Thirty-first Ohio both came gallantly up to my assistance, and we completely routed the rebels, they flying before us in the greatest confusion. What I had taken for a battery of the enemy proved to be five guns of the Fourth Indiana Artillery and two Parrotts of the First Michigan, which had been captured by the enemy ; the guns were immediately sent to our rear. The enemy were now reported as trying to turn our right flank. The Thirty-first Ohio was double-quicked by the right flank, leaving my regiment again on the extreme left. I now followed the Tenth Indiana by the right flank and joined the rest of the brigade, when we were again attacked by a large force and compelled to fall back, which was done in some disorder. Arriving on the crest of a small hill, my regiment and the Fourth Kentucky, Major Kelly commanding, faced about and opened a well-directed fire upon the enemy, checking his advance. The whole brigade rallied and we again drove the enemy back and held our position until relieved at 2 p. m. by General Johnson's division, of the Twenty-first Army Corps.

Upon being relieved I fell back as ordered about one-half mile in a southwesterly direction and rested until 4 p. m., when I received an order to march with the brigade. We proceeded in a southwest course until we struck the main Georgia State road, near which we took a position about 3 miles from the first position occupied by my regiment. Here we remained quiet until dark, when, by order of Col. John T. Croxton, I moved my men to the rear three-quarters of a mile and camped for the night.

On Sunday morning, September 20, I marched the regiment at 3 o'clock back to the position across the Georgia State road that we left the evening previous. The regiment was then formed in line of battle on the right of the brigade. At about 7 a. m. the brigade was moved about one-half mile to the left. My regiment was then formed on the right of the brigade, in rear of the Tenth Indiana. The battle opened on our front about 9 a. m., and continued until about 10.30 or 11, when the troops on our right gave way, the enemy completely flanking us on the right in large force. I immediately formed my regiment by filing to the right on a line perpendicular to the one just occupied, but held this position but a few moments. We were overwhelmed by numbers, and the enemy continued to flank us. Our loss at this point was very great. It was here that the gallant Captain Bevill fell mortally wounded. Col. John T. Croxton, our brigade commander, was wounded about the same time. I then moved the regiment to the left, near the house on the hill. Colonel Croxton's wounds not permitting him to remain on the field, I took command of the brigade, and Lieutenant-Colonel Wharton took command of the regiment.

The officers and soldiers of the regiment behaved with great gallantry and courage. They all did their duty nobly. We went into the fight with 421 men. A statement showing the number and names* of killed, wounded, and missing is forwarded with this report.

I am, very respectfully, your obedient servant,

WM. H. HAYS,
Colonel Tenth Kentucky Infantry.

Lieut. CHARLES V. RAY,
Acting Assistant Adjutant-General, Second Brigade.

No. 54.

Report of Lieut. Col. Gabriel C. Wharton, Tenth Kentucky Infantry.

HDQRS. TENTH KENTUCKY VOLUNTEER INFANTRY,
Chattanooga, Tenn., September 28, 1863.

SIR: In obedience to orders just received from you, I have the honor to make the following statement of the action of the Tenth Kentucky Volunteer Infantry during the battle of the 20th September, while under my command:

At about 11 o'clock on the 20th Col. John T. Croxton, commanding Second Brigade, was severely wounded at the head of his column, and the command of the brigade devolved upon Col. W. H. Hays, of the Tenth Kentucky Regiment, when I assumed command of the regiment. At this time the regiment, together with the Fourth Kentucky Regiment and the Fourteenth Ohio, were posted on the crest of a high hill on the west side of the Chattanooga and La Fayette road, which they were ordered to hold, which we succeeded in doing with slight loss, until 3 o'clock, when we were relieved by the divis-

---

* Embodied in revised statement, p. 172.

ion of General James B. Steedman. I then withdrew my regiment about 200 yards and replenished our exhausted ammunition, and rested the troops for about half an hour, when the Third Brigade, which was posted on this same hill to the left of position from which we had been relieved by General Steedman, was furiously assaulted by a large column of the enemy, and we were ordered forward to their support. The troops went forward with great determination at a double-quick, and took position behind a temporary fortification of rails, immediately on the left of the Third Brigade, Third Division, Fourteenth Army Corps, and poured a most destructive fire into the advancing columns of the enemy, which staggered them for a moment, but they rallied and advanced again and again. It seemed two or three times it would be impossible to hold our position, so overwhelming was the force of the enemy, but our troops, being partially screened by the rails, poured volley after volley into their masses, so well aimed that after three hours of most desperate fighting the enemy withdrew, just as our ammunition was exhausted and General Brannan had ordered the men to fix their bayonets and receive the enemy on their points if they again advanced. During the whole fight the men never wavered or gave an inch, and the officers of my regiment all were at their posts encouraging their men; several of them took the guns of their wounded men and shot away every cartridge in their boxes. The regiment suffered severely in this fight. The list of killed and wounded are reported in a report heretofore made by Col. W. H. Hays.

Lieut. H. H. Warren, of Company A, was here wounded in the ankle while doing his duty manfully, as was also Lieut. W. E. Kelly, who was shot while in the center of the regiment bearing the flag and encouraging the men. After night had well set in we, in obedience to orders received from General Brannan in person, withdrew the regiment from its position on the hill and marched to Rossville, reaching that place at 12 o'clock, where we rested for the night.

All of which is respectfully submitted.

I have the honor to be, your obedient servant,

G. C. WHARTON,
Lieut. Col. Tenth Kentucky Vol. Infantry, Comdg.

Lieut. CHARLES V. RAY,
Acting Assistant Adjutant-General, Second Brigade.

No. 55.

Report of Lieut. Col. Henry D. Kingsbury, Fourteenth Ohio Infantry.

HDQRS. FOURTEENTH OHIO VOLUNTEER INFANTRY,
Chattanooga, Tenn., September 26, 1863.

CAPTAIN: I have the honor to submit the following as a report of the part taken during the two days' engagement with the enemy by my command:

The morning of the 19th, before any firing was commenced, after moving in line, my command occupied the right of the second line, in rear of the Tenth Indiana, consisting of 18 commissioned officers and 442 enlisted men.

In this position we advanced 500 yards when we were ordered to the extreme right of the front line, where skirmishers were thrown out covering our front.

A heavy force of infantry were seen approaching our extreme right, and the Seventy-fourth Indiana were formed upon our right to meet them. The enemy advanced with three colums of infantry, without skirmishers, and forced us to retire.

In the afternoon, when the advance was again made more to the right, our position was still on the extreme right.

In this position we were ordered to [move] forward until we came to an open field or the left of the line should halt. In this position we advanced about 200 yards, when the enemy's skirmishers were met and driven back. We then charged upon their line and drove them for over 200 yards, when our line met a superior force and, being outflanked, retired fighting. We were then moved to the right, but without any more fighting. We lay in an open field near where the brigade was halted for breakfast till 6.30 p. m., when we were ordered to the rear for the night. Our loss during the day was 29 killed, 7 commissioned officers and 130 enlisted men wounded, and 31 reported missing.

At 3 o'clock the morning of the 20th we moved by the right flank to the right of the road, and took position in the second line, in rear of the Thirty-first Ohio and a battery, and on the right of the Tenth Kentucky.

We were in this position when the line on our right was turned, and held the position until the right was so far driven back that the enemy held position in our rear, and were forced to retire. We fell back across the field, and there rallied what men I could and formed them upon the hill. During the confusion my command became separated and were kept so during the day; but from what fell under my own observation I can report that I never saw men, disorganized as they were, fight better.

The major and several other of the officers, with what men they could rally, remained upon the hill to the right of the hospital (on the right), and fought until the enemy fell back and gave up the contest. It was 6.30 p. m. when they were withdrawn and moved to the rear.

The confusion which we were at times thrown into renders a more explicit report impracticable. Our colors were shot down three times on the 19th and twice on the 20th, but were bravely defended and brought from the field at night.

The loss on the 20th was 7 men killed, 1 commissioned officer and 29 men wounded, and 12 men missing.

I am, captain, very respectfully, your obedient servant,

H. D. KINGSBURY,
Lieutenant-Colonel, Commanding.

Capt. LOUIS J. LAMBERT,
Asst. Adjt. Gen., Third Div., 14th Army Corps.

No. 56.

Report of Lieut. Marco B. Gary, Battery C, First Ohio Light
Artillery.

HDQRS. COMPANY C, 1ST REGT. OHIO VOL. ARTILLERY,
Chattanooga, Tenn., September 28, 1863.

CAPTAIN: I have the honor to submit the following report of the part taken by Battery C, First Regiment Ohio Volunteer Artillery, in the late battle of the 19th and 20th instant, also the killed and wounded and *matériel* expended or abandoned.

At 8 o'clock on the morning of the 19th instant, by order of Colonel Croxton, commanding the Second Brigade, Third Division, of the Fourteenth Army Corps, I moved forward in the second line of the brigade then in the face of the enemy, and as soon as our skirmishers were engaged took a position indicated by Colonel Croxton in a small open field, supported on my right by the Fourteenth Ohio Volunteer Infantry and on my left by the Fourth Kentucky Volunteer Infantry. The infantry then advanced a considerable distance into the timber and engaged the enemy, who were in heavy force. Twenty minutes later, by order of Colonel Croxton, I moved to the front, and found the infantry already falling back before a superior force of the enemy; and before our infantry had uncovered my front so as to admit my fire upon the enemy, I received orders from Colonel Croxton to fall back and take position on a ridge to the right and rear of that first occupied. From this position I threw a few shells at a high elevation, and over the heads of the infantry, for effect only. Three successive times during the day I was ordered by Colonel Croxton to a position in the face of the enemy, and each time the infantry were driven back so rapidly that I was again ordered to the rear as soon as I had obtained a position bearing on the enemy.

The ground on which I maneuvered on the 19th was so densely covered with timber and underbrush as to render rapid movements of artillery exceedingly difficult and uncertain.

My loss in the first day's engagement was 1 man severely wounded and 1 horse killed.

On the morning of the 20th, at 7 o'clock, by order of Colonel Croxton, I took position on the rear line of the brigade, and as the enemy attacked the brigade I received orders from Colonel Croxton to send two 12-pounder pieces to the front. I accordingly ordered Lieutenant Turner forward, who took position in easy range and opened on the enemy with shell and spherical case with fine effect.

Thirty minutes later I received orders from Colonel Croxton to move forward on the front line with the balance of the battery, take position on the left of Lieutenant Turner, and open fire on the enemy as soon as he appeared in force. I immediately moved by piece into position leaving my caissons 50 yards in rear, partially covered by a ridge in front, and in charge of First Sergeant Shaw, by whom they were handled, as on the day previous, in a very efficient manner.

A heavy column of the enemy immediately appeared marching by the flank directly across my front, and at a distance of 600 yards from my pieces. I opened fire upon him with shell and spherical case. Changing direction to the right, he attacked in great force the line on which I was posted, and about 200 yards to my right, and after capturing nearly all of the Fourth Michigan Battery and driving away the infantry, he pushed to within 100 yards of my right piece. Changing the direction of my fire to the right oblique, I threw canister into his solid masses with great rapidity, and I have reason to believe with fine effect, my guns some portion of the time being double shotted with canister.

The enemy soon fell back so far as to allow the infantry on my right to regain their position on the front line.

Fifteen minutes later the support on my right again fell back, and the enemy again advanced on a line nearly perpendicular to my original front and to within 100 yards of the battery.

Ten to fifteen minutes later, having no support on my right, with a loss of 13 men killed and wounded, and 25 horses killed, and believing it impossible to save the battery, after further resistance I moved the battery without orders to the left and rear, where I fell in, and, by order of General Brannan, moved with the troops of Major-General Negley's command.

Of the conduct of the officers of the battery, Lieutenants Turner, King, and Stephens, to particularize that of either could only be to the prejudice of the others, they all having done their whole duty.

To the non-commissioned officers and privates too much credit cannot be given. To them mainly is due the credit of saving the battery from capture, for so great was the loss of horses that several of the pieces had to be drawn far to the rear by hand, and the only piece lost in the engagement was abandoned after being dismounted and the linch-pins thrown away 200 yards to the rear, the men becoming too much exhausted to drag it farther by hand.

My loss in the two days' engagement is 4 men killed, 9 men wounded, and 26 horses killed, 1 6-pounder James rifled gun and 1 caisson abandoned.

The following is a list of the killed and wounded, *matériel* expended or captured in the two days' engagements:

Killed, 1 sergeant and 3 privates; wounded, 9 privates.

Number of horses killed and captured, 26; number of 6-pounder James' rifled guns captured, 1; number of caissons captured, 1; number of rear parts of caissons captured, 2; number of rounds of ammunition expended, 498.

Very respectfully, your obedient servant,

M. B. GARY,
Lieutenant, Commanding Company.

Capt. Josiah W. Church,
Chief of Artillery, 3d Division, 14th Army Corps.

No. 57.

Report of Col. Ferdinand Van Derveer, Thirty-fifth Ohio Infantry, commanding Third Brigade.

HDQRS. 3D BRIGADE, 3D DIVISION, 14TH ARMY CORPS,
Chattanooga, Tenn., September 25, 1863.

CAPTAIN: I have the honor to report the part taken by the Third Brigade in the action of the 19th and 20th instant, near the Chickamauga.

My command consisted of the Second Minnesota, Colonel George; the Ninth Ohio, Colonel Kammerling; the Thirty-fifth Ohio, Lieutenant-Colonel Boynton; the Eighty-seventh Indiana, Colonel Gleason; and Battery I, Fourth Artillery, First Lieut. F. G. Smith. Our effective strength on the morning of the 19th instant was 1,788 officers and men.

After a fatiguing march during the night of the 18th, and without any sleep or rest, while halting near Kelly's house, on the Rossville and La Fayette road, I received an order from Brigadier-General Brannan, commanding Third Division, to move with haste along the road to Reed's Bridge over the Chickamauga, take possession of a ford near that point, and hold it. I immediately moved northward to McDonald's house, and thence at right angles eastward toward the bridge. A short distance from McDonald's I formed the brigade in two lines, sent skirmishers to the front, and advanced cautiously, though without losing time, 1½ miles. In the meantime brisk firing was progressing upon my right, understood to be maintained by the First and Second Brigades of this division.

Being without a guide and entirely unacquainted with the country, I am unable to state how near I went to Reed's Bridge, but perceiving from the firing upon my right that I was passing the enemy's flank, I wheeled the line in that direction and began feeling his position with my skirmishers.

About this time I received an order stating that the Second Brigade was gradually giving back, and that it was necessary I should at once make an attack. This we did with a will, the first line, composed of the Thirty-fifth Ohio on the right and the Second Minnesota on the left, moving down a gentle slope, leaving the Eighty-seventh Indiana in reserve on the crest of the hill. At this time the Ninth Ohio, which had charge of the ammunition train of the division, had not arrived. Smith's battery, composed of four 12-pounder Napoleons, was placed in position in the center and on the right of the line. The enemy having discovered our location, opened a furious fire of artillery and musketry, which was replied to promptly and apparently with considerable effect; for in half an hour the enemy slackened his fire, and his advance line was compelled to fall back. I took advantage of this moment to bring forward the Eighty-seventh Indiana, and by a passage of lines to the front carried them to the relief of the Thirty-fifth Ohio, which had already suffered severely in the engagement. This movement was executed with as much coolness and accuracy as if on drill. Scarcely was the Eighty-seventh Indiana in line before fresh forces of the enemy were brought up in time to receive a terrible volley, which made his ranks stagger and held him for some time at bay. The Ninth Ohio, which I had previously sent for, arriving at this moment, I placed it on the right of my line. Still farther to the right a section of Church's battery and the Seventeenth Ohio, which had been ordered to report to me, were in position.

As the enemy slackened his fire, Colonel Kammerling, chafing like a wounded tiger that he had been behind at the opening, ordered his men to charge. Away they went, closely followed by the Eighty-seventh Indiana and the Seventeenth Ohio, the enemy falling back precipitately. The Ninth in this charge recaptured the guns of Guenther's battery, Fifth Artillery, and held them.

In the meantime the enemy, massing his forces, suddenly appeared upon my left and rear. He came forward, several lines deep, at a double-quick, and opened a brisk fire, but not before I had changed my front to receive him. My new line consisted of the Second Minnesota on the right, next one section of Smith's battery, commanded by Lieutenant Rodney, then the Eighty-seventh Indiana, flanked by Church's and the other section of Smith's battery, and on the extreme left the Thirty-fifth Ohio. The two extremities of the line formed an obtuse angle, the vertex on the left of the Eighty-seventh Indiana, and the opening toward the enemy. The Second Minnesota and the Eighty-seventh Indiana lay on the ground, and were apparently unobserved by the enemy, who moved upon the left of my lines, delivering and receiving a direct fire, Church opening with all his guns and Smith with one section. He advanced rapidly, my left giving way slowly until his flank was brought opposite my right wing, when a murderous and enfilading fire was poured into his ranks by the infantry, and by Rodney's section shotted with canister. Notwithstanding this he steadily moved up his second and third lines. Having observed his great force as well as the persistency of his attack, I had sent messenger after messenger to bring up the Ninth Ohio, which had not yet returned from its charge, made from my original right. At last, however, and when it seemed impossible for my brave men longer to withstand the impetuous advance of the enemy, the Ninth came gallantly up in time to take part in the final struggle, which resulted in his sullen withdrawal. In this last attack his loss must have been very severe. In addition to the heavy fire of the infantry, our guns were pouring double charges of canister in front and on his flank, at one time delivered at a distance not exceeding 40 yards. During the latter part of the contest re-enforcements had arrived, and were by General Brannan, then present, formed in line for the purpose of supporting my brigade, but they were not actively engaged at this time.

Our dead and wounded were gathered up, and a new line, under the supervision of General Brannan, was formed. The enemy, however, made no further demonstration, and quietly withdrew. A small number of prisoners were taken, who reported that the force opposed to us was two divisions of Longstreet's corps, one commanded by General Hood. They fought with great obstinacy and determination, only retreating when fairly swept away by our overwhelming fire.

After the second withdrawal of the enemy, our empty cartridge-boxes were replenished from wagons sent on the field by the general commanding division. After resting my command for an hour or more, I was ordered to report to Major-General Reynolds. Immediately moving toward his position, we arrived near Kelly's house just before sundown, and there, by direction of General Brannan, went into bivouac.

At 8 o'clock the next morning, Sunday, the 20th September, 1863, my brigade was posted as a reserve in rear of the First and Second Brigades of the division, formed in two lines of columns closed *en masse*, where we remained for about an hour, slowly moving over toward the left for the purpose of occupying the space between the Third and Reynolds' divisions. Here I received an order to move quickly over to the left and support General Baird, who, it was said, was being hard pressed by the enemy.

I wheeled my battalions to the left, deployed both lines, and moved through the woods parallel to the Chattanooga road, gradually swinging round my left until when, in rear of Reynolds' position, I struck the road perpendicularly at a point just north of Kelly's house, near and back of his lines.

On approaching the road, riding in advance of the brigade, my attention was called to a large force of the enemy moving southward in four lines, just then emerging from the woods at a run, evidently intending to attack Reynolds and Baird, who were both hotly engaged, in the rear, and apparently unseen by these officers. I immediately wheeled my lines to the left, facing the approaching force, and ordered them to lie down. This movement was not executed until we received a galling fire delivered from a distance of 200 yards. At the same time a rebel battery, placed in the road about 500 or 600 yards in our front, opened upon us with two guns. My command continued to lie down until the enemy approached within 75 yards, when the whole arose to their feet, and the front line, composed of the Second Minnesota and the Eighty-seventh Indiana, delivered a murderous fire almost in their faces, and the Thirty-fifth and Ninth Ohio, passing lines quickly to the front, the whole brigade charged and drove the enemy at full run over the open ground for over a quarter of a mile, and several hundred yards into the woods, my men keeping in good order and delivering their fire as they advanced. The rebels fled hastily to cover, leaving the ground strewn with their dead and wounded. We took position in the woods, and maintained a determined combat for more than an hour. At this time I greatly needed my battery, which had been taken from the brigade early in the day by command of Major-General Negley.

Finding a force moving on my right to support us, and the enemy being almost silenced, I ordered a return to the open ground south of the woods; this movement was executed by passing lines to the rear, each line firing as it retired.

I learned from prisoners that the force we fought and put to flight this day was the division of the rebel General Breckinridge. That we punished them severely was proven by their many dead and wounded, among the former of which were several field officers, and among the latter one general officer of high rank.

I thence moved to a position on the road by the house near General Reynolds' center, and there remained resting my men and caring for my wounded for an hour or more. Although I had not reported to either General Reynolds or Baird, as ordered in the morning, I believe I rendered them very substantial assistance, and at a time when it was greatly needed.

About 2 o'clock, hearing heavy firing on the right of the line, and learning that the high ground in that direction was being held by General Brannan with a part of our division, I moved cautiously through the woods, and at 2.30 p. m. reported my brigade to him for duty. We were immediately placed in the front, relieving his troops, then almost exhausted. The position was well selected and one capable of being defended against a heavy force, the line being the crest of a hill, for the possession of which the enemy made desperate and renewed efforts.

From this time until dark we were hotly engaged. The ammunition failing, and no supply at hand, except a small quantity furnished by Maj. Gen. Gordon Granger, our men gathered their cartridges from the boxes of the dead, wounded, and prisoners, and finally fixed bayonets, determined to hold the position.

Here again the Ninth Ohio made a gallant charge down the hill into the midst of the enemy, scattering them like chaff, and then returning to their position on the hill.

For an hour and a half before dark the attack was one of unexampled fury, line after line of fresh troops being hurled against our position with a heroism and persistency which almost dignified their cause. At length night ended the struggle, and the enemy, having suffered a terrible loss, retired from our immediate front. During the latter part of the day the position directly on our right had been held by the division of Brigadier-General Steedman, but which early in the evening had been withdrawn without our knowledge, thus leaving our flank exposed. From the silence at that point Brigadier-General Brannan suspected all might not be right, and ordered me to place the Thirty-fifth Ohio across that flank to prevent a surprise. This had scarcely been done before a rebel force appeared in the gloom directly in their front. A mounted officer rode to within a few paces of the Thirty-fifth Ohio and asked, "What regiment is that?" To this some one replied, "The Thirty-fifth Ohio." The officer turned suddenly and attempted to run away, but our regiment delivered a volley that brought horse and rider to the ground and put the force to flight. Prisoners said this officer was the rebel General Gregg.

At 7 p. m. an order came from Major-General Thomas that the forces under General Brannan should move quietly to Rossville. This was carried into execution under the direction of Captain Cilley, of my staff, in excellent order.

During the whole of the two days' fighting my brigade kept well together, at all times obeying orders promptly and moving with almost as much regularity and precision as if upon drill. They were subjected to a very severe test on the 19th, when, being actively engaged with the enemy, another brigade (not of this division) ran panic-stricken through and over us, some of the officers of which shouted to our men to retreat or they certainly would be overwhelmed, but not a man left the ranks, and the approaching enemy found before him a wall of steel. Private Savage, of Smith's battery, struck one of the retreating officers with his sponge and damned him for running against his gun.

Our loss in the engagements of both days amounts to 13 officers and 132 men killed, and 25 officers and 581 men wounded, and 51 missing, the total loss being 802 men and officers.

Doubtless many of those enumerated among the missing will be found either wounded or killed. There was no straggling, and I have little doubt those not wounded or killed will be found prisoners in the hands of the enemy.

It is a noticeable fact that the Second Minnesota had not a single man among the missing or a straggler during the two days' engagement.

I cannot speak too highly of the conduct of my officers and men. Without exception they performed all that was required, much more than should have been expected. Where all did so well it seems almost unjust to make distinctions. More gallantry and indomitable courage was never displayed upon the field of battle.

The attention of the general commanding the division is particularly called to the conduct of Col. James George, Second Minnesota; Col. Gustave Kammerling, Ninth Ohio; Col. N. Gleason, Eighty-seventh Indiana; Lieut. Col. H. V. N. Boynton, commanding Thirty-fifth Ohio; and First Lieut. Frank Guest Smith, commanding Battery I, Fourth Artillery. These officers performed every duty required of them with coolness and great promptness, and by their energy and gallantry contributed much to the favorable result which attended every collision with the enemy. Such officers are a credit to the service and our country.

Smith's battery rendered great help in the action of the 19th, and was ably and gallantly served, Lieutenant Rodney being conspicuous in the management of his section.

Captain Church, of the First Brigade, with one section of his battery, fought well and is entitled to credit for the assistance he rendered me on the 19th. I cannot refrain from alluding to the reckless courage and dash of Adjutant Harries, Ninth Ohio. My staff upon the field consisted of Capt. J. R. Beatty, of Second Minnesota, acting assistant adjutant-general ; Capt. Oliver H. Parshall, of the Thirty-fifth Ohio, and Capt. E. B. Thoenssen, Ninth Ohio, acting aides; Capt. C. A. Cilley, Second Minnesota, brigade topographical engineer ; and First Lieut. A. E. Alden, brigade inspector.   For efficiency, personal courage, and energy their conduct deserves more than praise. They exposed themselves upon all occasions, watching the movements of the enemy, carrying orders, rallying the men, and by every means in their power contributing to the success of the brigade.   Captain Parshall was killed early in the action of the first day.   He was a brave, noble soldier, an upright gentleman, and carries with him to the grave the love and regret of many friends.   Captain Thoenssen was missing the evening of the second day, and I believe was captured. Captains Beatty and Cilley had each two horses shot under them. There are many names particularly commended for courage and good behavior, for which I respectfully refer to reports of regiments and the battery.

We have lost many gallant officers and men, a list * of whom is herewith furnished you.   In the charge made by the Ninth Ohio on the 19th, when they recaptured the battery of the regular brigade, their loss in killed and wounded was over 50.

I am, captain, very respectfully, your obedient servant,

FERDINAND VAN DERVEER,
Colonel, Commanding Third Brigade.

Capt. Louis J. Lambert,
Assistant Adjutant-General, Third Division.

No. 58.

Report of Col. James George, Second Minnesota Infantry.

Hdqrs. Second Regiment Minnesota Volunteers,
Chattanooga, Tenn., September 25, 1863.

General : I have the honor to transmit the following report of the part taken by the Second Regiment Minnesota Volunteers in the battle of the 19th and 20th instant, near Crawfish Spring, Ga. :

The regiment was placed in position at 10 a. m. on the 19th, on the extreme left of the brigade and next to Battery I, Fourth U. S. Artillery, facing the south.

A few minutes later the enemy approached in line in front to within about 300 yards and opened a heavy fire of musketry, which was returned with such effect as to repulse the attack in about ten minutes.   Another similar attack was soon after made and met with a like repulse, the enemy falling back in disorder entirely out of sight.   About half past 10 o'clock sharp firing of musketry was suddenly opened at some distance in our left and front, which soon began to approach us.   The cartridge-boxes had been replenished, and the regiment was laid down in line to await its time, the men having been admonished to withhold their fire until the enemy should be within close range.   There soon appeared, approaching in disorder from the left front, a line of our troops in full retreat and closely pursued by the enemy, who was cheering and firing furiously

---

* Embodied in revised statement, p. 173.

in their rear. It proved to be the regular brigade, the men of which passed over our line and were afterward partially rallied in our rear and on our left.

As soon as these troops had passed us the farther advance of the enemy was checked by a volley from our line. A sharp contest with musketry followed, which resulted in a few minutes in the complete repulse of the late exultant enemy, who fled from our front in confusion.

About 11 o'clock a large force was discovered advancing on us from the east and simultaneously from the north. Our front was immediately changed to the left to meet this attack, and after a few minutes' fighting, the enemy seeming to be moving around to the northward, our front was again changed to the left under a hot fire, so that the regiment faced the northeast, and again finally to face the north as the enemy massed his troops for an assault from that direction. The enemy charged desperately, and were finally and completely repulsed and routed after a brief but bloody contest. The fighting ended with us at about 11.30 a. m. Our loss was 8 killed and 41 wounded, including 2 commissioned officers; none missing. The regiment commenced the battle with 384 officers and enlisted men.

On the 20th the regiment took place in the brigade with 295 officers and men, 40 men having been detached for picket duty the previous evening and not relieved when the regiment marched. At 10 a. m. the regiment on the right of the brigade was advanced into an open field to the support of a battery which was in action immediately on our right, the line facing the north. Scarcely had the line been halted in its assigned place when a furious fire of musketry and artillery was opened on it from the edge of woods bordering the field on the west, and 300 to 400 yards distant. The brigade front was instantly changed to the left, the movement being made in good order, though under fire; and our line at once opened on the enemy. After a few minutes' firing a charge was ordered, and we advanced at the double-quick across the field and into the woods, driving the enemy back upon their supports. Here the engagement was continued for fifteen or twenty minutes, when the enemy moved off by their right flank, clearing our front and getting out of our range, even when firing to the left oblique. The regiment was then withdrawn and the brigade reformed, facing the south. Presently an artillery fire was opened on us from the east, and our front was changed to face it. After remaining here in position for about half an hour we were moved off a distance of a mile or more to a hill on the right of our general line of battle, where, at 2.30 p. m., we again became hotly engaged with musketry. The enemy charged repeatedly and desperately on our position here, but were always repulsed by the cool and deadly fire of our rifles. The firing here continued without any intermission until 4.45 p. m., when the enemy temporarily withdrew from the contest. Two other attacks were afterward made on us here, but both were repulsed, and darkness ended the fight at about 6.30 p. m.

Our loss on this day was 27 killed and 72 wounded, being more than one-third of our entire number; none missing. Some 8 or 10 men of other commands, who joined us temporarily, were killed while bravely fighting in our ranks. I regret that I cannot give their names and regiments. The conduct of the officers and men of my regiment was, on both days, uniformly gallant and soldier-like beyond praise. If any one of them failed in doing his whole duty I do not know it.*

Asst. Surg. Otis Ayer and Hospital Steward Frederick A. Buckingham were captured from the field hospital September 20, and are prisoners in the hands of the enemy. A good portion of our wounded were left lying on the field and are now prisoners in hands of the enemy.

I am, general, very respectfully, your most obedient servant,

JAMES GEORGE,
Commanding Second Minnesota Volunteers.

Brig. Gen. LORENZO THOMAS,
Adjutant-General, U. S. Army, Washington, D. C.

No. 59.

Report of Lieut. Col. Henry V. N. Boynton, Thirty-fifth Ohio Infantry.

HDQRS. THIRTY-FIFTH OHIO INFANTRY VOLUNTEERS,
Chattanooga, Tenn., September 24, 1863.

CAPTAIN: I have the honor to report the following as the part taken by the Thirty-fifth Ohio in the action of September 19 and 20 in this vicinity :

We were brought into action at 8 a. m. of the 19th, after a most fatiguing march begun at 5 p. m. of the previous evening, and only ended in time to allow of fifteen minutes' rest before the fight. The Thirty-fifth occupied the right of the first line, and the skirmishers of the command met the enemy after a very short advance in line. The engagement soon became very fierce, but the accurate fire of the line soon broke the rebel line. In this short fight our loss in thirty minutes was 60 killed and wounded. In a short time the rebels rallied and made another desperate assault on the line, but were again repulsed.

The next move of the enemy was an attempt to flank our position on the left. The regular brigade, which had been engaged on our right and to the front, were driven across our line, which was placed as a support to the Fourth Regular Battery, Lieutenant Smith commanding. Seeing this rapid approach of the enemy in four lines, the front of my regiment was immediately changed to the left, though without orders from the colonel commanding the brigade, it being perfectly apparent that this alone could save the battery.

The assault of the rebel lines proved terrific, but so soon as the confusion attending the passage of the regular brigade had in part subsided, the Thirty-fifth faced, advanced, and by a few moments of close fighting, in connection with the well-directed fire of Lieutenant Smith's double-shotted guns, repulsed that portion of the rebel line opposed to our immediate front. This closed the fighting of the day, it having continued for four hours with great fury. The rebel forces opposed [to] us were a portion of Longstreet's forces, as prisoners reported. Together with the other regiments of the brigade, we bivouacked upon the battle-field without blankets or tents, and although a white frost covered the ground, and being in an open

---

* List of casualties, here omitted, is embodied in revised statement, p. 173.

field, we passed the night without fires as best we could under the circumstances.

The rapid and fatiguing march of the night before had caused 21 men to fall behind; 25 were back sick. Seventeen cooks had been ordered to follow the teams to Chattanooga, and 10 men were left to guard the knapsacks when the fight opened, so that the regiment went into the fight with a total of 391 officers and men. Of this number 9 were killed, 97 wounded, and 4 reported missing. Three of the wounded were officers, Capt. Joel K. Deardorff, Company K, severely in the leg ; Capt. A. J. Lewis, Company I, severely in the bowels, and Lieut. L. P. Thompson, Company E, who received a flesh wound in the leg.

Capt. Oliver H. Parshall, of Company F, was shot dead immediately on the right of our line. He had only the day before returned from home and was detailed upon the staff of the colonel commanding the brigade. Notwithstanding the fact that he was detached, I cannot refrain from mentioning his great coolness and gallantry, which were constantly displayed along my own portion of the line. His course as an officer has always been such as to secure the confidence and esteem of all.

On the morning of the 20th, at 9 a. m., the brigade having taken its position in two lines as the reserve of the division, the Thirty-fifth was assigned its position on the right of the rear line in column of divisions closed *en masse*. At 11 a. m. the enemy attacked, in overwhelming numbers, the division in front and the one on the left. The brigade being ordered to support General Baird, our columns were deployed under a sharp fire of shot and canister. On reaching the rear of General Baird's position we met General Breckinridge's division advancing to attack General Baird's flank. Having no notice of the approach whatever, the flank of my regiment, without a moment's notice, was subjected to a galling fire from the main rebel lines at very short range.

Notwithstanding the difficulties of the position, the men of the Thirty-fifth immediately changed front, faced the enemy by orders, lay down until the first line should finish its fire; the second line then rose and charged, following the broken and retreating lines of the rebels. The second line followed in rear of the first; the Thirty-fifth in advance on the left, supported by the Ninth Ohio on the right, charged across an open field for a third of a mile and advanced a hundred yards into the woods beyond, the left of the regiment covering the road over which the rebels advanced, and in which they had planted a battery. The Thirty-fifth held its position until the brigade was ordered to retire to allow the advance of a relief brigade from our right. The withdrawal was accomplished in regular order by the successive passage of lines to the rear, but not without heavy loss to the regiment. We then returned with our brigade to the position occupied at the commencement of the charge. In this position we remained for about an hour, subjected for about half of the time to the fire of a rebel battery which had occupied the position held at the beginning of the action by the left of our division. From this point the brigade passed toward the right of our general line of battle.

Here we joined General Thomas, who had rallied, with the assistance of General Brannan, a portion of several brigades. Our own brigade came upon the hill unbroken and immediately took position in one line on the crest, the Thirty-fifth on the right. In a short time the Thirty-fifth advanced to a line of logs, hastily thrown together and just sufficient to cover the heads of the men when lying on the ground. The hill was twice attacked in overwhelming force, the first attack hardly ceasing before the second began with almost inconceivable fury and persistence. The fighting continued for nearly two hours, when our ammunition became exhausted. Nothing daunted, the regiment fixed bayonets and awaited the shock. Fortunately a load of ammunition arrived, and the firing was renewed with vigor; still the rebels pressed us hard and maintained their position at close quarters.

At this point our cartridges again gave out, when by the exertions of several of the officers—among whom were Major Budd, Captain L'Hommedieu, Captain Daugherty, and Lieutenant Bone—the line was supplied with cartridges from the boxes of the dead and wounded. The attack progressing, this supply was soon exhausted, when the officers and men of the Second Minnesota kindly supplied us with several rounds, for which I take this opportunity to thank them. These were ordered to be so distributed as to give each man 3 rounds, and the order given to cease firing, fix bayonets, and await the approach of the enemy. It was near dark. The troops having been removed on the right of our line, the Thirty-fifth was ordered to protect the right flank and was wheeled accordingly. The hill was immediately occupied by a rebel regiment, whose right flank rested only 50 yards from the front of the Thirty-fifth.

A rebel general, believed to be General Gregg, here rode up and asked whose troops we were; at the reply, "Thirty-fifth Ohio," he wheeled, but received a volley from the Thirty-fifth which riddled him and his horse and raked the line of the rebels, striking them at an angle of 30 degrees, breaking their line, and sending all but three companies down the hill in confusion. The three remaining companies poured a volley into our front and left. With this fire the engagement ceased, it being 7 p. m.

The order for retiring arrived just at this juncture, and together with the troops on the hill we fell back to Rossville.

The regiment went into the fight on the second day with a total of 280 officers and men. Of these 1 officer was killed, Lieutenant Harlan, Company F; 2 were severely wounded, Lieutenant Adams, Company G, and Lieutenant Sabin, Company A; Lieutenant Rothenbush, Company I, slightly; Lieutenant Cottingham, Company E, was captured. Eight enlisted men were killed, 51 wounded, and 21 missing, part of whom were captured in the charge. The loss of the regiment thus shows 50 per cent. as near as may be of the number engaged. This, taken in connection with the fact that the regiment never broke and constantly maintained its ground, shows its merits in a strong light and needs no comment. The present available force of the regiment for line of battle is 240 guns, 11 company and 2 field officers.

Dr. Charles O. Wright and Dr. A. H. Landis were left to take care of our wounded in the hands of the enemy.

Where all fought so nobly and so well it is impossible to make distinctions. Still I must be allowed to speak particularly of the excellent management of our skirmishers, first by Captain Daugherty, Company A, and subsequently by Lieutenant Miller, Company C, and the heroic conduct of our color-bearer, Sergt. Mark B. Price—to his coolness much of the good order that prevailed from first to last is owing; and to commend especially to your notice Orderly Sergt. William B. Mikesell, Company E, Orderly Sergt. Richard H. Ford,

Company K, and Sergt. William K. Van Horn, Company I, who commanded their respective companies with marked ability on the second day of the fight. Lieutenant Harlan's last words as he fell were a cheer to his company to press forward. Lieutenant Adams, though the youngest officer of the line, displayed great courage, and when he thought himself dying said, with a smile, "I shall die, but that is nothing if we whip the rebels." Captains Lewis and Deardorff fell in the thickest of the first day's fight, and Lieutenants Rothenbush and Sabin on the second. For them all it is enough to say that they fell at their posts facing the foe. Lieutenant Mather, commanding Company H, was ever conspicuous in the discharge of every duty. For Captain Henninger, Lieutenants Steele, Taylor, Cottingham, Houser, and Davidson I desire to say that they were ever at their post and performed their duty to my entire satisfaction. Half of the Thirty-fifth are dead or wounded, and to those who remain I can only say that their commanding officer looks upon them with feelings to which no language can give expression. To have belonged to the Third Brigade will hereafter be the crowning glory of your old age.

Returning our heartfelt thanks to our Heavenly Father, the God of Battles, that we were all able thus to discharge our whole duty, and sorrowing as soldiers only can over the deaths and wounds of our noble comrades fallen, we pray that the future may find us ever ready to combat treason both on Southern battle-fields and, when the war is over, among the vile traitors of the North.

Yours, respectfully,

H. V. N. BOYNTON,
Lieut Col., Comdg. 35th Ohio Volunteer Infantry.

Capt. J. R. BEATTY,
Acting Asst. Adjt. Gen., 3d Brig., 3d Div., 14th A. C.

No. 60.

Report of Lieut. Frank G. Smith, Battery I, Fourth U. S. Artillery.

HEADQUARTERS COMPANY I, FOURTH ARTILLERY,
Chattanooga, September 26, 1863.

CAPTAIN : In reply to your circular of this date, calling for report of part taken by this battery in the engagements of the 19th and 20th instant, I have the honor to report that when the action of the 19th began the first section of my battery, under First Lieut. G. B. Rodney, was placed in the front line, between the Second Minnesota and Thirty-fifth Ohio Volunteers (the Thirty-fifth Ohio Volunteers being on the right), and the second section, under Lieutenant Stephenson, on a hillside 60 yards in rear of the right wing of the Thirty-fifth Ohio Volunteers. The firing began before we had fairly taken our positions, and 4 of my men were disabled before I could open fire on the enemy. After a sharp engagement of half an hour's duration, the firing slackened on both sides. Lieutenant Stephenson's section having suffered severely from the musketry fired at the infantry in his front, and as it was impossible to use canister (should it become necessary to do so) without injury to our own men, I directed it limbered to the right, with the intention of placing it on the right of the line. At this time, however, the Ninth Ohio Volunteers advanced in line and took position on the right of the Thirty-fifth Ohio Volunteers; the firing recommenced, and Lieutenant Stephenson was obliged to go into action on the same ground. The rebels were soon repulsed, after which the second section was moved to the crest of the hill, 150 yards in rear of the line, and placed on the left of your battery, which had come up a short time previously with a regiment of infantry, under Colonel Connell.

On the completion of this arrangement the rebels renewed the attack; in about twenty minutes they were driven back, closely followed by the Ninth Ohio Volunteers and Seventeenth Ohio Volunteers at a charge. Before the firing here had fairly ceased, the enemy began a furious attack upon our left and rear. To meet this, both sections of my battery changed front where they stood. Your battery came into position on the right of Lieutenant Stephenson (your right thrown a little forward), leaving room for the Eighty-seventh Indiana between your battery and the first section of mine. The Second Minnesota was on the right and the Thirty-fifth Ohio Volunteers on the left of the line.

The battery was now formed so that Lieutenant Stephenson could deliver a direct and Lieutenant Rodney an oblique—almost an enfilade—fire into the ranks of the approaching rebels, but they still came on. When they had arrived within 100 yards of us, we gave them canister, double-shotted, two or three rounds of which, with the aid of a galling fire from our supports, sent them to cover at a double-quick. The fighting ended about noon. After several changes of position to the right, we bivouacked for the night 2 miles from our first position of the morning. My loss was 1 officer and 11 enlisted men wounded, 1 limber blown up, and 16 horses permanently disabled.

Early on the morning of the 20th instant I obtained a detail of 8 men from the brigade, and so partially filled up my gun detachments.

Between 9 and 10 a. m., while the Third Brigade was moving to the support of Baird's division toward the left of our line, a staff officer with the rank of major directed me, by command of Major-General Thomas, to move the battery to a certain hill and report to Major-General Negley. I did so and was placed by him, with other batteries and some infantry, near a hospital, on a ridge from which we could sweep the valley in rear of our front line, which was then hotly engaged.

This ground was occupied by me during the rest of the day, our front being changed from time to time to meet the different attacks of the enemy. Before noon part of the front line broke, and was rallied on the hill which we occupied. Not long afterward I found that General Negley had moved with all of his artillery but my battery, leaving no orders and no support but the men just spoken of, and such stragglers as had brought wounded from the front and were either unable or unwilling to rejoin their commands.

At about 3 p. m. General Granger joined us on the hill, and half an hour afterward the Third Brigade also came up. We fought almost constantly from noon until sunset, when we withdrew with but 6 rounds of ammunition to the gun, having suffered a loss of 1 man killed, 9 wounded, and 3 horses disabled, and bivouacked for the night near Rossville, 4 miles from the battle-field.

I inclose herewith a report* of most important losses sustained in the action. The baggage wagon containing all of my company

---

* Embodied in Church's report, p. 406.

papers was captured by the enemy on the 20th, otherwise I could give a more detailed report of the losses sustained in ordnance, stores, &c.

Where all did so well it may not seem proper for me to mention acts of individuals, but I cannot refrain from calling your attention to the gallantry displayed by First Lieut. G. B. Rodney; also to the coolness and bravery of Sergts. Thomas J. Myers and Charles Ellis, the latter of whom, though seriously wounded in the action of the first day, refused to leave his post until compelled to do so by a shot in the thigh.

I have the honor to be, captain, very respectfully, your obedient servant,

FRANK GUEST SMITH,
First Lieutenant Fourth Artillery, Comdg. Company.

Capt. JOSIAH W. CHURCH,
Chief of Artillery, Third Division.

No. 61.

Reports of Maj. Gen. Joseph J. Reynolds, U. S. Army, command-ing Fourth Division.

HDQRS. FOURTH DIVISION, FOURTEENTH CORPS,
Trenton, Ga., September 6, 1863.

COLONEL : I have to report movements and operations of my com-mand during the month of August, as follows, viz:

Division left Decherd, Tenn., on 16th, crossed Cumberland Mount-ains at University Place, and moving via Sweeden's Cove and Battle Creek, arrived at Jasper, Tenn., on the 21st. At University, de-tached the mounted brigade (Colonel Wilder's) of the division, send-ing them to a point on the Tennessee River opposite to Chattanooga, which position the brigade reached, and shelled Chattanooga (by Lilly's Eighteenth Indiana Battery) on the 21st. Also detached from University the Eighty-ninth Ohio Regiment, Co'onel Carlton, to occupy Tracy City, where that regiment still remains.*

On the 22d a portion of Col. E. A. King's brigade (Second) took posession of Shellmound Ferry and the south side of Tennessee River at that point; destroyed trestlework on railroad to prevent running of trains from Bridgeport to Chattanooga.

This brigade aided a battalion of pioneer brigade in finding and raising flat-boats, which, with one large boat made by pioneers, afforded ferrying facilities for the division, which was in readiness to cross, at the rate of 800 men per hour.

On night of the 30th crossed Colonel Ray's East Tennessee Cav-alry, and made reconaissance, supported by King's brigade, to within 2½ miles of Chattanooga, the brigade remaining on the south side of the river.

On the 31st crossed my ammunition train.

Respectfully submitted.

J. J. REYNOLDS,
Major-General.

Lieut. Col. GEORGE E. FLYNT,
Assistant Adjutant-General, Hdqrs. 14th Army Corps.

---

* But see p. 866.

HDQRS. FOURTH DIVISION, FOURTEENTH CORPS,
Chattanooga, Tenn., September 23, 1863.

COLONEL : I herewith submit a report of the operations of the Fourth Division, Fourteenth Corps, in the battle of Chickamauga Creek, Ga., September 19 and 20, 1863.

The division moved from Pond Spring about 4 p. m. on the 18th, and, having marched all night, halted one hour for breakfast near Osburn's, and thence proceeded, by order of General Thomas, commanding Fourteenth Corps, to take position in line of battle northeast of Glenn's house. While taking this position the division was ordered to advance immediately toward McDonald's and enter into the action then progressing on our left. I at once reported in person to the corps commander, and, in accordance with his instructions, directed the Third Brigade, Turchin's, to take position southeast of Kelly's Cross-Roads. The Second Brigade, King's, was about leaving the main road to take place on the right of the Third, when I met General Palmer in the road, who represented that his command had gained upon the enemy, but was nearly out of ammunition and in great need of assistance to enable him to hold what he had gained, at least until they could replenish ammunition. This, although not the precise position indicated to me for the Second Brigade, was very close to it, and appeared to be a place that it was essential to fill at once, and no other troops were in sight to take the position. Three regiments, under Col. E. A. King, were therefore ordered in at this point, leaving in my hands one regiment, Seventy-fifth Indiana, and Harris' battery. I had just arrived upon the field and found my division would occupy about the center of our line. No reserve force being anywhere apparent, I determined to form one of Harris' battery and Seventy-fifth Indiana, to which was shortly added Swallow's battery, which I found in the road unemployed, and the Ninety-second Illinois (temporarily dismounted). In a short time the Sixth Ohio came from the front, and took position near Harris' battery to resupply ammunition. General Palmer soon called also for the Seventy-fifth Indiana, temporarily; it was ordered to go, the Sixth Ohio serving in the interim as support to the guns. The Sixth having resupplied ammunition was subsequently ordered away, leaving the Ninety-second Illinois the only support for the batteries. The Seventy-fifth Indiana returned late in the day and in some disorder, having relieved an entire brigade and done efficient service.

Calls for support had been made from the right, to which it was impossible for me to respond. General J. C. Davis arrived and inquired where troops were needed. I gave him the substance of my information, and he led his division in on our right. Finally a call came direct from Col. E. A. King, who had drifted farther to the right, that he was hard pressed and wanted his own regiment, the Seventy-fifth Indiana. This regiment was gone, but I ordered to him the Ninety-second Illinois, trusting to regiments returning to the road to resupply ammunition for support to the batteries, or, that in case the forces to the front were driven back, of which I felt there was danger, I might rally them around the batteries and re-establish the line. The two howitzers of the Ninety-second Illinois were now added to the two batteries, and the Ninety-second started to King's support. Scarcely had it cleared the front of the guns when this regiment was struck in flank by our own forces retiring, followed closely by the enemy. I met our retiring regiments in person, pointed them to 14 guns in position as evidence that the enemy must be thrown back, and by great exertion succeeded in reforming several regiments in rear of the batteries.

Battery M, Fourth Regular Artillery, commanded by Lieutenant Russell, at this time came to our position, and was ordered into action on Harris' left.   These batteries fired with terrible effect upon the enemy, his progress was checked, and our line for a time prevented from yielding any farther.

The enemy now shifted farther to the right, where there was evidently an opening in our line, and coming in on their right flank our regiments again became disheartened and began to retire.   The batteries, following the regiments, changed front and fired to the right, and the line was reformed along a fence nearly perpendicular to its former position, with the batteries in the edge of the woods. The enemy pushing still farther to our right and rear, I rallied and formed into double line some ten or twelve other retiring regiments, which came in from the left center, and placing the front line under the immediate command of Colonel Croxton, Tenth Kentucky, ordered them to swing round on the left flank as a pivot. This order was well executed by both lines, and our rear thus entirely cleared of the enemy.

It was now nearly sundown, and operations on this part of the field ceased for the day.

On the 20th my division was posted at Kelly's Cross-Roads *en échelon*, the Third Brigade, Turchin's, in front and immediately on General Palmer's right, the Second Brigade, King's, slightly retired, to secure good ground, and facing the main Rossville and La Fayette road.   Two brigades of the Third Division, Fourteenth Corps, Brannan's, were on my right.   My division was formed in two lines, nearly one-half the infantry being in reserve.

During the early morning of the 20th temporary breastworks were erected of such material as could be found at hand, and were of great benefit.   The attack of the enemy on our position commenced about 10 o'clock, and was very heavy; he was successfully repulsed at all points in front of our position without calling upon the second line of infantry.

About 11 o'clock the two brigades of the Third Division, being heavily pressed in front and right flank, which had been left uncovered, began to yield.   Colonel Croxton reported this to me, and personal inspection verified the report.   The One hundred and fifth Ohio, Major Perkins commanding, and until this time lying in reserve, was ordered to face the enemy and go at them with the bayonet.   The order was gallantly executed; the enemy was thrown back, and the yielding regiments partly rallied, but the enemy returning with increased force and turning their right, these regiments were borne back, the One hundred and fifth Ohio with them. The latter regiment carried off the field the rebel General Adams, wounded, who had been previously captured by Captain Guthrie's company, of the Nineteenth Illinois.

After all of our troops had left the right of my division, and the enemy was silenced in front, a column of the enemy appeared on the main road in the prolongation of the line of battle of the Second Brigade; at the same time a rebel battery was firing into the rear of this brigade.   The position of the Second Brigade was therefore changed, so as to throw its left nearer the right of the Third Brigade and to face the enemy, who had taken position on our right and rear. At this time the division was out of ammunition, except such as was gathered from the boxes of the dead, and the enemy was between us and our ammunition train ; but for this circumstance we could have maintained our position indefinitely. The ammunition train by another route got safely to Chattanooga.

We remained in this position for some time, when orders were received from the corps commander to prepare to change our position, and the division in a short time received orders to initiate a movement toward Rossville. This was done with the brigades still formed in two lines and moving by flank in parallel columns, thus ready at a moment's notice to face with double line in either of the directions in which firing had lately been heard.

Arriving at the Rossville road, the command was met by the corps commander in person, and I was directed to form line perpendicular to the Rossville road. This done General Thomas pointed in the direction of Rossville and said, "There they are; clear them out."

The division was faced about and a charge ordered and executed in two lines at double-quick, through the rebel lines, dispersing them and capturing more than 200 prisoners under a fire of infantry in front and artillery in flank.

I understood that this movement was intended to open the way to Rossville for the army, and did not then know of any other road to that point. I therefore pressed right on in the charge, expecting the whole division to do the same until the rebel lines and batteries were cleared and the road opened, and found myself with only about 150 of the Third Brigade, under Colonel Lane, Eleventh Ohio, near the field hospital of the Fourteenth Corps.

The remainder of the division proceeded to the high ground on the left by order of General Thomas. The Third Brigade was reformed by Brigadier-General Turchin, who had his horse shot under him in the charge. The Second Brigade was reformed by Col. M. S. Robinson, who succeeded to the command of that brigade after the death of Col. E. A. King. The advanced party rejoined the division on the ridge to the west of the road, and the whole division marched to Rossville by the Valley road.

The First Brigade, Wilder's mounted infantry, was detached from the division by order of the department commander, except the Ninety-second Illinois, which was with the division on the 19th. The operations of this brigade will be reported separately.

The brigade commanders, Brig. Gen. J. B. Turchin and Col. E. A. King, handled their brigades with skill and judgment, and no instance of confusion or disorder occurred.

The batteries, Harris', Nineteenth Indiana, and Andrew's, Twenty-first Indiana, were skillfully and bravely managed, and did fine execution, the Nineteenth Battery on both days and the Twenty-first Battery more especially on the 20th. Captain Harris was wounded on the 19th; his battery was ably commanded on the 20th by Lieutenant Lackey. This battery lost two guns, one left on the field, the horses killed ; the other disabled by the enemy's fire.

Andrew's battery lost one gun, left from the breaking of the harness.

The untimely fall of Colonel King renders it impracticable to obtain a connected report of the operations of the Second Brigade.

The regiments were ably commanded as follows: One hundred and first Indiana, Lieutenant-Colonel Doan ; Seventy-fifth Indiana,

Colonel Robinson : Sixty-eighth Indiana, Captain Espy, wounded; One hundred and fifth Ohio, Major Perkins, wounded.

The division staff were at their posts and discharged their duties promptly and faithfully.

Maj. John Levering, assistant adjutant-general, sick in ambulance. Maj. O. Q. Herrick, medical director, in the hands of the enemy. Capt. F. T. Starkweather, assistant quartermaster ; Capt. J. L. Leech, commissary of subsistence; Capt. C. O. Howard, mustering officer, aide-de-camp, wounded in hand ; Capt. J. T. Floyd, One hundred and first Indiana, aide-de-camp ; Capt. R. B. Hanna, Seventy-second Indiana, provost-marshal, wounded; First Lieut. J. W. Armstrong, Seventeenth Indiana, ordnance officer ; Second Lieut. W. P. Bainbridge, One hundred and first Indiana, aide-de-camp, wounded in arm; Sergt. Daniel Bush, Company D, One hundred and first Indiana, orderly at headquarters, was badly wounded and has since died.

Among the deaths the country has to deplore the loss of Col. E. A. King, commanding Second Brigade, and Col. W. G. Jones, commanding Thirty-sixth Ohio, both superior officers.

Herewith are submitted lists of casualties,* from which it appears that the total loss of the division in killed, wounded, and missing is 963.

Very respectfully, your obedient servant,
J. J. REYNOLDS,
Major-General, Commanding Division.

Lieutenant-Colonel FLYNT,
Assistant Adjutant-General, Fourteenth Army Corps.

No. 62.

Report of Capt. Samuel J. Harris, Nineteenth Indiana Battery, Acting Chief of Artillery.

HEADQUARTERS NINETEENTH INDIANA BATTERY,
Chattanooga, Tenn., October 4, 1863.

Statement of the loss of men, matériel, and horses in the Nineteenth and Twenty-first Indiana Batteries, of the Fourth Division, Fourteenth Army Corps, during the action of the 19th and 20th September, 1863.

Batteries.	Men.			Guns and limbers.		Small-arms.			Rounds of ammunition expended.			Matériel.			
	Killed.	Wounded.	Missing.	3-inch Rodman.	12-pounder smooth-bores. Gun limber, 12-pounder.	Pistols.	Sabers.	3-inch.	12-pounder.	Friction primers.	Sponges and staves.	Sponge buckets.	Leather or watering buckets.	Trail handspikes.
19th Indiana Battery, Capt. S. J. Harris.	2	16	2	1	1	4	3	350	750	1,200	7	4	6	8
21st Indiana Battery, Captain Andrew.	....	10	....	....	1	1	....	....	....	442	560	2	....	4	....
Total................	2	26	2	1	2	1	4	3	350	1,192	1,760	9	4	10	8

* Embodied in revised statement, p. 173.

Statement of the loss of men, matériel, and horses, &c.—Continued.

Batteries.	Matériel.											
	Prolongs.	Gunners' haversacks.	Trays.	Saddles, cavalry.	Bridles, cavalry.	Bridles, artillery.	Nose bags.	Curry-combs.	Horse brushes.	Whips.	Halters.	Tow hooks.
19th Indiana Battery, Capt. S. J. Harris.........	2	2	6	4	5	6	25	10	10	10	15	10
21st Indiana Battery, Captain Andrew.............	....	2	....	1	1	1	....	....	....	....	12	....
Total..	2	4	6	5	6	7	25	10	10	10	27	10

Batteries.	Matériel.									Horses.		
	Priming wires.	Gunners' pinchers.	Thumb stalls.	Horse blankets.	Harness, sets.	Paulins.	Axes.	Fifth wheel.	Lanyards.	Lost and killed.	Wounded.	Wounded and abandoned.
19th Indiana Battery, Capt. S. J. Harris	6	3	6	25	10	....	....	....	....	15	6	....
21st Indiana Battery, Captain Andrew...........	2	....	2	....	1	4	4	1	2	....	....	12
Total..	8	3	8	25	11	4	4	1	2	15	6	12

S. J. HARRIS,
Capt. 19th Ind. Batty., Actg. Chf. of Arty., 4th Div., 14th A. C.

No. 63.

Report of Col. John T. Wilder, Seventeenth Indiana Infantry, commanding First Brigade (Mounted Infantry).

HEADQUARTERS DEPARTMENT OF THE CUMBERLAND,
Chattanooga, November 27, 1863.

Brig. Gen. LORENZO THOMAS, *Adjutant-General, U. S. Army:*

GENERAL: Inclosed herewith I have the honor to transmit the report of Col. John T. Wilder, Seventeenth Regiment Indiana Volunteers, commanding brigade of mounted infantry, of the operations of his brigade in co-operation with the main portion of the Army of the Cumberland before and after the evacuation of Chattanooga by the rebel army, including the battle of Chickamauga, and up to the time of the assembling of the army at Chattanooga.

For his ingenuity and fertility of resource in occupying the attention of an entire corps of the rebel army while our army was getting around its flank, and for his valor and the many qualities of a commander displayed by him in the numerous engagements of his brigade with the enemy before and during the battle of Chickamauga, and for the excellent service rendered by him generally, I would respectfully recommend him to the President of the United States for an appointment as brigadier-general.*

I am, sir, very respectfully, your obedient servant,
GEO. H. THOMAS,
Major-General, Commanding.

---
*See also Rosecrans to L. Thomas, p. 79.

HDQRS. 1ST BRIG., 4TH DIV., 14TH ARMY CORPS,
November 10, 1863.

GENERAL: On August 16, in accordance with orders received from headquarters Department of the Cumberland, my command, consisting of the Seventy-second Indiana, Col. A. O. Miller; Seventeenth Indiana, Lieut. Col. Henry Jordan; Ninety-second Illinois, Col. S. D. Atkins; Ninety-eighth Illinois, Col. J. J. Funkhouser; One hundred and twenty-third Illinois, Col. James Monroe; and the Eighteenth Indiana Battery, Capt. Eli Lilly, constituting the First Brigade of Mounted Infantry, commenced the ascent of the Cumberland Mountains on the road from Decherd to Tracy City. We camped that night at the Southern University, and early next morning started for Tracy City, arriving there at night, over roads very muddy and much cut up by the retreat of the rebels. The next morning we moved on toward Therman, in Sequatchie Valley, making about 20 miles, being delayed to repair the roads so that our artillery and trains could pass. Next day we descended into Sequatchie Valley at Therman, surprising and capturing a party of 14 rebels and releasing 5 Union prisoners they were about to hang, and proceeded to Dunlap, arriving there about an hour sooner than General Palmer's division, of General Crittenden's corps. The next morning we started over Walden's Ridge. Being delayed by General Hazen's brigade in going up the mountain we did not reach the summit until 1 p. m.; when, taking the lead, crossed the mountain, going down it at Poe's Tavern, surprising and capturing Captain Carson and a party of rebels, 11 in number, releasing 3 Union men whom they held as prisoners.

The next morning before daylight I put the command in motion, sending Colonel Funkhouser with the Ninety-eighth Illinois and Ninety-second Illinois and a section of Lilly's battery to demonstrate upon Harrison, 6 miles distant, and with the remainder of the command proceeded rapidly toward Chattanooga, 15 miles distant, sending a scouting party of two companies of the Seventeenth Indiana, under Captain Vail (Company H, Seventeenth Indiana), to examine the river between the mouth of North Chickamauga and Chattanooga. We approached Chattanooga so unexpectedly as to capture the animals and some of the men of a battery, and part of the picket stationed on the north side of the river, and wounding a number of the relief pickets who were crossing in a boat to the north side of the river before they could get beyond our fire. The troops and people in the town seemed to be in great consternation, running in all directions. Presently some guns in a battery on the west side of town opened upon us, and Captain Lilly replied to them, in a short time silencing their fire, when they opened upon us from a rifled 32-pounder, the first shot from which killed 4 horses and mortally wounded Corporal McCorkle, of the Eighteenth Indiana Battery. It, however, fired but four shots before Captain Lilly silenced it also, one of his shells exploding in the embrasure from which the gun was being fired, killing a captain and 3 men. He succeeded also in sinking the steamer Paint Rock, and disabling another lying at the landing, and sinking a number of their pontoons, which were laid in the stream preparatory to being swung across the river. We then commenced making feints as if trying to cross the river at different points for 40 miles above the town, and succeeded in so deceiving them as to induce them to use an entire army corps to prevent the execution of such a purpose, they working every night fortifying the south bank of the river at every feasible crossing for miles above. Details were made nearly every night to build fires indicating large camps, and by throwing boards upon others and hammering on barrels and sawing up boards and throwing the pieces in streams that would float them into the river, we made them believe we were preparing to cross with boats. This was kept up until Chattanooga was evacuated, when my command was immediately thrown across the river at the ford at Friar's Island, 8 miles above Chattanooga. The first across was Colonel Funkhouser with the Ninety-eighth Illinois, who gallantly crossed the ford at 12 m. in the face of the rebel cavalry on the south bank. This was on September 9.

Colonel Atkins had been previously ordered to report to General Thomas with his regiment (Ninety-second Illinois), and had crossed the river at Battle Creek several days before, and coming up Lookout Mountain from Lookout Valley had entered Chattanooga at 10 a. m. the same day, driving the rebel rear guard of cavalry before him, and moving up the south bank of the river joined the command near Friar's Island.

On the 10th we moved south toward Ringgold, and camped that night at Taylor's Gap, sending a party consisting of four companies of the Seventy-second Indiana, under Lieutenant-Colonel Kirkpatrick, Seventy-second Indiana, forward to Ringgold that night; they returning that night, reported no rebels. The next morning, 11th, we started forward at daylight, and when 2 miles from Ringgold met Scott's brigade of rebel cavalry, drawn up in line of battle, their left resting on Chickamauga Creek and their right on a ridge of hills. Colonel Atkins' regiment being in advance, immediately formed line, dismounted, and gallantly attacked them, while the Seventeenth Indiana, under Major Jones, was sent to flank their right.

They soon fell back, leaving 13 dead. We pressed them, hoping to cut them off from retreating through the gap at Ringgold, when General Van Cleve, coming up from the direction of Rossville, drove them in confusion through the gap before my flanking party could intercept them. We immediately passed General Van Cleve, and about 3 miles from Ringgold found them drawn up in line of battle in a strong position, with artillery. Here they made a stubborn resistance, but we flanked and drove them, pursuing them to Tunnel Hill, where we again found them in line of battle, re-enforced by another brigade under General Armstrong, all under command of General Forrest. We attacked them and drove them to within 4 miles of Dalton, wounding General Forrest and inflicting considerable loss on them. Night coming on, we camped in line of battle in a secure position near Tunnel Hill, expecting a fight in the morning.

In the night I received orders from General Crittenden to return to Ringgold at daylight. This we did, and I was then ordered to report to General Reynolds at La Fayette, Ga., by way of Leet's Tanyard. About 4 miles from Ringgold my advance encountered General Pegram's pickets. At the same time my rear guard reported an enemy in our rear. I immediately made preparation for battle, and advancing in line, found Pegram's force drawn up in line of battle, occupying a high wooded hill to the south of Leet's Tan-yard. I immediately attacked him. Being unable to use my artillery, on account of the woods, my left flank was now attacked by a force under Armstrong, while the force in our rear pressed us closely. With two regiments I boldly attacked Pegram, driving back toward

La Fayette the other two regiments holding my rear and left flank.
On our right, toward Pea Vine Church, a brigade of rebel infantry,
under General Strahl, occupied the road toward Gordon's Mills. I
immediately determined to cut my way through this and join General Crittenden at Gordon's Mills. Leaving a strong line of skirmishers facing the rear, left, and front, I, with the remainder of the
command, charged Strahl's command, driving back his left and
opening the road to Napier's Gap, in the Pea Vine Ridge, safely
withdrawing my command by that route, and joining General Crittenden at midnight.

On the next day my command made a reconnaissance to Pea Vine
Church, discovering a considerable number of rebels in that vicinity.
The day after we rejoined General Reynolds at Cooper's Gap.

On the 17th we were sent down Chickamauga Creek to guard the
crossing at Alexander's Bridge, 3 miles below Gordon's Mills.

On the 18th, at 10 a. m., we were attacked by a brigade of rebel
infantry, but our position being a strong one we repulsed them easily.
Colonel Minty, being at Reed's Bridge, 2 miles below, with a brigade
of cavalry, sent a pressing request for help. I sent Colonel Miller
with the Seventy-second Indiana and seven companies of the One
hundred and twenty-third Illinois and a section of the Eighteenth
Indiana Battery to his assistance. Soon after three brigades of
rebel infantry again attempted to carry my position. We repulsed
them, however, with severe loss to them. At 5 p. m. a picket stationed in my rear reported a strong force of rebel infantry in my
rear. Having driven the cavalry away from a ford below me, I
immediately commenced withdrawing my forces in the direction of
Gordon's Mills, and intercepted the force that was trying to surround
me, when, being re-enforced by two regiments of infantry from General Wood's division and Colonel Miller returning to my assistance,
we held the rebels from farther advance until morning, although
they made a desperate attempt to drive us at 9 o'clock at night.

On the morning of the 19th I received orders from department
headquarters to take up a position " on the right fighting flank of
our army, and keep the department commander advised of events in
that vicinity." I immediately occupied the woods at the edge of a
field on the west side of the road from Gordon's Mills to Rossville,
at a point where the road from Alexander's Bridge and the fords in
the vicinity of Napier's Gap intersect that road, being satisfied that
the rebels would attempt an advance in that direction. At about
1 p. m. heavy fighting was heard in my front, and by General Crittenden's order I advanced my line across the road, when, seeing a
rebel column in the act of flanking a battery of General Davis' command, I sent two regiments to the right to repel them. This was done
in handsome style by Colonels Monroe and Miller, with their regiments, when my skirmishers reported a heavy rebel column flanking
my left under cover of the woods. I now brought my entire command
double-quick back to their original position, changing direction to
my left with two regiments, and opened a deadly fire on a dense
mass of rebels, enfilading their left flank as they were making way
(across the road to Gordon's Mills) in the open ground in front of
Mrs. Glenn's house, first staggering them and soon routing them in
confusion, driving them back into the woods east.

In a few moments this or another column of rebels came out of
the woods near Vineyard's house, moving obliquely at and to my
right, driving General Davis' command before them. General Crit-

tenden at this point came near being captured in trying to rally these troops.   I immediately again changed front and enfiladed their right flank with an oblique fire, which soon drove them back with terrible slaughter.   General Davis now rallied his men, who gallantly advanced on my right under a galling fire, but were soon driven by overwhelming numbers back again to my right, being followed to the center of the field to a ditch in which the rebel advance took cover.   I at once ordered Captain Lilly to send a section of his battery forward on my left to a clump of bushes and rake the ditch with canister.   This was promptly done, with terrible slaughter, but very few of the rebels escaping alive.

In these various repulses we had thrown into the rebel columns, which attacked us closely massed, over 200 rounds of double-shotted 10-pounder canister, at a range varying from 70 to 350 yards, and at the same time kept up a constant fire with our repeating rifles, causing a most fearful destruction in the rebel ranks.   After this we were not again that day attacked.

On the morning of the 20th I was directed by General Rosecrans in person to take up a position on the right of General McCook's line, and ordered to report to General McCook.   I immediately did so, and he (General McCook) placed me in a very strong position on his right, on the crest of the east slope of Mission Ridge, about one-quarter of a mile to the south of Widow Glenn's house.   We lay here until about half past 11 a. m., when I received orders from General McCook to "close up on his right, and keep the line connected, and occupy the ground left vacant by him, as he was going to move to the left."   At this moment desperate fighting was heard down the line a mile or more to the left.   As the troops on my left moved from their position still farther to the left, a column of rebels, five lines deep, assaulted them, breaking and dispersing the troops at my left, and driving them by weight of numbers in great confusion into the woods in their rear.   My command was at this time advancing by regiments in line of battle.   The Ninety-eighth Illinois immediately changed front to the left, and charged double-quick at the rebels (who had taken a battery stationed at Mrs. Glenn's house) and retook the battery, their gallant colonel, Funkhouser, falling severely wounded while gloriously fighting in the front rank, still cheering his men forward after he fell.

The other regiments coming up in succession formed in their proper places into line, rapidly and without confusion, when the whole line was ordered to charge obliquely into the left flank of the rebels, and completely driving back their left down to the Gordon's Mills road, and taking two guns from them still loaded with canister, which was emptied into their fleeing ranks.

At this time a force of the enemy that had been menacing my right fell back with but little fighting, apparently under the impression that their right had been driven back, and that they were being flanked.   Captain Lilly was in the meantime pouring a heavy fire to the left down the rebel line, when word was brought me that a rebel line was advancing around my left.   I immediately transferred three regiments from my right to the top of the hill west of Mrs. Glenn's house, and with them and four pieces of artillery of Captain Lilly's battery, soon drove them northeast across the road north of Mrs. Glenn's.   I now organized my line on the top of Mission Ridge, so as to command the road to the rear of Rossville, and deploying skirmishers north and east of my position, I sent messengers to find General McCook.

Lieutenant-Colonel Thruston, chief of General McCook's staff, soon appeared and notified me that the line to my left was driven back and dispersed, and advised that I had better fall back to Lookout Mountain. I determined, however, to attempt to cut my way to join General Thomas at Rossville, and was arranging my line for that purpose when General Dana, Assistant Secretary of War, came up and said that "our troops had fled in utter panic; that it was a worse rout than Bull Run; that General Rosecrans was probably killed or captured;" and strongly advised me to fall back and occupy the passes over Lookout Mountain to prevent the rebel occupancy of it. One of my staff officers now came up and reported that he had found General Sheridan a mile and a half to the rear and left, who sent advice to me that he "was trying to collect his men and join General Thomas at Rossville, and that I had better fall back to the Chattanooga Valley." I now, at 4 p. m., did so with great reluctance, bringing off with me a number of wagons loaded with ammunition, a great many ambulances, a number of caissons, a great many stragglers, and quite a number of straying beef-cattle.

After reaching Chattanooga Valley at dark, my pickets were properly posted to guard all approaches to Chattanooga from that direction, when I sent a courier to you at Chattanooga informing you of my position and dispositions.

The list of casualties * in my command has been forwarded heretofore.

In conclusion, I am happy to state that through the entire campaign my commands were obeyed with cheerful promptness, men and officers seeming to fully appreciate our dangers and difficulties, and willingly submitting to the great privations incident thereto.

My subordinate commanders are entitled to the warmest praise for their gallantry and judgment in the numerous engagements, in all of which each did his whole duty.

I am, sir, very respectfully, your obedient servant,

                                           J. T. WILDER,
        Colonel Seventeenth Indiana, Comdg. Mounted Brigade.

Maj. Gen. W. S. ROSECRANS, U. S. Army,
                                           Commanding, &c.

No. 64.

Report of Col. Abram O. Miller, Seventy-second Indiana Infantry, commanding First Brigade (Mounted Infantry).

HDQRS. 1ST BRIG., 4TH DIV., 14TH ARMY CORPS,
                    Friar's Island, September 28, 1863.

SIR : I have the honor to report that on the afternoon of the 9th instant two regiments of this command, the Seventy-second Indiana, myself commanding, and the Ninety-eighth Illinois, Colonel Funkhouser, forded the Tennessee River at this point and bivouacked on the south bank for the night.

---

* During the campaign the loss was 1 officer and 20 men killed, 0 officers and 96 men wounded, and 1 officer and 18 men captured or missing; total, 145. For loss at Chickamauga, see p. 173.

On the morning of the 10th the One hundred and twenty-third Illinois, Colonel Monroe; the Seventeenth Indiana, Major Jones; the Eighteenth Indiana Battery, Captain Lilly, and the howitzer battery, four guns, under command of Sergeant Anderson, Seventy-second Indiana, crossed over. Here we were joined by Colonel Atkins, with his regiment, the Ninety-second Illinois, who the day before, in advance of General Wood's column, was the first to enter Chattanooga and unfurl the national colors. Some time was consumed in crossing the river and issuing rations to the command, so that before we were fully ready to take up the march it was 2 p. m. We then set out for Ringgold, Ga., and after marching 10 or 12 miles bivouacked for the night in a valley beyond Mission Ridge, 3 miles east of Graysville, and along the Georgia line, nothing of importance having transpired except the capturing of a large rebel mail at Tyner's Station by the One hundred and twenty-third Illinois.

We were now within 4 or 5 miles of Ringgold, and a scouting party from the Seventy-second Indiana was sent into the town who reported no enemy there.

At 6 a. m. on the 11th the command was on the march, moving steadily forward. Orders having been received during the night to have the Ninety-second Illinois report to Major-General Reynolds at La Fayette, Ga., they were accordingly placed in the advance with two howitzers. When within 2 miles of Ringgold they encountered the pickets of the enemy, driving them in. At this time they were a full mile in advance, and when the column came up were engaged in a brisk fight, part dismounted and part fighting on horseback. The Seventeenth Indiana were at once ordered up, dismounted, and sent to occupy the crest of a hill on the left of the line of battle of the Ninety-second Illinois. A section of Lilly's battery was then ordered into position and opened on the enemy with telling effect. In the meantime the Ninety-second Illinois, steadily advancing, drove the enemy through and beyond the town. By this time the Twenty-first Army Corps, moving on another road, reached the place. The enemy proved to be a brigade of Forrest's cavalry, with two pieces of artillery.

Here Colonel Atkins was ordered to join Major-General Reynolds, via Rossville, which he proceeded to do. When about 8 miles out he again encountered the enemy, about 600 strong, compelling his hasty retreat and saving a wagon train from falling into his hands.

The remainder of the command, in the meantime, moved on the Dalton road, driving the enemy, who retired slowly, stubbornly disputing our advance, and burning the railroad and other bridges as he fell back.

At one time, about 2½ miles beyond Ringgold, in a favorable position for defense, he formed line of battle, planted his artillery, and opened fire. Two of Lilly's guns were immediately put in position, when a sharp artillery duel ensued, which, lasting near an hour, the enemy again fell back. The command was then formed in three columns, and moved up the valley by the flank with a strong line of skirmishers well to the front, who advanced rapidly, keeping up a constant fire on the retreating enemy. That night we bivouacked at Tunnel Hill, 7 miles from Dalton.

During the night orders were received from Major-General Crittenden for the command to proceed to La Fayette, Ga., and join Major-General Reynolds, returning by way of Ringgold, and from there going forward by way of Rock Spring. In retiring to Ringgold the enemy hung upon our rear, annoying us but little, however. When within a mile of Rock Spring we came upon the outposts of the enemy, who gave us battle. At first their pickets were driven in, but being re-enforced they advanced in line. The Seventeenth and Seventy-second Indiana were now dismounted, formed in line, and the Ninety-eighth Illinois ordered to their support. Four companies of the Seventy-second Indiana were detached and thrown far to the left on the line of battle. This disposition being made, the enemy fell back after considerable skirmishing, and occupied a strong position on a ridge near a half mile in his late rear. The line was now ordered to advance, which it did under a sharp fire. Being in charge of the four companies on the extreme left, I soon discovered that the enemy's right extended beyond our left, and that he was falling back on the front and sending a column to gain our rear. I at once obliqued my four companies to the left, crossed an open field, and gained a ridge in the woods, when the enemy opened on me with a volley of musketry and two pieces of artillery. My men returned the fire promptly. Seeing they greatly outnumbered us, and being aware of the danger resulting from their gaining our rear, I ordered a charge. My men, who were now not 50 yards distant from the enemy, gave a yell and went forward, driving the enemy from the ridge. My dead, 7, and wounded, 8 in number, I brought off the field.

Darkness was now upon us. Taking the road from Rock Spring to Lee and Gordon's Mills, the command had not marched far when we came upon the enemy drawn up in line of battle across the road. After reconnoitering his lines it was found we could turn his left flank, and by passing down the Pea Vine Valley, join General Crittenden, which we did at midnight. The force encountered this day was Pegram's command, which we thought to be the rear of Bragg's army, but which proved to be his advance. The next day we moved off on the left flank of the army 4 miles, and lay in line of battle all day confronting a strong force of the enemy, and skirmishing with him at intervals from morning till night, when we withdrew and returned to camp at Lee and Gordon's Mills.

On the morning of the 14th we marched by way of Chattanooga Valley to join General Reynolds at or near Catlett's Gap, and reported to him that afternoon. Here we remained until the 17th, when orders were received from department headquarters to take position on the left flank of the army at Alexander's Bridge over Chickamauga Creek, 2 miles down the stream from Lee and Gordon's Mills. This we did, and bivouacked that night at the bridge. During the forenoon of the next day the enemy, in great force, advanced and gave us battle. About noon Colonel Minty, of the cavalry, engaging the enemy on our left, at Reed's Bridge, 2 miles below, sent to us for re-enforcements. The Seventy-second Indiana and the One hundred and twenty-third Illinois, with a section of Lilly's battery, were at once sent him. This done, there was left at Alexander's Bridge two regiments, the Seventeenth Indiana and Ninety-eighth Illinois, and four guns to hold the enemy in check. This we succeeded in doing until the enemy had succeeded in forcing a passage at a ford half way between Alexander's and Reed's Bridges, cutting our communications with Colonel Minty so that we could no longer act in concert, when it was deemed advisable to fall back on General Wood at Lee and Gordon's Mills, which we did in good order under a heavy cannonade at short range.

The enemy followed up his advantage, and after nightfall a close and spirited engagement took place in the woods along the lines of our new position. The enemy repulsed, we lay on our arms until near daylight, when the lines were withdrawn to a new position back of some fields, and established in the skirt of a heavy woods behind a fence, near to and on the right of the house of Mrs. Glenn, in form something after the manner of two sides of a square, forming with each other a right angle.

Upon falling back from the bridge, Major-General Crittenden, commanding the Twenty-first Army Corps, was at once advised of the movements of the enemy, and information was at the same time sent to department headquarters. With the appearance of day it was plain to us that a general engagement was about to take place. We were now ordered to hold our position. This we did until the after part of the day, when General Davis, moving from our right, threw his forces against the enemy in the woods immediately on our front, and soon became hotly engaged. Finding himself overpowered by superior numbers, and being hotly pressed, he sent to us for re-enforcements. Four regiments, all that were with us, went to his assistance, and, moving up in good order, entered the woods and checked the enemy. This done, General Davis again entered the woods, and we retired to our old position.

The enemy, having massed his forces here, soon drove General Davis back, who now took position on our right.

General Sheridan now advanced and took General Davis' position, confronting the enemy, but was at once compelled to retire his force, the enemy following him closely, with colors flying, to within 150 yards of our lines, when he was by us repulsed, Lilly's battery playing on him with deadly effect. It was now 5 p. m., and orders were received to throw our line of battle across a corn-field to our left, which we did. Here we were joined by Colonel Atkins, Ninety-second Illinois, who, taking position on our left, prolonged our line of battle into the woods, somewhat to the left and front of Mrs. Glenn's. In this position we lay on arms until morning.

Morning having come, we were ordered to hold our position until compelled to fall back. Afterward we received orders to report to General Mitchell, commanding cavalry, and to occupy a ridge to the right and rear of Mrs. Glenn's, filling an unoccupied space between the right of the infantry and the left of the cavalry. This we did, leaving one regiment to occupy our old line of battle. The command being disposed in its new position, nothing of note occurred until about noon, when the enemy hotly pressing the forces on our left, we were ordered to their support. We left our position on the hill and advanced at double-quick time to meet the enemy below in the woods. Here the contest was desperate for a half hour, when the enemy were driven back in great confusion. By this time the enemy had gained the rear of our position taken in the morning, and were firing on the men holding our horses. This necessitated the withdrawal of the command from the woods below, near Mrs. Glenn's house, and the formation of a new line of battle, facing to the rear of our position on the ridge. This being done, the enemy was driven away, and the horses brought off.

Finding we were cut off from the main army, we at once moved on a road leading into Chattanooga Valley, and bivouacked for the night 7 miles from Chattanooga. We recaptured two guns of a Missouri battery, which we brought off with us, beside gathering up a train of ambulances and wagons which were wandering in the woods, not knowing where to go, and which would have fallen into the hands of the enemy.

Our loss in killed, wounded, and missing is as follows:

[Command.]	Killed.	Wounded.	Missing.	Total.
Brigade staff	.....	2	.....	2
92d Illinois	2	26	2	30
98th Illinois	3	30	2	35
123d Illinois	1	13	10	24
17th Indiana	4	9	3	16
72d Indiana	10	23	2	35
18th Battery	1	2	.....	3
Total	21	105	19	145

Among the killed is the brave and generous McMurtry, captain Company I, Seventy-second Indiana. He fell in the thickest of the fight, in the full discharge of his duties.

Among the wounded whose loss will be greatly felt, not only in his regiment but in the brigade and division, is the steady, cool, and resolute Colonel Funkhouser, of the Ninety-eighth Illinois, who fell while leading his men most gallantly in the charge on Sunday afternoon.

Others are deserving of special mention here, but already this report is too long, and Colonel Wilder, who commanded the brigade during all the time reported, will, I have no doubt, mention their names and services in a manner that will do them the amplest justice.

A number of prisoners were taken at different times; 35 in the last charge on Sunday, the 20th.

All of which is respectfully submitted.

A. O. MILLER,
Colonel Seventy-second Indiana, Commanding Brigade.

Capt. C. O. HOWARD,
Acting Assistant Adjutant-General, Fourth Division.

No. 65.

Reports of Col. Smith D. Atkins, Ninety-second Illinois (Mounted) Infantry.

HDQRS. NINETY-SECOND ILLINOIS VOLUNTEERS,
Pond Spring, Ga., September 16, 1863.

CAPTAIN: By command of Colonel Wilder to report the movements of my regiment since I was first detached from the brigade, I have the honor to submit the following:

That on September 7, at 10 a. m., agreeably to orders I received at Poe's Tavern, I reported to Major-General Thomas, with my regiment, at the foot of Raccoon Mountain, and was ordered by him to report to Major-General Reynolds at Trenton, which I did at 11 a. m. same day.

On September 8, by order of Major-General Reynolds, Companies F and G made a reconnaissance on Lookout Mountain. Company E, Captain Van Buskirk, went to near Summertown, finding no enemy, and returned at 9 p. m.

On September 9, at 3 a. m., by order of Major-General Reynolds, I proceeded with my regiment to Chattanooga, passing many troops on the road, and taking the advance. Three miles on the west side of Lookout Mountain we drove the enemy's pickets in, and had sharp skirmishing with them in crossing the head of Lookout Mountain, but without loss on our side. At about 9.30 a. m. my advance, under Captain Dunham, entered Chattanooga, but, under my order, did not push up to the river bank, but followed the retreating enemy by Rossville on the La Fayette road 4 or 5 miles, but, owing to the jaded condition of his horses, could not overtake them. I followed with my regiment down the mountain, and immediately sent out scouting parties southward, knowing it to be the line of the enemy's retreat from the columns of dust plainly visible as I came down the mountain. I then went on with my regiment to the railroad depot in Chattanooga, and at 10 a. m. my regimental colors were planted on the third story of the Crutchfield House, the first to float over the evacuated town. I sent one company to patrol the town and reconnoiter, and learned that some of the enemy's forces had retreated up the river toward Harrison when we entered the other side of the town. At the depot I waited until 1 p. m., when Colonel Wilder ordered me to proceed up the river to cover the crossing of the remainder of his brigade at Chickamauga, which I did, capturing a few of the stragglers of the enemy and firing on his rear guard. We found the brigade already crossing the river on arriving at the ford.

On the 10th Colonel Wilder ordered me to proceed with the brigade, which I did, marching to within 5 miles of Ringgold with it.

On the morning of the 11th September received orders to report to Major-General Reynolds at La Fayette, Ga., and with my regiment and two mountain howitzers started to Ringgold in advance of the brigade. Two miles out drove in the enemy's pickets, and when within 1 mile of Ringgold dismounted Company E, Captain Van Buskirk, and steadily pushed the enemy. I sent Company G, Captain Schermerhorn, to protect the right flank, mounted, and Captain Dunham, Company I, to protect the left flank, mounted. Company E skirmished briskly, and rapidly advanced down the road driving the enemy; and Captain Dunham advanced mounted and deployed as skirmishers over an open corn-field on their left to the foot of a heavily wooded hill, drawing the enemy's fire, and defeating the enemy flanking my advance, which was evidently his intention. Captain Dunham having lost 6 horses, dismounted and joined the line of skirmishers, pushing the enemy through the woods. Colonel Wilder had just previously arrived and took command, and ordered me to protect the right, which I did by ordering up all my regiment except one company, but finding the right protected by the Chickamauga, Lieutenant-Colonel Sheets ordered them to re-enforce Companies E and F on the left of the road. The firing was brisk and lasted about twenty minutes. We were opposed by an entire brigade of Forrest's cavalry. My loss was 6 horses and 3 men wounded, all of Company F; Captain Dunham, Sergt. H. Ferrin, and Corporal Winslow severely, and Private Marl slightly. Private Petermier, Company F, had his horse shot under him and killed, the butt of his rifle shot away, and his pantaloons and coat flap and coat collar torn by bullets, and coolly remarked, "Now, I am tired to death running after them." The enemy's loss was 13 killed, left on the ground, they taking off their wounded in their retreat. Officers and men behaved with courage and coolness.

At Ringgold I left the brigade, continuing my march to La Fayette, but by order of Colonel Wilder proceeded via Rossville. About 8 miles out my advance was fired upon. I rode to the foot of the hill with Captain Van Buskirk, in command of the advance guard, and again drew their fire over our heads, and discovered the enemy were on a cross-road south of and leading into the road I was traveling. I ordered three companies forward dismounted, and one along the hill southward mounted. These dispositions were not completed when I discovered a wagon train approaching on our road from the direction of Rossville, and the rebels about 30 or 40 strong charging on to it with a yell as it crossed the intersecting point of the roads. My dismounted companies pressed rapidly forward over the open field to cut them off, but they discovered the movement, left the train, and retreated, receiving a volley from us as they passed. I ordered them followed by one company, Captain Hawk, who followed them 3 miles, but could not overtake them. Captain Preston sent to the left at first, reported seeing about 600 who all retreated on the return of the party that charged the train. We marched to Rossville that night.

On the 12th, after receiving orders through General Garfield, I started with my regiment to report temporarily to General Crittenden, at Gordon's Mills, but 7 miles out was overtaken by a courier with orders for me to countermarch and go via Summertown. I immediately countermarched, and reported in person at department headquarters and was ordered to establish a courier line from Summertown to Major-General Thomas' headquarters at Stevens' Gap. I left Summertown with my regiment after dark and marched along the top of Lookout Mountain, 20 miles, establishing a courier line, and reaching General Thomas' headquarters at 4 a. m. September 13.

September 14, by order Major-General Reynolds, I marched with balance of my command (seven companies) to Gordon's Mills, and opened communication with General Crittenden. I returned through the ridges of Mission Ridge, reaching Pond Spring at night, scouting the country well north and west of Chickamauga River, between Gordon's Mills and Pond Spring. I sent a large party of scouts toward Wicker's Gap, who drove in the enemy's pickets on the road from Gordon's Mills to La Fayette. My scouts were fired upon by the pickets of the enemy, at a bridge over the Chickamauga, 4 miles down from Pond Spring, and reported all the pickets of the enemy withdrawn across the Chickamauga from Gordon's Mills to Pond Spring.

Most respectfully, your obedient servant,

SMITH D. ATKINS,
Colonel Ninety-second Illinois Volunteers.

Capt. Alexander A. Rice,
Assistant Adjutant-General.

———

Hdqrs. Ninety-second Ill. Vol. (Mounted) Infty.,
Harrison's Landing, Tenn., September 27, 1863.

Captain: I have the honor, in continuation of my report, to state that on the 17th instant, while in camp at Pond Spring, Ga., I was ordered by Major-General Reynolds to send a company to report to

General Turchin, in front of Catlett's Gap. Company E, Captain Van Buskirk, was sent forward. He had a sharp skirmish, losing 1 man killed, 1 wounded, and 1 taken prisoner.

On the 18th I remained in camp at Pond Spring.

On the 19th left camp at daylight and overtook General Reynolds' division about 8 a. m. near Crawfish Spring, and was ordered to take position in rear of and support of Colonel Wilder. At about noon was ordered to headquarters of General Reynolds. At about 1 p. m. was ordered by General Reynolds to hitch all my horses in the woods, which I did, and moved up to and on the right of a battery planted by General Reynolds in reserve to King's brigade. Had just got into position when I was ordered by General Reynolds to the support of Colonel King's brigade, and immediately moved forward by the flank, a captain being sent to show me the way. He went to the road with me and told me to "keep down the road," when he left me. We were then moving by the right flank down the road in front of our first position, with timber and underbrush on the left of the road. King's brigade had already been pressed back, and the fire of the enemy was directly on my left flank from the timber ; in front of me the enemy were pressing over the road. I ordered the head of my column to the right along a fence facing the timbered hollow, into which the enemy were pressing. When two companies had filed to the right some mounted officer rode up and ordered my regiment to "get out of the road," which the regiment did by a right flank, and under fire the regiment fell back over the open ground to its old position on the hill. Here we reformed our line, not without some difficulty, as the center of the regiment was crowded by the previous movements, and some confusion was occasioned by the coming in of some of King's brigade, leading to the fear that we were firing on our own men. Order was soon restored, and my regiment lying down coolly received the fire of the enemy and returned it, gallantly maintaining our ground, until I perceived that the other regiment supporting the battery had given way, and men falling back from other regiments were taking our horses hitched in the rear, and that both batteries had limbered up and were leaving, while the enemy pressing up the wooded ravine to my right had completely flanked my regiment, subjecting it to an enfilading fire, when I ordered my regiment to fall back and mount their horses. The engagement lasted only a few minutes, and my loss was about 25 in killed and wounded, the names having been already furnished. To maneuver by the flank and to the rear under fire is ever attended with danger, and I am greatly indebted to all my officers for their heroic assistance in reforming our line. All did their duty manfully. Lieutenant McCamman, Company G, and Lieutenant Cox, Company A, were wounded while rallying their men.

After we were mounted I soon met a lieutenant on the staff of General Reynolds, and was informed that the general had not been seen recently, and supposing him killed or wounded, for I saw him in the thickest of the fight helping to rally the left of my regiment, I reported to Colonel Wilder, and was ordered by him into position on the left of his brigade. I immediately took the position assigned, and during the night built a slight breastwork of logs and rails.

At daylight on the 20th was ordered by Colonel Wilder to the right of his brigade. On the withdrawal of his brigade, was ordered to deploy my regiment mounted, and hold the ground he had held until pressed back, when I was to form on the right of Wilder's brigade. Here I remained until about noon, when the enemy had completely flanked my left and were pressing up in front with their skirmishers, when I fell back, passing around a heavy force of the enemy half a mile in rear of my left. I formed three different times in falling back, and faced the enemy, but could not check his advance, and when I fell back to the position assigned on the right of Wilder's brigade it was to find the brigade already moved away. As soon as possible I dismounted, sending my horses to the rear, and going with my regiment to where I supposed Colonel Wilder to be, but found him with his brigade falling back to mount. I immediately returned and mounted, and with the brigade marched to near Chattanooga, where we encamped.

Early next morning was ordered by Colonel Wilder with my regiment and Lilly's battery to take position and hold the McLemore's Cove and Summertown roads, but had not got into position when I was ordered to cross the river and proceed to Friar's Island.

Four mountain howitzers of Lilly's battery were with me on the 19th, and placed in position by General Reynolds, when I was ordered to dismount. The sergeant in command was wounded and I have no report, but cannot refrain from bearing testimony to the gallant manner in which their guns were manned, convincing me of their effectiveness at short range. One howitzer was left on the field.

In the various engagements many of my horses were shot, but I have not yet the official report from my companies.

I had during this time but eight companies, two of my companies being on courier duty, and remained so.

Most respectfully, your obedient servant,

SMITH D. ATKINS,
Colonel Ninety-second Illinois Volunteers.

Capt. ALEXANDER A. RICE,
Assistant Adjutant-General.

No. 66.

Report of Lieut. Col. Edward Kitchell, Ninety-eighth Illinois
(Mounted) Infantry.

HDQRS. NINETY-EIGHTH ILLINOIS VOLUNTEERS,
Near Chattanooga, Tenn., September 26, 1863.

SIR : I have the honor to report that on the 9th instant my regiment, in conjunction with the Seventy-second Indiana Volunteers, forded the Tennessee River at the mouth of Chickamauga Creek, and immediately went into camp on the Ringgold road.

On the 10th instant we advanced about 10 miles toward Ringgold, without noticing anything of importance.

On the 11th instant we skirmished smartly with the enemy during the greater part of the day, but lost no men.

On the morning of the 12th instant we returned to Ringgold, and moved out on the road to La Fayette.

The Seventy-second Indiana becoming engaged with the enemy's cavalry, we were ordered to the support of that regiment, but were not called upon to take any more active part.

On the morning of the 13th instant, the brigade having been ordered to reconnoiter the enemy's position, my regiment was ordered to take the advance.

After a march of about 4 miles we met the enemy's skirmishers, with whom a few shots were exchanged without loss.   At dark we returned to camp.

On the 14th instant we marched to camp near Stevens' Gap, where we remained until the morning of the 17th instant, when we moved out to Chickamauga Creek, near Alexander's Bridge.

Nothing of importance occurred until about 2 p. m. of the 18th instant, when five companies of my regiment, under command of Major Marquis, were ordered forward to engage the enemy (who were in position on the opposite side of the creek), which they did for about three hours, losing 1 man killed and 7 wounded.   The balance of the regiment was thrown out as skirmishers on the right.

About sundown fell back and took position east of and near the Chattanooga road, where we remained under arms until daylight of the 19th instant, when the position was changed to a piece of timber near the Chattanooga road facing north, where we remained until 5 p. m., when the position was again changed to a corn-field a little to the left, facing the road to the east.   During the night the regiment again remained under arms, and on the morning of the 20th instant moved back and took position on the right of Sheridan's division, on the edge of a piece of timber, where we erected temporary breastworks.

At 11 a. m. we were ordered to move by the left flank to the support of Sheridan, who was hotly engaging the enemy.   Upon arriving on the ground formerly occupied by Sheridan's right we moved forward by the right flank, driving the enemy's skirmishers before us across an open field to a strip of timber, where we met the enemy in force, charged him, and drove him back.

During this charge Colonel Funkhouser was severely wounded and compelled to leave the field, leaving the regiment under my command.

I was then ordered to fall back to a hill formerly occupied by a battery on Sheridan's right in order to check the enemy, who was coming up a ravine in our rear.

I immediately opened a hot fire upon him and drove him back. I remained on this ground until ordered to return to my horses, which I did, and then moved to within 4 miles of Chattanooga, where we camped until the morning of the 21st instant, when I crossed the river and took the road to Stevenson, Ala., in charge of 1,350 prisoners.

I take great pleasure in complimenting both officers and men of my regiment for the highly gratifying manner in which they behaved whenever called upon to meet the enemy.   I would particularly mention the name of Capt. Ira A. Flood, of Company E, who was in the hottest part of the engagement of the 18th instant, and conducted himself with coolness and bravery.

The loss of my regiment is 3 killed and 32 wounded.

I am, sir, very respectfully, your obedient servant,

E. KITCHELL,
Lieutenant-Colonel, Commanding.

Capt. ALEXANDER A. RICE,
Assistant Adjutant-General, First Brigade.

No. 67.

Report of Col. James Monroe, One hundred and twenty-third Illinois (Mounted) Infantry.

HDQRS. 123D ILLINOIS VOLUNTEER INFANTRY,
Friar's Island, September 26, 1863.

COLONEL: In compliance with your Special Orders, No. ——, I have the honor to submit the following report of the operations of my command from the 10th to the 21st day of September, 1863:

September 10, crossed Tennessee River at Friar's Island and captured a large rebel mail at Tyner's Station, and camped in the valley beyond Mission Ridge, 3 miles east of Graysville and 1 mile from the Georgia line.

September 11 moved at 8 a. m. The Ninety-second Illinois, having been sent forward some half hour in advance, found the enemy near Ringgold, and, after a sharp skirmish, in which my command took little part, drove them through the town, passed through Ringgold, now occupied by Van Cleve's division. Found the enemy (Forrest's command) in strong position on our front. The brigade was dismounted and formed in line, this regiment on the left, and compelled the enemy to retire after a sharp skirmish, in which the Seventeenth Indiana alone participated. The brigade, by direction of Colonel Wilder, was then formed in column of regiments, moving by the flank, with strong advance guards, and in this order moved forward to Tunnel Hill, driving the enemy before us, and skirmishing the entire distance, bivouacked for the night.

September 12, withdrew to Ringgold, this regiment covering the rear and closely followed by the enemy. Took the road to La Fayette; found the enemy near Wheeler's occupying a very strong position covering the road and a gap in the mountains; dislodged him after a sharp skirmish, in which the Seventeenth and Seventy-second Indiana lost severely. This regiment was now moved to the front, and the column moved forward on the La Fayette road. Found the enemy again in position, drove in his advance, but discovering a considerable force of infantry, and night having come on, Colonel Wilder, leaving the road, moved the command across the country to Gordon's Mills, this regiment covering the rear, and arriving late in the night.

September 13 moved to the left of General Crittenden's command, and skirmished with the enemy during the day. In the evening returned across the Chickamauga at Gordon's Mills, and camped 1½ miles down the stream.

September 14 rejoined our division at Pond Spring.

September 17 moved to the extreme left, passing down the Chickamauga and taking position at Alexander's Bridge.

September 18 the Seventy-second Indiana and this regiment, under command of yourself, were ordered to report to Colonel Minty, who with his cavalry brigade was guarding the fords of the stream, some 2 miles on our left, and who was being hard pressed by the enemy; moved rapidly, and upon reporting there were ordered to move some 2 miles farther down the stream to guard the fords, and and finally this regiment, with one piece of artillery, was ordered still farther to the left, and one company sent down to Red House Ford, which, upon arriving at that point, was ambuscaded by the enemy, who had already crossed the stream, and after a sharp skirmish driven back with loss. In a few moments I received orders to withdraw and report to Colonel Minty, which I did under a brisk fire. The entire command then fell back to a point on the road some 1½ miles from Gordon's Mills, where we found Colonel Wilder, who had been driven back from Alexander's Bridge, and formed in line to resist the farther advance of the enemy, who charged our right furiously, but was repulsed. Lay in line of battle all night.

September 19 large bodies of infantry were moved to our left during the night, and a general engagement was opened by sending Grose's brigade, of Palmer's division, on a reconnaissance down the road. We held our position during the day. Late in the afternoon the enemy appeared on our front in an open field and charged our line. They were met by the Seventy-second and Seventeenth Indiana, Lilly's battery, and the left of this regiment, and driven back with severe loss. Later in the evening the brigade was thrown forward to meet a flank movement on our right, and after driving back the enemy returned to our old position, where we passed the night.

September 20, the right of our line of battle having been withdrawn during the night, at 8 a. m. we moved to the right and rear and took position on the right of Sheridan's division on the crest of a ridge with open fields in front. The battle opened at 10 a. m. The enemy, feeling along our lines, arrived in front of General Sheridan, who moved his division forward down the slope, and was soon fiercely engaged. The enemy flanking him, we were ordered to charge, and headed by Colonel Wilder our men went in with a shout, driving and breaking the enemy's lines at once, this regiment taking 30 prisoners. Whilst pressing vigorously forward we found that the enemy had broken through Sheridan's line, and an entire brigade of rebels were passing to our left and rear. We were at once withdrawn, and after waiting two hours to bring up stragglers and artillery left on the field by Sheridan's division, were by an order of General McCook moved to the rear and into Chattanooga Valley, 7 miles south of Chattanooga, this regiment covering the rear and holding the gap by a heavy picket force.

September 21 crossed the Tennessee River at Chattanooga and moved to this point.

I cannot close this report without alluding to the gallant conduct of the officers and men of my command. All did their duty. My loss in the different engagements is 24 killed, wounded, and missing. The missing are, I fear, killed or wounded without exception, as there was no straggling from any part of the command.

I am, colonel, yours, truly,

JAMES MONROE,
Colonel, Commanding.

Col. ABRAM O. MILLER, *Commanding First Brigade.*

No. 68.

Report of Maj. William T. Jones, Seventeenth Indiana (Mounted) Infantry.

HDQRS. SEVENTEENTH INDIANA VOLUNTEERS,
North Chickamauga Creek, Tenn., September 26, 1863.

CAPTAIN: I respectfully submit the following report of the operations of the regiment under my command from the 10th to the 21st of the present month:

On the 10th instant, crossing the Tennessee River, I moved with the brigade on the Ringgold road to a point within 1 mile of the State line, and about 5 miles from Ringgold, where I remained during the night. Resuming the march toward Ringgold on the 11th at 8 a. m., we came up with the rear of the Ninety-second Illinois (that regiment having moved about forty-five minutes in advance of the rest of the brigade) when about $1\frac{1}{2}$ miles from town. Here rapid firing in front announced that Colonel Atkins had found the enemy.

My regiment was moved rapidly to the front and left, and having dismounted my men I was ordered to move along the crest of a hill which ran parallel with the road on which the command was moving. In the execution of this order I arrived at a point opposite the town, without opposition, to find it occupied by that portion of the command which had moved on the road, and by General Van Cleve's division. Here I was directed to mount my command and move in advance on the Dalton road. I found the enemy strongly posted on this road about $2\frac{1}{2}$ miles from Ringgold, where he checked my advance with a fire from two pieces of artillery. I halted my command until the other regiments of the brigade were thrown into position, the One hundred and twenty-third Illinois on my left, the Ninety-eighth Illinois on my right, and the Seventy-second Indiana closing up with me in the rear. We moved against the enemy, and after some skirmishing drove him from his position, and resumed the march toward Dalton, the regiments moving by the flank and parallel with each other, my regiment being to the left of the road, constantly skirmishing with the enemy. We moved in this order until we reached and occupied Tunnel Hill, where we bivouacked for the night.

On the morning of the 12th I moved with the brigade in retreat to Ringgold, thence on the La Fayette road to a point 1 mile from Rock Spring, where the scouts of the regiment were detached and sent by a circuitous route to gain the rear of a picket of the enemy, which was reported to be on the road in our front. Two companies were at the same time thrown forward on the road and encountered the enemy's outpost, driving him from his position to the foot of the hill near the spring. Here the enemy appeared in force, advancing toward our position, and was checked by the two companies in front until the regiment advanced, when he retired a short distance and took a position on a ridge about a half mile from our line. The brigade being thrown into position, my regiment being on the right and covering the road, we advanced, the enemy retiring, hotly pressed by the Seventy-second Indiana on my left. From this point the brigade moved in column by a road leading westward in the direction of Lee and Gordon's Mills, my regiment being ordered to follow and support the battery.

I marched in this order to within 2 miles of Lee and Gordon's Mills, where I bivouacked for the night.

On the 13th I moved my regiment with the brigade to a position on the left of General Van Cleve's division, expecting an attack from the enemy, who appeared in force in our front. We returned at night to the vicinity of Lee and Gordon's Mills, where we bivouacked until the morning of the 14th.

On the 14th my regiment, with the brigade, joined our division near Pond Spring.

On the 17th instant I marched with the brigade to Chickamauga Creek, near Alexander's Bridge, and threw out a line of skirmishers on the south bank of the stream.

At 12 m. of the 18th my line was attacked by the enemy's advance and the regiment was ordered to take position to support the battery. I held this position during the action and until the battery was withdrawn, when I was directed to cover the rear of the brigade in retreat. This I did under the fire of the enemy's artillery, and, following the brigade, I took position for the night on the left center of the brigade and on the right of the road leading from Lee and Gordon's Mills to Chattanooga, 1½ miles from the mills.

At 4 a. m. of the 19th I retired my regiment with the brigade across the road and took a position in the edge of a wood, fronting eastward. This position I occupied during the day. At about 3 p. m. the enemy, having repulsed the division of General Davis in our front, advanced on our position, but was checked by our fire at a distance of 150 yards from our line and retired in confusion to the cover of the wood on the opposite side of the road, my regiment, together with the Seventy-second and the right of the One hundred and twenty-third Illinois, pouring into him a destructive fire.

On the morning of the 20th I was ordered to retire about 1 mile, where I again took position in line with the brigade. At 10 a. m. of that day the action became general, and not long after that hour it became evident that the forces on our left were being driven back in confusion. At this time the command was given to charge the enemy. I followed the One hundred and twenty-third Illinois from our position and formed my regiment on its right. The men moved forward in good order, cheering and firing rapidly as they advanced. The enemy was driven about three-quarters of a mile with considerable loss, and the command was still moving forward when the order of recall was received. My command took some prisoners here, but, as they were sent rapidly to the rear and consigned to other commands, I cannot give the number.

Retiring with my command in good order, to the crest of the hill in our rear, I remained there until the order was given to move to our horses, 1½ miles farther to the rear. When the brigade mounted I was ordered to move on the flank of and to protect the battery and train. Disposing my command as required by this order, I reached a point in Chattanooga Valley about 4 miles from town, at 7 p. m. Here I remained until 11 a. m. of the 21st, when I recrossed the river at Chattanooga and marched to this point.

My entire loss during the time included in this report was as follows: Killed, 4; wounded, 10; missing, known to be prisoners, 3. Total, 17.

The small number of casualties I attribute to the fact that we in each of the positions occupied for any length of time constructed temporary breastworks which protected us from the fire of small-arms.

In concluding this report, I do but justice in bearing testimony to the gallantry of both officers and men of my command. All of them did their whole duty.

To Captain Vail, acting major, and Adjt. J. J. Howard, I am especially indebted for their invaluable assistance. Captain Boswell, who had been acting major, performed his duty well until the morning of the 19th, when he was accidentally wounded and retired from the field.

I am, captain, very respectfully, your obedient servant,.

WM. T. JONES,
Major, Commanding Seventeenth Indiana.

Capt. ALEXANDER A. RICE,
Assistant Adjutant-General, First Brigade.

No. 69.

Reports of Col. Abram O. Miller, Seventy-second Indiana (Mounted) Infantry.

HDQRS. SEVENTY-SECOND INDIANA VOLUNTEERS,
Camp at Pond Spring, Ga., September 15, 1863.

SIR: I herewith submit a report of the part taken by my command in the engagement at Rock Spring, Ga., on the 12th instant:

Immediately after the skirmishers of the Seventeenth Indiana engaged the enemy, in accordance with your orders, I directed Lieutenant-Colonel Kirkpatrick to proceed with four companies (A, F, D, and I) of my regiment to the left of the position occupied by the Seventeenth Indiana, across a hollow to an adjoining hill. Arriving on the hill, Lieutenant-Colonel Kirkpatrick dismounted these companies, formed line of battle, and advanced to a cross-roads a quarter of a mile farther front, where he halted and reported to me that he held possession of a road which lay at right angles, near the crossing with the one on which the main column was advancing. In the meantime I sent Company C, under Captain Robinson, some distance to the right of the Seventeenth to observe and hold in check any flank movement which might be made against us by the enemy from that direction. The four remaining companies were dismounted and formed on the left of the road, and to the left of the Seventeenth. The whole line was then advanced through the woods about a quarter of a mile, where I halted, placed the four left companies of my regiment in charge of Major Carr, then joined my four right companies at the point above stated, and by your orders advanced with my four left companies on my right through a dense copse of pine undergrowth, across a ravine, and ascended a ridge running parallel with the road leading from Ringgold to La Fayette. Sergeant Clark, with the mounted scouts of the Seventy-second Indiana, who had been sent out as flankers a distance of 200 yards to my left, at this time engaged the skirmishers of the enemy and drove them back a quarter of a mile, where he met their main [body] advancing toward us in line of battle. The scouts, after firing a volley upon them, returned and reported them advancing with their right extending a considerable distance beyond our left. To avoid the contingency of a flanking demonstration by the rebels, I moved my four right companies (now on the left) obliquely to the left across an open field, where I entered a woods covered with thick undergrowth. Here my command encountered the enemy, who opened upon us with a volley of musketry and two pieces of artillery, shouting along their whole line as they fired. I commanded my companies to commence firing, which order was promptly executed. The firing was incessant on both sides for some moments, the rebels advancing and showing a disposition to drive us from the ridge. At this juncture I gave the command, which was repeated by Lieutenant-Colonel Kirkpatrick, to raise a yell, charge firing, and stop their advance. This was successfully performed. Their center gave way, which was soon followed by both wings, leaving us in possession of the ridge, and the enemy running in confusion. Being separated from our right, and the force of the enemy greatly outnumbering my own, I did not pursue, but held the ridge until I received your order to collect and care for my dead and wounded and join the remainder of the command which was done by nightfall.

Our loss was 7 killed and 8 wounded. That of the enemy was much larger. Among their killed was the major of the Sixth Georgia Regiment. The following is a list* of the casualties in my regiment:

Company D, Captain Thomson, although in the midst of the fight, fortunately escaped without injury.

Three of my scouts had horses shot under them during the engagement.

While I sincerely regret the loss of any of my command, I cannot refrain from making special mention of Captain McMurtry, who had always shown himself a faithful and competent commander, and fell at the head of his company while gallantly leading it in the fight against his country's foes.

To Lieutenant-Colonel Kirkpatrick and Adjutant Byrns, of my regiment, I extend thanks for the efficient services rendered during the engagement. The officers and men fought nobly, and are deserving of much praise. Surgeon Morrow and Assistant Surgeon Cole performed the work appertaining to their positions in a skillful and very creditable manner.

Respectfully submitted

A. O. MILLER,
Colonel Seventy-second Indiana.

Capt. ALEXANDER A. RICE,
Assistant Adjutant-General.

HDQRS. SEVENTY-SECOND INDIANA VOLUNTEERS,
Friar's Island, Tenn., September 27, 1863.

SIR: I herewith submit a report of the part taken by my command in the fighting of the 18th, 19th, and 20th instant:

In pursuance of your order I proceeded with seven companies of the Seventy-second Regiment and the One hundred and twenty-third Illinois, under Colonel Monroe, and two pieces of the Eighteenth Indiana Battery across the Chickamauga, and reported to Colonel Minty, who was then skirmishing with the enemy.

In accordance with his orders I recrossed the river a few hundred yards below, over Baird's [Reed's?] Bridge, and proceeded down the river, stationing the Seventy-second Regiment at Dyer's Ford, sending Colonel Monroe with the One hundred and twenty-third Illinois to Dalton's Ford, with orders to send a scout to Red House Bridge on the road running from Ringgold to Chattanooga. In half an hour I received orders from Colonel Minty to draw back my force and form line of battle on his left, dismounting Nos. two and deploying them on foot as skirmishers. The enemy were at this time throwing shells very rapidly, the most of which passed over us and exploded in our rear. About 4 p. m. Colonel Minty ordered me to fall back in line on the right of the road leading to and intersecting the Chattanooga road in the vicinity of Gordon's Mills, at which point I joined the brigade, formed, and lay in line of battle on left and perpendicular to the Chattanooga road until the morning of the 19th, when, as ordered, I took position on right of the brigade, in the edge of the woods, some 200 yards from the Chattanooga road, and parallel with the same, and in support of the Eighteenth Indiana (Captain Lilly's) Battery.

---

* Nominal list omitted.

I soon formed a breastwork of rails and logs, which afforded great protection from the balls thrown from small-arms, and especially sharpshooters, who seemed to keep up a continuous firing on us.

About 3 p. m., as ordered, I moved my command across the Chattanooga road to the edge of the woods, and held my position there for half an hour, under a heavy fire, when I received your order to take my former position.   Shortly after gaining it I received your order to move to the left of the brigade, the execution of which I had just commenced when ordered by General Crittenden to remain and hold my position.   On stating to him your order he assumed the responsibility, and directed my attention to the advancing rebels in my front.   I then ordered my command to fire upon them, which they did promptly, checking their advance, and drove them from farther pursuit of those on my right, who were falling back, four guns having been placed in position near the center and a little to the rear of my regiment, and which I, as ordered by General Crittenden, remained to support.   On the morning of the 20th, about 7.30 a. m., in accordance with your order, I fell back about 1½ miles, and took my position on the right of the brigade, placing two companies some 400 yards to the right to guard against a flank movement of the enemy.

I at once proceeded to construct a breastwork of rails and logs, and soon had a formidable work against a fire from small-arms. About 12 o'clock I received your order to mount and charge the enemy.   My men had reached and prepared to mount their horses, when I received your order to advance on foot, which I did, marching by the flank until well over the hill, from which point I moved forward in line of battle, coming under and returning the fire of the enemy near a burning house which had been the headquarters of General Rosecrans.   A brisk firing was kept up until the enemy retired, when, according to your order, I moved back in line in rear of the battery.   After getting back to our horses I formed line of battle in rear of the train until reaching McCulloch's Mills, at which place we camped for the night, and, in connection with the One hundred and twenty-third Illinois, picketed the various roads leading to said mills.

Two of my companies, A and F, who were on picket on the 18th, and not taken with me to re-enforce Colonel Minty, but remained at their post, disputing the passage of the enemy across the Chickamauga, Company [?] losing 24 of their horses.   Company F, after falling back, joined the Ninety-eighth Illinois and was in a skirmish with the enemy after dark, both companies reporting to me next morning.   The following is a list of my killed and wounded.*

Making a total of killed :
    September 19 and 20.. 3
    September 12... 7
                                                   —— 10

Total wounded :
    September 19 and 20.. 15
    September 12 8
                                                   —— 23

Total missing :
    September 19 and 20.. 2

Making a total of lost on September 12, 19, and 20...................... 35

* Nominal list omitted.

To Lieutenant-Colonel Kirkpatrick, Major Carr, Adjutant Byrns, and all officers and men of my regiment, I extend thanks for their efficient services rendered and bravery shown during the battle.

Respectfully submitted.

A. O. MILLER.
Colonel Seventy-Second Indiana Volunteers.

Capt. ALEXANDER A. RICE,
Assistant Adjutant-General.

No. 70.

Report of Capt. Eli Lilly, Eighteenth Indiana Battery.

HDQRS. 18TH IND. BATTERY, 1ST BRIG., 4TH DIV., 14TH A. C.,
Friar's Island, Tenn., September 26, 1863.

CAPTAIN : In obedience to orders, I have the honor herewith to report operations of this battery since crossing the Tennessee River at this ford September 10, 1863:

After fording as above, the battery moved with the brigade on the Ringgold road and at nightfall camped near the Georgia line.

Eleventh instant marched at 7 a. m., and arriving within 2 miles of Ringgold, Ga., our advance was resisted and one section was taken forward and placed in position, which soon shelled the rebels out and the town was occupied. We from this point took the Dalton road, the enemy making a stand at a gap 2 miles out, and a sharp artillery duel ensued from which they retired after an hour and a half's fight, leaving 3 crippled horses and harness on the field. Our movement from this to Tunnel Hill was uninterrupted.

Twelfth, moved back to Ringgold and took the La Fayette road. Following the camps and marches of the brigade, nothing of note occurred till the 17th instant, when we marched from Pond Spring to Alexander's Bridge on Chickamauga Creek, 3 miles from Gordon's Mills.

Eighteenth instant, at 9.30 a. m., one section was sent with detachment from our brigade to re-enforce Colonel Minty, who was reported hard pressed on our left. At about 12.30 p. m. the enemy appeared in strong infantry force on our front and attacked our skirmishers. I immediately opened fire on them from my four remaining guns, doing fine execution on their ranks with long-range canister and shell at from 600 to 1,200 yards range. They soon planted two guns on an open hill in front and succeeded in throwing three shells at us before we silenced them. One of their shells fell near one of my guns when Private Sidney A. Speed, seeing the fuse still burning, picked it up from among my cannoneers and threw it over the house near by before it burst. This engagement lasted till 4.30 p. m., when Colonel Minty having been obliged to fall back, I was ordered to limber my pieces and move out, when we retired to the Gordon's Mills and Chattanooga road and rested for the night.

On the 19th instant I did not become engaged until about 2.30 p. m., when our brigade moved in support of Davis' division, at which time I shelled the enemy's lines to cover the movement. When our brigade was relieved by other troops and returned to its former line I ceased firing. My position at this time was on the west side of and facing the Gordon's Mills and Chattanooga road, four pieces near the right of an open field, two pieces at the left corner of the same field, all retired in the edge of the timber. A ravine crossed the field parallel to our line two-thirds of the way to the road. The troops in our front were now falling back, and as it was expected the enemy would fall on our left, the lines were extended in that direction and the four pieces on the right were moved to a corn-field on the left of the timber we had just left, and in a direct line with our former position. This was no sooner done than the enemy moved to the road in front of our center, when the section posted at the corner of the field opened lively, the pieces being double-shotted with canister. They advanced under this and a strong oblique fire from my pieces on the left, in addition to the fire of the infantry lines, until they reached the ravine, when they fell back in disorder. We remained on this part of the field all night.

On the 20th instant we took position with the brigade on the extreme right of our lines, and were posted on the first ridge west of the road running from Crawfish Spring to Chattanooga, near where department headquarters were the day before. At — o'clock Sheridan's division, on our left, was faltering and our brigade went to its support. The brigade moved in at double-quick, and the battery took position a few hundred yards to the left of our former post and opened very rapidly, shelling a field beyond a narrow strip of woods through which the enemy was moving. The brigade soon cleared the woods, and I took a section from the hill and planted it to the right of former department headquarters and opened with canister on the retreating enemy till out of range. We now moved to our former position and finally to Chattanooga Valley, 5 miles from Chattanooga, from which place on the 21st instant we recrossed the river at Chattanooga and took position at Friar's Island covering the ford. My four mountain howitzers were with the Ninety-second Illinois Volunteers detached from the brigade on Saturday, and under Sergeant Anderson, Seventy-second Indiana Volunteers, did good fighting. Sergeant Anderson was wounded severely, and Sergeant Edwards, Seventeenth Indiana Volunteers, took command and did good work till all support left them and the enemy were within a few yards of his pieces, when he succeeded in escaping with three of his pieces and the limber of the other. Either of these men would do honor to the commissions of the miserable shoulder-strapped poltroons who allowed the support to run away from the pieces in the hour of danger. Of my officers and men I can say they have behaved bravely whenever called on. They have never faltered in duty. There is a single exception of one man who has already suffered severe punishment for straggling from the field. I have met with a loss of 2 men killed and 8 wounded. I have also lost in action 6 horses killed, 1 horse wounded, and 1 mountain howitzer; ammunition expended, 778 rounds.

All of which is respectfully submitted.

I have the honor to be, captain, your most obedient servant,

ELI LILLY,
Captain, Commanding Eighteenth Indiana Battery.

Capt. ALEXANDER A. RICE,
Asst. Adjt. Gen., 1st Brig., 4th Div., 14th Army Corps.

No. 71.

Reports of Col. Edward A. King, Sixty-eighth Indiana Infantry, commanding Second Brigade.

HDQRS. 2D BRIG., 4TH DIV., 14TH ARMY CORPS,
In Camp, Jasper, Tenn., August 29, 1863.

SIR : In compliance with orders from Major-General Reynolds, to feel for the enemy in the direction of Chattanooga, I crossed the Tennessee River at Shellmound last evening at 10 o'clock with 200 men of the One hundred and first Indiana Infantry, under Lieutenant-Colonel Doan, and a squad of 9 mounted men under Captain Harris, of the Nineteenth Indiana Battery. I also crossed four companies of the Seventy-fifth Indiana Infantry, two of which I left at Shellmound under Lieutenant-Colonel O'Brien, taking two companies with me to post, if necessary, at the Narrows below Running Water, to hold that passage and secure my retreat should I encounter a very superior force of the enemy. At the upper end of the Narrows I came upon the enemy's pickets, received their fire without replying, and drove them in without firing, to avoid increasing the alarm in their camp. I sent the squad of mounted men up the Running Water Valley to a cross-road, and pushed with the infantry at double-quick forward and into the enemy's camp a half mile distant. We captured 6 prisoners, 11 horses, 7 saddles, 12 muskets, a bugle, and a surgeon's kit. I found that the camp had been occupied by Captain Edmondson's company, of the Third Confederate Cavalry. The troopers ran through the bushes and trees in the rear of their camp, and, of course, in the darkness were soon out of the reach of infantry. One of the prisoners taken is James M. Carroll, member elect of the Tennessee rebel Legislature for Marion County, and conscripting officer for the same county. Some of his conscription lists were also captured. He succeeded in getting out of camp, but ran into the hands of the mounted squad.

I returned by the Narrows to and crossed the river to the north side at Shellmound at 6 o'clock this morning, having before crossing added 2 fine mules and 1 horse to the captured stock.

The road from Shellmound to Running Water is in places quite bad, but could be put in fair condition in a short time.

Very respectfully, your obedient servant,

EDWD. A. KING,
Colonel, Commanding Second Brigade.

Maj. JOHN LEVERING,
Assistant Adjutant-General.

——

HDQRS. 2D BRIG. 4TH DIV., 14TH ARMY CORPS,
Shellmound, Tenn., August 31, 1863.

SIR : I have the honor to report that, in pursuance of orders, I crossed the Tennessee River last night with my brigade, and with 375 men of Second Tennessee Cavalry under Colonel Ray, who reported to me as directed by Major-General Reynolds. I sent Colonel Ray in advance, with instructions to proceed toward Chattanooga, and if he could, without exposing his regiment too much, to go within view of the enemy at Lookout Mountain, falling back upon my brigade if hard pressed, at the junction of the Trenton and Chattanooga road, where I supposed I could be in time. Colonel Ray carried out his instructions very handsomely, driving in the enemy's pickets at daylight, and approaching within view of a five-gun battery at Lookout Mountain, he captured a rebel acting commissary of subsistence, whose saddle-bags I examined and found $2,736.50, which, presuming to be public funds, I took possession of and will turn over to order.

I left Trenton road at 9 a. m. to-day, reaching Shellmound at 2 p. m. The Chattanooga road is, in many places, quite bad. I forward herewith Colonel Ray's report.

Respectfully, yours, obediently,

EDWD. A. KING,
Colonel, Commanding Second Brigade.

Maj. John Levering,
Assistant Adjutant-General, Fourth Division.

No. 72.

*Itinerary of the Second Brigade.**

August 1 the brigade encamped at University Place, Franklin County, Tenn.

August 2 Col. Edward A. King, Sixty-eighth Indiana Infantry, by order of Maj. Gen. J. J. Reynolds, assumed command of the brigade.

August 17 the brigade moved at 9.30 a. m., and encamped at Sweeden's Cove, 12 miles from University Place.

August 18 marched at 1 p. m., and encamped at Battle Creek, 5 miles from Sweeden's Cove.

August 21 ordered to break the enemy's railroad communications by the Chattanooga and Nashville Railroad with Bridgeport at Shellmound. Moved the Seventy-fifth Indiana Infantry and a section of the Nineteenth Indiana Battery to Tennessee River, opposite Shellmound. Shelled the enemy out after dark. Crossed a small party in a canoe and burned the Nickajack Bridge and captured the ferryboat.

August 26 crossed a party over the river, driving away the enemy's pickets, and made a reconnaissance of the vicinity of Shellmound. Moved the One hundred and first Indiana Infantry to the river.

August 28 crossed the river at Shellmound after dark with a detachment of the Seventy-fifth and One hundred and first Indiana Infantry and 9 mounted men, under Captain Harris, Nineteenth Indiana Battery. Moved up the river toward Chattanooga to feel for the enemy with 200 men of the One hundred and first Indiana and the mounted squad, two companies of the Seventy-fifth Indiana as a rear guard. Six miles up the river, at the upper end of the Narrows, the enemy's picket fired on the column; drove them in upon a double-quick, and charged into the enemy's camp. He, surprised, fled pell-mell, but we took 6 prisoners, 11 horses, 7 saddles, 12 rifles, a bugle, and surgeon's kit. The camp was occupied by a portion of the Third Confederate Cavalry. Fell back to Shellmound and recrossed the river.

---

* From returns for August and September.

August 30 crossed the Tennessee with my brigade and 375 men of Second Tennessee Cavalry, Colonel Ray, after dark by means of scows. The brigade over before midnight; moved toward Chattanooga upon a reconnaissance. Pushed the cavalry up to within view of the enemy's batteries at Lookout Mountain, driving in his outposts for 4 miles. Moved the infantry to Trenton Junction in support of the cavalry. The object of the expedition being fully accomplished, we fell back to Shellmound, reaching that point at 2 p. m. August 31. Headquarters at Shellmound. This brigade has driven the enemy's posts from Shellmound to Lookout Mountain, a distance of 20 miles, by its operations since August 22.

September 3 marched from Shellmound, Tenn., across Raccoon Mountain.

September 4 bivouacked at Squirreltown.

September 5 marched to Trenton, Ga.

September 7 moved to Empire Iron-Works, 3 miles south of Trenton.

September 10 marched to Johnson's Crook, at the foot of Lookout Mountain.

September 11 moved on to Lookout Mountain.

September 12 ordered to report to General Negley, at Stevens' Gap. Arrived at foot of mountain at 10 a. m. Took position in line of battle on the left of General Beatty's brigade, Negley's division.

September 13 moved to foot of Cooper's Gap.

September 14 moved to Pond Spring. Lay at this point the 14th, 15th, and 16th.

September 17 relieved Turchin's brigade, guarding Catlett's Gap.

September 18 was relieved by Johnson's division, Twentieth Corps, and took up the line of march for Crawfish Spring. Lay in the road most of the night.

September 19 at 9 a. m., took first position in line of battle, near Widow Glenn's house, about 3 miles from Crawfish Spring. Went into action at 3 p. m., engaging Cheatham's division; were pressed heavily; troops on right and left giving way, were forced by overpowering numbers to retire, losing one piece of artillery. At 7 p. m. took position in new line of battle to the left of former position, on ground occupied during the day by Van Cleve's division, Twenty-first Corps.

September 20 at 9.30 a. m., heavily engaged by troops of Longstreet's corps. Troops on the right giving way, thus breaking the line, the One hundred and fifth Regiment Ohio Volunteer Infantry, held in reserve, was ordered up for a charge on the column of the enemy about piercing the line. The regiment, numbering about 900 men, went in gallantly, cutting up and routing the enemy's troops of Adams' brigade, Johnston's army, bringing off General Adams, wounded, and 26 prisoners. During the engagement four of the five pieces of our artillery were disabled by great depression, double-shotting, and rapid firing. The axle-tree of one breaking, it was abandoned. From 12.30 to 4 p. m. comparative quiet. At 5 p. m. ordered to retire. Cut our way out under heavy fire of shot, shell, and canister. Retired to Rossville.

September 21 lay at Rossville in line of battle.

September 22 at 1 a. m., retired to Chattanooga, and took position on the right of General Negley's division, our left resting on Fort Negley. Remainder of the month remained in camp doing heavy picket and fatigue duty.

No. 73.

Report of Capt. Samuel J. Harris, Nineteenth Indiana Battery.

HEADQUARTERS NINETEENTH INDIANA BATTERY,
October 8, 1863.

SIR : I have the honor herewith to inclose inspection report* of the mounted batteries of artillery of the Fourth Division up to October 1, 1863, and also the operations of the Nineteenth Indiana Battery on Saturday, the 19th, under my command, in the action of the 19th September, 1863, which please find subjoined.

The battery left Pond Spring at 6 p. m. on the evening of the 18th, marched all night, halted at Crawfish Spring, on the morning of the 19th, about one hour and thirty minutes, advanced about 3 miles, and left the main road leading to Chattanooga, diverging to the right, and occupying, with the Second Brigade, several different positions, in anticipation of an attack by the enemy. About 3 p. m., the brigade having been sent forward, the battery was ordered to take position on a ridge running parallel to the Chattanooga road, separated therefrom by a thin growth of timber, and covering all the space intervening. About 3.30 we commenced the action by projecting spherical case over the heads of troops belonging to Van Cleve's division, who were now falling back, and when we could do so without endangering the lives of our own men, used canister, I think to good advantage. At 4.15 the battery and parts of batteries on our right and left having all retired, and receiving a close and destructive fire on my right, I ordered the piece on the right to retire, with the purpose of changing the front of the right half battery, so as to enable me to meet the fire of the enemy. These instructions were misapprehended. While endeavoring to execute this movement I was disabled by a contusion received on my right side. The bruise, though not serious, was very painful, and being unable to meet the flank movement of the enemy from the cause stated, and receiving no support from the infantry detailed for that purpose, the battery fell back toward the Chattanooga road, in the wooded space before referred to, with the loss of one 12-pounder smooth-bore, which was unavoidably left on the ground, in consequence of the number of horses killed and disabled in the limber of that piece, and the close proximity of the enemy.

Having established a new line, First Lieut. R. S. Lackey took command of the battery, who, if he has not already done so, will furnish you the report of the 20th September.

Too much praise cannot be awarded to First Lieut. R. S. Lackey and First Lieut. W. P. Stackhouse for their gallantry and general good conduct.

The loss of men and horses on the 19th : Enlisted men, killed, 2; wounded, 13; missing, 2. Horses killed and disabled, 15.

Respectfully,

S. J. HARRIS,
Captain Nineteenth Indiana Battery.

Maj. W. E. LAWRENCE,
Chief of Artillery, Fourteenth Army Corps.

* See p. 143.

No. 74.

Report of Lieut. Robert S. Lackey, Nineteenth Indiana Battery.

HEADQUARTERS NINETEENTH INDIANA BATTERY,
September 28, 1863.

SIR: I have the honor to report the following as the part taken by Nineteenth Indiana Battery in the action of the 20th September, 1863 (Captain Harris being disabled by a wound received in the action of the 19th, the command of the battery fell on myself):

In accordance with orders from Colonel King, commanding Second Brigade, Fourth Division, the battery took position on the right of Third Brigade, Fourth Division. The enemy commenced the action by opening out upon us with shell from two pieces of artillery, but we soon silenced them by concentrating our fire on them with solid shot and shell. In a short time thereafter the enemy approached in force, making several attempts to turn our right, but were as repeatedly repulsed with heavy loss. The battery, with the brigade, held their position until ordered to fall back by Major-General Reynolds, taking a new position in the rear of the Third Brigade, Fourth Division, and left flank of our first position. From this point we fired a few rounds of shell and solid shot, but thinking it a waste of ammunition, I asked and obtained permission of Colonel King to cease firing.

In the rapid and heavy firing through the action we disabled two of the guns by breaking the axle of a 3-inch rifled Rodman and the axle-straps of a 12-pounder Napoleon. In coming off the field we lost the 3-inch rifle by the axle coming entirely off from the axle-bed, making it impossible to bring it any farther. The piece was unlimbered and left in the road. The other disabled piece was brought off in safety.

Respectfully, yours,

R. S. LACKEY,
First Lieutenant Nineteenth Indiana Battery.

Maj. W. E. LAWRENCE,
Chief of Artillery, Fourteenth Army Corps.

No. 75.

Reports of Brig. Gen. John B. Turchin, U. S. Army, commanding Third Brigade.

HDQRS. 3D BRIGADE, 4TH DIVISION, 14TH ARMY CORPS,
Pond Spring, Ga, September 14, 1863.

SIR: Leaving Cooper's Gap with my brigade at 6 a. m. this day, I took the Pond Spring or Catlett's Gap road, driving in a rebel cavalry picket across the Chickamauga Cove road, toward Catlett's Gap.

Posting my brigade on the Chickamauga Creek and pickets along the Chickamauga Cove road, I took the Ninety-second Ohio Regiment forward, passing Widow Thomason's house, to a meeting-house about one-half mile from the gap.

Our few advanced men found the cavalry pickets posted beyond a corn-field at the gap, and when they came in sight of the pickets they saw a party of rebels on foot deploying along the edge of the woods to the right. Not wishing to bring on an engagement, I returned to camp, meeting General Reynolds, who decided on withdrawing the Ninety-second Ohio Regiment to this point. Shots were exchanged between my men and the rebels throughout the entire march and at the gap.

According to the statements of Mr. Hall, a Union citizen residing here and formerly a soldier under General Scott, the gap is 4 miles long, with high, wooded mountains on each side of the road.

The road is very good, with no steep grades; was blockaded by the rebels, but cleared again by them, and a large train of wagons passed from here through the gap the day General Negley was attacked.

There is no stream of water in the gap, but a few small springs at different places. There is but one small field of corn for 4 miles beyond the point we were at.

Very respectfully, your obedient servant,

J. B. TURCHIN,
Brigadier-General, U. S. Volunteers.

Maj. JOHN LEVERING,
Assistant Adjutant-General, Fourth Division.

HDQRS. 3RD BRIGADE, 4TH DIVISION, 14TH ARMY CORPS,
Chattanooga, Tenn, September 26, 1863.

SIR: After holding the opening of Catlett's Gap for two days with my brigade against the enemy, who tried to come out of it and occupy our position, I was relieved in the evening of the 17th of September by the Second Brigade, putting my brigade in the reserve.

On the 18th I received orders to march, and the division moved in the evening by the Chickamauga Cove road, and halted on the morning of the 19th to cook coffee at Osburn's house, north of Crawfish Spring.

At about 10 o'clock on the 19th the division moved toward Widow Glenn's house, northeast of which it was supposed to take position, but an order came from General Thomas to move to McDonald's house, and the division moved by a cross-road, my brigade being at the head of the column.

While approaching McDonald's house I received an order from the general commanding the division to face about and to return to Kelly's Cross-Roads, but immediately after that my assistant adjutant-general, Captain Curtis, brought me information that two of my regiments, the Ninety-second Ohio and the Eighteenth Kentucky, had been moved to the front already by General Reynolds, and that he (Captain Curtis) would take the balance of the brigade to the position.

While we were thus marching forward and backward heavy fighting was going on in the front and on our right flank.

At 3 p. m. I succeeded in finding my two regiments that were engaged, and took position with the other two regiments that were with me (the Thirty-sixth and Eleventh Ohio) in the second line, having the Twenty-first Indiana Battery on a low ridge at the right of the battalions.

The position was in the woods, two regiments fighting in the hollow in front supporting General Hazen's brigade, of Palmer's division ; on my left was General Willich's brigade, of Johnson's division. I had hardly taken the position when General Hazen requested me to send one of my regiments to relieve one or two of his regiments that were fighting in front, as they were out of ammunition. I sent the Eleventh Ohio to the front. Shortly afterward I relieved the Ninety-second Ohio with the Thirty-sixth Ohio, putting the former in reserve.

The enemy being repulsed on my front, the brigade of General Willich advanced to the front and left, and the brigade of General Hazen being withdrawn, my brigade was isolated from other troops. I decided to take to the right, and formed in two lines on the left of General Cruft's brigade, of Palmer's division.

Shortly afterward, at about 4.30 p. m., the enemy came in heavy columns on our front ; there was wavering and indecision, and I ordered a charge. The brigade yelled, rushed forward, and drove the enemy back in confusion, taking some prisoners. The brigade of General Cruft charged with us. After consulting General Cruft, we decided to fall back, to reform our line, on the original position. This being done, I received orders from the general commanding to join the Second Brigade, which I subsequently did, and that closed the day.

The charge was executed by the whole brigade most gallantly. We routed, as we learned from the prisoners afterward, Law's brigade, Hood's division, Longstreet's corps, a crack brigade of the rebel army of Richmond.

The position on the first day was so bad and so wooded that my battery could fire only three shots during the day's fighting, and those were fired at the rebel stragglers after we made the charge.

On the morning of the 20th I was ordered to shift my brigade to the left and move to the front to take the place of General Hazen's brigade, which moved to the left, the Second Brigade taking my place. I had the Thirty-sixth Ohio, Ninety-second Ohio, and a portion of the Eleventh Ohio in the first line, several companies of the latter and the Eighteenth Kentucky Regiment being in the reserve.

At about 10 o'clock we were attacked by the enemy, and for about one hour the infantry and the battery kept up a continual fire. The breastwork of rails and timber protected our men. The enemy suffered severely. At noon and after until 2 o'clock there was a comparative lull in our front, while the battle raged on the right and left of the position of the army.

Receiving orders to change front and to abandon a portion of the fortifications, to complete the line with the Second Brigade, I directed my battery to move back and take place on the left of Captain Harris' battery, of the Second Brigade, and the Thirty-sixth Ohio Regiment to support it, and was preparing to move other regiments when an order came from General Thomas to hold the position. I moved the Thirty-sixth and the battery to their original positions, driving the enemy's sharpshooters back.

Shortly after General Reynolds came with the Second Brigade and informed me that two brigades of Brannan's division, on the right of the Second Brigade, gave way, and the Second Brigade was obliged to change front, and that I must change my front to the right. I reformed my brigade, with the Thirty-sixth and Eleventh Ohio Regiments in the first line and the Ninety-second Ohio and Eighteenth Kentucky Regiments in the second, four pieces of artillery in front and two in the reserve, the Second Brigade being placed, *en échelon*, on my right and rear.

The roar of the battle on our right and left advancing more and more to our rear, the time was coming to retreat. At last the order came for us to retreat by the right flank. The brigade moved, then halted and faced to the front; then orders came to move to the rear. The brigade faced about, made a few paces and faced that portion of the enemy that had outflanked the left of our lines and was in the rear of Palmer's, Johnson's, and Baird's divisions.

The command "Forward" was given; some few shots were exchanged; I gave the order to charge. The brigade yelled, rushed forward, and broke to pieces the confronting columns of the rebels. They fled pell-mell; we took 250 prisoners, charged up hill, and, notwithstanding the flank fire of the rebel battery and the front fire of the two pieces, the regiments rushed on and took the two pieces, but for want of time and the horses being disabled, could not get them away.

I ordered the brigade to move by the left flank, and joined Colonel McCook's brigade, of the Reserve Corps, that was in position on our left.

As I learned afterward General Reynolds, with about 150 of my brigade, being on the extreme right and not noticing our movement to the left, was still moving on the main road; some rebel troops were met, but gave way, and the rest of the brigade joined us safely.

That charge relieved our troops of the left that were outflanked and partially surrounded. The charge was made most gallantly. It showed that we have soldiers on whom we may rely in the most difficult circumstances.

The Ninety-second Ohio Regiment, having never been in action before, behaved most gallantly during these two days. All the other regiments had seen fight before and they did admirably.

The officers and men of the brigade did nobly. The maneuvers were executed with precision and order. We did not flinch one inch from our position during both days' fight. My brigade formed the salient point of the position on the second day, and while on the right and left our troops were falling back we held our ground until we charged to the rear.

Colonel Lane and Major Higgins, of the Eleventh Ohio Regiment, most gallantly directed the movements of their regiment.

After Colonel Jones. of the Thirty-sixth Ohio, was mortally wounded, Lieutenant-Colonel Devol commanded the regiment with great skill and bravery. Major Adney being wounded, Lieutenant-Colonel Devol was the only field officer with the regiment.

After Colonel Fearing, of the Ninety-second Ohio, was wounded Lieutenant-Colonel Putnam commanded the regiment, and notwithstanding that he was wounded himself, remained faithfully with the regiment, nobly assisted by Major Golden and his brave and intrepid adjutant, Lieutenant Turner.

Lieutenant-Colonel Milward, of the Eighteenth Kentucky, received a severe bruise from a horse that overran him, but remained on the field of battle until Sunday afternoon, when Captain Heltemes took charge of the regiment. Major Wileman having been wounded in the first day's fight, Captain Heltemes conducted the regiment in the last charge bravely and took a two-gun battery of the enemy, showing thereby his bravery and coolness.

In conclusion, I must mention the gallant conduct of my staff officers on the battle-field.   Captain Curtis, my assistant adjutant-general, was my right hand during the two days' battle.   Captain Price, Eleventh Ohio, brigade inspector, and Captain Robbins, Eighteenth Kentucky, brigade provost-marshal, acted as my aides-de-camp and assisted me gallantly.

Our loss during the two days' fight is 1 officer and 29 men killed, 18 officers and 209 men wounded, and 6 officers and 80 men missing.

The Eighty-ninth Ohio Regiment having unfortunately been previously detached from the brigade, was during the fight serving in General Steedman's division of the Reserve Corps.

The entire regiment, as I understand, was captured by the enemy, excepting about 100 men and 3 officers, who were detailed to guard some train.   It was unfortunate for a brigade that came out of the campaign so nobly to lose one of its regiments by the fault of somebody else.

The list of the casualties is herewith submitted.*   The reports of the regimental commanders will be forwarded as soon as received.

An approximate sketch † of a portion of the battle-field and of the positions of my brigade is herewith forwarded.

I am, sir, very respectfully, your obedient servant,

> J. B. TURCHIN,
> *Brigadier-General, Commandiug.*

Maj. JOHN LEVERING,
> *Asst. Adjt. Gen., Fourth Division, 14th Army Corps.*

ADDENDA.

Itinerary of the Third Brigade for September, 1863.‡

September 1 moved from Jasper, Tenn., to Shellmound, Tenn., crossing Tennessee River at Shellmound Ferry.

September 4 moved across Raccoon Mountain to Squirreltown, Ga.

September 5 moved to Trenton, Ga.

September 10 moved to Johnson's Crook, Lookout Mountain.

September 11 moved across Lookout Mountain, Cooper's Gap, Ga.

September 14 moved to Pond Spring, Ga.

September 15, 16, 17, and 18, guarded the western opening to Catlett's Gap, Pigeon Mountain, skirmishing daily.   Loss, 6 wounded.

September 18, at 7 p. m., started toward the battle-field of Chickamauga, spending the night on the road, blockaded by trains of other commands.

September 19, at 7 a. m., passed Crawfish Spring.   Halted at Thomas Osburn's house at 8 a. m.   Moved at 10 a. m. to battle-field. Entered into action at 2 p. m.   At 4 p. m. charged a brigade of Hood's division, Longstreet's corps, driving them three-fourths of a mile, capturing two pieces of artillery.   Returned to position, and at 7 p. m. ordered to take place in new line of battle.

September 20, at 7 a. m., ordered to move to the left, taking the ground previously occupied by Hazen's brigade, Palmer's division, Twenty-first Army Corps.   At 9 a. m. heavily engaged.   From 12 m. to 3 p. m. comparatively quiet, during which a change of front was made, on account of the right wing of the army having been driven back.   At 5 p. m. a retreat ordered.   Brigade moved about one-third of a mile to rear, formed two lines, and charged the enemy, drawn

---

* Embodied in revised statement, p. 173.
† Not found.
‡ From return for September.

up to cut off our retreat, taking 300 prisoners and 2 pieces of artillery. After pursuing them about one-half mile, the brigade moved by the left flank and reached Rossville road. A small portion of the brigade, about 150 men, pursued the enemy about 1 mile farther, returned, and joined the command. At 8 p. m. the brigade moved to Rossville, Ga.

September 21, at 7 a. m., 4 officers and 93 men, the *débris* of the Eighty-ninth Ohio Volunteer Infantry, joined the command. This regiment was detached from the brigade and ordered to Tracy City, Tenn., August 17; ordered to join brigade September 1; at Bridgeport was ordered to escort a train to Chattanooga; at Chattanooga was placed in a brigade of Steedman's division of the Reserve Corps, and reached the battle-field of Chickamauga about noon of the 20th instant. Loss of the brigade in the battles of 19th and 20th : 1 officer and 29 men killed; 18 officers and 209 men wounded; 6 officers and 80 men missing ; total, 25 officers and 318 men. Loss of the Eighty-ninth Ohio Volunteer Infantry in the battles of the 19th and 20th : 2 officers and 17 men killed; 2 officers and 61 men wounded; 13 officers and 158 men missing ; total, 17 officers and 236 men ; aggregate loss of the entire brigade, 42 officers and 554 men. At 8 a m. brigade took position on the right of Negley's division.

September 22, at 1 a. m., brigade moved to Chattanooga, Tenn. At 7 a. m. took position on the left of the Twentieth Army Corps. At 8 a. m. ordered to fall back to the line of intrenchment traced for a line of permanent defense. Remainder of the month brigade remained at Chattanooga, doing heavy picket duty.

No. 76.

Report of Lieut. Col. Hubbard K. Milward, Eighteenth Kentucky Infantry.

HDQRS. EIGHTEENTH REGT. KENTUCKY VOL. INFANTRY,
Near Chattanooga, Tenn., September 26, 1863.

CAPTAIN : I herewith submit report of the part taken by my command in the engagement of Saturday and Sunday, 19th and 20th instant.

Saturday morning about 10 o'clock the regiment reached the camp of the brigade 2 miles northeast of Crawfish Spring, and after a halt of a few minutes moved with the brigade about a half mile up the road and formed in double column in the rear line of the brigade ; about 11 o'clock moved forward and up the Chattanooga road, the Eighteenth Kentucky in rear of the Ninety-second Ohio Volunteer Infantry, and at a point south of Kelly's house was ordered by Major-General Reynolds, commanding division, to form line of battle and support the Ninety-second Ohio Volunteer Infantry, which entered the woods east of road. After advancing 300 to 400 yards the regiment formed in the line and on the left of the Ninety-second Ohio Volunteer Infantry, and was immediately exposed to a heavy and well-directed fire from the enemy, which was warmly returned, and the enemy gradually pushed farther back into the woods. About 3 p. m. a charge on the left by a brigade of General Brannan's division caused the fire to cease from that flank and the regiment was half wheeled to the right and that position retained until 4.30 p. m., when the supply of ammunition being exhausted orders were received to fall back a short distance which was done ammunition distributed, and the remaining dead and wounded cared for. Soon after this the regiment was moved to the rear, formed line in rear of Ninety-second Ohio Volunteer Infantry, but immediately changed front to the right to resist an attack from that flank, and by order of Brigadier-General Turchin, commanding brigade, fixed bayonets and lay down; after the charge by the balance of the brigade was made, took position in the woods on the right of where we were engaged in the morning, and at dusk went into bivouac on the Chattanooga road south of Kelly's house. Details for guard duty, including the whole of Company A, has reduced the effective force of enlisted men to about 250 men, of whom there were 4 killed, 30 wounded, and 20 missing; commissioned officers wounded, 5, among them Maj. A. G. Wileman and First Lieut. and Actg. Adjt. Silas Howe, both of whom behaved with great gallantry on the field.

Surgeon Fithian, being acting brigade surgeon, was on duty at the hospitals. Assistant Surgeon Elliott was on the field and rendered aid to the wounded. To Capt. J. B. Heltemes, who, after Major Wileman was wounded, became acting major, great credit is due for his coolness and gallant bearing while under fire.

The line officers did their whole duty, and to name those deserving mention would be to name them all. I beg to make special mention of Color Sergts. Andrew Simmons, Company I, and Patrick Burns, Company B, neither of whom faltered or wavered, but bravely bore our starry emblems in the very front of the battle during the entire day.

I saw no cowards, nor does the report of any company commander speak of one.

Sunday morning, between 8 and 9 o'clock, the regiment moved from bivouac into the breastworks on the right and front, and took position in line of battle in the rear (50 or 75 yards) of the Ninety-second Ohio Volunteer Infantry. At 11 o'clock, I being so disabled from injuries received by being run over by a horse during the march of the Friday night previous as to be unable to walk, mount, or dismount without great assistance, and in the field contrary to the advice of Division Surgeon Herrick and Brigade Surgeon Fithian, by advice and consent of Brigadier-General Turchin, commanding brigade, left the regiment in command of Capt. and Actg. Maj. J. B. Heltemes.

I inclose his report covering operations of the balance of the day, and list of killed, wounded, and missing during the two days' fight.

I have the honor to be, very respectfully, your obedient servant,

> H. K. MILWARD,
> *Lieutenant-Colonel, Commanding.*

Capt. W. B. CURTIS,
  A. A. G., 3d Brig., 4th Div., 14th Army Corps.

No. 77.

Report of Capt. John B. Heltemes, Eighteenth Kentucky Infantry.

HDQRS. EIGHTEENTH KENTUCKY VOLUNTEER INFANTRY,
  Near Chattanooga, Tenn., September 26, 1863.

CAPTAIN: I have the honor to submit the following report of the part taken by the Eighteenth Kentucky Volunteer Infantry during the fighting of Sunday, September 20, 1863, after 11 a. m.:

At that time Lieutenant-Colonel Milward, being disabled, left the field, and the command devolved on me, the regiment being in line of battle, lying down about 75 yards in rear of Ninety-second Ohio Volunteer Infantry, which was in action at the works. About noon the regiment relieved seven companies of the Ninety-second Ohio Volunteer Infantry, and held the position against several heavy charges of the enemy until all the ammunition was exhausted, when it was withdrawn, formed in double columns, and fresh ammunition received; then took position about 50 yards in rear of Thirty-sixth Ohio Volunteer Infantry, holding position at the right end of the works; remained there about forty minutes, when front was changed by the brigade, and the Eighteenth took position, closed *en masse*, in rear of the left wing of the Thirty-sixth Ohio Volunteer Infantry. At 4 p. m. the brigade moved to the Chattanooga road and formed line of battle north of said road, facing west, then faced about and charged the enemy along the road and across a field into the woods, where the Eighteenth captured two pieces of artillery left by the enemy in their flight, but these pieces being turned the wrong way and no place to turn them, we took what prisoners we had and flanked to the left, to rally on the left of our brigade, which then began to form in the rear of a portion of Maj. Gen. Gordon Granger's corps on a hill north of the woods. Here a rest of about one and a half hours was given, and we moved with the brigade down the Chattanooga road to a point 2 miles east of Rossville and bivouacked.

The loss sustained in the day's fighting was : Enlisted men killed, 3 · commissioned officers wounded, 3; enlisted men wounded, 8; commissioned officers missing, 4; enlisted men missing, 12. Among the officers missing, Surgeon and Acting Brigade Surgeon Fithian, who was at the division hospital when it was captured by the enemy.

The officers of the line behaved handsomely, and too much praise cannot be awarded to Color Sergt. A. Simmons, Company I, and Corpl. J. W. Wiley, Company F, who in the absence of Color Sergeant Burns (who was sick) carried his stand of colors.

I am, very respectfully,

J. B. HELTEMES,
Captain Co. K, Actg. Major 18th Ky. Vol. Infty.

Capt. W. B. CURTIS,
   Asst. Adjt. Gen., Third Brigade, Fourth Division.

No. 78.

Report of Col. Philander P. Lane, Eleventh Ohio Infantry.

HDQRS. ELEVENTH REGT. OHIO VOLUNTEER INFANTRY,
       Chattanooga, Tenn., September 26, 1863.

SIR : I have the honor to report the following details of the part taken by the Eleventh Regiment Ohio Volunteer Infantry in the action of the 19th and 20th instant :

The effective strength of the regiment was 413 enlisted men and 20 commissioned officers, all our commissioned officers being present except Captains Duncan and Layman and Lieutenant Morris, absent on recruiting service in Ohio, and Lieutenant-Colonel Street, sick in hospital. We arrived on the battle-field at 9 a. m. on the morning of the 19th instant, and were soon after placed in a position to support the Ninety-second Ohio Regiment, then under fire.

Soon after General Hazen notified me that one of his regiments to my front and right was out of ammunition and were falling back, and wished me to occupy its position. I referred him to you, but in the meantime the regiment fell back, and I took the responsibility of ordering my regiment forward to fill the gap, but before the movement was completed I received your order to occupy the position. The Ninety-second Ohio was soon after relieved and the Thirty-sixth Ohio Regiment moved up on our left ; the enemy kept up a brisk fire on our front and right flank; my regiment was ordered to charge, which was done with spirit and we drove the enemy from a field in our front and captured a number of prisoners. At the commencement of the charge the color-bearer was struck by a spent ball and fell. The colors were seized by Lieutenant Peck, of Company E, and carried at the head of the line. We held the ground gained for half an hour or more, and then I moved the regiment by the left flank under cover of timber and to support the Thirty-sixth Ohio Regiment, which was then lying to the left and rear and exposed to a heavy fire on their right. We were then ordered to fall back to our first position and change our front more to the right to meet the enemy, who were making heavy demonstrations in that direction. The Eleventh [being] on the left and Thirty-sixth on the right, we were ordered to make a second charge, which was done successfully, cleaning the front of the enemy and taking a number of prisoners. We then fell back to our first position, which we held until dark.

On the morning of the 20th, we were stationed on the second line to support the Thirty-Sixth Ohio Regiment, in rear of a rude fortification on the left of the Second Brigade. We were kept alternately on left and rear until the afternoon, all the time under a brisk fire. During the hardest fire our rude fortification caught fire, and Second Lieutenant Hardenbrook, Company B, took a part of his company and separated the timber to prevent its spreading and destroying the protection it afforded us. Company D, deployed as skirmishers on the left of the line, lost 13 killed and wounded in a short time. We were withdrawn from this position to make a charge on the enemy, who were moving in our rear. The charge was made by the rear rank and the line became much broken, but it was made with spirit and success, taking a large number of prisoners. We followed up the enemy some 3 miles on the Rossville road ; by some misunderstanding more than two-thirds of the regiment marched by the left flank soon after the first line of the enemy was broken. The other third and about the same proportion of the Thirty-sixth kept to the front, led by Major-General Reynolds. We found the enemy in force on the Rossville road, about 3 miles from the point we started from. We halted here and formed the fragments of the Eleventh, Thirty-sixth, and Ninety-second Ohio Regiments, and marched by the left flank and joined General Granger's command, where we found our brigade. Our loss during the two days was 5 killed, 36 wounded, and 22 missing. The missing are probably nearly all prisoners, as they were sent to the rear with prisoners on our last charge, and the enemy being in that vicinity, our men and their prisoners were captured. Up to the time of our last charge not more than 6 of my men were missing.

The officers and men of my regiment endured every hardship and braved every danger with cheerfulness. Many of our men were without water for twelve or fifteen hours. Nearly all of our wounded of the 20th were left on the field.   Our hospital arrangements were a total failure ; neither surgeons, hospital corps, nor ambulances were to be found.

Very respectfully, your obedient servant,

P. P. LANE,
Colonel, Comdg. Eleventh Regt. Ohio Vol. Infantry.

J. B. TURCHIN,
Brigadier-General, Commanding Third Brigade.

No. 79.

Report of Lieut. Col. Hiram F. Devol, Thirty-sixth Ohio Infantry.

CAMP AT CHATTANOOGA,
September 23, 1863.

SIR : I have the honor to submit the following report of the Thirty-sixth Regiment Ohio Volunteer Infantry for the two days' battle, September 19 and 20, 1863:

On the morning of the 19th we went into position on the right of the road leading to Ringgold, and about 1½ miles east of Crawfish Spring.   From there we were ordered 1 mile to the east and front to relieve the Ninety-second Ohio Volunteer Infantry, who had been engaged in the woods on the right of the road.   About 3 p. m. the troops on our right were driven back by the enemy, which caused us to change front to the right and to the rear of the Ninetieth Ohio Volunteer Infantry and one other regiment.   In a short time they were driven back through our lines; we then engaged the enemy, who were in considerable force.   In a very few minutes, and when we were suffering terribly from the enemy's fire, I went to look for the colonel but did not see him.   I then ordered a charge, which was obeyed most gallantly by my regiment and the Eleventh Ohio Volunteer Infantry, who had formed on our left.   We drove the enemy from a quarter to half a mile, when I halted and reformed. We were then ordered back to our former position.   I then learned that Colonel Jones had been wounded in the early part of the engagement.   About 6 o'clock I took position in the road and to the right, where we camped for the night with the balance of the brigade.

On the morning of the 20th we moved to the position occupied by our brigade.   We held that position until 4 p. m., when the enemy had us nearly surrounded.   We were then formed on the west side of the road, fronting southeast.   We then faced about and charged the enemy about a mile, driving and routing them completely.   Passing one of their batteries, killed their horses and dismounted their guns.   We then formed on the hill where some of the Reserve Corps were posted, and marched to Rossville, arriving about 10 p. m.

Casualties in the two days' fighting : Killed, 12 ; wounded, 65, and missing, 14 (according to accompanying list*).

Too much praise cannot be awarded to both officers and men for their gallantry.   Without an exception they behaved nobly, driving the enemy, who were in greatly superior numbers, in every instance.

---

* Nominal list omitted.

The success of this regiment and brigade is not owing to its discipline and efficiency alone, but to its confidence in the skill of its brigade commander.

Very respectfully, your obedient servant,

H. F. DEVOL,
Lieutenant-Colonel, Commanding Regiment.

Capt. W. B. Curtis,
Assistant Adjutant-General.

No. 80.

Report of Lieut. Col. Douglas Putnam, jr., Ninety-second Ohio Infantry.

Hdqrs. Ninety-second Regiment Ohio Vol. Infty.,
Chattanooga, Tenn., September 26, 1863.

Captain : I have the honor to submit the following report of the part taken by the Ninety-second Regiment Ohio Volunteer Infantry in the battles of Saturday and Sunday, September 19 and 20, 1863:

At daylight on the 19th of September the Ninety-second Regiment Ohio Volunteer Infantry, Col. B. D. Fearing commanding, moved with the brigade from bivouac on the Chattanooga road, about 7 miles west of Ringgold, passed Crawfish Spring about 7 a. m., and halted for breakfast about 2 miles from the spring. About 10 a. m. the regiment moved with the Eleventh and Thirty-sixth Regiments Ohio Volunteer Infantry, Eighteenth Kentucky Volunteer Infantry, and Twenty-first Indiana Battery up the road about one-half mile, and formed in double column in the second column of the brigade for battle. About 11 a. m. the brigade was moved forward and up the Chattanooga road, the Ninety-second being ordered to follow the battery. As the regiment was moving along the road south of Kelly's house, it was ordered by Major-General Reynolds, commanding division, to form line of battle and advance into the woods east of the road, supported by the Eighteenth Kentucky Regiment, the remainder of the brigade passing along the road. The regiment, numbering in effective strength about 400 men, engaged a line of the enemy, relieving a regiment of General Palmer's division, and meeting a very severe fire of musketry and shell, under which they remained until 3 p. m., holding the enemy in check and pushing his line back some distance. A brigade of General Johnson's division charged the woods on our right about 3 o'clock, causing the enemy's cross-fire to cease. About this time Colonel Fearing was wounded and carried from the field, and the command, so skillfully commanded by him, fell to me. At 4 o'clock, the regiment being nearly out of ammunition, and the Thirty-sixth and Eleventh Ohio Volunteer Infantry having returned, the Ninety-second Ohio Volunteer Infantry was relieved by the Thirty-sixth Ohio Volunteer Infantry, and I took a position in support of the brigade. Soon after this the brigade, being now all together, changed front to the right, and charged through the woods, the Ninety-second Ohio Volunteer Infantry being in the second line. The brigade of the enemy (Law's brigade of Hood's division, Longstreet's corps) were routed and driven back. The regiment then went into position with the brigade, on the right of the woods, where we fought in the morning, and about dark went into bivouac on the Chattanooga road, south of Kelly's house. The regiment lost in the battle of Saturday 5 men killed, 3 officers and 50 men wounded, and 5 men missing. The smallness of the loss was due to the very skillful management of Colonel Fearing, and his coolness and bravery while under fire and in command.

Early on the morning of Sunday, the 20th, the regiment moved forward into the woods in front of their bivouac, and were placed behind a breastwork of logs and wood facing south, and kept up a brisk fire upon the enemy's line until noon, when firing almost ceased, and the regiment was drawn back and lay in double column unengaged till about 4 p. m. About this time the regiment moved with the brigade up the Chattanooga road, a short distance above Kelly's house, when line of battle was formed facing southwest. The line was then faced by the rear rank to the northeast and ordered to charge a line of the enemy drawn up in solid column across the road. The Ninety-second Regiment led the charge on the right, now become the left, and with the other regiments drove the rebels across the field and over the hill and came out at a battery stationed on the hill north of the woods, belonging to Granger's corps. After receiving a volley from the enemy, with bayonets fixed and a shout, [we] rushed forward and in utter confusion forced them to abandon a part of a battery and throw away their arms. A colonel and several officers were taken prisoners by my men. After resting in line of battle for an hour and a half the regiment moved with the brigade down the road to a point about 2 miles from Rossville, where we bivouacked for the night. We lost in the charge 3 commissioned officers wounded, 12 men wounded, 15 men missing. We sent back a number of prisoners, who were taken to Chattanooga. The entire loss of the two days' fight was as follows: Killed, 6; wounded, 62; officers, 6; missing, 20.*

Major Golden assisted me in every possible manner and did himself credit. Captains Grosvenor and Whittlesey are especially deserving of notice for bravery and coolness and for the manner in which their companies were managed. After Colonel Fearing was wounded, Captain Grosvenor took command of the left wing, Major Golden going to the right. I feel under obligations to Adjt. George B. Turner, whose assistance was invaluable to me, and whose coolness and forethought were manifested on every occasion. He is deserving of especial notice and commendation. Surgeon Colton was with us whenever it was possible for him to reach us, and left nothing undone for the comfort of the wounded. Quartermaster Priestley showed himself to be a brave man, and was on the field attending to the wants of the men.

Very respectfully, your obedient servant,

DOUGLAS PUTNAM, JR.,
Lieutenant-Colonel, Commanding.

Capt. W. B. Curtis,
Assistant Adjutant-General, Third Brigade.

---

*See revised statement, p. 173.

No. 81.

Report of Second Lieut. William E. Chess, Twenty-first Indiana Battery.

CHATTANOOGA, TENN., *September 27, 1863.*

SIR : I have the honor to report to you the part taken in the action of September 19 and 20, 1863, by the Twenty-first Indiana Battery ; also the loss of men and *matériel.*

The battery was first brought into position on the morning of the 19th in the center of the brigade, from which point some 180 rounds of ammunition were expended. When the troops on the right gave way the battery changed front, and after a few rounds of canister had been fired the brigade charged, followed by the battery. After advancing half a mile the battery again came into position and fired canister and case-shot. We were then ordered back to our old position and in a few minutes back to a high ridge, where we camped for the night.

On Sunday morning we were ordered to or near the position occupied on the previous day. After firing canister and case-shot for several hours, the battery was ordered to the rear, on the left of the Nineteenth Indiana Battery, from which point a few rounds were fired. At about 2 p. m. we were ordered again into position to the rear of Fourth Division Hospital. Our caissons having become separated from the battery and ammunition being scarce, but few rounds were fired from this position. When the brigade charged the battery got separated from it and reported to General Thomas, by whom it was assigned a position with the Second Brigade until the Third Brigade's position was ascertained. Captain Andrew then reported to General Turchin for orders.

LOSSES.

Men wounded *	10
Horses wounded and abandoned	12
Gun and limber, light 12-pounder	1
Ammunition chest	1
Fifth wheel	1
Rounds of canister	160
Rounds of shell	104
Rounds of spherical case	168
Rounds of solid shot	10
Friction primers	560
Gunners' pouches	2
Priming-wires	2
Thumb-stalls	2
Lanyards	2
Sponge-staves	2
Rubber buckets	4
Saddle, cavalry	1
Bridle, cavalry	1
Halters	12
Set harness, single	1
Artillery bridle	1
Axes	4
Tarpaulins	4

Hoping the above may prove correct, I am, yours, truly,

W. E. CHESS,

Second Lieut., Comdg. Twenty-first Indiana Battery.

Captain HARRIS,

Comdg. 19th Indiana Battery, Chief of Arty., 4th Div.

---

* See revised statement, p. 173.

No. 82.

Report of Maj. Gen. Alexander McD. McCook, U. S. Army, commanding Twentieth Army Corps.

HEADQUARTERS TWENTIETH ARMY CORPS,
Chattanooga, October 2, 1863.

GENERAL: I have the honor to submit a detailed account of the operations of the Twentieth Army Corps, from the date of constructing the pontoon bridge over the Tennessee River at Caperton's Ferry, on the 29th of August, 1863, until the occupation of Chattanooga by the Army of the Cumberland.

At 4 a. m., August 29, the pontoons were ready for the construction of the bridge over the Tennessee River. Heg's brigade, of Davis' division, of this corps, was placed in the boats and crossed to the opposite bank to cover its construction, to drive away the enemy's pickets, and to seize the heights of Sand Mountain. This duty was well performed, and the bridge completed at 1 p. m.

Carlin's brigade, assisted by 100 men and officers of the Pioneer Corps, guarded the bridge.

August 30, General Davis crossed his remaining two brigades, concentrating them at the foot of Sand Mountain.

Johnson's division, of the Twentieth Corps, stationed at Bellefonte, Ala., marched to the ford at Crow Creek, and Davis' entire division encamped on night of the 30th on top of Sand Mountain.

Sheridan's division assisted in building a bridge at Bridgeport, Ala., to enable it to cross the river at that point. His line of march was via Trenton, Ga., thence to Will's Valley.

August 31 Johnson's division crossed the river at Caperton's Ferry and encamped at foot of Sand Mountain.

September 1 headquarters of corps at Stevenson, Ala.

September 2 Davis' division advanced and encamped at the foot of Sand Mountain, in Will's Valley. Johnson's division moved up the mountain and encamped near the western summit. Sheridan's division crossed at Bridgeport and marched toward Trenton.

September 3 Davis in camp in Will's Valley. Johnson marched to near eastern summit of Sand Mountain. Headquarters of corps with this division. The First and Second Divisions of cavalry passed this point at 1 p. m.

September 4 Davis marched to Winston's, foot of Lookout Mountain, and seized the pass over the mountain at that place. Johnson's division marched down the Sand Mountain and encamped on the ground vacated by Davis.

Winston's is 42 miles from Chattanooga, 25 miles from Caperton's Ferry, 48 miles from Rome, Ga., and 45 miles from Dalton, Ga.

September 5 General Sheridan reported his command to be encamped a few miles southwest of Trenton, having been delayed by Negley's wagon train.

September 6 Sheridan encamped at Stevens' Mill, 12 miles from Winston's.

September 7 no movements.

September 8 Johnson's division marched to Long's Spring, on the Trenton road, and two brigades of Davis' division were ordered into Broomtown Valley, to support Stanley's cavalry.

September 9 Carlin's brigade, of Davis' division, marched on

Alpine, Ga., to support the cavalry. Heg's brigade of same division marched toward Broomtown Valley, by way of Neal's Gap. At 6 p. m. I received information from the general commanding, stating that the enemy had evacuated Chattanooga, and were retreating southward, and ordering me to move rapidly upon Alpine and Summerville, Ga., in pursuit; to intercept his line of retreat and attack him on flank.

September 10 Post's brigade, of Davis' division, was ordered to remain at Winston's, to guard trains, &c. Johnson's division marched at 5 a. m. from Long's Spring, and crossed Lookout Mountain, encamping at base near Henderson's. Sheridan's division marched at 5 a. m. from Stevens' Mill, and encamped on Little River, about 2½ miles from the western crest.

Headquarters of the corps moved to near Alpine.

On arriving at Alpine I discovered that the enemy had not retreated very far from Chattanooga, and not being able to communicate with General Thomas by way of the valley, I dispatched couriers by way of Valley Head and learned to my surprise that he had not reached La Fayette as ordered. His reasons for not having reached that place became more apparent as we progressed. Under these circumstances I did not move upon Summerville as ordered.

My corps was isolated at Alpine, and had it moved to Summerville it would have been exposed to the entire rebel army, which reconnaissance soon convinced me was being concentrated at or near La Fayette, Ga.

September 11, 9.30 p. m., I received communication from General Thomas, repeating his difficulties on the march, and that he could not reach La Fayette until the 12th. Believing that no co-operation could exist between General Thomas and myself by way of Broomtown Valley, I ordered all my wagon trains and *matériel* not absolutely necessary for the troops to be returned to the top of Lookout Mountain, and there to await the result of the cavalry reconnaissance sent by General Stanley to ascertain the whereabouts of the enemy, the general commanding being apprised of my movements and dispositions.

September 12 the Twentieth Corps rested in position near Alpine.

September 13 orders were received from General Thomas at midnight, directing two divisions of my corps to be moved to his support, and the other division to be left to guard the trains. This order was given by direction of General Rosecrans. It was my desire to join General Thomas by the Mountain road via Stevens' Gap, but not having any guide, all the citizens concurring that no such road existed, and General Thomas also stating that the route by Valley Head was the only practicable one, I determined to join him by that route. A brigade from each division was detailed as a guard for my trains and General Lytle placed in command. My corps was moved up the mountain at Alpine.

On the night of the 13th and on the night of the 14th my corps was again encamped in Lookout Valley, except the division guarding the trains, which was encamped at Little River, on the mountains. Sheridan's division marched down Lookout Valley to Johnson's Crook, and encamped at the base of the mountains.

Being informed that a good mountain road ran direct from Valley Head to Stevens' Gap, Generals Johnson and Davis were ordered to march on that road with the utmost expedition.

By direction of the general commanding, General Lytle was ordered to move with two brigades to the head of McLemore's Cove to observe Dougherty's Gap.

On the 17th my corps was concentrated in McLemore's Cove, Sheridan being posted at the foot of Stevens' Gap, Davis at Brood's [Brooks'], in front of Dug Gap, Johnson at Pond Spring, in front of Catlett's Gap, in Pigeon Mountain. My instructions were to concentrate my corps between Pond Spring and Gower's, on Chickamauga Creek. It was impossible for me to comply with these orders, as General Thomas' corps occupied the ground. My instructions were subsequently modified.

On the 18th General Lytle arrived with his two brigades, and on the night of the 18th my corps was closed up compactly upon the Fourteenth Corps with the exception of Post's brigade of Davis' division, which was by the direction of the general commanding ordered to hold Stevens' Gap, in Lookout Mountain, at all hazards.

Subsequently Colonel Post was ordered to report to General R. B. Mitchell, commanding the cavalry, and did not report to General Davis until his arrival at Chattanooga on the morning of the 22d of September.

September 19, at 12.15 a. m., I was ordered to move down to Crawfish Spring with the Twentieth Corps as soon as General Thomas' troops were out of the way.

In compliance with this order Johnson's division marched at early dawn, followed by Davis' and Sheridan's divisions. I arrived at Crawfish Spring at an early hour, and reported in person to the general commanding, who ordered me to mass my troops at that place and await further orders. This was done as General Johnson's troops arrived.

At 10.15 a. m. I was ordered to take command of the right and the cavalry, including Negley's division of the Fourteenth Corps, then observing two fords of Chickamauga Creek near Crawfish Spring, one brigade of this division being then engaged with the enemy. The same order directed me to send General Johnson's division forward to Widow Glenn's house to report to General Thomas. Immediately afterward I received instructions to send General Davis' division, also, to the Widow Glenn's house to report to General Thomas or the general commanding. These orders were at once complied with.

By this time the advance of Sheridan's division came up, and as soon as he was posted to support the right of Crittenden's corps at Gordon's Mills, General Negley's division was withdrawn from the fords of Chickamauga Creek, and by the direction of the general commanding ordered to report to General Thomas, which he did. This left me with but one division, Sheridan's, and the cavalry (which had not been heard from) to take care of the right.

Learning from an aide-de-camp of General Wood (Lieutenant Yaryan) that General Wood's troops had been withdrawn from Gordon's Mills, and appreciating the great importance of that point, General Sheridan's division was at once ordered to take position there, and arrived just in time to prevent the enemy from crossing.

Subsequently an order reached me from the general commanding to hold the position at Gordon's Mills.

At 3 p. m. I received an order to send two brigades of Sheridan's division to the Widow Glenn's house, leaving the First Brigade, General Lytle's, at Gordon's Mills; also directing me, should the right be secure, to go forward in person and take command of the troops of the corps already engaged.

General R. B. Mitchell reporting with his cavalry, I was enabled to obey this order at once, arriving upon the field at the close of the engagement of the 19th.

On the 19th General Johnson's division fought near the extreme left of the line of battle. His division fought gloriously, driving the enemy more than a mile, capturing seven of the enemy's guns and a large number of prisoners.

General Davis' division fought on the right of Widow Glenn's house against vastly superior numbers, maintaining the conflict gallantly until near nightfall, when it was relieved by Bradley's brigade, of Sheridan's division, which was hastily thrown forward and gallantly drove the enemy from the open ground and across the Chattanooga and La Fayette road, after a sanguinary engagement, recapturing the Eighth Indiana Battery, which had been previously captured by the enemy, and capturing also a large number of prisoners belonging to Hood's division, of Longstreet's corps. Darkness coming on the battle closed.

At midnight of the 19th of September I received the following order:

HEADQUARTERS DEPARTMENT OF THE CUMBERLAND,
Widow Glenn's, September 19, 1863—11.45 a. m.

Major-General McCook,
Commanding Twentieth Army Corps:

The general commanding directs you as soon as practicable after the receipt of this order to post your command so as to form the right of the new battle front, and hold this place. Leave your outposts and grand guard where they now are till they are driven in by the enemy, when they will fall back on the main body of your command, contesting the ground inch by inch.

Very respectfully,

J. A. GARFIELD,
Brigadier-General, and Chief of Staff.

The date of the above order should be read 11.45 p. m.

This order was strictly complied with. Lytle's brigade, of Sheridan's division, was posted on the strong position in rear of Glenn's house, Sheridan's other two brigades were posted on very strong ground to the right and rear of this position. Davis' division, consisting of two small brigades, was posted to the left and rear of this position, in reserve, his left resting on the right of Crittenden's corps. These movements were all completed by daylight of the 20th, when the general commanding visited my position in person. Johnson's division was still retained near the extreme left of the line of battle and not under my immediate orders.

At 6 a. m. of the 20th Col. J. T. Wilder, Seventeenth Indiana, commanding brigade of mounted infantry, reported in person to me, stating that he had with his troops been ordered to join my command and receive orders from me, also stating that he had two regiments armed with the Spencer rifle posted in the woods on the right of Negley's position, which was to the left and front of General Lytle's position. The remainder of Colonel Wilder's command, with its artillery, was posted on strong ground immediately to Sheridan's right.

At about 7 a. m. the following was received :

> HEADQUARTERS DEPARTMENT OF THE CUMBERLAND,
> *McDonald's, September 20—6.35 a. m.*
>
> Major-General McCOOK,
>   *Commanding Twentieth Army Corps:*
>
>   General Negley's division has been ordered to General Thomas' ieft.   The general commanding directs you to fill the space left vacant by his removal, if practicable. The enemy appears to be moving toward our left.
>   Very respectfully, your obedient servant,
>
>   J. A. GARFIELD,
>   *Brigadier-General, and Chief of Staff.*

Immediately upon receipt of this order, Major-General Sheridan and myself rode to the position vacated by General Negley's division. We found nearly all this space already occupied by General Wood's division.   He informed me that his left rested on General Brannan's right, and that his orders were to close up on General Brannan.

Discovering that a portion of the rude barricades on Wood's right was not occupied by our troops, I ordered General Sheridan to bring forward one of his brigades to fill up the space between Wood's left and Wilder.

On turning from this position I met General Davis' division marching toward and about 100 yards from the vacant barricades on Wood's right, he informing me that he had been ordered there by General Rosecrans.   Seeing his position and knowing the advantage of occupying the barricades at once, I directed him to place one brigade there, holding the other in reserve.

On the arrival of the brigade from Sheridan's division it was posted in column on Davis' right and rear as his support.   Davis' instructions were to keep well closed up to the left.

These instructions being just completed, the following order was received :

> HEADQUARTERS DEPARTMENT OF THE CUMBERLAND,
> *In the Field, September 20, 1863—10.10 a. m.*
>
> Major-General McCOOK,
>   *Commanding Twentieth Army Corps:*
>
>   General Thomas is being heavily pressed on the left.   The general commanding directs you to make immediate disposition to withdraw the right so as to spare as much force as possible to re-enforce Thomas.   The left must be held at all hazards even if the right is withdrawn wholly back to the present left.   Select a good position back this way and be ready to start re-enforcements to Thomas at a moment's warning.
>
>   J. A. GARFIELD,
>   *Brigadier-General, and Chief of Staff.*

Within five minutes after the receipt of the above order, and instructions given to carry it out, the following order was received :

> HEADQUARTERS DEPARTMENT OF THE CUMBERLAND,
> *In the Field, September 20, 1863—10.30 a. m.*
>
> Major-General McCOOK,
>   *Commanding Twentieth Army Corps:*
>
>   The general commanding directs you to send two brigades of General Sheridan's division at once and with all possible dispatch to support General Thomas, and send the third brigade as soon as the lines can be drawn in sufficiently.   March them as rapidly as you can without exhausting the men.   Report in person to these headquarters as soon as your orders are given in regard to Sheridan's movement.
>   Have you any news from Colonel Post?
>
>   J. A. GARFIELD,
>   *Brigadier-General, and Chief of Staff.*

This order was executed at once.   Two brigades of Sheridan's division, Lytle's and Walworth's, were taken from the extreme right, and were moving at the double-quick to the support of General Thomas. Simultaneously with this movement, and much to my surprise, Wood's division left the position it held in line of battle on Davis' left, marching by the left flank, leaving a wide gap in the line of battle. An attempt was made by General Davis to fill up the space thus vacated. Buell's brigade, of Wood's division, had scarcely marched more than its length when a most furious and impetuous assault was made by the enemy, in overwhelming numbers, on this portion of the line, the enemy's lines of battle extending from beyond Brannan's right to a point far to the right of the Widow Glenn's house, and in front of the strong positions just abandoned by General Sheridan's two brigades.

To resist this attack I had but two brigades of Davis' division (numbering about 1,200 men), and Colonel Laiboldt's brigade, of Sheridan's division, as a support. Finding the enemy pouring through the interval between Davis and Brannan, Lytle's and Walworth's brigades were deflected from their line of march to the left, and ordered to assist in resisting the enemy.

Colonels Wilder and Harrison, with their commands, closed in on Sheridan's right as speedily as possible, and did good service. General Davis' command, being overwhelmed by numbers, was compelled to abandon its position in order to save itself from complete annihilation or capture. Laiboldt's troops, moving up to Davis' support, met with a similar fate.

The other two brigades of Sheridan's division were illy prepared to meet such an attack. They struggled nobly, and for a time checked the enemy in their immediate front, but the position being turned far to the left they were compelled to withdraw from the unequal contest.

It was thus that these five brigades of the Twentieth Corps were cut off and separated from the remainder of the Army of the Cumberland. No troops fought with more heroism or suffered greater losses than these five small brigades, their loss being over 40 per cent. of the number engaged in killed and wounded.

In regard to the numbers of the enemy that attacked on the right I can make no estimate. General Sheridan captured prisoners from five different rebel divisions.

The Fifty-first Illinois, of Walworth's brigade, captured the colors of the Twenty-fourth Alabama.

The troops of Generals Sheridan and Davis' divisions were rallied a short distance in rear of the line of battle and marched toward Rossville to endeavor to form a junction with the troops under General Thomas. Their presence was reported to General Thomas by my chief of staff, Lieutenant-Colonel Thruston.

These troops were placed in position by order of General Thomas, on the road leading from the battle-field to Rossville. During the night they withdrew to Rossville with the remainder of the army. The Second Division of the Twentieth Corps, under General R. W. Johnson, fell back to Rossville with the Fourteenth Corps, Willich's brigade forming the rear guard.

On the night of September 20 the Twentieth Army Corps was united in good order at Rossville.

On the morning of the 21st, a short time after daylight, the corps was again put in line of battle, the left resting on Mission Ridge, covering the Crawfish Spring road, the right extending toward Chattanooga Creek and Lookout Mountain.

The corps remained in this position until 2 a. m. on the morning of the 22d of September, when it was withdrawn to Chattanooga with the rest of the army.

Since arriving at Chattanooga the Twentieth Corps has been engaged in performing heavy guard duty and erecting strong lines of intrenchments, which, in my opinion, can only be taken by regular approaches.

My thanks are due to Col. Joseph C. McKibbin, Capt. A. S. Burt, Capt. R. S. Thoms, and Lieut. George Burroughs, of General Rosecrans' staff, for valuable assistance in rallying the portions of Sheridan's and Davis' divisions which had been overwhelmed.

Brig. Gen. J. St. C. Morton, chief engineer of the Army of the Cumberland, being separated from his chief, reported to me for duty.

After ascertaining that the center of our line had been broken, my first object was to endeavor to find the general commanding to ascertain to what point he wished the rallied troops marched. Failing to find the general and believing that an efficient stand could not be made by the army until it reached Chattanooga, the firing on the left retiring toward Rossville, from the statements of General Rosecrans' guides, and from observations by General Morton, I was satisfied that the enemy was endeavoring to cut our army off from Rossville. At this juncture, Lieut. Col. Lyne Starling, of General Crittenden's staff, rode up and reported to me that his chief had gone to Chattanooga to report to General Rosecrans. I then decided to report to General Rosecrans at once for instructions as my last order from his headquarters required.

Finding the general commanding at Chattanooga, he directed me to go out on the road to Rossville, collecting all the troops possible, and report to General Thomas.

Leaving Chattanooga at midnight I arrived at Rossville at about 4 a. m. on the morning of the 21st, when the line of battle above referred to was formed, and strong barricades erected.

The conduct of the troops of the Twentieth Corps was everything that could be expected of men.

During the two days' battle Johnson's division fought on the left, separated from the corps. All acknowledge the gallantry of his division. He never attacked that he was not successful, and the enemy never assaulted him without being handsomely repulsed. I depend upon General Thomas and the official reports to do this gallant division justice.

The troops of Sheridan's and Davis' divisions, behaved with great courage, never yielding except to overwhelming numbers when it would have been suicidal to have contested the ground longer.

To the families of the heroic dead the sympathies of the nation are due. Such names as Lytle, Heg, Baldwin, brigade commanders, Colonels Alexander, Gilmer, McCreery, and many other distinguished field and line officers, who fell upon this memorable field, will make a brilliant page in our history as a nation.

These expressions should also extend to the many non-commissioned officers and privates who gave their lives in defense of their country and flag.

To Maj. Gen. P. H. Sheridan, commanding Third Division ; Brig. Gen. R. W. Johnson, commanding Second Division ; Brig. Gen. Jeff. C. Davis, commanding First Division of the Twentieth Corps, my thanks are due for their earnest co-operation and devotion to duty.

Major-General Sheridan is commended to his country.   Brigadier-Generals Johnson and Davis are commended to their country, and recommended to my superiors for promotion.

Brig. Gen. August Willich, commanding First Brigade, Second Division, and Col. W. W. Berry, Fifth Kentucky Volunteers, commanding Third Brigade, are strongly recommended by General Johnson for promotion.

Col. L. P. Bradley, Fifty-first Illinois, commanding Third Brigade, of Third Division, and Col. Bernard Laiboldt, Second Missouri Volunteers, commanding Second Brigade, Third Division, are strongly recommended for promotion by General Sheridan.

It affords me pleasure to add my testimony as to the gallantry of these distinguished soldiers, and commend them to my superiors for promotion.

The Twentieth Army Corps, during the two days' battle, lost five pieces of artillery and captured seven from the enemy, also retaking the Eighth Indiana Battery lost on Saturday.

Two guns lost by Johnson's division were so disabled by shot and the killing of horses that it was impossible to remove them.

Davis' division did not lose a gun or wagon during the conflict.

To my staff, Lieut. Col. G. P. Thruston, assistant adjutant-general and chief of staff ; Maj. Caleb Bates, aide-de-camp ; Capt. B. D. Williams, aide-de-camp ; Capt. F. J. Jones, aide-de-camp ; Capt. J. H. Fisher, volunteer aide-de-camp ; Lieut. Col. H. N. Fisher, assistant inspector-general ; Lieut. Col. J. F. Boyd, quartermaster ; Lieut. Col. G. W. Burton, commissary of subsistence ; Maj. G. A. Kensel, chief of artillery ; Capt. A. C. McClurg, acting assistant adjutant-general and ordnance officer ; Capt. I. C. McElfatrick, topographical engineer ; Surg. J. Perkins, medical director ; Capt. A. T. Snodgrass, provost-marshal, my thanks are due for their devotion to duty, gallantry in action, and intelligence on the field.

Throughout the entire campaign, since the corps left Stevenson, the Thirty-ninth Indiana Mounted Infantry, under its efficient commander, Col. T. J. Harrison, has performed the most arduous and important service.   On the morning of September 20, when the enemy was endeavoring to turn our extreme right, this fine regiment made a most gallant charge, driving the enemy several hundred yards and inflicting terrible punishment upon them.

The brigade of Colonel Wilder charged the rebel lines at the same time very handsomely, capturing nearly 200 prisoners.

I desire also to speak in terms of the highest commendation of the conduct of my escort from the Second Kentucky Cavalry, commanded by Lieutenant Batman, and of the provost guard attached to corps headquarters, and under command of Captain Richards, of the Eighty-first Indiana Volunteers.

The signal corps, under Lieut. B. R. Wood, jr., has also been useful and efficient during the entire campaign.

For particular instances of individual bravery I refer you to the inclosed reports of division and brigade commanders.

A list of killed and wounded and missing will be forwarded as soon as it is completed.

All of which is respectfully submitted.

A. McD. McCOOK,
Maj. Gen. of Vols., Comdg. Twentieth Army Corps.

Brig. Gen. JAMES A. GARFIELD,
Chief of Staff.

HEADQUARTERS TWENTIETH ARMY CORPS,
Chattanooga, Tenn., October 2, 1863.

GENERAL : I have the honor to submit the following statement showing the casualties* of the Twentieth Army Corps during the late battles, also the number of rebel prisoners captured by the corps :

[Command.]	Commissioned officers.				Enlisted men.				Aggregate.	Rebel prisoners captured.
	Killed.	Wounded.	Missing.	Total.	Killed.	Wounded.	Missing.	Total.		
First Division............										
First Brigade					1	5	19	25	25	48
Second Brigade............	4	27	13	44	46	276	287	609	653	2
Third Brigade	8	30	5	43	57	484	110	651	694	6
Total....................	12	57	18	87	104	765	416	1,285	1,372	56
Second Division..........	1			1			2	2	3	64
First Brigade.............	7	15	3	25	47	340	110	497	522	169
Second Brigade.............	3	17	28	48	23	184	283	490	538	300
Third Brigade.............	4	24		28	50	421	67	538	566	63
Total........	15	56	31	102	120	945	462	1,527	1,629	596
Third Division...............										5
First Brigade...	4	20	5	29	45	236	171	452	481	50
Second Brigade.............	2	16	13	31	37	180	241	458	489	
Third Brigade.............	7	19	10	36	57	241	213	511	547	17
Total....................	13	55	28	96	139	657	625	1,421	1,517	72
Grand total.............	40	168	77	285	363	2,367	1,503	4,233	4,518	724

I am, general, very respectfully, your obedient servant,
A. McD. McCOOK,
Major-General.

Brig. Gen. JAMES A. GARFIELD,
Chief of Staff.

ADDENDA.†

HEADQUARTERS DEPARTMENT OF THE CUMBERLAND,
Chattanooga, Tenn., October 3, 1863.

Major-General McCook :

I have received your letter‡ inclosing and calling my attention to a newspaper paragraph which says that in my official dispatches I attribute our failure to overthrow the enemy in the battle of Chickamauga to your disobedience of my orders. I take pleasure in saying to you that no official or other dispatches of mine have warranted a charge of disobedience of orders by you on either of the days of the battle of Chickamauga.

Very respectfully, your obedient servant,
W. S. ROSECRANS,
Major-General.

---

* See revised statement, p. 173.
†See also record of Court of Inquiry, p. 930.
‡ Not found.

No. 83.

Report of Surg. Jabez Perkins, Tenth Kentucky Infantry, Acting Medical Director.

HEADQUARTERS TWENTIETH ARMY CORPS,
MEDICAL DIRECTOR'S OFFICE,
Chattanooga, October 1, 1863.

SIR: I have the honor to transmit the following report of field operations in the medical department of Twentieth Army Corps during the campaign that recently terminated in the battle of Chickamauga.

We left Stevenson, Ala., on the 2d day of September last, with 105 available ambulances and 8 wagon loads of reserve medical and hospital supplies. Among these were 12 hospital tents entire, which I procured of the post quartermaster at Stevenson, our former supply having been exhausted in the organization of a general hospital at Tullahoma in pursuance of orders from the medical director of the department.

On the eve of starting from Stevenson an order was issued from corps headquarters, without my knowledge or consent, limiting the amount of medical and hospital supplies to be carried by each regiment to 500 pounds. On learning the fact I procured such modification of the order as permitted the regular hospital wagons, of which we had 11 in the corps, to be taken along with their contents unreduced, and also 1 additional wagon to each division for the transportation of such supplies as, in the judgment of the division medical directors, were most needed.

The health of our troops on starting was good, considering the season and locality. Malarial fevers prevailed to some extent, but they were generally of a mild character.

The First and Second Divisions crossed the Tennessee River at Caperton's Ferry, 4 miles from Stevenson, and the Third at Bridgeport, 12 miles above.

The former arrived at Valley Head on September 4, at which place they were joined by the Third Division on the morning of September 10.

The command had just received orders to cross Lookout Mountain, and as an early engagement with the enemy was deemed probable, I ordered the sick to be left at Valley Head, where a wagon train was parked, and Colonel Post's brigade left as a guard. Such cases as were likely to be protracted were subsequently sent by supply trains to Stevenson, and the remainder came forward with Colonel Post's brigade and joined their command at this place September 23.

On the morning of September 10 we ascended Lookout Mountain, crossed over into Shinbone Valley, and camped near Alpine, Ga.

On the 14th we recrossed Lookout Mountain and passed down Will's Valley to Stevens' Gap, where we again crossed the mountain and joined General Thomas' command on the 16th, at Pond Spring.

On the morning of the 19th the entire corps moved forward on the Rossville road, about 8 miles, in the direction of Chattanooga, where they were ordered into line of battle, preparatory to a general engagement, which opened on our left about 11 a. m.

In the disposition of troops the Twentieth Corps was divided, the Second Division being posted on the extreme left of our army and the First and Third on the right.

The wounded of the Second Division were removed to a temporary hospital immediately in their rear, and those of the First and Third to the vicinity of Crawfish Spring, on the right and rear of our line of battle. At this point we occupied a large brick building, with a number of outhouses, for hospital purposes, and to these were added such hospital tents as were in our possession.

In addition to the wounded of the Twentieth Corps a large portion of those from the Fourteenth were brought here, it being the nearest point at which they could obtain water.

By 8 o'clock in the evening every place of shelter was full, and a large number were yet unprovided for. The night was extremely cold for the season, yet those compelled to remain out were rendered comparatively comfortable by large fires and such bedding as we could command. An abundance of nourishment, in the form of beef soup, coffee, &c., was provided for all, and their wounds were dressed as rapidly as was possible under the circumstances.

Our wounded at the Second Division hospital were well cared for during the night, but soon after the battle was renewed, on the morning of the 20th, our forces on the left were compelled to fall back, and it became evident that the hospital would fall into the hands of the enemy. Dr. Schussler, acting medical director of the division, immediately ordered all his available ambulances to be filled with such cases as were transportable, and sent in the direction of Chattanooga. Those who were able to do so walked to a place of temporary safety, while about 40 of the more severely wounded fell into the hands of the enemy.

About 1 o'clock of the same day, our right having given way, the enemy placed themselves between us and our hospitals at Crawfish Spring.

General Mitchell with a large cavalry force was guarding the spring, but it was evident that he would be compelled to abandon the position. I was on the left at the time and cut off by the enemy from our hospitals on the right. Surgeons Waterman and Griffiths, however, made their arrangements as judiciously and as rapidly as possible for leaving, and Colonel Boyd, our corps quartermaster, being present, with commendable promptness collected a large number of empty wagons, which, having been partly filled with straw, were, with the available ambulances, loaded with wounded and conducted across Missionary Hills to the Lookout Valley road, and thence to Chattanooga.

About 250 men were left in hospitals occupied by the First and Third Divisions, but many of them were from the Fourteenth Corps.

Our forces, after giving way on the right and center, fell back in confusion for some distance; but they were finally rallied, and the reserve, under General Granger, coming up about that time, the enemy were again held in check, and severe fighting continued until dark. The First and Third Divisions, however, of the Twentieth Corps were not again engaged. The Second Division was engaged during the evening, and such of the wounded as we had the means of removing were sent to Rossville, 4 miles in the rear, and from thence to Chattanooga the next morning.

During the night our forces fell back on Rossville, thus leaving the entire field, and with it our dead and the greater part of the more severely wounded, in the hands of the enemy.

The field on which occurred the greater part of the fighting is slightly rolling and covered with timber.

Artillery entered somewhat extensively into the battle, but the fighting was mostly done with musketry at short range and with conical leaden bullets.

Judging from my own observation I would say that the proportion of slight wounds is greater than usually occurs.

We left with our wounded 11 medical officers, with the necessary medical supplies and about 3,000 rations.

We lost during the battle 14 ambulances and all the hospital tents in the reserve supply, with 5 belonging to the First and 2 to the Third Division, left at Crawfish Spring. Besides the hospital tents, the only issues on the field from the corps supplies were 250 tin cups, 250 tin plates, 250 table spoons, and 100 woolen blankets. The balance was brought to Chattanooga.

During the night of the 21st our army fell back to Chattanooga, at which place, in pursuance of orders from the medical director of the department, division hospitals have been established in which such of the wounded as have not been sent to the rear are now being treated, and are generally doing well.

The fortunes of war have placed it beyond our power to furnish a report of the killed, and at present it is impossible to procure a list of the wounded that will even approximate accuracy as to numbers. Accompanying this report will be found a reliable list,* as far as it goes, and a more complete one will be forwarded as soon as it can be obtained.

In conclusion, I am desirous of bearing testimony to the zeal and conscientious regard for duty that have characterized the conduct of our medical officers throughout the entire campaign, but more especially during and since the battle. Of the division medical directors of this corps I wish to speak in terms of special commendation, as very much of the good that we have been able to accomplish is due to the prompt and efficient manner in which they have performed their duties.

Many of the regimental surgeons and assistant surgeons are deserving of special notice, for which I beg leave to refer you to the reports of the division medical directors, which are herewith transmitted.

Very respectfully, your obedient servant,

J. PERKINS,
Surg. 10th Regt. Ky. Vol. Inf., Act. Med. Dir., 20th A. C.
Surg. G PERIN, U. S. Army,
Medical Director, Dept. of the Cumberland.

No. 84.

Report of Brig. Gen. Jefferson C. Davis, U. S. Army, commanding First Division.

HDQRS. FIRST DIVISION, TWENTIETH ARMY CORPS,
Chattanooga, Tenn., September 28, 1863.

COLONEL : The following report of the operations of this division since breaking up camp on the Big Crow Creek, near Stevenson, Ala., August 28, 1863, is respectfully submitted for the information and consideration of the corps commander :

On the morning of the 28th ultimo, in accordance with instructions, the Third Brigade, commanded by Col. Hans C. Heg, Fifteenth

---

* See revised statement, p. 173.

Wisconsin Volunteer Infantry, was ordered to move forward as an escort to the pontoon train intended to establish the bridge to be thrown across the Tennessee River at Caperton's Ferry at daylight on the morning of the 29th, under the personal supervision of the corps commander. This brigade crossed in the boats and effected a successful landing on the opposite bank of the river. The work of constructing the bridge was at once commenced, and in a few hours the entire brigade with its baggage was crossed and encamped at night on the summit of Sand Mountain, 5 miles from the river, at the fork of the Trenton and Winston roads. The energy and gallantry exhibited by the troops on this occasion were highly commendable, and have been specially noticed by both the department and corps commanders.

The Second Brigade, commanded by Brig. Gen. W. P. Carlin, moved at an early hour on the morning of the 29th to Caperton's Ferry, and on the 30th ascended the mountain and joined the Third Brigade. The First Brigade, commanded by Col. P. Sidney Post, Fifty-ninth Illinois Volunteer Infantry, following the Second Brigade, went into camp on the evening of the 30th.

The division remained in camp at this point until the morning of September 2, during which time reconnoitering and working parties were sent out on the different roads to ascertain their practicability and prepare them for our advance. Resuming the march at an early hour on the 2d instant, the whole division moved on the road leading to Rome, Ga., via Winston's, and went into camp at the foot of the mountain 3½ miles from Winston's.

The division remained in this camp until the afternoon of the 4th, when it moved across Valley Head and went into camp at Winston's, taking possession of and picketing the gap and roads over Lookout Mountain at that place.

During the night of the 8th and early on the morning of the 9th the Cavalry Corps, under command of Major-General Stanley, ascended Lookout Mountain and moved to the front with the object of making a reconnaissance in the direction of Alpine and Summerville.

In obedience to orders from General McCook, I moved forward with the Second and Third Brigades in support of this movement, leaving the First Brigade behind to hold the mountain pass at Winston's, and to guard the baggage train of both corps ordered to be left at that place.

After ascending the mountain in compliance with instructions, Heg's brigade was ordered to march across the mountain and take possession of Neal's Gap, on the southeast side of Lookout Mountain, while Carlin's followed the main cavalry column and encamped at the base of the mountain near Alpine, Ga.

During the night it was ascertained that General McCook's whole corps would be concentrated at this point, and after consultation with General Stanley as to its propriety, I ordered Colonel Heg to move from Neal's Gap at once and report to me at Henderson's Gap. This movement was made on a mountain road leading direct from Neal's to Henderson's Gap by the succeeding forenoon.

September 10 the corps commander arrived at Henderson's Gap, bringing with him Generals Johnson's and Sheridan's divisions, and the whole remained in bivouac until the morning of the 13th, at which time the whole corps commenced its retrograde march to join General Thomas, near Stevens' Gap. The greater part of the day was occupied in getting the artillery and baggage trains up the mountain.

On the morning of the 14th the division following General Johnson's crossed Lookout Mountain, and went into camp at Long's Spring, in Valley Head, 4 miles in advance of Winston's.   In the afternoon of the 15th I received orders to reascend Lookout Mountain and proceed to Stevens' Gap by the most direct road to be found on the mountain.   Three days' rations of provisions were issued to the command during the night, and the artillery taken up the mountain.

The march was commenced at an early hour in the morning, and Stevens' Gap reached about dark, after a hard day's march of 25 miles, 15 of which was without water.   During the night I received orders from General McCook, who had already established his headquarters at the foot of the mountain, to move with my command in the morning down the mountain and report to him, which I did about 10 a. m.   The signal officers at this time reported the enemy advancing toward Stevens' Gap in heavy force.   The general commanding the corps immediately gave orders for the proper disposition of the troops to receive an attack.   After a few hours spent in awaiting their approach, it was ascertained that no serious attack would probably be made and the division marched for Pond Spring, at which place it was intended to take position for the night, closely following the baggage train of General Brannan's division.   On arriving near Pond Spring, however, its destination was changed, and, under the personal direction of the corps commander, moved back to Brooks' farm, and took a strong position in front of Dug and Blue Bird Gaps.   In this position it was supported by General Sheridan's division, on the right, at Bailey's Cross-Roads.   The division held this position until late in the evening of the 18th, when it moved and went into camp 1½ miles in advance of Pond Spring.

During the night instructions were received to follow the division of General Johnson, which was ordered to the support of General Thomas, whose corps then formed our extreme left.

The column had advanced but a few miles when the roar of artillery in the direction of Thomas' corps announced the opening of the coming struggle.

As the fire increased and gave assurances of a general engagement, the troops closed their ranks and moved steadily forward with that firm step and soldierly alacrity which characterizes the actions of determined men on the eve of battle.

On approaching the vicinity of the battle-field I received orders from the corps commander to move forward and to report my command to Generals Rosecrans or Thomas for orders.

Arriving near Widow Glenn's, at whose house General Rosecrans had established his headquarters, I reported my command ready for action.   The rapid and increasing fire of musketry gave indications of the necessity of re-enforcements being pushed forward, and General Rosecrans ordered me to place one of my batteries in position on a commanding point in front of his headquarters, and to move forward as speedily as possible in the direction of the heaviest firing, and to make an attack with a view, if possible, to turn the enemy's left flank.   A few minutes' march brought the head of my column to the right of our lines, and Heg's brigade was at once formed into line of battle and ordered to advance and form on the right of our lines then engaged.

The enemy, in strong force, was at once met, and both sides opened fire with great fierceness and determination.

Carlin's brigade was immediately deployed on Heg's right, and his left regiments became at once engaged in the conflict.   Carlin's right rested in a small open field, which presented an admirable position for a light battery, and the Second Minnesota was rapidly brought into position a little in rear of our line of infantry, which was soon drawn back so as to give as free range as possible to the guns.   The enemy soon showed himself in heavy force on our front, and was evidently making an effort to turn our flank with a view to getting possession of the road leading to Gordon's Mills, over which a part of the troops of General Crittenden's command had yet to pass in reaching the battle-field.

My lines of infantry as now formed ran through a thick oak forest, a few hundred yards in advance of and parallel to the road leading to Gordon's Mills, my right a little refused.   The action commenced about half past 12 p. m., and was sustained with great stubbornness on both sides for a half to three-quarters of an hour, when Heg reported his left as being very hard pressed and asked for re-enforcements, informing me at the same time that he had ordered his reserve regiment into the front line and was still unable to hold his position much longer.   I immediately ordered Carlin's reserve regiment, which proved to be the Twenty-first Illinois, to his support.

This distinguished regiment moved promptly into position under its indomitable leader, Colonel Alexander, and engaged with great spirit in the contest then pending and of doubtful issue.   My lines thus arranged, with the admirable position taken, and efficient working of the Second Minnesota Battery on my right, I was enabled to repel the repeated assaults of the enemy, and to prevent him from flanking our position, until about 4 p. m., when re-enforcements arrived.   Colonel Harker's brigade, of General Wood's division, first arrived and was quickly formed in line, and moved forward in support of my troops.

Generals Crittenden, Wood, and Sheridan arrived at this time upon the field, followed by their respective commands.   As soon as fresh troops could be placed in position to do so, my command was relieved from further participation in this part of the engagement, and ordered into bivouac a few hundred yards in rear of the field they had held for so many hours against almost overwhelming odds, over one-third of their number having fallen, killed or wounded, among whom was the gallant leader of the Third Brigade, Colonel Heg.

The approach of night was fast bringing a close to the contest, and I ordered my troops to stack their arms, in order that they might get refreshments and replenish their exhausted cartridge boxes.

About 3 o'clock in the morning of the 20th, in compliance with orders from the corps commander, I ordered my command under arms and moved it to the forks of the road in rear of the Widow Glenn's house, where it remained awaiting orders until daylight. My position by this time having been determined upon, I at once formed my lines and put my batteries in position on a high wooded hill a few hundred yards north of the road leading to Crawfish Spring.

General Lytle's brigade, of General Sheridan's division, was formed immediately in my front a short distance in advance of the base of the hill.

Remaining in this position until near 10 o'clock, I received orders from General McCook (through Captain McClurg) to move to my left and close upon General Crittenden's right.   This movement was immediately commenced, and I soon discovered that General Crittenden's troops were moving to the front, a fact of which I had not been informed. Closing my left on General Van Cleve's right I moved forward, conforming my lines to his, until the open field a few hundred yards in front of my original position was reached, when I received orders from General Rosecrans, through Captain Morrison, of my staff, to move forward and take position along the skirt of timber bordering the field in my front. On reaching this point I received orders from General McCook to move forward into the timber and take position on General Wood's right, occupying a line of rude breastworks erected by troops previously occupying this position.

Carlin's brigade was ordered to and at once took position on the right of Colonel Buell's brigade, then forming the right of General Wood's division.

Heg's brigade, now commanded by Colonel Martin of the Eighth Kansas Volunteer Infantry, took position, in accordance with my instructions, in rear of Carlin's brigade as a reserve.

Colonel Buell at this time informed me that he had just received orders to move to his left in order to close up with our lines in that direction. Colonel Buell's brigade commenced the movement, and, in compliance with orders from General McCook, I directed Martin to move his brigade into the position thus being vacated. This brigade moved promptly into position, but had scarcely reached the line when the enemy, advancing in heavy force, opened fire on its and Carlin's front. These brigades received the fire with veteran coolness and returned it with deadly effect for several rounds, and in some instances the musket was used in beating back the enemy before the position was yielded.

The sudden withdrawal of troops from my left and the absence of any support on my right, just as the attack was being made, made my position little better than an outpost and perfectly untenable against the overwhelming force coming against it. Nothing but precipitate flight could save my command from annihilation or capture. Observing the critical condition of my flanks I rode up to Colonel Laiboldt, commanding one of General Sheridan's brigades posted in an open field a few hundred yards to my rear and right, and informed him that if he was there for the purpose of supporting my troops it must be done immediately. He at once commenced deploying his troops to form line on my right, but before the movement was fully completed his brigade received a heavy attack from that part of the enemy's line which had passed thus far unopposed around my right flank. My troops were by this time compelled to abandon their position, falling back rapidly. A few hundred yards brought them into the open field and exposed them to the full effect of the pursuing enemy's fire.

Laiboldt's brigade did not seem sufficiently strong to check the enemy's advance, and a general rout of our troops on the right was manifest.

Ineffectual attempts were made by the different commanders to reform the lines on a rocky ridge in the open field a few hundred yards to the rear.

The heavy loss sustained by my troops in the two days' conflict, particularly among the commissioned officers, rendered a reformation of my command very difficult, and was only accomplished after falling back to a small farm some 2½ miles to the rear. This place offered a suitable position for the use of artillery, and I ordered one of my batteries to be posted there and the troops to be formed with it. General Negley's division at this time passed to the rear, in the direction of Rossville, and I understand took position at that place.

General Carlin and Colonel Martin had also by this time succeeded in reforming their troops as far as was possible, and reported.

Colonel Ward, commanding the Tenth Ohio Infantry, reported to me with his regiment for duty, and after allowing the men a few minutes to procure water, I ordered them again under arms, and moved for the battle-field, with a view to support General Thomas' corps, which was still maintaining its position. It is proper here to add that several detached battalions and commands reported to me and accompanied my command to the battle-field, making in all a force of 2,500 to 3,000 men.

On arriving near the field, a staff officer from Colonel Post arrived and informed me that his brigade was yet in the vicinity of Crawfish Spring, and would not, as I had anticipated, be able to join me before night.

While in the act of forming my lines near Thomas' right I received information from General Garfield that Thomas was falling back, and orders to repair to Rossville. Following General Johnson's division I arrived and went into bivouac at Rossville about 9 p. m. Thus ended the 20th September and the conflict.

The list of casualties herewith transmitted shows a loss in the division of 1,372 officers and enlisted men in killed, wounded, and missing during the time above described. The loss in the two brigades that participated in the engagement is 1,369 officers and enlisted men killed, wounded, and missing, exceeding 50 per cent. of the number engaged.

The following field officers are reported, as follows:

Col. J. W. S. Alexander, Twenty-first Illinois Volunteers, supposed to be killed.

Lieut. Col. W. E. McMackin, Twenty-first Illinois Volunteers, supposed to be killed.

Col. D. H. Gilmer, Thirty-eighth Illinois Volunteers, supposed to be killed.

Maj. H. N. Alden, Thirty-eighth Illinois Volunteers, wounded, present.

Maj. B. B. McDanald, One hundred and first Ohio, supposed to be killed.

Lieut. Col. John Messer, One hundred and first Ohio, wounded, present.

Col. Hans C. Heg, commanding Third Brigade, killed.

Capt. Henry Hauff, acting assistant adjutant-general, Third Brigade, missing.

Lieut. Col. O. C. Johnson, Fifteenth Wisconsin Volunteers, missing, supposed to be killed.

Maj. Samuel D. Wall, Twenty-fifth Illinois Volunteers, wounded, present.

The heavy list of casualties shows with what determination and pertinacity the battle was contested, and what noble sacrifices our troops will make for their country's preservation and glory.

The reports of the brigade commanders are herewith transmitted and attention called to them for many details necessarily omitted in this report.

In the report of General Carlin I regret to notice a spirit of factious fault finding exhibited, and a mischievous introduction of insinuations and reflections against myself and staff, as well as others, uncalled for and out of place in his report, and which cannot be properly noticed in a report of this kind without lowering its dignity and changing its purport.

This division sustained no loss whatever in artillery or baggage train.

Throughout the entire campaign the efficiency and gallantry of my staff, consisting of Capt. T. W. Morrison, assistant adjutant-general; Capt. T. H. Daily, aide-de-camp; Lieut. F. E. Reynolds, aide-de-camp; Surg. L. D. Waterman, medical director; Capt. W. A. Hotchkiss, chief of artillery; Capt. H. N. Snyder, assistant commissary of musters; Capt. H. W. Hall, inspector; Capt. J. P. Pope, commissary of subsistence; Lieut. J. E. Remington, acting assistant quartermaster; Lieut. J. P. Kuntze, topographical engineer, and Lieut. J. M. Butler, ordnance officer, were well tested, and to them I desire to express my many obligations.

I am, very respectfully, your obedient servant,

JEF. C. DAVIS,
Brigadier-General, Commanding Division.

Lieut. Col. G. P. THRUSTON,
Asst. Adjt. Gen., and Chief of Staff, 20th Army Corps.

[Inclosure No. 1.]

Casualties in the First Division, Twentieth Army Corps, in the engagements of the 19th and 20th of September, 1863.

Command.	Killed.			Wounded.			Missing.			Aggregate.
	Commissioned officers.	Enlisted men.	Total.	Commissioned officers.	Enlisted men.	Total.	Commissioned officers.	Enlisted men.	Total.	
First Brigade.(a)										
22d Indiana Volunteer Infantry		1	1		2	2		4	4	7
59th Illinois Volunteer Infantry					1	1		1	1	2
74th Illinois Volunteer Infantry					1	1		4	4	5
75th Illinois Volunteer Infantry								10	10	10
Total		1	1		4	4		19	19	24
Second Brigade.										
21st Illinois Volunteer Infantry	1	19	20	6	64	70	9	139	148	238
38th Illinois Volunteer Infantry	1	13	14	9	79	88	2	76	78	180
81st Indiana Volunteer Infantry		4	4	4	56	60	2	21	23	87
101st Ohio Volunteer Infantry	2	10	12	7	76	83		51	51	146
Total	4	46	50	26	275	301	13	287	300	651
Third Brigade.										
8th Kansas Volunteer Infantry	3	30	33	8	152	160		25	25	218
15th Wisconsin Volunteer Infantry	2	3	5	6	47	53	4	49	53	111
25th Illinois Volunteer Infantry		10	10	11	160	171	1	23	24	205
35th Illinois Volunteer Infantry	3	14	17	5	125	130		13	13	160
Total	8	57	65	30	484	514	5	110	115	694
Total infantry	12	104	116	56	763	819	18	416	434	1,369
Artillery.										
5th Wisconsin Battery					1	1				1
2d Minnesota Battery				1	1	2				2
8th Wisconsin Battery										
Total artillery				1	2	3				3
Total artillery and infantry	12	104	116	57	765	822	18	416	434	1,372

a The loss in this brigade occurs from picket duty and skirmishing, not being in the battles of the 19th and 20th.

[Inclosure No. 2.]

Return of ordnance and ordnance stores lost and expended in action on the 19th and 20th instant by First Division, Twentieth Army Corps.

[Command.]	Guns, number.	Bayonets, number.	Accouterments, number.	Ammunition, rounds.
Infantry	1,156	1,159	1,159	117,915
Artillery				369
Total	1,156	1,159	1,159	118,284

No. 85.

Report of Capt. William A. Hotchkiss, Second Minnesota Battery, Chief of Artillery.

HDQRS. CHIEF OF ARTY., 1ST DIV., 20TH ARMY CORPS,
Chattanooga, September 26, 1863.

CAPTAIN: I have the honor to report the part taken by the batteries of First Division, Twentieth Army Corps, in the marches and expeditions prior to and during the late battle of the 19th and 20th instant.

The 5th Wisconsin Battery, Captain Gardner commanding, was detached from the division with the First Brigade, on duty at Valley Head, near Mr. Winston's, Ala., and did not arrive in the vicinity of the battle-field until the afternoon of the 20th instant, too late to take part in the action. Following a road near the base of Lookout Mountain, it reached Chattanooga, with Colonel Post's brigade, on the morning of the 22d instant without loss.

The Second Minnesota and Eighth Wisconsin Batteries accompanied the division on all its movements after crossing the Tennessee River, and arrived with it at Widow Glenn's house, near the right of our line of battle, a little after meridian the 19th instant, when, by order of General Davis, I put the Eighth Wisconsin Battery, Lieutenant McLean commanding, in position a little to the right of Mrs. Glenn's house, and followed the division into the field with Second Minnesota Battery, Lieutenant Woodbury commanding. General Davis led his troops by the right flank through a dense woods under a heavy fire, and, regarding the movement and use of artillery at any point where the line of the division was being established impracticable, I reported to the general for further orders, when he directed me to move the battery, with as much speed as possible, to the right and establish it on the first eligible ground that could be found. At the extreme right of the line of the division a small field in front of the enemy's left was found. The battery was promptly brought into position, under a brisk fire from the enemy's skirmishers, and soon drove in not only his skirmishers but his main line. The service the Second Minnesota Battery did at this point was of great importance. Three successive times it prevented the enemy from forming and extending his left with the evident purpose of flanking General Davis' right. Between 4 and 5 p. m., after holding its ground for nearly three hours against a superior force, the division began to fall back, according to my observation, in very good order. I immediately determined to retire the Second Minnesota Battery and a section of an Indiana battery, then on the left of the Minnesota battery, slowly and in line with the troops, about 250 yards across the only open ground in our rear. An unforeseen and very unnecessary circumstance prevented the accomplishment of my purpose. The drivers and men of the section of the Indiana battery above alluded to became panic-stricken, and stampeded with their caissons and gun limbers through the Second Minnesota Battery, endangering the safety of its guns, very nearly causing the loss of the left section. I am indebted to the courage and coolness of Lieutenant Harder for its safety.

After a brief consultation with the lamented Colonel Heg, commanding Third Brigade, I ordered Lieutenant Woodbury to put his guns in position on the right of the new line and again engage the enemy, which was promptly done. A few minutes later Colonel Heg was mortally wounded and Lieutenant Woodbury was disabled by a severe wound in the left arm. About this time General Davis' division was relieved by General Wood, when, in accordance with instructions, I retired the Second Minnesota Battery out of range.

I have heard of a report that an occasional shell from the Second Minnesota Battery wounded men in General Carlin's brigade. Of my own knowledge the statement is unfounded; in fact, in the course of the engagement General Carlin rode up to me, a little to the left and in front of the battery, and stated that he had extended his lines partially across the front of the battery; that his men were occupying an undulation in the ground about 100 yards distant, and remarked, "If your fire is well directed it can do no harm to my troops." I immediately pointed out General Carlin's line to Lieutenant Woodbury, and to each lieutenant commanding sections, and ordered that all firing over them should be at a range not less than 700 or 800 yards; also I rode up to the commanding officer of a battery that had just gone into position on my right and pointed out to him General Carlin's line, and cautioned him against firing into his men. At this juncture the section of the Indiana battery heretofore alluded to commenced firing. I rode up to the lieutenant commanding it, told him our own troops were immediately in front of him, and as, from his position, he could not see the enemy, I ordered him to cease firing. From this time up to the moment the division was retired I remained near the guns of the Second Minnesota Battery, watched closely the movements of the troops in front, and directed the fire of the battery. I repeat, of my own knowledge, not one man of our own was injured by shot or shell from my guns. I did think an occasional shot from other guns lodged in or near our lines, and so reported to a lieutenant of the battery on my right.

Early in the morning of the 20th General Davis was ordered to occupy a position as a reserve, and the Second Minnesota and Eighth Wisconsin Batteries were assigned positions covering the Chattanooga road and did not fire over half a dozen shots during the day. After the divisions of General Davis and General Sheridan had been repulsed, and it had become evident to General Davis that the infantry could not be rallied for the support of his batteries, he ordered them retired out of range of the enemy's guns, himself remaining on the field with the hope that something might still be done to retrieve the fortunes of the right wing. When I drew off my batteries I found the gap on the road leading through the hills to Chattanooga so thoroughly blockaded with batteries and ammunition trains as to (in the confusion) prevent their farther progress. I turned my attention to extricating the artillery from the jam by drawing them out in columns, piece by piece, on either side of the road until I had the satisfaction of seeing every carriage of all kinds in motion. While this was being done one of the enemy's guns was throwing solid shot into the gap. About 300 or 400 yards to the rear 800 or 1,000 men had been collected, for whose support I put one section of the Second Minnesota Battery in position so as to cover the road from the farther advance of the enemy, and remained there myself until General Davis came up and announced his intention to overtake the advance of the scattered troops going to the rear, where he would rally them for the purpose of marching them to the support of General Thomas, who was then holding the enemy in check. In less than two hours General Davis had collected about 1,500 men, with whom and the Eighth Wisconsin Battery he marched toward the front, but night closing in before he could reach the field, in obedience to orders, he countermarched and bivouacked his troops near Rossville about 11 p. m. The Second Minnesota Battery was the only battery of the division that was under fire on the 19th and 20th instant.

The number of casualties were: Wounded, First Lieut. A. Woodbury, severely; Private Fordis Averill, slightly.

The men of the battery without exception behaved well. Lieutenant Woodbury's conduct was particularly commendable.

Respectfully submitted.

WM. AUGUSTUS HOTCHKISS,
Captain and Chief of Arty., 1st Div., 20th Army Corps.

Capt. T. W. Morrison,
Assistant Adjutant-General, First Division.

No. 86.

Report of Col. P. Sidney Post, Fifty-ninth Illinois Infantry, commanding First Brigade.

HDQRS. FIRST BRIG., FIRST DIV., 20TH ARMY CORPS,
Chattanooga, Tenn., September 28, 1863.

CAPTAIN: I have the honor to submit the following report of the operations of the First Brigade, First Division, Twentieth Army Corps, since crossing the Tennessee River:

On the 30th day of August, in compliance with the order of Brigadier-General Davis, commanding division, I crossed the pontoon bridge at Stevenson, and made the laborious march over Sand Mountain, camping September 4 at Valley Head.

On the 9th, the infantry of the Second and Third Brigades having moved forward on Lookout Mountain for the purpose of making a reconnaissance toward Alpine, in accordance with General Davis' instructions to guard and hold the several roads belonging to this mountain pass, I moved the Twenty-second Regiment Indiana Volunteer Infantry, commanded by Col. M. Gooding; the Seventy-fifth Illinois Infantry, commanded by Lieutenant-Colonel Kilgour (Colonel Bennett being at the time sick, though with the regiment), and the Fifty-ninth Regiment Illinois Infantry, commanded by Lieutenant-Colonel Winters, up the mountain and posted them so as to secure all the roads. The Seventy-fourth Regiment Illinois Infantry, commanded by Col. Jason Marsh, remained in the valley guarding the trains and artillery of the division.

At 11 p. m. I received an order from Major-General McCook, Brigadier-General Davis having gone forward with the reconnoitering force, assigning to this brigade "the onerous and important duty of moving all the trains of this corps and the Cavalry Corps to the front."

Major-General Sheridan's ammunition train reached the top of the mountain about dusk the evening of the 10th. I immediately commenced pushing forward the several trains in the order indicated by my letter of instructions. The night was very dark, but by detailing seven companies from my command to assist them, the trains were kept steadily moving forward during the whole night. During the following day and night all the trains of the corps and cavalry cleared the ascent.

Learning from scouts and citizens, and also being warned by a communication from Major-General McCook, that a force of Confederate cavalry was near Lebanon threatening our communication and trains crossing Sand Mountain, I dispatched the Seventy-fifth Regiment of Illinois Infantry toward Stevenson to meet and escort a large cavalry supply train which I had learned was on the way to the front without a guard. This regiment returned on the 13th with the train for which it had been sent, having made, with much endurance and spirit, a march of 28 miles in less than twenty hours, half of the way in the night and over a rough road.

Having been temporarily assigned to the command of Brigadier-General Lytle, I communicated with him in person on the evening of the 15th, and was informed by him that he should leave his position at 3 o'clock the next morning for Dougherty's Gap. I immediately ordered the Fifty-ninth Regiment Illinois Infantry on the mountain to defend the approaches by the Alpine road, which position it reached, near the Falls of Little River, about 1 a. m. of the 16th.

As Brigadier-General Lytle had warned me that the enemy were in some force on the mountain, I moved the Seventy-fifth Regiment Illinois Infantry, now commanded by Col. John E. Bennett, early in the morning to strengthen my force on Little River. During the time that I had been stationed at Valley Head the sick of this corps and of the Cavalry Corps had been constantly accumulating on my hands. Surg. C. N. Ellinwood, Seventy-fourth Regiment Illinois Infantry, acting as brigade surgeon for this brigade, did much to alleviate their condition. Under his supervision a temporary hospital was established, and everything done for their comfort possible under the circumstances. The efforts of Surgeon Ellinwood were such as humanity and professional skill dictate. As many as possible were loaded upon the only supply train which returned to Stevenson.

Having received orders from Major-General McCook to come on as soon as the road was clear, on the morning of the 18th I sent up the ammunition train left with me and the Fifth Wisconsin Battery, commanded by Capt. G. Q. Gardner, leaving such of the sick as had not been sent away to be provided for by Colonel Watkins, commanding a brigade of cavalry still remaining at Valley Head. I reached the top of the mountain with my command at 12 o'clock, and pushed on to within a mile of Stevens' Gap, where I bivouacked at 11 p. m., having marched 23 miles.

At 2 o'clock the next morning I received a communication from Major-General McCook inclosing a letter of instructions from department headquarters directing me to remain at Stevens' Gap and " to hold that position at all hazards, but if compelled to abandon the gap, to retire along the mountain road to Chattanooga, contesting the ground inch by inch." I accordingly made the proper dispositions to hold the mountain pass from whatever direction it might be assailed, and also to afford protection to the large cavalry train collected there.

About 4 o'clock of the morning of the 20th I received an order from Major-General McCook to move forward to the battle-field by way of Crawfish Spring, and to send all the trains by the Mountain road to Chattanooga. I put the trains in motion immediately, sending with them 67 prisoners of war, under charge of Sergeant McCune, commanding the provost guard of this brigade. At the same time I passed down the mountain, and, procuring some guides, I pressed forward with all possible speed toward Crawfish Spring. As I advanced the cannonading in my front and attacks upon my front and flank warned me of my critical position and the danger of being cut off from the main body of the army. I thoroughly informed myself concerning all roads and by-ways leading back into the Valley of Chattanooga Creek by which I could reach the army under shelter of Lookout Mountain if the enemy should be found in such force in my front as to render it impossible to cut my way through.

At the Ringgold road I found the enemy apparently in considerable force. I caused a heavy line of skirmishers to be deployed, under charge of Capt. Robert Hale, provost-marshal on my staff, and drove them from the front up the road leading toward Ringgold, while at the same time throwing my advance guard well out, I kept my column moving forward toward Crawfish Spring as rapidly as possible. The skirmishers on my right flank engaged and kept the enemy at bay, following the column in succession as it passed, and in this manner we reached Crawfish Spring, where I reported to Brig. Gen. R. B. Mitchell, commanding Cavalry Corps, at 1 o'clock in the afternoon.

My men had borne up under the dust and heat of this rapid march with admirable spirit, and the alacrity and success with which they had contended with the enemy gave promise of what might be expected of them in the contest in which I anticipated soon to lead them.

Brigadier-General Mitchell informed me that all communication was cut off with Major-General McCook's corps, and that it was impossible to move to the point indicated in my orders. He therefore assumed command of my brigade and directed me to take a position to repel an attack which he apprehended on his front. After I had placed my men in position, being extremely anxious to rejoin the division, or, if that should be impossible, at least to inform my division and corps commanders of my arrival at Crawfish Spring, I dispatched Capt. Robert Hale, a resolute and discreet officer, to communicate with you, if possible, in which undertaking you are aware he was quite successful. Brigadier-General Mitchell being fully satisfied that direct communication could not be opened with Major-General McCook's corps, directed me to move back upon Chattanooga Creek along with his corps. We bivouacked near McCulloch's house almost one hour before daylight.

The next morning Brigadier-General Mitchell informed me that he had received orders from department headquarters to retain my brigade, and directed me to take a position with General Crook's division to prevent the enemy coming down the valley. I accordingly placed my men in the most defensible position for the purpose, Captain Gardner's battery covering every approach, and awaited the enemy, who advanced to within a short distance of us but did not attack.

At 1 o'clock the next morning I was ordered by General Mitchell to quietly withdraw my command and to take a position near the cross-road leading to Rossville. I accordingly selected a position admirably adapted for defense, with my left resting upon a mill-pond and my right secured by the steep heights of Lookout Mountain. I remained in this position, the cavalry passing on toward Chattanooga, until General Mitchell, becoming aware that the enemy had penetrated to the mountain in our rear and had possession of the road leading to Chattanooga, ordered us to retire toward that place. We soon found the enemy in considerable force with a battery of artillery commanding the road. I formed my line on the side of the mountain, prepared to contest the farther advance of the enemy and to regain the road. Captain Gardner opened with his entire battery with good effect, and soon succeeded in driving away the enemy's battery and clearing the road.

At this time I received an order from Major-General McCook to retire by the main road to Chattanooga. Knowing that the enemy was in force and had a battery of artillery on the right of the road on which I was to retire, I moved by the left flank on the right of the road while my battery kept the road, being in position to instantly engage him and to protect my artillery. The enemy opened upon us with his artillery, but without effect, and we crossed the bridge over Chattanooga Creek, rejoining the division at 1 o'clock in the afternoon of the 22d.

For three days I had been in close proximity with the enemy's heavy force and in constant danger of being completely cut off, and had marched a distance of 30 miles almost through the enemy's camp, without loss of *matériel* or men. The endurance of my men, their willing and uncomplaining perseverance on this tedious march and during the watchful nights, deserves particular mention. Never have I seen men more desirous of doing their whole duty, and their success was equal to their desire. When I say of the officers that they executed my orders with spirit and in good faith, I say that which expresses that they did their full duty well.

Upon reporting to Brigadier-General Davis, I was ordered to relieve with my command the Third Brigade of his division doing duty upon the skirmish line. During the afternoon and night I thoroughly intrenched my position. Notwithstanding the great fatigue under which the men were suffering, they worked with astonishing alacrity to shelter themselves from the enemy's fire. In the afternoon of the 22d the enemy opened a battery on my left, but a few shots from Lieutenant McKnight's section of Captain Gardner's battery made it necessary for him to withdraw it.

In the afternoon of the 24th, by order of Major-General McCook, a reconnaissance was made for the purpose of ascertaining the strength and character of the force in our front. The Twenty-second Regiment Indiana Infantry and the Seventy-fourth Regiment of Illinois Infantry, under the command of Colonel Gooding, advanced about half a mile, when their skirmishers developed a heavy force of infantry in a defensible position, upon which the reconnoitering force was withdrawn.

Too much praise cannot be awarded to the officers and men of this command for the energy and vigilance which they have constantly exhibited during the laborious operations of the month. I have received the most cordial support at all times from the regimental commanders, and the thorough discipline of Colonel Gooding, the coolness and determination of Colonel Marsh, and the activity and prudence of Colonel Bennett and Lieutenant-Colonel Winters are especially commended. Captain Gardner and his lieutenants have exhibited great zeal and ability in the management of the Fifth Wisconsin Battery. Sergt. Charles Allen, of the Seventy-fourth Regiment Illinois Infantry, in the performance of a delicate and important duty, displayed much tact and gallantry. I am particularly indebted to the several members of my staff for the efficient assistance which they have rendered day and night throughout the campaign.

The conduct of Capt. Samuel West, acting assistant adjutant-general, at all times prompt, able, and discreet, and Capt. Robert Hale, who, with his usual intrepidity, twice succeeded in communicating with you when none of the Cavalry Corps were able to do so, was worthy of their high reputations. Both officers have endeared themselves to the command by their services on other battle-fields, and their behavior, as well as that of Captain Hatch, brigade inspector, and Lieutenant Mason, aide-de-camp, deserves the highest praise.

I inclose a list of the killed, wounded, and missing from the brigade.

I have the honor to be, very respectfully, your obedient servant,

P. SIDNEY POST,
Colonel, Commanding Brigade.

Capt. T. W. MORRISON,
Assistant Adjutant-General, First Division.

[Inclosure.]

List of Casualties in the First Brigade since crossing the Tennessee River.*

Command.a	Killed.		Wounded.		Missing.		Aggregate.
	Enlisted men.	Total.	Enlisted men.	Total.	Enlisted men.	Total.	
5th Wisconsin Battery	.....	.....	1	1	.....	.....	1
22d Indiana Volunteer Infantry	1	1	2	2	4	4	7
59th Illinois Volunteer Infantry	.....	.....	1	1	1	1	2
74th Illinois Volunteer Infantry	.....	.....	1	1	4	4	5
75th Illinois Volunteer Infantry	.....	.....	.....	.....	10	10	10
Total	1	1	5	5	19	19	25

a The loss in the brigade occurs from picket duty and skirmishing, not being in the battles of the 19th and 20th.

* Nominal list omitted.

No. 87.

Report of Lieut. Col. Joshua C. Winters, Fifty-ninth Illinois Infantry.

HDQRS. FIFTY-NINTH REGIMENT ILLINOIS INFANTRY,
Chattanooga, Tenn., September 27, 1863.

SIR: I have the honor to submit the following report of the part taken by the Fifty-ninth Regiment Illinois Infantry in the operations since crossing the Tennessee River:

The regiment left their camp on south side of Tennessee River on Monday, August 31, at 1 p. m., and ascended the Raccoon Mountain; halted at summit and assisted the brigade battery and train to ascend. Then moved forward 4 miles and went into camp. Remained in camp September 1, at which time, by General Orders from corps headquarters, the transportation of the regiment was cut down to 3 wagons.

September 2 crossed Raccoon Mountain and descended into Lookout Valley and went into camp. Remained in camp until 2 p. m. of September 4, when marched 4 miles to Winston's and went into camp. Remained in camp at Winston's until the evening of September 9; then marched to the top of Lookout Mountain, and picketed roads leading to valley until Sunday, September 13, when moved back to Winston's.

Remained in camp at Winston's until 11 p. m. of the 15th of September, when marched again to top of mountain and went into camp at Falls of Little River. Remained in camp until 3 p. m. of September 17, when moved back to old camp on top of mountain.

September 18 marched from camp on top of mountain with balance of brigade; continued march all day and until 11 o'clock at night, when reached Stevens' Gap.

September 19 remained with balance of brigade at Stevens' Gap, guarding roads and train.

September 20 marched with balance of brigade, at 6 a. m., from Stevens' Gap in a northeasterly direction toward battle-field; when within 3 miles of the division hospital established at [the] big springs [Crawfish Spring] were fired upon by the enemy. I immediately deployed Companies H and K as skirmishers, who pressed back the enemy until the brigade and the train had passed. At the hospitals at [the] big springs joined General Mitchell's corps of cavalry, which had been cut off by the enemy from the right of our main army. Formed line of battle to support the cavalry in the attempt to reopen communication, which was, however, abandoned, and at or about 4 p. m. marched from the hospitals, with the balance of brigade and General Mitchell's cavalry, on road to Chattanooga.

September 21 arrived at McCulloch's farm, in Chattanooga Valley, at about 2 a. m., and bivouacked at or about 9 a. m., the brigade and cavalry having been formed in line of battle across the Chattanooga Valley to hold the road leading to Chattanooga. The Fifty-ninth Illinois was placed in reserve formed in close column by division.

September 22, at 2 a. m., marched with balance of brigade 4 miles in the direction of Chattanooga, then halted until about 9 a. m., when again moved forward toward Chattanooga. After marching about 3 miles were attacked by the enemy with infantry, cavalry, and artillery, who were in position on the east side of the road.

The Fifty-ninth moved forward and formed in line of battle on hill-side west of the road fronting the enemy, and supported a section of the Fifth Wisconsin Battery which took position on hill above and commenced firing upon the enemy's battery.

The Fifty-ninth was subsequently moved back on line with balance of brigade on second range of hills, and remained until the enemy's batteries were silenced, when again moved on to the road, formed line of battle, and moved about 300 yards in the direction of the enemy, and remained in position until the battery and General Mitchell's cavalry crossed the bridge over Chattanooga Creek; then the regiment moved back upon the road and crossed the bridge and came within the lines of our main army. The regiment was placed in position on the outposts facing the Chattanooga Creek to the south and east, and was engaged in building breastworks until noon of September 23, when the regiment was moved to the left facing the east. Engaged in building breastworks on the east front balance of the 23d and all of the 24th.

September 25 the regiment moved back to the second line of fortifications, and have been engaged in building earth-works and other fortifications up to this date.

On the 20th instant, while on march from Stevens' Gap, Private Andrew Abner, of Company G, was fired upon and wounded by the enemy, and Private Thomas Slattery, of Company K, taken prisoner; both of them were straggling from the column at the time.

I have the honor to be, very respectfully, your obedient servant,

J. C. WINTERS,
Lieut. Col., Comdg. Fifty-ninth Illinois Infantry.

Capt. SAMUEL WEST,
Acting Assistant Adjutant-General, First Brigade.

No. 88.

Report of Col. John E. Bennett, Seventy-fifth Illinois Infantry.

HDQRS. SEVENTY-FIFTH ILLINOIS VOLUNTEERS,
Chattanooga, September 27, 1863.

CAPTAIN: In accordance with the order of Colonel Post, commanding brigade, we broke up camp at Stevenson, Ala., on the morning of August 30, 1863, and marched through town to the Tennessee River, halted on the bank near the pontoon bridge till 4 p. m., when we moved over the river and camped on the opposite bank.

The next day we took a position on the side of the mountain to help the teams up, and at 8 p. m. went into camp on the mountain.

On September 2 we were ordered to resume the march and at night camped at Sand Valley, where we remained till 1.30 p. m. of September 4, then marched to Lookout Valley and camped on Winston's plantation. We remained in camp in the valley and on the mountain till September 18, doing picket duty, foraging, &c.

On September 12, at 6 p. m., in obedience to the order of Colonel Post, Lieutenant-Colonel Kilgour (Colonel Bennett being sick at the time) started with his command in the direction of Stevenson to meet the cavalry supply train and escort it to camp.

The train was reached at about 3 a. m. of the 13th at Rock Creek. After resting two hours Colonel Kilgour moved back with his command as directed with the train in charge, and arrived in camp at about 4 p. m. same day, having marched 40 miles in less than twenty-three consecutive hours, more than half the distance in the night, through a dark forest and very rough road.

On September 18, at noon, we again moved on as rear guard to the train. The march was slow and tedious, arriving at Stevens' Gap late in the night. We remained in camp to hold that place till September 20, when we were ordered to the front.

We accordingly moved on and came up to the main army at Crawfish Spring.

At dark marched about 4 miles, halted to draw rations, then moved on about 4 miles farther, and rested until morning.

On September 21 moved a short distance, formed line of battle, and remained in line till 3 a. m. of the 22d, when we moved about 4 miles in the direction of Chattanooga, and again formed in line.

We soon found that the enemy were trying to get into our rear. After a short skirmish we moved safely over Chattanooga Creek and joined the main body at about 12 m. same day; immediately commenced work on the intrenchments, and lay behind them till the morning of the 25th, then moved silently behind the works where we now are.

On September 20, 10 men of the different companies were unable to keep with the command and are now missing—probably captured by the enemy at Crawfish Spring—this being the only loss while on the movement to this place.

Of the officers and men I can only say they are willing to do their whole duty as patriotic soldiers without murmur or complaint, and I now realize what was at first confidently expected of Illinois soldiers.

I have the honor to be, very respectfully, your obedient servant,

JOHN E. BENNETT,
Colonel, Commanding Regiment.

Capt. SAMUEL WEST,
Acting Assistant Adjutant-General, First Brigade.

No. 89.

Report of Lieut. Col. William M. Kilgour, Seventy-fifth Illinois Infantry.

HDQRS. SEVENTY-FIFTH ILLINOIS VOLUNTEERS,
Winston's Plantation, Ala., September 14, 1863.

COLONEL: In obedience to your order, received at thirty minutes past 5 o'clock on Saturday, the 12th, directing me to move with my command in the direction of Stevenson, I did at 6 p. m. of the same day move from camp in the direction indicated in your order with my command, consisting of 200 men.

On arriving outside the picket lines I ordered a halt, an inspection of arms, the pieces loaded and primed; time occupied, ten minutes. I at the same time ordered Capt. A. S. [Vorrey], of Company F, to take and keep a position about 40 rods in advance of the main body, to act as skirmishers in case of attack in the front and to prevent surprise or ambuscade.

Near Young's plantation we met the quartermaster of the train in question, who, not giving satisfactory answers at first and attempting to draw his pistol, was promptly arrested by Captain Vorrey, of the advance. He finally explained satisfactorily that he was quartermaster of the train, and stated that his train was camped at Rock Creek, distance about 12 miles from the foot of the mountain. He was then released.

I passed on with my command, under your instructions to, if possible, camp with the train, and reached them in camp at Rock Creek at a few minutes before 3 a. m. of the 13th. I found the camp, of some 100 wagons, entirely unprotected—no pickets out, no camp guard, no preparations of any kind for defense.

I rested with my command for two hours, when, with the train in our charge, we moved back as directed, and arrived at your headquarters at 3.30 p. m. of the 13th, having entirely and successfully accomplished the object of our march without any casualties of any kind excepting blistered feet.

I wish to make particular mention of Capt. Addison S. Vorrey as a prompt and most efficient officer; also Adjutant French, of the Seventy-fifth Illinois, who accompanied the advance with Captain Vorrey; also Capt. A. McMoore, Company D, and Captain Frost, Company E. Of the men and officers, all, I can only say they performed their duty as Illinois soldiers usually do. This is the highest encomium I know how to bestow.

We marched 40 miles in twenty-three consecutive hours, near half the distance in the night, through a dark forest and very rough road.

I am, colonel, very respectfully, your obedient servant,

W. M. KILGOUR,
Lieut. Col., Comdg. Seventy-fifth Illinois Volunteers.

Col. P. SIDNEY POST,
Comdg. 1st Brigade, 1st Division, 20th Army Corps.

No. 90.

Report of Col. Michael Gooding, Twenty-second Indiana Infantry.

HDQRS. TWENTY-SECOND REGIMENT INDIANA VOLUNTEERS,
Camp in the Field, September 27, 1863.

CAPTAIN: Agreeable to your order, I submit to you the following report of my regiment since leaving Tennessee River:

According to orders received, we marched from camp near Stevenson, Ala., on the 30th day of August, and crossed the Tennessee River same day, from whence we marched over the Sand Hill Mountains and arrived at Valley Head or Winston's farm on the evening of the 4th of September.

From thence we marched over Lookout Mountain and guarded the road. We left the top of the mountain on the 18th, marched to Stevenson, where we guarded the gap.

On the morning of the 20th we marched from thence; crossing Missionary Ridge, we arrived at Crawfish Spring about 3 p. m. and took up position with the cavalry forces commanded by Brig. Gen. R. B. Mitchell, and marched from there about 5 p. m. same day, and arrived in the valley at the foot of Lookout Mountain about 8 p. m., and took position on the right of the brigade, the right of my regiment resting against the mountain.

On the 22d of September we arrived within 1 mile of Chattanooga, and same day took position in front on the banks of a small creek.

On the evening of the 24th I received orders to proceed across the creek with my regiment and the Seventy-fourth Illinois (commanded by Col. Jason Marsh) for the purpose of making a reconnaissance. I advanced a strong line of skirmishers, who came upon the rebel pickets immediately after leaving our line of pickets. Only a few shots were fired and the rebels fell back about a half mile, where their front line was concealed behind a fence near the edge of the woods. As soon as my skirmish line advanced within 200 yards the rebels rose in force and fired a volley into the skirmishers, killing 1, mortally wounding 1, and slightly wounding 2. The skirmishers then fell back, bringing the wounded into the edge of the woods, where I placed my forces in position and reported to Colonel Post, commanding brigade, that the enemy were in force in our front, whereupon I received orders to bring in the wounded and return to the picket line.

In the meantime the enemy advanced a regiment and a battery on my right flank, and attacked my skirmishers on the right, evidently with the intention of gaining my rear, when I withdrew and took up my former position.

During the entire skirmish and march my officers and men conducted themselves with decorum and bravery, seemingly willing to endure anything to insure our success. I especially recommend Asst. Surg. N. J. Beachley for the energy he displayed in the discipline of the infirmary corps, and providing for the sick and wounded on the march, in consequence of which there has not been a man lost during this time from straggling.

I am, captain, very respectfully, your most obedient servant,

M. GOODING,
Colonel, Comdg. Twenty-second Regiment Indiana Vols.

Capt. SAMUEL WEST,
Acting Assistant Adjutant-General, First Brigade.

No. 91.

Report of Capt. George Q. Gardner, Fifth Wisconsin Battery.

HEADQUARTERS FIFTH WISCONSIN BATTERY,
Behind Breastworks, Chattanooga, Tenn., Sept. 27, 1863.

COLONEL: In accordance with instructions from your headquarters, I herewith respectfully submit to you the following report of the part performed by the Fifth Wisconsin Battery in the late campaign since leaving the Tennessee River:

Until we arrived at a point about 2 miles from this point nothing worthy of note transpired, excepting the hardships endured by both men and horses.

As above stated, when we reached the point where the Trenton road descends the mountain, a skirmish ensued, during which a section of my command under command of Lieutenant McKnight and one under Lieutenant Lafferty engaged and silenced a rebel battery. After the enemy were driven off my command moved down the hill, joined the brigade, and marched safely into Chattanooga.

After joining the division, the right half of the battery engaged a battery and some rebel skirmishers in our immediate front, and soon caused both battery and skirmishers to move off. I am perfectly satisfied with the deportment of both officers and men under my command while on the march and under fire.

In conclusion, I would say that at the present time the battery is in an admirable position and the men in good spirits.

I am, colonel, your very obedient servant,

GEO. Q. GARDNER,
Captain, Commanding Fifth Wisconsin Battery.

Col. P. SIDNEY POST,
Commanding First Brigade.

No. 92.

Report of Brig. Gen. William P. Carlin, U. S. Army, commanding Second Brigade.

HDQRS. SECOND BRIG., FIRST DIV., 20TH ARMY CORPS,
Chattanooga, September 27, 1863.

CAPTAIN : I have the honor to report as follows on the part taken by my command in the battles of the 19th and 20th instant, near Gordon's Mills:

Under the direction of Brig. Gen. J. C. Davis, commanding the division, the brigade was brought into action on the right of the Third Brigade, Colonel Heg commanding, and in the following order: The Thirty-eighth Illinois Volunteers, Lieutenant-Colonel Gilmer commanding, on the left; the One hundred and first Ohio Volunteers, Lieutenant-Colonel Messer commanding, in the center; the Eighty-first Indiana Volunteers, Capt. N. B. Boone commanding, on the right; the Thirty-eighth Illinois being in the timber, the other two regiments in an open field. The Twenty-first Illinois, Colonel Alexander commanding, was first ordered by General Davis to remain in reserve, and was placed about 100 yards to the right and rear of the Eighty-first, in the edge of a forest which lay directly in front of it. This regiment had no sooner reached the position described than an order came from General Davis for it to report to Colonel Heg to support his brigade, and went accordingly to the Third Brigade.

About the same time the general commanding the division ordered me to send a regiment to support the artillery of the division, and in obedience to this order the Eighty-first Indiana was detached from my command. The Second Minnesota Battery had previously been withdrawn from my brigade, and was serving under the direction of Captain Hotchkiss, chief of artillery. My command during the fight was therefore reduced to two regiments of infantry. The incompetency displayed by Captain Boone early in the action induced me to supersede him by Maj. James E. Calloway, Twenty-first Illinois Volunteers, a gallant and very efficient officer.

When my line was formed, General Davis rode along my regiments and ordered them to lie down, without giving me or them additional instructions. The firing then was heavy on my left, and from the enemy. When my line was first formed Colonel Wilder informed me that two of his regiments were on my right in the timber. Shortly after this I discovered troops in front of my right swinging around at right angles to my line. Not knowing whose they were I galloped over to them, under fire from the enemy, and ascertained that they were Colonel Barnes' brigade. They continued their wheel to the left, until they masked half of the One hundred and first Ohio, when, to prevent them masking both my regiments, I ordered Lieutenant-Colonel Messer to advance and half wheel to the left and open fire into the woods, where the enemy was posted. This movement was completed when a volley from the enemy caused the left of Barnes' brigade to break, and in doing so they carried away the right of the One hundred and first Ohio. The Thirty-eighth Illinois maintained its position till the Third Brigade had been driven back, when that regiment gave way. The One hundred and first Ohio fell back in better order, fighting over every step, under the efficient command of the gallant and chivalric Messer, aided by the brave Major McDanald. The two regiments fell back across the road and across the open field west of the road into the edge of the timber occupied by a part of Wood's division. During this retreat there were many instances of individual gallantry observed, the most conspicuous of which was in the commander of the One hundred and first Ohio, Lieutenant-Colonel Messer, who always kept his colors and a part of his regiment facing the enemy. In the open field west of the road I succeeded in rallying men enough from all the regiments of the Second and Third Brigades, and some from other divisions, to form a respectable line. This was a very arduous and very perilous service, and there were many brave officers and soldiers whose assistance was invaluable at that critical moment, but whose names I do not know. The lamented Colonel Heg and Lieutenant-Colonel Chandler, Thirty-fifth Illinois, were among them. With the hope of recovering the ground we had lost, I led them in a charge across the field to the road, but the want of regimental organizations prevented me from getting them farther. At that moment a brigade of Sheridan's division took the front but was soon driven back. It was now about sundown, and orders were received from General Davis to fall back to an open field half a mile to the rear, and bivouac for the night.

The Eighty-first Indiana and Twenty-first Illinois not having fought under my directions, I can make no special report upon their conduct.

Major Calloway, however, speaks in terms of great praise of the Eighty-first Indiana, and judging from the severe loss in the Twenty-first Illinois it must have done as well as could have been expected. It is proper here to remark that during the action of the 19th repeated complaints were made by the One hundred and first Ohio that our batteries were killing and wounding our men. I immediately informed Lieutenant Woodbury, commanding Second Minnesota Battery, of this fact, and he replied that the charge was probably true as he had received repeatedly orders from Captain Hotchkiss and General Davis to shorten his fuse and burst his shells nearer, and that he really had not been informed where our troops were. This battery was immediately in rear of the One hundred and first Ohio. So much for the 19th September.

Early on the 20th the brigade was moved up on a high ridge near Widow Glenn's. About 9.30 a. m. I received orders again to move forward. Passing over a rocky ridge a position was assigned to my brigade by General Davis and Major-General Crittenden. The position seemed strong, having been improved by rude breastworks. The Third Brigade was again on my left; there were no troops on my right.

The Thirty-eighth Illinois was held in reserve behind breastworks 100 yards in rear of the brigade. The Twenty-first Illinois was on the right, the Eighty-first Indiana in the center, and the One hundred and first Ohio on the left. Skirmishers were thrown out to the front, and twice I rode out beyond the skirmishers and beyond the main road leading up the valley to reconnoiter. Not the least sign of an enemy could be seen. I had just returned from the second visit to the front of my skirmishers when firing commenced and the skirmishers ran into the main line. The firing on both sides immediately became terrific, and ours I know was very destructive. The front line of the assaulting column of the enemy was everywhere driven back or shot down except where it overlapped my right, but soon I discovered a few men running on the right of the Twenty-first Illinois.

I immediately rode up to Lieutenant-Colonel Gilmer, Thirty-eighth Illinois, and ordered him to move his regiment to the right of the Twenty-first Illinois. From some cause not now ascertainable he hesitated, but finally succeeded in giving an order to his men to rise; it was now too late. A column of the enemy had come directly on my right flank and nearly against it, and opened a most destructive enfilading fire. This enabled the storming column in front of my right to reach the breastworks, and many of the enemy were on our side of them before a retreat was ordered. Seeing that the position could not be held I ordered a retreat, intending to reform on the rocky ridge in rear about 400 yards. But in this design I was utterly disappointed. But one field officer of my brigade succeeded in getting away from the position, and but few company officers; I believe nearly if not quite all of them were killed or wounded, and many of our men shared the same fate. When assistance was too late a part of Sheridan's command came up on my right, but fell back in disorder at the first fire of the enemy. I remained near the position for half an hour or more endeavoring to collect scattered men to hold the enemy in check, and the scattering fire from a few brave men that could be induced to halt checked the enemy for a long time. The officers of my staff had gone to the rear to rally the regiments of the brigade, and succeeded in collecting about 400 men, with a few officers.

Until about 4 o'clock in the evening I remained near the position endeavoring to collect men and to do the best that circumstances would permit. It was too evident that but little more fighting could be procured from this division. I had received no instructions from General Davis for an emergency of this kind, and could find neither him nor his staff ; finally I discovered a column headed by General Sheridan and followed by the remnants of the Second and Third Brigades. Sheridan sent word to me that he was conducting the column, and I replied that I would follow him.

The flag of the division commander was delivered to me by a staff officer of General Davis (Lieutenant Reynolds I believe). Placing Major Calloway in command of the Second Brigade, I assumed command of the division and conducted it to Rossville, where I found General Davis, who there resumed command. On approaching Rossville Major-General Negley, with sword in hand, came to me and informed me that General Thomas was still fighting. That the rebel cavalry pickets were between us and him, and that we should go to his relief. He then remarked, "If you will go to his relief I will support you." Considering that I had but about 600 men in the two brigades and having heard that the major-general had almost his entire division intact in the vicinity, I felt compelled to refer him to General Sheridan, commanding the column.

On the 19th I took into action 85 officers and 1,130 enlisted men; aggregate, 1,215. I lost 43 officers and 608 enlisted men; aggregate, 651. Among these officers were many of the bravest and best of my brigade, including every field officer engaged of the four regiments except one, viz, Col. J. W. S. Alexander and Lieutenant-Colonel McMackin, Twenty-first Illinois; Lieutenant-Colonel Gilmer and Maj. H. N. Alden, Thirty-eighth Illinois; Lieutenant-Colonel Messer and Major McDanald, One hundred and first Ohio. Lieutenant-Colonel Messer and Major Alden, having been wounded on the 19th, did not fall into the hands of the enemy. All the others I believe were killed or wounded and captured.

I have now to perform the pleasing duty of mentioning those officers who proved themselves brave and efficient under the most terrible fire. The most conspicuous of these were Lieut. Col. J. Messer and Maj. B. B. McDanald, One hundred and first Ohio; Maj. James E. Calloway, Twenty-first Illinois, commanding Eighty-first Indiana; Maj. Henry H. Alden, Thirty-eighth Illinois; Capt. Leonard D. Smith, One hundred and first Ohio. The conduct of these officers was truly admirable, and nothing better for the public service could be done than to promote those who survive to the command of regiments.

After our division was scattered and not another officer could be seen on the field Major Calloway remained with me and assisted me in halting men and causing them to fire back at the enemy, and I am confident that but for these efforts the pursuit of the enemy would have been far more rapid and consequently more destructive. Every officer of my staff deserves credit for gallantry and efficiency during the struggle.

Capt. W. C. Harris, Thirty-eighth Illinois, provost-marshal, acted as aide-de-camp on the field, and frequently volunteered to perform the most perilous duty. Capt. S. P. Voris, Thirty-eighth Illinois, acting assistant adjutant-general, had one horse killed under him; Lieut. W. E. Carlin, Thirty-eighth Illinois, aide-de-camp, had one killed and another wounded under him. Lieut. J. W. Vance, Twenty-first Illinois, inspector, was constantly under fire with me, and was at all times zealous and efficient in the execution of my orders.

The attention of my superior officers is respectfully called to the reports of regimental commanders which are inclosed herewith. As the aggregate of this brigade is now less than 700, and many companies have not an officer with them, I most earnestly recommend a thorough reorganization of every regiment.

I could have little confidence in their usefulness if taken into battle in their present condition.

Respectfully submitted.

W. P. CARLIN,
Brigadier-General, Commanding.

Capt. T. W. Morrison,
Asst. Adjt. Gen., Hdqrs. First Div., 20th Army Corps.

[Indorsements.]

Respectfully forwarded.

General Carlin was called upon for a report of the part taken by his brigade in the late action. He has seen fit to introduce a number of uncalled-for and out-of-place insinuations and reflections upon myself, staff, and others; these reflections and insinuations, so far as myself and staff are concerned, are false representations throughout, and the undersigned is constrained to believe they were introduced from motives of malice. Good taste or the good of the service certainly did not authorize their insertion in a report of this kind.

With these remarks this report is respectfully submitted to my superiors for their consideration.

JEF. C. DAVIS,
Brigadier-General, Commanding Division.

HEADQUARTERS TWENTIETH ARMY CORPS,
October 4, 1863.

This report is respectfully forwarded.

I am sorry such feeling exists between General Carlin and his division commander. I respectfully recommend that General Carlin be transferred to some other command.

A. McD. McCOOK,
Major-General, Commanding.

No. 93.

Report of Capt. Chester K. Knight, Twenty-first Illinois Infantry.

HDQRS. TWENTY-FIRST REGIMENT ILLINOIS VOLUNTEERS,
Chattanooga, Tenn., September 27, 1863.

CAPTAIN: In accordance with orders received from brigade headquarters, First Division, Twentieth Army Corps, I have the honor to report that on the morning of the 19th instant, this regiment, in command of Colonel Alexander, moved from where it bivouacked near the McLemore road in the direction of Crawfish Spring, and [had] passed said spring about 3 miles, when Colonel Alexander received orders to double-quick forward in the direction of where heavy firing was heard, which was a distance of about three-quarters of a mile, where the regiment was formed in line of battle, and immediately moved to the front, a distance of about 200 yards, where the enemy was engaged in great fury. The fire was continued about twenty minutes, when the troops on our left gave way, and Colonel Alexander ordered the regiment to retire about 100 yards, which was done in good order, when the temporary confusion which had existed on our left flank was quickly restored, and we again advanced in the face of a galling fire, about 100 yards in advance of our former line, and held the position for about half an hour, when the regiment on our left again retired, and the enemy following rapidly poured a deadly fire upon our left, and Colonel Alexander ordered the regiment to retire to a position near an open field, which was the ground upon which we first formed, where we were relieved by a brigade from General Sheridan's division, which was quickly repulsed, when we retired beyond the field and remained about half an hour, and again advanced to the front about 400 yards on the right of the Thirteenth Michigan Regiment and left of the Fifty-eighth Indiana Regiment. This regiment held its position about fifteen minutes, when the fire of the enemy increased in front and on our left, so that our regiment was driven from the field in some confusion to the woods in the rear, a distance of 150 yards, when orders were received from General Davis to form and bivouac in a field 200 yards to the rear of the field from which we had been last repulsed.

On the morning of the 20th instant orders were received to move at 3 a. m., which we accordingly did, stopped at General Rosecrans' headquarters, a distance of about 1 mile from where we bivouacked. At daylight we moved to the crest of a hill half a mile farther to the rear and remained until 10 a. m., when we moved in advance along said hill a distance of about 1 mile to the road, when we crossed into an open field and advanced about a half mile, and took position behind some rudely constructed wooden breastworks, where skirmishers were immediately deployed, their left resting on the right of the Eighty-first Indiana Regiment, all of which were quickly engaged and driven in, when the enemy appeared in heavy force in our front, into which our regiment poured a destructive and well-directed fire, which seemed to entirely destroy the front lines, but they quickly rallied and renewed the assault with terrible fury, with lines of immense depth, judging from the number of flags to be seen. Our regiment bravely stood the shock until the enemy approached to within 20 paces in front, and our right flank being turned and a terrific fire being poured in from that direction, further resistance seemed hopeless, and we rapidly, and with broken ranks, retired to the second hill in the rear, where we made a last desperate attempt to rally, which was in part successful, and a continual fire continued for about ten minutes, when the troops on our right again gave way, and we were once more driven from our position. We again formed about 1½ miles in the rear under the direction of General Carlin, when the command of the regiment fell to myself, being the senior officer present (Major Calloway being detached on the 19th to command the Eighty-first Indiana Regiment). Orders were then received to move to a position 2 miles in the direction of Chattanooga, which place we reached at night, and the roll being called showed a loss of—

Officers and men.	Killed.	Wounded.	Missing.	Total.
Commissioned officers	1	6	9	16
Enlisted men	21	64	139	224
Total	22	70	148	240

The companies were commanded by Captains Eaton, Welshimer, Jamison, Reed, Freeland, Blackburn, George, Harlan, Knight, and Wilson. Captains Reed, George, Harlan, and Wilson were wounded, the three former severely, while at their post gallantly endeavoring to check the solid columns of the advancing foe. Lieutenant Weitzel was killed at his post, heroically encouraging his men. Lieutenants Hunter and Austin fought with marked gallantry until wounded. Colonels Alexander and McMackin are among the miss-

ing, both of whom acted as brave men only can act.   In short, suffice it to say that, without exception as to officers and with few as to
the men, all behaved with becoming coolness, gallantry, and courage during the entire engagement; and to Adjutant Steele great
praise is due for his encouragement to the men by word and deed,
fearless, daring, during the entire conflict.   Chaplain Wilkins is deserving of special mention for his untiring efforts to alleviate the
sufferings of the wounded and dying and assisting to reform the
broken ranks of the regiment.

I am, captain, your obedient servant,

CHESTER K. KNIGHT,
Captain, Commanding.

Capt. S. P. VORIS,
Acting Assistant Adjutant-General, Second Brigade.

No. 94.

Report of Capt. William C. Harris, Thirty-eighth Illinois Infantry.

HEADQUARTERS THIRTY-EIGHTH ILLINOIS INFANTRY,
Chattanooga, Tenn., September 28, 1863.

CAPTAIN : I have the honor to report the part taken by the Thirty-
eighth Illinois Infantry in the battle of the 19th and 20th of September, near Crawfish Spring.

September 18 broke camp near Dug Gap about dark ; marched
about 4 miles to the left, relieving General Brannan's division.

On the 19th moved to the left about 10 o'clock.   Passed Crawfish
Spring about 3 miles and filed right into the woods, double-quicked
about a mile and a quarter, filed right and formed on the left, by
file into line, on the right of Colonel Heg's brigade.   The regiment
was under a very heavy fire ; were ordered to lie down.   Company
K was lying in the road and was very much exposed ; they suffered
severely.   The men, ordered not to fire, stood their ground without
flinching.   In a short time the men were ordered to their feet and
the line was moved forward ; the right and left became entangled
with other regiments.   For a few moments the firing was heavy,
when it became evident that the troops on our left had given way,
exposing the left flank.   We were ordered to fall back, which we
did, firing as we went, to a road at the edge of the timber, where a
stand was made till, being heavily pressed on the left and front, the
line retired across an open field to the woods.   Here the men were
rallied at a fence, the batteries playing over their heads.   The enemy
was checked.   A line was formed and charged across the open field
to the woods from where we were first driven, and held it under a
heavy fire until a brigade of General Sheridan's division came to
our relief.   The regiment was then reformed and bivouacked in an
open field in rear of the battle-field.   The regiment entered the fight
at 2 o'clock and was relieved at half past 5 ; loss very heavy.

At 3 o'clock the morning of the 20th took position near General
Rosecrans' headquarters on Chattanooga road.   About 7 a. m. moved
to a range of hills on the west side of Chattanooga road.   Formed in
close column by division at half distance and stacked arms.   At 10
o'clock moved by the left flank a quarter of a mile, then by the right
flank, and halted in a valley east of the Chattanooga road.   After a

short rest were moved about 200 yards to a hill in front and deployed into line; moved forward into the valley, and took position behind a slight barricade 75 yards in rear of the Eighty-first Indiana, in an open wood on the right of General Wood's division. Colonel Heg's brigade came up and formed on our left, filling up a gap between our left and General Wood's division.

The line in front was already heavily engaged, and Colonel Heg's brigade was driven back almost as soon as it reached the line. At the same time the right of General Carlin's brigade was turned by a heavy force. General Carlin ordered the regiment to fall back. The line in front came over us; the men fired one volley and retired. Colonel Gilmer, who commanded (supposed wounded), fell into the hands of the enemy at this point. For a mile the men were exposed to a flank fire. It was impossible to rally men in open ground under such heavy fire. When some three-fourths of a mile from the battle-field in the woods, the men were rallied and marched with the division toward Chattanooga; bivouacked in a valley near Rossville; stacked 56 guns. Captain Whitehurst, [who] was senior officer, was in command.

On the morning of the 21st were moved to a position on the right of the brigade, commanded by Colonel Martin. There threw up breastworks. Sick and detached men increased the regiment to about 100 men.

At 3 o'clock the morning of the 22d we marched to Chattanooga. By order of Brigadier-General Carlin, commanding brigade, I was placed in command of the regiment, being senior officer.

Our casualties were:

Officers and men.	Killed.	Wounded.	Missing.	Total.
Officers	1	12	2	15
Enlisted men.	12	79	77	168
Total ...	13	91	79	183

Officers and men behaved very well, and did all that could be done against such unequal force. The list of casualties shows the men fought gallantly. Many of the missing are probably killed or wounded. The regiment went in the action with 20 commissioned officers and 281 enlisted men.

I am, respectfully, your obedient servant,

W. C. HARRIS,
Captain, Commanding Regiment.

Capt. S. P. Voris,
Acting Assistant Adjutant-General, Second Brigade.

No. 95.

*Report of Maj. James E. Calloway, Twenty-first Illinois Infantry,
commanding Eighty-first Indiana Infantry.*

HEADQUARTERS EIGHTY-FIRST INDIANA VOLUNTEERS,
Chattanooga, September 28, 1863.

CAPTAIN: In accordance with orders from headquarters Second Brigade, First Division, Twentieth Army Corps, I have the honor to report that about 2.30 p. m. on the 19th instant, while with the Twenty-first Illinois Volunteers, and being hotly engaged with the enemy at a point about 3 miles north of Crawfish Spring, on a line west of and near Chickamauga Creek, and east of and parallel to the La Fayette road, leading to Chattanooga, I received an order to immediately report to Brigadier-General Carlin, commanding brigade.

Upon reporting, General Carlin directed me to at once assume command of the Eighty-first Indiana Volunteers, of his brigade. I immediately obeyed the order, and, upon assuming command, found the regiment (Eighty-first Indiana Volunteers) lying about 50 yards in rear of and supporting the Second Minnesota Battery, the regiment not yet having engaged the enemy. The regiment then numbered, in fighting men present for duty, 15 officers and 240 enlisted men. About five minutes thereafter I received an order in person from Brigadier-General Davis, commanding division, to move my command about 200 yards to the right and front of the Second Minnesota Battery and support a regiment there severely engaged with the enemy, saying at the time he thought it was the Thirty-eighth Illinois Volunteers. Upon taking position, the right resting behind and shielded by a point of timber with heavy undergrowth, the left resting on the crest of and being covered by a slight elevation, I had discovered a regiment (Seventeenth Kentucky Volunteers) to my right and a little to my front slowly giving way to the right, and steadily contesting the ground under a most withering fire from a very heavy column of the enemy briskly advancing and not over 300 yards distant. We immediately opened a well-directed fire, first by volley and then by file, causing the enemy to recoil and give way in much confusion, thereby relieving the regiment to our right. The firing had not yet ceased when a large body of the enemy was seen moving to our left, and soon attacked the Second and Third Brigades of Davis' division. The enemy in our front again took courage and advanced upon our position, but, being shattered, was easily repulsed. The brigades to our left and the Second Minnesota Battery, together with the Fifty-eighth Indiana Volunteers, immediately joining the Eighty-first Indiana on the left, though most stubbornly and bravely resisting the terrible onsets of most overwhelming numbers, were driven from their po ition, leaving the Eighty-first Indiana entirely without support on the left. I had in the mean time made a partial change of front to the rear by throwing back the left wing of the regiment, and continued our fire, somewhat enfilading the lines of the enemy and partially checking his farther progress.

About this time a vigorous attack was made on our front and right, causing the Seventeenth Kentucky to farther withdraw.

The Eighty-first Indiana Volunteers, owing to the admirable position occupied, was not suffering very greatly, but the position was so flanked as to endanger my entire command, exposing it to capture. It was then withdrawn in good order about 200 yards to a thin curtain of timber covering the road. After again halting and reopening fire, I was informed by an officer that 50 yards to our rear and across the road was a fieldwork that had been hastily constructed of rails. I accordingly faced the regiment about and took position within the works, when we again opened and continued a most galling and deadly fire upon the enemy, who had advanced within short range, and after long and hard fighting he was dislodged from his position with heavy loss.   We immediately followed his retreating forces and retook our former position at the front, that we had been compelled to abandon, and held it during the remainder of the day.   The Fifty-eighth Indiana Volunteers again came up to our left, and about the same time I observed Brigadier-General Carlin, still to the left of the Fifty-eighth Indiana Volunteers, most fearlessly moving forward a body of troops I then supposed to be the remainder of this brigade to the attack of the enemy, again moving up in double lines and well supported to our attack.   The general and his command made a most gallant and heroic resistance, but being overpowered, were shattered and driven back with fearful loss, leaving the colors of the Twenty-first Illinois Volunteers in the hands of the color-sergeant, who was shot dead on the field.   I immediately ordered the Eighty-first Indiana Volunteers to open an oblique fire to the left, completely enfilading the lines of the enemy, and repulsed him with immense slaughter, recovering the colors of the Twenty-first Illinois Volunteers and protecting the One hundred and first Ohio while it most gallantly recovered the Eighth Indiana Battery taken by the enemy.   The Third Brigade of Sheridan's division came to the relief of General Carlin, and formed on the left of the Fifty-eighth Indiana Volunteers; and though the brigade, together with the Fifty-eighth Indiana Volunteers, was twice driven from their position, the Eighty-first Indiana Volunteers stubbornly holding its position, never losing an inch of the ground, the Fifty-eighth Indiana Volunteers recoiling each time, but seeing the Eighty-first Indiana standing firmly, would rally and return to our assistance.

Hearing a heavy roll of musketry and much cannonading on our right, and not knowing who occupied the position, I had fears that my position might be flanked, as the forces seemed to recoil and the firing was growing to our rear.   Upon information received, and after making a personal inspection of the right, I learned that a brigade commanded by a Colonel Barnes had been repulsed on our right, but the colonel had so posted his battery as to command his front and our right, enfilading the enemy's approach in attempting to turn our position.   During the engagement Captain Eaton and Lieutenant Gross and about 60 men of the Twenty-first Illinois Volunteers either reported to me or were rallied upon the Eighty-first Indiana Volunteers, and continued fighting most gallantly under my command, several of them being wounded; Sergeant Russell, Company G, and Private John Jones, Company F, Twenty-first Illinois, severely.

Being still on the front line and our ammunition nearly exhausted, I was endeavoring to obtain a supply, when, about sunset, an order came from General Davis, and immediately thereafter from General Carlin, to withdraw my command and join the division about 800 yards in rear.

During the engagement on that afternoon we fired an average of 54 rounds to each man of my command, and suffered the following losses: Officers wounded, 4, Captain Mitchell mortally; enlisted men, killed, 4; wounded, 58; making a grand total of 66 killed and wounded.

In obedience to orders received I rejoined the brigade about dusk, with the Eighty-first Indiana Volunteers and 3 officers, the regimental colors, and with about 50 men of the Twenty-first Illinois Volunteers, when we bivouacked for the night.

At 3 a. m. next morning, on the 20th instant, I received orders to move my command left in front, following the One hundred and first Ohio. Marched about half mile and stacked arms at General Rosecrans' headquarters, remaining until about sunrise. At that hour we moved to the rear about 600 yards and formed a line on an elevated ridge, running west of and parallel to the Chattanooga and La Fayette road. At about 10 a. m. I received orders from Brigadier-General Carlin to form my command into double column at half distance and follow the One hundred and first Ohio, moving by the left flank. We moved steadily along the apex of the ridge in a northeasterly direction about 1 mile, when we came into an extended glade and halted. The Twenty-first Illinois Volunteers was ordered to deploy and move forward in line, the Eighty-first Indiana moving in column abreast with the Twenty-first Illinois, and to deploy on reaching the apex of the hill in our front, and take position in line on the left of the Twenty-first Illinois Volunteers.

Having deployed my command and the enemy not being immediately in range, though heavy firing was progressing on our left, I was ordered to form my command into close column by division, right in front, and follow the Twenty-first Illinois Volunteers. Following on this line we marched about 800 yards, ascending to a somewhat elevated position, and was ordered to deploy my command and take position on the left of the Twenty-first Illinois Volunteers, behind some rude and illy constructed fieldworks erected upon our line of battle. I then threw forward Company A, Eighty-first Indiana Volunteers, Lieut. S. H. McCoy commanding, and relieved the skirmishers of another command, then retiring.

While posting the skirmishers, I observed the Third Brigade on our left was heavily attacked and driven back before getting into position. In a few moments thereafter the enemy appeared emerging from a body of thick timber about 150 yards in our front and moving to our attack without skirmishers and in most overwhelming numbers, massed by battalions, and, as near as I could judge from the battle-flags exhibited, four lines in depth. Our skirmishers came flying in, and, according to previous instructions, rallied on the right of the regiment.

As soon as my battalion front was unmasked by the skirmishers we opened a terrible and deadly fire upon the advancing foe. The firing was continued with unabated fury on both sides, the enemy steadily advancing and our men determinedly resisting until but 3 men of the enemy's first line and about half of his second line were standing; their comrades apparently had fallen in windrows and his farther progress seemed checked, perhaps impossible. Being near the right of the Eighty-first Indiana Volunteers and the left of the Twenty-first Illinois Volunteers, I saw to my inexpressible surprise and horror the right of the Twenty-first Illinois Volunteers was breaking and rapidly melting away. After a second and more careful observation I noticed the enemy was actually crossing the breastworks on the right and extending his left flank far to our rear, completely flanking our position, at the same time pouring a deadly fire from the rear on the Twenty-first Illinois Volunteers. Seeing the desperate and critical state of affairs, having no opportunity of obtaining orders, and knowing further delay would surrender my entire command, I gave orders for a hasty retreat. The fire being most terribly destructive our lines were entirely broken and the command was temporarily disorganized. In company with Brigadier-General Carlin, commanding brigade; Captain Smith, One hundred and first

Ohio; Captain Varner, Twenty-fifth Illinois, and Captain Wheeler, and several other officers of the Eighty-first Indiana Volunteers, we made several efforts with partial success to rally our scattered commands. We made three several stands, and on a rise about 1,200 yards to the rear of the fieldworks, made the last and desperate resistance with a few hundred men, checking the progress of the enemy and enabling our batteries to be taken safely from the field. We then withdrew from the field quietly and sullenly with every regimental color and field piece of the brigade, and retired about 1½ miles to the rear, reaching there about 2 p. m., and reformed our remnant of a command. We then, in company with the brigade and division to which we are attached, together with several other divisions of the army, moved to a position about 2 miles nearer Chattanooga, and bivouacked for the night.

Upon calling the roll of the Eighty-first Indiana Volunteers 2 officers and 19 enlisted men were reported missing. We have good evidence for knowing that several among the missing were killed or wounded, but owing to the great uncertainty enveloping the case they are all reported on the sad list of missing. We expended in the two days' fighting about 61 rounds of ammunition per man, and sustained the following casualties: Six officers and 81 enlisted men, a correct list of the names having preceded this report.

It is due, under the circumstances, that I should speak of the conduct of the officers and men of the Eighty-first Indiana Volunteers. With scarcely an exception they behaved in the most gallant and admirable manner, and though comparatively a young regiment, conducted themselves with the coolness, steadiness, and precision of veterans on the field of battle. Captain Mitchell, a brave and efficient officer, was mortally wounded, and Lieutenants Northcutt, Cummings, and Zimmerman were wounded while gallantly leading their men in the discharge of their duties. They battled as brave men worthy of the best Government ever instituted among men, and the Republic may feel confident when its interests rest in the hands of such defenders. It would be deemed little less than invidious were I to mention one officer or man as excelling another in gallantry and efficiency, but I cannot close this report without thanking Adjutant Schell for the aid and courtesies he has shown me in the discharge of my duties, and tendering all the officers and men my thanks for the cheerfulness and universal promptness with which they have obeyed my orders. I desire to offer no eulogium upon the conduct of the officers and men of the Eighty-first Indiana Volunteers. I wish to say they shared no higher honor than that they "fought in Carlin's brigade of the Army of the Cumberland, obeyed orders, and did their duty in the great battle of Chickamauga, 'the Creek of Death,'" and when the long sad list of killed, wounded, and missing is published the shadows of gloom that will gather around many of the hearthstones of our homes will show that there also they were loved and appreciated.

I am, sir, your obedient servant,

J. E. CALLOWAY,
Major Twenty-first Illinois Volunteers, Commanding.

Capt. S. P. VORIS,
  Actg. Asst. Adjt. Gen., Second Brigade, First Division.

No. 96.

Report of Capt. Leonard D. Smith, One hundred and first Ohio Infantry.

HDQRS. 101ST REGIMENT OHIO VOLUNTEER INFANTRY,
Chattanooga, Tenn., September 25, 1863.

SIR : On the morning of the 19th the One hundred and first Regiment Ohio Volunteer Infantry, under command of Lieutenant-Colonel Messer, moved with the balance of the brigade toward Crawfish Spring, near which the battle was already progressing. Between 1 and 2 p. m. the regiment left the pike, and after moving about a mile at double-quick obeyed the order of "On left by file into line,' and were in line of battle in a corn-field and woods, while the movements of the enemy were concealed by heavy timber in our front. A few moments after 2 o'clock the regiment was ordered forward to the fence dividing the corn-field and woods. By this time the Thirty-eighth Illinois on our left had become engaged; also, a Kentucky regiment of General Wood's division to our right, a portion of which covered the front of our right wing. The regiment had but reached the fence and taken position before the Kentucky regiment on our right gave way, a portion of it running through the right wing of the One hundred and first, thus temporarily breaking its organization, and compelling the regiment to fall back over the ridge to our rear, and from here to fall back in some confusion. The regiment was rallied and again moved forward, driving the enemy back through the corn-field, and in turn were again driven back to the ridge. Colonel Messer took the colors (the color-bearer having been killed), and leading the men forward drove the enemy before them. Here the fighting ceased, it being after 5 o'clock. Skirmishers were thrown forward, and the regiment moved back behind the ridge.

About dark the regiment was ordered to the rear of General Sheridan's division. There were found present Major McDanald, in command; Captains Fleming and Smith, Adjutant Neff, Lieutenants Hosmer, Bryant, Taggart, Read, Roberts, McGraw, Myers, Cline, Petticord, and Jay C. Butler, with 119 enlisted men.

Early on Sunday morning, September 20, we were moved to a position to the rear of the Chattanooga pike and opposite General Rosecrans' headquarters, on a high range of hills At 8 o'clock we moved to the left, and then forward, recrossing the Chattanooga pike, and took a position on a ridge near a peach orchard. We were soon moved forward in close column by division about 1 mile and then deployed, taking a position behind some logs which had been used as a breastwork. Skirmishers were thrown out, relieving those we found there, and the men ordered to lie down. While in this position, a regiment not belonging to this brigade moved up and lay down among our men, thus rendering the management of the regiment almost impossible. At 11 o'clock the skirmishers were driven in, closely followed by the enemy in force. They were driven back in our immediate front, but before the men had delivered half a dozen rounds the enemy were found coming over the logs within a short distance of our left, while the right was being turned from the effect of a severe flank fire. The regiment was compelled to retreat, and, being mingled with another regiment (I think of Sheridan's division), lost its organization for the time. During the retreat Major Mc Donald was severely wounded, and the command devolved upon me.

I collected as many of the men as possible together and reported to you, and with the balance of the brigade moved back to Rossville, where a new position was chosen and occupied till the night of September 21, when we were moved to Chattanooga.

Early on the morning of the 22d Colonel Kirby arrived and took command. Major McDanald, Lieutenants McGraw, Read, and Petticord, were wounded on the 20th. There are with the regiment who were actually engaged 87 enlisted men and 10 commissioned officers. Praise is due officers and men for the prompt manner of doing their duty. For those who have lost their lives we mourn; they died while nobly doing their duty. Bright on memory's pages will remain the many virtues of our comrades, who have laid down their lives for free government and the restoration of the Union.

Respectfully,

LEN. D. SMITH,
Captain, Commanding Regiment.

Capt. S. P. VORIS,
Acting Assistant Adjutant-General, Second Brigade.

No. 97.

Report of Col. John A. Martin, Eighth Kansas Infantry, commanding Third Brigade.

HDQRS. THIRD BRIG., FIRST DIV., 20TH ARMY CORPS,
Chattanooga, September 28, 1863.

CAPTAIN: I have the honor to report the following account of the action of this brigade from the time of crossing the Tennessee River up to the present date, including its participation in the engagements on the 19th and 20th instant.

As I did not assume command of the brigade until the 19th instant, when the brave and gallant Colonel Heg was mortally wounded, and as Capt. Henry Hauff, acting assistant adjutant-general of the brigade, was taken prisoner, and none of the official records of headquarters are in my possession, the report of our movements prior to the 19th may contain inaccuracies of memory, which the general commanding will readily correct.

On the 28th of August the brigade was ordered to march from Stevenson, Ala., and at 5 p. m. started, reaching the banks of the Tennessee River at 11 p. m. We bivouacked for the night, and at daylight next morning were ordered to cross the river in pontoon barges and occupy the other side. The crossing was supposed to be a dangerous enterprise, as the enemy had pickets in plain sight on the farther shore and might be in force. The Pioneer Brigade had during the night unloaded and got the pontoons in order. The regiments of the brigade were divided into squads of 25 men, each commanded by a commissioned officer, and as soon as everything was in readiness the boats were launched down the banks and into the river. They were rapidly filled with men and started across, occupying but a few moments in the passage. As soon as the opposite bank was reached the regiments were rapidly formed, the Twenty-fifth and Thirty-fifth Illinois left on the bank to protect the shore, while Colonel Heg advanced the Eighth Kansas and Fifteenth Wisconsin across the bottom to the foot of Sand Mountain, keeping a strong line of skirmishers in front. Reaching the mountains, the Fifteenth was left at the foot and the Eighth Kansas advanced up the mountain road, occupying the summit at 10 a. m. The Fifteenth Wisconsin was ordered up at 3 p. m., and at dusk the two regiments advanced about 3 miles across the mountain and camped, remaining in this position until the 2d instant. The Twenty-fifth and Thirty-fifth came up on the evening of the 30th. Frequent scouts were sent out from the brigade during the time we occupied the mountain; one under Lieutenant-Colonel Abernathy, Eighth Kansas, penetrating to near Trenton, Ga., discovering the enemy in force.

On the 2d we marched 16 miles to Will's Valley; 4th, marched 5 miles to Winston's; 9th, ascended mountain and marched across 14 miles, bivouacking at the entrance of Lafourche [Neal's ?] Gap; 10th, marched south along summit of mountain and descended into the valley through Henderson's Gap, bivouacking near Alpine; 14th, crossed back over mountain to Lord's farm; 15th, marched back to Winston's; 16th, marched over mountain to Stevens' Gap; 17th, descended into valley and bivouacked near Lee's Spring; 18th, marched 4 miles north on Chattanooga road.

On the 19th instant we marched at 8 o'clock, and at 11.30 o'clock reached a point near General Rosecrans' headquarters. The brigade filed through the woods to the right, and after marching about a mile was rapidly formed in line of battle, the Fifteenth Wisconsin, Eighth Kansas, and Thirty-fifth Illinois being in line, and the Twenty-fifth Illinois a reserve directly in their rear. The brigade then moved three-quarters of a mile to the right, then by the left flank forward. We had not advanced more than a hundred yards when the enemy, concealed in the timber and behind fallen logs, opened a destructive fire on us. The men replied with promptness and effect, and pushed forward vigorously. The roar of musketry at this time was deafening.

The Twenty-fifth Illinois was ordered forward and came gallantly into line. The stream of wounded to the rear was almost unparalleled. Still the brigade held its ground, cheered on by the gallant, but unfortunate, Colonel Heg, who was everywhere present, careless of danger. The enemy was constantly re-enforced, and at last flanked us on the left, pouring a destructive fire down our line. We had then held the ground three-quarters of an hour. Colonel Heg gave the order to fall back, and the men slowly retreated, taking shelter behind the trees, firing at the advancing enemy, and stubbornly contesting every inch of the ground. Fifty yards to the rear they were again formed and again advanced, almost gaining their original ground, but were again compelled by overwhelming numbers to fall back. Again and again they formed and advanced, only to be driven back. Almost half of the brigade was killed or wounded. Colonel Heg was mortally wounded; but the remnants of the brigade, falling back to a fence a short distance in the rear, held the enemy in check until re-enforcements came up and relieved them, when they fell back across an open field, taking position in the edge of a forest behind a log barricade. What remained of the brigade I reformed here, with the assistance of Captain Morrison, assistant adjutant-general of the division, and again advanced across the field, taking our old position behind the fence, and remaining there until nearly dusk, when the ammunition of the men was exhausted, and we withdrew to the barricade in the edge of the woods again. Just at dark we were withdrawn by order of General Davis, and went into bivouac near the battle-field.

During the night of the 19th the brigade changed its location, crossing the Chattanooga road, and occupying a strong position on a ridge in the woods to the north. Our ammunition was replenished to 60 rounds. At noon we received an order to support General Sheridan on the right. We advanced across the road again and formed in line of battle, and then advanced to near a small barricade in the woods, fronting an open field. Finding the barricade already occupied by our troops, the brigade was moved by the right flank to the rear of General Carlin's brigade, and was ordered to lie down in a small ravine.

This order had hardly been executed when I received an order to move back by the left flank and take position on the left of General Carlin's brigade, the troops that had occupied the ground having been moved away to the left. I directed the movement, passing General Carlin and moving by the right flank forward to the barricade. The three regiments on the right of the brigade reached their position, but the Thirty-fifth Illinois, the regiment on the left of the line, had not reached its position, when the enemy rose up from the tall weeds in front and advanced on us four columns deep, pouring in a destructive fire. The left flank of the brigade was entirely exposed, as the troops that had occupied that position had moved so far to the left as to be out of sight, and we were soon flanked and exposed to a destructive enfilading fire. The enemy in front was terribly punished as he came up. Our men fired coolly from behind the barricade and with terrible effect, the closed ranks and heavy columns of the enemy making their loss very heavy. The brigade held the position until the enemy had mounted the barricade, when, flanked on the left and overpowered by numbers in front, the men fell back in confusion, partially rallying about 200 yards in rear, but, finding all support gone and the line on the left in disorder, breaking again.

On the brow of the hill in the woods across the road they were again rallied, formed in line, and left the field by order in the rear of Sheridan's division, which had rallied at the same point.

I inclose herewith a list of killed, wounded, and missing of the brigade during the two days' engagement. By far the larger number were lost the first day; our loss on the 20th being light. On the second day we had hardly 600 men left in the brigade when we were thrown into the fight. These were opposed by at least a full division of the enemy's army. The list accompanying shows the loss to be fully 60 per cent. of those engaged, and amply attests the courage, stubborness, and determination with which the troops fought.

Where all behaved so gallantly it would be invidious to mention individuals as particularly conspicuous for their actions. The vacant ranks, eloquent with heroic memories of the dead and wounded, speak for our absent comrades; the living, who fought by their sides through the terrible storm of two days' conflict, have again established the invincible courage of the defenders of the Union.

The effective fighting force of the brigade, when it went into the engagement of the 19th, was as follows:

Command.	Present.		
	Commissioned officers.	Enlisted men.	Aggregate.
25th Illinois Volunteer Infantry...	17	320	337
15th Wisconsin Volunteer Infantry...	19	157	176
8th Kansas Volunteer Infantry	24	382	406
35th Illinois Volunteer Infantry...	18	281	299
Total	78	1,140	1,218

The loss of the brigade during the two days' engagement was as follows, viz:

Command.	Commissioned officers.			Enlisted men.			Aggregate.
	Killed.	Wounded.	Missing.	Killed.	Wounded.	Missing.	
25th Illinois Volunteer Infantry	......	11	1	10	160	23	205
15th Wisconsin Volunteer Infantry	2	6	4	3	47	49	111
8th Kansas Volunteer Infantry	3	8	......	30	154	25	220
35th Illinois Volunteer Infantry............................	3	5	......	14	125	13	160
Total *	8	30	5	57	486	110	696

Since the battles on the 19th and 20th the brigade has been re-enforced by a number of returned convalescents and by two companies of the Fifteenth Wisconsin Volunteers, which joined us on the 21st from detached service at Island No. 10. Many of the men slightly wounded have bravely returned to duty, considerably augmenting our force.

I am, captain, very respectfully, your most obedient servant,

JNO. A. MARTIN,
Colonel, Commanding Third Brigade.

Capt. T. W. MORRISON,
Asst. Adjt. Gen., First Div., Twentieth Army Corps.

No. 98.

Report of Lieut. Col. James L. Abernathy, Eighth Kansas Infantry.

HEADQUARTERS EIGHTH KANSAS VOLUNTEERS,
Chattanooga, Tenn., September 29, 1863.

CAPTAIN: I have the honor to make the following report of the part taken by my regiment in the action of the 19th and 20th instant:

I was not in command of my regiment until the evening of the

---

* See revised statement, p. 174.

19th, when the loss of our brave brigade commander threw the command of the brigade upon Colonel Martin.

On the morning of the 19th, after marching nearly 8 miles, most part of the way on double-quick, we were suddenly turned to the right and marched nearly 1 mile into the timber, when we were formed into line of battle, facing east.   Soon after being formed in line we were ordered forward, but had scarcely advanced 50 yards, when the enemy poured a terrible fire upon us from behind a ledge of rocks, where they lay concealed.

Many of the men fell at the first fire, but the others, promptly returning the fire, pressed forward vigorously, and not only maintained their ground, but had nearly penetrated the lines of the enemy, when our brigade commander, seeing the terrible fire to which the line was exposed, gave the order to fall back.

Reforming the line, we again advanced under a perfect shower of bullets, sometimes driving the enemy and in turn being driven by them, until we had fought the ground over and over again, and almost half of our number lay dead or wounded upon the field.

The enemy being largely re-enforced, we took a position farther to the west, on the edge of the timber, where we resisted every effort of the enemy, and finally drove them entirely from that part of the field.

We encamped with the rest of the brigade that night close to the battle-field.

Before dawn next morning we were moved into position on the road to Chattanooga, where we remained until near 12 m., when we crossed the road and took position behind a low rail fence.

Scarcely had we taken our position, however, when the enemy rose up in front of us, where they had been concealed in the tall weeds, and poured upon us a heavy enfilading fire.

The fire was quickly returned, and with good effect, whole lines of the enemy falling at every discharge.   This continued for a short time, and the enemy was almost effectually checked in our front, when the troops upon our right and left gave way, and before I was aware of the danger, the enemy appeared in heavy force upon both flanks, when, unsupported and almost surrounded, we were compelled to leave the field or fall into the hands of the enemy.   We fell back in disorder until we reached the ground formerly occupied by us in the morning.   From here we were ordered to the support of the right of General Thomas, but before reaching the field were ordered forward to this point.

There were many instances of personal bravery and valor displayed upon the field, but all did their duty well.

I submit a list* of the killed and wounded, which speaks for itself of the severity of the contest and the heroic bravery with which our men contested the field.   The regiment entered the battle with 406 officers and men.   Our loss, as you will perceive by the list, is 217.

Very respectfully,

J. L. ABERNATHY,
Lieut. Col. Eighth Kansas Volunteers, Commanding.

Capt. JNO. CONOVER,
Actg. Asst. Adjt. Gen., Third Brigade, First Division.

---

* Embodied in revised statement, p. 174.

No. 99.

Report of Capt. Mons Grinager, Fifteenth Wisconsin Infantry.

HDQRS. FIFTEENTH REGIMENT WISCONSIN VOLS.,
Chattanooga, Tenn., September 29, 1863.

SIR : I have the honor herewith to transmit the following report of the part taken by the Fifteenth Wisconsin Volunteers in the battle of Chickamauga Creek, Ga., on the 19th and 20th instant:

About 1 p. m. on the 19th we were ordered into line of battle on the south side of the Chattanooga road, 3 miles east of Crawfish Spring, our left resting on the Eighth Kansas Volunteers. We marched by the right flank through some heavy underbrush till our right rested on a corn-field about three-quarters of a mile from the road. We then advanced in line of battle over a slight elevation of ground, and on ascending the top the enemy's skirmishers opened fire on us, but with little effect. We drove them in. After advancing a short distance farther, we received a heavy volley from the enemy's line immediately in our front.

The engagement now became general. We held our position for some minutes, and had fired about 6 or 7 rounds, when we were ordered back 10 or 15 paces, on account of being exposed to a heavy cross-fire from infantry on our right and a rebel battery on our left.

This position we held for some time, and had fired about 10 or 12 rounds, when we were ordered to fix bayonets and charge the line immediately in our front. The order was complied with; but our right being so hard pressed, they could make but little headway, having no support to the right, and the Eighth Kansas to the left had partly broken and were a short distance in our rear, being thus exposed to a raking cross-fire. We then received orders to fall back, which was done slowly and in good order, holding the enemy in check until we were relieved by the Second Brigade, General Carlin's, which advanced and engaged the enemy. We reformed in rear of the Second Brigade, which soon was forced back behind us, and we again fired some rounds, but were met with such overwhelming force that we were forced to fall back across an open field immediately in our rear. On our arrival at the edge of the timber, on the north side of the field, the Third Brigade of Sheridan's division advanced on our right and engaged the enemy. We twice tried to recross the field, and succeeded the second time in getting as far as to the log-house on the south side of the field, where we retook a few pieces of artillery, and which position we held until fresh troops arrived.

We then were ordered about three-quarters of a mile to the rear, where we reformed with the division, and bivouacked until 3 o'clock the next morning.

Our loss the 19th in killed, wounded, and missing was : Commissioned officers, 7 ; enlisted men, 59.

Among our killed was Capt. John M. Johnson, Company A. Among our wounded, Col. Hans C. Heg, commanding brigade, since dead. Capt. Hans Hansen, Company C, severely wounded and left on the field ; Maj. George Wilson and Capt. A. Gasman, severely ; Lieut. C. E. Tanberg, Company D, slightly wounded, and Capt. Henry Hauff missing.

At 3 a. m. on the 20th we were ordered a short distance to the left, and took up our position on a hill on the north side of the Chattanooga road, where we were held as reserve until about 11 a. m., when the battle was renewed, and we were ordered to the front. We formed line of battle on the south of the road, and advanced through an orchard and a parcel of timber. After having changed positions several times, took up our final position behind some hastily constructed barricades, our left resting on the Eighth Kansas Volunteers and right on the Twenty-fifth Illinois. We were not fully into our position when the enemy advanced on us from the timber on the opposite side of the field in our front; when they got in short range, we fired and drove the first line back, but they soon advanced again with overwhelming numbers. We held our position until we were outflanked on the left, exposed to a raking cross-fire and almost surrounded, when we got orders to fall back. We then made a hasty retreat to the hill on the north side of the Chattanooga road, in which the battalion soon became scattered. At about 4 p. m. the brigade was sent to the rear.

Our loss on the 20th was:

Commissioned officers	3
Enlisted men	32
Our loss on the 19th	66
Total*	101

Among our loss on the 20th was Lieut. Col. Ole C. Johnson, commanding regiment; Capt. C. Gustaveson, Company F, and Lieut. O. Thompson, Company A, missing.

I had not the honor to command the regiment during the battle, as our lieutenant-colonel, Johnson, was not missing until we fell back from our last position on the 20th, but I observed that both officers and men behaved bravely during the battle, and it is but justice to mention the following officers, who showed more than ordinary courage and bravery during the battle: Lieut. Col. Ole C. Johnson, Maj. George Wilson, Adjt. L. G. Nelson; Capt. John M. Johnson, Company A; Capt. H. Hansen, Company C; Lieutenant Simonson, Company F; Lieutenant Clement, Company K, and Lieutenant Brown, Company H.

I have the honor to be, sir, very respectfully, your obedient servant,

MONS GRINAGER,
Captain, Comdg. 15th Regt. Wisconsin Infty. Vols.

Col. JOHN A. MARTIN,
Comdg. Third Brigade, First Division, 20th Army Corps.

No. 100.

Report of Brig. Gen. Richard W. Johnson, U. S. Army, commanding Second Division.

HDQRS. SECOND DIVISION, TWENTIETH ARMY CORPS,
Chattanooga, Tenn., September 28, 1863.

COLONEL: I have the honor to submit the following report of the operations of my division in the battle of the 19th and 20th instant:

Early in the morning of the 19th, while in camp near Catlett's Gap, a passage through Pigeon Mountain, I received an order to move forward on the Chattanooga road to the support of the left. On my arrival at Crawfish Spring, I received an order from the major-

---

*See revised statement, p. 174.

general commanding the corps to move forward and report to Major-General Thomas, from whom I would receive orders.   I at once sent Capt. E. T. Wells, of my staff, to report to General Thomas, and to receive from him such orders as he might have for me.   The instructions I received were to move in the direction of the cannonading. Arriving near the battle-field, I met Major-General Thomas, who ordered me to form line of battle and move forward and attack.   My division was formed with Willich's brigade on the right and Baldwin's on the left, with Dodge in reserve.   In this order the command moved forward, though oblique to the general line.   Soon the skirmishers became engaged and the enemy forced back.   General Hazen's brigade, at this time on my right, was reported heavily pressed, and I ordered Dodge's brigade to his relief.   The brigade moved forward at double-quick, and soon engaged the enemy.

The contest was severe, but soon the enemy was forced from my entire front, but unfortunately the troops on my right and left did not move forward.   After driving the enemy for at least a mile, Willich sent me word that there were no supports on his right.   I ordered him not to move forward, but to hold his ground.   Everything remained quiet on my front until about 5 p. m., when my entire line was attacked by an overwhelming force in front, flank, and rear. Here the assault was terrific, but darkness soon prevented us from recognizing friend from foe, and in hand-to-hand contest the enemy was repulsed, and the Second Division remained master of the field.

A short time before dark I received an order from Major-General Thomas to fall back at dark and encamp in a position which he designated.   This order was sent to brigade commanders.

My staff officer delivered this order to Colonel Baldwin, soon after which he fell, and Colonel Berry, his successor, was not made aware of the movement until he saw it being executed by the troops on his right.   By this movement many of our wounded fell into the hands of the rebels.   I established my line at the point designated by General Thomas, by placing Berry's brigade on the right and Dodge's on the left, with Willich posted in strong position as a reserve.   In this position my right rested against Palmer and my left on Baird.

Early in the morning of the 20th breastworks were hurriedly thrown up, behind which my men were well sheltered.   At 10 a. m. the enemy advanced in force, attacking my entire front.   I have not heard heavier musketry during the war than we had for one hour, when the enemy was handsomely repulsed in great confusion, leaving the ground literally covered with their dead and dying.   Before the repulse I ordered Willich in with his brigade, to resist to the last extremity.   After the repulse he withdrew a portion of his brigade to his former position, to support his battery in reserve.   There was comparative quiet on my front, with occasional shots only, until about 4 p. m., when we were again vigorously attacked.   General Baird appealed to me in person to send him re-enforcements, or to make a demonstration in his behalf.   The Ninth, Fifteenth, and Forty-ninth Ohio, Fifth Kentucky, and Thirty-second Indiana were sent, under Willich.   Soon after the troops on my left gave way, and the troops above mentioned charged, driving the enemy back with terrible slaughter.   After this movement Willich assembled his regiments in their former position.

While the attack on my immediate front was progressing well, I received an order from Major-General Thomas for the withdrawal of the entire army ; Reynolds first, then Palmer, and I was to follow the latter. I at once sent a staff officer to General Thomas, to say to him that I supposed his order was given based upon the belief that all was quiet on my front, whereas I was fearfully attacked, though I felt confident of being able to hold my position, yet a retreat at that time might be disastrous. Before the return of the staff officer Reynolds and Palmer commenced the movement, followed by a heavy force of the enemy, thus exposing my right. I barely had time to send word to my command to save them from complete destruction. They, however, withdrew in good order. By having Willich in reserve he was enabled to engage the enemy in four different directions, and by his prompt movements he saved the troops from annihilation and capture.

At the time the order was received to withdraw he was engaged with the enemy immediately in my rear. I did not send him the order to withdraw, believing that he was then engaged with General Granger [?]. He withdrew, however, in fine style, and with his brigade covered the retreat of the army.

To each of my brigade commanders I am under many obligations for their good and gallant conduct and their valuable suggestions. Brig. Gen. A. Willich, commanding First Brigade, was always in the right place, and by his individual daring rendered the country great service. This gallant old veteran deserves promotion, and I hope he may receive it. Col. J. B. Dodge, commanding Second Brigade, handled his brigade well, and is worthy and deserving of promotion. He is a brave and gallant soldier. Col. W. W. Berry, who took command of the Third Brigade, behaved with so much coolness and displayed so much skill and ability in the management of his brigade after the fall of the lamented Baldwin, that I hope he may be promoted at once. Colonel Berry first joined the troops under Rousseau at the first outbreak of the rebellion, and has participated in all the battles and skirmishes of his regiment (Fifth Kentucky Infantry) with distinguished gallantry. Col. P. P. Baldwin, than whom a more gallant or accomplished officer is not in the service, fell in the night attack on the 19th. His loss will be seriously felt to his regiment and the service. At one time before his fall one of his regiments became somewhat disorganized, owing to the fall of its colonel. Baldwin seized the colors, and calling out, "Rally round the flag, boys!" the effect was electrical; the men rallied, and this gallant regiment moved magnificently forward.

My thanks are due for coolness and distinguished gallantry to Lieutenant-Colonel Langdon and Major Stafford, First Ohio; Major Gray and Captain Strong, Forty-ninth Ohio; Lieutenant-Colonel Askew and Major McClenahan, Fifteenth Ohio; Lieutenant-Colonel Hall and Major Williams, Eighty-ninth Illinois; Colonel Buckner, Lieutenant-Colonel Rives, and Major Van Deren, Seventy-ninth Illinois; Major Collins, Twenty-ninth Indiana; Lieutenant-Colonel Hurd and Major Fitzsimmons, Thirtieth Indiana; Colonel Rose, Lieutenant-Colonel Pyfer, and Major Phillips, Seventy-seventh Pennsylvania; Colonel Strong, Lieutenant-Colonel Martin, and Major Birch, Ninety-third Ohio; Major Thomasson, Captain Huston, Fifth Kentucky; Lieutenant-Colonel Tripp and Major Campbell, Sixth Indiana.

For individual mention of subaltern officers reference is respectfully made to regimental and brigade reports: but I take this occasion to thank every officer and soldier in the division for their good conduct. No troops ever behaved better. I wish it were possible for me to mention each member of the division by name in this report.

To my staff, Captains Bartlett, Wells, Metzner, Taft; Lieuts. A. S. Smith, J. J. Kessler, Edward Davis, I owe my thanks for their efficiency and gallantry on the battle-field. Captains Bartlett and Wells were with me all the time, and were frequently sent to points of danger; their duties were faithfully and fearlessly performed.

Lieut. F. N. Sheets, of my staff, was killed. He was a brave and gallant young man, and died as heroes wish to die.

My thanks are due to Captain Simonson, my chief of artillery, and all the artillery officers, for good and gallant service. My thanks are due to my medical director, Surg. Charles Schussler, and the other medical officers of the division. They were untiring in their exertions to alleviate the pain of the suffering.

My escort and orderlies performed their duties well. Among them I mention Sergeant Miles, Third Kentucky Volunteer Cavalry, and Private Robert Hays, Thirtieth Indiana.

The country must mourn the loss of gallant spirits who offered their lives upon her altar. For a list, reference is made to sub-reports.

The First Brigade captured five pieces of artillery, and the Third Brigade two pieces. About 600 prisoners were captured by the division and sent to the rear.

It is a source of great pleasure to me to know that the Second Division did not yield an inch; that it defeated every force, whether attacked or attacking.

The list of casualties shows that it did hard fighting.

Respectfully submitted.

R. W. JOHNSON,
Brigadier-General of Volunteers, Commanding Division.

Lieut. Col. G. P. Thruston,
Chief of Staff, Twentieth Army Corps.

[Inclosure.]

Command.	Commissioned officers.				Enlisted men.				Aggregate.
	Killed.	Wounded.	Missing.	Total.	Killed.	Wounded.	Missing.	Total.	
Division staff	1	.....	.....	1	.....	.....	2	2	3
First Brigade	7	15	3	25	47	340	110	497	522
Second Brigade	3	17	28	48	23	184	283	490	538
Third Brigade	4	24	.....	28	50	421	67	538	566
Total *	15	56	31	102	120	945	462	1,527	1,629

No. 101.

Report of Capt. Peter Simonson, Fifth Indiana Battery, Chief of Artillery.

Camp at Chattanooga, Tenn.,
October 10, 1863,

Colonel : In answer to your order of yesterday, I have the honor to report that I was not in command of the batteries of this division during the battle of the 19th and 20th. General Willich, command-

---

* See revised statement, p. 174.

ing the First Brigade of this division, some time previous to the fight, desired to have entire control of the battery in his brigade, and it was so ordered by General Johnson. This relieved me, and I took command of my own battery on the 1st of September. I herewith transmit the reports of the battery commanders of this division, and can only add that Battery A, First Ohio Light Artillery, did nobly. I saw from my position the fight described in Captain Goodspeed's report, and have never seen a battery better handled or fought than he did then.

Captain Grosskopff did not do much. Saturday night he fired a few rounds, which endangered our own troops, and he was stopped. During Sunday he early disappeared from the field, and I can give no additional information than that afforded by his report.

I am, very respectfully, your obedient servant,

PETER SIMONSON,
Captain, and Chief of Artillery.

Col. JAMES BARNETT,
Chief of Artillery.

No. 102.

Report of Brig. Gen. August Willich, U. S. Army, commanding First Brigade.

HDQRS. FIRST BRIG., SECOND DIV., 20TH ARMY CORPS,
Chattanooga, Tenn., September 28, 1863.

SIR: I have the honor to forward report of part taken by my command in the battle of the 19th and 20th instant.

On the 19th instant, at 5.30 a. m., the brigade marched (from the right of the army) with the rest of the division, and the brigade leading, behind the line of battle toward the left, to the support of General Thomas. Arrived at a gap in the line, I halted under orders, and formed the brigade, the Thirty-second Indiana Volunteers, Lieutenant Colonel Erdelmeyer, commanding, and Forty-ninth Ohio Volunteers, Major Gray, commanding, protected by their skirmishers in front; Eighty-ninth Illinois Volunteers, Lieutenant-Colonel Hall commanding; and Fifteenth Ohio Volunteers, Lieutenant-Colonel Askew, commanding, in second line; the battery under Captain Goodspeed in the rear of the brigade. The ground being wooded and hilly, it would not allow free maneuver for artillery, and I gave Captain Goodspeed instructions to keep his battery out of musket-range and in the rear of the infantry until further orders. As soon as the Third Brigade of this division was formed on my left, both brigades advanced, under directions from General Thomas, in a direction which diverged from the advancing line of troops on my right at an angle of about 45 degrees.

My skirmishers soon engaged the enemy, who opened with shell and then with canister from a point right in front, so that the fire did not reach the Third Brigade. After having re-enforced the skirmish line, and having brought to bear two sections of my battery, and having sufficiently shaken the enemy's infantry line, I ordered a bayonet charge, and took the Eighty-ninth Illinois into a line with the Forty-ninth Ohio and Thirty-second Indiana, keeping the Fifteenth Ohio in reserve. The charge was executed in splendid order, and with such an energy that everything was swept before it for about a mile. Five pieces of the enemy's artillery, which had done us much damage, were taken, brought to the rear, and delivered by my assistant adjutant-general at the headquarters of the army. Fearful to lose all connection with other troops, I halted my brigade in a good position, and endeavored to find that connection. The Third Brigade was on my left; on the left of the Third Brigade was nothing. Calling on General Johnson, commanding division, and inquiring for our connection with other troops, I was assured by the division inspector that a division of another corps was on our left. Colonel Rose, Seventy-seventh Pennsylvania, on my wish, reconnoitered the right along the enemy's skirmish line, and reported the next troops on our line a mile distant. To the left of the Third Brigade was an open field, inclosed by woods. After some hours of light skirmishing in front, Colonel Baldwin, commanding Third Brigade, communicated to me that the enemy was turning his left flank toward the rear. I advised him to take his two rear regiments and charge to the rear and left; at the same time I threw the Forty-ninth Ohio Volunteers along the fence inclosing the open field on the right of the First Ohio Volunteers (Third Brigade). As soon as the enemy entered the open ground he received a murderous fire, which he could not stand; at the same moment Colonel Baldwin attacked his right, and drove the enemy with great slaughter before him, capturing two pieces of artillery.

The particular feature of this attack and repulse of the enemy on our left flank and rear was that it took place directly in front of that division of our army which had to make connection with our left, but which did not move along with us in our first advance, and thereby created an opening of 1¼ to 1½ miles between their front and our own. As we had discovered the flank of the enemy in our first forward move, the great consequence for the success of the day presents itself to every military mind which would have resulted from a spontaneous advance of the division to our left with our own advance, and by which we could have attacked the enemy's broken flank by changing front to the right. As it was, all I could do was to keep my position and be on the lookout for other attacks in the flank and rear. I received a written order from General Johnson to fall back at 6.30 p. m. to our general line of battle. With dusk the attack looked for took place. The enemy had succeeded in bringing his batteries and masses of infantry into position. A shower of canister and columns of infantry streamed at once into our front and both flanks. My two front regiments were swept back to the second line. This line for a moment came into disorder. Then they received the command, "Dress on your colors;" repeated by many men and officers; and in no time the four regiments formed one solid line, sending death into the enemy's masses, who immediately fell back from the front, and there did not answer with a single round.

On my left, the Third Brigade had also been successful; on my right, the Second Brigade appears to have lost ground, because, at once, a line of rebels poured from the right and rear a volley in my right flank. One regiment only, the Thirty-second Indiana, faced them, and the enemy soon disappeared. Then I fell slowly back in two lines, and coming to the general line of battle, I found General Johnson, who designated the place for the brigade to bivouac.

Though our loss in this last attack was heavy, I take it as a very happy incident that the Second Division was able to break the fury of the charge before it could reach the general line of battle on the left of our army. By the skillful and well-timed action of Captain Goodspeed, the battery had reached the bivouac ground before the regiment.

On the 20th September the other two brigades of our division were ordered into temporary breastworks erected during the night in our front, my brigade in reserve. I took my position, in rendezvous formation, behind a slope in an open field in the rear of the breastworks. From here I could support the front and be prepared for the flanks and rear ; after a short stay in this position, at 9 a. m. I was ordered forward, and directed by General Johnson to engage the enemy immediately in our front. I obeyed, and advanced the Eighty-ninth Illinois and Thirty-second Indiana over the lines, not engaged, up to the skirmishers, with whom they mixed, and helped to drive back the charging enemy. Feeling sure that the enemy would fall on our flank, I ordered the Fifteenth Ohio back to the support of the battery, where they arrived in the brink of time, the enemy advancing in triple lines on the flank toward the rear. The battery had changed front, and Captain Goodspeed poured double-shotted canister into the enemy, who left some of his dead 50 yards in front of the battery. The Fifteenth Ohio gave a volley, and formed on the left of the battery.

The Ninth Ohio (General Brannan's division) deployed into line under heavy fire, and made, supported by the Fifteenth Ohio, a glorious charge.

The same glorious charge was made on the left flank of the enemy's advancing columns by the Forty-ninth Ohio, with rear rank in front, supported by the Louisville Legion, of the Third Brigade. The rebel columns were driven with heavy slaughter, and the enemy was routed. Our army, whose very existence would have been endangered by a success of this bold and powerful charge, was for the time safe. My battery behaved splendidly, and suffered heavy losses. The enemy was driven half a mile, when he to some extent rallied and brought the fight to a stand. The Forty-ninth Ohio reported that their ammunition gave out. On my inquiry, Colonel Berry, commanding Third Brigade after the fall of Colonel Baldwin, declared he could hold the breastworks with his own command. At this I took the Thirty-second Indiana, leaving the Eighty-ninth Illinois in its old position, advanced with it through the Forty-ninth Ohio, charged and drove the enemy for 1¼ miles, leaving the ground strewn with dead and wounded, and taking numerous prisoners; then I swept, with the Thirty-second Indiana, to the left through the woods, where I fell in with the enemy's cavalry, and on the Chattanooga road to the open field, where my battery was planted. Here I assembled my whole brigade, and took a position in the northwest corner of the field, which, in my judgment, then was the most threatened point. My skirmishers caught some prisoners (100) in front of my new line, and I learned that a whole brigade of Longstreet's corps was about 500 yards in my front, concealed and quietly lying down in a gap between the line of battle of our wing and General Thomas' position. The enemy's artillery was playing on my brigade, though partly silenced by Captain Goodspeed, and I could do no more than watch his intentions. At this time I perceived heavy clouds of dust moving through the woods to the left of our intrenchments. The intentions of the enemy's troops in my front was then clear. They would break in with the attack to be made on our breastworks and cut their defenders off in the rear. I called the attention of General Johnson several times to the approaching thunder-storm. Just when it was on the point of breaking forth, one or two of our divisions on the right of our breastworks left this portion of the battle-field under higher orders, each regiment cheering as they left, which cheering did not at all cheer us, who kept the position under a heavy fire. Then the storm broke loose; first in small squads, then in an unbroken stream, the defenders rushed without organization over the open field, partly over and through my brigade, which was formed in two lines. At the same time the enemy's artillery in front of me and in the rear of our lines advanced within canister range, swept my position, and entered into a canister duel with Captain Goodspeed. The enemy's infantry did not attempt to force me.

When the fugitives had reached the cover of the woods, I ordered the battery to retire and to join the troops under General Thomas; then I slowly withdrew the brigade in two lines, exposed to heavy artillery fire, but not pressed by the enemy's infantry. On the other side of the woods, formerly General Thomas' ground, I took a good position, reported to General Thomas, and received orders to cover the retreat in connection with General Reynolds.

I sent my battery, which had made good its retreat without loss and had faithfully waited for me, ahead on the Rossville road, took a new position, permitted all troops to pass, and followed as rear guard, driving many stragglers before us, and reached camp unmolested at 12 p. m. Here I found General Johnson, with the other two brigades of the division; we received rations for the men, and tried to calm our sore feelings over the apparent non- uccess of our fighting, marching, and suffering, and over the great havoc death had worked in the ranks of our friends and brothers in arms. Though our loss can only be a percentage of the loss inflicted on the enemy, in no instance he resisted [repelled ?] our charges or was able to force our lines.

I do not feel competent to bestow praise on the officers and men of my command; for their bravery and self-denial they are above praise. They have again and again proven that they are true sons of the Republic, who value life only so long as it is the life of freemen, and who are determined to make the neck of every power, slaveratic [sic] or monarchical, bend before the commonwealth of the freemen of the United States of America. Young and brave Lieutenant-Colonel Hall, Eighty-ninth Illinois, sealed, dying, his political creed with the words, "Tell my regiment to stand by the flag of our country.' Captain Whiting, Eighty-ninth Illinois, the beloved brother and leader of his men; Capt. William H. Rice, Captain Spink, Lieutenant Adams, all Eighty-ninth Illinois; Captain Ritter, Thirty-second Indiana, good and brave to the last moment; brave Lieutenant Fowler, Fifteenth Ohio, and all those brave men whose bodies now molder in Southern ground—they are so many columns in the arch of this Republic, and every Northern traitor who tries to make their glorious deaths useless for the cause of humanity should be led to the little mound of earth which covers their remains and learn penitence.

All the regimental commanders—Lieutenant-Colonel Erdelmeyer, Lieutenant-Colonel Askew, Lieutenant-Colonel Hall. and Major Williams after the fall of Colonel Hall, and Major Gray came fully up to all that men in high positions merit in judgment, skill, and bravery.

Captain Goodspeed and his brave officers and men have still more endeared themselves to the brigade.   I have the more to pay my compliments to Captain Goodspeed, as during the most of the time, and during the most trying circumstances, I could give him very little advice, partly on account of the formation of the ground, partly on account of the character of the battle, the enemy charging on us alternately from all directions of the compass; several times charging from several sides at the same time.   My adjutant, Capt. Carl Schmitt, deported himself, as in all former engagements and battles, so actively and skillfully, that he took a great deal of my labor on his shoulders.   So did Lieutenant Butler, aide-de-camp, who was wounded on the first day and missed after the last attack.   I sincerely hope that he is only prisoner, and that his valuable services will be preserved to his country.   Lieutenant Green, inspector; Lieutenant McGrath, aide-de-camp; and Lieutenant Blume, engineer, distinguished themselves, as on all previous engagements, by their judgment and cool bravery.   For the names of the other officers I must refer to the regimental and battery reports.   Orderly G. Hirshheurser distinguished himself greatly, and fell, wounded, in the enemy's hands.

Looking back on the manner this brigade and so many others have done their duty, I cannot repress a regret to see our best troops melt away to a mere nothing.   My brigade now numbers scarcely 800 rifles, instead of 3,500.   Why have not the old regiments been filled up, instead of forming new ones ?   Then the new men would have got a good school, instead of being intrusted to new and inexperienced officers; then the new troops would have been veterans in a short time.   Now the veterans day by day die out.

Annexed please find summary of losses.*

A. WILLICH,
Brigadier-General of Volunteers.

Lieutenant SMITH,
    Acting Assistant Adjutant-General, Second Division.

No. 103.

Report of Maj. William D. Williams, Eighty-ninth Illinois Infantry.

HDQRS. 89TH ILL. INF., 1ST BRIG., 2D DIV., 20TH A. C.,
In the Trenches, Chattanooga, Tenn., September 25, 1863.

SIR: In compliance with orders received this day, I present a brief outline of the operations of the Eighty-ninth Regiment Illinois Infantry Volunteers since breaking up camp in Tullahoma, Tenn.:

On the 16th of August, 1863, the Eighty-ninth Regiment received orders to march at 4 p. m.   We started at the appointed time under the command of Lieut. Col. D. J. Hall (Col. C. T. Hotchkiss, 5 line officers, and 10 sergeants being absent on special recruiting service). The regiment in company with the brigade marched all night, passing through Winchester and Salem, and thence by easy marches over the mountains to Bellefonte, Ala.   The regiment and brigade encamped at Bellefonte six days awaiting orders.

On the morning of August 30 we broke up camp, and proceeded up the Tennessee River road to a point opposite Stevenson, Ala.

---

* Embodied in revised statement, p. 174.

On the 31st the brigade and regiment crossed the Tennessee River on a pontoon bridge, thence by easy marches over the Sand Mountain to Broomtown Valley, thence back again to Winston's, thence up the mountain again and along the ridge to Stevens' or Frick's Gap, through the same to a point 4 miles south, opposite the enemy's extreme left. The operations of the regiment, from the crossing of the Tennessee River to striking the enemy's left, embraces a period of some sixteen days, which was employed in marching and countermarching over mountains and through valleys.

On the 18th of September the regiment stood picket opposite the enemy's left and about 800 yards distant therefrom.

At daylight on the morning of the 19th of September we marched with the brigade about 4 miles to a point opposite the left of General Thomas' corps, it being understood we were to re-enforce the left of our line of battle. We arrived about 11 a. m. at Gordon's [Crawfish] Spring, formed in double column, marched with the brigade 2 miles toward the left of General Thomas' corps, wheeled to the right, deployed column within easy musket range of the enemy, the Eighty-ninth Illinois and Fifteenth Ohio forming the second line, the Thirty-second Indiana and Forty-ninth Ohio forming the first line. The Eighty-ninth Illinois occupying the right of the second line, we had no connection, so far as I could discover, on our right. We lay flat on the ground, without firing, about forty minutes, subject in the meantime to the heavy musketry and artillery fire of the enemy, which wounded 5 of our men, at the expiration of which time the brigade bugle sounded "Forward;" the officers and men obeyed with alacrity, starting forward on a double-quick, driving the enemy almost without stopping (at least not stopping more than five minutes) upward of a mile. About a mile from where we started to charge the enemy, the right and left companies of the Eighty-ninth encountered two of the enemy's batteries; the left, Company C, Eighty-ninth, captured one of the pieces opposite them (a 6-pounder Parrott and caisson), the enemy escaping with the balance. The three right companies were checked by the murderous discharges of grape and canister from the enemy's battery opposite them. It was here that Capt. W. H. Rice, Company A, Capt. John W. Spink, Company D, Lieutenant Warren, Company E, and Lieutenant Ellis, Company B, fell with many of our men. Lieutenant-Colonel Hall, seeing the right thrown into some confusion (caused by an over-zeal of the three right companies to capture the only remaining rebel piece, which was being dragged off by hand), ordered the regiment to halt and fall back 20 yards, firing.

In the meantime order was restored on the right. At this point Brigadier-General Willich came forward, and, standing in front of the regiment and amid the shower of bullets poured into us, complimented the regiment for its impetuous advance, calmed their excitement, instructed them how to advance firing and maintain their alignment with the advance of the brigade, and by his own inimitable calmness of manner restored order and confidence in the regiment, and after dressing them and drilling them in the manual of arms for a short time, ordered them to advance about 30 paces to the edge of an open space. They did so in good order; lay down and kept the enemy in check for the next two hours.

In the meantime the enemy kept up a constant fire, which was vigorously returned by our men. About 5.30 p. m. the enemy, having been re-enforced and somewhat recovered from the severe fright and punishment we had inflicted upon him, advanced in heavy force and pressed our regiment and brigade back some 250 yards, where the brigade made a determined stand in an advantageous position, checked the advance of the enemy, but not without severe loss in killed and wounded.   By this time it was pitch dark; prudence suggested a withdrawal to maintain connection with the brigades on our right and left.   General Willich led the Eighty-ninth Illinois, Thirty-second Indiana, Forty-ninth and Fifteenth Ohio, his brigade, to a position in the rear near to the position occupied in the morning, when we deployed column.   Here we bivouacked for the night, exultant in our success, proud of our brigade and its incomparable commander, but saddened with the sight of our thinned ranks and the loss of personal friends.   Thus ended the eventful 19th of September, 1863.

Early on the morning of the 20th, the brigade took a rendezvous position in double column about the center of a large open field and about the center of the left of our entire line of battle, which, at this point, partook of the convex order of battle, around which the enemy was in heavy force.   The Eighty-ninth and Thirty-second formed the first line, the Forty-ninth and Fifteenth the second line.   After considerable maneuvering the brigade was faced to the east and ordered to advance to the support of the Third Brigade, then hotly engaged with the enemy.

The Eighty-ninth and Thirty-second moved straight forward over two lines of temporary breastworks to the Third under a heavy fire.   The Forty-ninth and Fifteenth obliqued to the left.   The attack of the enemy, after a fierce contest, was handsomely repulsed. After lying at this point perhaps two hours the Eighty-ninth and Thirty-second, together with the Forty-ninth and Fifteenth, were ordered to the support of Goodspeed's battery, near a log-house at the southwest corner of the field, the enemy having swung around to the rear of our position.   At this point, while lying in support of this battery, which played vigorously on the enemy, and was fiercely shelled and played upon in return, about 3 p. m. fell Lieut. Col. D. J. Hall, commanding Eighty-ninth Illinois Infantry, pierced through the bowels by a musket-ball at the hands of a rebel sharp-shooter.   I cannot let the opportunity pass without adding my humble tribute to the many excellences of this young and promising officer and accomplished gentleman.   "None knew him but to praise."   His death at this juncture is an irreparable loss to the regiment and the service.   His last words were, "Tell my parents I died for my flag and my country ; tell my regiment to stand by their flag and their country."   On the happening of this dreadful misfortune I assumed the command of the Eighty-ninth Regiment.

About 5 p. m. it was observed that regiments and brigades on our right and left were giving way in inextricable confusion; at the same time the enemy were shelling us furiously on our front, right, and rear, mingled with terrific musketry.   General Willich ordered the battery to take position about 100 yards to the left of original position.   They did so.   The Eighty-ninth moved in good order by the left flank, fronted, and laid down, the Thirty-second, Forty-ninth, and Fifteenth doing the same on our left.   During this change of front a stream of fugitives was running through and over us, but the brigade stood firm and undaunted.   It was during this trying ordeal that the First Brigade of the Second Division, Twentieth Army Corps. earned its sobriquet of the "Iron Brigade of the Cumberland Army." After the battery had withdrawn and the cloud of fugitives had passed to the rear, the First Brigade about-faced, and halting and fronting every 50 yards, presented a bold and defiant front, effectually checking the enemy. The Eighty-ninth, with the other regiments of the brigade, halted about half a mile to the rear of original position in the morning, confronting the enemy and holding him in check, while the balance of the Army of the Cumberland filed by our rear in full retreat to Chattanooga, some 10 or 12 miles distant.

The First Brigade formed the rear guard of the Army of the Cumberland; the Eighty-ninth Illinois formed the rear guard of the brigade. We marched about three hours, picking up countless stragglers, and forcing them on to Chattanooga. The enemy did not molest us. We halted with the brigade about 8 miles from the battle-ground of Chickamauga.

The next morning, September 21, we took position about 4 miles in front of Chattanooga, remaining there in line of battle until 1 a. m., September 22, when we withdrew to within a mile of Chattanooga, formed in line of battle, threw up a temporary breastwork, and are, at the moment of writing, awaiting the enemy.

In the above sketch I have endeavored to give a truthful account of the operations of the Eighty-ninth Illinois Infantry from my standpoint, but the operations of the regiment are so mingled and mixed with the brigade, that it is necessarily more or less imperfect, desultory, and obscure. It remains for me but to say the men and officers of the Eighty-ninth Illinois Infantry are, in my judgment— and, I trust, in the judgment of my superiors—worthy to belong to the First Brigade, and to be under the command of such a general as A. Willich. I trust the time will come when we can all sit by our peaceful firesides (when great command shall have been awarded him), and recount the time when he was our brigade commander, standing in front of our regiment, amid the rain of bullets and shells, and drilling us into steadiness and confidence.

Of the officers of the Eighty-ninth, during the memorable two days of historic Chickamauga, I cannot speak in too high praise; of the gallant dead, Captains Rice, Spink, and Whiting, and Lieutenant Adams, they fell gloriously at the head of their companies. Can language furnish a more eloquent epitaph for a soldier's tomb? Of the wounded, Adjt. E. F. Bishop added new laurels to the chaplet won at Stone's River; Lieutenants Warren, Ellis, and Darcy led their commands with distinguished bravery and coolness.

It would ill become me to speak of the merits of such officers as Capt. John M. Farquhar, Capt. H. L. Rowell, Captain Hobbs, Lieutenants Dimick, Sampson, Young, and Harkness; it would be a feeble and pitiable attempt to "gild refined gold or paint the lily;" their praise should be a general's encomium and a nation's gratitude.

Of the non-commissioned staff, Sergt. Maj. E. J. Stivers deserves especial mention for brave and intrepid conduct. The men fought like veterans, and proved themselves worthy of the title. I did not see a single enlisted man of the Eighty-ninth flinch from his duty. Where such is the case it would seem invidious to discriminate, yet the conduct of Private Beecher, of Company D, deserves especial notice. All the commissioned and non-commissioned officers present with his company were either killed or disabled in the early part of the action of the 19th. Private Beecher assumed the command, the men instinctively obeying his orders; his intrepidity, coolness, and excellent judgment kept the company together, and stamped him as worthy of command. Sergeant Friday, the color-bearer, stands out a hero, and has no superior for the position he holds. But space admonishes me to close.

Appended please find exhibit marked A, which attests the severity of the actions of the 19th and 20th of September, 1863, and which exhibits the casualties* of the Eighty-ninth Illinois Infantry. The missing are undoubtedly killed, wounded, or prisoners.

All of which is respectfully submitted.

W. D. WILLIAMS,
Major, Comdg. Eighty-ninth Regiment Illinois Infantry.

Capt. CARL SCHMITT,
Assistant Adjutant-General, First Brigade.

No. 104.

Report of Lieutenant-Colonel Frank Erdelmeyer, Thirty-second Indiana Infantry.

HDQRS. THIRTY-SECOND REGIMENT INDIANA VOLS.,
Chattanooga, Tenn., September 27, 1863.

GENERAL: I have the honor to report to you the part which the Thirty-second Indiana Volunteers took in the battle of Chickamauga Creek.

The regiment marched at the head of the brigade on Saturday, the 19th instant, from the right wing of the army toward its left wing; reached the scene of action at 10 a. m. The regiment advanced with skirmishers in the front and soon was wholly engaged. Our right flank being exposed by our advanced position, could not proceed any farther until the evil was remedied. We then, in connection with the other regiments of your brigade, charged the enemy and drove him from his position, taking 2 pieces of artillery and 3 caissons and many prisoners; also recaptured the men's baggage of the Thirty-third Ohio Regiment. Having been relieved by the second line of brigade, we remained quiet until nightfall, when our line was fiercely attacked and repulsed. We slowly fell back, keeping a well-directed fire upon the enemy. Night having come on, we ceased firing and slowly returned from the field to the bivouac of the division. Our loss on this day was heavy, especially in wounded, of which 4 were commissioned officers.

On the morning of the 20th of September the regiment, with the brigade, was in a reserve position, and was ordered to engage the enemy at 9 a. m. Our lines being placed behind a breastwork, we could do no more than stand at ease and repulse one attack which was made against it, most of the time nothing but a few sharpshooters being in our front. As the enemy's attack upon the left wing of the army was becoming desperate, the Thirty-second Indiana marched to the support. We formed a line toward the left flank of the original line of battle, and, in connection with collections of men from different regiments, charged on the advancing lines of the enemy, and drove them under continual fire over a mile.

---

* Nominal list omitted; see revised statement, p. 174.

Passing over the field, we found the dead body of General Walker, commanding a division of the so-called Confederate army, also a Colonel von Zinken, of the First [Twentieth] Louisiana, and a great many officers killed during this fight. I would also claim a rebel flag, which was passed over by our men during the engagement, and picked up by some stragglers in the rear of my regiment.

We returned from this charge, and again returned to a reserve position on the road and in the rear of General Reynolds' division. There remained quiet until about 5 p. m., exposed, however, to the fire of the enemy's sharpshooters.

At this time the enemy, being invited by the withdrawal of General Reynolds' division, recommenced throwing shells upon us and over us in such a manner as to make our position not maintainable; we therefore changed front and fell back across the road. Hardly in position, the left wing of the army commenced falling back, and after the most of the troops were gone and the enemy had taken possession of the breastworks in our front, we fell back through the woods, taking possession of a hill in the rear of the woods, covering the Chattanooga road, and then followed the brigade as rear guard of the army. The total loss of my regiment during the two days was 21 killed, 81 wounded, and 20 missing, supposed to be partly killed or wounded. The above includes 1 captain killed, and 1 captain and 3 lieutenants wounded.

Before closing this, my report, I cannot abstain from mentioning that my full praise and most sincere thanks are due to all my officers and men for their promptness in obeying my orders, as well as for the courage displayed during the whole of the battle and under such trying circumstances.

I have the honor to remain, general, your obedient servant,

FRANK ERDELMEYER,
Lieutenant-Colonel, Commanding 32d Indiana Volunteers.

Brig. Gen. A. WILLICH,
Commanding First Brigade.

No. 105.

Report of Col. Thomas J. Harrison, Thirty-ninth Indiana (Mounted) Infantry.

HDQRS. THIRTY-NINTH REGIMENT INDIANA VOLS.,
Chattanooga, September 28, 1863.

On Thursday evening, 17th instant, I was ordered with my regiment to Bailey's Cross-Roads, in McLemore's Cove, which is opposite and 2½ miles from Dug Gap and 3 miles from Blue Bird Gap. Those gaps were occupied at the time by a strong force of the enemy. About 3 p. m. my regiment was attacked by a brigade of rebel cavalry at Davis' Ford, on Chickamauga Creek. The fight lasted two hours. The field was left in our possession. We had 2 men slightly wounded; none killed. The enemy had 2 killed, one of whom was Colonel Estes, of the Third Confederate Cavalry, and 8 wounded.

On the next day we skirmished at the Widow Davis' Cross-Roads, retaining the ground without loss. The enemy's loss unknown.

On the night of the 18th instant we were ordered to Pond Spring.

On the morning of the 19th, were directed to protect the right and rear of General Sheridan's division. My regiment was delayed in its movements by demonstrations made by the enemy on the La Fayette and Ringgold roads, thereby throwing us in rear of General Mitchell's cavalry. About meridian, the enemy attacked our right flank, and succeeded in cutting off the Second Indiana Cavalry, the cavalry train, and my regiment from the main body of troops. But after considerable fighting, we drove the enemy and rejoined our army; we reached Crawfish Spring at sunset. I learned that our soldiers on the field were suffering greatly for water. I directed my regiment to press all the canteens that could be found, and, with our own, we were enabled to deliver 1,000 canteens of water by midnight to our suffering soldiers on the battle-field.

On Sunday, the 20th, we were again assigned a position on the extreme right of the infantry. Dismounting, we moved our horses to a secure position in the rear. At 11 a. m. we moved forward, meeting an advancing enemy. Colonel Laiboldt's brigade, of General Sheridan's division, was on our left; Colonel Wilder's mounted infantry on our right. The enemy met us at the top of a high ridge, and neither party discovered the other until within 30 paces. The struggle was brief, but desperate; yet the enemy was unable to withstand our Spencer rifles, and gave way, running in disorder before both Colonel Wilder's and my commands. At the same time Colonel Laiboldt's command was driven back, entirely changing the direction of our line and bringing the enemy directly between us and our army, entirely cutting Colonel Wilder and myself off. At that juncture we were ordered to take a train, which was also cut off, and make our way in the direction of Lookout Mountain and thence to Chattanooga, which we did, reaching the neighborhood of Chattanooga at dark.

On the evening of the 21st I was ordered to take position with my regiment on Missionary Hill, 5 miles east of Chattanooga, and to hold the enemy in check as long as I could safely do so. On reaching the ridge I found the Forty-fourth Indiana and Thirteenth Ohio occupying the same position I was directed to hold. I arranged the three regiments to the best advantage, and on the next morning at 10 o'clock a division of the enemy attacked us. Company B, commanded by Lieutenant Noble; Company C, Captain Crowell; Company D, Captain Herring, and Company F, temporarily commanded by Dr. Connett, received and withstood the attack for some time. But I thought it best to draw them back on the reserve line, where the action became general. Lieutenant-Colonel Aldrich, in command of the Forty-fourth Indiana, made a gallant fight; and I am pleased to call attention to the conduct of Lieutenant Norvell, in command of Company H, of my regiment. Late in the evening, the superior force of the enemy, enabling him to outflank us, compelled a retreat;

In these engagements we had 5 men killed and 32 wounded. Captain Potts was wounded on the 20th, and fell into the hands of the enemy. Lieutenants Garboden and Clark were both wounded. I was much pleased with the gallant conduct of Maj. J. D. Evans and Adjutant Fortner. Drs. Gray and Connett acquitted themselves with honor in their department. My line officers all discharged their duty in a most commendable manner. My non-commissioned officers and private soldiers were generally prompt and brave.

All of which I respectfully submit.

THOMAS J. HARRISON,
Colonel Thirty-ninth Indiana Volunteers.

[Brig. Gen. R. W. JOHNSON.]

HDQRS. SECOND DIVISION, TWENTIETH ARMY CORPS,
September 29, 1863.

Respectfully forwarded, commending Colonel Harrison, his officers, and men, for their good and gallant conduct.

R. W. JOHNSON,
Brigadier-General.

No. 106.

Report of Lieut. Col. Frank Askew, Fifteenth Ohio Infantry.

HDQRS. FIFTEENTH REGT. OHIO INFANTRY VOLS.,
Chattanooga, Tenn., September 26, 1863.

SIR: I have the honor to report the part taken by this regiment in the battles of the 19th and 20th instant:

On Saturday, the 19th, the regiment, having been on picket duty, was not able to march with the rest of the brigade, but under orders marched as soon as the men got their breakfasts and as soon as the pickets could be drawn in, and after a very rapid march came up with the brigade several miles south of Crawfish Spring; thence we moved in the rear of the brigade, the battery being before us until we reached the place where the brigade went into action. We formed the second line, in rear of the Forty-ninth Ohio, which was on the left. We followed the front line closely in their brilliant and rapid advance, ready to support them if necessary, until the brigade was halted, when we were formed in double column on the center. We were lying in this position when the enemy made the attack about dark on Saturday evening. The stragglers from the first line, of which there was a considerable number, threw the regiment into some confusion, but they were soon rallied, and the regiment deployed into line on the left of the Forty-ninth Ohio, when the enemy was checked and the firing ceased. We then moved into camp with the brigade.

On Sunday, the 20th instant, the brigade being in reserve in rendezvous position, we were formed in double column on the center, in rear of the Eighty-ninth Illinois Volunteers, and to the left of the Forty-ninth Ohio, fronting the line occupied by the Second and Third Brigades of this division. We remained in this position for some time, when the brigade, advanced to the first line of barricades, deployed into line. Here I received an order from the general to go to the support of Captain Goodspeed's battery and to form on its left. The battery at that time was near the house on the road, and a little to the right and considerably to the rear of our line. I immediately moved by the right flank. When the head of my column had nearly reached the battery, though we were still on the right of it, we received a sharp volley from a body of the enemy who were advancing down the road, and on the left flank of our general line of battle, and who had driven our troops that were protecting that flank before them. I immediately halted and faced by the rear rank, and gave the enemy a volley. By this time the Ninth Ohio, which had been formed parallel to the road and fronting our general line of battle, changed front forward on their tenth company, which threw their line in front of ours, and this attack of the enemy was repulsed with the assistance of two other regiments of the brigade, which were in line along the barricades, and which faced, I supposed, by the rear rank, and gave the enemy a fire in his flank. As soon as possible I proceeded to form on the left of the battery, as before ordered, my right resting on the road and fronting up the road or in a northerly direction, and in the direction from which the last attack was made. While here General John Beatty came to me and informed me that the enemy were again directly on our front, and requested me to advance the regiment with some other troops which were formed on our right and left. I told him I would do so if I got permission of the general. He obtained the permission, and we advanced through the woods, driving the enemy before us until we reached the point where the field on the right of the road terminated and the woods began. The regiments on our right and left having halted before this, and being considerably in advance of the line without support, I did not deem it prudent to advance farther, and the regiment was halted here. I then sent Major McClenahan to inform the general where we were and to ask for orders. The major returned with the order to rejoin the brigade. Before this order was begun to be executed the enemy again advanced to the attack.

Our flanks being exposed we fell back slowly and gradually, firing in retreat; we fell back perhaps 100 yards in this way, when the enemy appeared to have been satisfied, as he did not follow us up. I formed the regiment here and moved back over the ground which we had retreated over, the enemy falling back rapidly before us. We gathered up our wounded, and then joined the brigade near the house, forming on the left of the Thirty-second Indiana Volunteers and fronting to the west. The movements of the regiment during the remainder of the day having been with the brigade and directly under the eye of the general, I do not think it necessary to go into an extensive account of it. I cannot speak in terms of too high praise of the conduct of the officers and men of the regiment; under the hottest fire they were cool, collected, and determined. The men fired deliberately, never firing unless they saw something to fire at, and then with good aim. Lieutenant Fowler, commanding Company F, a gallant officer, was killed. Captain Byrd and Lieutenant Updegrove, both commanding companies, were wounded. Major McClenahan, although quite unwell, remained on the field to the last, and rendered gallant and efficient service in the management of the regiment. Out of 325 with which we went into action we lost as follows:

Officers and men.	Killed.	Wounded.	Missing.	Total.
Officers...	1	2	......	3
Enlisted men.	9	75	33	117
Total...	10	77	33	120

I am, very respectfully, your obedient servant,

FRANK ASKEW,
Lieutenant-Colonel, Commanding Regiment.

Capt. CARL SCHMITT,
Assistant Adjutant-General, First Brigade.

No. 107.

Report of Maj. Samuel F. Gray, Forty-ninth Ohio Infantry.

HEADQUARTERS FORTY-NINTH OHIO VOLUNTEERS,
Chattanooga, Tenn., September 26, 1863.

SIR : I have the honor to submit the following official report of the part taken by this command in the battle of the 19th and 20th instant :

The facilities for making a report at this time are such that it must necessarily be imperfect in some respects, but I shall endeavor to make it a history of facts as far as I go.

We marched with the brigade from our bivouac at 5 o'clock on the morning of the 19th. After marching about 9 miles toward the left, and parallel with the general line of battle, we arrived at 12 o'clock near the left of the line, where a heavy fight was progressing. The brigade was immediately thrown into position and marched to the front, the Forty-ninth Ohio on the left in the first line, with the Thirty-second Indiana on my right ; my left connecting with the First Ohio, Third Brigade, and supported by the Fifteenth Ohio in column on the center. In this order we advanced across a corn-field and entered an open wood. My flanking companies, commanded by Captain Hartsough, Company A, and Captain McCormack, Company B, were at once deployed as skirmishers to cover our front, with Company F, Lieutenant Wolf, and Company G, Lieutenant Pool, as supports. They immediately went bravely forward, and advancing about 300 yards over level ground, found the enemy, when light skirmishing at once commenced, growing hotter until it became necessary to throw forward the support companies. They also moved up in fine style. The fight now became general along the whole line, and by order of the general commanding brigade the first line advanced to the work under a heavy fire of musketry. Arriving at a place where the ground gradually descended from our front, the enemy opened on us with a battery planted directly in front of my right wing, and at close range, throwing much grape and canister. Here my command was ordered to lie down, while a portion of Captain Goodspeed's battery moved up on my left and opened on the enemy's guns. After a brief artillery duel the general commanding brigade ordered a charge. We responded, going forward at double-quick, capturing two Parrott field pieces, and driving the enemy before us. Having thus gained nearly a mile, and being much in advance of the troops on the right of our brigade, we halted, and held this position until nearly dark, when the enemy, having pressed back the troops on either flank of our brigade and division, massed in our front, and compelled us to relinquish a portion of the ground gained during the afternoon. It was now dark, and having been relieved by other troops, we returned to bivouac in the corn-field through which we first advanced. Our entire loss during the first day's engagements was as follows : Killed and wounded, 51 ; missing, 10 ; including 2 commissioned officers.

At daylight on the morning of the 20th the division went into position on the field of our operations on the preceding day, our brigade in reserve, the Forty-ninth on the right in the second line. About 8 a. m. the enemy made a furious attack on some temporary breastworks thrown up in front during the night, and were handsomely repulsed. The other brigades of the division then advanced, and we were thrown forward to occupy them. In this movement my command was changed to the left flank of the brigade. We had occupied this position but a short time when the enemy drove back the brigade on my left, commanded by General Beatty, and came pouring into the open field directly in our rear. I immediately faced by the rear rank, and, wheeling half to the right, opened on them a galling cross-fire. This, in connection with the fire from Captain Goodspeed's battery, in position directly fronting the advancing rebels, soon caused them to waver. At this moment I ordered a charge. This was executed under the eyes of the generals commanding brigade and division, who can testify to the prompt and enthusiastic manner in which it was done. The Sixth Regiment Ohio Volunteers having rallied, now joined us in the charge, and the enemy was completely routed. In this charge the regiment captured 50 prisoners and sent them to the rear. After driving the enemy about one-half mile and exhausting our ammunition, we were relieved by the Thirty-second Indiana Volunteers, under Colonel Erdelmeyer, charging through our lines and again driving the enemy, who had partially rallied. I take pleasure in testifying to the gallant charge made by this noble old regiment. Early in our charge I was struck on the head by a glancing ball and compelled to leave the field for half an hour in the hottest part of the engagement. During this time the command devolved upon Capt. L. M. Strong, acting field officer, who distinguished himself for gallantry and capacity to command. During the remainder of the day and until the close of the fight we acted with the brigade and were constantly under fire, but did not again become closely engaged. A full report of our operations during Sunday afternoon will no doubt be made by the general commanding brigade.

To the officers and men of the Forty-ninth Regiment my thanks are due for their heroism and unflinching bravery exhibited throughout the protracted struggle. My thanks are especially due Captain Strong for valuable assistance rendered on the field. Sergt. Maj. D. R. Cook, acting adjutant, was conspicuous for gallantry, always at his post of duty and in the thickest of the fight.

In closing this brief report allow me to congratulate the general commanding brigade upon the successful operations of his entire command, its perfect organization from the beginning to the end of the fight, and to tender him, on the part of every officer and man in my command, his heartfelt thanks, feeling that we owe to his superior courage and skill our preservation and any honor we may have won.

I am, very respectfully,

S. F. GRAY,
Major, Comdg. Forty-ninth Ohio Volunteer Infantry.

Capt. CARL SCHMITT, *Asst. Adjt. Gen. First Brigade.*

No. 108.

Report of Capt. Wilbur F. Goodspeed, Battery A, First Ohio Light Artillery.

HDQRS. BATTERY A, FIRST OHIO LIGHT ARTILLERY,
Chattanooga, Tenn., September. 27, 1863.

SIR: In compliance with orders, I have the honor to report the part taken by my battery in the battles of the 19th and 20th instant.

I marched with the brigade to the battle-field, and the brigade being ordered into action, I took a position in the rear of the brigade, leaving my caissons still farther in the rear.

The brigade having captured a battery from the enemy, I was ordered to haul the pieces off the field. I sent for my caisson teams, and took off three 10-pounder Parrott and two 12-pounder Napoleon guns and one caisson; I also got one limber from the front of the brigade, but, owing to the fact that the enemy opened a terrific fire, I had to abandon it.

The infantry advanced farther, and General Willich sent me orders to bring up one section, which, under Lieutenant Scovill, took a position on the right and rear of the brigade. Toward evening the brigade was attacked by the enemy in force, and another section, under Lieutenant Belding, was ordered to the left and rear of the infantry, while shortly afterward the whole battery was formed in the rear and center of the brigade. In these positions we opened on the enemy's lines with solid shot and shell, and were replied to by one battery. The brigade withdrew and I was ordered to bring my battery to the rear, where we took a reserve position in an open field, my battery forming in the rear of the infantry. Here we bivouacked during the night.

On the morning of the 20th the brigade changed position, facing south. I changed front with the brigade, keeping my battery still in the rear of the infantry. In this position I remained when the brigade was ordered into action.

At about 10 a. m. one of the enemy's batteries opened on me from the left in front. I changed front and replied with three pieces, throwing shells, soon silencing the enemy. At about 11 o'clock a heavy column of the enemy was discovered about 1,000 yards from my position. Crossing the road, I immediately changed front. At this time the Fifteenth Ohio Volunteers came up, and was ordered to the left of my battery. A few minutes later the enemy charged on us, and got up to within 50 yards. My battery then opened, double-shotted with canister, and, being gallantly supported by the Fifteenth Ohio Volunteers, we succeeded in routing the enemy, and driving him back with great slaughter. The enemy having disappeared from my front and showing himself in the rear, my battery, with the Fifteenth Ohio Volunteers, moved to the small log houses which were temporarily used as hospitals, and was faced to the rear. At about half past 1 p. m., the rest of the brigade having formed near my position, the enemy opened on me in my new front with artillery. I replied with about 50 rounds, when he ceased firing. My battery remained in this position until nearly dark, when a general retreat began. The troops on our left giving way, the enemy threw shell and canister into the position of the brigade from that side. I answered with the same projectiles.

After the other troops had passed us, General Willich ordered the brigade to fall back. I attached the prolonges to my pieces and retreated firing. The enemy closed in from three sides, and his batteries came so near that we fired at each other with canister. Under orders I limbered up and moved back to a hill in the rear, where I awaited the arrival of the brigade. Here General Willich ordered me to move on to the Rossville road, and follow the other troops. My battery arrived at Rossville at 12 p. m. and went into camp.

I brought into camp my battery complete. In the engagements of the two days my battery sustained the following loss :

Officer wounded, 1; enlisted men killed, 2; enlisted men wounded, 13; enlisted men missing, 4, supposed to be wounded. Horses wounded, 15, and, in consequence of not unharnessing for six days and the hardship they have undergone, I will lose 25 more horses.

I cannot close this report without speaking in terms of the highest praise of the gallantry displayed by First Lieuts. E. B. Belding and C. W. Scovill. My heartfelt thanks are due to the non-commissioned officers and men of my battery for the promptness with which they executed every order, and the coolness they preserved under the hottest fire. I feel in duty bound to acknowledge the obligations I am under to the general commanding the brigade for the able manner in which he handled and the care he took of my battery, and to the regiments composing the brigade for the cheerful support accorded to me under such trying times.

Respectfully submitted.

W. F. GOODSPEED,
Captain, Comdg. Battery A, First Ohio Light Artillery.

Capt. CARL SCHMITT,
Assistant Adjutant-General, First Brigade.

No. 109.

Report of Col. Joseph B. Dodge, Thirtieth Indiana Infantry, commanding Second Brigade.

HDQRS. SECOND BRIG., SECOND DIV., 20TH ARMY CORPS,
Chattanooga, September 27, 1863.

SIR : In compliance with your circular of the 25th instant, I have the honor to submit the following report of the part that this brigade took in the recent battles near this place:

After a tedious and laborious march, we reached a point about 4 miles from Crawfish Spring, in the direction of Stevens' Gap, on the 18th instant, where my brigade was placed on picket and staid all night.

On the morning of the 19th I marched at about 7 o'clock with the rest of the division, and passed Crawfish Spring, in the direction of Chattanooga, about 3 miles, when we filed off the road to the right. My brigade, being on the left of the division, was, agreeably to your order, here deployed into column; the Seventy-seventh Pennsylvania, Col. Thomas E. Rose, commanding, and the Seventy-ninth Illinois, Col. Allen Buckner, commanding, in the first line; and the Twenty-ninth Indiana, Lieut. Col. D. M. Dunn, commanding, and the Thirtieth Indiana, Lieut. Col. O. D. Hurd, commanding, in the second line, in rear of the First and Third Brigades, and ordered to govern myself by their movements, and to support them.

After moving in this manner a short distance, I received an order to move to the right, until I reached General Hazen's brigade of General Palmer's division, and relieve him, as his men were getting short of ammunition. I accordingly moved my whole command by the right flank about 400 yards, when I found a very brisk engagement going on, and the enemy's line formed in an oblique direction to the one I was in. I immediately changed front forward with my first line, and seeing that the enemy were well sheltered, while my command was badly exposed to their fire, and my men being comparatively fresh, I ordered a charge. The whole column had previously deployed into line, that having been necessary in order to keep from making too wide an opening between my left and the right of General Willich's brigade.

The order was most gallantly obeyed by both officers and men, and the enemy gave way in utter rout and confusion. In this charge the Twenty-ninth Indiana was on the right, the Seventy-seventh Pennsylvania next, the Seventy-ninth Illinois next, and the Thirtieth Indiana on the left. We drove them in this manner nearly or quite 1 mile (some officers think farther), when, finding that my line was getting broken in consequence of losses in killed and wounded, and that I had no support on either flank, I ordered a halt. On this charge my command passed some 30 or 40 yards to the right of a battery belonging to the enemy, which was nearly deserted by them, and a part of which was captured by one of the other brigades to my left (General Willich's, I believe). I then reformed my command in its original order and moved about 400 yards to my left and rear, and formed a connection with the right of General Willich's brigade, refusing my right slightly, so as to protect my flank as much as possible, and threw out a heavy line of skirmishers in my front and on my flank. There was no force (of ours) on my right in sight, and I was fearful that the enemy would attack us on that flank.

In order to be certain, about 4 p. m. I sent out a detachment under Lieutenant-Colonel Pyfer, Seventy-seventh Pennsylvania, to examine the position of the enemy, if possible, and to ascertain the position of the nearest troops on our own line. He reported a heavy picket force of the enemy about 500 yards to my front and right, and that it was about three-fourths of a mile from my right to the left of General Turchin's brigade, and that his were the nearest of our troops on that flank. I strengthened my line of pickets, and made all the preparations possible to resist an attack from that quarter. Just before dark the enemy made an attack some distance to my left, and gradually swept round to my front, when I was informed that a heavy column was moving directly against my flank. It was now quite dark, so that it was impossible to distinguish any person a few feet off. I immediately withdrew my battery to the rear, just in time to save it, as this column swept round on my right and rear, delivering at the same time a very heavy fire, and capturing nearly the whole of the Seventy-seventh Pennsylvania and about one-half of the Seventy-ninth Illinois. A large portion of the men succeeded, in the confusion and darkness, in making their escape, but Colonel Rose, Lieutenant-Colonel Pyfer, and Major Phillips, all of the Seventy-seventh Pennsylvania, and Major Fitzsimmons, of the Thirtieth Indiana, who had previously been wounded, but was near the Seventy-seventh Pennsylvania, together with quite a number of line officers, were captured, or wounded so that they were unable to get away.

My second line returned their fire and held their position. I was as yet not aware of the extent of the loss of my brigade, owing to the darkness, and while endeavoring to move my left more to the front got into the enemy's lines and was taken prisoner, but succeeded in making my escape, and on my return found that my brigade, with the rest of the division, was being withdrawn from its perilous position, as it was almost entirely surrounded by a force largely its superior in numbers. We bivouacked that night about 300 yards to the right of the Chattanooga road.

Early on the morning of the 20th instant, by your order, I took a position with the remnant of my brigade in rear of the Third Brigade, forming the second line.

Shortly afterward I received an order to move to my left, when I found that I was detached from the division—General Baird's division, of the Fourteenth Army Corps, being between the right of my line and the left of the rest of this division and one brigade on my left, forming the extreme left of our line. About 9 o'clock the enemy made an attack on our front, which was repulsed after a severe fight. From that time until about 5 p. m. we were under a constant fire, at times one of great intensity, but every attack was repulsed, and some of them were attended with great slaughter to the enemy.

At about 5 o'clock, during a very severe attack, and which we were repulsing with our usual success, I received an order from General Johnson in person to withdraw my command, fighting the best way I could, as our whole line was to do the same. I immediately moved my command by the left flank, in rear of the brigade that had been on my left, toward the Chattanooga road, and then across the hills in the direction of Rossville. Some little confusion took place in this movement, owing to the terrific fire we received from infantry and artillery on our flank and rear while crossing a corn-field ; but with the assistance of Colonel Buckner, of the Seventy-ninth Illinois Volunteers, I succeeded in getting into good order again, and retired in that manner to near Rossville, where we bivouacked for the night. During this terrible engagement I am proud to say that all, men and officers alike, behaved in such a manner as to make distinctions between them invidious ; but all will pardon me for mentioning in an especial manner Col. Allen Buckner, of the Seventy-ninth Illinois Volunteers, for coolness and bravery under the heaviest fire. Major Collins, of the Twenty-ninth Indiana Volunteers, is among the missing. He was with his regiment when it commenced to move to the rear, and I fear that he is either killed or severely wounded. He behaved in a very gallant manner.

The loss of my brigade is shown by the following table.* It will be seen that out of an aggregate of 1,130 who went into the engagement there remain but 598 effective men.

The list of missing, as will be seen, is quite large. A large majority of those reported in that manner, I am satisfied, are either killed or wounded, as much of the heaviest loss, I suppose, was during the attack of the night of the 19th. As we received a very heavy cross-fire from the enemy, there must have been a great many struck down by the enemy's balls. Very nearly all that were lost at that time are reported as missing, and will have to stand that way until we receive more definite information. Lieut. C. P. Butler, Twenty-ninth Indiana Volunteers, provost-marshal of the brigade, was wounded in the leg at the commencement of the attack in the evening, and was taken prisoner. Lieutenants McGowan, Twenty-ninth Indiana Volunteers, topographical engineer, and Culbertson, of the Thirtieth Indiana Volunteers, acting aide-de-camp on my staff, were both captured also while gallantly assisting me in the discharge of my duties. It is impossible to tell whether they were wounded or not.

---

* Omitted ; embodied in revised statement, p 174.

I am under great obligations to them and to Lieut. S. T. Davis, Seventy-seventh Pennsylvania Volunteers, brigade inspector (who was severely hurt by a spent grape-shot on Sunday), and Capt. E. P. Edsall, Thirtieth Indiana Volunteers, acting assistant adjutant-general of the brigade, for their promptness and efficiency under the most trying circumstances during this most terrible battle.   I feel it a duty to report also the gallant conduct of my orderlies, they being detached from their commands and having no opportunities to be noticed in any other way.   Orderly Black, Seventy-seventh Pennsylvania Volunteers, was severely wounded (if not killed) on the evening of the 19th, while accompanying Lieutenant Davis, of my staff, in collecting men that, owing to the darkness, had become separated from their commands.   Richard Sloane, Thirtieth Indiana Volunteers, was severely wounded in the hand and head on Saturday, while carrying an order, and was compelled to go to the rear; but he reported again to me for duty on the morning of the 21st. Orderlies Marr, Twenty-ninth Indiana, and McCarty, Thirty-fourth Illinois, by their coolness and courage, showed that they were worthy of holding commissions.   It is but an act of justice to say that the Thirty-fourth Illinois Volunteers, Lieutenant-Colonel Van Tassell, commanding, of this brigade, were detached at the crossing of the Tennessee River, and have been detained there since; so that that regiment had no opportunity to take a part with those whom they have hitherto accompanied in every fight in which this brigade has been engaged.   I regret this deeply, as I know that regiment was anxious to be with us.

I have the honor to be, very respectfully, your obedient servant,

J. B. DODGE,
Colonel, Comdg. 2d Brigade, 2d Division, 20th Army Corps.

Lieut. A. S. SMITH,
Acting Assistant Adjutant-General, Second Division.

P. S.—Accompanying this please find reports of regimental commanders, and of Captain Grosskopff, commanding Twentieth Ohio Battery.

No. 110.

Report of Col. Allen Buckner, Seventy-ninth Illinois Infantry.

HEADQUARTERS SEVENTY-NINTH ILLINOIS VOLUNTEERS,
Chattanooga, Tenn., September 27, 1863.

SIR: In compliance with an order, I proceed at once to make my report, as follows:

On Saturday, the 19th instant, this regiment was in the rear of the Second Brigade, Second Division, Twentieth Army Corps. It marched 7 or 8 miles, came near the point where the left of the army was hotly engaged, and doubled its column at half distance, formed on the left of the Seventy-seventh Pennsylvania Volunteers as a reserve, the Twenty-ninth and Thirtieth Indiana Volunteers being in front. Threw out a strong line of skirmishers to protect our left flank, moved forward a short distance, made a half right wheel, advanced about 200 yards and made a left quarter wheel, then deployed into line of battle and formed the right on the left of the Seventy-seventh

Pennsylvania Volunteers, charged upon the enemy and drove them before us nearly 1½ miles, halted, dressed up the line, found that the brigade did not connect on the right or left and had gone quite a distance beyond our line on either side, moved by the left flank from 200 to 400 yards, then about-faced and moved back near 40 rods, halted and rested a short time, still under fire of grape and canister from the enemy, and constantly losing in killed and wounded. Here General Willich came up, and, as I learned, suggested that you join your left on his right in two lines; therefore the Seventy-seventh Pennsylvania and Seventy-ninth Illinois were placed in front, the Twenty-ninth and Thirtieth Indiana in reserve. When this movement was executed the sun was nearly down, we having been engaged with the enemy almost all of the time since 1 p. m., and constantly under fire, the Seventy-ninth Illinois still on the left of the Seventy-seventh Pennsylvania. After this disposition had been made, Colonel Rose and myself went to see what connection we made with General Willich's line; as near as we could ascertain the Eighty-ninth Illinois was to the left and in front as skirmishers, our own skirmishers being on their right, and no line of battle connecting with us whatever; soon the skirmish line was heavily attacked, and fell back, whereupon we opened a heavy fire, holding our position and kept it up until the enemy was silenced. It was now quite dark, and in a few moments we were surprised to find the rebel skirmishers coming into our line, and while we were taking them prisoners we found that a heavy line of the enemy had outflanked and were closing around the Seventy-seventh Pennsylvania, also a heavy line had formed in our immediate front, at once opening upon us a dreadful fire, under which we had to fall back. Our greatest loss during the whole battle amongst officers and men occurred here, in the space of ten minutes, 4 captains and 8 lieutenants being left at this point; add to this, we fell back under a heavy cross-fire from the enemy and our friends. I found the colors of the Thirtieth Indiana and rallied as many as possible and made an effort to form on the right of General Willich's brigade, constantly moving back until we reached the rear of our battery and followed it into camp, where we formed upon the remainder of the brigade.

My officers and men did well during this terrible day. As soon as we got into camp I was ordered to take the Seventy-ninth Illinois and the Thirtieth Indiana, and go on picket. With the assistance of my adjutant I formed the best line possible.

On the morning of the 20th I formed my regiment and the remainder of the Seventy-seventh Pennsylvania on the left of the brigade, and by your direction took command of the line, you superintending the general movement. We then moved back in reserve, threw up temporary fortifications, and waited until the front lines were attacked all along our lines, right and left. This attack seemed to be repulsed, whereas, under your immediate direction, we moved by the left and right flanks, until we formed on the left of General King's brigade of regulars. Here we were heavily attacked by the enemy and replied, driving the enemy and keeping up a heavy fire for nearly three hours, emptying our cartridge boxes and replenishing on the line. After the enemy was completely driven we moved back, under your immediate direction, about 100 yards, where we halted and rested. Shortly after, we sent out a line of skirmishers to ascertain the movements of the enemy, and as to their report I am not advised. We then moved a little forward and to the left, when we threw up temporary fortifications a short distance in the rear of the line which had been our reserve in the morning.   We remained here until near 4 o'clock in the afternoon, not knowing that the right had given way.   About this time we were heavily attacked.   The line in our front kept up a tremendous fire, holding the enemy in check, who seemed to be determined to break our lines.   Our brigade was constantly cheering and encouraging the line in front of us, though we were exposed to a terrible fire of artillery and musketry.   This was kept up about an hour, when an officer came up and ordered us back.   We would not retire until we heard from you. · In a moment you came in person, giving the order to fall back; this we did in the best possible manner, and after getting back to the hill assisted in getting the brigade together, and, under your direction, moved back to Rossville.

On the 21st I formed my regiment on the extreme right of the brigade and threw up breastworks, where it remained until 1 o'clock next morning, when, by your order, we moved back to Chattanooga. I will not eulogize my officers and men one by one, but it is sufficient to say they are good and true.   The above is as near a correct history of the part the Seventy-ninth Illinois took in the battle as I can remember.   I submit it for your consideration, and have the honor to remain your obedient servant,

ALLEN BUCKNER,

Colonel, Commanding Seventy-ninth Illinois Volunteers.

Capt. E. P. Edsall,
    Acting Assistant Adjutant-General.

No. 111.

Report of Lieut. Col. David M. Dunn, Twenty-ninth Indiana Infantry.

Hdqrs. 29th Regiment Indiana Volunteers,
Chattanooga, Tenn., September 27, 1863.

Sir : I herewith hand you, as per your order, my report of the part taken by the Twenty-ninth Regiment Indiana Volunteer Infantry in the battle of the 19th and 20th instant, near Crawfish Spring, Ga.

This regiment, after marching 200 miles (after leaving Tullahoma), arrived and encamped at the foot of Lookout Mountain, at Will's Gap.   On the morning of the 18th instant we marched and rejoined the division, and relieved the Thirty-second Indiana on picket duty about 4 a. m.

On the morning of the 19th instant I was ordered to withdraw my pickets silently, and to act as rear guard to the brigade into camp.

After arriving in camp and drawing rations we took the advance of the brigade toward the left of our army, where heavy cannonading could be distinctly heard.   We marched about 12 miles, when we arrived in rear of General Thomas' line of battle (about 1 p. m.), upon which the enemy was making a heavy attack.   Our brigade was directed to relieve General Hazen's brigade.   My regiment, being on the right and front, was soon deployed, and I was ordered to charge the enemy at double-quick.   I gave the order, and the men rushed forward cheering lustily, and never stopped until they had routed the enemy from his temporary fortifications, killing many and taking a large number of prisoners. We pursued them about 1½ miles, when we were ordered to halt, having no protection on our right from a flank movement of the enemy. After we halted our brigade was again formed in two lines, my regiment in the first line and on the left of the brigade (the two regiments forming the second line at the commencement of the engagement having been brought to the front in our pursuit of the enemy participated freely in the fight), my left resting on the supposed right of the Eighty-ninth Illinois Volunteers. We remained in this position, having our front protected by a line of skirmishers, until near the close of the evening, receiving occasional shots of musketry and grape from the enemy. About dark my regiment was relieved and placed in the second line, and joined to the Thirty-second Indiana on the left. We were lying in this position, when shortly after dark we were all startled by a furious attack of the enemy on our front and right flank. The attack was so sudden, though not unexpected, that my men became somewhat confused, but immediately regained their places in line and assisted in silencing the fire of the enemy. I was then ordered to move my regiment to the right to protect our flank. I remained in this position until about 9 p. m., when we returned into camp in rear of First Brigade. On the morning of the 20th instant built breastworks in front of our line as we were encamped (being in reserve), and remained there until about half past 10 a. m., the enemy attacking our first line and being repulsed. About half past 10 a. m. our line was changed, forming to the front on the left company, and marched forward about 200 yards and joined on the left of the Sixteenth Regulars. While in this position we poured a galling fire in the enemy's attacking column, that passed our front about 100 or 150 yards' distant, disorganizing them very much. They tried to plant a battery but were prevented by our well-directed fire. We then moved back about 15 rods and formed in rear of the Second Ohio, and built breastworks. In this position we were very much annoyed by sharpshooters, and remained in this position until 4 p. m., when the enemy came up in our front and poured into us a very destructive fire of musketry and artillery. We, however, held the enemy in check until ordered to retreat, and fell back over an open field under a severe fire from the enemy. We reformed on a hill three-quarters of a mile to our rear, and marched from there to camp near Rossville, in charge of Capt. J. H. M. Jenkins.

Our losses are as follows: First day—killed, 9; wounded, 69; missing, 35. Second day—killed, 2; wounded, 22; missing, 33. Total, 170.

I cannot speak too highly of both officers and men, and must notice especially the praiseworthy conduct of Major Collins and Capt. J. H. M. Jenkins.

I am, captain, very respectfully, your obedient servant,

D. M. DUNN,
Lieutenant-Colonel, Commanding Regiment.

Capt. E. P. EDSALL,
Acting Assistant Adjutant-General, Second Brigade.

No. 112.

Report of Lieut. Col. Orrin D. Hurd, Thirtieth Indiana Infantry.

HDQRS. THIRTIETH REGIMENT INDIANA VOLUNTEERS,
Chattanooga, Tenn., September 27, 1863.

SIR: In compliance with instructions, I have the honor to make the following report of the part taken by my regiment in the late battle:

On the morning of the 19th instant, I moved with the brigade from Stevens' Gap, at the foot of Lookout Mountain, at about 9 a. m. to Crawfish Spring, where the battle was then going on. We arrived on the battle-ground at about 1 p. m. and after a rest of ten minutes, took position in the line which was on the extreme left. My regiment was placed on the left of the brigade, in the reserve line, the Twenty-ninth Indiana in my front and the Seventy-ninth Illinois on my right. I was ordered to throw a platoon on my left as skirmishers, as that part was unprotected. As soon as this was done the line moved forward on double-quick, immediately coming in sight of the enemy, and driving him by a charge a distance of at least 1 mile, when it was halted and again formed. In this charge my regiment suffered severely, losing several commissioned officers and a large number of men, most of which were but slightly wounded. We were from here ordered to move by the left flank and formed on the right of the First Brigade of this division; my front was slightly changed to the right.

This movement I have since learned left a gap of some extent on the right of this brigade, giving the enemy a partial chance to flank us. At 5 p. m. the firing had ceased in our front, but was still kept up on our left, or in front of General Willich's brigade—however not to such an extent as to attract a great deal of our attention—and the men were ordered to lie down on their arms. At dark all was quiet, appearance showing the fight ended for that day. After dark the enemy charged our front and the right flank of the brigade with such an overwhelming force that the front rank was completely annihilated by his first fire, while our reserve dare not fire on account of our own men. The reserve now moved up and held him until he came directly upon our right flank, and within talking distance, when we fell back to near the point where we first formed, where we lay during the night.

In consequence of the extreme darkness and the dense forest, the enemy captured quite a number of men and officers. Among the latter were Major Fitzsimmons, Lieutenants Sterling and Foster, all of whom had conducted themselves with great coolness and bravery.

The next morning a temporary work of logs was thrown up, and preparations made for a hard battle, as it became evident that the enemy greatly outnumbered us. There was no firing of any consequence until about 9 o'clock, when the enemy again made his appearance along our whole front and again charged us, but was repulsed with heavy loss. I was now moved to the left into a gap and became engaged, but in a few moments the enemy fell back and firing again checked. Part of my regiment was sent on the skirmish line, and troops kept forming on our left, as it became evident from the cloud of dust that the enemy was massing on that point. At about 12 m. our suppositions were confirmed by his making a heavy assault upon our front and left, driving the latter back a short distance, when we rallied and checked him, afterward regaining our position. All was now quiet in our front until about 3 p. m. when the enemy again attacked, and a fight of about one hour took place, after which we were ordered to fall back to Pigeon Gap, where we lay during that night.

On the morning of the 21st instant we again built a temporary work and remained in it during that day, but nothing of importance took place in our front. At about 10 o'clock that night a retreat was ordered, and our line, except pickets, was quietly withdrawn as far as Chattanooga, where my regiment arrived about 4 a. m. on the 22d.

Here the men took the first two hours of undisturbed sleep they had had since the night of the 17th, but at 6 o'clock we were again under arms, and at about 7 moved farther to the right, and again formed line. I was now placed on the left of the brigade, the Twenty-ninth Indiana on my right and the Twenty-first Illinois, of General Davis' division, on my left. Rifle-pits were immediately commenced, but were constructed into a heavy breastwork capable of keeping off heavy shot. Nothing of importance in which my regiment had part took place until the morning of the 25th instant, when we were again withdrawn from our work and moved about three-quarters of a mile to the rear, where we now lie. There have been no casualties in my regiment since the 20th instant, which I have already reported.*

This has proved the hardest battle in which the regiment ever had part, as at Shiloh and Stone's River we had more than twice the number of men engaged, while the total loss of each was not as great as this.

There is no record that will show harder fighting and better behavior of men than was displayed in this battle under the most trying circumstances. The officers (excepting two) and men were as cool as though on parade. I might mention many deeds of daring and bravery, but to note all would lengthen the report and to mention part would do injustice to others. I heartily thank them for their conduct, assuring them that they have again merited the names of true soldiers and patriots. The friends and relatives of the wounded and dead have my heartfelt sympathy, and I feel proud to say that their brothers and sons fell true soldiers, with not a stain upon them.

Respectfully submitted.

O. D. HURD,
Lieut. Col., Comdg. Thirtieth Regiment Indiana Vols.

Capt. E. P. EDSALL,
Acting Assistant Adjutant General, Second Brigade.

No. 113.

Report of Capt. Edward Grosskopff, Twentieth Ohio Battery.

CAMP OF 20TH BATTERY OHIO VOLUNTEER ARTILLERY,
Near Chattanooga, Tenn., October 11, 1863.

CAPTAIN: I have the honor to report the part which the Twentieth Battery Ohio Volunteer Artillery took in the late fight at or near Crawfish Spring, September 19 and 20.

---

* Embodied in revised statement, p. 174.

The Twentieth Battery Ohio Volunteer Artillery was ordered, September 19, in the afternoon, to take up position on a hill in the rear of Second Brigade, Second Division; Twentieth Army Corps, near Crawfish Spring. I did remain there until 5 p. m., when I was ordered forward to a clearing. This position I was ordered to change soon after, and took up another one more to the left, near the Seventy-seventh Regiment Pennsylvania Volunteer Infantry, and opened fire on the enemy. After this, as night had set in, I fell back to the aforementioned clearing, but was ordered to again change my position still farther to the rear. In the act of carrying out this order I received a cross-fire from the enemy, whereby one of my men and several of the horses were wounded. Soon after I joined the Fifth Battery Indiana Volunteer Artillery, commanded by Captain Simonson, and took up camp after the firing had ceased in an open field, near the headquarters of the Second Division, Twentieth Army Corps.

On the 20th of September, in the morning at 5 o'clock, I received orders from Colonel Dodge, commanding Second Brigade, Second Division, Twentieth Army Corps, to remain with my battery where I was until further orders. I waited for orders until 9 a. m., when a division of the Fourteenth Army Corps was ordered to take up a position where I stood, and therefore I had to move the battery and station myself on the right of Battery A, First Ohio Volunteer Artillery, and in the rear of Second Division, Twentieth Army Corps. Here I remained and held out an attack on our left flank until about 11 or 11.30 a. m., when I was ordered by a staff officer to take a position more to the right; but I had hardly moved toward that place and not yet in position when the troops stationed there gave way, and, being without any support, I fell back about 500 yards and took up a position near an open field. There I reported to Lieut. Sidney Smith, acting assistant adjutant-general Second Division, Twentieth Army Corps, and received orders from him to remain there. I did so until the army in general fell back; then I took up a position on a hill near the gap, to protect, in case of need, the retreat. This position I held until about 4 p. m., when I was ordered by Colonel Barnett, chief of artillery of the Army of the Cumberland, to report at the cross-road which General Sheridan held with his infantry and where my battery could be supported by them. Here I remained until the whole army commenced moving; then I fell in, as ordered by the adjutant of General McCook's staff, and marched to a field where the different corps had assembled, and reported to Second Division, Twentieth Army Corps, when Captain Bartlett, inspector-general of Second Division, ordered me to move the battery to Rossville.

I lost 2 men wounded, 2 men missing, 11 horses (9 dead and 2 wounded). I shot away 85 rounds of ammunition and lost 1 caisson.

In general my men behaved very well, excepting 2, who behaved very cowardly—John Hutchins, detailed from the Twenty-ninth Regiment Indiana Volunteer Infantry, and Charles White, detailed from the Seventy-seventh Regiment Pennsylvania Volunteer Infantry, who left their posts.

I remain, very respectfully, your obedient servant,

E. GROSSKOPFF,
Captain, Comdg. 20th Battery Ohio Volunteer Artillery.

Capt. PETER SIMONSON,
  Chief of Artillery.

No. 114.

Report of Col. William W. Berry, Fifth Kentucky Infantry, commanding Third Brigade.

Hdqrs. Third Brig., Second Div., 20th Army Corps,
Chattanooga, September 27, 1863.

Lieutenant: I have the honor to submit the following report of the part taken by this command in the battles of 19th and 20th instant:

The brigade is composed of the following regiments: Fifth Kentucky, First and Ninety-third Ohio, and Sixth Indiana Volunteer Infantry, together with the Fifth Indiana Battery, Captain Simonson.

Moving, on the morning of the 19th instant, from our bivouac, 4 miles west of Crawfish Spring, to the extreme left of the army, 3 miles east of the spring, the brigade, Col. P. P. Baldwin commanding, took position on the left of General Willich's command, the formation being in two lines; the First Ohio, Lieutenant-Colonel Langdon commanding, on the right, and the Fifth Kentucky, Colonel Berry commanding, on the left of the front line; and the Sixth Indiana, Lieutenant-Colonel Tripp commanding, on the right, and the Ninety-third Ohio, Colonel Strong, on the left of the second line; the battery in the rear. The ground in our front was heavily timbered and had been fought over before we reached it. The advance was sounded, and in a few moments the skirmishers were engaged. A battery of the enemy's opened on us, but was soon silenced by Simonson. Advancing steadily, a portion of the time on the double-quick, we drove the enemy a full mile, thus occupying ground farther to the front than the Federal forces had yet held. At this point, with an open field in our front, the brigade was halted, maintaining its original formation. Scarcely half an hour elapsed before the enemy advanced with infantry and artillery and attacked with his usual vigor. So far outflanked that we were almost enveloped, Colonel Baldwin ordered the Ninety-third Ohio to deploy on the left of the Fifth Kentucky. In a few moments Colonel Strong was wounded. The Ninety-third staggered slightly under the blow, when Colonel Baldwin, riding up with the cry, "Rally round the flag, boys!" seized the colors and ordered the regiment to charge, which was done with a will, and so effectually that the enemy fled, leaving two guns in our possession, one of which was brought away by the Ninety-third Regiment, but the other was so knocked to pieces by Simonson's shells that it was impossible to move it. The Fifth Kentucky and First Ohio, standing stock-still, swept their front as with a broom. In the meantime the Sixth Indiana, having been deployed on the left of the original line, moved up on the double-quick, and successfully engaged the enemy, who was thus driven entirely from our portion of the field. There was perfect quiet for an hour and a half, and then burst upon us one of the most furious assaults of this or any other battle; but the brigade drove the enemy completely from its front and ceased firing. Just here the regiment on the right of the First Ohio broke, and in a moment the enemy was on the flank of that regiment, which fell back and formed on the right of the Sixth Indiana, which had some time before this been ordered to the rear to support the battery. Simonson coolly extricated his pieces, with the exception of one, which in the crowded state of affairs became entangled in the top of a fallen tree and was abandoned.

About this time Colonel Baldwin was shot, and we at this critical point were without a commander. The loss was irreparable; the value to his troops of his courage and devotion was incalculable. For the good and glory of his country it is to be hoped that he is only wounded. The Fifth Kentucky was completely cut off, the enemy's line of battle being between it and the reserve; but it was so dark that friend could not be distinguished from foe, except by the direction of the fire. While the First Ohio and Sixth Indiana were engaging the enemy, the Fifth Kentucky and Ninety-third Ohio silently passed the enemy on the double-quick, connected with the reserve, faced about, and here occurred the most terrific fighting ever known by this brigade. The two lines were but a few yards apart, and at some points it was a hand-to-hand fight. But the enemy was repulsed after thirty minutes of this work, and there stood the brigade like a wall of iron, its commander gone, its connections broken. Up to this time I did not know of Colonel Baldwin's fate, but here his staff, coming up, reported him missing and asked me for orders. I had none to give except to hold the lines till I could communicate with General Johnson. Soon General Baird rode up and informed me that his division was there ready to join on my left, but General Willich had fallen back to a new line, thus exposing my right. It was impossible to remain thus detached, so we concluded to fall back, which was done with the utmost quiet and order. I soon met General Johnson, who ordered me into position on the left of General Palmer's division. I disposed the brigade in two lines, the Sixth Indiana and Ninety-third Ohio in front and the Fifth Kentucky and the First Ohio in rear. The battery was ordered to a commanding position between the lines. Very early next morning I ordered the construction of such works as we had facilities for building—rude barricades of logs. At 9 o'clock the enemy attacked, and after an hour's hard fighting was whipped and driven from the field, the Sixth Indiana and Ninety-third Ohio in the front line, doing the fighting in conjunction with the battery. At thirty minutes past 10 I received an order from General Johnson to hold my position at every hazard; at the same time an attack was made on the extreme left of the army—four brigades lying to the left of this command. Supposing that the attack would gradually extend to me, I determined to move up to the front line, for the purpose of strengthening it, the two rear regiments. They had advanced but a few yards when I perceived that the left was giving way. Instantly I changed the front of the First Ohio and Fifth Kentucky, then commanded by Captain Huston, throwing their line perpendicular to my front facing to the left. But the enemy, pursuing the troops who had broken, had gotten into a field in my original rear. Quickly executing another change of front with my second line, I ordered them to charge the enemy in their flank. I recalled the First Ohio, however, in a few moments, fearing to leave my front line entirely without support. The Fifth Kentucky charged under the lead of Captain Huston with an impetuosity never excelled, struck the enemy in their flank, and drove them pell-mell for a mile and a half, capturing many prisoners, among them General Adams. In this charge Lieutenant Huston, of the Fifth Kentucky, was killed. He was a great loss to the regiment, one of its best officers, and a young man of unusual promise. The Fifth Kentucky returned to its place in the course of an hour.

At times during the afternoon there was strong skirmishing in my front.   Lieutenant-Colonel Tripp, of the Sixth Indiana, was badly wounded in the midst of the morning's fight.   I regretted greatly the absence of so brave an officer, but Major Campbell from this time on handled the regiment in a manner highly creditable to himself. At 5 p. m. the enemy made a final attack on my lines, and this was repulsed as handsomely as the others had been.   While finishing the thing off with the battery the question was asked me, "What had become of the troops on my right?"   Upon looking in that direction, to my utter amazement, not a soldier was to be seen.   I at once supposed that General Palmer's division had gone to re-enforce the right of the army, and ordered up my second line to take the place of that division.   While leading it up I received an order from General Johnson to fall back, and this was the first I knew of the army retreating.   I ordered the battery ahead, and followed with the infantry to Rossville in the most perfect order.   There was not a particle of confusion or panic in the command, but all appeared nonplussed at the movement, when in every single fight of the two days' battle, whether attacked or attacking, we had uniformly defeated the enemy and driven him like a whipped dog.   Of course our loss is severe.   Such fighting as this brigade did cost heavily.

We marched from Rossville to Chattanooga on the morning of the 22d, and that evening were ordered to the front lines, where we remained under the fire of artillery and sharpshooters until the evening of the 25th instant, when for the first time for eight days the men took off their accouterments.

The endurance and patience of the soldiers were remarkable, and is but another proof of their courage.   I would respectfully call the attention of the commanding general to the worth of the following officers: Lieutenant-Colonel Langdon, whose sagacity, vigilance, and courage deserve well of the Government; Lieutenant-Colonel Martin, of the Ninety-third Ohio, who with an unhealed wound attests his devotion by his presence in the field; Lieutenant-Colonel Tripp and Colonel Strong, most efficient officers; Major Stafford, First Ohio, Major Birch, Ninety-third Ohio, Major Campbell, Sixth Indiana, and Captain Huston, who, when an example of daring is required, are always ready to set it; Captain Prather, Sixth Indiana, in the night fight of the 19th displayed the highest qualities of an officer; Captain Simonson handled his guns with skill and effect and displayed great spirit in the work before him.

I would respectfully ask the consideration of the general to the regimental reports for other cases of special mention.

To the officers of the brigade staff I am under many obligations. Comparatively a stranger to them, they rendered me most important service.

Capt. F. P. Strader received a painful wound in the knee on the 20th instant, but like a true soldier refused to leave the field.   Capt. J. E. Jones, Lieut. W. N. Williams, and Lieut. J. J. Siddall are among the most brave, energetic, and earnest officers of the army. Sergt. Lambert Schile (of the escort), with the other orderlies, and Thomas Dunn were always where their duties called them.

Very respectfully, your obedient servant,

WM. W. BERRY,
Colonel, Commanding Brigade.

Lieut. A. S. SMITH,
Actg. Asst. Adjt. Gen., 2d Division, 20th Army Corps.

No. 115.

Report of Maj. Calvin D. Campbell, Sixth Indiana Infantry.

HDQRS. SIXTH REGIMENT INDIANA VOLUNTEERS,
September 28, 1863.

SIR: I have the honor to submit the following report of the part taken by this command in the actions of the 19th and 20th instant:

On the morning of the 19th instant, Lieutenant-Colonel Tripp in command, we marched from near Catlett's Gap, 4 miles west of Crawfish Spring, to 3 miles east of Crawfish Spring, where the brigade was put into line of battle in two lines, we forming the right of the second line. We had advanced but a short distance when the first line engaged and drove the enemy a short distance, when the enemy again rallied (it being about 1 p. m) and made a more decided stand, during which time we were lying down, and exposed to a perfect shower of shot and shell for three-quarters of an hour. Captain Simonson coming up at this time, the enemy were soon driven, and we then advanced to the ground where Loomis' battery had stood in the morning. Intimations being received at this time of an attempt of the enemy to flank us upon the left, the Ninety-third Ohio, forming the left of the second line, was deployed to the left, and moved up on the first line, and we then changed direction to the left, and deployed upon the line and then charged at double-quick, driving the enemy for half or three-quarters of a mile, charging past a burning battery and getting one gun. We were then ordered to move by the right flank and go to the support of the battery, receiving a heavy volley from the enemy on our right as we moved off, losing several men. We then took position in rear of battery, deployed in line, men very much exhausted. It was then near 4 o'clock and the firing had ceased. We remained in this position until near dark, when a heavy volley was poured into our right, and the first line was seen falling back hotly pressed by the enemy. As the battery limbered to the rear, and was again wheeling into position, the right of the regiment was ordered forward at double-quick by Colonel Baldwin, Colonel Tripp or myself not being advised of the movement. The right moved forward some 50 or 75 paces, when it struck the heavy columns of the enemy, and a portion forced back, while another portion remained between the enemy's fire and our own.

On this charge Colonel Baldwin fell, his horse dashing back through our lines. When the right was seen to advance, in the absence of orders, the remainder of the regiment was held in its position, Colonel Tripp riding along the line and encouraging them to stand firm. At this time the left of the regiment received a volley from our left and rear, doing us but little damage. As soon as our front was clear of our own men we opened fire upon the enemy, the Fifth Kentucky rallying on our left and the Ninety-third Ohio on our right. We held our position and kept up this fire until the enemy withdrew. Colonel Tripp immediately threw Captain McKeehan's company to the front as skirmishers to watch the movements of the enemy, who were found to be maneuvering a heavy force as if to bivouac for the night. We were then ordered back to the road, where we remained until the following morning.

On the morning of the 20th we occupied the right of the first line, the Ninety-third Ohio upon our left and the left of Palmer's division upon our right.   Temporary breastworks of logs were thrown up, and our works were scarcely finished when the enemy made his attack, in three heavy lines.   Remaining concealed until he was in easy range, we opened upon him, and kept up an unremitting fire for two hours and forty minutes, at which time the enemy fell back. We threw a heavy skirmish line to the front, and during the day took quite a number of prisoners.   We held the ground until near 5 p. m., when I received your order to withdraw my command, which was done under a heavy fire from the enemy's skirmishers, leaving the field in good order.

Of the officers and men of the regiment I cannot speak too highly. Every man was at his post and every man did his duty.   Colonel Tripp was wounded early in the engagement of the morning, but remained upon the field until the heavy firing had ceased.   Both officers and men were cool and calm under the heaviest fire, and there was no straggling from the regiment; their bravery is unquestioned, and their record is one of which I am proud.   Appended find list of casualties.*

I have the honor, captain, to be, your obedient servant,
CALVIN D. CAMPBELL,
Major, Commanding Regiment.
Capt. Frank P. Strader,
Acting Assistant Adjutant-General, Third Brigade.

No. 116.

Report of Col. William W. Berry, Fifth Kentucky Infantry.

Headquarters Fifth Kentucky Volunteers,
Chattanooga, September 27, 1863.

Captain : I have the honor to submit the following report of movements of my command in the action of the 19th instant :

Early on the morning of the 19th we marched with the brigade from the extreme right to the left of the army, and were then thrown forward to retake ground from which a portion of the army had been driven before we arrived.   The brigade was formed in two lines, my regiment being on the left of the front line and the extreme left of the army.   Skirmishers were thrown out and the command moved forward.   The skirmish line was soon engaged.   The brigade took the double-quick, charged the enemy, and drove him a mile, retaking fully the ground lost in the morning.   Here we were halted in the edge of a field, my command forming, with the First Ohio, an obtuse angle, with the opening toward the front.   The enemy were soon seen working round toward our left.   I notified Colonel Baldwin of this, when he ordered the Ninety-third Ohio to deploy on my left.   It had scarcely gotten into position before the attack opened on us, with infantry and artillery.   Colonel Strong, of the Ninety-third, was wounded at almost the first fire and his regiment slightly recoiled, thus leaving my flank exposed; but the left companies poured in an oblique fire, and in a moment the Ninety-third came dashing forward under Colonel Baldwin, kept it up, charged and drove the enemy in their front, and captured two guns.

The enemy had already been repulsed in my front, and this was

---

* Embodied in revised statement, p. 174.

the last we heard of them for an hour and a half, when they again advanced, attacked, and were driven back in more confusion than before. Captain Hurley and Lieutenant Ayars had command of the skirmish line up to this time, and merit the highest commendation for their skill and courage. The enemy repulsed, I ordered the command to cease firing, and for a few moments the utmost quiet reigned, when just at dusk an officer called my attention to the right, where the First Ohio had been, and there stood a rebel line of battle pouring its fire into the second line of the brigade. A slight ridge had cut the line of vision between me and the First Ohio, which regiment I could not see without going on the top of this ridge. It seems that the troops on their right had given way, thus letting the enemy in on their flank, and they had fallen back to the second line. I had no notice of this till I saw the direction of the fire. It was so dark, that except by this direction of the fire, you could not tell friend from foe. I was completely cut off. I ordered the regiment to move off silently. The enemy thought us a part of their line and did not fire into us, but a Federal brigade (Starkweather's, I believe) coming up just then, poured a volley in my ranks and killed many of my men. We not stopping they ran away, fortunately for us. Upon reaching the second line I faced the regiment about and opened instantly on the enemy, who, thinking their own line was firing on them, soon retreated, leaving us in full possession of the ground. In this half-hour's work I lost 100 men and 7 officers killed and wounded. Major Thomasson, Captain Lovett, and Captain Lucas have been since missing; but it is to be hoped that they are only wounded and prisoners, as there are no better officers in this army. Here the brigade staff rode up, and informing me that Colonel Baldwin could not be found, reported to me for orders, and I took command of the brigade. For a further report of the part taken by the brave men of the Fifth Kentucky, I respectfully refer you to the report of Captain Huston, simply adding that harder fighting was never done and truer officers and men were never known.

Respectfully, your obedient servant,

WM. W. BERRY,
Colonel Fifth Kentucky Volunteers.

Capt. FRANK P. STRADER,
Acting Assistant Adjutant-General, Third Brigade.

No. 117.

Report of Capt. John M. Huston, Fifth Kentucky Infantry.

HEADQUARTERS FIFTH KENTUCKY VOLUNTEERS,
September 27, 1863.

SIR: I make, by order, the following report of the operations of the Fifth Regiment Kentucky Volunteers in the battle of the 20th instant:

Upon Colonel Baldwin's disappearance, Colonel Berry assumed command of the brigade, and I took command of the regiment, Lieutenant-Colonel Treanor being on detached duty, and Major Thomasson shot. The regiment at this time was standing in line of battle, having just repulsed the enemy in a night fight. Presently I was ordered to move my command to the rear to get connection with the general line of the army.   Reaching this point, the brigade was formed in two lines, the Fifth Kentucky was on the right of the second line.

At 9 o'clock on the morning of the 20th the enemy attacked, but was repulsed all along the line.   At 10 o'clock, as I was moving my command forward to strengthen the front line, the left of the division on our left was seen to give way.   Colonel Berry halted me, and ordered a change of front forward on the left company, which was promptly executed, thus throwing my line perpendicular to the front. The troops on the immediate left of the brigade stood fast, but those on the extreme left fled in the utmost confusion, the enemy pursuing till he was in our original rear.   Another change of front was ordered and executed, and being commanded to charge the enemy in his flank, I did so, fell upon him, and drove him a mile and a half. I suppose in this charge we captured 200 prisoners, among them Brigadier-General Adams, besides inflicting heavy loss upon the enemy in killed and wounded.   Here Captain Moninger was wounded, and my oldest son, Lieutenant Huston, was killed.   He died like a soldier, with sword in hand, in the midst of a victorious charge upon a fleeing enemy.   I was ordered back to the brigade, and joined it immediately, where I lay in the second line till evening, when I was ordered to fall back with the brigade to Rossville, which we did in the utmost order and regularity.

The officers and men conducted themselves in a manner to reflect great credit upon themselves and their country, the only difficulty being to restrain them from going too far.   Lieutenant Zoller, though wounded, kept his place with his company and behaved most manfully.   Captains Hurley, Lindenfelser, and Wilson, and Lieutenants McCorkhill, Miller, Powell, Thomas, and Jones are gallant soldiers.   The conduct of Adjutant Johnstone was conspicuous for courage, and I thank him for the assistance given myself.   I am under great obligations to Dr. Barr, of the First Ohio, detailed to take charge of my wounded, which duty was discharged fearlessly and energetically.   The men of the Fifth Kentucky are soldiers; this is not only proven by their bravery on the field, but by the patience and forbearance with which they endured the most extraordinary labor, exposure, and privation.   John T. Steele, of Company B, especially deserves mention.   Struck four times, he still stuck to his gun, and was with the Ninety-third Ohio when the cannon was captured, he himself reaching the pieces first and capturing the battery battle-flag.   Corpl. William Murphy, of Company I, when the color-bearer was shot, seized the flag and thenceforth bore it.

Respectfully, your obedient servant,

JOHN M. HUSTON,
Captain.

Capt. FRANK P. STRADER,
Acting Assistant Adjutant-General, Third Brigade.

No. 118.

Report of Lieut. Col. Bassett Langdon, First Ohio Infantry.

HDQRS. FIRST REGIMENT, OHIO VOLUNTEER INFANTRY,
In the Field, September 27, 1863.

CAPTAIN : By direction of the colonel commanding the brigade, the following report of the operations and losses of the First Regiment Ohio Volunteer Infantry is respectfully submitted from the 18th instant to the present time:

On the morning of Friday, the 18th instant, the regiment moved to the front under my command and took position in line of battle, relieving the One hundred and fifth Ohio. Three companies were at once advanced as skirmishers to within sight of the enemy, and shortly after, it being ascertained that no connection existed on our left, five more companies were moved out and a regular picket line established, connecting the Ninety-third Ohio Volunteer Infantry on our right with a shifting line of infantry pickets on our left.

This position was occupied until the morning of Saturday, the 19th instant, our picket line sustaining most of the time during the day an irregular and distant fire from the pickets of the enemy without returning it. The regiment withdrew from this position early Saturday morning, under marching orders, and moved about 10 or 12 miles up the valley to the north and east, and were halted in an open field near a tannery, under fire of the enemy's cannon. During the few minutes that we lay there, 1 man, belonging to Company K, was mortally wounded and died next morning.

Being ordered forward we moved rapidly to the front, in double-quick time, and a quarter of a mile farther on I deployed in line of battle on the left of General Willich's brigade, my regiment forming the right of the first line of the Third Brigade. A platoon of skirmishers from each of my flank companies (B and G) was deployed in front of the regiment and moved forward to find and feel the enemy. Two hundred yards sufficed to bring them under the enemy's fire, and I moved the regiment up rapidly, keeping even with the first line of General Willich, halting when his line halted and advancing as he advanced.

The enemy fell back steadily and rapidly before our advance, and were hotly followed up and pressed by the skirmish line. The enemy abandoned a battery on the right of my line, which was taken in charge by General Willich's brigade, in whose immediate front it was situated. After pressing the enemy back about a mile and a half in this manner, I halted my regiment, agreeably to orders, in an open field of weeds, with my right near the woods and my left advanced diagonally across the field fronting to the east, with from 100 to 300 yards of open descending ground in my front, terminating in a ravine, beyond which was an open forest into which my skirmishers had followed the enemy. Colonel Baldwin shortly afterward ordered me to change front to rear on the first company and retire behind the fence on my right, information having been received from Major Stafford, in command of the skirmish line (now strengthened by the remaining platoons of the two flank companies), that the enemy was moving to our left.

But a short time elapsed after this disposition was made till the enemy precipitated a heavy force upon the regiments on our left, closely followed by an attack in our front and upon the brigade on our right. I opened fire by file as soon as our own skirmishers were clear of our front, and soon drove the enemy back from the open field and well into the woods, when, finding myself free from fire, and that the enemy was directing his whole attention to the regiments on my right and left, I sounded the signal to cease firing and again moved into the open field where my fire would be more effective against the enemy.

This position was held till the enemy was repulsed all along the

line and had fallen back beyond our fire, when, by order of Colonel
Baldwin, I again took position behind the fence, and strengthened
it by a hastily constructed barricade of rails. Major Stafford was
again sent forward with skirmishers into the woods beyond the
open field. Companies A, C, and G were detailed on this duty,
under the respective commanders, Captain Hooker, First Lieutenant Boyer, and Captain Trapp. Company G, which had skirmished
from the beginning of the action, was soon after relieved by Company E, under command of Captain Dornbush. Information was
sent me that the enemy were now moving to our right, which was
promptly communicated to Colonel Baldwin. About sunset my
skirmishers were pressed back with serious loss to within a few yards
of the regiment, where they were exposed to so hot a fire from the
enemy that I recalled them to tempt the enemy into the open field.
In this skirmish Captain Dornbush was seriously wounded in the
thigh, and the command of his company devolved on First Lieutenant Leonard.

Finding the enemy not disposed to enter the open, and the firing
having increased on my right, I sent Company A again into the
field as skirmishers to prevent the enemy's getting too close to my
front unobserved, the nature of the ground being such as to raise
an apprehension of that character. This company was in the act
of deploying when it found itself exposed to a very hot fire on its
right flank, and immediately took position to meet it and opened
fire warmly in return. At this instant General Willich's regiment,
on my immediate right, opened fire in line, and warned by all these
indications where the real attack would come, I hastily recalled the
skirmishers, intending to meet it by a volley at short range. Unfortunately the recall of the skirmishers, who fell back firing, and
the heavy roll of musketry on our right, with the whistling of the
enemy's bullets, set the guns of my right company going and an
irregular file fire ran along my front from right to left, mainly directed to the enemy in my front. Meantime, I strove in vain to make
myself heard to stop the firing and to call the regiment to attention.
In thirty seconds the regiment on my right was broken and running
to the rear in great confusion, and while I was striking my men (who
were lying down) with the flat of my sword to get their attention,
the rebel line was seen within 40 yards of my right flank moving
rapidly up perpendicularly to it. I was barely able to get my men
to their feet in time to see the rebel colors flaunted almost in their
faces, and their guns being mostly unloaded I directed them to retire. The regiment fell back about 150 yards, and rallying handsomely upon the colors, delivered a withering fire upon the enemy,
which checked his advance and drew in return a storm of grape,
canister, and musketry. The contest raged till long after darkness
and the dense smoke of battle had shut out everything from view
but the flash of the enemy's guns, and only terminated when the
enemy ceased to return our fire.

During the fight the sound appeared to indicate that the regiments
on our left were being pressed back, and I sent First Lieutenant
Chappell to ascertain the state of facts there and assure those troops
of our intention and ability to hold our own. I sent the same officer
to the right to communicate with General Willich, and his report
relieved me from apprehension in both directions. On the termination of the fight I learned from General Willich that an order had
been issued for the Second Division to fall back, which I communi-

cated to Captain Strader, of Colonel Baldwin's staff, and in half an hour the regiment retired at the head of the brigade to the place where the knapsacks had been deposited on entering the fight. Bivouacking there till morning, I was ordered to take position in line of battle on the left of the brigade in the second line and construct a breastwork for defense. A substantial work was soon built and hardly completed when the enemy opened a fierce attack in our front. So suddenly did it burst upon us, that Captain Hooker, in command of Company A, as skirmishers, was unable to get back to the regiment, and fought till the enemy was repulsed behind the breastwork of the first line. Twenty men were detailed from my command to man the guns of the Fifth Indiana Battery, who fought with it during the day. In the intervals between the attacks of the enemy in our front on Sunday I had usually one or more companies of skirmishers covering the front, under the command of Major Stafford, who had charge of the skirmish line of the brigade.

About the time the enemy made his second attack in our front, and while my command was moving to relieve the Ninety-third Ohio on the first line, it was discovered that the enemy had broken through General Baird's line on our left, and filled the woods to our left and rear with his troops. The open field between us and these woods was covered with fugitives in Federal uniform fleeing from the victorious enemy. Under the command of Colonel Berry, I at once about-faced, and changed front to oppose them, and almost immediately afterward moved forward, recrossing the breastworks of the second line into position on the right of the Louisville Legion, and opened fire upon the enemy, checking his advance and driving him instantly to the cover of the woods. With one impulse, and apparently without command, the entire line rushed for the woods.

I turned to see if the movement had been ordered, and received Colonel Berry's order to halt and return my regiment to its proper position at the breastwork. My voice could not be heard in the confusion, and, seizing the colors, I had the halt and "to the colors" sounded by my bugler, and succeeded in getting about two-thirds of my regiment into line and back to position. The remainder went on ignorant that a halt had been ordered, and took part with the legion and Fifteenth Ohio in the brilliant charge which cleared the woods in our rear and taught the rebels a lesson of caution which saved us from molestation, when later in the day they again broke General Baird's line and entered the same woods.

Among the losses attending this charge I have to report Second Lieutenant Hallenberg, seriously wounded in two places; First Sergeant Burgdorf, Company B, mortally wounded, and a number of my bravest men killed and wounded. When ordered to retire in line of battle, my regiment moved off in double-quick and in good order, and although subjected to an enfilading fire from the enemy's batteries, accomplished the movement with a loss which, though unknown, was certainly smaller than would have been thought possible. A half hour sufficed to place us safely on the hills to the rear, and no further loss was sustained by the regiment till the following Tuesday, when it was placed in an exposed position on the bank of the creek south of Chattanooga, and endured the fire of rebel shells and solid shot from batteries on our flanks and front for the space of about one hour's time. By this fire or by the fire of two guns of the Second Minnesota Battery, situated in rear of our right flank, 2 sergeants and 4 privates were wounded. The wound of Sergeant Miller, of Company C, was terrible and mortal. He died in a few hours after. On that evening the regiment was retired to a better position, and a strong breastwork constructed on that night and the following day.

On Thursday a reconnaissance of the front was twice made by Major Stafford, Captain Hooker, with Company A, forming, part of his force on the last, and Captain Patterson, with Company H, on the first occasion. The first was without loss, but the last cost the death of John McCarthy, private Company A, and the wounding of John Shannon, also private of same company. The regiment continued in front till Friday evening, when it was ordered to the rear, and, after eight days and nights of duty under arms and under fire, was permitted to enjoy the rest it so much needed.

In all these varied duties of picket reconnaissance, skirmish, battle, and siege which the experience of these eight days covers, my command behaved admirably; always vigilant, patient, active, and brave. Officers and men deserved victory and obtained it, for they were successful throughout—uniformly so. Some cowards there were among us, it is true, but only enough to make brighter the example of the brave men of the command.

To the officers and men of the regiment generally I tender my sincere thanks for their good conduct. To the valuable services of Major Stafford and Captain Trapp, the senior captain present, I am much indebted; both are experienced soldiers, of tried courage and ability. The regiment sustained a heavy loss. First Lieutenant Jackson was killed by a grape-shot on Saturday night while gallantly waving his sword and encouraging his men. Captain Dornbush and First Lieutenant Grove were wounded seriously on Saturday afternoon. The latter rejoined his command on Sunday morning, but was unable to continue with it. Second Lieutenant Hallenberg, whose conduct is always admirable, was separated from his command in the pursuit on Sunday and wounded in the woods to our rear. He rejoined his company afterward, but was compelled to leave it on the retreat. Fourteen in all are known to have been killed, 80 are wounded, and 1 officer, First Lieut. and Actg. Adjt. Charles N. Winner, and 40 men are missing. Among the missing are doubtless many killed and wounded, and probably some prisoners. Among the killed are Sergt. Andrew Losh, Sergt. William B. Riddle, and Corpl. Robert M. Taylor, of Company G; Sergt. William D. Miller, Company C; Private J. H. Springher, Company I.

Privates Caleb Copeland, Company A, and John McCarthy, Company A, deserve special mention for their gallantry. We need not stint their praise. No after act can sully the brightness of the record they have left.

Please find accompanying list containing names of killed and wounded, marked A.* Thirty-eight prisoners were taken by my skirmishers on Saturday and turned over to the provost-marshal of the brigade.

I have the honor to be, captain, very respectfully,

BASSETT LANGDON,
Lieut. Col. First Ohio Vol. Infantry, Comdg. Regt.

Capt. FRANK P. STRADER,
Acting Assistant Adjutant-General, Third Brigade.

---

* Nominal list omitted; see revised statement, p. 174.

No. 119.

Report of Lieut. Col. William H. Martin, Ninety-third Ohio Infantry.

Camp near Chattanooga, Tenn., *September* 26, 1863.

Sir : The following is an unvarnished report of the action taken by the Ninety-third Ohio Volunteer Infantry in the battle of the 19th and 20th instant :

On the morning of the 19th instant the Ninety-third Ohio Volunteers, under command of Col. Hiram Strong, was ordered as a support to the Fifth Kentucky Volunteers, then marching in line of battle. The advance becoming engaged with the enemy, the enemy's batteries opened fire with shell, one shell exploding directly between Companies G and C (as we then lay at double column at half distance), wounding 6 men. After driving the enemy about a mile, met him strongly posted in the edge of a corn-field and thick woods. The Ninety-third Ohio was ordered to deploy in line of battle and take position on the left of the Fifth Kentucky. Companies A and K, in command of Maj. William Birch, were deployed as skirmishers and were immediately engaged with the enemy, and forced to fall back, losing several men killed, wounded, and missing. Great credit is due Maj. William Birch for his gallantry and bravery during the several engagements ; he was always wherever duty called him, and I cheerfully recommend him to the notice of our commander-in-chief.

After taking our position we were attacked by a superior force. The coolness and bravery of our men repulsed the enemy. In this engagement our brave and heroic colonel (Strong) was severely wounded and carried from the field. Upon the wounding of Colonel Strong I took command of the regiment. At this time the enemy had returned to our front with a battery of two 12-pounder guns, strongly supported by infantry, and undertook to plant his battery within 75 yards of my front. At the first volley from my regiment every horse was killed, and a large number of the gunners killed or wounded. They succeeded in firing one round of grape into my regiment over their dead horses, which killed and wounded several of my men. By this time our gallant and lamented colonel (P. P. Baldwin, commanding Third Brigade) ordered my regiment to charge the battery, he (Colonel Baldwin) leading the charge in person, with the flag streaming high over his head, which resulted in the complete rout of the enemy and capture of his battery of two guns. Lieut. John R. Gallup, acting adjutant, with 12 men, drew one of the guns to the rear, and delivered it to Captain Simonson, commanding Third Brigade battery. I was then ordered to return to my position, where I was first attacked, and ordered to build temporary breastworks, where we were soon attacked again by a superior force on our front and right flank ; nevertheless we kept them at bay about half an hour.

The enemy being in such overwhelming numbers, I was ordered to fall back a short distance, my left flank forming on the right of the Sixth Indiana Regiment. By this time it was quite dark ; nevertheless the battle raged furiously from forty minutes to one hour, which terminated in a repulse of the enemy. I then received orders to fall back with the brigade and take possession of a hill one-half mile to the rear, where we bivouacked for the night.

The casualties of my regiment to this time were heavy, having 5 commissioned officers wounded and not less than 100 enlisted men killed and wounded.

Sunday morning, September 20, 1863, at daylight, I received orders from Captain Strader, of brigade staff, to build breastworks connecting on my right with the Sixth Indiana. About 8 a. m. we were attacked by a large force; my regiment, with the Sixth Indiana, held their fire until the rebel lines were within 100 yards, when the Ninety-third Ohio and Sixth Indiana raised up and poured a volley into their front line (which was one of three) nearly demolishing it; nevertheless they pressed forward new lines, which met with the same fate. This engagement lasted one hour and a half. The enemy was completely routed with great slaughter, leaving his dead and wounded (which were numerous) on the field. Our skirmishers were pressed forward, and report finding at least 300 dead and wounded in front of the Sixth Indiana and Ninety-third Ohio, and a greater number of small-arms. The casualties of my regiment in this engagement were 5 wounded and 1 killed. Nothing more of importance occurring through the day until 3.30 p. m., the enemy again attacked us. We held them at bay for one hour, when it became necessary, by movements on other parts of the field, to fall back, which ended the fight for the day.

The casualties of my regiment in the two days' hard fighting were as follows, as near as opportunities would permit of ascertaining:

Commissioned officers wounded, 5; enlisted men killed, 15; enlisted men wounded and missing, 110. Aggregate, 130.

I cannot draw any line of distinction between the bravery of officers and men of my regiment. All stood up alike to the work before them. But cases present themselves of such a character that I must make special mention of them for their coolness, bravery, and determination, who were wounded slightly but remained with their companies and performed duty: Sergeant Holmes, Company B; Abia C. Zearing, Company B; John Sloan, Company B; John Drewry, Company B; Henry Linn, Company B; Isaac C. Snavely, Company B; Samuel Rohrer, Company B; Allen Dodge, corporal Company C; George Rosscoe, Company C; G. W. Gifford, John McClay, William Armstrong, and James M. Logan, of Company D; Sergt. John H. Parks, of Company D, I would mention especially on account of his gallant conduct in the hottest of the battle, he having to my knowledge two guns shot from his hands, two bullets passing through his hat, and one through the bottom of his pants, cutting his sock, and left the field with the regiment fully equipped; Sergts. John H. Atherton, Company F; John Murphy and John Eberts, Company G; Chris. J. Sensenbaugh, Company I; Corpl. James E. Fairchild and Private David Kinsey, Company K. Private Kinsey deserves especial mention for gallant conduct while skirmishing, capturing important maps and papers.

I cheerfully recommend Sergt. Maj. Oscar M. Gottschall for a commission; he was wounded by a piece of a shell, but was ever present and ready to do any duty he was called on to perform.

I could not help but notice the bravery and coolness of our brigade staff; wherever duty called they were present, rendering important aid in every instance.

Respectfully submitted.

Your obedient servant,

WM. H. MARTIN,
Lieut. Col., Comdg. 93d Ohio Volunteer Infantry.

Capt. Frank P. Strader,
Acting Assistant Adjutant-General, Third Brigade.

No. 120.

Reports of Capt. Peter Simonson, Fifth Indiana Battery.

HDQRS. FIFTH BATTERY INDIANA VOLUNTEERS,
Chattanooga, September 26, 1863.

CAPTAIN: I have the honor to report the part taken by this command in the action of the 19th and 20th:

The battery was first put in position, on Saturday at about 1 o'clock, with the brigade in the woods to the front and left of the corn-field, from which point it advanced with the brigade about half way through the woods, when I was ordered to take a position on a slight ridge, and commenced firing at a battery of the enemy's, which was shelling our line at this point. We fired about 130 rounds, when the opposing battery ceased firing and the brigade charged. I was ordered to follow the brigade, which I did changing front and firing to the left twice, until I reached nearly the point of the woods, where we lay quietly in position until nearly dark, when our line was heavily attacked with both infantry and artillery. The battery opened fire immediately and continued until our left flank broke, when, fearing that the guns would be captured, we retired with the brigade.

On this retreat one gun was lost by first getting the limber lodged on a tree and then having a horse shot. On Saturday night the battery bivouacked in line of battle with the brigade in the woods in front of the corn-field.

Early Sunday morning the battery was ordered to slightly change its position, which it did, and commenced building log breastworks. Before these were quite completed the enemy attacked the line about 9 o'clock, which lasted but a short time. After it was repulsed, we continued work on the breastworks until the general attack·was made, at about 11 o'clock. The battery fought in this position during the entire day, drawing out of it twice; once on account of the left being turned and once for want of ammunition. At a time when the left was turned we left this position, when the brigade was ordered back, and in leaving lost one more gun by a solid shot from the enemy's battery, disabling it. This gun I spiked.

On the night of the 20th we camped with the division at Rossville, and were in line of battle during the day and night of the 21st at that place, falling back to Chattanooga toward morning of the 21st. The command has been in line since reaching this place until this morning, during which time it has fired a number of shots in support of the line and drove a battery of the enemy from its position on our front, on the afternoon of the 23d, by firing about 40 rounds. The loss of the command during the fight was 1 killed, 7 wounded, and 1 missing, among whom was First Lieut. Alfred Morrison, whose conduct up to the time of receiving his wound was an example to the whole command, and who, by remaining with the command since he was wounded, has greatly inspirited the men. I also desire to favorably mention Lieutenants Briggs and Ellison, especially the former, who saved the battery by his coolness and good judgment.

On the afternoon of Sunday, when the final retreat was made, our loss in horses was 30; we also lost some of our harness. The battery fired during the engagement over 1,200 rounds of ammunition.

I also take this occasion to express my obligation to Lieutenant

Williams, of the brigade staff, who, with Lieutenant Ellison, of this command, brought forward ammunition to the battery under a very heavy fire.

I am, very respectfully, your most obedient servant,

PETER SIMONSON,
Captain, Commanding Fifth Battery Indiana Volunteers.

Capt. FRANK P. STRADER,
Acting Assistant Adjutant-General, Third Brigade.

—

CAMP AT CHATTANOOGA, TENN.,
October 10, 1863.

COLONEL: The Fifth Indiana Battery was first put in position with the Third Brigade, Second Division, on the ground previously occupied by General Baird's division at 1.30 o'clock Saturday, when I opened fire on two batteries and a line of infantry firing in our front. After firing about 50 rounds their firing ceased, when the brigade charged and drove the enemy about half a mile out of the woods to a field. Upon reaching the batteries with which we were engaged, I found one of them to be three guns of the First Michigan Battery, which the enemy had captured and were using on us. Fighting continued at this place at intervals until dark, when a heavy force was massed on our left flank, which turned it, and the division was driven back. I lost a gun on this retreat by having a horse shot at a time when the gun was caught on a tree.

That night the battery was put in position in the line of battle with the brigade between Palmer's division on our right and Baird's division on the left. The battery staid there all the next day (Sunday), and was hotly engaged from 10 o'clock in the morning until 5 o'clock in the afternoon. We fired in this position over 1,000 rounds of ammunition, and during the two days 1,247 rounds. In getting away from this position I lost another gun by having it disabled by a solid shot. From this position we moved slowly to Rossville, arriving there at about 10 o'clock. My thanks are due to Lieutenants Morrison and Briggs for gallantry.

The loss in the battles was: Officers wounded, 1; men killed, 1; men wounded, 7; men missing, 1; horses shot, 30; guns and caissons lost, 2.

I am, very respectfully, yours, &c.,

PETER SIMONSON,
Captain, and Chief of Artillery.

Col. JAMES BARNETT, *Chief of Artillery.*

———

No. 121.

Report of Maj. Gen. Philip H. Sheridan, U. S. Army, commanding Third Division.

HDQRS. THIRD DIVISION, TWENTIETH ARMY CORPS,
Chattanooga, Tenn., September 30, 1863.

COLONEL: I have the honor to report the following as the operations of my command from September 2 to September 23, 1863:

On the 2d and 3d of September this division crossed the Tennessee River at Bridgeport, and encamped at Moore's Spring, in the little valley at the base of Sand Mountain, some delay having occurred in consequence of the giving way of the bridge.

On the 4th I ascended the mountain and encamped at Warren's Mill, about half way across.

On the 5th I descended the mountain and encamped near Trenton, Ga., in Lookout Valley.

On the 6th I moved south and encamped at Colonel Easley's, 5 miles from Trenton.

On the 7th I moved to Stevens' Mill, a distance of 5 miles, where I remained during the 8th and 9th.

On the 10th I moved to Valley Head, ascended Lookout Mountain, and encamped at Indian Falls.

On the 11th I crossed and descended the mountain, and encamped at Alpine, in Broomtown Valley.

On the 12th I remained at Alpine.

On the 13th and 14th I recrossed Lookout Mountain and encamped again at Stevens' Mill.

On the 15th and 16th I recrossed Lookout Mountain at Stevens' Gap, and encamped at the base of the mountain, in McLemore's Cove.

On the 17th the division remained in line of battle during the day and night, the enemy having made demonstrations on my front, and the rest of the army having moved to the left.

On the 18th I marched to the left, encamping at Lee's Mill, on the extreme right of the army. During the night of the 18th I followed the army to the left, camping at Pond Spring.

On the 19th I was again ordered to resume the march, coming into line of battle at Crawfish Spring.

Immediately after forming my line, I was ordered to hold the ford at Gordon's Mills with my whole division, the troops on my left having moved to the left, and again isolating me.

In a short time after occupying the position at Gordon's Mills, and after having driven the enemy's skirmishers from my immediate front, I was directed to support General Crittenden with two brigades of my division.

Moving rapidly to the left, I came in to the support of Generals Wood and Davis, who were being hard pressed and their troops nearly exhausted. The brigade of Colonel Bradley, consisting of the Twenty-second, Twenty-seventh, Forty-second, and Fifty-first Illinois, was hastily formed, and gallantly drove the enemy from the open ground and across the Chattanooga and La Fayette road, after a sanguinary engagement, in which it recaptured the Eighth Indiana Battery, which had previously been captured by the enemy, and captured a large number of prisoners belonging to Hood's division, of Longstreet's corps.

While Colonel Bradley was thus driving the enemy, Colonel Laiboldt, with his brigade, formed upon his right. Darkness coming on, the opposite lines lay down upon their arms, ready to renew the contest in the morning.

In this engagement Colonel Bradley received two severe wounds while gallantly leading his brigade. Lieutenant Moody, his acting assistant adjutant-general, was mortally wounded at the same time.

About 11 o'clock that night I was again directed to move to the left and occupy a position at Glenn's house. This was successfully accomplished by strengthening the picket lines and moving the brigades from right to left until the point designated was arrived at. The picket lines were then withdrawn.

On the morning of the 20th I rearranged my lines and found myself in a strong position on the extreme right, but disconnected from the troops on my left.

About 9 o'clock the engagement again opened by a heavy assault upon the left, while everything was quiet in my front. To resist the assault that was being made on the left the interior divisions were again moved.

About 11 o'clock the brigade of Colonel Laiboldt, composed of the Second and Fifteenth Missouri, Forty-fourth and Seventy-third Illinois, was directed to move to the left and occupy a portion of the front which had been covered by General Negley. Before getting into this position, however, the ground was occupied by Carlin's brigade, of Davis' division, and Laiboldt was directed to take position on a very strong ridge in his rear, with directions to deploy on the ridge and hold it, so as to prevent Davis' flank from being turned. Word was then sent to General McCook of the disposition which had been made, which he approved.

Immediately afterward I received orders to support General Thomas with two brigades. I had just abandoned my position, and was moving at a double-quick when the enemy made a furious assault with overwhelming numbers on Davis' front, and, coming up through the unoccupied space between Davis and myself, even covering the front of the position I had just abandoned, Davis was driven from his lines, and Laiboldt, whose brigade was in column of regiments, was ordered by Major-General McCook to charge, deploying to the front. The impetuosity of the enemy's charge, and the inability of Laiboldt's command to fire on account of the ground in his front being covered with Davis' men, who, rushing through his ranks, broke his brigade, and it also was driven [sic]. In the meantime I had received the most urgent orders to throw in my other two brigades. This I did at a double-quick, forming the brigade of General Lytle, composed of the Thirty-sixth and Eighty-eighth Illinois, Twenty-fourth Wisconsin, and Twenty-first Michigan, and Colonel Bradley's brigade, now commanded by Col. N. H. Walworth, to the front under a terrible fire of musketry from the enemy. Many of the men were shot down before facing to the front. After a stubborn resistance, the enemy drove me back nearly to the La Fayette road, a distance of about 300 yards. At this point the men again rallied and drove the enemy back with terrible slaughter, regaining the line of the ridge on which Colonel Laiboldt had originally been posted. The Fifty-first Illinois captured the colors of the Twenty-fourth Alabama. A number of prisoners were also captured at the same time.

Here, unfortunately, the enemy had strong supports, while I had none to relieve my exhausted men, and my troops were again driven back to the La Fayette road after a gallant resistance.

In this engagement I had the misfortune to lose General Lytle, commanding my First Brigade, and many of the best and bravest officers of my command.

After crossing the road my division was again formed on the ridge which overlooked the ground where this sanguinary contest had taken place, the enemy manifesting no disposition to continue the engagement further. I here learned positively what I had before partially seen, that the divisions still farther on my left had been driven, and that I was completely cut off.   I then determined to connect myself with the troops of General Thomas by moving on the arc of a circle until I struck the Dry Creek Valley road, by which I hoped to form the junction.   In the mean time I was joined by a portion of the division of General Davis, under command of General Carlin, and a number of stragglers from other divisions.

On reaching the Dry Creek Valley road I found that the enemy had moved parallel to me and had also arrived at the road, thus preventing my joining General Thomas by that route.   I then determined to move quickly on Rossville and form a junction with him on his left flank via the La Fayette road.   This was successfully accomplished about 5.30 p. m.   Before undertaking this movement I disencumbered myself of sixteen pieces of artillery, forty-six caissons, one entire battery, and a portion of another battery, belonging to other divisions, which I found in wild confusion and collected where I first reformed my lines.

After forming the junction with General Thomas on his left, his command was ordered to fall back to Rossville, and I was directed to fall back to the same place, where the command rested during the night.

On the 21st I formed my command in line of battle at Rossville, and remained in that position until during the night of that day, when I fell back to Chattanooga, forming the rear guard of our corps.

The above is a brief narrative of the operations of my division, which numbered before going into action on the 19th about 4,000 bayonets.

The battle of the 20th was fought under the most disadvantageous circumstances, without time being given to form line of battle, without supports, and contending against four or five divisions.   The division gave up its ground after a sanguinary contest, with a loss of 96 of its gallant officers and 1,421 of its brave men.

Among the killed early in the engagement of the 20th was Brig. Gen. W. H. Lytle, who was three times wounded, but refused to leave the field.   In him the country has lost an able general and the service a gallant soldier.

Colonel Bradley, commanding my Third Brigade, who had greatly distinguished himself, was twice severely wounded in the action of the 19th; Colonel Laiboldt, commanding my Second Brigade, behaved with conspicuous gallantry in the action of the 20th.   I respectfully recommend both of these officers for promotion.

Col. N. H. Walworth, Forty-second Illinois, succeeded Colonel Bradley in the command of the Third Brigade, and Col. Silas Miller, Thirty-sixth Illinois, succeeded General Lytle in the command of the First Brigade.   They both behaved with great skill and bravery.

The following regimental officers were especially distinguished: Col. J. F. Jaquess, Seventy-third Illinois, for skill exhibited and great personal courage—he is almost the only officer left with his regiment, 17 of them having been either killed or wounded; Col. W. W. Barrett (Forty-fourth Illinois), Lieut. Col. John Weber (Fifteenth Missouri), Lieut. Col. John Russell (Forty-fourth Illinois), and Lieut. Col. J. I. Davidson (Seventy-third Illinois) were all wounded; Maj. J. Leighton, Forty-second Illinois, was killed on the 19th, and Col. W. B. McCreery, Twenty-first Michigan, killed on the 20th; Major Smith, Seventy-third Illinois, killed; Maj. S. Johnson, Twenty-second Illinois, mortally wounded; Lieut. Col. T. S. West, Twenty-fourth Wisconsin, wounded and captured; Lieutenant-Colonel

Wells, Twenty-first Michigan, killed; Col. J. R. Miles, Twenty-seventh Illinois; Col. Joseph Conrad, Fifteenth Missouri; Lieut. Col. S. B. Raymond, Fifty-first Illinois; Maj. H. A. Rust, Twenty-seventh Illinois; Lieut. Col. J. A. Hottenstein, commanding Forty-second Illinois; Lieut. Col. F. Swanwick, commanding Twenty-second Illinois; Lieut. Col. W. A. Schmitt, Twenty-seventh Illinois; Maj. Arnold Beck, commanding Second Missouri; Lieut. Col. A. S. Chadbourne, commanding Eighty-eighth Illinois; Major Chandler, Eighty-eighth Illinois; Lieut. Col. P. C. Olson, commanding Thirty-sixth Illinois; Maj. George D. Sherman, Thirty-sixth Illinois, and many other officers of lesser grades, whose names cannot be given without undue length to this report.

I respectfully bring to the notice of the general commanding the following officers of my staff; Surg. D. J. Griffiths, medical director; Maj. F. Mohrhardt, topographical engineer; Capt. H. Hescock, chief of artillery, who was probably wounded and fell into the hands of the enemy; Capt. George Lee, assistant adjutant-general; Capt. A. F. Stevenson, inspector; Capt. W. L. Mallory, commissary of subsistence; Capt. P. U. Schmitt, acting assistant quartermaster; Capt. J. S. Ransom, provost-marshal; Lieut. A. J. Douglass, ordnance officer; Lieuts. F. H. Allen, M. V. Sheridan, and T. W. C. Moore, aides-de-camp, and Lieut. J. Van Pelt, acting aide-de-camp, all of whom rendered me valuable service, both on the march and in action. After the death of General Lytle, Col. J. F. Harrison, volunteer aide-de-camp, and Lieut. Alfred Pirtle, aide-de-camp, of his staff, reported to me for duty, and subsequently behaved very handsomely.

The total casualties—officers and men—in this division are as follows:

Killed, 152; wounded, 1,037; captured, 328. Total 1,517.* Of the 1,037 wounded, 325 were left in the hospital at Crawfish Spring and fell into the hands of the enemy.

I am, sir, very respectfully, your obedient servant,

P. H. SHERIDAN,
Major-General, Commanding.

Lieut. Col. G. P. THRUSTON,
Asst. Adjt. Gen., and Chief of Staff, 20th Army Corps.

No. 122.

Report of Col. Silas Miller, Thirty-sixth Illinois Infantry, commanding First Brigade.

HDQRS. FIRST BRIG., THIRD DIV., 20TH ARMY CORPS,
Chattanooga, Tenn., September 28, 1863.

SIR: I have the honor to submit the following report of the operations of this brigade since crossing the Tennessee River:

The command crossed at Bridgeport, Ala., about noon on Wednesday, September 2, 1863, and remained in Hog Jaw Valley, at the foot of Sand Mountain, until afternoon of the 4th, when it moved up the mountain and back 5 miles, camping at Warren's Mill.

Saturday, 5th, marched early, passing down the mountain and camping at Trenton, Ga.

Sunday, 6th, moved at 12 m., 5 miles up the valley.

---

* See revised statement, p. 175.

At 5.30 on the morning of the 7th marched 6 miles up the valley, camping at Benham's, 11 miles from Trenton. Remained there until the morning of the 10th, then marched 15 miles, via Winston's, to Little River Falls, on Lookout Mountain.

September 11 moved at 6 a. m., passing down the mountain and camping at Alpine, Ga., in Broomtown Valley, where we remained until 3.30 p. m. of Sunday, the 13th, when the command, having been detailed as part of the rear guard of the corps train, moved to the foot of the mountain.

Monday, 14th, started up the mountain at 5 a. m., and after a tedious, dusty march, camped at Little River Falls.

Wednesday, 16th, moved at 5 in the morning in company with the Second Brigade, Second Division, making camp at Dougherty's Gap, 10 miles. 17th, marched along the ridge of the mountains and down Stevens' Gap into McLemore's Cove, camping near the gap. 18th, moved cautiously, joining the division. The Eighty-eighth Illinois reconnoitered, under direction of General Sheridan, in advance of the column as far as Lee's Mill, at which place arrangements were made for camping, but at sunset the general sounded, and after a tedious night's march halted at Mitchell's, near Pond Spring.

At 11 a. m. of the 19th the command moved toward Gordon's Mills, near which point the action was then in progress. This brigade was placed in position to hold the ford at the mills, the Eighty-eighth Illinois, Twenty-first Michigan, with two sections of the Eleventh Indiana Battery, being posted at the ford, the Thirty-sixth Illinois and Twenty-fourth Wisconsin, with the remaining section, being farther to the left, near the barricade erected the previous night by the division of General Wood, on the Chattanooga road near Chickamauga Creek.

Sunday, the 20th, at 3.30 a. m., the command moved via Chattanooga road, and by sunrise had taken a strong position near Lee's Mills, at the house occupied by General Rosecrans during the night as his headquarters. The battle having been some time in progress toward the left, at 11.30 a. m. this brigade was moved a short distance to the left, along the road, to occupy the ridge, supporting the Second Brigade. The Eighty-eighth Illinois and Thirty-sixth Illinois moved first, the Eighty-eighth on the right forming in double-quick time along the ridge to the right of the road under a heavy fire. They were almost immediately followed by the Twenty-first Michigan and Twenty-fourth Wisconsin, forming the second line; also by the battery, one section of which was posted with much difficulty near the base of the ridge in rear of the left of the Thirty-sixth Illinois. This position was flanked by the enemy both on the right and left shortly after it was taken, and the fire poured in by the enemy from the flanks soon drove the first line from its place. The second line advancing held the front while the first regiment re-formed, having changed front oblique to the rear, protecting the flanks of the remaining line as well as possible. While rallying the men to the formation of this line our noble and beloved commander fell (two or three times wounded previously). During this action he had persistently refused to leave the field, but gallantly doing more than his duty to the men he loved, and who worshiped him, he sacrificed himself without reluctance. No words or eulogies of men can add any luster to his deeds of heroic daring or render more honored and revered among men the name and memory of William H. Lytle.

This position having become entirely untenable the command was compelled to fall back somewhat precipitately. The rifled section of the battery under Lieutenant Williams, after doing splendid execution, had finally to be abandoned. The caissons were brought off, and the remainder of the battery was saved only through the almost superhuman efforts of Captain Sutermeister and his men.

The command was rallied in a disorganized condition, being united with portions of other brigades and divisions on the ridge in rear of our position. A large force having been rallied, it was moved by a mountain road toward the center, to a point on the Chattanooga and La Fayette road, 3 miles from Rossville, when it was reformed and took up position. By your order it soon removed, this brigade in advance, passing via Rossville on the Ringgold road 3 miles to —— Church, arriving about dusk. Here the column halted until about 9 o'clock, when, by your order, it returned to Rossville.

Monday, the 21st, remained at Rossville erecting strong barricades. Some skirmishing, in which the brigade was not engaged.

At 2.30 o'clock on the morning of the 22d the command fell back from that place upon Chattanooga, taking position with the right resting upon the river, near the rolling mill, at daylight in the morning.

Some embarrassment in making this report results from the fact that orders received by General Lytle for movements while on the march in command of the rear guard were upon his person when he fell, and cannot therefore be obtained for reference, and from the fact that during the active part of the battle and until advised of his death, I only received orders concerning the disposition of my own regiment.

Herewith is forwarded a list* of casualties in the brigade. While it is painful to reflect that such men must be sacrificed, it is a glorious consolation to know that none fell but in the discharge of the highest and holiest duty which can devolve upon man as a citizen or a soldier. Col. William B. McCreery, of the Twenty-first Michigan, fell mortally wounded while gallantly leading his regiment. Lieutenant-Colonel Wells, of the same regiment, was killed while bravely performing his duty. Major Chase, upon whom the command then devolved, performed his duties with signal efficiency and bravery. Captain Bishop and Adjutant Morse, of this regiment, particularly distinguished themselves. Lieutenant-Colonel West, of the Twenty-fourth Wisconsin, was also wounded while at the head of his regiment in the thickest of the fight, and fell into the hands of the enemy. Major von Baumbach, thus placed in command, acquitted himself with credit and honor. Lieutenant-Colonel Chadbourne, of the Eighty-eighth Illinois, distinguished himself by his perfect calmness in the most trying circumstances in the discharge of his duties. He was ably assisted by Major Chandler. Lieutenant-Colonel Olson and Major Sherman, of the Thirty-sixth Illinois, deserve special mention for their skill and daring; both had their horses shot under them, and were very efficient in leading the men in the fight and rallying and reforming the lines. Adjutant Miller, of the Eighty-eighth Illinois, Adjutant Clark, of the Thirty-sixth Illinois, and Adjutant Balding, of the Twenty-fourth Wisconsin, rendered themselves conspicuous by their bravery and usefulness.

For further mention of meritorious conduct on the part of officers and men I refer to reports of regimental commanders. The conduct

---

* Embodied in revised statement. p. 175.

of the brigade staff after I came in charge was unexceptionable. Not having been in command during the heat of the action, I cannot speak of each separately.

After having reported to me, Lieutenant Turnbull, brigade inspector; Lieutenant Boal, topographical engineer; Lieutenant Jackson, provost-marshal; Lieutenant Pirtle, aide-de-camp, and Lieutenant Eaton, aide-de-camp, signalized themselves by their usefulness and recklessness of danger in the performance of duty. Of Capt. James A. Grover, assistant adjutant-general, I can speak from observation, during the heat of the action having continually found him in the thickest fire and wherever his presence was most needed in the action; also of Col. J. F. Harrison, volunteer aide-de-camp to General Lytle. During the rallying for the formation of the second line, being wounded, he seized a stand of colors and, under the influence of his example, the men rapidly went forward, again forming under a terrible fire.

The greatest credit and highest praise of all is due to the enlisted men of the command.

Respectfully submitted.

SILAS MILLER,
Col. 36th Ill. Vol. Inf., Comdg. 1st Brig., 3d Div., 20th A. C.

Capt. GEORGE LEE,
Assistant Adjutant-General, Third Division.

No. 123.

Report of Maj. Seymour Chase, Twenty-First Michigan Infantry.

HEADQUARTERS TWENTY-FIRST MICHIGAN INFANTRY,
Chattanooga, Tenn., September 28, 1863.

CAPTAIN: In compliance with orders I have the honor to report the part borne by this regiment in the action of the 20th instant at or near Crawfish Spring, Ga.

Before daylight on the morning of the engagement the regiment, under the command of Col. William B. McCreery, took position on the extreme right of the brigade, near the house occupied the evening before by General Rosecrans as his headquarters. Here it remained, the men throwing up temporary breastworks, until about twenty minutes past 11 a. m., when it was ordered into action. Colonel McCreery, according to orders, moved by column of companies about 400 yards to the left and deployed it in line. Fixing bayonet on the double-quick, the regiment steadily advanced under fire to the crest of a small hill and took position on the extreme right of the brigade. Here the men were ordered to lie down until our troops in front could pass through to the rear.

As the enemy neared our position the regiment rose and poured a withering volley into them, which checked their advance for a time. At one time quite a large number of the enemy, who had worked around our right flank, were driven back in full retreat by the constant fire and unerring aim of Company A, armed with the Colt revolving rifle. A fresh regiment, however, appearing in their places. After a terrible contest of about twenty minutes, the right wing of the regiment was forced back, and the whole compelled to retire to escape capture.

At this time both Colonel McCreery and Lieutenant-Colonel Wells, while encouraging the men, were badly wounded, and left on the field in the hands of the enemy. After falling back about half a mile the regiment was rallied and brought off the field in good order.

I take pleasure in mentioning the gallant conduct of Company B (numbering 30 men), under Lieut. A. E. Barr, and also of 7 men and Lieut. C. E. Belknap, of Company H. They were thrown forward as skirmishers early in the morning in the corn-field directly in front of the first position taken by the regiment. When the regiment was ordered into action these skirmishers were not called in. Cut off from the main body of the command and attacked by an overwhelming force of the enemy, they rallied and made a stand behind the buildings before mentioned.

Here they held the enemy in check for nearly an hour, and successfully joined the regiment with the loss of but 1 man, and he killed instantly.

On account of the command not devolving upon me until the retreat began, I cannot speak with accuracy of the orders received or whether they were implicitly followed.

Permit me to testify to the coolness and gallantry of both officers and men of the command. Every one seemed to know his whole duty, and I believe the loss of the regiment and the small number missing not known to be wounded, will show that each performed it. And particularly conspicuous for their courage and daring were the two colonels, McCreery and Wells, who left their bodies on the field to testify to their devotion and well-doing.

The casualties of the regiment were as follows : Known to be killed, 10 enlisted men ; wounded and within our lines, 2 officers and 58 enlisted men ; wounded and missing, 3 officers and 16 enlisted men ; missing, 2 officers and 15 enlisted men ; making a sum total of 7 officers and 99 enlisted men.

On the 24th instant we had 1 man mortally wounded by the explosion of a shell from the rebel battery on Lookout Mountain.

I am, captain, very respectfully, your obedient servant,

SEYMOUR CHASE,
Major, Commanding Twenty-first Michigan Infantry.

Capt. JAMES A. GROVER,
Asst. Adjt. Gen., 1st Brig., 3d Div., 20th Army Corps.

No. 124.

Report of Maj. Carl von Baumbach, Twenty-fourth Wisconsin Infantry.

HDQRS. 24TH REGIMENT WISCONSIN VOL. INFANTRY,
Camp near Chattanooga, September 29, 1863.

GENERAL: I have the honor to submit the following report of the part taken by this regiment in the late engagements, September 19 and 20, before Chattanooga, viz:

On the morning of the 19th instant the regiment marched from camp near Pond Spring at 11 a. m., under the command of Lieut. Col. T. S. West, to a short distance beyond Gordon's Mills, where it was formed in line on the right of the Chattanooga road, fronting the Chickamauga Creek, the right resting on the barricades built by

General Wood's division the previous night, our regiment and the Thirty-sixth Illinois forming the first line, and the Eighty-eighth Illinois and the Twenty-first Michigan the second line.

In accordance with orders from Brigadier-General Lytle, we here sent 1 commissioned officer and 10 men to deploy as skirmishers along the edge of the creek to watch the movements of the enemy. We had not remained long in this position before the enemy opened on us with one piece of artillery, but which fortunately did us no harm. We remained in this position until shortly after dark, when we received orders from General Lytle to move about 200 paces to the rear in the edge of a piece of timber, where we bivouacked for the night.

At 3 a. m. on the morning of the 20th the regiment assembled under arms, and shortly after were marched directly in the rear of the Eleventh Indiana Battery down the Chattanooga road to Lee's Hill, where we formed in line to the right and rear of Widow Crane's house (General Rosecrans' former headquarters), the Eighty-eighth Illinois and the Twenty-first Michigan forming the first line, and the Twenty-fourth Wisconsin and Thirty-sixth Illinois the second line.

We remained in this position until half past 10 a. m., when we were moved about one-fourth of a mile farther down the Chatta-nooga road at a double-quick, where we formed line on the right of the road facing the Chickamauga Creek, under a terrific fire from the enemy, our right resting on the Twenty-first Michigan and our left on the Thirty-sixth Illinois; here we fought the enemy for nearly half an hour, driving him entirely from our front.

We here lost our brave and gallant Brig. Gen. W. H. Lytle, who was shot down while in the rear of the center of our regiment encouraging the men. About that time the enemy moved a heavy column upon our left flank, and the regiment on our left having given way, we were exposed to a severe enfilading fire. Our two left companies were swung to the rear and poured an effective fire into their ranks, but they still moving up in overwhelming numbers, we were at last forced to give way. We retreated in some disorder, but quickly reformed on a hill some 400 yards to our rear. Our brave and gallant young commander, Lieut. Col. T. S. West, being among the missing, I here assumed command, and in accordance with orders received from Col. S. Miller, I moved my regiment with the rest of the brigade down the Chattanooga and La Fayette road, and thence up the Chattanooga and Ringgold road about 5 miles, where we halted for a short time, and then marched back to Rossville, where we bivouacked for the night.

On the morning of the 21st, in obedience to orders, I marched my regiment to the front and took my position in line. We here threw up some breastworks and occupied them until about 1 a. m. of the 22d, when I marched with the rest of the brigade to our present position near Chattanooga.

I cannot speak too highly of the conduct of both officers and men; they advanced and formed into line under a terrific fire from the enemy with a coolness and celerity that was most admirable, and when driven from their position by overwhelming numbers quickly reformed and were as eager as ever to be led on again.

Where all did so well it is hard to discriminate, but I would make especial mention of Lieut. Thomas E. Balding, acting adjutant, for his gallant conduct and efficient aid as acting field officer after I assumed command. I would also tender my thanks to Surg. H. E. Hasse for his care and attention to the wounded men.

Inclosing a list of the casualties, and tendering in behalf of the officers of the regiment my thank to Col. S. Miller for his untiring exertions for our welfare and comfort, I have the honor to be, general, your most obedient servant,

CARL von BAUMBACH,
Major, Comdg. Twenty-fourth Wisconsin Volunteers.

Aug. Gaylord,
Adjutant-General, State of Wisconsin.

No. 125.

Report of Capt. Arnold Sutermeister, Eleventh Indiana Battery.

Headquarters Eleventh Indiana Battery,
Chattanooga, October 2, 1863.

Colonel : I have the honor to transmit to you according to your orders the following statement of the operations of this battery during September 19 and 20:

The battery started from the neighborhood of Joliet under the direction of Brigadier-General Lytle, commanding First Brigade, to Lee and Gordon's Mills, on Chickamauga Creek. From here we were ordered down the road toward our center, and the two 12-pounder sections were stationed on a little eminence commanding the fields beyond the stream, the rifle section kept in reserve. During the afternoon the 12-pounder sections were ordered back to Lee and Gordon's Mills, to guard the ford.

At 3 a. m. of the 20th the battery was ordered off and took position in front of two log-houses occupied, I believe, by General McCook as his headquarters the previous day. Here we awaited the approach of the enemy till about noon, when we were ordered by General Lytle to fall in, in regular brigade order, and march with the brigade. Advancing at a round trot we soon reached a field, where I received orders to station the battery, which was done at once, the rifle section taking the right.

After getting in position we had to remain inactive and wait till our scattered and retreating troops cleared the field; as soon as this was done we opened a rapid fire of canister on the enemy. Finding, however, that our infantry was nowhere supporting us, and the enemy drawing very close, I ordered the battery to limber up and retreat. At this moment the horses of the limbers of the rifle section were shot down, 5 drivers wounded, also several canoneers. Lieut. H. M. Williams, commanding the section, also disabled, and the section had to be abandoned. The two 12-pounder sections, as also all the caissons, came out safe with the loss of a few horses.

On the hill in rear of this position to which we retreated we opened fire once more, but were ordered by general officers to withdraw.

Soon after I received information that General Sheridan was forming a new line of battle, and I hastened to report to him, General Lytle having been killed; but I found that the division was retreating, and Captain Stevenson, inspector of Third Division, ordered me to follow with the battery. After a short march I rejoined our brigade.

Officers and men fought like soldiers, and to their bravery I have to give the credit of saving the two sections and bringing them out of that most unfavorable position in which they were placed.

The casualties during the battle are as follows.*

I also annex the loss of *matériel* and ammunition.

Very respectfully, your most obedient servant,

A. SUTERMEISTER,
Captain, Eleventh Indiana Battery.

Col. JAMES BARNETT,
Chief of Artillery, Department of the Cumberland.

[Inclosure.]

LOSS OF MATÉRIEL.

Ordnance: Two 3-inch rifled guns, with all the implements, as hand-spikes, prolonges, sponges, and rammers, water and tar buckets, sights, pouches, priming wires, punches, &c., belonging to the section; 2 limbers for same; 4 sets of lead harness complete, with blankets, nose-bags, &c., belonging to it; 2 sets of wheel harness complete, with blankets, nose-bags, &c., belonging to it; 2 sergeant's saddles complete; 3 revolvers, with belts and pouches; 2 sabers, with belts; 3 sponge buckets; 100 rounds of 3-inch rifled ammunition expended and lost; 20 rounds of 12-pounder ammunition, canister, expended.

Quartermaster stores: 19 horses, 20 shelter tents, 2 tarpaulins, knapsacks, haversacks, and canteens.

A. SUTERMEISTER,
Captain, Eleventh Indiana Battery.

No. 126.

Report of Col. Bernard Laiboldt, Second Missouri Infantry, commanding Second Brigade.

HDQRS. SECOND BRIG., THIRD DIV., 20TH ARMY CORPS,
In Trenches before Chattanooga, September 29, 1863.

SIR: In compliance to circular from corps headquarters, I have the honor to submit to you the following report of the movements of my brigade since crossing the Tennessee River, and of the part it took during the late engagement:

After crossing the Tennessee River, on September 2, 1863, we proceeded to Hog Jaw Valley, from where we ascended the Raccoon Mountain on the 5th and marched to Gunther's Mill.

On the 6th we marched over Trenton to Lookout Creek, and on the 7th to Stevens' Mill on Stuart's Creek.

On the 10th we proceeded through the Lookout and Will's Valleys to Rock Creek, and on the 11th reached Alpine, Ga.

On the 13th, returning we crossed the Lookout Mountain and camped on Little River. Reached Stevens' Mill on the 14th. Left there at 2 p. m., on the 15th, and arrived at Johnson's Crook at 6 p. m. Ascending Lookout Mountain on the 16th, we took position

----

*Nominal list omitted; see revised statement, p. 175.

in McLemore's Cove, which position we held till the 18th. Starting at 9 a. m. that day we marched to Lee's Mill and Pond Spring.

On the 19th we proceeded to Crawfish Spring, where we arrived about 1 p. m. My brigade was the first formed in line of battle on the crest of the hill, from where it was ordered to take position near Gordon's Mills, and to guard a ford of Chickamauga Creek. At about 4.30 p. m. my brigade was ordered to the battle-field to support General Davis.

On arriving there a line of battle was formed along a road and the regiment ordered to advance, but the enemy having already been driven by Colonel Bradley's brigade, my brigade took no further part in the struggle of that day, and kept their position until near daybreak of the 20th, when we were ordered to the extreme right of the right wing, where the brigade took a position on a hill near the Chattanooga road, having Colonel Bradley's brigade as reserve.

At 11.30 o'clock we were ordered toward the center to support General Davis, and took a very favorable position on the slope of a hill. After a short interval, when General Davis' division was already routed, Major-General McCook ordered the brigade to charge in rear of the flying troops, and promptly obeying the command the position on the hill slope was abandoned, and the regiments, with charged bayonets, rushed into the thicket of woods, parting them yet [farther] from General Davis' command, unable to fire effectually without injuring our own men. Thrown in confusion by the fleeing troops and finally exposed to the scathing fire of the enemy in front, as also a fire in the flank, my troops gave way, and after rallying them once more, but not being able to hold a position, I fell back to the mountains, where, after the lapse of about three quarters of an hour, I succeeded in collecting the remaining portion.

You will please find annexed the list* of casualties during the engagement.

In connection with the official report of the participation of my brigade in the late engagement, I have the honor to remark that the commanding officers of the Second Missouri Volunteers and the Seventy-third Illinois Volunteers make no especial mention in their respective reports of cases of courage and bravery, as, in their opinion, officers and men alike sustained their former reputation of true courage and unflinching valor.

The commanding officer of the Fifteenth Missouri Volunteers mentions especially his adjutant, First Lieut. Friedrich Lipps, and the commanding officer of the Forty-fourth Illinois Infantry, Major Sabin; Captains Freysleben and Knappen, and acting adjutant, First Lieutenant Weyhrich, for gallant conduct. Lieutenant Schueler, commanding Battery G, First Missouri Artillery, mentions Second Lieut. John Miller and Sergt. S. H. Jennings for brave behavior.

I take great pleasure to state that Lieut. Col. A. Beck, Second Missouri Volunteers ; Colonel Conrad, Fifteenth Missouri Volunteers ; Colonel Barrett, Forty-fourth Illinois Volunteers, and Colonel Jaquess, Seventy-third Illinois Volunteers, and First Lieutenant Schueler, commanding Battery G, First Missouri Artillery, entitled themselves, by their unflinching courage and gallant behavior during the engagement, to the highest commendations. The company of sharpshooters (Captain Ernst) did the work assigned to them faithfully. While the members of my staff, Major Spinzig, brigade surgeon ; Captain Fuelle, acting assistant adjutant-general ;

---

* Embodied in revised statement, p. 175.

Captain Morgan, brigade inspector; Captain Carroll, provost-marshal; Captain Gale, assistant quartermaster and commissary of subsistence; First Lieutenant Neudorff, aide-de-camp, and Second Lieutenant Heydtman, topographical engineer, merit my acknowledgment of their zeal and activity during the campaign and in battle, I feel it incumbent on me to especially mention Capt. B. A. Carroll and Lieutenant Neudorff, whose untiring efforts in assisting me to rally the brigade, I shall always thankfully remember.

I have the honor to sign, your obedient servant,

B. LAIBOLDT,
Colonel, Comdg. 2d Brig., 3d Div., 20th Army Corps.

Capt. GEORGE LEE,
Assistant Adjutant-General, 3d Div., 20th Army Corps.

No. 127.

Report of Maj. Arnold Beck, Second Missouri Infantry.

HDQRS. SECOND INFANTRY MISSOURI VOLUNTEERS,
Camp Lytle, near Chattanooga, Tenn., October 7, 1863.

SIR: I have the honor to hereby most respectfully transmit to you a report inasmuch as the Second Missouri Infantry Volunteers was concerned in the battle in front of Chattanooga, Tenn., September 19 and 20, 1863.

On the 19th the Second Infantry Missouri Volunteers, forming a part of the Second Brigade, Third Division, Twentieth Army Corps, was ordered by Col. B. Laiboldt, commanding brigade, into position in the rear of the Third Brigade, Third Division, Twentieth Army Corps, which position, without firing a shot, we maintained until the following morning, September 20, 1863. The regiment was then ordered to re-enforce a brigade of our corps. Having arrived into an open field on the left of General Johnson's division, line of battle was formed in rear of the Fifteenth Missouri Volunteers. About fifteen minutes after being formed the command was given by Col. B. Laiboldt to "advance with charge bayonets," and arriving at the edge of the woods, about 1,000 yards in front of us, we were received by a terrific fire from the enemy. Suffering very severely, we were obliged to fall back, leaving our dead and wounded on the field in the hands of the enemy. The Second Missouri, being in the rear of the brigade, had no chance whatever to return the fire of the enemy without running the risk of killing our own men. After several fruitless attempts to rally the men, I at last succeeded in doing so at a place about 1 mile from the battle-field, where we formed the remains of the division. I am sorry to be obliged to acknowledge the loss of 2 of our regimental flags, which, under the circumstances, could not be avoided, as the bearers and entire color guard were shot down at once, as also several others who attempted to take their places.

A special denomination of gallant conduct I do not make, as I feel confident every one did his duty to the full extent of his abilities.

I am, colonel, very respectfully, your obedient servant,

ARNOLD BECK,
Major Second Infantry Missouri Vols., Comdg. Regt.

Col. JOHN B. GRAY,
Adjutant-General, State of Missouri.

No. 128.

Report of Col. Joseph Conrad, Fifteenth Missouri Infantry.

HDQRS. FIFTEENTH REGIMENT MISSOURI INFANTRY,
Camp at Chattanooga, September 30, 1863.

SIR: I have the honor to respectfully report the movements and active part of this regiment in the late campaign and battle of Chickamauga, September 19 and 20, 1863.

After the fall of Chattanooga we marched with the Twentieth Army Corps, to which this regiment belongs, through the Valley Head Pass, 45 miles south of Chattanooga, across Lookout Mountain range, and arrived on the 11th September at Alpine, a little village about 20 miles east [northwest] of Rome, Ga.

On the 13th we received orders to fall back to the rest of the army. We had to make the same way again over the Lookout Mountain. We arrived September 16 at McLemore's Cove, where our corps formed connection with the Fourteenth Army Corps.

On the 17th report came in that the enemy was approaching. Our corps was drawn in line of battle. I was ordered with my regiment to hold Stevens' Gap at all circumstances. My regiment was stationed there until September 18 at 9 a. m., when we moved about 5 miles farther on to McLemore's Cove. Moved again that night at 10 p. m. to Pond Spring, 18 miles south of Chattanooga, where we arrived at 2 a. m. on the 19th.

At 9 a. m. of the 19th we heard heavy cannonading to our left. The battle had commenced. We left camp at 11 o'clock, marched at double-quick to Crawfish Spring, and took position about 1 mile farther in the woods, but had to move again at double-quick to Gordon's Mills, where we took position in line of battle, my regiment on the right of Battery G, First Missouri Artillery, to support said battery. Here we lay for an hour, but the firing on the right of our line getting heavier, and two brigades under General Wood being in confusion, we were moved again at double-quick to the battle-field, where the Second and Fifteenth Missouri were drawn up in line of battle at the edge of the timber, on the right of Battery G, First Missouri Artillery, under a most appalling fire of the enemy, as a support of the Third Brigade of our division. We laid in this position all night in much discomfort, as the cold was very severe and fires were not allowed.

Before daylight next morning, September 20, the enemy having changed position, we also changed our line. Our brigade was marched about a mile to the rear and right, General Sheridan's division holding the extreme right and our brigade the extreme right of General Sheridan's division. Companies I and K of my regiment were thrown out as skirmishers. We held this position until about 12 o'clock, when our brigade was relieved by the Third Brigade of our division. We were marched about a half a mile farther to the left, took position on a side-hill stubble-field in column of regiments at company distance, facing a belt of woods at the foot of the hill. We were hardly in position when the enemy, after a fruitless attempt to break our left and center, massed his troops on our right and broke two brigades to our left.

At this critical point we received orders to charge on the enemy with the point of the bayonet. Nobly was the order carried out. The men went in good order in the woods in column of regiments ;

wheeling on the march to the right, a murderous fire received us. The rebel forces that had been engaged with the brigades to our right and left closed in on our flanks, keeping up a heavy fire, and still the men did not give way—not until we were nearly surrounded and the alternative was either to get killed or be taken prisoners ; then the men retreated, but still fighting. In going up the hill again the rebels had an excellent opportunity to do us much harm, which they failed not to improve. Their bullets swept the hill from three sides, and many of our brave men fell there, or were wounded and taken prisoners. I am in much uncertainty as to the fate of many of my men, as the rebels held the field. Our division marched that night to Rossville, about 10 miles from the battle-field, where we arrived about 11 o'clock and encamped there.

Monday, the 21st, we were all drawn up in line of battle, our division again on the extreme right, a renewal of the fight [being] again expected. Monday night the army fell back to Chattanooga, our brigade forming the rear guard. The retreat was successfully and safely accomplished. We reached Chattanooga at about 6 o'clock in the morning.

On Tuesday, the 22d, our brigade was thrown again to the advance, and took position near the railroad and turnpike bridge over a creek, near its junction with the Tennessee River, at the foot of Lookout Mountain, which formed our right ; which position we still hold, my regiment having daily heavy picket duty to do. The men are all in good spirits ; they all know that the enemy failed in accomplishing his object, and are willing and anxious to try the enemy again.

I have the honor to be, your excellency's most obedient servant,

JOSEPH CONRAD,
Colonel, Comdg. Fifteenth Regiment Missouri Infantry.

Governor H. R. GAMBLE,
Of Missouri.

No. 129.

Report of Lieut. Gustavus Schueler, Battery G, First Missouri Light Artillery.

CHATTANOOGA, TENN.,
October 2, 1863.

SIR : I herewith submit a statement of the part taken in action of Battery G, First Missouri Light Artillery, on September 20 (not having been in action on the 19th).

The battery being in position on the hills with the Third Brigade, the enemy approaching in strong force, attacking our division, I was ordered to report to Colonel Walworth, of the Forty-second Illinois Volunteers, commanding Third Brigade, which brigade left its position on the hills and formed on the edge of the corn-field to check the attack of the enemy, and just arriving there, the brigade met the enemy, who poured a deadly fire into our lines, and the battery came into action under a most destructive fire of musketry. During this engagement officers and men behaved bravely and cool, and particularly I have to mention Capt. H. Hescock (who was taken prisoner in the engagement) and Lieut. John Miller.

Of the non-commissioned officers, I have to report for his coolness and bravery Sergt. S. H. Jennings.

I remain, very respectfully, captain, yours,

GUSTAVUS SCHUELER,
First Lieut. First Mo. Light Arty., Comdg. Battery G.

Capt. A. SUTERMEISTER.

P. S.—You will find inclosed losses sustained and expenditures of ammunition.

[Inclosure.]

CHATTANOOGA, TENN., *October* 2, 1863.

Loss in action September 20, 1863.—Capt. Henry Hescock, taken prisoner; Private Richard Reading, killed by musketry; Corpl. Christian Anthes, wounded by musketry in shoulder; Private James Donahue, wounded by musketry in shoulder; Private John O'Brien, wounded by musketry in leg.

Loss in matériel.—Wheel harness, 1 set; lead harness, 2 sets; limber of light 12-pounder gun, 1 limber (disabled).

Ammunition expended in action.

	Rounds.
Light 12-pounder gun:	
Case-shot	94
Canister	9
Shell	86
Solid shot	26
10-pounder Parrott gun:	
Case-shot	5
Shell	57

I certify that the above is a correct statement.

GUSTAVUS SCHUELER,
First Lieut. First Missouri Arty., Comdg. Battery G.

No. 130.

Report of Col. Nathan H. Walworth, Forty-second Illinois Infantry, commanding Third Brigade.

HDQRS. THIRD BRIG., THIRD DIV., 20TH ARMY CORPS,
Chattanooga, September 26, 1863.

CAPTAIN: In pursuance of orders this day received, I would respectfully make the following statement of the operations of the brigade under my command during the action of September 19 and 20, 1863:

Col. L. P. Bradley, of the Fifty-first Illinois, had command of the brigade until about 4 p. m. of the 19th, when he fell gallantly leading it against the enemy. At that time the enemy had attacked a brigade of General Wood's division and driven it from its position, compelling them to leave four guns and two caissons on the field. In pursuance of orders from General Sheridan, Colonel Bradley formed his brigade in two lines, as follows: The Twenty-seventh Illinois on the right and the Twenty-second Illinois on the left of the first line, with the Forty-second Illinois on the right and the Fifty-first on the left of the second line. In this manner he ordered the brigade forward to attack the enemy. The brigade moved steadily forward across a piece of open, level ground and ascended a gentle slope, when the enemy opened with a most withering fire of musketry, which cut down Colonel Bradley and Lieutenant Moody, his acting assistant adjutant-general, at the outset.   I had command of the second line, and seeing that the first line wavered under the deadly fire of the enemy, who were posted along the whole front and in the woods to the left, I ordered the second line to pass the first.   This was splendidly done, and I retired the first line to the shelter of the rising ground. The enemy could not withstand the steady fire of the Forty-second Illinois (Lieutenant-Colonel Hottenstein) and the Fifty-first Illinois (Lieutenant-Colonel Raymond) and quickly retired in great disorder and with heavy loss, leaving the captured battery (the Eighth Indiana) in our possession.   This battery was subsequently turned over to its officers.

During this action the Twenty-second Illinois and Fifty-first Illinois lost many officers and men from a heavy fire poured into them from the woods on their left flank.   The enemy constantly threatened us until dark, but did not again attack us, except with skirmishers, who were repulsed by our own.

In pursuance of orders the brigade followed the brigade of Colonel Laiboldt in its movement to the hill (three-fourths of a mile north), at 4 a. m. on the 20th, and was placed in reserve in column of regiments on its summit until ordered to take position as support to General Lytle's brigade, on the road at the base of the hill.   Soon after we were ordered to replace Laiboldt's brigade on the side of the hill to the right and rear of Lytle's brigade.

After remaining in this position some thirty minutes, I received orders from General Sheridan to move the brigade rapidly toward the left.   I moved it at once by the left flank at double-quick, and when nearing the position of Lytle's brigade we were assailed by a heavy fire of musketry from the right.   I immediately ordered the Twenty-second Illinois, which was in advance, to face the enemy and check them if possible, but the numbers were too great for our line, lengthened as it was by a flank march at double-quick, and they were compelled to give ground which they contested strongly until their left flank was exposed by the movements of the troops on their left, when they were compelled to retire up the hill.   The same remarks apply to the Fifty-first Illinois, which was immediately on the right of the Twenty-second.   The Forty-second Illinois was ordered to advance by General McCook and General Sheridan immediately on the right of the Fifty-first Illinois, although I had sent orders for them to form in rear of where the Twenty-second Illinois were fighting, intending them, together with the Twenty-seventh Illinois, to form the second line.   Moving to the right I found them gallantly fighting, refusing to give ground after the regiments on their left had given way.   The loss which they here sustained, which was nearly one-half of the force engaged, is evidence enough of the numbers with which they had to contend.   The Twenty-seventh Illinois was posted to the right of the Forty-second Illinois, and suffered but little, as the force of the attack was more to the left, and they were protected somewhat by buildings.   To withstand the numbers which the enemy brought against us was impossible, and the brigade retired up the hill, resisting the enemy until it had gained the crest, when the enemy fell back.

In pursuance of orders from General Sheridan, I then ordered the brigade to march by the left flank to rejoin the center of the army, which we were compelled to do, by way of Rossville, as the enemy held the other road. The battery attached to this brigade (Captain Prescott's) was ordered by Captain Hescock, chief of artillery, to report to Colonel Laiboldt's brigade, and was posted by him in the rear of that brigade. It lost three guns and one caisson during the engagement. Three of the regiments, the Twenty-second Illinois, Forty-second Illinois, and Fifty-first Illinois, lost nearly one-half of their whole force engaged in the two days' action. Maj. James Leighton, of the Forty-second Illinois,* and Maj. Samuel Johnson, of the Twenty-second Illinois, both fell gallantly fighting. Such men deserve the thanks of their country, if they live to receive them, or an honorable place in history should they die of their wounds. The former is still missing. To Col. J. R. Miles, of the Twenty-seventh Illinois, to Lieutenant-Colonel Swanwick, of the Twenty-second Illinois, to Lieutenant-Colonel Raymond, of the Fifty-first, and to Lieutenant-Colonel Hottenstein, of the Forty-second Illinois, I owe my sincerest thanks for their ready co-operation and zeal. Lieut. A. O. Johnson, Lieut. L. Hanback, and Lieut. C. Montague, of my staff, all fearlessly and gallantly carried my orders under the heavy fire and assisted greatly in the operations of the brigade.

Of all the officers and men of this brigade I have to report that they did their duty, and although it was a repulse still it was before too great a force to permit of holding our position.

The subsequent movements of the brigade are those of the whole division.

I am, captain, very respectfully, your obedient servant,

N. H. WALWORTH,
Colonel Forty-second Illinois, Commanding Brigade.

Capt. GEORGE LEE,
Asst. Adjt. Gen., Third Division, 20th Army Corps.

No. 131.

Report of Col. Jonathan R. Miles, Twenty-seventh Illinois Infantry.

HDQRS. 27TH REGT. ILLINOIS VOLUNTEER INFANTRY,
THIRD BRIG., THIRD DIV., 20TH ARMY CORPS,
Chattanooga, Tenn., September 30, 1863.

SIR: I have the honor to report the part taken by my regiment in the battles of the 19th and 20th instant on Chickamauga River and Missionary Ridge, Ga.

The regiment had, upon the morning of the 18th instant, been detailed to remain at Stevens' Gap until the division train should make the descent of the Lookout Mountain, then to constitute its guard while joining the division. The train was all down the mountain at 5 p. m. of said day, and the regiment escorted it to the division (a distance of 4 miles), which was then just moving out; and the regiment took its place in the column and continued the march until 10 p. m., when it, together with all the other regiments of the division, bivouacked for the night, the regiment having marched 7 miles since last joining the division.

At 8 a. m., 19th instant, the regiment took its assigned position in the brigade column, and marched toward Crawfish Spring, Ga. (a point 8 or 9 miles distant), which place we reached at noon, having had a dusty, rapid, and necessarily fatiguing march, all the while hearing heavy cannonading, and for the last 2 or 3 miles distinctly hearing musketry in the direction in which we were marching. Here we rested a half hour, then marched a mile to the top of a wooded hill, where we halted and lay in line of battle a half hour, when we again moved, and in an easterly direction, at a double-quick, about 1 mile to an open field, where we were placed in position, in which, however, we remained but a few minutes, when we were again put in motion, and marched 1 mile in a northerly direction (during the last half mile wounded men were continually passing us to the rear), which brought us in close proximity to the fierce battle then raging.

Our brigade was then formed in two lines, my regiment being the right of the front line, and the brigade was promptly and gallantly led forward by Colonel Bradley, Fifty-first Illinois Infantry, commanding, about 60 rods over an open field and up a gentle slope, where it met a fierce fire from the advancing enemy, whose advance was checked and they repulsed. Our front line was halted upon the eminence, where was posted the Eighth Battery Indiana Artillery, whose infantry support (troops not belonging to our division) had almost abandoned the position entirely. The artillerymen worked their guns for a few minutes after our arrival, but they soon entirely abandoned their pieces, although my regiment was at the time supporting them in an unbroken line. Their guns, four in number, were all secured by our brigade and taken to a place of safety, my own regiment assisting in the removal of three of them. The horses attached to a caisson became unmanageable, and wheeling around, ran across my line, dragging the caisson over and injuring 1 or 2 men thereby. The regiment was, by order, lying flat upon the ground.

My regiment was in line upon said eminence about a half hour, delivering its fire and receiving a heavy fire from the enemy, when it was retired some 15 rods, just under the crest of the eminence, the firing having nearly ceased, and the Forty-second Illinois Infantry passed to our front and occupied the line from which we had retired.

In this action the regiment suffered the loss of 1 officer killed and 1 enlisted man killed, and 1 officer and 47 enlisted men wounded.

The regiment remained in position last described during the whole of the night of the 19th instant, which was freezing cold, so that the men lying upon their arms and without fires suffered severely.

At about 4.30 a. m., 20th instant, the regiment, as well as the brigade, retired from its position to a point about 1 mile to the left and rear upon a hill (where the entire division was assembled), where it remained until 9 a. m., when the sound of battle was heard and it was ordered to the foot of the hill on Rossville road, where it lay until 11 a. m., when, receiving orders, I marched it one-quarter of a mile by the left flank, then brought it by the right flank into line of battle, and it was instantly under a heavy fire. The right of the regiment rested at a log-house, near which was posted three guns of Battery G, First Missouri Light Artillery. In front of the six right companies was an open field and the four left companies were in thick woods and underbrush. The enemy advanced through the open field in heavy force, but were driven back in confusion by the battery and my regiment, and must have suffered very severely from our fire. After a time the enemy were seen to have broken through the lines of our forces upon the left of the regiment, and to have passed in force across the road and apparently up the ridge, which movement, of course, isolated my regiment from the main forces. At about 1.30 p. m., the regiment having held its original position in spite of many and desperate onslaughts (though no longer pressed), was retired to the summit of a hill one-eighth of a mile to the rear, where it was reformed, and, in company with Colonel Wilder's mounted infantry (a portion of whom, it should be stated, had dismounted and formed upon our right near the said log-house and assisted in repelling the assaults of the enemy), immediately started to effect a junction with our main forces.

The column, composed of Colonel Wilder's command, my regiment, a portion of the Fifty-first Illinois Infantry, under command of their major, and squads of the Twenty-second and Forty-second Illinois Infantry, also men from nearly every regiment in the division, making an aggregate of probably 600 (aside from Wilder's command) who joined my regiment and of whom I assumed command, was led by Colonel Wilder, whose troops were remounted about 1 mile to the rear. We marched some 3 miles, when we came upon our division ammunition train, ambulance train, &c.; here we replenished our nearly empty cartridge-boxes from the ammunition train, and here we received information that Major-General Sheridan was about 1½ miles distant, leading the majority of his command, and I should have immediately joined him had not Capt. W. E. Merrill, chief topographical engineer, on Major-General Rosecrans' staff, earnestly advised, which also seemed to me decidedly necessary, that my command should guard the heavy and valuable train to a place of safety. I acted upon said advice, and, in accordance with my own views of duty, and marched my command abreast of the train to a point on the Chattanooga Valley road some 5 miles out from Chattanooga, where, the train being considered safe, I halted my command at 6 p. m. and caused supper to be cooked. Meanwhile, I reported to Major-General McCook, at Chattanooga, for orders, sending Lieut. Lewis Hanback, our brigade inspector, upon that duty. He returned at about 8 p. m. with orders from Major-General McCook that my command move to the tannery, 2½ miles nearer to Chattanooga, and there bivouac for the night, which instructions were complied with, and at 10.30 p. m. we reached the place designated.

On the morning of the 21st instant, having learned the position of the division, I sent Lieutenant Hanback to Major-General Sheridan for orders, and in response thereto was ordered to join the division at Rossville, 4 miles distant, which order was immediately obeyed, and at 10.30 a. m. I reported with my command at Rossville, there joining the brigade and division.

In the engagement Saturday evening, 19th instant, Capt. W. S. Bryan, commanding Company I, was shot through the heart while he was, with true soldierly magnanimity and self-forgetfulness, assisting his mortally wounded orderly sergeant to retire from his advanced position, where he (sergeant) received his wound. In the death of Captain Bryan the service has lost a brave officer and the country a patriotic defender, while his company and regiment are mourners. In the same action Capt. A. J. Bozarth, Company K, was slightly wounded.

In the engagement of Sunday, 20th instant, Capt. Horace Chapin, commanding Company D, was shot in the ankle, and amputation of foot, it is feared, will be necessary. In the same engagement Capt. L. French Williams, commanding Company C, was shot through the head, and the wound can hardly fail to prove mortal. In the same engagement First Lieut. Joseph Voellinger, Company A, received a musket shot just below the knee, breaking the bone, necessitating amputation of limb. Captain Williams and Lieutenant Voellinger were both taken to a field hospital, and are now in the hands of the enemy. In the same engagement Second Lieut. Isaac Nash, Company K, was struck by a fragment of shell, but is now doing duty. Captains Chapin and Williams and Lieutenant Voellinger are lost to the service, and it is but justice that I record the manly virtues of Captain Chapin, the endearing social qualities of Captain Williams, and the faithful performance of duty by them all during a period of military service of more than two years, and particularly do I mention their intrepid and gallant conduct during the engagements of the 19th and 20th instant up to the moment of their receiving their respective wounds.

The losses of the regiment during both engagements are as follows, viz:

[Casualties.]	Commissioned officers.	Enlisted men.	Total.
Killed	1	1	2
Wounded	5	75	80
Missing		9	9
Total	6	85	91

Of the wounded doubtless several are already dead and others will die, while a large number are but slightly wounded.

The missing are mainly those who assisted the wounded to hospitals and remained to attend upon them, thus naturally falling into the hands of the enemy. The regimental ambulance and its driver on the 20th instant were captured.

Of the conduct of all the officers and men of my command during the battles aforesaid, it is fitting that I speak in terms of commendation and express my satisfaction for the firmness with which they stood at their posts and their efficiency in executing their respective duties. Where all performed their entire duty, it would be invidious to give any person especial prominence in this report.

Respectfully submitted.

J. R. MILES,
Colonel, Commanding.

Maj. S. L. COULTER,
Actg. Asst. Adjt. Gen., 3d Brig., 3d Div., 20th Army Corps.

No. 132.

Report of Capt. Mark H. Prescott, Battery C, First Illinois Light Artillery.

HDQRS. BATTERY C, FIRST ILLINOIS, LIGHT ARTILLERY,
Chattanooga, Tenn., October 2, 1863.

COLONEL : In obedience to orders requiring a report of the operations of my battery during the engagements of the 19th and 20th instant, I have the honor herewith to transmit the following report :

On the morning of the 19th, being in camp on the Chickamauga Creek, I was ordered by Colonel Bradley, commanding Third Brigade, Third Division, Twentieth Army Corps, to take up line of march in rear of the Twenty-seventh Regiment Illinois Infantry Volunteers, and in advance of the Forty-second Regiment Illinois Infantry Volunteers.   Having marched as far as Crawfish Spring the column was halted, where we rested about thirty minutes and again resumed the march.   Having passed Crawfish Spring about 1 mile, I was ordered by Colonel Bradley to bring my guns into battery to the right of the road on a high point of timber commanding the east slope of the hill and within easy shelling distance of the woods in the valley in front of my present position.

I remained in this position some thirty minutes when I was ordered to limber up my pieces and fall in the rear of the Twenty-seventh Illinois Infantry, when we advanced to the front and took up line of battle on the right of Second Brigade, Third Division. Here, on a slight eminence in the open field, I was ordered by Colonel Bradley to bring my guns into battery, being in easy canister range of the Chickamauga Creek to my front and left oblique, remaining in this position some ten or fifteen minutes, when I was again ordered to limber up and take my original position in line of march.   We then passed in rear of Second and First Brigades of Third Division and marched to the left.   I was ordered to bring my guns into battery in the edge of the woods fronting an open corn-field.   I remained in this position until the morning of the 20th ultimo, when, before daylight, I was ordered by Captain Hescock, chief of artillery, Third Division, Twentieth Army Corps, to quietly withdraw my battery and march about half a mile farther to the left and place my guns in battery on the right of the Second Brigade, Third Division, fronting to the south, which I did, and remained in this position some two or three hours, when I was ordered by Captain Hescock, chief of artillery, to limber up, have the cannoneers mount and move as rapidly as possible and take up position in the rear of General Davis' division, in line, and remain so until further orders, which I was to receive from Colonel Laiboldt, whose brigade (Second) was now in my immediate front.

The enemy was now pressing General Davis so hard that he was obliged to fall back.   Colonel Laiboldt charged forward with his brigade, leaving me without orders what to do.   I, however, brought my guns into battery, reserving my fire until I was sure that I should not fire into our own line, which by this time had become badly broken up.   I fired some 8 or 10 rounds, when the line in front was so badly broken and the men were coming through my battery in such a confused mass that it was impossible to fire without killing our own men.   The fire under which I was by this time exposed, receiving showers of bullets, from both my front and left flank, I thought it prudent to withdraw my battery to the next hill in rear of the present position.   As soon as I had reached the crest of the hill I brought my guns into battery and fired some 6 or 8 rounds.   Having no support and the enemy already upon me, I limbered up and moved in a left oblique direction, when the wheel horses of the right piece of each section were shot down.   I was obliged to abandon them and to save the other pieces, if possible, which I succeeded in doing.   I reported as soon as possible with the remainder of my battery to General Sheridan, who ordered me to fall into the column then marching in the direction of Chattanooga. I camped that night with the Third Brigade, Third Division, in camp near Chattanooga.

My officers and men all performed their duties well. Total expenditure in ammunition was 19 rounds. Loss in ammunition by being captured was 175 rounds. Had two rifled Rodman guns captured, and one 12-pounder howitzer, three limbers lost, and the rear part of one caisson was lost by a tree falling across it. Twelve horses were also lost, and had 4 men wounded and none killed.

I am, colonel, respectfully, your obedient servant,

M. H. PRESCOTT,
Captain Battery C, First Illinois Artillery.

Col. N. H. WALWORTH, *Comdg. Third Brigade.*

No. 133.

Report of Maj. Gen. Thomas L. Crittenden, U. S. Army, commanding Twenty-first Army Corps.

HEADQUARTERS TWENTY-FIRST ARMY CORPS,
Chattanooga, October 1, 1863.

SIR: In obedience to directions from department headquarters, dated 25th ultimo, requiring me to forward, as soon as practicable, a report of the operations of my command during the late engagements, including a brief history of its movements from the time of crossing the Tennessee River up to the beginning of the battle, I have the honor to report:

First. The movements of the Twenty-first Army Corps from the time of its crossing the Tennessee River, terminating on the morning of the 19th ultimo, when the battle of Chickamauga opened.

August 31.—My command stationed in Sequatchie Valley, at Pikeville, Dunlap, and Therman, respectively, excepting General Wagner's brigade, First Division, opposite Chattanooga, and General Hazen's at Poe's Tavern, the latter 15 miles north of Wagner, and both in Tennessee Valley. My command had been thus stationed since the 19th of August, having left Manchester, Tenn., on the 16th of August, crossing the mountains at three different points, in obedience to orders received from department headquarters at 12.30 a. m. of the 16th. At 2.15 p. m. of this day I received your orders of the 30th, dated 12.30 p m., to move my entire command, excepting the brigades of Generals Hazen and Wagner, as soon as practicable down the Sequatchie Valley, and to supply myself with everything necessary for an active campaign. The orders further directed me to cross my trains at Bridgeport and my troops at Bridgeport, Shellmound, and Battle Creek. Should Chattanooga be evacuated, Hazen and Wagner were to cross the river and occupy the place and close down upon our left. Colonel Minty, with his brigade of cavalry, and Colonel Wilder, with his brigade of mounted infantry, were to co-operate with Hazen and Wagner.

September 1.—My command all in motion. General Wood and his command arrived at Jasper. General Palmer within 3 miles of Jasper and General Van Cleve to within 5 miles of Dunlap.

September 2.—Received orders to cross the river with one brigade at Jasper crossing and one at Battle Creek. Other part of the command to follow as soon as the way is open.

Colonel Buell's brigade (First Division) marched at dark to Shellmound, where he crossed the river in flats during the night.

September 3.—General Wood, with his other brigade (Harker's), moved down early this morning to Shellmound, and was across the river by 8 p. m., having been delayed till 2 p. m. by General Reynolds' train. Colonel Grose and his brigade (Palmer's division) moved down early this morning to Battle Creek, but were unable to secure the ferry, being used all day by General Brannan's division. General Cruft and his brigade (Palmer's division) was therefore ordered to Shellmound, and he, following close on General Wood, succeeded in crossing his command by 4 a. m. next day.

General Van Cleve, with his two brigades, arrived at Jasper and went into camp to await the crossing. Received from the general commanding orders for my movements and position after crossing the river, viz, to move up the Valley of Running Water Creek to Whiteside's, where I was to post one regiment, and send one division along the Nashville and Chattanooga Railroad to the Trenton road, and to push forward as near to Chattanooga as practicable and threaten the enemy in that direction. The remainder of the command to occupy a position near the junction of the Murphy's Valley road with road marked on the map as "Good wagon road to Naylor's." The movement to be completed on the evening of the 4th instant.

September 4.—At 3.30 a. m. received word from General Cruft that his brigade was all over. Moved General Van Cleve down at once, and at 1 p. m. moved headquarters to Shellmound, which crossed before night.

General Palmer succeeded in crossing with his one brigade at Battle Creek to-day. Thus the whole command was over the river.

September 5.—At 2.30 p. m., after having the command organized and in position, and with all of the ammunition and most of the transportation up, troops all moved out light to Whiteside's, General Wood in the advance, General Palmer center, and General Van Cleve rear, taking with them their ammunition trains; regimental and supply trains to move up at 5 a. m. to-morrow.

September 6.—Road up Running Water Creek rough but passable. At 9.30 a. m. I arrived at junction of Murphy's Valley and Nickajack roads, and encamped there as ordered, Generals Palmer and Van Cleve and their divisions following us, and General Wood and his division pursuing road up Running Water Creek and encamping 7 miles from Chattanooga, reporting that the enemy was close before him in force.

September 7.—Colonel Harker, with his brigade, made very satisfactory reconnaissance to spur of Lookout Mountain. Drove the enemy's pickets and light advance 2 miles, and returned by dark, believing the enemy to be in force in his front.

September 8.—Gave orders to make two reconnaissances to-morrow morning; the one up Lookout Mountain via Nickajack Trace, and for which General Beatty and his brigade were detailed, the other up same mountain to Summertown, for which Colonel Grose and three regiments were detailed, both to unite if practicable on top of the mountain, and to start at or before day on the morrow.

September 9.—At 2.20 a. m. received dispatch from the general commanding the army, approving the two reconnaissances ordered, and directing that the whole command be held in readiness to move round the point of Lookout Mountain to seize and occupy Chattanooga in the event of its being evacuated; to move with caution and not to throw my artillery around the point of Lookout Mountain till I am satisfied that the evacuation is not a ruse. Should I occupy Chattanooga, I am to order General Wagner and all his force across to join me.

At 5.45 a. m. further dispatches from department headquarters, apprising me of the evacuation of Chattanooga and ordering that the whole command be pushed forward at once with five days' rations, and to make a vigorous pursuit. This latter dispatch was too late to stop the reconnaissances ordered, but I lost no time in putting the balance of the command in motion and arrived at Chattanooga with General Wood's division at 12.30 p. m., having taken peaceable possession of same.

It was nightfall, however, before the troops were well up, owing to the great delay in getting the artillery and ammunition train up this very rough and precipitous hill. It was thus impossible to make any pursuit to-day. I, however, ordered Generals Palmer and Van Cleve to turn off south after having passed the spur of Lookout Mountain and encamp at Rossville, distant 5 miles from Chattanooga. General Wood I placed in command of the town.

At 2.15 p. m. received further instructions from department headquarters ordering me to leave a light brigade to hold Chattanooga, and with the balance of my command to pursue the enemy with the utmost vigor. The line of march will probably lead me near Ringgold, and from thence in the vicinity of Dalton.

September 10.—Generals Palmer and Van Cleve with their divisions ordered to make vigorous pursuit early this morning, marching on road from Rossville to Ringgold, thence to Dalton. General Wood, after leaving one brigade at Chattanooga, to follow with his two brigades in the same direction. General Wagner with his brigade having crossed during the night, was left as post commander. At 4 p. m. received report from General Palmer that owing to want of supplies, troops only marched 6 miles, the advance encamping on Chickamauga Creek, 5 miles from Ringgold. The rear, General Wood, on Pea Vine Creek, 2 miles to rear of advance ; also, that the enemy's cavalry was in his front and that a portion of it had charged his advance ; rode over four companies of the First Kentucky Infantry and captured 50 men and 2 officers, without any one on either side being hurt. At night received from the front several reports going to show that the enemy was in force this side of La Fayette and threatening to retake Chattanooga.

September 11.—At 1 a. m. the general commanding, feeling uncertain as to the position and strength of the enemy in our front, ordered me to proceed to the front at once. Was misled by the guide, and did not reach my command till 6 a. m., and 2 of my orderlies on duty with Captain McCook in search of me, thinking I had taken the wrong road, were captured, he narrowly escaping. Early in the morning Colonel Harker, with his brigade, was moved back to Rossville, and by night made a reconnaissance up the Rossville road as far as Gordon's Mills, driving squads of the enemy before him. At 2.30 p. m. gave General Wood his orders, through one of my staff, who received them in person from department headquarters, to move his other brigade at once to Gordon's Mills to support Colonel Harker, and at 5 p. m. my staff officer reported to me at Ringgold. My entire

Second and Third Divisions were then at Ringgold. General Hazen, with his brigade, having crossed the river yesterday, rejoined his division (Palmer's) to-day. Colonel Dick, with Second Brigade, Van Cleve's division (left at McMinnville to guard stores, &c.), rejoined his command on the 9th. Your instructions received at this time, and dated 9.15 a. m., were to move with the balance of my corps on the Chickamauga and Pea Vine Valley roads, keeping in view two objects: first, to support General Thomas in case the enemy is in force in the vicinity of La Fayette, or, second, to move eastward and southward toward Rome in case he has continued his retreat. Other verbal instructions received by my staff officer urged upon me the importance of keeping my separate divisions in supporting distance of one another.

At 8.30 a. m. I received your dispatch of 3.30 p. m., informing me that the enemy was in heavy force in the Valley of Chattanooga, and instructing me to move my whole force across, by the most available route and as quickly as possible, to the Rossville and La Fayette road to some defensible point between Gordon's Mills and Shields' house, and to close Wood up with me or myself to him.

I at once called my general officers together, and after a long consultation and diligent inquiry of citizens as to the nature of the roads and country, gave orders to move the command in the direction ordered at 5 in the morning.

September 12.—Sent word early this evening to Colonel Wilder, who was in the advance and near Tunnel Hill, to return to Ringgold with his command, and to follow on my line of march, covering my left flank. He moved promptly and met me at Ringgold, and reported that the enemy was in force in his front last night, and that he learned from deserters that Forrest was to leave to-day to flank and cut off this command, and Wharton in opposite direction for same purpose. General Van Cleve, with the train, moved to Peeler's and met no enemy; General Palmer to Gilbert's, where he met some squads of the enemy and skirmished with him. After opening communication with General Van Cleve and General Wood, moved the whole command to Gordon's Mills, Colonel Wilder also coming in after night, having had a severe skirmish during the day near Leet's Tan-yard, and losing 30 men killed and wounded.

September 13.—In the morning the Fourth U. S. Cavalry, 650 strong, reported to me for duty. The three divisions were put into position for defense. General Cruft and Colonel Wilder sent out to reconnoiter on the left, Fourth Cavalry on the right to McLemore's Cove, and General Van Cleve to the front and center on La Fayette road. The latter only found the enemy (cavalry with artillery), who retired skirmishing a distance of 3 miles, when the brigade was halted, and soon after returned to camp. In this skirmish Captain Drury, chief of artillery, Third Division, was severely wounded. At 2.30 p. m. received your two dispatches of 12.20 and 12.25 p. m., respectively, former ordering me to post General Wood in a strong defensible position at Gordon's Mills for him to resist stoutly the enemy's advance, and in case of extremity, and if Granger's force (a division of infantry) has not arrived at Chattanooga so as to support Wood at Rossville, and he (Wood) should be compelled to fall back farther, he must take his position at a point guarding the road to Chattanooga and around the point of Lookout Mountain, and hold them at all hazards. To move the balance of my command during the evening and night to a position on Missionary Ridge so as to cover the road along the Valley of Chattanooga Creek, and also that running up the Valley of West Chickamauga Creek, and to send Wilder with his command up Chattanooga Creek to feel his way carefully, and who is to join General Thomas as soon as possible, the latter ordering me to hold myself in readiness to execute to-night the orders sent me at 12.20 to-day.

September 14.—At 6.30 a. m. received dispatch from Colonel Goddard, stating that it was the intention of the general commanding that I should move before daylight to Missionary Ridge, and that it was perhaps his unfortunate wording that prevented it. I at once commenced the movement. In the night Colonel Minty, with the balance of his cavalry brigade, reported for duty. I sent him in the rear of my two divisions ; Wilder, with his command, I sent to join General Thomas, then in Chattanooga Valley. Arrived at the position soon after 9 a. m. and staid there all day, being unable to have communication with department headquarters. Saw nothing of the enemy. At 7.40 p. m. received orders to return with the command, placing it at Crawfish Spring and along the Chickamauga Valley near Gower's. Too late to make the movement to-day.

September 15.—The two divisions moved, as directed last night, the left, Van Cleve's division, at Crawfish Spring ; right, Palmer's, near Gower's, and supported on its right by the Seventh Pennsylvania Cavalry. Balance of the command, under Minty, sent to reconnoiter the whole front and left. At 11.30 p. m. Colonel Minty reported that the enemy was in force at Dalton, Ringgold, Leet's, and Rock Spring Church.

September 16.—Nothing occurred of peculiar interest this day except that department headquarters were established at Crawfish Spring. At 9.30 p. m. received orders to issue to the men three days' rations in haversacks and 20 rounds of ammunition in the pocket of each man, in addition to having his cartridge-box full. There are indications that the enemy is massing for an attack on our left.

September 17.—General Thomas, with his corps, arrived on our lines to-day. In afternoon moved General Palmer's division farther to the left, in order to make room for General Thomas' troops and to concentrate my own. Toward dark, in obedience to orders, moved corps headquarters to vicinity of department headquarters.

September 18.—At 10.30 a. m. General Wood, holding position on Chickamauga at Gordon's Mills, sent in word that a strong force of skirmishers was advancing on his left. Soon after another of his staff rode up reporting his line very thin and asking for a brigade. At 11 a. m. a third staff officer rode up reporting the enemy advancing on his right and Van Cleve's left. At 11.45 a. m. an orderly came reporting that the enemy—infantry, cavalry, and artillery—were advancing on the La Fayette road. At same moment General Van Cleve was moving up to General Wood's left and General Palmer was ordered to take Van Cleve's position on Wood's right. At 3.45 p. m. Colonel Wilder sent word that Colonel Minty, with his cavalry, after being re-enforced with two regiments of his, is falling back ; that the enemy is getting in his (Wilder's) rear, and that he is also falling back on Wood. No firing to be heard. In afternoon Palmer was ordered up to form on the left of Van Cleve's new position on line of the Chickamauga River, which, from Gordon's Mills, runs in an easterly direction, whilst the road to Chattanooga, via Rossville, is nearly north and south. We hold the river at Gordon's

Mills, but on our left the enemy's pickets were reported to be between the road and the river.

I was informed by the general commanding that we also occupied the bridge across the Chickamauga with one brigade of infantry at Reed's Mill, situated northeast from Gordon's Mills, and distant about 3½ miles, and thus the space between the two mills was in a great measure open to the enemy.

REPORT OF THE OPERATIONS OF THE TWENTY-FIRST ARMY CORPS, DURING THE ENGAGEMENTS OF THE 19TH AND 20TH OF SEPTEMBER, ON CHICKAMAUGA RIVER, GA.

Battles.—In continuation of my report of the movements of the Twenty-first Army Corps, since crossing the Tennessee River and ending the 18th ultimo, the day preceding the battle, I have now the honor to report the operations of my command during the late engagements. It was 4 o'clock on the morning of the 19th before the last brigade of Major-General Palmer's division arrived at its position on the left of Brigadier-General Van Cleve. During the evening and night of the 18th of September, my command was placed in position as directed by the general commanding the department, the right resting at Gordon's or Lee's Mills, and the left running northeasterly along the Chickamauga and the road to Rossville.

On the morning of the 19th I rode to the extreme left of my line, and there being no appearance of the enemy in my front, at 7.40 a. m. I ordered Colonel Grose, Major-General Palmer's division, with his brigade, then in reserve, to make a reconnaissance down the road and in direction of Reed's Mill, on the Chickamauga, to ascertain if the main road from Gordon's Mills to Rossville was clear, and if practicable to ascertain if Colonel McCook with his brigade held the bridge at Reed's Mill, from which direction I had just heard the report of four or five cannon.

On arriving at this position I found all quiet, Colonel Wilder, with his command, supported by two regiments of Brigadier-General Van Cleve's division, being on the extreme left. I found Colonel Wilder in the edge of the woods some 150 yards west of the road leading to Rossville, his men dismounted, and behind a breastwork of rails.

It was here reported to me that the command of General Thomas had been heard passing in our rear toward Chattanooga. I immediately directed an officer to go to the rear until he came to the road on which these troops were passing, and to report at once the character of the country which intervened, the distance, &c. I remained until the officer returned and reported. All still being quiet, I rode rapidly to department headquarters with this information, which I thought important, and which I believed would be gladly heard by the commanding general. I promptly returned, and on my arrival at the left of my lines, about 11 a. m., I heard heavy cannonading about 1½ to 2 miles to my left. Musketry firing began and soon became so heavy that I was satisfied the battle had commenced. For a moment I felt embarrassed. The general commanding the department had inquired of me several times if I could hold my position, and I knew the importance to the movements of the army then going on of my ability so to do. I was on the left and thrown forward, covering a movement by which the entire army was to pass in my rear, leaving me on the right should the movement take place without interruption.   I hesitated but for a moment as to whether I should weaken myself by sending aid to Major-General Thomas, who, having passed to my rear, was already engaged to my left.   All being quiet on my front, I ordered Major-General Palmer to the support of Major-General Thomas.   I at once informed the general commanding the army of this movement, who approved of it in his note of 12.20 p. m., when he informed me that, from present appearances, General Thomas will move *en échelon*, his left advanced, threatening the enemy's right.

At 11.20 I received a note from Captain Willard, aide-de-camp to Major-General Thomas, dated McDaniel's [McDonald's] house, September 15 (intended for 19th), 10.15, stating that if another division can be spared it would be well to send it up without any delay.   At the time of the receipt of this note I heard very heavy musketry in the direction of Major-General Palmer, then advancing to the fight, and I at once sent Major Mendenhall, my chief of artillery, and Colonel Mc-Kibbin, of General Rosecrans' staff, to see Major-General Palmer and learn particulars.   They returned quickly without seeing him, having been halted and shot at by the enemy, which led me to believe that Major-General Palmer was not only fighting in his front, but was attacked in his rear and perhaps surrounded.   I at once dispatched Lieutenant-Colonel Lodor, my inspector-general, and Colonel McKibbin to department headquarters (which at this time had been moved to the Widow Glenn's, distant about a mile from my position) to report facts and ask permission to bring up Brigadier-General Van Cleve to support Major-General Palmer, as I was then well satisfied that the enemy was crossing the Chickamauga at several points, and at one near my position.   During their absence I sent to Brigadier-General Van Cleve to move up to where I then was stationed, and just at the time of his arrival Lieutenant-Colonel Lodor returned with permission to send Brigadier-General Van Cleve in, which I immediately did.   He brought with him but two brigades, Brigadier-General Beatty's and Colonel Dick's, leaving his Third Brigade, Colonel Barnes, in position on the left of Brigadier-General Wood.

At 12 m. I received your note of 11.10 a. m. ordering me to send Colonel Minty with his cavalry brigade to Chattanooga, and to report for orders at Widow Glenn's, which I at once complied with. It was then stationed in the woods in reserve.

At 12.50 p. m. I received a note from General Palmer, dated 12.35 p. m., stating that his "division was just going in; enemy said to be in heavy force; fight is raging, but principally on his left flank."

At 1.15 p. m. I wrote to Brigadier-General Wood, reporting the heavy fight that Van Cleve and Palmer were hotly in, and that he must look out for his left.

I then sent Colonel Starling, my chief of staff, to department headquarters, reporting Brigadier-General Van Cleve heavily in the fight, and asking that I might move Brigadier-General Wood up to assist. He shortly returned with the request granted, and I dispatched Major Mendenhall to bring him up.   The enemy appeared to have troops enough to fight us everywhere, and to fill up every interval as soon as my divisions passed.

At 2 p. m. I received your dispatch of 1.45 p. m., advising me that you had ordered Major-General McCook to relieve me, to take command of my corps, and to make the best dispositions possible; also, that Major-General Sheridan would come in if necessary on my right, and to take care of my right.

On receipt of this note, the firing having ceased for a time, I immediately rode rapidly to headquarters, hoping to get final instructions before Brigadier-General Wood's command arrived, and returned just as General Wood with his two brigades came up to a position that Brigadier-General Davis, of Major-General McCook's corps, was fighting over on the right of Brigadier-General Van Cleve. Colonel Barnes' brigade, Brigadier-General Van Cleve's division, had been left back with General Wood; it came up just in advance of General Wood's two brigades, and had gone into position through the woods to the right of Brigadier-General Davis.

I rode forward to a battery which I understood belonged to General Davis, where I was told I would find both him and General Wood ; neither of them was there, and I rode back in search of General Wood. I had instructed Lieutenant-Colonel Starling to say to General Wood, that in coming to the field he might have an opportunity, by leaving the road before he reached our position and moving to his right, to strike the enemy on the flank. I should regret that I had not sent an order instead of a mere suggestion but that the commanding general condemned the movement when I informed him that I had suggested it to General Wood. Colonel Barnes moved in this direction, and Colonel Harker, of General Wood's division, was going into position on the right of Colonel Barnes, when Lieutenant-Colonel Starling, chief of staff, at the solicitation of Brigadier-General Davis, who was then being pressed by the enemy, recalled Colonel Harker, and in this way he was brought down the road beyond the position that Colonel Barnes had taken in the woods on General Davis' right, and Colonel Buell with his brigade followed after Colonel Harker.

General Wood reached the field but a short time before the enemy attacked our right, on Saturday evening, and had General Wood been in the position I suggested, he would have been on the flank of the enemy, and, I think, would have punished him severely.

Colonel Buell went into position just off the road on the right and to the rear of Brigadier-General Davis' battery, which was firing across an open field at the enemy in the woods, who could be plainly seen by their bayonets glistening. In the meantime General Wood, with Harker's brigade, had passed still farther down the road and went into position on Colonel Buell's left, striking the woods as he left the road. In Colonel Buell's front there was a large gap in the woods, recently a corn-field.

The enemy in Colonel Buell's front came out at this time, and he, with his men, lying down supporting General Davis' battery, fell back in some confusion. All crossed the road ; thence across another open field, in which I and my staff were on a high point, when they came into the woods again, along the edge of which Colonel Wilder, with his brigade, was lying. His men soon opened fire, and when I ordered the artillery that was at hand to be put in position along the edge of the woods, under the superintendence of Major Mendenhall, he opened fire rapidly from twenty-six guns, and soon checked and drove the enemy to the cover of their own woods. Our loss in this brief conflict was quite severe. Brigadier-General Wood and Colonel Buell were present, and were very active in rallying the men and restoring them to order.

Soon after accomplishing this, Colonel Buell's brigade again advanced, Brigadier-General Carlin and his command co-operating, and reoccupied their former position. About this time General Sheridan came up through the woods I was in, and promptly sent in a brigade to support these troops.

Soon after this I received your note of 3.45 p. m., at 4.35 p. m., stating that Davis was heavily pressed, and ordering me to assist him if I could with some of my command. At 4.45 p. m. I received your note of 3.10 p. m., stating that Johnson was driving the rebels handsomely in the center; that he had taken many prisoners, and expected to drive the enemy across Chickamauga to-night.

Colonel Barnes, with his brigade, I had heard from, as being in a commanding position, and in good order. Generals Palmer and Van Cleve I had not heard from since they went in. Night was coming on, and I left for department headquarters, where, after sitting in council with the general commanding the army, other corps commanders, and some general officers, I received at midnight the following order:

HEADQUARTERS DEPARTMENT OF THE CUMBERLAND,
Widow Glenn's House, September 19, 1863—11.20 p. m.

GENERAL: The general commanding directs me to inform you that General Mc-Cook has been ordered to hold this gap to-morrow, covering the Dry Valley road, his right resting near this place, his left connecting with General Thomas' right. The general places your corps in reserve to-morrow, and directs you to post it on the eastern slope of Missionary Ridge to support McCook or Thomas. Leave the grand guard from your command out, with instructions to hold their ground until driven in, and then to retire slowly, contesting the ground stubbornly.

I proceeded at once to move General Wood back to the reserve position, leaving the grand guards as directed, and by daylight, 20th September, found General Van Cleve in the valley very near his new position. Major-General Palmer, with my strongest division, having been sent to Major-General Thomas the day before, was to remain with him. About 8 or 9 o'clock on the morning of the 20th I was ordered to move General Wood's division up to a position in front, which had been occupied by General Negley, and to keep General Van Cleve in reserve and in supporting distance of General Wood. This order had been executed but a short time when I was ordered to move General Van Cleve, with two brigades (his other brigade having been sent with General Wood, who otherwise could not have filled the place General Negley occupied), several hundred yards to the left, and some 200 yards to the front. His guns were placed in position on the crest of the ridge, and his command placed near the foot of the slope, formed in column, doubled on the center, and halted. The general commanding the department was at this time in the field near by.

I was now ordered to move General Van Cleve directly to the front to take part in the battle now raging in that direction. The order was immediately given, and I said to the commanding general, as this was the last of my corps not already disposed of, I should accompany it. I rode immediately after Brigadier-General Van Cleve, whose troops were already in motion. On reaching the woods I was surprised to find General Van Cleve's command halted ; on inquiry I was informed that General Van Cleve had run up on General Wood's command. I directed him to take ground to the left, to pass through the first interval he could find, and engage the enemy. At this moment an officer rode to me from General Thomas, saying that the general still wanted support on his left. I directed this officer to General Rosecrans' position, then not far distant, and did not stop the movement of General Van Cleve, as he was going in the right direction if the general commanding the department should change my orders and send me to General Thomas' left. In a few moments I received orders to move General Van Cleve's division with the utmost dispatch, not exhausting the troops, to the support of General Thomas' left. I gave the order immediately to General Van Cleve and its execution was at once begun.

At this moment I received a message from General Wood that it was useless to bring artillery into the woods. The chief of artillery of this corps was ordered to put the batteries back on the ridge, in a commanding position with several hundred yards of open country in front, where I hoped, in the event of any reverse, these guns could cover our retiring troops. I now received a message from General Wood informing me that he had received an order direct from headquarters of the department to move at once to the support of General Reynolds. Looking at the artillery which Major Mendenhall had just put in position, and not knowing exactly what to do with it under my last order, my difficulty was suddenly removed by the enemy. While we had been steadily, from the beginning of the battle, and very properly, in my judgment, weakening our right and strengthening our left, the object of the enemy being clearly to throw himself between us and Chattanooga, the enemy had been receiving accessions of fresh troops, and now made a sudden attack on our right and right center, driving these attenuated lines from the field.

Upon turning from the batteries and looking at the troops I was astounded to see them suddenly and unaccountably thrown into great confusion. There was but little firing at this moment near the troops, and I was unable until some time afterward to account for this confusion. In a moment, however, the enemy had driven all before them, and I was cut off from my command though not 100 yards in rear, and in full view. The enemy had attacked and run over our extreme right at the same moment of time. I was now cut off entirely both on the right and left from all our troops. The way, however, was open to the batteries, and I rode immediately there, hoping that stragglers enough, both from right and left, would rally there to hold the position, or at least enable me to carry off the guns. Upon reaching the batteries, I found them without the support of a single company of infantry. It was a time of painful anxiety. I still hoped that support would come from somewhere or be driven to me. But the signs grew rapidly worse. Lieutenant Cushing, commanding Battery H, Fourth U. S. Artillery, rode up to me at this moment and said he thought the enemy's cavalry had got in our rear. Upon asking him his reason, he answered that a shell had just been thrown from our rear. I started to look if this could possibly be so, stating to Lieutenant Cushing that I did not think it possible. He asked me in case he was driven which way he should go. I replied he must not be driven, still hoping for support. He said he would like to know what road to take in case he should be driven, and I pointed out the direction.

A short distance in rear of the guns, just at this moment I met about 60 or 70 men, apparently rallied and led up to the batteries by a young officer whom I did not recognize, but who were really rallied and brought up by that pure-hearted and brave officer, Brigadier-General Van Cleve.

It will be best here to explain the cause of the confusion and consequent disaster which but a little while before had befallen two brigades of his division.   While in the act of passing to the support of
General Thomas, troops in his front—I do not know of what division—broke and ran in great confusion, and a battery at great speed
was driven through the ranks of his men, wounding several seriously.
This, of course, threw his command into great confusion, and before he could possibly restore order, the enemy was upon him.   This
accident, for which the troops who suffered by it were not responsible, and which could scarcely have been avoided by any precaution,
is deeply deplored by the officers and men of that gallant division,
whose steady courage and discipline has been too often and well
tested to be doubted now.   Notwithstanding this disaster, three
regiments of the eight composing these two brigades, viz, Forty-
fourth Indiana Volunteers, commanded by Lieutenant-Colonel Aldrich ; Ninth Kentucky, commanded by Colonel Cram, and Seventeenth Kentucky, commanded by Colonel Stout, rallied and formed
on the right of our main line, and, fighting all day, only left the field
when ordered.

The little force brought by General Van Cleve to the support of
the battery was insufficient.   I rode rapidly toward the next ridge,
hoping to find some general officer and to obtain support for my batteries.   I had ridden but a few steps down the hill when I heard the
batteries moving quickly away.   Nothing but the greatest energy
enabled the officers commanding these batteries to save any of their
guns.

The enemy had come close up to the batteries on the left while
pouring in a severe fire of sharpshooters from the front.   All the
horses attached to one of the guns of Lieutenant Cushing were shot
almost at the same moment; yet he succeeded in bringing away three
guns, losing but one.   For the good conduct of artillery officers in
this and other positions during the day, I refer you to the report of
Major Mendenhall, chief of artillery, and to the reports of their
division commanders.

On reaching the crest of the next hill I found only a small number of men, less than 100, who had been rallied by a captain of the
Eighteenth Regulars, as he told me, and whom he kept in line with
great difficulty.   I remained here for some time, probably a half
hour, expecting to meet some officers from the commands which had
been posted to my right.   After this lapse of time Major Mendenhall informed me that the enemy had turned our own guns upon us
from the hill we had just left.   I then determined to go immediately to Rossville or Chattanooga, if it was practicable.   I could
hear nothing of General Rosecrans, nor of Generals McCook, Sheridan, or Davis, and I greatly feared that all had fallen into the hands
of the enemy.   I should have ridden rapidly to Rossville or Chattanooga to apprise whoever was in command of the actual state of
things on our right, but that I feared to add a panic to the great
confusion.

The road was filled with soldiers, wagons, cannon, and caissons
all the way to Rossville.   All were moving without organization,
but without undue haste and without panic.   After leaving the hill
and riding slowly about a mile and a half, I met Colonel Parkhurst
with his regiment and with men enough—whom he had stopped—to
make another regiment of the ordinary size, and who seemed to be
well organized.   The colonel rode up to me and asked if I would

take command. I told him no, that he was doing good service; and I directed him to hold his position and let the artillery, wagons, &c., pass, and then follow on, covering the rear.

About this time I learned the general commanding had not been captured, but that he had gone to Chattanooga. I rode to Rossville where I expected to find some troops and to learn something of the locality of the main army, and its condition, but finding no one who could give me any information, I rode to Chattanooga where I found the general commanding the department, and reported briefly to him.

The general commanding having ordered the army to withdraw to Rossville, directed me to report to Major-General Thomas at that place for orders. I rode that night to Rossville, reported to General Thomas, and early in the morning of the 21st, placed the two divisions of my command which were at this place (General Palmer's and Wood's) in the position assigned them. General Van Cleve, having collected about 1,200 of his men, sent me word that he was encamped a few miles distant on the road leading from Chattanooga to Bridgeport, and that he had received orders from the general commanding the army. The enemy made some demonstrations during this day on my front, which covered the road leading from Ringgold to Rossville, but was easily made to keep a respectful distance; and after night, in obedience to orders, my command withdrew so quietly to Chattanooga that our own pickets were not aware of the movement.

General W. C. Whitaker had reported to me on this day with two brigades, and occupied the extreme left of my line. His were the last troops to withdraw, and I remained until he moved away with his command. On reaching Chattanooga I was assigned to the position I now hold.

It is a source of much regret to me that circumstances made it impossible, with any regard to the interests of the service, for my corps to act as a unit in these battles. The pride of the corps was such, that I think its attack would have been irresistible; and an attack upon it, fatal to the enemy. But the great object of the battle was obtained: We foiled the enemy in his attempt to reoccupy Chattanooga; we hold the prize for which the campaign was made, and if nothing has been added to the fame of the corps, it is only because its noble blood has been shed in detachments on every part of the field where an enemy was to be encountered, instead of flowing together as at Stone's River. The people will look with hissing and scorn upon the traducers of this corps when they learn with what stubborn bravery it poured out its blood in their cause.

The Army of the Cumberland matched itself against one army, and for two days we disputed the field with three veteran armies, and then, unmolested by them, were moved to the coveted place, which we now hold and where they have not ventured to assail us.

The conduct of the various detachments from the Twenty-first Army Corps in these battles fully sustains their reputation.

With pride I point to the services of Major-General Palmer and his splendid division. Starting from Gordon's or Lee's Mills, they fought their way to General Thomas, and participated in all of the terrible struggles in that part of the field, and when ordered to withdraw came off with music and their banners flying. Such was the conduct of this part of my command, all of which has been published to the country as having "disgracefully fled from the field." With pride I call attention to the distinguished services of Brigadier-General Cruft, Brig. Gen. W. B. Hazen, and Col. William Grose, commanding the brigades of this division.

With pride I point to the services of Brig. Gen. H. P. Van Cleve and his gallant division, which followed General Palmer into the fight. With daring courage they attacked the enemy on Saturday, capturing a battery, from which, however, they were driven by overwhelming numbers, but rallying they maintained themselves, and soon again advancing captured another battery, which they brought off.

With pride I mention the name of Brig. Gen. Samuel Beatty for his conduct on this occasion.

On this day, and, indeed, whenever he was engaged, General Van Cleve's command was but two small brigades; his largest brigade, Colonel Barnes commanding, being detached. The accidental and unavoidable disaster of Sunday, which threw out of the fight altogether five regiments, cannot tarnish the fame of this division. Such was the conduct of this part of my command, all of which has been published to the country as having "disgracefully fled from the field."

With pride I point to the services of Brigadier-General Wood and his gallant command. The last of my corps ordered to the scene of conflict, they became engaged almost at the very moment of their arrival.

Unexpectedly run over by a portion of our troops, who were driven back upon them, the brigade of Colonel Buell was thrown into confusion, and borne along with the fleeing for a short distance, but were soon and easily rallied by General Wood and Colonel Buell, and though the loss had been very heavy for so short a conflict, these brave men were led back by their division and brigade commanders to the ground from which they had been forced.

On Sunday, when our lines were broken, Brigadier-General Wood, with the brigades of Colonels Harker and Barnes and that part of Colonel Buell's brigade not cut off by the enemy, reached Major-General Thomas, as ordered, and participated in the battle of the day with honor to themselves. Such was the conduct of this, the last part of my command, all of which has been published to the country as having "disgracefully fled from the field."

With pride I most respectfully call attention to the brilliant conduct of Col. C. G. Harker, commanding Third Brigade of Brigadier-General Wood's division. On Saturday evening he skillfully avoided being thrown into disorder ; with good judgment pressed the enemy, captured near 200 prisoners, and withdrew his command in good order. On Sunday he equally distinguished himself by the skill with which he managed his command, and more than all by the gallantry with which he fought.

It is proper that I should mention the conduct of Colonel Barnes, commanding Third Brigade of Brigadier-General Van Cleve's division, for his conduct on Saturday evening. Colonel Barnes was at this time separated from his division, and in the fight of Saturday evening was posted on our right. He had a very severe engagement with a superior force, and, in my judgment, prevented the enemy from attempting to turn our right at this time by the firmness with which he fought. He suffered a severe loss, but withdrew his command in good order before night. The names of those in this corps who particularly distinguished themselves have been mentioned by their respective commanders, and I most earnestly commend them to the commanding general and the Government.

With deep sorrow, yet not unmixed with pride, I call attention to the terrible list of casualties, amounting to nearly 28 per cent., of my entire command. The tabular statement, herewith inclosed, will show how small a proportion of this percentage is missing or unaccounted for.

For a more detailed account of the operations of my command in this campaign I refer you to the able reports of division, brigade, and regimental commanders. I also inclose report by Major Mendenhall of the operations of the artillery of this corps.

Captain Bradley, Sixth Ohio Battery, acted with great energy and effect in repelling the advance of the enemy on Saturday ; and Captain Swallow, with his battery, and Lieutenant Cushing, with his (Company H, Fourth Artillery), acted with great coolness and decision, saving nearly all their pieces on the ridge (Sunday) while the enemy was among them. Of the artillery commanders in the Second Division—Captain Standart, Captain Cockerill, Lieutenant Russell, and Lieutenant Cushing—I refer to Major-General Palmer's very honorable mention of their conduct throughout both days' fight.

My warmest thanks are due to my staff. Lieut. Col. Lyne Starling, chief of staff, as always on the battle-field, was courageous and active. Capt. P. P. Oldershaw, assistant adjutant-general, discharged his duties with promptness and ability, displaying both coolness and bravery, and who has earned and deserves promotion. Of Lieutenant-Colonel Lodor, inspector-general of the corps, I can say no more than that he was as brave, as active, and as useful as at Stone's River. Major Mendenhall, chief of artillery of the corps, has fairly earned, and I hope will receive, promotion. My aides-de-camp—Maj. L. M. Buford, Capt. George G. Knox, and Capt. John J. McCook—were active and attentive to their duties, freely exposing themselves throughout the battles.

I call particular attention to the efficiency and good judgment of the medical director of the corps, Surg. A. J. Phelps. By his judicious arrangements nothing that could be done for our wounded was neglected.

Asst. Surg. B. H. Cheney, medical purveyor of the corps, managed his department creditably.

Lieut. Col. A. Sympson, quartermaster, and Lieut. Col. G. C. Kniffin, commissary of subsistence of the corps, were not on the field, but were where I ordered them, performing their duties, as always, effectively, in their respective departments.

Capt. Henry Kaldenbaugh, my very efficient provost-marshal, aided very materially in facilitating the movements of ambulances during the battles and in the removal of the wounded from the field. I have rarely seen an officer of his department so thoroughly efficient as he has proved himself to be in camp and on the battle-field.

Capt. William Leonard, Lieut. Burch Foraker, and Lieut. C. H. Messenger, of the signal corps, were with me frequently during the battles and made themselves useful.

It gives me much pleasure to call attention to Captain Sherer, Lieutenant Harvey, and the company they command, as my escort. To habitual good conduct in camp they have added good conduct on the field of battle ; also to John Adkins, Company D, Second Kentucky Volunteers, senior clerk in the assistant adjutant-general's office, who remained on the field with my staff both days', and aided as much as any one in rallying the men. He is a good clerk, well educated, and in everything competent to command, and is deserving of a commission.

The same may be said of George C. James, private Company A, Sixth Ohio Volunteers, clerk to my chief of artillery and topographical engineer, who, when detailed as a clerk, stipulated to join his regiment when on a march with the prospect of an engagement. On the march from Murfreesborough to Manchester he joined his regiment, and also from the time of crossing the Tennessee River until the termination of the late engagements, in both of which he participated. If promotion cannot be had in their regiments, some distinguishing mark of honor should be bestowed on both of these men.

I am, sir, very respectfully, your obedient servant,

T. L. CRITTENDEN,
Major-General, Commanding Twenty-first Army Corps.

Lieut. Col. C. GODDARD,
A. A. G., Dept. of the Cumberland, Chattanooga, Tenn.

[Inclosure.]

Report of the Casualties in Twenty-first Army Corps in the engagements of September 19 and 20, 1863.

Command.	Taken into action.			Casualties.								
				Killed.		Wounded.		Missing.		Total.		
	Commissioned officers.	Enlisted men.	Total.	Commissioned officers.	Enlisted men.	Commissioned officers.	Enlisted men.	Commissioned officers.	Enlisted men.	Commissioned officers.	Enlisted men.	Aggregate.
FIRST DIVISION.												
First Brigade headquarters...	....	....	....	....	....	....	....	....	....	....	....	....
100th Illinois Volunteers ..	26	313	339	....	23	6	111	2	22	8	156	164
26th Ohio Volunteers	26	336	362	4	23	6	134	2	48	12	200	212
13th Michigan Volunteers	25	195	220	2	11	6	61	2	24	10	96	106
58th Indiana Volunteers .	30	370	400	2	14	5	96	1	24	8	134	142
Total First Brigade	107	1,214	1,321	8	71	23	402	7	113	38	586	624
Third Brigade headquarters ..	7	38	45	....	....	....	....	....	....	....	....	....
125th Ohio Volunteers	16	298	314	1	16	2	81	....	5	3	102	105
64th Ohio Volunteers	26	299	325	1	5	2	41	....	16	3	62	65
65th Ohio Volunteers	21	285	306	3	12	5	65	....	18	8	95	103
3d Kentucky Volunteers.	26	375	401	1	12	8	70	....	22	9	104	113
Total Third Brigade.....	96	1,295	1,391	6	45	17	257	....	61	23	363	386
Artillery:												
6th Ohio Battery	5	114	119	....	....	1	5	....	3	1	8	9
8th Indiana Battery.......	5	129	134	....	....	.....	8	....	7	......	15	15
Total artillery	10	243	253	....	....	1	13	....	10	1	23	24
Total First Division	213	2,752	2,965	14	116	41	672	7	184	62	972	1,034
SECOND DIVISION.												
Division headquarters	17	86	103	....	1	2	....	2	1	4	2	6
First Brigade headquarters...	7	17	24	....	....	....	....	....	....	....	....	....
31st Indiana Volunteers...	25	355	380	1	4	2	59	....	17	3	80	83
1st Kentucky Volunteers	7	111	118	....	2	1	25	....	3	1	30	31
2d Kentucky Volunteers	20	347	367	1	9	5	59	....	18	6	86	92
90th Ohio Volunteers......	22	393	415	2	5	2	60	1	14	5	79	84
Total First Brigade	81	1,223	1,304	4	20	10	203	1	52	15	275	290

Report of the Casualties in Twenty-first Army Corps, &c.—Continued.

Command.	Taken into action.			Casualties.								Aggregate.
				Killed.		Wounded.		Missing.		Total.		
	Commissioned officers.	Enlisted men.	Total.	Commissioned officers.	Enlisted men.	Commissioned officers.	Enlisted men.	Commissioned officers.	Enlisted men.	Commissioned officers.	Enlisted men.	
SECOND DIVISION—continued.												
Second Brigade headquarters.	7	17	24	....	....	....	....	....	....	....	....	
124th Ohio Volunteers	22	431	453	....	15	4	88	....	34	4	137	141
41st Ohio Volunteers	23	337	360	....	6	5	95	....	9	5	110	115
9th Indiana Volunteers	30	298	328	3	22	6	59	....	18	9	99	108
6th Kentucky Volunteers	22	280	302	5	9	5	88	....	11	10	108	118
Total Second Brigade...	104	1,363	1,467	8	52	20	330	....	72	28	454	482
Third Brigade headquarters ..	8	35	43	1	....	....	3	....	....	1	3	4
36th Indiana Volunteers ..	25	322	347	1	13	8	89	....	17	9	119	128
24th Ohio Volunteers	19	258	277	....	3	3	57	....	16	3	76	79
6th Ohio Volunteers	25	337	362	1	13	7	94	1	16	9	123	132
84th Illinois Volunteers ...	26	356	382	1	12	2	81	....	9	3	102	105
23d Kentucky Volunteers	25	249	274	1	10	3	49	....	6	4	65	69
Total Third Brigade	128	1,557	1,685	5	51	23	373	1	64	29	488	517
Artillery:												
Battery F, First Ohio Volunteer Artillery.	4	106	110	1	1	....	8	....	2	1	11	12
Battery B, First Ohio Volunteer Artillery.	2	130	132	...	1	....	8	....	4	....	13	13
Battery H, Fourth U. S. Artillery.	2	85	87	....	4	1	16	....	....	1	20	21
Battery M, Fourth U. S. Artillery.	2	115	117	....	2	....	6	....	....	....	8	8
Total artillery	10	436	446	1	8	1	38	....	6	2	52	54
Total Second Division	340	4,665	5,005	18	132	56	944	4	195	78	1,271	1,349
THIRD DIVISION.												
First Brigade headquarters...	....	....	....	....	....	....	....	....	....	....	....	
19th Ohio Volunteers	27	357	384	....	7	2	58	....	23	2	88	90
79th Indiana Volunteers...	18	282	300	....	1	2	42	1	9	3	52	55
9th Kentucky Volunteers	26	187	213	....	2	4	41	1	12	5	55	60
17th Kentucky Volunteers	20	467	487	1	5	2	103	....	15	3	123	126
Total First Brigade	91	1,293	1,384	1	15	10	244	2	59	13	318	331
Second Brigade headquarters.	8	30	38	....	....	....	....	....	....	....	....	
13th Ohio Volunteers	18	286	304	2	3	4	41	....	22	6	66	72
59th Ohio Volunteers	17	273	290	2	5	1	40	2	28	5	73	78
86th Indiana Volunteers	20	241	261	....	1	3	28	....	21	3	50	53
44th Indiana Volunteers ..	27	202	229	1	2	7	52	....	10	8	64	72
Total Second Brigade...	90	1,032	1,122	5	11	15	161	2	81	22	253	275
Third Brigade headquarters ..	....	....	....	....	....	....	....	....	....	....	....	
51st Ohio Volunteers	21	298	319	....	8	1	34	4	51	5	93	98
8th Kentucky Volunteers	21	297	318	....	3	2	29	....	2	2	34	36
99th Ohio Volunteers	24	333	357	....	3	2	19	....	33	2	55	57
35th Indiana Volunteers ..	31	198	229	....	5	3	20	2	35	5	60	65
Total Third Brigade. ...	97	1,126	1,223	...	19	8	102	6	121	14	242	256
Artillery :												
Independent Pennsylvania Battery.	5	107	112	1	1	1	13	....	1	2	15	17
3d Wisconsin Battery	3	116	119	....	2	....	13	....	12	....	27	27
7th Indiana Battery	5	117	122	....	....	....	8	1	2	1	10	11
Total artillery	13	240	353	1	3	1	34	1	15	3	52	55
Total Third Division	291	3,791	4,082	7	48	34	541	11	276	52	865	917

Report of the Casualties in Twenty-first Army Corps, &c.—Continued.

RECAPITULATION.

Command.	Taken into action.			Casualties.								
				Killed.		Wounded.		Missing.		Total.		
	Commissioned officers.	Enlisted men.	Total.	Commissioned officers.	Enlisted men.	Commissioned officers.	Enlisted men.	Commissioned officers.	Enlisted men.	Commissioned officers.	Enlisted men.	Aggregate.
First Division..............	213	2,752	2,965	14	116	41	672	7	184	62	972	1,034
Second Division............	340	4,665	5,005	18	132	56	944	4	195	78	1,271	1,349
Third Division.............	291	3,791	4,082	7	48	34	541	11	276	52	865	917
Total Twenty-first Army Corps.*	844	11,008	12,052	39	296	131	2,157	22	655	192	3,108	3,300

CHATTANOOGA, *October* 1, 1863.

T. L. CRITTENDEN,
Major-General, Commanding.

Capt. P. P. OLDERSHAW,
Assistant Adjutant-General.

ADDENDA.

Itinerary of the Twenty-first Army Corps.†

August 16.—Command stationed at Manchester, McMinnville, and Hillsborough, Tenn., with a brigade outpost at Pelham. Moved out under orders for Sequatchie Valley ; crossed the Cumberland Mountains at three different points.

August 19.—At 3 a. m. arrived in the valley, occupying Pikeville; the Second Division, Dunlap, and the Third Division, Therman.

August 20.—One brigade sent to occupy and hold Poe's Tavern, about 15 miles north of Chattanooga. Another brigade sent to threaten the enemy opposite Chattanooga, the latter co-operating with Colonel Wilder's mounted infantry, and all located in the Tennessee Valley.

August 31.—Received orders for the whole command to move down the Sequatchie Valley quietly and at once, and cross the Tennessee River at Shellmound, Battle Creek, or Bridgeport. Movement commenced next day.

———

FRANKFORT, KY., *December* 22, 1863.

Maj. Gen. H. W. HALLECK, *General-in-Chief:*

GENERAL : The New York Herald of the 12th instant contains what purports to be your report on the late operations of the armies of the United States.

I would most respectfully call the attention of the General-in-Chief to the following sentences contained in this report referring to the Army of the Cumberland :

Our right and part of the center had been completely broken, and fled in confusion from the field, carrying with them, toward Chattanooga, their commanders, Generals McCook and Crittenden, and also General Rosecrans, who was on that part of the line.

———

* See revised statement of losses, p. 177.　　　† From the return for August.

In another place you say :

As most of the corps of McCook and Crittenden had retreated toward Chattanooga, it was deemed advisable to withdraw the left wing to that place.

I deem it my duty to the Twenty-first Army Corps, and my duty to you, sir, to say not only that no part of my corps was in Chattanooga, but that all except five regiments fought with the left wing in the close of the battle, and that these five regiments were cut off from the main army, which the left wing had grown to be, in the act of going to its support.

I did go to Chattanooga, and this, to some extent, may have misled the General-in-Chief ; but no confused troops carried me there, nor did I carry with me any troops; in truth, I had none to carry.

Whatever counter reports or statements have been made to the General-in-Chief I engage to disprove by the general testimony of the army, officers and all.

Under these circumstances I most respectfully and earnestly entreat the General-in-Chief to examine further into the matter ; then I am sure he will correct a report which does such cruel injustice to a corps justly proud of its reputation.

I have the honor to be, very respectfully, your obedient servant,

T. L. CRITTENDEN,
Major-General, U. S. Volunteers.

—

COMMONWEALTH OF KENTUCKY,
OFFICE SECRETARY OF STATE,
Frankfort, Ky. [*January* —], 1864.

His Excellency the PRESIDENT OF THE UNITED STATES:

DEAR SIR: I inclose you an attested copy of resolutions of the Kentucky Legislature adopted on the 14th of December, 1863, in regard to the investigation of the conduct of Maj. Gen. Thomas L. Crittenden at the battle of Chickamauga. The apparent delay in not forwarding the copy at an earlier day was produced by the press of business.

With the kindest regards for your health and prosperity, I remain, your obedient servant,

E. L. VAN WINKLE.

[Inclosure.]

RESOLUTIONS IN RELATION TO MAJOR-GENERAL CRITTENDEN.

The fame of its true, brave, and patriotic men is a part of the wealth of a nation; that of patriots which has been tested in battle is doubly prized by a grateful people. The people of Kentucky are grateful; they honor and love those gallant sons who in this terrible civil war have been found struggling to maintain the nationality of the Government of the United States and the ancient renown of the Commonwealth.

In the list of those living worthies prominent among all is the name of Thomas L. Crittenden; his unshadowed patriotism, his modesty, and his courage have been signalized from the beginning of this rebellion, while his fitness for military command and his dauntless courage were conspicuous and eminently recognized at Shiloh, Stone's River, and many other battle-fields. This Legislature has heard that he has been relieved of his command and ordered to report to a military court for the examination of his conduct at Chickamauga. No such court has been convened, and none, so far as they have learned, has yet been ordered. They have no doubt that the result of a fair investigation will not only exonerate him from all censure but brighten his fame.

The soldiers of Kentucky in the field demand his trial.

Be it therefore resolved by the General Assembly of the Commonwealth of Kentucky, That the President of the United States be, and is hereby, respectfully requested to convene a court for the investigation of the conduct of Major-General Crittenden at the earliest possible day.

Resolved, That a copy of these resolutions be forwarded to the President of the United States, and to each of our Senators and Representatives in Congress.

H. TAYLOR,
Speaker of the House of Representatives.
RICHARD P. JACOB,
Speaker of the Senate.

Approved December 14, 1863.

THO. E. BRAMLETTE,
Governor.

A copy.
Attest:

E. L. VAN WINKLE,
Secretary of State.

[Indorsements.]

JANUARY 5, 1864.

I ask the respectful attention and consideration of the Secretary of War and General-in-Chief.

A. LINCOLN.

Referred to Major-General Halleck, with directions to detail a Court of Inquiry as speedily as possible.*

EDWIN M. STANTON,
Secretary of War.

No. 134.

Report of Surg. Alonzo J. Phelps, U. S. Army, Medical Director.

HDQRS. 21ST ARMY CORPS, MEDICAL DIRECTOR'S OFFICE,
Chattanooga, Tenn., September 29, 1863.

SIR: I have the honor to submit the following report of the medical department of this corps previous to and at the battle of the Chickamauga:

Before leaving Murfreesborough, in June last, this corps was placed in a good and effective condition to meet the enemy; the train of 10 wagons for reserve hospital supplies had been replenished, each regiment was supplied with 1 good ambulance, and each division with 30 additional ambulances, every 10 of which were placed under the charge of an ambulance master. The medical officers of each division were organized in such a manner as to give to each officer a specific duty to perform, and certain of the medical officers were designated to remain with the wounded in the event of a retreat.

---

*See record of Court of Inquiry, p. 971.

Thus prepared we marched against the enemy at Shelbyville, Tenn., who declined battle and precipitately retreated to the south side of the Tennessee River. In the skirmishing that took place at this time our corps scarcely fired a gun. The army then halting for several weeks it became necessary for us to establish hospitals for the temporary care of our sick at Manchester and McMinnville, which was done by your order. Hospitals to accommodate 250 patients were established at these points, and requisitions were made upon my corps reserve supplies for this purpose.

Finally, on the 16th of August, we took up our line of march to Chattanooga, and crossed the Tennessee River at Shellmound on the 4th and 5th of September, and occupied Chattanooga on the 9th with but little skirmishing. Immediately upon arriving at this place I examined the hospital accommodation it afforded, a report of which I made to you at the time.

Our corps was ordered to make immediate pursuit, and skirmished daily with the enemy with a total loss of 40 wounded besides the killed until Saturday, the 19th of September, when the battle opened in earnest.

The day previous to the battle the most favorable sites were selected for our division field hospitals. They were selected within 1½ miles of Crawfish Spring, which was the only accessible water, and with a view to the possibility of retreat were placed upon roads that led to the rear across Missionary Ridge to Chattanooga Valley. These points were directly in the rear of our line of battle in the morning, but as the battle seemed to be tending to the left, about noon I received an order from the medical director of the department to remove my hospitals in that direction, which order was subsequently countermanded. Accordingly they were restored to their original position, and during the day and night about 1,200 wounded were received into these hospitals.

On Sunday morning, the 20th September, I directed my corps purveyor to issue his supplies equally to each of the three hospitals, to be used at the discretion of the surgeons in charge. Toward noon it was discovered that the wounded ceased to come in and that our communication was cut off with the army. The Cavalry Corps only remained, which had been posted for the protection of the hospitals and the right flank of our line of battle. At about 2 p. m. it became apparent that we were finally separated from our forces, and that the cavalry was being slowly forced back upon us. I then gave the order to remove the hospital over the ridge to Chattanooga Valley. Upon arriving there I discovered that it was not prudent to stop short of Chattanooga, at which place all arrived in the course of the succeeding night. The enemy, I have since learned, were in possession of the ground occupied by our hospitals within a few minutes after we had left.

Every means of transportation was seized upon to carry away our wounded, and but about 200 were left behind. Fourteen medical officers of the corps were detailed to remain and attend to these and to the wounded left upon the field, and a liberal supply of hospital stores was left for their use, besides a number of hospital tents, which it was impossible to bring away.

On Monday morning, by direction of the medical director of the department, I assisted in the selection of a safe point beyond the Tennessee River for a general field depot for the wounded, which was placed under the charge of W. W. Blair, chief surgeon of the First

(Wood's) Division, and at the present time each division of this corps has its own surgeons in professional charge of its own wounded not sent forward to Bridgeport, all of which are doing well.

The strictly professional report of this battle must necessarily be very unsatisfactory in consequence of our having lost the field, and with it the severest wounded in the Sunday's fight. The list furnished by the division surgeons will be made out with all possible care, giving the location and character of wound, &c.

The firing was chiefly musketry at short range, with conical ball; the cannonading was not proportionally as severe as at Stone's River.

The following is a statement of the number of killed and wounded reported in the corps. I am of the opinion that 150 in addition will cover our losses.

Officers killed, 33; officers wounded, 142; total officers killed and wounded, 175. Privates killed, 269; privates wounded, 2,015; total privates killed and wounded, 2,284. Grand total, 2,459.

I wish to speak in terms of high commendation of the services rendered by Surg. Samuel D. Turney, U. S. Volunteers, medical director, Third Division (Van Cleve's); W. W. Blair, surgeon Fifty-eighth Indiana Volunteers, medical director, First (Wood's) Division, and S. G. Menzies, surgeon First Kentucky Volunteers, and medical director Second (Palmer's) Division.

The promptness with which they located their hospitals and received and cared for the wounded, and the efficiency that they exhibited throughout, even to the final removal of their hospitals and wounded from the dangers of capture, recommend them to your high confidence. Also, I am desirous to speak of the services of Asst. Surg. B. H. Cheney, Forty-first Ohio Volunteers, and corps medical purveyor, who was prompt in issuing his supplies and rendering professional assistance to the wounded.

I know of no case of neglect of duty on the part of regimental medical officers of this corps; on the other hand, all evinced a desire to do their part well. For special mention of such and other matters especially connected with the divisions, I beg to refer you to the accompanying reports* of the division surgeons.

In a few days I expect to be able to forward a list of the names of the killed and wounded of the corps.

Very respectfully, your obedient servant,

A. J. PHELPS,
Surgeon, U. S. Vols., Medical Director, 21st Army Corps.

Surg. G. PERIN, U. S. Army,
Medical Director, Department of the Cumberland.

No. 135.

Report of Maj. John Mendenhall, U. S. Army, Chief of Artillery.

HEADQUARTERS TWENTY-FIRST ARMY CORPS,
OFFICE CHIEF OF ARTILLERY AND ORDNANCE,
Chattanooga, Tenn., September 28, 1863.

SIR: I have the honor to make the following report of the operations of the artillery of this corps on the 19th and 20th instant:

On the morning of the 19th the batteries were posted with the

---

* Not found.

divisions to which they belonged, overlooking West Chickamauga River from Gordon's Mills along the road toward Rossville. One battery (the Eighth Indiana) was above the mills with Colonel Buell's brigade, of General Wood's division.

About 11.30 o'clock, the firing being very heavy on the left, General Crittenden ordered General Palmer, with his division, to move to his (General Thomas') support. All the batteries of the division (H and M, Fourth U. S. Artillery, and B and F, First Ohio Artillery) went with it, and I saw nothing more of them during the battle, except Battery H, Fourth Artillery (Lieutenant Cushing commanding), a short time before it left the field on the 20th.

From one to two hours later General Van Cleve, with two of his brigades, was also ordered to the support of General Thomas. The Independent Pennsylvania Battery (Captain Stevens) and four guns of the Seventh Indiana (Captain Swallow) accompanied General Van Cleve, and I saw nothing more of them that day.

I think it was 2 o'clock when the other brigade of General Van Cleve's division and General Wood, with his two brigades, were ordered to the left. I directed Lieutenant Livingston, with Third Wisconsin Battery, to take a position in a corn-field on the right of a battery of General Davis' division. He remained in this position until compelled to fall back a short distance with the rest of the troops, when he took a new position. Before retiring he punished the enemy severely, and again, from his new position (which was on our right, with Colonel Barnes' brigade, Third Division), he aided in checking their advance. He kept this second position till evening.

While General Wood's command was coming up, I discovered the section of Swallow's battery which had not gone with the division, and I posted it in the field in the rear of where General Wood's head of column was entering the woods. I saw nothing more of this section till next morning, when it had rejoined its battery.

The batteries of the First Division had not gotten into position before our troops fell back. When I saw them falling back I directed the Sixth Ohio Battery (Captain Bradley) to take position in the edge of the woods, so as to check the enemy as he advanced across the open ground. The Eighth Indiana Battery (Captain Estep) got into position on the right of the Sixth Ohio Battery. In a little while our troops charged back over the open ground, and drove the enemy back into the woods, the Eighth Indiana Battery accompanying them. Our men were again driven back, and the Eighth Indiana Battery suffered severely, being compelled to leave one gun behind them, which they recovered during the afternoon. The Sixth Ohio Battery remained where I had posted it, and did excellent service in repelling the enemy as he attempted to cross the open ground.

These batteries (Sixth Ohio, Eighth Indiana, and Third Wisconsin) moved to the foot of Missionary Ridge, along with their commands, before daylight next morning. About 9 o'clock the First Division moved forward and the Third (which was now together) soon followed, each brigade having a battery. General Wood soon became engaged, and Colonel Barnes, with a brigade of the Third Division, moved forward to his support. General Wood ordered the Third Wisconsin Battery, which was with Colonel Barnes, not to follow, stating that there was no position there to put a battery in (only a portion of the guns he had with him were then in position).

This battery took a position in rear on a ridge, and the other batteries of the Third Division took position on the same ridge as they came up, the infantry moving forward.   A little later the Third Division moved to the left, and I had the artillery move parallel to it.   The batteries got a good position some 400 yards in rear of the division (which latter was in low ground in same field).   The fighting was quite heavy in front, but the artillery could be but little used for fear of injuring our own troops.   The Eighth Indiana Battery, and Battery H, Fourth Artillery, fell back and took position on same ridge.

Some rebel sharpshooters got into a point of woods to our right and front and began firing at the artillery, and soon some of the pieces began to retire without orders.   I rode back and ordered them to return, and while I was so employed a stampede took place in our front, and in a few moments the rebels were in among the guns. How they got by our troops I have no idea.   A gap must have been left, through which, I suppose, they passed.

I considered our position the best we could get in case the troops fell back, and the batteries were ready to move forward should they advance.

We lost 15 out of 26 guns at this time : One from Seventh Indiana, 2 from Independent Pennsylvania, 5 from Third Wisconsin, 6 from Eighth Indiana, and 1 from Battery H, Fourth Artillery.

Captain Swallow and Lieutenant Cushing deserve credit for getting away with as many guns as they did; they each lost one.   Captain Stevens, Independent Pennsylvania Battery, was killed here.

I did not leave the ground till the enemy was among the guns, and was agreeably surprised that any got away.   I believe that every officer did his duty well here, as well as at every other point on the field where they were engaged during the battle.

The following is a list of casualties, losses, &c.:

Command.	Commissioned officers.		Enlisted men.			Horses.	
	Killed.	Wounded.	Killed.	Wounded.	Missing.	Killed.	Wounded.
6th Ohio Battery, Captain Bradley	....	1	1	5	....	....	2
8th Indiana Battery, Captain Estep	....	1	1	7	9	56	......
Total	....	2	2	12	9	56	2
Battery M, 4th Artillery, Lieutenant Russell	....	....	2	6	......	7	6
Battery H, 4th Artillery, Lieutenant Cushing	....	1	4	14	2	19	6
Battery B, 1st Ohio, Lieutenant Baldwin	....	....	1	4	4	13	......
Battery F, 1st Ohio, Lieutenant Cockerill	1	....	1	8	2	2	10
Total	1	1	8	32	8	41	22
7th Indiana Battery, Captain Swallow	....	....	....	8	......	8	6
Independent Pennsylvania Battery, Captain Stevens	1	1	1	13	1	37	......
3d Wisconsin Battery, Lieutenant Livingston	....	....	2	13	11	32	......
Total	1	1	3	34	12	77	6
Grand total	2	4	13	78	29	174	30

Command.	Guns and carriages.	Gun limbers.	Caissons.		Harness sets.		Horse equipments.	Battery wagons.	Ammunition expended, rounds.
			Limbers.	Bodies.	Wheel.	Lead.			
6th Ohio Battery, Captain Bradley.................	....	....	2	2	......	......	......	1	336
8th Indiana Battery, Captain Estep.............	6	6	3	5	......	......	......	....	750
Total...	6	6	5	7	......	......	......	1	1,086
Battery M, 4th Artillery, Lieutenant Russell........	....	1	2	3	......	......	1	....	511
Battery H, 4th Artillery, Lieutenant Cushing........	1	1	......	......	2	5	2	....	760
Battery B, 1st Ohio, Lieutenant Baldwin	2	....	......	......	......	......	6	....	1,145
Battery F, 1st Ohio, Lieutenant Cockerill..........	....	....	......	......	......	3	......	....	......
Total.......................	3	2	2	3	2	8	9	....	[2,416]
7th Indiana Battery, Captain Swallow	1	1	......	......	1	2	......	....	250
Independent Pennsylvania Battery, Captain Stevens	4	4	1	......	5	10	......	....	......
3d Wisconsin Battery, Lieutenant Livingston.......	5	5	......	......	5	10	......	....	......
Total.......................................	10	10	1	......	11	22	......	....	[250]
Grand total	19	18	8	10	13	30	9	1	[3,752]

In the Seventh Indiana there is 1 officer missing.

I subjoin the reports from each of the batteries.

I am, very respectfully, sir, your most obedient servant,

JOHN MENDENHALL,

Major, and Chief of Artillery.

Col. JAMES BARNETT,

Chief of Artillery, Department of the Cumberland.

ADDENDA.

Itinerary of the artillery of the Twenty-first Army Corps, commanded by Maj. John Mendenhall, U. S. Army, for the month of September, 1863.[*]

FIRST DIVISION.

September 1.—The batteries of the First Division marched from Therman, Tenn.

September 10.—Arrived at Chattanooga.

September 12.—Moved to Lee and Gordon's Mills, Ga.

September 19 *and* 20.—Engaged the enemy for several hours each day.

September 21 *and* 22.—Moved to Chattanooga and encamped.

September 19 *and* 20.—This division lost six guns, captured by the enemy.

SECOND DIVISION.

September 1.—The batteries of the Second Division marched from Dunlap, Tenn.

September 12.—Arrived at Lee and Gordon's Mills.

September 19 *and* 20.—Engaged the enemy, losing three guns.

September 21 *and* 22.—Moved to Chattanooga and encamped.

---

[*] From return for September.

THIRD DIVISION.

September 1.—The batteries of the Third Division marched from Dunlap, Tenn.

September 12.—Arrived at Lee and Gordon's Mills.

September 19 *and* 20.—Engaged the enemy, losing ten guns.

September 21 *and* 22.—Moved to Chattanooga and encamped.

No. 136.

Report of Brig. Gen. Thomas J. Wood, U. S. Army, commanding First Division.

HDQRS. FIRST DIVISION, 21ST ARMY CORPS,
Chattanooga, East Tenn., September 29, 1863.

SIR: At early dawn of the morning of Sunday, the 16th August, I received an order to move with my division from Hillsborough, in Middle Tennessee, by the most practicable and expeditious route across the Cumberland Mountains to Therman, in the Sequatchie Valley. Wednesday evening, the 19th, was the time fixed for the division to arrive at the destination assigned to it. The Second Brigade (Wagner's) had for a month previously occupied Pelham, near the foot of the mountains, and General Wagner had been ordered to repair the road up the mountains known as the Park road. As the order of movement left to my discretion the route by which my division should cross the mountains, I determined to make the ascent by the Park road, thence to Tracy City, thence by Johnson's to Purdons, whence I would fall into the road leading from McMinnville by Altamont to Therman.

Immediately on receiving the order I dispatched instructions to General Wagner to commence the ascent of the mountains, and to insure his being out of the way of the other two brigades, I directed he should continue the work of getting up his train during the night of the 16th. This was done, and early in the morning of the 17th, the road being free, the First and Third Brigades, with their baggage trains and the ammunition and supply trains of the division, began to ascend the mountains. The work was continued unintermittingly through the day and entire night of the 17th, and by 10 o'clock of the 18th the whole was up. Wagner's brigade had advanced to Tracy City Monday morning, the 17th, with orders to move forward as far as the Therman and Anderson road.

On Tuesday, the 18th, I allowed the First and Third Brigades (Buell's and Harker's) to rest till 1 p. m., and then moved to Tracy City. Wagner was ordered to advance on the Therman road to Therman Wednesday morning, select a good encampment, and await my arrival there with the other two brigades and heavy trains. The distance from Tracy City to Therman is 28 miles, which had to be accomplished in one day with First and Third Brigades, their batteries, and the trains, to be at the rendezvous assigned me at the designated time.

At 4 a. m. on the 19th the march was commenced, and a little after nightfall the brigades encamped at Therman. The order for the general movement directed me to take with me ten days' subsistence for the men and ten days' grain for the animals. I descended into the Sequatchie Valley with twenty-five days' subsistence for the men and sixteen days' grain for the animals. I do not mention this fact in a spirit of egotism, but simply to show what can be accomplished by intelligence, good judgment, energy, and a willingness to make some sacrifice of personal comfort by commanders. Every educated and experienced soldier knows that one of the greatest drawbacks on the mobility and activity, and consequently on the offensive power of an army, is to be found in the immense baggage and supply trains which usually accompany its movements; hence, whatever lessens the number of vehicles required for the transportation of baggage and supplies by so much increases the efficiency of the army. I transported all the supplies I took into the Sequatchie Valley in the wagons originally assigned to my division for the transportation of regimental and staff baggage. I was then prepared with my division for a campaign of twenty-five days on full rations, or fifty days on half rations. The additional forage required beyond what I brought with me could have been found in the country. In conformity with the order for the general movement, I dispatched Wagner's brigade early Thursday morning, the 20th, to the eastern slope of Walden's Ridge, to make something of a show of force, and at the same time closely to observe, and if opportunity permitted, to threaten the enemy. With the other two brigades, First and Third, I remained encamped at Therman till the early morning of the 1st of September. I then moved in conformity to orders to Jasper, lower down in the valley.

Late in the afternoon of the 2d I received an order to send one of my brigades to Shellmound to cross the Tennessee River. The First Brigade was immediately put in motion under this order, and under the skillful management of Colonel Buell was thrown across the river rapidly, and without accident, during the night. Early in the morning of the 3d I moved with the Third Brigade, and the ammunition and ambulance trains, to the crossing, and with the energetic and judicious assistance of Colonel Harker had everything passed rapidly across without accident. I remained encamped at Shellmound till Saturday afternoon, the 5th, awaiting orders, the delay being occasioned by the necessity of waiting for the arrival of the supply train, which had been sent to cross the river at Bridgeport.

During the afternoon of the 5th I received an order to move, with the two brigades of my division with me, via Whiteside's and the River road, to the junction of the Nashville and Chattanooga Railway with the Trenton and Chattanooga Railroad, for the purpose of observing and threatening the enemy posted on the spur of Lookout Mountain. I advanced as far as Whiteside's Saturday afternoon and evening. Early Sunday morning I continued to advance, Harker's brigade leading. Soon very light parties of the enemy were encountered, but they rapidly fell back before my sturdy, onward movement, though the country through which my line of march led me is most favorable to a prolonged and obstinate resistance by a small force.

Crossing Raccoon Mountain, I descended into Lookout Mountain Valley, and then followed down the valley northward to the junction of the two railways. As I moved down the valley the enemy's signal stations on the crest of Lookout Mountain were in full and perfect view, evidently watching my advance, and actively communicating the result of their observations to the rear. At the junction of the railways my command was about 2 to 2½ miles from the enemy's advanced works, but the outposts and pickets were much nearer to each other ; in fact, in hearing distance. As I was well aware that the enemy had been able to learn from his signal stations with very close approximate correctness the strength of my command, and hence would most probably be disposed to take advantage of my inferiority of force to attempt to crush me by a sudden blow, I immediately made the best possible dispositions to foil such an effort. In making these dispositions I soon became convinced of the utter untenableness of the position at the junction of the railways for an inferior force to receive an attack from a superior one. The position is entirely open, capable of being assailed simultaneously in front, on both flanks, and in the rear. I was well satisfied that I was in the immediate proximity of a very large force of the enemy (which could be still further swelled in very short time). This information I had gained satisfactorily during my advance, and it was strengthened and corroborated during the afternoon and early evening of the 6th. At 2 p. m. I communicated to the corps commander my position, 7 miles from Chattanooga (being at the junction of the railways), informed him of my immediate proximity to the enemy, and attempted to describe briefly the obstacles which barred my farther progress to Chattanooga.

At 4 p. m. I communicated to him the result of further observations and some facts omitted in my note of 2 p. m. In my note of 2 p. m. I suggested that he should move part of the force immediately with him to cover my rear from a reverse attack. This he declined to do on the ground of a want of authority, and indicated that in case I should be attacked by a superior force, I would have to fall back on him ; also indicating that if I should have to retreat, I had better do so by the Trenton road. I had already opened communication with him by that road. Not intending to retreat except as a matter of the last and direst extremity, and as the evidences continued to thicken and multiply during the evening that I would be attacked in heavy force early next morning, I determined to shift my command a mile and a half to the rear, to a very strong and highly defensible position, in which I was satisfied I could maintain myself against almost any odds for a long time, and if finally overpowered could draw off my command to the rear. From this position I could maintain my communication by the Trenton road with the force immediately with the corps commander.

The movement was commenced at 10 p. m., the 6th, and made with perfect success, though my pickets were at the time in hearing of the enemy's pickets. My command was thus safely extricated from immediate imminent danger. I learned satisfactorily during the afternoon of the 6th that the spur of Lookout Mountain was held by Cheatham's division, supported immediately in rear by Hindman's (late Withers') division, being the whole of Lieutenant-General Polk's corps. My two small brigades confronted this force.

About 8 a. m. in the morning of the 7th I received a copy of a communication addressed by the commanding general to the corps commander, saying that he thought it would be safe (judging from some indications he had obtained of the movements of the enemy) to threaten the enemy on the spur of Lookout Mountain with a part of my force. This communication the corps commander appears to have interpreted into an order to make a reconnaissance in force, and accordingly ordered that I should make such a reconnaissance without loss of time. I accordingly commenced at once to make my preparations for making the reconnaissance, and actually made it at the earliest possible moment compatible with the safety of my command and the assurance of the success of the reconnaissance itself.

As the results of the reconnaissance have hitherto been reported, I will not recapitulate them. After taking the necessary precautions to insure, as far as possible, the safety of the command to be engaged in the reconnaissance and the success of the reconnaissance, I committed the conduct of it to that gallant and accomplished officer, Colonel Harker, commanding the Third Brigade of my division. I instructed him to proceed with the utmost circumspection, but to force his command as near to the enemy's position as he might deem prudent.

This point I was, of course, compelled to submit to his judgment. It affords me the greatest satisfaction to record in a permanent official manner that Colonel Harker conducted the reconnaissance in exact conformity to my wishes and instructions. Securing well his flanks and rear from being assailed without timely notice, he drove his solid line to within some thousand yards of the enemy's batteries (and his line of skirmishers to within some 600 yards), whence twelve guns opened on him, and then drew off his command with the loss of but one man. I know no parallel in military history to this reconnaissance. My command being much jaded and worn by the labors of the several preceding days, I allowed it to rest during the 8th, but I was on the alert to gain information of the movements and designs of the enemy. Near nightfall I obtained some information which led me to suspect the enemy was evacuating Chattanooga, but the indications were by no means positive. With a view to verify, this information, I addressed a note to the corps commander, informing him that I had observed some mysterious indications on the part of the enemy, of which I proposed to compel a development by a reconnaissance in force early next morning. During the night I received a reply to my note, saying the corps commander could not approve the making of the reconnaissance on account of some indications of a general movement of the army, but that he would refer the note to the commanding general. Confidently believing the commanding general would approve my proposition to make the reconnaissance, I held my command in readiness for the movement. In the meantime General Wagner, having with him the Second Brigade of my division, had received information on the north side of the river that the enemy was evacuating Chattanooga. The information having been communicated to the commanding general of the army, an order was dispatched to me to move my command to Chattanooga, prepared for a vigorous pursuit of the enemy.

This agreeable order was joyfully obeyed, and in a very few minutes my command was in rapid motion. Between my late camp in Lookout Mountain Valley and the spur of the mountain my command was overtaken by the Ninety-second Illinois Mounted Infantry, commanded by Colonel Atkins, who informed me he had been ordered to press forward to Chattanooga with all haste, to secure any property the enemy might have left behind, and to discover something of his lines of retreat. I allowed his regiment to pass my command, but on the spur of the mountain I overtook the regiment, halted, when the colonel informed me that the enemy's skirmishers outflanked his, and his farther progress was debarred. I immediately threw forward the Twenty-sixth Ohio, Lieutenant-Colonel Young commanding, to the right and higher up the mountain side than the skirmishers of Colonel Atkins extended, and rapidly drove the enemy's skirmishers from the mountain side. No further opposition was encountered in occupying Chattanooga, and the Ninety-second Illinois pushed rapidly into the town, followed by my First and Third Brigades. The Second Brigade crossed from the north side of the river during the afternoon and evening of the 9th.

The colors of the Ninety-seventh Ohio, of the Second Brigade of my division, were the first planted on the works of Chattanooga, having been brought across the river by a few men in a small boat early in the morning. Thus was this great strategic position, the long-sought goal, gained to us and occupied by our troops. Placing myself as soon as possible after the occupation in communication with the most intelligent and reliable citizens, I learned that a portion of the enemy's troops had retreated by the Cove road, and that the remainder, with the baggage and material of war, had retreated by the Rossville and La Fayette road. I was informed further, that Buckner's command, which had been posted at Tyner's Station on the railway, had retreated by Johnson toward Ringgold, but I subsequently learned he did not go so far eastward as Ringgold, but passed through Graysville and thence to La Fayette. The bulk of these facts I reported to the commander of the corps immediately on his arrival, and by him I am informed they were communicated to the commanding general.

My division remained in Chattanooga till the morning of the 10th. I then received an order to detail one brigade to occupy the town, and move with the other two in pursuit of the enemy by the Rossville and Ringgold road. The Second Brigade was detailed to remain in Chattanooga. At 10 a. m. of the 10th I led the First and Third Brigades out of Chattanooga to commence the pursuit of the enemy. At 2 p. m. of that day I advised the corps commander of the reported presence of a considerable force on my right flank, and at 7 p. m. I further advised him that I had taken a contraband during the late afternoon, who reported the bulk of the rebel army, with General Bragg in person, at Gordon's Mills on the Chickamauga where it is crossed by the Rossville and La Fayette road. I was incredulous of the story, and so expressed myself; but if true, it was so important it should be known that I deemed it my duty to report his narrative. It is due to the humble person who furnished me this invaluable information to record that subsequent developments proved his report to be singularly accurate and correct. Based on my note of 7.30 p. m. of the 10th, a communication was sent me by the commanding general to send a brigade by the way of Rossville to make a reconnaissance in the direction of Gordon's Mills with a view to verifying the truth of the contraband's report. The order was received at early daylight of the morning of the 11th. Colonel Harker's brigade was immediately sent to execute this service. About the time Harker's brigade was moving the corps commander arrived at my camp. I was directed by him to move forward with my remaining brigade 2 miles on the Ringgold road and then to await further orders. The order was obeyed. At 3.30 p. m., while awaiting further instructions, I received an order from the commanding general to move across the country, by the shortest and most expeditious route, to the Rossville and La Fayette road to support Colonel Harker. Near the same hour I received a note from Colonel Harker, informing me that he had been driving the enemy all day and had arrived within 3 miles of Gordon's Mills.

I immediately sent him an order to press forward to the mills, and informing him that I would make a junction with him during the evening. The junction was made and fortunately, for Harker had been driving his little brigade all day against a vastly superior force, the rear guard of the enemy's great army. A full report of this brilliant and dangerous reconnaissance has been already made, and it is not now necessary that I should say more than that it was superbly made. When I arrived at Gordon's Mills, at 8.30 p. m. of the 11th, the enemy's camp fires could be distinctly seen on the other side of the creek. Their light, reflected over a wide section of the horizon, and, extending upward on the heavens, told that the foe was present in considerable force.

It was my intention to continue the pursuit early next morning, the 12th, but till 8 a. m. the atmosphere was so loaded with haze, fog, and smoke that it was difficult to see a hundred yards in advance. While I was waiting for the atmosphere to become sufficiently clear to continue the pursuit, I received an order to remain at Gordon's Mills till the corps commander arrived there with the other two divisions of the corps. This was done during the afternoon of the 12th. My two brigades remained quiet during the 13th, enjoying much-needed rest.

During the evening of the 13th a copy of a letter of instructions from the commanding general to the corps commander was furnished me by the latter, in which he was directed to leave my command at Gordon's Mills and proceed with the other two divisions to a position on Missionary Ridge, with a view of facilitating the concentration with the other corps of the army. My orders directed me to try stoutly to maintain the position at Gordon's Mills, but if attacked by a superior force, to fall back slowly, resisting stoutly, to Rossville, where it was supposed I would be supported by Major-General Granger's force. In case of extremity, and in case also I should not be supported by General Granger at Rossville, I was directed to select a position guarding the roads leading to Chattanooga and around the point of Lookout Mountain, and hold them at all hazards.

Resolved to make the most stubborn resistance at Gordon's Mills, I took advantage of the creek, a very strong defensible feature in the position, and barricaded my entire front and flanks strongly. So strengthened, I could have successfully resisted a front attack of a vastly superior force. With the exception of an occasional firing on my pickets, the enemy left me undisturbed at Gordon's Mills till between 11 a. m. and 12 m. of Friday, the 18th instant. A rapid advance of his light troops, supported by troops in a solid line, on my right front drove in my pickets as far as the creek, but no effort was made to pass the stream. Such an attempt would have been foiled and cost the enemy dearly.

At about 1 p. m. a force, apparently about a brigade of four regiments, emerged from the wood on the southern side of the creek, nearly opposite the center of my position, apparently with the intention of forcing a passage at the ford near the mills. A few well-directed shots from Bradley's battery soon forced him to relinquish this design and seek the shelter of the woods. The enemy continued to hover in my front during the whole afternoon, making however no serious attempts, and accordingly I became reasonably satisfied that his demonstrations were only a mask to his real design, that of passing a heavy force across the creek lower down, with a view of turning our left and cutting off our communication with Chattanooga.

I communicated my opinion on this point to the commanding general at his headquarters during the evening of the 18th. It was verified by the opening of a terrific engagement on our left as early as 8.30 a. m. on the 19th. Troops had been moved to our left during the night of the 18th to meet the emergency. The battle continued throughout the forenoon and into the afternoon, but my command was left at Gordon's Mills until 3 p. m.

At this hour, I received a verbal order from the corps commander through one of his staff to move with my command and take position, as well as I now remember, on the right of some part of General Van Cleve's division. Throughout the entire preceding part of the day I had distinctly observed a considerable force in front of my position at Gordon's Mills, and just before I received the order to move into action a contraband came into my lines, from whom I learned that this force was the division of General Bushrod R. Johnson. Knowing it would pass the creek immediately I vacated my position, if it should not be occupied by some other troops, I dispatched one of my aides-de-camp to the commanding general, to inform him of the presence of this force in my front, and to suggest that at least a brigade should be sent to occupy the position as soon as I should vacate it. On his way to the headquarters of the commanding general my aide-de-camp encountered Major-General McCook, to whom he communicated the object of his mission to headquarters. General McCook immediately ordered a brigade from his corps to move into position at Gordon's Mills. My aide-de-camp rode on to headquarters and reported what had been done to the commanding general, who approved the dispositions. No delay, however, had occurred on this account in the movement of my command from Gordon's Mills.

Immediately on the receipt of this order my command was put in rapid motion for the scene of the great conflict.

As already remarked, the order directed me to take position on the right of General Van Cleve's command, but as I was totally ignorant of his position in the battle, and met no one on my arrival on the field to enlighten me, I found myself much embarrassed for the want of information whereby I could bring my command judiciously and effectively into action. It should be borne in mind that many of the troops were engaged in the woods, and that it was next to impossible to gain information by sight of the arrangement of the troops already engaged. This information could only be given by general and staff officers, posted in advance to aid in bringing the troops arriving freshly on the ground into action properly. Fortunately, shortly after my arrival on the field I met General Davis, from whom I received some useful information in regard to the status of the conflict. From him I learned that his left brigade (Heg's) was sorely pressed and needed assistance. While I was in conference with him a staff officer informed him that Colonel Heg reported that he could not maintain his position, and at the same instant I saw a stream of fugitives pouring out of the woods, across the Rossville and La Fayette road and over the field to the west of it. These, I learned, belonged to Heg's brigade, of Davis' division. It was evident a crisis was at hand. The advance of the enemy, before which these men were retiring, must be checked at once, or the army would be cut in twain.

Desiring Major Mendenhall, of the corps commander's staff, who chanced to be near me at the moment, to go and rally the fugitives rushing across the field on the west of the road, I at once commenced my dispositions to check the advancing foe. When I first met General Davis on the field I had inquired of him where the fight was. He pointed into the woods, whence the roar and rattle of a very sharp musketry fire resounded, and told me that Heg's brigade was heavily engaged in there. I immediately directed Colonel Harker to form his brigade in battle array nearly parallel to the Rossville and La Fayette road, advance into the woods, and engage the enemy. But the evidence immediately brought to my notice that Heg's brigade was retiring, made a change in this disposition necessary. I consequently directed Colonel Harker to throw forward his right, holding his left as a pivot on the road, thus giving his line an oblique direction to the road, and then advance his whole line. By this disposition I hoped to be able to take the enemy's advancing force in flank. These dispositions, though most expeditiously made, were scarcely completed when a staff officer rode up and reported that the enemy had gained the road and was advancing up it, i. e., in the direction of Gordon's Mills.

This information rendered necessary a further change in the arrangement of Harker's brigade. I ordered him to refuse his left, which brought the left half of his line at right angles with the road and gave to his whole front the form of a broken line, with the apex toward the enemy. In this shape he advanced rapidly, engaged the enemy and drove him between a half and three-fourths of a mile. I followed his advance nearly half a mile, and finding he was doing well, as well as having perfect confidence in his ability to handle his brigade, I remarked to him that I would leave him and go to look after my other brigade, Colonel Buell commanding, which had followed Harker's to the field of battle. For the details of the severe conflict through which Harker's brigade passed in this stage of the battle, for an account of the valuable services it rendered in checking the force which threatened to cut the right of the army from the left, for a report of the heavy loss of gallant officers and men which occurred here, and for a description of the skillful manner in which the brigade was extricated from the perils by which it became environed from encountering in its advance a vastly superior force, I must refer to the more detailed report of the brigade commander. The list of casualties attests the severity of the fighting. The gallant commander himself had 2 horses shot under him. Bradley's battery, attached to Harker's brigade, owing to the density of the woods into which the brigade advanced, did not accompany it. The signal service which this battery rendered at a little later period of the action will be chronicled at the proper time. Leaving Harker's brigade, I returned to where I had ordered Colonel Buell to halt and form his brigade.

When I first met General Davis on the field of battle I was informed by him that Carlin's brigade, of his division, was hotly engaged in the woods in advance or eastward of the corn-field in which our meeting occurred. The sharp and quick rattle of musketry fully assured the correctness of the statement. Seeing no other reserves at hand, and assured that both Harker and Carlin were severely engaged, I determined to hold Buell's brigade in hand to meet emergencies. And it was fortunate I did so, for ere long Carlin's brigade was swept back out of the woods, across the corn-field and into the woods beyond the field on the western side of the road, carrying everything away with it. When I observed the rush across the corn-field I was near the One hundredth Illinois.

With a view of checking an exultant enemy, I ordered Colonel Bartleson, commanding One hundredth Illinois, to fix bayonets and charge the foe. The bayonets were promptly fixed, and the regiment had just commenced to advance, when it was struck by a crowd of fugitives and swept away in the general *mélange*. The whole of Buell's brigade was thus carried off its feet. It was necessary for it to fall back across the narrow field on the western side of the road to the edge of the woods, under whose cover it rallied. As soon as possible it was formed along the fence separating the field from the woods, and with the aid of a part of Carlin's brigade, and a regiment of Wilder's brigade, dismounted there, repulsed the enemy. This result was greatly contributed to by the heavy and most effective fire, at short range, of Bradley's and Estep's batteries. At this critical moment these two batteries were most splendidly served. The narrow field separating the woods on the west from the Rossville and La Fayette road is scarcely 200 paces wide. Buell's brigade was formed just east of the road when it was struck by Carlin's brigade. It, hence, had to retire but the distance of less than 200 yards to get the shelter of the woods for reforming. But in crossing this narrow space it suffered terribly. The killed and wounded were thickly strewn on the ground. Captain George, Fifteenth Indiana, of my staff, was struck by a ball by my side and knocked from his horse. So soon as the enemy was repulsed, I addressed myself to reforming Buell's brigade, for the purpose of advancing it to recover the lost ground.

Order being restored and a sufficiently solid formation acquired to warrant an advance, I led the brigade back in person, and reoccupied the ground from which it had been forced—the site on which it had been originally formed. In this advance my horse was twice shot, the second time proving fatal. I dismounted one of my orderlies near me and took his horse.

In this advance a portion of Carlin's brigade participated, led by General Carlin. Estep's battery, attached to Buell's brigade, accompanied the advance. Scarcely had the lost ground been repossessed than the enemy emerged from the woods on the eastern side of the corn-field, and commenced to cross it. He was formed in two lines, and advanced firing. The appearance of his force was large. Fortunately re-enforcements were at hand. A compact brigade of Sheridan's division, not hitherto engaged, was at the moment crossing the field in the rear of the position then occupied by Buell's brigade and the portion of Carlin's. This fresh brigade advanced handsomely into action, and joining its fire to that of the other troops, most materially aided in repelling a most dangerous attack. But this was not done until considerable loss had been inflicted on us. The enemy advanced near enough to cut down so many horses in Estep's battery that he could not bring off his guns; but as our infantry held its ground, they did not fall into the hands of the enemy. After the attack had been repelled some of the men of the brigade of Sheridan's division kindly drew the pieces to the ravine, or rather dip in the ground, in rear of the ridge on which the battery was posted, where Captain Estep retook possession of them. For this act of soldierly fraternity and kindness I desire publicly and officially to return my thanks and those of my division to the troops who rendered it, and I regret that I do not know the number of the brigade and the name of its commander, that I might more distinctly signalize them in my report.

The day was now far spent; in truth, it was near sunset. No further serious demonstration was made by the enemy on our immediate front. The troops were posted in a strong position to resist a night attack, the brigade of Sheridan's division and Buell's brigade being in juxtaposition, the former on the right and the latter on the left. Harker's brigade was held as a reserve in the edge of the woods on the western side of the road, and Bradley's battery was posted near to it, covering the troops in the front line.

Just after nightfall a sharp fire ran along the line, caused by some movement of the enemy, which at first was taken for an advance, but in the end proved to be nothing more than a picket demonstration. Jaded, worn, and thirsty, the men lay down on their arms to pass a cheerless, comfortless night on the battle-field.

It affords me much pleasure here to record a Samaritan deed rendered to my division during the night by Colonel Harrison, of the Thirty-ninth Indiana and a part of his mounted regiment. The men were very thirsty, but the distance to water was so great that but few could hope to get permission to go for it. During the night Colonel Harrison brought to us some 400 canteens of good water. They were distributed among my men as equitably as possible, and proved the cooling drop to the thirsty soldiers.

Estep's battery was refitted during the night and was ready for service the next morning.

Between midnight and daylight of the morning of the 20th I received an order to move my command to a position on the slope of Missionary Ridge, to be held there as part of the reserve of the army in the coming conflict of the morning. The movement was quietly and successfully made. In the early morning I was directed to move my division eastward from the slope of Missionary Ridge and take the position hitherto occupied by Negley's division, keeping my left in constant communication with General Bran an's right. Colonel Barnes' brigade, of Van Cleve's division, was ordered to report to me for service during the day. Placing his brigade on the left, Harker's in the center, and Buell's on the right (the whole formed in two lines, the front one deployed, the second one in double column closed *en masse*, with their batteries following and supporting), I advanced my command and occupied the position assigned. In doing so I met with no opposition from the enemy. I was instructed not to invite an attack, but to be prepared to repel any effort of the enemy. In throwing out skirmishers to cover my front I aroused the enemy, and had quite a sharp affair with him. By a very imprudent advance of his regiment, done without an order, Colonel Bartleson (moving himself in advance of his troops) was shot from his horse, and either killed or very severely wounded; it was impossible to decide which, on account of the proximity of the place where he fell to the enemy's lines. He was an accomplished and gallant officer, and a high-toned, pure-minded gentleman. His loss is a serious disadvantage to his regiment and to the service:

The position my command then occupied closed the gap in our

lines between Sheridan's left and Brannan's right. Although I had not been at all seriously engaged at any time during the morning, I was well satisfied the enemy was in considerable force in my immediate front. Consequently I was extremely vigilant. Such was the status of the battle in my immediate vicinity when I received the following order:

HEADQUARTERS DEPARTMENT OF THE CUMBERLAND,
September 20—10.45 a. m.

Brigadier-General WOOD,
  Commanding Division, &c.:
  The general commanding directs that you close up on Reynolds as fast as possible, and support him.
  Respectfully, &c.,

FRANK S. BOND,
Major, and Aide-de-Camp.

I received the order about 11 o'clock. At the moment of its receipt I was a short distance in rear of the center of my command. General McCook was with me when I received it. I informed him that I would immediately carry it into execution, and suggested that he should close up his command rapidly on my right to prevent the occurrence of a gap in our lines. He said he would do so, and immediately rode away. I immediately dispatched my staff officers to the brigade commanders with the necessary orders, and the movement was at once begun. Reynolds' division was posted on the left of Brannan's division, which, in turn, was on the left of the position I was just quitting. I had consequently to pass my command in rear of Brannan's division to close up on and go in to the support of Reynolds.

So soon as I had got the command well in motion, I rode forward to find General Reynolds and learn where and how it was desired to bring my command into action. I did not find General Reynolds, but in my search for him I met General Thomas, to whom I communicated the order I had received from the commanding general, and desired to know where I should move my command to support General Reynolds. General Thomas replied that General Reynolds did not need support, but that I had better move to the support of General Baird, posted on our extreme left, who needed assistance. I exhibited my order to him, and asked whether he would take the responsibility of changing it. He replied he would, and I then informed him I would move my command to the support of General Baird. I requested General Thomas to furnish me a staff officer who could conduct me to General Baird, which he did. Taking this staff officer with me, I rode at once to Barnes' brigade and directed the staff officer to conduct it to and report it to General Baird. I then rode to the other two brigades for the purpose of following with them in the rear of Barnes' brigade to the assistance of General Baird. When I rejoined them I found the valley south of them swarming with the enemy.

It appears that when I moved my command to go to the support of General Reynolds, the gap thus made in our lines was not closed by the troops on my right, and that the enemy poured through it very soon in great force. The head of his column struck the right of Buell's brigade, and cutting off a portion of it, forced it over the adjacent ridge, whence it retired, as I have subsequently learned, with the vast mass of fugitives from the troops on our extreme right toward Rossville. In moving to the support of General Reynolds,

naturally following the shortest route, I moved through the woods.
My two batteries, Estep's and Bradley's, could not follow their brigades through the woods, and consequently were compelled to make
a short *détour* to the left to get into the open fields on the slope of the
ridge, intending to move thence parallel to their brigades. But they
were caught in this movement by the rapidly advancing columns of
the enemy. Estep's guns were captured (in the neighborhood as I
understand of infantry on the right, which might have supported him
if it had stood), while Bradley's battery, more fortunate, succeeded
in getting over the ridge and drew off toward Rossville with the tide
of fugitives setting strongly in that direction.

For further details in regard to the movements of these batteries
at this stage of the action, I must refer to the reports of Captains
Bradley and Estep.

I will only remark that while their movements did not occur under my immediate observation, but took place beyond the reach of
my infantry support, I am fully satisfied from all I have learned
that neither Captains Bradley nor Estep can be censured for what
occurred. When I discovered the enemy in force in the valley south
of my command, I at once divined his intention, and appreciated the
terrible hazard to our army and the necessity for prompt action.
His object was clear.

Having turned our right and separated a portion of our forces from
the main body, he was seeking the rear of our solid line of battle,
to attack it in reverse, hoping thus to cut our communication with
Chattanooga and capture and destroy the bulk of our army. I had
with me at the time but one brigade (Harker's) and a portion of
Buell's. I immediately formed a line across the valley facing southward, determined, if possible, to check the advance of the enemy.
He was in full and plain view in the open fields, and it was evident
his force far outnumbered mine. But I felt that this was no time
for comparing numbers. The enemy, at all hazards, must be checked.
I was without the support of artillery and knew I had to depend
alone on the musket. I formed my line in a skirt of woods reaching across the valley. In front of me was the open fields across
which the enemy was advancing. It was a matter of great importance to get possession of the fence which bounded this field on the
northern side. My line was some 150 or 200 yards from the fence on
the north of it, while the enemy's lines were perhaps as much as 350
yards south of it. In person I ordered the One hundred and twenty-
fifth Ohio, Colonel Opdycke commanding, to advance and seize the
fence. There was a momentary hesitation in the regiment to go forward. Its gallant colonel immediately rode in front of the center of
his regiment, and taking off his hat, called on his men to advance.
His regiment gallantly responded by a prompt advance, as men ever
will under the inspiration of such leadership. The regiment quickly
lined the fence, whence a sharp fire was opened on the enemy. Soon
the Sixty-fourth Ohio, Colonel McIlvain commanding, followed and
formed along the fence on the left of the One hundred and twenty-
fifth Ohio.

This bold and rapid offensive movement seemed to take the enemy
by surprise and disconcert his movements, for his hitherto advancing lines halted. The other regiments, Sixty-fifth Ohio and Third
Kentucky (Major Brown commanding the former and Colonel Dunlap the latter), of Harker's brigade, with the Fifty-eighth Indiana,

of Colonel Buell's brigade, Lieutenant-Colonel Embree commanding, were formed on the right of the One hundred and twenty-fifth Ohio, higher up the fence and on a hill dominating the field in which the enemy had halted. The One hundred and twenty-fifth and Sixty-fourth Ohio again advanced, and took position behind a copse of woods near the center of the field, the now debatable ground of the contending bodies.

The movements of the enemy at this moment were so singular, and his blurred and greasy and dusty uniform so resembled our own when travel-stained, coupled with the fact that it was expected a part of McCook's command would come from that direction (the terrible disaster to his force on the right not then being known to us), that for a few minutes the impression prevailed and the cry ran along the line that the troops in front of us were our own. I ordered the firing to cease, the thought of firing on our comrades in arms being too horrible to contemplate. In a few moments, however, the delusion was dispelled, the enemy commencing to advance again in a way that left no doubt of his identity, for he advanced firing on us. I do not mention this singular mistake on account of its possessing any particular importance *per se*, but rather to record it as an instance of the strange delusions that sometimes occur on the battle-field without any sufficient cause and without the possibility of a reasonable explanation. This mistake was the more remarkable as the enemy was probably not more than 300, certainly not over 350 yards distant, and was halted in a broad open field. But for the mistake we could have punished him most severely at the time he was halted. The hour was now about high noon; possibly it may have been as late as 12.30 p. m. When the One hundred and twenty-fifth and Sixty-fourth Ohio advanced to the copse in the open field, I ordered Colonel Opdycke to line the southern side of the copse with skirmishers, with a view of annoying and delaying the progress of the enemy. As he advanced, he inclined to his left, evidently with the intention of outflanking my line and turning my right. This movement of the enemy made it necessary I should gain a position in which I could form a shorter and more compact line, in which my right would be more protected by natural obstacles.

I accordingly retired my command to a narrow and short ridge which shoots out nearly at right angles as a spur from the general ridge which is parallel to the Rossville and La Fayette road. The short and narrow ridge extends athwart the valley in a nearly east-and-west course. The abruptness of the declivity on either side of it almost gives to this ridge the quality of a natural parapet. Troops holding it could load and fire behind it out of reach of the enemy's fire, and then advance to the crest of it to deliver a plunging fire on the advancing foe. In addition there was a moral effect in its command over the ground south of it which inspired the courage of the troops holding it. Here I determined to make an obstinate and stubborn stand. When General Brannan's right was turned (by the opening of the gap in our lines by the movement of my division to support General Reynolds), he had been compelled to fall back to the general ridge inclosing, on the west, the valley in which the great battle was fought, which ridge, as already remarked, runs nearly parallel to the Rossville and La Fayette road. When I took position with Harker's brigade on the narrow ridge extending partially across the valley, General Brannan formed his command on my right and higher up on the main ridge, thus giving to our united lines something of the shape of an irregular crescent, with the concavity toward the enemy. This disposition gave us a converging fire on the attacking column. Colonel Buell formed his command with General Brannan's. When my arrangements in this position were concluded it was probably 1 p. m. or a little after.

The enemy did not leave us long in the quiet possession of our new position. Soon a most obstinate and determined attack was made, which was handsomely repulsed. Similar attacks were continued at intervals throughout the entire afternoon. To describe each one in detail would be unnecessary and only add useless prolixity to my report. But I deem it proper to signalize one of these attacks specially. It occurred about 4 o'clock, and lasted about 30 minutes. It was unquestionably the most terrific musketry duel I have ever witnessed. Harker's brigade was formed in two lines. The regiments were advanced to the crest of the ridge alternately, and delivered their fire by volley at the command, retiring a few paces behind it after firing to reload. The continued roar of the very fiercest musketry fire inspired a sentiment of grandeur in which the awful and the sublime were intermingled. But the enemy was repulsed in this fierce attack, and the crest of the ridge was still in our possession.

Finally the evening shades descended and spread the drapery of moonlight over the hardly contested field. The battle ceased, and my command still held the position it had taken about 1 o'clock, maintaining with glorious courage a most unequal contest in point of numbers. But our inferiority of strength did not appall my men. Their courage and steadfast resolution rose with the occasion. I do not believe that history affords an instance of a more splendid resistance than that made by Harker's brigade and a portion of Buell's brigade, from 1 p. m. on the 20th to nightfall. A part of the contest was witnessed by that able and distinguished commander, Major-General Thomas. I think it must have been near to 2 o'clock when he came to where my command was so hotly engaged. His presence was most welcome. The men saw him, felt they were battling under the eye of a great chieftain, and their courage and resolution received fresh inspiration from the consciousness.

At a most opportune hour in the afternoon, probably between 2 and 3 o'clock, Major-General Granger arrived on the field with two brigades of fresh troops of the division of General Steedman. They were brought into action on the right of General Brannan (who was on my right), and rapidly drove the enemy before them. This movement very considerably relieved the pressure on my front. The gallant bearing of General Granger during the whole of this most critical part of the contest was a strong re-enforcement. It affords me much pleasure to signalize the presence with my command for a length of time during the afternoon (present during the period of the hottest fighting) of another distinguished officer, Brigadier-General Garfield, chief of staff. After the disastrous rout on the right, General Garfield made his way back to the battle-field (showing thereby that the road was open to all who might choose to follow it to where duty called), and came to where my command was engaged.

The brigade which made so determined a resistance on the crest of the narrow ridge during all that long September afternoon had been commanded by General Garfield when he belonged to my division. The men remarked his presence with much satisfaction, and were delighted that he was a witness of the splendid fighting they were doing.

Early in the afternoon my command was joined by portions of two regiments belonging to Van Cleve's division, the Seventeenth Kentucky, Colonel Stout commanding, and the Forty-fourth Indiana, Lieutenant-Colonel Aldrich commanding. The fact that these parts of regiments, preserving the form of a regimental organization, did not leave the field after this disaster on the right, where so many other troops fled from the contest, is certainly most creditable to them.

The fact also affords very just ground for the inference that if a more determined effort had been made by the officers, many other regiments that left the field might have been kept on it. The remains of the two regiments most nobly and gallantly aided my command in repulsing the repeated attacks of the enemy. The Forty-fourth Indiana bore itself with special gallantry.

I should do injustice to my feelings were I to omit to record my testimony to the splendid resistance made on my right by General Brannan and his command. It was the *ne plus ultra* of defensive fighting.

About 7 p. m. I received an order from General Thomas to withdraw my command from the field and retire to Rossville. The order was executed without noise, without confusion, and without disaster. My command left the field, not because it was beaten, but in obedience to an order. With a fresh supply of ammunition it could have renewed the contest next morning. And here I can appropriately return my thanks to Major-General Granger for a timely supply of ammunition given me during the afternoon, when that in the cartridge-boxes and men's pockets was reduced to 2 or 3 rounds per man, and when the prospect of being reduced to the bayonet alone as a means of defense seemed inevitable. My own ammunition train had been carried off by the rout from the right. My command reached Rossville about 10 p. m., where it bivouacked for the night.

Early next morning, the 21st, in obedience to orders, I took a strong position on Missionary Ridge. Strong barricades against an infantry assault were at once made. During the day there was some light firing on my picket front, but nothing serious. The enemy was, however, evidently in considerable force in my front.

At 10 p. m. of the 21st my command, in obedience to orders, left its position on Missionary Ridge and withdrew to this place.

Early Tuesday morning, the 22d, it occupied its present position in the line of defenses, and has since been most constantly and actively engaged in strengthening them.

To the officers and men of my command I return my thanks for their gallant bearing, soldierly conduct, and steadfast courage, exhibited both in the contest of Saturday, the 19th, and Sunday, the 20th. Their conduct on both days deserves all praise, and I commend it to the consideration of the commanding general. There were undoubtedly instances of individual misconduct, which deserve reprehension, but as a whole the behavior of the command was most satisfactory.

Of the numerous killed and wounded I would gladly speak by name, but the list is too numerous. To do so would extend my report beyond all reasonable compass. I can only here express my sincere condolence with the relatives and friends of the gallant dead and wounded. The regiments and batteries in my command represented the States of Ohio, Indiana, Illinois, Michigan, and Kentucky. The citizens of these great and loyal States have much cause to be proud of their representatives in the late great conflict. They may safely trust their honor and the public weal to such representatives. For the special commendation by name of the more subordinate officers and men who distinguished themselves, I must refer the commanding general to the reports of my brigade commanders, Colonels Harker and Buell, with their accompanying documents, the sub-reports of regimental commanders.

Where so great a portion of my command behaved well, it is difficult to distinguish officers by name, and perhaps may be regarded as making an invidious distinction. Nevertheless, I consider it my duty, on account of their distinguished services, to commend to the notice of the commanding general Colonel Dunlap, commanding Third Kentucky; Colonel McIlvain, commanding Sixty-fourth Ohio; Colonel Opdycke, commanding One hundred and twenty-fifth Ohio, and Captain Bradley, commanding Sixth Ohio Battery.

I desire to commend Colonel Opdycke, especially, to the favorable consideration of the commanding general. The record of his regiment (a comparatively new one and never before in a general engagement) in the late battle will, I am sure, compare most favorably with that of the most veteran regiments engaged. The credit is mainly due to the colonel commanding. His untiring zeal and devoted attention to his regiment has brought forth fruit worthy of his efforts. I commend him to the commanding general as an officer capable and worthy of commanding a brigade.

Colonel Buell, commanding the First Brigade of my division, has exercised this command about three months. He bore himself with great gallantry on the field both on Saturday, the 19th, and Sunday, the 20th. With a little more experience he would make an excellent brigadier-general, and should receive the promotion.

In my report of the battle of Stone's River I especially signalized the services of Colonel Harker, commanding the Third Brigade of my division, and earnestly recommended him for promotion, both as a reward for his merits and as an act of simple justice. In the late campaign he has peculiarly distinguished himself. He made two of the most daring and brilliant reconnaissances during the campaign—reconnaissances almost without a parallel in the annals of warfare; and his personal gallantry on the battle-field, the skillful manner in which he handled his brigade, holding it so well together when so many other troops broke, and his general good conduct, are beyond all praise. To speak of his services in the language of what I conceive to be just encomium might be considered fulsome praise. I earnestly recommend him for immediate promotion to the rank of brigadier-general.

Returns herewith submitted show that I went into action on Saturday with an effective force of men and officers of 2,965. The return of casualties shows that my command lost in killed and wounded, absolutely known to be such, 844, and in killed, wounded, and missing, 1,035. Taking the number of the killed and wounded actually known, it will be found to be 28.80 per cent. of the effective force with which I went into action. But it is fair to presume as we retired from the field Sunday evening, that many of the 191 reported missing were either killed or wounded, and that their bodies fell into the hands of the enemy. Taking the number of the killed, wounded, and missing it will be found to be 34.90 per cent. of my whole command. These figures show an almost unparalleled loss. They attest the severity of the conflicts through which my command passed on the 19th and 20th. The record of its participation in the great battle of the Chickamauga is written in blood.

Before closing my report I deem it my duty to bring to the notice of the commanding general certain facts which fell under my observation during the progress of the conflict on the 20th. As I was moving along the valley with my command to the support of General Reynolds, in conformity with the order of the commanding general, I observed on my left (to the west of me) a force posted high up on the ridge. I inquired what force it was, and was informed it was a part (a brigade, perhaps) of General Negley's division. I was informed that General Negley was with this force in person. I remember distinctly seeing a battery on the hillside with the troops. At the time it was certainly out of the reach of any fire from the enemy. This was between 11 and 12 o'clock in the day. A little later in the day, perhaps half or three-fourths of an hour, when I became severely engaged, as already described, with the large hostile force that had pierced our lines and turned Brannan's right, compelling him to fall back, I looked for the force which I had seen posted on the ridge, and which, as already remarked, I had been informed was a part of General Negley's division; hoping, if I became severely pressed, it might re-enforce me, for I was resolved to check the enemy, if possible. But it had entirely disappeared. Whither it had gone I did not then know, but was informed later in the day it had retired toward Rossville, and this information, I believe, was correct. By whose order this force retired from the battle-field I do not know, but of one fact I am perfectly convinced, that there was no necessity for its retiring. It is impossible it could have been at all seriously pressed by the enemy at the time; in fact I think it extremely doubtful whether it was engaged at all.

Near sundown of the 20th I met General John Beatty not far from where I had fought the enemy all the afternoon. He was entirely alone when I met him and did not seem to have any special command. I at once came to the conclusion that he had not retired from the battle-field when the bulk of the division he is attached to did. At the moment I met him I was engaged halting some troops that were crossing the valley north and west of my position, and who appeared to have straggled away from the front on which General Thomas' command had fought all day. General Beatty desired to know where I wished these troops reformed. I pointed out a position to him and desired him to reform them, which he said he would do. I then rode back to my command. It is proper that I should remark that I did not see the corps commander from about 9.30 a. m. of Sunday, the 20th, to some time after sunrise of the 21st, when I met him at Rossville.

The officers of my staff performed their duties well in the late arduous campaign, as well on the march and in camp as on the battle-field. I deem it due to them to record their names in my official report, and to thank them individually for their valuable assistance and co-operation. Capt. M. P. Bestow, assistant adjutant-general; Lieut. J. L. Yaryan, Fifty-eighth Indiana, aide-de-camp; Lieut. George Shaffer, Ninety-third Ohio, aide-de-camp; Lieut. Col. T. R.

Palmer, Thirteenth Michigan, inspector-general; Surg. W. W. Blair, medical director; Capt. L. D. Myers, assistant quartermaster; Capt. James McDonald, commissary of subsistence; Capt. William McLoughlin, Thirteenth Michigan, topographical engineer; Capt. J. E. George, Fifteenth Indiana, assistant commissary of musters; Lieut. P. Haldeman, Third Kentucky, ordnance officer; Capt. M. Keiser, Sixty-fourth Ohio, provost-marshal up to the occupation of Chattanooga, when his leg was accidentally broken, since which time his duties have been well performed by Lieutenant Ehlers, of the same regiment; Capt. Cullen Bradley, Sixth Ohio Battery, who, in addition to commanding his own battery, ably performed the duties of chief of artillery.

It affords me much pleasure to mention in my official report the true courage and faithful devotion exhibited throughout the entire conflict by two members of my personal escort. Early in the conflict of Sunday my color-bearer was wounded. The colors were then taken by Sergt. Samuel W. Goodridge, Company A, One hundredth Illinois, who bore aloft my standard through the remainder of the day, remaining with me all the time. Private Robert Lemon, Company I, Fifty-eighth Indiana, a member of my escort, rode immediately in rear of me through the whole conflict of Sunday, the 20th. Whenever I called, this brave and devoted boy, a youth of not more than sixteen or seventeen years of age, responded.

I have the honor to forward herewith as accompaniments to my report: First, official report of Colonel Harker, commanding Third Brigade (with sub-reports of regimental commanders), marked A; second, official report of Colonel Buell, commanding First Brigade (with sub-reports of regimental commanders), marked B; third, return of effective force taken into action on the 19th September, 1863, marked C; fourth, return of casualties in the battles of the 19th and 20th, marked D; fifth, map showing the various positions of command in the battles of the 19th and 20th, marked E.

I cannot conclude my report of the participation of my command in the great battle of the Chickamauga—a battle in which the fate of the proud Army of the Cumberland hung trembling in the balance; in truth, a battle in whose result the great nation's life seemed involved—without returning thanks to Almighty Providence for His merciful deliverance vouchsafed to us from the hosts of our enemies. For His protection of myself through all the dangers of the bloody conflict I am humbly thankful.

I am, very respectfully, your obedient servant,

TH. J. WOOD,
Brigadier-General of Volunteers, Commanding.

Capt. P. P. Oldershaw,
Assistant Adjutant-General, Twenty-first Army Corps.

[Inclosure C.]

Effective force of the First Division, Twenty-first Army Corps, September 19, 1863.

Command.	Officers.	Enlisted men.	Total.
First Brigade...	107	1,214	1,321
Third Brigade	96	1,295	1,391
Total	203	2,509	2,712
Artillery:			
6th Ohio Battery	5	114	119
8th Indiana Battery	5	129	134
Total	10	243	253
Grand total..	213	2,752	2,965

TH. J. WOOD,
Brigadier-General, U. S. Volunteers.

CHATTANOOGA, TENN., *September 30, 1863.*

[Inclosure D.]

Report of Casualties in the First Division, Twenty-first Army Corps, Department of the Cumberland, in the engagement of September 19 and 20, 1863.

Command.	Commissioned officers.				Enlisted men.			
	Killed.	Wounded.	Missing.	Aggregate.	Killed.	Wounded.	Missing.	Aggregate.
First Brigade, Col. G. P. Buell commanding:								
100th Illinois Volunteers............................	.....	6	2	8	23	111	22	156
26th Ohio Volunteers...............................	4	6	2	12	23	134	43	200
13th Michigan Volunteers.........	2	6	2	10	11	61	24	96
58th Indiana Volunteers............................	2	5	1	8	14	96	24	134
Total.........	8	23	7	38	71	402	113	586
Third Brigade, Col. C. G. Harker commanding:								
125th Ohio Volunteers..............................	1	2	......	3	16	81	5	102
64th Ohio Volunteers...............................	1	2	......	3	5	41	16	62
65th Ohio Volunteers...............................	3	5	......	8	12	65	18	95
3d Kentucky Volunteers...........................	1	8	......	9	12	70	22	104
Total...	6	17	......	23	45	257	61	363
Artillery :								
6th Ohio Battery *a*..................................	......	1	......	1	......	5	3	8
8th Indiana Battery *b*..............................	......	....	......	....	1	8	7	16
Total...	......	1	......	1	1	13	10	24

a Two horses lost, 2 caissons, and 1 battery wagon.
b Fifty-six horses lost, 6 guns, 5 caissons, and 9 limbers.

RECAPITULATION.

	Killed.	Wounded.	Missing.	Aggregate.	Killed.	Wounded.	Missing.	Aggregate.
First Brigade	8	23	7	38	71	402	113	586
Third Brigade	6	17	......	23	45	257	61	363
Artillery	......	1	......	1	1	13	10	24
Aggregate	14	41	7	62	117	672	184	973

Total killed, 131 ; total wounded, 713 ; total missing, 191.   Grand total, 1,035.*

HDQRS. FIRST DIVISION, TWENTY-FIRST ARMY CORPS,
Chattanooga, Tenn., September 29, 1863.

TH. J. WOOD,
Brigadier-General, U. S. Volunteers, Commanding.

Capt. M. P. BESTOW, *Assistant Adjutant-General.*

* See revised statement, p. 176.

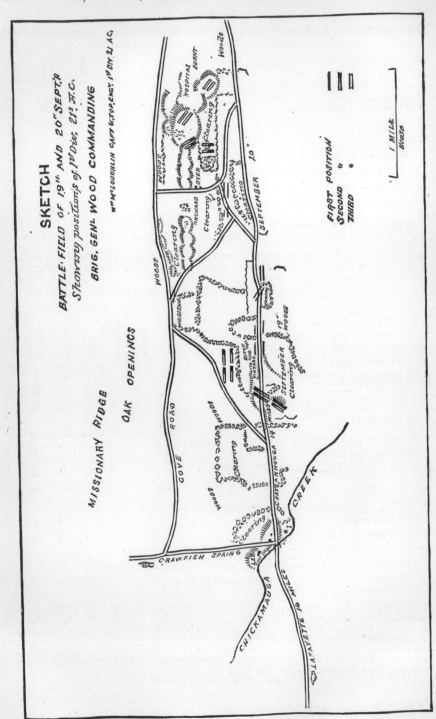

SKETCH

BATTLE-FIELD OF 19ᵗʰ AND 20ᵗʰ SEPTᴿ

Showing positions of 1ˢᵗ Div, 21ˢᵗ A.C.

BRIG. GENˡ WOOD COMMANDING

Wᵐ McLOUGHLIN CAPT 8ᵗ TOP. ENGᴿ 1ˢᵗ DIV. 2ˡ A.C.

MISSIONARY RIDGE

OAK OPENINGS

FIRST POSITION
SECOND
THIRD

1 MILE
Scale

ADDENDA.

Semi-weekly report of effective force of the First Division, Twenty-first Army Corps, Brig. Gen. Thomas J. Wood commanding.

Command.	Headquarters.			Infantry.		
	Commissioned officers.	Enlisted men.	Total.	Commissioned officers.	Enlisted men.	Total.
First Division, Brigadier-General Wood..........	12	66	78			
First Brigade, Col. G. P. Buell	10	47	57	99	1,225	1,324
Second Brigade, Brig. Gen. G. D. Wagner	8	28	36	107	1,334	1,441
Third Brigade, Col. C. G. Harker	7	41	48	89	1,228	1,317
Artillery Battalion						
Total............................	37	182	219	295	3,787	4,082

Command.	Artillery.			Total.			Number of horses.	Number of guns.
	Commissioned officers.	Enlisted men.	Total.	Commissioned officers.	Enlisted men.	Aggregate.		
First Division, Brigadier-General Wood..........				12	66	78		
First Brigade, Col. G. P. Buell				109	1,272	1,381		
Second Brigade, Brig. Gen. G. D. Wagner.........				115	1,362	1,477		
Third Brigade, Col. C. G. Harker				96	1,269	1,365		
Artillery Battalion	12	309	321	12	309	321	301	18
Total..............................	12	309	321	344	4,278	4,622	301	18

MONDAY, *September* 14, 1863.

TH. J. WOOD,
Brigadier-General of Volunteers, Commanding.

Capt. M. P. BESTOW,
Assistant Adjutant-General.

HDQRS. THIRD DIVISION, FOURTH ARMY CORPS,
Chattanooga, October 21, 1863.

Brig. Gen. LORENZO THOMAS,
Adjutant-General, U. S. Army:

GENERAL: The following extract is taken from the official report of Maj. Gen. W. S. Rosecrans, late commander of the Army of the Cumberland, of the battle of the Chickamauga:

General Wood, overlooking the order to "close up on" General Reynolds, supposed he was to support him by withdrawing from the line and passing to the rear of General Brannan, who, it appears, was not out of line, but *en échelon* and slightly in rear of Reynolds' right. By this unfortunate mistake a gap was opened in the line of battle, of which the enemy took instant advantage, and, striking Davis in flank and rear, as well as in front, threw his whole division into confusion.

In the foregoing extract there is the positive statement:

First. That I overlooked the direction to "close up on" General Reynolds.

Second. There is an entire omission to state that I was positively ordered by the commanding general, in a written order, to support General Reynolds, leaving it to be inferred that the effort to support General Reynolds was a movement made on my own supposition of necessity.

Third. There is an obvious attempt to produce the impression that General Reynolds might have been "closed up on" by some other movement than by withdrawing from the line.

Fourth. Characterizing the withdrawing from the line to close up on and support General Reynolds as an unfortunate mistake, the plain intention and object of the entire paragraph are to shield General Rosecrans from the responsibility of the unfortunate mistake and its still more unfortunate consequences, and to fix the responsibility on myself.

The following statement of facts, with accompanying copy of order from General Rosecrans, will show conclusively the incorrectness of statement of the extract, as also establish the injustice of its object and intention:

At 10 o'clock and 45 minutes, on Sunday morning, the 20th of September, ultimo, the following was the position of my division in line of battle: The left of my division was closed up on and rested firmly against the right of General Brannan's division, which in turn had its left fully closed up on and resting on the right of General Reynolds' division (General Brannan assures me that his division was in line with General Reynolds' division, with his left closed on and resting firmly on General Reynolds' right); on the right of my division was General Davis' division.

At the time my division was not engaged at all—not a shot was being fired on its front. Half an hour previously there had been some skirmishing, but it had subsided. There was, however, satisfactory reason for believing that the enemy was in considerable force in my front; hence I was keenly on the alert. But while the enemy was quiescent on my front he was not so elsewhere. The roar of artillery and the rattle of musketry borne to us from the left, told unmistakably that our comrades in that direction were heavily engaged with the foe.

A few minutes, perhaps five, before 11 a. m. on the 20th, I received the following order:

HEADQUARTERS DEPARTMENT OF THE CUMBERLAND,
September 20—10.45.

Brigadier-General WOOD,
    Commanding Division, &c.:

The general commanding directs that you close up on Reynolds as fast as possible, and support him.

Respectfully, &c.,

FRANK S. BOND,
Major, and Aide-de-Camp.

This order was addressed as follows: "10.45 a. m. Gallop. Brigadier-General Wood, commanding division."

At the time it was received there was a division (Brannan's) in line between my division and General Reynolds. I was immediately in rear of the center of my division at the time. I immediately dispatched my staff officers to the brigade commanders, directing them to move by the left, passing in the rear of General Brannan's division, to close up on and support General Reynolds, and as the order was peremptory I directed the movement to be made at the double-quick. The movement was commenced immediately.

As there was a division between General Reynolds and mine, it was absolutely physically impossible for me to obey the order by any other movement than the one I made. How was I to close up on General Reynolds and support him (as my division was then situated in reference to General Reynolds' division) but by withdrawing from the line and passing in rear of General Brannan's division ? I maintain that I have clearly established—

First. That I did not overlook the direction to close up on General Reynolds, but moved to do so as promptly as possible after I had received the order to do it.

Second. That I was ordered to support General Reynolds, and that the movement was not made on any supposition of mine of the existence of a necessity therefor.

Third. That I moved to close up on General Reynolds to support him in the only way it was possible to do so ; namely, by withdrawing my division from the line and passing to the rear of General Brannan.

Fourth. That however unfortunate the mistake was that opened a gap in the line, the responsibility for the gap rests on General Rosecrans, who gave the order which produced it, and not on the subordinate who executed it.

I respectfully request that this communication be put on file in the War Department, in conjunction with General Rosecrans' report, and that in case the Department should have the report published, this communication be published with it. I respectfully submit that this course is due to myself, due to this army, due to the country, and to the truth of history.*

Very respectfully, your obedient servant,
TH. J. WOOD,
Brigadier-General of Volunteers.

—

LOUISVILLE, KY.,
February 6, 1864.

Brig. Gen. LORENZO THOMAS,
Adjutant-General, U. S. Army :

SIR : I am informed that General Rosecrans has, under date of the 12th [13th] January, filed an answer to my comments of the 23d [21st] October last on his official report of the battle of the Chickamauga. I am further informed that this communication of General Rosecrans does me great injustice. I have the honor, therefore, most respectfully to request to be furnished with a copy of it. As I will leave here in the morning to rejoin my command in the front, I ask you will address your answer to me as commanding Third Division, Fourth Army Corps, Army of the Cumberland.

I am, very respectfully, your obedient servant,
TH. J. WOOD,
Brigadier-General of Volunteers.

P. S.—An early favor is respectfully requested.

---

*See Rosecrans to L. Thomas, pp. 101, 102 ; Rosecrans to Townsend, p. 104, and Townsend to Rosecrans, p. 105.

WAR DEPARTMENT, ADJUTANT-GENERAL'S OFFICE,
Washington, March 1, 1864.

Brig. Gen. T. J. WOOD, *U. S. Volunteers:*

GENERAL: I have the honor to acknowledge the receipt of your communication, and to inclose an official copy of the letter of General Rosecrans as requested.

I am, general, very respectfully, your obedient servant,

JAS. A. HARDIE,
Assistant Adjutant-General.

(Copy inclosed of General Rosecrans' letter addressed to the Adjutant-General, dated Cincinnati, Ohio, January 13, 1864.*)

—

HDQRS. THIRD DIV., FOURTH ARMY CORPS,
ADJUTANT-GENERAL'S OFFICE,
In the Field in East Tennessee, March 11, 1864.

[Col. JAMES A. HARDIE,
Assistant Adjutant-General:]

SIR: I am just in receipt to-day of your communication of the 29th ultimo [1st instant], inclosing me a copy of General Rosecrans' communication of the 13th of January last, in reply to my comments (under date of the 23d [21st] October last) on his official report of the battle of the Chickamauga.

I made my application for a copy of this communication on the 7th [6th] of last month, and I regret sincerely your letter inclosing the copy has not reached me earlier. Had it done so it would have found me possessed of the leisure to reply irrefutably to General Rosecrans' communication; now it finds me in an active campaign without leisure and with all my time and energies absorbed in looking after the enemies of the country, the Union, constitutional liberty, and free government for all mankind. My answer, therefore, to General Rosecrans' misstatement of facts and fallacies of conclusion must be delayed necessarily till the termination of the present active operations.

When these are terminated I pledge myself to make an answer which will show that General Rosecrans' communication of the 13th January last is replete with misrepresentations of facts and errors of military principles.

I request that this communication be laid before the Commander-in-Chief and the honorable Secretary of War.

I am, sir, very respectfully, your obedient servant,

TH. J. WOOD,
Brigadier-General of Volunteers.

———

No. 137.

Report of Capt. Cullen Bradley, Sixth Ohio Battery, Chief of Artillery.

HDQRS. ARTY. BATTALION, 1ST DIV., 21ST ARMY CORPS,
Camp at Chattanooga, Tenn., September 26, 1863.

SIR: I have the honor to make the following official report of the operations of the artillery belonging to the First Division, Twenty-

———

*See p. 102.

first Army Corps, during the engagements of the 19th, 20th, and 21st days of September, 1863, on the Chickamauga River, Ga., the batteries engaged being the Sixth Ohio Independent Light Battery, commanded by myself, and the Eighth Indiana Light Battery, commanded by Capt. George Estep:

The batteries of this division have been attached to and acted with the different brigades for the last sixteen months—the Eighth Indiana Battery, Capt. George Estep, attached to the First Brigade, Colonel Buell commanding, and the Sixth Ohio Battery with the Third Brigade, Col. Charles G. Harker commanding. The other battery of this division being attached to the Second Brigade, General Wagner commanding, was stationed at Chattanooga, Tenn., and did not participate in the engagement before mentioned.

It will thus be seen that I was only chief of artillery in name and did not have actual command of any battery but my own.

On the 19th of September we were at Lee and Gordon's Mills. At daylight firing was heard on our extreme left (the army), and as the day advanced the firing became heavier, and seemed to be working around to the right flank. About 3.30 p. m. received orders from Colonel Harker to get ready to move at once to re-enforce our right (Colonel Wilder's men, I believe). Our brigade moved in splendid style, at a double-quick, about 1½ miles, when we arrived on the ground where several batteries were firing into the woods some 300 or 400 yards obliquely to the right and front. I received orders from Colonel Harker at this place to remain in the road until further orders. I halted the battery as directed, and rode some distance after the brigade to observe the direction as well as the nature of the ground on which our brigade was moving.

After the brigade entered the woods in front, I lost sight of them until they fell back. As soon as they had disappeared I rode up to the batteries on the right that were firing, to see what was up in that direction, but could see nothing in the shape of an enemy. I returned to the battery, which was still standing in column of pieces in the road. I had hardly time to reach my battery before the enemy came pouring out of the woods in every direction, and at the same point where my brigade had entered the woods not more than ten minutes previous. I had to act at once, as there was no time to think. I ordered the leading section to the left of the road, and then placed the others on the best ground, but we could not open on the enemy here without inflicting as much damage on our own men as on the enemy, as they all seemed to be mixed up in one mass. Lieuts. James P. McElroy and George W. Smetts did splendid execution on the enemy here, using case and canister. Lieutenant Ayres had moved his section into the edge of the woods by direction of Major Mendenhall, and was now opening on the enemy with telling effect. I ordered Lieutenant McElroy, with his section, to the left of Lieutenant Ayres, where he again opened the section on the advancing enemy.

During this time Lieutenant Smetts had been firing, retiring with prolonges fixed, using canister out of the 12-pounder Napoleons with splendid effect, the enemy still advancing, but not in very good order. I should think that they came within 50 yards of our battery before they gave way. They retired (the enemy) in anything but good order, but not discouraged, for in less than ten minutes they reappeared in the field again and rushed forward, but our battery, in conjunction with others and some of Colonel Wilder's men that were formed behind a fence, gave them such a warm reception that they retired in the greatest confusion, and did not make their appearance again that evening. During this day's engagement there were 209 rounds of ammunition used; of this some 20 rounds were canister.

The casualties were very slight considering the heavy infantry fire that we were under. There was 1 killed (Private Weeks). I have every reason to believe this man to be dead, but cannot say positively. Lieut. George W. Smetts, severely wounded, Privates Welker, Tryon, Point, and Sharnel wounded. Sharnel has served with the battery since he was wounded. Only 2 horses slightly wounded. All did their duty well and nobly, with but two exceptions, Privates James G. Earle and William Barr; both these men ran and abandoned their guns and comrades in the most cowardly manner.

The remainder of the night we passed in taking care of our horses and getting ready for the next day. About 2 a. m. on the 20th September I received orders to get ready to move at once. We moved out, and I should say that we marched about 2½ miles and encamped, and the men were permitted to get some coffee. At 8 a. m. we moved forward and took position in rear of General Negley's division; did not remain long before I received orders to move up with the brigade on the main line of battle. Our skirmish line was thrown forward and soon felt the enemy in force. They (the enemy) opened on us with one piece of artillery. Colonel Harker ordered up one section of my battery, which opened on the enemy. I then ordered up the center section, and it opened on the woods in which the enemy were totally concealed from view. I fired some 32 rounds here, and I have every reason to believe that they did good execution, as they were fired very low with 2½-second fuses. Both case and shell were used.

At this time the firing was very heavy on our left, for the purpose, as I learned, of supporting General Negley. I limbered to the rear, and received orders from Colonel Harker to move in rear and opposite the center of the brigade. I took the position designated and was moving at about quick time. We had not moved more than a half or three-quarters of a mile when there occurred a perfect stampede—guns, caissons, fragments of regiments all came out in one disordered mass, and the enemy closely pursuing. I was entirely cut off from my brigade. I flanked to the left, which threw me face to the rear. I did this to gain an elevated position so that I could play on the enemy should I get an opportunity. My caissons I had placed in charge of my first sergeant, George W. James, and had instructed him to keep well in the rear, so as to supply ammunition should it be necessary. When the enemy turned our right flank they were on him before he had time to get out of the way; he was forced to leave two of the caissons and battery wagon, but saved the horses. He would not have abandoned them at all but in the general confusion they got foul with other carriages, and I give him great credit for saving as many of my caissons as he did, as whole batteries were lost where he only lost two caissons and battery wagon.

After being cut off from my brigade and seeing no prospect of rejoining it, I reported to General Negley, who told me to place my guns in battery on the crest of the hill, which I did, and remained there until all had fallen back entirely to the rear. I saw there was no use of remaining longer without support or any prospect of a stand being made, and I followed the troops and other batteries on over to the main road. I there found Colonel Palmer, who had been directed to take ammunition to the division. He started back on the road, and I followed him, determined to rejoin my brigade and division if possible, but we had proceeded but a short distance when the colonel discovered that the enemy were on the road in force. We then turned back, and I again reported to General Negley for orders, and he directed me to follow his men into Rossville. I also informed him that our division ammunition train was there, and he directed that it should follow his troops also. We followed the troops in and encamped below Rossville for the night.

On the morning of the 21st September I reported to Colonel Harker for orders and rejoined the brigade. We then moved on the Ringgold and Chattanooga road, and took position on the left of the road and on the top of Missionary Ridge. At about 2 p. m. the enemy advanced and opened on us with one section; we replied, expending 127 rounds ammunition. I cannot even conjecture what amount of damage we did the enemy, if any. At 7.45 p. m. I received orders to move down the hill toward Chattanooga, and at 11 p. m. was joined by the brigade and moved into Chattanooga, arriving about 3.45 a. m., September 22.

To the officers and men of the battery great credit is due for their manly bearing and coolness under fire; where all did their duty so well it would be unjust to particularize.

Recapitulation.—The effective strength on the 19th day of September was:

Commissioned officers, 4; enlisted men, 107. Aggregate, 111.

Killed: Enlisted men, 1.

Wounded: Commissioned officers, 1; enlisted men, 5. Aggregate, 6.

Run off, enlisted men, 2. Horses wounded, 2. Total rounds of ammunition expended, 336.

Herewith inclosed please find Capt. George Estep's report.

I am, major, very respectfully, your obedient servant, &c.,

CULLEN BRADLEY,

Capt. 6th Ohio Lt. Batty., and Chief of Arty., 1st Div., 21st A. C.

Maj. John Mendenhall,
    Chief of Artillery, Twenty-first Army Corps.

ADDENDA.

Itinerary of the Artillery Battalion, First Division, Twenty-first Army Corps, commanded by Capt. Cullen Bradley, Sixth Ohio Battery, for September, 1863. [*]

September 1.—At 6 a. m. the artillery of the First Division, Twenty-first Army Corps, left camp, near Therman, East Tenn., marched 17 miles, and encamped near Jasper, Tenn., at 4 p. m.

September 3.—Marched at 6 a. m., 9 miles, crossed the Tennessee River, and encamped at Shellmound, on the Chattanooga and Nashville Railroad.

September 5.—At 3 p. m. left camp, marched 9 miles, and encamped at 8 p. m. on the River road to Chattanooga.

September 6.—At 8 a. m. marched 6 miles to Trenton Junction, on the Chattanooga and Nashville Railroad.

September 9.—Marched 9 miles, and encamped at Chattanooga, Tenn., at 2 p. m.

---

[*] From return for September.

September 10.—Moved on the Chattanooga and Ringgold road 9 miles, and encamped at 5 p. m.

September 12.—Moved to Lee and Gordon's Mills, Ga., on the Chickamauga River, at the crossing of the Chattanooga and La Fayette road.

September 19.—Moved 1½ miles toward Chattanooga, Tenn. Engaged the enemy from 4 p. m. until 6.30 p. m.

September 20.—At 2 a. m. moved 2 miles in the direction of Chattanooga. Engaged the enemy two hours, from 10 a. m. until 12 m. Moved 7 miles, to Rossville, and encamped at 7.30 p. m.

September 22.—At 1 a. m. moved 3½ miles, to Chattanooga, Tenn.

No. 138.

Reports of Col. George P. Buell, Fifty-eighth Indiana Infantry, commanding First Brigade.

TRACY CITY, *August* 24, 1863.

SIR: About 11 a. m. of the 22d instant I received orders to take a force of about 400 men and march to the Tennessee River, for the purpose of capturing the steamer Paint Rock, there disabled, and lying partially guarded somewhere between Suck and Skillet, on said river. Immediately selected 100 men from each regiment, Twenty-sixth Ohio, Fifty-eighth Indiana, One hundredth Illinois, and Thirteenth Michigan, well officered and equipped with three days' rations. In accordance with my request Lieutenant-Colonel Embree accompanied me as second in command, accompanied by 8 or 10 mountain scouts. We started on the expedition. When 3 miles from camp we received orders to halt a short time, news having been received of the probable approach in force of the enemy. We again received orders to advance at 5 p. m. We marched about 10 miles down the Sequatchie Valley road to Keller's Mill, thence 8 miles on a very indistinct trail over Walden's Ridge to Bob White's house, on the road known as Haley's road, leading from Jasper to Chattanooga, which point we reached at 3 a. m. of the 23d.

We were then within 2 miles of shore. The steamboat had been disabled. We had intended capturing it before daylight of this morning, but the enemy had within the preceding twenty-four hours secured and passed the vessel above the Suck and out of our reach.

During the morning of the 22d the enemy crossed to the north side of the river four companies of cavalry at Kelley's Ferry, but recalled them and all their pickets in the afternoon of the same day.

There were this morning about 100 men on the south side of river guarding Kelley's Ferry. It could be surprised and taken without the loss of a half dozen men. The river from the point up to the Suck is from 400 to 500 yards wide. A scout, who came from the south side of the river, reported that the enemy were being re-enforced, and that he was intrenching Lookout Mountain.

Having obtained what information we could, we retraced our steps and reached camp at 8 o'clock this evening. Too much praise cannot be given to the officers and men of my command for their prompt obedience to orders, their endurance of so fatiguing a march, and their energy and zeal in the undertaking.

GEO. P. BUELL,
Colonel Fifty-eighth Indiana Infantry.

Brig. Gen. JAMES A. GARFIELD.

HDQRS. FIRST BRIG., FIRST DIV., 21ST ARMY CORPS,
September 27, 1863.

SIR : I have the honor to submit the following report of the movements of this brigade since crossing the Tennessee River :

My command commenced crossing the Tennessee River about 11 p. m. of the 2d instant. The crossing was completed and the brigade in camp near Shellmound, on the south side of the river, by 6 a. m. of the 3d instant.

We remained in this camp until 2 p. m. of the 5th instant, when, by order of General Wood, we took up the line of march toward Chattanooga, my command following Colonel Harker's brigade till dark, when we encamped for the night at Whiteside's Junction, on the railroad leading from Nashville to Chattanooga. We again marched, on the morning of the 6th instant (with slight skirmishing in front), till we reached the junction of the Nashville, Chattanooga and Trenton Railroad. At this point we took position in line of battle at about 4 p. m. Colonel Harker formed on the right and my brigade on the left. On minute examination of this position we found that we were liable to be flanked, and knowing that there was no support near, we fell back about 2 miles, early in the night, to a point we could far easier defend. During the next day (7th instant) we remained in this camp, while Colonel Harker, commanding Third Brigade, made a reconnaissance to the front, finding the enemy in strong force on the point of Lookout Mountain nearest the river.

My brigade remained in this camp until the morning of the 9th instant, when, by order of General Wood, it led the advance on Chattanooga. At the point of Lookout Mountain we met a small picket force of the enemy which we soon dislodged, and marching on entering Chattanooga about 12 o'clock of the 9th instant. My brigade was the first that entered the city.

About 9 a. m. of the 10th instant I received orders from General Wood to march my command out on the Rossville road, following Colonel Harker's brigade, which I did, and encamped the same night on the east side of the Chickamauga, on the road leading from Rossville to Ringgold. Soon after we had encamped on the night of the 10th a dash was made on my right flank by a small squad of cavalry, but to no avail. My command was immediately called to arms, skirmishers deployed, and the enemy dispersed. Just here 2 stragglers of my command were captured.

Early on the morning of the 11th instant Colonel Harker's brigade was detached for the purpose of making a reconnaissance on the La Fayette road. In order that our small force (one brigade) might not be surprised, a commanding position was chosen about 1 mile to the front where all preparations were made for defense under General Wood's immediate supervision. Here my command remained until about 4 p. m., when, by order of General Wood, we took up the line of march for the La Fayette road, by way of Reed's Bridge, a distance of 8 miles, thence south on this road to Gordon's Mills, on the Chickamauga River, where we rejoined Colonel Harker's command, my brigade taking position on the right. It was now generally conceded that the enemy were in strong force in our front and that we should probably fight a battle somewhere in the vicinity of Gordon's Mills, hence all preparations were made for a strong defense at this point to prevent the enemy's getting north of the Chickamauga. We remained quietly here without anything of importance transpiring until the morning of the 18th instant, when the enemy was seen approaching us in heavy force on the La Fayette road, and when within 1 mile filing off as if to pass round our left.

Although various demonstrations were made by the enemy in my front, lines of battle formed, &c., there was nothing more than slight skirmishing and some little cannonading during the afternoon of the 18th instant.

The 19th day of September opened with a severe battle on our left, which continued throughout the day. About 2.30 p. m. of this day (19th instant) I received orders to move my command at the double-quick up the La Fayette road toward the scene of action. After marching about 2 miles I was directed by General Wood to form my command fronting to the east and parallel to the road. My brigade was formed in two lines, the front line east of and the rear line on the west side of the road, with a distance of about 75 yards between the two; the Eighth Indiana Battery in the front line, with the Twenty-sixth Ohio, commanded by Lieutenant-Colonel Young, on the left, and the One hundredth Illinois Regiment, Col. F. A. Bartleson, on the right. The rear line was composed of the Fifty-eighth Indiana, Lieutenant-Colonel Embree, on the right, and the Thirteenth Michigan, Colonel Culver, on the left.

With my command formed thus, the Twenty-sixth Ohio and a part of the battery were in heavy timber, while the other regiments and remainder of the battery were in open ground. Just in front of the One hundredth Illinois was another battery, already engaged with the enemy.

While my troops were being formed the enemy's balls were whistling about our ears, and the battle, raging most fiercely, seemed approaching nearer, although I had been informed several times by staff officers that we were driving the enemy, and that our force was only needed to finish the rout. I was not yet informed as to the positions of troops around me, whether we had troops in front and on my left flank. The formation of my command was not yet complete, when everything on my immediate front and left gave way, and hundreds of our own men ran through my ranks crying, "Fall back! Fall back!" as they themselves were in shameful rout toward the rear. My command was cautioned particularly to lie down, hold fire, and countercharge the enemy. Immediately following the mass of panic-stricken men of our own army and parts of two batteries (all of which passed through and over my men) came the enemy in heavy force on my front and left flank. Knowing my front regiments could not long withstand such a shock, I ordered a charge bayonet with my rear regiments.

The attempt was manfully made. They met hundreds of our own men on the fence in front of them; they met artillery and caissons, besides the enemy's fire, so that it was impossible to keep any kind of a line, but notwithstanding such obstructions, they gained some distance to the front. At this period my brave men, both front and rear lines, strove desperately to hold their ground. The Twenty-sixth Ohio and One hundredth Illinois, being in front, had already lost nearly one-half. Just here the slaughter was completed; the Fifty-eighth Indiana and Thirteenth Michigan men fell by scores. Colonel Culver, Thirteenth Michigan, stunned by a shell; Lieutenant-Colonel Waterman, of the One hundredth Illinois, fell wounded; Captain Ewing, acting major of the Twenty-sixth Ohio, fell wounded; Captains Davis and Bruce, Fifty-eighth Indiana, Cap-

tains Fox and Hosmer, Thirteenth Michigan, Captain Ross, Lieutenants Burbridge and Williams, Twenty-sixth Ohio, all fell pierced
with bullets. Overpowered on both front and flank, my men faltered and finally fell back about 200 yards across a field in our rear.
Here my men were rallied, and again they charged forward, retook
the ground, and also three pieces of artillery that were lost in the
first part of the action. Again the enemy came forward like an
avalanche, and forced my men back a short distance ; again my men
rallied, and retook the same position they had formerly held. The
enemy came forward a third time, but were effectually repulsed,
and the sun went down with my command holding the field a short
distance in advance of its original position. My command had
been engaged since about 3 o'clock and had lost most heavily. During the whole of these three hours' fighting, the Eighth Indiana Battery, Captain Estep, had done fine execution, and had suffered
severely, the captain himself slightly wounded in the neck and arm.
The wounded of my brigade were all gotten off the field by 10 p. m.
Over 100 wounded men were taken out of a ditch in the field where
we had fought.

The whole of this afternoon's fighting was done under the eye of
General Wood, who was ever present.

When night finally closed the scene the position of my command
was as follows: The Fifty-eighth Indiana on the left and the Twenty-
sixth Ohio on the right in the front line; the Thirteenth Michigan
and One hundredth Illinois were placed in reserve, and the Eighth
Indiana Battery still farther in reserve, undergoing repairs. The
troops on my immediate left and rear were, I believe, of General
Sheridan's command. Colonel Barnes' brigade of General Van
Cleve's division was on my immediate right.

The men of my brigade lay on their arms in this position until
about 3 a. m. of the 20th instant, when, by order of General Wood,
my brigade was moved (leaving the skirmishers to follow at daylight) to the left about 1½ miles. Here we were permitted to make
coffee and draw rations.

At about 9 a. m. of the 20th instant, by order of General Wood,
my brigade was moved forward and put in position behind some
temporary works of rails and logs, my brigade being on the immediate right of Colonel Harker. About this time I was informed
that General McCook's corps would join me on my right. My brigade at this time was formed in two lines of battle with skirmishers
about 75 yards to the front. I soon learned that the enemy was massing immediately in my front and perhaps on my right. Staff officers
were immediately sent off to my right with a heavy line of skirmishers, for the purpose of learning if there were yet any of our
own troops on my immediate right. Soon the report came there
were none as yet. My two reserve regiments, Fifty-eighth Indiana
and Thirteenth Michigan, were immediately deployed on my right
with a heavy line of skirmishers, so that my right might not be
turned without timely knowledge of the fact. My battery (Eighth
Indiana) was placed so as to sweep the crest of a low ridge in my
front. Very soon after this, perhaps 10.30 a. m., one brigade of
General Davis' division reported to join me on the right. I immediately drew in two regiments from the right, so that my brigade
would have but two regimental fronts, allowing General Davis' left
to rest against the right of the Twenty-sixth Ohio, which was my
right front battalion, the One hundredth Illinois the left front, the

Fifty-eighth Indiana left rear, and Thirteenth Michigan right rear battalions.

At this time the enemy was making bold demonstrations in my front, so much so that whenever one of my skirmishers moved or rose to his feet he was shot at. Now that my right flank was protected I felt confident that we could hold our position.

About this time I received notice from a staff officer that the One hundredth Illinois, Col. F. A. Bartleson, had charged to the front, and that the colonel asked to be supported. Thinking perhaps a general charge had been ordered by General Wood and that the left of my brigade was moving to the front with Colonel Harker's, and that the officer bearing me the order might have fallen (I then being at the extreme right of my brigade), I ordered the Twenty-sixth Ohio to charge as far as the crest of the low ridge or bench in front, but to go no farther without further orders until I could investigate the cause of the One hundredth Illinois being in front of the position assigned it by me. The Twenty-sixth Ohio had hardly gotten to the front as ordered when the One hundredth Illinois came back without its colonel and resumed its former position. Colonel Bartleson leading his regiment had run into a masked battery and heavy line of the enemy, and is supposed was himself wounded and captured. In him we lost a most gallant and efficient officer and gentleman; his brigade and regiment will ever mourn his loss.

About half past 11 a. m. of the 20th instant I received orders to move my brigade by the left flank at the double-quick, following Colonel Harker's brigade, for the purpose of supporting some portion of the line to our left. The orders for this purpose were immediately issued; before moving the brigade, however, orders were issued for the skirmishers to remain and hold their position until relieved by the command still on my right, and to be certain that this would be done without a doubt I sent two staff officers to attend personally to it. Orders were also issued to my battery commander, Captain Estep, to move his battery around on my left flank, which would be in my rear when facing the enemy. I was fearful of making the movement, with the enemy not over 200 yards distant, closely watching every maneuver.

Two brigades on my left had already moved off, and of course my command must move by the gap left by them. Having my line of skirmishers secure, and, as I thought, my battery safe, the movement was commenced, myself leading the direction.

We had scarcely moved one brigade front when the shock came like an avalanche on my right flank. The attack seemed to have been simultaneous throughout the enemy's lines, for the entire right and part of the center gave way before the overpowering numbers of the foe. My own little brigade seemed as if it were swept from the field. Captain Estep with all speed moved his battery about 400 yards to the rear, on the crest of a hill, where he opened on the enemy with great effect. The greater portion of my brigade was cut off from me and driven to the rear. My staff, who were executing orders at this time, were also cut off ; the orderly carrying my headquarters flag, who was in the rear at the time, was captured. That portion of my command that was near me, the Fifty-eighth Indiana and some stragglers of other regiments that were rallied, remained on the field, and while we were still in front of and to the left of the battery the enemy came around my right flank and shot down 35 horses of my battery, thus capturing the same. I retreated with a portion of my command to the left oblique, fighting at the crest of every hill for a distance of at least three-fourths of a mile. At one point we advanced again from one hill to the next in front, and fought the left flank of a long line of battle (all of which was in full view) until we were almost surrounded and flanked on our right. Just here Lieutenant-Colonel Embree was cut off from his command and very nearly captured, which left Major Moore, of the Fifty-eighth Indiana, the next in rank to myself.

About this time I discovered General Wood with Colonel Harker's brigade, several hundred yards to my left, also on the retreat. I continued to retreat with the remnant of my brigade until we came up to the right flank of General Brannan's division, which was in position on the top of a high hill. Here I reported to General Brannan, and we remained in this position until the sun went down. The remainder of my brigade, being unable to find me, went to the rear with thousands of others who had not even fired a gun, nor had their lines been broken. If my battery commander had done as I saw several other batteries doing, he would have saved his battery, but as long as there was any chance to fight he fought, and then it was too late to start for Rossville.

During the afternoon of the 20th instant my command was on the right of General Brannan, while Colonel Harker's was on his left. About 4.30 o'clock our ammunition entirely failed ; we had already taken all from the dead and wounded around us. Just at this time Colonel Stout, of the Seventeenth Kentucky, came up with about 100 men, having 60 rounds each. He gladly relieved my men, while they remained in his rear with fixed bayonets to help hold the hill; this, as a last resort. Soon after 4 p. m., as the enemy was again coming round our right flank, General Steedman's division, of General Granger's corps, came up on the right. Happy were we to see them. They held the right till night. As night closed the scene, the whole rebel army, then almost surrounding us, gave one long and exultant cheer. Our few thousand exhausted men, who, without ammunition, had so long struggled and held the trying position, being by no means disheartened, answered their cheers with bold and defiant shouts. Soon after dark I was ordered to follow Colonel Harker's command with mine. We marched to the rear, and reached Rossville about 11 p. m.

Early in the morning of the 21st instant my brigade took position on Missionary Ridge on the left of Colonel Harker's brigade. The Seventeenth Kentucky reported to me, and occupied my extreme left. We remained in this position till 10 p. m., when we retreated and took up our present position around the city. We are intrenched and can hold our works forever.

I take pleasure in commending to their superiors Colonel Culver, Thirteenth Michigan ; Lieutenant-Colonel Young, Twenty-sixth Ohio; Lieutenant-Colonel Embree, Fifty-eighth Indiana; Lieutenant-Colonel Waterman, One hundredth Illinois; Major Moore, Fifty-eighth Indiana; Major Eaton, Thirteenth Michigan; Major Hammond, One hundredth Illinois, and Captain Estep, Eighth Indiana Battery, for their endurance and bravery throughout the whole conflict.

In Col. F. A. Bartleson, One hundredth Illinois, and Captain Ewing, Twenty-sixth Ohio (acting major), our country lost two most valuable officers. My personal staff, Capt. James G. Elwood, acting assistant adjutant-general; Lieuts. J. C. Williams and Zach. Jones, aides-de-camp; Capt. William Baldwin, assistant inspector-general; Captain Gardner, provost-marshal, and Lieutenant Ludden, topographical engineer, and Horace A. Hall and John Scheck, two of my orderlies, were ever efficient and ready, being in the hottest of the fight. Lieut. Zach. Jones and Orderly Hall were both slightly wounded. Captain Warner, acting commissary of subsistence, and Lieutenant Sterne, are also entitled to much credit for the faithful discharge of their respective duties. For more minute particulars I respectfully refer you to regimental and battery reports accompanying this.

I herewith submit a list of casualties in this brigade, which is over 40 per cent. The command entered the action with:

Command.	Officers.	Enlisted men.	Total.	Officers.				Enlisted men.			
				Killed.	Wounded.	Missing.	Total.	Killed.	Wounded.	Missing.	Total.
100th Illinois	26	313	339	.....	6	2	8	23	111	22	156
13th Michigan	25	195	220	2	6	2	10	11	61	24	96
26th Ohio	26	336	362	4	6	2	12	23	130	39	192
58th Indiana	30	370	400	2	5	1	8	14	96	24	134
8th Indiana Battery	5	119	124	...	...	...	...	1	9	7	17
Aggregate	112	1,333	1,445	8	23	7	38	72	407	116	595

SUMMARY OF LOSS.

Command.	Killed.	Wounded.	Missing.	Total.
Officers	8	23	7	38
Enlisted men	72	407	116	595
Total loss*	80	430	123	633

All of which is respectfully submitted.

GEO. P. BUELL,
Colonel Fifty-eighth Indiana Vols., Comdg. Brigade.

Capt. M. P. BESTOW,
Assistant Adjutant-General, First Division.

—

HDQRS. FIRST BRIG., FIRST DIV., 21ST ARMY CORPS,
Chattanooga, Tenn., October 5, 1863.

SIR: I respectfully request to make the following additions to my report of the actions of the 19th and 20th September, the facts of which have come to my knowledge since the date of that report:

On Saturday night nearly every wounded man of my brigade was removed from the scene of battle to the division field hospital and left there in charge of Surgeon Ewing, Thirteenth Michigan; Assistant Surgeons Holtzman and Downey, Fifty-eighth Indiana; Surgeon McGavran, Twenty-sixth Ohio, and Asst. Surg. H. T. Woodruff,

*See revised statement, p. 175.

One hundredth Illinois.   From the wounded men that have arrived from that hospital I am pleased to learn that these officers have conducted themselves in the execution of their duties with great credit and honor.   Through no fault of theirs these officers are now in the hands of the enemy awaiting exchange.

Your acceptance of this short tribute to them as faithful and efficient officers, will be but conferring upon them what is justly their due.

I would respectfully request that this may be attached to my report forwarded September 28, 1863.

I have the honor to remain, respectfully, your obedient servant,

GEO. P. BUELL,
Colonel, Commanding Brigade.

Capt. M. P. Bestow,
Assistant Adjutant-General, First Division.

No. 139.

Report of Maj. Charles M. Hammond, One hundredth Illinois Infantry.

Headquarters One Hundredth Illinois Volunteers,
Chattanooga, September 26, 1863.

Sir: I have the honor to report that on the 19th of September, at about 3 p. m., this regiment (Col. F. A. Bartleson, commanding) lay in position on the right of the Third Brigade (Wood's division), which was protecting the ford at Lee and Gordon's Mills.   Orders were received to move at once in the direction of Chattanooga on the Chattanooga and La Fayette road.   As a part of the First Brigade, this regiment in the advance, it proceeded rapidly about 2 miles and formed in line of battle on the right of the road, a battery of Davis' division, and the Twenty-sixth Ohio Volunteers, on our right and left, respectively, to support the right of Davis' division, which was being heavily pressed and giving way.   But a few moments intervened for our front to be cleared of our own troops, when the order to advance and charge the enemy was given and promptly complied with, under a heavy fire of musketry, and with a loss of nearly 100 men in killed and wounded, including Lieutenant-Colonel Waterman, who was severely wounded in the right arm.

On the order to retreat being given, the regiment fell back and made a stand, first behind a breastwork of rails on the left of the road, and afterward advanced to the right of the road, driving the enemy before us, making a stand which was maintained until relieved by troops of Sheridan's division, when we again retired to the rear of the breastworks and lay down on our arms for the night.

On the morning of the 20th, at about 3 o'clock, we moved to the left on a road in the rear about 1¼ miles, and at 8 a. m. to the front and relieved a part of General Negley's division, our left resting on Harker's brigade, and our right supported by the Twenty-sixth Ohio Volunteers, and occupied a position behind a light breastworks.   Skirmishers were now thrown out, and as they met with slight opposition they were quickly followed by the regiment, which charged across an open field and through a small ravine up to a masked battery supported by infantry, both of which opened a fire so deadly that the main portion of the regiment fell back to its original position behind the breastworks. A part of it, however, was rallied, by the colonel commanding, behind a picket fence near the ravine, checking the advance of the enemy until overpowered, when it hastily retreated, leaving the colonel and several of the men dead or wounded upon the field. At this juncture, I had just returned from the line of skirmishers of the First Brigade, which I had located by order of Colonel Buell, and found the regiment in a disorganized state without their commander. I rallied and formed them behind the rude rail breastworks, and after remaining in that position five or ten minutes, in the meantime, I called for volunteers to go and recover Colonel Bartleson, whereupon Adjutant Rouse, Lieutenant Wicks, and 4 men volunteered and went. Soon after I was ordered by Colonel Buell to move the regiment by the left flank and follow the Fifty-eighth Indiana Volunteers, and [we] moved across an open piece of ground to the top of a hill under heavy fire. I here lost sight of the Fifty-eighth Indiana, but discovered a long line of the enemy swinging around on our right, which I held in check a short time, but was forced by superior numbers to fall back. Here portions of other regiments of the First Brigade became intermingled with my own. Of these I took command and attached them to a portion of General Negley's division, which was drawn up in line of battle, but eventually fell back with them and a portion of General Reynolds' division to a point near Rossville, where I found Lieutenant-Colonel Young, of the Twenty-sixth Ohio Volunteers, to whom I turned over the command of all those of the First Brigade I had succeeded in gathering up. I was then ordered into camp by Colonel Young with my regiment, now numbering 98 officers and men.

Respectfully submitted.

Your most obedient servant,

C. M. HAMMOND,
Major, Commanding Regiment.

Capt. J. G. ELWOOD,
Acting Assistant Adjutant-General, First Brigade.

No. 140.

Report of Lieut. Col. James T. Embree, Fifty-eighth Indiana Infantry.

HDQRS. FIFTY-EIGHTH REGIMENT INDIANA VOLS.,
September 26, 1863.

SIR: I have the honor to report the following as the action of this regiment in the late battle fought on the 18th, 19th, and 20th instant on the Chickamauga River:

About noon of the 18th instant, when the regiment was in camp at Gordon's Mills, the enemy was discovered approaching our position and moving to the left.

By order of George P. Buell, colonel commanding the brigade, the regiment was stationed in line of battle on the right of the brigade, facing southward and nearly perpendicular to the line formed by the other regiments of the brigade, and to the rear of that line, for the purpose of opposing any attempt on the part of the enemy to cross the river in that quarter.

Strong lines of skirmishers were here advanced to the front and along the banks of the river, and this position held until about 2 p. m. of the 19th instant, no attack having been made at this point by the enemy.

About this time orders were received from the colonel commanding the brigade to call in the skirmishers and hasten to the left, there to rejoin the brigade, which was about moving in that direction for the purpose of entering into action.

The skirmishers were recalled and the regiment moved as ordered with 369 men with arms, 27 commissioned officers, and 1 of the non-commissioned staff, making a total of 397 officers and men, who actually were engaged in action.

When the regiment arrived at the spot where it was supposed that the other regiments of the brigade would be found, these regiments had already moved to the left; whereupon this regiment moved at a double-quick and soon came upon the rear of the brigade.

During this time the battle was furious in the direction in which we were moving, and conflicting reports as to the fortune of the hour were circulating.

Having arrived in front of the enemy, this regiment was posted in the second line of battle about 75 paces in rear of the One hundredth Illinois Regiment and on the right of the Thirteenth Michigan. The line thus formed was immediately in rear of the caissons of some unknown battery and of the Eighth Indiana Battery, and within 5 paces of these caissons.

At the time this position was taken, the report was current that the enemy were falling back before our forces, who were fighting a short distance to our front.

To the rear of this line was a large open field; on the front of the left wing about 50 paces distant was a dense wood, while the right wing was covered by an open field, and the whole front of the regiment covered by fencing, but a short distance forward of the line and to the rear of the One hundredth Illinois Regiment.

At ten minutes before 3 p. m. our forces who were engaged immediately in front of this position fell back in disorder before the enemy and rushed through the lines thus formed, and the enemy advanced near the edge of the wood above mentioned, and poured a destructive fire upon the whole brigade.

At this moment the brigade was ordered to charge the enemy. While the regiment was attempting to execute this order the horses of the caissons above mentioned became frightened and unmanageable, and were directed toward this regiment and driven madly through the line, crushing several men and utterly destroying all line or order in the regiment, and cutting off three companies on the left of the regiment.

In this condition the regiment undertook to execute the order to charge. No enemy could be seen, they being concealed by the fence, brush, horses, men, and dust in front.

Having advanced on this charge into the field in front, the regiment was ordered to halt, lie upon the ground, and fire upon the enemy then in the wood.

Within ten minutes after this position was taken the regiments on the right, left, and front gave way, and, so far as could be seen, there was no friendly force within supporting distance of the regiment except the Sixth Ohio Battery, then posted about 150 paces to the rear.

The enemy were then moving without opposition around the left flank of the regiment, and pouring a destructive, enfilading fire into the ranks. Seeing that the position was untenable, and that there was a certainty of being overpowered if the attempt was made to remain longer, the order was given to retreat and support Bradley's (Sixth Ohio) battery, which was done, and the regiment formed about this battery in rear of a small defense made of rails. Here, again, fire was opened upon the enemy, who were advancing over the field from which the regiment had retreated.

In this position the regiment, together with a part of the One hundredth Illinois Regiment, which had joined them, were hotly engaged with the enemy for about one hour, and succeeded in driving the enemy from the field and back to the woods.

During this time Colonel Buell, commanding the brigade, was busily engaged in bringing together the other regiments of the brigade, which seemed to have formed in some other part of the field not far distant.

At the close of about one hour's fighting at this point, Colonel Buell gave orders to this force to charge the enemy with the bayonet, which was attempted with good will, but with no other result than driving the enemy back from view in the woods, save, perhaps, a few killed or wounded by the firing which was done while advancing.

Having advanced into the field about 50 paces beyond and a short distance to the right of the point from which the regiment had retreated, a halt was called and the men ordered to lie down. About this time a small force was collected and formed on the left of the regiment, but I cannot say of what it consisted. Soon after reaching this point the enemy again opened a heavy fire upon the regiment, and the forces on the left, above spoken of, gave way in disorder. Soon the panic reached this regiment, and they too broke from their lines and retreated in disorder to about 75 paces to the rear.

At this time Joseph Moore, major of the regiment, gallantly seized the colors, planted them in the ground, and called upon the men to rally about them, and thus succeeded in forming the nucleus about which the whole regiment was in a short time rallied, and from thence advanced to the point just abandoned. Here, also, at the same time, Brigadier-General Wood, commanding the division, came upon this part of the field, urged the troops forward to the work, and gave renewed confidence to all.

From this time until about 7 p. m. the regiment was engaged during the greater part of the time.

A short time before sunset the whole brigade was concentrated at this place by George P. Buell, colonel commanding, and formed into line of battle in a strong position, and the Forty-second Illinois Regiment, of General Sheridan's division, had joined our line on the left and the Eighty-first Indiana on the right.

While in this position two of the guns of the Eighth Indiana Battery were recovered by the men of this regiment, they having been abandoned from loss of horses a few hours before, and also the colors of the Twenty-first Illinois Regiment were recovered by Lieutenant Behm, of this regiment, and returned to their regiment, these colors having been found in front of the line then occupied by this regiment.

During the engagement of this day the regiment suffered the following loss, to wit :

Killed : Commissioned officers, 1 ; enlisted men, 12. Wounded : Commissioned officers, 4 ; enlisted men, 73. Missing : Enlisted men, 21. Total, 111.

Of this loss all but 10 occurred before the regiment was ordered to retreat to Captain Bradley's battery ; in fact, in less time than one-quarter of an hour. During this day Capt. Charles H. Bruce was killed, and the regiment now mourns the loss of a brave and most efficient officer, a kind friend, and most gallant gentleman.

Here, too, were wounded while bravely discharging all their duties: Capt. William Davis, Capt. James M. Smith, Lieut. James D. Foster, and Lieut. Samuel L. Snyder.

Lieutenant Foster is counted among the wounded, but there are strong grounds for believing him killed. Captain Davis is a prisoner in the hands of the enemy, and it is feared is mortally wounded. He was captured with the division hospital.

About 3 a. m., 20th instant, orders were received from the colonel commanding the brigade to retire from the position thus held as above stated, and join the other regiments of the brigade then posted in the second line, leaving the skirmishers in front with directions to follow the regiment at daybreak. This having been done, the whole brigade was moved about 1 mile and a half to the left, and the men allowed to build fires, get their breakfast, and warm themselves, the night having been intensely cold.

At this time the attempt was made to issue to the regiment two days' rations, but about 9 a. m., before the issue was completed, the regiment was ordered to move to the front, and after carrying these rations from place to place after the regiment, they were finally by force abandoned and lost.

The brigade moved about 9 a. m. of this day and took position behind some defenses built of logs in the front line of battle, with the One hundredth Illinois and Twenty-sixth Ohio Regiments on the left, and the Thirteenth Michigan on the right of this regiment, and the Eighth Indiana Battery in the rear.

Skirmishers were sent forward and were warmly engaged with the enemy when orders were received to vacate this position, leaving the skirmishers still in the front, and follow the rear of the second line of Colonel Harker's brigade (which was then moving by the left flank), the One hundredth Illinois following the rear of the first line of that brigade.

This order was obeyed; Colonel Harker's brigade moved to the left, followed by Colonel Buell's brigade. About the time this regiment had moved to the left, say 500 paces, the skirmishers who were left behind were overpowered, Company B of this regiment there losing 12 men, having lost on the previous day 28 men. Thus the flanks and rear of the brigade were wholly uncovered, and the enemy rushed through the opening thus made in great force. The remaining regiments of the brigade gave way, indeed, all the Federal forces within view of this regiment fell back before this host, a part rushing through the lines of this regiment. On the left of this regiment, while marching by the left flank, there was a large field with a knoll on the farther side, on which was then posted artillery, which was being fired at the enemy. All other forces within sight having given way, the command was given to this regiment to march by the left flank, thus moving in line faced to the rear. Having moved in this direction about 50 paces toward the artillery, the regiment was halted and faced to the front.

Our fleeing men were then so numerous in front that it was dangerous to fire upon the enemy; hence the regiment did not fire, although themselves subjected to a severe fire.

While in this position, Colonel Buell, who was working energetically to maintain the brigade in order, rode up to the regiment and ordered the position to be held, if possible, until the brigade was united, or until further orders should be received.

Colonel Buell then sought for the remaining regiments without success, and shortly afterward ordered this regiment to be moved toward the battery above mentioned. In executing this order it was attempted to move the regiment by the right flank into position to the left and forward of the artillery to repel an attack then about being made by the enemy upon the unsupported artillery. This position could not have endangered the regiment by reason of the artillery, but so soon as the movement was begun some officer unknown to me called from the rear, urging the men not to move in the direction indicated, that "the artillery would tear them to pieces." By this the regiment was caused to file to the right and some confusion caused, and almost instantly afterward the artillery was captured by the enemy.

This regiment was then placed in position to the left of the field on a ridge commanding the knoll and field. Here also were collected by Colonel Buell and Major Moore a number of stragglers from other regiments, In this position fire was opened upon the enemy, who occupied the knoll and field, and in about one hour the enemy were driven from their position.

The enemy having been driven back, the regiment, with those collected with it, was ordered to advance to the top of the knoll in the field, which was done, Colonel Buell conducting the movement. Seeing at this time the colors of two regiments to the left, I went to them and sought aid in this movement. I there found the Twenty-first or Thirty-first Ohio Regiment (I cannot remember which), or rather about 40 or 50 men of the regiment, under command of a captain, who readily consented to join in the movement, and did so. The other was the Sixty-fifth Ohio, which was separated from its brigade, or seemed so to be. This regiment held a good position at the time, to assist in clearing the lower part of the field, and prepared readily for the work when the object was explained.

I then hastened to rejoin my regiment, which at this time had almost reached the top of the knoll. I arrived at the top with them.

At this time the enemy were prolonging their lines to the left of our lines in the valley below, with four regiments dressed in dark uniform and carrying dark-red flags immediately in our front. There was also at the same time another line moved by the enemy against the right flank of the regiment, but which at the time was concealed by the hill and brush.

Here arose conflicting opinions as to the character of this opposing force, some officers contending that they were friends, some that they were enemies. At this I advanced to the front of the line, and was satisfied that they were enemies, and gave the order to fire, while other officers on the right of the line (I being on the left) countermanded the order. These officers were unknown to me.

While this parley was going on, the regiment was struck on the right flank by this flanking force, above mentioned, and before I could be aware of it the whole line had given way, and the enemy were on the knoll. I followed as well as I was able (being on foot, exhausted and lame from a hurt received on the previous day), but I was too slow to overtake the regiment and was compelled to stop at the bottom of the hill. Soon I sought the regiment, but failed to find any part of it, I happening to move to the left while they went, or a part of them went, to the right. This was at 1.15 p. m. I did not succeed in finding any great part of the regiment until late in the afternoon, when I found 113 men, who, with parts of every other regiment of the brigade, were moving to the rear, under command of Lieutenant-Colonel Young, of the Twenty-sixth Ohio Volunteers.

The remainder of the facts connected with the action of the 20th instant I received from Maj. Joseph Moore, who at the time the regiment was forced to retreat from the knoll was a short distance in the rear moving up the knoll with a small force which he had rallied to the aid of the regiment. Seeing the line about giving way, the major gallantly met the colors as they were being borne way, and succeeded in rallying about 150 men in support of two pieces of artillery, then under command of Brigadier-General Brannan, and was then engaged, except at short intervals, until night. About 4 p. m. this force was re-enforced by General Steedman's division, and had previously been joined by Colonel Buell.

On the left was General Brannan's division, then Colonel Harker's brigade, the force under Major Moore being the only part of this brigade on that part of the field. Here also were General Thomas, General Brannan, General Wood, General Steedman, and Colonel Harker.

In this position the portion of the regiment with the major fought most bravely, discharging all their cartridges, replenishing from cartridge boxes scattered over the field, and finally prepared to hold the position with the bayonet. This position was maintained until dark, when by order of George P. Buell, colonel commanding the brigade, these troops were retired in good order to the rear and were camped at Rossville, about one-fourth of a mile from the force then under my command.

While I would not have it understood as detracting from the valor and good service of others, I feel that I cannot perform my duty in making this report without specially commending certain officers and men of the regiment.

And, first, I would call attention to Maj. Joseph Moore, who, by his conduct during the entire battle, has proved himself as brave and efficient a man and officer as any in the Army of the Cumberland.

I would specially mention Sergt. Maj. William R. Fowler, who, by his conduct, proved himself worthy of a better position and richly deserves promotion.

Also I would beg to mention Color Sergt. Jesse B. Miller, who, although sick and almost unable to move about the field, stood bravely to his post, and proved that so long as he bears them, the colors of his regiment will not be lost.

I would also commend Capts. Green McDonald and George Whitman, Adjt. Charles C. Whiting, and Second Lieut. Jacob Davis.

It also becomes my duty to record the death of another brave and good officer, Hugh J. Barnett, second lieutenant of Company F, who was killed in the action on the 20th instant. Than him there were none braver.

Capt. William E. Chappell, of Company I, did much for the cause of his country in this engagement, and should be highly esteemed by all patriots.

The loss on the 20th instant was as follows:

Killed: Commissioned officer, 1; enlisted men, 2. Wounded: Commissioned officer, 1; enlisted men, 23. Missing: Commissioned officer, 1; enlisted men, 3. Total, 31.

The commissioned officer above mentioned as wounded is Second Lieut. Robert Cromwell, who was severely wounded in discharge of his duty.

In addition to the above-mentioned loss (which has reference only to those actually engaged) there was the following loss in the hospital corps of the regiment, to wit:

Captured: Commissioned officers (surgeons), 2; enlisted men, 7. Total, 9. Making the aggregate loss of the regiment in the action as follows:

Killed: Commissioned officers, 2; enlisted men, 14. Wounded: Commissioned officers, 5; enlisted men, 96. Missing: Commissioned officer, 1; enlisted men, 24. Captured: Commissioned officers (surgeons), 2; enlisted men, 7. Total loss, 151.

In addition to the above loss there are 18 enlisted men who were slightly wounded, but have since returned to duty.

Respectfully submitted.

JAMES T. EMBREE,
Lieutenant-Colonel, Commanding Regiment.

Capt. J. G. ELWOOD,
Acting Assistant Adjutant-General, First Brigade.

No. 141.

Reports of Col. Joshua B. Culver and Maj. Willard G. Eaton, Thirteenth Michigan Infantry.

HDQRS. THIRTEENTH REGIMENT MICHIGAN VOL. INFTY.,
Chattanooga, Tenn., September 26, 1863.

SIR: I have the honor herewith to report the actions of the Thirteenth Regiment Michigan Infantry in the sanguinary battles of the 19th and 20th instant:

On the morning of the 18th, the regiment was ordered to the south of Messrs. Lee and Gordon's Mills, on the north bank of the Chickamauga, where it was deployed as sharpshooters, excepting one company as a reserve. About 4 o'clock the enemy opened a battery upon our line from the right, with shell and grape-shot, but did us no damage. This battery was soon silenced by Bradley's Sixth Ohio and Estep's Eighth Indiana Batteries. At about 2 p. m. on the 19th instant, I received orders to ploy my regiment and join the brigade, which was ordered into action on the Chattanooga road, about 1½ miles north of Lee and Gordon's Mills, where we formed in line of battle in an open field in front of a belt of timber on the right of the road, and on left of the Fifty-eighth Indiana, and immediately in rear of the Twenty-sixth Ohio.

We had barely taken our position when we received the enemy's fire, who were steadily advancing, pressing back the troops in our front, many of whom passed through our lines. Finding it impossible to use our fire in this position without injuring our own troops, we charged across the field about a hundred yards to the edge of the timber occupied by the enemy, which position we held about ten minutes, delivering a destructive fire into the enemy's massed columns, but as our left flank had been turned, and being raked by an enfilading fire, we were compelled to retire. About this time I was disabled by a shell, and the command devolved upon Major Eaton, whose report is subjoined:

The regiment fell back to the position from which we made the first charge, and then rallied and made a second charge, and were again flanked and obliged to retire, which we did, and took a position a little to the right and in front of the position from which we made the first and second charges, where we remained during the night.

On the morning of the 20th, we were ordered with the brigade to Missionary Ridge, where, after drawing rations, we were assigned a position in rear of the One hundredth Illinois, in which position we advanced about a mile, and at 10 a. m. were ordered to the extreme right of the brigade and deployed behind a line of temporary breastworks, Company A being thrown out as skirmishers in advance. Our right being exposed by the withdrawal of the troops with which our line first joined, we threw out Company F to protect it. Holding this position until a few minutes before 11 a. m., we were then ordered to the left, and to follow the Eighth Indiana Battery. While making this movement to the left we were attacked. Finding the Twenty-sixth Ohio on our left, joined them and succeeded in holding the enemy in check for a short time, and, being obliged to retire, we fell back in good order about 100 yards. Here being pressed by the enemy in superior numbers, and an open field of about 100 yards in width in our rear, I determined to charge the enemy's advance and drive them back for the purpose of gaining time to cross the field, which I believed we should be obliged to do. In this charge we were successful, and gained a position in the woods, but our right was immediately turned, and we were again obliged to retire. I then determined to fall back to the woods on the brow of the hill to the rear of the open field where a battery was then stationed, but received orders to take position at a fence about midway in the field, where we held the enemy in check about twenty minutes, and were again compelled to retire.

On arriving at the brow of the hill I found no support, the battery being abandoned, and, our right continually turned, we moved to the left and succeeded in joining a portion of our brigade at 6 p. m. near Rossville. Companies A and F, our skirmishers and flankers, in retiring fell in with the troops on our right, and did not join the balance of the regiment until the next day.

I desire to call your attention to the gallant and soldierly bearing of Maj. W. G. Eaton, Adjt. A. B. Case, and the officers and men generally during the battle. Inclosed please find list* of killed, wounded, and missing.

All of which is respectfully submitted.

I am, sir, very respectfully, your obedient servant,
                                        J. B. CULVER,
                                        Colonel, Commanding.

Col. GEORGE P. BUELL,
    Commanding First Brigade.

No. 142.

Report of Lieut. Col. William H. Young, Twenty-sixth Ohio Infantry.

HDQRS. TWENTY-SIXTH REGT. OHIO VOL. INFANTRY,
            Chattanooga, Tenn., September 26, 1863.

SIR: I have the honor herewith to report the part taken by the Twenty-sixth Regiment Ohio Volunteers, of Colonel Buell's brigade, under my command during the series of battles recently fought between the Union and rebel forces on and near Chickamauga Creek, Ga.

During the 16th and 17th instant, while Colonel Buell's brigade was occupying the left bank of the Chickamauga at Gordon's Mills, Ga., and holding the tongue of land between the creek and the La Fayette road, my regiment was posted near the sharp bend of said creek, convex to our position one-half mile from the mill.

On the 15th, being somewhat annoyed by the enemy's cavalry scouts approaching by the road and firing into my camp from the high ground beyond the creek, I stationed, by Colonel Buell's direction, a line of sharpshooters along the left bank of the creek to hold them off. But on the 16th, as they became bolder, I threw a footway over the creek and advanced a line of sharpshooters as pickets over the creek, extending them across the neck of land formed by the bend in the stream. This last position was within musket range of the main road to La Fayette, on which the enemy's cavalry was continually showing itself with increasing boldness. On the same evening a detachment from my regiment was thrown still farther to the front, holding a point on the La Fayette road about 1 mile from the mills. On the evening of the 17th, a dash was made by a few rebel cavalrymen on this post, but was promptly repulsed, with the loss of 1 wounded on the part of the enemy.

This detachment was now immediately increased to 30 men, another post established one-quarter of a mile farther out on the road, and my whole line on the right bank of the creek considerably strengthened; about 100 men of my regiment now guarding this, the enemy's point of approach. During the night of the 17th, there was considerable movement on the road in front of this advanced line, and a systematic effort to draw the fire of the sentinels as if to ascertain their position.

On the morning of the 18th, the enemy made an unsuccessful attempt to surround and surprise my advanced post, 34 men, and at the same time my lookouts reported him advancing in heavy force. Shortly after, my sharpshooters were driven back by a heavy line of skirmishers covering the movements of the enemy now advancing in two lines of battle. In obedience to orders, my force beyond the creek was withdrawn to the left bank, the crossing cut away, and my regiment covered by a double line of sharpshooters and skirmishers posted on the creek, and facing the enemy's lines. During the remainder of this day, the night, and the 19th up to 3 p. m., I held the last-described position, skirmishing occasionally with the enemy at long range, and without casualty on my side. The enemy in the meantime passing heavy columns of troops along our front from right to left in the rear and under cover of his troops who had taken position in my immediate front.

At about 2.30 or 3 p. m. of the 19th, when the brigade was ordered to the left on the Chattanooga road, my regiment took the road in the rear of the One hundredth Illinois, and moved with the rest of the brigade at a double-quick some 2 miles to where the battle seemed to be raging with the utmost fury. Arriving at this point, where the conflict seemed fiercest, and the enemy was apparently pushing back our lines, my regiment was immediately thrown into line at double-quick on the right of, parallel to, and about 40 yards off the road, the Eighth Indiana Battery being on my right, my left resting in the woods.

In my immediate front, and for 75 yards in front of the prolongation of my line, to the right, was heavy timber, thickly grown with jack-oak bushes, making it utterly impossible to see what was going on 20 yards distant. Seventy-five yards to my right this timber made a right angle to the front, leaving on its right and in front of the road an inclosed field extending about 500 to 600 yards along the road and 600 to 700 yards to the front, being limited in each direction by timber and thickets. On my left and at my flank the line of timber in my front made a right angle to the rear, crossing the road and forming a dense cover for several hundred yards, and then opening into a half cleared, but bushy and thickly weeded field ; 30 to 40 yards in the rear of, and parallel to, my line, as before mentioned, was the road, and in the rear of this another inclosed field, extending about 400 yards to the rear of, and 600 to 700 yards parallel with, the road toward the right, and being bounded by timber in both directions. This last field descends with an easy slope from the road about 100 to 150 yards to a narrow ditch or gully and then rises with a slight grade to the timber in its rear. The gully varies in depth from $1\frac{1}{2}$ to $3\frac{1}{2}$ feet and in width from 3 to 6 or 8 feet, its border at intervals being slightly fringed with weeds and willows. This description and the accompanying sketch* will, I trust, make plain the movements of my regiment during the battle on the 19th p. m.

Having been originally posted in my first position under Colonel Buell's immediate supervision, as above described and as shown in the sketch, I immediately caused my men to lie down and simultaneously received instructions from General Wood that the position must be held. Even while receiving his instructions, and before the men had been allowed a moment to recover their wind after the rapid march, it became manifest the lines in our front were broken and the enemy pressing them rapidly back. In a moment more dozens, then scores, and finally hundreds, of straggling soldiers came rushing through the woods and over my line in the wildest disorder and most shameful confusion, there seeming to be no effort to either check or control the retreat, and at the same time a most galling fire began to reach and take effect upon my men, though lying close upon the ground.

In the meantime, I was holding my fire until our own men should be out of the way, intending, when the rebel line should show itself, to deliver my fire by volley and meet him at a charge with bayonets (previously fixed). As I was about executing this intention, a mounted officer came galloping to the rear calling out, "for God's sake, don't fire; two lines of our own troops are still in the woods." At the same instant I discovered a rapid fire enfilading my line from the timber on the left, most cruelly cutting my command. My horse fell under me pierced, as afterward appeared, with nine balls ; my acting major was dismounted and wounded, and the rebel line appeared in front within 20 yards, advancing firing. I immediately commenced firing and ordered a charge, but the command could be only partially heard, and the charge was not made. The rebel advance in front, however, was momentarily checked and his fire weakened ; but the battery on my right had already been withdrawn; a heavy line of rebels were already on my left, and rapidly gaining my rear, making it impossible to hold my position even for a moment longer except with the certainty of capture. I reluctantly gave the command to retire across the road to the fence immediately in my

---

* Not found.

rear. This was done in tolerable order but under a most galling fire, Lieutenant Burbridge, Company H, and a number of men being killed, and Captain Ewing, acting major, with perhaps 30 to 35 men, too badly wounded to get away, being left on the ground. This conflict was short and bloody, begun at a great disadvantage, kept up with the highest heroism, and the ground only yielded when the bayonet had been freely used and defense had become hopeless.

On retiring to the fence to position No. 2 the regiment was in great part promptly rallied, though under a severe direct and cross fire and the loud cheers of the advancing rebels. From this position an effective fire was poured back into the enemy, and he was compelled to retire to the timber for cover. But now a most terrible fire was concentrated upon us, direct and right and left oblique, there being no support on either of my flanks. The officers and men conducted themselves most heroically; many of the latter and all of the former, particularly those of the left wing, to whom my attention was more closely directed, disdaining the cover of the low fence and defiantly receiving and returning the concentrated fire of more than twice their front.

Again the enemy was closing up on my left flank not 30 yards from it and rapidly gaining my rear. I still hoped, though I had not seen it, there was some support on the left, and, depending for support for my right upon a rally that was being made around some old buildings 250 yards distant on the prolongation of my right, as well as upon a few brave heroes scattered along the fence between me and those buildings, I determined to hold the fence a few minutes longer; but it seemed of no avail. There was now almost a semicircle of fire around us; it was growing hotter every moment; we were beginning to receive the fire of our own troops rallied in the ditch below us and in the woods beyond. The five left companies had lost from one-half to three-quarters of their numbers. The left center company had but 5 men left from 24, and 1 of its officers was killed. Lieutenants Morrow, Ruley, and Williams, each commanding a left wing company, had been cut down while most gallantly cheering on their men in the unequal contest. Lieutenant Platt, of Company G (the Ninth), though still commanding his company, was painfully wounded, and already too many noble privates had written themselves heroes with blood stains upon the sod. It was a proud thing to have died there with those that were dead; it was duty to save the remnant of the living for still another struggle.

I now gave the command to fall back to the ditch. Many wounded had already sought this as a place of refuge from the storm of musketry, grape-shot, and shell now sweeping the field from the edge of the timber on both sides. Many others had also rallied here from the troops that had retreated over my line as above mentioned. Many of my own men had rallied here when the line first fell back and were fighting bravely from the imperfect cover the shallow ditch afforded. From this third position another defense was now opened, and for a few moments vigorously and effectually maintained. But this line, like the others, was flanked and raked with a murderous fire. Many of the wounded were again struck, even the second and third time. The enemy had not yet attempted to cross the open field. Our own artillery and infantry were already pouring into them an effective fire from the timber in the rear. The troops collected around the old buildings before mentioned were successfully holding the enemy's left, and under cover of their fire a brave remnant of my command with myself made good our retreat by the right and rear, many others moving directly to the rear through a very storm of bullets.

I immediately proceeded to reform my regiment, and after moving my colors into the open field, succeeded—with the assistance of my officers, conspicious among whom were Captains Ross, Adair, Hamilton, and Acting Adjutant Grafton—in rallying the bulk of my surviving men. Supported by a few men of the Thirteenth Michigan bravely rallied around their colors, and another fragmentary regiment of, I think, Davis' division, and a few brave spirits of various regiments under the immediate command of General Wood, we charged across the field under cover of Bradley's and Estep's batteries, but in the face of a galling fire. We were joined as we charged by many brave fellows who had staid in the ditch, and a few others who had remained by the fence. But here Captain Ross and Lieutenant Shotwell, both of the color company, fell mortally wounded, and many others less conspicious, though equally brave, were stricken down. Our little line staggered for a moment under the concentrated fire opened upon it from the woods, but pressing quickly forward firing we entered the woods at the point where the Eighth Indiana Battery had formerly stood, and nearly parallel to our original line, driving the enemy steadily before us. We entered the woods 200 yards, when, perceiving a rapid cross-fire on my left flank, I changed front to the rear on my first company, and, taking cover behind the fence at the edge of the woods, soon beat off the enemy in that direction. At this juncture I perceived a compact rebel line 500 to 600 yards distant advancing across the field from the woods in front of the road. I now changed front to the rear on my tenth company and ordered my men to lie down until the enemy should approach; other troops of our brigade then being on my right, somewhat to my rear, and a strong line of Sheridan's division at the same time coming up in my rear across the field in the rear of the road, this line halted near the road just as the enemy's fire was becoming severe, and commenced firing into my rear. I promptly moved back to the fence, and taking position under its cover awaited the onset. It was opened with a most murderous fire, driving back upon me a Kentucky regiment (of Sheridan's division, perhaps), which was advancing in line obliquely across my front. The entire line was broken by the shock. I held my command for a few minutes at the fence, but seeing the uselessness of attempting to hold the position, fell back to the ditch, where I rallied a few men, and from which Captain Potter and Lieutenant Renick, with their companies, A and F, gallantly advanced and drew off one of Captain Estep's guns which had been left behind. In this effort Captain Potter was badly hurt by being run over by the gun.

At this point Captain Hamilton was wounded. We drew back in tolerable order to the timber, when the regiment was again formed, mustering about 147 men out of 335 who had entered the battle, and 14 officers out of 24. Our ammunition was here replenished, and in obedience to Colonel Buell's orders, we were moved to a position in the woods near the road and on the right of the field in front of the road. It was now night, and movements for the day were over with. While moving to and after getting into our last position about 40 more men joined me who had become separated from the command during the progress of the battle, but the most of them gave sufficient evidence of having acquitted themselves well, fighting under the colors of other regiments of the brigade. The casualties of the day were very heavy. The officers and men behaved excellently, in many instances heroically. I know not a single instance of bad conduct on the part of an officer, nor can I say that a man was clearly guilty of misconduct, a few perhaps might have rallied better, despite the stampeding around them.

Immediately when all was quiet for the night, I detailed Lieutenant Foster and 10 men to go carefully over the battle-field and see that all my wounded were gathered up. He found many who had been overlooked by the hospital attendants and saw them carried away. Four musicians were wounded carrying off the wounded during the action.

Lieutenant Platt, of Company G, though wounded almost at the first fire, remained with his company until the close of the action, and when urged to go to the hospital consented, but first found his way back to the battle-field, where he remained until midnight until his last wounded man was cared for, and at the hospital gave his attention to his men rather than to himself during the night.

About 3 a. m., Sunday, my regiment, with the rest of the brigade, was moved about a mile to the left, where breakfast was taken, rations issued, and then again to the front, and put in position, under Colonel Buell's immediate supervision, on the crest of a hill on the right of the brigade. After resting there perhaps half an hour, about 8.30 or 9 a. m. we were again moved to the front one-half to three-quarters of a mile, and posted behind a rude breastwork of logs on the extreme right of the first line of the division, having the One hundredth Illinois on my left, the Thirteenth Michigan in my rear, and Davis' division, Twentieth Army Corps, on my right. We seemed to be occupying the middle line of a valley about one-half to three-quarters of a mile wide, between two parallel ridges. From this point I threw forward a line of skirmishers, who almost immediately drew the fire of the enemy. A few minutes later I was ordered to the front to support the One hundredth Illinois, which had gone forward. I immediately moved to the front to my line of skirmishers, but not knowing exactly where to find the One hundredth, halted a moment, had my men lie down under the fire they were receiving, and endeavored to discover Colonel Bartleson's position.

At this moment Colonel Buell ordered me to remain where I was until further orders. A half hour later I was ordered to leave four companies on the line of skirmishers and return to the breastwork. This movement drew upon me the enemy's fire, by which were wounded Second Lieutenant Mathias, commanding Company I, and 3 men. From this time, while we held this position, my skirmishers were more or less actively engaged with the enemy.

About three-quarters of an hour later I received an order from one of the brigade staff—Lieutenant Williams or Jones, I think—to move my command off by the left flank, and to follow the One hundredth Illinois. As my skirmishers (four companies) were then engaged, I asked if they were to be called in, and was told they were. I hesitated a moment lest there might be some mistake, but was told the order was imperative and the movement to be executed promptly and rapidly. I at once ordered my skirmishers in. The movement I since learned was made by the whole division. My skirmishers were scarcely drawn in until their line was occupied by the enemy's, and before I had marched a regimental front stray shots came whistling through the trees. I was marching in very quick time to keep in sight of the One hundredth. The battery marching in a parallel line on my left found much difficulty in making its way over the rocks and through the timber, and the enemy's fire was rapidly approaching nearer and increasing in rapidity. At this time we received orders to double-quick, which tended much to increase the excitement of the moment, the artillery dashing along against trees and over stones at a headlong rate. The One hundredth rapidly gaining the rear, first by a left oblique, and then by the rear rank, and the growing unsteadiness of my own men made me extremely anxious for the issue. I immediately fell back from the head of the column to gain a position on its left flank, as it was now very sensibly inclining to the rear, but at the same moment a mass of fugitives from the front struck my command on its right flank, and, becoming completely mingled with it, carried the whole to the rear about 50 or 75 paces into a corn-field before we could extricate ourselves and rally. This, however, was soon effected under fire, the command faced to the front, and ordered to charge back into the woods. It was gallantly done, but revealed an extended rebel line rapidly approaching and already considerably advanced on my right. I immediately retired my regiment to low ground in the corn about 200 paces from the edge of the timber from which we had emerged and just at the foot of the hill in our rear, but finding myself supported neither on the right nor left, and the position being untenable by reason of timber 150 yards to the right from which the enemy was already firing upon me—striking down several of my men, and Lieutenant Hoge, commanding Company H—I retired half way up the hill to a fence now parallel to my line.

Rallying behind this, I hoped, with the support of several batteries posted on the crest of the hill several hundred yards above and another regiment rallied under cover of the same fence row with mine 100 yards to my left, to hold the position. Captain Baldwin, of Colonel Buell's staff, here joined me and assisted in rallying the men of various commands who were falling back from the woods below.

He could give me no information of Colonel Buell's whereabouts. I remained at this fence about fifteen minutes, maintaining and receiving a steady fire. The enemy in front was held in the timber below, but meeting no opposition he advanced on the right under cover of a tongue of timber stretching part way up the hillside, and being entirely hidden from view by the weeds and bushes along a fence row perpendicular to my line and at the edge of the timber, had almost turned my right flank before he became visible. At the same time I discovered the regiment on the left had fallen back before a heavy line advancing on its left, and that the guns above were being retired. I promptly fell back rapidly, but in tolerable order, halting for a moment in rear of the Eighth Indiana Battery; but the enemy had already gained the timber crowning the prolongation of the ridge to the right, and scarcely 150 yards distant, from which position he had forced back a portion of the Thirteenth Michigan; he was also coming up in heavy lines on the left.

There was no support anywhere in sight; every man in the command saw and felt the hopelessness of attempting a stand at this point, and as the batteries were already moving off, finding it impossible to rally my command in any force, I fell back into the woods, assisting one of the batteries as we retired. The woods here were filled with fugitives from various commands (utterly disordered, and, in spite of [the efforts of] my own and other officers of Colonel Buell's brigade, both of the staff [and] line), making their way to the rear. With the assistance of Major Hammond and several line officers of the One hundredth, my own officers, still all together, and Lieutenant Lillie, of the Thirteenth Michigan, bearing his regimental colors, my own men and a few of the One hundredth Illinois and Thirteenth Michigan, [were rallied] at a point on the crest of another hill perhaps 200 yards in rear of the first. With my command [and] another battalion made up of the men of various regiments rallied on the ground under command of a colonel unknown to me, and a battery or parts of batteries near by, it was determined to hold the position. But being entirely cut off from any organized support, ignorant of the extent of the disaster, Captain Baldwin, Lieutenant Jones, Lieutenant ———, of Colonel Buell's staff, being unable to indicate the position of brigade or division headquarters, I thought it my duty to establish communications with the troops who still seemed fighting to the left and front. Accordingly, instructing my officers to pick up and keep together any men who should be found, I went in the direction of the firing, and for some time, perhaps a half hour, sought to make my way to our troops, but found myself completely cut off from them by the enemy. Returning to where my command was left, I found the ground likewise occupied by the rebel skirmishers. (I have since learned that soon after I left the command the artillery was all withdrawn, and the battalion of infantry, commanded by the colonel of whom I have spoken, had been removed by the rear, whereupon, after consultation, my own officers and those already mentioned of the Thirteenth Michigan and One hundredth Illinois and Colonel Buell's staff, finding themselves entirely unsupported and with no object to remain longer where nothing could be effected, and capture was almost certain, determined to retire.)

Making my way out with much difficulty, and under frequent fire, from skirmishers, I finally gained the road, finding it filled with soldiers, artillery, trains, line, staff, and field officers. Learning by inquiry that a stand was being made several miles to the rear, I rode rapidly for this point in order to rally the greatest possible number of my command.

Arriving here about 4 p. m., I found the most of my regiment detachments of the other regiments of the brigade, a few of the Third Brigade, the most of Colonel Buell's, and a part of Colonel Harker's and General Wood's staffs, and the colors of the Third Brigade. Assuming command of the whole, I took immediate measures to pick up and collect any others of the division who should come in, and reported to Colonel Lodor, of General Crittenden's staff. He ordered me to fall back to Rossville, where I arrived after dark and went into camp. On the next morning (the 21st), I turned over the command, numbering about 600 officers and men, to Colonel Buell and resumed command of my own regiment. My regiment has since remained with the brigade, without further action or casualty, to the present time.

Subjoined is a schedule report of the casualties on the 19th and 20th; the most of them occurred on the 19th. The left wing, it will be observed, suffered most severely, both in officers and men, not less than one-third being left on the ground of our first position. I think no prisoners were taken except the wounded, among whom was Capt. S. H. Ewing, Company B, acting major. Surgeon Mc-

Gavran, Hospital Steward Dunnen, and 4 musicians were captured at the field hospital, near Gordon's Mills.

The command was most unfortunate in its positions on both days, but, under all the circumstances, behaved with the most commendable valor where valor could be available for good. I cannot wonder that after more than half its officers and men were killed and wounded up to noon of the 20th, and many others were unavoidably separated from the command during the terrible struggle of the 19th, and by the overwhelming force thrown upon the flank of the brigade while marching to the left on the 20th, completely crushing it, and dashing it to atoms, as it were, against the hill in the rear, the remnant of the men, still gathered around their colors with their officers, pressed farther and farther back by continued flank attacks, left entirely without support, and nearly surrounded, should fall in with the immense columns of troops moving to the rear, and seek, with the rest, a place of safety. It might have been wiser to have done so sooner.

The following are the casualties of the command during the actions of the 19th and 20th: The staff surgeon, McGavran, captured at field hospital; Captain Ewing, Company B, acting major, wounded and captured; non-commissioned Staff Serg. Maj. B. A. Rabe wounded; Hospital Steward V. E. Dunnen captured at field hospital.

Company.	In action.		Killed.		Wounded.		Missing.		Aggregate loss.	
	Officers.	Men.	Officers.	Men.	Officers.	Men.	Officers.	Men.	Officers.	Men.
A	3	38	.....	.....	.....	13	.....	2	.....	15
B	2	41	1	4	1	16	.....	5	2	25
C	3	34	2	2	.....	17	.....	7	2	26
D	2	44	.....	.....	.....	13	.....	4	.....	17
E	2	32	1	3	.....	14	.....	2	1	19
F	2	36	.....	.....	.....	8	.....	4	.....	12
G	2	40	.....	5	2	13	.....	7	2	25
H	3	24	1	3	2	17	.....	1	3	21
I	3	34	.....	4	1	10	.....	5	1	19
K	1	31	.....	2	.....	12	.....	6	.....	20
Total	23	354	5	23	6	133	.....	43	11	196

Aggregate loss of officers 12
Aggregate loss of enlisted men... 201

I am, sir, very respectfully,

W. H. YOUNG,
Lieutenant-Colonel, Commanding.

Capt. J. G. Elwood,
Acting Assistant Adjutant-General, First Brigade.

No. 143.

Reports of Capt. George Estep, Eighth Indiana Battery.

CAMP IN THE FIELD,
Near Chattanooga, September 23, 1863.

CAPTAIN: The following report of the Eighth Indiana Light Battery, on the 19th and 20th days of September, 1863, at the battle on

Chickamauga Creek, is as near correct as it is possible for me to make it at present:

I lost on the 19th, 21 horses killed and disabled; 1 man killed, and 5 others severely wounded; 2 missing. I received a slight wound in the left arm. Lost one gun limber and the rear part of one caisson. Worked nearly all night in repairing losses. Joined my brigade (First) soon after daylight on 20th. Was engaged in but two positions, and at the second lost my six guns and limbers, two 12-pounder howitzers, and four 6-pounder smooth-bores, two caissons, and the rear carriages of two others; 35 horses killed and disabled; 2 men wounded and 7 missing—suppose that some of them were wounded and are in the hands of the enemy. I had no support at the time the battery was charged and taken. There was no infantry on my right or rear.

My officers and men did their whole duty during the different engagements we were in. I would make a statement to show that losing the battery was no fault of mine, and that I could not have prevented it, but for the reason that I believe my brigade and division commanders will fully exonerate me.

Very respectfully submitted.

I am, very respectfully, your obedient servant,

GEORGE ESTEP,
Captain, Commanding Eighth Indiana Battery.

Capt. Cullen Bradley,
Chief of Artillery, First Division.

P. S.—I am unable to tell the exact number of rounds of ammunition expended in consequence of the loss of limbers and caissons, but believe it to be between 700 and 750 rounds.

—

Camp in the Field,
Near Chattanooga, September 23, 1863.

Sir: I have the honor respectfully to submit the following report of the Eighth Indiana Light Battery in the recent battles on Chickamauga River, Northern Georgia, on the 18th, 19th, and 20th days of September, 1863:

I put my battery in position on the left bank of the river, by order of Col. George P. Buell, commanding brigade, about 11 a. m. of the 18th. The enemy soon made his appearance in force, moving to our left on the La Fayette road. As soon as the head of his column came within range, I ordered one section to commence firing. I could not, in consequence of the timber in front on the banks of the river and the heavy clouds of dust, discover the effect of the fire, but supposed I did the enemy no serious damage. He was compelled, however, to file his troops to the right and move off the road.

On the morning of the 19th, I opened fire on a line of sharpshooters that had crept up in our front during the night. A few shells only were required to send them in the direction from which they came. We then remained quiet till afternoon, when I was ordered by one of Colonel Buell's staff to move with the brigade to the left on the Chattanooga road. When about 1½ or 2 miles from Lee and Gordon's Mills, was ordered into position with the brigade on the right of the road, the left half of my battery resting in woods and the right in an open field. I had been in position but a moment (in battery) till I learned that the enemy were driving our troops (do not know

whose they were) back on the line we had just formed.   Hurried into
position as I was, I feared to fire on account of destroying our own
men.   I then rode to a battery commander on my right who was in
position when we came up, to learn, if possible, the location of the
enemy as well as that of our own forces.   He told me that he had
been firing at a range of 800 yards, but that the distance was growing
less very fast.   I rode back and ordered the right half to commence
firing shell at a range of 700 yards, believing from the information
I had received that the shell would not interfere with our troops in
front.   A moment after this and the battery was filled with men
falling back through it in great confusion.   I was compelled to cease
firing till our men passed from my front.   I thought I would then
be able to deal a destructive fire on the advancing line of the enemy,
but he was pressing so close upon our line, delivering his fire as he
advanced, his shots taking effect on my horses, I was compelled to
retire the battery.   This I succeeded in doing by leaving one piece of
the left section on the field, 5 horses being killed and disabled belonging to the piece.   The limber was upset and rendered worthless.
The piece was afterward drawn to the rear by hand by my own men
and by some of the men belonging to the Twenty-sixth Regiment
Ohio Volunteer Infantry.   I moved five pieces of the battery to the
rear with the regiments of the brigade across the road and field to
the timber, and again opened fire with other batteries on my left on
the enemy, who did not attempt pursuit over the open field.   The
brigade suffered severely in killed and wounded.   I received a painful
wound in the left arm, but fortunately not serious enough to prevent
me from remaining with the battery.   The brigade was soon ordered
forward over the field near the position first taken.   I was ordered
by Colonel Buell to move with it.   I did so promptly, got into position, and commenced firing at a range of 90 or 100 yards at the enemy's lines, then lying down in the woods.   I am positive that while
in this position I did the enemy serious injury, but his musketry
fire became so heavy, terrible, and galling that to remain there longer
was only to insure me that I would not have a horse left.   I gave the
order to limber to the rear.

The execution of the order had scarcely begun when the infantry
began to fall back, being charged by the enemy *en masse*, who came
yelling like devils.   Three of my pieces were left on the field, but
the enemy was again charged by our troops and my pieces retaken.
I then moved to the rear and worked nearly all night in repairing
carriages and harness, and supplying with extras, and from my battery and forge teams, the horses killed and disabled during the day.

On the morning of the 20th, before daylight, I was ordered by
Captain Baldwin, of Colonel Buell's staff, to move about 1 mile
and a half to the left.   Here we got some breakfast and I think two
days' rations were issued to the men.   About 9 a. m. I moved the
battery with the brigade (Colonel Buell's) nearly east to the front,
where a little work had been made of rails, limbs, and logs ; here I
put the pieces in position in battery with the brigade for support;
fired but three or four shots from this position ; received an order
after some time to move to the left, the infantry moving by the left
flank.   I limbered to the left and moved as I was ordered by Colonel
Buell to do with them.   We had gone but a short distance till I
thought it might become necessary to again form in battery to
fire nearly to the rear.   I formed my pieces forward into line, left
oblique, leaving the infantry between me and the enemy, who was

then advancing on our right. I moved in line as far as I possibly could, then broke into column of sections and finally into column of piece. When moving in this position the enemy burst upon us in such force as to render our holding (I mean the brigade) them back impossible. I then turned the head of my column to the left, moved across a corn-field to the crest of a hill about 400 yards distant. I then formed in battery and was told by Colonel Starling, of Major-General Crittenden's staff, to hold my fire till our own men got out of the timber. I immediately cautioned my lieutenants about holding fire till ordered, but a few moments elapsed, however, till the enemy came up in splendid style in heavy lines to the right of my front. I ordered firing to commence with shell and canister. I am confident that we killed and wounded hundreds of them as they came up. Other batteries were in the same line with mine and dealing perhaps equal destruction to the enemy, but just then when I supposed that we were going to drive them back, we received a galling fire from the enemy who had got position in force on our right flank and rear; but a moment more and the enemy was charging us from the right. My horses were killed and disabled, and I could do nothing but leave the battery in his possession.

The following casualties occurred during the 19th and 20th: 1 man killed, 8 wounded, and 7 missing.

I am of the opinion that most of the 7 missing are wounded and in the hands of the enemy. I cannot tell the exact number of rounds of ammunition expended, but believe it to have been between 700 and 750 rounds. I lost 56 horses killed and disabled, 21 on the 19th, 35 on the 20th. I have only 35 serviceable horses left and some 10 or 12 unserviceable, battery and forge wagons, 1 caisson, and 2 limbers. The enemy got with my caissons and limbers about 350 rounds of ammunition.

My officers and men I believe did their whole duty. Lieutenants Voris, Winsor, Stokes, and Eldred for the service rendered at all times, have my thanks. Lieutenant Eldred had charge of the line of caissons and I believe did as well as could have been done under the circumstances. Lieutenants Winsor and Stokes behaved with a coolness and bravery that was certainly commendable.

I am, sir, very respectfully,

GEORGE ESTEP,
Captain, Commanding Eighth Indiana Battery.

Capt. J. G. Elwood,
Acting Assistant Adjutant-General, First Brigade.

No. 144.

Report of Brig. Gen. George D. Wagner, U. S. Army, commanding Second Brigade.

HEADQUARTERS,
Chattanooga, Tenn., September 29, 1863.

Sir: I have the honor to report that on the 16th of August, I received orders to move with my command. The route was by way of Tracy City to Therman, in Sequatchie Valley, where it arrived on the evening of the 18th. This was a very difficult road, as the mountain was very steep and rocky; the men had to push the wagons and artillery for a mile, working all night ; bridges had also to be repaired on the way.

On the 19th, I was ordered by General Wood, who came up with the remainder of his command, to take three days' rations without baggage and move in the direction of Chattanooga by the Anderson road as far as the eastern edge of Walden's Ridge, which is some 5 miles from Chattanooga, and from which the town and fortifications were in plain view.   On the next day, Colonel Wilder, with his mounted infantry, arrived in front of the city, and opened upon it with artillery and was replied to by the enemy.   In the evening he fell back near my camp, where he remained until we entered the city. About the same time, General Hazen, with a brigade, had advanced from Dunlap to the Tennessee Valley, at Poe's Tavern, some 12 miles from Chattanooga and about 10 miles above my position and some 6 miles from Harrison, while Colonel Minty, with a brigade of cavalry, was posted at Smith's Cross-Roads.   Colonels Wilder and Minty guarded the river from Williams Island to Washington, a distance of about 50 miles, having strong pickets at the fords and crossings, and constantly patrolling the entire distance.   The enemy had at Chattanooga a pontoon bridge, ready to swing around, and could have in a short time been ready to cross a column of troops.   This made the utmost vigilance necessary; and on one or two occasions it was thought they were about to do so [to cross troops], and I think it was intended and would have been done had they not been kept in continual doubt as to our intentions by the continual changing of our troops, and by making demonstrations at other places so as to entirely mislead them as to our real design.   During the time that my command was in front of Chattanooga, the city was frequently shelled, which had little effect except to frighten the citizens.

On the 8th of September, I became convinced that the enemy were evacuating, and dispatched to General Rosecrans the fact.   Later in the day I informed him they had left and that I would take possession next morning, and which was done by the Ninety-seventh Ohio Volunteers by crossing the river in boats, which we had prevented the enemy from destroying by posting artillery on the bank of the river supported by sharpshooters.

On the 8th, Colonel Wilder, who was at Friar's Island, 7 miles above, reported that the enemy had withdrawn.   I sent him word to throw across the river a light party to reconnoiter and to support them, and if it should prove true that they had gone, to cross his entire force.   This there was not time to do.   That day he crossed the Seventeenth Indiana Volunteers on to the island, where they remained all night, ready to cross early in the morning, but by daylight the enemy had returned with some artillery, and opened from some works on the opposite side of the river and the right was withdrawn. The crossing was made in the evening, the enemy retiring as we had possession of Chattanooga and General Crittenden's corps had marched in the direction of Rossville.   General Hazen was directed to cross at Friar's Island.   Colonel Minty was also directed to cross at once and report to General Crittenden.

On the 10th, I took command of Chattanooga.

　　　Your obedient servant,

　　　　　　　　　　　　　G. D. WAGNER,
　　　　　　　　　Brigadier-General, Commanding.

Lieutenant-Colonel GODDARD,
　　　Assistant Adjutant-General.

ADDENDA.

Semi-weekly report of effective force at the post of Chattanooga, Tenn., Brig. Gen. George D. Wagner, commanding.

Command.	Headquarters.			Infantry.			Cavalry.		
	Commissioned officers.	Enlisted men.	Total.	Commissioned officers.	Enlisted men.	Total.	Commissioned officers.	Enlisted men.	Total.
Headquarters post, Brig. Gen. G. D. Wagner.	10	28	38						
15th Indiana Volunteers, Col. G. A. Wood.				28	323	351			
40th Indiana Volunteers, Col. J. W. Blake.				30	345	375			
57th Indiana Volunteers, Lieut. Col. G. W. Lennard.				27	251	278			
97th Ohio Volunteers, Lieut. Col. M. Barnes.				25	409	434			
Battalion 110th Illinois Volunteers, Capt. E. H. Topping.				11	244	255			
Company B, 14th Ohio Volunteers, Capt. George W. Kirk.				3	46	49			
3d Battalion, 3d Indiana Cavalry, Lieut. Col. Robert Klein.							8	151	159
10th Indiana Battery, Lieut. W. A. Naylor.									
Total	10	28	38	124	1,618	1,742	8	151	159

Command.	Artillery.			Total.			Aggregate.	Number of horses.	Number of guns.
	Commissioned officers.	Enlisted men.	Total.	Commissioned officers.	Enlisted men.				
Headquarters post, Brig. Gen. G. D. Wagner.				10	28		38	28	
15th Indiana Volunteers, Col. G. A. Wood.				28	323		351		
40th Indiana Volunteers, Col. J. W. Blake.				30	345		375		
57th Indiana Volunteers, Lieut. Col. G. W. Lennard.				27	251		278		
97th Ohio Volunteers, Lieut. Col. M. Barnes.				25	409		434		
Battalion 110th Illinois Volunteers, Capt. E. H. Topping.				11	244		255		
Company B, 14th Ohio Volunteers, Capt. George W. Kirk.				3	46		49		
3d Battalion, 3d Indiana Cavalry, Lieut. Col. Robert Klein.				8	151		159		
10th Indiana Battery, Lieut. W. A. Naylor.	4	118	122	4	118		122	100	6
Total	4	118	122	146	1,915		2,061	128	6

G. D. WAGNER,
Brigadier-General, Commanding Post.

September 14, 1863.

No. 145.

Reports of Col. Charles G. Harker, Sixty-fifth Ohio Infantry, commanding Third Brigade.

HDQRS. 3D BRIG., 1ST DIV., 21ST ARMY CORPS,
*Camp on Trenton and Chattanooga Road, 1½ miles
from junction of Trenton Branch Railroad with Nashville and Chattanooga Railroad, September 8, 1863.*

SIR: I have the honor very respectfully to submit the following report of the reconnaissance made by my brigade in the direction of Chattanooga on yesterday, the 7th instant:

My command, consisting of four regiments of infantry, the One hundred and twenty-fifth, Sixty-fifth, and Sixty-fourth Ohio, and Third Kentucky, and two pieces of artillery, left the camp at 1 p. m. yesterday. My instructions from the general commanding the division were, in substance, as follows: To proceed in the direction of Chattanooga, feeling my way very carefully, and not to push my reconnaissance beyond the point where the wagon road crosses Lookout Creek, and not so far as that point if I should deem it unsafe, and to return to camp before nightfall.

After leaving our pickets I disposed of my force to the best of my judgment and advanced with great caution. About 300 yards beyond the junction of the Trenton Railroad with the Nashville and Chattanooga Railroad, I first encountered the enemy's vedettes, which retreated rapidly before our skirmishers. We soon after reached a thin line of the enemy's infantry skirmishers which were driven rapidly by our own.

The general width of the valley between the secondary ridges was about half a mile. My skirmishers covered this entire distance, and there was more or less skirmishing along the entire line.

At a point about three-quarters of a mile northeast of the Trenton and Chattanooga Railroad, there is a ford on Lookout Creek, and a road leading thence along Lookout Mountain to Chattanooga. Near this I left four companies in charge of a field officer to guard the crossing and keep me apprised of any movement upon my right. I also sent four companies in charge of a field officer to take a strong position on the Kelley's Ferry and Wauhatchie road to guard against any demonstration upon my left. I then marched on until my advance reached Parker's house. At this point a road from Kelley's Ferry comes into the main Trenton and Chattanooga road. From Parker's house there are two wagon roads to Chattanooga, the right fork running north 65° east to the base of Lookout Mountain, the left fork running nearly due north until it intersects the main wagon road to Kelley's Ferry, about half a mile from Parker's house. This road then takes a winding northeasterly course toward the base of Lookout Mountain, crossing Lookout Creek at a bridge 1 mile from Parker's house and 4 miles from Chattanooga. I took the right fork.

When the most of my force had reached the vicinity of Parker's house, the enemy opened upon me with artillery located on the western slope of Lookout Mountain. The battery or batteries were estimated to be from 300 to 400 feet above the level of the railroad and about 1,100 yards from my main command, though my skirmishers were much nearer, having arrived at the crossing of Lookout Creek. I could not ascertain the number of his pieces, but from the extreme right to the left the distance was about 200 yards. These batteries command all the ground in the vicinity of the right fork, or the road upon which I was at the time. Their pieces were light 6 and 12 pounders. They had our range quite accurately, dropping their shells (many of which did not explode) quite near us, but, taking advantage of the ground, my casualties were very light.

I found the map furnished me very incorrect. I herewith inclose a more correct one* based upon my own observation and the best information I could gather from the citizens, &c.

The strength of the enemy must only be inferred from circumstances. They presented a strong line of skirmishers in the vicinity of the crossing of Lookout Creek, and when so hotly engaged by our own as to be unable to resist us longer, they were ordered to "fall back on their regiment or regiments," supposed to be not far from the right of the creek at the ford. But as the battery opened upon us shortly after this, and as I was ordered not to go beyond Lookout Creek, the regiments did not become engaged. From Mr. Parker (who has the reputation of being a Union man) I learned that one brigade (Strahl's) was encamped about 1 mile to the east of his house as late as the 5th instant. Mr. P[arker] has a pass dated "Headquarters Strahl's brigade, on outpost duty, September 3, 1863."

Mr. P[arker] states that he was in Chattanooga on the 3d; that the mountain is strongly fortified to guard the approaches from this direction; that he saw but few troops in the town and no artillery there, but from the indication of the woods in the surrounding country, and from what he could learn, he believed the enemy were there in strong force. A prisoner whom we captured stated that Bragg was being re-enforced from Johnston's command, and also from South Carolina. The battery which opened upon me commands all the ground in the vicinity of the road upon which I was approaching. A column cannot approach from this direction without being subjected to great slaughter, and should it succeed in approaching so near as to make the guns which opened upon me ineffective from their great elevation, it is reasonable to suppose that there are lower batteries which might be brought to bear upon us. Should it be designed to approach from this direction, I would recommend another reconnaissance by the left fork of the road from Parker's house. It is possible that new facts might thus be developed in regard to the nature of the ground, the position and strength of the enemy's batteries, which from the late hour of the day and the nature of my instructions, safety of my command, &c., did not permit me to ascertain.

I regard his position, however, as a very formidable one, if he intends making a stubborn resistance.

Having pushed my reconnaissance as far as ordered, and carried out my instructions to the best of my ability, I returned to camp, arriving about nightfall.

My loss was 1 man killed by the bursting of a shell.

I have the honor to be, very respectfully, your obedient servant,

C. G. HARKER,
Colonel, Commanding Brigade.

Capt. M. P. BESTOW,
Assistant Adjutant-General, First Division.

---

* Not found.

[Indorsements.]

HDQRS. 1ST DIVISION, 21ST ARMY CORPS,
Junction of Road via Whiteside's and Trenton Road,
September 8—1.30 p. m.

Respectfully forwarded, through corps headquarters, for the information of the commanding general of the army.

I sent in the substance of Colonel Harker's verbal report last evening, immediately on his return, but time was necessary this morning for the preparation of the written report and map.* The arrangements made for the reconnaissance, and the time of its moving, were well adjusted, and the reconnaissance itself was most brilliantly and successfully conducted by Colonel Harker. I do not believe that military annals offer an instance of a more daring reconnaissance made by so small a force against an intrenched position, strongly garrisoned, attended with so little loss.

TH. J. WOOD,
Brigadier-General, &c., Commanding.

HEADQUARTERS TWENTY-FIRST ARMY CORPS,
September 8, 1863.

Respectfully forwarded, commending Colonel Harker for his conduct and his report.

T. L. CRITTENDEN,
Major-General, Commanding.

—

THREE MILES FROM GORDON'S MILLS ON RECONNAISSANCE.
General WOOD :

GENERAL : I have been driving the enemy's cavalry to this point. Jackson's brigade of infantry encamped here last night. We have mortally wounded one cavalryman, who reports himself belonging to an Arkansas regiment of Forrest's command. They have resisted my skirmishers somewhat stubbornly, and have opened upon me with two pieces of artillery. I believe it the rear guard of the enemy. I do not believe he will stand this side of La Fayette. I will push the reconnaissance about 2 miles farther, and if I do continue to meet with more resistance, will return to the gap near Rossville and await orders.

C. G. HARKER.

[Indorsement.]

HDQRS. FIRST DIVISION, TWENTY-FIRST ARMY CORPS,
September 11, 1863.

Respectfully forwarded for the information of the commanding general.

I have ordered Colonel Harker to press forward to Gordon's Mills, where I will make a junction with him.

TH. J. WOOD,
Brigadier-General, Commanding.

—

HDQRS. THIRD BRIGADE, TWENTY-FIRST ARMY CORPS,
Gordon's Mills, September 11, 1863—3.30 p. m.

GENERAL : I have driven the enemy's cavalry beyond the crossing

———————————————————————

* Map not found.

of the stream at this place. I have taken up a strong position, and will await orders two hours, giving my men an opportunity to rest and make coffee.

From Captain Oldershaw, assistant adjutant-general, Twenty-first Army Corps, I learned that General Wood was ordered over to my support, but have not heard from him yet. If I do not hear from him by 6 p. m., I will return to Rossville. Bragg, Hill, and Polk left here last night, with infantry and artillery; retreated on La Fayette road. It is believed by citizens, prisoners, and contrabands that the enemy have gone to Rome. There is no good water for a camp between here and Rossville.

Very respectfully, your obedient servant,

C. G. HARKER,
Colonel, Commanding Brigade.

Brigadier-General GARFIELD,
Chief of Staff, Chattanooga.

—

HDQRS. THIRD BRIG., FIRST DIV., 21ST ARMY CORPS,
September 11, 1863.

GENERAL: In my dispatch of 3.30 p. m. I stated that I should fall back to Rossville at 5.30 p. m. if I received no further orders. If we are to pursue the enemy by this route it will be unwise to fall back, as I can hold this position until re-enforced, being persuaded that there is no considerable force except in my front, and that only a large force of cavalry, which I do not fear. There is heavy cannonading just commenced in the direction of Stevens' Gap, 12 miles from this place. Please send me orders. Prisoners and contrabands represent the cavalry force in my front at two brigades, one of which is Armstrong's, under Forrest. All agree that a very large force of infantry and artillery left here last night and early this morning.

Respectfully,

C. G. HARKER,
Colonel, Commanding Brigade.

Brigadier-General GARFIELD,
Chief of Staff.

P. S.—Having just received dispatch from General Wood, I shall remain here until he comes. No cannonading toward Stevens' Gap for fifteen minutes.

—

HDQRS. THIRD BRIG., FIRST DIV., 21ST ARMY CORPS,
Gordon's Mills, on Chattanooga and La Fayette Road,
September 12, 1863.

SIR: I have the honor to submit the following report of the reconnaissance made by my brigade on the Chattanooga and La Fayette road:

At 5 a. m., on the morning of the 11th instant, while my brigade was encamped on Chickamauga Creek on the road leading from Chattanooga to Ringgold, via Rossville, and about 5 miles east of the latter place, I was ordered by General Wood, commanding First

Division, Twenty-first Army Corps, to move my brigade and make a reconnaissance toward La Fayette, Ga., in obedience to orders received from department headquarters, of which the following is an extract:

The general commanding directs you to move immediately a brigade and battery back to Rossville, and post it in advance of the pass so as to command the La Fayette road, and in the morning to make a reconnaissance out on the La Fayette road far enough to ascertain whether there be any force threatening our communication.

I understood that I was expected to return to the gap at Rossville and await further orders. At 5.30 a. m. I left camp for Rossville with my brigade, consisting of the Sixty-fourth, Sixty-fifth, and One hundred and twenty-fifth Ohio, and Third Kentucky Regiments of Infantry, and the Sixth Ohio (Independent) Battery. About 2 miles from camp my flankers discovered 2 or 3 of the enemy's cavalry on my left flank, evidently a small scouting party. Arriving at the gap in Missionary Ridge, on the Rossville and La Fayette road, via Gordon's Mills, I left my train and caissons in a secure position on the western slope of the ridge with a guard of two companies, and placed four pieces of artillery in position to command the gap from the southeast. These pieces were supported by a regiment of infantry, under command of Colonel Opdycke, One hundred and twenty-fifth Regiment Ohio Volunteers. This force was intended to hold the gap and cover my retreat, in case I was compelled to fall back by the large force reported in my front. I had proceeded about three-fourths of a mile from the gap when my advance encountered a small number of the enemy's cavalry, which retreated rapidly before my skirmishers. The skirmishing was light until I had proceeded about 3 miles from the gap, when it became more spirited, the enemy resisting with dismounted cavalry supporting two pieces of artillery, which opened upon my advance. They were soon driven from their position, and my advance resumed.

While presenting a large front of skirmishers, I kept the main body of my command well to the right until arriving at the vicinity of the gap in Missionary Ridge, through which the Rossville and La Fayette road, via Couch's, passes. This disposition, while it secured my right flank, enabled me, from prominent points, to observe the country to my left, and in case of encountering a superior force to fall back along the ridge. Near Cloud's Store, about 3½ miles from Rossville, a private of the enemy's cavalry fell in our hands, mortally wounded. He reported himself as belonging to the Third Arkansas Regiment, of Armstrong's brigade, Forrest's division. He stated that two brigades were in my front—Armstrong's and another brigade made up of detached battalions—that this force was covering a large infantry force in the vicinity of Gordon's or Lee's Mills. As this man was in a dying condition, I attached much importance to his information. This information was but a corroboration of the statement made by a contraband captured by my command the evening previous, and which was taken by me to the general commanding the division. My movements were therefore made with great caution, in order to prevent a sudden encounter with a superior force.

I reconnoitered carefully every eminence near my line of march, and changed successively the position of my command from right to left, in order best to secure with safety the object of my mission. After passing that portion of Missionary Ridge between Rossville and the gap through which the La Fayette road, via Couch's, passes, my right became endangered by any force of the enemy that might be on the latter road.   I therefore took a commanding position on an eminence near the ridge, and reconnoitered the ground to my right and front.   A short distance from the latter position, and about $2\frac{1}{2}$ miles from Gordon's Mills, I learned from a citizen that a brigade of infantry had encamped there the night previous, but had left some time in the night or early in the morning.   This information was at once sent to the general commanding the department, and also to General Wood, commanding the divison.

I inferred from the information I now had that there was no infantry force of the enemy on the road I was reconnoitering north of of Gordon's Mills.   I, however, moved with greater caution, as I was now about 11 miles from Chattanooga, and was not aware that any troops had been ordered to my support up to that time.   A dense column of dust appeared on my right.   I moved a portion of my force in that direction, which, being perceived by the enemy, he retreated in haste.   I then pushed on toward Gordon's Mills, which I reached about 4.30 p. m., the enemy resisting more stubbornly as I approached the crossing of the Chickamauga.   Taking up a strong position near the mills, and throwing a strong cordon of outposts and pickets completely around my command, I allowed my men to rest and make coffee.   I again reported to department and division headquarters, intimating my intention of returning to Rossville about 6 p. m., unless I should receive orders to the contrary.   I learned that Generals Bragg, Polk, and Hill had been in the vicinity of Gordon's Mills until a late hour the evening previous, and that the great bulk of the enemy's forces were encamped in this vicinity at the same time, but had left some time during the night of the 10th, excepting the cavalry, which had harassed my front and flanks for a distance of 8 miles.   The enemy simply retired as I advanced, and, after taking up my position near the mills, his cavalry could be seen in the skirt of timber on my front, about one-half mile distant, watching my movements, and apparently endeavoring to learn my strength.

About 6 p. m. I received a dispatch from General Wood stating that he would join me that night, which decided me to remain in my position and await his arrival.   I sent a request to have Colonel Opdycke ordered up with the balance of my command.   General Wood arrived with Buell's brigade about 10 p. m., Colonel Opdycke about 1 a. m. on the 11th.

A short time before nightfall heavy cannonading was heard southwest of me, I presumed in the direction of Stevens' Gap.   I at once reported the circumstances to the general commanding the department.   I believe it to have been most fortunate that I was re-enforced during the night, as I cannot doubt that the enemy was in considerable force very near me.   At least one brigade (Wright's) encamped at Crawfish Spring, $1\frac{1}{2}$ miles from my right, that same night.   My isolated condition was, therefore, a precarious one.

I have great reason to believe that my very broad front of skirmishers (I had sixteen companies deployed a part of the time), and the frequent changing of my position from right to left, had a happy effect in deceiving the enemy in regard to my numbers.   I have learned since that my force was estimated to be very large.   I found that the impression upon the citizens was that most of the enemy's infantry and artillery were below or to the southeast of Pigeon

Mountain, and that they would probably endeavor to hold the gaps leading through the same to La Fayette, where they presumed a battle would be fought.   Others seemed to think that the enemy would fall back as far as Rome, Ga.   Though I endeavored to gain information from every possible source, I relied but little upon the statements of citizens who had either been subjected to such a system of despotism and tyranny that they were afraid to answer directly the most simple question, or who, from an ill-disguised sympathy with the enemy, were unwilling to give an unbiased opinion as to his strength, movement, &c.

I have the honor to be, very respectfully, your obedient servant,

C. G. HARKER,
Colonel, Comdg. Third Brig., First Div., 21st Army Corps.

Capt. M. P. BESTOW,
   Assistant Adjutant-General.

[Indorsements.]

HDQRS. FIRST DIVISION, TWENTY-FIRST ARMY CORPS,
   Gordon's Mills, September 17, 1863.

Respectfully forwarded for the information of the commanding general of the army.

The service of Colonel Harker's brigade was extremely hazardous, and was performed with great judgment, skill, and gallantry combined.   The men and officers of his command deserve great praise.

TH. J. WOOD,
Brigadier-General of Volunteers, Commanding.

HEADQUARTERS TWENTY-FIRST ARMY CORPS,
   Chattanooga, September 26, 1863.

Respectfully forwarded.

This report of Colonel Harker furnishes another convincing proof of his great value to the service.

T. L. CRITTENDEN,
Major-General, Commanding.

HDQRS. THIRD BRIG., FIRST DIV., 21ST ARMY CORPS,
   Chattanooga, Tenn., September 28, 1863.

SIR : In obedience to orders from the general commanding the division, I have the honor, very respectfully, to submit the following report of the operations of my command since crossing the Tennessee River, on the 3d of September, 1863 :

The troops, artillery, and ammunition of the First and Third Brigades, of the First Division, Twenty-first Army Corps, completed the crossing of the Tennessee, at Shellmound, about 9 p. m. on the 3d of September, 1863.   The troops bivouacked on the left bank of the river and awaited the arrival of the baggage train, which, having been ordered to cross the river at Bridgeport, Ala., joined the command about 8 a. m. on the 5th instant, nothing of interest occurring on the 4th.

About 1 p. m. on the 5th instant, my brigade, consisting of the One hundred and twenty-fifth Ohio Infantry Volunteers, Col. E. Opdycke commanding ; the Third Kentucky, Col. H. C. Dunlap commanding; the Sixty-fourth Ohio, Col. Alexander McIlvain commanding; the Sixty-fifth Ohio, Lieut. Col. H. N. Whitbeck commanding, and the Sixth Ohio (Independent) Light Battery, Capt. Cullen Bradley commanding, started from Shellmound on the left bank of the Tennessee, with three days' rations in haversacks, and one wagon for brigade headquarters, and one wagon per each regiment, and moved by the River road in the direction of Lookout Valley, via Whiteside's. My brigade having the advance of the division, the skirmishers and flankers of the leading regiment exchanged a few shots with the enemy's scouting parties, but suffered no casualties. We encamped about nightfall in the vicinity of Running Water Brook near Whiteside's. Whiteside's is a railroad station in a gorge of Raccoon Mountain, and is about 8 miles from Shellmound.

About 6 a. m. on the morning of the 6th instant, my brigade was again ordered to take the advance and proceed in the direction of Wauhatchie Station. This station is located in Lookout Valley at the junction of the Trenton and Chattanooga Railroad with the Nashville and Chattanooga Railroad, and about 8 miles from Chattanooga.

We had scarcely left our camp in the Running Water Valley when our skirmishers became engaged with those of the enemy. We drove the foe steadily before us, the resistance becoming more stubborn as we approached the vicinity of Wauhatchie Junction, which we reached about 1 p. m. Soon after entering Lookout Valley the signal stations of the enemy on Lookout Mountain were plainly to be seen. From these stations all of our movements could be observed, and from the lively manner in which the signal officers of these stations appeared to be engaged we inferred that information concerning our number, movements, &c., was being transmitted to the enemy at Chattanooga. The position taken up by the division near Wauhatchie, though the strongest in that vicinity, was an untenable one against a superior force. As this division was in the immediate vicinity of what was reported to be an overwheming force of the enemy and 14 miles from any re-enforcements, and as the best information that could be obtained, and the inference to be drawn from the enemy's signaling all seemed to indicate that an attack upon our little command was imminent, the general commanding very wisely resolved to fall back a short distance to a stronger position.

About 10 p. m. on the night of the 6th, the retrograde movement commenced, and the division took up a position on the Whiteside's road a short distance west of the junction of the same road with the Trenton and Chattanooga road and about 1½ miles south of Wauhatchie. We remained in this position until the following morning, when, after a little reconnoitering of the ground, a much stronger position was found near by and on the direct wagon road from Trenton to Chattanooga.

From this point my brigade started about 1 p. m. on the 7th instant to make a reconnaissance in the direction of Lookout Mountain. As I have already submitted a detailed report of said reconnaissance, I would respectfully request that the same be considered a part of the operation of my brigade, and will not encumber this with a repetition of it.

Nothing of special interest occurred on the 8th instant. The trains coming up, the haversacks were replenished with three days' rations.

On the evening of the 8th instant, the general commanding the division ordered me to start the following morning at 6 a. m. on a second reconnaissance toward Lookout Mountain. This order, I learned, was countermanded by the major-general commanding the corps. About 8 a. m., information having arrived of the evacuation of Chattanooga by the enemy, the division was ordered forward to occupy the place, the First Brigade, Colonel Buell commanding, having the advance. The place was occupied by our troops, without severe opposition, about 11 a. m.

Early on the morning of the 10th, the First and Third Brigades were ordered to be ready to move with the "light train" and three days' rations in haversacks. About 9 a. m. my brigade was put in motion on the road leading from Chattanooga to Ringgold. After a dusty and fatiguing march, we arrived about 1 p. m. at the crossing of a branch of the West Chickamauga, about 7½ miles from Chattanooga. As our advance was upon the rear of General Palmer's train, it was deemed expedient to make a halt, water our animals, and permit the men to make coffee.

While the command was thus at a halt my topographical engineer, Lieutenant Willsey, in making some observations in the front, discovered 2 contrabands with empty wagons. They reported to him that they belonged to Mr. Baird, who lived near by, and that they were returning from General Bragg's camp, having been sent there by their master with provisions for the enemy. One of the negroes —and, as it happened, the least intelligent of the two—was at once taken to the general commanding the division, but he told such a confused story that the general was loth to place confidence in it, and dismissed the matter for the time being. As the owner of the teams had clearly forfeited them, I directed that they be turned over to the quartermaster and that the contrabands be taken along as teamsters. About 3 p. m. the march was resumed, and continued until we arrived at the crossing of the West Chickamauga, which is about 10 miles from Chattanooga. It was then about 4 p. m., and we went into camp for the night. Some members of my staff having more fully questioned the contrabands above referred to, reported the result to me. I immediately sent for the more intelligent of the two, and after carefully questioning and cross-questioning him I became convinced that the enemy was either in great force near by or that this negro had been bribed to enter our camp as a spy. In either case his case required a minute investigation. I took him to the general commanding, who became equally impressed with the importance of the negro's statement, and conveyed the same in substance to the general commanding the department.

I desire respectfully to call the attention of the general commanding the department to the fact that information of such vital importance to our safety was derived from a negro slave driving a team on the highway. This negro was doubtless permitted to leave the enemy's lines through the inadvertency of the latter, or perhaps he imagined that a poor, ignorant slave would be incapable of conveying correct information; but I found his statements verified in every respect. It has taught me that in these critical times we should endeavor to elicit information from every conceivable source, and that the most humble may be profitably used in the promotion of our great cause.

About 5 a. m. on the morning of the 11th instant, I was ordered to return to Rossville and make a reconnaissance on the La Fayette road. The details of that reconnaissance having been forwarded on the 17th instant, I would respectfully refer the general commanding to my report of the same, and request that it be incorporated in this report.

On the morning of the 12th instant, as the enemy's cavalry was still hovering around our front and flanks, a part of my brigade was sent out and drove them about 1½ miles to the front, where we formed a junction with Brigadier-General Hazen's brigade, which had made a reconnaissance from the Pea Vine Valley to the Chickamauga. We then returned to the crossing at Lee and Gordon's Mills.

On the 13th, but little of interest occurred in my front, and the time was spent in strengthening my front by temporary breastworks made of rails, logs, and other material, to resist an attack of musketry from the front and flanks.

On the 14th, I again took two regiments, and went about 2 miles to the front, encountering but a small force of cavalry, and had 1 man slightly wounded. I discovered a light column of dust about 5 miles to the left, and after carefully questioning a citizen, who evidently sympathized with the enemy, but who was apparently afraid to commit himself either way, I inferred that the enemy were in force beyond Pigeon Mountain. This opinion was communicated to the general commanding the department. From this time until Friday, the 18th instant, everything was comparatively quiet on my front. About 12 m. on the latter day, Lieutenant-Colonel Palmer, inspector-general of the division, reported that the enemy were advancing upon the front of the First Brigade, then located on my right. A short time after, I perceived a column of dust approaching my front on the main La Fayette road. The ground in that direction from Gordon's Mills is comparatively level for a space of a thousand yards square, and free of timber; beyond that space the timber is large and quite dense. As the head of the column debouched from the skirt of timber, I perceived something white, which I first mistook for a flag of truce. I therefore sent immediate word to the pickets not to fire. I soon perceived my mistake, and as the column approached it deployed. When in effective range of my artillery, I directed the battery to open upon the enemy, and he at once gave way and sought refuge in the timber. A short time after a battery of the enemy opened upon Colonel Buell's brigade on my right. As it was within effective range of my own battery, I directed Captain Bradley to open with his guns, which soon silenced those of the enemy. From this time throughout the day, all was comparatively quiet on my front, except an occasional shot from the enemy's sharpshooters. Artillery was heard upon my left and east of the Chickamauga; it was apparently receding toward Rossville. From that we inferred that our troops were being driven.

This was reported to department headquarters, and General Van Cleve's division was sent to take position on my left. About nightfall sharp musketry could be distinctly heard, and I learned that a part of General Van Cleve's force had been sent to the relief of Colonels Wilder and Minty, who had been engaged, and that the enemy had steadily driven our forces until he had possession of the main La Fayette road. At dark the firing ceased, and all was quiet until the morning of the 19th, when firing of artillery and musketry commenced on our left, which became more general as the day advanced. There was also some cannonading on our right, apparently in the vicinity of Crawfish Spring. Except the shots from the enemy's sharpshooters, all was quiet on my front. About 3 p. m. I was ordered by the general commanding the division to move my brigade down the Rossville road toward the scene of action. In a short time my troops were under arms. As I arrived in the vicinity of the battle-field, about 1½ miles from Gordon's Mills, I was first directed by Lieutenant-Colonel Starling, of General Crittenden's staff, to take position on the right of Colonel Barnes' brigade, of General Van Cleve's division. I learned that Colonel Barnes' brigade was to go into action on the extreme right of our lines, and to strike the enemy in the flank. As the latter was supposed to be retiring (though stubbornly contesting the ground) in a southeasterly direction, I sent Major Coulter, of my staff, ahead to ascertain the right of Colonel Barnes' brigade, which being found I proceeded to move in position. I was soon stopped, however, by Lieutenant-Colonel Starling, who told me that Brigadier-General Davis (then on the left of Colonel Barnes) was hotly pressed, and requested the assistance of a brigade, and directed me toward his lines. I soon found General Davis, who showed me the direction to go into action, desiring me to relieve one of his brigades.

The One hundred and twenty-fifth Ohio Volunteers, Col. E. Opdycke commanding, was ordered in position nearly parallel to the La Fayette road, with its left resting near a small log-house on the east side of the road. The Sixty-fourth Ohio was ordered to go into position on the right of the One hundred and twenty-fifth Ohio Volunteers. I intended to go into action with a formation of two lines, keeping the Third Kentucky and Sixty-fifth Ohio in the second line.

The ground on my immediate front was slightly rising, and covered with a dense thicket and undergrowth. The enemy, therefore, had every advantage over us, as he could perceive our own movements, though his were concealed from us. I cautioned the regimental commanders that our own troops were in our immediate front, and not to allow our men to fire until they had passed our own lines. It soon became apparent that our own troops in my immediate front were yielding; at the same time a report reached me that the brigade upon my left was being repulsed, and that the enemy was advancing down the main road toward Gordon's Mills. This movement would expose my left flank and rear.

About this time there was very great confusion among the troops which had been engaged, and no one seemed to have any definite idea of our own lines or the position of the enemy. I was compelled, therefore, to resort to my own judgment alone and be guided by the general direction of the firing. The One hundred and twenty-fifth and Sixty-fourth Ohio Volunteers appeared to be advancing quite handsomely, though they were laboring with disadvantageous circumstances. As we were now attacked on my left, I quickly threw the Sixty-fifth Ohio Volunteers and Third Kentucky in position almost perpendicular to the road and to the general direction of my front line. It appeared now that we were attacked on both front and flank, and so fiercely that it required the utmost care to prevent the confusion in my own troops, which existed among those around me. Seeing the position of affairs, I directed the Third Kentucky to change its front in order to repel the attack on its right flank. This movement was performed most handsomely by Colonel Dunlap; the regiment moved through a heavy fire with a coolness and precision which merit the highest praise. So dense was the thicket that I afterward learned that a hand-to-hand fight occurred between some of the Third Kentucky and the enemy, the latter demanding a surrender, but our own troops proved victorious in the short encounter, taking a few prisoners. After changing direction, the Third Kentucky gave the enemy a volley which cleared its immediate front. At this time the Sixty-fifth Ohio Regiment was a litt'e to the rear of the Third Kentucky, with a view of making use of it as circumstances might require.

As what was at first my front line, to wit, the One hundred and twenty-fifth Ohio and Sixty-fourth Ohio, were now some distance obliquely to my right and front, and as from the denseness of the wood I could not have a direct supervision over my entire line, I sent an order to Colonel Opdycke to take command of the Sixty-fourth Ohio Regiment in connection with his own regiment, and to clear his own front of the enemy, as he had previously sent me word that a regiment of rebels was on his front, and I confined myself for the time being to the Third Kentucky and Sixty-fifth Ohio.

Again a more furious attack was made upon the left of the Third Kentucky; again the direction of the latter was changed, and the Sixty-fifth Ohio formed upon its left. My troops were now nearly all on the same general front, making, so to speak, a broken curved line with the convexity toward the enemy, with a short interval between the right of the Third Kentucky and the left of the One hundred and twenty-fifth Ohio Regiment, and stretching partly across the main road and making an angle of about 60° with it. In this position there was some of the most brilliant fighting that it has ever been my fortune to witness. Though its grandeur surpasses description, its severity may be imagined when I state that every mounted officer in the vicinity of this line except the adjutant of the Third Kentucky was dismounted by the enemy's musketry. Here the gallant Lieutenant-Colonel Whitbeck was most dangerously wounded while nobly commanding his regiment, and 5 officers of the line in the same regiment were stricken down, while in the ranks a great many of the enlisted men fell while bravely fighting. Never discouraged by their losses, they pressed forward most handsomely, and entirely dispersed the foe in front, and taking 204 prisoners. I then sent word to Colonel Opdycke to gain distance to the left and join me. This gallant officer brought up his regiments to me, closing the gap that had heretofore necessarily existed with but slight loss, while he did good service in punishing the enemy.

It will be seen from this hasty description that, from the troops having given way in General Davis' front, there was a wide gap, embracing the distance from the point where my troops first went into action to the right of the troops under General ———; that the rebels were rapidly advancing through this gap; that my brigade by sweeping across this gap checked their progress, and giving the troops on our right time to reform added greatly toward preventing a movement on the part of the rebels similar to that which proved so disastrous to the army on the following day, to wit, breaking through our lines and separating the right from the left.

Being now completely detached from my division, and having cleared everything on my front and left, and having pushed beyond the right of General ———, I resolved to rejoin my division, which was now about one-half mile to my right. I moved up and took position on the left and rear of Colonel Buell's brigade, and my troops were not again engaged during the night. When I was first ordered into action, I at once perceived that we would be compelled to fight in a perfect jungle, and that artillery could not be used to advantage; but, on the contrary, would be subject to capture should our troops meet with a sudden reverse. I therefore ordered Captain Bradley to remain on good ground in our rear, and await my orders. General Wood, after seeing my own brigade well engaged, remarked to me that he would now return and look after Colonel Buell and other troops on my right. I have learned that Colonel Buell's brigade, being overrun by fugitives, was compelled to fall back to the rear of the position, where my command first went into action. Captain Bradley, with the eye of a true soldier, selecting the best ground in his vicinity, opened with telling effect upon the enemy, inspiring our own troops with confidence and causing dismay among the rebel hordes. As our own troops fell back, the battery retired with prolonges fixed until it got a good position in the woods to the rear, where it was supported by our own troops. It here did great execution in repulsing the enemy, and remained in this position until I rejoined it. In this engagement, the brave and gallant Lieutenant Smetts was severely wounded while retiring his pieces with prolonges fixed, and firing at the enemy until the latter got within 50 yards of his section. This young officer is deserving of the highest praise for gallantry and daring.

About 1.30 a. m. on the 20th, I received orders to retire and take up a position in reserve on Missionary Ridge. My brigade was put in motion about 2 a. m., and arrived at a position on the ridge about one-fourth mile to the left and rear of the Widow Glenn's house on the La Fayette and Rossville road, via Couch's. We here permitted the men to build fires and make coffee.

Early in the morning of the 20th, both officers and men were supplied with three days' rations in haversacks, and with spirits buoyant with the success of the previous day, the command was again ready to go forth, and as we thought, finish the well-begun work. At 8 a. m. we were again ordered forward to an eminence about one-fourth mile in our immediate front, and, as I understood, the rear of a position occupied by General Negley's command. We soon took up the position indicated, the Third Kentucky and Sixty-fourth Ohio Regiments occupying the front in line of battle, with a strong line of skirmishers in front, the One hundred and twenty-fifth and Sixty-fifth Ohio Regiments in double column at half distance on the second line about 200 yards in rear, the battery having a very commanding position near the front line. My brigade was then on the left of the First Brigade, commanded by Colonel Buell. We had been in this position but a short time when we received orders to move forward and relieve General Negley's division. I understood that General Negley was ordered farther to the left, and that General Wood's division, now composed of three brigades, viz, the First Brigade (Colonel Buell's) on the right and my own (the Third) in the center and Colonel Barnes' brigade of General Van Cleve's division on my left. In this order we marched in battle array to the front and relieved General Negley's division, which was posted immediately on the left of General Brannan's division, and was a continuation of the main or front line of battle. We were advised that General Brannan had marched obliquely to the left and front, and that we must bear well to the left and "keep well closed up on Brannan." I kept well closed up on the right of Colonel Barnes.

The position to be occupied was pointed out to me by Major Lowrie, of General Negley's staff.   The line of battle on my front was in a wooded valley east of a by-road leading to the Rossville road and nearly parallel to it.   Temporary breastworks of wood, rocks, &c., had been erected by our troops, affording fair protection against infantry.   Immediately on my front there was an open field about 400 yards wide, bounded by timber on the south and east.   My skirmishers were thrown out in this field, and at once an exchange of shots with those of the enemy occurred.   We got well into position about 10 a. m.

For some time previous, light firing of artillery and infantry was heard on our left, which continually grew heavier and appeared to extend toward the right.   I had previously directed Captain Bradley to keep well to the rear with his battery.   I kept well apprised of movements, and told him to conform his own to mine, moving to the right or left as he might be directed, but not to bring it into the woods where it could not be used to advantage.

About 10.15 a. m., a section of the enemy's battery opened upon my front.   I ordered up a section of Bradley's battery, which silenced the enemy's.   I again ordered his section to the rear, as it was but a useless expenditure of ammunition to continue the fire longer.   About 11 a. m., I received orders, through General Wood, to move to the left, and support General Reynolds, in obedience to orders from the general commanding the department.   I immediately got my command in readiness, and sent word to Captain Bradley to conform himself to my movements.   Though we well knew that the enemy was immediately in our front ready to take advantage of any false step that we might make, yet as a part of General McCook's corps was immediately on our right, and, as I understood, ready to fill the gap which our removal would make, we at once moved to the left and rear in search of General Reynolds' division.   Having passed General Brannan's division, we were halted, as I understood that General Wood was not advised as to the exact position of General Reynolds.   I was soon directed by General Wood to move to the right again, as General Brannan was being pressed.   While executing this move, Lieutenant Germain, of General Brannan's staff, came up, laboring under great excitement, and requested me to hasten to General Brannan's relief.   He stated that Brannan's right had been turned, that Van Cleve's division, which had come to their relief, had broken.   I had moved but a short distance from this point before I was fired upon from the right.   I immediately formed line of battle, facing to the right and nearly perpendicular to the general line of battle heretofore existing, all of my regiments on the same line.

We had moved but a short distance, when we perceived a line of battle about 600 yards to our front, stretching across a corn-field.   This line was facing, and nearly parallel to our own.   The uniform of these troops was blue, and though we could not see their colors distinctly, many of us thought they were our own troops.

I could not conceive it possible that our troops had been so suddenly routed by an enemy who had thus far been repulsed at every point.   I was therefore in the most painful state of uncertainty that it is possible to conceive a commander to be placed in.   The idea of firing upon our own troops was a most horrible one to me, yet if perchance they should be rebels, valuable time was being lost to me, and they would take advantage of it; but to be on the safer side, I restrained my men from firing for the time being. About this time General Wood came up to me. He was likewise in doubt. Leaving the general with my brigade, I went to the left and front to satisfy myself. I was soon fired upon, and seeing their colors, I was assured that they were the enemy. Before I had returned to my position they had advanced and fired upon my brigade, which was promptly returned, but as they were now on my flanks, as well as front, I retired, by battalions, to the crest of a hill, running nearly perpendicular to the general line of battle. General Brannan, having rallied a part of his command, it, together with fragments of other commands, formed on the hill at my right, while my brigade formed in two lines to the left of Brannan, fronting to the south and nearly perpendicular to Reynolds' division, then on my left.

It will be seen that the right and a part of the center and Van Cleve's division being completely swept away, our line now reduced and in the form of a crochet, must resist nearly the whole rebel force in our front, or itself be swept away, and the great Army of the Cumberland—the pride of the nation—be utterly routed. Our brave troops, appreciating the importance of their position, promised to hold to the last. Nobly did they redeem their promise. From about 1 p. m. until nightfall this line was repeatedly attacked, but remained unbroken. The enemy failing to carry our line from the front, gradually worked around our right and must finally have succeeded but for the timely appearance of a part of Steedman's division of Maj. Gen. Gordon Granger's corps. These troops, taking position on the right of General Brannan, did most excellent service, and ultimately prevented our right from being turned. It affords me great pleasure to refer to the grand volley firing of the regiments of my brigade on the afternoon of the 20th. I have remarked before that while occupying a part of the " key of the position " they were formed in two lines.

They were lying a little below the northern or eastern crest of the hill; the front line firing by volley would retire, when the rear would move forward and execute the same movement. Thus a continuous volley fire was kept up for some length of time. This system was resumed whenever the rebels made their appearance in force, and repulsed them on every occasion. It had never before been my fortune to witness so grand an example of effective musket firing. Twice we nearly exhausted our ammunition, but were furnished with new supplies by Maj. Gen. Gordon Granger, and by Lieutenant Lyster, aide-de-camp to General King, to whom my thanks are due and most cordially extended. I should mention that soon after taking our position on the hill referred to, we were joined by about 40 men and stand of colors of the Forty-fourth Indiana Volunteers, Lieutenant-Colonel Aldrich commanding. This little squad of men behaved most handsomely and Lieutenant-Colonel Aldrich deserves great praise for his conduct. As night closed upon us the firing ceased, and my men were in the same position they had taken near midday and which they had held with such heroic tenacity. About dark we received orders to fall back to Rossville, throwing a strong line of skirmishers about 50 yards to the front with orders to remain at least one-half hour. After we had left the field we retired quietly and in excellent order, arriving at Rossville about 11 p. m.

I may here be permitted to remark that the presence of such tried and experienced officers as Major-Generals Thomas and Gordon Granger and Brigadier-Generals Wood and Garfield at the important position held by our troops, did much to inspire them with confidence during the eventful afternoon of the 20th.

On the morning of the 21st the First Division, Twenty-first Army Corps, was ordered to take a position on the left of General Palmer on the crest of Missionary Ridge. My brigade, including the battery, was soon placed in position. The troops were placed at work to construct temporary breastworks of rails, &c., while a fatigue party constructed a good road leading from the rear into Chattanooga Valley. About noon the enemy from the Ringgold road attacked our skirmishers, but did not drive them in. Soon after a battery from an eminence to the right and front of us opened upon my brigade. Bradley's battery replied and soon silenced the enemy. No loss on our side.

About 10 p. m. we were ordered to leave a force on our front, while the main body was to fall back on Chattanooga. Lieutenant-Colonel Bullitt and 200 picked men were left behind, with orders to remain until 2 a. m. on the 22d, if unmolested, but if attacked by overpowering numbers, to make a most stubborn resistance and fall back slowly toward Chattanooga. Our troops withdrew quietly and in good order. The rear, with Lieutenant-Colonel Bullitt commanding, arrived at the vicinity of our present position about 3 a. m. on the 22d instant. About 6 a. m. on the same day we were directed to our present position, where, after a little delay, our lines were marked out and our present breastworks commenced.

I have already stated in my report that I had directed Captain Bradley to keep well to the rear, but to conform his movements to my own. I did this partly from prudential considerations and partly from, as I conceived, a proper appreciation of the artillery arm of the service. While I have no disposition to criticise the conduct of others, and particularly my superiors, I nevertheless consider it my duty to state that I believe in many instances batteries in the late engagement were placed in positions where artillery could not be effectively used, and, from the nature of the country, could not easily be extricated. I believe that it was in this way that most of our artillery was lost in the late engagement. In other instances, from a want of judgment and knowledge of our lines, some of our artillery injured many of our own men. I submit this question as one of such great importance in the science of battles as to merit the serious consideration of the general commanding the department.

After the enemy had broken through our lines Captain Bradley, being some distance from me, and seeing from the nature of the country that he could not safely rejoin me, very wisely retired some distance to the rear. In doing this he acted upon the discretionary power conferred upon him by me. By his coolness, judgment, and skill, he succeeded in saving his battery, while so many in his immediate vicinity lost theirs. Captain Bradley states in his report that finding himself severed from my command, he reported to General Negley for orders. The latter directed him to follow his (General Negley's) troops into Rossville.

For details of the operations of my brigade, I most respectfully refer the general commanding to the official reports of my regimental commanders and of Captain Bradley.

In closing this report, I desire to call the attention of the general commanding to the good conduct, judgment, and skill evinced by regimental and battery commanders. To Colonels Opdycke, Dunlap, McIlvain, and Lieutenant-Colonel Whitbeck (wounded in action), to the memory of the lamented Major Brown, and to Captain Powell, commanding the Sixty-fifth Ohio after the fall of Major Brown, the country is indebted for gallant and distinguished services. Ever ready and willing to execute every order, and ever at their post in the hour of danger, they, by their lofty courage and intelligent conception of their duties, inspired their men with a confidence which nothing could shake. For their hearty co-operation, in every effort of mine, since I have had the honor to command them, my thanks are due, and most cordially extended. To them, and to the brave officers and men under their commands, is due whatever praise my brigade may have merited during the late perilous campaign. Without desiring to particularize where all did not only well, but handsomely, I still desire to refer briefly to the conduct of Colonel Opdycke, of the One hundred and twenty-fifth Ohio. The Third Kentucky and Sixty-fourth and Sixty-fifth Ohio Regiments had been tried at the sanguinary battle of Stone's River, and had acquitted themselves most admirably. We therefore had reason to expect much of them in the late battle on the Chickamauga. They exceeded my most sanguine expectations. But the One hundred and twenty-fifth remained to be tried. They moved on the field of battle with a precision and apparent indifference to danger which challenged the admiration of veterans. Their good conduct as a regiment may be inferred when it is stated that after passing through this terrible battle of two days' duration but one man was missing not accounted for as killed or wounded. The good conduct of this regiment must be attributed entirely to the untiring energy and superior military characteristics of their gallant leader, Colonel Opdycke. As second in command, he has rendered me great service in the late engagements. For the intelligent performance of every duty devolving upon him since he has been in my command, and for gallant and distinguished service in the late battle, I most cordially recommend that he be assigned to the command of a brigade. To reward such skillful officers by giving them higher commands will greatly add to the efficiency of this army. I would likewise especially mention Capt. Cullen Bradley, the commander of my battery. This experienced soldier has served his country most faithfully for seventeen years. He greatly distinguished himself in the battle of Stone's River, and maneuvered his battery with matchless skill in the late battle on the Chickamauga, saving his guns and nearly all his caissons when deserted by the infantry, and when almost any other officer would have lost his entire battery. Captain Bradley is a candidate for a position in the Regular U. S. Artillery. I most cordially recommend that he be rewarded with a commission which he has so worthily earned.

To the junior field officers of the brigade, Lieutenant-Colonel Bullitt, Third Kentucky, and Lieutenant-Colonel Brown, Sixty-fourth Ohio, and Major Brennan, Third Kentucky, the highest praise is due for their excellent conduct during the late battle, and the movements of my brigade previous to the engagement. They were all at different times in command of the skirmish lines, and were placed at different times in very responsible positions. They were ever found more than equal to the occasion; they have my warmest thanks. And here I must pay a just tribute of respect to the lamented Major Brown, of the Sixty-fifth Ohio. This heroic officer fell on Sunday while most gallantly leading his regiment. Well might his regiment waver for an instant as they saw his noble figure stricken down.

He belonged to that type of the true hero, who, without appearing to seek danger, is animated with lofty pride when placed in hazardous and responsible positions. He was ever ready to lead where brave men would follow, and ever went forth with that confidence of accomplishing his mission which manhood and true courage alone inspires. In him the regiment has lost a brave leader and benefactor, the service a valuable officer, and the nation a worthy citizen. May his name be indelibly inscribed upon his country's roll of honor.

To Maj. S. L. Coulter, acting assistant adjutant-general; Capt. Joseph M. Randall, acting assistant quartermaster, and to Capt. G. W. Roberts, acting commissary of subsistence, of my staff, my thanks are due for the prompt, efficient, and cheerful manner in which they have performed the duties of their respective departments since they have been serving on my staff. I desire particularly to commend Private Samuel Morris, of the First Ohio Cavalry, one of my orderlies, for his soldierly behavior throughout Saturday and Sunday. Through the thickest of the fight this brave youth was ever at my side ready for the performance of his duty. For his excellent conduct in battle, I shall recommend him to the Governor of Ohio for promotion.

I have the honor to be, sir, very respectfully, your obedient servant,

C. G. HARKER,
Colonel, Commanding Brigade.

Capt. M. P. Bestow,
    Assistant Adjutant-General, First Division.

ADDENDA.

HEADQUARTERS ANDERSON CAVALRY,
Chattanooga, September 11, 1863.

GENERAL : In obedience to your order, early this morning I took 20 men of my company to Rossville for the purpose of picketing the roads, arriving there at daybreak. Ascertaining that General Crittenden had passed with his corps on the Ringgold road at 2 a. m. the previous morning, I directed attention only to the La Fayette road about 2½ miles out, on which we encountered the enemy's pickets with an exchange of shots. Only a short time elapsed before I was requested by the colonel commanding Third Brigade of General Wood's division to accompany him with my men on that road, as he had been ordered to make a reconnaissance. I complied with his request and acted with his skirmishers with his advance for some time, when, finding it was his intention to push on toward La Fayette, I deemed it my duty to return. At that time (about 11 a. m.) we were pushing them, they occasionally firing a cannon shot. Our artillery was posted about a mile out on the road, but had not fired. In all probability it has been detached parties from this force which has given color to the rumors from Rossville for the last day or two. I presume they will vacate that section immediately.

With great respect, your obedient servant,

WM. P. ROCKHILL,
Captain Co. C, 15th Pennsylvania Volunteer Cavalry.

Major-General Rosecrans,
    Commanding Department of the Cumberland.

No. 146.

Report of Col. Henry C. Dunlap, Third Kentucky Infantry.

HEADQUARTERS THIRD KENTUCKY INFANTRY,
Fort Harker, Chattanooga, Tenn., September 27, 1863.

SIR: I have the honor to submit the following report of the movements and service rendered by my regiment under the orders and immediate supervision of our gallant brigade commander, from the period of crossing the Tennessee River at Shellmound, which was effected with the usual promptness peculiar to my ever ready mountain boys:

On September 5, at 2 p. m., we marched upon the River road to Chattanooga, leading the front of the Twenty-first Army Corps. Bivouacked 9 miles from Shellmound, resumed the march early on the 6th, again honored with the front. Skirmishers in charge of Lieutenant-Colonel Bullitt. Sharp skirmishing throughout the day with cavalry. No casualties except great fatigue of the column in following the rapid skirmishers, who emptied several saddles and captured their horses and equipments. Bivouacked on the night of the 6th, at junction of railroad at Wauhatchie; at 8 p. m. retired under orders 3 miles. On afternoon of the 7th, made reconnaissance within 3 miles of Chattanooga. No skirmishers from my regiment; but Major Brennan was placed in charge of the front line and led them vigorously forward, driving their cavalry, and confronted a battery on the point of Lookout Mountain. When the battery opened fire, our gallant and omnipresent Harker disposed every company, placing my command at three points, guarding every possible approach of the enemy. Constrained by orders to go no farther, we returned to camp, Third Kentucky covering the rear. Rested on the 8th; occupied Chattanooga on the 9th at 11 a. m. Marched on the 10th in direction of Ringgold, Ga., and bivouacked on East Chickamauga; marched on the 11th back to Rossville, and took road south to Gordon's Mills upon a reconnaissance desperate for any other brigade than one commanded by Colonel Harker. Sharp skirmishing all day with cavalry and artillery, but, with a bold front of skirmishers from the brigade, and the gallant Bullitt to cheer them on, with eight companies from my regiment forming part of the line, we successfully reached the limit of our orders at Gordon's Mills, with a loss of but 1 man wounded. I beg here to remark that the small loss is attributable to the long range which the retreating enemy were prudent to secure between us. Our skirmishers bravely did their duty, for, unlike the usual custom, the more rapid the firing the more vigorously they pressed forward.

At 4 p. m. of the 12th, a company from my regiment, with three others from the brigade, again in charge of Colonel Bullitt, made a reconnaissance across the Chickamauga. Soon they found the enemy, and with the usual vigor of the gallant Bullitt, pressed them until he developed a battery and heavy force in line of battle. When the cannonading commenced, I was ordered to re-enforce the skirmishers with my regiment, which was done at double-quick, fording the river, and coming so promptly to the relief that officers not of our command dubbed us Harker's cavalry. My regiment was moved to the right through bogs and swamps to flank the apparent foe, but issued from the woods to find no enemy to pay the tax of the trip. Returned to camp at the mills, built breastworks, moved to the left, constructed rail fort, ordered back to the mills with orders to hold the ford. Skirmishing in front. About noon of the 19th, ordered to the front where the battle was raging. Soon found the foe on every front; fought at every point of the compass; no confusion; changed front forward and to the rear in good order under fire. My guides took their position upon the line, as was their duty upon drill, and gallant sergeants of Companies A and B were wounded while in their positions with their guns inverted. My men were steady and obeyed my orders. My loss was 1 killed and 9 wounded. We captured 118 prisoners and sent them to the rear in charge of Lieutenant Newton, Company B, without a missing man unaccounted for. We fell back to our line and slept upon arms on the left of Bradley's battery and the right of the Seventeenth Indiana Mounted Infantry.

At 3 a. m. on the 20th, moved 1½ miles to the left, near department headquarters. At 6 a. m. moved to the front on general line of battle; deployed Companies A and B in charge of Major Brennan, who commanded the entire brigade line of skirmishers; severe fighting of skirmishers and conspicuous gallantry of Captains Powell and Barnett, and their officers and men, in driving the enemy; advancing through open ground, and the enemy, under cover of heavy timber, freely adding canister to the rapid musketry, and just at the juncture when my bold skirmishers had quieted our front, we were ordered to move by the left flank to the support of wavering lines in the neighborhood of Brannan or Van Cleve. Thousands of stragglers passed through our lines, but, every line officer being at his post and having no dodgers in difficulties, we escaped the avalanche until it struck my extreme right with a column of artillery and a pell-mell mob. But, with their usual clannishness, the dissevered parts of Companies A and C clung together under command of Lieutenant-Colonel Bullitt, assisted by Adjutant Hunt.

And just here I must remark that both of these officers behaved gallantly in gathering from the retreating mass some 400 stragglers, which they rallied upon the hill, which developed itself as part of the important key to the safety of the army. Being at the head of my regiment, I was not aware (at the time) of the aforesaid unavoidable rupture on my right. We moved onward to the left until we reached the right of Palmer (I believe). There we halted and built a barricade of rails. But as fate decrees for us, we never await the enemy, but go in search of him.

Under orders, and with the cheering presence of the peerless Harker, we moved by the flank to the right and entered the fatal field where a crouching enemy awaited us with a cross-fire. We moved forward in line of battle (by order) and halted at a fence, and instantly discovered the enemy in heavy lines upon our right flank. As promptly as possible we changed direction by file to the right at a double-quick, but before I could effect the disposition, we received a galling fire from two sides of a right-angle triangle, we confronting both faces. We returned the fire with deadly effect, but there was necessary confusion consequent upon the position and the fatality of the enemy's fire, which is evinced by the fact that just upon this ground I lost about 80 officers and men killed and wounded. Being overrun by hundreds of stragglers and the confusion increasing, so soon as the enemy were driven from this field, I took my flag and formed my regiment in the woods immediately adjacent, and moved, under Colonel Harker's orders, to the right upon the hill-top, and found a heavy force advancing, upon which we fired and ceased firing alternately by order, doubtful whether they were the enemy. This doubt encouraged their advance, and just here an avalanche of retreating hordes overran us, and compelled us to rally at the key-point 100 yards to the left. Here we resolved to do or die, and, buoyed by the presence and command of Generals Thomas and Wood and Colonel Harker, we did stay, occupy, and hold, and then and there expended the last of 130 rounds of ammunition, fixed bayonets, and coolly awaited the test of whether flesh will stand to take the steel. At this point, for four hours in the afternoon, our firing was by volley, marching to the crest of the hill, and at the command more than 50 deadly volleys we directed at short range upon the enemy. The effect is evidenced by their check upon the massive column. About 8 p. m. I was ordered to call my regiment to attention; with no ammunition, but every bayonet fixed, we were ready for a charge, and expected nothing less, but to our surprise, were ordered to file to the rear, where hordes had gone without orders. Until this order we held our position. No enemy was firing upon us when we left, and in perfect order we retired with our beloved commander, numbering 235 enlisted men.

I lost 1 officer killed and 8 officers wounded. Aggregate loss, 113 killed, wounded, and missing.

We retired to a position at Rossville, thence to this place, and are yet willing, ready, and feel able to hold " Fort Harker " until further orders.

With great respect, your obedient servant,

H. C. DUNLAP,
Colonel, Commanding.

Maj. S. L. COULTER,
Acting Assistant Adjutant-General, Third Brigade.

No. 147.

Report of Col. Alexander McIlvain, Sixty-fourth Ohio Infantry.

HDQRS. SIXTY-FOURTH OHIO VOLUNTEER INFANTRY,
Chattanooga, September 26, 1863.

SIR : I have the honor to report to you the part my regiment took in the advance on Chattanooga and subsequently, up to the time it occupied its present position.

The command, consisting of 27 officers and 296 men, crossed the Tennessee River at Shellmound on the afternoon of September 3, where it remained until noon of the 5th. It then marched with the brigade toward Chattanooga 8 miles and bivouacked for the night.

On the morning of the 6th, resumed the march in the following order : Third Kentucky, One hundred and twenty-fifth Ohio Volunteers, Sixty-fifth Ohio Volunteers, a section of Sixth Ohio Battery, and Sixty-fourth Ohio Volunteers. The command marched about 9 miles, but had no part in clearing the obstructions interposed by the enemy during the day. In the course of the night, the command was retired about 2 miles to a more advantageous position.

On the 7th, the regiment accompanied the brigade on the reconnaissance toward Chattanooga, in rear and supporting the section of the Sixth Ohio Battery, except Companies E and K, in charge of Lieutenant-Colonel Brown, who were detached toward Kelley's Ford to guard the left flank from an attack. The command, though exposed at times to the enemy's fire without having an opportunity of returning it, manifested the utmost willingness to discharge whatever duty was assigned it throughout the expedition.

On the 8th, remained in camp.

On the 9th, marched into Chattanooga.

On the 10th, marched 9 miles toward Ringgold.

On the 11th, returned 4 miles to Rossville and marched to Lee's Mills, 13 miles from Chattanooga, on the La Fayette road. During this advance, in the face of the enemy's skirmishers, my regiment had the right of the road, Companies G and K, in command of Lieutenant-Colonel Brown, as skirmishers. The troops during this severe march suffered greatly from heat and thirst, but the conduct of the men during this hazardous advance was praiseworthy.

On the 12th, lay at the ford near the mills.

On the 13th, worked at breastworks on the river bank.

On the 14th, made a reconnaissance with the One hundred and twenty-fifth Ohio Volunteers about 2 miles toward La Fayette. During this expedition, Companies D and I, under Lieutenant-Colonel Brown, were deployed as skirmishers, but only met with slight resistance. Joseph Laloe, of Company I, was severely wounded by a musket-ball in the arm.

On the 15th, 16th, and 17th, the command remained measurably quiet, but on the 18th, was ordered into line to defend the crossing at the mills, and remained there during the day and following night. Andrew Laird, of Company A, in charge of an ambulance, was shot in the foot, similar to a shot received at Stone's River in the same foot. Nothing further occurred to the regiment until 3 p. m. of the 19th, when it was ordered to the left about 2 miles. My command, being placed on the right in the front line, advanced into the woods, soon encountered a considerable body of the enemy, apparently somewhat detached from their main line. I immediately engaged them, and after a brisk fight of nearly half an hour, they fled in confusion, leaving in our hands about 20 prisoners, a majority of whom subsequently escaped by the mistake of those having them in charge taking the wrong direction to find the rear. The regiment soon after joined the brigade, from which it had been separated in the temporary confusion of establishing our lines under a heavy fire. In this contest, my regiment lost 5 wounded and 3 missing, 2 of whom were in charge of prisoners.

On Sunday, the 20th, the regiment moved with the brigade, and with it fought wherever and whenever an opportunity offered in the execution of its orders. On three several occasions, it was exposed to a severe fire from a greatly superior force of the enemy, and on each occasion behaved with great coolness and bravery.

The loss of the day was 1 captain killed, 1 captain wounded and left upon the field, 1 lieutenant wounded; 7 men killed, 43 wounded, and 10 missing. In the death of Captain Ziegler the regiment has lost a brave and good officer, and the army one of its faithful servants. Samuel A. Hayes, of Company F, who had lost his speech and had not spoken a word for nearly six months, on seeing a rebel fall that he shot at, exclaimed in a clear voice, "I've hit him!" and after that talked freely, being greatly rejoiced at his fortune. The brave fellow was later in the day wounded and left on the field.

On the evening of this eventful day, the regiment fell back in good order to Rossville, and on the following day, took a position on Missionary Ridge, where it remained till the night of the 21st, when it moved to its present position, and has since been engaged in the defenses of the situation.

The colonel commanding, in submitting this imperfect review of a campaign crowded with extraordinary incidents and gallant exploits, feels his inability to do justice to the endurance, courage, and unsurpassed bravery of those in his command who have so nobly sustained the honor of their State and flag, through such a severe ordeal, but he would beg leave to assure you that the regiment has, scarcely without an exception, justified the high expectations of its friends and country.

Your most obedient servant,

ALEXANDER McILVAIN,
Colonel, Commanding.

Col. C. G. HARKER,
Commanding Third Brigade.

No. 148.

Report of Capt. Thomas Powell, Sixty-fifth Ohio Infantry.

HDQRS. SIXTY-FIFTH REGIMENT OHIO VOLUNTEERS,
Chattanooga, Tenn., September 26, 1863.

SIR: I have the honor to submit the following as a report of the movements and actions in which the Sixty-fifth Regiment Ohio Volunteers has been engaged since leaving Shellmound, Tenn.:

At noon, September 5, 1863, the regiment received orders to march. Moved out on the Chattanooga road, and about 12 m., September 6, bivouacked within 7 miles of Chattanooga, in the Lookout Valley. At 10 p. m., on that date, the regiment fell back 2 miles and took position on a ridge to the west of the Trenton and Chattanooga Railroad, where it remained till 8 o'clock next morning, when it was moved off the ridge, and was stationed on the right of the road in the rear of the Third Kentucky Volunteers, with its left resting near the road.

At 10 a. m. on the 7th, the regiment was ordered down the valley on a reconnaissance, taking nothing along but guns, accouterments, and canteens. After advancing 1½ miles, three companies (B, F, and G), under Major Brown, were sent forward as skirmishers, and the regiment moved forward on the center. The skirmish companies from this regiment had the right of the line, and drove the enemy till they crossed the creek at the foot of Lookout Mountain, when the enemy opened on them with one or two pieces of artillery. The regiment was formed into line about three-quarters of a mile from the creek, advancing on the right of the One hundred and twenty-fifth Ohio, with its right resting on Nashville and Chattanooga Railroad. When within about one-half mile of the creek, the regiment crossed the railroad and formed in the woods on the right and to the rear of the One hundred and twenty-fifth Ohio, when the enemy commenced shelling.

After lying under their fire for about fifteen minutes, in which 1 man from Company F of this regiment was killed by the explosion of a shell, we were ordered to retire.

The regiment fell back until out of range of the enemy's shells, where it was formed across the road, and when the skirmishers came up marched back to camp, which was reached about 7 p. m.

The next day, September 8, lay in bivouac, and on the 9th, marched into Chattanooga, going into camp about 3 o'clock, a mile to the southwest of town. Moved out the next morning at 9 o'clock, and camped about 3 p. m. within 8 miles of Ringgold, Ga., near the Chickamauga.

On the 11th, marched back to Rossville, and moved out on the La Fayette road about 1½ miles, where the regiment formed on the left of the Third Kentucky Volunteers and opposite side of the road. The left and three companies (G, C, and D), under Major Brown, were sent to the front as skirmishers, their right resting on the road.

Afterward Companies A and E were sent forward to strengthen the right of the skirmish line under Lieutenant-Colonel Bullitt, Third Kentucky Volunteers. The regiment arrived at Lee and Gordon's Mills at 4 p. m., skirmishing all the way, and camping on the left bank of the Chickamauga Creek.

From the 12th to the 18th, we remained at Lee and Gordon's Mills, strengthening our position by breastworks, and awaiting an attack by the enemy, our pickets skirmishing with them as they would make their appearance.

On the afternoon of the 19th, about 2 o'clock, we were ordered to move to the left, which we did, following the Third Kentucky Volunteers and marching on the double-quick till meeting and engaging the enemy. The regiment was engaged most of the time till sundown.

During the engagement on Saturday, we took about 70 prisoners, among them a major. Lieutenant-Colonel Whitbeck having been wounded, Major Brown succeeded him in command. The regiment remained in front during the night until 3 a. m. of the 20th, when we moved to the left and rear to breakfast and draw rations, again moving to the front at 8 a. m., and taking part in the engagement up to 10 o'clock, when, being flanked by the enemy, we moved by the right flank and took position on the right of the Third Kentucky Volunteers, our right resting on the hill. We held our position till the regiment on our right (who occupied the extreme summit of the hill) broke in confusion, thus enabling the enemy to take possession of the hill. Our right being thus flanked, we suffered a severe fire from the enemy, and were forced to fall back. While occupying the position on the hill, Major Brown was wounded, the command falling on me, the senior captain having been reported to me as being wounded. The regiment fell back to the rear of the log-house, where it rallied, and I was ordered by Colonel Harker, our brigade commander, to take position on the summit of the hill to the right of the log-house. Captain Tannehill took command of a number of men who had become separated from their companies, and took position at the left of the house. The regiment, though having lost many of its best officers, and its ranks having been thinned by the loss of over one-third of its men, still held its position and did so for an hour and a half, when we were joined by Lieutenant-Colonel Bullitt with two companies of the Third Kentucky, who, at my request, took command and held the enemy in check till ordered by Colonel Harker to fall back to the rear of the log-house. Here the regiment was formed, having been joined by Captain Tannehill and the men under his command. We were at this time supplied with cartridges to make up 40 rounds to the man.   After a rest of about thirty minutes, I was ordered to take position on the left of the Sixty-fourth Ohio. The engagement then being renewed, we fired by volley, alternately, with the One hundred and twenty-fifth Ohio, until the enemy were repulsed, when I was ordered to take position on the right of the log-house, still occupying position in the line on the left of the Sixty-fourth Ohio.   This position was occupied till after dark, or about 7 p. m., when, with the rest of the brigade, we fell back to Rossville, and camped for the night.

The next morning, the 21st, the regiment moved out and took position on the Missionary Ridge, to the left of the road, the Sixty-fifth forming the second line, in rear of the Sixty-fourth, until ordered to report to Colonel Buell, commanding First Brigade, where the Sixty-fifth was formed in the rear as reserve.   After lying in this position for two hours, we were ordered to report to our brigade, and were formed on the right of the One hundred and twenty-fifth Ohio.   At 7.30 p. m. we moved to the front, relieving the Sixty-fourth Ohio, which was occupying breastworks of rails, our left resting in the woods and connecting with the One hundredth Illinois.   We left the works at 11 p. m., and arrived near Chattanooga at 2 a. m. on the 22d, where we bivouacked till about 7 o'clock, when we were moved to this position and have been engaged since in throwing up fortifications and strengthening the fort.   Lieutenant-Colonel Bullitt, of the Third Kentucky Volunteers, took command of the regiment, by order of Colonel Harker, on the 23d instant.

During the engagements on the 19th and 20th, the following-named officers of the regiment were killed and wounded : Maj. Samuel C. Brown, wounded on the 20th, from the effects of which he died on the 21st ; First Lieut. Nelson Smith, killed instantly ; Second Lieut. S. C. Henwood, killed.

Wounded : Lieut. Col. H. N. Whitbeck, First Lieut. Asa A. Gardner, First Lieut. Wilbur F. Hinman, First Lieut. Joel P. Brown, and Second Lieut. Otho M. Shipley.

Casualties among the enlisted men were as follows : Killed, 12 ; wounded, 65 ; missing, 18.   Total killed, wounded, and missing, officers and men, 103.

The foregoing report can be but very incomplete from the fact that the position in which I was placed was of such a character that many things transpired that escaped my notice.

Where all did so well (inasmuch as the Sixty-fifth never gave back before the enemy until ordered by its commanding officer, neither was it ordered to take any position that it failed to plant its colors there) it may seem out of place to mention individual cases, yet there are those who acted with that coolness and bravery under the most trying circumstances, that to especially mention them cannot detract from the merit due others.   First among this number is our lamented Major Brown, who, with so much coolness and bravery, demonstrated every characteristic of the true hero, realizing the magnitude of the cause in which he was engaged.   From the commencement of the engagement up to the time he fell, he was ever found where the danger was greatest, and by his noble daring imbued every heart in the regiment with a determination to conquer.   Among the non-commissioned officers, Sergt. Maj. S. G. Pope deserves special credit for the manner in which he labored to keep the men together, and the promptness with which he conveyed orders to the line officers, during the entire engagement. First Sergt. Samuel P. Snider commanded Company D on the 20th and bravely led his men, whom he was encouraging by precept and example to stand by the flag at the time he fell. Sergeant Harlam, the color bearer, bravely faced the storm of bullets that greeted him on every side, and, even after being severely wounded, stood at his post till ordered to the rear.

I have the honor to be, sir, very respectfully, &c.,

THOMAS POWELL,
Captain Sixty-fifth Regiment Ohio Volunteer Infantry.

Maj. S. L. COULTER,
Acting Assistant Adjutant-General, Third Brigade.

No. 149.

Report of Col. Emerson Opdycke, One hundred and twenty-fifth Ohio Infantry.

HEADQUARTERS 125TH OHIO VOLUNTEER INFANTRY,
Chattanooga, Tenn., September 26, 1863.

SIR: I have the honor to submit a report of the operations of my regiment since crossing the Tennessee River.

At 3 p. m., 5th instant, we marched with the brigade from Shellmound, Tenn., toward Chattanooga on the River road. The next day, p. m., we bivouacked 7 miles distant from Chattanooga. At 10 p. m., same day, we retired 2 miles to a strong position.

On the 7th, we formed a part of the force under Colonel Harker, who made a reconnaissance till we developed and drew the fire of the enemy's batteries, which were in position to dispute our entrance to the city.

The skirmishers of my Company D, led by Lieut. E. P. Evans, made a gallant charge and cleared a house of a very troublesome fire of the enemy. This reconnaissance was deemed hazardous, and the colonel commanding directed me to be prepared to fight to the last man, and if surrounded to cut our way out, but nothing serious occurred and we returned without molestation.

At 1 p. m. on the 9th, we entered Chattanooga and bivouacked in its suburbs.

On the 10th, at 8 a. m., we moved toward Ringgold, Ga., bivouacked again at dusk. We countermarched, on the 11th, to the La Fayette road, and made a reconnaissance upon it. The One hundred and twenty-fifth, two companies of the Sixty-fourth Ohio Volunteers, and four guns of the brigade battery were placed under my command as reserve near Rossville. The colonel commanding ordered me to be prepared to cover a retreat, should one become necessary. Suitable dispositions were made but not needed, as at 6 p. m. I received Colonel Harker's report from Gordon's Mills, with orders to send a copy of it to General Wood, and the original to department headquarters at Chattanooga. This was done with the utmost dispatch.

At 9 p. m. I received orders from Colonel Harker to join him with my command without delay. This was accomplished by 1 a. m. of the 12th instant. The same day we were on a reconnaissance across the West Chickamauga River.

On the 13th, the colonel commanding made a reconnaissance with my regiment to the vicinity of Crawfish Spring, where we were left on detached picket duty till the a. m. of the 14th. In the p. m. of the same day we were out again on the La Fayette road.

The 15th and 16th were partially spent in making barricades along the north bank of the West Chickamauga.

At night we were ordered to be ready to march at daylight with 60 rounds of ammunition to each man.

At daylight on the 19th, my regiment was ready for action with the following organization : Emerson Opdycke, colonel command-ing ; Capt. E. P. Bates, acting major ; Lieut. E. G. Whitesides, ad-jutant ; H. McHenry, surgeon ; J. E. Darby, assistant surgeon ; J. G. Buchanan, assistant surgeon ; Freeman Collins, acting sergeant major ; H. N. Steadman, commissary sergeant.

Command.	Commissioned officers.	Enlisted men.	Aggregate.
Company A, Capt. Joseph Bruff	2	46	48
Company B, Capt. A. Yeomans	1	43	44
Company C, Lieut. M. V. B. King	1	39	40
Company D, Capt. R. B. Stewart	2	31	33
Company E, Lieut. A. Barnes	1	39	40
Company F, Lieut. D. Humphreys	1	42	43
Company H, Lieut. Charles T. Clark	1	36	37
Company G, Lieut. William W. Cushing	1	20	21
Field and staff	6	2	8
Total	16	298	314

At 11 a. m. heavy firing of all arms was heard 2 or 3 miles to our left, and at 1 p. m. we were rapidly moved to the scene of conflict. Our attack was made with the Third Kentucky on our left and the Sixty-fourth Ohio on our right. The enemy seemed surprised at our appearance, and after a sharp encounter, in which I lost the first sergeant of Company A, killed, and 11 men seriously wounded, he disappeared from view, leaving 9 prisoners, one an officer, in our hands. The growth of small timber was so dense we could see but a few rods in any direction. I then received orders from Colonel Harker by an aide to assume command of the Sixty-fourth Ohio, and with it and my own regiment to disperse any enemy we might find. We were then on the right of the road upon which we came out from Gordon's Mills. Firing upon us soon commenced from our front, right, and rear. I immediately ordered scouts and skirmishers out to develop our surroundings. Their deployment had only com-menced when I received orders from the colonel commanding, by an aide, to bring the two regiments out and join him, which was done without serious interruption. We were then joined to the balance of the division, and in line lay upon our arms, without fires, until 2 a. m. of the 20th. We then moved about 1½ miles, and at an early hour were placed in position for the impending battle. Colonel Barnes' brigade, of Van Cleve's division, was on our left, the Sixty-fourth Ohio in front, and the Sixty-fifth Ohio on our right. This and my own regiment formed the second line, and Colonel Harker directed me to have general charge of it, and have its movements conform to those of the first line. I then directed Major Brown, commanding the Sixty-fifth, to maintain his relative position to the

One hundred and Twenty-fifth and to the Third Kentucky, which was in his front, as far as possible.

A sharp skirmish and artillery firing occurred to our front, when we were marched on the double-quick, by the left flank, to re-enforce Reynolds, where a heavy roar of all arms had been heard a short time. We had only come under the outskirts of the enemy's fire in our new position, when we were vigorously attacked on our right flank and rear by superior numbers. A change of front to rear on our left, which was executed under a severe fire, placed us (the Sixty-fourth on our left, Third Kentucky on our right, the Sixty-fifth still farther to the right, the whole nearly perpendicular to Reynolds' line) facing to the south and to the enemy. The line stretched nearly across a long open field. One hundred yards to our rear was a ridge running parallel to the line, which ascended into quite a timbered hill 200 yards to my right. The enemy's line, which was 200 yards distant, reached beyond our flanks, and was advancing upon us. A severe encounter with small arms raged for a short time, when General Wood in person ordered us to move forward. My regiment fixed bayonets and charged on the double-quick.

The enemy fled in confusion, and disappeared for a time. We pursued 400 yards and lay down behind a prostrate fence, which was upon another less tenable, but parallel ridge to the first one. This ridge also rose into a wooded hill 150 yards to our right. The other regiments of the brigade soon prolonged my line to the right and left. Another line of the enemy, more formidable than the first, appeared in the distance, moving upon us. The terrible splendor of this advance is beyond the reach of my pen. The whole line seemed perfect and as if moved by a single mind. The musketry soon became severe and my losses heavy; the color-sergeant severely wounded, the standard shot in two the second time, and the colors riddled with balls. The regiment to my left gave way, and then that upon my right. My Company A, thinking this meant for all to retire, arose and faced to the rear, but almost instantly resumed their position. The enemy came on and themselves prolonged my line to the right, occupied the wooded hill there, and enfiladed my line with a destructive fire. Lieutenant King, commanding Company C, fell dead, when Sergt. Alson C. Dilley assumed command of his company. Lieutenant Barnes, commanding Company E, went down with a broken thigh, and Lieut. E. P. Evans was placed in command. Captain Yeomans carried off a ball in his upper leg, but he remained with his company during the battle under severe pain. Numbers fell dead and more were seriously wounded, but the line was firmly maintained. Lieutenant Clark coolly remarked, "They can kill us, but whip us never." Seeing no relief, I retired the regiment to the ridge in rear. In doing so, some troops passed obliquely through my right wing, which caused a little confusion there, but the ranks were closed immediately, and the crest occupied where ordered by General Wood. This position was repeatedly assaulted during the day in the most terrific manner by heavy forces of Longstreet's corps, but it was triumphantly maintained until the battle was ended and till after dark, when we were ordered to retire, which we did without molestation. Late in the afternoon two pieces of the Eighteenth Ohio Battery were placed at my command. They aided much to repulse the enemy. The Forty-first Ohio and Ninth Indiana, of General Hazen's brigade, Palmer's division, filed 2 rods to my rear, and added their veteran fire in repulsing the last assault.

On the 21st, we were in position near Rossville and on the 22d, we occupied our assigned position in the lines around Chattanooga.

Capt. E. P. Bates acted coolly and efficiently as acting major. My adjutant, Lieut. E. G. Whitesides, was almost indispensable to me; his gallant daring was conspicuous, and his horse was shot under him. Sergts. Alson C. Dilley, Company C; Rollin D. Barnes, Company B; H. N. Steadman, of the non-commissioned staff, and Charles C. Chapman, of Company G, distinguished themselves for cool courage and capacity to command under the severest tests. I have recommended them to the distinguished consideration of the Governor of Ohio.

My casualties were:

| Company. | Killed. | | Wounded. | | | | Missing. | | Aggregate. |
| | | | Seriously. | | Slightly. | | | | |
	Commissioned officers.	Enlisted men.	Commissioned officers.	Enlisted men.	Commissioned officers.	Enlisted men.	Commissioned officers.	Enlisted men.	
A	....	2	....	8	....	1	....	....	11
B	....	2	1	11	....	....	....	1	15
C	....	1	....	7	....	4	....	1	13
D	....	1	....	5	....	1	....	....	7
E	....	1	1	12	....	....	....	3	17
F	....	3	....	9	....	2	....	....	14
G	1	2	....	3	....	1	....	....	7
H	....	4	....	16	....	1	....	....	21
Total	1	16	2	71	....	10	....	5	105

Justice demands that the facts in favor of 4 of the missing be officially noted. Two of them had just joined from hospital; 1 had no shoes, and on crossing a burning turf, on the 19th, his feet became so burned that he and the other two, not being able to keep up, were ordered back by their officer. The fourth one was left to take care of Lieutenant Barnes, which leaves the fifth the only case without excuse in the regiment.

Very respectfully, your most obedient servant,

EMERSON OPDYCKE,
Colonel, Commanding 125th Ohio Volunteers.

Maj. S. L. COULTER,
Acting Assistant Adjutant-General, Third Brigade.

No. 150.

Report of Maj. Gen. John M. Palmer, U. S. Army, commanding Second Division.

HDQRS. SECOND DIVISION, TWENTY-FIRST ARMY CORPS,
Chattanooga, Tenn., September 30, 1863.

CAPTAIN: I have the honor to report that on the 1st day of September, the brigades of Cruft and Grose, with Standart's, Russell's, and Cushing's batteries, marched from Dunlap down the Sequatchie

Valley toward the Tennessee River. Hazen's brigade, with Cockerill's battery, was at the time at Poe's Tavern, in the Tennessee Valley, and not then subject to my orders.

On the 3d of September, Grose's brigade reached the mouth of Battle Creek, and the following night and next day crossed the river on rafts. Cruft was sent, by order of the general commanding, by way of Shellmound; found good boats, and crossed without difficulty.

During the afternoon of the 4th of September, both brigades were brought together at Shellmound.

On the 5th of September, I received orders to march to Whiteside's Station, on the Nashville and Chattanooga Railroad, following Wood's division to that point, and then to move up the Valley of Running Water Creek. In the afternoon of that day, I followed Wood closely and reached Whiteside's at 9 p. m., and the next day marched up Running Water, clearing the road of trees felled by the enemy, and reached Cole's Academy, in Lookout Valley, near noon. My command remained at Cole's Academy until 4 o'clock in the morning of the 8th of September, and then moved down the Trenton and Chattanooga Railroad to Hawkins' Station, 1½ miles to the rear of Wood. At Hawkins' information was received from General Wood that the enemy occupied Lookout Mountain in strong force. I at once sent two regiments to reconnoiter the face of the mountain, to ascertain if it could be ascended, and found a gap accessible to infantry and cavalry, and applied to the general commanding the corps for his approval of an expedition to the top of the mountain to learn what the enemy was doing. I received his approval, and ordered Colonel Grose, with three regiments, to attempt the ascent at 3 o'clock next morning. At about 8 o'clock in the evening, Brigadier-General Wood called at my quarters and told me that he had received information that on the night before the enemy had relieved his infantry pickets along our front with cavalry, and proposed to make a reconnaissance toward Chattanooga with his own division early next morning, to be supported by me. I had already, with the approval of the general commanding the corps, ordered Colonel Grose to the top of the mountain, and was not able to meet General Wood's wishes.

At 3 o'clock on the morning of the 9th, Colonel Grose marched in execution of his order, and ascended the mountain with but little difficulty, and at 4 o'clock Captain McCook, of the staff of the general commanding, reached my quarters, and gave me information of the evacuation of Chattanooga.

Under orders from the general commanding the corps, at 8 o'clock on the 9th instant, with Cruft's brigade, two regiments of Colonel Grose's, all the artillery and baggage of both brigades, I marched toward Chattanooga, following Wood's division and all his transportation. The road around the spur of the mountain was rough and blocked by the wagons of the First Division; in consequence, the march was slow and fatiguing. Upon reaching the eastern base of the mountain, I directed my march to Rossville, without passing through Chattanooga, and when near there drove a small cavalry force before me, and halted at Rossville for the night.

At 5 o'clock on the morning of the 10th, I received orders from the general commanding the corps directing me to take 100 rounds of ammunition per man and five days' rations, and march on the Dalton road by the way of Ringgold in pursuit of the enemy. I was ordered not to wait for my train, but leave that under a sufficient escort to follow me.   I was then separated from my supplies and had with me but one day's rations.   I determined, therefore, to make a short march on that day, with the hope that the supply train would reach me during the night.   Accordingly, I marched to Pea Vine Creek, within 5 miles of Ringgold, and halted.   Upon reaching this point, a small mounted force of the enemy was seen in front, and Captain Norton, an officer of great firmness and experience, was sent forward with my personal escort, and a small detachment of cavalry (Fourth Michigan), to drive them off.   This small party attacked with great spirit, drove the enemy a mile, and as it was quite obvious that the parties of the enemy near were numerous and comparatively strong, it rejoined the column.

A few minutes after the return of our cavalry, a force of the enemy, under cover of a cloud of dust, charged the advance guard (four companies, First Kentucky) at full speed, threw it in confusion, and captured 2 officers and 56 enlisted men.   The pressure of other duties has prevented a full investigation of this unfortunate affair. None of the excuses yet tendered are satisfactory to me.   I will, for that reason, as soon as time will allow, bring the officers responsible to trial for what seems to me gross negligence in the performance of their important duties.   It is due to the regiment and all its officers that I should say that on all subsequent occasions during the late operations, all behaved most creditably.

The five days' rations required by the order of the 10th reached me during the night, and at 6 o'clock next morning the march was resumed by the way of Graysville in charge of the baggage of my own and Van Cleve's division, he having taken the more direct route to Ringgold over the hills.   At Graysville, Hazen's brigade united with the division, and the whole moved to Ringgold and bivouacked that night.

It was apparent on the 10th instant that the enemy were numerous on our front and right, but were rapidly drifting south.

On the 11th, Colonel Wilder, supported by Van Cleve, pushed a large cavalry force through Ringgold in the direction of Dalton. Reports from a hundred sources, citizens, deserters, &c., all pointed to Rome, Ga., as the point fixed for the concentration of the whole rebel army.

At 6 o'clock on the morning of the 12th of September, in pursuance of orders received during the previous night, I marched in the direction of Gordon's Mills, by the way of Gilbert's, on Pea Vine Creek. Upon reaching the road on Pea Vine citizens gave the information that a heavy cavalry force of the rebels had passed down toward La Fayette in the course of the night.   The bridge was cut down and the ford blocked, and signs of the recent passage of retreating troops abundant.

In accordance with the orders of the general commanding the corps, before referred to, my command was halted at the junction of the Gordon's Mills road with the La Fayette road for several hours to cover the march of Van Cleve's division, which had crossed the Pea Vine Valley lower down in charge of the transportation.

A few troops of the enemy were seen watching our movements. About 1 o'clock it was reported to me that firing was heard toward Gordon's Mills.   I pushed Hazen forward to learn the cause and effect a junction with our forces at the mills.   This he did with but little trouble.   About 2 o'clock I sent a portion of Cruft's brigade up the valley toward Pea Vine Church to clear that flank of the enemy, and learn the cause of firing heard in that direction.   This was handsomely done by Colonel Sedgewick and Colonel Rippey, with their respective regiments and one section of Standart's battery.   About dusk the whole division bivouacked at Gordon's Mills.

September 13, early in the morning, Grose's pickets were fired upon by the enemy.   After a noisy skirmish the enemy fell back. Grose remained in position during the day, watching a reconnaissance made by Van Cleve to the front, and Cruft marched back to Pea Vine Valley to support a reconnaissance by Colonel Wilder.

September 14, marched at 6 o'clock across Missionary Ridge to Henson's, in Chattanooga Valley; pushed one brigade 2 miles up the valley to Mitchell's.

September 15, started at daylight for the Chickamauga Valley. Marched by way of Crawfish Spring, and then up the valley to Gower's, two brigades occupying and covering the crossing at Gower's, and one was posted at Matthew's, near Owens' Ford.

September 16, Grose, with two regiments and one section of artillery, crossed the creek and drove a party of the enemy over the hills.

September 17, early in the morning, the enemy's cavalry attacked our pickets at Gower's.   After a sharp skirmish, were repulsed with some loss in wounded and 1 prisoner.   In the afternoon, marched down the creek toward Crawfish Spring, giving way to the Fourteenth Army Corps.

September 18, orders were received in the afternoon to relieve Colonel Barnes, of Van Cleve's division, at the ford near Glenn's, with one of my brigades.   After putting Grose in position there I reported at department headquarters, and received orders to march to Gordon's Mills as soon as relieved by General Negley.   While receiving these orders I was called upon by a staff officer of General Negley for information as to the position of the brigade on the creek to be relieved, and sent with him a staff officer (Lieutenant Scarritt) to guide him.   I then, by written order, directed Colonel Grose, as soon as relieved, to march toward Crawfish Spring and await orders. Brigadier-General Hazen was ordered to follow Grose, and Cruft to move in the rear.   These orders were promptly issued and delivered, and, placing the movement under the directions of General Cruft, I started soon after to Gordon's Mills to select a position for my command, but Grose was not, in fact, relieved before midnight. Hazen and Cruft were justified by my orders in awaiting his movement, and I have no doubt if Grose had been relieved by 7 o'clock, as I had every reason to believe would have been done, my whole command would have been in position at Gordon's Mills by 10 o'clock at the latest.   These delays, however, made it nearly daylight before my command was in position on the left of Van Cleve's division, and about 1 mile north of Gordon's Mills.

At daylight the cavalry of Minty's brigade passed from the front to the left, giving me the information that the woods along the creek to my right front were occupied by the enemy.   At about 9 o'clock by the orders of the general commanding the corps, Colonel Grose was ordered with his brigade to reconnoiter the Rossville road as far as McDonald's Cross-Roads, ascertain if the road was clear and communicate with General Thomas.   Soon after this brigade had marched, firing was heard in the direction of Rossville, which excited some apprehension for its safety, and about half past 10 o'clock a messenger came in from Colonel Grose in charge of one of General Bragg's orderlies taken prisoner.   From this prisoner, who was sent forward to headquarters, enough was learned to satisfy me that the enemy was near in force.   In answer to Colonel Grose's inquiry as to whether he should engage the enemy reported near him—without information of the plans of the general commanding, beyond the contents of my orders, and under the belief that the defense of the position at Gordon's Mills was of vital importance—I ordered him not to engage unless there was a very clear prospect of doing good, but to return.

About noon I received orders to move my whole division to the assistance of our troops then engaged.   I moved at once, and met Grose's brigade returning.   After marching quickly for perhaps a mile and a half, guided by the sounds of the firing, and forming lines to the right of the road, ordered Hazen, who was on the left, to march in the direction of the firing, Cruft to keep well closed up to him on his right, and Grose in reserve re-enforcing the right and engage as soon as possible.

At this moment I received a note from the general commanding the army, which led to a slight, but what turned out to be a most advantageous, change of formation.   He suggested an advance en échelon by brigades, refusing the right, keeping well closed up on Thomas.   This suggestion was adopted.   The brigades, at about 100 paces intervals, pushed forward and engaged the enemy almost simultaneously.   At once the fight became fierce and obstinate.   From the character of the ground, but few positions could be found for the effective use of artillery ; my batteries were used as well as was possible, but the work was confined mainly to the musket.   Our men stood up squarely without faltering, and, after a struggle of perhaps an hour, the enemy were driven from the ground and pursued for a considerable distance.   The firing along the line ceased and skirmishers were thrown forward, and as the ammunition of the Sixth and Twenty-fourth Ohio Regiments was completely exhausted, and all efforts to get a supply to them had so far failed, they were ordered back to the open ground in the rear, with the hope that they would meet the ammunition, which was known to be coming, and be ready to assist in checking the enemy's force, which was obviously driving some troops, of what command I am not able to say; and, passing the right, giving orders to close up the lines, I rode back to the open ground from which my command had marched upon the enemy.   I had hardly reached the road when some troops driven out of the woods crossed the road, pursued to the edge of the woods by the enemy.   At that moment one brigade of General Reynolds passed going to the right, but as they seemed likely to go too far, I requested Colonel Robinson, of the Seventy-fifth Indiana, to meet the advancing enemy.   He did so in fine style, and drove him back for a considerable distance.   The officers and men of that regiment deserve great credit for their gallantry in this affair. After Robinson's regiment had moved off under my orders, General Reynolds suggested that his withdrawal had left his battery without support.   I then ordered Colonel Anderson, with the Sixth Ohio, to fill his boxes and remain there until relieved, and returned to my own lines.   Upon reaching them I found my men resting, and every means was being used to fill the cartridge-boxes.   Hazen had been relieved by General Turchin, who had formed on Cruft's left, and he (Hazen) had retired to fill his boxes and protect some artillery which was threatened from the rear, and I then committed the error of directing Grose to move to the right to engage in a severe fight going on in that direction. I only for the moment saw that our troops were hard pressed and that mine were idle, but did not observe for a short time that one brigade was not enough to relieve them.

While riding toward Cruft's brigade, to order him to move to the right to support Grose, a heavy force came down upon him and Turchin. For ten minutes or more our men stood up under this fire, and then the enemy charged them and bore them back. Cruft, Turchin, and all their officers exerted themselves with distinguished courage to arrest the retreat, and I gave them what assistance I could. It seemed as if nothing would prevent a rout, but as if by magic the line straightened up, the men turned upon their pursuers with the bayonet, and as quickly they turned and fled, and were in turn pursued. Many prisoners were brought to me at this point by soldiers for orders. I told them to break their muskets and let them go, and then go back to their places in the ranks. By this time the enemy had passed to the rear, and I felt much apprehension for Hazen. I rode in the direction of heavy firing near the Rossville road, and found him with a part of his own brigade and a large conscription of stragglers and several pieces of artillery resisting an attempt of the enemy to cross an open field in his front. His fire was too hot, and they abandoned the effort. Very soon other troops of Reynolds' division came up; Grose collected his troops, who were somewhat scattered; Cruft was ordered to fall back to this point; our lines were reformed, and the battle seemed over. Major-General Thomas, who had been upon the ground all day, gave orders for the disposition of my command for the night, and the men suffering from cold built fires. About dusk the enemy made a furious attack upon General Johnson's command, which I then learned was upon my left. I at once ordered Cruft and Hazen to proceed rapidly to his support. They moved off with great alacrity, but did not reach the scene in time to participate in the affair.

About 8 o'clock I visited department and corps headquarters, and learned that from the difficulties of changing the positions of troops, it was expected, in the anticipated battle of the next day, my command would be subject to the immediate orders of Major-General Thomas, and this information was reiterated in orders received on the morning of the 20th from the headquarters of the corps.

Early on the 20th, I was directed by Major-General Thomas to form along a ridge running from northeast to southwest and terminating near the Rossville road, closing on the left upon Johnson's division. Intending to avoid what seemed to me the common error of the day before (too extensive lines), Hazen and Cruft were put in position in two lines, and Grose in double column in reserve. The men hastily constructed barricades of logs, rails, and other materials, and awaited the attack. The engagement commenced by a furious assault upon the position of Baird on the extreme left, and soon extended along the whole front. This was repulsed with great slaughter. Then a more persistent attack was made, the chief weight of which fell upon the extreme left; some troops posted there fell back. By order of General Thomas, my reserve brigade was moved in that direction, and took part in the obstinate contest there. The enemy were repulsed, but Grose suffered very severely. I respectfully refer to his report in reference to the share his brigade took in that bloody affair.

The positions held by the divisions of Reynolds, Johnson, Baird, and my own were frequently assailed during the day, but were maintained firmly by the willing men behind the barricades. A glance at the field along the front proved what these efforts were costing the enemy. At 2 o'clock unusually heavy firing was heard on the right of our position, which seemed like a determined effort on the part of the enemy to force the center of our line. Hazen was ordered by me to go in that direction. He moved off rapidly in obedience to the order. I heard his volley when he went in, and saw him no more that day. That his command did its duty, I have no doubt. I refer to his report for the details.

The remains of Grose's brigade had by this time returned, and now took Hazen's position in the line, but no formidable attempt was made upon us afterward. The enemy's sharpshooters were busy, and killed and wounded several officers, and some of our adventurous men tumbled—some of them from the trees upon which they were perched.

At about 5 o'clock I received an order from Major-General Thomas, by a staff officer, to retire. Under the impression that it was intended that I should, after retiring toward the rear of the center, form to resist the attacks which were coming on both flanks, I sent my orders to my brigade commanders, and rode to the Rossville road to await the head of the column. I reached the road and looked back across the field some 400 yards; my men were half way across. The enemy had already discovered the movement, and were crossing the barricades and firing. Batteries opened on us from the left and right, sweeping the road and field from opposite directions. It seemed impossible to bring men across the field in anything like good order. Grose was thrown into confusion, but Cruft came off in good style, and both with little loss. Cruft's brigade was retired slowly after leaving the field, frequently halting to serve as a nucleus for the reformation of our scattered troops. These brigades were conducted to the top of the ridge, formed and held until large crowds of stragglers passed, and, as I received no orders from any quarter, at late dusk I gave orders to the brigades to descend into the valley, throw out strong guards in the rear and front to resist any possible attack, and march to Rossville. The head of the column reached there at 8.40 p. m.

On the 21st instant, my command was placed in position on the ridge to the left of the Ringgold road, near Rossville. Barricades were constructed and the position occupied until 9 p. m., when, under orders, it was abandoned, and the troops retired to their present position. I can only say, in conclusion, that I am satisfied with the conduct of Brigadier-Generals Cruft and Hazen and Col. William Grose, commanding brigades; they have earned a new title to my respect and confidence, while subordinates of all grades maintained the character for hardy courage and endurance which has been won by good service upon many fields.

The artillery, under the general control of Captain Standart, chief of artillery, was used skillfully and, under all the circumstances, effectively. Standart had two and Cushing one gun disabled and abandoned. Captain Standart and Lieutenants Russell, Cushing, Cockerill, and Baldwin, skillful, gallant men, deserve well of the country. Lieutenant-Colonel Morton, aide-de-camp, and Capt. J. R. Muhleman, assistant adjutant-general, are missing, probably wounded, in the hands of the enemy. Captain Bartlett, of Seventh Illinois Cavalry, commanding my escort, Lieutenant Shaw, of the same company, ex hibited commendable courage. Capt. D. W. Norton was wounded. Lieutenants Scarritt and Thomas, aides, behaved with great gallantry. Captain Steele, Forty-first Ohio, topographical engineer, rendered most important services on the whole march from Dunlap to the battle-field, and on both of the days of the battle was on all occasions where duty called, exhibiting the highest courage and the most ready intelligence.

My thanks are due to Captain Howland, assistant quartermaster of the division; Lieutenant Chilton, commissary; the indefatigable Lieutenant Peck, who had charge of the transportation, and that model ordnance officer, Lieutenant Croxton, for the faithful manner in which they discharged their duties. Dr. Menzies, medical director, aided by Dr. Sherman and all the medical officers of the division, did all that was possible for skill, animated by humanity and sense of duty, for the relief of the wounded. Private Eby, Seventh Illinois Cavalry, remained with me all day as orderly, but at the close of the battle on Sunday was wounded and fell into the hands of the enemy.

I forward herewith the reports from brigades and regiments, and cordially approve the special mentions contained in them. Many of the instances of gallantry and good conduct adverted to in them occurred under my personal observation. I add, Colonel Sedgewick, Second Kentucky Regiment, remained with his regiment during both days' battles, kept it in good order under the heaviest fire, and brought it off the field ready to turn upon the enemy effectively at any moment. I recommend his promotion. Colonel Rippey, Ninetieth Ohio Regiment, remained with his regiment during both days' battle, kept it in good order, exhibiting great gallantry in resisting a charge of superior numbers on the 19th instant. Colonel Smith, Thirty-first Indiana Regiment, behaved with great courage and coolness. Lieutenant-Colonel Neff, of the same regiment, received a painful wound in the arm on the 19th, but refused to quit his post. He fought through both days and accompanied his regiment on its retreat. Colonel Wiley, Forty-first Ohio, for courage and coolness on the 19th and 20th. He kept the fire of his regiment under his control, firing by order and by volley. Colonel Suman, Ninth Indiana Regiment, for dauntless, steady courage. Colonel Waters, Eighty-fourth Illinois Regiment, for courage and steady composure in battle and vigilance in camp. Lieutenant-Colonel Carey, Thirty-sixth Indiana Regiment, was wounded on Saturday; remained with his command during the day; behaved with great courage. Colonel Anderson, Sixth Ohio Regiment, received a painful wound on Saturday; remained with his regiment until night; his courage and prudence deserve high praise. Major Erwin, Sixth Ohio Regiment, assumed command after Colonel Anderson was disabled, and acquitted himself well. Lieutenant-Colonel Foy, Twenty-third Kentucky Regiment, exhibited great courage and devotion to duty.

These special references to officers are based upon my own observations of their conduct, and are not to be understood to reflect upon others who did not act under my eye.

I am, very respectfully,

J. M. PALMER,
Major-General.

Capt. P. P. OLDERSHAW,
    Assistant Adjutant-General, Twenty-first Army Corps.

[Inclosure.]

Casualties of the Second Division, Twenty-first Army Corps, in the battle of 19th and 20th September, 1863.

Command.	Killed.		Wounded.		Missing.		Aggregate.		Horses killed.
	Commissioned officers.	Enlisted men.	Commissioned officers.	Enlisted men.	Commissioned officers.	Enlisted men.	Commissioned officers.	Enlisted men.	
Headquarters Second Division	......	1	2	....	2	1	4	2	......
Headquarters First Brigade.............									
31st Indiana Volunteer Infantry............	1	4	2	59	......	17	3	80	......
1st Kentucky Volunteer Infantry..........	..	2	1	25	......	3	1	30	......
2d Kentucky Volunteer Infantry........	1	9	5	59	......	18	6	86	......
90th Ohio Volunteer Infantry..............	2	5	2	60	1	14	5	79	......
Total First Brigade..............	4	20	10	203	1	52	15	275	......
Headquarters Second Brigade.............									
124th Ohio Volunteer Infantry.................	......	15	4	88	......	34	4	137	......
41st Ohio Volunteer Infantry	......	6	5	95	......	9	5	110	......
9th Indiana Volunteer Infantry........	3	22	6	59	......	18	9	99	......
6th Kentucky Volunteer Infantry.........	5	9	5	88	......	11	10	108	.....
Total Second Brigade..............	8	52	20	330	......	72	28	454	......
Headquarters Third Brigade..............	1	......	......	3	......	......	1	3	......
36th Indiana Volunteer Infantry..........	1	13	8	89	......	17	9	119	......
24th Ohio Volunteer Infantry.........	......	3	3	57	....	16	3	76	......
·6th Ohio Volunteer Infantry.	1	13	7	94	1	16	9	123	......
84th Illinois Volunteer Infantry	1	12	2	81	......	9	3	102	......
23d Kentucky Volunteer Infantry.	1	10	3	49	......	6	4	65	......
Total Third Brigade..................	5	51	23	373	1	64	29	488	......
Battery F, 1st Ohio Artillery..............	1	1	......	8	......	2	1	11	12
Battery B, 1st Ohio Artillery	......	1	......	8	......	4	......	13	13
Battery H, 4th U. S. Artillery	......	4	1	16	......	......	1	20	23
Battery M, 4th U. S. Artillery..............	......	2	......	6	......	......	......	8	14
Total artillery...........	1	8	1	38	......	6	2	52	62
Grand total Second Division *	18	132	56	944	4	195	78	1,271	62

J. M. PALMER,
Major-General, Commanding.

Capt. D. W. Norton,
  Acting Assistant Adjutant-General.

* See revised statement, p. 176.

ADDENDA.

Semi-weekly report of effective force of the Second Division, Twenty-first Army Corps, Maj. Gen. John M. Palmer commanding.

Command.	Headquarters.			Infantry.			Cavalry.		
	Commissioned officers.	Enlisted men.	Total.	Commissioned officers.	Enlisted men.	Total.	Commissioned officers.	Enlisted men.	Total.
Second Division, Major-General Palmer..	15	48	63	....	....	....	1	37	38
First Brigade, Brig. Gen. C. Cruft........	8	12	20	90	1,471	1,561	....	....	....
Second Brigade, Brigadier-General Hazen	9	38	47	117	1,652	1,769	....	....	....
Third Brigade, Col. William Grose (36th Indiana).	11	36	47	116	1,562	1,678	....	....	....
Battalion 110th Illinois, Capt. E. H. Topping.	....	....	....	11	235	246	....	....	....
Total infantry.....................	43	134	177	334	4,920	5,254	1	37	38
Battery B, 1st Ohio Artillery, First Lieut. N. A. Baldwin.									
Battery F, 1st Ohio Artillery, First Lieut. G. J. Cockerill.									
Battery H, 4th U. S. Artillery, First Lieut. H. C. Cushing.									
Battery M, 4th U. S. Artillery, First Lieut. F. L. D. Russell.									
Total artillery..................									
Grand total.........................	43	134	177	334	4,920	5,254	1	37	38

Command.	Artillery.			Total.		Aggregate.	Number of horses.	Number of guns.
	Commissioned officers.	Enlisted men.	Total.	Commissioned officers.	Enlisted men.			
Second Division, Major-General Palmer..	....	....	....	16	85	101	51	....
First Brigade, Brig. Gen. C. Cruft..... ...	....	....	....	98	1,483	1,581	5	....
Second Brigade, Brigadier-General Hazen	....	....	....	126	1,690	1,816	5	....
Third Brigade, Col. William Grose (36th Indiana).	....	....	....	127	1,598	1,725	5	....
Battalion 110th Illinois, Capt. E. H. Topping.	....	....	....	11	235	246	....	....
Total infantry.....................	....	....	....	378	5,091	5,469	66	....
Battery B, 1st Ohio Artillery, First Lieut. N. A. Baldwin.	3	130	133	3	130	133	112	6
Battery F, 1st Ohio Artillery, First Lieut. G. J. Cockerill.	4	104	108	4	104	108	100	6
Battery H, 4th U. S. Artillery, First Lieut. H. C. Cushing.	2	84	86	2	84	86	75	4
Battery M, 4th U. S. Artillery, First Lieut. F. L. D. Russell.	2	117	119	2	117	119	98	6
Total artillery	11	435	446	11	435	446	385	22
Grand total......	11	435	446	389	5,526	5,915	451	22

J. M. PALMER,
Major-General, Commanding.

Monday, *September 7, 1863.*

Special report of effective force of the Second Division, Twenty-first Army Corps, Maj. Gen. John M. Palmer commanding.

Command.	Headquarters.			Infantry.			Cavalry.		
	Commissioned officers.	Enlisted men.	Total.	Commissioned officers.	Enlisted men.	Total.	Commissioned officers.	Enlisted men.	Total.
Second Division, Twenty-first Army Corps, Maj. Gen. J. M. Palmer.	15	48	63	......	......	......	......		
First Brigade, Second Division, Twenty-first Army Corps, Brig. Gen. C. Cruft.				74	1,206	1,280	......		
Second Brigade, Second Division, Twenty-first Army Corps, Brig. Gen. W. B. Hazen.				92	1,336	1,428	......		
Third Brigade, Second Division, Twenty-first Army Corps, Col. William Grose.				130	1,556	1,686	......		
Total	15	48	63	296	4,098	4,394	......		
Company C, 7th Illinois Cavalry, escort, Captain Bartlett.							2	34	36
Battery B, 1st Ohio Artillery, Lieut. N. A. Baldwin.									
Battery F, 1st Ohio Artillery, Lieut. G. J. Cockerill.									
Battery H, 4th U. S. Artillery, Lieut. H. C. Cushing.									
Battery M, 4th U. S. Artillery, Lieut. F. L. D. Russell.									
Total									
Grand total	15	48	63	296	4,098	4,394	2	34	36

Command.	Artillery.			Total.		Aggregate.	Number of horses.	Number of guns.
	Commissioned officers.	Enlisted men.	Total.	Commissioned officers.	Enlisted men.			
Second Division, Twenty-first Army Corps, Maj. Gen. J. M. Palmer.	......	......	......	15	48	63	......	
First Brigade, Second Division, Twenty-first Army Corps, Brig. Gen. C. Cruft.	......	......	......	74	1,206	1,280	......	
Second Brigade, Second Division, Twenty-first Army Corps, Brig. Gen. W. B. Hazen.	......	......	......	92	1,336	1,428	......	
Third Brigade, Second Division, Twenty-first Army Corps, Col. William Grose.				130	1,556	1,686	......	
Total				311	4,146	4,457	......	
Company C, 7th Illinois Cavalry, escort, Captain Bartlett.	......	......	......	2	34	36	51	......
Battery B, 1st Ohio Artillery, Lieut. N. A. Baldwin.	3	132	135	3	132	135	101	6
Battery F, 1st Ohio Artillery, Lieut. G. J. Cockerill.	3	104	107	3	104	107	98	6
Battery H, 4th U. S. Artillery, Lieut. H. C. Cushing.	2	81	83	2	81	83	73	4
Battery M, 4th U. S. Artillery, Lieut. F. L. D. Russell.	2	119	121	2	119	129	90	6
Total	10	436	446	10	436	446	[362]	22
Grand total	10	436	446	323	4,616	5,339	413	22

[J. M. PALMER,
Major-General, Commanding.]

MONDAY, *September 14, 1863.*

Semi-weekly report of effective force of the Second Division, Twenty-first Army Corps, Maj. Gen. John M. Palmer commanding.

Command	Headquarters.			Infantry.			Cavalry.		
	Commissioned officers.	Enlisted men.	Total.	Commissioned officers.	Enlisted men.	Total.	Commissioned officers.	Enlisted men.	Total.
Second Division, Twenty-first Army Corps, Major-General Palmer.	15	48	63	.....	.....	.....	2	38	40
First Brigade, Second Division, Brig. Gen. C. Cruft.	7	17	24	74	1,206	1,280	.....	.....	.....
Second Brigade, Second Division, Brig. Gen. W. B. Hazen.	7	17	24	97	1,346	1,443	.....	.....	.....
Third Brigade, Second Division, Col. William Grose.	8	35	43	120	1,522	1,642	.....	.....	.....
Total	22	69	91	291	4,074	4,365			
Battery H, 4th U. S. Artillery, Lieut. H. C. Cushing.									
Battery M, 4th U. S. Artillery, Lieut. F. L. D. Russell.									
Battery B, 1st Ohio Volunteer Artillery, Lieut. N. A. Baldwin.									
Battery F, 1st Ohio Volunteer Artillery, Lieut. G. J. Cockerill									
Total									
Grand total	37	117	154	291	4,074	4,365	2	38	40

Command.	Artillery.			Total.			Number of horses.	Number of guns.
	Commissioned officers.	Enlisted men.	Total.	Commissioned officers.	Enlisted men.	Aggregate.		
Second Division, Twenty-first Army Corps, Major-General Palmer.	.....	.....	.....	17	86	103	51	.....
First Brigade, Second Division, Brig. Gen. C. Cruft.	.....	.....	.....	81	1,223	1,304	.....	.....
Second Brigade, Second Division, Brig. Gen. W. B. Hazen.	.....	.....	.....	104	1,363	1,467	.....	.....
Third Brigade, Second Division, Col. William Grose.	.....	.....	.....	128	1,557	1,685	.....	.....
Total	.....	.....	.....	313	4,143	4,456	.....	.....
Battery H, 4th U. S. Artillery, Lieut. H. C. Cushing.	2	85	87	2	85	87	73	4
Battery M, 4th U. S. Artillery, Lieut. F. L. D. Russell.	2	115	117	2	115	117	109	6
Battery B, 1st Ohio Volunteer Artillery, Lieut. N. A. Baldwin.	2	130	132	2	130	132	113	6
Battery F, 1st Ohio Volunteer Artillery, Lieut. G. J. Cockerill.	4	106	110	4	106	110	90	6
Total	10	436	446	10	436	446	385	22
Grand total	10	436	446	340	4,665	5,005	436	22

[J. M. PALMER,
Major-General, Commanding.]

SEPTEMBER 19, 1863.

[Indorsement.]

Respectfully returned.
The report is wanted by regiments, giving brigade totals.

[P. P.] OLDERSHAW,
Assistant Adjutant-General.

[P. S.]—Don't delay this regimental return.

No. 151.

Report of Capt. William E. Standart, First Ohio Light Artillery, Chief of Artillery.

CHATTANOOGA, *September* 28, 1863.

CAPTAIN: I have the honor to submit the following report of the batteries of Second Division, Twenty-first Army Corps:

On the 16th of August, left Manchester; arrived at Dunlap August 19.

On the 20th, Brigadier-General Hazen's brigade being ordered to Harrison's Landing, Battery F, Lieutenant Cockerill, moved with the brigade.

September 1, was ordered to move with the brigade that the batteries were temporarily attached [to] down the Sequatchie Valley.

On the 3d, Batteries H and M, with the Third Brigade, Colonel Grose, moved to Battle Creek, crossing the Tennessee River by 3 p. m. of the 4th, camping that night at Shellmound, Battery B crossing at Shellmound with First Brigade, General Cruft.

On the 5th, moved to Whiteside's; 6th, to Cole's Academy; 7th, in camp, and on the 8th, moved down the Trenton Valley road.

On the 9th, moved on to Chattanooga, passing Lookout Mountain spur, going into camp at Rossville.

On the 10th, moved to Pea Vine Creek; some skirmishing, the First Kentucky losing some men by capture; the 11th, moved on to Ringgold, General Hazen joining the column at Graysville with Battery F.

On the 12th, moved to Lee and Gordon's Mills; 13th, in camp; 14th, Second and Third Brigades moved to foot of Lookout Mountain with Batteries H and F; M and B remained with First Brigade at Lee's Mill; 15th, moved back to Crawfish Spring, then to Owens' Ford, First Brigade going with Batteries M and B; 16th and 17th, moved along, changing positions often.

On the night of the 18th, moved to Gordon's Mills.

On the morning of 19th, Battery B was posted in position in an open lot to the left of General Wood's light fortifications. Battery F was in position near an open lot in front of General Hazen, Colonel Grose being ordered on a reconnaissance. One section of Battery F, in command of Lieutenant Cockerill, went to the front. Generals Cruft and Hazen being soon ordered to move out, Batteries H and M were ordered to join. Moving in column, with heavy skirmish line on our right, General Hazen being in front with Battery F, moved to the east and was soon engaged with the enemy. General Cruft, with Battery B, was soon engaged on General Hazen's right. Colonel Grose was soon in position with Battery M, H being held in reserve, facing south of east. The right of Colonel Grose being in danger of being flanked, the Sixth Ohio, Colonel Anderson, and one section of Battery H, were ordered to support the right, enemy moving on and around our right, Generals Reynolds and Van Cleve at the time being engaged on our right.

Soon the enemy made their appearance on the road, Generals Van Cleve and Reynolds' troops falling back rapidly. I then showed Captain Harris where they were, he opening his full battery. The Sixth Ohio at this time returned from the woods and took position to support Harris' battery. Batteries M and H [were] soon ready and in position to the left of Harris' battery, but being outflanked and nearly surrounded, retired from the ridge. At this time General Hazen's column was crossing the road from what had been his position, moving up to check the enemy. [He] reported to Lieutenant Cockerill where he could get a good position. Battery H coming up at this time, they were posted so as to command an open space. The enemy checked at dark, had all the batteries in park ready to move. Batteries B and F were soon ordered to the line that was held by the Second Division on the 20th.

On the morning of 20th, got good position for Battery M. Colonel Grose's brigade being ordered on the reserve, placed H and M in reserve to the rear of Second Division. The Third Brigade, Colonel Grose, being ordered to support the left, Battery H moved with it [and] was soon hotly engaged. Lieutenant Cushing, not having a good position for his battery, retired, and reported the enemy on the left of the road in force, with a battery on the road. I sent to the reserve batteries of General Johnson's division, asking them to change front—to fire to the left. For some reason they did not. I then ordered Lieutenant Russell, Battery M, to change front and fire to the left, shell the woods to the left of the road, and silence the battery at the road, which was soon done. At this time [we were] getting a fire from front and rear from artillery, mostly passing over our position. Lieutenant Cushing reported his ammunition expended in his limbers; retired to his caissons; did not see him after that for the day. Soon afterward heard that the caissons had gone from where they had been. I went in search of them. General Brannan's division at this time was in full retreat. I was cut off from the division.

In going up the ridge I found the caissons of Battery B [and] one limber of caisson of Battery M. At this time General Negley ordered all to the rear, as he was going to form a new line on the ridge. Found three Parrott guns and carriages abandoned that I had limbered, one spare limber, and one on the rear of caisson of Battery B. To the right and near an old field saw one 12-pounder Napoleon [and] one 12-pounder howitzer. Sent a sergeant with his limber for [them], as he had lost his pieces. All of which were taken to Rossville.

The officers of the batteries and all of the men behaved with remarkable coolness and did their full duty, especially Lieutenants Russell and Butler, of Battery M; Lieutenants Cushing and Floyd, of Battery H (Lieutenant Floyd being wounded on the 19th); Lieutenants Baldwin and Throup, of Battery B; Lieutenants Cockerill, Osburn, Patton, and Lynch, of Battery F (Lieutenant Lynch was wounded and died on the 19th).

Casualties.—Battery M: Enlisted men killed, 2; enlisted men wounded, 6. Caissons abandoned, 3. Horses killed and abandoned, 14.

Battery H: Commissioned officer wounded, 1; enlisted men killed, 5; enlisted men wounded, 16. One 12-pounder howitzer, carriage, and limber abandoned. Horses killed and abandoned, 23.

Battery B: Enlisted man killed, 1; enlisted men wounded, 8; enlisted men missing, 4—1 voluntarily. Six-pounder James rifles and gun carriages abandoned, 2. Horses killed and abandoned, 13.

Battery F: Commissioned officer killed, 1; enlisted man killed, 1; enlisted men wounded, 8; enlisted men missing, 2. Horses killed and abandoned, 12.

All of which I respectfully submit.

W. E. STANDART,
Captain Company B, First Ohio Vol. Arty.,
and Chief of Arty., 2d Div., 21st Army Corps.

Capt. D. W. Norton, *Actg. Asst. Adjt. Gen., Second Div.*

No. 152.

Reports of Brig. Gen. Charles Cruft, U. S. Army, commanding First Brigade.

NEAR MATTHEWS' HOUSE, *September* 16, 1863.

CAPTAIN : The fact of an attack by cavalry of the enemy on the picket guard of this brigade, which occurred on the 10th instant, near Pea Vine Creek, Ga. (on the road leading from Rossville to Ringgold), has been heretofore promptly reported, with a list of officers and men captured. The matter has been since more fully investigated than was possible at the time of the occurrence and a detailed report thereof is now respectfully submitted.

The brigade left Rossville on the morning of the 10th instant, at 6 a. m., in advance of the division column. On leaving camp an advance guard was detailed and properly posted, with skirmishers, road party, and reserve, to precede the column. This advance consisted of a battalion of four companies of the First Kentucky Volunteer Infantry, to wit, Companies B (Lieutenant Hammond commanding), D (Captain Jones commanding), G (Lieutenant Brown commanding), K (Lieutenant Hornung commanding), the whole under command of Maj. A. R. Hadlock. Lieut. John A. Wright, my aide-de-camp, accompanied the party, and was charged with the execution of my instructions.

After crossing Missionary Ridge and the west fork of Chickamauga River, the road passed over a considerable range of hills, at the foot of which, on the east, was a valley of near 2 miles in width, through which ran Pea Vine Creek. When the head of the column reached the top of the hill, above the valley, it was halted, by command of Major-General Palmer (who happened to be riding with me at the time), for the purpose of exploring the valley. From this point a large portion of the valley could be overlooked, and something could be seen of the roads running through it. Dust was observed at points along these roads indicating movements of the enemy's cavalry. General Palmer furnished me with a small mounted force to precede the infantry battalion and explore the valley. This force consisted of a portion of the division escort (Lieutenant Shaw, Company C, Seventh Illinois Cavalry, commanding), and a portion of Company —, Fourth Michigan Cavalry (Captain ——— commanding), in all numbering some 60 or 70 men. Captain Norton (and perhaps others), of General Palmer's staff, accompanied the cavalry. The battalion of the First Kentucky was ordered by me to follow the cavalry, and take post within supporting distance of it beyond Pea Vine Creek, and there hold the road at all hazards. The skirmishing became quite spirited shortly after the cavalry crossed the creek, but the retiring reports of the carbines indicated that our men were driving the enemy. The brigade column passed down the hill, crossed the creek, and, in accordance with orders from General Palmer, was passing into camp. It had been expressly enjoined that the flanks of the camp should be well explored and speedily protected. A few hundred feet east of the creek the woods became dense. Along the margin of the woods two good roads intersected the main road nearly at right angles, the one on the left leading to Graysville, about 2½ miles distant, that on the right southward toward La Fayette. At the time the column crossed the creek the firing at the front had diminished and soon altogether ceased.

A messenger was sent to the front, who speedily returned with the information that our cavalry had driven off the enemy (which was represented to be a few mounted men), and that the infantry guard was in position. Colonel Sedgewick, with the Second Kentucky, was ordered to reconnoiter the right-hand road for the distance of a mile, and there await further orders. Two companies were ordered up the Graysville road for half a mile, with similar instructions. After these dispositions, the Thirty-first Indiana and Ninetieth Ohio were placed in line of battle on the right of the main road, under cover of the woods, and the men kept to their arms. The battery was placed in position in rear of the line, with orders not to unhitch. It was intended that the Third Brigade (Colonel Grose commanding) should encamp on the left of the road, in prolongation of my line, and this brigade was following down to its position. Skirmishers had been detailed, and were being posted in front of my line. During the few moments occupied in making these dispositions the skirmish firing again commenced well to the front, but at such intervals in reports as not to call for any special attention or indicate any sharp work; straggling shots merely were being exchanged. Attracted, however, by this, I waited a few moments for the battery to get into position and then started to the front. Captain Norton met me a few yards from the cross-roads. He was returning with the cavalry. He reported, substantially, that he estimated the enemy's force at about 200, but that it was too strong for his party to skirmish with successfully. Something was said expressing an apprehension that the enemy had artillery. Captain Standart, coming up at this moment, was requested to go to the front with me. We had been started but a few moments when Lieutenant Wright was met returning. He stated the enemy were maneuvering in the front, with a force which he supposed to be 150 to 200, and which he thought might be easily repulsed with a section of artillery. Lieutenant Wright was ordered to return rapidly to the front, and generally look after things there, and to say to Major Hadlock that I had perfect confidence in his holding the road against any column of cavalry until re-enforcements could be brought up if needed. Captain Standart was directed to have a section of his battery ready to move at a moment's notice. He replied that such was the case already. Lieutenant Wright galloped away, and we followed more leisurely. After going a short distance Adjutant Atkinson, First Kentucky, rode rapidly back, and, meeting us, said the enemy were about charging the line, and asked for re-enforcements.

Simultaneously with this request, a volley of musketry was heard and some yelling, and a cloud of dust was seen about the place occupied by the battalion and drifting down the road. We soon saw our people running back and a few of the enemy's cavalry dashing down the road toward us. Captain Standart was ordered to put his guns in shape to rake the road. Orders were immediately sent to the two regiments standing in line to advance. Before reaching the flank of the line, however, two of the enemy's cavalry passed me, coming at full speed, one of them turning into the woods on the right; the other dashed up close to the battery, fired a shot, wheeled his horse, and turned to the Graysville road. Lieutenant Hill, of the battery, returned the shot from a pistol almost instantly, but apparently without effect. The Thirty-first Indiana and Ninetieth Ohio advanced rapidly in line, and were within musket range of the point of attack within about five minutes after the volley, and the section of artillery followed them right up. The picket had all scattered, and no organized force could be seen in the road. The enemy had also all retired. The regiments were pushed immediately up to the place of attack and beyond, and the artillery planted on a commanding position, but no enemy could be seen. The line was halted for a few moments, during which Colonel Grose brought up a regiment (the Twenty-third Kentucky) of his command and reported to me. This was placed on the left of the road, prolonging my line.

Upon consultation, it was not deemed prudent to advance the line without looking to the Graysville road, which was a short distance from our left flank. At my request Colonel Grose ordered up another regiment of his brigade (Thirty-sixth Indiana) to cover the Graysville road. The lines then advanced over 1 mile, and some sharp skirmishing had with the enemy, who was finally driven off. The line remained in the latter position until about 4.15 p. m., when it was ordered back to camp. Colonel Rippey, of the Ninetieth Ohio, reports to have killed one of the enemy's cavalry in front of his skirmish line. There were no casualties on our part.

The attack on the battalion of the First Kentucky was made about 11 a. m. The battalion numbered 9 commissioned and non-commissioned officers and 144 effective men. The presence of the enemy in its immediate front was well known; the force was ample to resist the attack. The ground was unfavorable to cavalry, requiring any charge to be made in narrow column. There was not a steady resistance made, so far as can be learned. The attacking column consisted of about 80 volunteer troopers of General Pegram's command as is said by prisoners subsequently captured. The same authority states that his whole brigade was within supporting proximity. Be this as it may, but a small force was engaged or was seen. The attacking party fired but a few straggling shots. The troopers of the enemy are reported to have had scarce any sabers. Our skirmishers do not appear to have fired on the advancing column, or at most but a shot or two. The reserve of two companies fired a single volley, which, though said to have been well delivered and at short range, proved so ineffectual as not to have injured the enemy in any way.

In view of these facts, I have asked of the officers in charge of the guard a solution of the following queries:

First. How a force of 200 cavalry could break their line if posted as directed?

Second. How a volley could be fired at short range without hurting anybody?

Third. Why firing at will did not occur after the volley?

Fourth. How 58 men could be captured by cavalry without sabers in a narrow road with thick underbrush on each side?

Fifth. Why steady resistance with the bayonet was not made?

These inquiries were propounded conversationally at an interview with the officers, and reports in writing subsequently ordered from each. I herewith hand you the reports of Major [Lieutenant-Colonel] Hadlock commanding, Lieutenant Hammond, Lieutenant Brown, and Lieutenant Hornung, hereto appended and marked, respectively, A, B, C, and D.*

---

* See, respectively, pp. 742, 748, 749, and 750.

I also herewith submit the report of Lieutenant Wright, aide-de-camp, accompanied with the plat of the locality where the affair occurred, marked E.*

I also append a corrected list of the 58 officers and men captured, marked F.†

On the whole matter, it is difficult for me to express an opinion which may not unjustly reflect on those whom I esteem good soldiers, or on the other [hand] reflect harshly on companions in arms whom I believe to be good officers. The First Kentucky Regiment is one of the oldest in the service, and is composed of brave officers and men. Its record is good, and has been earned by bold acts on the battle-field. To account for the affair of the 10th, above reported on, we are forced to one of three conclusions, either that the officers and men were careless, that they became panic-stricken, or that there is some want of confidence between officers and men hitherto unsuspected.

Very respectfully, &c.,

CHARLES CRUFT,
Brigadier-General, Commanding.

Capt. J. R. Muhleman,
Assistant Adjutant-General, Second Division.

—

HEADQUARTERS FIRST BRIGADE, SECOND DIVISION,
In the Field, Chattanooga, Tenn., September 28, 1863.

CAPTAIN: I herewith submit a summary report of the movements and operations of this brigade from the 3d to the 18th instant, inclusive.

Thursday, September 3.—The command was encamped on the Little Sequatchie, 5 miles north of Jasper. At 11 a. m. it took up line of march, following General Van Cleve's division, then passing. My orders were to march to mouth of Battle Creek and join the division and cross there. On arriving at Jasper, about 1.30 p. m., General Crittenden ordered a change in the direction of the march, and directed the brigade to cross the Tennessee at Shellmound. The column reached the river about 7 p. m. March of the day, 12 miles. The rear of Colonel Harker's brigade, of General Wood's division, was crossing on my arrival. The ferry was in charge of a detachment of the pioneer corps. It consisted of seven flats, and was well managed by the pioneer officer in charge. He was an accommodating, gentlemanly, and hard-working officer, and I regret to have forgotten his name.

My column commenced ferriage at 10 p. m. At 1 a. m. all the infantry and half the battery was in bivouac on the opposite shore. The passage of the rest of the battery, my escort, &c., consumed some two hours more. The whole passage of the river was effected in about five hours.

Friday, September 4.—Lay in bivouac at Shellmound all day.

Saturday, September 5.—At 3 p. m. moved out on the Chattanooga road to near Whiteside's, and encamped for the night on Running Water Creek. Marched 9 miles.

Sunday, September 6.—Marched at 6 a. m. southward along Murphy's Valley road to the intersection of Nickajack road. Cut the felled timber out of the road at places where it had been obstructed

—

*See p. 739.   † Omitted.

along for some 4 miles.   Met General Brannan's column at Nicka-jack road.   Went about a mile south from the intersection and en-camped near Cole's Academy, called by the people Squirreltown. Marched 6 miles.

Monday, September 7.—Lay at Squirreltown all day; sent a com-pany (K, Thirty-first Indiana, Captain Hager) to establish a signal station on Lookout range.   It discovered the locality of Nickajack Gap—say 3 miles east of our camp—and attempted to reach the top of the mountain.   A sharp skirmish was had with the enemy near the top of the gap.   The force of the enemy was too heavy to effect the purpose, and the company fell back.   The only casualty was 1 man wounded.   The reconnaissance established the fact that the pass was practicable for troops.   I was ordered to take two regi-ments to the support of the company.   Took Thirty-first Indiana (Col. J. T. Smith) and Ninetieth Ohio (Colonel Rippey), and marched to base of mountain.   Finding Captain Hager's company safely re-tired, and orders not permitting any attempt farther on the pass, I returned.

Tuesday, September 8.—At 4 a. m. marched to Hawkins' Station, on Trenton Railway, and went into camp at 7 a. m.; march, 5½ miles. Sent Major Mitchell with battalion of five companies, First Ken-tucky Volunteers, as guard to the supply train back to Bridgeport. Sent Second Kentucky (Colonel Sedgewick) to make reconnaissance along base of Lookout Mountain.   Discovered locality of Powell's Gap.

Wednesday, September 9.—Left Hawkins' Station at 9 a. m., and marched over spur of Lookout Mountain, leaving Chattanooga to the left, to Rossville; march, 16 miles.   Had a short skirmish with the enemy's cavalry at Rossville, resulting in their retreat with no casualties.

Thursday, September 10.—Left Rossville at 6 a. m. and marched to Pea Vine Creek, 7 miles, arriving at about 10.30 a. m.   Encoun-tered enemy's cavalry at Pea Vine and had some skirmishing.   My picket guard on Ringgold road, consisting of four companies of First Kentucky, under Major Hadlock, was attacked by enemy's cavalry, and 58 officers and men captured (a report in detail of this affair has been rendered).   The residue of the afternoon was spent in skirmishing with Pegram's cavalry.   Colonel Sedgewick, by my order, with Second Kentucky, made a reconnaissance down the road leading to the right, for 1½ miles, immediately after crossing creek without results.

Friday, September 11.—Marched at 7 a. m., via Graysville, to Ring-gold, 8 miles, and encamped on south bank, east fork, of Chicka-mauga River, above the town.

Saturday, September 12.—Marched at 5 a. m. toward Lee and Gordon's Mills.   Skirmished with enemy's cavalry and went into line, say 3½ miles east of mills, near Pea Vine Church.   In the even-ing took camp near the mills, on east side Chickamauga; march of the day, 12 miles.

Sunday, September 13.—Sharp skirmishing on picket line at 7 a. m. Formed line of battle and lay till, say, 10 a. m.   Was then sent on reconnaissance on the road of yesterday to support Wilder's brigade of mounted infantry.   Sent the Ninetieth Ohio (Colonel Rippey) south on the cross-roads leading from Pea Vine Church, and posted it on a ridge.   The other three regiments were posted farther east, and nearly as of yesterday.   Had some skirmishing with enemy;

pretty sharp along Colonel Rippey's line, who reports to have killed 4 of the enemy's skirmishers. Wilder's men took line on my right; put out skirmishers, who had some skirmishing, and otherwise all rested quietly till 5 p. m., when we returned to the mills, crossed the river, and went into camp.

Monday, September 14.—Brigade lay at Lee and Gordon's Mills all day, guarding the transportation of the corps. Sent Second Kentucky (Colonel Sedgewick) to Chattanooga in guard of supply train.

Tuesday, September 15.—Marched, at 2 p. m., 6 miles on the road leading up to McLemore's Cove, and took camp near Matthews' house at 5 p. m., bringing up the transportation.

Wednesday, September 16.—Lay in camp. Supply train came up at 7 a. m. At 5 p. m. broke camp, and moved back along the road about 1½ miles, to Abercrombie's (called Crummy's by the inhabitants), and encamped.

Thursday, September 17.—Lay in camp near Abercrombie's all day.

Friday, September 18.—Left Abercrombie's at, say, 2 p. m., and marched back to Crawfish Spring, putting men in bivouac about 5.30 p. m. Marched 2½ miles. Left Crawfish Spring at 10.30 p. m., and marched beyond Lee's and Gordon's Mills, say 1 a. m., and went into line of battle. Marched, say, 3 miles.

Very truly, &c.,

CHARLES CRUFT,
Brigadier-General, Commanding.

Capt. D. W. Norton,
Acting Assistant-Adjutant-General, Second Division.

—

HEADQUARTERS FIRST BRIGADE,
In Field, Chattanooga, Tenn., September 29, 1863.

CAPTAIN: The following report of the part taken by the brigade under my command in the battle of the 19th and 20th instant, on the eastern slope of Missionary Ridge, Ga., is herewith submitted:

The brigade consisted of Second Kentucky Volunteers, Col. T. D. Sedgewick, commanding; Thirty-first Indiana Volunteers, Col. John T. Smith, commanding; Ninetieth Ohio Volunteers, Col. Charles H. Rippey, commanding; battalion of (four companies) First Kentucky Volunteers, Maj. A. R. Hadlock, commanding; Standart's battery, B, First Ohio Volunteer Light Artillery, Lieut. N. A. Baldwin commanding.

The effective strength of the brigade on the morning of the 19th instant was as follows:

Infantry:
Field, staff, and line officers.. 74
Enlisted men 1,206

Total infantry 1,280
Artillery:
Commissioned officers... 2
Enlisted men 126

Total artillery.. 128

Aggregate force of both arms 1,408

On the afternoon of the 18th instant, the brigade was bivouacked on the left of the road leading south from Lee and Gordon's Mills, up McLemore's Cove and near Crawfish Spring, Catoosa County. At 6.30 p. m. the brigade column rested on the road ready to march, as ordered, but was detained in this position for some three hours, awaiting the passage of commands belonging to other corps. About 10 p. m. the brigade was in motion, pretty closely followed by the Second Brigade and later by the Third Brigade of the division. The column reached Lee and Gordon's Mills about 1 a. m. of the 19th instant. The brigade was here placed in line of battle by Major-General Palmer, with its right resting on the left fork of the Chickamauga River, near a battery on a slightly fortified hillock, constituting General Van Cleve's left, and extending northwest across the Rossville road. In this position the men rested until daylight. About 9 a. m. the Third Brigade (Colonel Grose) was ordered to the front on a reconnaissance. All was quiet at the front until about 10.40 a. m., when a discharge of artillery and volleys of musketry off in a northerly direction indicated the commencement of a battle. It soon became evident that a portion of General Thomas' corps had become engaged with the enemy. The Second Brigade (General Hazen) was ordered up by General Palmer, and immediately (at 11 a. m.) my brigade was ordered to follow, bringing up with it the artillery of the division.

After marching a short distance, this brigade was ordered past the Second Brigade and down the road. After having passed along the Rossville road to the house of McNamara, distant about 1½ miles from the mills, the brigade was thrown to the right into an open woods and formed in line, facing the direction of the sound of battle, which was nearly east. Here General Palmer indicated the order of battle and superintended the formation of his division lines. The Second Brigade (General Hazen) passed me and formed on the left, the Third Brigade (Colonel Grose) on the right. The division line was to advance *en échelon* by brigades, retiring the right. This order threw the Second Brigade some hundred paces to the front of my left and the Third Brigade the same distance to the rear of my right, and made this brigade for the time being the center of the movement. Skirmishers were thrown out rapidly, and the advance of the division soon commenced in steady line. After advancing about 400 yards, the skirmishers engaged those of the enemy and drove them in. The line pressed steadily up. The Second and First Brigades engaged the enemy nearly simultaneously, at about 12.30 p. m., and the Third Brigade soon also became engaged.

The general orders were to press off in an east or rather northeasterly course, in the direction of the sound of the battle then progressing, and endeavor to connect on the right of the line of our troops that were fighting. The sound of the fire when first heard at the mills, seemed to be to the left of the Rossville road (looking north), and then speedily changed to the right or east of it, becoming constantly more intense.

My command encountered the enemy's line at a point about three-quarters of a mile east of the Rossville road. The ground between the road and the enemy's line was, at first, an open woodland, with an undulating surface, which terminated in a small ridge, parallel with the road and about half a mile back from it, below which lay a level plateau about a quarter of a mile across. On the east side of this plateau the ground broke off abruptly and disclosed a level, cleared spot of ground, forming a small semicircular cove in our immediate front. At the latter place the enemy made a stand. He had the advantage of position against a line formed on the margin of the plateau. My line was therefore thrown down the side of the bank and rapidly formed on the same level with the enemy. Three of the regiments of the brigade were placed immediately in the fight, the battalion of the First Kentucky for the time being having been placed in support of the artillery of the division, a service which it performed well. The brigade was formed in single line, the Second Kentucky on the right, Thirty-first Indiana in the center, and Ninetieth Ohio on the left. Half the battery was opened on the enemy with canister, from the plateau immediately over the heads of the troops, and the other half battery was placed on the ridge, a quarter of a mile to the rear, to shell the woods in our front and flanks. At this point the line of battle stood N. 20° E. The fight became very severe in my front at 12.40 p. m., and lasted until 2.20 p. m., an hour and forty minutes, with but little intermission in the musketry on both sides. During the action the half battery to the rear was brought up to the left flank of the line, and rendered excellent service by a left oblique fire on the portion of the rebel line which was attacking General Hazen. The enemy made three very obstinate attempts to break my line by charges, and at each time was re-enforced from the woods in their rear. They were on each occasion repulsed, with apparently heavy losses. My command behaved bravely, and steadily held the line. Not a straggler was observed going to the rear. The file-closers did their duty and every officer and man stood to his work. The cartridges of the men, however, began to fail, and the ill-success of attempts to procure a supply from the rear excited for the moment great apprehension as to our ability to hold the position. A few well directed volleys at the crisis drove the enemy from our front, and at 2.20 p. m. his fire had ceased. Skirmishers were now thrown forward and occupied a margin of the wood, beyond the cleared space, some 300 or 400 yards to our front. A general cessation of the firing now also occurred on the flank, during which ammunition arrived from the rear and was served to the men.

About 3.50 p. m. a very severe attack commenced on what appeared to be our extreme right, and rolled along the line toward the left, apparently concentrating its force on the Third Brigade (Colonel Grose) of this division. His line retired rapidly in direction from my right and occupied the extension of the ridge in a southwesterly direction. This position brought his front to the right and rear of my line. The fight became momentarily more critical on the right, and orders were now received from General Palmer to move such portion of my command as was possible to Colonel Grose's aid. The Second Kentucky and Thirty-first Indiana were ordered from my front line (leaving the Ninetieth Ohio and battery alone to hold it); their front rapidly changed perpendicularly to the old line, and moved off to the south along the plateau to Colonel Grose's relief at double-quick. The battalion of the First Kentucky was already in the action in support of the batteries. These two regiments reached Colonel Grose's line only to find it overpowered and giving way, stubbornly, under a most impetuous attack by overwhelming numbers, with its supporting lines on the right wholly gone. They became involved for a moment in the confusion that surrounded them, moved off to the right a short distance to avoid the retreating mass, and engaged the enemy sturdily, checking him sufficiently, perhaps, to prevent a rout. The moment was critical. Soldiers and officers ran to the rear, mingled with guns and caissons, in much disorder, and the whole plateau was rapidly being commanded by the enemy's musketry. At this time orders reached me to withdraw my command. The battery was ordered from its position, and the Ninetieth Ohio changed front, covering it, and the retrograde movement commenced. After proceeding about a hundred yards, my command encountered the head of General Turchin's brigade column coming up on my flank from the left and rear. The Ninetieth Ohio was halted and faced to the front, and the artillery ordered to the right upon the ridge. The Ninetieth was ordered to fix bayonet and charge the enemy, which was responded to with a yell of enthusiasm by the men, and the regiments started back at double-quick. General Turchin hurried up a regiment from the head of his column, which formed rapidly on the left, rushed forward with the Ninetieth Ohio, and he otherwise cheerfully assisted in the charge so far as his column could do from its position. In sweeping to the front, the Ninetieth caught a portion of the Thirty-first Indiana and Second Kentucky, and the whole mass rolled down on the enemy, making a most successful charge. The rout of the enemy was complete, and the line was restored. Great credit is due to the officers and men of the Ninetieth Ohio for the cheerful and gallant manner in which they made this charge, and the zeal in which they pursued the enemy after he had fled.

The brigade was now formed in line covering part of the ground which we had previously lost and holding it firmly until 5 p. m., when orders were received to fall back and bivouac for the night. The brigade was accordingly marched back, in good order, to the Rossville road, near Kelly's house, about a mile to the northward from where it had turned off in the morning. It had now become dark. The men had scarcely got their camp fires lighted when heavy musketry was heard in the woods to the northeast, indicating, as was said, a night attack upon General Johnson's division. The brigade was ordered by General Palmer to his relief. The men were got to arms quickly, and the column marched out a narrow road in the direction of the firing. After proceeding east a short distance, the road turned pretty squarely to the north. Passing the curve a short distance, the brigade was formed in line of battle, facing the east, and an advance ordered. Owing to the darkness of the night and the inequality of the ground, it was found almost impossible to advance in order. Sending to the front, it was ascertained that a line of fires of our troops was between the brigade and General Johnson's forces. Firing now ceased, and the arrival of officers from the front, who explained the cause, obviated the necessity for attempting a farther advance. Upon reporting my position to the general commanding division, orders were received to bivouac for the night. The ground was selected as carefully as could be done in the darkness, and the regiments posted in line. During the early part of the night, General Johnson's division returned from the front and took position in extension of my line on the left, and General Hazen's brigade moved in on the right.

During the preceding night and by daylight of the morning of 20th, the various regiments of the brigade had constructed rough log breastworks along the front. There were but few tools in the hands of the men, but they worked cheerfully and industriously with what they had, and availed themselves of every device to provide some protection. The ground was favorable for a line. It lay along a crest which fell off gradually to the front for the distance of about good musket range, and then rose up to a corresponding ridge, lower, however, than that which we occupied. A narrow road ran along the crest. The position of the troops on the flanks was the same as on the night before.

The attack commenced on our front at 7.40 a. m. It was very sharp and determined, and consisted of a series of persistent assaults with musketry and occasional artillery, continuing until about 12 m. Musketry and artillery were required almost constantly along the brigade line, during these four hours, to repel the enemy.

At the commencement of the fight the brigade was disposed in two lines. The Second Kentucky and Thirty-first Indiana comprised the first line, the Ninetieth Ohio and battalion of First Kentucky, the reserve line. The direction was N. 10° E. The battery was on the right flank. The lines were passed at 11 a. m., and the Ninetieth Ohio and battalion of the First Kentucky became the front line. This position was held firmly against every attack, and with but few casualties on our side, and apparently with considerable losses on the part of the enemy. So complete was the protection afforded by the rude breastworks which had been constructed, that not an enlisted man was killed while the brigade occupied this position, and but very few wounded. The enemy's sharpshooters constantly fired from trees at long rifle range at officers, and it was exceedingly hazardous for them to move about. One officer was killed and several wounded here during the morning.

At 11.30 a. m. a very severe attack was made on the troops upon our left. Their line curved around toward the Rossville road. The attack seemed to be made at a point about midway between the road and the front of my line. The musketry indicated a heavy engagement, and our lines seemed to give way under it to such a degree as seriously to threaten my left flank and rear. The reserve line of the brigade was faced to the rear, and marched a short distance with change of direction so as to be opposite the line of the enemy's fire, and the battery placed in position to be speedily withdrawn in case we should be flanked. The arrival of re-enforcements, however, soon repelled the attack.

At 12 m. another and apparently more determined attack was made in the same quarter. About 12.30 p. m. the sound indicated heavy work upon the extreme right of our lines. Occasional attacks were made on the skirmish lines in my front from 12 to 2 p. m., but the lines, having been strengthened, were sufficient to resist them successfully.

About 2 p. m. the fighting to the right of our position again became severe. At 2.40 p. m., General Hazen's brigade having been withdrawn from my right, orders were received to occupy the breastworks which had been held by his line. The Thirty-first Indiana and Second Kentucky were taken from my reserve line and thrown into them. At this time the enemy commenced using artillery freely on the position held by the brigade from three directions. Their range, however, was imperfect, and their shells generally passed over the men. At this time, and during the balance of the time that we occupied the line, it is most probable that no heavy force of the enemy lay on our immediate front. A very considerable force of sharpshooters was there, which kept up a continuous and irregular fire.   At 3.55 p. m. terrible musketry opened on the extreme right of our lines, and continued without intermission until 4.40 p. m.

At 5.12 p. m. orders were brought me to abandon the position in which the brigade then was, and retire across the Rossville road to the wood beyond.   There was no intimation given that the line was falling back generally, and officers and men of the brigade supposed when the movement commenced that they were marching to relieve our troops on the extreme right who were being so hotly engaged. The regiments were marched out from behind the breastwork, formed in line, and, moving out separately, formed in column of regiments at long intervals, and marched across the open field to our rear under a most severe artillery fire from two directions, Standart's battery and Russell's battery following the column in good order.   But very few casualties occurred while passing through this fire.   Upon reaching the woods to the west of the Rossville road Lieutenant Thomas, of General Palmer's staff, communicated to me the design of the movement and the direction which should be taken.   The brigade was then halted.   At this time Lieutenant-Colonel Foy, of the Twenty-third Kentucky, Third Brigade, reported to me, having become separated from his brigade and was placed in my column. Here also a large lot of stragglers were picked up and put in my line.   The regiments were ordered to double column on the center, which was quickly done, and the line moved through the woods down a slope, across a field, and up to the summit of Missionary Ridge in very good order, and with but little straggling, although still under the artillery fire of the enemy until it had crossed the field.   The batteries were sent around to the right into the cross-road which led into the ravine that passed through the ridge, with instructions to halt after passing beyond the enemy's artillery range. They were subsequently ordered forward.

When the brigade reached the top of Missionary Ridge, it was aligned regularly and faced to the front in line of battle.   There was no other organized command to be seen upon the ridge.   There was a multitude of stragglers.   An attempt was made to force or persuade them to form a line in extension of the brigade line.   Very many commissioned and non-commissioned officers assisted me in trying to restore order and form a line.   The brigade was halted in position for about an hour, during which time I met the general commanding the division and received his order to move the brigade out the road and halt there, which was executed.   Subsequently, it was ordered to march to Rossville, which was accordingly done in as good order as on any ordinary march.   An advance and rear guard were posted, and all the ordinary discipline of marches was observed.

The brigade reached Rossville about 8.15 p. m., and was placed in line and arms stacked, and details sent for water.   After the men were supplied with water, it was marched to a convenient camp and bivouacked for the night, the ordinary roll-calls were had, and camp guard posted.

On the morning of the 21st, the brigade was marched east to the top of Missionary Ridge, on the Ringgold road, and took position on the right of the division, with its right resting near the road. Breastworks were constructed in front of the brigade line by 9 a. m., and the command rested during the day behind these.   A large party of skirmishers were sent to the front, and considerable skirmishing had with the enemy during the day without any casualties whatever.

The brigade was subjected during the day to the shelling from the enemy's guns and to annoyance from his sharpshooters, but without any losses. At 9 p. m., in compliance with orders, the brigade marched from camp to Chattanooga. Three companies and the picket were left in position during the night, and to await orders to leave. Orders were subsequently sent to the officer in charge of the force left behind (Lieutenant-Colonel Hurd, Second Kentucky) to leave just before dawn of day, which was accordingly done, and the entire force rejoined its command shortly after sunrise without any casualty. Colonel Hurd performed this duty very gallantly.

The following is a summary of the casualties of the brigade in the battles of the 19th and 20th:

Command.	Killed.		Wounded.		Missing.		
	Officers.	Men.	Officers.	Men.	Officers.	Men.	Total.
31st Indiana	1	4	2	59	......	17	83
1st Kentucky	......	2	1	25	......	3	31
2d Kentucky	1	9	5	59	......	18	92
90th Ohio	2	5	2	60	1	14	84
Total infantry	4	20	10	203	1	52	290
Standart's battery	......	1	......	8	......	4	13
Aggregate	4	21	10	211	1	56	303

The greater part of the casualties occurred in the battle of the 19th instant. The officers killed were: Capt. William I. Leas, Thirty-first Indiana Volunteers; Capt. James M. Bodine, Second Kentucky Volunteers ; Capt. R. D. Caddy and Adjt. D. N. Kingery, Ninetieth Ohio Volunteers. All of these officers fell in the discharge of their duties and in their places, bravely doing their work.

The officers wounded were : Lieutenant-Colonel Neff, Thirty-first Indiana ; Major Baldwin, Second Kentucky ; Captains Martin, Stacey, and Hurd, Second Kentucky ; Lieutenants Tilly, First Kentucky ; Haviland and Connelly, Thirty-first Indiana ; Patterson, Ninetieth Ohio, and Bryant, Second Kentucky.

The number of prisoners captured from the enemy and sent to the rear by this brigade, from first to last, during the battles, was 41.

A plat of the portions of the battle-field over which this brigade fought, prepared by Lieut. George R. Crow, topographical engineer, of my staff, is hereto appended, marked A.* This plat shows the positions occupied by the brigade during the battles, together with somewhat of the topography of the surrounding country.

The reports of Colonel Sedgewick, Second Kentucky Volunteers; Colonel Smith, Thirty-first Indiana Volunteers; Colonel Rippey, Ninetieth Ohio Volunteers, and Lieutenant-Colonel Hadlock, First Kentucky Volunteers, are also submitted and attached hereto, marked, respectively, B, C, D, and E. These reports are in the main prepared with care and furnish a history of the operations of the regiments with as few minor discrepancies perhaps as arc pos sible in the description of battles. Appended to each of these reports is a detailed statement of the casualties of the regiment.

The regimental commanders make numerous special mentions of

---

*See p. 737.

officers for gallant conduct which I know to be well merited.   With one accord they also commend the behavior of the enlisted men of their commands.   This commendation was well earned.   Almost every non-commissioned officer and soldier of the brigade deserves notice for his good conduct on the field during the recent battles. Though suffering from loss of rest and want of water (in common with the rest of the army), the soldiers of the brigade exhibited a cheerfulness and willingness in the discharge of their duties during the two days of the fight which merits high commendation.   A list of these special mentions is collated and hereto appended, marked F.

The report of Maj. James W. Mitchell, First Kentucky Volunteers, who was absent on detailed service with five companies of that regiment from the 7th to the 24th instant, is hereto attached, marked G.   Though near the battle-fields of the 19th and 20th the character of his detail prevented his command from taking an active share in the engagements.   The report furnishes a detailed account of the operations of his battalion during the time above specified.

The detailed report of Surg. W. C. Hendricks, Thirty-first Indiana Volunteers, acting brigade surgeon, is herewith submitted, marked H, containing all the required surgical information in regard to the casualties of the battles.   The hospitals of the division were so far to the rear of the battle-fields as to render it impossible to visit them. A good account was brought to me of the efforts of the brigade surgeon and the entire medical staff of the regiments to care for and relieve the wounded during the engagements.   The lack of transportation, however, compelled us to leave many wounded on the field.

It is not within the province of this report to mention by name all the field, staff, and line officers who distinguished themselves during the late battles by good service.   These are covered by the regimental lists to which reference is made.   With regard to commanders of regiments and detachments of the brigade, I will say that the personal carriage of Colonels Sedgewick, Rippey, and Smith in the field was courageous and at all times proper.   These officers handled their commands well.   They are soldiers of long service, and have been frequently mentioned in official reports of other fields for good conduct.   Meritorious service placed each of them in their present position, and they should not be omitted in the roll of honorable names which will spring from the recent sanguinary battles.   I recommend the promotion of Colonel Sedgewick.   Lieutenant-Colonel Hadlock behaved well upon the field and managed his battalion with skill and bravery.   It did good work, though it was small in numbers and sustained the well-earned reputation of its regiment.

Lieut. N. A. Baldwin, commanding Standart's battery, handled his guns well, and by the promptness and fearlessness with which his battery was at all times maneuvered, as ordered, contributed largely to repelling the enemy.   Lieut. D. H. Throup nobly seconded his commander, and managed his pieces with judgment and courage.   The battery fully sustained the good reputation which it has hitherto enjoyed.   During the action of the 20th instant, one of the pieces became disabled and was sent to the rear and probably fell into the hands of the enemy; another was also injured by a premature discharge, and on the march from the field was compelled to be left on the road owing to the breakage of the carriage.   No other property of the battery was lost.   Upon the withdrawal of the two guns from Standart's battery, on the 20th instant, Lieutenant Russell, Battery

M, Fourth U. S. Artillery, then lying in reserve, kindly replaced them with two howitzers from his battery, which were gallantly served with my command during the afternoon. Lieutenant Russell's battery retired from the field with my command.

I recommend that a certificate of honor be given by the general commanding to Corpl. Jesse R. Dodd, Company F, Thirty-first Indiana, for gallant conduct in seizing the colors of his regiment upon the fall of the color-bearer and bravely bearing them during the residue of the battle; and also to Corpl. James J. Holliday, Company H, Ninetieth Ohio Volunteers, for a similar act in respect to his regimental colors.

The following officers of the staff were with me constantly on the field, to wit: Capt. W. H. Fairbanks (Thirty-first Indiana Volunteers), acting assistant adjutant-general; Lieut. John A. Wright (First Kentucky Volunteers), acting aide-de-camp; Lieut. H. Weinedel (Second Kentucky Volunteers), acting brigade inspector; Lieut. J. B. Socwell (First Kentucky Volunteers), acting brigade commissary, and Lieut. George R. Crow (Ninetieth Ohio Volunteers), acting topographical engineer. These staff officers were much exposed during the battles, and each acquitted himself in a faithful and soldierly manner, and has my gratitude for his assistance and good conduct.

I am, captain, very truly, &c.,

CHARLES CRUFT,
Brigadier-General, Commanding.

Capt. D. W. NORTON,
Acting Assistant Adjutant-General, Second Division.

[Appendix F.]

LIST OF SPECIAL MENTIONS FROM REGIMENTAL REPORTS.

Report of Thirty-first Indiana Volunteers.—Lieutenant-Colonel Neff and Adjutant Noble, wounded but continued at post. Lieutenants Connelly and Haviland, wounded and carried to the rear. Company commanders, Captains Waterman, Pickins, Brown, Hager, Hallowell; First Lieutenants Morris, Mason, Brown, Scott; also Second Lieutenants Roddy, Hatfield, Ford, Powers, Fielding, Douglas, Wells, and McKinzie, for good conduct, acquitted themselves gallantly. Chaplain Hiram Gillmore, "constantly on field attending to wounded; much exposed; had his horse killed." Assistant Surgeon McKinney, "on the field and rendered all assistance in his power." Corpl. Jesse K. Dodd, Company, I, "seized the colors when color-sergeant was shot and bravely carried them the remainder of the day."

Report of the Ninetieth Ohio Volunteers.—Major Perry, Captains Rains, Witherspoon, Hitchcock, and Angle; First Lieutenants Felton, Sutphen, and Cook, "for coolness, fortitude, and bravery." J. A. Wright, aide-de-camp on general's staff, "for gallant services rendered on Saturday, 19th instant." Corpl. James J. Holliday seized the colors when color-sergeant was shot and carried them the remainder of the day.

Report of Second Kentucky Volunteers.—Lieut. Col. John R. Hurd "displayed the greatest gallantry." Maj. O. L. Baldwin "was wounded while gallantly encouraging the line during a heavy attack."

Report of the First Kentucky Volunteers.—"Great praise is due to Companies B, D, G, and K for coolness and bravery on the field."

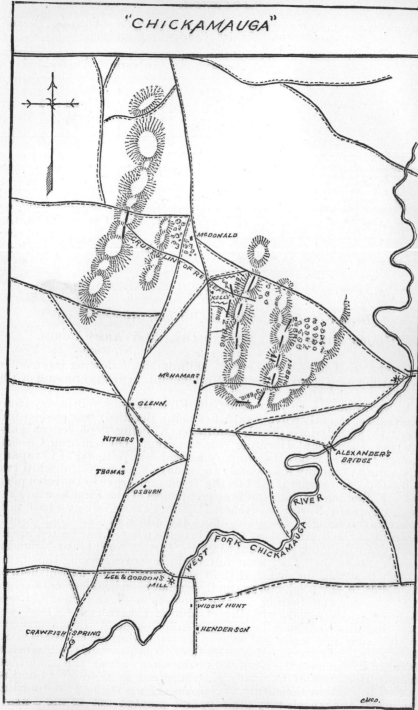

"CHICKAMAUGA"

ADDENDA.

Semi-weekly report of effective force of the First Brigade, Second Division, Twenty-first Army Corps, Brig. Gen. Charles Cruft commanding.

Command.	Headquarters.			Infantry.			Total.		
	Commissioned officers.	Enlisted men.	Total.	Commissioned officers.	Enlisted men.	Total.	Commissioned officers.	Enlisted men.	Aggregate.
First Brigade, Brigadier-General Cruft.	7	17	24	....	....	....	....	....	....
1st Kentucky, Lieutenant-Colonel Hadlock.	....	....	....	7	111	118	....	....	....
2d Kentucky, Colonel Sedgewick.	....	....	....	20	347	367	....	....	....
31st Indiana, Colonel Smith	....	....	....	25	355	380	....	....	....
90th Ohio, Colonel Rippey	....	....	....	22	393	415	....	....	....
Total	7	17	24	74	1,206	1,280	81	1,223	1,304

CHARLES CRUFT,
Brigadier-General, Commanding.

September 18, 1863.

No. 153.

Report of Lieut. John A. Wright, Aide-de-Camp.

Hdqrs. First Brig., Second Div., 21st Army Corps,
September 11, 1863.

General: I have the honor to submit the following report of a skirmish which occurred, on the 10th instant, near the crossing of the La Fayette and Ringgold roads:

In accordance with your order, the First Kentucky Infantry (four companies, the other five companies being detailed) was pushed forward as an advance guard, Company K being deployed as skirmishers, Lieutenant Hornung commanding. On reaching Chickamauga Creek, I relieved Company K, and sent out part of Company B, holding Company K as an advance guard. Shortly afterward two companies of cavalry passed to the front and drove in the rebel pickets. Following up with the four companies of the First Kentucky, I found Captain Norton, of General Palmer's staff, about a half mile from the crossing of the above-named roads, and about half a mile in front of the line occupied by the brigade where I had halted the infantry, not deeming it prudent to go any farther until I heard from the cavalry in front. They soon fell back, however, saying the enemy were too strong for them. I then strengthened the skirmishers on each side of the road, but as the firing had been heaviest on the right of the road, and fearing a flank movement of the enemy, I sent Lieutenant Hammond with the residue of Company B to that side, ordering him to deploy his men and take charge of the skirmishers, at the same time sending Company K to the front (on the road) about 150 yards, and ordering Major Hadlock, commanding the reserve, to form in line across the road, which he did. About this time Lieutenant Hornung, of Company K, came back from the front and reported to me that the enemy were bringing up artillery, stating that he heard the wheels very plainly, and pointed out to me a heavy cloud of dust. Ordering the reserve to lie down so they would be

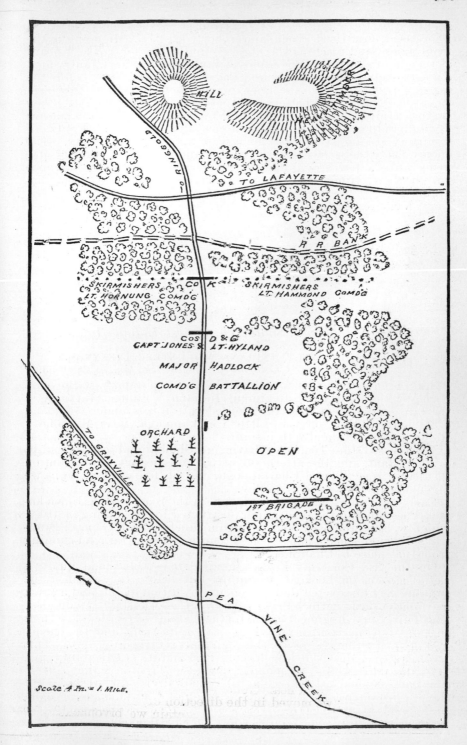

sheltered by the slight rise in their front from the enemy's artillery if he used any, I rode back and reported to you. In going to the front again, and reaching the high ground at the log-house, I heard a tremendous cheering, and almost simultaneously the infantry fired a good steady volley. The sound had scarcely died away before the cavalry dashed through the lines, one of them coming up to within 20 yards of Standart's battery. As soon as the line was first broken by the cavalry the firing ceased, and by some unaccountable means 2 commanding officers (Captain Jones and Lieutenant Kautz, of Company D), and 56 enlisted men were taken by the enemy. The enemy made their charge at full gallop and with great impetuosity, firing only a few straggling shots. The position of the advance will be better understood by reference to the accompanying diagram.*

Very respectfully, your obedient servant,

JNO. A. WRIGHT,
First Lieutenant, and Aide-de-Camp.

Brigadier-General CRUFT,
Commanding First Brigade, Second Division.

No. 154.

Report of Col. John T. Smith, Thirty-first Indiana Infantry.

HDQRS. 31ST REGT. INDIANA VOLUNTEER INFANTRY,
Camp near Chattanooga, Tenn., September 28, 1863.

SIR : I have the honor to submit herewith a report of the part borne by the Thirty-first Regiment Indiana Volunteer Infantry in the late engagement with the Confederate forces under command of General Bragg, on the Little Chickamauga, near Missionary Ridge, on the 19th and 20th instant.

We crossed the Tennessee River at Shellmound on the night of 3d instant, and the afternoon of the 5th instant moved out on the River road toward Chattanooga, and at 10 o'clock at night we bivouacked in Whiteside's Valley.

Early next morning we moved out on the road leading to Nickajack Pass, finding the road much obstructed by the felling of trees, which we soon removed, and formed a junction with General Brannan's division, some 4 miles from Trenton, near the railroad running from that place to Chattanooga.

On the 7th, Company K was detailed to establish and guard a signal station on Lookout Mountain, but before they reached the summit they discovered that the enemy held that point, and a brisk skirmish ensued, in which Private Andrew Case was slightly wounded. The Thirty-first Regiment and Ninetieth Ohio were ordered to their support, but the company having cleared its front and the enemy making no further resistance, the regiments returned to camp. This reconnaissance discovered Nickajack Pass and its practicability.

On the 8th instant, we moved down the Trenton Valley some 5 miles and bivouacked near General Wood's division. At 9 a. m. of the 9th instant, we moved in the direction of Chattanooga ; leaving the main road at the base of the mountain we bivouacked for the night at Rossville, some 5 miles south of Chattanooga.

*See p. 739.

On the morning of the 10th, at 3 o'clock, the Thirty-first was thrown forward to the summit on the left-hand or Ringgold road.   Here we captured 3 prisoners, and at 7 a. m. we rejoined the brigade, which was moving in the direction of Ringgold.   We halted at Pea Vine Creek at 11 a. m., and had scarcely stacked arms when the advance guard was driven in.   The Thirty-first was immediately moved forward, Companies G and I in advance as skirmishers, who engaged the enemy and drove him some 2 miles, the regiment following in supporting distance.   We then returned to Pea Vine Creek and bivouacked for the night.   Early next morning we moved out via Graysville to Ringgold, where we again bivouacked and passed the night.

At 6 o'clock on the morning of the 12th instant, we moved out on the La Fayette road and came to the enemy's pickets, some 3 miles from Lee and Gordon's Mills, which, after considerable maneuvering, were driven back, and we passed on to the mill, where we bivouacked for the night.   Early next morning our pickets were driven in and the day was spent in line of battle and maneuvering, but the enemy making no further demonstration, we retired to the mill, and passed the night and remained until the afternoon of the 15th, when we moved some 3 miles south of Crawfish Spring near Matthews' house.

The afternoon of the 17th, we moved back to Abercrombie's house, a distance of 1½ miles, where we remained until the evening of the 18th, when we moved to a position one-half a mile north of Lee and Gordon's Mills.

At 11 a. m. of the 19th, we moved down the Chattanooga road some 1½ miles, or to McNamara's, when we moved by the right flank or in line, Company E deployed as skirmishers, the Second Kentucky on our right and the Ninetieth Ohio on our left.

We had moved in that direction but a few rods when our skirmishers engaged those of the enemy, driving them some three-quarters of a mile to an open field, beyond which we found the enemy in line of battle, and we were soon engaged in a close contest for some two hours, expending on an average 50 rounds of ammunition per man and driving the enemy from our front.   We then retired some 50 paces to the woods, where we rested and filled up our cartridge boxes.

By this time the enemy was pressing the forces on the right of our brigade.   We were ordered to change front perpendicularly to the right, but just as this movement was accomplished, the troops on our right and front gave way, and were precipitated on the right of our regiment, closely followed by a heavy column of the enemy.   We then attempted to withdraw, but in doing so the regiment became somewhat scattered, but were soon rallied, and joined in a charge against the enemy, repulsing him handsomely.   After holding the ground for some time, we were moved to the Chattanooga road, near Kelly's house, where we prepared to bivouac for the night, but the enemy making an assault on a division to our left, we were moved to its support.   On getting into position, we found the enemy repulsed, and we were ordered to rest on arms for the night.

Early on the morning of the 20th, we prepared some hasty defenses of logs and trees, and at one-quarter before 8 a. m. the enemy made his appearance on our immediate front and made a vigorous assault on our feeble works.   He was, however, soon repulsed, but renewed the attack three different times, but was forced to retire severely punished.

We continued to hold our position during the day until near 5 p. m., when we were ordered to retire, and in doing so, had to pass through an open field under a most terrific shower of shot and shell. This movement was conducted with perfect order and self-possession. After gaining the wood, the regiment was formed in line with the brigade facing the enemy amid a perfect mass of scattered and disordered troops. Here we rested for near an hour, when we marched leisurely to Rossville.

During the engagement of the 19th, Capt. William I. Leas fell mortally wounded while leading his command in a charge against the enemy. He was a brave and faithful officer, and had, by his bravery on this and other occasions, won the esteem of his command and of the entire regiment. Color-Sergt. John West was killed while bearing the colors before the enemy. No sooner, however, had he fallen than the colors were gathered up and unfurled by Corpl. Jesse R. Dodd, of Company F, who bravely carried them during the remainder of the day. Lieutenant-Colonel Neff was struck on the elbow with a spent canister, disabling his arm, but he remained on the field, always at his post. Adjutant Noble was slightly wounded, but continued at his post until the close of the engagement. Lieutenant Connelly was severely wounded and carried off the field. Lieutenant Haviland received a slight but painful wound and was sent to the rear.

The company commanders, Captains Waterman, Pickins, Grimes, Brown, Hager, Hallowell, and Lieutenants Morris, Mason, Brown, and Scott, all maneuvered their commands successfully, and acquitted themselves with much gallantry. Lieutenants Roddy, Hatfield, Ford, Powers, Douglas, Fielding, Wells, and McKinzie were all cool, faithful, and brave, and rendered much efficient service.

Chaplain Gillmore was constantly on the field attending to the wounded, and was much exposed, having his horse killed.

Assistant-Surgeon McKinney was on the field and rendered all the assistance in his power.

I cannot express terms of praise too high for the conduct of my entire command. During the entire campaign they evinced a spirit of endurance and bravery unexcelled, which was truly gratifying to myself as well as creditable to them.

Appended you will find a list of casualties.*

All of which is respectfully submitted.

I am, sir, your most obedient servant,

JOHN T. SMITH,
Colonel, Commanding.

Capt. W. H. FAIRBANKS,
Acting Assistant Adjutant-General, First Brigade.

No. 155.

Reports of Lieut. Col. Alva R. Hadlock, First Kentucky Infantry.

HDQRS. FIRST REGIMENT KENTUCKY VOLUNTEERS,
September 10, 1863.

SIR : I have the honor to transmit the following report of skirmish of First Kentucky Infantry:

On the morning of the 10th, took up line of march, proceeding to-

---

* Embodied in revised statement, p. 176.

ward Ringgold, Ga.   Having advanced near three-quarters of a mile, two companies (B and K) were ordered to the front as skirmishers, and Companies G and D, the remaining part of the regiment, were held in reserve.   Company K was deployed to the right and left of the road, while B was held as first reserve.   The two companies were under the immediate command of Lieutenant Wright, aide-de-camp. The skirmishers advanced slowly and cautiously until the advance arrived near Pea Vine Creek, when the cavalry advanced, dismounted, and deployed to the right and in front of my line of skirmishers. Scarcely had they advanced 200 yards before they encountered the advance picket post of the enemy, driving them slowly before them for over a mile, my regiment (four companies) keeping within supporting distance; here the cavalry, encountering a superior force of the enemy, were obliged to retire.   The line of skirmishers (First Kentucky) was now re-enforced, Company K being deployed to the right of the road, 10 men from Company B were thrown forward to the left, and 10 men to the left on the right of Company K, while the reserve (two companies) were drawn up in line across the road ; at — p. m. the enemy's cavalry, supported by infantry, made a dash, breaking through my lines and throwing the men into confusion. To take the cover was now the only measure left, but the enemy advancing on another road on my right flank, a great many of the men broke cover and were captured.

It is needless to say, had we been properly supported, the enemy might have been checked and the shameful occurrence of to-day might have been guarded against.   The skirmishers were at least a mile in advance of the column.   I took into the skirmish 9 officers and 144 effective men, whom I must say exhibited courage, and obeyed all my orders with cheerfulness and alacrity until it became known to them that they were not supported.

The following table will show the casualties of regiment: Missing, commissioned officers, 2 ; enlisted men, 56. Aggregate, 58.

Respectfully submitted.

A. R. HADLOCK,
Major,* Commanding First Kentucky.

Brigadier-General CRUFT.

HDQRS. FIRST REGT. KENTUCKY VOLUNTEER INFANTRY,
Near Chattanooga, Tenn., September 24, 1863.

SIR: In accordance with orders, I have the honor to transmit the following report of the part taken by four companies of the First Kentucky Volunteers during the engagements of September 19 and 20 :

On the morning of the 19th, I was ordered by General Cruft to take a position in the rear of and act as escort to three batteries (B, First Ohio, H and M, Fourth United States), and to proceed with them until further orders.

After marching with them about 2 miles, I was ordered by General Palmer to take position in the rear of Cushing's battery, which was about engaging the enemy, and to support it.   I remained there under a terrible musketry fire until the battery was forced from its position and Colonel Grose's brigade was obliged to retire to a new line.

---

* Promoted lieutenant-colonel to date from September 14.

Allowing the battery sufficient time to take a new and safer position, I formed my four companies with the Twenty-third Kentucky Volunteers on the new line of Grose's brigade, there engaging the enemy desperately until the entire line was broken, when I fell back in good order, keeping up a continual fire on the advancing enemy. Up to this time I had lost 1 officer and 18 men wounded and 2 men killed, out of 111. Soon after, having again formed with Colonel Grose's brigade, I was ordered by General Cruft to resume my place in the First Brigade. After dark I was ordered out to assist in the action then waging on our front and left, but was not engaged, and went into camp shortly after.

On the morning of the 20th, I was ordered to throw up breastworks to protect my position. Immediately before the attack commenced I was ordered to leave them and take position in the second or reserve line of the brigade. Here I remained under a very heavy musketry fire, and had 5 men severely wounded before I was ordered to relieve the Second Kentucky in the breastworks. After taking position in the breastworks, I remained there until late in the afternoon, when I was ordered to retreat with the rest of the brigade, which I did in very good order. Since then I have remained and taken position with the brigade in all instances.

Too much praise cannot be given to the four companies, B, D, G, and K, which were engaged during the 19th and 20th. Acting with coolness and deliberation at all times, and obeying orders fearlessly and with promptitude during the heat of action, they fully sustained the fair reputation which was won by them at Shiloh, Corinth, and Stone's River.

I am, your obedient servant,

A. R. HADLOCK,
Lieutenant-Colonel, Comdg. First Kentucky Regiment.

Capt. W. H. FAIRBANKS,
Acting Assistant Adjutant-General, First Brigade.

No. 156.

Report of Maj. James W. Mitchell, First Kentucky Infantry.

CHATTANOOGA, TENN.,
September 28, 1863.

GENERAL: I would most respectfully submit the following report of the performance of duties of train guard assigned to five companies of the First Regiment Kentucky Infantry by your order of September 7, and which I had the honor to command. The details consisted of Companies A, C, F, and I. They were ordered to be ready to march at 4 a. m., September 8. Everything being in readiness at that time, I started from our camp 5 miles north of Trenton, Ga., and, after disposing the men in the wagons (of which there were 50), gave orders to go to Shellmound, Tenn., 13 miles distant, which was reached about 9 a. m. Lying over at that place until 12 m., the train was started again, and that night I camped my command at Bridgeport, 21 miles from the place of starting.

September 9.—Started from Bridgeport and arrived at Stevenson, Ala., 10 miles distant, at 10 a. m.; the balance of the day was spent in loading the train with provisions for the division. Camped this night at Stevenson.

September 10.—Started the train on the return at 4 a. m., but did not get as far as I anticipated, on account of the blocking up of the road by troops and trains of the First Reserve Corps, which was moving to the front. Camped this night at Shellmound.

September 11.—Left Shellmound and camped at 4 p. m. at Squirreltown. I found the road between these two points exceedingly rough and rocky, and met with less accidents from broken wagons, &c., than I had anticipated.

September 12.—Left Squirreltown and camped, 2.30 p. m., at Chattanooga, 16 miles. I found the condition of the road traveled much better than that traveled the day before.

The accompanying quartermaster, Lieutenant Grubbs, Thirty-first Indiana, afforded me all the assistance in his power during this trip, and is deserving of mention.

I reported my command at 4 p. m. to General Wagner, commanding post, for orders to go to the front, when I received orders from him to hold myself and command in readiness to march at 6 a. m. on the following day.

September 13.—Reported myself and command to General Wagner, and was given charge of 30 wagons of First Division and 50 wagons of Second Division, also 439 prisoners of war, with instructions to guard them (the prisoners) to Stevenson, Ala., and turn over to provost-marshal, and return with train and provisions to Chattanooga as soon as possible, crossing Raccoon Mountain, a different route from that previously traveled, but found it impracticable for to return upon with loaded wagons.

September 14.—Started at daylight and reached Stevenson at dark. Was obliged to have the train stop here next day, to load and to have the mules shod, as they were unfit for traveling over the rocky roads we were traveling.

September 16.—Started on return trip, and, passing Bridgeport, camped at Shellmound.

September 17.—Left Shellmound at 3 a. m., and, passing Whiteside's and Squirreltown, reached a point 10 miles from Chattanooga.

September 18.—Started at 5 a. m., and after reaching Lookout Mountain, experienced considerable trouble and delay from trains coming in opposite direction, and also from trains having the precedence of mine. Reached Chattanooga at 4 p. m. and reported again to General Wagner, commandant of post, who ordered me to report at 8 a. m. on the following day. Reported myself September 19, and ordered to be ready to move my command to the front at 2 p. m., in charge of supply train of Second Division. Started from Chattanooga at 4 p. m. in charge of train previously under the charge of Lieutenant Chilton, acting commissary of subsistence, Second Division, Twenty-first Army Corps, taking the La Fayette road. Traveled until 10 p. m., when various and confused rumors of an engagement having occurred on the road leading into the rebel lines reached us.

Adopting the necessary precaution, I sent forward horsemen to ascertain the truth of the statements, and delayed here two hours. I then learned that an engagement had occurred, but the road was still open, and accordingly proceeded and camped one-half mile from Crawfish Spring.

I was next morning getting my command in readiness to join my regiment when I received orders from General Palmer, per Captain Howland, assistant quartermaster, Second Division, to take the train back to Rossville. Started at 8.30 a. m. toward Rossville, and had but just gotten the train upon the road when the battle commenced directly upon my right and front.

I got the rear of my train through just in time. After experiencing various difficulties from other trains traveling the same road and going to the rear, finally arrived at Rossville at 12 m., and at 2.30 p. m. concluded that under the circumstances it was best to move to Chattanooga with train, which I did accordingly and camped.

September 21.—Crossed the Tennessee River, and parked the train one-quarter mile from it.

September 22 *and* 23.—Remained with the train according to orders; and at 2.30 o'clock, September 24, received orders from yourself to join regiment, which I did accordingly on that day. During the time I had charge of detail, I received the hearty co-operation of both officers and men.

Submitting this for your approval, I am, general, very respectfully,

JAMES W. MITCHELL,
Major First Kentucky Infantry.

Brigadier-General CRUFT,
First Brigade.

No. 157.

Report of Capt. David J. Jones, First Kentucky Infantry.

OOLTEWAH, TENN.,
April 20, 1864.

SIR: In accordance with your request, I have the honor to make the following report of the circumstances connected with the capture of myself and 22 of my company, near Pea Vine Creek, Ga., on the 10th of September, 1863:

In the advance from Chattanooga, four companies of my regiment, under Major Hadlock, constituted the advance guard, disposed as follows: Company K, under Lieutenant Hornung, deployed across the road and on either side as skirmishers; Company B, under Lieutenant Hammond, marching by the flank in the road as a reserve for the line of skirmishers; and the remaining two (D and G) also marching by the flank some distance in rear. During the morning a body of mounted men were sent to the extreme front. These came across the enemy near Pea Vine Creek, and commenced skirmishing with them. The advance was halted, and our column moved up to its support. It being apparent that the enemy were in considerable force in our front, and that they intended an offensive movement, dispositions were at once made to meet the contemplated attack.

Three companies of the battalion were formed in line across the road, Company B in the woods to the right; my company (D), with the colors and color-guard on its right, and about seven files of Company G on its left, occupied the road; the remainder of Company G in the woods to the left. The line, thus formed, was advantageously posted behind the crest of a hillock in the road, and commanded the road as far as the fork, perhaps 600 yards. Company K was still in front deployed as skirmishers.

We remained half an hour or so, slight skirmishing going on between our cavalry and the enemy, until the former withdrew and went to the rear, leaving our skirmishers directly opposed to the enemy.

Soon the dust to our front and right plainly indicated an advance of the enemy, and, unaccountably, Company K fell back upon our main body, and resisted the utmost endeavors of their commander to drive them to their duty. Seeing that there was no probability of the skirmishers being advanced to cover our front, I suggested that they establish a new line where we then stood, and the main body be withdrawn about 100 yards to the rear.

Major Hadlock acted upon my suggestion so far as to move the main line about 50 yards to the rear, in such a position that we could see the road no farther than the crest of the hillock before mentioned, a distance of not more than 60 yards at farthest. A cloud of dust in front told plainly the enemy were coming, and not far off. The line of skirmishers fell back on their appearance; the main line, with pieces ready, awaiting orders with a coolness and determination I never saw surpassed. As the enemy came up we could hear the clatter of the horses' hoofs (they were cavalry), but could not see them on account of the elevation in front.

At this time Major Hadlock was on a slight elevation in our rear, and, being mounted, could see the enemy as they approached much sooner than any of his command could. While we were still waiting, no enemy yet in sight, we were surprised by an order from Major Hadlock to fire, accompanied with some such remark as that we will give them one volley anyhow. There can be no mistaking that there was no enemy in sight when my company fired in obedience to the order thus given. Though the men aimed very low, the volley, of course, proved ineffectual, as it passed over their heads. We were thus with empty pieces when a moment after the head of the enemy's column appeared on the crest in front, and halted to observe the position of things. On their appearance Major Hadlock ordered a retreat in quick time, the men reloading as they fell back. The enemy, quick to profit by the advantage thus given them, charged us. Seeing the new danger, the major ordered a double-quick, and being thus thrown into confusion, we fell an easy prey. My company, being altogether in the road with no advantages for escape, suffered a greater loss than the rest, while the companies in the woods suffered slightly. None of the men captured were wounded, and but 2 of the enemy were struck, both hurt slightly. These and the 2 horses wounded were shot by the file leaders and such others of my company who did not fire with the body of the company.

After my capture I learned that one regiment of cavalry, the Sixth Georgia, under Colonel Hart, was the attacking force, but that one company of the regiment, Company A, under Captain Brown, made the charge and routed our four companies.

I would be doing a gross injustice to the men with whom I have shared the fortunes of war for the last three years did I close this report without bearing testimony that throughout this most disgraceful affair the alacrity with which they obeyed orders, and the coolness they evinced, I never saw surpassed, and that, though sharing the disgrace, and, many of them, with myself, the suffering consequent, they do not deserve any part of the blame.

I trust, general, that, having the facts at length before you, you will procure, at an early day, an investigation of the affair, that the blame may rest where it properly belongs.

I remain, sir, very respectfully, your obedient servant,

D. J. JONES,
Captain Company D, First Kentucky Volunteers.

Brig. Gen. CHARLES CRUFT,
Commanding Brigade.

[Indorsements.]

HEADQUARTERS FIRST KENTUCKY REGIMENT,
Ooltewah, April 21, 1864.

Respectfully forwarded, approved.

D. A. ENYART,
Colonel, Commanding Regiment.

HDQRS. FIRST BRIGADE, FIRST DIVISION,
FOURTH CORPS, ARMY OF THE CUMBERLAND,
Ooltewah, April 22, 1864.

Respectfully forwarded.

A report of the affair mentioned within was made a few days after its occurrence through headquarters, Major-General Palmer, commanding Second Division, Twenty-first Army Corps, to which the brigade was then attached. This report should be appended to that one as it furnishes some facts which do not come out in any of the sub-reports of the other officers. My report was dated September 28, 1863, and this is forwarded as an appendix thereto.* The enlistment of the regiment expires on the 8th June proximo, but for which fact I would favor the granting of Captain Jones' request for a proper investigation.

CHARLES CRUFT,
Brigadier-General, Commanding.

No. 158.

Report of Lieut. George Hornung, First Kentucky Infantry.

CAMP FIRST KENTUCKY VOLUNTEERS,
September 16, 1863.

SIR: In compliance with an order from brigade headquarters to report, the part taken by me in the skirmish on the 10th instant is as follows:

After leaving camp on the morning of the 10th of September, 1863, and marching some 2 miles, the column (First Brigade, Second Division, Twenty-first Army Corps) was halted. I received orders from the adjutant of my regiment (First Kentucky) to deploy my company, K, as skirmishers, one platoon on each side of the road leading to Ringgold, Ga. I immediately ordered the first platoon of the company on the right of the road, and the second platoon on the left of the road, commanded by Second Lieut. Alexander Tilly. I assumed command of the first platoon. I advanced with the company de-

* See p. 726.

ployed as skirmishers some 5 miles, running on to a creek which it was impossible to ford. About that time I received an order from John A. Wright, aide-de-camp to General Cruft, to march by the left flank, which I executed, assembling my men on the road (the creek course at that place was on a right angle with the road). From thence I crossed a bridge and marched forward, not as skirmishers, but as an advance guard. This was ordered by John A. Wright, aide-de-camp, until getting to the next creek; the distance I estimated about 2 miles.

We halted for a temporary rest of some fifteen minutes; having our rest, we resumed our march forward.

The escort of Major-General Palmer had passed us some twenty minutes previous, and commenced firing about 1 mile ahead of us. We moved on cautiously and halted on the road, with a thick pine underwood on each side of the road. The escort soon came back and reported them coming, some 200 strong.

First Lieut. John A. Wright, aide-de-camp, then ordered 5 of my company forward on the road as far as the cross-roads (some 200 yards ahead). After selecting the 5 men, I in person went with them, but was fired on half way. I immediately posted the men behind trees, with instructions to keep a good lookout.

Shortly after the firing I saw the enemy forming and coming down the road, which caused me to go back to the company to be prepared for an attack. I formed a line on a right angle with the road, my left resting on the road. This done, the enemy's cavalry charged down on two roads, the road the company was on and a road some 100 yards on my right. As the cavalry approached close enough, the company fired and appeared to break ranks with the intent to get behind trees. I wanted to rally them, but without success. My company, together with Company B (of the First Kentucky Regiment), fell back through the woods. Company B was formed in the rear of my company. The formation of the company was according to Lieut. John A. Wright's (aide-de-camp) instructions.

Respectfully submitted.

GEO. HORNUNG,
First Lieutenant, Comdg. Co. K, 1st Ky. Vols.

Capt. W. H. FAIRBANKS,
Acting Assistant Adjutant-General.

No. 159.

Report of Lieut. Patrick J. Brown, First Kentucky Infantry.

CAMP FIRST KENTUCKY VOLUNTEERS,
September 16, 1863.

CAPTAIN: I have the honor to submit the following report of the part taken by this company under my command—Company G—in the skirmish of the 10th instant near Graysville, Ga.:

Shortly after the return of General Palmer's escort, who had been skirmishing with the enemy's pickets, my company was ordered into line in conjunction with Company D. I formed the company in accordance with orders, the right resting on the edge of the road, the left and center in the woods; were ordered to lie down, which the men did; remained thus for about five minutes, when the order was given to fall back. Reformed a new line some 30 yards in rear of the former one, and waited probably five minutes before my company fired. The company on my right fired first, my command discharging their guns directly afterward. After the discharge of the first volley, I discovered that the company on my right was falling back. Supposing that that company, with mine, had been so ordered to do, I gave the command to fall back, which was executed with considerable confusion, as the underbrush and briars made our way to the rear next to impossible. Such being the case, I ordered the company out on the road. When reaching it, the cavalry were within 30 yards of us, on a full charge. My men not having had sufficient time to reload their pieces, I saw no other alternative but to gain the woods on the opposite side of the road, and thereby prevent capture. Those who did not succeed in crossing the road, or remain hidden in the underbrush on the left, were mostly all captured.

Respectfully submitted.

P. J. BROWN,
Lieutenant, Commanding Company G, First Kentucky.

Capt. W. H. FAIRBANKS,
Assistant Adjutant-General, First Brigade.

No. 160.

Report of Lieut. David Hammond, First Kentucky Infantry.

CAMP FIRST REGIMENT KENTUCKY VOLUNTEERS,
September 16, 1863.

SIR : In compliance with orders, I have the honor to forward the following report of the part taken by Company B in the recent skirmish of the First Kentucky Volunteers :

On the morning of the 10th instant, the companies with regiment (four companies, under command of Maj. A. R. Hadlock) took up line of march, proceeding toward Ringgold, Ga., by the direct route. When about three-quarters of a mile from Lookout Creek, where we last bivouacked, two companies (B and K) were taken from the right and ordered forward as skirmishers. Company K was deployed to the right and left of road, while my company (B) was held as reserve. The skirmishers were thrown forward about 40 yards in advance of regiment. We continued to advance slowly and cautiously, and when near Pea Vine Creek the skirmishers were halted and two or three companies of cavalry were sent forward, and their skirmishers were deployed to right and left of road and in front of Company K's line of skirmishers. Company K's skirmishers were now called in, and 12 men and 2 sergeants taken from Company B and deployed to right and left of road, Sergeant Cannon in command of 6 men on the right and Sergeant Conklin in command of 6 men on the left.

The skirmishers were again ordered forward to support the cavalry, who continued slowly driving the enemy for over a mile, and when near Graysville they encountered the enemy in force and were obliged to retire. The remainder of my company was now ordered by Lieutenant Wright (aide-de-camp) into the woods to support the line of skirmishers on the right, having advanced into the woods about 30 yards, when Company K commenced falling back, and immediately after a volley was fired by the two companies that were drawn up across the road. Owing to the thickness of the underbrush, it was impossible for me to see anything of the enemy. I now fell back to where the right of the reserve rested on the road, and could plainly see the enemy in my rear. I now moved my company to the right, where we were ordered to remain by General Palmer.

Casualties in company : Missing, 2.

Respectfully submitted,

DAVID HAMMOND,
First Lieutenant, Comdg. Company B, First Kentucky.

Capt. W. H. FAIRBANKS,
Acting Assistant Adjutant-General, First Brigade.

No. 161.

Report of Col. Thomas D. Sedgewick, Second Kentucky Infantry.

HEADQUARTERS SECOND KENTUCKY INFANTRY,
Chattanooga, Tenn., September 29, 1863.

SIR: In compliance with orders, I have the honor to submit the following report of the part taken by the Second Kentucky Infantry in the actions on the 19th and 20th instant, and also of its movements since crossing the Tennessee River:

At 11.30 p. m. of the 3d instant, we crossed the river at Shellmound, and bivouacked on the south side until 3.30 p. m. of the 5th, when we moved forward and halted at 9 p. m. at Whiteside's.

September 6.—Division moved at 8 a. m., my regiment in advance. Marched to junction of Murphy's Bottom and Nickajack roads, where we halted several hours to allow Brannan's division to pass, then moved on about three-quarters of a mile and went into camp at Cole's Academy.

September 8.—Left camp at Cole's Academy at 3 a. m., and marched with division 5 miles to Hawkins' Station, where we went into position to support General Wood. At 3 p. m. I was ordered to take my regiment and make a reconnaissance around the base of Lookout Mountain, which I did, marching 7 miles and developing all the facts and gaining all the information desired.

September 9.—Learning that Chattanooga had been evacuated, we moved at 9 a. m. for that place, passed by, and about dark went into camp at Rossville, Ga., 6 miles south of Chattanooga.

September 10.—Moved at 7.30 a. m., and at 10 a. m. arrived at Pea Vine Creek, where the division halted to go into camp, and I was sent with the regiment to make a reconnaissance to the right. After advancing about 1 mile, I was ordered to return, as the rebel cavalry had attacked our front in large force. I did so, put the regiment in line of battle, and remained so until nearly dark, when we bivouacked for the night.

September 11.—Moved at 7 a. m., and at 1 p. m. went into camp at Ringgold, Ga.

September 12.—Moved at 6 a. m. in direction of Gordon's Mills, 4 miles out. The enemy's cavalry appearing on our flanks and in front, the brigade was halted, formed in line, and skirmishers thrown forward, who drove the enemy from our immediate front. About 3 p. m. I was ordered forward with the Second Kentucky, First Kentucky, and one section of artillery to make a reconnaissance to the front and right. The Ninetieth Ohio Volunteer Infantry furnished the skirmishers. We advanced, under direction of Major-General Palmer, to a road about one-half mile to the front, when, finding no enemy, we were ordered to return. After rejoining the brigade we moved on, and went into camp at Gordon's Mills at dark.

September 13.—About daylight the regiment was called to arms by heavy firing on the picket line. We remained under arms, changing position to the front, until 10 a. m., when we moved forward with the brigade to support Colonel Wilder's brigade at the point of the skirmish on the previous day. We remained here during the day, and at nightfall returned to Gordon's Mills.

September 14.—Remained in camp at Gordon's Mills until 4 p. m., when I was ordered with my regiment to escort the corps supply train to Chattanooga and back. Started at 6 p. m. and arrived at Chattanooga at 2 a. m.

September 15.—Started from Chattanooga with supply train at 1 p. m., and reached Gordon's Mills, without accident, at dark; found that the brigade had moved. Went into camp by order of General Wood.

September 16.—Moved with trains of Palmer's and Van Cleve's divisions at daylight. Reached the latter at Crawfish Spring at 5.30 a. m., and turned over his train; then moved on and joined the former at Matthews' house at 7.30 a. m.

September 17.—Moved with division about 1 mile to the left.

September 18.—At 7.30 moved with brigade to Gordon's Mills, where we arrived at 1 a. m., and were placed in position by General Palmer.

September 19.—The regiment was under arms at daylight and two companies, under direction of Major Baldwin, thrown out on the right as skirmishers. We remained in this position until 11 a. m., when the firing in our front becoming very heavy, we were ordered forward in that direction. We moved down the Rossville road to a point about 1½ miles distant, and were here placed in order of battle. The order to the division was to advance by brigades *en échelon* by the left, at 80 paces, General Hazen's (Second) brigade being on the left, General Cruft's (First) in the center, and Colonel Grose's (Third) on the right, my regiment forming the right of the first line of First Brigade; Company A, Captain Martin, was advanced as skirmishers.

The order to advance being given, I moved forward about 400 yards, when our skirmishers became warmly engaged; they pressed onward, however, causing those of the enemy to retire before them. We moved forward a short distance, when the command was given for the brigade to halt. This left my regiment in a very undesirable position, on low ground and exposed to a terrible fire from three sides from the enemy, who had now opened upon us. Ere the regiment could be placed in proper position, the skirmishers had been driven in, 2 captains wounded, and 9 men killed and wounded. I soon rectified the alignment, and then opened fire upon the enemy with such effect as to drive back the first line, which we followed up a short distance, but he returned re-enforced and we were forced to halt, yet bravely held the ground obtained up to this moment. Colonel Grose's brigade had not joined me on the right, and in consequence the rebels were pouring in a deadly enfilading fire from that quarter and endeavoring to turn our flank. My men were falling fast and the position was becoming untenable, when the Twenty-third Kentucky, of Grose's brigade, moved up and joined me on the right; together we succeeded in checking them; they, however, kept up a bold front and steady fire for one and a half hours, when their line apparently being repulsed on the left, they appeared to withdraw from our immediate front and move off toward our right. Taking advantage of the lull in the firing, I replenished the ammunition and had the killed and wounded removed a short distance to the rear.

In a short time, as I had anticipated, the firing opened with redoubled fury on the right of our line, soon sweeping around to Colonel Grose's brigade, now formed on our right and occupying a ridge, with his right retired. Finding that the enemy was evidently gaining ground on the right, I changed front perpendicularly to the rear, to be ready as a support, but had scarcely got my line reformed before we were completely thrown into disorder by retiring troops, and forced to fall back about 200 yards, the enemy following so closely as to allow us to bring back some 15 of them as prisoners. The regiment was here rallied, reformed, and faced to the front. The enemy halted and retired a short distance beyond the brow of the hill. Our position now was not a very enviable one, being far in advance, separated from the remainder of the brigade, and without support, but in a few moments General Turchin moved up rapidly with his brigade; he placed his battery in front of my regiment and moved his infantry to the left. The latter advanced and we remained as a support to the battery. I was here joined by the remaining regiments of the First Brigade.

The enemy having withdrawn from our front, the order was given to retire, which we did in line and in good order. Moved out to a point on the Rossville road, where we remained until 7.30 p. m., when we were ordered to move to the left to the support of General Johnson. Moving down the road about 500 yards we were halted, and after having thrown out a strong skirmish or picket line, we bivouacked for the night.

On the 20th, one hour before daylight found my regiment under arms, and the picket line relieved, strengthened, and advanced. Immediately upon learning that we would occupy the same position during the anticipated battle of the day, I set heavy details to work to build a temporary breastwork in front of the line occupied by the regiment. My position was on the left of the front line of the brigade, connecting with the right of General Johnson's division, the Thirty-first Indiana on my right. About 7 a. m. heavy firing commenced on our left; it gradually increased and drew nearer; at 7.40 a. m. our skirmishers became engaged and were soon driven in, the enemy following closely. The action now became general, and the enemy advanced boldly up to our slight work. Their first line was driven back, but again and again they advanced, and each time were repulsed by the withering fire of the men, who, protected by their work, coolly and deliberately loaded and fired without suffering materially from the enemy's fire. The firing was incessant on both sides until about 11 a. m., when it gradually ceased. The ammunition of my regiment being exhausted, as was that of the Thirty-first Indiana, the front line of the brigade was retired, my regiment being relieved by the Ninetieth Ohio Volunteer Infantry. We moved back about 100 yards and took position below a slight crest, where we received a fresh supply of ammunition. No heavy firing taking place in our immediate front, we were not again called into action. About 5

p. m., it being evident that the right of our line was giving way, the order was given to retire. I moved about 100 yards by the flank, and was about entering a large corn-field immediately in our front, when I received an order to cross it in line.

I at once formed the regiment forward into line, and under a terrific fire of musketry and artillery, we at common time and in perfect order retired across the field, maintaining our position in the brigade. Gaining the cover of the woods on the opposite side, we were halted and faced toward the enemy. Remaining thus for some moments, we were formed in double column, faced to the rear, and again retired; reaching the top of a high ridge, about 1 mile distant, we were again halted and faced about; here remained until the arrival of General Palmer, when we took up our line of march for Rossville, which place we reached about 9.30 p. m. in perfect order. The conduct of the officers and men of the regiment during the battles of both days was of the most heroic character. I have never seen men act more coolly or deliberately, or obey orders more promptly under any circumstances. The loss of the regiment, which occurred entirely on the first day, will attest the bravery of the men. I had no stragglers. The missing are in the hands of the enemy. Lieutenant-Colonel Hurd and Major Baldwin, as on all previous fields, displayed the greatest gallantry. Captain Bodine received his death wound while coolly directing the fire of his men. Major Baldwin was wounded while gallantly encouraging the line during a heavy attack. All of my officers deserve special mention, but neither time nor space will admit it. Subjoined please find a list of the casualties of the regiment.*

I have the honor to be, with respect, yours, &c.,

T. D. SEDGEWICK,
Colonel, Commanding Second Kentucky Infantry.

Capt. W. H. Fairbanks,
Acting Assistant Adjutant-General, First Brigade.

No. 162.

Report of Col. Charles H. Rippey, Ninetieth Ohio Infantry.

Hdqrs. 90th Regiment, Ohio Volunteer Infantry,
September 28, 1863.

Sir: I have the honor to submit the following report of the part taken by the Ninetieth Regiment Ohio Volunteer Infantry in the battles of the 19th and 20th instant, on the eastern slopes of Missionary Ridge, together with a summary of its marches, reconnaissances, &c., since crossing the Tennessee River. The regiment was transported across the river on the night of the 3d instant, between the hours of 11 and 12, and bivouacked at Shellmound. The crossing was attended with no accident or mishap whatsoever.

On the 4th, it encamped at Shellmound, awaiting the arrival of the train with supplies.

On the evening of the 5th, it moved with the brigade to Running Water Creek, distant 9 miles; thence, on the 6th, to the intersection of the Murphy's Bottom and Nickajack roads, near which it encamped.

---

* Embodied in revised statement, p. 176.

On the 7th, it was ordered on a reconnaissance to Nickajack Gap, for the purpose of relieving a signal escort, which had been attacked on the side of the mountain. No skirmishing occurred.

On the 8th, it marched to Hawkins' Station, on the Trenton Railroad; thence, on the 9th, to Rossville, 16 miles, leaving Chattanooga on the left.

On the 10th, it marched to Pea Vine Creek, 7 miles, where it encamped at about 10.30 a. m. A few moments after arms had been stacked an attack was made by a body of rebel cavalry upon the skirmish line of the brigade still thrown to the front, and the line driven in. The regiment was formed at the time on the right of, and at right angles to, the road leading to Ringgold, the Thirty-first Indiana Volunteers being formed between the left and the road. I was immediately ordered to move forward in line, which I did, throwing a company of skirmishers to the front. After advancing about half a mile in a direction parallel with the road, my skirmishers became engaged with the skirmishers of the enemy who had retired thus far. As fast as was thought advisable by the brigade commander, I allowed my skirmish line to advance upon the enemy, who retired whenever a fire was opened upon them. In this manner I followed them, until about 3.30 p. m., over a distance of several miles, when I received an order to fall back to camp and bivouac. My skirmishers succeeded in killing 1 horse and 1 man, besides severely wounding one other. No casualties happened among my men.

On the 11th, the regiment moved to Ringgold, distant 8 miles; thence, on the 12th, to Gordon's Mills.

When within 3½ miles of Gordon's Mills, to the east, I was ordered by General Crittenden to deploy a battalion as skirmishers and clear out a piece of woods to the left of the road. A small squad of cavalry, which had been observing our movements, retired as my skirmishers advanced. As I commenced withdrawing my line to rejoin the brigade, they returned and opened fire, which was returned by my skirmishers. I immediately halted and adjusted the line so as to cover the front of the brigade, which had halted and formed line of battle. During the afternoon, under an order from General Palmer, I advanced my skirmish line, well supported by the First and Second Kentucky Regiments, down a valley leading toward La Fayette. Finding no considerable force in that direction, I was ordered back to the road, and immediately afterward rejoined the brigade and resumed the march to Gordon's Mills, where we encamped. The casualties of this day were said to be one rebel major killed by my regiment.

On the 13th, the brigade being ordered on a reconnaissance to the aforesaid valley, I was ordered with my regiment down a by-road leading toward La Fayette, for the purpose of protecting the right and rear of the brigade against a flank movement. After advancing about 1 mile, I halted, formed across the hollow, and threw out a heavy skirmish line to the front. After remaining in this position about one hour, my skirmishers were attacked by a considerable force of rebel cavalry, dismounted. Three separate times within an hour the enemy advanced upon my skirmish line, but were each time handsomely repulsed. They finally retired, leaving several dead and wounded on the field, 6, as I afterward learned from prisoners. Just at this time I was ordered to join the brigade, which I did, retiring in line and covering the rear with a heavy line of skirmishers.

The reconnaissance being completed, I moved with the brigade to Gordon's Mills, where the regiment encamped.

On the 14th, the regiment remained in camp, the brigade being left in charge of the corps transportation.

On the 15th, it marched to Matthews' house, distant 6 miles, where it remained encamped during the 16th.

On the 17th, it moved back 1½ miles to Abercrombie's house, where it remained until 9.30 o'clock on the evening of the 18th, when it moved to Gordon's Mills, and went into line of battle at 1 a. m. on the morning of the 19th.

At 11 a. m. on the 19th, the division being ordered to engage the enemy on the right of ———— division, our brigade took the advance, moving by the left flank up the Rossville road, the Ninetieth Ohio leading. Having marched about 1½ miles to McNamara's house, I turned obliquely to the right and formed line of battle. The Second Brigade having passed up in the rear formed to my left. At 12.30 o'clock I advanced, keeping my left well closed on the right of the Second Brigade, though 80 paces in the rear, the brigades moving *en échelon* by the left. The Second Brigade soon became hotly engaged and halted, and before I could move up on to the line, my skirmishers were driven in and I received the fire of one of the enemy's battalions. I immediately moved forward in double-quick, driving the enemy before me, and took position on a line with the Second Brigade, my right somewhat advanced so as to form an angle slightly enfilading the enemy. The other regiments of the brigade moved on to the same line about the same time.

The fight then opened fiercely with both musketry and artillery. I had gained for my regiment rather an advantageous position on the crest of a swell in the ground along which was some fallen timber and other cover. The enemy made four separate attempts to dislodge the regiment from this position, but were each time repulsed with heavy loss.

A battery of artillery posted directly in my front were so harassed by the sharp practice of my men that they were unable to work their pieces, save to deliver a few straggling shots. After the third assault of the enemy, my men having expended all their ammunition except about 2 rounds per man, I retired the regiment about 20 yards, so as to gain the cover of the woods, in case it became necessary to retreat. By permission of General Cruft, there was also brought from the right of the brigade a section of Standart's battery, and I posted it so as to enfilade the column which was pressing the front of the Second Brigade. The last attack of the enemy was a feeble one. The volley which I had instructed my men to reserve for them scattering them in every direction. At the same time, the section of artillery which had been posted assisted very materially in creating confusion in the enemy's lines, and in a few moments they were fleeing in every direction over the open country in our front. This fight lasted about two hours and was very hot.

The casualties in my regiment amounted to 4 killed and 57 wounded. The enemy having retired from our front, there was a lull of about two hours, during which time the men were supplied with fresh ammunition and their guns cleansed and put in order. At about 3.30 p. m. heavy firing was again heard upon the right and rear of our position, and rapidly approached us, until it seemed the right of our brigade was attacked in flank. Under orders from General Cruft, I quickly changed front to the right and formed, supporting the battery. The Thirty-first Indiana Volunteers attempted to form on my right, but before they were in position a mass of disorganized troops came rushing across our lines in great disorder, the enemy pressing closely upon them, and pouring in heavy volleys of musketry. An order was given me to retire, by General Cruft. The battery, in order to pass to the front of the retiring column, was obliged to pass directly through my regiment, which, together with the fleeing fugitives upon the right, threw my regiment into a moment's confusion. As soon, however, as we were clear of the battery and the fugitives, I rallied the regiment and faced to the front, under directions from the general commanding brigade. The enemy still pressed closely upon my front, and as I feared we might not be able to hold them in this position, I, on request of general commanding brigade, ordered a charge. Many of my officers sprung gallantly to the front, and, with a cheer, the men followed, fixing their bayonets as they ran. Quick as thought, they were upon the enemy, who, scarcely waiting to discharge their pieces, turned and fled in utter confusion. My color-sergeant was shot down, but one of the escort seized the flag, and the men, seeing the discomfiture of the enemy, and knowing that support was coming up on the left, rushed forward with a wild cheer, literally outrunning and capturing many of the retreating foe. The pursuit continued for a full half mile, when, seeing that we had left the supports far in the rear, and fearing lest the regiment should be cut off, I halted them, and marched back slowly to join the brigade.

Having taken position on the left of the brigade, the regiment remained in line until nearly dark, when, no enemy appearing in our front, the brigade was moved off to the right and rear, and took position on the left of General Brannan's division, which had formed across the Rossville road.

Shortly after we had taken this position, an attack was made upon General Johnson's division, some distance to the left. The brigade was ordered out to his support and moved off by the left flank, but by the time it had arrived within supporting distance, the firing ceased, and we were immediately ordered to bivouac for the night. While moving to this position, the regiment was exposed to a severe fire from the enemy's artillery posted on the opposite ridge, but fortunately no one was injured.

On the morning of the 20th, the regiment was under arms by 4 o'clock and in line of battle, occupying the right of the brigade, which was formed in single line. Having ascertained that this would probably be our position during the day, the men were ordered to stack arms and construct such defenses as were practicable. In less than one hour, without the aid of axes or other intrenching tools, a strong breastwork of logs and stones was built, which would effectively protect the men against all light missiles. Before any attack was made, however, the brigade was formed in two lines, my regiment occupying the right of the reserve line. About 8 o'clock a fierce attack was made upon the front line, which lasted for several hours, but was successfully resisted. My regiment being ordered to lie down behind the crest of a rising piece of ground, met with but few casualties.

At about 11 a. m. I was ordered forward to relieve the Thirty-first Indiana and a portion of the Second Kentucky. Being obliged to pass over high ground, several of my regiment fell before they reached the defenses. But few volleys were fired by my regiment after they reached the defenses, as shortly afterward the enemy withdrew, leaving only a line of sharpshooters in our front. This position was held by my regiment during the remainder of the day until 5 p. m., when orders were sent me to retire. The brigade had moved some moments before I received the order. I marched out by the right flank and was enabled to overtake the right of the Thirty-first Indiana moving in line. After reaching the open fields to the rear, I thought it advisable to march in this order since the brigade was exposed to a cross-fire of artillery from the flanks. Although this fire was very severe, the regiment moved steadily and in good order. One officer and several men fell here, and could not be brought off the field. Having reached the ridges on the left of the Rossville road, I halted with the brigade and formed line of battle. After resting here about one hour, the regiment moved back with the division to Rossville and encamped.

During the whole of this engagement and the skirmishes preceding it, the most of my officers and men behaved as well as soldiers could, obeying every order cheerfully, promptly, and with judgment. A very few left the field before the engagement ended, but I will not disgrace the history of those gallant men who remained, by mentioning their names among these pages. Among the officers who deserve special credit for their coolness, fortitude, and bravery, I might mention Major Perry, Captain Rains, Captain Witherspoon, Captain Hitchcock, and Captain Angle, together with Lieutenants Felton, Sutphen, and Cook. Indeed, all the officers, with two or three exceptions, conducted themselves as well as I could desire.

My especial thanks are due Lieut. J. A. Wright, of the staff, for gallant services rendered me on Saturday afternoon. It affords me great pleasure to notice the conduct of Corpl. James J. Holliday, who, when the color-sergeant was shot down in the charge on Saturday afternoon, seized the colors and waving them over his head sprang to the front with a cheer which seemed to inspire every soldier on the line. I should be pleased to mention many others if time and space permitted. Attached you will find a list * of the killed and wounded of the regiment, which I consider remarkably small considering the severity of the fire to which the regiment was so often exposed.

Very respectfully,

C. H. RIPPEY,
Colonel, Commanding.

Capt. W. H. FAIRBANKS,
Acting Assistant Adjutant-General, First Brigade.

No. 163.

Report of Lieut. Norman A. Baldwin, Battery B, First Ohio Light Artillery.

CHATTANOOGA,
September 27, 1863.

SIR: I have the honor of submitting to you the following report of Battery B, First Ohio Volunteer Artillery, in the engagement of the 19th and 20th of September, 1863 :

September 17.—Encamped at Mission Church ; sent one section,

---

* Nominal list omitted; see revised statement, p. 176.

under command of Lieutenant Throup, on picket; it remained there till about 4 p. m., when it was relieved by General Baird's division. At about 6 o'clock moved the battery, with our brigade, about 10 miles toward Crawfish Spring. Bivouacked for the night.

September 18.—At about 2 p. m., moved to Crawfish Spring; remained there until about 11 p. m., when we moved with our brigade to about 1½ miles this side of Lee's Mills; bivouacked for the remainder of the night.

September 19.—Took position on a hill with cleared field in front, supported by the Second Kentucky and Thirty-first Indiana Regiments. At about 10 a. m. heavy firing was heard to our left. Was ordered with the brigade in that direction; moved down the road about 1½ miles, and formed our line, battery in rear and center of the brigade; moved forward into the woods; had not proceeded more than 500 yards before we met the enemy. Fought till nearly dark; held our position all the afternoon. Fired 159 rounds; had 3 men wounded, and 2 horses shot. The ground fought over was very unfavorable for artillery, being thickly covered with timber and underbrush. At dark fell back to cleared field and prepared to bivouac for the night. At about 7 p. m. heavy firing was heard to the left of us; was ordered with our brigade in that direction. Moved about 600 yards, and took position in center of brigade, and bivouacked for the night.

September 20.—At daylight, commenced building a high breastwork of logs in front of the battery; had it finished by 6 a. m. At 8 a.m. was attacked by the enemy in strong force, who fought with great determination for two hours, but did not succeed in moving us. We held our position till 5 p. m., when we were ordered to fall back with our brigade; we fell back across the open field, where we were ordered by Major-General Thomas to report at Rossville. Arrived there about 7 p. m. Casualties this day, 1 man killed, 5 wounded, and 4 missing. Horses killed and disabled, 11. Three 6-pounder rifled guns disabled, 2 left on the field. Fired 986 rounds.

Number of guns lost	2
Number of horses lost	13
Number of men wounded	8
Number of men killed	1
Number of men missing	4
Number of rounds fired	1,145

Very respectfully, &c.,

N. A. BALDWIN,
First Lieut. Battery B, First Ohio Vol. Arty., Commanding.

Capt. W. E. STANDART,
Chief of Artillery, Second Division.

No. 164.

Reports of Brig. Gen. William B. Hazen, U. S. Army, commanding Second Brigade.

HDQRS. SECOND BRIG., SECOND DIV., 21ST ARMY CORPS,
Chattanooga, October 1, 1863.

SIR : In obedience to orders received at Poe's Tavern, September 3, 1863, from headquarters of the department, I assumed command of all the troops in the Tennessee Valley, embracing Wagner's and my own brigade of infantry, Minty's brigade of cavalry, and Wilder's brigade of mounted infantry—in all, between 6,000 and 7,000 men— with orders to keep these forces well in hand, to closely watch the movements of the enemy at all the crossings of the Tennessee River, to make such dispositions of the forces as should lead the enemy to believe that the valley was occupied by a large force, and to cross ourselves and occupy Chattanooga at the earliest opportunity. The forces were scattered from Kingston to Williams' Island, a distance of 75 miles, watching the entire line of the river for this distance, and guarding at least twenty ferries and fords. I at once visited in person the entire length of the line, making such dispositions as I thought best for carrying out the design of the command, with-drawing as much as possible the left of the line, and giving orders for the construction of boats in the North Chickamauga to be floated down and used for crossing when needed at the mouth of that stream.

Troops were made to appear simultaneously at three or four dif-ferent crossings, and, by ingeniously arranging their camp fires and beating their calls and the dexterous use of artillery, were made to represent a division of troops at each place.

The object designed was fully attained. I also placed all heavy stores on Walden's Ridge, and as the enemy threatened to cross his cavalry in heavy force, made preparations to receive him, and, failing to destroy him, to drive him up the valley beyond Pikeville, where he could be met by General Burnside. A battery and two regiments of infantry were placed opposite Chattanooga, and the enemy at that point annoyed and two of his boats disabled. I also established communication by signal between all the crossings near me and my headquarters.

On the 2d, the enemy burned the Loudon Bridge, and Buckner's corps commenced moving slowly down the river, making strong demonstration upon its banks as if to cross at several places. They moved on Tyner's Station, reaching that point on the 6th and 7th, followed by a heavy cavalry force that took the place of the infantry on the river as they were relieved, and, from their numbers, Colonel Minty reported that indications made it pretty certain that a cross-ing was about to be attempted. At the same time, the pontoon bridge of the enemy was moved at Chattanooga as if to cross over troops at that point.

All the crossings were closely watched, and the troops held in readiness for any movement.

On the 8th, the river was cleared of all rebel troops above Chatta-nooga, and I directed Minty to cross over at the mouth of Sale Creek, reconnoitering the country well in his front, and move cautiously down to Harrison, always controlling one of the fords near him so as to cross back if it should be found necessary.

Before the order could be obeyed, a heavy cavalry force confronted him on the opposite side of the river and the crossing was not at-tempted. On that night, however, they all retired from above Friar's Island, and at 11 a. m., the 9th, from their works opposite that island.

The city of Chattanooga was also evacuated the same morning, and the troops of General Wagner crossed over and occupied the city, a portion of Wilder's force crossing at Friar's Island, reconnoitering thoroughly the country opposite and toward Chattanooga.

Colonel Minty was at once ordered down to cross and report to Colonel Wilder, while all the troops not already over, were, on the night of the 9th, concentrated at Friar's Island, and on the morning of the 10th crossed by fording, which was accomplished within the space of six hours without loss of life or *matériel*.

The boats, although completed, were not required. I found in the Tennessee Valley an abundance of subsistence for my troops, and brought out of it 70 beeves for the army. The casualties in all these operations were 2 killed, 1 drowned, and 5 or 6 wounded. Several hundred prisoners and deserters were sent to the rear.

I have earnestly to commend to the attention of the Government the services of Colonels Wilder and Minty, commanding cavalry brigades.

I am, very respectfully, your obedient servant,

W. B. HAZEN,
Brigadier-General, Comdg. Troops in Tennessee Valley.

Lieut. Col. C. GODDARD,
Asst. Adjt. Gen., Department of the Cumberland.

—

HDQRS. SECOND BRIG., SECOND DIV., 21ST ARMY CORPS,
Chattanooga, September 28, 1863.

SIR : In obedience to instructions, I have the honor to submit the following report of the part taken by the troops under my command in the battles of the 19th and 20th instant :

The narrative commences with the crossing of the Tennessee River, September 10, when the brigade consisted of the One hundred and twenty-fourth Ohio Volunteers, Col. O. H. Payne ; Forty-first Ohio Volunteers, Col. Aquila Wiley ; Ninth Indiana Volunteers, Col. I. C. B. Suman ; Sixth Kentucky Volunteers, Col. George T. Shackelford, and Battery F, First Ohio Volunteer Artillery, Lieut. G. J. Cockerill ; in all, an effective aggregate of 1,531 officers and men.

My brigade moved to Graysville and there joined its proper division on the 11th. We reached Ringgold the same day, and the next day moved over to Gordon's Mills, skirmishing a portion of the way, losing 2 men and wounding and capturing 3 from the enemy. In the evening of this day, the brigade made a reconnaissance about 3 miles in the direction of La Fayette, meeting the enemy and skirmishing briskly with him, when we returned to the mills. The next day the division marched to Chattanooga Creek, and the day after to Gower's Ford, on the West Chickamauga, where we remained quietly until the morning of the 17th, when my pickets on the La Fayette road were vigorously attacked. They, however, repulsed the enemy with a loss to him of 1 captain and several men.

On the evening of this day, we marched to within 2 miles of Crawfish Spring, and in the night of the 18th, to a position 1 mile north of Gordon's Mills, where we formed in line of battle, on the left of General Cruft and near the La Fayette and Rossville road. Here we remained, with an occasional shot in our front, until about 11 a. m. of the 19th, when I received orders to move in the direction of the firing, then growing severe, about 1½ miles to our left in front of the position of General Thomas.

On reaching McNamara's house, on the La Fayette and Rossville road, the brigades of the division were formed in two lines facing the east, the second line being doubled by regiments on the center. My brigade was on the left of the division, General Cruft being on my immediate right. The line was then moved forward *en échelon* by brigades, my brigade commencing the movement. The enemy was struck after advancing about three-quarters of a mile, when a terrific contest here was added to the already severe battle on our left. The enemy gave ground freely, and the left at this juncture making an advance, all the ground desired on the left was carried, extending to the right as far as the *échelons* of the Second Division had been placed.

I was at this time relieved by General Turchin and ordered back to the road to fill my boxes with ammunition, already twice exhausted, and take charge of some batteries left there without supports. This I had just accomplished when a vigorous attack appeared to be going on upon that part of our lines immediately to the right of the ground fought over by the last *échelon* of our division. I at once moved my brigade to the right, and forming it so as to face the sound of battle, moved forward and placed it in position as a support to some troops of General Reynolds, my left resting on the La Fayette and Rossville road near a small house, the right thrown forward, forming an angle of about 45° with the road. The battle neared my position rapidly. At this moment I met General Van Cleve, whose division the enemy had engaged, and who told me his men had given way and that he could no longer control them. The enemy continued to advance steadily, and the line in my front gave way. My men then advanced to the top of the crest, and withstood the shock until they were completely flanked upon their left, then obliqued well to the right and took position upon a high elevation of ground, confronting the left flank of that portion of the enemy which had broken our center. The advance of the enemy was now steady, and northward nearly in the direction of the La Fayette and Rossville road. I found myself the only general officer upon that part of the field, and to check the farther advance of the enemy was of the utmost importance. I hastily gathered and placed in position all the artillery then in reach, including portions of Standart's, Cockerill's, Cushing's, and Russell's batteries, in all about twenty pieces, and with the aid of all the mounted officers and soldiers I could find, succeeded in checking and rallying a sufficient number of straggling infantry to form a fair line in support of the artillery. My brigade could not be brought into position in time, there being but about two minutes to make these dispositions before the blow came, when the simultaneous opening of all the artillery with grape checked and put to rout the confronting columns of the enemy. It is due Lieutenants Baldwin, First Ohio Volunteer Artillery, commanding Standart's battery, Cockerill, of the same regiment, commanding battery, and Cushing and Russell, Fourth U. S. Artillery, commanding batteries, to state that for accuracy in maneuvering and firing their guns in the immediate presence of the enemy on this occasion, the army and country are placed under lasting obligations.

Major-General Reynolds came to this position at this time and made further disposition of troops, but the fight was closed for the day except a fierce attack made at nightfall upon General Johnson. A short time after the above repulse General Thomas came to this place and took command of all the troops in this part of the field.

It would appear that all the troops except General Johnson's division had been withdrawn from the portion of the field he occupied, leaving him well advanced and entirely unsupported. When the attack was made upon him, my brigade was sent with the residue of the division to his assistance, but the firing ceased when we had marched some 400 yards east of the La Fayette and Rossville road opposite Kelly's house, and we were placed here in position for the fight of Sunday.

Although my losses this day had been great, including Colonels Payne and Shackelford wounded, and Lieutenant-Colonel Rockingham killed, besides the loss of 439 officers and men, the brigade, with the exception of the Sixth Kentucky, was in good condition, with few absentees. The latter regiment, from the great mortality among its officers, was very much broken, its fragments being attached to the other regiments of the brigade.

On the morning of the 20th, the men were roused at 3 a. m. and directed to make coffee where they had water, and at daybreak a breastwork of logs and rails was commenced which was taken up on my right and left, and carried through our entire division and that of Reynolds on our right, and Johnson and Baird on our left. Wherever this work was done, the line remained the entire day with firmness and with little loss. At about 8 o'clock the attack commenced upon the left of this line and swept along toward the right, arriving at my position about fifteen minutes afterward, passing on but producing no effect until it had passed General Reynolds. This assault was kept up without intermission till about 11 o'clock with a fury never witnessed upon the field either of Shiloh or Stone's River. The repulse was equally terrific and finally complete. A few light attacks upon this front were made from time to time up to 1 p. m., after which everything was comparatively quiet. The value of this simple breastwork will be understood since my loss behind it this day was only about 13 men during a period of more stubborn fighting than at Shiloh or Stone's River, when the same brigade at each place lost over 400 men. Our left flank was twice turned and partially driven this day, but the enemy was easily checked and our lines speedily restored.

At about 10 a. m. our couriers for ammunition, previously prompt to return, failed to come back, and it soon came to be believed that our trains had been captured. I at once cautioned my colonels, who fired only by volley, not to waste a single round of ammunition, and my battery was similarly cautioned.

During the quiet that afterward settled upon us, several officers were struck by sharpshooters from distant trees. Ascertaining the proper direction, I caused volleys to be fired into the tops of the trees, and thus brought several of them from their hiding places, checking for a time this species of warfare. Skirmishers sent out along this front reported the execution of our arms during this engagement to have been terrible beyond anything before seen in this war, as I believe the fight from 8 to 11 o'clock to have been.

The stillness that now hung over the battle-field was ominous. We had four divisions in line that, although they had withstood one of the most terrific assaults on record, had hardly felt the breath of the battle. There were four more upon our right, with General Thomas, as fresh as we were, but the feeling that our ammunition was gone was like a leaden weight in the breasts of many. The men, however, felt confident of success. It afterward appeared that the breaking up of the troops on our right had swept away our ammunition—and much else along with their fragments—to Chattanooga.

No new dispositions of troops on our part of the line were made, except that General Reynolds' right was somewhat withdrawn to cover that flank. General Wood, General Brannan, and two divisions of the Reserve Corps were formed in a line at right angles with and directly in rear of the position before described, the left of this line being about one-half mile from and opposite Reynolds' right.

At about 3 p. m. a fearful onslaught was made upon this line. The battle raged for one hour with apparently varying fortunes, when several general officers at our position expressed a sense of the necessity for a brigade to move over and strike the deciding blow. No one appeared to have any ammunition. I found, upon examination, that I still had 40 rounds per man, and immediately moved my men over at double-quick with a front of two regiments. Arriving near the scene of action, I caused a partial change of direction to the left, and was quickly pouring in volleys, my second line alternating with my first, the action lasting but a few minutes, the enemy retiring.

There was no more fighting. At dusk I received orders from General Thomas to retire on Rossville, which I did quietly and in perfect order, the pickets of the enemy following mine closely as they were withdrawn, and confronting an officer sent to see that it was thoroughly done.

There are several lessons to be learned from this fight, and to me none more plainly than that the iron hand that strikes justly, yet firmly, can alone make the soldiers that can be relied upon in the hour of trial. The effect of firing by volleys upon the enemy has invariably been to check and break him. It further gives a careful colonel complete control of his fire. The effect of sending in fractions to battle with an entire army is to waste our own strength without perceptibly weakening the enemy.

My entire brigade has my warmest thanks for its services. Colonel Payne, One hundred and twenty-fourth Ohio Volunteers, and Colonel Shackelford, Sixth Kentucky Volunteers, both of whom fell early in the fight of Saturday, carried in their commands bravely and at the opportune moment. The One hundred and twenty-fourth Ohio Volunteers, though in its maiden engagement, bore itself gallantly and efficiently. Major Hampson, who commanded this regiment after the fall of its colonel, bore his part with ability and success. Colonels Wiley, Forty-first Ohio Volunteers, and Suman, Ninth Indiana Volunteers, with their regiments, are veterans of so frequent trial that it would be mockery to praise them with words. The country cannot too highly cherish these men. Colonel Wiley had his horse shot from under him. The services of Lieutenant-Colonels Kimberly, Forty-first Ohio Volunteers, and Lasselle, Ninth Indiana Volunteers, were conspicuous and valuable. Lieutenant-Colonel Kimberly had two horses killed under him.

Of the noble dead, there are Lieutenant-Colonel Rockingham, Captains McGraw, Johnston, and Marker, Lieutenants Lockman and Eubanks, all of the Sixth Kentucky; Lieutenants Criswell, Nickerson, and Parks, of the Ninth Indiana, with a long list of others as brave and true, but bearing no title. Many tears are shed for them.

My staff were efficient, performing every duty assigned them with promptness and accuracy.

Capt. H. W. Johnson, Forty-first Ohio, acting assistant quartermaster, was with me the entire day on Saturday, and at night brought upon the battle-field such portions of his train as were needed for the comfort of the command, taking them away before daylight the next morning.

Capt. John Crowell, jr., assistant adjutant-general; my aides, Lieuts. William M. Beebe and E. B. Atwood, Forty-first Ohio; my inspector-general, Capt. James McCleery, Forty-first Ohio;

my provost-marshal, Capt. L. A. Cole, Ninth Indiana; my commissary of subsistence, Lieut. F. D. Cobb, Forty-first Ohio; and
my topographical officer, Lieut. A. G. Bierce, Ninth Indiana, were
with me at all times, doing valuable service. My surgeon, M. G.
Sherman, Ninth Indiana, was, as he always is, in his place.

Of my orderlies, Waffle, Bierce, Morrison, and Sweeney, deserve
special mention. Shepherd Scott was particularly distinguished for
bravery and good services. He on two occasions brought brigades
to my assistance when greatly needed. His horse was shot, and he
killed or captured. Should he be restored, I recommend that he be
appointed a second lieutenant. Quite a number of horses were
killed and disabled in the service of my staff.

The casualties of the brigade were as follows:

| Command. | Killed. | | Wounded. | | Missing. | Aggregate. |
	Officers.	Men.	Officers.	Men.		
124th Ohio Volunteers	......	15	4	88	34	141
41st Ohio Volunteers		6	5	95	9	115
9th Indiana Volunteers	3	22	6	59	18	108
6th Kentucky Volunteers	5	9	5	88	11	118
Battery F, 1st Ohio Volunteer Artillery	1	1	......	8	2	12
Total*	9	53	20	338	74	494

The commander of the brigade was twice struck but not injured.
Two or three members of my staff were also struck, but without effect.

Attention is called to accompanying reports of regimental commanders.

I am, very respectfully, your obedient servant,

W. B. HAZEN,
Brigadier-General.

Capt. D. W. Norton, *A. A. A. G., Second Division.*

———

HDQRS. 2D BRIG., 2D DIV., 21ST ARMY CORPS,
Camp at Chattanooga, September 24, 1863—8 p. m.

In obedience to orders from my division commander, I moved with
my brigade, without artillery, at about 4 p. m. to-day, to reconnoiter
the country in front of our line occupied by the Twenty-first Army
Corps.

After passing about one-half mile beyond the line of our pickets,
I met a strong line of the pickets of the enemy, who fell back through
an oak wood upon a low ridge, then about 300 yards across a field,
firing all the time, when they came upon their reserves, posted in
the edge of a wood, and just at the foot of the low ridge, situated
about 1 mile this side of Missionary Ridge.

The reserves fell back upon the crest of this ridge, when they were
joined by several hundred other troops. A halt was here called, and
a column organized to crown the hill, and orders were given for the
movement, when I received a dispatch from General Palmer, directing me to retire, which I at once obeyed

———

*See revised statement, p. 176.

I could not see beyond the ridge mentioned, but from the smokes believe them to be only a small force there, say two or three brigades. Artillery was seen to come down the road from Missionary Ridge as I approached, as if to be placed in position to check my advance. My casualties were 1 killed and 5 wounded.

I am, very respectfully, your obedient servant,

W. B. HAZEN,
Brigadier-General.

Capt. W. D. NORTON,
Acting Assistant Adjutant-General.

[First indorsement.]

Respectfully forwarded.

The orders for the movement were received at 2.45 p. m., and commenced as soon as possible. Details for fatigue were out and had to be recalled. General Hazen was withdrawn, as there was, at the time, not daylight for farther advance, and because the party of the Fourteenth Corps had returned.

J. M. PALMER,
Major-General.

[Second indorsement.]

HEADQUARTERS TWENTY-FIRST ARMY CORPS,
September 24, 1863.

Respectfully forwarded.

The reconnaissance was very handsomely conducted by General Hazen, and he got back, as ordered, just at dark.

T. L. CRITTENDEN.

ADDENDA.

Semi-weekly report of effective force of the Second Brigade, Second Division, Twenty-first Army Corps, Col. Oliver H. Payne, One hundred and Twenty-fourth Ohio Volunteers, commanding.

Command.	Headquarters.			Infantry.			Total.		
	Commissioned officers.	Enlisted men.	Total.	Commissioned officers.	Enlisted men.	Total.	Commissioned officers.	Enlisted men.	Aggregate.
Second Brigade, Second Division, Twenty-first Army Corps, Col. O. H. Payne.	9	38	47	....	....	....	9	38	47
124th Ohio Volunteer Infantry, Captain Aumend.	....	....	....	20	346	366	20	346	366
41st Ohio Volunteer Infantry, Major Williston.	....	....	....	21	330	351	21	330	351
9th Indiana Volunteer Infantry, Col. I. C. B. Suman.	....	....	....	26	266	292	26	266	292
6th Kentucky Volunteer Infantry, Colonel Shackelford.	....	....	....	26	302	328	26	302	328
Total	9	38	47	93	1,244	1,337	102	1,282	1,384

O. H. PAYNE,
Colonel 124th Ohio Vol. Infantry, Comdg. Brigade.

MONDAY, *September 7, 1863.*

Semi-weekly report of effective force of the Second Brigade, Second Division, Twenty-first Army Corps, Brig. Gen. William B. Hazen commanding.

Command.	Headquarters.			Infantry.			Total.		
	Commissioned officers.	Enlisted men.	Total.	Commissioned officers.	Enlisted men.	Total.	Commissioned officers.	Enlisted men.	Aggregate.
Second Brigade, Second Division, Brigadier-General Hazen.	7	17	24	.....	.....	.....	7	17	24
124th Ohio Volunteer Infantry, Col. O. H. Payne.	.....	.....	.....	22	431	453	22	431	453
41st Ohio Volunteer Infantry, Col. A. Wiley.	.....	.....	.....	23	337	360	23	337	360
9th Indiana Volunteer Infantry, Col. I. C. B. Suman.	.....	.....	.....	30	298	328	30	298	328
6th Kentucky Volunteer Infantry, Col. George T. Shackelford.	.....	.....	.....	22	280	302	22	280	302
Total	7	17	24	97	1,346	1,443	104	1,363	1,467

W. B. HAZEN,
Brigadier-General, Commanding.

SATURDAY, *September 19, 1863.*

No. 165.

Report of Col. Isaac C. B. Suman, Ninth Indiana Infantry.

HEADQUARTERS NINTH INDIANA VOLUNTEER INFANTRY,
In Camp at Chattanooga, Tenn., September 29, 1863.

CAPTAIN: I have the honor to submit the following report of the marches made and the part taken in the late action by the Ninth Indiana Volunteer Infantry since leaving camp at Poe's Tavern, Tenn., September 9, 1863:

In compliance with orders, the regiment marched for Friar's Island, on the Tennessee River, at 8 p. m., and arrived at the landing, a distance of 12 miles, at 2 a. m. Shortly after daylight on the morning of the 10th, the regiment forded the river (the water being waist deep and very swift), and, after a short rest, the regiment pushed forward, through a deep dust, with the brigade a distance of 11 miles, and went into camp at a large spring, the water of which was cold and clear.

Friday, September 11.—Weather clear and very hot; marched at daylight; crossed the Memphis and Charleston Railroad at 9 a. m. at Graysville Station; from thence marched with the division to Ringgold, Ga., where the regiment camped for the night, having marched during the day 11 miles.

September 12.—Marched shortly after daylight in a westward direction. Shortly after starting, the Ninth, with the Forty-first Ohio Volunteers, threw forward two companies as skirmishers, who soon succeeded in driving the rebel cavalry that had threatened to retard our advance. At 3 p. m. arrived at Lee and Gordon's Mills, where General Wood's division was encamped. At 5 p. m. the regiment with the brigade made a reconnaissance to the front. After driving the rebels about 2 miles, night coming on, the regiment with the brigade fell back and encamped near Lee and Gordon's Mills.

September 13.—Remained encamped during the entire day.

September 14.—Marched 5 miles in a southwest direction and encamped in Chattanooga Valley.

September 15.—Marched 8 miles in a southeast direction and encamped on Fisher's Creek.

September 16.—Regiment on picket.

September 17.—A regiment of rebel cavalry made a charge on the
outpost pickets at daylight and a brisk skirmish ensued. They were
handsomely driven back, with a loss on their part of 1 man captured
and 4 horses killed. I afterward learned by a prisoner that their
loss in the charge was 2 killed, 7 wounded, and 1 captured, and that
the regiment that made the charge was the Fourth Georgia Cavalry.
There was no loss on our side. Late in the evening the regiment,
with the brigade, marched 4 miles, and camped 1 mile south of Crawfish Spring.

September 18.—In camp during the day. At dusk heavy cannonading and musketry was heard upon our extreme left. On going to
bed we received orders to be ready to move at a moment's notice.
At 10 p. m. the regiment was aroused and marched to the road, where
it was halted until 1 p. m. waiting for General Thomas' corps to pass.
Immediately after it had passed, we started and marched 4 miles,
and bivouacked 1 mile north of Lee and Gordon's Mills, in line of
battle.

September 19.—The morning opened clear, and with an ominous silence, "The quiet which precedes the storm." At an early hour the
regiment was placed in a good position on a ridge to the left of the
Forty-first Ohio Volunteers. At 9 a. m. cannonading and constant
volleys of musketry were heard upon our extreme left. About 11 a.
m. the brigade was moved to re-enforce the left, and, taking a circuitous route, came down upon the rebel right flank. The Ninth
and Forty-first Ohio Volunteers, being the advance regiments (the
Ninth being upon the left of the Forty-first Ohio Volunteers), engaged the rebels in a thin skirt of woods with great fury. About 1
p. m., after an engagement of an hour, and after driving the enemy
before us, the regiment, by order of General Hazen, was drawn off
to procure more ammunition, replenish canteens, and clean the guns—
this after firing about 100 rounds of cartridges per man. While here
General Hazen passed along the lines and was heartily cheered by
every man in the regiment. At 3 p. m. the regiment took a position
in an open stubble-field and there opened fire upon the enemy, and
there held its position about twenty minutes, when, our support upon
the right and left giving way, the regiment was forced to retire,
which it did in some disorder; but, on retiring 40 or 50 rods, it promptly
rallied to again give battle to the enemy. Night coming on, however, ended the conflict for the day with a loss to the Ninth Regiment of First Lieut. Lewis S. Nickerson, killed; Second Lieut. Seth
B. Parks, killed. They were brave and efficient officers and true soldiers. First Lieutenant Criswell, Captain Merritt, First Lieutenant
Creviston, Second Lieutenants Shipherd and Franklin, and Captain
Craner were wounded, making a total loss of 8 commissioned officers
and 69 enlisted men, of whom 16 were killed or mortally wounded,
and 8 missing, of whom 5 are supposed killed. During the engagement of the 19th, the regiment fired 140 rounds of ammunition per
man.

Early on the morning of the 20th, my regiment was set to work
building a temporary breastwork of logs and rails on a ridge in the
timber. Shortly after they were completed, and about 9 a. m.,

firing commenced on my left.   It was near 10 a. m. when the enemy advanced in line of battle on my front, determined to drive me from my position.   By a steady fire, the regiment, assisted by Captains Andrew's and Cockerill's batteries and the brigade on the left, not only checked the rebels' advance, but repulsed them with great slaughter.   The enemy afterward repeatedly advanced to charge our position, but in every instance were driven back with heavy loss.   Notwithstanding the heavy shower of shot and shell poured upon my command, owing to the shelter afforded by the breast-works, my loss was very light.   The whole loss at this point was First Lieutenant Marshall and 2 enlisted men wounded.   About 3 p. m. I moved my regiment to the right about a quarter of a mile, into a thick clump of pines, and threw out three companies as skir-mishers.   One of the skirmishers was mortally wounded by the enemy's sharpshooters.

About 4 p. m. my command was moved still farther to the right to support the One hundred and twenty-fifth Ohio Volunteers.   The Forty-first Ohio Volunteers, Ninth and One hundred and twenty-fifth Ohio Volunteers for a short time fired alternately, which was very destructive to the enemy, speedily driving him from his posi-tion, and compelling him to abandon his position in front of that portion of our lines entirely.   My regiment was then ordered still farther to the right, on a high hill.   It was while in this position that my attention was drawn to my right by an unnecessary amount of talking.   I went over to see what it meant, and, to my surprise, I found the enemy demanding our troops to surrender.   At that moment a rebel officer pointed a pistol at my head and demanded my surrender.   I informed him that I had surrendered some time ago.   He appeared satisfied with my explanation.   At that moment something drew his attention, and I slipped away from him and brought two of my right companies to bear, and opened fire on them and scattered the party.   Our men ran one way and the rebels ran another.   The officer with whom I talked reported himself as colonel of the Thirty-fifth [Fifty-fourth?] Virginia Regiment, and said he was attached to Buckner's corps.   He said he was only off of the cars seven hours.   One of my lieutenants went over to see what was going on, and the same officer took his sword from him.   One of his men fired on the rebel colonel and killed him, retook the lieuten-ant's sword, and took the rebel's sword and pistol.   At this moment the officer came up that I had reported to at that point.   He ap-peared to think it impossible that the enemy had gained that point. I informed him that he had but 30 steps to walk to convince him-self, but he seemed not inclined to convince himself by going to see. Immediately afterward I was ordered to retire with my command, which I did in good order.   My loss on the 20th was 1 lieutenant wounded, 1 enlisted man killed and 6 wounded, 1 mortally, and 6 missing.

About the time of leaving the breastworks, Lieutenant-Colonel Lasselle asked permission to visit the left of the lines, which was granted, since which time he has not been heard from.   Fears are entertained that he has been killed or taken prisoner.

The officers and men of my command behaved most gallantly during the engagement, and too much praise cannot be awarded them for the bravery and zeal manifested by them throughout the entire engagement.   The medical department of the regiment was efficiently conducted, and the musicians did all in their power to carry off the wounded and alleviate their sufferings and assist the surgeon in seeing to their wants. I noticed during the entire engagement but one man (a sergeant) who skulked; this was on the 19th. I promptly tore his chevrons from his arms, but, owing to his good conduct on the 20th, I permitted him to retain his position.

On the night of the 20th, we fell back 3 miles and camped for the night.

On the morning of the 21st, we again moved to the front, and took a position on a high ridge to the left of the Chattanooga road, and immediately began to fortify the position. Nothing of importance occurred during the day, and on the night of the 21st, the regiment fell back with the brigade to Chattanooga, where nothing of importance occurred until the evening of the 24th, when the regiment, with the brigade, made a reconnaissance to the front, in which reconnaissance my regiment was deployed as skirmishers. Shortly after deploying, my regiment became engaged with a considerable body of the enemy's sharpshooters, when, after driving them a short distance, I was ordered to retire, having lost 1 man killed and 7 wounded.

The following is the loss in the Ninth Indiana Volunteer Infantry since the morning of the 19th:

Officers and men.	Killed.	Wounded.	Missing.	Total.
Officers	3	6	1	10
Enlisted men	22	59	17	98
Total	25	65	18	108

I remain, with great respect, your obedient servant,

I. C. B. SUMAN,
Colonel Ninth Indiana Volunteer Infantry.

Capt. JOHN CROWELL, Jr.
Assistant Adjutant-General, Second Brigade.

No. 166.

Report of Maj. Richard T. Whitaker, Sixth Kentucky Infantry.

HDQRS. SIXTH REGIMENT KENTUCKY VOL. INFANTRY,
Camp at Chattanooga, Tenn., September 29, 1863.

SIR: I respectfully submit the following report of the part taken by the Sixth Kentucky Volunteer Infantry in the battles of the 19th and 20th September, 1863:

Having bivouacked in a dense thicket in the latter part of the night of Friday, September 18, 1863, about 1 mile north of Lee and Gordon's Mills, about sunrise on the morning of the 19th, the regiment was called to attention and moved forward to the road running parallel with Chickamauga Creek, leading to Lee and Gordon's Mills, the regiment in double column at half distance. At 8 a. m. the regiment was ordered forward to the crest of a hill in a rag-weed field, on the line of the Ninth Indiana skirmishers, and deployed in line of battle, Company A, Capt. John McGraw commanding, having been thrown out as flankers on the left. Company F, Capt. Robert H. Armstrong, was ordered forward as skirmishers. The regiment remained in this position until about 10 a. m., during which time a lively fight had been progressing about 1 mile to our left. At 10 a. m. the regiment moved by the right flank, countermarching to the road previously occupied, along which it marched about 1 mile, and was faced to the front, moving forward in double column as reserve to the Forty-first Ohio Volunteers; the Ninth Indiana also in the second line in reserve to the One hundred and twenty-fourth Ohio Volunteers. The movements of the Sixth Kentucky Volunteers were now double-quick, and the regiment after advancing a half mile, and 30 paces beyond the crest of a hill, was halted and ordered to lie down. While in this position our gallant colonel, George T. Shackelford, was severely wounded in the right shoulder. Capt. Peter Marker, Company G, lost his right leg by a cannon-shot, and quite a number of the regiment were killed and wounded, among whom were Second Lieutenant Lockman, Company C, since dead; First Lieut. Thomas R. Danks, Company C, wounded; and Corporal and Color-Guard Abraham Souther, Company B, killed. Lieut. Col. Richard Rockingham, having just reached the regiment from an absence on sick leave, now took command, and in a few moments the regiment took the place of the Forty-first Ohio Volunteers in front. At this point the regiment remained about one hour and a half exposed to a galling fire, to which they gallantly replied and drove the enemy back. Here Captain McGraw fell mortally wounded, and the regiment suffered severely in killed and wounded. The regiment was then relieved by the Eleventh Ohio Volunteers, and retired to the crest of the hill. In this position the regiment remained about one hour in support of a battery, and replenished ammunition.

At this point Second Lieut. Thomas Eubanks, of Company B, was killed by canister shot. A heavy assault being made upon our right, the regiment was moved to the right by the flank, a distance of half a mile, double-quick. We were fronted and marched some 400 yards, where we met the enemy in strong force, pressing our right. Here we fought them, until, finding we were about to be flanked upon the right, the regiment retired behind the road, forming a new line. During this engagement, Lieut. Col. Richard Rockingham was wounded by a Minie ball in the left leg; Capt. Isaac N. Johnston, Company H, wounded and missing. In this position, the regiment remained about one hour, when the brigade was moved to the left, down the Chattanooga road about half a mile, then moved to the east side of the road some 400 yards to the crest of the hill fronting the enemy, where we camped for the night. During the night a detail from the regiment, in command of Capt. William Frank, Company E, was sent out as skirmishers to the left of the Forty-first Ohio Volunteers. Generals Palmer and Hazen, aided by the officers of their staffs, were at all times during the day along the lines; and when it seemed likely that the command of General Palmer would be flanked, he, with General Hazen and their staffs, were encouraging the men to support the battery, and by their presence and active encouragement animated them with fresh courage, when they succeeded in driving the enemy back.

Sabbath morning, September 20, 1863, General Hazen retired his brigade some 100 paces, and with the vigilance and thorough discipline that characterizes him as a commander, ordered temporary breastworks to be thrown up, which were held by the Forty-first Ohio Volunteers and Ninth Indiana Volunteers in the first line, and the One hundred and twenty-fourth Ohio Volunteers and Sixth Kentucky in the second line, against several desperate charges of the enemy until 2 p. m. In the afternoon, when every man from commanding general to private seemed to say, "What next?" an attack raging upon our right, and threatening to cut off our access to the road to Chattanooga, was met by sending General Hazen's brigade in support of Colonel Harker's command of Wood's division. In crossing a belt of woods to join the brigade, the Sixth Kentucky lost some 6 men wounded. Having crossed the woods we fell in with the brigade, in reserve to the Forty-first Ohio Volunteers, then actively engaged with the enemy. Our front line, Forty-first Ohio Volunteers and Ninth Indiana, having driven the enemy, the brigade formed upon the crest of the hill, facing the late rear, about dark. After dark, Sixth Kentucky was ordered to deploy as skirmishers to our then front, obeyed the orders received, and the right flank of the regiment deployed as skirmishers came in contact with a rebel regiment camped for the night Owing to the presence of mind of Capt. Robert H. Armstrong, commanding Companies A and F, Sixth Kentucky, an engagement with the enemy was avoided. I having sent word to the general commanding of the proximity of the enemy, was ordered to assemble the regiment and rejoin the brigade, which then moved by the Dug Gap road to Rossville.

In the afternoon of the 19th, when the Sixth Kentucky and Ninth Indiana were driven by overpowering numbers to retire, the safety of the Army of the Cumberland was secured by the indomitable and almost superhuman energy and exercise of will displayed by Generals Palmer and Hazen, aided by their staffs.

In the actions of the two days, 19th and 20th, the regiment sustained the following casualties, to wit: 1 colonel, 1 captain, 3 lieutenants, 88 enlisted men, wounded; 1 lieutenant-colonel, 2 captains, 2 lieutenants, 9 enlisted men, killed; 1 captain, 10 enlisted men, missing. Total, 118.

R. T. WHITAKER,
Major, Commanding Sixth Kentucky Infantry.

Capt. John Crowell, Jr.,
Assistant Adjutant-General, Second Brigade.

No. 167.

Report of Col. Aquila Wiley, Forty-first Ohio Infantry.

Camp of Forty-first Regiment Ohio Volunteers,
Chattanooga, Tenn., September 25, 1863.

Sir: In compliance with your order, I have the honor to submit the following report of the part taken by this regiment in the operations terminating in the general engagement on the Chickamauga River on the 19th and 20th instant:

On the morning of September 10, the regiment forded the Tennessee River at Friar's Island, at which place it had been on outpost duty for two days previous, and marched the same day to Tyner's Station, on the Knoxville and Chattanooga Railroad.

On the 11th, it marched thence to Ringgold, via Graysville, at which place we joined the rest of the division.

On the 12th, it marched from Ringgold to Gordon's Mills, acting as advance guard of the division. During the day's march, a body of rebel cavalry attempted to cut off a portion of the advance guard by charging on its flank; but the vigilance of Lieutenant-Colonel Kimberly, commanding it, frustrated their object, a volley from the skirmishers killing 1 horse and wounding 1 man (who, with two others, fell into our hands), caused them to retreat precipitately. After going into bivouac the same day at Gordon's Mills, the enemy's cavalry exhibiting great audacity in approaching our position, the brigade was ordered on a reconnaissance, the regiment again forming the advance. Four companies, deployed under command of Lieutenant-Colonel Kimberly, drove them easily and without loss a distance of 2½ miles, when we were ordered to return to camp. Remained in bivouac on the 13th at Gordon's Mills; marched thence to Chattanooga Valley on the 14th; thence on the 15th to a position on the Chickamauga River, about 5 miles from Gordon's Mills, and — miles from La Fayette; remained in bivouac here, receiving supplies of clothing, &c., until the evening of the 17th, when we went into position in line of battle about 3 miles farther north on the same road.

In the night of the 18th, took up a new position about 4 miles farther north, on the same road ; bivouacked here in line of battle, covering the front of the regiment with skirmishers.

On the 19th, the engagement began still farther on the left. As the firing of musketry became brisk, the regiment, with the rest of the brigade, was again moved to the left. About 1 p. m. we advanced in line of battle to the attack, being on the right of the first line of the brigade, with two companies deployed as skirmishers. Passing through an open wood, our skirmishers soon became engaged with those of the enemy and drove them. On emerging from the wood, we came to an open field about 400 yards in width, with another skirt of woods beyond. Through this woods the enemy started in line across the field to meet us. Near the middle of this field, and a little to our left, was a narrow strip of timber. The enemy had advanced but a short distance when he delivered his fire, and then sought to gain the cover of this strip of timber. We were too quick for them, gaining it first, and delivering our fire by battalion at short range, sent them back to the woods from which they started. As soon as they began to retreat, a battery, planted in the edge of the wood, opened fire, inflicting considerable loss. As soon as the retreating forces gained the cover of the woods a heavy infantry fire was also opened on us. This position the regiment maintained till about 4 p. m., replying to the enemy's fire and repelling three attempts to dislodge us. In repelling the last assault we were supported and assisted by two companies of the One hundred and twenty-fourth Ohio Volunteers. The regiment was then relieved by the Sixth Kentucky, and ordered to retire to procure ammunition and clean their arms. While replenishing our boxes we were again ordered forward to the right, to the support of a portion of Van Cleve's division. We had barely got into position in rear of the line when it began to fall back. The regiment remained in position until the troops to whose support we had gone had retired. Those on the left retiring toward the left, created an interval through which the enemy advanced.   We fired one volley by battalion, and then retired slowly, halting, facing about, and firing by battalion as soon as the regiment had loaded, and effectually holding the enemy in check in our front.   Finally, the advance of the enemy on the left having been checked, and the troops to whose support we had been sent having been reformed on a ridge in our rear, the regiment again moved off to the left and joined the rest of the brigade.   It was now sundown, and our part in the engagement for the day was ended.   The regiment bivouacked for the night in the first line on a ridge on the east side of the road, and maintained the same position on the 20th till about 3 p. m.   A small parapet of logs, hastily constructed on the morning of the 20th, enabled us to repel two assaults on the position during the day without loss to ourselves.

About 3 p. m. it was moved to the right, to the support of a portion of Harker's brigade, Wood's division, which was in position on the crest of a hill which the enemy was endeavoring to carry.   The possession of the hill was maintained, the regiment losing about a dozen wounded in this part of the action.   As soon as it became dark we withdrew from this position, marched to Rossville, where the regiment bivouacked, and on Monday morning again went into position in the first line on Missionary Ridge, throwing up a parapet of rails and covering our front with skirmishers.   The enemy soon afterward engaged our skirmishers, and later in the day opened with one piece of artillery, evidently for the purpose of feeling our position.   The main line, however, did not become engaged, and at night we were again withdrawn, and the next day took up the position in the present line, which we now occupy.   The following is the list of casualties.*

Total killed: Enlisted men, 6; wounded, commissioned officers, 5; enlisted men, 95 ; missing, enlisted men, 9.   Aggregate: Killed, 6; wounded, 100 ; missing, 9.

Number engaged, commissioned officers, 23 ; enlisted men, 337. Aggregate, 360.

Lieutenant-Colonel Kimberly had 2 horses and Maj. J. H. Williston 1 horse wounded and disabled in the engagement.   My own horse was killed.   I cannot speak too highly of the gallantry and fortitude of both officers and men, nor of the enthusiasm that two days' hard fighting and their thinned ranks failed to depress.   My thanks are especially due Lieut. Col. R. L. Kimberly and Maj. J. H. Williston, as well for their untiring vigilance and zeal, as for their gallantry in action.   Lieutenant Fisher, acting adjutant, deserves and has my thanks for promptness in communicating orders under severe fire.   Late on the 19th, he was severely, and it is supposed mortally wounded, while going to the rear to bring up ammunition.   He is supposed to be in the hands of the enemy.   Lieut. J. N. Clark performed the duties of adjutant during the remainder of the engagement, and deserves mention for zeal and gallantry. Among company officers, while I can commend all for their cheerful and steady courage throughout the engagement, Lieut. C. W. Hills deserves special mention for deliberation and coolness, which attracted my attention in the heat of the engagement on Saturday, and for the obstinacy with which he held his ground on Monday, while commanding a line of skirmishers that was vigorously attacked by the enemy.   Corporal Strock, of Company E, also deserves

---

* Nominal list omitted ; see revised statement, p. 176.

notice for pursuing and bringing in 2 prisoners who took refuge in a house when the regiment repelled the last attack on their position on Saturday afternoon. They belonged to the Twelfth Tennessee, Colonel Watkins, Smith's brigade, Cheatham's division. Corporal Strock's name had previously been placed upon the roll of honor, and his conduct in this engagement shows that the confidence of his comrades has not been misplaced.

Of the 9 men missing, should any prove skulkers or cowards, I shall take the same interest in having them punished that I shall always take in securing to good soldiers the reward due gallant and noble conduct.

I have the honor to be, your obedient servant,

AQUILA WILEY,
Colonel, Commanding Forty-first Ohio Volunteers.

Capt. JOHN CROWELL, Jr.,
Assistant Adjutant-General, Second Brigade.

No. 168.

Report of Maj. James B. Hampson, One hundred and twenty-fourth Ohio Infantry.

HEADQUARTERS 124TH OHIO VOLUNTEER INFANTRY,
Camp near Chattanooga, Tenn., September 28, 1863.

CAPTAIN : As commander of the One hundred and twenty-fourth Regiment Ohio Volunteer Infantry, I have the honor to submit the following report of the part taken by this regiment in the recent engagements of the 19th and 20th instant:

At 3 o'clock on the morning of the 19th, we went into bivouac on the left of the State road, about 2 miles north of Lee and Gordon's Mills, in double column at half distance. At half past 6 a. m. we moved forward to the road, the Forty-first Ohio Volunteer Infantry deployed in our front, and stood to arms in that position until 11 a. m., during which time heavy firing was heard on our left. At half past 11 o'clock, in obedience to orders, we moved to the left along the State road, with Company B thrown out as flankers, until we reached a left-hand road, which we followed about half a mile, and then moved to the right half a mile, when we again came into position on the State road in rear of the Forty-first Ohio Volunteer Infantry in double column at half distance. The forward was then sounded, and we had advanced but a short distance when the firing commenced in our front, and the regiment was deployed into line of battle under a heavy fire of musketry from the enemy. After lying down in this position for some time on a gentle rise of ground, exposed to a severe fire and meeting with some losses, orders were received to move the regiment by the left flank and form a continuation of the line of battle of the Forty-first Ohio Volunteer Infantry. It was at this time, when confused by a galling fire from the enemy, that Companies A and H and a part of D, not understanding the order from the commanding officer, became detached, and they were unable to rejoin the regiment until late in the afternoon, having in the meantime done gallant service on the right of the Sixth Kentucky. After moving by the left flank about 400 paces, we were moved by the right flank with Company B, commanded by Capt. George W. Lewis, deployed to the front as skirmishers, the enemy's fire, which had now become very heavy, telling fearfully in our ranks. The colonel at this time fell severely wounded and was carried to the rear. The firing had now become so heavy in my immediate front that I ordered my skirmish line to assemble on the left of the regiment, and fired by volley until the cartridges were nearly expended, when I was temporarily relieved by the Ninety-second Ohio. After refilling cartridge boxes, the regiment immediately retook position in the front, relieving the Ninety-second and remaining under a severe fire for nearly an hour, when, after a very heavy loss, we were again relieved by one of General Turchin's regiments and ordered to join our brigade, which had been moved to the right.

This engagement was in an open wood, with little shelter on either side, in full view of the enemy, who advanced repeatedly in line against us, the combined fire of artillery and infantry being for a long time incapable of breaking either line; but the superior valor and energy of our troops at last triumphed, and as the regiment retired it was evident the line of the enemy was giving way. This was the first severe fire my regiment had ever sustained, and too much cannot be said in praise of the skill and courage of the men, for few troops have ever met a heavier and more resolute fire. We were placed on the left of the brigade about half a mile to the right of our former position, with our left resting on the State road, and were here rejoined by Companies A and H of the regiment. We were hardly in position when the brigade which we were ordered to support fell back, and we received the full force of a terrible fire before being aware that the line just to our front in the woods was that of the enemy and not our own troops. The regiment delivered a most telling volley in return, when, being greatly outnumbered and unsupported on its flanks, it retired in line to the crest of a hill in the rear, regaining position just as the enemy were checked by the fire of batteries massed on the left. It was now sundown, and the fighting for the day having apparently ceased, we went into bivouac in line of battle about one-half a mile to the left of the position last held.

At about half past 7 o'clock heavy firing was heard on our left, and we were again ordered to move in that direction, taking up our position in the front line, and bivouacking in line of battle immediately in front of Johnson's division.

On the morning of the 20th, we threw up a slight breastwork of logs and rails on a slight crest immediately in front of our lines, behind which we fought without loss until afternoon, resisting several most desperate charges of the enemy, who vainly tried to capture our works and our battery, of which we were the left support. Our fire, which was by volley, was delivered with marked precision and rapidity, my regiment being for a short time assisted by the Twenty-third Kentucky, who alternated with us in pouring most deadly discharges into the enemy's ranks, which were repeatedly broken and finally repulsed. About 3 o'clock we were ordered to move to the right to support Colonel Harker's brigade, which was being hard pressed, and we suffered a loss of several killed and wounded in performing the movement, Company A being thrown out as skirmishers. But the enemy were soon driven, the regiment firing by battalion and performing several evolutions under fire. The firing at this point was for a short time very severe. Heavy firing was soon developed on the left, and I was ordered to change front from right to rear, which was done promptly and without loss.

At twilight all firing ceased, and our regiment was formed with the brigade in a hollow square on the crest of the hill about which we had fought, where we remained until after dark, when we were ordered to retreat on the road to Rossville, which was done in perfect order, Company A being thrown out on the right as flankers. We went into bivouac at Rossville in line of battle, and remained there until 8 o'clock on the morning of the 21st, when we were moved to the front and placed in position in the front line of the brigade on Missionary Ridge. There we threw up a slight breastwork of rails and stone, with our front well covered with skirmishers, and remained under cover during the day, exposed in the afternoon to a light fire from a rebel battery.

We were moved from this position on the night of the 21st, and took up the position we now occupy on the morning of the 22d.

I hereby submit a list of casualties:

Companies.	Killed.	Wounded.	Missing.	Total.
Officers		2		2
A	2	19	5	26
B	1	13	1	15
C		6	4	10
D		11	1	12
E	1	11	3	15
F	3	3	1	7
G	1	5	3	9
H	4	11	5	20
I	2	9	4	15
Unassigned	1	2	7	10
Total	15	92	34	141

The early loss of the colonel at a moment of great danger was most keenly felt by the regiment, and cannot be too sincerely deplored. Unbounded confidence was felt in his skill and courage, and his gallant conduct during the brief exposure before his wound gave evidence of what might have been expected in the subsequent encounters. Officers and men unanimously lamented his loss, regarding the absence of a respected and beloved leader as no small calamity for a regiment just undergoing its first trial, from which the memory of his example and the fruit of his thorough and patient drill could alone rescue it. My adjutant, C. D. Hammer, displayed tact and courage in a marked degree, and I gladly take the occasion to mention his efficiency in all his duties, both in the field and at the desk, a deserved compliment in which all my officers will most heartily join.

My line officers, with one or two exceptions, merit unqualified praise for their coolness, bravery, and gallant conduct, which enabled them to control and inspire their men in moments of severe trial and great danger. Nearly all my non-commissioned officers exhibited gallantry of a high order, meeting with an unusually large number of losses, which is a proof at once of their courage and devotion.

I am, captain, very respectfully, your obedient servant,

J. B. HAMPSON,
Major, Commanding Regiment.

Capt. JOHN CROWELL, Jr.,
Assistant Adjutant-General, Second Brigade.

No. 169.

Report of Lieut. Giles J. Cockerill, Battery F, First Ohio Light Artillery.

HDQRS. BATTERY F, FIRST OHIO VOL. ARTILLERY,
Chattanooga, Tenn., September 27, 1863.

SIR : I have the honor to submit the following report of the part taken by my battery in the late battle of Crawfish Spring, Ga:

On the morning of the 17th instant, I was encamped on the La Fayette road at [Gower's] Ford, on Chickamauga Creek, with General W. B. Hazen's brigade. About 6 a. m. the enemy drove in our pickets; heavy skirmishing until 12 m. same day. At 4 p. m. received orders from General Hazen to move to Gordon's Mills. Took up line of march at sunset. Bivouacked 1 mile from Crawfish Spring for the night. Moved up in line of battle on eve of the 18th, battery occupying a high ridge in front of General Hazen's brigade. Took up line of march same night at 12 m. by order of General Hazen. Marched 5 miles. Went into position on right of Chattanooga road at daylight of the 19th, supported by the Ninth Indiana and Forty-first Ohio. Made a reconnaissance early in the morning with one section, supported by Colonel Grose's brigade, to the left of our position. Heavy firing was heard on our left, but we did not participate. Moved and joined our division. I moved with General Hazen's brigade on Chattanooga road about 1 mile, formed line of battle on the right of the road ; then, moving forward one-half mile, we met the enemy in strong force. Battery taking position in rear of General Hazen's brigade, opened fire on the enemy at 12 m., firing at intervals for about three hours. The brigade having been relieved, I was ordered to fall back to the Chattanooga road. We lost here 2 men wounded.

Having halted on the road, I received orders from General Hazen that our right was being driven back, and, if it was possible, to check the enemy. I changed front from our original position to fire to the right. The enemy showing himself in strong force in our front, I opened a heavy cannonade upon him, which, with the assistance of Lieutenants Russell's and Cushing's batteries, succeeded in putting him to flight. In coming into position here, Second Lieut. John Lynch fell from his horse, mortally wounded, expiring next day at 2 p. m. The firing having ceased in our front, we moved down the Chattanooga road about one-half mile, bivouacked on the left of the road to allow my men to prepare supper. Received orders from General Hazen at 7 p. m. to move to our left and front with his brigade as support for General Johnson (who was on our left), he being engaged. But before we reached him the enemy had withdrawn, and we bivouacked for the night one-quarter mile from, and on the right of, the Chattanooga road.

Sunday morning, the 20th, the infantry supporting me, changed front to the right, throwing up temporary works, having replenished with 200 rounds in the meantime. Near 9 a. m. the enemy attacked us in strong force, when we opened upon him. Succeeded in maintaining our position, notwithstanding the repeated desperate charges made by him during the day. Near 2 p. m. the fire on both sides gradually ceased, with the exception of a few sharpshooters. Received orders at 4 p. m. from one of General Palmer's aides to withdraw to the Rossville road. Battery limbered up and withdrew, having expended all my ammunition but 15 rounds. Held the position we had taken the evening before. During this day's fight, had 1 man killed, 6 wounded, and 2 missing. Had 2 horses killed and 10 wounded. Halted for the night at the spring near Rossville.

Monday morning, 21st, firing in front. Took position near road by your order. Did not do any firing during the day. At 4 p. m. received orders from Major Mendenhall to move toward Chattanooga. Bivouacked in a large field on the right of the road for the night.

Tuesday morning, the 22d, received orders to march from General Hazen. Moved in rear of his brigade to the right of town, and took position on the ridge. Pieces, limbers, and caissons were all brought off the field safely.

Casualties during the entire battle were: One commissioned officer killed, 1 enlisted man killed, 8 enlisted men wounded, 2 enlisted men missing, 2 horses killed, and 10 wounded.

All of which is very respectfully submitted.

Very respectfully,

G. J. COCKERILL,
First Lieutenant, Commanding.

Capt. W. E. STANDART,
Chief of Artillery, Second Div., 21st Army Corps.

No. 170.

Reports of Col. William Grose, Thirty-sixth Indiana Infantry, commanding Third Brigade.

HEADQUARTERS THIRD BRIGADE,
September 16, 1863—6.15 p. m.

SIR: I have just returned from Green Worthen's farm, about 2 miles out. We met the enemy's pickets about 600 yards from our picket line, and skirmished the balance of the way. The route is very difficult to advance over, with everything in favor of the party in position. The enemy first took position behind the crest of a ridge on the farther side of a large farm, at which place, only, we were compelled to move them by a couple of shells. At Worthen's house they made a determined stand, but our skirmishers here could reach their flanks, and in this way drove them beyond the pass at Worthen's house. The enemy had but cavalry—perhaps about 200 strong—which had been encamped at the pass spoken of in Colonel Wheeler's inclosed torn note* to Major McDonald, which was picked up in the road at the last position of the enemy.

We obtained about 20 bushels potatoes, 4 small cattle, and about 60 bushels of wheat in sacks, all at Worthen's What shall I do with the wheat? The other items are disposed of. There is more wheat there, but we had but two wagons.

Worthen and family have left, and their premises were only occupied by the rebel troops.

I had but 1 man wounded, and he not dangerous.

I am, most respectfully,

WM. GROSE,
Colonel, Commanding Brigade.

Capt. J. R. MUHLEMAN, *Assistant Adjutant-General.*

---

* Not found.

HDQRS. THIRD BRIG., SECOND DIV., 21ST ARMY CORPS,
Camp at Chattanooga, Tenn., September 27, 1863.

SIR : I have the honor to make a brief report of the part this brigade took in the recent engagement with the enemy.

I crossed the Tennessee River at the mouth of Battle Creek, on the night of the 3d of September, by means of log rafts, sending most of my train by way of Bridgeport, 6 miles below, to cross on the bridge. I passed over without any loss of either men or property. My command consisted of the Sixth Ohio, Col. N. L. Anderson; Eighty-fourth Illinois, Col. L. H. Waters; Twenty-fourth Ohio, Col. D. J. Higgins; Thirty-sixth Indiana, Lieut. Col. O. H. P. Carey; Twenty-third Kentucky, Lieut. Col. James C. Foy. Aggregate officers and men, including staff, 1,687 ; to which were attached Batteries H and M, Fourth U. S. Artillery, commanded by Lieutenants Cushing and Russell (ten pieces). In conjunction with the division we marched thence to Shellmound, to Squirreltown Creek, and thence to Lookout Valley, and on the morning of the 9th instant, with the Twenty-fourth Ohio, Twenty-third Kentucky, and Eighty-fourth Illinois, I ascended or rather climbed upon Lookout Mountain near Hawkins' farm, 9 miles to the right of Chattanooga, and met and drove the enemy from the mountain with no loss to my force. The enemy left the mountain to the northeast via Summertown. Cavalry was all that I found on the mountain. As I reached the point of the mountain overlooking Chattanooga, the remainder of my brigade, with the First Brigade, General Cruft, and General Wood's division were entering the city. I may here notice Capt. Isaac N. Dryden, of the Twenty-fourth Ohio, and his company, for daring bravery in the advance in ascending the mountain and driving and punishing the enemy. With light but successful skirmishing near Graysville, Ringgold, and Chickamauga Creek, and a reconnaissance from the latter to Worthen's farm to a pass in Pigeon Mountain, I was directed on the morning of the 19th instant to make a reconnaissance below Lee and Gordon's Mills, on the Chickamauga Creek, in the State of Georgia, which I did and found the enemy in force, and on receiving orders I withdrew the brigade, joined the column, and with it moved upon the enemy into an open woodland to the right of the road leading toward Chattanooga. My position happened to be on a small elevation, General Cruft's brigade to my left, and General Reynolds' division on my right.

We met the enemy's lines about 12 m. My brigade was formed in double lines, the Twenty-fourth Ohio, Colonel Higgins, and the Twenty-third Kentucky, Lieutenant-Colonel Foy, in the front line; the Thirty-sixth Indiana, Lieutenant-Colonel Carey, and the Eighty-fourth Illinois, Colonel Waters, in the rear line ; the Sixth Ohio, Colonel Anderson, in reserve. On meeting the enemy with the front line the troops on the right of my brigade gave way, and the Thirty-sixth Indiana was immediately changed to the right to defend the flank, and in a very few minutes the enemy passed so far to my right and rear that the Sixth Ohio, as well as the Thirty-sixth Indiana, Twenty-fourth Ohio, and Twenty-third Kentucky, were all desperately engaged and so continued for two long hours. Here was the best fighting and least falling out (except the killed and wounded) that I ever witnessed. Finally the ammunition of these four regiments gave out, and there being none at hand (bad luck) they had to be retired. Now came the time for the Eighty-fourth Illinois to come into the breach. The colonel changed front to the right, and with his brave and hitherto-tried regiment contested every inch of ground until compelled to give way before overwhelming numbers, the enemy having reached his then right flank (our former rear). All was retired in tolerably good order, which ended my fighting for the day.

General Cruft's brigade, which had not yet exhausted its ammunition nor been seriously engaged, now changed front to the enemy, engaged him, and came off master of that part of the field.

The ensuing night we lay upon our arms without water or rest, and though the fatigues had been great, yet there was more to endure upon the coming day. Ammunition replenished, we were again in position for the fearful labors that awaited us on the holy Sabbath.

Early I was ordered to take position on the right of General Hazen's brigade on the right of our division, which was done, and each regiment quickly threw before it barricades of logs and such materials as could readily be obtained, but before the action on our part of the line commenced, one of my regiments, the Twenty-third Kentucky, had been loaned to General Hazen to fill out his lines, and with the other four, about 9 o'clock, I was ordered to the left of General Baird's division (General Rousseau's old division) to strengthen his left. Before we arrived at the intended position in the line, the enemy came upon Baird's division, and consequently upon my command, in fearful numbers. I formed the four regiments under a destructive fire from the enemy in a woodland covered with a heavy underbrush, fronting nearly north and at right angles with the main line of battle, the Thirty-sixth Indiana and Eighty-fourth Illinois in the front line, the Sixth and Twenty-fourth Ohio in the second line. Thus formed we met the enemy, and had a desperate struggle with fearful loss on both sides. The brigade advanced and was repulsed, advanced a second time and was again repulsed, and, with some forces that now came to our assistance, advanced the third time and held the woodland.

In this contest for mastery over the woodland, fell many of my best and bravest officers and men. The dead and dying of both armies mingled together over this bloody field. Here I parted with many of my comrades forever, particularly old mess-mates of the Thirty-sixth Indiana, and whose remains I was unable to remove from the field. In this conflict and amid the shifting scenes of battle, Colonel Waters, of the Eighty-fourth Illinois, with a part of his regiment became detached from the brigade to the west of the road and became mingled with the division of General Negley, who, it seems, shortly after ordered that portion of Colonel Waters' regiment, with at least a portion of his own command, toward Chattanooga, on the pretext of sending off Colonel Waters as train guard, for particulars of which, reference is made to the report of Colonel Waters. The residue of the Eighty-fourth Illinois Regiment, under the command of Capt. William Ervin, of Company C, with Lieutenants McLain, Scoggan, and Logue, with parts of four companies, remained with the brigade, and, on the left of and with the Thirty-sixth Indiana, did efficient and good service. Captain Ervin deserves notice for coolness and bravery during this fight as well as the lieutenants above named. After the fighting had ceased, and with seeming success to our arms, on this portion of the line, now about 1 or 2 p. m., I withdrew the Thirty-sixth Indiana. Twenty-fourth and Sixth Ohio, with that portion of the Eighty-fourth Illinois, under command of Captain Ervin, to near the position we had taken in the forenoon near the right of General Hazen's brigade, and put my men in position to rest and to await further developments. The Twenty-third Kentucky having remained with General Hazen at that point where I had left it in the morning, the enemy's sharp-shooters and occasional cannonading kept up amusement for us in the meantime. It was here, near by me, that Colonel King, of the Sixty-eighth Indiana, fell a victim to the aim of a sharpshooter.

In these two days, 19th and 20th, my command took a considerable number of prisoners and sent them to the rear; among them was Capt. E. B. Sayers, chief engineer of General Polk's corps. He surrendered to me in person, was put in charge of Lieutenant Scott, my engineer, and sent back to General Thomas' corps hospital. Sayers was one of the Camp Jackson prisoners and formerly a citizen of Saint Louis, Mo. I presume many of the prisoners taken on Sunday escaped. About 4 o'clock a deserter came in and informed us that Breckinridge's division of the rebel army was advancing toward the same point where we had been in such deadly strife during the forepart of the day, which statement was soon verified by the roar of artillery and small-arms in that direction, again moving upon Johnson's and Baird's shattered divisions. About the same time, a heavy force of the enemy commenced an attack to our right and rear, from toward Lee and Gordon's Mills and from the direction we had come in the morning, and opened the most terrific cannonading I had heard during these battles, and in a few moments completely enfilading our entire rear. At fifteen minutes before 5 o'clock, Lieutenant Thomas, Major-General Palmer's aide, brought me the order to retire my command. Which way or where to retire to was not an easy question to solve, the enemy fast approaching from right and left toward our rear, their artillery fire meeting. I, however, immediately sent orders to the regiments there with me to retire across the farm to our rear, passing to the right of the farm-house in the following order: Sixth Ohio, Thirty-sixth Indiana, and that portion of the Eighty-fourth Illinois with me, the Twenty-third Kentucky to bring up the rear; portions of the Twenty-fourth Ohio were with each of these regiments. My artillery had been retired to the west of the farm. The forces that were to my left, when faced about, had to retire farther to my right and cross the farm farther north. When I commenced the move, it seemed evident that my now small command would be swept away by the artillery fire of the enemy.

To prevent breaking of ranks or any further panic, and to indicate to the men that this was a time for coolness and steady habits, with Lieutenant Boice, one of my aides-de camp, he carrying the brigade flag at my side, we rode on the left of the front regiment and in the direction from which the most terrific fire of the enemy emanated, until we passed the ordeal of danger. As soon as we passed the point of greatest danger, I halted the two front regiments, Sixth Ohio and Thirty-sixth Indiana, and into line faced them to the rear to defend and cover the retreat. This was done coolly and deliberately. General Palmer was here to consult with me and give directions. Here was the last I saw of Capt. J. R. Muhleman, assistant adjutant-general of the division, and, I presume, he fell near this place, for we were yet under a sharp fire. As soon as all was closed up and had passed this line, I again retired the force across another farm about one-half mile, and ascended a high wooded hill and reformed, faced as before, now out of range of the enemy's fire. It was now dusk, and as soon as all was closed up, and meeting General Cruft with his brigade here, we consulted together with our division commander, and retired to Rossville, about 4 or 5 miles distant on the Chattanooga road, and rested for the night.

It is due that I mention in this place an act of bravery and danger of my aide, Lieutenant Boice. After we had passed over the first farm, fearing that my orders to Captain Ervin, of the Eighty-fourth Illinois, had not been definitely understood, and that he with his command might be left behind and lost, I directed Lieutenant Boice to return again over the field of death and see that the captain was coming with his command. The direction was promptly obeyed, and the lieutenant made the trip and returned unharmed. My fears for his safety were inexpressibly relieved when I saw him safely return. For this and similar efficient services during all these battles Lieutenant Boice deserves the most favorable notice. In the position assigned me with my command at and near Rossville on the 21st, although I did no fighting, and a better situation could not have been given me, yet I lost 1 man killed and 1 wounded from the enemy's artillery. From thence we withdrew to our present position without further harm.

Lieutenant Russell, in command of M Company, Fourth U. S. Artillery, on Saturday, the 19th, was placed in position in the center of my front line, and did effective service. On Sunday he, as well as Lieutenant Cushing, commanding H Company, Fourth U. S. Artillery, played a heavy part upon the enemy's columns. Those lieutenants, although they look like mere boys, yet for bravery and effective service they are not excelled if equaled in efficiency by any artillerists in the army. They have the credit of being in the last of the fighting, and then retiring with but the loss of one piece of Lieutenant Cushing's that had been disabled during the engagement.

Colonel Waters, with his brave regiment, deserves great credit for the manner in which the one commanded and the other performed the perilous duties devolving upon them during the battle.

The brave Col. Nick Anderson, with his regiment, Sixth Ohio, performed his whole duty up to the evening of the 19th. He having been wounded during that day, was compelled to be relieved. The command thereafter devolved upon Major Erwin, who performed it highly satisfactorily.

Lieutenant-Colonel Carey, Thirty-sixth Indiana, brave to the last, received a severe wound during the battle on the 19th, and was succeeded by Major Trusler in command, who deserves a high meed of praise for continuing the good management of the regiment. Brave old regiment! your country will remember you when these trying times are over.

Lieutenant-Colonel Foy and Twenty-third Kentucky, side by side with your comrades and brothers in arms from Ohio, Illinois, and Indiana, you did your duty well.

Colonel Higgins and Twenty-fourth Ohio can boast of as brave and dutiful officers and men as can be found in any army. Capt. George M. Graves, my acting assistant adjutant-general, a brave and good officer, fell by my side, mortally wounded, on the 19th, while rendering efficient service. He has since died. Rest in peace, brave soldier.

Isaac Bigelow and George Shirk, two of my orderlies, were wounded on the 20th, the latter seriously, and who was carrying the brigade flag when he fell. Corpl. Dorsey A. Leimin, of Company I, Twenty-fourth Ohio, seeing the flag fall, rushed to it, rescued it, and bore it off the field, as he did his own regimental colors on two occasions the day before when the color guards had been shot down. Such bravery and high bearing as this is highly deserving the notice of the appointing power. My grateful thanks are due to the brave officers and men of the brigade for their noble conduct through these trying scenes in behalf of the right and to put down the wrong.

My staff officers, Major Kersey, medical director; Captain Peden, provost-marshal; Captain Brooks, inspector; Lieutenant Scott, topographical engineer; Lieutenant Livezey, aide-de-camp, with those heretofore mentioned, as well as my non-commissioned staff, have my grateful acknowledgments for their kind and efficient help during these laborious battles, and they, with me, unfeignedly lament the fall of our comrade and brother, Capt. George M. Graves. Many officers and men of my command that it is impossible to refer to specially, are equally deserving with the best of soldier patriots. Captain Adams, Eighty-fourth Illinois; Captain Tinker, Sixth Ohio; Captain Wadsworth, Twenty-fourth Ohio; Lieutenant Patterson, Thirty-sixth Indiana; Lieutenant Hoffman, Twenty-third Kentucky, with 57 brave enlisted men, fell on these battle-fields a sacrifice upon their country's altar. My heart sickens to contemplate these irreparable losses. To the suffering wounded, may the God of Battles soothe their afflictions, heal, and restore them again to usefulness.

The following table shows the casualties of the brigade as nearly as is possible to ascertain at the present time:

Command.	Killed.		Wounded.		Missing.		Total.		
	Commissioned officers.	Enlisted men.	Commissioned officers.	Enlisted men.	Commissioned officers.	Enlisted men.	Commissioned officers.	Enlisted men.	Aggregate.
Headquarters, Col. William Grose	1			3			1	3	4
36th Indiana Infantry, Lieutenant-Colonel Carey.	1	13	8	89		17	9	119	128
24th Ohio Infantry, Colonel Higgins		3	3	57		16	3	76	79
6th Ohio Infantry, Colonel Anderson	1	13	7	94	1	16	9	123	132
84th Illinois Infantry, Colonel Waters	1	12	2	81		9	3	102	105
23d Kentucky Infantry, Lieutenant-Colonel Foy.	1	10	3	49		6	4	65	69
Battery M, 4th Artillery, Lieutenant Russell.		2		6				8	8
Battery H, 4th Artillery, Lieutenant Cushing.		4	1	16		1	1	21	22
Total *	5	57	24	395	1	65	30	517	547

Add to this the 659 loss at Stone's River, with many other casualties in smaller engagements; it shows a fearful destruction of human life in one small command. For further and more minute particulars, reference is made to the reports of regimental commanders herewith forwarded.

I have the honor to be, your most humble servant,

WM. GROSE,
Colonel, Commanding Third Brigade.

Capt. D. W. Norton,
Acting Assistant Adjutant-General, Second Division.

---

* See revised statement, p. 176.

ADDENDA.

Semi-weekly report of effective force of the Third Brigade, Second Division, Twenty-first Army Corps, Col. William Grose commanding.

Command.	Headquarters.			Infantry.			Total.			Number of horses.
	Commissioned officers.	Enlisted men.	Total.	Commissioned officers.	Enlisted men.	Total.	Commissioned officers.	Enlisted men.	Aggregate.	
Headquarters, Col. William Grose...........	11	36	47	....	....	....	11	36	47	5
36th Indiana Volunteers, Lieutenant-Colonel Carey.	....	....	....	24	336	360	24	336	360	....
24th Ohio Volunteers, Colonel Higgins	....	....	....	19	277	296	19	277	296	....
6th Ohio Volunteers, Colonel Anderson.....	....	....	....	25	329	354	25	329	354	....
84th Illinois Volunteers, Colonel Waters....	....	....	....	23	357	380	23	357	380	....
23d Kentucky Volunteers, Lieutenant-Colonel Foy.	....	....	....	25	263	288	25	263	288	....
Total.........	11	36	47	116	1,562	1,678	127	1,598	1,725	5

SEPTEMBER 7, 1863.

WM. GROSE,
Colonel, Commanding Brigade.

Semi-weekly report of effective force of the Third Brigade, Second Division, Twenty-first Army Corps, Col. William Grose commanding.

Command.	Headquarters.			Infantry.			Total.			Number of horses.
	Commissioned officers.	Enlisted men.	Total.	Commissioned officers.	Enlisted men.	Total.	Commissioned officers.	Enlisted men.	Aggregate.	
Headquarters, Col. Willam Grose	10	35	45	....	....	....	10	35	45	5
36th Indiana Volunteers, Lieutenant-Colonel Carey.	....	....	....	25	322	347	25	322	347	....
24th Ohio Volunteers, Colonel Higgins	....	....	....	19	258	277	19	258	277	....
6th Ohio Volunteers, Colonel Anderson.....	....	....	....	25	337	362	25	337	362	....
84th Illinois Volunteers, Colonel Waters....	....	....	....	26	356	382	26	356	382	....
23d Kentucky Volunteers, Lieutenant-Colonel Foy.	....	....	....	25	249	274	25	249	274	....
Total.............................	10	35	45	120	1,522	1,642	130	1,557	1,687	5

SEPTEMBER 16, 1863.

WM. GROSE,
Colonel, Commanding Brigade.

Semi-weekly report of effective force of the Third Brigade, Second Division, Twenty-first Army Corps, Col. William Grose commanding.

Command.	Headquarters.			Infantry.			Total.		
	Commissioned officers.	Enlisted men.	Total.	Commissioned officers.	Enlisted men.	Total.	Commissioned officers.	Enlisted men.	Aggregate.
Headquarters, Colonel Grose.....	8	35	43	....	....	....	8	35	43
36th Indiana Volunteers, Lieutenant-Colonel Carey.	....	....	....	25	322	347	25	322	347
24th Ohio Volunteers, Colonel Higgins.......	....	....	....	19	258	277	19	258	277
6th Ohio Volunteers, Colonel Anderson	....	....	....	25	337	362	25	337	362
84th Illinois Volunteers, Colonel Waters	....	....	....	26	356	382	26	356	382
23d Kentucky Volunteers, Lieutenant-Colonel Foy.	....	....	....	25	249	274	25	249	274
Total	8	35	43	120	1,522	1,642	128	1,557	1,685

SEPTEMBER 19, 1863.

WM. GROSE,
Colonel, Commanding Brigade.

No. 171.

Report of Col. Louis H. Waters, Eighty-fourth Illinois Infantry.

HDQRS. EIGHTY-FOURTH ILLINOIS VOLUNTEERS,
Chattanooga, September 26, 1863.

SIR: I have the honor to report, for the information of the colonel commanding, the part taken by the Eighty-fourth Regiment Illinois Volunteers in the recent engagements with the enemy.

On the 3d instant, we crossed the Tennessee River at the mouth of Battle Creek, and proceeded from thence with the Third Brigade to Chattanooga, via Shellmound, Whiteside's, Hawkins' Station, and Summertown, on Lookout Mountain, arriving at the latter place in the forenoon of the 9th instant, and in time to see the rear guard of the enemy leaving Chattanooga. During the afternoon we moved to Rossville and encamped for the night.

At daylight on the morning of the 10th, in pursuance of orders received about midnight, I moved my command down the La Fayette road for the purpose of guarding the pass or gap near McFarland's house. About 1½ miles from camp we came upon an outpost of the enemy, consisting of two companies of cavalry, which were soon driven beyond the point I was to occupy, and with a loss to the enemy, as I have since learned, of 1 killed and 1 wounded. Our skirmishing had scarcely ceased when we could distinctly hear numerous drums in the direction the outpost had retreated. These facts were promptly reported to Lieutenant Livezey, who about this time came to me with orders for me to return to the Ringgold road and follow the brigade.

On the morning of the 19th, we arrived a second time at Gordon's Mills, and marched thence out the road leading to Chattanooga, to the position assigned our brigade (the Eighty-fourth being on the left of the second line) composed of the Thirty-sixth Indiana and Eighty-fourth Illinois. The steady advance of the enemy on our right made it necessary for that regiment to change front to the right, and most gallantly did it go into the fight, soon checking the enemy on that flank. I moved my command to the front, relieving the Twenty-third Kentucky, and was soon engaged with the enemy advancing upon the angle formed by the Eighty-fourth Illinois and Thirty-sixth Indiana, the former regiment fronting the east, the latter the southeast. The regiments on our right as their ammunition was exhausted, withdrew, and soon the Eighty-fourth and Thirty-sixth were left alone, the enemy meanwhile steadily pushing around our right. We maintained this position until the ammunition of the Thirty-sixth was entirely exhausted and it was withdrawn. This isolated my regiment and left me the alternative of withdrawing or having my command, as I then believed, captured, and I accordingly withdrew. Both regiments behaved splendidly, and Lieutenant-Colonel Carey and Major Trusler are entitled to much credit for their conduct during the engagement. My command, although much broken by the retreat, was soon reformed, and without water or supper we rested for the night in the woods near the road, and took arms next morning but little revived by the night's rest, and suffering much from thirst.

We moved early in the morning to support General Beatty, who held the left and was having a brisk skirmish. Our entire brigade moved in a single line, and by the left flank, to position in rear of General Beatty's brigade, on General Baird's left, my regiment in advance, and scarcely had I reached General Beatty's right before the enemy, now engaging his brigade in front and flank, sent into my ranks a galling fire, under which we had to advance the length of the battalion and to form, and we had but just formed when the enemy appeared well around our left flank, and the brigade at the works in our front as promptly disappeared, leaving the works in the hands of the enemy and our men in a slaughter pen. The other regiments had formed in my rear. To enable me to change front obliquely to the left and to avoid the useless sacrifice of my men, I ordered my command to retire. In our rear was a dense growth of brush, around which I was compelled to ride, and by the time I had done so, something more than half of my regiment—but as I then thought all of it—thrown into confusion by passing these obstacles, had passed on to the woods beyond. I gathered them up, soon reformed them (another officer added some men thereto), and then I left them in charge of my adjutant near some troops that seemed to be a part of General Negley's command, and rode back to report to Colonel Grose.

In the meantime, his brigade had so changed its position that I could not find him, and I hastened back to my men, determined to take them into the fight whenever I should see a good opportunity, of which there seemed to be no scarcity, and found when I had returned that they had been ordered to Chattanooga to guard a train, the order coming, as I was informed, through Major-General Negley. Left without a command, I co-operated with several gentlemen of the staffs of Major-General Palmer and Colonel Grose, in getting together such portions of our division as had been separated from their commands, and with them assisted in getting off two pieces of artillery that otherwise would have been lost. Our party being entirely cut off from the division, upon consultation, we concluded to follow that portion of the army with which we then were to Rossville, which place we reached at dusk and found General Negley in position. Here I found that portion of my command, and portions of the other regiments of our brigade, which had been sent in at the same time, and at about 10 o'clock I had the pleasure of joining the rest of the brigade. Captain Ervin, with a portion of the regiment that passed to the left of the brushwood when we fell back in the morning, stopped with the Thirty-sixth Indiana, and deserves much credit for the manner in which he conducted himself during the day.

I herewith inclose a list of the casualties* of the Eighty-fourth Illinois. I have to regret the loss of Capt. Thomas D. Adams, a brave Christian gentleman and an efficient officer. My command lost 13 killed, 83 wounded, and 9 missing. All of the missing I am satisfied are in the hands of the enemy.

Very respectfully, your obedient servant,

L. H. WATERS,
Colonel, Commanding Eighty-fourth Illinois Volunteers.

Lieutenant BOICE,
   Actg. Asst. Adjt. Gen., Third Brigade.

---

*Embodied in revised statement, p. 176.

No. 172.

Report of Maj. Gilbert Trusler, Thirty-sixth Indiana Infantry.

HEADQUARTERS THIRTY-SIXTH INDIANA VOLUNTEERS,
Chattanooga, Tenn., September 27, 1863.

SIR: As commander of the Thirty-sixth Regiment Indiana Volunteers, I have the honor to report the movements of the regiment since the afternoon of September 3, 1863, at which date we arrived on the north bank of the Tennessee River. The crossing was effected between 10 p. m. of the 3d and daylight of the 4th, at the mouth of Battle Creek. Lieut. Col. O. H. P. Carey was at this time commanding the regiment. The strength of the regiment was 25 commissioned officers and 322 enlisted men. We moved to Shellmound, 5 miles up the river, on the afternoon of the 4th. Our marches from that time forward, until we crossed the Lookout Mountain, 2 miles south of Chattanooga, on the 9th instant, were slow, though men and officers suffered from exposure, the nights being quite cool, and nearly everything in the shape of baggage and bedding being left behind.

From the 9th to the 16th, we marched with the rest of your brigade a distance of some 60 miles, skirmishing with the enemy's cavalry frequently, suffering no loss.

On the 16th, we had another skirmish with the enemy's cavalry, Companies G and H, as skirmishers, with Companies A and C, thrown out as flankers, driving them pell-mell into and partly through Worthen's Gap of the Pigeon Mountain, where we captured a quantity of forage. We had none killed or wounded.

From the 16th to the evening of the 18th, we were moving along the banks of the Chickamauga River, always in presence of the enemy, but by whom we were not molested, excepting the wounding of 1 man of Company F from a stray shot on the afternoon of the 18th. In the memorable battles of Saturday and Sunday, the 19th and 20th instant, the part taken by the Thirty-sixth regiment was an active one. It was our fortune to be thrown into the engagement of Saturday immediately after the firing began, 11 a. m. Though suffering terribly in killed and wounded, [we] were able to hold our position on the right of the brigade, in support of a section of artillery, until 3 p. m., at which time our ammunition gave out, and we were compelled to fall back. This was accomplished in good order and with small loss. During the engagement the enemy, pressing us closely at all points, was punished severely. Lieutenant-Colonel Carey retained command of the regiment from the beginning of the engagement until 1 p. m., when he was severely wounded in the ankle and compelled to retire from the field. After falling back a distance of perhaps 200 yards, our men were reformed, and, although unable to secure ammunition, stood up before the enemy's fire with fixed bayonets, supporting a battery of artillery, which was showering shot and shell into his ranks.

The rebel charge being checked, we moved a short distance forward, and to the rear and left of the position occupied during the day, where we bivouacked for the night.

At daylight on the morning of the 20th, we again shifted our position to the left, throwing up breastworks of logs and brush, in anticipation of an early attack. We remained at this place but a short time when we were relieved by a regiment of another division. At 8 o'clock the enemy's column was advancing upon us, and we at once moved forward to the combat, our position being the extreme left regiment of the line. The enemy charged three times to our front, and was as often repulsed with heavy loss. On the fourth attack his column moved around our left, and we again got an opportunity, which we gladly improved, to punish him severely. The men of my regiment, with 100 men of the Eighty-fourth Illinois Volunteers, under Captain Ervin, attaching themselves to our left, rushed vigorously to the assault, but it was like the ocean spray beating against the rock-bound coast. We were utterly powerless to check the surging and powerful columns of a foe outnumbering us three to one; and, regardless of the slaughter to which he was exposing his men, onward and still onward he moved, until our position was passed and our flank turned. By your order we then withdrew, and awaited the order to retire from the field, on which our men had displayed the greatest heroism and valor, and which, from being vastly outnumbered, they were compelled to yield to the desperate foe. We came off in good order about 5 p. m., being exposed to a concentrated fire from the enemy's artillery, who appeared to anticipate the movement.

Our losses in the battles of the two days are hereto appended.[*]

I cannot conclude, colonel, without calling especial attention to the heroism and bravery displayed by the officers and men of my command, from the commencement to the end of these most terrible conflicts of the war. They were brave beyond what may ordinarily be expected of men, and no one can but be proud that his name is identified with the Thirty-sixth Indiana Volunteers.

Very respectfully,

G. TRUSLER,
Major, Commanding Thirty-sixth Indiana Volunteers.

Col. W. GROSE, *Commanding Third Brigade.*

No. 173.

Report of Lieut. Col. James C. Foy, Twenty-third Kentucky Infantry.

HDQRS. TWENTY-THIRD REGT. KENTUCKY VOL. INFTY.
Camp near Chattanooga, Tenn., September 27, 1863.

SIR: About 2 a. m. of the 4th instant, Lieutenant Livezey, aide-de-camp to Col. William Grose, commanding our brigade, came to me as we lay in bivouac near Battle Creek, with orders for me to arouse my men and proceed to cross the Tennessee River. My instructions were to cross one-half the regiment at that point and march with the remainder some 1½ miles below to Battle Creek, where Colonel Grose had crossed most of the brigade. The same orders were repeated to me in a few minutes by Captain Brooks, inspector of our brigade. The men were instantly awoke and formed in marching order. The evening before, I, according to orders received through Lieutenant Boice, aide-de-camp to Colonel Grose, had sent three companies to the river to assist the battery in crossing. The companies on that duty were Company D, Capt. William Boden; Company E, Capt. John Barnes, and Company F, First Lieut. J. P. Duke. On arriving at the river I found that one of these companies had already crossed, and immediately ordered out

---

[*] Nominal list omitted; see revised statement, p. 176.

Company H, Captain Tifft, and Company I, Captain Black, to cross here, and placed the whole under the command of Capt. T. J. Williams, who was assisting me in the capacity of acting major. With the other four companies, A, B, K, and C, I proceeded down to the designated point, Company G being detached as guard to the ammunition train.

We soon arrived at the crossing, and reported to Colonel Grose, whom I found superintending the crossing of the brigade in person. We were ordered to get an old scow loose that had been run on a snag, which was not accomplished without some difficulty. In the meantime, as soon as any of the small boats would arrive, I had them filled, and placed the first load in charge of Maj. G. W. Northup. I remained behind myself to assist the others off until every man had crossed except the chaplain and a few of the hospital department.

On arriving at the opposite bank a little before sunrise, Captain Williams reported to me that the companies under his charge had all crossed in safety. I ordered him to remain where he was until I could get word from Colonel Grose. I then marched the four companies that were with me back from the river into a grove of trees, where we got breakfast about 8.30 a. m. I received orders, through Capt. G. M. Graves, acting assistant adjutant-general of Colonel Grose's brigade, to collect my men together. I immediately dispatched Maj. G. W. Northup for the four companies in charge of Captain Williams. They joined us about 9.30 a. m. We lay there until about 1 p. m., when we, in connection with the other regiments of the brigade, went into camp close to Shellmound, 7 miles distant from the place of crossing the river.

September 5.—Left Camp Shellmound about 3.30 p. m. and marched toward Chattanooga on the road running along the river. Passed the burned bridge and camped about 8 miles, at 9.30 p. m., in a cornfield, called Camp Whiteside.

September 6.—Continued our line of march, starting about 7 a. m. Halted about 12 m. Bivouacked in an orchard on the left of the road. Were now within 4 miles of Trenton, Ga. The place of our camp was called Squirreltown Spring. We crossed the Tennessee line into Georgia about 9 a. m. this day.

September 7.—Remained at this place all this day.

September 8.—Reveille at 2 a. m. We were in motion precisely at 3 a. m. Marched until 6.30 a. m., when we halted and kept the men under arms all day. Hawkins' Station about 4 miles distant. That night I received orders from Colonel Grose in person that he intended to start the next morning on a reconnaissance up the Lookout Mountain; that he would start at 4 a. m., and would expect to take my regiment with him in connection with the Twenty-fourth Ohio and Eighty-fourth Illinois. Accordingly, at 4 a. m. we fell in line and moved off. On our arrival at the foot of the mountain, distant from our place of bivouac 2 miles, the Eighty-fourth Illinois was left there to protect our rear, while the Twenty-fourth Ohio led the advance up to the summit, followed close by my regiment. The skirmishers of the Twenty-fourth Ohio drove in the enemy's outposts, wounding 1 man that we know of. On hearing the enemy's fire I hastened my men up the mountain. Colonel Grose ordered me to take my position on the right of Twenty-fourth Ohio, and to throw out one company as skirmishers, which I immediately did. I ordered Captain Hardiman, commanding Company B, to deploy his company well to the right, which he did. We now stood in line of battle for a few moments. Not seeing or hearing any more from the enemy, Colonel Grose ordered me to throw up temporary breastworks. This was quickly done. After lying there about two hours, we moved forward along the crest of the mountain, arriving at Point Lookout about 11.30 a. m. We found no enemy in force on the mountain, and now from this point could be distinctly seen the dust from the enemy's column moving out from Chattanooga. The colonel commanding decided on giving us a little rest for a few hours. We started down the mountain between 1 and 2 p. m., leaving Chattanooga to our left. Went into bivouac near Rossville, distant about 4 miles from Chattanooga, and in the State of Georgia.

September 10.—Marched from camp on the Ringgold road. The skirmishers of the First Brigade were driven back by the rebels at ——. My regiment was ordered forward at double-quick. I threw out Company B, Captain Hardiman, and Company D, Captain Boden, as skirmishers here. We proceeded forward in line of battle with our right resting on the road, connecting with the left of the Thirty-first Indiana, in General Cruft's brigade. We skirmished all the afternoon, driving the enemy's skirmishers before us. Returned and bivouacked on the enemy's camp ground 1½ miles west of Graysville.

September 11.—Left camp about 6.30 a. m. Started on the Ringgold road, via Graysville. Arrived at Ringgold about 12 m. Halted and went into bivouac close to the town.

September 12.—Left camp a little after sunrise by the road to La Fayette. At 10 a. m. halted, distant 5 miles from Ringgold, and formed line of battle, with our left resting on the road. I sent out the two left companies forward on the road as outposts. They were stationed by Colonel Grose. Heard skirmishing to our left. We were under arms here all the time until about 4 p. m., when we marched out, bivouacked some 3 miles ahead in a corn-field, where it was said that General Polk's corps had passed the night before. This was on the Chickamauga Creek, which was about one-quarter of a mile from the camp, and immediately opposite Lee and Gordon's Mills on the east side.

September 13.—We were up and stood in line of battle from 3 a. m. until daylight, when we proceeded to get breakfast. About 7 a. m. we were startled by heavy skirmishing in our front. The regiment formed line of battle instantly, and was ordered by Colonel Grose to take position about 200 yards to the rear of the Eighty-fourth Illinois, with our left almost connecting with the Thirty-sixth Indiana. We remained in this position and under arms all day.

September 14.—Received orders from Colonel Grose to be ready to march at a moment's notice. This was about 3.30 a. m. Started in connection with the brigade about sunrise. Crossed the Chickamauga at Lee and Gordon's Mills, marched about 10 miles in a southwesterly direction, and bivouacked in Chattanooga Valley, about 12 miles from Chattanooga.

September 15.—Reveille at 3 a. m. Started at 5 a. m., retracing our way toward Lee and Gordon's Mills, but turned off to the right. Halted about 9.30 a. m. for water at Crawfish Spring. After resting a short time, resumed the march and halted at 12 m. on the bank of Chickamauga Creek, south of Lee and Gordon's Mills and 6 miles above.

September 16.—Prospect of staying here. Had the camp well cleaned up under the supervision of Lieut. J. P. Duke, as officer of the day.

September 17.—There was considerable firing on our pickets last night and early this morning. The rebel pickets made a heavy dash on General Hazen's brigade, which was camped on our right. I was immediately on my horse and had the regiment ready to move. Colonel Grose came down, and the firing not continuing, we were ordered to get our breakfast and be ready to move. Not hearing anything new of the enemy, I had a hastily constructed breastwork of logs thrown up on the bank of the stream. This evening moved camp about 3 miles toward Lee and Gordon's Mills and bivouacked in an open field.

September 18.—Lay here until 3 p. m. Moved out and relieved the Eighth Kentucky, of General Van Cleve's division. We formed line of battle to the left of the Sixth Ohio, our right resting close to a farm-house 4 miles from Lee and Gordon's Mills. According to orders, I sent out Company H, Captain Tifft, and Company F, First Lieut. J. P. Duke, to relieve two companies of the Eighth Kentucky, who were out as skirmishers. Our skirmishers saw the rebels plainly and drove their line back, until I had to send word for them to fall back and act as pickets for the regiment. At 12 o'clock midnight we were relieved by the Fifteenth Kentucky. After some little delay, the brigade proceeded toward Lee and Gordon's Mills, where we arrived about daylight on the morning of the 19th.

September 19.—We had scarcely breakfasted when our brigade was in motion again, going out the Rossville road. We numbered for duty 240 enlisted men, 23 officers; aggregate, 263.

(I should have mentioned above, that on crossing the Tennessee River I had 300 men; [but] through sickness and [those] necessarily with the teams left behind, the regiment [was reduced] to the above number.)

We proceeded down this road about 3 miles, throwing out Company I, Captain Black, and Company C, First Lieutenant Hudson, as skirmishers, when we turned to the right of the road, marching down 700 yards and formed line of battle on the right of the Thirty-sixth Indiana, and 350 yards to the rear of the Eighty-fourth Illinois, battery being behind the Eighty-fourth Illinois, and they had proceeded but a short distance when the battle commenced by some other troops on our left and front. We proceeded cautiously along in the direction of the battle-ground, but just before we reached the conflict I was ordered to march my regiment by the left flank back to the road we had come on, the other regiments of the brigade following. Colonel Grose had just received orders from General Palmer, commanding the division, to march his brigade back. Before we had got quite back we were met by General Palmer and were turned toward the field of battle again. We arrived on the battle-ground a little before 11 a. m. My regiment was posted to the left of the Twenty-fourth Ohio, about 30 paces, Russell's battery a little to our rear, the Second Kentucky about 100 yards in advance and to our left. The battle was now raging warmly. The battery to our rear was pouring a destructive fire into their ranks, while the Second Kentucky to our left, the Twenty-fourth Ohio on our right, and the Twenty-third Kentucky poured in volley after volley. After we had been in this position about one-half to three-quarters of an hour, I noticed that the enemy were renewing the attack with redoubled vigor. The Second Kentucky retired step by step and inch by inch until they arrived on a line with us. At this instant I noticed the Twenty-fourth Ohio giving slowly back. I immediately sent an officer to see what was the matter. He brought the word back "all right," and that they intended to hold their ground. We now fought, I suppose, for about an hour longer, but right in the midst of the fighting, finding out that the artillery to our rear was wounding some of the men in the right companies, I moved the regiment by the left flank until they formed with the Second Kentucky. The storm of battle now somewhat ceased. We renewed our ammunition, marched to pass lines to the rear, which was done in good order, the Eighty-fourth Illinois relieving us. We had scarcely fallen back when the enemy redoubled their attack with great fury.

It was now plain that they were moving men to our right. We immediately changed front toward our right with the left company resting where the right had been. This threw the Twenty-fourth Ohio in our front about 100 yards. We were ordered to lie down. The attack was now made on the Twenty-fourth Ohio, this time still stronger than before, and here allow me to bear testimony to the bravery of that little regiment. I do not think any regiment that day was under a more galling fire than they were; yet they stood as if every man was a hero for the space of half an hour; then they fell back step by step until they were in the rear of our regiment. I then ordered my men to rise up and open fire, which they did with a cheer. The Twenty-fourth Ohio halted in our rear, and now, side by side and shoulder to shoulder, did the Twenty-fourth Ohio and Twenty-third Kentucky stand up and successively repulse the enemy in all his attacks.

The fire now was very hot. It appeared to me as though every third man in the regiment was struck. I was struck on the right breast, the bullet going through the lapels of my overcoat, and struck a large button, glancing off, doing no injury. I kept my eyes watching well the enemy, while the two regiments were there bravely fighting. I noticed the enemy had worked round our right, we having no protection there, and were now pouring a heavy cross-fire into our ranks. One or two of the captains had suggested to me that we had better retire. I thought we would have to, but hesitated about giving the command.

Finally, seeing we were outnumbered, as I thought by the length of their line of battle, at least five to one, I very reluctantly gave the command to retire, which we did, and took a new position about 300 to 400 yards to the rear, and close to Cockerill's battery, belonging to General Hazen's brigade. We now rested until sundown, marched down into the woods, and bivouacked for the night. I found my loss to be 1 officer killed, 3 officers wounded, and 42 enlisted men wounded and 9 killed.

Next morning, September 20, we threw up some slight breastworks, but about 8 a. m. we had to march out to an open field, and then formed in double column on the center, about 350 yards to the rear of General Hazen's brigade. I had not been in this position more than twenty minutes, when I was ordered, through Lieutenant Livezey, aide-de-camp to Colonel Grose, to report with my regiment to General Hazen. On reporting to the general, he ordered me to extend the line of the Sixth Kentucky on their right, which placed me to the rear of the One hundred and twenty-fourth Ohio, about 100 yards, whom we were to support, they being stationed behind some breastworks that General Hazen had had the prudence to erect, I suppose, the night before. The battle now commenced by a terrific attack on our front and left. We lay flat on the ground, the bullets flying over us in all directions. The regiment at the breastworks did well, and successfully repulsed the enemy.

After about three-quarters of an hour we were ordered up to the works. I had 3 men wounded while we were lying down. The men knelt down behind the breastworks, and volley after volley did we pour into the enemy's ranks, one regiment always reserving its fire until the other had loaded. The whole left of our army was turned at one time in the morning, but so well did this brigade do its duty behind the line of breastworks the general had erected, that I have no doubt they saved a portion of the army from premature rout. We remained in this position until about 4 p. m., successfully repulsing every attack made on us. We were now ordered to change front to the right. After being in this position half an hour we were ordered back to the breastworks. The storm of battle had now ceased on our left and front, but off to the right it was renewed with increased vigor. There was now considerable changing round of troops. General Hazen, with his entire brigade, moved off in the direction of the enemy's left to attack them, leaving orders with me to hold the breastworks at all hazards. We were now joined by the Seventy-fifth Indiana. At this time there was no firing where we were, only by the sharpshooters of the enemy. The battle on our right now waxed warmer and warmer. At times it would seem as if it would recede from us, and then again it would come up nearly to where we lay. By this time it was plain that the tide of battle was going against us. The Seventy-fifth Indiana had been moved away to another part of the field, and our little regiment was all that was left in the breastworks, where a whole brigade of five regiments had done battle in the morning.

After receiving my orders from General Hazen, General Palmer rode along and told us about the same thing, adding that we were not to leave there until he gave the order. Soon we could see our men, line after line, give way on the right. At length the whole line to my right appeared to be falling back fast. The battery that was with us at this instant hitched up and drove off. I looked toward the left. General Cruft was slowly retiring his brigade.

Maj. G. W. Northup now came up to me with an order from Colonel Grose to follow the battery that had just left. I proceeded to move off by the right flank by file right. I soon saw there was great danger of being thrown into confusion in marching by the flank. I then formed into columns of companies as we marched, and proceeded across the field. I could see no organized body of troops but our regiment, and General Cruft with his brigade, who were retiring in excellent order on our then right. I approached the general and asked him what was best to be done. He told me he intended to halt as soon as he reached the woods, and try and rally some of the broken regiments that were leaving the field in disorder. I told him then that I would report to him with my regiment for duty. As soon as we reached the edge of the woods we halted. The general finding this was too close to the enemy's fire to rally any of the scattered men, he moved on with his brigade to the top of a high hill about 1½ miles from the battle-field, where he halted for the space of one or two hours, collecting the remains of different regiments together. We now proceeded down the hill. At the foot of the hill I saw Colonel Grose, and then joined our brigade and proceeded to the vicinity of Rossville, near Chattanooga, where we bivouacked for the night.

September 21.—We marched out the Rossville road about 2½ miles, ascended a point of the mountain to the north of the road. We lay on the west side of the mountain until about 3 p. m. ; were ordered to the top of the mountain and placed behind some breastworks to the left of the Forty-first Ohio. Very little firing was done here, except by an occasional sharpshooter. About midnight we moved down the hill and bivouacked in our present camp from that time until now. Since then our duty has been varied, such as picket and outpost duty, standing at arms, resting, and working on the breastworks.

I have forgotten to mention the casualties of the 20th. They were as follows : One man killed, 3 wounded, which make a total of casualties of 1 officer killed, 9 enlisted men killed, 3 officers wounded, and 45 enlisted men wounded and 9 enlisted men missing. There are 10 or 12 others wounded in the regiment, but their wounds being so slight, they being all able for duty, I thought it unnecessary to report them. There are only nine companies of the regiment, the other company being detached as train guard.

And now, in conclusion, allow me to express publicly my warmest thanks to both men and officers for the promptness and alacrity with which they obeyed every order; also, for the cool courage with which they faced the enemy in the battles of the two days.

Where all did well it is hard to particularize. I must thank Captain Tifft for his undaunted courage on both days. I also return my thanks for the assistance rendered me in the management of the regiment by Maj. G. W. Northup, Capt. T. J. Williams, acting major, and Adjt. W. H. Mundy. I feel grateful to Captain Hardiman and Lieut. J. P. Duke for the prompt assistance rendered me. Lieut. Henry G. Shiner, of Company B, who was wounded in Saturday's fight, I cannot speak too highly of—his qualities as a soldier and an officer, ever ready to obey and yield me all the assistance in his power, whether it was on the march or in the bivouac. I know that the services of an officer like him can never be repaid, but he has my best wishes for his speedy recovery. For Lieut. J. C. Hoffman and the brave men who fell I drop a silent tear.

One word now for the enlisted men. No men could fight better ; not only my own men, but all that came under my observation, and too much credit cannot be given to the private soldiers for the fortitude, bravery, and unparalleled heroism displayed by them. I had almost forgotten our worthy chaplain, Rev. William H. Black, whose place here, as at Stone's River, was in hospital and visiting wounded soldiers. I know that many of the wounded, both in this and the battle of Stone's River, have had cause to bless his name, as he worked with his own hands to administer to them what relief was in his power. In the name of the sick and wounded soldiers, I publicly return him my thanks for favors bestowed on them; also, to Surgeons Morrison and Hasbrouck, who, in their department, I know labored to alleviate the suffering of the wounded soldiers consigned to their charge. Herewith I inclose you a list of the casualties.*

I remain, sir, very respectfully, yours, &c.,

JAS. C. FOY,

Lieutenant-Colonel, Comdg. 23d Regt. Kentucky Vols.

Col. W. GROSE, *Commanding Third Brigade.*

* Embodied in revised statement, p. 176.

No. 174.

Report of Maj. Samuel C. Erwin, Sixth Ohio Infantry.

CAMP SIXTH REGT. OHIO VOLUNTEER INFANTRY,
Near Chattanooga, Tenn., September 27, 1863.

COLONEL: I have the honor to submit the following report of the part taken by the Sixth Ohio in the recent battles of Missionary Ridge:

On the morning of the 18th instant, the effective force of the regiment was 23 officers and 324 enlisted men. On the evening of the 18th, while on outpost duty, Private Hooth, of Captain Thatcher's company, was shot by the enemy's pickets and instantly killed.

On the morning of Saturday, the 19th, after returning from a reconnaissance made by the brigade under your personal direction, we were posted in the second line of the brigade, two or perhaps more of the right companies extending beyond our front line, the right company detached and posted on the right of Cushing's battery. We had been thus placed for a short time when the engagement began and soon became general, the enemy pushing toward our right. Our regiment was extended in that direction and all were hotly engaged. The loss of our regiment was very severe. Captain Gilman, Adjutant Throop, and Sergeant-Major Mellon were all severely wounded. We held our position until the enemy was repulsed, when, our ammunition being entirely exhausted, we retired, by order of General Palmer, across the road to the rear of the Seventeenth Indiana Battery to get a fresh supply of ammunition. Having received it, we were moving in order to join the brigade when the troops in our front and on our right gave way in confusion and the enemy made a dash for the battery, which had been placed in reserve and was without infantry support. We immediately formed in the rear of the battery for its defense, under as hot a fire of musketry as I ever saw. The enemy in front was held in check by a furious discharge of grape and canister from the artillery, but in a few minutes gained our right flank and poured in a destructive fire. We then changed front to the rear on tenth company and held them while five of the six guns were safely retired, when we fell back through the woods in rear of Brannan's division, coming into the Rossville road at a point where Cushing's battery was stationed, from where we reported to you and rejoined the brigade.

Our loss in this fight was heavy. Colonel Anderson was struck by a musket ball in the shoulder and severely wounded. Captain Tinker fell mortally wounded; Captain Montagnier was shot through both legs. Lieutenant Holmes was missed here, and I fear is either dead or wounded and a prisoner. Lieutenant Choate was also slightly wounded. The behavior of all these officers was above all praise. Night having now fallen and the fight ceased, Colonel Anderson, for the first time, retired to have his wound dressed, when it was found to be of such a nature as to preclude the possibility of his remaining longer in the field, and he was sent to the rear and the command of the regiment devolved on me.

Early the next morning we were employed, under your direction, in constructing defenses on an eminence on the east of the Rossville road, and nearly parallel with it, in an open wood. When these were about finished, they were occupied by other troops (whose I do not know), and we were retired and placed in reserve. The brigade being in two lines, my regiment in the second line, formed in double column at full distance, on the right of the Thirty-sixth Indiana, formed in like manner, and in rear of the Eighty-fourth Illinois, deployed in line of battle. We rested here, I should think, over half an hour, when we were moved to the left and formed at nearly right angles with our former position, and facing a little east of north, in a cornfield just east of the Rossville road ; we were on the extreme left of the brigade, with the Twenty-fourth Ohio on our right. The enemy were attempting to turn our left and were delivering a hot fire in front of our position, when our batteries in the field opened upon the rebels (I suppose, though I then thought they mistook my regiment for the enemy), but firing too low they killed and wounded numbers of my men and officers, among them Captain Bense, senior captain and acting major, and Lieutenant Cormany. It was a trying position, the enemy's fire in our front and our own in the rear, and more danger in retiring than in remaining. At length the fire of the battery ceased, and I moved my regiment by the right flank to a little hollow, near where we reformed, and were then placed on the right of the Twenty-fourth Ohio, and between that regiment and the regular brigade, my left a little retired from my former direction, and a part of my front covered by one of the regiments of our brigade. We here met the full force of the enemy's advancing column and were forced back in some confusion, but rallied and drove the enemy. The pursuit was broken and irregular on the part of all our troops, who, however, inflicted severe punishment on the flying rebels. My regiment became divided, and in retiring a portion, with some of my officers, got to the west side of the Rossville road and were for some time separated from me.

When I returned from the pursuit, I reformed on the right of a portion of the Sixteenth Regulars at the breastworks to the right of my last position and was joined by a portion of the Eighty-fourth Illinois, under Captain Ervin, and a few of the Twenty-fourth Ohio, with Lieutenant Kies and the colors of their regiments. We remained there until the brigade was reformed under your direction and moved to the right in support of Reynolds' troops, and, though under fire more or less all the time until we were retired from the field, were not again actively engaged. We retired in good order under a heavy cross-fire of the enemy's artillery, losing but 1 man, and camped with the brigade at Rossville.

With a single exception the behavior of my officers was all that could be desired. I would especially mention Captain Bense, acting major ; Captains Thatcher and Russell, and Lieutenants Choate, Irwin, Lewis, Meline, and Glisan, whose gallantry was conspicuous. Lieutenant McLean, after behaving badly on the field, absented himself on Sunday morning and did not return until Monday afternoon. I placed him in arrest, and have preferred charges against him.

Among the non-commissioned officers and privates, instances of gallant conduct were numerous, but space prevents their mention. During the whole of the two days' fight the men suffered severely from the want of water.

I am happy to be able to report my regiment in fine condition and good spirits.

I annex herewith a statement in detail of all casualties* in my command.

Very respectfully,   S. C. ERWIN,
                          Major 6th Ohio Vol. Inf. Comdg. Regt.
Col. W. Grose, *Commanding Third Brigade.*

---

* Embodied in revised statement, p. 176.

No. 175.

Report of Col. David J. Higgins, Twenty-fourth Ohio Infantry.

CAMP TWENTY-FOURTH OHIO,
Chattanooga, Tenn., September 28, 1863.

SIR: I have the honor to report the following marches and engagements in which my command has borne a part since September 4, 1863, together with a list of casualties which have occurred during that time:

This command being detached as escort to wagon train crossed the Tennessee River with 19 commissioned officers and 310 enlisted men. Of these 27 were detailed in quartermaster's department and as company cooks, and 6 sick, leaving an effective force of 277 enlisted men and 19 commissioned officers.

Rejoining the brigade on the morning of the 5th September, we marched by the way of Nickajack and Squirreltown Creek to within 10 miles of Chattanooga.

On the morning of the 9th September, the Twenty-fourth Ohio, Twenty-third Kentucky, and Eighty-fourth Illinois Regiments, under your command, made a reconnaissance of Mount Lookout by a steep bridle-path, the Twenty-fourth Ohio in advance. Reached the top at 6 a. m., my skirmishers meeting and driving in the enemy's cavalry pickets. There we received orders to march upon Chattanooga. This we did, meeting no enemy, he having evacuated that place the night previous. We camped at Rossville, where we were joined by the remainder of the brigade.

On the 10th, advanced on the road to Ringgold, skirmishing with the enemy and passing Graysville, reaching Ringgold, in conjunction with the whole of Second Division, on the 11th.

From the 12th to the 18th, were engaged in daily skirmishing with the enemy, feeling for his position and strength, in the neighborhood of Gordon's Mills.

On the morning of the 19th, the enemy showed himself in strong force in the Chickamauga Valley, north of Gordon's Mills. The army was put in motion to meet him, my command, a part of your brigade, receiving and returning a heavy fire throughout the day, never shrinking from the deadly contest except when outnumbered and crushed by mere weight of numbers. The battle was renewed on the 20th, and fought gallantly, when, after repeated successes and repulses, the Twenty-fourth Ohio being on the extreme left, was crushed, and with other regiments of the brigade was forced to give way, torn and bleeding at every part. The whole loss of this regiment is 3 commissioned officers wounded, 3 enlisted men killed, and 57 wounded, and 16 missing. The heaviest loss was on the 19th, and yet as severe fire was received on the 20th.

My present command is, for duty, commissioned officers, 15; enlisted men, 184; aggregate, 199. Enlisted men sick, 7; present, detailed, 30. Total aggregate present, 236.

Loss: Commissioned officers wounded, 3; surgeon, in hands of enemy, 1; enlisted men killed, 3; enlisted men wounded, 57; enlisted men absent without leave, 9; enlisted men missing in action, 16; enlisted men sent to hospital, 4. Aggregate, 93.

Where all did their duty so faithfully it would seem invidious to mention particular cases. The brave Captain Wadsworth fell in the action of the 20th, pierced with two balls, and was captured by the enemy. Captain Dryden and Lieutenant McCoy, equally as brave, were borne from the field severely wounded. When the gallant Corporal Ogle, who bore the regimental colors, fell, Corpl. D. A. Leimin seized and bore them safely from the field.

A list of the killed, wounded, and missing appended.*

Respectfully submitted.

DAVID J. HIGGINS,

Colonel, Comdg. Twenty-fourth Ohio Volunteer Infantry.

Col. W. Grose, *Commanding Third Brigade.*

No. 176.

Report of Lieut. Harry C. Cushing, Battery H, Fourth U. S. Artillery.

Battery H, Fourth U. S. Artillery,
Chattanooga, September 26, 1863.

Major : I have the honor to submit the following report of the part taken by my battery during the battle of the 19th and 20th instant :

On the morning of the 19th, by direction of Captain Standart, chief of artillery Second Division, I moved it from its temporary position on the road near Gordon's Mills and joined Colonel Grose's brigade. I was immediately moved into action. I sent Second Lieut. Robert Floyd, with one section, to the left center of the brigade, and took the other to the right myself. Fighting commenced immediately and was very severe. The enemy endeavored to drive our right, but the vigorous action of Colonel Anderson and the Sixth Ohio and a liberal use of short-fused case-shot and canister by my section caused them to retire, and the arrival of General Reynolds' troops completed their discomfiture. This gave me time to refill my limbers, and, fighting being discontinued in our immediate front, we lay quiet about a quarter of an hour, but increased firing in General Reynolds' front decided me to go to his assistance. At a gallop I took the whole battery and reported to General Reynolds, and took position on the left of his battery. His troops were retiring before the heavy force of the enemy, but the quick and well-sustained fire of these batteries gave the troops time to recover and the enemy was repulsed there. The enemy, foiled there, gained ground to the left and precipitated themselves in tremendous force on the right of these troops and enfiladed our line of batteries. The whole line was thrown back, and this throwing the batteries back in the hollow, I reported to General Hazen, who was forming a new line across the road. M, of the Fourth Artillery, F, of the First Ohio, and my battery were massed obliquely across the road covering the rebel approach. Their appearance was the signal for a most rapid and destructive fire from these batteries and driving the rebels. This closed the fight for me that day, my ammunition being totally exhausted. The next morning our ordnance train arrived and we filled up. Lieutenant Floyd had been wounded the evening before and sent to General Johnson's hospital. Our brigade was in reserve, but as soon as the fighting commenced, it was ordered to re-enforce General Johnson, my battery accompanying it. Hardly had we reached the ground when the left of General Johnson was

---

* Embodied in revised statement, p. 176.

pushed back. Colonel Grose swung to the rear on his right and I placed one section commanding the road. The enemy had gained possession of the road, and as soon as I opened on them at about 350 yards with case-shot they left it, but opened a full battery of 12-pounder guns on me. Their fire was rapid and effective and I was compelled, by the exhaustion of my ammunition, to call on Lieutenant Russell for assistance. That officer relieved me while I got off a disabled gun and retired to refill. My caissons had been ordered back by some one from the place I left them in, and I was ordered by General Thomas to take my guns and find them and refill. I found them back on a hill, but their limbers were coming up at a gallop. I was refilling and fixing up when I met you, and was by you ordered to join the batteries massed on the hill in the rear of the center. This was done, but hardly had I formed in line when the rebels broke the line in front, and, under the supposition that our troops were to fall back on us, I did not come into battery until the whistling of bullets and the appearance of the enemy from the woods in our front. I gave the command, "Action front," but before the pieces could be unlimbered a volley shot all the horses on my right piece, and I saw that, instead of forcing our troops back, they had pierced through and were coming right at us.

There being no support, I got the three other pieces to the left-about, and, directing the sergeant where to take them, gave my attention to the other. The horses on this piece were perfectly ungovernable and in inextricable confusion, and, to complete the thing, the pole was broken, 1 man killed, and 4 wounded. I endeavored to unlimber the piece to draw it off by hand, but it was so jammed up that the united strength of myself and 2 of my men was powerless to do it, and the rapid approach of the enemy and their heavy fire, combined with solicitude for the fate of the other guns, made me reluctantly abandon it. On reaching the others, I found the wheelhorse of one dead, and, amid all the confusion, he was taken out and his place supplied. This closed the fight for my battery.

I marched to Chattanooga by the Cove road, so called. I regret the probable capture of Lieut. Robert Floyd, while lying wounded in Johnson's division hospital, prevents me from subjoining his report of detached operations, but the voice of every witness is loud in praise of his cool, determined, and most gallant conduct. He was wounded, I think, severely in the hip and body while endeavoring to pull off the piece of another battery, on the evening of the 19th. I cannot too highly compliment his bravery and efficiency as an officer, and sincerely hope my fears are groundless as to his capture.

The conduct of the non-commissioned officers and men was admirable throughout, cool, steady, and collected, and maintaining that high reputation for efficiency which they have gained under my predecessors.

In conclusion, I would state that personal experience proves to me that too much care cannot be taken in depriving a battery of its proper complement of officers. Had I had more, or even one, I am firmly of the opinion that I could have brought off my gun. Subjoined is a list of casualties in men,* horses, and *matériel.*†

I am, major, very respectfully, your most obedient servant,

HARRY C. CUSHING,
First Lieut. Fourth U. S. Artillery, Comdg. Battery.

Maj. John Mendenhall, *Chief of Artillery, 21st A. C.*

---

* Embodied in revised statement, p. 176.   † See Mendenhall's table, p. 623.

No. 177.

Report of Lieut. Francis L. D. Russell, Battery M, Fourth U. S. Artillery.

CAMP NEAR CHATTANOOGA,
September 27, 1863.

SIR: I have the honor to submit the following report of the part taken by my battery (M), of the Fourth U. S. Artillery, in the battle of the 19th and 20th of this month:

About 10 o'clock on the morning of the 19th, I received orders from Colonel Grose, commanding the brigade to which I am attached, to follow his command, which was then marching in the direction of heavy firing, which I learned proceeded from General Brannan's division, then engaged with the enemy.

After marching some distance Colonel Grose ordered me into position on the crest of a ridge covered with a dense wood. Immediately on my coming into battery, Colonel Grose's command was attacked, and I was ordered to fire down the hill. The impossibility of getting a clear view rendered my fire very uncertain, and I was still in doubt whether I gave any material assistance. The enemy were finally driven back and the firing ceased for over an hour.

About 2 o'clock in the afternoon the enemy moved up a second time in heavy force. At this period I could see them distinctly, and, loading with canister, I fired as rapidly as possible. The attack was too heavy to be resisted, and, the infantry falling back, left me exposed to capture.

Thinking that to remain longer without a sufficient support would be sacrificing my battery, I limbered up and retired to a better position, about 600 yards to the rear. I there found Lieutenant Cushing, who had placed his battery in position. I formed immediately on his right, with an open field in front. The enemy advancing, Lieutenant Cushing and I opened with canister and speedily repulsed them.

The battle for that day was ended, and toward evening I went into camp with Colonel Grose's brigade.

Early the next morning Captain Standart, chief of artillery, of General Palmer's division, placed me in an open field in rear of General Cruft's brigade, holding me in reserve. I remained there throughout the day, firing but once, when Colonel Grose's brigade was driven out of the woods on the left. I then changed front, and, firing over the infantry, drove the enemy back. I had left my caissons in the woods, about 200 yards in rear of the battery, under charge of my first sergeant. They remained there but a short time, being ordered by some officer back with the transportation wagons.

When the wagons were ordered to fall back to Chattanooga, my caissons were ordered to go too. On the road, three of them being crowded on one side, the poles broken and the enemy firing upon them, the sergeant in charge took the responsibility of abandoning them.

About 5 o'clock in the afternoon of the 20th, I received orders to retreat to Rossville, and arrived at 8 o'clock in the evening.

The next morning I joined my command. My casualties in the two days' fight were 2 men killed, 6 wounded, 14 horses killed and wounded, and 3 caissons abandoned.

My men behaved admirably throughout the fight, and were every-thing I could wish. Lieutenant Butler, the only officer with me, distinguished himself by his cool and gallant conduct, and rendered me the most essential service.

Hoping this will prove satisfactory, I am, very respectfully, your obedient servant,

F. L. D. RUSSELL,
First Lieut., Fourth Artillery, Comdg. Company M.

Major MENDENHALL,
Chief of Artillery, Twenty-first Army Corps.

No. 178.

Report of Brig. Gen. Horatio P. Van Cleve, U. S. Army, command-ing Third Division.

HDQRS. THIRD DIVISION, TWENTY-FIRST ARMY CORPS,
Chattanooga, Tenn., September 30, 1863.

COLONEL: I have the honor to submit the following report of the operations of this division from the 4th to the 21st of September:

On the 4th, by your order, I crossed the Tennessee at Shellmound with the First and Third Brigades, the Second Brigade being at McMinnville.

On the 5th, we marched to Whiteside's. Then, by your order, I left Colonel Price, with the Twenty-first Kentucky, to guard the road, and we marched a few miles southeast with the balance of the command.

On the 9th, we marched toward Chattanooga, and learning that it had been evacuated by the enemy, we turned to the left, after cross-ing Lookout Mountain, and marched to Rossville.

On the 10th, we marched toward Ringgold, and encamped in the valley of Pea Vine Creek. Was joined by Colonel Dick, with the Second Brigade, on the 11th. We continued our march, and at Ringgold, meeting the rebels, under Forrest, drove them before us. At this time Col. Sid. M. Barnes was in the advance, and handled his brigade very handsomely. At Ringgold, while waiting for General Palmer, who was marching by way of Graysville, Colonel Wilder passed me, following the enemy toward Dalton.

The rebels destroyed the railroad bridges across the Chickamauga, some four or five, as they fell back before us. I encamped that night 3 miles beyond Ringgold, on the road toward Dalton. The next day, the 12th, I marched back to Ringgold, and, by the way of Peeler's Factory, went to Gordon's Mills, on the Chattanooga and La Fayette road. Here I found General Wood, with his division, and in the evening was again joined by General Palmer.

On the 13th, by your order, I made a reconnaissance with my division 3 miles toward La Fayette. We met the rebel cavalry im-mediately after passing our picket line, and with sharp skirmishing drove them back. Two privates of the Nineteenth Ohio were mor-tally wounded by a solid shot. Captain Drury, chief of artillery, and Lieutenant Clark, Company G, Seventy-ninth Indiana Volun-teers, were seriously wounded. The loss of the enemy is not known. In this reconnaissance, General Beatty was in advance and managed his command well.

On the 14th, I marched to Chattanooga Creek Valley, and on the

15th, back to Chickamauga River Valley, and encamped at Crawfish Spring.

On the 18th, by your order, I marched to Gordon's Mills. Toward evening I received a communication from Colonel Wilder, who was about a mile in front, that he needed support or would be compelled to fall back. I sent to his aid Colonel Dick, with two regiments of his brigade.

On the 19th, about 1 p. m., I was ordered to have one brigade in position near Gordon's Mills and move forward rapidly with the rest of my command to support General Palmer on our left, who was then hotly engaged with the enemy. I immediately ordered General Beatty, with the First Brigade, to move to the left at double-quick, and at the same time ordered so much of the Second Brigade as was not with Colonel Dick to move forward, sending an order to Colonel Dick to join us as we passed him. Colonel Barnes, with the Third Brigade, was left in position in the road.

With the First and Second Brigades I formed on the right of General Palmer, and immediately engaged the enemy fiercely, drove him rapidly, and captured four guns. The enemy, however, soon threw re-enforcements on his left, flanked my right, which was not supported, and compelled me to retire and leave the guns we had captured. We soon rallied and again charged him, driving him as before, and captured four more guns, which were brought off the field by the First Brigade. Again we were driven back, and again we rallied and drove the enemy, till, overwhelmed by masses on our unsupported right, we fell back in some disorder. I sent successively two officers of my staff to inform General Crittenden of my situation. The first reached him, but was unable to return; the second could not reach him, communication being cut off by the enemy. On the left of the road a battery was stationed. I fell back to that point; and there attempted to rally my men, with only partial success. Here Capt. Thomas F. Murdock, of my staff, was struck down by my side while cheering those who rallied.

While the First and Second Brigades were thus engaged, the Third Brigade, Colonel Barnes, which had been left in position in the road near Gordon's Mills, was ordered forward by you to take part in the action, and to engage the enemy wherever he should be met. He encountered the enemy in a wood about three-quarters of a mile to the right of the position occupied by the First and Second Brigades, and after a sharp contest for about a half hour, being overpowered by superior numbers, was compelled to fall back to a more commanding position, where he threw up barricades and remained, till ordered to join the rest of the division on the following morning. Our losses this day were very heavy.

On the morning of the 20th, my division took position on the left of the First Division, General Wood, on the eastern slope of Missionary Ridge, and on the west side of the road running from Crawfish Spring to Rossville. Here we issued rations and replenished our stock of ammunition. About 10 a. m. I was instructed by you to order Colonel Barnes to move his brigade forward to the support of General Wood. With the First and Second Brigades I was ordered to the front and left, and [to] take position by my batteries on a hill about 400 yards distant. The eastern slope of this hill was a clear field, at its foot a strip of timber, beyond which was a large cornfield bordered by timber. I had no sooner gained my position than I was ordered by General Rosecrans in person to form my regiments in double column on the center, move rapidly to the foot of the hill, cut roads through the wood for my artillery, and there hold myself in readiness for any emergency.

Immediately after taking this position, I was ordered by you to move forward and engage the enemy wherever I should find an open space in our front lines. After passing the strip of timber in my front, my lines were deployed, and coming upon General Wood's command in line of battle, they were ordered to lie down. I was now ordered to move rapidly to the left to the support of General Thomas. The Second Brigade being in the rear and near at hand, soon received the order and moved off at double-quick. Before the First Brigade could execute the order, its right was uncovered. General Wood having moved to the left, and a brigade of infantry with a battery of artillery, driven in confusion by the enemy, [having] passed diagonally across my line, throwing my men into confusion—some of whom were crippled and otherwise injured by horses and gun carriages—caused this brigade to fall back toward Rossville. The Second Brigade moving to the left, joined General Thomas' command, as ordered, when it soon became engaged with the enemy, and after a short action, being overwhelmed by superior numbers, it was compelled to retire in some confusion. After rallying, a portion of this brigade, under Colonel Aldrich, went to the support of General Wood, and did good service. The remainder of the brigade, under its commander, Colonel Dick, for a time supported a battery, and afterward General Brannan, whom he found hard pressed. Being again overpowered by superior numbers, Colonel Dick fell back to the Chattanooga road toward Rossville.

Colonel Barnes, as ordered, joined General Wood in the morning, and was actively engaged with the enemy on the field at various points several times in the course of the day till evening, when he retired fighting. The First and Second Brigades bivouacked on the night of the 20th about a mile south of Rossville ; on the morning of the 21st, marching into Chattanooga. The batteries of my command, the Seventh Indiana, Captain Swallow; the Third Wisconsin (Captain Drury's), commanded by Lieutenant Livingston, and Twenty-sixth Pennsylvania, Captain Stevens, were very active, did effective service, and suffered heavy loss both in men and *matériel*. Captain Stevens was killed on the 20th while bringing off his guns.

I would respectfully invite your attention to the reports of commanders of brigades, regiments, and batteries, which are herewith inclosed. My loss is 57 killed, 601 wounded, and 295 missing.* I inclose lists of casualties of the separate commands.

I cannot close this report without commending to your especial notice the conduct of my brigade commanders, General Samuel Beatty, Col. Sid. M. Barnes, and Col. George F. Dick. Colonel Barnes, cool, intrepid, and judicious, has proved himself on all occasions an able commander, and has well earned promotion. To Col. P. T. Swaine, Ninety-ninth Ohio, I gave command of two additional regiments on the 18th, to take a commanding position on our front. In posting his troops, he displayed, as I have noticed on other occasions, much judgment and skill. His conduct on the field received the commendations of his brigade commander. I commend him to your notice. In this last action I was deprived of the valuable services of my chief of artillery, Capt. L. H. Drury, he having been wounded in battle on the 13th. The commanders of my batteries, Captains

---

* See revised statement, p. 177.

Swallow and Stevens, the latter killed on the 20th, and Lieutenant Livingston, deserve particular notice for their good conduct. The non-commissioned officers and privates of the batteries have my warmest thanks for the pertinacity with which they stood by their guns when surrounded by the enemy. I am happy to inform them that their praise is on the tongues of all who witnessed their conduct.

I am also happy to bear testimony to the good conduct of my infantry, that although overpowered and driven back by superior numbers, they held to their arms and there was no skulking.

To the members of my staff, I am indebted for the promptness and faithfulness with which they discharged their duties. Surg. S. D. Turney, medical director, by his prudence, skill, and industry had so arranged the division field hospital, that the wounded were readily attended to without loss of time, provision being made to send them to the rear in case of reverse. To this we owe the present safety of many of our brave wounded. To Capt. E. A. Otis, assistant adjutant-general; Capt. Carter B. Harrison, inspector-general; Capt. J. O. Stanage, commissary; Capt. A. K. Robinson, topographical engineer; Captain Sheafe, provost-marshal ; Lieut. W. H. H. Sheets, ordnance officer, I am sincerely indebted for the promptness and readiness with which they rendered me every aid and performed every duty.

On the 19th, Capt. T. F. Murdock, commissary of musters of my staff, a noble young man, a true soldier and patriot, was struck down by my side while gallantly assisting me to rally my disordered ranks. Lieutenant Knoble, my aide, who had ever been faithful and true, cheerfully and unhesitatingly conveying orders in the midst of danger, was sent on the 20th to one of the brigades with an order and never returned. It is feared he too was struck down.

The brigade, regimental, and battery commanders in their reports bring to notice meritorious individuals to which I earnestly invite your attention.

May God heal our wounded and comfort the friends of our dead.

I am, colonel, very respectfully, your most obedient servant,

H. P. VAN CLEVE,
Brigadier-General, Commanding Division.

Lieut. Col. LYNE STARLING,
Asst. Adjt. Gen. and Chief of Staff, 21st Army Corps.

ADDENDA.

Semi-weekly report of effective force of the Third Division, Twenty-first Army Corps, Brig. Gen. Horatio P. Van Cleve commanding.

Command.	Headquarters.			Infantry.		
	Commissioned officers.	Enlisted men.	Total.	Commissioned officers.	Enlisted men.	Total.
Headquarters Third Division, Brigadier-General Van Cleve.	9	15	24	....	....	....
First Brigade, Brigadier-General Beatty.	9	20	29	106	1,378	1,484
Second Brigade, Col. George F. Dick.	8	30	38	92	1,097	1,189
Third Brigade, Col. S. M. Barnes.	7	31	38	113	1,168	1,281
Artillery Third Division, Capt. George R. Swallow.	......	......	......	......	20	20
Total.	33	96	129	311	3,663	3,974

Semi-weekly report of effective force, &c.—Continued.

Command.	Artillery.			Total.				
	Commissioned officers.	Enlisted men.	Total.	Commissioned officers.	Enlisted men.	Aggregate.	Number of horses.	Number of guns.
Headquarters Third Division, Brigadier-General Van Cleve.	......	......	......	9	15	24	......	......
First Brigade, Brigadier-General Beatty	......	......	......	115	1,398	1,513	......	......
Second Brigade, Col. George F. Dick	......	......	......	100	1,127	1,227	......	......
Third Brigade, Col. S. M. Barnes	......	......	......	120	1,199	1,319	......	......
Artillery Third Division, Capt. George R. Swallow.	13	320	333	13	340	353	337	18
Total	13	320	333	357	4,079	4,436	337	18

SEPTEMBER 14, 1863.

H. P. VAN CLEVE,
Brigadier-General, Commanding.

Capt. E. A. OTIS,
Assistant Adjutant-General.

No. 179.

Report of Capt. George R. Swallow, Seventh Indiana Battery, Chief of Artillery.

HDQRS. ARTILLERY BATTALION, THIRD DIVISION,
September 29, 1863.

CAPTAIN: I have the honor to submit herewith copies of the official reports of the commanding officers of the batteries of this division, and also a list of the names * of the killed, wounded, and missing.

The Independent Pennsylvania Battery went into the action with:

Commissioned officers.. 5
Enlisted men.. 107
Total... 112

The Third Wisconsin Battery went into the action with :

Commissioned officers.. 3
Enlisted men.. 116
Total... 119

The Seventh Indiana Battery went into the action with :

Commissioned officers.. 5
Enlisted men... 117
Total... 122

I submit these reports without comment, as the batteries were acting and moving under the orders of yourself and the different brigade commanders, almost as often as they were from [under] mine, and a detailed report from me would be simply a copy of their several reports. It is, however, my painful duty to note the death of Capt. A. J. Stevens. As an artillery officer he had few equals and no superiors. His only fault was in being too brave and fearless. By his own personal labors, he saved two of his guns on both Saturday

* Omitted.

and Sunday, and that, too, when most of batteries would have saved nothing. He fell trying to bring the third piece off by hand. Long will the artillery of the Third Division mourn the loss of this brave and efficient officer and true gentleman. I would make special mention of Private Frank Wyman, Fourteenth Regiment Ohio Volunteers, as rendering valuable assistance to the Seventh Indiana Battery on the 20th instant. Without his help this battery would probably have lost two guns instead of one.

All of which is most respectfully submitted.

Most respectfully, your obedient servant,

G. R. SWALLOW,
Captain, and Chief of Artillery.

Capt. E. A. OTIS, Asst. Adjt. Gen., Third Division.

No. 180.

Reports of Brig. Gen. Samuel Beatty, U. S. Army, commanding First Brigade.

HDQRS. FIRST BRIG., THIRD DIV., 21ST ARMY CORPS,
Chattanooga, September 28, 1863.

CAPTAIN : I have the honor to submit the following report of the operations of my command, from the time of crossing the Tennessee River, to include the late engagements :

In obedience to orders from Brig. Gen. H. P. Van Cleve, commanding Third Divison, Twenty-first Army Corps, I moved my command from Jasper, Tenn., to cross the Tennessee River at Shellmound, on the morning of September 4, 1863, and bivouacked 1 mile from the Shellmound depot.

At 3 p. m., September 5, received orders and marched with the division on the Chattanooga road to Whiteside's, arriving in bivouac at 1 a. m. of September 6. From that date until the 8th, marched by short stages to Lookout Valley, to occupy ground that had been vacated by Major-General Palmer's division.

On the morning of the 9th, under orders of Brigadier-General Van Cleve, I marched my command at 3 a. m. to make a reconnaissance to the top of Lookout Mountain, by the way of Nickajack Trace. Finding no enemy I advanced, according to directions, to communicate with a similar reconnaissance sent out by Major-General Palmer, at Summertown, and met orders from General Van Cleve to march to join the other brigades of the division at Chattanooga, and before arriving at that place met other orders from him, which changed my course toward Rossville.

On the 10th, marched toward Ringgold. Camped for the night at Pea Vine Creek. One man of my command was wounded while on outpost duty at this place ; 11th, advanced beyond Ringgold 3 miles in the direction of Dalton ; 12th, returned through Ringgold and marched to Lee and Gordon's Mills; 13th, with the division, my brigade in advance, marched to make reconnaissance toward La Fayette. I deployed three regiments, Nineteenth Ohio, Seventy-ninth Indiana, and Seventeenth Kentucky, with skirmishers in advance of each, and, with the Nineteenth Ohio on the left and the Seventy-ninth Indiana and Seventeenth Kentucky on the right of the road, drove the enemy, who were a force of perhaps three regiments of cavalry and three pieces of artillery. After driving the enemy's forces 3 miles, by order of General Van Cleve I returned to camp. The enemy did not return that night. In this reconnaissance I lost 2 men of the Nineteenth Ohio, killed, and 1 lieutenant of the Seventy-ninth Indiana Volunteers, wounded.

On the 14th, marched with the division to Chattanooga Creek, and on the 15th back to Crawfish Spring, where we remained doing heavy picket duty until the 18th, when, by orders from the general commanding the division, I marched my brigade to take position on the left of General Wood at Lee and Gordon's Mills. With slight modifications of position, we remained on the left of the First Division, Brigadier-General Wood commanding, until 1 p. m. of the 19th, when I received orders from General Van Cleve to march at double-quick to the support of General Palmer, who was heavily engaged with the enemy.

Under direction of Generals Crittenden and Van Cleve, I formed by brigade in two lines on the right of General Palmer's division, with the Nineteenth Ohio Volunteers, Lieut. Col. H. G. Stratton commanding, on the right, and the Seventy-ninth Indiana Volunteers, Col. Fred. Knefler commanding, on the left, in the front line, and the Ninth Kentucky Volunteers, Col. George H. Cram commanding, on the left, and Seventeenth Kentucky Volunteers, Col. Alexander M. Stout commanding, on the right in the second line. Advancing about 200 yards, we met and engaged the enemy, driving him steadily for some distance. My front line charged upon and took possession of two rebel batteries, but a heavy flanking movement and fire of the enemy upon our right compelled it to fall back a short distance, when two regiments of the Second Brigade, Colonel Dick commanding, formed on our right, and detachments of the different regiments of my brigade, chiefly of the Seventy-ninth Indiana, brought off the battery of four guns, which was taken to the rear and saved. The capture of this battery was timely, as it had fired a few rounds of shell and was, when taken, double-shotted with canister. The enemy continued to extend his lines past our right, and the falling back of the Second Brigade again exposed my right to a galling and destructive fire, under which I caused a change of front to the rear, on the left, in which position my men were exposed to the fire not only of the enemy, but of a battery of our own (reported to be the Nineteenth Indiana Battery, Captain Harris) upon my lines, which were falling back to take a new position, and killing some of my men, broke the lines into disorder. (Upon being informed that he was firing upon our own men, the commanding officer reported that he was ordered to do so.) A large portion of my command rallied in rear of this and the battery of Capt. George R. Swallow, Seventh Indiana, which were posted in a cleared field to the right of the road, but was soon again outflanked by the enemy, and retired to the crest of a hill in rear of that position and about 600 yards from the road, where, by order of the general commanding the division, we bivouacked for the night.

About 7 o'clock on the morning of the 20th, I was ordered to move my brigade to position on the left of the First Division, a little retired from our bivouac of the night previous, in reserve. Rations were here drawn, and ammunition distributed.

About 9 o'clock by orders from General Van Cleve, I formed battalions in double column, and advanced in a direction forward and to the left nearly a half mile, where I was ordered to deploy in support of batteries posted in a commanding position on a hill, and soon again by his order formed double column to advance and engage the enemy.   Arriving near the woods east of the road, I threw forward skirmishers, who soon came upon two lines of infantry and artillery of Colonel Harker's brigade, First Division.   I immediately reported to the general commanding the Third Division that there were two lines of our troops before us, and was ordered by him to move my command to the left until I should find an opening in our lines, and occupy it.   The line being reported intact, I was ordered by General Van Cleve to move by the left flank and support any weak place in the line.   When in rear of the division of General Brannan, which was heavily engaged with the enemy, I received orders from General Van Cleve to halt, deploy, and have my men lie down.   The lines of my brigade were at this time but a few yards in rear of those of the troops in my front, and the four lines resembled more a column in mass than supporting lines, the rear line being exposed to the heavy fire directed on the front line.   The moving of the First Division from its position in line on our right to the left, caused a gap to be made, through which the enemy's forces poured in great numbers, and opened heavy on my flank.   At the same time the brigade in my front, reported to be of General Brannan's division, gave way, and before my men could rise to their feet, a battery of artillery and a disordered mass of infantry rushed obliquely through and over them, and completely broke my lines and confused my men with those of other brigades and divisions which were compelled to fall back at the same time.   Some of my men were wounded and disabled by being run over by the artillery and trampled by the infantry.   The Ninth Kentucky Volunteers, Col. G. H. Cram commanding, after retiring 25 or 30 yards, faced about and charged forward 150 yards, capturing a rudely constructed breastwork of logs, which they held until, completely flanked and enfiladed by the enemy, they were compelled to fall back to the line of hills, afterward held by them and in connection with other troops.

The penetration of our lines by the enemy separated me from the major part of my command and a part of my staff.   With the rest of my staff, I used every effort in my power to rally my men, but the rapid advance of the enemy on my right, rendered it impossible to effectually organize them.   Parts of the Ninth Kentucky and Seventeenth Kentucky, under their commanding officers, were rallied, and in connection with officers and men of the Nineteenth Ohio and Seventy-ninth Indiana Volunteers of my brigade, and detachments of many other regiments of other commands, made a stand and held possession of a hill by most terrific fighting until dark, when they withdrew by order and joined the army at Rossville.   The detachment of the Seventeenth Kentucky not being able to find the brigade, reported to Brigadier-General Wood, commanding First Division, until the 22d, when it rejoined the brigade and reported to me at this place.   Officers of my staff collected and organized a portion of my men at Missionary Gap, and, under direction of Major-General Negley, marched them to Rossville, where I reported them to General Van Cleve.

At 2 a. m., 21st, by orders from him, I marched my command to the cross-roads at the foot of Lookout Mountain, and later to ground we now occupy on the left flank of the defenses of Chattanooga.

My officers and men acquitted themselves with credit on Saturday, the 19th, as evidenced by the fact that two batteries were taken possession of by them, one of which was secured, but were overpowered and outflanked by greatly superior numbers and compelled to retire.

On Sunday they were thrown into confusion before brought into action, being so close to the lines they were in support of as to be swept into disorder with a mass of troops of other brigades. My regimental officers exerted themselves to their utmost to rally their men, but being constantly subject to the enemy's fire, were unable to do so effectively. The officers of my personal staff, Capt. O. O. Miller, assistant adjutant-general; Lieut. W. A. Sutherland, inspector; Lieut. Edgar J. Foster, aide-de-camp; Lieut. George G. Earl, aide-de-camp, and Lieut. Henry H. Townsend, topographical engineer, are entitled to credit for their coolness and steadiness under fire and active cheerfulness in obtaining information and carrying orders, as well as for their efforts in rallying and organizing the command. Capt. Thomas Stackpole, acting commissary of subsistence, by great exertions, brought forward supplies and issued rations on the battlefield.

My escort, under Sergt. Ezra Buchanan, of the Seventy-ninth Indiana Volunteers, carried themselves bravely and accompanied me in the thickest of the battle. For more specific items I beg to refer to the accompanying reports of regimental commanders, and for a report of casualties to the inclosed list of casualties *

I have the honor to be, very respectfully, your obedient servant,

SAMUEL BEATTY,
Brigadier-General of Volunteers, Commanding.

Capt. E. A. OTIS, *Asst. Adjt. Gen., Third Dvisiion.*

———

HDQRS. FIRST BRIG., THIRD DIV., 21ST ARMY CORPS,
Chattanooga, September 29, 1863.

CAPTAIN: In accordance with circular from headquarters Third Division, Twenty-first Army Corps, of September 28, 1863, I have to report by regiments the number of men and officers of my command taken into action on September 19, to wit:

Command.	Commissioned officers.	Enlisted men.	Total.
19th Ohio Volunteers	27	357	384
79th Indiana Volunteers	18	282	300
9th Kentucky Volunteers	26	187	213
17th Kentucky Volunteers	20	467	487
Total	91	1,293	1,384

Officers of brigade, general and staff, 6.

I respectfully state that since the battle a sufficient number of my men, who were on temporary detached duty and convalescent from hospitals, have returned, as to nearly raise my effective force to the standard before the engagements.

I am, very respectfully, your obedient servant,

SAMUEL BEATTY,
Brigadier-General, Commanding.

Capt. E. A. OTIS, *Asst. Adjt. Gen., Third Division.*

———

* Nominal list omitted; see revised statement, p. 177.

No. 181.

Report of Col. Frederick Knefler, Seventy-ninth Indiana Infantry.

HDQRS. SEVENTY-NINTH REGIMENT INDIANA VOLS.,
Before Chattanooga, Tenn., September 28, 1863.

CAPTAIN: I have the honor to report that on the 18th of September, 1863, the regiment left camp at Crawfish Spring, and marched with the brigade to Gordon's Mills, on Chickamauga Creek. The regiment was then placed in position in reserve of the Ninth and Seventeenth Kentucky Regiments, which were posted on the bank of the creek on the left of the brigade of General Wood's division. Remaining there for a short time the regiment was ordered to take a position on the left of a hill occupied by artillery. Toward dusk the regiment was ordered to move forward and take position on the left of the Thirteenth Ohio Regiment, which was supporting a section of artillery. The regiment remained there during the night. No firing occurred during all that time.

On the morning of the 19th, the regiment was again moved back to its original position, in reserve of the Ninth and Seventeenth Kentucky Regiments. About 1 o'clock on Saturday the brigade moved forward toward the left of the army. Upon arriving near the position, the regiment was placed in the front line of the brigade on the left of the Nineteenth Ohio, supported in the rear by the Seventeenth Kentucky, and ordered to keep on the line with the Nineteenth Ohio. After penetrating the woods, and shortly after the firing commenced, my attention was directed by Lieutenant Mounts to a battery in front and covering the left wing of my regiment. The order was given to disable the men and horses; the battery was covered with a heavy fire; the order to charge was given, which was promptly obeyed, and the battery captured. It consisted of four guns and caissons. The artillery officer commanding it surrendered to me, and, together with the men who were not killed or wounded, were sent to the rear as prisoners. The horses with but few exceptions were killed or wounded, lying in the traces perfectly unmanageable. The regiment here suffered considerable loss, but not what it might have been had opportunity been given the enemy to discharge the pieces, as upon examination by our artillery officers they proved to be double shotted with canister.

Before we had time to remove the guns, the brigade was flanked on the right and compelled to give way. The regiment fell back on a line with the Nineteenth Ohio, which was on the right, but immediately making a stand, I sent men to haul out the guns to prevent the enemy, who were rapidly approaching, from taking possession and using them. We succeeded in bringing them out by hand, with the assistance of a few men from the Ninth and Seventeenth Kentucky, and placing them on the road in rear of the brigade. After a short time, the enemy attacked the whole line in force and drove it back upon the road. The Seventh Indiana Battery and some others opened a heavy fire; a force was rallied to support the batteries, which did good work until our artillery was compelled to abandon the position, when all fell back. By dint of hard exertion I succeeded in rallying a large number of men of different commands, and placed them upon the roads in rear of the hospital, from which they were ordered by General Beatty to occupy the crest of the hill, where they remainded for the night, and were organized and put in shape. We succeeded in bringing the captured guns under a very severe fire in safety to the rear. The regiment did its duty well under the circumstances.

On Sunday morning, the 20th, the regiments of the brigade being formed in double column at half distance, were ordered to advance from the crest of the hill toward the road, being almost the same point occupied before the repulse on the preceding day. Arriving near the road the regiments were deployed and immediately marched up the hill again. Shortly afterward double column was formed again, and the brigade advanced once more upon the road, where the skirmishers reported the front covered by our troops. We were then moved by the left flank to a considerable distance, being halted several times at intermediate points. Upon arriving at the proper place the regiments were deployed in rear and only about a distance of a few yards from the lines in front of them, who commenced firing at that time. I could not ascertain to what command the front lines belonged. After some heavy firing, the lines in front gave way, throwing the brigade in confusion, making it an impossibility to keep our lines, as the men were literally trampled down and overrun by artillery. Had a sufficient space intervened, a stand could have been promptly made, but under the circumstances it was impossible to do anything. Every effort was made to rally the men, but all efforts were utterly unavailing in the confusion. After doing everything in my power, I reported to the general commanding the brigade, with whom I remained for some time aiding him in his efforts to rally the men, and with him left the field in the afternoon. I reformed the scattered men of my regiment at the crossing of the roads, when we left for Chattanooga at 2 a. m.

Inclosed I send a list of the killed, wounded, and missing.*

I have the honor to be, captain, very respectfully, your obedient servant,

FRED. KNEFLER,
Colonel Seventy-ninth Regiment Indiana Volunteers.

Capt. O. O. MILLER,
Assistant Adjutant-General, First Brigade.

No. 182.

Report of Col. George H. Cram, Ninth Kentucky Infantry.

HDQRS. NINTH REGIMENT, KENTUCKY VOL. INFTY.,
Chattanooga, Tenn., September 26, 1863.

CAPTAIN : Below you will please find a report of the part my regiment took in the battles at Chickamauga Creek.

On Friday, September 18, I was ordered by General Beatty to hold my regiment in readiness to move at a moment's notice, the division then being in camp at Crawfish Spring, Ga.

About 12 o'clock I moved with the brigade to Lee and Gordon's Mills, about 2 miles from the spring, when I was ordered to take a position a few yards from and facing toward Chickamauga Creek, about 300 yards north of the mill and behind a barricade of rails that had been previously built. The Seventeenth Kentucky was on my left and Colonel Harker's brigade, of General Wood's division, on my right. About dark I was ordered to move to the left to sustain a

---

* Embodied in revised statement, p. 177.

portion of the line, which, as the firing indicated, was receiving a heavy attack. I moved at double-quick and arrived at the point indicated just as the firing ceased, the enemy having been repulsed. I remained there until next morning, September 19, when I was ordered back to the position near the mills. Skirmishing began early in the day, extending along our entire front, and about 11 o'clock the battle seemed to open very heavy on our left, and about 12 o'clock I was ordered by General Beatty to move by the left flank and at double-quick. I was conducted to the left about 2 miles, halted in the road, ordered to form on the left of the Seventeenth Kentucky, and move on as it did. We moved forward and to the left for about a quarter of a mile, when the Seventeenth opened fire. I moved up quickly to the position assigned me, but found that the Seventeenth Kentucky in moving forward had somewhat changed the direction of its line. I also found the Seventy-fifth [Seventy-ninth?] Indiana engaged on my left and partially covering my front. To take a position between the two regiments, it was necessary to change front; as the firing was very heavy, I did not think it safe to attempt it, so I ordered the men to lie down. The Seventy-fifth [Seventy-ninth?] Indiana soon changed its position, leaving sufficient space for my regiment between it and the Seventeenth Kentucky. I accordingly made an oblique change of front forward on my first company, moved forward to the line of battle, and commenced firing. We fired by volley and the enemy soon disappeared from our front. After firing the first volley I discovered a full battery of the enemy's artillery about 150 yards to our front, which was disabled and had been abandoned by the enemy. A rebel regiment was attempting to remove the guns, but abandoned them after our first volley. The guns were soon moved to the rear by men from the Seventy-ninth Indiana, a few of my men assisting them.

Everything appeared to be going on well with us, when the enemy made an attack along our entire front (brigade). We repulsed them and thought our success was certain, but I soon saw our troops breaking away from our right and then from the left till my regiment stood alone. We held our position for a short time, but the enemy poured in on our right and we received a terrible flank fire. I gave the order to fall back, which we did in tolerably good order. We fell back across the road where a battery (Fourth U. S. Artillery) had taken position on a slight rise which commanded the woods in front, but here the same scene was enacted as before. The enemy poured in on our right, forcing us back over the ridge, sweeping everything before them. We fell back to the Chattanooga road and there halted. I afterward moved about three-quarters of a mile to the right and rejoined our brigade. This ended the fight of this day (Saturday).

The regiment fought splendidly and did not fall back one step without orders from me. The men were cool and their officers had the most perfect control of them. The cause of all the trouble seemed to be that there was a gap in the line of battle some distance to our right, through which the enemy could move at pleasure, flanking us.

On rejoining the brigade I was ordered by General Beatty to a position overlooking the battle-field, on a ridge some 500 yards to the rear of the road, where we bivouacked for the night.

On Sunday morning, the 20th, the division was moved from its position to one farther to the rear and right, and apparently placed in reserve. About 9 o'clock the division moved forward, the regiments in double column. The First Brigade was in two lines, the Nineteenth Ohio on the right, in the front line, the Seventy-ninth Indiana on the left, the Seventeenth Kentucky supporting the Seventy-ninth, my regiment supporting the Nineteenth Ohio. The battle was then raging fiercely, the artillery fire being very heavy. I was ordered by General Beatty to move with the brigade, maintaining my relative position to the other regiments. We moved forward and to the left until we had crossed the road before spoken of, and over which we had fallen back the day before, some 300 yards. When we seemed to be but a short distance to the rear of the line that was firing, we were ordered to lie down, which order was scarcely executed before the troops in front of us gave way and literally ran over us, carrying us back with the retreating mass some 25 yards, when we rallied and moved forward at double-quick about 150 yards and took possession of a rude breastwork of logs which had been thrown up during the night by General Davis' division.

The enemy here made a most desperate attack with infantry and artillery, but did not succeed in driving us from the position. The work did not extend but a few yards to our right, and the troops to the right of it, if there were any there, soon gave way, and we again found ourselves flanked on the right, receiving a terrible fire of infantry and artillery. After an unsuccessful attempt to change front, I ordered the regiment to fall back, which it did, pursued by the enemy. We moved to the left and rear nearly half a mile, and took position on the crest of a hill overlooking the road and a flat valley, and with the fragments of several other regiments made a most desperate and successful resistance against all attempts to take the hill. From about 1 until 4 o'clock the enemy kept up an almost constant fire of musketry. Taking advantage of a short lull in the firing, I ordered barricades of such material as was most convenient to be built on the crest of the hill, and logs, stumps, and rails were scarcely piled up to the height of 2 feet before the enemy again made a most desperate attempt to take the hill. For half an hour the firing was the most terrific I had ever heard, my men firing during that time 60 rounds of cartridges, and it was only when the last cartridge was expended that I ordered my men to fall back. The enemy did not occupy the hill until the next morning. We moved off a short distance to the right, intending to rejoin the division, or such part of it as I might be able to find, but after getting to the Chattanooga road found that the army had fallen back to Rossville. I moved on to Rossville that night and the next day to Chattanooga, and reported to General Beatty.

The officers and men, without an exception, did their duty splendidly, and taking everything into consideration, they could not have done better. We entered the fight with but 187 guns, our largest company (A) having been detailed but two or three days before the fight came up as provost guard at division headquarters, and having a detail of 30 men absent with a supply train. Our loss sums up as follows :

Commissioned officers wounded... 5
Enlisted men killed.. 1
Enlisted men wounded... 40
Enlisted men missing 10

Total.. 56

This list of wounded only includes such as were disabled ; almost as many more were struck by spent balls and more or less injured. The majority of the wounds are slight.   All of our first day's wounded were brought to Chattanooga, and many of those who were wounded on Sunday, leaving but few in the hands of the enemy.   I have to regret the loss of my adjutant, Lieut. J. H. Shepherd, who was wounded in the first day's fight, and I suppose fell into the hands of the enemy.

Respectfully submitted.

GEO. H. CRAM,
Colonel, Comdg. Ninth Kentucky Volunteer Infantry.

Capt. O. O. MILLER,
Assistant Adjutant-General, First Brigade.

No. 183.

Report of Col. Alexander M. Stout, Seventeenth Kentucky Infantry.

HDQRS. 17TH REGIMENT KENTUCKY VOLUNTEERS,
Chattanooga, Tenn., September 24, 1863.

CAPTAIN: The following report of the operations of the regiment which I have the honor to command, from the 18th instant, when your brigade left Crawfish Spring, Ga., to the 22d instant, when my regiment rejoined the brigade at this place, is respectfully submitted:

You will recollect that, on the evening of the 18th, we took position on the north bank of Chickamauga Creek, and heard heavy skirmishing on our left during the evening and next morning until near the middle of the day.   It became evident from the roar of firearms not only that the battle had begun in earnest, but from the change in the direction that our forces were yielding ground.

Then, by your order, we moved quickly to the scene of conflict, near 2 miles distant.   Arrived there, the brigade was formed in two lines, the Seventy-ninth Indiana Volunteers on the right in the first line, and the Nineteenth Ohio Volunteers on the left, the Seventeenth Kentucky Volunteers on the right in the second line, the Ninth Kentucky Volunteers on the left.   The first line at once engaged the enemy.   The Seventy-ninth Indiana (Colonel Knefler), finding a battery of the enemy in its front, charged upon it and silenced it, but was almost immediately repulsed by the enemy and driven back through my regiment, which at once opened upon the enemy, who was partially concealed by a dense cover of underbrush. The firing on both sides was very severe, and continued for near a half hour, when the enemy fell back, still leaving the battery.   We here captured 5 prisoners, and the company skirmishers which I had thrown out on my right captured 3 more.   An order was then received from General Van Cleve, as I understood it, to advance. And I did advance to within 50 paces of the battery, when seeing that the regiment on my left had halted, my own was halted also. But a little before this advance, and after the firing had ceased, some officers and men of the Seventy-ninth Indiana advanced to take the captured artillery to the rear, when a portion of my command did likewise, and wheeled two of the pieces with the flag of the battery to the rear through my lines. The detachments from the Seventy-ninth Indiana wheeled the other two or three pieces through in the same way. In the meantime, the enemy were seen and heard moving to my right, as if to turn it; and two or three regiments from some other brigade moved from our rear to my right, when the enemy attacked them with great fury, and almost immediately turned their right, advancing and firing with great rapidity; they broke to the left and rear in great disorder. My regiment at once felt the enemy's fire upon the right flank and rear, and to escape capture fell back to the left and rear by companies; the first company first, then the second, and so on, until all were in retreat to the left and rear, the enemy in greatly superior numbers advancing and firing with great rapidity.

It was here that First Lieut. John D. Millman, a faithful and gallant officer, was killed, and Capt. J. W. Anthony was shot through the right hand. We fell back through a dense wood to a small open field of high ground, from which one of our batteries was playing upon the advancing enemy, and there we ourselves confronted him in support of the battery. We, with the aid of others, succeeded in checking his advance in our front, but we hardly had time to become aware of this success before we felt the fire right across the battery upon our right and rear.

Being again compelled to retire, we pursued the same course as before, until we reached a high and commanding ridge about 1 mile from the battle-field, where the brigade formed again and we rested for the night. By 7 o'clock on the morning of the 20th, we became aware that some of our troops had moved in our front at least a mile distant, and had engaged the enemy. The firing increased in intensity, and by 9 o'clock it became manifest that our forces were being driven. We were moved down the slope, by the general's order, in double columns, the Nineteenth Ohio on the right, and the Seventy-ninth Indiana on the left, in the first line, the Ninth Kentucky on the right, and the Seventeenth Kentucky on the left, in the second line.

When we reached a road in the valley running parallel with our line, we were quickly deployed into line of battle; the first line came at once under fire, while the second, being only about 40 paces to the rear, became almost equally exposed. The enemy in overwhelming numbers were advancing and firing rapidly, and at the same time turning our right. Our retreating forces in our front were running over us; we were between the enemy and open ground, while they were concealed by a dense cover of underbrush. The Nineteenth Ohio soon broke to the left and rear across my right, while the shots of the enemy began to pour into my right and rear directly down the road. It was impossible then to change my front, for a battery of our artillery was passing through my line to the rear, and the uproar was so great, and the dust and smoke so dense, that the officers could scarcely be seen or heard. We were compelled to fall back or be captured, as we were without support. Here Lieutenant-Colonel Vaughan received a shot through the leg, while gallantly doing his duty, and was carried off the field. Sergeant-Major Duncan was here shot through both legs, and was saved. With the major, adjutant, and colors, and about 100 men I moved to the left and rear, several times halting and firing a volley at the enemy, but in every instance outflanked until we reached the crest of a high ridge running from north to south and then turning at right angles and running westward. There we found fragments of various commands, including a small portion of General Brannan's division. These were hastily formed along the crest and preparations made to hold the position. It was immediately between the battle-ground and this place. The enemy soon appeared, when our little force opened fire upon him with great spirit—the most of the company officers of my regiment were with me. Captain Nall and several others, who had picked up guns, fought with their men. The men as well as officers seemed to be sensible of the importance of holding the position. Our little force, increased to some 1,500, Colonel Cram and Lieutenant-Colonel Bailey, of the Ninth Kentucky, with a small portion of that regiment, took a position and held it until dark. A few men of the Nineteenth Ohio and Seventy-ninth Indiana were also with my small command. By hard, determined fighting, the enemy was held back until late in the evening, when a part of General Granger's command arrived and took position on our right and engaged the enemy just as he was about to turn our right. A desperate fight ensued and lasted until nearly dark. Our little fight on the crest I must consider as the most brilliant of the two days' battle. Thousands of the enemy were there driven against us.

Colonel Walker, of General Brannan's command; Col. George P. Buell, of the Fifty-eighth Indiana, commanding First Brigade, First Division, Twenty-first Army Corps; Lieutenant-Colonel Stoughton, commanding Twenty-first Ohio, and Maj. D. M. Claggett, of my own regiment, attracted my attention and excited my admiration by the fearless manner in which they encouraged and directed officers and men along our line. Colonel Walker had no command of his own, Colonel Buell a very small one, but rendered great service to all commands by their confidence and enthusiasm. Of my own regiment, I am unwilling to single out by name any company officers when all did so well during the two days. I cannot name one of them who acted badly. The men fought gallantly when they had a chance to fight, as I knew they would. While fighting for the rebel battery, they stood without flinching under a most deadly fire. There one company (D, Captain Gist), of 41 men, had 11 wounded.

We went into battle on both days under great disadvantages. Each day we were thrown suddenly under fire to support troops who were being driven pell-mell over us by the enemy in superior numbers and flushed with success, and always outflanked.

The firing having ceased, at night on the 20th, not knowing where to find our brigade, I reported to Brig. Gen. T. J. Wood, commanding First Division, Twenty-first Army Corps, who had moved his command near us. At his instance I joined myself to his First Brigade, commanded by Colonel Buell. In a few minutes we commenced to move in this direction, and bivouacked near Rossville that night.

Next morning we moved to the left up and along the mountain range bounding the Chattanooga Valley on the east; took position and remained until 11 o'clock that night, when we moved within a mile of this place and camped.

On the morning of the 22d, we joined you here. I had sent out an officer on the 21st to find you, and he returned after night with an order from you to join the brigade at once, but General Wood detained us. General Wood and Colonel Buell treated us with great kindness. My men had shot away their 60 rounds of ammunition, and were out of rations. They bountifully supplied us with both, and made us feel at home.

My losses are as follows: One officer killed; 2 wounded severely. Of enlisted men, 7 killed, 95 wounded, and 16 missing. Total casualties, 121. I send herewith a list of them.*

Respectfully,

A. M. STOUT,
Colonel, Commanding.

Capt. O. O. MILLER,
Assistant Adjutant-General, First Brigade.

No. 184.

Report of Lieut. Col. Henry G. Stratton, Nineteenth Ohio Infantry.

HDQRS. NINETEENTH OHIO INFANTRY VOLUNTEERS,
Chattanooga, Tenn., September 24, 1862.

CAPTAIN: I have the honor to submit the following report of the operations of my regiment in the battles of the 19th and 20th, and up to the 23d instant:

Near midday of the 18th instant, we left our bivouac near Crawfish Spring under orders received from General S. Beatty, marching to the vicinity of Lee and Gordon's Mills, and taking position in line of battle upon the left of General Wood's division, upon the Chattanooga and La Fayette road. We remained in this position until dark, when we moved under orders to a position about one-half mile to the left and down the same road, in rear of a barricade hastily constructed of rails. Here we remained under arms during that night and until about 1 p. m. of the 20th, supporting the Third Wisconsin Battery stationed on our right.

About 1 p. m. of the 20th, under orders received from Brigadier-General Beatty, I moved my regiment in quick and double-quick time down the Chattanooga and La Fayette road, in the direction of heavy firing, artillery and musketry, a distance of about 2 miles. Here I formed line of battle in the skirts of a thick woods, and immediately moved forward, engaging the enemy, driving them steadily before us under a heavy fire of infantry and artillery. Obtaining sight of the battery, I immediately gave the order to charge upon it, which was promptly and gallantly responded to by the men, and in connection with the Seventy-ninth Indiana Volunteers, of our brigade, formed on our left, we took possession of this battery of six guns. My regiment captured about 20 prisoners, who were sent to the rear. Discovering the enemy passing in force to my right, I ordered a halt, and was very soon joined on the right by troops from the Second Brigade of our division. My right support giving way, I was ordered to fall back and take position in rear of the Ninth Kentucky Volunteers, then in line a few rods to my left. I remained in this position under a heavy fire of rebel infantry until ordered to fall back, the enemy having again succeeded in turning our right flank. I was retiring my men in good order until one of our batteries stationed upon the hill across the road in our rear opened fire, several of their shots striking the center of my battalion

---

*Omitted; see revised statement. p. 177.

and killing and wounding a number of my men. This created considerable confusion in the ranks and the men became somewhat scattered. I succeeded in rallying most of the regiment in rear of the batteries, from which place we were forced again to retire, and take position upon a second crest near the Rossville road. Here we bivouacked and remained until the morning of the 20th.

Early on the morning of the 20th, our forces being engaged with the enemy, we moved in column of divisions at half distance to the front one-half mile, under orders from Brigadier-General Beatty. After changing position to the left several times, I was finally ordered to deploy column in rear of two lines of troops and a battery. The troops in our front shortly afterward became warmly engaged with the enemy, but, after a brief resistance, retired in confusion, the battery breaking through and disorganizing my line. My men became confused and scattered as a consequence, and I did not succeed in rallying them again in a body until evening. They rallied in squads, however, and remained on the field until dark, fighting with fragments of other regiments. Having collected my command, less the killed and wounded, at Missionary Gap near Rossville, on the evening of the 20th we bivouacked until 2 a. m. of the 21st, when we moved under orders from General S. Beatty to the outskirts of Chattanooga upon the east side of the town.

On the morning of the 22d, commenced throwing up earthworks for the defense of our position, the labor on which has been diligently prosecuted until this evening, September 23, night and day, when they were pronounced finished.

The casualties in my command, during the period mentioned in this report, will be found in the tabular statement hereto annexed.*

To Maj. James M. Nash, for his valuable aid, assistance, and advice, and to the officers generally for their hearty support, I return my sincere thanks. To the non-commissioned officers and privates, with very few exceptions, all praise is due. I cannot forbear mentioning the gallant conduct of the color guard. Nobly they stood to their post; 6 out of 7 were wounded.

Respectfully, yours,

HENRY G. STRATTON,
Lieut. Col., Comdg. 19th Regiment Ohio Vol. Infty.

Capt. O. O. MILLER,
Assistant Adjutant-General, First Brigade.

No. 185.

Report of Lieut. Samuel M. McDowell, Twenty-sixth Pennsylvania Battery.

CHATTANOOGA, *September* 26, 1863.

SIR: After the Third Division reached Crawfish Spring, on Tuesday, the 15th, the Third Brigade, with the Pennsylvania battery, marched 2 miles beyond that place, where they lay in camp until Friday, the 18th, when we were ordered by Colonel Barnes, commanding the brigade, to be in readiness to move out quickly, as the enemy's pickets were closing in on ours. We had barely got hitched up when

---

* See revised statement, p. 177.

the enemy commenced shelling us. We instantly moved back on a high hill, where we remained for orders. In a short time the section I commanded was ordered to the extreme right, to cover a hill where it was feared the rebels would plant a battery. In a short time the enemy's skirmishers advanced and drove ours back. I was then told to fire, which I did, and our men soon had possession of the hill again, which we held until relieved by a brigade from another division. We were then ordered back to join our division, which we found at Gordon's Mills. The Pennsylvania battery was ordered into line with the First Brigade and remained in that position until daylight Saturday, when it was ordered to move farther to the right by Captain Swallow, chief of artillery. After remaining here for some two hours there was a rebel battery posted in the woods opposite, which commenced firing. As soon as its position was known, the Pennsylvania battery was ordered to silence it, which was soon done, as it left shortly after firing a few rounds.

After this we lay still until noon, when the captain received orders to move to the front with the First Brigade. When there we moved by the right flank and formed in line in the rear of the Seventeenth and Ninth Kentucky Regiments.

I was told by Captain Stevens to follow up closely, but not to fire, as there was another line of infantry in front of us. We followed on in this way for a quarter of a mile, always obliquing to the left when the enemy seemed to make a stand. Captain Stevens then ordered the four smooth-bore guns, by hand, to the front, to be ready to open with canister should they drive our first line back. We had scarcely got the first guns forward when we found we were in the front line and always had been there since leaving the road.

We commenced firing canister as fast as we could, but it was impossible to check them. The regiment on the right of us fell back through the battery, and by the time the battery had limbered up, the horses of three pieces were nearly all shot and one limber blown up. The right half battery, being a little in the rear, had time to limber up and fall back with the infantry. When out of the woods, I met General Beatty, who ordered me to form on a small hill in front and open on them. We remained here until our ammunition was all expended, and not being able to find any more, were compelled to fall to the rear. One of the pieces here, in getting away, had the pole broken or shot away, and not having men enough to pull it off, had to be left. When we were back in the woods, I was ordered to follow the Ninth Kentucky Regiment, and fell back on the Chattanooga road about a mile, but in a short time moved up to the front again, where we found the Seventh Indiana Battery, and went into camp for the night. At this place we received two smooth-bore cannon, which had been taken from the rebels.

Sunday, 20th, the Pennsylvania battery, about 9 o'clock, was ordered to the right in rear of the First Brigade, but in a short time was moved over to the left in a line with the Seventh Indiana Battery, and with it moved forward after the infantry for about 500 yards, when the battery was ordered by the left flank and moved at a double-quick for nearly a half a mile, but, before we came into position, we were ordered to countermarch and come back about half the distance, when we went into position, but were ordered not to fire by Major Mendenhall until we could see the rebels coming out of the woods, and by that time we were receiving a galling fire from the rebel infantry on our right flank.

We fired all the canister we had and were ordered to limber up, but it was too late; 11 horses of the right section were killed and wounded, and the bushes so thick that we could not draw off the pieces by hand. One piece on the left got out with the limber, and to the fourth we fixed the prolonge, and with the help of some infantry we succeeded in getting out, thus saving two pieces of the four we took into action in the morning. The losses of the Pennsylvania battery are as follows:

Officers killed, 1 (Capt. A. J. Stevens); enlisted men killed, 1; officers wounded, 1; enlisted men wounded, 13; enlisted men missing, 1; horses killed, 37; guns lost, 4; limbers lost, 5; sets wheel harness lost, 5; sets lead harness lost, 10.

I cannot tell how much ammunition was expended, as Captain Stevens drew a supply on Sunday morning of which I have no account.

Yours, respectfully,

S. M. McDOWELL,
First Lieutenant Independent Pennsylvania Battery.

Capt. G. R. SWALLOW,
Chief of Artillery, Third Division.

No. 186.

Report of Col. George F. Dick, Eighty-sixth Indiana Infantry, commanding Second Brigade.

HDQRS. SECOND BRIG., THIRD DIV., 21ST ARMY CORPS,
Chattanooga, September 28, 1863.

CAPTAIN: I have the honor to submit the following as a report of operations of my brigade since the 7th instant (having previously been detached from division to hold the post of McMinnville):

On the afternoon of the 7th, I crossed the Tennessee River at Bridgeport, Ala., and encamped on its eastern bank.

On the 8th, I marched 14 miles, and halted for the night at a narrow gap in Raccoon Mountain called Whiteside's. On the following day a march of 16 miles on the Trenton road brought me within 10 miles of Chattanooga.

On the 10th, I crossed the Lookout Mountain after a considerable delay, occasioned by the difficulty of getting a large supply train, which was moving in front of my column, over the road.

At the Widow Gillespie's, I halted until my brigade train should come up, for the purpose of complying with the order for the reduction of baggage. This caused a delay until 4 p. m., when I again moved forward, reaching Rossville at sunset. Here a courier came in, reporting that about 60 rebel cavalry had attacked a portion of General Wood's supply train about 2 miles ahead. I immediately ordered the Thirteenth Ohio, Fifty-ninth Ohio, and Forty-fourth Indiana Regiments, with a section of the Third Wisconsin Battery, on the double-quick, to drive back the raiders, leaving the Eighty-sixth Indiana as guard to my own train. After double-quicking a little more than 2 miles, the Fifty-ninth Ohio, being in front, came up to the train, when the enemy withdrew. The road being now clear, I moved my column forward, and at 11 p. m. I came up to General Wood's encampment on the Chickamauga Creek, where I bivouacked for the night.

At 5 o'clock next a. m., I was ordered forward to rejoin the division, which order I complied with, arriving at division headquarters, 5 miles from Ringgold, Ga., at about 7 a. m., when I reported to Brigadier-General Van Cleve.

At 9 a. m. I moved with the division in the direction of Ringgold. Marching with the division, I went with it into camp on Dogwood Creek, 2½ miles south of Ringgold, on the Dalton road.

On the morning of the 12th instant, I marched with the division to Gordon's Mills, 15 miles from our camp of the night previous, and encamped.

On the morning of Sunday, 13th, I was ordered to follow the First Brigade in the direction of La Fayette. After marching a mile and a half, the First Brigade becoming engaged with the enemy's cavalry, under Wheeler, I was ordered to deploy my brigade in an open field, in front of the house of Mr. Henderson, to be ready to support General Beatty, if necessary. After having driven the enemy 2½ miles, the First Brigade was ordered to withdraw, when I was ordered to deploy a regiment to protect the division in its retrograde movements. Having deployed the Thirteenth Ohio, under Lieut. Col. E. M. Mast, as skirmishers, I withdrew my other three regiments and followed the division into camp north of Gordon's Mills.

On the 14th, I marched with the division down the Chattanooga Valley, 6 miles, and encamped.

On the 15th, I marched with division to Crawfish Spring, where we lay in camp that and the two following days and nights.

On the 18th, I was ordered to move back to Gordon's Mills, where I was ordered to form entire lines, fronting toward the southeast, in order to support General Wood, who was engaging the enemy with infantry and artillery. I had been in this position scarce an hour when I was ordered to support General Wood on his extreme left, which was exposed and threatened, with two of my strongest regiments. After placing the Thirteenth Ohio in support of a section of artillery, in a barricade constructed of rails, on the brow of a hill about 300 yards east of the Chattanooga road, and the Fifty-ninth Ohio on their right, a little retired, I was ordered to report with the Forty-fourth Indiana and Fifty-ninth Ohio (the Eighty-sixth Indiana, under command of Maj. J. C. Dick, taking the late position of the Fifty-ninth Ohio) to Colonel Wilder, whose brigade had fallen back from the Chickamauga fords to within a mile of General Wood's left, "to support him and hold the road at all hazards." I reported forthwith to Colonel Wilder, who ordered me to his right, to hold the approaches from the two fords which intersected the main road at the house of Mr. McDonald. I immediately placed the Forty-fourth Indiana on the fork of the road leading from the lower ford, and the Fifty-ninth Ohio upon the other (in the woods, 500 yards east of the main road), leaving an interval of 150 yards between the regiments. I remained quietly in this position until an hour after dark.

The advance of the enemy then showed themselves to the cavalry skirmishers, who had been thrown out in front of my regiments. They were immediately driven back. Another half hour of quiet elapsed, when the enemy again appeared, and in force of at least one brigade, on foot, in front of the Fifty-ninth Ohio. Having first driven in the mounted skirmishers, the Fifty-ninth, commanded by

Lieutenant-Colonel Frambes, permitted him to approach within 50 yards, when they poured a deadly volley into him and broke his line in front; but the enemy's superior numbers enabled him to sweep around on Colonel Frambes' flanks, when the colonel retired in good order to a ravine in a corn-field 150 yards in rear of his first position. There being little or no firing in front of the Forty-fourth Indiana, Lieutenant-Colonel Aldrich commanding, kept his position until I ordered him in line with Colonel Frambes. The line thus formed remained undisturbed until 4 a. m. of the 19th, when Colonel Wilder ordered me to fall back to the Chattanooga road in order that daylight might not discover my exposed position to the superior force of the enemy. I then placed my two regiments on the left of the road in the edge of a dense wood, fronting an open field, toward the north. I immediately ordered the position to be strengthened by throwing up a barricade of rails and logs in front of my line, and remained there until 1 p. m., when the Thirteenth Ohio and Eighty-sixth Indiana were ordered to rejoin me, when I was ordered forward with the division.

At this time, General Thomas being hard pressed, I was ordered forward on double-quick, and to form in two lines in rear of and to support the First Brigade on General Thomas' right. But the First Brigade having obliqued to the left, and my front line, composed of the Fifty-ninth Ohio and Forty-fourth Indiana, being uncovered, was immediately engaged and gallantly drove the first line of the enemy back to his second, where he made a stand. I again charged him until I found a superior force from his rear was marching rapidly past my right flank through an interval of more than a half mile, occasioned by General Davis' division swinging too far off in that direction. I was then compelled to retire my first to my second line, composed of the Eighty-sixth Indiana and Thirteenth Ohio, which was done with but little confusion and under a most galling fire. My brigade being now in one line, with the Fifty-ninth Ohio on the right and the Thirteenth Ohio on the left, I was ordered to form on General Beatty's second line, which was immediately done. The enemy was soon advancing upon us, but received a withering volley which confused and halted him in my immediate front, but again he brought from his rear a heavy column, by the right flank and on double-quick, and threw it upon my right. I was now under fire on my front, right, and rear, and was compelled again to fall back, this time, more rapidly and in more confusion than at first. At this critical moment, Lieut. Frank H. Woods, my efficient and energetic acting inspector-general, was mortally wounded by a Minie ball while gallantly endeavoring to rally the crumbling ranks on my right. Here also was the brave Lieutenant-Colonel Mast, commanding the Thirteenth Ohio Volunteers, instantly killed while encouraging his men to hold their ground, and Major Snider, of the same regiment, severely wounded; thus leaving the regiment in command of the senior captain (Cosgrove). I now rallied my command 400 or 500 yards west of the road on a ridge, and for a short time supported a part of the Twenty-sixth Pennsylvania Battery. Having the enemy still on my right, I was compelled to fall still farther back to another and higher ridge, taking advantage of a thin wood on its top. Here I soon collected the greater part of the brigade, when, the firing having nearly subsided, I marched back in good order to the Crawfish Spring road to rejoin the division. The division having reformed, I marched with it to the support of batteries on the ridge.

Sunday, the 20th, early in the morning, I was ordered to form in column in rear of the First Brigade as reserve on the side of a ridge on the west side of the road, and one-half mile farther south than the position of last night. Here I supplied my command with rations and rested until 9 a.m. I was now ordered to form in close column of division in two lines and move with General Beatty—on his left. The division then moved back to the barricade on the first ridge east of the Crawfish Spring road, and advanced through an open field down the eastern slope of the ridge. After marching thus about 500 yards, and on entering a wood, I was ordered to move by the left flank in order to get in supporting distance of General Thomas' right. In accordance with an order from General Van Cleve, I then deployed my column and formed in two lines, with the Fifty-ninth Ohio Volunteers and the Forty-fourth Indiana in the first line, and the Thirteenth Ohio and Eighty-sixth [Indiana] in the second line, and moved forward until my first line came up with General Brannan's second line.

I was then ordered to move on double-quick by the left flank to the support of some artillery said to be in position in the woods. I moved thus on double-quick 500 or 600 yards, when, seeing no artillery and receiving no further orders from General Van Cleve, I halted in rear of, and forming a second line to, and supporting Colonel Van Derveer. Colonel Stanley's brigade on the left of Colonel Van Derveer being soon hard pressed, I went to his support, but after firing a short time his line gave way in confusion, and retreated in disorder over my command lying on the ground. This uncovered my line and caused it to become somewhat confused, but having partially recovered, I gave the enemy a galling fire for more than fifteen minutes. I was soon overwhelmed by a far greater force of the enemy; and the troops on my right having been withdrawn, I fell back in some disorder. Here the worthy Captain Gunsenhouser, of the Forty-fourth Indiana, was killed instantly while fearlessly keeping his company together under the most severe fire. Here Brigadier-General Adams, of Texas [Louisiana], was wounded and captured.

Again I rallied a portion of my command on the brow of a hill 500 yards to the rear, while Lieutenant-Colonel Aldrich, of the Forty-fourth Indiana, rallied the remainder in another part of the field. He immediately went to the support of General Wood, which I understand he did with much skill and gallantry, doing much credit to himself and good service to his country. With my portion of the brigade, I remained in support of a battery in position on the hill for an hour, when I marched farther to the left, in order to reform and get my command in better organization. This occupied but little time, when I went to the support of General Brannan, who was hard pressed on a ridge between the two roads and fronting toward the south, being on the extreme right of our whole line. Here I held the enemy in check until he succeeded in planting a battery still farther to my right on a ridge commanding my position, with which he raked my line with an enfilading fire, while he again threw a fresh line of infantry upon my exposed flank, which compelled me to again fall back. I now found the greater part of our army falling back, and I myself fell back through the woods, gathering as many stragglers from the Twenty-first Army Corps as possible. Having gone nearly 1 mile, I struck the Chattanooga road, where my disordered troops were again attacked by the enemy's cavalry. I then marched down the Chattanooga road another mile, and, halting in a large open field on the left, I succeeded in collecting together nearly 600 men of the division, and was ordered by Lieutenant-Colonel Lodor, of General Crittenden's staff, to march into Chattanooga. On nearing Rossville, I learned that General Van Cleve had established his headquarters there, and sent forward to notify him of my approach. I then received orders and went into camp with division at Rossville.

At 1 a. m. of the 21st instant, I marched with the division on the Valley road, arriving at Chattanooga at 4 a. m., and bivouacked until daylight, when I again moved with the division to a ridge on the left of Fort Cheatham and 1 mile east of town, resting in line until 1 p. m. Three of my regiments were then ordered to occupy and hold the approaches to the town; respectively, the Thirteenth Ohio on Missionary Ridge at the gap of same name, the Forty-fourth Indiana at Shallow Ford Gap, one-half mile to the left of the Thirteenth Ohio, each 4 miles from town, and the Fifty-ninth Ohio at Chickamauga Bridge, 6½ miles out and 3 miles to the left of the Forty-fourth Indiana, the first two regiments being in command of Lieutenant-Colonel Aldrich, of the Forty-fourth Indiana, and the latter in command of Lieutenant-Colonel Frambes, while the Eighty-sixth Indiana, in command of Maj. J. C. Dick, was placed as a reserve to the line of pickets in our front. For the operations of my regiments while thus detached, you are referred to the reports of their commanding officers, copies of which are herewith forwarded. The Forty-fourth Indiana and Thirteenth Ohio, under Colonel Aldrich, held the gaps until noon of the 22d unmolested, when they were attacked by a brigade of the enemy's cavalry, dismounted. The Thirty-ninth Indiana, in command of Colonel Harrison, mounted infantry, being unable to protect his flanks, Colonel Aldrich retired from his position, in accordance with orders from Colonel Swaine, commanding the outposts, and fell back in good order, fighting, reaching our picket line at 1 p. m. I then assigned the two regiments of Lieutenant-Colonel Aldrich positions behind the railroad, with the Eighty-sixth Indiana, about 100 yards in rear of the line of sentinels. I remained quietly in this position until about 4 p. m., at which time the enemy was observed getting a battery in position on the railroad, about 600 yards to my left, and immediately opened upon my line. This caused some confusion, when I was ordered by Colonel Swaine to fall back inside the fortifications, which I did in good order. I was then ordered to relieve the pickets with the Forty-fourth Indiana and Eighty-sixth Indiana. I went forward and deployed the Eighty-sixth Indiana as sentinels or skirmishers, relieving the old line, and left the Forty-fourth Indiana in reserve in two battalions. Soon heavy skirmishing commenced along my whole line, but I maintained my position until 12 p. m., when I was relieved by the Ninety-ninth Ohio and Seventy-ninth Indiana, and marched within the fortifications and bivouacked, finding my command in an exhausted condition.

At 2 p. m., finding my enemy in considerable force in the valley west of Missionary Ridge, I endeavored to communicate with the Fifty-ninth Ohio at the Chickamauga Bridge in order to have them fall back, knowing he would soon be in Colonel Frambes' rear. To this end I sent one of my staff officers with Colonel Harrison and 200 mounted infantry, who offered to go to Colonel Frambes' assistance. He was enabled to go out but a mile, when he came upon a force of the enemy. His ammunition being exhausted, he could not go farther.   Colonel Frambes was then left to fight his way back as best he could, which he did with bravery and remarkable coolness, cutting his way through two lines of the surrounding enemy, composed of dismounted cavalry and artillery, and leaving only 14 men and 2 officers in his hands.

Of my command, as a whole, it is due to say that during the whole of the different engagements in which they bore a part, they acted nobly, and fought with the greatest coolness and bravery— but very few were found skulking in rear of their places—always driving the enemy in their front, and only falling back when he succeeded in gaining their flank, which was so often exposed, or were thrown into disorder by our own men running over and through them.   When thus driven back, each man seemed to seek only a position where he might do something to check the enemy or rejoin his command.

Of my officers I think I am saying much when I can report each of them as having done his whole duty.   I am under especial obligations to the officers commanding my different regiments: Lieutenant-Colonel Aldrich, Forty-fourth Indiana; Lieutenant-Colonel Mast, Major Snider, and Captain Cosgrove, Thirteenth Ohio; Lieutenant-Colonel Frambes, Fifty-ninth Ohio, and Maj. Jacob C. Dick, Eighty-sixth Indiana, for their hearty co-operation and promptness with which they executed every order given them.   I must here particularly mention the respective members of my staff: Capt. C. F. King, acting assistant adjutant-general; Lieut. Frank H. Woods, acting inspector-general (until mortally wounded at 4 p. m. of the 19th), and Lieut. F. F. Kibler, topographical engineer, were ever active in using their utmost exertions to assist me in carrying my brigade through its many evolutions, and each was ever ready to and did carry orders to the different regimental commanders in the thickest of the fight.   Through the energetic action of Surg. A. C. McChesney my wounded and those of the division that came under his charge were well cared for, and in the retreat but few were left in the hands of the enemy.

Although the battle of Chickamauga has been the severest and bloodiest in which my command has been engaged, and although it has suffered greater than ever and was driven back by superior forces, their spirits are unbroken, and they are now ready to again meet the enemy whenever called upon.

The following is the aggregate of casualties and losses sustained by my command during the time included in this report:

Officers and men.	Killed.	Wounded.	Missing.	Total.
Commissioned officers	5	15	2	22
Enlisted men	11	161	71	243
Total	16	176	73	265

All of which is respectfully submitted.

G. F. DICK,
Colonel, Comdg. 2d Brig., 3d Div., 21st Army Corps.

Capt. E. A. Otis,
    Assistant Adjutant-General, Third Division.

[Inclosure.]

Report of the effective force of the Second Brigade taken into action on the 19th day of September, 1863, Col. George F. Dick commanding.

Command.	Headquarters.			Infantry.			Total.		
	Commissioned officers.	Enlisted men.	Total.	Commissioned officers.	Enlisted men.	Total.	Commissioned officers.	Enlisted men.	Aggregate.
[Headquarters]...	8	30	38	.....	.....	......	8	30	38
44th Indiana Volunteers, Lieut. Col. S. C. Aldrich.	..	.....	....	27	202	229	27	202	229
59th Ohio Volunteers, Lieut. Col. G. A. Frambes.	.....	.....	....	17	273	290	17	273	290
13th Ohio Volunteers, Lieut. Col. E. M. Mast.....	.....	.....	....	18	286	304	18	286	304
86th Indiana Volunteers, Maj. J. C. Dick.........	.....	.....	....	20	241	261	20	241	261
Total	8	30	38	82	1,002	1,084	90	1,032	1,122

G. F. DICK,
Colonel, Commanding.

No. 187.

Report of Lieut. Col. Simeon C. Aldrich, Forty-fourth Indiana Infantry.

CAMP 44TH REGT. INDIANA INFANTRY VOLUNTEERS,
Chattanooga, September 27, 1863.

COLONEL : In compliance with orders, I herewith submit a report of the part my regiment took in the series of battles near this point. I shall not notice minor points, but confine myself to important acts and facts :

On the 18th, my regiment and the Fifty-ninth Ohio were ordered about 3 miles to the left of our camp at Crawfish Spring, to support Colonel Wilder. We reached the point designated and formed in line of battle, in the after-part of the day, in a wood in front of an open field. Here our cavalry was driven in a little after dusk. I kept my line, expecting to see the enemy's cavalry approach, but they not showing themselves, and being left alone, you ordered me to fall back to a new line that was forming in the field. Here we remained till near daylight next morning. When the rest of our division came up we were ordered still to the left, in line of battle, when we engaged the enemy in large force, my regiment and Fifty-ninth Ohio in front, and Thirteenth Ohio and Eighty-sixth Indiana in second line. We had a severe fight, contesting the ground inch by inch. The enemy succeeded in getting around the right flank of the Fifty-ninth Ohio, which obliged them to fall back. My regiment being on their left, and the timber thick, I did not discover the movement of the enemy till some time after the Fifty-ninth left, when, discovering that the left had also fallen back, I ordered a slow retreat, fighting our way back to a small ravine, where I rallied my men again, brought them to an about face, and advanced a short distance and poured a destructive fire into the enemy's ranks. We were again obliged to leave the field. This we did in tolerable good order, joining the remainder of our brigade on the hill opposite and to the rear of the battle-ground.

These are the main points of the engagement on Saturday, 19th. Sunday morning, after drawing rations (which part of my men did not have time to do), we were ordered to the front again. We were ordered to double column on the center, and proceed by flank and forward movements till we reached a point near where the battle was raging. We advanced along a low piece of ground, making distance to the left, till [where] we made a short halt till the enemy approached. A regiment had been engaged in our front, which was falling back, and when they came up with our brigade, being very much scattered, caused a panic with most of our brigade. I succeeded in holding the most of my men, and fought the enemy at great odds. We held them in check for some time, but on their breaking round our left I ordered a retreat, which we made in good order and went in search of our brigade.

On our march to the rear we heard to our (then) left quite heavy firing and directed our march to that point; found it to be General Wood's command contesting the possession of a hill, a very important point. We arrived very opportunely and took position with General Harker's brigade. Placing our flag on the brink of the hill, our men nobly rallied and fought like veterans. We repulsed the enemy three times with great slaughter. They finally abandoned the ground. I must say I never saw troops handled better or fight more determinedly than did Colonel Harker's brigade. We remained here till after dark, some time after the firing ceased, till the enemy fell back, when we also proceeded to the rear and reached Rossville about 10 or 11 o'clock at night.

On hearing that General Van Cleve was near the forks of the road, we moved, on the morning of the 21st, to find him and our brigade. I had found some of the Thirteenth Ohio, which I took command of the night before. I collected quite a number from different regiments by the time we reached the springs near the Chattanooga road. Here we received orders from Captain Otis to march to town, which we did. Soon after reaching town, I was ordered by you to take my regiment and Thirteenth Ohio and proceed to two gaps on Missionary Ridge. This I did, and threw up a breastwork on the right of the road on the top of the ridge. I also placed the Thirteenth Ohio in a very commanding position. We were supported by Colonel Harrison's regiment of mounted infantry.

On the 22d, about 10 a. m., our vedettes exchanged shots with the enemy's advance, which was driven back by Colonel Harrison's men. Between 11 and 12 o'clock the enemy advanced again, drove in our pickets, and appeared in force. I reserved my fire till they came in very short range, my men being completely hid. When we opened fire, the enemy were taken completely by surprise and retreated in great disorder. We repulsed them in this manner twice, with considerable loss, when, our mounted infantry giving way and the enemy appearing on our flanks, we were obliged to fall back to prevent being surrounded. This we did in good order, skirmishing all the way to the railroad.

This ended all the important engagements in which my regiment took part. I must say for my officers and men that I never saw men fight better or so few scattered. Captain Gunsenhouser, Company F, fell nobly fighting at the head of his company. No braver man ever fought; his life has been laid on the altar of his country; his example in the regiment has ever been worthy of imitation. Adjutant Hodges nobly assisted me in the management of the regiment. Captain Curtis deserves especial mention; he fought like a hero. Captains Wilson, Burch, Hildebrand, Grund, and Getty did nobly. Lieutenants of the several companies did nobly with but few exceptions. The ever faithful Surg. J. H. Rerick followed us from point to point, assisted by Dr. Carr, and I am pleased to say that no regiment had better care for their wounded than did ours. He succeeded in getting all our wounded from the hospital, which was captured on Sunday evening by the enemy. My men, with but very few exceptions, deserve great praise and have earned additional honor and glory.

I also transmit herewith a detailed statement of the casualties in the regiment:

Killed... 3
Wounded.. 59
Missing... 10
                                                                           ___
  Total *... 72

I have the honor to be, your obedient servant,
                                                S. C. ALDRICH,
          Lieutenant-Colonel, Comdg. 44th Indiana Volunteers.

Col. GEORGE F. DICK,
     Comdg. Second Brigade, Third Division.

No. 188.

Report of Maj. Jacob C. Dick, Eighty-sixth Indiana Infantry.

HDQRS. EIGHTY-SIXTH INDIANA VOLUNTEERS,
                    Chattanooga, Tenn., September 26, 1863.

CAPTAIN : I have the honor to report the following as the operations of the Eighty-sixth Indiana Volunteers since the 7th instant, on the evening of which it crossed the Tennessee River with the brigade at Bridgeport. The 8th, 9th, 10th, 11th, and 12th, as you are aware, were only occupied in marching. Nothing occurred worthy of note until we reached Lee and Gordon's Mills, and during the 13th, 14th, 15th, 16th, and 17th nothing occurred in our regiment that was not common to the brigade.

On the 18th, we were ordered out and occupied various positions in line of battle with the brigade until evening, when we were left in line on the left-hand side of the road about 1 mile north of the mills, where we remained with the Ninety-ninth Ohio and Thirteenth Ohio, all under command of Colonel Swaine, of the Ninety-ninth Ohio, until 2 p. m. of the 19th, when we were ordered forward, and joined the brigade about 2 miles up the road, leading to this place, and with it went into action, and came out with the following casualties : 24 four wounded and 8 missing.

On the 20th, we went into action again with the brigade and came out with a loss of 1 killed, 13 wounded, and 7 missing ; the regiment was considerably scattered, and did not get together entirely until the next day (21st), at this place.

---

* See revised statement, p. 177.

We rested in camp here until the morning of the 23d, when we were ordered out on picket about a mile in front of our present position, where we skirmished almost continually with the enemy until relieved on the evening of the 23d. During the night of the 23d large details from our regiment worked upon the fortifications, inside of which we are still stationed.

All I can say of the conduct of the regiment as a whole, during the recent battles, is, that it has done apparently as well as good regiments with which it has been, and of individual officers and men, that many have acted admirably.

By order of Maj. J. C. Dick, commanding Eighty-sixth Indiana:

E. D. THOMAS,
Adjutant.

Capt. CHAS. F. KING,
Acting Assistant Adjutant-General, Second Brigade.

No. 189.

Report of Capt. Horatio G. Cosgrove, Thirteenth Ohio Infantry.

HDQRS. 13TH REGT. OHIO VOLUNTEER INFANTRY,
Near Chattanooga, September 26, 1863.

SIR: I have the honor to submit the following report of the part taken by the Thirteenth Regiment Ohio Volunteer Infantry, in the battles of the 18th, 19th, and 20th instant:

At 10 a. m. we were ordered, in company with the balance of the brigade, to a position near Lee's Mills, where my regiment was detached to support a section of the Seventh Indiana Battery, on the crest of a hill near the mills, where we were relieved on the 19th by the Ninety-ninth Ohio Volunteer Infantry and ordered to the front. We joined the remainder of the brigade and division at 2 p. m. and soon after took position, with the Fifty-ninth Ohio Volunteer Infantry on our right and the Eighty-sixth Indiana Volunteers on our left. Sharp skirmishing took place between our skirmishers and the enemy until 4 p. m., when, the enemy having by a flank movement compelled the regiment on our right to give way, and having completely flanked our position, we were compelled to fall back in some disorder. The regiment was rallied near the road, when, the enemy coming upon us in overwhelming force, we were compelled again to fall back, losing many commissioned officers and men, killed or wounded, Lieutenant-Colonel Mast being of the former and Major Snider of the latter.

The commanding officer being killed, the command of the regiment devolved upon me, and I formed the regiment on the crest of a hill to the rear of our former position, and lay in line until the morning of the 20th, when the regiment occupied a position in the second line and on the left of the Eighty-sixth Indiana Volunteers, and we were marched to a position about 1 mile to the left of our position of the day before. We here lay in position nearly an hour, when my regiment was ordered to move forward and charge a battery; but the order was countermanded before the movement could be put into execution. The enemy at this time pressing us in overwhelming numbers, our line fell back, and nearly 100 of the regiment, with the colors, took position on the crest of a hill to the right of the general hospital, where we had many men killed or wounded. At dark we were ordered to vacate the hill, and fell back, in company with part of General Brannan's division, to a point 4 miles to the rear. The next morning, at daylight, we were ordered to join the division, and at 8 a. m. did so at Chattanooga. At 3 p. m. we were ordered to take possession of and hold Missionary Gap, 3 miles east of the town, and at 4 p. m. took position on the hills at and around the gap. At 8 a. m., 23d, we were attacked by the enemy's skirmishers. We held them in check until 12 m., when the enemy, by throwing a strong force on our right flank, compelled us to fall back to the foot of the hill. I had attempted to communicate with Colonel Aldrich, Forty-fourth Indiana Volunteers, on our left, but found that the enemy had cut off our communication on that side. I found the Forty-fourth Indiana nearly at the foot of the hill, having been, like ourselves, driven back by a superior force. We fell slowly back, when we were ordered by Col. G. F. Dick, commanding Second Brigade, to take position along the railroad, where we lay in line nearly an hour, when the enemy planted a piece of artillery on our left flank, completely raking us, and we were again compelled to fall back, this time to the breastworks near Chattanooga, where we still lay, with the enemy confronting us.

The men, with some exceptions, behaved nobly, and it would scarcely be just to the officers to mention only a part; but I cannot refrain from mentioning the following as especially deserving of great praise, viz: Capt. John E. Ray, for gallantry and untiring efforts in rallying the men and encouraging them; this, too, at a time when he was excused from field duty; Second Lieut. Emery Malin, acting adjutant, for invaluable services and gallant conduct on the field in rallying the men; and to Lieutenants Sieg and Henderson, for gallant and meritorious conduct.

The following officers served with the regiment during the engagement with credit to themselves: Lieutenants Smith, Schart, Coe, Thompson, Rutan, Dorman, and Blackburn.

I have the honor to be, very respectfully, your obedient servant,

H. G. COSGROVE,
Captain, Comdg. 13th Regt. Ohio Volunteer Infantry.

Capt. Chas. F. King,
Acting Assistant Adjutant-General, Second Brigade.

No. 190.

Report of Lieut. Col. Granville A. Frambes, Fifty-ninth Ohio Infantry.

Hdqrs. Fifty-ninth Ohio Volunteer Infantry,
Chattanooga, Tenn., September 26, 1863.

Captain: I have the honor to report the part which my regiment took in the late engagements since crossing the Tennessee River at Bridgeport, on the evening of the 7th instant:

On the 8th, we pushed forward and overtook the division on the 11th instant, within 8 miles of Ringgold, Ga., while in pursuit of the enemy. My regiment was with the division on the 13th instant, when it made a reconnaissance of 2 miles on the La Fayette road beyond Lee and Gordon's Mills, in which some sharp skirmishing and cannonading took place. I was deployed in line with brigade in rear of First Brigade as support, but was not actually engaged. Nothing particular occurred from this time till the 18th instant, when we were at Crawfish Spring. Then the division was ordered down to Lee and Gordon's Mills to support General Wood. I was ordered by Colonel Dick to take position on the right-hand side of the road leading from Crawfish Spring to Lee and Gordon's Mills, near the mills, with the Thirteenth Ohio on my left. I had not remained here over an hour, when Colonel Dick ordered my regiment and the Thirteenth Ohio to move down the Chattanooga road and cover the left of our line, entirely unprotected.

In the course of an hour I received an order from Colonel Dick to move my regiment, together with the Forty-fourth Indiana, down the Chattanooga road and report to Colonel Wilder, who was being hard pressed by the enemy, with orders that that road must be held at all hazards. Colonel Dick, our brigade commander, having reported to Colonel Wilder, he ordered my regiment to take position in the woods on the east side of the Chattanooga road, and on the right-hand fork on a road leading to Ringgold, just in the edge of the woods, with a corn-field between me and the Chattanooga road in my rear. I had just gotten into position when the enemy advanced on a detachment of Colonel Wilder's mounted infantry, placed in our front as skirmishers. It being but the advance of the enemy, the skirmishers succeeded in driving him back. But the enemy soon sent up a brigade of infantry, who drove the skirmishers back, but not without strong resistance.

In the meantime, my regiment was lying upon the ground in line of battle waiting his approach. When he advanced within 50 yards of my line, I gave the order to rise, fire, and charge, cheering loudly, the effect of which threw him into confusion, checked his advance, and caused him to fall back a short distance. After firing several rounds, on account of his being under cover of the woods and it now being dark, I gave the order to fall back about 100 yards to a ravine in the field, which was done in good order. I then threw out my skirmishers and remained until 4 o'clock in the morning, skirmishers occasionally firing at each other during the night. Thus ended the day, with 1 man severely wounded and 2 in the hands of the enemy, who, fortunately, effected their escape in the night. During the night circumstances convinced me that the enemy was in our immediate front in force. I reported these facts to Colonels Wilder, Dick, and Minty, and stated that our line was too weak to hold the position we then occupied, and that we had better fall back across the open field to the Chattanooga road before daylight and avoid the necessity of being driven back in the morning. Colonels Wilder and Dick then ordered me to fall back and take position on the west side of the Chattanooga road in the edge of the woods and put my skirmishers along the road.

At daylight of the 19th instant, sharp picket firing commenced across the open field. I constructed temporary breastworks of logs and rails to protect myself in the front (in case of an attack, which was ominous) to the best advantage possible. In this position, I remained until about noon, when Colonel Dick ordered me to fall in with the balance of the brigade and move out with the division to meet the enemy, who had engaged a part of our force on the extreme left. We had not moved over half a mile down the Chattanooga road till I received an order from Colonel Dick to form my regiment on the right by file into line, with the Forty-fourth Indiana on my left, and to advance in line of battle into the woods, and be sure to keep my left in line with and joined to the Forty-fourth Indiana.

I had not advanced over 300 yards when my regiment became engaged with the enemy, well positioned in a depression in the woods. I kept up an incessant fire, and advanced steadily all the time, driving the enemy slowly before me until he reached his second line, when he came to a stand. I then ordered my regiment forward on double-quick, cheering heartily as we went, which caused the enemy to give way in confusion in my front. I then observed that my line was in advance of the remainder of the line, and my right flank was unprotected by an interval of half a mile caused by the force on my right not connecting with me. I then halted and had to lie down and fire at will. Shortly after I gave this order I discovered that the enemy was flanking me on my right and the line on my left was falling back rapidly, which left me in great danger of being captured. I then gave the order to fall back. My regiment fell back in order about half way to the road, when I moved it by the left flank a short distance and then forward and joined the Thirteenth Ohio on its right and engaged the enemy vigorously, but my right flank being exposed, the enemy took advantage of it and charged upon us with an overwhelming force, which caused my regiment to fall back with the whole line in confusion. I succeeded in rallying a part of the regiment behind a line of artillery stationed on a ridge in an open field on the west side of the Chattanooga road. Here we succeeded in checking him by the aid of artillery and the stubborn fighting of the fragments of several different regiments for some time, but was finally forced to give way. I then fell back to the Crawfish Spring road, about a half mile, where, with the brigade, I camped during the night. Thus closed the day's fighting of my regiment, in which I had 1 officer and 2 men mortally wounded, 1 officer and 32 men wounded, and 5 men missing.

Sunday, 20th, after drawing rations for my regiment, I moved out in column of division by order of Colonel Dick, with the brigade in column, and on the right of the Forty-fourth Indiana, and, crossing the field in our front, bearing to the left to support our forces on the left, who were being pressed hard by the enemy. After moving forward about 1 mile, I deployed into line and took position in the rear of the advance line of troops. I remained here about half an hour, when I was ordered to follow the Forty-fourth Indiana by the left flank at double-quick. I moved by the left flank about 1 mile. I was then ordered to take position in the rear of the line of the extreme left, with the Thirteenth Ohio on my left.

During all these movements, I was under a hot and galling fire. I had not been in rear of this line more than twenty minutes, when it was driven back in confusion over my regiment, and, in fact, over the whole brigade. I immediately threw out skirmishers and endeavored to hold our position. We succeeded in checking him in our front, but, to our great surprise, we soon discovered that our brigade was cut off, the troops on our right having fallen back. Colonel Dick attempted to cut through and join them again, but it was impossible; we were greatly outnumbered. Colonel Dick then moved us off in the direction of the place we left in the morning, but we soon discovered that the enemy had possession of it, and we were forced to move farther to the right in the direction of the Crawfish Spring road. After moving about 1 mile, Colonel Dick ordered his brigade to form in line under cover of the hill and move up to support Brannan (he being cut off at that time from the main part of the army as I understood). Here my regiment did good service with the brigade in aiding Brannan in his critical position until we were completely outflanked on the right by infantry and artillery, and compelled to fall back, by superior numbers, completely cutting us off from Brannan and the rest of the army. Colonel Dick made another attempt to gain the hill at a point about a half mile to the right, but did not succeed. Here I got separated from Colonel Dick, who was cut off from me in attempting to occupy the hill in the second effort, leaving his acting assistant adjutant-general and the most of the brigade that was left under my command. Finding it impossible to regain the ridge, I moved down the hollow in the direction of the Crawfish Spring road, intending to move back round the ridge to the position we occupied in the morning and rejoin our forces, but when I reached the road I found that one or two divisions had passed, and Sheridan was passing, falling back in the direction of Chattanooga. I then ordered my command to fall in with Sheridan's troops and move with them. I had gone about 3 miles when I found General Van Cleve with a part of the division. I fell in with the division and moved to within 4 miles of Chattanooga, where we bivouacked in an open field for the night. Thus ended the fight of my regiment for the day, in which I had 1 man killed, 5 wounded, 4 missing, and 2 taken prisoners.

September 21, the division moved to town and took position beyond the cemetery on the Harrison road. I had received an order from Colonel Dick to move my regiment out to the Chickamauga River on the Harrison road, and hold the bridge over the river and prevent the enemy from crossing. I moved out and took my position in about a quarter of a mile of the bridge in the woods, and put out three companies on picket, and made every disposition necessary for safety. All quiet through the night.

September 22, sharp firing along the picket line about 9 o'clock. I had made ready to burn the bridges, provided I could not hold them. My pickets reported a heavy force of infantry and cavalry, with artillery, in my front. I gave orders to burn the bridges if they could not hold them, and about 12 m. I was forced to burn them. The enemy was then reported moving round on my flank. I sent a statement of the facts to Colonel Dick and told him that our cavalry had all been ordered in, and that I would not be able hold the place without re-enforcements. Receiving neither re-enforcements nor orders, I held my position until about 3 p. m., when I found that I could not hold it any longer. I ordered my pickets to fall back slowly and cover my retreat. I sent out an advance guard, and threw out flankers on each side, and marched my regiment left in front in quick time for Chattanooga. The enemy effected a crossing above me, and came over the ridge, and was firing on my rear guard from three sides. I had not gone more than 1 mile when I halted my regiment and fronted it, to wait for the rear guard to come up and give the enemy fight. I do not think I had been halted a minute before the enemy opened out on my rear with a masked battery of four guns, not over 100 yards distant in the bushes. Discovering that I was cut off from town. I immediately double-quicked my regiment, leaving the battery to my left.   I succeeded in cutting their line and getting between them and town; that is, their infantry force, which I think was about one brigade.   I had now nothing to do but to fight and fall back toward town.   I had not gone far before I discovered a large force of cavalry deployed across the road and field in my front.   I then gave orders for the regiment, except about 50, to move to the right and gain the woods and work their way down the river.   I moved on down the railroad with about 50, driving their cavalry from the road, and drawing their attention to me while the rest should gain the woods.

By taking advantage of the railroad as a breastwork I succeeded in foiling the enemy.   A portion of their cavalry charged upon my men in the field, but by the coolness of my officers and men they took advantage of the skirmish drill and soon repulsed them, with a loss to them of 2 men killed and 1 horse.   During all this time they were shelling us rapidly, and their infantry making strong efforts to flank me.   I had to leave the railroad once with my horse in order to get along.   I rode around a curve in the dirt road, and was forced to run my horse through a small squad of rebels in order to pass.   They demanded me to halt, but I rode along rapidly, and compelled them to give way or be run over.   They fired at me, but did no harm.   I rode round to the railroad, halted my advance guard, and held the enemy in check till my 50 who came along the railroad had passed. I was now near our line, and fell back inside the line, having with me the colors and 50 men; the remainder kept coming in during the evening.   Thus closed the day, with 1 man wounded and 2 officers and 14 men missing.

I have now given a statement of the facts as they occurred during the whole engagement.   I am certain that I have not exaggerated in the least.   I consider that we have just passed through one of the hottest battles of the war, and I can say that my regiment has done its whole duty.   I have carried out every order I received promptly, and have had the hearty co-operation of every officer and soldier of my command, for which they have my heartfelt thanks.   It is true we mourn the loss of a gallant Woods, Ellis, Ferree, Downing, Eckland, Howard, and Laycock, but we have the satisfaction of knowing that they fell at their posts while in the discharge of their duty, in behalf and in honor of their country.

In behalf of the regiment, I tender our sympathy to the wounded, and trust that God in His providence will restore them and heal their wounds, and return them to us again, with increased vigor, to battle for their country.

Respectfully submitted.

GRANVILLE A. FRAMBES,
Lieut. Col., Comdg. 59th Regt. Ohio Vol. Infantry.

Capt. Chas. F. King, *A. A. A. G., Second Brigade.*

No. 191.

Report of Capt. George R. Swallow, Seventh Indiana Battery.

[September —, 1863.]

About 12 m., 18th instant, the battery received orders to march immediately, with our division, to Lee and Gordon's Mills, where we bivouacked for the night.

Saturday, 19th instant, one section was placed in position on a commanding knoll, and fired a few shells at a gun the enemy were placing in position on the east bank of the river. This section was detached, and remained with the Third Brigade the remainder of the day.

The remaining four guns were ordered to the front with the Second Brigade, took position several times on the right of the road leading from Lee and Gordon's Mills to Chattanooga, but could do no firing, and seeing part of our line falling back I retired, and took position on the left of the road in a small field; had been in position but a short time until our line fell back to, and across, the road. I then opened upon the enemy a rapid fire with canister, and kept it up until two regiments fell back through the battery, in confusion and disorder; part of the Thirteenth Ohio then rallied on my right and rear, but their lieutenant-colonel being killed, they, too, fled in disorder. My canister being exhausted, and the enemy in force in front and on the right, I, with some difficulty, withdrew the battery to the rear, and soon after bivouacked for the night.

Sunday, September 20, took position with two brigades of our division; they soon advanced to the front, and the battery advanced to a position in an open field, where we remained a short time and were ordered by Major Mendenhall to move to the left, and when upon a high ridge halted for further orders, taking position on the ridge a little retired. The enemy had now opened a heavy fire of musketry in our front. Our infantry soon fell back, and we opened fire upon the enemy's advancing storming column, composed of, I should think, one brigade of infantry—one regiment of which were sharpshooters. Our fire, although very rapid, failed to check them, and on they came, with bayonets fixed, on our right and front until they reached the guns, when we, with great difficulty, limbered up and retired in great haste and much confusion, leaving Lieutenant Fislar, 1 sergeant, 1 man, and 1 gun complete, in the enemy's hands; took position in rear of the former one, collected our guns and men, expecting another attack, but they failed to come. Some troops of General Negley's division passed near me, and I was informed that a new line was being formed in the rear. Marched with General Negley's troops until near Rossville, when we joined our division.

The battery went into action with 5 officers and 117 men. Lost 1 officer, missing, and 8 men wounded (2 of them missing and probably dead), and one 10-pounder Parrott gun.

All of which is most respectfully submitted,

G. R. SWALLOW,
Captain, Commanding Seventh Indiana Battery.

No. 192.

Report of Col. Sidney M. Barnes, Eighth Kentucky Infantry, commanding Third Brigade.

HEADQUARTERS THIRD BRIGADE, THIRD DIVISION,
Chattanooga, Tenn., September 28, 1863.

CAPTAIN: In obedience to orders, I herewith submit to you my report of the part my brigade took in the action of the 19th and 20th instant, and also a history of the operations of the brigade after crossing the Tennessee River up to the commencement of the fight, which is as follows, to wit:

The Third Brigade crossed the Tennessee River on Friday, the 4th day of September, 1863, at Shellmound, camping 1 mile east of that place, where we remained until 3.30 p. m. on the 5th, when we marched eastward toward Chattanooga, over a very rough road, continuing our march until 12 p. m. and camping near Whiteside's.

Early on the morning of the 6th, leaving the Twenty-first Kentucky at Whiteside's by order of General Van Cleve, we moved 3 miles on the Trenton road, camping at the base of Raccoon Mountain, where we remained till the morning of the 8th, when we moved around the southern base of Raccoon Mountain and camped in the edge of Lookout Valley.

At 6 a. m. on the 9th, we moved down Lookout Valley toward Chattanooga, crossed Lookout Mountain, leaving Chattanooga to our left, and proceeded on the Ringgold road beyond Chattanooga Creek, where we camped for the night.

On the 10th, we still marched southwesterly, camping at Foster's, on Pea Vine Creek.

Early on the morning of the 11th, my brigade being ordered to take the advance of the army, we moved forward in line of battle, with a strong line of skirmishers thrown forward and on each flank. Soon after I advanced the enemy's cavalry began to annoy us on the right of the road, but after a slight skirmish, they retired on our right along a range of hills, while we moved forward rapidly toward Ringgold. On arriving at Chickamauga Creek, 1 mile from Ringgold, our skirmishers were fired at from the opposite bank of said creek, but the enemy fled as we approached, and when we arrived in position beyond the creek, a line of battle was seen beyond the town, about 1,000 yards distant. We advanced until our skirmish line was within 200 yards of the enemy's position, who had begun to retreat, when our battery opened•upon them. But having got too short a range, they shot among our own skirmishers, to some extent disarranging both our skirmish line and line of battle, which were both put in peril by our shells. However, the advance was rapidly continued, and the enemy driven in great confusion from the town. My men being greatly exhausted, we halted beyond the town, by order of General Van Cleve. Perceiving a dense smoke ahead of us on the railroad, we were ordered to press rapidly forward to save the bridge, which order was promptly complied with, but on reaching the bridge we found it in flames and destroyed. The enemy, still retreating and skirmishing with our advance, burned three other railroad bridges. At the second bridge, we were relieved by Colonel Wilder's command, who took the advance and drove the enemy several miles. We proceeded 3 miles beyond Ringgold and camped for the night. We sustained no loss during the day. The enemy lost 1 killed and several wounded severely, besides several horses.

On the 12th, my brigade marched in rear through Ringgold in charge of the transportation of the Twenty-first Army Corps, and of Wilder's command also. From Ringgold we moved westward, crossing West Chickamauga Creek and striking the Chattanooga and La Fayette road. Thence turning south we proceeded to Lee and Gordon's Mills.

On Sunday, the 13th, the Third Brigade was ordered out with the Third Division on a reconnaissance, the Third Brigade acting as the reserve of the division. We advanced some 2 miles rather south, in the direction of Pigeon Mountain, and after heavy skirmishing on the part of the advance brigade (General Beatty's) and considerable artillery firing, the division returned to camp.

On the 14th, we moved west, over a ridge to Chattanooga Valley, camping on Chattanooga Creek and remaining there until 11 a. m. on the 15th, when we returned 4 miles toward Gordon's Mills and turned south, passing Crawfish Spring and camping 2 miles above it, on West Chickamauga Creek, near Glass' Mill. We remained in camp there during the 16th and 17th without perceiving any demonstrations of the enemy. Several reconnoitering parties reported the enemy in force about 1 mile or 1½ miles southeast, on Pigeon Mountain.

At 9 a. m. on the 18th, the pickets reported the enemy in force on the opposite bank of the creek. Soon after, the enemy threw some shells into our camp, injuring no one, however, but slightly wounding a horse. I immediately put my command in motion, retiring them some 200 yards to a better position, formed two lines of battle, and posted the artillery on commanding ground, so as to control both front and flank, and threw forward, and on each flank, skirmishers and detachments, to prevent the enemy from gaining such positions with artillery as would enable them to expel me from my position. Here we skirmished with the enemy nearly all day, killing and wounding several near a house on the opposite side of the creek, where they attempted to plant a battery and signally failed. We lost none. My entire command, both officers and men, behaved well on this occasion, and is entitled to praise. I have no means of knowing the number of the enemy before me and around me on that day, but it consisted of a considerable force of mounted infantry and artillery. Soon after taking my position, I received an order from Brigadier-General Van Cleve to hold my position until relieved by a brigade from General Palmer's division, which I did. I was relieved late in the evening of the 18th by Colonel Grose, of General Palmer's division, having under his command five regiments of infantry and ten pieces of artillery. Being ordered, when relieved, to join my command at Gordon's Mills, I proceeded with all possible dispatch to obey said order; passing Crawfish Spring about dark, and proceeding direct to Gordon's Mills, I joined my division, camping west of the road and adjacent to General Wood's command. I succeeded in getting in position about 9 p. m., forming two lines of battle, the right of each line resting near the road and running rather diagonally to the road. I remained in this position until the morning of the 19th, when Colonel Swaine's (Ninety-ninth Ohio) regiment was temporarily detached from the brigade and moved several hundred yards across the road, and he placed in command of two or three regiments and a battery. I changed position two or three times, by order of my division commander, remaining on the same side of the road.

Toward the middle of the day, General Van Cleve went forward to the battle-field with the First and Second Brigades, leaving my brigade and eight pieces of artillery under my command, with instructions to take care of myself, hold my position, and repel any assault of the enemy. Colonel Swaine, with his (Ninety-ninth Ohio) regiment, again joined my command. Lest the enemy should attempt to turn our right flank and get in rear, I placed the artillery in position to command the ground to the right of the road, and formed on each side of the battery, a strong line of skirmishers

being thrown forward to guard against any advance or surprise of
the enemy. In this position I remained until 1.30 p. m., when I
was ordered forward with my command, infantry and artillery, into
action. I asked to whom I should report, and upon whom I should
form, and where was the enemy. I was informed by Colonel Starling, Major-General Crittenden's chief of staff, that I was needed
immediately to go forward at once and engage the enemy, that they
were on the right of the road toward the creek as we went from
Gordon's Mills to the battle-field, that our army was driving them,
that I could take them in flank; to go in and act on my own judgment. I accordingly did go in. I formed line of battle at once,
Col. R. W. McClain, of the Fifty-first Ohio, having charge of the
first line, composed of the Fifty-first Ohio and Eighth Kentucky,
Col. P. T. Swaine having charge of the second, composed of the
Ninety-ninth Ohio and Thirty-fifth Indiana.

The timber and underbrush being thick, I moved for a considerable
distance by the right of companies to the front, the road being the
center of the line for a considerable distance. The artillery moved
along the road until within the vicinity of the enemy, when it became
necessary to move the brigade to the right of the road over rough
ground and into thick timber. Not being able to find a suitable position for the battery, it was not moved into the timber, but halted in
rear, near the road, on a commanding position, the enemy being on
the right of the road and our army on the left. The fight appearing
to drift to the right, I caused my line of battle to bear in the direction of the enemy's flank, in order, if possible, to strike him in the
flank, as I was advised I could. I sent aides-de-camp forward to find
out where my division commander was. Not finding him, I endeavored to find and report to my corps commander. Not being able to
find either, and the fight waxing hotter, I determined to engage the
enemy, which I did. We entered the woods to the right of General
Carlin's brigade, as I was informed, having no support on the right,
expecting, however, to be supported on the right by Colonel Harker's
brigade, of General Wood's division, but, as I afterward learned, he
was ordered to the left. No sooner had we entered the woods than
we met the enemy. A regiment of Colonel Wilder's command, just
after we had commenced the action, retired through my command
and produced some little confusion. Recovering from this, we continued to advance steadily and rapidly upon the enemy through
heavy timber and thick underbrush, fighting our way all the time.
My brigade drove the enemy several hundred yards (perhaps 1,000
yards) until the first line, composed as before stated of the Fifty-
first Ohio and Eighth Kentucky, became very hotly engaged in front.
Soon the enemy appeared in overwhelming force in front and on the
right flank, when the right of the first line (Colonel McClain) Fifty-
first Ohio, gave way, then the entire regiment, and then the Eighth
Kentucky (Colonel Mayhew). They both retired fighting, passing
the second line, which was then lying down. When they passed, the
second line was ordered to rise, advance, and fire, by Colonel Swaine,
who was in command of it, by my order. They obeyed the order
and maintained their position as long as they could, when they were
outflanked and compelled to retire.

The officers of the brigade assisted me faithfully in rallying the
command. When rallied we fell back to a strong position on the
road on which we had advanced. I caused the Eighth Kentucky
and Thirty-fifth Indiana to form in two lines on the left of the

battery, and the Fifty-first and Ninety-ninth Ohio on the right, and then ordered Lieutenant Livingston to fire into the enemy and hold them in check and prevent them from crossing the road or turning our right, which he did.   This was kept up until near night, the enemy not gaining any farther ground.   Learning that the enemy was endeavoring by a considerable circuit to gain my flank and rear, I changed front, faced rather east, threw out skirmishers and threw up a barricade, and held my position until ordered away at 2 a. m. on the 20th.   My line during the night connected with Colonel Buell, of Wood's division, on the left.

When ordered to join my command on the morning of the 20th, I left my skirmishers and pickets, by order of Colonel Starling, chief of General Crittenden's staff.   They joined me on the 20th.   The fight of the 19th lasted about twenty-five minutes from the time it commenced until the brigade was forced to retire to the position named, where it remained until 2 a. m. on the 20th.

From there we marched to the eastern slope of Missionary Ridge and rejoined the Third Division.   About 9 a. m. we were ordered to advance.   In obedience to orders I formed two lines of battle, the first deployed and the second in column of division, doubled on the center, with Livingston's battery in the center of the first line, and advanced rapidly, forming on the left of General Wood's division, Colonel Harker's brigade, and connecting with General Brannan on his right.   Being under the command of General Wood, I formed and acted in concert with the forces named, being instructed not to put my battery in peril nor attempt to use it, unless I could do so to advantage.   Not being able so to use it, and it being left on a different part of the field from where I operated in the main, I did not see it after 12 m. of the 20th.

After advancing a considerable distance we were ordered to lie down, which we did.   Soon I was ordered by General Wood to quit my position and move on the double-quick by the left flank, and, passing General Brannan, to report to General Reynolds for action.   This order I complied with as far as I could.   I double-quicked my command a mile or more, sent aides-de-camp in every direction in quest of General Reynolds, but could find neither him nor his command. Being ordered by General Wood to halt near the foot of a hill and throw up a barricade, we did so.   We were then ordered to report to General Baird, of General Rousseau's command, for action.   I accordingly ordered my command forward through a dense wood and galloped forward with a guide, an officer of General Baird's command, to be shown my position.   Finding it on the left and at the edge of a large open corn-field, I returned to my command through a shower of balls and conducted them to a position behind a barricade.   Just before completing this order, the enemy drove back a body of our troops, apparently a brigade, in disorder through the open field on my left.   I was then ordered to change front, charge the enemy, and drive them back.   This order I obeyed, the Fifty-first Ohio and Eighth Kentucky, with great spirit and promptness, driving the enemy in great confusion a long distance back and punishing them severely.   They then maintained their position, built a barricade, and occupied it amid shot and shell all the rest of the day until ordered to retire fighting.   The Ninety-ninth Ohio and Thirty-fifth Indiana did not get up in time to participate to much extent in this charge, having missed their way and getting behind in coming through the wood before reaching the corn-field.   But when they did arrive, they entered with great spirit into the charge, and would have gone forward as far as the first two regiments named, but were ordered to return and form behind a barricade, which they did promptly. There they remained under charge of Colonel Swaine until the final assault, late in the evening, in which they gallantly participated, both officers and men, and where they faithfully remained until ordered by me, under instructions from General Baird, to retire my command fighting, which I did.

I have to report, in the actions of the 19th and 20th, the loss of 299 killed, wounded, and missing, 163 on the 19th and 136 on the 20th.

The number and names of officers and men in each regiment will appear in the reports of the respective regimental commanders, herewith filed and marked 1, 2, 3, and 4. Said reports give in detail the part each regiment took in the actions named, with their versions of the whole affair, which I forward in justice to said commands. From the said reports it will appear that the Fifty-first Ohio (Colonel McClain) lost in killed, wounded, and missing 98 officers and men, to wit, 1 commissioned officer wounded, Lieutenant Wood; 4 missing; 8 enlisted men killed, 34 wounded, and 51 missing. The Ninety-ninth Ohio lost 2 commissioned officers wounded, 3 enlisted men killed, 19 wounded, and 33 missing; making in all, 57 killed, wounded, and missing. The Eighth Kentucky lost 2 commissioned officers wounded, 1 missing; 4 enlisted men killed, 45 wounded, and 27 missing; making in all, 79. The Thirty-fifth Indiana lost 2 commissioned officers wounded, 2 missing; 5 enlisted men killed, 21 wounded, and 35 missing; making in all, 65.

The following is the number of officers and men carried into action on the 19th:

Command.	Commissioned officers.	Enlisted men.	Total.
35th Indiana	31	198	229
8th Kentucky	21	297	318
51st Ohio	21	298	319
99th Ohio	24	333	357
Total	97	1,126	1,223

And on the 20th, it was as follows, to wit:

Command.	Commissioned officers.	Enlisted men.	Total.
35th Indiana	30	160	190
8th Kentucky	19	251	270
51st Ohio	21	216	237
99th Ohio	23	280	303
Total	93	907	1,000

I regret to report the loss of Col. R. W. McClain and Lieut. Col. James D. Mayhew. They were gallant, efficient, and very valuable officers. I fear they are killed. Colonel Mayhew was missing in the battle of the 19th, in the charge made by the brigade. Colonel McClain was lost late in the evening of the 20th, after the order to retire fighting. He could not be excelled for genuine coolness and bravery. He obeyed all orders with great promptness.

It gives me the greatest satisfaction to say that Col. P. T. Swaine acted well his part, and gave evidence of undoubted courage and ability to command.   Also Major Clark, Eighth Kentucky ; Lieutenant-Colonel Cummins and Maj. Ben. F. Le Fever, Ninety-ninth Ohio; Maj. John P. Dufficy, Thirty-fifth Indiana, and Lieutenant-Colonel Wood, Fifty-first Ohio, all behaved well and deserve well of their country.   I gladly testify in behalf of all the officers and men of each of said regiments under my command, subject to the qualifications of regimental commanders, in their respective reports herewith filed.   They all behaved so well it is impossible to name all separately.

I cannot close this report without mentioning my adjutant-general, Capt. William H. Catching, Eighth Kentucky ; Lieut. J. P. Phipps, Eighth Kentucky, senior aide-de-camp; Lieut. Jerry R. Dean, Twenty-first Kentucky, aide-de-camp ; Capt. John North, Fifty-first Ohio, brigade inspector, and Lieut. T. M. Gunn, Twenty-first Kentucky, topographical engineer, all of whom rendered me most important aid, and carried my orders fearlessly wherever and whenever required, and aided in rallying the command when forced back on the 19th.   They each deserve the respect of all brave men and the gratitude of their country and promotion.

After the brigade was ordered to fall back on the evening of the 20th, I used my utmost exertions to rally and reform my command, and also to rally and encourage all others to reform and stand by their colors.   I am happy to say that Colonel Swaine and many other officers were prominent in advising the men to rally.

The Twenty-first Kentucky was not present in the actions of the 19th and 20th, not having been relieved from duty at Whiteside. They have this day rejoined my command.

Dr. Turney acted as volunteer aide-de-camp to me in the skirmish and advance on Ringgold, and behaved well and rendered me good service.

The reason why the number of officers and men appear so small on the 20th is, that those left on picket and as skirmishers had not been relieved when we advanced in the morning ; they, however. rejoined me during the day.

All of which is most respectfully submitted.

SIDNEY M. BARNES,
Colonel Eighth Kentucky, Commanding Third Brigade.

Capt. E. A. OTIS,
  Assistant Adjutant-General, Third Division.

No. 193.

Report of Maj. John P. Dufficy, Thirty-fifth Indiana Infantry.

HDQRS. (FIRST IRISH) 35TH REGT. IND. VOL. INFANTRY,
Chattanooga, Tenn., September 27, 1863.

COLONEL: I have the honor to report the following as the operations of this command since crossing the Tennessee River, together with the skirmishes and battles in which my regiment has been engaged; also a list of the killed, wounded, and missing, giving as far as known particulars in each case:

This command crossed the Tennessee River at Shellmound on the 4th September, 1863, and went into camp near that place and at the foot of Raccoon Mountain; had no opposition or accident on crossing.

September 5.—Received orders to march at 3.30 p. m., and proceeded without interruption about 9 miles, and went into camp.

September 6.—Marched about 4 miles and camped in the valley at the base of Whiteside's Mountain; all quiet at this point.

September 8.—Received orders to march at daylight, and encamped about 3½ miles from Trenton.

September 9.—Took up line of march at 6 a. m., and passed Chattanooga on our left, encamping about 4 miles south of that place.

September 10.—Resumed march at 9 a. m. in the direction of Ringgold, Ga., and encamped about 6 miles north of that point.

September 11.—Took up line of march, the Thirty-fifth Indiana supporting the Eighth Kentucky; skirmished briskly with the enemy, following closely to their rear until about 3 o'clock, when we went into camp.

September 12.—Marched back through Ringgold, leaving Chattanooga on our right, and encamped on the Rome road at 8 p. m. and 14 miles from Chattanooga.

September 13.—Formed line of battle at daylight; at 11 a. m. our division (the Third) was ordered to the front; found the enemy, and drove him about 4 miles, and returned to camp, near Lee and Gordon's Mills.

September 14.—Resumed line of march at 7 a. m., direction west; went about 5 miles, and halted in a thick covering of woods until about 6 p. m., when the march was taken up, and went into camp at the cross-roads in Chattanooga Valley, at the base of the south side of Lookout Mountain. No enemy seen on this march.

September 15.—Marched at 11 a. m., going south. Marched 6 miles and went into camp, our brigade (the Third) in advance. At this point could distinguish the enemy's camp fires, but experienced no interruption.

September 16.—Rested all day in camp near Lee and Gordon's Mills. At this point Privates Donahue, Barrett, and O'Donnell, of Company B, were taken prisoners, when absent without leave.

September 17.—Remained in camp; occasional firing on the picket line; no other demonstrations.

September 18.—Heavy skirmishing in front with our pickets. The enemy appeared in force along the line, and commenced shelling us, a few of which reached our camp, but did no injury. At this juncture we were preparing to form line of battle; shells occasioned some confusion, but good order was immediately restored. Relieved by a brigade of General Palmer's division, when we fell back and took up a position near to Lee and Gordon's Mills; heavy fighting to-day on our left.

September 19.—Fighting commenced about 8 a. m., the right and left becoming heavily engaged, and continued without intermission the whole of the day. At about 3 o'clock, our left being heavily pressed, we were ordered to support it, and moved in that direction in line of battle, double-quick. The fighting here was desperate, and continued without intermission until the darkness of night veiled the contending columns. Here we were ordered to take position near the left center, supporting a battery; built some rude breastworks of logs and rails, which were of material benefit in affording shelter to the men. During this action my regiment was exposed to a cross-fire so severe and destructive that orders were again given by Colonel Swaine, of the Ninety-ninth Ohio (who was then in command of our line), to fall back; this order was obeyed in as prompt a manner as possible, but not until the enemy was completely on our flank.

Our loss in killed, wounded, and missing in this engagement amounted to 29.

Their names will be found in the list of casualties appended to this report, embracing these engagements:

September 20.—About 2 a. m. were ordered to change position, and moved left to Missionary Ridge; here we rejoined the rest of our division, who had been separated from us in the action of the previous day. About 8 a. m. we received orders to move to the front to support General Wood's division. Heavy and unceasing fighting commenced about 9 o'clock. About 10 o'clock were ordered farther to the right to support General Baird; in this movement our brigade, led by Colonel Barnes, made a desperate charge on the enemy, through a corn-field on the left of General Johnson's division, and drove them from the woods in that vicinity, where they were in considerable force. As soon as this noble piece of work had been accomplished, we formed in line of battle, in rear of some works which had been erected by General Johnson's forces, and immediately on the left of the second line of his division. The enemy in the meantime massed a heavy force in our front, and about 4 o'clock opened a heavy fire of artillery and musketry upon us, which continued until near sundown, when we received orders from General Thomas to retire. This was accomplished under a most destructive fire, and in which it is feared many of our men reported as missing may have been either killed or wounded. Our line was reformed on a hill in our rear, from whence we marched toward Chattanooga, and encamped within 4 miles of that place.

The conduct of both officers and men during these engagements was all that could be desired. It would be impossible for me to make any distinction, as each officer and man in my command behaved with distinguished bravery. I must, however, except First Lieut. John Dugan, of Company K, who basely deserted his company on the 19th instant, and has not since been heard from. I recommend his dismissal from the service for cowardice.

Appended is a list of the casualties* of my command, giving particulars in each case as far as known.

Very respectfully, your obedient servant,

JOHN P. DUFFICY,
Major, Commanding Regiment.

Col. SID. M. BARNES,
Commanding Third Brigade.

No. 194.

Report of Maj. John S. Clark, Eighth Kentucky Infantry.

HDQRS. EIGHTH KENTUCKY INFANTRY REGIMENT,
Chattanooga, Tenn., September 26, 1863.

CAPTAIN: I have the honor to report that, on 4th instant my regiment, then under command of Lieut. Col. James D. Mayhew, crossed the Tennessee River at Shellmound, Tenn., and encamped a mile above the crossing.

---

* Embodied in revised statement, p. 177.

On 5th, marched 7 miles; camped near Whiteside's.

On 6th, marched 3 miles, and camped on Running Water Creek, in Dade County, Ga., where we remained until the morning of the 8th, when we moved 3 miles, and on the 9th marched over Lookout Mountain, passing Chattanooga (it having been evacuated by the rebels and occupied by our troops on the morning of same day), and encamped on the Chattanooga and Rome dirt road, at a distance of 6 miles from the former place.

On 10th, marched about 6 miles.

On 11th, the Fifty-first Ohio and Eighth Kentucky Regiments marched in advance, each furnishing three companies as skirmishers. The skirmishers of my regiment, which I commanded, advanced on the left, and those of the Fifty-first Ohio, under command of Lieutenant-Colonel Wood, on the right of the road. We drove the enemy, consisting of two regiments of rebel cavalry, through and beyond Ringgold without very stubborn resistance, and with no loss on our side in either killed, wounded, or missing, and with a loss to the enemy of 1 killed and 3 or 4 wounded. My skirmishers behaved gallantly.

From 10th until 15th nothing important characterized our marches. We remained in camp on Chickamauga Creek, 2 miles beyond Crawfish Spring, from the 15th until the morning of the 18th, when our camp was shelled by the enemy, whereupon, and in obedience to orders, we retired 200 yards to the rear and occupied a commanding position in an open field. After skirmishing with them until late in the evening, and being relieved by Twenty-third Kentucky Regiment, we marched to Lee and Gordon's Mills, where we rejoined our division and camped for the night.

On the morning of 19th, the battle opened briskly on the left. My regiment remained in position until 1 p. m., when it was ordered into the fight. After engaging the enemy for five or ten minutes, I discovered that the Fifty-first Ohio, which occupied a position on our right, was flanked by the enemy and was retiring. After that regiment had retired 20 or 30 paces, I ordered the Eighth Kentucky to fall back, which it did, and in as good order as possible.

We retired 400 or 500 yards to the rear, fighting as we retired to an elevated position on the Ringgold and La Fayette road, where we formed on the left of the Third Wisconsin Battery, and remained during the night.

The casualties during the day's battle were as follows :*

In the actions of both days, both officers and men of the Eighth Kentucky behaved with great coolness and bravery. There are probably two or three who did not conduct themselves as soldiers should, and these men I propose to deal with the first opportunity. I would make special and favorable mention of some of the officers and men of the regiment, but my report should have been handed in before this, and I have not the time now.

Engaged on 19th: Officers, 23; enlisted men, 297.

Engaged on 20th: Officers, 18; enlisted men, 245.

I am, very respectfully, your obedient servant,

JNO. S. CLARK,
Major, Commanding.

Capt. WILLIAM H. CATCHING,
Actg. Asst. Adjt. Gen., Third Brigade, Third Division.

---

* Nominal list omitted ; see revised statement, p. 177.

No. 195.

Report of Lieut. Col. Charles H. Wood, Fifty-first Ohio Infantry.

HDQRS. 51ST REGIMENT OHIO VOLUNTEER INFANTRY,
September 26, 1863.

CAPTAIN : I have the honor to report the operations of the Fifty-first Regiment Ohio Volunteers, from the time it crossed the Tennessee River up to the present date :

The Fifty-first Regiment Ohio Volunteers, commanded by Col. Richard W. McClain, crossed the Tennessee River with the balance of the Third Brigade, Third Division, Twenty-first Army Corps, on Friday, the 4th day of September, 1863, at Shellmound, and proceeded by the way of Whiteside's, Murphy's Valley, Lookout Mountain, to a point 10 miles south of Chattanooga without encountering the enemy.

On the morning of September 11, the Fifty-first Regiment Ohio Volunteers marched in the advance, and had not proceeded over 1 mile before it encountered the rear guard of the enemy, composed of cavalry. Colonel McClain immediately formed the regiment on the right of the road, the Eighth Kentucky forming on the left. We drove the enemy with but very little resistance to Ringgold, a distance of 6 miles, at which place they attempted to make a stand, but we immediately charged upon them, driving them about 3 miles beyond the town, killing 1 and wounding several. We sustained no loss.

On the 12th instant, we marched, with the balance of the brigade, to Lee and Gordon's Mills.

On the 13th instant, the Third Division made a reconnaissance in force. We took no part, remaining in reserve.

September 14, we marched with the division to Chattanooga Valley, and from thence 2 miles south of Crawfish Spring, where the Third Brigade went into camp.

Friday, at 10 a. m., the enemy fired into our camp with artillery, and the Eighth Kentucky and Fifty-first Ohio skirmished with them till 4 p. m., at which time we received orders to march to Lee's Mills and camp.

Saturday morning, September 19, Colonel McClain received orders to form line and prepare for battle.

The Fifty-first Ohio formed on and parallel to the Chattanooga road one-half mile north of Lee's Mills, the Eighth Kentucky forming on our left, thus completing the first line. We remained in this position until 2 p. m., at which time Colonel McClain received orders to advance.

Crossing the Chattanooga road, the first line advanced by the right of companies north and parallel to said road, and after proceeding nearly a mile encountered the enemy in a thick wood. Line of battle was immediately formed, and we drove the enemy rapidly 500 yards.

At this juncture they were re-enforced, and we, having no troops on our right, were soon flanked by an overwhelming force and compelled to retire, which we did, contesting the ground inch by inch till we reached a high piece of ground, and, taking position with the assistance of the Third Wisconsin Battery, checked the enemy. We remained in this position till dark, when we changed front to the right and bivouacked for the night. At 2 a. m. Colonel McClain received orders to march with the balance of the brigade to Missionary Ridge, which place we reached at 5 a. m.

We here drew rations and breakfasted.

At 8 a. m. we again formed line of battle in the same order as the day previous. Moving eastward, we were ordered to connect on the right with Harker's brigade, Wood's division, and on the left with Brannan's division, Fourteenth Army Corps.

Throwing Companies B and G forward as skirmishers, the line advanced, and after proceeding about three-fourths of a mile encountered the enemy's skirmishers. Quite a brisk fire was kept up for one hour, assisted on both sides by artillery. Orders were then received to move by the left flank to the support of General Reynolds' division, which was reported being hard pressed by the enemy.

After moving double-quick nearly 1 mile, we took position in the edge of a woods and awaited twenty minutes, but no enemy made their appearance. We then received orders to move to the support of General Baird, commanding First Division, Fourteenth Army Corps. Moving forward double-quick by the right flank we came to an open corn-field, where we found our forces on the left closely pursued by the enemy.

Forming line immediately we awaited the retreating forces to pass by, then raising the cheer we charged on the enemy, repulsing him and driving him back. Several attempts were made by the enemy to rally, but all in vain. A few well-directed volleys from our ranks and they broke in great confusion, throwing away their arms and accouterments. We charged them three-fourths of a mile, killing, wounding, and capturing many. We also captured the colors of the Twenty-sixth South Carolina Regiment.*

After completely routing the enemy on the left, we took position on the left of General Starkweather's brigade, and no firing occurred in our front except occasional skirmishing until 5 p. m., at which time the engagement became general. The right of the line falling back, the enemy opened a terrific fire of musketry and artillery on the left, completely enfilading the Fifty-first Ohio and Eighth Kentucky. Having no support, we were compelled to fall back in some disorder. Several attempts were made to rally the men immediately, but it proved impossible to do so under such a murderous fire with no support. Falling back about one-half mile, we rallied and reformed with the balance of the Third Brigade.

On reforming we were sorry to learn that Col. R. W. McClain and 4 line officers were missing, supposed to be badly wounded or killed.

From Missionary Ridge we were ordered with the balance of the brigade to Rossville, where we bivouacked for the night, and at 2 a. m. received orders to proceed to Chattanooga and go into camp, at which place we are now, on the bluffs east of town near the river.

Before closing this report, I take pleasure in stating that both officers and men of this regiment behaved with great coolness and bravery. As regards the general conduct and bearing of the regiment during the action I will not speak, but leave it for criticism of the commanding officers, under whose eyes it fought.

The regiment entered the fight with 21 commissioned officers and 297 enlisted men. The loss sustained during the entire action was 5 commissioned officers and 93 enlisted men.

---

* This regiment was serving in South Carolina.

Attached to this report I forward you a full and complete list of the casualties,* with rank, &c.

I have the honor to be, captain, very respectfully, your obedient servant,

C. H. WOOD,
Lieut. Col., Comdg. Fifty-first Ohio Volunteers.

Capt. WILLIAM H. CATCHING,
Actg. Asst. Adjt. Gen., Third Brigade, Third Division.

No. 196.

Report of Col. Peter T. Swaine, Ninety-ninth Ohio Infantry.

HDQRS. NINETY-NINTH OHIO VOLUNTEERS,
Chattanooga, Tenn., September 26, 1863.

SIR : In giving a report of the operations of my command, I must preface by saying it varied from a regiment to a brigade.

On the 4th instant, my regiment crossed the Tennessee River (Lieut. Col. John E. Cummins being back with 139 officers and men escorting a train).

Marched on the 5th to Whiteside's; 6th, to Murphy's Valley; 8th, to Trenton Valley; 9th, to Rossville, Chattanooga Valley; 10th, to within 6 miles of Ringgold ; 11th, through Ringgold and 3 miles beyond, fighting rear guard of enemy all day (was joined by Colonel Cummins' command that night); 12th, to Gordon's Mills; 13th, made part of a reconnoitering force under the division commander to feel the enemy, the reconnaissance resulting in a sharp skirmish with the enemy ; 14th, to within 16 miles of Chattanooga, in Chattanooga Valley ; 15th, to a position about 2 miles beyond Crawfish Spring, on the West Chickamauga Creek ; there we remained on the 16th, 17th, and 18th, our pickets on the latter day having a very lively skirmish with the cavalry and artillery of the enemy.

That night we were marched back to Gordon's Mills, and on the morning of the 19th we participated in the great battle.

Soon after daylight I was placed in command of the Thirteenth Ohio, Lieutenant-Colonel Mast ; the Eighty-sixth Indiana, Major Dick ; Stevens' (Twenty-sixth Pennsylvania) battery ; a section of Swallow's (Seventh Indiana) battery, and the Ninety-ninth Ohio, Lieutenant-Colonel Cummins, and occupied a very prominent and commanding position on the creek, from which point the batteries did good execution in silencing the enemy's guns and preventing them from establishing batteries. This command was ordered by detachments farther to the left, and I was ordered with my regiment to join my brigade, then on its advance upon the enemy. I was placed in command of the second line, the Thirty-fifth Indiana, Major Dufficy, and the Ninety-ninth Ohio, Lieutenant-Colonel Cummins.

The first line soon got hotly engaged with the enemy, driving them for about 1,200 yards, part of the distance through a dense thicket of trees and underbrush. Suddenly a heavy force of the enemy appeared in their front and, as I afterward heard, on their flank, compelling those two brave regiments (the Eighth Kentucky and Fifty-

---

* Nominal list omitted ; see revised statement, p. 177.

first Ohio) to fall back.   The second line was in supporting distance, lying on the ground.   I ordered the men to lie still until the colors of the advance regiments should fall to our rear, and as soon as our front was cleared of our own men, I ordered an advance, which was gallantly made in the face of a deadly fire of musketry, the Irishmen and Buckeyes keeping up a perfect flame of fire and shower of lead. Our line staggered for a moment, the command "Lie down" was promptly obeyed, and the volley from the enemy's re-enforcements sped harmlessly over their backs.   In an instant they obeyed the command to advance again, and were dealing terrific punishment to the foe, when another line opened upon our right flank, doing us more injury than we had suffered before.   The time had come to retreat, and I cautioned them in retiring to fight their way back. The line fell back in good order, fighting, and retired to the battery in our rear, where the brigade was ordered to remain and [hold] the position, a commanding one.

That night we were ordered to march to the left, leaving our pickets, and next day were pushed early into action, moving hither and thither to the support of our troops wherever they were hard pressed, our last position being with General Baird's division, of the Fourteenth Army Corps.   This division received the order to fall back, fighting, late in the afternoon, after all the support on the right had been driven from the field.

On the top of the ridge to our rear, I halted my retreating force, and seeing that a general rout had taken place from all the forces in our vicinity, I assumed command and ordered all the bugles to blow the assembly.   The color-bearers of some twenty regiments planted their colors, and at the cry "Rally round the flag, boys!" the tide of retreat was checked, and I found myself commanding a force worthy to be led by one of much higher rank.   I formed to resist cavalry, requiring the men to divide their cartridges with those out of ammunition.   Knowing, however, the command was too much disorganized to resist a further attack from infantry, I directed that it should fall back to Rossville and there reorganize.

At this juncture we were joined by general officers and brigade commanders, relieving me from further responsibility, but they accomplished my suggested movement.

The next morning we took position on the left of the works at Chattanooga, and I was placed in command of the advance forces of the division composed of the Second Brigade, Colonel Dick, and detachments from the First and Third Brigades.   The enemy that day massing troops in the valley, compelled me to withdraw the troops from Missionary Hill, the Thirteenth Ohio and Forty-fourth Indiana making a good resistance under the command of Lieutenant-Colonel Aldrich, and falling back in good order as a grand guard on the picket line.   The Fifty-ninth Ohio, Lieutenant-Colonel Frambes, came near being cut off, but forced their way in with a loss of 2 officers and 14 men.   Since that day nothing of importance has occurred except skirmishes on the picket line.

My regiment entered into battle with 24 officers and 333 enlisted men.   Aggregate loss, 57, as follows: Killed, 3 enlisted men; wounded, 2 officers and 19 men ; wounded and missing, 9 men; missing, 24 men.

(See report* in full herewith inclosed.)

---

* Nominal list omitted.

In closing my report, it becomes my duty to speak of the conduct of the troops I commanded in battle, the Ninety-ninth Ohio and Thirty-fifth Indiana. They behaved with coolness, bravery, and daring, were obedient to a fault, and maneuvered in the hottest of the fight as handsomely as on drill. Lieutenant-Colonel Cummins, who knows not what fear is, managed his men with coolness and judgment, particularly on Saturday, when he changed front with two companies—Captain Bopes' and Lieutenant Davidson's—to resist an enfilading fire on his men. Major Dufficy could always be found at his post giving commands, and anticipating my orders very anxiously. I must leave for his report a particular mention of those of his regiment who behaved most gallantly. Lieut. William Zay, Ninety-ninth Ohio Volunteer Infantry, held his post on the picket line all Saturday night with 15 men of Captain Bopes' company, unsupported by any of our troops, and only left next day when orders were sent to him. He captured one of General Bragg's escort, who had a fine revolving pistol. I recommend that he be allowed to keep this pistol as a compliment to him and the brave little band he commanded.

Capt. Harrison Strong volunteered to advance skirmishers upon the enemy when they were reported marching upon us at a certain point, and he with Captain Barnd and Lieutenant McConnell were very efficient as commanders of skirmishers. Color-Serg. William Duncan deserves the warmest praise for the gallant manner in which he bore the Stars and Stripes in the strife, and was cool and collected, holding the colors aloft even in retreat, that the men might "Rally round the flag." Major Le Fever was with us through the battle, but was absent four days after, reporting sick, and that his leg was bruised by a piece of shell. Captain Persinger left us in the battle Sunday morning reporting sick. Lieutenant Richards the same, Lieutenant Goble and First Sergeant Bennett, Company G, were not in the battle, but left before a shot was fired; their conduct reflects on themselves and regiment. The absence of Captain Persinger and Lieutenant Goble left Company H without an officer. Lieutenant Harper, of Company K, ably commanded it in Sunday's battle. Lieutenant Shaw, Company C, was not in the battle on account of sickness.

With the exceptions mentioned, my whole regiment did their duty well and proved themselves soldiers.

I remain, captain, very respectfully, your obedient servant,

P. T. SWAINE,
Colonel Ninety-ninth Ohio Volunteer Infantry.

Capt. WILLIAM H. CATCHING,
Acting Assistant Adjutant-General, Third Brigade.

No. 197.

Report of Lieut. Cortland Livingston, Third Wisconsin Battery.

HEADQUARTERS THIRD WISCONSIN BATTERY,
Near Chattanooga, Tenn., September 27, 1863.

CAPTAIN: I have the honor herewith to transmit a report of the operations of the battery under my command, during the two days' battle of the 19th and 20th September:

I occupied the position taken with the First Brigade on the afternoon of the 18th, until about 12 m., when I was ordered to report to Colonel Barnes, commanding Third Brigade, who moved me to a position in an orchard about 300 yards to the left, and on the right of the road. Remained in battery for about one-half hour, when I was ordered forward with the brigade. We moved to the left about a quarter of a mile, and took commanding position in an open field. Major Mendenhall then rode up and ordered me still farther to the left. I took position in corn-field on right of another battery. The brigade, which had gone into the woods from their last position, was driven back, when I opened my battery on the advancing lines of the rebels. They came in front and on the left flank. I continued the fire until the battery on my left was captured by the enemy, when I limbered up, and got back to my position in the field on the right, when I opened fire on the woods, filled with the enemy, with great effect, stopping their advance. This position gave me an enfilading fire. The Third Brigade rallied and took position on my flanks. From this position I opened a very effective enfilade fire on the enemy, did them much injury, during several successive charges they were making to their front, in the corn-field. They (the enemy) brought up their artillery, which was soon silenced by our guns. This position was retained, with slight variation of the line, for the night.

About 3 a. m. of the 20th, word came that the enemy had been cutting roads through the woods all night, that they might be able to bring their artillery to bear upon our position, and we were ordered to follow the brigade to another position, which we did, joining our division about 3 miles to the left. About daybreak I filled up my ammunition chests and moved forward into line with Third Brigade, when we were ordered to report to General Wood. It was almost impossible to follow the brigade through the woods on account of the difficult road for artillery, but I finally reached my position in line by a circuitous route, and reported, with Colonel Barnes, to General Wood, who immediately ordered me out of the woods. I then returned to the open field in the rear and took position in battery. I was soon ordered by Major Mendenhall to take position on a hill, about one-fourth of a mile to the left, with the batteries of Captain Stevens, Captain Swallow, and Lieutenant Cushing, Lieutenant Cushing being on my right and Captain Stevens on my left. There was great embarrassment in opening fire from this position on the woods in front, where it was well known the enemy was heavily massed, on account of the impossibility of obtaining any certain information in regard to where the lines of our troops were. We were ordered to reserve our fire until we could see the lines of the enemy. The field and a long strip of woods to our left flank had been left without any infantry support, and the enemy, seeing this, advanced in the woods, and their musketry was soon telling with fearful effect upon our cannoneers and horses. They also brought two masked guns to bear upon us. I opened my whole battery upon these woods. The enemy made rapid movement under cover of a corn-field, and completely flanked us, pouring volleys of musketry. I lost 30 horses belonging to my first five pieces, which were also lost. One piece was pulled by hand into the woods, but we could not get away with it. I lost 1 horse in getting away with the sixth piece, which was the only piece saved.

My loss in killed, wounded, and missing is as follows: One sergeant, 6 corporals, and 19 privates. My caissons being in the rear under the conduct of my stable sergeant, Edward Downey, into whose hands their care was committed (we being short of commanding officers) and who deserves special notice for his coolness and bravery, seeing the charge, made their escape. I collected my command together and moved on the ridge of the mountains until I struck the Chattanooga road.

We were flanked by the enemy twice during our march, but escaped notice. We arrived in Chattanooga about daylight of the 21st. Lieutenant Hubbard commanded the left half battery and Lieutenant Currier the right. Their conduct was that of brave and efficient officers. I wish to express the greatest satisfaction in the good fighting qualities of our men, for greater bravery under such severe circumstances could not have been shown. If particular mention was admissible, I would notice the cool conduct of Corpl. John W. Fletcher, in command of the fifth piece, who though taken prisoner at his gun, by his coolness escaped his captors.

Great praise is due to our non-commissioned officers and privates, whose terrible loss in the short space of ten minutes testifies the terrible fire under which they were while working their guns. I cannot mention an instance of cowardice during the action.

For several days prior to the battle I had been suffering with neuralgia and severe sick headache, which continued, and I was hardly able to sustain myself in saddle, and nothing but an overpowering desire to be with my men in the struggle kept me from leaving the field.

Very respectfully, your obedient servant,

CORTLAND LIVINGSTON,
Lieutenant, Commanding Third Wisconsin Battery.

Capt. G. R. SWALLOW,
Chief of Artillery, Third Division.

No. 198.

Reports of Maj. Gen. Gordon Granger, U. S. Army, commanding Reserve Corps.

HEADQUARTERS RESERVE CORPS,
ARMY OF THE CUMBERLAND,
Chattanooga, September 30, 1863.

COLONEL : I have the honor to submit the following report of the recent operations of a part of the Reserve Corps :

On the 6th instant, I received orders from the general commanding the Army of the Cumberland to concentrate at Bridgeport, Ala., as much of my corps as could be spared from the duty of guarding the railroad, depots, exposed points north of the Tennessee River, &c., and from that point to move them to the support of the main body of the army.

McCook's brigade, which was relieved by Colonel Mizner, was ordered from Columbia to Bridgeport, where it arrived on the 10th instant. Two brigades of General Steedman's division, which were relieved from duty along the lines of railroad from Murfreesborough to Cowan, and from Wartrace to Shelbyville, by other troops from the rear, arrived at Bridgeport on the 11th instant. The Twenty-second Regiment Michigan Infantry, under command of Colonel Le Favour, was sent direct to Bridgeport by railroad from Nashville, and was there attached to General Steedman's command. The Eighty-ninth Regiment Ohio Infantry was also attached to the same command, having been sent to Bridgeport from Tracy City.

The difficulties to be overcome in forwarding and in concentrating these troops, and in bringing forward others to partially supply their place in so short a period, can only be appreciated when the large space of country over which they were scattered, the great distance from which relief had to come, and the necessity of leaving no point of communication exposed, is fully known.

On the 12th instant, McCook's brigade, with Barnett's battery, was pushed to Shellmound.

At 7 o'clock on the morning of the 13th instant, I started the following-mentioned forces, under the immediate command of Brig. Gen. James B. Steedman, on a forced march from Bridgeport, Ala., for Rossville, Ga., viz: the First Brigade, First Division, Reserve Corps, commanded by Brigadier-General Whitaker; Second Brigade, First Division, Reserve Corps, commanded by Col. J. G. Mitchell; the Twenty-second Regiment Michigan Infantry, Eighty-ninth Regiment Ohio Infantry, Eighteenth Ohio Battery, and Company M, First Illinois Artillery, and at the same time I started Colonel McCook's command from Shellmound for the same place.

These forces arrived at Rossville, a distance of 35 miles from the place of starting, the next day at 10 a. m., having marched the whole distance through a suffocating dust and over a very rocky and mountainous road, on which it was exceedingly difficult for troops to travel.

I established my headquarters at Rossville, and there remained awaiting orders from the general commanding the Army of the Cumberland.

At 3 o'clock on the morning of the 17th instant, in accordance with orders that I had given him, General Steedman started from his camp at Rossville, with six regiments of infantry and a battery of artillery, for the purpose of making a reconnaissance in the direction of Ringgold. In this undertaking he met with no resistance from the enemy until within 2 miles of that place. Here he encountered the enemy's pickets, whom he drove rapidly across the East Chickamauga, following them one mile and a quarter. He then halted and planted a section of artillery, by the fire of which he soon drove the enemy, who appeared to be in force, out of and beyond the town. Having accomplished the object of the reconnaissance, and discovering large clouds of dust arising from the Tunnel Hill and La Fayette roads, and which were approaching his position, he deemed it prudent to return to Rossville, and at once marched back to within 8 miles of that place, where he halted for the night.

The enemy advanced and shelled his camp before midnight, but they fell back and disappeared before morning. At daylight he broke up camp, started back to Rossville, and arrived there at 1 p. m. of the same day.

At 4 p. m. on the 18th instant, I ordered Brigadier-General Whitaker to move at once with his brigade, and take possession of the crossing of the Chickamauga at Red House Bridge, and at the same time Col. Daniel McCook was ordered to march to the support of Colonel Minty, who was disputing the crossing of the Chickamauga at Reed's Bridge with the enemy. Colonel McCook arrived within 1 mile of the bridge at dark, where he encountered the enemy, and with whom he had a slight skirmish, taking 22 prisoners.

At 5 p. m. of the same day, I sent Colonel Mitchell, with his brigade, to strengthen and support Colonel McCook, and he joined him during the night.

General Whitaker was prevented from reaching the Red House Bridge by coming in contact with a superior force of the enemy on the road leading thereto. He had a severe skirmish, losing 60 men killed and wounded, but he held his ground until the next morning, when he received re-enforcements. The enemy, however, withdrew from his immediate front before daylight.

The enemy obtained possession of Reed's Bridge on the afternoon of the 17th [18th].

At daylight on the morning of the 18th [19th], Colonel McCook sent Lieutenant-Colonel Brigham, with the Sixty-ninth Ohio Infantry, to surprise the enemy and gain possession of it. He gallantly charged across the bridge, drove the enemy from it, and, in accordance with instructions received from General Steedman, destroyed it by fire. As the enemy were gathering in force around Colonel McCook, I sent him an order, at 6 o'clock on the morning of the 19th instant, to withdraw from that position. This order was executed by 7 a. m.

I now posted Colonel McCook's brigade at the junction of the Cleveland and Ringgold roads, covering the approaches to the rear and left flank of that part of my forces which were then on the road leading to the Red House Bridge, while Colonel Mitchell's brigade was led by General Steedman to the assistance of General Whitaker. Nothing further than slight skirmishing occurred in our front during the remaining part of the day. Yet all indications led us to believe that a large force of the enemy confronted us.

The position of my forces on the morning of the 20th instant, and up to the hour of battle, was as follows: Colonel McCook's brigade was moved to a point near the McAfee Church, and was placed in such a position as to cover the Ringgold road; General Whitaker's brigade, together with Colonel Mitchell's, retained the same position that they had the evening before; and Colonel Minty, who reported to me at daylight on the morning of the 20th, with a brigade of cavalry, was posted at Missionary Mills, which positions completely covered our extreme left flank.

The enemy did not make his appearance in our immediate front during the morning, but large clouds of dust could be seen beyond our position arising from the La Fayette and Harrison roads, moving in the direction of the sound of battle.

At 10.30 a. m. I heard heavy firing, which was momentarily increasing in volume and intensity on our right, in the direction of General Thomas' position. Soon afterward, being well convinced, judging from the sound of battle, that the enemy were pushing him hard, and fearing that he would not be able to resist their combined attack, I determined to go to his assistance at once. It was now about 11 a. m. I started with General Whitaker's and Colonel Mitchell's brigades, under the immediate command of General Steedman, and left Colonel McCook's brigade at the McAfee Church in position to cover the Ringgold road.

General Thomas was at this time engaging the enemy at a point between the La Fayette and Dry Valley roads, in the vicinity of ———————— house, about 3½ miles from our place of starting. We had not proceeded more than 2 miles when the enemy made his appearance in the woods on the left of our advancing column, about three-fourths of a mile from the road.

They opened upon us quite briskly with their skirmishers and a section of artillery. I then made a short halt to feel them, and becoming convinced that they constituted only a party of observation, I again rapidly pushed forward my troops.

At this juncture, I sent back and ordered up Colonel McCook's brigade to watch the movements of the enemy at this point, to keep open the La Fayette road, and to cover the open fields on the right of the road, and those that intervened between this point and the position held by General Thomas. As rapidly as possible, Colonel McCook brought up his brigade, took the position assigned to him, and held it until he marched to Rossville from the field of battle at 10 p. m. At 6 p. m. the enemy opened an artillery fire upon Colonel McCook, but he soon silenced their battery, which had done little or no damage to his troops. At about 1 p. m. I reported to General Thomas. His forces were at that time stationed upon the brow of and holding a "horseshoe ridge." The enemy were pressing him hard in front and endeavoring to turn both of his flanks.

To the right of this position was a ridge running east and west, and nearly at right angles therewith. Upon this the enemy were just forming. They also had possession of a gorge in the same, through which they were rapidly moving in large masses, with the design of falling upon the right flank and rear of the forces upon the Horseshoe Ridge. General Thomas had not the troops to oppose this movement of the enemy, and in fifteen minutes from the time when we appeared on the field, had it not been for our fortunate arrival, his forces would have been terribly cut up and captured.

As rapidly as possible I formed General Whitaker's and Colonel Mitchell's brigades, to hurl them against this threatening force of the enemy, which afterward proved to be General Hindman's division.

The gallant Steedman, seizing the colors of a regiment, led his men to the attack. With loud cheers they rushed upon the enemy, and, after a terrific conflict lasting but twenty minutes, drove them from their ground, and occupied the ridge and gorge. The slaughter of both friend and foe was frightful. General Whitaker, while rushing forward at the head of his brigade, was knocked from his horse by a musket-ball, and was for a short time rendered unfit for duty; while 2 of his staff officers were killed, and 2 mortally wounded.

General Steedman's horse was killed, and he was severely bruised, yet he was able to remain on duty during the day. This attack was made by our troops, very few of whom had ever been in an action before, against a division of old soldiers, who largely outnumbered them; yet with resolution and energy they drove the enemy from his strong position, occupied it themselves, and afterward held the ground they had gained with such terrible losses. The victory was dearly won, but to this army it was a priceless one.

There was now a lull in the battle. It was of short duration, however, for within thirty minutes after we had gained possession of the ridge, we were impetuously attacked by two divisions of Longstreet's veterans.

Again the enemy was driven back, and from this time until dark the battle between these two opposing forces raged furiously.

Our whole line was continually enveloped in smoke and fire. The assaults of the enemy were now made with that energy which was inspired by the bright prospect of a speedy victory, and by a consciousness that it was only necessary to carry this position and crush our forces to enable him to overthrow our army and drive it across the Tennesse River.   Their forces were massed and hurled upon us for the purpose of terminating at once this great and bloody battle. But the stout hearts of the handful of men who stood before them as a wall of fire quailed not.   They understood our perilous position and held their ground, determined to perish rather than yield it. Never had a commander such just cause for congratulation over the action of his troops.

The ammunition which was brought in our train to this part of the field was divided with Generals Brannan's and Wood's divisions early in the afternoon, and we soon exhausted the remainder.   All that we could then procure was taken from the cartridge boxes of our own and the enemy's dead and wounded.   Even this supply was exhausted before the battle was over, and while the enemy was still in our front, hurling fresh troops against us.   It was almost dark ; the enemy had been driven back, but we had not a round of ammunition left.   All now seemed to be lost if he should return to the contest.   Anticipating another attack, I ordered the command to be given to the men to stand firm, and to use the cold steel.   After an ominous silence of a few minutes, the enemy came rushing upon us again.   With fixed bayonets our troops gallantly charged them and drove them back in confusion.   Twice more were these charges repeated and the enemy driven back before darkness brought an end to the battle.   Night came, and the enemy fell back whipped and discomfited.

At 3 p. m. Brigadier-General Garfield, chief of staff, appeared upon that part of the field where my troops were then hotly engaged with the enemy.   He remained with us until dark, animating and cheering both officers and men.

Although they were not under my command, I cannot refrain from herein noticing the troops that held the Horseshoe Ridge, and from testifying to their heroic bravery and unflinching steadiness under the heaviest fire.   Their commanders, Generals Brannan and Wood and Colonel Harker, behaved with unqualified bravery and gallantry.

At 7 p. m. I received instructions from Major-General Thomas to withdraw my troops from the position they held at dark, to march back to Rossville and to cover the rear of the forces falling back upon that place with McCook's brigade.   These instructions were promptly carried out, and I went into camp that night in accordance therewith.   My two brigades numbered 216 commissioned officers and 3,697 men when they went into this action.   Between the hours of 1 p. m. and dark there were killed, wounded, and missing 109 commissioned officers and 1,623 men, a total of 1,732.

These losses are subdivided as follows :

Killed, 235 ; wounded, 936 ; missing (all of whom, with the exception of a very small fraction, were taken prisoners), 561.

Herewith is filed a tabular statement showing the strength of each regiment as they went into battle on the 20th instant, and the casualties in the same.

Among the gallant dead who fell upon the field of battle was Capt. William C. Russell, my assistant adjutant-general.   He fell with his face to the enemy, in the thickest of the battle, while discharging an important duty.   His loss is severely felt.   Through his sterling qualities of heart and head he became the idol of his corps.   All who knew him now lament the loss of an accomplished soldier and sincere gentleman.

It is with pleasure that I call the attention of the commanding general to the bravery and gallantry displayed during the battle by Brig. Gen. James B. Steedman. He fearlessly rushed into the midst of danger, and was ever present with his troops, handling them with ease and confidence, rallying and encouraging them, and established order and confidence.

General Whitaker and Colonel Mitchell, commanding brigades, were also conspicuous for their bravery and activity. They managed their troops well, and contributed much to our success during the day.

Col. Daniel McCook, commanding Second Brigade, Second Division, Reserve Corps, properly and promptly carried out all orders and instructions I gave him. Although his brigade was not engaged in the battle, it held a very important position, protecting the rear of those who were fighting.

The aid and assistance rendered me by Col. James Thompson, my chief of artillery, was timely and of great importance. His well-known ability and former experience rendered him a most efficient officer on the field.

The commanding officers of all my regiments, with but one exception, and of all of my batteries, behaved nobly. Below I give a list of those most conspicuous for efficiency and bravery, and deserving special mention.

Colonel Champion, Ninety-sixth Regiment Illinois Infantry; Colonel Moore, One hundred and fifteenth Regiment Illinois Infantry; Colonel Le Favour, Twenty-second Regiment Michigan Infantry; Colonel Carlton, Eighty-ninth Regiment Ohio Infantry; Lieutenant-Colonel Banning, One hundred and twenty-first Regiment Ohio Infantry; Lieut. Col. Carter Van Vleck, Seventy-eighth Regiment Illinois Infantry; Lieutenant-Colonel Warner, One hundred and thirteenth Regiment Ohio Infantry; Major Broaddus, Seventy-eighth Regiment Illinois Infantry (killed); Major Yager, One hundred and twenty-first Regiment Ohio Infantry; Lieutenant-Colonel Sanborn, Twenty-second Regiment Michigan Infantry (wounded); Captain Urquhart, commanding Ninety-eighth Regiment Ohio Infantry (wounded).

Captain Thomas, who succeeded to the command of the Ninety-eighth Ohio Infantry, and who was killed; Captain Espy, [acting] commissary of subsistence, First Brigade, First Division, Reserve Corps, killed; Captain Hicks, Ninety-sixth Illinois; Adjutant Hamilton, One hundred and thirteenth Ohio Infantry, and Captain Moe, assistant adjutant-general, Major Smith, Lieutenant Blandin, and Captain Hays, all on Brigadier-General Steedman's staff.

All of General Whitaker's staff officers were killed or wounded in the commencement of the battle. Their names have not been given to me.

I desire to return my thanks to the following mentioned members of my own staff who were with me, and who rendered me efficient aid and service during the two days of battle, viz: Maj. J. S. Fullerton, Capt. J. Gordon Taylor, Capt. William L. Avery, and Lieut. T. G. Beaham.

Respectfully submitted.

G. GRANGER,
Major-General.

Lieut. Col. C. GODDARD,
Assistant Adjutant-General, Army of the Cumberland.

[Inclosure.]

Tabular statement of the killed, wounded, and missing of the First and Second Brigades of the First Division, Reserve Corps, Department of the Cumberland, also Twenty-second Michigan and Eighty-ninth Ohio Volunteer Infantry, temporarily attached thereto, in the battle of the Chickamauga.

Regiments.	In battle.		Killed.		Wounded.		Missing.		[Remarks.]
	Commissioned officers.	Enlisted men.	Commissioned officers.	Enlisted men.	Commissioned officers.	Enlisted men.	Commissioned officers.	Enlisted men.	
96th Illinois Volunteers......	21	380	1	43	8	125	......	11	First Brigade, commanded by Brigadier-General Whitaker.
115th Illinois Volunteers......	26	400	2	32	7	130	......	2	
84th Indiana Volunteers.....	25	349	2	21	7	91	......	8	
40th Ohio Volunteers........	29	508	1	17	8	94	1	11	
18th Ohio Volunteer Battery.	4	91	......	......	2	5	......	......	
[Total]..................	105	1,728	6	113	32	445	1	32	
22d Michigan Volunteers....	23	432	......	36	2	89	15	247	Temporarily attached to First Brigade.
89th Ohio Volunteer Infantry.	20	369	2	17	2	61	13	158	
[Total]..................	43	801	2	53	4	150	28	405	
78th Illinois Volunteers......	19	334	1	17	7	69	4	58	Second Brigade, commanded by Colonel Mitchell.
98th Ohio Volunteers........	11	170	2	7	3	38	1	12	
121st Ohio Volunteers........	21	214	2	7	7	76	......	7	
113th Ohio Volunteers........	15	340	3	20	6	90	......	12	
Battery M, 1st Illinois Artillery.	2	110	......	2	......	9	......	1	
[Total].................	68	1,168	8	53	23	282	5	90	
Grand total............	* 216	3,697	16	219	59	877	34	527	

[RECAPITULATION.]

	Commissioned officers.	Enlisted men.	Total.
Killed....................	16	219	235
Wounded..................	59	877	936
Missing...................	34	527	561
Total *................	109	1,623	1,732

Respectfully submitted.

G. GRANGER,
Major-General.

ADDENDA.

HEADQUARTERS FOURTH ARMY CORPS,
Loudon, Tenn., March 9, 1864.

Maj. A. J. NEFF,
Comdg. Eighty-fourth Indiana Infantry Volunteers:

Owing to very pressing business engagements, I have not been able before now to answer your letter, asking what officer was referred to in the statement that all officers behaved well with but a

---

* See revised statement, pp. 177, 178.

single exception, made in my official report of the operations of the Reserve Corps in the battle of Chickamauga, and asking why your name did not appear in the list of "special mentions."

I was not aware that your name had been so left out until my attention was called to this fact by your letter. After receiving it I examined a copy of the report as it appears on my letter-book, thinking that it might have been left out of the printed copy through a mistake of the compositor, and I was pained to find that it was not there. I can only account for the fact by supposing that it happened through the negligence of the person who copied the original of my report (which was destroyed), or by some such accident. I certainly mentioned your name, or at least intended to mention it, in my report, and to testify therein to your soldierly conduct and gallantry in the hottest part of one of the hardest fought battles of the age.

You certainly were not the person referred to.

Very respectfully, your obedient servant,

[G. GRANGER,]
Major-General, Commanding.

No. 199.

Report of Brig. Gen. James B. Steedman, U. S. Army, commanding First Division.

HEADQUARTERS FIRST DIVISION, RESERVE CORPS,
ARMY OF THE CUMBERLAND,
Chattanooga, September 26, 1863.

SIR: I have the honor to report the part taken by my command in the late battle of Chickamauga Hills.

In obedience to the order of the major-general commanding the corps, my command, consisting of the First and Second Brigades of the First Division of the Reserve Corps, the Twenty-second Regiment Michigan Volunteers, and Eighty-ninth Regiment Ohio Volunteers (serving temporarily under my command), and the Eighteenth Ohio Battery, and Company M, [First] Illinois Artillery, marched from Bridgeport, Ala., at 7 a. m. on the 13th, and reached Rossville, Ga., a distance of nearly 40 miles, at 11 a. m. on the 14th.

At 3 a. m. on the 17th, I moved, under the orders of the major-general commanding the corps, with six regiments and a battery, to reconnoiter the road in the direction of Ringgold. I moved without opposition until within 2 miles of Ringgold, where we encountered and drove in the enemy's pickets. Crossing the East Chickamauga within three-fourths of a mile of Ringgold, I placed a section of artillery on the crest of the ridge commanding the town, and drove the enemy out of it. Discovering from the heavy clouds of dust rising from the roads leading to Tunnel Hill and La Fayette that large bodies of troops were moving, I deemed it prudent to return with my command as speedily as I could without indicating to the enemy an intention to retire hastily, and recrossing the Chickamauga, returned 6 miles toward Rossville, bivouacking for the night at Battle Spring. At 11 p. m., the enemy having followed us, threw 6 shells into my camp, and then, under the cover of darkness, speedily retired.

At 8 a. m. on the 18th, discovering no signs of an enemy, my command moved and reached Rossville at 1 p. m.

At 4 p. m. on the 18th, in obedience to the order of Major-General Granger, I sent Colonel McCook's brigade (serving temporarily under my command) to Reed's Bridge, and General Whitaker's brigade to Red House Bridge. At 5 o'clock Colonel Mitchell's brigade was sent to re-enforce Colonel McCook, who had reached Reed's Bridge without opposition, where Colonel Mitchell's brigade joined him. General Whitaker met resistance, and lost 60 men, killed and wounded, in a severe skirmish with the enemy's cavalry.

On the morning of the 19th, having received orders from Major-General Granger to do so, I withdrew Colonel McCook's and Colonel Mitchell's brigades from Reed's Bridge, which had been burned by my order before the troops were withdrawn. I moved with Colonel Mitchell's brigade to the support of General Whitaker, and posted Colonel McCook's brigade at the junction of the Cleveland and Ringgold roads.

On the morning of the 20th, McCook's brigade was ordered on to the road leading from the Ringgold road to Dyer's Mill. At half past 11 o'clock, General Granger becoming satisfied, from the heavy and receding sounds of artillery, that the enemy was pressing the left of our line severely, ordered me to move to the battle-field as rapidly as possible with two brigades of my command, General Whitaker's and Colonel Mitchell's. I moved at once, and after marching 5 miles, with the enemy's cavalry on my left flank and shelling my troops for 2 miles of the distance, reached Major-General Thomas and reported to him at half past 1 p. m. Immediately after reaching General Thomas, I received orders to move on the enemy on the left of General Wood's division. After getting in position to execute this order, Major-General Granger ordered me to move to the right of General Brannan's division, which order was promptly executed, and the moment my troops were in position they moved on the enemy, and after a severe fight of about twenty-five minutes the enemy was driven from his position, and my troops occupied the ridge from which they had forced the enemy. Slight skirmishing was kept up for about three-quarters of an hour, when the enemy attacked us furiously, and after severe fighting for about half an hour we repulsed him, but in a few moments he renewed the attack with increased force, and was again repulsed. Determined to get possession of the ridge, he immediately attacked us again, and for about one hour fought desperately, my troops maintaining their position against superior numbers until 6 o'clock, when, having expended our ammunition (the extra ammunition which I had with my command—95,000 rounds—having been taken to supply General Brannan's troops, who were out), my troops fell back, under orders, slowly and in good order. After retiring to the second ridge in rear of the one on which they had fought, and resting half an hour, finding the enemy did not attempt pursuit—all firing having ceased on both sides—they retired under orders to Rossville, and occupied their former camp.

The officers and men of my command behaved well, fought bravely, and I am proud to say did all that could have been expected of them to insure the success of our arms, to win and hold the bloody ground on which they fought. I beg leave to reassure the major-general commanding the corps of my confidence in the willingness and ability of the division to meet his highest expectations.

Under other circumstances it might be proper for me to make a more elaborate and detailed report of the part taken by my command in the terrible conflict of Sunday, but as my troops fought under the eye of the major-general commanding the corps, I have deemed it proper to just briefly state in general terms the prominent features of the engagements.

I respectfully submit herewith a tabular statement * of the killed, wounded, and missing in my command, together with statements † of the losses in the quartermaster's and ordnance departments.

With esteem, respectfully submitted.

JAMES B. STEEDMAN,
Brigadier-General, Comdg. First Division, Reserve Corps.

Maj. J. S. FULLERTON,
Assistant Adjutant-General.

No. 200.

Report of Brig. Gen. Walter C. Whitaker, U. S. Army, commanding First Brigade.

HDQRS. FIRST BRIG., FIRST DIV., RESERVE CORPS,
September 28, 1863.

SIR: On the 18th of September, 1863, I was ordered by Major-General Granger to proceed with my command, the First Brigade, First Division, Reserve Corps, composed as follows: Ninety-sixth Illinois, Colonel Champion commanding; One hundred and fifteenth Illinois, Colonel Moore commanding; Eighty-fourth Indiana, Colonel Trusler; Fortieth Ohio, Lieutenant-Colonel Jones commanding, to occupy the bridge over the Chickamauga, on the Ringgold road from Rossville, if it could be done without bringing on a general engagement.

At 4 p. m. I took up the line of march, and had progressed about 3 miles, when, crossing Spring Creek, or Little Chickamauga, the advance was fired upon by the enemy. The skirmishers of the Ninety-sixth Illinois and one section of Aleshire's (Eighteenth Ohio) battery engaged the enemy and drove him before them with some loss, losing 1 killed and 3 wounded. Night terminated the skirmish.

Having good reason to believe during the night that the rebels were changing their position to the rear of my command, I changed position, occupying the hills at McAfee's Church.

On the morning of the 19th, being ordered by the general commanding the division to maintain my position, skirmishers were sent forward from the Eighty-fourth Indiana, under Major Neff, supported by the regiment, who very spiritedly skirmished up to the camp of the enemy and fired into their camp. They were found to be infantry, mounted infantry, and cavalry in considerable force, supported by artillery, and occupying the south side of the Chickamauga. The skirmishers retired with some loss to their support, and rested upon the bank of the Little Chickamauga. The country [is] covered with heavy undergrowth, with few fields intervening. About 1 p. m. the rebels in large force made an attack upon the Eighty-

---

* See inclosure to Granger's report, p. 858.   † Not found.

fourth Indiana, which was firmly sustained.   The Fortieth Ohio was sent to its support, the enemy still continuing to increase their numbers and the vigor of their attack, and having orders to maintain my position only, I cautiously withdrew the Fortieth Ohio and Eighty-fourth Indiana, covering their withdrawal by the One hundred and fifteenth Illinois and one section of Captain Aleshire's battery, which was ably and efficiently done.

The enemy rashly exposed himself, and was severely punished, the fight being maintained with great spirit from about 2 until 5 p. m., when the rebels were driven from the field.

They numbered, as far as I could ascertain from prisoners, about 3,500 of Scott's, Forrest's, and Wheeler's forces, with one or two regiments of infantry.   Notifying the commander of the division, General Steedman, of the strength of the enemy, re-enforcements, consisting of the Twenty-second Michigan and Eighty-ninth Ohio, commanded by Colonel Le Favour, the Second Brigade of the First Division, and the Second Brigade of the Second Division, under his command in person, promptly arrived at about half past 5 o'clock.

Disposition of the force was made to resist any attack the enemy might make.   The loss of my command was 5 killed and 36 wounded.

I have to regret the loss of Captain Rowan, who was taken prisoner or killed in the thick undergrowth.   He was a brave, efficient officer.   The enemy lost very heavily, being exposed to a continuous fire from two regiments and a section of artillery, while advancing across an open field.

On the morning of the 20th (Sunday), General Granger visited the command.   About 9 o'clock firing was heard in the direction of Crawfish Spring, on the Chickamauga.   About 10 o'clock the firing of cannon and musketry took such direction as to force us to the conclusion that our forces were being driven.

Orders were given to me to march my brigade, and the Twenty-second Michigan and Eighty-ninth Ohio, which were then attached to my command for the day, to the aid of General Thomas, on the Chickamauga, near Crawfish Spring.   With alacrity and enthusiasm the men marched under a hot sun, and through clouds of dust, up the La Fayette road, until they found the rebel mounted infantry drawn up in line of battle to intercept our progress.   They had already reached the rear of General Thomas' command and had possession of the field hospital, which they had most inhumanly shelled while filled with our wounded, killing my personal friend, the gallant Dick Rockingham (lieutenant-colonel of my brave old regiment, the Sixth Kentucky Infantry), who was lying in it wounded.

Line of battle being formed by us, and advancing, the enemy retreated.   My command was then moved by the flank in two lines, three regiments in the first and three in the second line, at nearly double-quick time, up the valley for near a mile, under a heavy fire of shell from a rebel battery.   Several were killed and wounded.

Arriving between 12 and 1 p. m. at the point occupied by General Thomas, we found him sorely pressed, and yielding stubbornly to superior numbers.   I was directed to drive the enemy from a ridge on which he had concentrated his forces in great numbers, supported by artillery, and was seriously threatening the destruction of our right by a flank movement, forming my command in two lines, the Ninety-sixth Illinois on the right, the One hundred and fifteenth Illinois in the center, the Twenty-second Michigan on the left of the first line; the Fortieth Ohio on the right, the Eighty-fourth Indiana in the center, and Eighty-ninth Ohio on the left of the second line.

Both lines advanced at a double-quick pace against the enemy. The conflict was terrific. The enemy was driven near half a mile. Rallying, they drove my command a short distance, when they in turn were driven again with great loss. Both lines had been thrown into the conflict on the second charge, and the whole line kept up a deadly and well directed fire upon the enemy, who fought with great determination and vigor.

The Ninety-sixth Illinois, Colonel Champion, fought with bold impetuosity, efficiency, and gallantry.

The Twenty-second Michigan, Colonel Le Favour, after fighting for near three hours, having exhausted their ammunition, boldly charged into the midst of overwhelming numbers with the bayonet, driving them until overcome by superior strength.

The One hundred and fifteenth Illinois, Colonel Moore, deserves notice for its courage and bearing. The entire command bore themselves like veterans, under a most withering, murderous fire of musketry, grape, and canister for over three hours, firmly maintaining their ground until we were directed to retire, which was done in fair order, the enemy retiring also at the same time.

My command has the honor of bringing from that gory field the flags of our brave corps commander and of our gallant division commander, all proudly floating by that of the First Brigade. Our loss was heavy. It could not be otherwise. We fought, as I have been informed by prisoners, three divisions of the enemy, two of which were from Longstreet's corps. They fought like tigers, and with a zeal and energy worthy of a better cause.

I specially commend Colonel Champion and Captain Hicks, of the Ninety-sixth Illinois, and Colonel Le Favour, of the Twenty-second Michigan, for gallantry and bravery. Captain Aleshire, commanding Eighteenth Ohio Battery, attached to my command, both officers and men, behaved with great gallantry and courage through the engagements of Saturday and Sunday, and rendered effective service. Their loss was 2 commissioned officers and 5 men wounded. The service and our country has to regret the loss of Lieutenant-Colonel Clarke, of the Ninety-sixth Illinois, and Lieutenant-Colonel Kinman, of the One hundred and fifteenth Illinois, who fell bravely cheering their men on to victory.

Lieutenant-Colonel Sanborn was badly wounded. He demeaned himself with great credit.

The effective strength of my brigade was 106 officers and 1,843 enlisted men, making a total of 1,949; deduct from this the loss experienced in the battle of Saturday, 45 killed and wounded, and the available force of my brigade in Sunday's fight, with the addition of the Twenty-second Michigan and Eighty-ninth Ohio Regiments, was 2,877 rank and file (see exhibit* herewith filed, marked Exhibit Whitaker's brigade, for particulars); of the number there were killed, wounded, and missing in the battle of the 20th, Sunday evening, rank and file, 1,225, making from my command of 2,922 men in the Saturday and Sunday's engagements a loss of 1,270 killed, wounded, and missing, 1,225 of which was incurred on the evening of the 20th September, 1863. The enemy's loss far exceeded ours. We took many prisoners; the number I cannot give, as they were

---

* Not found; but see p. 858.

hurried to the rear without being numbered. My command received able support from the Second Brigade, which was ably commanded by Colonel Mitchell.

Conspicuous in its ranks I noticed Colonel Banning and Adjutant Hamilton in the fight.

My entire command fought well and ably. My staff suffered severely. There were but 7, 8 with myself. Lieut. Jerome B. Mason, aide-de-camp; Capt. S. B. Espy, commissary, but volunteer aide, were killed on the field. Braver men never lived. Lieut. J. M. Moore, [acting] assistant adjutant-general, was shot through the body. Lieutenant Hanon was mortally wounded and taken prisoner. Capt. James Allen was severely wounded. Captain Rowan was taken prisoner; but one escaped—Lieutenant Pepoon. The honored dead I mourn.

To the living I tender my warmest thanks, in behalf of our country, for their courage and faithfulness in the face of the foe.

The general commanding received a severe flesh wound, but continued in command, bringing his men from the field.

I hope it will not be considered beyond the scope of a report to congratulate the great States of Illinois, Ohio, Michigan, and Indiana upon the courage, efficiency, and fidelity with which their sons, composing my command, have sustained the honor of their respective States and served our common country.

I have the honor to be, yours, respectfully,

W. C. WHITAKER,

Brigadier-General, Comdg. First Brigade, First Division.

Capt. S. B. MOE,
  Assistant Adjutant-General, First Division.

ADDENDA.

Itinerary of the First Brigade for September, 1863. *

September 7.—The brigade marched from Estill Springs, Tenn., by order of Brigadier-General Steedman, commanding division.

September 9.—Arrived at Stevenson, Ala.

September 10.—Marched to Bridgeport.

September 13.—Left Bridgeport in the morning for Rossville, Ga.

September 14.—In the evening, arrived at Rossville.

September 17.—General W. C. Whitaker rejoined the brigade and resumed command at Rossville, Ga.

September 18 (*Friday*).—The brigade was ordered by Maj. Gen. Gordon Granger to move and occupy the bridge over the Chickamauga, on the Ringgold road from Rossville, if it could be done without bringing on a general engagement. In crossing Spring Creek had a skirmish, which resulted in driving back the enemy, with the loss of 1 killed and 3 wounded to ourselves. In the night I changed my position, occupying the hills at McAfee's Church.

September 19.†—In the morning, had an engagement with a largely superior force of the enemy, which lasted from 2 until 6 p. m., in which I lost 5 killed and 36 wounded, but maintained my position, and was re-enforced.

September 20 (*Sunday*).—Fought the battle of Chickamauga with

---

* From return for September.
  † For a clearer account of this day's operations, see p. 861.

honor and credit to itself. The losses of the command in the engagements were 1,270 in killed, wounded, and missing.

September 22 (Tuesday).—The command was ordered to occupy the hill opposite Chattanooga, and accordingly marched over and took that position. The Ninety-sixth Illinois Volunteers was sent to guard the ferry and crossing on the river at Williams' Ferry.

September 24.—The rebels opened fire on Colonel Champion's men and took the ferry-boat, which was being floated down the river. The balance of the brigade was moved down to the ferry, the boat was retaken, and the command was distributed along the river between Brown's and Williams' Ferries. Has since done a heavy duty and has been much exposed to the enemy's sharpshooters. When the brigade was withdrawn from its position near McAfee's Church, on the Ringgold road, on the night of the 21st, by order, Lieutenant Long, aide-de-camp at division headquarters, was sent by General Whitaker to withdraw three companies which were on picket duty, viz, one from the Fortieth Ohio and two from the Ninety-sixth Illinois; but he failed to find them, and they, being left alone, were captured. There was gross negligence on the part of the lieutenant, or the officer to whom he reported.

No. 201.

Report of Col. Thomas E. Champion, Ninety-sixth Illinois Infantry.

HDQRS. 96TH REGT. ILLINOIS VOL. INFANTRY,
Camp in the Field, near Chattanooga, Tenn., Sept. 22, 1863.

SIR : I have the honor to report that on Sunday, the 20th instant, my regiment lay in line of battle during the forenoon, near the Little Chickamauga, about 3 miles from Rossville. About noon I received orders to move, with the balance of the brigade, in a southwest direction, toward Missionary Ridge, going to the assistance of General Thomas. We arrived on the field of battle at 2 p. m., and immediately went into action. My regiment occupied the extreme right of our front line. We charged the enemy's left in the face of a murderous fire of infantry and artillery at short range, and maintained our position until every regiment on our left and in our rear had given way. We then fell back about 500 or 600 yards, and reformed. In the meantime a section of our artillery had been planted about 600 yards to the right of our previous position, and we were ordered up to repel a charge of the enemy. We repulsed the enemy after about twenty minutes' desperate fighting. We then moved to the left of the battery and again charged the enemy, driving him down the ridge running nearly parallel with our first line nearly half a mile, until we received an enfilading fire from the Eighty-fourth Indiana and One hundred and fifteenth Illinois Volunteers, and were compelled to retire. At this time if I had had 500 men, I could have driven the enemy completely from the field.

We then fell back and reformed with the remnant of the regiment, on the right of the first line of the brigade, and as the left of the line successively gave way, we fell back with it until night ended the contest.

Officers and men behaved with great gallantry, and where all did so well discriminations would seem to be invidious. I cannot, however, forbear to mention Capt. George Hicks, Company A, and Lieut. Charles W. Earle, Company C, for their persistent and determined efforts in rallying and encouraging the men during the entire conflict. Others did as well until they became engaged in attending to the wounded.

Our loss was heavy in both officers and men, including Lieut. Col. Isaac L. Clarke, killed on the field. He behaved with great gallantry. On a carefully amended report I find our loss to be, killed, 42; wounded, 121; missing, 11; total, 174. Of the missing, 5 are probably killed. We took from 30 to 40 prisoners; exact number not known.

Very respectfully, your obedient servant,

THOS. E. CHAMPION,
Colonel, Commanding Ninety-sixth Illinois Volunteers.

Lieut. J. R. Boone, ·
Acting Assistant Adjutant-General, First Brigade.

No. 202.

Report of Capt. Isaac C. Nelson, Eighty-ninth Ohio Infantry.

HDQRS. 89TH REGIMENT OHIO VOLUNTEER INFANTRY,
Chattanooga, Tenn., September 28, 1863.

SIR: I have the honor to transmit my official report of the action of the Eighty-ninth Regiment Ohio Volunteer Infantry in the battle of the 19th and 20th of September, 1863.

The regiment at the time of the battle was brigaded with the Twenty-second Regiment Michigan Volunteers, in Steedman's division, of the Reserve Corps. The regiment left camp at Rossville, Ga., early on the morning of the 19th, and were in the battle on Chickamauga Creek, where 9 of the regiment were wounded.

The regiment remained on picket at that place the night of the 19th, and moved to re-enforce troops on the right about 10 a. m.

About 2 p. m. of the 20th, they became engaged in a most terrific musketry fight, which lasted over an hour, during which time they drove the enemy from their position on a hill, and held the place. A short time before dark they became engaged again and fought superior numbers until after dark, when their ammunition gave out and they were surrounded and captured.

The casualties in the regiment are, as far as can be ascertanied, as follows: Officers killed, 2; wounded, 2; missing, 13. Enlisted men killed, 17; wounded, 61; missing, 158.

I am, very respectfully, your obedient servant,

I. C. NELSON,
Captain, Comdg. Eighty-ninth Ohio Volunteer Infantry.

Lieut. J. R. Boone,
Acting Assistant Adjutant-General, First Brigade.

No. 203.

Report of Col. John G. Mitchell, One hundred and thirteenth Ohio Infantry, commanding Second Brigade.

HDQRS. SECOND BRIG., FIRST DIV., RESERVE CORPS,
Camp near Chattanooga, Tenn., September 26, 1863.

SIR: I have the honor to submit herewith a report of the operations of this command in the late series of engagements in this department.

In accordance with instructions, the command left camp opposite Bridgeport, Ala., at 7 o'clock on the morning of the 13th instant, for Chattanooga, taking with them only blankets and five days' rations.

At 9 o'clock the next morning Chattanooga was passed on our left, and at 11 o'clock we bivouacked at Rossville, Ga., having marched a distance of nearly 40 miles in thirty consecutive hours.

On the morning of the 17th instant, the brigade formed a part of the force which marched to Ringgold, 16 miles from Rossville, drove in the enemy's pickets, and planted a battery on the crest of a hill commanding the town.

On the morning of the 18th instant, the command returned to Rossville, and in the evening of the same day was ordered to the support of Col. D. McCook, commanding the Second Brigade, Second Division, Reserve Corps, who had taken a position between the Ringgold and the La Fayette roads.

On the morning of the 19th instant, our skirmishers engaged the enemy's advance, and the engagement was fast becoming general when a peremptory order recalled us to Rossville, to place three days' rations in haversack, and proceed to the support of Brigadier-General Whitaker, whose command was lying on the Ringgold road, 4½ miles southeast of Rossville. Here the command rested on their arms during the night of the 19th.

At 11 o'clock on the morning of the 20th, we were ordered across to the La Fayette road, thence to the proximity of the Fourteenth Army Corps. During the last mile of this march, our left flank was constantly threatened by the enemy's cavalry, and our column endangered by the continued firing from masked batteries. After having reached the extreme right of the center, Fourteenth Corps, we found the country one series of ridges separated from each other only by a few hundred yards of thick woods.

At 1 o'clock an order was received to form line of battle, which was arranged as follows: One hundred and Twenty-first Ohio, Lieut. Col. H. B. Banning commanding, on the right; the Ninety-eighth Ohio, Capt. M. J. Urquhart, on the left, with the Seventy-eighth Illinois, Lieut. Col. Carter Van Vleck, and the One hundred and thirteenth Ohio, Lieut. Col. D. B. Warner, in the center. Battery M, First Illinois Artillery, Lieut. Thomas Burton commanding, took position on the extreme right, supported by two companies of the One hundred and thirteenth and One hundred and twenty-first Ohio Regiments.

When the line, thus formed, reached a point half way up the last of the mentioned ridges, the enemy appeared in force on the crest, and opened a murderous fire.

The order to charge was given, and in response the solid line rushed to the crest, drove the enemy from his position, and held it.

Three several times the enemy rushed upon us to hurl back our line, but in each instance he was met, and gallantly repulsed. In one of these charges, when the conflict had become hand-to-hand, the One hundred and twenty-first Ohio captured the flag of the Twenty-second Alabama Regiment, and bore it with them from the field.

For five hours the command remained in the position first gained, holding it against the repeated assaults of greatly superior numbers, and at sundown, after the last cartridge was fired, fell back to the ridge first in our rear.

At half past 6 o'clock we were ordered to Rossville, where we remained until the morning of the 21st, when we went to the support of General Wood's division, Twenty-first Army Corps.

On the morning of the 22d, we were ordered to Chattanooga, where we have remained in the intrenchments up to this period.

An official list of the killed, wounded, and missing is herewith transmitted,* showing that more than one-third of our brave comrades are gone. This list will tell more plainly than any words of mine can the manner in which the men of this command bore themselves in the trying hour.

Every officer, and almost every single man, did his whole duty.

The splendid manner in which their several commanders handled the individual regiments, deserves your special commendation. No men could have done more than they did.

My most cordial thanks are thus publicly due the members of the brigade staff for the gallant and efficient manner in which they performed every duty assigned them: Adjt. J. K. Hamilton, Lieut. J. T. Collins, and Capt. R. M. Black.

I have the honor to remain, very respectfully, your obedient servant,

JOHN G. MITCHELL,
Colonel, Commanding.

Capt. S. B. Moe,
Assistant Adjutant-General, First Division.

No. 204.

Report of Lieut. Col. Carter Van Vleck Seventy-eighth Illinois Infantry.

OFFICERS' HOSPITAL,
Chattanooga, Tenn., September 22, 1863.

COLONEL: Pursuant to your request, I improve the first opporⱼunity to make you an official statement of the part taken by my regiment in the battle of Chickamauga.

We were not engaged in the battle of Saturday, except to protect the right flank of our division lines while the First Brigade were engaging the enemy on the Rossville and Ringgold road.

Sunday morning soon after light we were posted in line with the Ninety-sixth Illinois on said road and remained thus until about 10 a. m., when we received orders to move in haste to the support of General Thomas, some 4 or 5 miles to the right, whither we went with the other regiments of the division under the command of General Steedman.

The last mile and a half of this march was made over an open plain under a continuous fire of artillery and musketry. No serious casualties occurred, but the temper of the men was well tried and proved to be of the right material.

From this open plain we passed into a dense piece of timber, where our brigade was formed in two lines, the One hundred and thirteenth and Ninety-eighth Ohio Volunteer Infantry making the front line, and the Seventy-eighth Illinois and One hundred and twenty-first Ohio Infantry making the rear line, and advanced in this order

---

*See revised statement, p. 178.

in the direction of the enemy. Our lines very soon became separated and the rear line found itself confronted by the enemy, posted in strong position on the crest of a high ridge. We immediately charged upon him and drove him from his position and occupied the crest ourselves, capturing several prisoners. In this charge our loss in wounded was severe, but we lost none killed, excepting Major Broaddus, who received a fatal shot through the neck.

The knowledge of his death stung every heart with bitter grief. As an officer and soldier he was the pride of the regiment; as a Christian and a patriot he had no superior; as a man he was beloved by all who knew him. His loss to his friends, the regiment, and the service, is irreparable.

We maintained the admirable position we had gained from about 1 o'clock until after 4, under one of the most terrible fires on record; it was emphatically a hand-to-hand musketry fight. Time and again did the enemy charge upon our lines in superior force, often getting as near as 20 or 30 yards, but he was as often hurled back into the ravine from which he vainly struggled to ascend.

After maintaining this fearful contest for more than three hours an overwhelming force was thrown against our left wing, which left us no alternative but to retire or be overpowered and captured. Such a shower of grape, canister, and musket-balls as was at this time poured over the regiment can hardly be imagined. We put forth every energy in our power to drive back, or at least hold in check, the massive columns that moved steadily against us, but in vain. Our only salvation was in retreat. The order was reluctantly given and still more reluctantly obeyed. While communicating this order I received a severe wound in my left [arm]. I nevertheless conducted the regiment to the crest of another ridge some 300 yards to the rear. This retreat was made and the line reformed under a heavy fire, without the least disorder, when we resumed our fire with the same determined energy as before. I remained with the regiment for nearly half an hour after I received the wound, when I became so much exhausted from loss of blood as to be compelled to leave the field, having first committed the command of the regiment to Adjt. George Green, which was done with the consent of all his superior officers because of his recent election as major, in consideration of the resignation of Colonel Benneson and the consequent promotion of the other field officers. The regiment could not have been committed to better hands. During the entire engagement he exhibited the most undaunted courage and perfect self-possession. He took command with the composure of a veteran and a hero, and kept the regiment at its deadly work until darkness put an end to the strife, when he withdrew it in perfect order to Rossville. I should very much like to mention the gallant conduct of different officers, but to mention one would involve the necessity of mentioning all, for every one did his duty, his whole duty, and nothing but his duty, and did it most nobly.

The soldiers, too, were not a whit behind the officers in the gallant and noble discharge of their whole duty. Sufficient to say that our hearts were all filled with gratitude and pride to know that, having been most severely tried, not one craven or coward [is] to be found in our ranks; there were no stragglers from the Seventy-eighth Illinois. We went into action with about 370 men (Company F having been previously detailed to guard the field hospital), and we lost in killed, wounded, and missing 142 men, besides 54 that were taken prisoners while doing picket duty Monday night.

A detailed statement* of these losses is herewith sent.   We captured 30 prisoners and 1 stand of regimental colors.   Our regimental and brigade alignments were not broken by us from the time we entered the field until we left it.   That we were not utterly destroyed is owing in a great measure to the protection afforded by our excellent position.

I am, colonel, with great respect, your most obedient servant,

CARTER VAN VLECK,
Lieut. Col., Comdg. 78th Illinois Volunteer Infantry.

Col. J. G. MITCHELL,
Commanding Brigade.

No. 205.

Report of Lieut. George Green, Seventy-eighth Illinois Infantry.

HDQRS. SEVENTY-EIGHTH ILLINOIS INFANTRY,
Near Chattanooga, Tenn., September 25, 1863.

SIR : On the morning of the 19th instant, the regiment was moved 4 miles on the Ringgold road.   A line of battle was formed, the Seventy-eighth Illinois placed on the right of the brigade, and supporting Company M, First Illinois Artillery ; Companies D and K thrown out as skirmishers.   We remained in that position during the night.

On the morning of the 20th, our position was changed to the left of the line of battle formed across the Ringgold road, and were temporarily under the command of Colonel Champion, Ninety-sixth Illinois Volunteers.   At 10 a. m. we were marched to the right wing of the army, some 4 or 5 miles distant, where Thomas' corps was fighting.   We became engaged with the enemy about 1 p. m.   We charged and drove them from their position on the crest of a hill, and maintained our position until sundown, when our ammunition became exhausted and we were compelled to retire, and were withdrawn from the field to Rossville, where we bivouacked for the night.

Our loss was quite severe, amounting to 91 killed, wounded, and missing.   Prior to the engagement Company F was detailed to guard prisoners at field hospital.

We went into the battle with 334 men and 19 officers.

On the 21st, we moved up the Chattanooga road and went on Mission Hill, where we threw up breastworks and put out skirmishers and let them remain as a picket.   At midnight we left the hill and marched into Chattanooga, leaving 30 men and 3 officers, of Company F, and 19 men and 1 officer, of Company I, as pickets, who were not relieved, and are supposed to be in the hands of the enemy.

Our whole loss from the 19th instant to the 22d was : Officers killed, 1 ; wounded, 8 ; captured, 4 ; total, 13.   Enlisted men killed, 16 ; wounded, 52 ; wounded and missing, 5 ; captured and paroled, 9 ; captured, 51 ; total, 146.†

All of which is respectfully submitted.

GEORGE GREEN,
Lieutenant, Commanding Regiment.

Lieut. J. T. COLLINS,
Acting Assistant Adjutant-General, Second Brigade.

---

* Not found ; see revised statement, p. 178.
† See revised statement, p. 178.

No. 206.

Report of Col. Daniel McCook, Fifty-second Ohio Infantry, commanding Second Brigade, Second Division.

HEADQUARTERS SECOND BRIGADE,
Chattanooga, Tenn., September 23, 1863.

SIR: I have the honor to report that on the afternoon of the 18th instant my command, then consisting of the Eighty-fifth, Eighty-sixth, and One hundred and twenty-fifth Regiments Illinois Volunteers, the Fifty-second and Sixty-ninth Ohio, and Barnett's battery, was ordered to march from Rossville to support Colonel Minty, who was then disputing the passage of the Chickamauga at Reed's Bridge. Arriving within a mile of the bridge just at dark, the head of my column ran into the rear of McNair's rebel brigade, capturing 22 prisoners. I quietly got into position, allowed no fires to be built, threw out strong pickets, and awaited daylight. During the night Colonel Mitchell, of General Steedman's division, joined me with his brigade.

Before daylight I sent Lieutenant-Colonel Brigham, of the Sixty-ninth Ohio, to surprise and burn Reed's Bridge, which had been carried, about 4 p. m. the day before, by the enemy, after a severe resistance by Colonel Minty.

Colonel Brigham gallantly charged across the bridge, drove the enemy from it, and set it on fire; thus one division of Longstreet's corps was cut off from the two other which had already crossed.

At 7 a. m. on the 19th instant, I received orders to withdraw to Rossville. This order came not a minute too soon, for I have since learned that one division of Longstreet's corps was in my front, another in my rear, only three-quarters of a mile distant, and the third on my left flank, just across the creek.

That afternoon I was ordered to cover the Cleveland road, which I did.

On the morning of the 20th instant, I received orders from General Steedman to join him at McAfee's Church. I lay near this point until I was ordered to march for the battle-field. As I arrived opposite Cloud's Hospital the enemy began shelling my column on the Chattanooga road. To avoid being delayed from arriving on the field, I turned the head of my column to the right to go around some open fields which the enemy commanded by their artillery. While passing around these fields I was ordered by Major Fullerton, of your staff, to form line of battle behind them and cover the Chattanooga road. About 6 o'clock the enemy opened upon me with artillery and some musketry. I soon silenced their batteries. At 10 p. m., by order of General Thomas, I withdrew from the field to Rossville, and was the last brigade to leave the field. The next day my brigade was ordered into position on Mission Ridge. Two guns of Barnett's battery, commanded by Lieutenant Coe, had a severe affair defending the Ringgold and La Fayette Gaps. He repulsed with canister three attempts of the rebels to charge him. At 8 p. m. I was ordered to withdraw to Chattanooga.

My officers and men behaved well under all circumstances, particularly Barnett's battery. To the members of my immediate staff, Captains Anderson and Swift, Fifty-second Ohio, Dr. Hooton, Lieutenants Rogers and Deane, Eighty-sixth Illinois, I return my thanks for their attention to duty and coolness in action. My casualties are very slight—2 killed, 14 wounded, and 13 prisoners.

I am, very respectfully, your obedient servant,

DAN'L McCOOK,
Colonel, Commanding Brigade.

Lieut. T. G. BEAHAM,
Acting Assistant Adjutant-General, Reserve Corps.

—

HEADQUARTERS SECOND BRIGADE,
North Chickamauga, October 10, 1863.

GENERAL : According to promise, I send you a map* of the left part of the battle-field and the country as far down the Chickamauga as Mission Mills. It is taken off the basis of one of the engineer maps furnished me. The roads and situation of houses on that map are in many places corrected, while many other roads are added, and corrections made in the range of Mission Hills. The position of the rebels upon the night of the 18th is partly taken from what I saw, and partly from reports of prisoners and correspondence from Southern papers. You will find it very rough, for I only have one pencil, but in its main features correct. If referred to General Thomas, he can correct any little inaccuracies or place the line Sunday.

I am, very respectfully, your obedient servant,

DAN'L McCOOK,
Colonel, Commanding Brigade.

Major-General ROSECRANS, *Commanding.*

ADDENDA.

Itinerary of the Second Brigade, commanded by Col. Daniel McCook, Fifty-second Ohio Infantry, for September, 1863.†

September 1.—The brigade left Blowing Springs, marched toward and arrived at Athens, Ala., the following day. From Athens it marched to Huntsville, remained one night, and then moved to Bridgeport, via Stevenson, Ala.

September 14.—It reached Chattanooga by a forced march from Bridgeport.

September 15.—Marched to Rossville in the morning, where it remained until the 18th, when it was ordered to destroy Reed's Bridge, which it accomplished in the face of the enemy.

September 19 *and* 20.—During the battles the brigade was held in reserve on the left.

September 21.—In the afternoon the battery was engaged. In the evening the brigade entered Chattanooga. It lay there until the 23d, when it was ordered up to this point to guard the ford at the mouth of North Chickamauga Creek.

———

No. 207.

Report of Col. Caleb J. Dilworth, Eighty-fifth Illinois Infantry.

HDQRS. EIGHTY-FIFTH ILLINOIS VOLUNTEER INFANTRY,
North Chickamauga, October 11, 1863.

SIR : In reporting to you that part which the Eighty-fifth Regiment Illinois Volunteers took in the bloody conflict of September 19 and

———

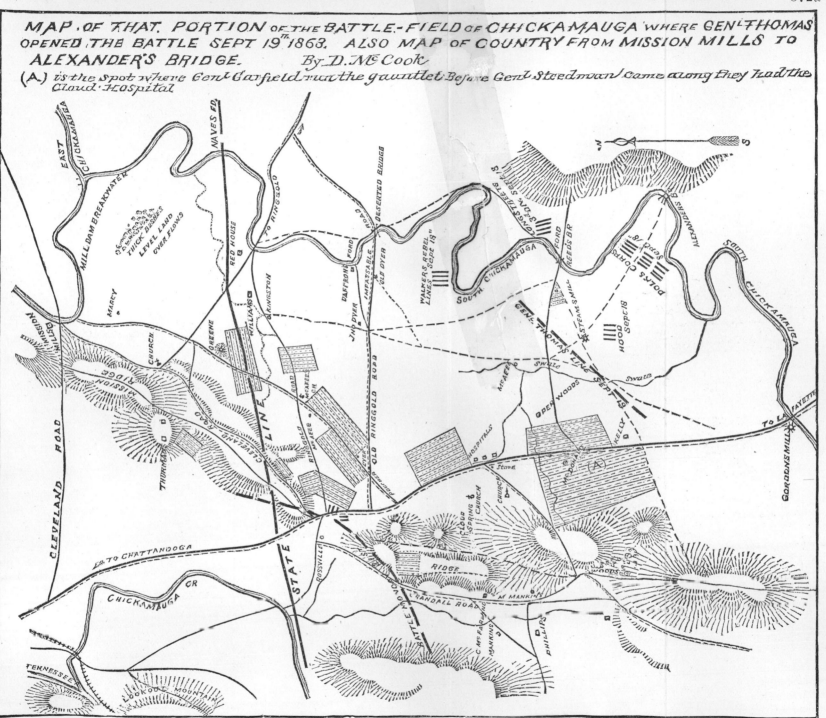

MAP . OF . THAT. PORTION OF THE BATTLE.-FIELD OF CHICKAMAUGA WHERE GEN'L THOMAS OPENED THE BATTLE SEPT 19TH 1863. ALSO MAP OF COUNTRY FROM MISSION MILLS TO ALEXANDER'S BRIDGE. By D. McCook

(A) is the spot where Gen'l Garfield ran the gauntlet before Gen'l Steedman came along they had the Cloud Hospital

20, I have the honor to report that the regiment under my command, consisting of Company D, Captain Houghton ; Company B, Captain Griffith ; Company C, Captain Blanchard'; Company A, Lieutenant Havens ; Company E, Lieutenant Trent ; Company F, Captain Kennedy; Company G, Captain Latourrette; Company H, Captain McNeill ; Company I, Captain Halsted, and Company K, by Captain Yates, marched out of camp at Rossville, Ga., about 3 p. m., September 18, 1863, and took its place in rear of the Eighty-sixth Regiment Illinois Volunteers, commanded by Lieutenant-Colonel Magee, and in advance of the One hundred and twenty-fifth Illinois Volunteers, commanded by Colonel Harmon, and in this order we marched out from Rossville, and proceeded along the old La Fayette road about — miles until we reached the [Ringgold] road, and then proceeded along this road until we arrived at about — miles from [Reed's] Bridge, where we halted for the night, and took position fronting to the north, and a prolongation of Battery I, Second Illinois Artillery, commanded by Captain Barnett, with my right resting on his left piece and my left thrown a little forward.   I immediately sent Company D, commanded by Captain Houghton, and Company K, Captain Yates, forward as skirmishers, with instructions to cover my front and flanks as well as that of the battery.

In this condition we rested on our arms, without fire, for the night. Near morning we were aroused by the sound of musketry, but it not being followed up by any further attack, we rested quietly until daylight.   During the night I could distinctly hear the rattle of wagons or artillery.   At daybreak I received orders from Colonel McCook (who is always on the alert to get the advantage of the enemy) to change my position farther to the east and 150 yards in the rear of Eighty-sixth Illinois, with my left resting on the road.   In this position I stacked arms, made fires, and sent out water details, and commenced to get breakfast.   While the men were drinking their coffee I saw the Eighty-sixth fall in and file to the left.   Slight firing had commenced with the skirmishers, and as the enemy were approaching my rear and left flank, I ordered the men to fall in and take arms. At this instant Captain Anderson, acting assistant adjutant-general to Colonel McCook, came riding down, and gave me orders to move along parallel to the road and take position in rear of the Eighty-sixth, which regiment was then facing to the road, with their left toward me.   I immediately filed to the left and commenced moving to the new position assigned me, and had marched about half the length of the battalion, when I saw the Eighty-sixth face to the right and move off by the flank over a rise in the ground.   I continued to march in the same direction, and sent my adjutant, C. N. Andrus, forward to learn and report the location of the Eighty-sixth.   He soon returned with the intelligence that it was three regiments in advance on the road toward Rossville, and that all the other troops, together with the battery, had left the field.   At this time the firing had become severe, and I directed Captain Griffith, Company B (he being in the advance), to take the rear of the One hundred and twenty-fifth Illinois (which was moving) as a guide, while I rode back to the rear of the regiment to ascertain the situation of affairs at that point.

There I found the enemy advancing upon my rear and left flank, also making an attempt upon my right.   At the same time they galloped up with two pieces of artillery, drawn by mules, unlimbered within 200 yards of my skirmishers, and opened fire upon us with grape and canister, but, their range being too high, their shot passed harmlessly over our heads. I directed my skirmishers to fall back upon and cover the rear of the regiment, which order was executed in a splendid manner, but not without some loss. Willard Hicks and Robert Neider, Company D, were wounded and taken prisoners. Captain Houghton's servant was shot by his side. We returned to Rossville, where we arrived about noon, rested about three hours, and encamped on the hill east of Rossville for the night.

Early next morning we moved out the Ringgold road about 4 miles, and filed to the left until we came to the farm of Mr. ———. There we remained until about 10 a. m., and then returned to the [McAfee] Church, and remained there until 1 p. m., then moved out the road past the Dyer farm, and continued our march until we passed the residence of Mr. ———, about one-half mile, when the Eighty-sixth Illinois (which was in the advance) was fired upon by a rebel battery from the left of the road. We were then ordered to take position upon the hills which were directly on our right, but in doing so we had to pass through burning woods 200 or 300 yards wide, the flames in many instances almost suffocating us. The woods being cleared, we moved up and took position on the hill, with the Eighty-sixth on our right and the battery on our left, forming a line on the crest of the hill, while the grape, canister, and shells of the enemy fell around us at every step. The blaze and smoke of the grass and dead timber were so great that nothing could be done until half past 3 p. m., when we succeeded in extinguishing the flames so that the battery could open fire, which was immediately replied to from a battery of the enemy, and a very severe cannonading was kept up until dark, the shells of the enemy bursting around us in all directions. When we first arrived upon the top of the hill, I again sent Company K to the right, under command of Captain Yates, as skirmishers, who took a position upon the right of the Eighty-sixth, and kept up a brisk fire upon the enemy during the afternoon, and in the evening they were thrown in front.

A short time after dark we were ordered back to Rossville, which place we reached in the night, and next day took position on the mountain east of Rossville on the right of the Eighty-sixth, where we remained until after dark, when we were ordered back to Chattanooga, which place we reached during the night.

It is with great pleasure that I am able to state, that during the several engagements referred to every officer and man under my command behaved with the utmost coolness and bravery, and in every manner conducted themselves to my entire satisfaction.

I am glad to call particular attention to the gallant officers and men of Companies D and K for their particularly good conduct while acting as skirmishers on the 19th and 20th of September, 1863.

I am glad to call particular attention to Sergt. William Delong, of Company F, for capturing and bringing into camp 2 prisoners; also John R. Gardner, of Company C, for capturing and bringing into camp prisoners on the night of the 18th September. To Maj. R. G. Rider and the adjutant, C. N. Andrus, I am much indebted for their assistance in the field.

I am, sir, very respectfully, your obedient servant,

C. J. DILWORTH,
Colonel, Commanding Eighty-fifth Illinois.

Capt. E. L. ANDERSON, *Actg. Asst. Adjt. Gen.*

No. 208.

Report of Lieut. Col. David W. Magee, Eighty-sixth Illinois Infantry.

HDQRS. EIGHTY-SIXTH REGIMENT ILLINOIS VOLUNTEERS,
Camp North Chickamauga, Tenn., October 10, 1863.

SIR: I have the honor of making the following report of the part taken by the Eighty-sixth Regiment Illinois Volunteer Infantry in the battle of the Chickamauga, on the 19th, 20th, and 21st of September, 1863, which was as follows, to wit:

On the evening of the 18th of September, we marched with the brigade (then encamped at Rossville, Ga.) on the old La Fayette road to the point where it intersects or crosses the Ringgold road, which road we then followed for perhaps 1 mile. I was then ordered into position on the extreme right of the brigade, in a thick woods, with an open field on my front. Immediately after getting into position I deployed two companies as skirmishers, covering my front and right flank, commanded as follows: Company I, Capt. A. L. Fahnestock, and Company B, Capt. J. P. Worrell.

We remained in this position, sleeping on our arms, until about 12 or 1 o'clock, at which time we were aroused by quite a sharp fire opening on our right, which proved to be skirmishing between the independent scouts belonging to our brigade and some rebel cavalry. Nothing further occurred to break the stillness of the morning. About half an hour before daylight I received an order to move my regiment by the left flank and take up a new position on the left of Captain Barnett's battery (I, Second Illinois), then posted on the north side of the road leading to Reed's Mill. We remained in our new position but a short time, when a brisk fire was opened by my skirmishers. These two companies did splendid work, Captain Worrell having advanced his left about one-fourth of a mile, or until his line was parallel with Captain Fahnestock's, who covered the right flank during the night. You will readily understand by the description of our movement that my skirmishers were not withdrawn when the regiment moved to its new position on the north of the road leading to Reed's Mill. The firing now became quite severe, the rebels advancing in line of battle.

About this time I detailed 2 men from each company, which detail I placed under command of First Lieut. William D. Faulkner, Company D, to procure water from a spring immediately outside of our line of skirmishers. He proceeded on this perilous duty and succeeded in reaching the spring and filling a few canteens with water, but did it under a galling fire from the rebel line, then advancing upon our skirmishers, who stood like a wall of fire between the enemy and our front. The water party were soon compelled to fall back, which they did in good order, as the rebels opened artillery upon them, compelling them to seek shelter in the woods; not, however, until they had paid their compliments to them in the shape of a few well-directed fires from their Enfield rifles. Lieutenant Faulkner succeeded in joining the regiment again with all his command except Andrew W. Peters, a private in Company H, who continued too long in the good work, and allowed the rebels to approach him so close as to capture him, and is now a prisoner in their hands. The firing now became severe and continuous, the rebels having advanced their second line.   This compelled our skirmishers to fall back and take a new position.

The advance of the rebels had now become so formidable and rapid that, before our skirmishers were well aware of it, they had turned our right and threatened to cut them off entirely from the regiment.   But becoming aware of their perilous position, they jumped from tree to tree, retreating the while, until Captain Fahnes-tock (who held the right) got his company within reach of the rear of our column, which was then moving by the flank (by order of General Steedman) toward the old La Fayette road.   Captain Worrell, however, was not so fortunate, his left being so far advanced, and acting under an order to "hold his position until he heard Barnett's battery open on the enemy," remained too long, and when forced to retreat, found his right covered by the enemy in force.   This compelled him to move rapidly to the rear and left, but he was so nearly surrounded by the enemy that he lost 4 men : Sergeant Kingsley, M. V. Birdine, private, wounded and taken prisoners; Lewis L. Lehman and Alexander Bennett, privates, missing (condition not known). Captain Worrell succeeded in joining the regiment with the remainder of his company.

The conduct of Captains Fahnestock and Worrell, with their companies, on this occasion, I am proud to say, was that of brave and true soldiers, and worthy of the great cause for which we are battling.

The regiment then moved with the brigade to Rossville, where we were again drawn up in position to support Captain Barnett's battery (I, Second Illinois), which had taken position on the mountain on the left of the gap leading south from Rossville, where we remained during the night of the 19th.

Early on the morning of the 20th, I moved with the brigade on the Ringgold road, and took up position on an elevated piece of ground near McAfee's Church, where we remained for about two hours.

My position was then changed to ground immediately in front of McAfee's Church, in which position we remained until about 1 o'clock in the afternoon, when we moved with the brigade, in compliance with an order, to report to Maj. Gen. Gordon Granger, on the north side of Chickamauga Valley, in prolongation of Generals Steedman's and Whitaker's line of battle.   In moving into this position my regiment was in the advance.

After passing the field hospital on the old La Fayette road, and the whole column being enveloped in a thick cloud of dust, we were suddenly brought to a halt by a rebel battery opening upon us with shell from the left of the road.   Being ordered to leave the main road, which I did by marching by the right flank, which brought us in line of battle by the rear rank.   In this order we passed through a narrow skirt of woods and across a field which had been fired by the shells in previous conflict on that ground early in the day.   A more desolate sight never met the eye.   The entire country seemed to be one smoking, burning sea of ruin.   Through this blazing field we marched, while the rebel battery played upon us with spherical case, shell, and almost every conceivable missile of death.   Under this fire we moved quietly into the woods skirting the field on the north, where we remained until we extinguished the fire.   We then moved into position, my regiment being on the right of the brigade.   My line was formed on the crest of the ridge, with my left resting on the Eighty-fifth Illinois, commanded by Colonel Dilworth. I immediately deployed a company (A, Capt. William S. Magarity) as skirmishers, covering my right flank. The enemy being beyond musket range, all that we could do was to quietly lie down, and for three and a half hours were the pastime of the rebel battery, which paid its addresses alternately to Barnett's battery and the line of infantry.

A new danger suddenly made its appearance in the shape of a 12-pounder solid shot from a battery on our right, which, mistaking us for rebel troops, sent in two enfilading fires, which admonished us to display our colors and to move a little farther under cover.

Our casualties while in this position were 1 man killed and 1 wounded, Companies I and B being again the sufferers. As night closed in upon us the firing ceased. I then deployed a company (G, Captain Bogardus) as skirmishers, covering my front.

Soon after dark I received an order to call in my skirmishers and form in the rear of the brigade, which had been ordered to return to Rossville.

Immediately after the column was formed I deployed a company (K, Capt. John F. French) as flankers, covering my right flank. We moved in this order to Rossville, where we arrived about 10 o'clock in the evening, and where we bivouacked for the remainder of the night.

About 11 o'clock on Monday morning, September 21, I received an order from our brigade commander, Col. Daniel McCook (who is always ready when the time comes to meet the enemy), to form my regiment immediately and march in the rear of the Fifty-second Ohio Volunteer Infantry, to take up a position on the mountain to the right of the gap leading south from Rossville. We moved to the position assigned us by the flank, my left resting on the One hundred and twenty-fifth Illinois Volunteer Infantry, and my right on the Eighty-fifth Illinois Volunteer Infantry, and were held in reserve to support the Fifty-second Ohio Volunteer Infantry, commanded by Major Holmes.

We remained in this position until 9 o'clock in the evening, at which time I received an order to form my regiment in the rear of the brigade, and move through Rossville to Chattanooga, where we arrived at 1 o'clock on Tuesday morning, September 22, 1863.

In conclusion, captain, permit me to say that the conduct of the officers and men composing my regiment on the three days we were connected with the troops engaged in the conflict referred to was such as to reflect credit upon themselves and the State they represent, and especially Captain Worrell, commanding Company B, and his brave officers and men, I most cordially thank for the heroism displayed on Saturday morning, the 19th, and Captain Fahnestock, acting major (Maj. O. Fountain being in arrest), as well as Adjt. C. D. Irons, for the brave and officient manner in which they assisted me on that occasion. For coolness and bravery and the patient endurance of the fatigues incident to battle-fields my regiment could not be excelled.

I am, sir, your obedient servant,

D. W. MAGEE,
Lieutenant-Colonel, Commanding Eighty-sixth Illinois.

Capt. E. L. ANDERSON,
Acting Assistant Adjutant-General, Second Brigade.

No. 209.

Report of Col. Oscar F. Harmon, One hundred and twenty-fifth Illinois Infantry.

HEADQUARTERS 125TH ILLINOIS VOLUNTEERS,
In the Field, near Chattanooga, September 24, 1863.

SIR: In pursuance of orders, I have the honor to report the part taken by my command in the battle of Chickamauga, September 19 and 20.

At 3 p. m., September 18, I was ordered to march from Rossville in the rear of the Eighty-sixth Illinois Volunteer Infantry by the left flank. A rapid march of two hours brought the brigade of which my regiment is a part within a half mile of Reed's Bridge, across Chickamauga River. It being then dark, the brigade took position upon a low hill gently descending to the north and east. Two lines were formed, of which my command formed the right of the second. The men slept upon their arms without fires, the night being intensely cold.

Standing to arms at 3 a. m., at early dawn two new positions were taken without relative changes in the brigade.

A spring had enticed several of the men to the front for water; they, being discovered by the enemy, were fired upon, but no one was injured; 1 man losing his gun in the hasty retreat. The enemy advanced rapidly, engaging and driving our skirmishers, the bullets from the enemy's guns passing over our heads.

At this moment, 8 o'clock, I noticed Barnett's battery and the Eighty-sixth Illinois Volunteer Infantry falling back on the double-quick to my right. Having no orders, I remained until Lieutenant Rogers, aide to Colonel McCook, informed me the brigade was ordered to retreat, when I fell back by the right flank in the rear of the Fifty-second Ohio Volunteer Infantry, the march being continued until the brigade reached the crest of Missionary Ridge to the left of the Rossville road.

A double line was here formed, I being placed upon the left of the second line and in double column. By sunrise the brigade was again marching down the road leading to the front and enemy's right, my regiment in the rear.

At 10 a. m., having advanced several miles and the scouts having reported the enemy near, the brigade filed back a half mile, and occupied a hill cleared and owned by Mr. Green. My regiment was posted upon the right of first line, supporting Barnett's battery. Here General Granger joined us and made extended observations, but no enemy appeared.

At 12 m. was ordered to march by the right flank with flankers to my left, the brigade not changing in the march its order in line. Coming up to General Steedman's command, an opening was occupied on slightly elevated ground; my command held the left of the first line. No enemy appeared. The brigade remained at this place until about 2.30 p. m., when it again moved toward General Thomas' left by the right flank, One hundred and twenty-fifth in rear.

In approaching the enemy's right their skirmishers appeared and fired upon us, when the brigade moved on double-quick to a strong position on the crest of a high hill, facing the enemy in two lines, I being upon the left and rear. A heavy fire was opened upon us from two batteries, which was vigorously answered by Barnett's battery.

The cannonading continued for an hour and a half; but so hot was Barnett's fire, that he silenced the enemy's guns and their infantry dared not advance. Protected by the hill, I lost no men.

At 8 p. m. I marched by the left flank in rear of Fifty-second Ohio Volunteer Infantry to Rossville.

The next day, September 21, at 12 m., was ordered to move up the western slope of Missionary Ridge to the right of the Rossville road and take position in rear of Fifty-second Ohio Volunteer Infantry. The three left companies—H, I, and K—were refused, to keep clear of the road, making an angle of about 60° with the line. My position was discovered by the enemy, and he opened fire upon me, using case-shot. His fire was directed at the angle referred to chiefly, though he swept the whole line. I moved the regiment to the rear twice to avoid his range, but not soon enough to escape injury. Two men were wounded, 1 mortally, many others narrowly escaping. The fire continued for about two hours. I was ordered to move into the road at 9 o'clock, and from thence marched to Chattanooga.

It affords me pleasure to report that during the battle neither man nor officer deserted his post. The men were calm, and under the enemy's fire of Monday self-possessed and determined. Two men in Company G, Corpl. William Flougher and Private John L. Smith, who carried off a wounded man, immediately returned to their places. I am pained to report that Capt. Stephen D. Conover and Privates John F. Leonard and William Chandler, Company B, and Jacob Poulson, Company H, are missing. Under orders from General Granger, Captain Conover was, on the 17th of September, stationed upon a high point in front of Rossville, to observe and report the movements of the enemy, [with] the privates named as a guard. I entertain serious apprehensions that his position, when captured, so far compromised him in the judgment of a relentless foe that he was cruelly slain, together with his brave comrades.

My casualties are: William Means, Company H, mortally wounded, now dead; Richard Clearwater, Company G, wounded, foot amputated; Capt. S. D. Conover, missing; John F. Leonard, Company B, missing; William F. Chandler, Company B, missing; Jacob Poulson, Company H, missing; Corporal Ray, Company H, wounded in the arm.

Very respectfully, your obedient servant,

O. F. HARMON,
Colonel, Commanding.

Capt. E. L. Anderson,
Acting Assistant Adjutant-General, Second Brigade.

No. 210.

Report of Maj. James T. Holmes, Fifty-second Ohio Infantry.

Hdqrs. Fifty-second Ohio Volunteer Infantry,
Chickamauga Creek, Tenn., October 10, 1863.

Sir: I have the honor to make the following report of the part taken by this command in the battle of Chickamauga:

At Rossville, Ga., between 2 and 3 p. m. of Friday, September 18, I was ordered to see that every man of the command has 60 rounds of ammunition and be ready to march at a moment's notice. Following Battery I, Second Illinois, Captain Barnett commanding, as ordered, about 3 o'clock the regiment moved out. Our march lay along the La Fayette road a distance of 5 miles, at which point we struck a road to the left leading to Reed's Bridge. After following this road a mile I was ordered to take position at right angles with the road, the left of the regiment resting near it. The position was not reached until nightfall.

The men were ordered to lie down by their guns and preserve strict silence. I was ordered to send a picket force 300 or 400 yards in front, extending the line beyond the right of the regiment to protect the left of the Eighty-sixth Illinois.

It was sent forward and took the position ordered as nearly as the denseness of the woods and undergrowth would permit in the darkness.

At daylight on the morning of the 19th, I was directed by a staff officer from Colonel McCook to change front to rear on the first company, afterward to move by the right flank 100 paces.

Very soon slight skirmishing commenced with the pickets in front of our original position, and also at the spring some distance to the left of the position then occupied.

About 8 a. m. I was ordered to march my command by the right flank on the left of the battery, as it was then moving toward the La Fayette road. Striking this road I was directed to follow, with the regiment, that portion of the battery moving toward Rossville. At this point the pickets sent out the night before rejoined the regiment. We reached Rossville at noon. In the afternoon the regiment, as directed, took up position on the Ringgold road at the top of Mission Ridge, where it remained through the night.

After passing McAfee's Church early on the morning of the 20th, Company D, Captain Neighbor commanding, and Company B, Lieutenant Duff commanding, were thrown forward as skirmishers, and Company I, Lieutenant Marsh commanding, was deployed to cover the right flank of the regiment. Thus disposed, the regiment moved over a mile toward the Chickamauga, when I was ordered to halt, face it about, and follow the column. The skirmishers and flankers were at the same time ordered to march in retreat.

Upon the hill seized by the brigade immediately afterward, I was ordered to form line of battle 100 paces in rear of the Eighty-sixth Illinois, upon the left of the battery. The skirmishers, by direction of a staff officer from the colonel commanding, were deployed in front and upon the left flank of the position, 1,000 yards distant.

Later in the day, 10 a. m., the skirmish companies having been ordered in, I was ordered to march the regiment in rear of the Eighty-fifth Illinois, and when the position near McAfee's Church was taken up I was directed with the regiment to take position on the left of the battery in rear of the One hundred and twenty-fifth Illinois. From here, as ordered, I sent two companies to join the skirmishers of the One hundred and twenty-fifth Illinois. They were Company C, Captain Thomas commanding, and Company H, Lieutenant Summers commanding.

At noon, being ordered to have the skirmish companies of the regiment recalled quickly, I directed Adjutant Masury to apprise them of the order to move and conduct them to the regiment. In the march from the church to Cloud's house, according to order, I followed the battery with the regiment.

When suddenly fired upon in the low grounds near that house the command was marching by the right flank.   It was halted instantly, the rear carriages of the battery having halted a moment before. Without delay the colonel commanding in person directed me to move the regiment behind the crest of the hill on our right.

Facing the regiment from flank to front, and as quickly facing it to the rear, I ordered it forward.   The distance over which the regiment must march with the backs of the men unavoidably exposed to the fire of the enemy's battery could not have been short of 300 yards.   Shots were flying and shells were bursting in front and rear of the regiment, upon its right and left flanks, and over it, and yet, strange as it might appear to those who witnessed it, not a man was injured.   The movement was steadily executed, save the slight interruption of a fence that lay obliquely in our way.

The crest of the hill gained, a new enemy confronted the position we were ordered to take on the left of the battery.   The tall grass and the weeds down the slope in front of us had been fired through the day, and a line of flame driven by the breeze directly in the faces of the men compelled a withdrawal of a few paces, until a detail should brush away the new foe.   The task was speedily completed ; we moved to our position.

After lying under fire of the enemy's guns almost or quite an hour, I received an order to have the men rise, as the enemy were thought to be on the point of charging.   The order " Rise up " was no sooner given than as one man and instantly the regiment sprang to its feet.   The enemy's skirmishers appeared on our left and fired, but were quickly driven back to the woods for shelter.   Such was the excellence of our position at this time, that while shot and shell, with occasional grape and rifle balls, hummed and whistled close to the line of heads along that crest, the open field in front was completely commanded by our arms.

With the advent of night the sounds of battle died away.   I received an order immediately after dark to move quietly out by the left flank, as soon as I could recall the pickets that had been first posted 300 yards in front of the command.   It was done, and after a brisk march of about 5 miles the regiment bivouacked at Rossville.

On the following morning Company F, Captain Hutchison commanding, rejoined the regiment, having been left on picket when the command was ordered out on the 18th.   Every company was now present ; besides those already mentioned were Company G, Captain Rothacker commanding ; Company E, Captain Mansfield commanding ; Company A, Lieutenant Lane commanding ; Company K, Lieutenant James commanding.

At noon, 21st, I was ordered to move the regiment up Missionary Mountain, and by the personal directions of the colonel commanding occupied the side of the mountain, the right of the regiment resting near the crest, and the left slightly refused near the road ; the Eighteenth Ohio upon our left ; the One hundred and fourth Ohio* upon the right.   In one-half hour a line of breastworks was formed of logs and bushes from the mountain side.   It covered the entire regiment.

About 2 p. m. our skirmishers, Company A, were attacked by those of the enemy.   This firing was continuous for four hours.   Our skirmish line was 50 yards in front of the temporary breastworks, in which many of the enemy's balls lodged.   Shells from the enemy's guns were constantly bursting and flying over the regiment, until

---

* So in original ; but it was probably the One hundred and fourth Illinois.

darkness came on, when the order was received to withdraw from the mountain without noise or confusion at 8 p. m. precisely, and march into Chattanooga, which place the regiment reached at 11 p. m.

On the morning of the 23d, the regiment was ordered from its position in the outskirts of the city to form line behind the fort and rifle-pits to the east.

After noon of the 25th, ordered to move across the pontoon and 4 miles up the river.

Evening of the 27th, ordered to the present camp.

Our loss was 3 men on the 19th and 2 on the 20th.

I could not make special mention of any officer or officers of this command that would not be injustice to the others in it whose names could not appear in a report of this length.

It will suffice to say that through all, both officers and men bore their parts with a steady firmness and brave endurance that must ever reflect upon them with honor. In the midst of rumors of terrible disaster to our arms, they never were disheartened, but believed that, although temporary reverses might befall us, in God and right is our strength, and we cannot fail of ultimate and permanent success.

I am, captain, very respectfully, your obedient servant,

J. T. HOLMES,
Major, Commanding Regiment.

Capt. E. L. Anderson,
Acting Assistant Adjutant-General, Second Brigade.

No. 211.

Report of Capt. Charles M. Barnett, Battery I, Second Illinois Light Artillery.

Battery I, Second Illinois Artillery,
North Chickamauga Creek, Tenn., October 12, 1863.

Sir: I have the honor to make the following report in regard to my participation in the action of September 20 and 21, ultimo:

On the morning of the 20th September, I moved south (with the brigade to which I am attached) from my camp, at the fork of the roads, about three-quarters of a mile south of Rossville, Ga., and after going into position twice, marched 2 miles southwest and found the enemy posted in the woods on the west side of West Chickamauga Creek, near Gaines' Mill. The enemy immediately opened upon us (while we were in column of march, through the burning woods), and we were compelled to move by the right flank into an open field, on the east side of Missionary Ridge, the enemy in the meanwhile shelling us vigorously. Upon the crest of the ridge I went into battery, but the fire in the meantime had extended all over the field, which prevented me from commencing the action until it was extinguished in our front, which duty was performed by the brigade.

At 2 p. m. I opened upon the enemy in my front, and was engaged about one hour, firing very slow, when the enemy brought another battery in position on my right, getting an oblique fire upon me. To these guns I instantly directed my fire, and silenced them in about fifteen minutes. At this time General Turchin came with his brigade from the extreme left of our army, and I assisted him to advance by shelling the enemy from his front, so that he succeeded in gaining shelter, and reformed in the rear of our brigade. I continued firing at intervals until 6 p. m., when I closed the action by two successive six-gun discharges. About 7.30 p. m. we commenced falling back toward Rossville, Ga., which place we reached about 11 p. m., having been engaged four hours, and fired 165 rounds, without any casualties worth mentioning in the battery.

On the 21st, at 12 m., the enemy commenced firing from the heights south of Rossville, and I received orders to move forward from where I was camped a half a mile north of Rossville, on the Chattanooga road. At Rossville I was ordered by General Thomas to place two guns on the hill in the forks of the road, a quarter of a mile above that place. I immediately proceeded with Lieutenant Coe's section, and placed them in the designated position, leaving the remainder of the battery under the hill, in column of pieces faced toward Chattanooga.

About 2 o'clock the enemy opened upon the position with four guns, and continued firing for half an hour, when they ceased, and their infantry came down in line, yelling and shouting, but upon giving them a few rounds of canister (some of them double-shotted) they retreated, nor did they make another charge that day, although their artillery kept up a slow though steady fire until about 5.30 p. m., when we again silenced them after firing 129 rounds. At 8.30 p. m. we withdrew from the hill and arrived at Chattanooga at 11 p. m., no casualties happening upon our side.

My officers and men behaved as usual, doing all that could be done.

Lieutenant Coe commanded the section under fire on the 21st.

I remain, very respectfully, your obedient servant,

CHAS. M. BARNETT,
Captain, Commanding Battery.

Capt. E. L. ANDERSON,
Acting Assistant Adjutant-General.

No. 212.

Reports of Brig. Gen. James G. Spears, U. S. Army, commanding Third Brigade, Third Division.

HDQRS. 3D BRIG., 3D DIV., RESERVE ARMY CORPS,
Chattanooga, Tenn., September 27, 1863.

SIR: I respectfully submit the following as my report of the movements of this brigade from McMinnville to this point:

On the night of the 12th of September, 1863, I received orders from Maj. Gen. Gordon Granger to march the Tennessee troops to Jasper, Tenn., leaving the Fifth Iowa Cavalry at McMinnville and Stokes' cavalry at Tracy City. Accordingly early on Sunday morning, 13th, tents were struck and line of march taken up and reached Beersheba Springs, on Cumberland Mountains, that night and rested until morning.

September 14, 5 a. m., line of march resumed by way of Therman, and camped that night 9 miles short of Therman and rested until next morning.

September 15, 5 a. m., line of march resumed by way of Therman, in Sequatchie Valley, and thence down the valley to Cheeksville, and there camped for the night.

September 16, 5 a. m., line of march resumed for Jasper, which point, with my command, I reached at noon, and then went into camp, as ordered. The average distance of march each day was about 20 miles. The road was extremely dusty and in many places water was very scarce, and the troops and stock suffered considerably. No accidents or casualties occurred on this march worthy of note.

September 17, remained in camp all day and night.

September 18, at 10 a. m., received orders from Maj. Gen. G. Granger to march my command to mouth of Battle Creek. The line of march was immediately taken up and mouth of Battle Creek reached at noon same day, and rested there that night; however, the transportation was all the time busily engaged in bringing in forage and supplies. During that night an order was received from Maj. Gen. G. Granger directing me to march my command to Wauhatchie. Accordingly early on next morning I took up the line of march for that point.

September 19, marched on until night at or near Gardenhire's Old Ferry, near Running Water, and then halted to get something to eat, feed and rest the teams. At 11 o'clock that night orders were received from Major-General Granger to move my command directly on to Chattanooga.

September 20, 1 a. m., line of march resumed for Chattanooga and Chattanooga reached with my infantry at noon same day. When near Chattanooga I received orders from Maj. Gen. G. Granger to march my command to Rossville, Ga. My transportation was unable to get across the point of the mountain until night, the road having been all day so blockaded with other trains that it was difficult to get them along at all. At night I was ordered by Major-General Rosecrans to occupy with my force a position near the bridge across Chattanooga Creek, at the steam tannery, and to halt all officers and soldiers coming into Chattanooga below the rank of major-general, and to forward the wounded and transportation into Chattanooga. Accordingly I ordered Colonel Cooper, commanding Sixth [Tennessee] Regiment, with his command to take position at said bridge, and to halt all such persons as directed. Colonel Shelley, commanding Fifth [Tennessee] Regiment, with his command was located at the cross-roads at the point of the mountain on the south side, and Colonel Cross with his command [Third Tennessee] was located at Gillespie's, on the Rossville road; the whole night was employed in executing said orders, and by next morning I had halted and encamped, of different corps and divisions, between 8,000 and 12,000 officers and soldiers, who were on next morning all thrown to the front again.

Thus my command rested until Monday evening at dusk, when I received orders to leave the First Middle Tennessee Battery (Captain Abbott) and one regiment in a commanding position at the cross-roads, and proceed with the other two regiments down the Chattanooga Valley road, and join Brigadier-General Mitchell, commanding cavalry (a distance of about 5 miles). This I at once did, and informed General Mitchell of my arrival. Here my men rested until about 2 a. m., September 22, when I received orders from Major-General Rosecrans to return with my command and reoccupy my old position, with all but one regiment, which I was ordered to throw on the mountain at Summertown. I accordingly ordered Colonel Cross, commanding Third Regiment, with his command to Summertown, on Lookout Mountain, with proper instructions, and Colonel Cooper with his command was marched to the cross-roads, near where the battery and Colonel Shelley's regiment were. All this was accomplished before daylight.

On Tuesday morning, September 22, about 8 o'clock, orders were received from Major-General Rosecrans to send all the transportation and First Middle Tennessee Battery into Chattanooga, and, in the event I was attacked by the enemy, to contest the ground inch by inch and foot by foot, and to fall back across the mountain and cross the river at Brown's Ferry, where a steamboat would be in waiting.

Accordingly, I immediately sent the transportation and battery as ordered. I was also ordered to send three companies upon the railroad along the river at the point of the mountain, which I did from Colonel Shelley's regiment; and the Sixth Regiment, Colonel Cooper's, and five companies of Fifth Regiment, Colonel Shelley's (two other companies having been left at Carthage, and not yet having arrived), I had drawn up in line of battle at the cross-roads awaiting the enemy's attack.

At about noon the enemy, with one regiment of skirmishers and sharpshooters, supported by three regiments of infantry or mounted infantry, and with artillery and cavalry, attacked my line. The attack was made principally upon the Sixth Regiment (Colonel Cooper). The command of Colonel Shelley (five companies) was immediately upon the right of Colonel Cooper and connecting therewith.

The engagement lasted about one hour and a half, when the contest in numbers being so unequal, I ordered my command to slowly fall back to a more favorable position on the first bench on the point of the mountain, which was done in good order, and the enemy declined to pursue. This contest was severe, and my command, officers and men, all behaved well, and fought gallantly, and deserve much praise.

The casualties were as follows:*

Here my command remained, holding the point of the mountain that evening, night, the next day (23d), and that night, until orders were received to march off the point of the mountain with two regiments, and to leave one regiment on the point of the mountain as a picket. This order was received from Major-General Rosecrans at about 2 o'clock on morning of 24th of September.

On the evening of the 23d, a considerable force of the enemy appeared on the mountain near Summertown, and demanded a surrender of Colonel Cross and his command. This information was immediately dispatched to me by Colonel Cross, upon receiving which I ordered Colonel Cross not to comply, but to fight the enemy stubbornly. Accordingly the enemy attacked Colonel Cross and his command, which was resisted, and the enemy repulsed. This was in the evening and prior to the order to march the Third Regiment from the top of the mountain.

---

* Nominal list (omitted) shows 3 killed, 19 wounded, and 2 missing.

The casualties of Colonel Cross in this engagement were as follows: Private Alexander C. Walker, of Company F, wounded with a minie ball in the thigh; Company G lost 4 men missing, to wit, Corpl. William Hickman and Privates James M. Hair, Alexander Hair, and James A. Jenkins; Company B lost, missing, 9 men, to wit, Sergt. J. A. Brown, Corpl. Thomas D. Woods, and Privates John Baley, Callaway Beets, Wiley Parker, Foster E. Brown, John McClannahan, four of whom have since returned, but without arms or accouterments, to wit, John Baley, Callaway Beets, Wiley Parker, and John McClannahan; and W. G. Anderson, of Company A, was left sick upon the mountain.

The Third and Fifth Regiments were marched off the point of the mountain into Chattanooga between the hours of 2 o'clock and sun-up on the morning of the 24th instant to present camp in Chattanooga. Colonel Cooper, Sixth Regiment, who was, with his command, left on the point of the mountain as a picket, was flanked and attacked by a superior force of the enemy early in the morning of September 24, but resisted the attack stubbornly until compelled to yield the ground and march his command to my present encampment, which he successfully did, losing 1 man, missing, to wit, Private John Harris, of Company B.

In the engagement on Tuesday my whole command, officers and men, acted well, gallantly, and bravely. Major Gamble, of Sixth Regiment, had a minie-ball hole shot through his hat, the ball cutting the skin on the top of his head, but he remained on the battle-ground throughout. Two companies of Colonel Shelley were left at Carthage and three were on the railroad.

Very respectfully, your obedient servant,

JAMES G. SPEARS,
Brigadier-General, Commanding, &c.

Lieut. Col. C. GODDARD,
Asst. Adjt. Gen., Dept. of the Cumberland.

—

HDQRS. THIRD BRIG., THIRD DIV., RESERVE CORPS,
On First Bench of Lookout Mountain Point, September 22, 1863.

GENERAL: The enemy attacked us to-day at 12.30 with four regiments of infantry and artillery. My forces fought well and never yielded the ground until they were overpowered and compelled to fall back, which was done in good order, and we now have our position on the first bench of the mountain. The enemy seems to be reluctant in advancing. I have several men killed and many wounded. I will contest it according to your order this day, inch by inch and foot by foot.

Respectfully, your obedient servant,

JAMES G. SPEARS,
Brigadier-General, Commanding.

Major-General ROSECRANS.

[P. S.]—I am informed the enemy is endeavoring to flank me across the mountain beyond; whether true or not I am unable to state. The enemy holds the position I occupied this morning.

No. 213.

Reports of Maj. Gen. David S. Stanley, U. S. Army, Chief of Cavalry, Army of the Cumberland.

HEADQUARTERS CHIEF OF CAVALRY,
Near Winston's, Ala., September 6, 1863—10 p. m.

GENERAL: Yesterday Crook went into the Broomtown Valley, sixteen miles east of this. He found the enemy at the descent of the mountain, chopping or commencing to cut timber into the road. He followed the rebels into the valley; they fled in all directions south. Five miles from this, McCook's scouts crossed at Davis' Gap, found the pickets at the descent of the mountains, drove them within 6 miles of Alpine, capturing a sergeant and 10 men of the Fourth Georgia, Crews' brigade. Five regiments of cavalry are at Alpine. The prisoners say that a large force of cavalry is at La Fayette, with artillery. Wharton's division is picketing between this and Rome. The road by Winston's Gap is the best to Rome. Eleven miles from Rawlingsville, at a little place called Porterville, a road crosses the mountains. From Porterville to Rome is about 40 miles, a good road and a very little mountain. By this road it is about 20 miles farther to Rome than by the Winston's Gap road.

I send you a sketch* of the vicinity by Greenwood and the road across the mountains by Crook's.

The prisoners say they are told that Johnston is at Chattanooga and that his force is all expected. A citizen, who is reliable, says that citizens he could vouch for had been to Chattanooga to learn, and came back with the story that Bragg is ordered to retreat. I give this for what it is worth. We will try and prevent this, blocking the descent from the mountains. Our supply trains have been sadly delayed, having had to fall in behind the trains of McCook.

We are anxious to hear from you.

Very respectfully, your obedient servant,

D. S. STANLEY,
Major-General, and Chief of Cavalry.

Brig. Gen. JAMES A. GARFIELD,
Chief of Staff.

—

HDQRS. CHIEF OF CAVALRY, DEPT. OF THE CUMBERLAND,
Henderson's Gap, near Dorsey's Tan-yard,
September 9, 1863—6.30 p. m.

GENERAL: I received your dispatch directing me to make a reconnaissance to Summerville, and another by the route General Crook crossed the mountain. At the time I received the dispatch we were near the barricade the enemy had thrown across the gap. We here first struck their pickets and continued to fight them back through Alpine, where they took the Rome road, some going on the Blue Pond road.

We took about a dozen prisoners. They all say there is infantry at Summerville. One man says it is Johnston's old division of the Virginia army ; another, that it is a part of Polk's corps.

I send you the dispatches taken from one of Wheeler's couriers.

---

* Not found.

I do not understand their import, excepting that he is concentrating at La Fayette.

The labor getting down the mountain to-day, and the fight, brought us to nightfall. I have sent a scout within 5 miles of Summerville, not yet returned. I occupy Alpine. I have rumors that Bragg is retreating south of the Oostanaula ; I have not definite information. The enemy fought stubbornly from the foot of the mountain. The country is well adapted to their mode of warfare.

We have had 2 men killed and 7 wounded.

Since writing the above, General Davis has arrived at my head-quarters.

A brigade is at the Broomtown Gap, which I will re-enforce with cavalry at early dawn.

I am, your obedient servant,

D. S. STANLEY,
Major-General, and Chief of Cavalry.

Brigadier-General GARFIELD,
Chief of Staff.

P. S.—One of the enemy captured to-day says Forrest was here to-day, and that he saw him and knows him.

[Inclosure No. 1.]

HEADQUARTERS CAVALRY CORPS,
La Fayette, Ga., September 9, 1863.

Maj. W. E. HILL,
Commanding Élite Battalion.

MAJOR : I am directed by General Wheeler to instruct you to move with your command to La Fayette, Ga., immediately upon receipt of this dispatch. In moving you will send a courier in advance to the commanding officer at Alpine to notify him of your approach.

Respectfully, major, your obedient servant,

D. G. REED,
Assistant Adjutant-General.

[Inclosure No. 2.]

HEADQUARTERS CAVALRY CORPS,
La Fayette, Ga., September 9, 1863.

Commanding Officer, Gadsden, Ala. :

General Wheeler directs me to say that you will send out scouts toward the Tennessee River to ascertain if there is any movement of the enemy in that direction. Any information that may be gained by these scouts will be promptly transmitted to General Wheeler at La Fayette.

The scouts sent to the river will be instructed to have all boats on the river brought to the south side of river, and the owners will be given peremptory orders, under pain of being treated as disloyal citizens, not to bring any Yankees to this side of the river, and to burn their boats in case the enemy attempt to obtain possession of them.

Respectfully, your obedient servant,

D. G. REED,
Assistant Adjutant-General.

[Inclosure No. 3,]

HEADQUARTERS CAVALRY CORPS,
La Fayette, September 9, 1863.

Colonel ——,
Commanding at Alpine, Ga. :

COLONEL : I am directed by General Wheeler to say that he desires you will not fail, in case you are forced back from Alpine, to cause a portion of your force to fall back in the direction of La Fayette, sending a courier to the general at La Fayette, with a statement of the force of the enemy which drove you from Alpine. This latter fact—that is, the force of the enemy which opposes itself to you—you will endeavor to ascertain by any means in your power, as it is important that the commanding general should know it.

The Élite Corps, under Major Hill, is now at Cedar Bluff, but will receive orders by this courier to move to La Fayette.

Respectfully, colonel, your obedient servant,

D. G. REED,
Assistant Adjutant-General.

—

HDQRS. CHIEF OF CAVALRY, DEPT. OF THE CUMBERLAND,
Near Alpine, Ga., September 10, 1863—7 p. m.

GENERAL : I have made three reconnaissances to-day. One toward Rome, crossing the Chattanooga River at Milville—this developed the fact that there are no troops excepting 6 miles this side of Rome. A boy direct from there says there are troops of all arms. An intercepted letter says Walker's division of infantry is there. The reconnaissance of General Crook to within 10 miles of La Fayette learned that all the cavalry force of Bragg's army was assembling at La Fayette ; commenced concentrating yesterday. Armstrong's brigade, of Forrest's division, was south of Chattanooga and went back to La Fayette last night. Forrest went through here with nothing but his escort at 10 o'clock yesterday, going toward La Fayette, via Summerville.

Colonel Watkins, with the Third Brigade, of First Division, made reconnaissance to Summerville. He found their pickets 4 miles this side of the town, and charged them, driving them through the town without serious resistance. He had 1 man killed and 1 wounded ; captured a captain and about 20 prisoners. His information is that Forrest, Armstrong, Wheeler, and Wharton were there yesterday, with their commands, and moved in the afternoon and during the night to La Fayette, and giving as a reason that the Yankees were attacking their forces at that point.

The Second and Third Georgia, however, retreated on the road to Rome, which from Summerville is 23 miles. From La Fayette to Summerville it is 16 miles. I have been very sick and confined to my bed all day, but hope to be up to-morrow or next day.

I am, your obedient servant,

D. S. STANLEY,
Major General, and Chief of Cavalry.

Brig. Gen. JAMES A. GARFIELD,
Chief of Staff, &c.

HDQRS. CHIEF OF CAVALRY, DEPT. OF THE CUMBERLAND,
Henderson's Gap, Ala., September 13, 1863—8 p. m.

GENERAL : The reconnaissance sent to La Fayette to determine the position of the enemy returned this evening. General Crook went within 3 miles of there this a. m., and charged and drove their cavalry through their infantry, and captured about 20 of their infantry pickets belonging to the Thirteenth Louisiana. They say they belong to Breckinridge's division, and that all of Johnston's army, excepting one division (Loring's), which has been sent to Charleston, had re-enforced Bragg. As soon as he struck their infantry pickets they opened upon him with artillery, and he immediately fell back, having accomplished the object for which he was sent.

Colonel McCook moved his force on the Summerville and La Fayette road as far as Trion Factory, and sent one regiment from there to reconnoiter toward La Fayette. He reports a column of something moving off from the Summerville and La Fayette road toward Rome, but I can learn from him nothing definite in regard to it. The reconnaissance was very unsatisfactory, and if I can hear anything more definite in regard to it, I will dispatch it to you at once. I will carry out your instructions in regard to the passes, and put myself in closer communication with the right of the army to-morrow. Our marching had been very heavy, and our horses are very much jaded.

I am, very respectfully, your obedient servant,

D. S. STANLEY,
Major-General, and Chief of Cavalry.

General JAMES A. GARFIELD,
Chief of Staff, &c.

No. 214.

Report of Brig. Gen. Robert B. Mitchell, U. S. Army, Chief of Cavalry.

HEADQUARTERS CHIEF OF CAVALRY,
Island Ferry, October 3, 1863.

GENERAL : I have the honor to report that in accordance with orders received from department headquarters, I crossed the Tennessee River at and above Caperton's Ferry with parts of the First Division Cavalry, Col. E. M. McCook commanding, and Second Brigade, Second Division Cavalry, Brigadier-General Crook commanding, and September 3 moved across Sand Mountain, camping the night of the 3d on Town Creek, having left at the Tennessee River one regiment from each brigade to guard our trains and assist them in getting up the mountain.

September 4.—General Crook moved with his command to Winston's, at Valley Head, and Colonel McCook with his division moved 4 miles farther down the valley in the direction of Rawlingsville, sending a scout to that place which discovered no enemy.

September 5.—The Second East Tennessee, which had been posted at Jasper when the movement across the river began, had the day previous to our crossing been ordered down to Bridgeport, and orders were left at Bridgeport for it to follow on and join the brigade. It reached the brigade on the morning of the 5th.

The Second Michigan, which had also been temporarily detached from its brigade, having crossed the river several days previous at

Bridgeport, and been scouting under orders from Generals Sheridan and Thomas, also arrived and joined its brigade the same morning. General Crook with his command made a scout to-day over to Lookout Mountain into Broomtown Valley; discovered only 150 or 200 of the enemy, and returned the same night to Valley Head. Colonel McCook's command scouted in the direction of Lebanon and on the mountain (Lookout), finding small parties of the enemy's cavalry, and capturing 10 of them.

September 6.—Sent scouting parties in various directions, mostly down Will's Valley, finding but little indications of the enemy and meeting no resistance.

September 7.—The trains having begun to arrive, the day was spent in shoeing up the command.

September 8.—Moved General Crook's command, the artillery and ambulances, up into Lookout Mountain, at Winston's Gap, where it encamped for the night. The trains were parked in the vicinity of General McCook's corps, and all the dismounted men started back to Nashville for a remount.

September 9.—At daylight, the command, First Division, and Second Brigade, Second Division, moved across Lookout Mountain in the direction of Henderson's Gap, General Crook's command having the advance. As they neared the gap the advance struck the enemy's pickets, which were easily driven back down the gap. The gap was found to have been obstructed by them by felling timber across the road, which is a narrow pass, and rolling large bowlders of rock into it. It took about an hour to clear out the gap, when the command moved into Broomtown Valley.

General Crook's command soon engaged the enemy and a severe skirmish ensued, the enemy resisting stubbornly, having occupied the timber skirting some large fields. However, as soon as Colonel McCook's command came up, by sending strong parties on their flanks they were forced to retire, fighting us, however, from the time we struck them in the valley until we drove them through Alpine, some retreating on the Rome road, but the most of them on the road to Summerville. For the details of the engagement I refer you to the reports of the division, brigade, and regimental commanders. The command, after pursuing till dark, bivouacked at night in line of battle in the vicinity of Alpine, standing to horse at 3 a. m. in the morning.

September 10.—Sent scouts in the direction of Rome, La Fayette, and Summerville. Colonel Watkins with his brigade (Third Brigade, First Division) moved on the Summerville road, striking the enemy's pickets about 5 miles from Summerville. He instantly charged them, driving them easily through Summerville. From prisoners taken he learned that Wheeler, Forrest, Wharton, and Armstrong had left the night before on the La Fayette road, leaving only a small force at Summerville. The scout in command of General Crook (Second Brigade, Second Division), which went on the La Fayette road, confirmed what the prisoners captured at Summerville reported. Colonel Watkins captured 1 captain and 15 men. He had 1 man killed—killing also 1 rebel. The scout of Colonel Campbell's brigade (First Brigade, First Division), which went in the direction of Rome, met no enemy, but found out in various ways that the enemy had a large force of all arms at Rome. All of the scouts returned the same night.

September 11.—Another scout was sent this morning toward

Rome, consisting of two brigades, under command of Colonel Mc-Cook, with directions not to return until the next day. Same day, sent the brigade commanded by Colonel Watkins to the support of the Thirty-ninth Indiana Mounted Infantry, which General McCook had sent out toward La Fayette to communicate with General Thomas, who was supposed to have reached La Fayette with his command the night previous. Learning that the main part of Bragg's army was still at La Fayette instead of General Thomas' corps, the whole party were ordered back.

September 12.—Colonel McCook returned early from scout on Rome road, bringing reliable information that Bragg's and Johnston's armies are both at La Fayette.

All the trains of the cavalry command that had got down the gap were ordered immediately back on top of the mountain.

General Stanley, who had been too unwell to keep the saddle for several days previous, ordered General Crook to make a strong reconnaissance toward La Fayette, and find out the truth of the reports and rumors we had obtained.

He started at 1 o'clock with two brigades on the La Fayette road, sending Colonel McCook at the same time with two more brigades on the Summerville road. General Crook with his command moved to what is called Valley Store, 10 miles from La Fayette, and bivouacked for the night, having met with no resistance whatever. Colonel McCook moved to Trion Factory, on the La Fayette and Summerville road, found the enemy's cavalry in strong force, but drove them before him, and at night fell back to Summerville, where he bivouacked.

September 13.—General Crook with his command moved forward toward La Fayette this morning slowly, their cavalry pickets fighting him as they fell back, and when within 4 miles of La Fayette sent the Ninth Pennsylvania forward at a charge and captured the infantry picket belonging to Breckinridge's division, and coming out with slight loss. Having gone as far as it was prudent, and having accomplished the object for which the reconnaissance was sent, viz, to find out positively the position of the enemy, the whole command moved back to Alpine.

September 14.—The whole command moved up on top of the mountain and bivouacked at Little River.

September 15.—Being absent on sick leave up to the evening of the 14th, and consequently not being with the command, cannot give a detailed statement of the doings of the cavalry prior to the 14th from personal observation.

On my arrival at Valley Head, I found Major-General Stanley dangerously sick. On the morning of the 15th, he was compelled to turn over the command of cavalry to me, and return to Nashville for treatment.

General Crook's command moved to Dougherty's Gap and took post.

McCook's division returned down the mountain, via Winston's Gap, and encamped near Valley Head.

September 16.—McCook's division, except Colonel Watkins' brigade, moved up Winston's Gap over Lookout Mountain, and took post at Dougherty's Gap.

September 17.—Colonel McCook's command (the Second Brigade, stationed at Dougherty's Gap) moved down into McLemore's Cove and camped.

September 18.—Moved Colonel McCook's command up to within 2 miles of Blue Bird Gap and bivouacked.

September 19.—Received orders during the night of the 18th to draw in all cavalry from Valley Head and Dougherty's Gap, and keep closed up on right of Twentieth Army Corps, Major-General McCook commanding. Orders were sent at daylight to the detached portions of the command at the places above-mentioned in accordance with the instructions received from department headquarters, and at daylight that portion of the command stationed at Blue Bird Gap was in motion up McLemore's Cove.

The whole army was found to be in motion and the command moved rapidly up the valley, with some slight skirmishing, until it arrived at Crawfish Spring, where it was halted, formed in line of battle, and remained posted at this point during the remainder of the day.

September 20.—Command was engaged all day in guarding fords on Chickamauga Creek. General Crook, with his command, reported about 10 a. m. from Dougherty's Gap. The enemy attacked the forces at the various fords in strong force, and after severe fighting succeeded in effecting a crossing, but gained but little ground afterward, for they were stubbornly resisted at every step, and finally gave up the attempt to get in on our right through the cavalry. About 3 p. m. I received verbal orders from an orderly from General McCook to fall back, as our right had been turned. Not deeming an order of so important a nature as that, coming in such a manner, valid, I did not move, as I had been ordered in the morning to hold Crawfish Spring at all hazards, but sent staff officers to ascertain the position of affairs, and, if possible, communicate with either General McCook or Rosecrans. From them I learned that our right had been driven round and that everything on the right was moving toward Chattanooga up Chattanooga Valley. I therefore, after moving out all trains and loading into ambulances all wounded able to ride from the vicinity of my position, about 5 p. m. commenced falling back up Chattanooga Valley, bringing off on my retreat two pieces of artillery which had been abandoned by the troops of General McCook's corps, and collecting about a regiment of stragglers from the same command. The command bivouacked on Chattanooga road during the night.

September 21.—The whole command stood in line of battle all day in Chattanooga Valley, with frequent skirmishing. The enemy's cavalry were in sight all day, but no severe attack was made.

September 22.—In accordance with orders from department headquarters, at daylight whole force, with exception of one brigade, which was left to keep up show in front, moved into Chattanooga. The brigade left at the front fell back about 10 a. m., fighting hard as they came.

For the detailed reports of the many skirmishes on several occasions I respectfully refer you to the detailed reports of brigade, division, and regimental commanders.

Among the missing on the 20th is Capt. James Hawley, Second Michigan Cavalry, acting assistant inspector-general at headquarters chief of cavalry. While rallying the Fourth Ohio at Crawfish Spring he fell from his horse wounded, and probably killed. Information through Surgeon Vaile, medical director of First Cavalry Division, who fell into the hands of the enemy that day, renders this probable, that he was killed. He was a young man of sterling worth. Beginning poor in life, by industry and economy he had sought to gain for himself an education. At the fall of Fort Sumter he was at college, and about to graduate. Throwing aside all thoughts of completing his course, he entered the ranks. Because of his previous scholarly qualities, by unanimous consent of the faculty he was granted a diploma. Soon after entering the service he was promoted to a second lieutenancy; from this he gradually arose to the rank of captain, earning his promotions as he went. In battle he was brave almost to a fault. A stranger to fear, his delight was to be amid the strife. Thoroughly patriotic, with no motive but duty to his country and his God, he has fallen where he often expressed his desire to fall, if fall he should during the war, in battle, his feet to the foe, and nobly performing his duty in a trying hour.

I cannot close this report without calling to the attention of the general commanding, the gallantry and daring of the cavalry command during the two days' battle, as well as the following two days on our retreat to Chattanooga, each regiment, brigade, and division trying to outstrip each other in deeds of daring.

Brigadier-General Crook, commanding Second Division, deserves the gratitude of the country for the gallant manner in which he discharged his duty throughout the entire advance, as well as on the battle-field of Chickamauga.

Col. E. M. McCook, commanding the First Division, as well as Colonels Campbell, Long, and Ray, brigade commanders, deserve a full share of the praise awarded to the cavalry. I must here tender my thanks to Major Sinclair, Lieutenant-Colonel Gwynne, Captains McCormick and Warner, and Lieutenants Osgood, Rankin, Hosea, Greenwood, and Arthur, members of my staff, for the gallant manner in which they each and every one discharged their duty.

I must, in conclusion, say that there was never work more opportunely done on the battle-field than the work of the cavalry on the 20th of September at Chickamauga.

I am, general, very respectfully, your obedient servant,

ROBT. B. MITCHELL,
Brigadier-General, and Chief of Cavalry.

Brig. Gen. James A. Garfield, U. S. Army,
Chief of Staff, &c.

No. 215.

Report of Col. Edward M. McCook, Second Indiana Cavalry, commanding First Division, Cavalry Corps.

HEADQUARTERS FIRST CAVALRY DIVISION,
Bridgeport, Ala., September 30, 1863.

MAJOR: I have the honor to forward a report of the operations of this division in the engagement at Crawfish Spring, Ga., on the 19th and 20th instant, together with a brief minute of its marches, &c., since crossing the Tennessee River and prior to the dates mentioned above.

On the 3d instant, the division left its bivouac at Caperton's Ferry, crossing the pontoon bridge and ascending Sand Mountain; arrived that night at a small spring run in Lookout Valley.

September 4.—Marched into Will's Valley, encamping at Allen's house, 4 miles from Valley Head, Ala.

September 5.—The First Brigade, Colonel Campbell commanding, proceeded on a reconnaissance down the valley, destroyed rebel salt-works, and took some few straggling rebel soldiers prisoners. Detachment of the Fourth Kentucky Cavalry, Major Welling commanding, sent across Lookout Mountain; at Davenport Gap, came up with the enemy at the eastern crest and charging, captured the enemy's picket, 13 in number.

September 6.—Supply train arriving, issues were made.

September 7.—In camp.

September 8.—Sent back train with guard to Big Will's Valley.

September 9.—Left Allen's house at daylight, ascending Lookout Mountain at Winston's Gap, and found the eastern descent blockaded by felled trees. After a spirited skirmish with the enemy's cavalry we gained possession of the town of Alpine at the foot of the mountain and bivouacked.

September 10.—Detachments were sent on all the roads to reconnoiter; the Third Brigade, First Division, with part of the Second Division, encountered a small force of rebel cavalry on the Summerville road. The First Brigade, First Division, proceeded as far as the Chattooga River on Rome road and found nothing of importance.

September 11.—Reconnaissance of the division on Rome road to Melville; discovered a large force of infantry and artillery at the junction of Chattooga and Coosa Rivers.

September 12.—Marched at daylight, returning to Alpine; received orders to proceed at once on the La Fayette road; marched as far as and across Chattooga River; encountering Wheeler's cavalry command, drove them for some distance. Returned to Summerville and bivouacked, communicating with General Crook on Broomtown Valley road.

September 13.—Advanced again to the Chattooga River with whole command. The Fourth Indiana Cavalry being sent across the river, discovered a large column of the enemy's cavalry, infantry, and artillery moving to our left; crossed over to Broomtown Valley, joining General Crook, and returned to camp at Alpine.

September 14.—Reascended Lookout Mountain through Henderson's Gap and encamped on Yellow Fork of Little River.

September 15.—Marched to Allen's Spring in Little Will's Valley.

September 16.—Marched through Winston's Gap across Lookout Mountain to Dougherty's Gap and bivouacked in McLemore's Cove.

September 17.—Moved 5 miles to Cedar Grove Church.

September 18.—Moved 7 miles to Blue Bird Gap.

September 19.—The Second Brigade with our train was attacked near Crawfish Spring by the enemy's cavalry and artillery, and after about an hour's heavy skirmishing, repulsed them. I afterward received orders to distribute my command as follows: Colonel Campbell, with two regiments of his brigade, in Dry Valley to protect ammunition and supply trains; the Second Indiana Cavalry immediately on the left of Colonel Wilder's mounted infantry, and the remainder of the division in front and on the left of Crawfish Spring.

September 20.—Part of the division only was with me personally, and was formed in the following manner: The Ninth Pennsylvania on the left, the First Wisconsin on the right, and the Second Indiana in reserve. The rest of the division acted under the immediate supervision of the general commanding the corps, farther to the right. Our line of skirmishers connected with the mounted infantry, who were on the right of our infantry. The enemy's cavalry was in our front during the whole day, in line of battle on the other side of Chickamauga. My orders were not to cross, but during the whole day the skirmishing was continuous and at times heavy. About 3 o'clock in the afternoon General McCook's adjutant-general met me with an order for all the cavalry to come up at once, as the mounted infantry had been compelled to fall back, and the enemy was turning his right. I immediately started on a gallop with the First Wisconsin and Ninth Pennsylvania Regiments, and after proceeding one-quarter mile, Captain McCormick, of General Mitchell's staff, overtook me and ordered me back to the right to re-enforce the rest of the command, as the enemy had attacked in force and were pressing us hard. I moved back and formed a line in front of Crawfish Spring. My division covered the withdrawal of the trains to Chattanooga, and although isolated and almost surrounded by the enemy's infantry and cavalry, accomplished it in good order, and without the loss of a wagon, bringing off also all the cavalry wounded. None of our cavalry moved from the field of Chickamauga until after General Mitchell had ascertained that the infantry lines on our left had been entirely broken, and the safety of all our trains had been assured.

On the morning of the 21st, in pursuance of orders, I sent the Second Michigan to Chattanooga as an escort to the ammunition and supply trains brought off the day previous from Crawfish Spring. I then proceeded, with the balance of the division, to Dry Valley for the purpose of opening communication with the right of the main line of the army, which was, up to this time, broken or imperfectly established, and also to hold the gap through Missionary Ridge, as it had become evident that the enemy intended forcing a passage to our right in the direction of Chattanooga. The First Brigade was disposed upon the right of my line, and with the Second Brigade I connected my line with that of General McCook's right, sending one regiment from this brigade (the Second Indiana) to hold a road leading from the main Crawfish road through Wood's Gap, and intersecting the Chattanooga road between that place and Rossville. After forming this line I communicated personally with Major-General Thomas, and reported the disposition of my force. Skirmishing was kept up continuously at different points during the day, and the design of the enemy to gain possession of Chattanooga Valley successfully frustrated. About 4 p. m. long and heavy columns of dust indicated that a large force was massing in my front and upon the right of the infantry line, and an hour later a more determined attempt was made to force my position. The enemy were promptly repulsed by the First Wisconsin and Second East Tennessee. During the night I sent one squadron of the Second Indiana and one squadron of the First Wisconsin to reconnoiter in front as far as the Crawfish road. This battalion passed through the lines of the enemy and proceeded as far as the field hospital, near the spring, where they learned that General Bragg and escort had left a short time before.

On the morning of the 22d, I received orders to fall back, covering the retreat of the army upon Chattanooga. I immediately ordered Colonel Campbell to move the First Brigade up the Chattanooga Valley road in the direction of Chattanooga, covering the rear with the First Wisconsin. An officer from my staff was dispatched to the left, with orders to move the Second Indiana over upon the Rossville road, and, if attacked, to hold the enemy in check until the rear of the infantry column had reached Chattanooga. This regiment arrived at Rossville about sunrise, and found that the place had been entirely abandoned except by a few stragglers, who were at once sent to the rear. As soon as the retrograde movement of the army was discovered, the enemy made a spirited attack upon the Second Indiana with cavalry and artillery in large force, threatening to cut off the infantry brigade of General Spears and the cavalry moving up the Valley road in the direction of Chattanooga. This regiment repulsed the enemy's cavalry and maintained their position under a heavy fire of grape and canister until re-enforced by the First Wisconsin.

By this time the column moving up the Chattanooga road had passed the intersection of the Rossville road, and both regiments were ordered to fall back across the creek into Chattanooga. This movement was executed in splendid order under a continuous and heavy fire from a largely superior force of the enemy. After bringing my command across Chattanooga Creek in safety, and finding that the enemy were advancing a heavy line of skirmishers through the woods, I ordered a sufficient force to dismount and deploy across the creek and hold the enemy in check, where they remained until the lines of the Twentieth Army Corps had been formed. My skirmishers were relieved by the infantry. The men and officers throughout displayed uniform good conduct, courage, and endurance, and are entitled to the thanks of the country for their soldierly bearing and firmness in the face of disaster that tried the nerves of the boldest. Although they knew our army had suffered disaster, if not defeat, and that they were surrounded by the enemy, there was no wavering, no haste; they retired from the field slowly and orderly, as though on parade.

List of casualties.—The First Brigade lost 3 enlisted men killed, 9 wounded, and 1 missing. The Second Brigade lost 1 enlisted man killed, 10 wounded, and 11 missing. The Third Brigade lost 5 commissioned officers and 211 men; making a total of 5 commissioned officers and 246 enlisted men killed, wounded, and missing.

In conclusion, I cannot speak too highly of the efficient manner in which Colonel Campbell, commanding First Brigade, and Colonel Ray, commanding Second Brigade, handled their commands and executed the orders given them. The gallant conduct of Captain Pratt, assistant adjutant-general; Lieutenant Miller, mustering officer; Major Helveti, inspector-general; Captain Hancock, Captain Mitchell, Captain Porter, and Lieutenant Cunningham, officers of my staff, and the prompt manner in which they performed their arduous duties throughout all the march, greatly contributed to our success.

I refer you to reports of brigade commanders herewith inclosed for information as to details.

I have the honor to be, major, very respectfully, your obedient servant,

EDWARD M. McCOOK,
Colonel, Commanding First Cavalry Division.

Maj. W. H. Sinclair,
Assistant Adjutant-General, Cavalry Corps.

ADDENDA.
Itinerary of the First Cavalry Division.*

September 15.—Descended the mountain into Will's Valley, en-camping again at 4 miles from Valley Head, Ala.

September 17.—Reascended, with the First and Second Brigades, Lookout Mountain at Winston's Gap (Third Brigade being left at Winston's Gap). Crossed to Dougherty's Gap, and, descending, bivouacked at head of McLemore's Cove.

September 18.—Moved 5 miles, to Cedar Grove. Same date moved to Blue Bird Gap.

September 19.—Moved to Crawfish Spring, in which direction heavy musketry and cannonading was heard. Near Crawfish Spring the Second Brigade, with the train, was attacked by the enemy's cavalry in large force. One hour's fighting found them repulsed. Disposition of this division was made under the orders of General Mitchell, acting chief of cavalry, for the morrow's continuance of the battle of this date.

September 20.—The division joined the right wing of Major-General McCook's Corps, which was hotly engaged from 10 a. m., and the Second Cavalry Division on the right. The enemy was constantly pressing us in front. General McCook was apparently being over-powered. General Crook, with the Second Cavalry Division, was in hot and close engagement on the right, when it was discovered that the former had been obliged to fall back, and that the enemy were between our left and main army. Communicating with General Mitchell, he ordered, after observation, the falling back to Chick-amauga Valley, which was accomplished safely, all transportation of the cavalry and Twentieth Army Corps being brought over without the loss of a wagon. Marched to bivouac 7 miles from Chattanooga.

September 21.—In position in Dry Valley, communicating with the right of the army at Rossville. Enemy constantly pressing our line to force a passage, but were repulsed.

September 22.—Under orders from General Mitchell, retired from the position at Dry Valley. Sent the Second Indiana Cavalry, via Rossville, to keep up communication with the infantry, and fell back to Chattanooga. The Second Indiana Cavalry was warmly engaged with the enemy's cavalry and artillery. Arrived at Chattanooga, crossed Tennessee River, joined by the Third Brigade, which had marched from Winston's with its train and suffered severely. The losses of the division in the campaign amount to 265 killed, wounded, and missing. Crossed the Tennessee River and remained in bivouac.

September 25.—On the north side of the river, when, crossing Wal-den's Ridge, the division marched to Bridgeport, arriving September 27.

No. 216.

Report of Col. Archibald P. Campbell, Fourth Michigan Cavalry, commanding First Brigade.

Headquarters First Brigade, First Division,
Camp near Stevenson, Ala., September 30, 1863.

Sir: In compliance with orders received from the colonel commanding, I have the honor to report the operations of this brigade since leaving Stevenson, Ala., September 3.

---

* From return for September.

The Second Michigan Cavalry having been detached and sent to Bridgeport, I marched with the balance of my brigade, First East Tennessee and Ninth Pennsylvania Cavalry. I marched at daylight from Caperton's Spring up Sand Mountain, thence across the mountain on the direct road to the head of Will's Valley, a distance of 22 miles. My pickets took 2 prisoners.

September 4.—Marched at daylight through Winston's Gap, 3 miles into Little Will's Valley at Valley Head, thence down the valley 4 miles to Allen's farm. My pickets took 2 prisoners.

September 5.—Ordered on a scout; proceeded to 1 mile south of Rawlingsville, where I met some rebel cavalry; Lieutenant-Colonel Brownlow, First East Tennessee Cavalry, charged them 2 miles through a heavy cloud of dust, but failed to capture them and they fled. I then proceeded to Lebanon, which place I found evacuated the night before by the enemy. I then returned to Allen's farm, having marched in all 28 miles.

September 9.—Marched at daylight up Little Will's Valley to Winston's Gap, through the gap across Lookout Mountain to Henderson's Gap, thence down the gap or mountain to Alpine, Ga., where we bivouacked for the night, having marched 18 miles over mountain roads.

September 10.—Marched to Melville, on the Rome road, on a scouting expedition, took 4 prisoners and obtained valuable information of the enemy's movements; returned to Alpine, making a march of 15 miles.

September 11.—Marched at 12 m. to Melville and sent out scouts within 12 miles of Rome, who ascertained that a large force of the enemy were encamped 6 miles north of that place; also sent scouts to Galesville, 13 miles, and found no enemy.

September 12.—Returned to Alpine, where I received orders to join General Crook's division and proceed toward La Fayette. After marching 12 miles up Broomtown Valley I camped for the night.

September 13.—Marched at 6 a. m. toward La Fayette; 5 miles from that place I encountered the enemy's pickets and skirmished with them 1 mile, when I ordered the Ninth Pennsylvania Cavalry to charge the enemy in column; leading the charge in person, which they obeyed most gallantly, capturing 18 prisoners from the grand guard of the enemy's infantry. The Ninth Pennsylvania and First East Tennessee and Second Michigan Cavalry pressed on rapidly a short distance and found the enemy in large force with artillery, who fired a number of volleys, killing 2 men and wounding 3. I immediately formed my command in line to charge the rebels, but at that moment received orders from General Crook to return, that the enemy was in our rear, and that, the object of the reconnaissance being effected, I should make no further demonstrations with my brigade, and in compliance with these orders I returned to Alpine.

September 14.—Marched up Lookout Mountain through Henderson's Gap and encamped at Little River.

September 15.—Marched to Allen's farm in Will's Valley, 12 miles.

September 16.—Marched through Winston's Gap across Lookout Mountain to Dougherty's Gap, and camped in McLemore's Cove, 18 miles.

September 17.—Moved 5 miles to Cedar Grove Church.

September 18.—Moved 7 miles to Bailey's Cross-Roads.

September 19.—Marched via Pond Spring to Crawfish Spring. A slight skirmish occurred on our right flank, but without loss. The enemy's skirmishers retreated rapidly. The Second Michigan Cavalry skirmished the enemy in front and to the right of Crawfish Spring during the afternoon, driving the enemy across Chickamauga River, holding the fords.

September 20.—In accordance with orders from the general commanding, I occupied the crest of the ridge, 1 mile to the rear and to the right of Crawfish Spring, with the First East Tennessee and Fourth Indiana Cavalry. The Second Michigan Cavalry skirmished during the day in front of Crawfish Spring, driving and being driven by the enemy with slight loss, and the Ninth Pennsylvania Cavalry of my command was to the left of Crawfish Spring and was not seriously attacked. At 3 p. m. the discovery was made that the cavalry command was not in communication with any other part of the army, and a part of my brigade, consisting of the First East Tennessee and Fourth Indiana Cavalry, was ordered to Chattanooga Valley, to hold any enemy that should attempt to approach Chattanooga by that route. Upon arriving in that valley I found that General McCook's corps was driven back in disorder and that the right flank of the army had been turned. I formed a regiment of infantry and a battery of artillery in the valley beside my two cavalry regiments, and kept my line of battle across the valley until the whole wagon train and column of wounded soldiers had passed on toward Chattanooga. At dusk, in accordance with orders from the general commanding, I sent the Second Michigan Cavalry as a guard with the wagon train to Chattanooga, and with the balance of my command bivouacked 6 miles from Chattanooga.

September 22.—The Ninth Pennsylvania Cavalry and First East Tennessee were ordered to Chattanooga at daylight, and in pursuance of orders from General Mitchel, the Second Indiana and First Wisconsin Cavalry reported to me for duty. I marched 2 miles toward Crawfish Spring, and met the enemy's pickets. The Second Indiana passed a few shots among them and proceeded along Missionary Ridge toward Chattanooga, and the First Wisconsin Cavalry marched down the valley toward the same place. Upon nearing Chattanooga the Second Indiana was attacked by the enemy, and a brisk skirmish ensued. I immediately went to their support with the First Wisconsin Cavalry, but having to march this regiment by file along a narrow path of the mountain, in the face of the enemy and a continuous fire from the enemy's artillery, I did not reach the Second Indiana until they had commenced driving the enemy, but with the aid of our artillery the rebels were driven out of sight by the Second Indiana Cavalry. I was then ordered to cross the Tennessee River without delay, which I did at the ford.

September 25.—In compliance with orders from the general commanding, I marched at 10 p. m. with the First East Tennessee Cavalry and Ninth Pennsylvania and Fourth and Sixth Kentucky Regiments of Cavalry to Bridgeport, via Jasper, and arrived 11 a. m. next day.

September 27.—Marched to Stevenson and camped at Pond Spring, throwing out patrols and pickets along the river from Cox's Ferry to Bellefonte.

September 28.—I directed Colonel Cooper to march with the Fourth and Sixth Kentucky Cavalry to Bellefonte, at 2 a. m. At 11 a. m. I received a dispatch from him, saying that the enemy were crossing the river in that vicinity on rafts. I immediately marched with the Ninth Pennsylvania and First East Tennessee Cavalry to prevent their crossing. But after marching 6 miles toward that point I received a second dispatch from Colonel Cooper, saying that he had driven the enemy back across the river in great haste, killing 1 of their number. No further demonstrations being made, I returned with my command to Pump Spring, near Stevenson, Ala.

List of casualties is as follows : Ninth Pennsylvania Cavalry, 2 privates killed, 3 wounded at La Fayette ; First East Tennessee Cavalry, 1 private missing ; Second Michigan Cavalry, 1 private killed, 6 wounded at Crawfish Spring.

Very respectfully submitted.

Your most obedient servant,

A. P. CAMPBELL,
Colonel, Commanding.

Maj. W. H. SINCLAIR,
Assistant Adjutant-General, Cavalry Corps.

No. 217.

Report of Maj. Leonidas S. Scranton, Second Michigan Cavalry.

HEADQUARTERS SECOND MICHIGAN CAVALRY,
Winchester, Tenn., November 3, 1863.

LIEUTENANT : I have the honor to report the operations of this regiment for the month of September, 1863.

The 1st of the month found us bivouacked on the left bank of the Tennessee River opposite Bridgeport, having forded the river and scouted up as far as the Running Water on the last days of the last month.

September 2, ascended Raccoon Mountain at Moore's Gap and scouted out 12 miles and back ; 3d, marched to Caperton's Ferry, 18 miles ; 4th, crossed Raccoon Mountain to Winston's, near Valley Head ; 5th, moved up Little Will's Valley 5 miles and joined the brigade; 6th, 7th, and 8th, at same place; Privates Henry Edding and Martin Degroot straggled from camp and were captured ; 9th, crossed the Lookout Mountain to Alpine, Ga. ; 10th, scouted toward Rome 6 miles and back ; 11th, scouted to same point and remained until near morning ; 12th, returned to Alpine and marched out toward La Fayette, 10 miles ; Private Bernard Bourassa, missing, having stopped to attend to calls of nature, was not seen or heard from after ; marched 16 miles ; 13th, advanced to within a short distance of La Fayette. The Ninth Pennsylvania being in advance, drove the enemy's pickets 4 miles, when they encountered a strong force in a strong position. This regiment was ordered forward to cover the field while the wounded were removed, then covered the retreat, taking several prisoners ; marched back to Alpine ; 14th, moved to the summit of Lookout Mountain, 8 miles ; 15th, recrossed the Lookout Mountain to Little Will's Valley, 12 miles ; 16th, crossed the Lookout Mountain again to McLemore's Cove, 16 miles ; 17th, moved 4 miles down the cove ; 18th, First Battalion scouted to Blue Bird Gap, found the enemy in possession of the gap ; 19th, moved down the cove and joined the infantry line at Pond Spring, remained in line two hours, then moved briskly down to Crawfish Spring ; was there detached from the brigade, scouted southeasterly to the fords on the Chickamauga at Bird's Mill and Morgan's place ; remained on picket during the night 1 mile from the fords, marched 16 miles, the enemy in sight more or less all day, and fired some shots at long range, but we wasted no powder; the enemy made a dash on our train, but we sustained no damage; 20th, moved forward at daylight and drove the enemy's pickets over the ford at Bird's Mill, Companies D, I, C, M as skirmishers, the Third Battalion as support; this detachment, except Companies D and I, remained to guard this ford, Companies C and M remaining close to the ford and exchanging shots with rebels continually; Private Patrick Dooley was here wounded.

The First Battalion was formed three-quarters of a mile to the west and fronting south, as support to Companies H and L guarding the other ford, while the other detachment fronted east.

Remained in these positions until about 10 a. m., when the enemy, having planted a battery on a high bank on the opposite side of the stream just to the right and nearly in line with the skirmishers of the first detachment, opened with grape and canister, driving the skirmishers back to the support and all back to a more secure position. Our artillery having now come up, an artillery duel ensued. The enemy having now crossed the stream, this detachment, consisting of 100 men, was ordered to drive them back again, but were themselves soon driven back by the enfilading fire of enemy's artillery on the right, and the flank fire of their musketry from the woods on the left. As we fell back we were met by other regiments moving forward to form on our left, when we again advanced, forming the right of the whole line. The line on the left of us, with one company of the detachment, after a sharp engagement which reached only part way on our front, gave way, and had fallen back 300 or 400 yards, when the detachment retreated under a sharp flank fire of the enemy. At the edge it was halted, but, finding no support, fell back, halting frequently, to the led horses. In the meantime, the First Battalion had been ordered back, but Companies A and F, not hearing the order, still remained in their position, and were enabled to punish those of the enemy that, in their too eager pursuit, had ventured into the woods. Companies H and L passed farther to the west and joined the regiment at Crawfish Spring. Joined the brigade at Crawfish Spring, and, with the Ninth Pennsylvania Cavalry, covered the retreat into Chattanooga Valley. From there guarded the train into Chattanooga, arriving there at 3 a. m. of 21st.

Casualties of this day: Captain Hawley, acting assistant inspector-general on General Stanley's staff, supposed to be killed; Lieutenant Ranney, assistant surgeon, captured; Sergeant Loomis and Private W. W. Wright, Company A, slightly wounded; Private Thomas O'Brien, Company E, missing; Private James M. McCullough, Company F, slightly wounded; Private Thaddeus L. Waters, Company G, prisoner; Corpl. James Burt, same company, slightly wounded; Sergt. Albert M. Spaulding and Private Patrick Dooley, Company M, severely wounded.

On 21st, crossed the river and went to the Harrison's Ferry, 14 miles above Chattanooga; 22d to 27th, guarded ferries and fords from the Harrison Ferry to Thatcher's Ferry, 15 miles. [From] there up Company I made a scout on the 22d to Ooltewah, 10 miles distant, on the enemy's side of the river. Corporal Cook, of that company, severely wounded. Company L made a scout on the 25th farther up on the same side. Sergt. Job Reynolds and Private Nathan Jenne, Company B, and Private G. Carlisle, Company E, were taken prisoners while doing some blacksmithing; 28th, marched to Chattanooga, 14 miles; 29th, marched over Walden's Ridge to Rankin's Ferry, 25 miles; 30th, at Rankin's Ferry.

Recapitulation of casualties: Commissioned officers, 2; Captain Hawley, probably killed, and Lieutenant Ranney, assistant surgeon, prisoner. Enlisted men, prisoners, 9; wounded, 7.

I am, respectfully, your obedient servant,

L. S. SCRANTON,
Major, Commanding Second Michigan Cavalry.

Lieut. E. HOYT, Jr.,
Actg. Asst. Adjt. Gen., 1st Brig., 1st Div., Cav. Corps.

No. 218.

Report of Lieut. Col. Roswell M. Russell, Ninth Pennsylvania Cavalry.

HEADQUARTERS NINTH PENNSYLVANIA CAVALRY,
Winchester, Tenn., November 3, 1863.

COLONEL: In compliance with your directions, I hereby submit the following report of the marches, skirmishes, &c., of the Ninth Pennsylvania Cavalry, during the month of September, 1863:

Shortly after daylight, September 3, I left Caperton's Spring, Ala., with ten companies of my command, and, crossing Raccoon Mountain, encamped for the night at a point on the Trenton road equidistant between that place and Lebanon.

At sunrise of the 4th, left camp on Trenton road, and went into camp at 8.30 a. m., 4 miles south of Valley Head.

September 5.—Left camp at 8.30 a. m. on a scout to Lebanon, 15 miles distant, and returned to camp at 9 p. m.

September 9.—Left camp at daylight, and crossing Lookout Mountain, encamped at 9 p. m. near Alpine, Ga.

September 10.—Left camp near Alpine, and marched to Melville, 8 miles distant. From that place (by order of Colonel Campbell, commanding brigade) I sent a squadron, in command of Major Savage, to reconnoiter the Rome road as far as the crossing of the Oostanaula River. On the return of Major Savage, the command moved back to Alpine.

At noon of the 11th, left camp near Alpine, and advanced on the Rome road as far as Melville, where the command was halted until 3 a. m. of the 12th, when it returned to Alpine.

At 11 a. m., September 12, left camp near Alpine, and moved out on the La Fayette road, encamping at 7 p. m. near Valley Store, 7 miles south of La Fayette.

September 13.—Resumed the march to La Fayette. When about 3 miles from that place, my advance guard, consisting of Companies A, C, and E, under command of Captain Porter, came in sight of the enemy's vedettes and advanced picket posts. The enemy, when pressed, fell back upon his reserves, until sufficiently strong to offer a show of resistance, and then delivered a volley into my line of skirmishers on the left, killing one man of Company E. He then fell back, and occupied the crest of a knoll, densely covered with underbrush. On reaching this point the enemy again opened a severe fire. Colonel Campbell now directed me to push forward a squadron to re-enforce the skirmishers and clear the road.   In compliance therewith I ordered two companies, H and F, under Major Savage, to charge.   The command was promptly obeyed; but the charge met with a momentary check by the complete obscurity of the road, caused by clouds of dust concealing a deep gully running across the road, which tripped the horses and dismounted the first set of fours.   The débris of horses and men removed, the charge was continued; but had not advanced more than 200 yards when the enemy opened a withering enfilading fire, killing 1 man, mortally wounding 2 others, and disabling 8 horses.   Captain Shriver, of Company H, had 2 horses shot under him; Lieutenants Shuman and Jordon, each, 1.   Following closely with the balance of the regiment, upon the heels of the battalion engaged, and finding Major Savage recalling his men, the road encumbered with his prisoners (18 in number), and the enemy still keeping up a rapid fire, at close range, I ordered the fences to be torn down on both sides of the road. Then deploying the regiment, I was slowly driving the enemy from his cover, when orders were received to withdraw and form on the flanks of the Second Michigan Cavalry, then being deployed on foot across the road.   Shortly after the whole command fell back to Alpine, which it reached at 9 p. m.

September 14.—Left camp at 8 a. m., marched to and encamped for the night near Little River, on the table-land of Lookout Mountain.

September 15.—Left camp near Little River at 8 a. m. as escort to cavalry division train, reaching camp near Valley Head, in Will's Valley, at 5 p. m.

September 16.—Moved out of camp at noon and, crossing Lookout Mountain, encamped in McLemore's Cove, at the foot of Dougherty's Gap, at 8 p. m.

September 17.—Left camp at 3 p. m. and halted for the night at Cedar Grove.

September 18.—Left camp at Cedar Grove at 2 p. m.; encamped at 8 p. m. near Bailey's Cross-Roads.

September 19.—Left camp at sunrise and moved in line of battle along the left of Crawfish Spring road until reaching Cowan's Ford, on the Chickamauga Creek.   At this point I was ordered to cross the creek and disperse a squad of rebel cavalry posted in the edge of a corn-field.

On the approach of the two companies, under the command of Captain Longsdorf, sent in compliance with this order, and to reconnoiter an adjacent wood, the enemy fired a volley and hastily retreated.   On the return of Captain Longsdorf the command recrossed the Chickamauga, halting at Crawfish Spring.   About 4 p. m. I was ordered to take position along the western bank of the Chickamauga, with instructions to hold the ford and keep a line of pickets and patrols connecting and keeping up communication between the right of General Wilder's mounted brigade and my left. This position I held (with occasional exchanges of shots with the enemy) until 3 p. m. of the 20th September, when I was ordered by General Mitchell to push my regiment at a trot along the old Chattanooga road and open communication, if possible, with General Sheridan.

Proceeding about 2 miles I found the enemy strongly posted upon the crest of a hill around which the road passed, and which his artillery completely commanded.   Whilst making the necessary dispositions to ascertain the strength and length of his line, for the purpose of forcing or turning it, I received orders from General Mitchell to return immediately to Crawfish Spring. Reporting to Col. E. M. McCook, commanding Second Division, I was ordered to remain with my regiment in rear of the column and keep the enemy in check. Shortly after leaving Crawfish Spring a body of rebel cavalry made a dash on my rear guard, in command of Major Kimmel, but was instantly repulsed, and I proceeded without further annoyance to a point on the Chattanooga and —— road, going into camp at midnight.

September 22.—Left camp at daylight and entered Chattanooga at 8 a. m. Here I remained until 6 p. m., when I crossed the Tennessee River, the command going into camp on the bank of the river opposite the town.

September 24.—Left camp opposite Chattanooga at 7 p. m., encamping near Sevely Springs, 6 miles from Chattanooga.

September 25.—Left camp near Sevely Springs at 9 p. m., making a forced march, by Haley's Trace, to Bridgeport, near which went into camp at 11 a. m. of the 26th.

September 27.—Left camp near Bridgeport at 7 a. m. and encamped near noon at Pump Spring, Ala.

September 28.—I was ordered to proceed with my regiment to Bellefonte and re-enforce Colonel Cooper, commanding Third Brigade. When within 4 miles of Bellefonte received orders to encamp for the night convenient to forage. Returned to Pump Spring early on the morning of the 29th.

Very respectfully,

R. M. RUSSELL,
Lieutenant-Colonel, Comdg. Ninth Pennsylvania Cavalry.

Col. A. P. CAMPBELL,
Comdg. 1st Brig., 1st Div. Cavalry, Winchester, Tenn.

No. 219.

Report of Lieut. Col. James P. Brownlow, First Tennessee Cavalry.

HEADQUARTERS FIRST TENNESSEE CAVALRY,
Winchester, Tenn., November 3, 1863.

LIEUTENANT: I have the honor to submit the following report of operations of the First Tennessee Cavalry for the months of September and October:

After crossing the Tennessee River on the 1st of September, we encamped at Caperton's Spring, Ala. Squadrons F and G, ordered to report to General Jeff. C. Davis for picket, were placed in advance of a reconnoitering party, and after skirmishing with the enemy's advance for some time, drove them into and through Trenton, Ga., without any loss.

On the 4th, crossed Sand Mountain; encamped in Will's Valley, 4 miles from Valley Head.

On the 5th, in advance of the First Brigade, we moved on the Will's Valley road in the direction of Lebanon, and after skirmishing with the enemy for a distance of 3 miles, drove them several miles beyond the town and returned to camp.

On the 9th, crossed Lookout Mountain and entered Alpine, Ga. The entire command stood picket on the night of the 9th, and on the 10th remained in line of battle.

On the 11th, with the brigade, we proceeded to Chattooga River. Here I was ordered to make a scout in the direction of Rome, Ga. After proceeding 5 miles I divided the command, sending a portion in command of Majors Dyer and Flagg on the main road, in which direction they proceeded as far as the Narrows, within 10 miles of Rome, where they drove in the pickets, capturing and destroying all the arms and equipments of one company. I proceeded with the other battalion, in command of Major Thornburgh, to the main road leading from Rome to Dalton as far as Dirt Town, within 10 miles of Rome. This move was made in between the divisions of Generals Forrest and Wharton.

After skirmishing with the enemy for two hours I captured 4 prisoners, from whom I gained very valuable information, and returned to camp with my entire command at midnight without the loss of a man in killed, wounded, or missing.

On the 12th, we returned to Alpine.

On the 13th, we proceeded to La Fayette, Ga., where our brigade engaged the enemy; here I was shelled by the enemy at short range for some time, and returned with the rest of Campbell's brigade as a rear guard to Alpine.

On the 14th, left Alpine and bivouacked on Lookout Mountain; 15th, returned to Will's Valley; 16th, recrossed Lookout Mountain into McLemore's Cove; 17th, proceeded to Cedar Grove; 18th and 19th, moved to Crawfish Spring, and remained in line of battle till the evening of the 20th, when we fell back, to guard the Chattanooga Valley road, where we remained in line of battle until 10 p. m. of the 20th, at which time we fell back to within 5 miles of Chattanooga.

On the 21st, advanced 4 miles in the direction of Chickamauga, and remained in line of battle until the morning of the 22d, when we fell back into Chattanooga; remained in line of battle till evening, when we crossed the Tennessee River.

On the night of the 25th, we crossed Walden's Ridge, and proceeded to Caperton's Ferry, Ala.*

I am, very respectfully, your obedient servant,

JAS. P. BROWNLOW,
Lieutenant-Colonel, Commanding.

Lieut. E. HOYT, Jr.,
Acting Assistant Adjutant-General, First Brigade.

No. 220.

Report of Col. Daniel M. Ray, Second Tennessee Cavalry, commanding Second Brigade.

HDQRS. SECOND BRIGADE, FIRST CAVALRY DIVISION,
Bridgeport, Ala., September 30, 1863.

SIR : I have the honor to report the part taken by my brigade in the several skirmishes during the recent march from the time of

---

*For remainder of this report, see Wheeler and Roddey's Raid, Part II, p. 680.

crossing the Tennessee River on the 2d instant, to the time of our arrival at Chattanooga.

We crossed the river on the 2d day of September, and moved in the direction of Winston's Gap, arriving at that place on the 6th. Here we left our extra horses, wagons, &c., and crossed the mountain into Broomtown Valley.

My brigade was not actively engaged with the enemy during the march, although supporting the First Brigade in several sharp skirmishes. We returned to Winston's and remained in camp one day and moved with our transportation up the mountain to McLemore's Cove, arriving at the head of the cove on the night of the 18th.

On the morning of the 19th, we marched in the rear of First Brigade down the cove and met the division supply train near Stevens' Gap. Soon after crossing West Chickamauga Creek, about 1 mile from Stevens' Gap, the rear of the supply train was attacked by the enemy's cavalry, consisting of about four regiments and two pieces of artillery. The Second Indiana Cavalry, under command of Major Presdee, being in the rear, immediately formed in line and repulsed the first attack.

The First Wisconsin Cavalry and the Fourth Indiana Cavalry were sent to support the Second Indiana Cavalry, and after a spirited skirmish of about one hour repulsed the enemy and brought the train through in safety.

On the morning of the 20th, the brigade was formed in line near Crawfish Spring and continued skirmishing with the enemy until 4 o'clock, when we were ordered to fall back to Dry Valley.

On the morning of the 21st, I was ordered to send a detachment to open communication with Major-General McCook near Rossville, which was accomplished about 10 a. m. My brigade was formed as follows : First Wisconsin on the left flank, Second Indiana left of center, Second East Tennessee on the left of First Brigade, Fourth Indiana on a reserve to support Lieutenant Newell's battery. About 10 o'clock a sharp skirmish commenced on the left of the line, and a strong effort was made by the enemy to cut off communication between us and the infantry. The attack was promptly repelled by the First Wisconsin, and after two or three attempts, the enemy retired. We remained at this point until daylight the next morning, when we fell back to Chattanooga with the Fourth Indiana and Second East Tennessee. The Second Indiana and First Wisconsin were under the immediate command of Brigadier-General Mitchell on the morning of the 22d, and I cannot report the result of the skirmish during the retreat.

The following is the report of the casualties :*

I am under many obligations to regimental commanders and officers for the prompt and energetic manner with which they obeyed all orders given, and especially to the soldiers for their bravery and endurance during the long and tedious march.

I am also under obligations to my staff for the promptness with which they executed my orders during the different engagements, also my orderlies for their bravery in carrying dispatches.

I am, colonel, your obedient servant,

D. M. RAY,
Colonel, Commanding Second Brigade.

Col. E. M. McCook,
Commanding Cavalry Division.

---

* Nominal list omitted; see revised statement, p. 178.

ADDENDA.

Itinerary of the Second Brigade, for September, 1863.*

September 2.—The brigade left Larkinsville and crossed Tennessee River; passed though Trenton, and arrived at Winston's Gap, Valley Head, Ga.

September 7.—Crossed the mountain to Alpine, and went toward La Fayette. Found the enemy in force with cavalry, infantry, and artillery. Had several skirmishes and fell back to Valley Head.

September 17.—Went up the mountain road to McLemore's Cove and passed down Dougherty's Gap to the head of the cove.

September 18.—Met the wagon train at Stevens' Gap. Sent the Second East Tennessee Cavalry to the top of the mountain to hold the gap until Colonel Post's brigade, of Davis' division, should arrive. When about 6 miles from Stevens' Gap the wagon train was attacked by six regiments of the enemy's cavalry, with two small howitzers. The Second Indiana Cavalry, acting as rear guard, held the enemy in check until re-enforced by the First Wisconsin and Fourth Indiana, when the enemy fell back across the Chickamauga Creek, and the train was brought to Crawfish Spring.

September 19.—Skirmished all day.

September 20.—Skirmishing, and, being cut off from the main column of infantry, fell back to the foot of Lookout Mountain, and went into camp at Rocky Ford. At daylight went out on the Rossville road and were attacked on the right, about noon, but the First Wisconsin repulsed the enemy. At 2 a. m. we fell back toward Chattanooga. Severe skirmishing with the enemy.

September 22.—Crossed the river.

September 25.—Marched to Bridgeport, Ala., with transportation.

No. 221.

Report of Maj. David A. Briggs, Second Indiana Cavalry.

HEADQUARTERS SECOND INDIANA CAVALRY,
Winchester, Tenn., November 7, 1863.

COLONEL: I have the honor to submit the following report of the part taken by my regiment in the late campaign:

Leaving Larkinsville on the 31st of August, 1863, and moving southward, crossing the river on the 2d September, 1863, and proceeding in the direction of Alpine, Ga., arriving at the foot of Lookout Mountain on the 9th, formed my regiment in line of battle and moved in the direction of Rome, Ga.

On the 11th, I sent Company M, of my regiment, on a reconnaissance toward Summerville, Ga. They finding nothing to excite suspicion, the command moved on the 12th 4 miles beyond Summerville and returned to Alpine. Then recrossing Lookout Mountain to Little Will's Valley, where we remained one day. Again taking up line of march proceeded across Lookout Mountain in the direction of Stevens' Gap, where we arrived on the 17th September.

On the 18th, moved out to Davis' Cross-Roads, where I found the Thirty-ninth Indiana posted.

---

* From return for September.

On the 19th, moved in the direction of Crawfish Spring; when I arrived to within 3 miles of the spring, I found my regiment, together with the division supply train, had been cut off by the enemy from the main column. I then sent Sergeant Edwards, of Company B, with one other, with a dispatch to the main column stating my situation and asking for relief. The sergeant delivered the dispatch, although a dangerous undertaking, being exposed to the enemy's fire from all sides. I ordered Company K, Captain Barr commanding, to the rear of the train to guard it, at the same time dismounting Companies A, C, D, and sending them to the front and right of the road; deploying Company M on the right flank to protect the train on that side; Companies E, F, H, I in the center. In this manner I held my position until assistance arrived, saving the train, supplies, &c. I have to thank both the officers and men of my command for the coolness, daring, and bravery which they exhibited on this occasion.

On the 20th instant, my regiment was held in reserve for a saber charge on the enemy; 21st, moved forward in the direction of Chattanooga, skirmishing continually with the enemy.

In these three days' engagements I had 1 man killed, of Company L, and 4 wounded, 2 of Company E, 1 Company F, and 1 Company L.*

I am, colonel, respectfully, your obedient,

DAVID A. BRIGGS,
Major, Commanding Regiment.

Col. D. M. RAY,
Commanding Brigade.

No. 222.

Report of Maj. George H. Purdy, Fourth Indiana Cavalry.

MAJOR : On the 2d of September, 1863, the Second and Third Battalions, under Col. John A. Platter, crossed the Tennessee River and camped for the night.

On the morning of the 3d, the command marched to the foot of the mountains, having in charge the wagon train of the Second Cavalry Brigade ; the horses were tied and fed, and dismounted [men] were sent to assist the train.

On the morning of the 4th, the command marched up the mountain and halted, the colonel sending back a sufficient number of men to assist the train.

The 5th and 6th were spent in getting the train over the mountain. On the 7th, the command descended the mountain and camped near a large spring, 4 miles from Valley Head, where it remained until the morning of the 9th. While at this camp Col. J. A. Platter sent his resignation papers to headquarters department.

On the 9th, Colonel Platter, Adjutant Anderson, Chaplain Hendricks, and a number of non-commissioned officers and privates were sent to hospital sick. We were also joined at this place by Lieutenant Young with a party of men, having in charge about 45 horses. At an early hour the command crossed the mountain and entered Alpine, and marched in line of battle for several miles, when night

---

* For remainder of report, see Wheeler and Roddey's Raid, Part II, p. 681.

came on and the command returned to Alpine and went in camp ; 10th, scouted toward Rome, Ga., but found no enemy ; returned to camp, distance 12 miles ; 11th, on picket 6 miles east of Alpine ; 12th, marched to Summerville, Ga., distance 12 miles ; 13th, marched 5 miles east of Summerville, skirmishing with the enemy, drove them 4 miles (Companies F and G in advance); lost 1 man in Company G mortally wounded and left at private house near 4 miles from Summerville. The command then returned to Alpine, accompanied by the First Battalion, under Maj. J. P. Lesslie; 15th, recrossed mountains to Valley Head and went in camp (12 miles) ; 16th, crossed over Lookout Mountain and camped in McLemore's Cove ; 17th, marched toward La Fayette, 6 miles, and camped ; 18th, marched 3 miles near Blue Bird Gap and stood in line of battle all night; 19th, marched toward Gum Spring, had a skirmish with the rebels, lost 2 men missing ; 20th, regiment stood in line of battle all morning, changing position several times. At 1 o'clock fell back 6 miles toward Chattanooga, and stood in line of battle till 8 o'clock, when the command again fell back to Chattanooga Valley ; 21st, remained in line all day and night ; 22d, fell back to Chattanooga, remained a short time near the city, then forded the river and camped opposite Chattanooga. Private Ed. Hurst accidentally shot himself. In line of battle all night ; 23d, in line all day ; 24th, went back to wagon train, 3 miles in the rear ; 25th, in camp all day ; 26th, crossed the mountain and camped in Sequatchie Valley ; 27th, remained in camp all day waiting for train to get down the mountain ; 28th, marched to Bridgeport, distance 20 miles ; 29th and 30th, remained in camp at Bridgeport.*

G. H. PURDY,
Major, Commanding Fourth Indiana Cavalry.

Maj. W. H. SINCLAIR,
Assistant Adjutant-General Cavalry Corps.

No. 223.

Report of Lieut. William G. Anderson, Adjutant Fourth Indiana Cavalry.

HEADQUARTERS FOURTH INDIANA CAVALRY,
Paint Rock Bridge, Ala., August 25, 1863.

SIR: Under instructions from Colonel Platter, I would respectfully report that Major Lesslie returned last evening from the scout to Deposit and Tennessee River, bringing in 6 prisoners, several horses and mules.

Major Lesslie reports as follows regarding a skirmish he had at Tennessee River:

My advance moved on the ferry, and observing a man beckoning across the river a charge was ordered in hopes of capturing the ferry-boat, but on reaching the river the boat had got half way over. Our men on appearing at the river were greeted with a heavy fire from about 30 rebels on the opposite side and those on the ferry-boat, which was at once effectually returned, our men killing and wounding all in the ferry-boat save 1 man before it reached the other side. Two men fell over the side of the boat in the river. Two horses were on the boat. One was

---

* For remainder of this report, see Wheeler and Roddey's Raid, Part II, p. 682.

killed, and the other jumped overboard, swam back, and was captured by our men. This horse was owned by the notorious conscript agent, Cooper. There seems no doubt but what Cooper was one of the men killed.

Of the effect of our fire on the other side of the river nothing can be definitely stated, only that 1 horse fell dead from the river bank, and the rebels fled in haste after our second volley.

The only injury inflicted on our side was 1 mule shot through the shoulders.

The ferry-boat would undoubtedly have been captured with all in it but for the exertions of a preacher named Poarch (who is sent up as a prisoner to you) to warn the rebels of our approach.

Four refugees who have been hid in the mountains have come in and joined this regiment. They seem to be good men. From all appearances several others will join.

Last evening 6 men, deserters from Bragg's army at Chattanooga, came into our camp. They report Bragg's army completely demoralized, desertions taking place by hundreds, and the officers making little or no efforts to restrain or keep their men.

These men report further that Bragg is evacuating Chattanooga and moving toward Atlanta.

I thought it advisable to allow them to go on their way, as they expressed a wish to take the oath, and appeared very desirous to get out of the rebel service. They belonged to Arkansas regiments.

Eleven prisoners go up in charge of Captain Rosencranz. I inclose a list* of them.

Captain Rosencranz takes the list of prisoners for Captain Hancock.

I am, colonel, very respectfully, your obedient servant,

WM. G. ANDERSON,
Adjutant Fourth Indiana Cavalry.

Col. E. M. McCook,
Commanding First Cavalry Division.

No. 224.

Report of Col. Daniel M. Ray, Second Tennessee Cavalry.

HDQRS. SECOND EAST TENNESSEE CAVALRY,
August 31, 1863.

COLONEL: I have the honor to report to you that, in pursuance to orders received from Major-General Reynolds, I proceeded to Shellmound to report to you. I commenced crossing my regiment about dark, and by 10 o'clock my regiment was all safely landed on the south side of the river. At 10.30 o'clock I moved out on the Chattanooga road. I proceeded to within 2 miles of Chattanooga without meeting with any opposition. At this point I came on the rebel pickets. I drove them before me to the point of Lookout Mountain, where I came in sight of a battery of artillery and infantry. Not thinking it prudent to go any farther I moved back in the direction of Shellmound. On my return I captured R. L. Hawkins, a Confederate agent, with $2,736.50 of Confederate money.

I am, colonel, very respectfully, your obedient servant,

D. M. RAY,
Colonel Second East Tennessee Cavalry.

Col. E. A. King,
Comdg. Second Brig., Fourth Div., 14th Army Corps.

---

* Not found.

No. 225.

Report of Col. Oscar H. La Grange, First Wisconsin Cavalry.

HDQRS. FIRST REGIMENT WISCONSIN CAVALRY,
Winchester, Tenn., November 6, 1863.

MAJOR : I have the honor to transmit the following report of campaign of First Regiment Wisconsin Volunteer Cavalry, from September 1 to October 31, 1863 :

September 1, the regiment was moved to the north bank of Tennessee River, near Stevenson, Ala.

On the 2d, crossed on the pontoon bridge.

On the 3d, crossed Raccoon Mountain.

On the 4th, reached the foot of Little Will's Valley.

On the 9th, crossed Lookout Mountain into Broomtown Valley.

From the 10th to the 14th, inclusive, there was frequent skirmishing in this valley.

On the 15th, crossed Lookout Mountain westward into Little Will's Valley.

On the 17th, recrossed the same range eastward into the head of McLemore's Cove.

On the 18th, moved about 8 miles southward and camped in line of battle.

On the 19th, moved northward and had a brisk skirmish with the enemy's cavalry, which attacked one of our wagon trains about 4 miles south from Crawfish Spring. One half of the regiment was dismounted, and drove the enemy from his concealment in the woods across the Chickamauga River, when the remainder executed a flank movement that compelled him to fall still farther back and allowed the train with its escort to pass in safety. In this affair Private Northrop, of Company G, was severely wounded in the arm, and Private Wixson, same company, reported missing. Regiment camped in line of battle at Crawfish Spring.

On the 20th, took an active part in the cavalry movements on the extreme right of our army line. In the afternoon moved toward Chattanooga, followed by the enemy's cavalry, and camped in line of battle 9 miles from the town. Corporals Byers, of C, and Eldridge, of E, reported missing. Supposed to have been wounded and captured by the enemy.

On the 21st, skirmished nearly all day, holding the position until the morning of the 22d, when we were ordered to Chattanooga. Forded the river and camped upon the north bank.

On the 25th, marched 5 miles and encamped.

On the 26th, crossed Walden's Ridge and camped in the Sequatchie Valley.

On the 28th, marched to Bridgeport, Ala.*

Very respectfully,

O. H. LA GRANGE,
Colonel First Wisconsin Cavalry.

Maj. W. II. SINCLAIR,
Assistant Adjutant-General, Cavalry Corps.

───────────────

*For remainder of report, see Wheeler and Roddey's Raid, Part II, p. 682.

No. 226.

Reports of Col. Louis D. Watkins, Sixth Kentucky Cavalry, commanding Third Brigade.

HDQRS. THIRD BRIGADE, FIRST DIVISION CAVALRY,
Summerville, Ga., September 10, 1863.

I have taken possession of this place.   There were two companies of Second Georgia here when we entered.   They immediately fled.
I have captured about a half dozen and killed and wounded several.
I lost 1 man killed in the engagement.
I learn that there is one regiment encamped about 7 miles from here on La Fayette road.   The rebels ran toward Rome and La Fayette.
We learn from citizens that all the force which was stationed here left last night.
The party found here had come on a scout from the camp 7 miles from here.
The prisoners captured say that it is 23 miles from here to Rome, and 16 to La Fayette ; 33 to Dalton, and Ringgold 28.
I shall remain here two hours to feed.
Respectfully, your obedient servant,
LOUIS D. WATKINS,
Colonel, Commanding.

Major-General STANLEY, or
Col. E. M. McCOOK.

—

NEAR KNOX'S HOUSE,
September 11, 1863.

CAPTAIN : I have the honor to report that when I returned from Summerville last night I was met on the road by an orderly from General Stanley, who directed me to put my brigade in camp near the headquarters of the commanding general.
We captured at Summerville 1 captain and 11 privates, most of them of the Third Georgia Cavalry.   They stated to us yesterday that two regiments of rebel cavalry were encamped about 3 miles from Summerville on the La Fayette road.   Major Cheek, Fifth Kentucky Cavalry, with about 80 men, went in the direction they said the camp was and got within a mile of the camp.   He could plainly see their camp fire, and thought from the bustle they were expecting an attack from the force we had at Summerville.   A large storehouse was discovered filled with baled cotton ; also about 20 barrels of flour, some vinegar, a small quantity of bacon, and some hard bread were found, none of which was brought away, as we had no transportation.   In the skirmish the Sixth Kentucky lost 1 man killed and 3 or 4 slightly wounded.   One of the escort of General Stanley, who was with the Sixth, was shot in the shoulder.   Two of the rebels are known to have been killed ; their bodies were found lying in a field.   We got from the prisoners about 5 or 6 pretty good horses and several Belgian rifles.
Respectfully submitted.

I have delayed making this report longer than I should, but fully intended to send it in early this morning, and so instructed my adjutant, and he forgot it.

I am, captain, very respectfully, your obedient servant,

LOUIS D. WATKINS,
Colonel, Commanding.

Capt. JOHN PRATT,
Asst. Adjt. Gen., First Cavalry Division, Alpine, Ga.

[P. S.]—This report was sent two hours ago; the orderly could not find your headquarters. A partial report was sent yesterday from Summerville.

—

HDQRS. THIRD BRIGADE, FIRST CAVALRY DIVISION,
Near Knox's House, Half Mile from Alpine, Ga.,
September 12, 1863.

CAPTAIN: I have the honor to report that, in obedience to an order from Major-General Stanley, I moved out with my brigade and one piece of Newell's artillery on the La Fayette road at 5.30 o'clock yesterday evening, for the purpose of opening the road between this place and a point 10 miles from here, at which Colonel Harrison with his regiment (Thirty-ninth Indiana Mounted Infantry) had halted, he being unable to proceed farther with the force he had.

Having arrived at the point to which I was directed to go, I halted the column, threw out strong picket guards, and had my horses fed. Colonel Harrison was not there when I arrived, and did not come up until about 12 o'clock. We passed him on the road. I remained there till 4 o'clock this morning, when, learning that the rebels were in front of us in heavy force, and that General Thomas had not possession of La Fayette, I returned, arriving at my old camp at 7.30 o'clock this morning. Just before I left the place at which I stopped last night, I sent out a strong patrol, with instructions to proceed cautiously on the La Fayette road for a mile and a half, and then to return.

The result of their scout was, no sign of the enemy within 2 miles of where we bivouacked. Colonel Harrison returned with me, covering the rear of my brigade.

I am, captain, your most obedient servant,

LOUIS D. WATKINS,
Colonel, Commanding.

Capt. JOHN PRATT,
Assistant Adjutant-General, First Cavalry Division.

[P. S.]—Negroes reported last night that Forrest and Wheeler were both just ahead of us, and were coming to collect all the negroes in that part of the country this morning and run them off.

—

HDQRS. THIRD BRIGADE, FIRST CAVALRY DIVISION,
Camp near Chattanooga, Tenn., September 25, 1863.

MAJOR: I have the honor to make the following report of the operations of my brigade since its departure from Winston's house, Ala., where I was ordered to remain to take charge of the sick and prisoners of war who were turned over to me by Colonel Post, commanding First Brigade, First Division, Twentieth Army Corps, on the 18th instant :

On the 19th instant, I received your order to march, and at daylight next day, with 400 sick and 4 prisoners of war (commissioned officers), I took up my line of march to Stevens' Gap. On arriving at that place I received a second order from you, dated battle-field, Crawfish Spring, September 19, directing me to bring forward my whole command that night, excepting one battalion to be left at Stevens' Gap; also to bring forward the Second East Tennessee Cavalry then at that place. The Second East Tennessee Cavalry had left in the morning, just before my arrival.

To comply with your order, I left one battalion of the Fifth Kentucky Cavalry, under command of Major Cheek, to remain and hold the gap at all hazards.

I left the foot of the mountain near Stevens' Gap and took the main road to Crawfish Spring. About 3 miles from the gap I struck a small picket-post of the enemy, who fled after firing their guns. When within 3 miles of Crawfish Spring, I came across another picket post, which I drove in. I then drew up the Fourth, Fifth, and Sixth Kentucky Cavalry in line of battle, parked the train and sent 20 men, under command of Lieut. Joseph A. Cowell, Fourth Kentucky Cavalry, to Crawfish Spring to ascertain the position of the Federal army. In an hour he returned and reported the spring in possession of the rebels. I forthwith pressed a guide and crossed over to the Chattanooga road, the distance across being 4 miles.

On reaching the main road I halted to let the train close up. While in this position, Capt. James O'Donnell, Fourth Kentucky Cavalry, reported to me that the rebels were advancing down upon us in three columns.

I immediately ordered the train around in the direction of Cooper's Gap, and ordered Lieutenant-Colonel Hoblitzell to take his regiment (Fifth Kentucky Cavalry) to the gap, some 4 miles distant, to cover the retreat.

I then took the Fourth and Sixth Kentucky Cavalry, about 400 in number, and proceeded to meet the enemy. About 1¼ miles I came up with the enemy's skirmishers. I then placed the Sixth Kentucky Cavalry (Major Gratz commanding) in line on the left of the road, and the Fourth Kentucky Cavalry (Colonel Cooper commanding) on the right. The two regiments now commenced falling back slowly under cover of their skirmishers, when the Fourth Kentucky Cavalry formed across the road at Lookout Church, and the Sixth Kentucky Cavalry passed on, but being flanked on both sides by overwhelming numbers, the Fourth Kentucky Cavalry was compelled to fall back slowly, fighting with desperation, and rallied on the Sixth Kentucky Cavalry, when the two regiments combined held the enemy in check for fully twenty minutes. Then they were again flanked.

Now commenced a running fight, but the wagons (as they only got as far as the foot of the mountain) blockaded the road and threw all into confusion. All efforts of the officers to form and rally the men proved only partially successful ; enough so to keep the main column of the enemy from advancing too rapidly.

As I ordered Lieutenant-Colonel Hoblitzell to cover the retreat, I expected to find his regiment formed at the foot of the mountain, which would have effectually checked the enemy and saved the whole brigade ; but I discovered that he had retreated through Cooper's Gap at a very rapid rate. Here the enemy's column, flanking on my right, ran in and intercepted a portion of the Fourth and Sixth Kentucky Cavalry, and after considerable slaughter on both sides the enemy captured a large number of prisoners. I sent Captain Farris and Lieutenant Kelly, of my staff, forward to form the men on the top of the mountain to resist the enemy, if possible. On reaching there myself I found some men of the Fourth, Fifth, and Sixth Kentucky Cavalry.

I then proceeded to rally and form the men (dismounted) as they came up, behind a ledge of rocks, and repulsed the enemy.

I then ordered Colonel Cooper to go in search of Lieutenant-Colonel Hoblitzell, and order his command back; also to bring up a company of infantry that I learned was on the mountain.

In the meantime I learned that the enemy were not disposed to follow me too closely.

I ordered Major Welling, Fourth Kentucky Cavalry, to take command of the force at the entrance and hold it until ordered to return. I then started for the Chattanooga road. I found on the mountain a small train of wagons, belonging to General Thomas' corps. I told the captain in charge that I would place two regiments in front and one in the rear of his train, and make for Chattanooga.

I then ordered Colonel Cooper to bring his regiment forward, and Lieutenant-Colonel Hoblitzell to remain in the rear of the train. I felt a great deal of uneasiness on the march, as I had every reason to believe that the enemy would attempt to cut off my command by the Nickajack Gap. About 10 p. m. of the 21st instant, the head of the column reached Chattanooga.

Too much credit cannot be given to the officers of the Fourth and Sixth Kentucky Cavalry; also to the officers of my staff, Lieut. H. B. Kelly, acting assistant adjutant-general; Capt. Fleming Farris, acting assistant inspector-general; Lieuts. James R. Meagher, and A. K. Collins, aides-de-camp, and Lieut. J. V. Conrad, acting assistant quartermaster; Lieut. J. G. McAdams, acting commissary of subsistence, and Sergt. Maj. Harcourt F. Berkeley, Sixth Kentucky Cavalry, for their services during the day.

The total number missing* are 5 commissioned officers and 200 enlisted men. Lieut. H. B. Kelly and Serg. Maj. H. F. Berkeley are both missing. The Fourth Kentucky Cavalry lost 4 commissioned officers, Capts. Adam Rodgers, Company B, and John W. Lewis, Company I; Lieuts. Max Cohen, Company E, and Rudolph Curtis, Company G (slightly wounded in the arm), and 80 men missing.

The Sixth Kentucky Cavalry lost 1 commissioned officer, Lieutenant Mead, Company F, and 120 men missing. Stragglers are occasionally coming in, and it is supposed that there [are] quite a number still on the mountain concealed in the rocks.

Total number missing, 6 commissioned officers and 211 enlisted men.

There were 36 wagons (brigade and regimental) lost, besides 17 wagons belonging to Captain Dudley, assistant quartermaster.

I have the honor to be, major, very respectfully, your obedient servant,

LOUIS D. WATKINS,
Colonel, Commanding Brigade.

Maj. W. H. SINCLAIR,
Assistant Adjutant-General, Cavalry Command.

---

* See revised statement, p. 178.

[Inclosure.]

HDQRS. THIRD BRIGADE, FIRST CAVALRY DIVISION,
Battle-field, Crawfish Spring, Chattanooga Road,
Between Stevens' Gap and Chattanooga, September 19, 1863.

Colonel WATKINS,
Comdg. Third Brigade, First Division Cavalry:

Bring up to-night your entire brigade, excepting one battalion to be left at Stevens' Gap; also bring with you the Second East Tennessee, left there to-day by my order. The battalion to be left there is expected to hold the gap at all hazards.

By command of General Mitchell:

L. M. HOSEA,
First Lieut., and A. C. M. Cav., A. A. A. G.

P. S.—Look out for the enemy. We have been fighting all along the line.

No. 227.

Reports of Brig. Gen. George Crook, U. S. Army, commanding Second Division.

HDQRS. SECOND CAVALRY DIVISION,
Camp Big Will's Valley, Ala., September 8, 1863.

MAJOR : In accordance with orders received from the major-general commanding Cavalry Corps, on the morning of the 5th of September, I marched from camp at Winston's with two regiments (First and Third Ohio) of the Second Brigade of this division, and proceeded up the mountain at Winston's Gap, and then moved forward across the mountain toward Broomtown Valley.

From information gained from citizens and residents, it appeared that a body of the enemy's cavalry, supposed to be three companies, had crossed the mountain that evening in the direction of Winston's Gap, for the purpose of blockading the road up the mountain, but upon meeting with our pickets, or learning of their whereabouts, returned upon the road in the direction of Broomtown Valley, with the intention of blockading the road leading down the mountain into the valley.

When within 3 miles of the top, and 5 miles from the valley, our advance guard was fired into by the enemy's pickets. We skirmished to the top of the mountain, the enemy making little or no resistance. Here we found the road leading into the valley partly blockaded, the work having been left unfinished on account of our advance.

I ordered 100 men to be dismounted and proceed to the foot of the mountain, it being impracticable for horses on account of the fallen timber. No enemy was found at the foot of the mountain, and after a rest the command proceeded to climb the mountain.

Finding little grain on top of the mountain, and water in a large stream called Little River, 3 miles from Winston's Gap, and a stream 3 miles from the top of the mountain at Broomtown Valley, and our men being out of rations, I deemed it best to return to the old camp at Winston's, where we arrived at 7 p. m. the evening of the 5th. The distance is said to be 16 miles over the mountain from foot to foot. The country on top of the mountain is barren and sandy, being cultivated but little. A good stream of water, called Little River, is to be found upon the top of the mountain suitable for infantry camping grounds. There is not a sufficiency of grain near to make it available for cavalry.

Broomtown Valley is represented as from 5 to 10 miles wide and 50 miles long, very fertile, with abundance of water and plenty of grain.

Very respectfully, your obedient servant,

GEORGE CROOK,
Brigadier-General, Commanding.

Maj. W. H. SINCLAIR,
Assistant Adjutant-General.

—

HEADQUARTERS SECOND CAVALRY DIVISION,
Camp near Washington, East Tenn., September 29, 1863.

MAJOR: In obedience to the circular issued by the general commanding the department, dated September, 1863, requiring reports of operations since leaving Stevenson, I have the honor to make the following report of the cavalry under my command during that period:

On the 2d of September, I left camp at Widow's Creek with Colonel Long's brigade, consisting of First, Third, and Fourth Ohio, and Second Kentucky Regiments, and Stokes' battery, and marched into Will's Valley. From this point I made several small expeditions.

On the 9th of September, my command, being the advance of General Stanley's expedition into Broomtown Valley, met the enemy at Alpine, where a skirmish ensued; the enemy retreated toward Rome; my loss there was 3 killed and 11 wounded; could not tell what damage was done to the enemy.

On the 13th of September, General Stanley being sick, I was ordered with all the cavalry force to make a reconnaissance to La Fayette, to ascertain what force the enemy had at that place. I sent Colonel McCook with two brigades to march on La Fayette by the Summerville road, when I would march with the other two brigades on the direct road, intending the two commands to march abreast. Colonel McCook, meeting too heavy a force, swung around on my road in my rear. (See his report.)

With my column I struck their pickets some 10 miles from La Fayette, driving them steadily without firing, until within some 3½ miles of town, when I saw by their actions I was near their force, and I ordered a regiment to charge and pick up their pickets, when Colonel Campbell, at the head of the Ninth Pennsylvania, made a most gallant charge and picked up all the pickets in front of their line of battle. They fired several volleys into him, but the dust was so thick that there were only 3 wounded and 2 missing. He brought out 17 of their pickets. From this point we moved to Dougherty's Gap, which we held until September 19, when we were ordered to the front and arrived at Crawfish on the evening of the 20th. At this point I found General Mitchell, who ordered me to take post at once in front of the fords of the Chickamauga and hold that point at all hazards. The only point I could occupy was a thick, rocky woods with heavy underbrush. The enemy were already across the river occupying a very strong position. About 11 o'clock I was attacked by Hindman's division of infantry, a battalion of sharpshooters, and a large body of cavalry. They drove us back steadily, contesting every inch of ground, about 200 yards, where we held our ground. At this time I received an order from General Mitchell to fall back to the hospital, 1½ miles distant. Our entire force consisted of Colonel Long's brigade, about 900 strong. The entire command, both officers and men, behaved very gallantly. Among the list of casualties was Lieutenant-Colonel Cupp, First Ohio Cavalry.

Command.	Killed.		Wounded.		Missing.	
	Officers.	Enlisted men.	Officers.	Enlisted men.	Officers.	Enlisted men.
1st Ohio Cavalry		1	1	13		7
3d Ohio Cavalry		2		7		8
4th Ohio Cavalry		3		9	3	19
2d Kentucky Cavalry		11	5	45		2
Total		17	6	74	3	36

Officers	9
Enlisted men	127
Aggregate	136

Officers wounded: Lieut. Col. Valentine Cupp, First Ohio Cavalry; First Lieut. George W. Griffiths, Second Kentucky Cavalry; First Lieut. Edward B. Ayres, Second Kentucky Cavalry; Capt. Charles A. Zachary, Second Kentucky Cavalry; First Lieut. John Calder, Second Kentucky Cavalry; First Lieut. Bird P. Brooks, Second Kentucky Cavalry.

Officers missing: First Lieut. Richard W. Neff, Fourth Ohio Cavalry; Second Lieut. Greenleaf Cilley, Fourth Ohio Cavalry; First Lieut. Charles D. Henry, Fourth Ohio Cavalry.

The latter-named officer, Lieutenant Henry, was left near Crawfish Spring in a gross state of intoxication, so as to be perfectly helpless and immovable. From this point we joined the remainder of the cavalry force, and fell back to McCulloch's Cross-Roads and moved to Chattanooga.

I am, major, very respectfully, your obedient servant,

GEORGE CROOK,
Brigadier-General, Commanding.

Maj. W. H. Sinclair,
Assistant Adjutant-General, Cavalry Command.

ADDENDA.

*Itinerary of the Second Cavalry Division, commanded by Brig. Gen. George Crook, for September, 1863.**

During the first part of the month the division was active in moving about the country, scouting through Tennessee and the northern portion of Georgia, picking up many stragglers and deserters.

---

* From return for September.

September 20.—One brigade, the Second of the division, was engaged upon the right of the army at Chickamauga, under the immediate command of the general. The First Brigade was upon the left of the army. During the latter portion of the month the division was stationed near Washington, Tenn., guarding the fords between Chattanooga and Loudon.

No. 228.

Report of Col. Robert H. G. Minty, Fourth Michigan Cavalry, commanding First Brigade.

HDQRS. FIRST BRIGADE, SECOND CAVALRY DIVISION,
Smith's Cross-Roads, Tennessee Valley, August 26, 1863.

SIR: At 2 a. m., on 17th instant, in accordance with orders from Major-General Rosecrans, through Brigadier-General Van Cleve, I marched for Pikeville, via Sparta.

I sent my artillery and wagons direct with the infantry train. At 2 p. m. my advance struck General Dibrell's pickets 2 miles from Sparta.

I sent the Seventh Pennsylvania and Fourth Michigan up the east side of Calfkiller Creek to Sperry's Mill, where they found Dibrell's brigade and quickly drove it across the creek. With the Third Indiana and Fourth Regulars, I moved up the west side of the creek with the intention of cutting off their retreat, but the nature of the ground was so much in the enemy's favor that they had no difficulty in escaping.

I followed them to within a short distance of Yankeetown, and then moved back toward Sparta, for the purpose of going into camp for the night.

About 4 miles above Sparta the road runs close to the creek with a high bluff (thickly wooded) on the opposite side.

Here about 200 men lay in ambush, and as the head of the column was passing they poured in a volley, wounding Lieutenant Vale, the brigade inspector, and 2 of my orderlies.

Part of the Fourth Michigan and one squadron of the Fourth Regulars were quickly dismounted and engaged the enemy across the creek.

In an attempt to cross the creek a little higher up, the Fourth Regulars lost 1 man drowned and a few wounded. The Seventh Pennsylvania and Third Indiana crossed lower down, and, with slight loss, succeeded in dislodging the rebs.

It being now after 8 o'clock, and quite dark, I bivouacked for the night. In the morning I could not find any trace of the enemy, except a couple of them dead, which the citizens were ordered to inter.

The enemy's force was estimated by the citizens at 1,500. I placed it at 1,200, but every foot of the ground over which we fought was familiar to them. It was wooded, hilly, broken, and intersected by half a dozen branches or creeks, with plenty of good positions, all of which they were able to take advantage of.

My force numbered about 1,400, and the country was to us *terra incognita*, notwithstanding which we drove them at a gallop.

I had 1 man drowned, and 15 wounded, including 3 commissioned officers. I took 23 prisoners, including 1 lieutenant, and representing four regiments.

The enemy's loss in killed and wounded I have no means of ascertaining. I know of only 2 who were killed. A few badly wounded were left at the houses of citizens.

I will send in regular report of casualties in a day or two.

I am, respectfully, your obedient servant,

ROBT. H. G. MINTY,
Colonel, Commanding.

Capt. R. P. KENNEDY,
Assistant Adjutant-General.

—

HDQRS. FIRST BRIGADE, SECOND CAVALRY DIVISION,
Pikeville, Tenn., August 20, 1863.

SIR: I left McMinnville at 2 a. m. on 17th instant, and arrived at Sparta at 2 p. m. General Dibrell had his own regiment and Starnes' and one other. The citizens said from 1,200 to 1,500 men. I fought them until after dark, driving them steadily. Camped near Yankeetown. In the morning rebels had disappeared. Cannot say what their loss was ; saw only 2 dead, but a good many wounded ; a few by sabers.

Took 1 lieutenant and 13 privates prisoners ; our loss pretty heavy.

Regiments.	Men killed.	Wounded.		Total.	
		Officers.	Men.	Officers.	Men.
Brigade headquarters		1	1	1	1
4th Michigan			3		3
7th Pennsylvania		2	5	2	5
4th United States	a1		3		4
3d Indiana					
Total	1	3	12	3	13

a Drowned.

I march in about half an hour for Morganstown, &c.; will send in regular report when I return.

I left about 200 men in McMinnville for want of horses.

Third Indiana are at Rock Island. I wish I could get them back, as I can turn out only about 1,200 men.

Yours, in haste,

ROBT. H. G. MINTY,
Colonel.

Major SINCLAIR,
Assistant Adjutant-General, Cavalry.

[P. S.]—My roan mare was hit twice.

—

MURFREESBOROUGH, TENN.,
December 26, 1863.

SIR : I beg to hand you the following report of the operations of the First Brigade, Second Cavalry Division, from the 13th September to and including the battle of Chickamauga:

September 13.—With the Fourth U. S. Cavalry, Fourth Michigan

Cavalry, Seventh Pennsylvania Cavalry, and one section of the Chicago Board of Trade Battery, I marched from Chattanooga to Gordon's Mills and reported to Major-General Crittenden, commanding the Twenty-first Army Corps.

September 14.—Under orders from Major-General Crittenden, I crossed Missionary Ridge into Lookout Valley.

September 15.—Marched back to Gordon's Mills where General Crittenden ordered me to proceed to Pea Vine Valley and encamp at or near Leet's Cross-Roads.   I crossed the Chickamauga at Reed's Bridge, and shortly before dark encamped on Pea Vine Creek, near Peeler's Mill, and sent out scouts toward Graysville, Ringgold, Leet's, and Rock Spring.   Same night I reported to Major-General Crittenden the information brought in by these parties, and in answer received a letter from Captain Oldershaw, assistant adjutant-general, Twenty-first Army Corps, of which the following is an extract :

The major-general commanding directs me to acknowledge the receipt of your report of this date informing him that Forrest is at Ringgold, Longstreet at Dalton, Pegram at Leet's, and Buckner at Rock Spring ; all this would indicate infantry, which the major-general commanding cannot believe.

September 16.—Strong scouting parties from toward Ringgold and Leet's advanced on me ; they were promptly met, driven, and followed.   The pickets on the La Fayette and Harrison road, which lies between Pea Vine Ridge and Chickamauga, were attacked from toward La Fayette and my rear threatened.   I fell back to the west side of the ridge, thus covering Reed's Bridge, but at same time held all the roads in Pea Vine Valley by strong pickets.   The force which followed the rebel scout to Leet's crossed the line of march of a column of infantry moving from toward Rock Spring to Ringgold and lost 1 man shot through the head.   On being reported to General Crittenden, he answered that " it could be nothing but dismounted cavalry."

September 17.—Slight skirmishing between my scouts and those of the enemy.   The scout to Graysville reported that General Steedman's brigade had passed through there on a reconnaissance toward Ringgold.   The courier to Gordon's Mills reported that Colonel Wilder's brigade of mounted infantry was encamped on the west side of Chickamauga Creek, at Alexander's Bridge, about 2 miles above me.

September 18.—At 6 a. m., I sent 100 men, Fourth United States, toward Leet's, and 100 from Fourth Michigan and Seventh Pennsylvania toward Ringgold.   About 7 a. m. couriers arrived from both parties with the information that the enemy was advancing in force. I strengthened my pickets on the La Fayette road and moved forward with the Fourth Michigan, one battalion of the Fourth Regulars, and the section of artillery, and took position on the eastern slope of Pea Vine Ridge.   I dispatched couriers to Major-General Granger, at Rossville ; Colonel Wilder, at Alexander's Bridge ; General Wood, at Gordon's Mills, and Major-General Crittenden, at Crawfish Spring. The enemy—infantry in force—advanced steadily, driving my skirmishers before them.   The head of a column getting into good range, I opened on them with the artillery, when they immediately deployed, and also strengthened their skirmish line.   At this moment I observed a heavy column of dust moving from the direction of Graysville toward Dyer's Ford.   I wrote to Colonel Wilder asking him to send a force to hold the ford and to cover my left flank.   As the force from Graysville advanced, I fell back until I arrived on the ground which I had occupied in the morning.   Here Colonel Miller, with two regiments and two mountain howitzers from Colonel Wilder's brigade, reported to me. I directed Colonel Miller to take possession of the ford, and again advanced and drove the rebel skirmish line over the ridge and back on their line of battle in the valley, where a force was now visible which I estimated at 7,000 men. The rebel line advanced and I was steadily driven back across the ridge.

My only means of crossing the creek was Reed's Bridge, a narrow, frail structure, which was planked with loose boards and fence-rails, and a bad ford about 300 yards higher up. I masked my artillery behind some shrubs near the ford, leaving one battalion of the Fourth Regulars to support it, and ordered the remainder of that regiment to cross the bridge, holding the Seventh Pennsylvania and Fourth Michigan in line to cover the movement. Before the first squadron had time to cross, the head of a rebel column, carrying their arms at right shoulder shift, and moving at the double-quick as steadily as if at drill, came through the gap not 500 yards from the bridge. The artillery opening on them from an unexpected quarter evidently took them by surprise and immediately checked their advance, causing them to again deploy. The Fourth Michigan followed the Fourth Regulars and the Seventh Pennsylvania the Fourth Michigan, one squadron of the Fourth Regulars, under Lieutenant Davis, most gallantly covering the passage of the Seventh.

One squadron of the Fourth Michigan, under Lieutenant Simpson, on picket on the Harrison road, was cut off by the rapid advance of the rebels. They made a gallant resistance and eventually swam the creek without the loss of a man.

The artillery crossed the road in safety, and I placed them in position to dispute the passage of the bridge, from which Lieutenant Davis' men had thrown part of the planking. Here I was soon hotly engaged, and was holding the rebels in check, when I received a note from the officer in charge of my wagon train, which I had sent back to Gordon's Mills, stating that—

Colonel Wilder has fallen back from Alexander's Bridge to Gordon's Mills and the enemy are crossing at all points in force.

I sent an order to Colonel Miller to join me without delay, and on his arrival I fell back to Gordon's Mills, skirmishing with the enemy, who followed me closely.

With 973 men, the First Brigade had disputed the advance of 7,000 rebels from 7 o'clock in the morning until 5 in the evening, and at the end of that time had fallen back only 5 miles.

On arriving at Gordon's Mills my men were dismounted, and, together with Colonel Wilder's brigade and a brigade from General Van Cleve's division, repulsed a heavy attack at about 8 p. m.

We lay in position all night, and were without fires, although the night was bitterly cold. At break of day Major-General Palmer's division relieved us. I then moved to the rear and procured forage for the horses and rations for the men, who had been entirely without since early the previous morning.

September 19.—Moved along the rear to the left, to protect the trains going into Chattanooga, and camped near Rossville for the night.

September 20.—Under orders from Major-General Granger, I proceeded to the ford at Missionary Mills, and sent strong patrols to Chickamauga Station and Graysville without meeting the enemy.

Toward the afternoon I received orders from General Granger to take possession of the position then occupied by him on the Rossville and Ringgold road.

On arriving on the ground I found that General Granger had already marched to the assistance of General Thomas. Being anxious to know what was in front of me, I pushed forward toward Red House Bridge, and found Scott's brigade of cavalry and mounted infantry, about 1,500 strong, moving into position on our side of the creek. I immediately attacked them. After a spirited skirmish of about an hour's duration, drove them across the creek with considerable loss.

September 21.—During the night, General Thomas fell back to the heights of Missionary Ridge at Rossville, and this morning I found myself about 2 miles directly in front of the center of his line of battle.

The rebels advanced in three columns from the direction of Missionary Mills, Red House Bridge, and Dyer's Ford. I skirmished with their advance for a couple of hours and then fell back to Rossville, with the loss of 1 officer and 9 men killed, and 1 officer and 13 men wounded. I was then ordered to the left to watch the movements of the enemy.

September 22.—Under orders from Major-General Thomas, the Fourth Regulars moved during the night to Rossville and took possession of the gap vacated by our retiring infantry.

At 6 a. m. I heard firing in the direction of Rossville. Leaving strong pickets in the passes over the ridge, I marched with the Seventh Pennsylvania and Fourth Michigan to support the Fourth Regulars, but found that Captain McIntyre had judiciously fallen back, the enemy having turned his flank by advancing on the road from Gordon's Mills. I retreated to Chattanooga, skirmishing sharply.

September 23.—With the Fourth Michigan and Seventh Pennsylvania, I worked in the trenches all night, and at 5 a. m. crossed the Tennessee with the brigade. I camped on Opossum Creek, and from thence picketed the Tennessee River from Washington to Sandy Shoals.

The loss in my brigade from the day on which I was detached from the division until I recrossed the Tennessee River, on the 24th, was under 100 men, of whom only 15 were reported missing. Of these 15, 9 are known to be either killed or wounded. In that time I have taken 439 prisoners from the enemy.

Herewith I hand you report of officers and men deserving special mention.

I am, respectfully, your obedient servant,

ROBT. H. G. MINTY,
Col. 4th Mich. Cav., late Comdg. 1st Brig., 2d Cav. Div.

Major SINCLAIR,
Assistant Adjutant-General.

[Inclosure.]

MURFREESBOROUGH, TENN., *December* 26, 1863.
Major SINCLAIR,
Assistant Adjutant-General:

SIR : I have the honor to call the attention of the major-general commanding to the following officers, whom I consider entitled to special mention for their gallant conduct during the battle of Chickamauga:

Second Lieut. Wirt Davis, Fourth U. S. Cavalry, commanded the squadron of his regiment which covered the retreat of the Seventh Pennsylvania Cavalry over Reed's Bridge, on the afternoon of the 18th September. This officer has invariably performed his duties in the most satisfactory and gallant manner.

Second Lieut. J. H. Simpson, Fourth Michigan Cavalry, commanded a squadron of his regiment on picket duty on the Harrison road, on the 18th September, and was cut off by the rapid advance of the enemy. After fighting as long as possible, he swam the Chickamauga, and brought in his squadron with no casualties but 1 man and 1 horse slightly wounded.

I am, respectfully, your obedient servant,

ROBT. H. G. MINTY,
Col. 4th Mich. Cav., late Comdg. 1st Brig., 2d Cav. Div.

ADDENDA.

*Itinerary of the First Brigade, Second Cavalry Division, commanded by Col. Robert H. G. Minty, Fourth Michigan Cavalry, for September, 1863.**

September 1 to 5.—The brigade remained at Smith's Cross-Roads, in the Tennessee Valley, picketing and guarding different fords and ferries on the Tennessee River.

September 6.—Moved to McDonald's Mill, on Sale Creek, 6 miles down the river toward Chattanooga, where we remained until the 11th.

September 11.—Moved to within 2 miles of Chattanooga.

September 12.—Crossed the Tennessee River at Friar's Ford and encamped at Chattanooga.

September 13.—Marched to Gordon's Mills, Ga.

September 14.—Moved to McLemore's Cove with the command of General Crittenden.

September 15.—Marched back by Gordon's Mills to near Reed's Bridge, over Chickamauga River, 4½ miles from Ringgold.

September 16 and 17.—Remained at Reed's Bridge, sending scouting parties toward Ringgold and La Fayette, who reported large bodies of the enemy on our front.

September 18.—At 8 a. m. the enemy drove in two of our scouting parties and our pickets. The brigade, consisting of the Fourth United States, Fourth Michigan, and Seventh Pennsylvania Cavalry, the Third Indiana being temporarily in Chattanooga, skirmished with the rebels at Pea Vine Ridge, but were compelled to fall back across the Chickamauga, disputing every foot of the ground, when we were re-enforced by two regiments of Colonel Wilder's brigade. From there we were driven back slowly to Gordon's Mills, where we arrived at dark.

September 19.—Remained at Gordon's Mills until noon, when we were ordered to report to General Granger, at Rossville. Did so that p. m., and bivouacked.

September 20.—At 5 a. m., by General Granger's order, went to Missionary Mills, on Missionary Ridge, to watch the left flank of the army. About 3 p. m. moved from Missionary Ridge down the road

* From return for September.

toward Ringgold, where we met and drove Scott's rebel cavalry 2 miles across the West Chickamauga Creek.

September 21.—About 9 a. m. the enemy advanced and drove the brigade, after a sharp skirmish, through the gap in front of Rossville, where our infantry was stationed. After passing through, the brigade moved back to Missionary Ridge and rested until night. Then, when the main army was withdrawn to Chattanooga, the First Brigade guarded the gap at and above Rossville.

September 22.—The enemy advanced early in the morning and gradually drove us back from Missionary Ridge to Chattanooga. Loss of the brigade from September 18 to 22, 1 officer killed and 2 wounded; 10 men killed and 39 wounded; missing, 4.

September 23.—Remained at Chattanooga. The Seventh Pennsylvania and Fourth Michigan Regiments were put into the intrenchments to throw up breastworks.

September 24.—Moved across the Tennessee River and encamped up the valley about 10 miles from Chattanooga.

September 25.—Marched to Sale Creek, where we remained until September 28, when we marched to near Washington, Rhea County. There remained during the 29th.

September 30.—The rebel cavalry under Wheeler crossed the Tennessee River, the Fourth Michigan and one battalion of the Fourth U. S. Cavalry disputing his passage. After he had crossed, the command was gathered together and moved to Smith's Cross-Roads.

No. 229.

Report of Col. Eli Long, Fourth Ohio Cavalry, commanding Second Brigade.

HDQRS. SECOND BRIGADE, SECOND CAVALRY DIVISION,
Camp near Bridgeport, Ala., September 1, 1863.

SIR: I have the honor to submit to you the following report:

On the morning of August 29, 1863, after leaving you, I accompanied the Second Regiment Kentucky Cavalry on the march in the direction of Caperton's Ferry. After proceeding about 2 miles, the advance guard captured a courier with dispatches for Colonel Estes, C. S. Army. From the dispatches we learned that there was a company of about 50 rebels at [or] near the ferry. We continued on at a gallop, hoping to capture these men, but upon arriving at the river we met some infantry troops belonging to Brigadier-General Davis' division.

We then commenced the ascent of Raccoon Mountain. The road going up the mountain is very bad, but upon arriving at the summit, we found the face of the country to be level, and the road very fair. On the mountain the advance captured 4 prisoners, 3 of them belonging to the Third Confederate Cavalry, the other had been engaged in collecting niter for the C. S. Government. We met with no opposition on the march whatever, and rejoined you near Price's place on the mountain, having marched since morning between 25 and 30 miles.

The country over which we marched had not been much cultivated, and forage is very scarce.

Very respectfully, your obedient servant,

ELI LONG,
Colonel, Commanding Second Cavalry Brigade.

Capt. R. P. KENNEDY,
Assistant Adjutant-General, Second Division.

ADDENDA.

Itinerary of the Second Brigade, Second Cavalry Division, commanded by Col. Eli Long, Fourth Ohio Cavalry, for September, 1863. *

September 2.—Colonel Long moved with the First, Third, and Fourth Ohio Volunteer Cavalry, and Second Kentucky Cavalry Regiments from camp, near Bridgeport, Ala., and crossed the Tennessee River in the general movement of the army toward Chattanooga.

September 3.—Crossed Sand Mountain and arrived in Will's Valley. Remained in camp here until September 8, when the brigade, with one section of Stokes' battery, crossed Lookout Mountain and engaged four regiments of rebel cavalry at Alpine, in Broomtown Valley, driving them from the field. Loss: Killed, 4; wounded, 8.

September 13.—Marched on reconnaissance toward La Fayette, in conjunction with Campbell's brigade, First Cavalry Division. Found Bragg's main army intrenched at that place. Falling back, reascended Lookout Mountain and proceeded to Dougherty's Gap.

September 19.—Marched through Rape's Gap into McLemore's Cove.

September 20.—Participated in the battle of Chickamauga, having position on the extreme right of the army at Crawfish Spring. The brigade encountered Hindman's infantry division and a small force of cavalry, and was forced back after a severe fight, with a loss of 122 men killed, wounded, and missing; 7 officers wounded, and Lieut. Col. V. Cupp, First Ohio, and First Lieut. R. W. Neff, Fourth Ohio, killed.

September 22.—Fell back with the army to Chattanooga and recrossed the Tennessee river to the north side.

September 26.—Colonel Long moved with brigade and Stokes' battery to guard the fords up the river, and arrived at Washington, Tenn., on the 28th. The Second Kentucky regiment went to Luty's, 5 miles, and the Fourth Ohio to Kelley's Ford, 10 miles distant.

September 30.—General Wheeler, with a large force of rebel cavalry and several pieces of artillery, crossed the river at Cottonport, protecting his crossing with his guns and shelling the pickets from the river. The brigade fell back as the enemy advanced, and the Fourth Ohio Regiment was cut off from the command. Lieut. William H. Scott, First Ohio Volunteer Cavalry, ordnance officer, Second Brigade, and Lieut. A. D. Leib, First Ohio Volunteer Cavalry, who had been sent to bring up this regiment and the Second Kentucky, were captured by the enemy. Colonel Long retired with the command to near Smith's Cross-Roads, and bivouacked with the balance of General Crook's command.

No. 230.

Report of Lieut. Col. Valentine Cupp, First Ohio Cavalry.

HEADQUARTERS FIRST OHIO CAVALRY,
Camp Crook, September 1, 1863.

COLONEL: I have the honor to submit to you the following report of the First Ohio Cavalry on the scout, August 29, 1863:

In compliance with orders received from Col. Eli Long, command-

---

* From return for September.

ing Second Brigade, Second Division, cavalry command, I proceeded up the river to Moore's Spring (9 miles), meeting with no resistance until within 1 mile of Moore's Spring, but observed numerous picket posts the enemy had just left, the citizens on the route informing me the enemy's pickets were on the road just in advance of my advance guard.

When within 1 mile of Moore's Spring, Mr. Moore informed me that Captain Rice, in command of a company of 150 men of the Third Confederate Cavalry, were encamped on the side of the mountain on the road leading from Bridgeport to Trenton, Ga., and that Colonel Estes, of the Third Confederate Cavalry, was encamped 2 miles on same road with his regiment, supposed to number 400. While in conversation with Mr. Moore my advance guard was fired on by the enemy. Captain Frankeberger, Company G, who had the advance, immediately ordered a charge, completely routing and demoralizing them to such an extent that the company on the side of the mountain fled in such confusion as to leave a great many of their arms, &c., stacked against the trees, and made no resistance to prevent me gaining possession of top of the mountain, save, perhaps, ten or twelve shots.

After gaining the top of the mountain, I pursued them as fast as possible (keeping my flanks well protected) until within half a mile of Colonel Estes' camp, when my advance was again fired on. My advance charged them again and charged into the camp, but the colonel had left with his command a few moments before my advance reached the camp, leaving clothing, cooking utensils, commissary stores, and their dinners cooking on the fire ; everything indicating a very hasty evacuation. I pursued them until I reached John E. Price's farm, the point at which I was ordered to join the brigade.

I destroyed 20 stand of arms (short rifles), killed 1 man, and captured 6 prisoners.

Respectfully submitted.

VALENTINE CUPP,
Lieutenant-Colonel, Comdg. First Ohio Cavalry.

Col. ELI LONG,
Commanding Second Brigade.

No. 231.

*Itinerary of the Pioneer Brigade.**

The Pioneer Brigade remained at Elk River railroad bridge during the month of August until the 16th, and during that time were engaged in building block-house, cutting cord-wood for railroad, and unloading cars, &c. Two of the four companies reported to Major-General McCook, Twentieth Army Corps, [and] remained with said corps for pioneer duty.

August 15.—Four companies of the First Battalion reported to Major-General Thomas, Fourteenth Army Corps, for pioneer duty. Six companies of the Third Battalion reported to Captain Mallory, commissary of subsistence, at Stevenson, Ala., to build platforms for commissary and quartermaster's stores. Two hundred men from the Second Battalion were sent to Nashville to forward pontoon boats and bring forward pontoon train. One company from the

---

* From returns for August and September.   The brigade was commanded by Capt. Patrick O'Connell, First Ohio Infantry.

First and one company from the Third Battalion were sent to Murfreesborough to complete fortifications. The remainder of the brigade left camp at Elk River at 7 a. m., going via Winchester. Went into camp at 5 p. m. 2 miles from Salem. Roads bad, on account of heavy rain that day.

August 17.—At 6 a. m. broke camp, taking the Bellefonte road. Traveled down Larkin's Fork of Paint Rock River. Crossed the same twenty-eight times. Roads bad and stony. Encamped 7 miles from Hinche's Crossing at 6 p. m.

August 18.—Broke camp at 5 a. m., crossed Paint Rock, and commenced the ascent of the mountain. Got only a small portion of the train up and encamped on the mountain side.

August 19.—Spent the entire day in getting the train up.

August 20.—At 6 a. m. broke camp, and, going down the mountain, reached Bellefonte at 6 p. m. Went into camp.

August 21.—At 5 a. m. left camp, and, crossing Mud and Crow Creeks, reached Stevenson, Ala., at 1 p. m., and went into camp 1 mile north of town. The most of the time was spent by the effective force of the brigade in pontoon drill.

August 28–29.—Forwarded pontoons to the river and laid the bridge.

August 31.—At 9 a. m. left camp, leaving one company with bridge at Stevenson. Reached Bridgeport at 7 a. m.

The brigade remained in camp at Bridgeport, Ala., up to the 14th of the month [September] engaged in constructing one pontoon and two pontoon-and-trestle (combined) bridges, and working on fortifications for defense of bridges, building platforms for commissary and quartermaster's stores, &c.

On the 14th, the brigade broke camp at 4.30 a. m., and, crossing the river, marching over rough, mountainous roads, camped near Running Water railroad bridge, 16 miles from Chattanooga, at 6 p. m.

Left camp on the 15th, at 5 a. m., and, crossing Lookout Mountain, reached Chattanooga [and] encamped at 5 p. m. Throughout the entire length of the route the roads were rough and dusty.

The brigade has been very busy during the remaining time constructing two trestle bridges across the Tennessee River, repairing and running steamboats and saw-mills, repairing roads, and working on fortifications, &c.

ADDENDA.

Semi-weekly report of effective force of the Pioneer Brigade, Capt. Patrick O'Connell, First Ohio Volunteer Infantry, commanding.

Command.	Headquarters.			Infantry.			Total.		
	Commissioned officers	Enlisted men.	Total.	Commissioned officers.	Enlisted men.	Total.	Commissioned officers.	Enlisted men.	Aggregate.
Headquarters Pioneer Brigade	13	22	35				13	22	35
First Battalion, Capt. C. J. Stewart				21	374	395	21	374	395
Second Battalion, Capt. Correll Smith				6	56	62	6	56	62
Third Battalion, Capt. R. Clements				20	427	447	20	427	447
Total	13	22	35	47	857	904	60	879	939

P. O'CONNELL,
Captain First Ohio Vol. Inf., Comdg. Pioneer Brigade.

THURSDAY, September 10, 1863.

No. 232.

Record of the McCook Court of Inquiry.

RECORD OF THE PROCEEDINGS OF A COURT OF INQUIRY, INSTI-
TUTED BY THE FOLLOWING ORDER:

SPECIAL ORDERS, } WAR DEPT., ADJT. GENERAL'S OFFICE,
    No. 13.   }   *Washington, January 9, 1864.*

*   *   *   *   *   *   *

20. By direction of the President of the United States, a Court of
Inquiry is hereby appointed to meet at Nashville, Tenn., on the 15th
instant, or as soon thereafter as practicable, to investigate the conduct of Maj. Gens. A. McD. McCook, T. L. Crittenden, and James
S. Negley, U. S. Volunteers, at the battle of Chickamauga, and in
leaving the field, and also to give their opinion upon the facts which
may be developed. The Court will adjourn from place to place, as
may be deemed necessary to procure the testimony of witnesses,
without taking them away from their appropriate duties, and will
sit without regard to hours.

Detail for the Court: Maj. Gen. David Hunter, U. S. Volunteers;
Maj. Gen. George Cadwalader, U. S. Volunteers; Brig. Gen. J. S.
Wadsworth, U. S. Volunteers; Col. Edmund Schriver, inspector-
general, recorder.

*   *   *   *   *   *   *

By order of the Secretary of War:

E. D. TOWNSEND,
Assistant Adjutant-General.

FIRST DAY.

NASHVILLE, *January 29, 1864.*

The Court met, pursuant to the above order, at 10 a. m., in the
Saint Cloud Hotel.

Present, Maj. Gen. David Hunter, U. S. Volunteers; Maj. Gen.
George Cadwalader, U. S. Volunteers; Brig. Gen. J. S. Wadsworth,
U. S. Volunteers; Col. Edmund Schriver, inspector-general, re-
corder.

Maj. Gen. A. McD. McCook, U. S. Volunteers, whose conduct is
ordered to be investigated, was also present.

The order appointing the Court was then read. Major-General
McCook being asked if he had any objection to the officers named in
the detail, and replying in the negative, the members and recorder
were sworn in his presence.

The Court then proceeded with the investigation, and directed the
recorder to make the following communication to Maj. Gen. George
H. Thomas:

NASHVILLE, *January 29, 1864.*

Major-General THOMAS,
    Commanding Department of the Cumberland, Chattanooga:

The Court of Inquiry instituted by Special Orders, No. 13, War Department, for
the investigation of "the conduct of Major-Generals McCook, Crittenden, and Negley. U. S. Volunteers, at the battle of Chickamauga, and in leaving the field," desire

you to send to me at the Galt House, in Louisville, as soon as possible, certified copies of all the reports which may be in your possession bearing on the conduct of those officers on the occasion referred to, and also the best map you have of the battle-field and the surrounding country. It is most desirable to have these reports and the map sent by an officer capable of explaining to the Court the position of the troops engaged. They wish you, also, to send any officers of your command who may have knowledge of the matter to be investigated, to report to the Court in Louisville, the names of whom you are desired to communicate to me. Please acknowledge this.

> ED. SCHRIVER,
> *Inspector-General, Recorder.*

On being questioned by the Court whether any papers or communications touching the matter to be investigated had been furnished, the recorder stated as follows:

Only one communication, that of General W. S. Rosecrans to the Adjutant-General of the Army, dated October 14, 1863, relative to Major-General Negley. That he addressed to the Adjutant-General of the Army the following communications:

> LOUISVILLE, *January* 27, 1864.

The ADJUTANT-GENERAL OF THE ARMY.

GENERAL: I have the honor to acquaint you that General Hunter has arrived here, and that the officers detailed for the Court instituted by Special Orders, No. 13, to investigate the conduct of Major-Generals McCook, Crittenden, and Negley, will repair to Nashville to-morrow. At an informal meeting had, it was seen that no papers respecting the conduct of those officers have yet been furnished to the Court, and I was, therefore, directed to request that any reports or communications on the subject which may be on file in the War Department, as well as the names and addresses of any persons who are known to be acquainted with the transactions ordered to be investigated, be sent to me at this place, whither the Court will return for the purpose of receiving the testimony of Major-General Rosecrans on 1st February.

Very respectfully, &c.,

> ED. SCHRIVER,
> *Inspector-General, Recorder.*

> NASHVILLE, *January* 29, 1864.

The ADJUTANT-GENERAL OF THE ARMY:

GENERAL: In my communication of the 27th instant, written by order of the Court of Inquiry instituted by Special Orders, No. 13, of 1864, I asked for all reports on file in the War Department bearing on the conduct of Major-Generals McCook, Crittenden, and Negley at the battle of Chickamauga. I am now directed to ask particularly for the following:

Certified copies of the official reports of the battle of Chickamauga made by Brigadier-Generals Wood, Brannan, and Davis, and Colonel Harker (Wood's division); also the supplementary report and papers appended which Major-General Negley forwarded October 9, 1863, at the request of and through Major-General Rosecrans, the same being required by Major-General Negley in his letter of 22d January. Please send them to the Galt House, Louisville.

Very respectfully, &c.,

> ED. SCHRIVER,
> *Inspector-General, Recorder.*

The Court here desired General McCook to furnish the recorder, from time to time, as far as possible, a list of the witnesses whose evidence he may wish to submit to the Court.

A recess of half an hour was taken, and subsequently an adjournment till 7 p. m. was ordered.

7 p. m.

The Court met pursuant to adjournment.

Present, Major-Generals Hunter and Cadwalader, Brigadier-General Wadsworth, Colonel Schriver, recorder, and Major-General McCook.

Capt. THOMAS C. WILLIAMS, Nineteenth U. S. Infantry, aide-de-camp to General Rousseau, being duly sworn, says to questions

By the COURT:

Question. Were you present at the battle of Chickamauga on 19th and 20th September, 1863?

Answer. I was.

Question. Please state what you know respecting the conduct of General McCook on that occasion.

Answer. I did not see General McCook on the 19th or 20th.

Question. Do you know of your own knowledge anything about the position of General McCook's troops on either day?

Answer. One division of General McCook's command, commanded by General Johnson, reported to General Thomas. They were engaged on 19th and 20th September, and behaved both days with the utmost gallantry.

Question. Do you know under what orders the division reported to General Thomas?

Answer. No.

Question. Do you know anything about the other divisions?

Answer. No.

By General McCOOK:

Question. Who organized the division that behaved with the utmost gallantry from raw levies?

(This question was objected to by the Court as not relevant to the subject.)

The Court adjourned to meet at 11 o'clock on 1st February, at Louisville, Ky.

SECOND DAY.

LOUISVILLE, *February* 1, 1864.

The Court met, pursuant to adjournment, in the supreme court-room.

Present, Major-Generals Hunter and Cadwalader, Brigadier-General Wadsworth, and Colonel Schriver, recorder, and Major-General McCook.

The proceedings of the first day were read and approved.

Maj. CALEB BATES, aide-de-camp to Major-General McCook (appointed under the act of July 17, 1862), being duly sworn, says to questions

By the COURT:

Question. What was General McCook's command at the battle of Chickamauga on the 19th and 20th September, 1863, and how was it posted?

Answer. On the morning of the 19th, the Twentieth Army Corps, composed of three divisions, under the command of Major-General Sheridan, Brigadier-General Johnson, and Brigadier-General Davis, one brigade of General Davis' being detached, guarding the train. The corps was in position immediately on the right of

General Thomas' corps, and in readiness to follow General Thomas as soon as his troops had moved out of the way. The headquarters of the corps on the night of the 18th were at Pond Spring. At early daylight on the 19th, General Thomas' troops having moved forward, the corps was put in motion and General McCook moved on and reported in person to General Rosecrans' headquarters, then at Crawfish Spring. On arriving there General McCook received instructions to take command of the right, and proceeded to examine the ground around about there. On returning toward General Rosecrans' headquarters, General Johnson's division was met, having just reached that point. The division was at rest, and it was ordered to move up and report to General Thomas by General McCook. After General Johnson's division had passed, General Davis' division came up, and was also ordered forward to report to General Thomas or the general commanding, who was then at the Widow Glenn's house. General Negley's division was then engaged, and was on the right of the troops then engaged. General McCook had received orders from General Rosecrans to take General Negley's division in his command. On General Sheridan's division arriving, it was ordered to take position on the right of General Wood's division, then stationed at Gordon's Mills. General Wood being moved from his position just as General Sheridan was going into position, General Sheridan was put in his place, and General Negley, being withdrawn from his position, was ordered up to report to General Thomas. General Robert B. Mitchell commanding the cavalry, General McCook proceeded to General Rosecrans' headquarters, two brigades of General Sheridan's command having been ordered to the left. General Johnson, on the night of the 19th, I believe, was on the extreme left of the line of battle. General Sheridan was near the Widow Glenn's house, and General Davis in reserve near by. About midnight General McCook rode round to Generals Sheridan and Davis and gave them instructions, and the line in the morning by daylight was withdrawn, General Sheridan's division being posted at and to the right of the Widow Glenn's house. General McCook's command on Sunday morning was three brigades of General Sheridan, two brigades of General Davis. General Davis' command was very much reduced by the casualties on the 19th. I don't know the strength of the command. There were no field returns that I saw.

Question. Were the orders which you state were given by General McCook to Generals Johnson and Davis to move forward and to report to General Thomas, then at Widow Glenn's house, given in consequence of orders which he received from General Rosecrans?

Answer. Such I understood to be the case.

Question. Was General McCook ordered to assume command of the whole of the right, including General Crittenden's command?

Answer. I heard nothing of General Crittenden's command, as I understood it included only his own command, General Negley's, and the cavalry.

Question. Was not General Crittenden's corps still farther on the right, and would not that have placed General McCook in the center?

Answer. I only saw one division of General Crittenden's command, commanded by General Wood, and posted at Gordon's Mills. I think it was to the left of General McCook's.

Question. At what time were you attacked on Sunday morning?

Answer. I think it was in the neighborhood of 11 o'clock.

Question. Did the troops break ; and, if so, at what hour ?

Answer. When the attack first commenced, I had gone to the extreme right of the line to Colonel Wilder's command, to notify him that the line was being moved toward the left, and to hold himself in readiness to move and keep closed up to the left. On my return to General McCook, I found the line broken and falling back fast. I think it was about half past 11.

Question. Where was General McCook when you returned, and what was he engaged in?

Answer. I found him on my return to the rear of the line endeavoring to reform the stragglers and get them into some order. I think the first I saw of him he had a flag in his hand trying to get the men together and rally them round him.

Question. Were the troops under the fire of the enemy at that moment?

Answer. They were. Musketry shot came in that struck near where I was, and must have come to him who was farther in front than I was.

Question. When did General McCook leave the field?

· Answer. After being driven from this position, the general fell back with the others until out of fire, and there stopped and appeared to be listening to the sound of the musketry and artillery. He went on again, till we reached an eminence, where we met some of General Rosecrans' staff, and also a guide that I understood to belong to General Rosecrans. He was with General Morton. A heavy cloud of dust could be distinctly seen toward Rossville, this guide stating that a road ran from that point, or near that point, to the road in the other valley, and he believed that the enemy were endeavoring to get on that road with their cavalry to cut off our stragglers.

Question. How long did General McCook remain on this eminence?

Answer. I suppose from ten to fifteen minutes.

Question. Where did he go when he left it?

Answer. He went toward the road leading to Chattanooga.

Question. Did any troops accompany him?

Answer. No; not from this position.

Question. Did he rally any troops, and what became of them?

Answer. A few were rallied but soon broken again by the heavy fire.

Question. Having struck the road to Chattanooga, where did he go?

Answer. To Chattanooga.

Question. At what hour did all this occur?

Answer. Half past 1 or 2, and between half past 4 to 5 he arrived at Chattanooga. I am not positive as to the time; it is the best I can remember.

Question. You have stated that you returned and found General McCook· rallying troops at about half past 11 o'clock. How soon after this did you reach the eminence where you met a staff officer and guide of General Rosecrans?

Answer. I cannot state positively; our movements were slow off the field, making frequent stops. I think in the neighborhood of an hour and two hours.

Question. About how far is it from that eminence to Chattanooga?

Answer. From 13 to 14 miles; I do not know.

Question. Did you make any halts between the eminence and Chattanooga?

Answer. Yes; I think we did. We met, after we left, Captain Sheridan, of General Sheridan's staff, and General McCook told him to tell General Sheridan that he was going to Chattanooga to find General Rosecrans for orders.

Question. What became of those troops which you say were broken? Why did General McCook leave them, and where did they go when he went to Chattanooga?

Answer. The troops were very much scattered, and it seemed almost impossible, if not impossible, to rally them. General McCook bore off toward the left of our line. I think his intention was to go to General Thomas' headquarters to find him, and, in bearing in that direction, became separated from the troops that were falling back.

Question. Do you know why he did not go to General Thomas?

Answer. I think it was the action of the guide of General Morton and General Morton himself, who, during the conversation, got down from his horse and examined the maps. The conversation I did not hear. We had met stragglers from a division occupying a position on our left, in the line of battle, which made it seem doubtful if we could get through to General Thomas.

Question. What did General McCook do when he got to Chattanooga?

Answer. He went to General Rosecrans' headquarters and remained there till sent out by General Rosecrans, at midnight, to Rossville.

Question. Was this the first General McCook had seen of General Rosecrans that day?

Answer. No; General Rosecrans visited the right of our line in the morning. I do not know the time, but it was before the attack was made on our right.

Question. Do you know when and where any portion of General McCook's troops were rallied, or got together, and by whom?

Answer. General Sheridan rallied part of his command in the rear of the line, as did also General Davis; but I do not know where.

Question. When did General McCook learn as to where these troops were rallied?

Answer. I do not know; but when we went back in the night we found them at Rossville, which was the first I knew of the fact.

Question. What staff officers of General McCook went to the rear with him?

Answer. His three aides, Major Bates, Captains Williams and Jones, and Lieutenant-Colonel Fisher, inspector-general. I believe that was all. I am not positive.

By General McCook:

Question. During the battle of Chickamauga, did General McCook command any of General Crittenden's troops?

Answer. Not that I know.

Question. Did or did not General McCook do all in his power to rally the portion of his command that had broken?

Answer. I think he did all that a man could do.

Question. Did or did not General McCook hunt for General Rosecrans on the field of battle for over two hours after the line was broken?

Answer. I heard General McCook make inquiries of General Rosecrans' staff officers, and ask where the general was. I do not know about the time.

Question. What position did General Morton hold in the army, and did he not report to General McCook for duty after being separated from his chief?

Answer. General Morton was chief engineer on the staff of General Rosecrans, and he joined General McCook, and went into Chattanooga with him.

Question. Did or did not General Morton take an observation on the field, and did he not report to me that the enemy were endeavoring to cut us off from Chattanooga?

Answer. I saw General Morton examining his maps, and point toward a cloud of dust, but could not hear the conversation, that I remember.

Question. What did Mr. McDonald, General Rosecrans' guide, say about the movements of the enemy?

Answer. He appeared to be under the impression that they would endeavor to cut off our right, which was broken, and judged that the cloud of dust was the enemy's cavalry coming down to endeavor to do so.

Question. Were the troops to the left of General McCook's position broken, and was not the enemy between General McCook's position in rear of the battle-field and General Thomas' position?

Answer. I would judge from the firing they were; the firing was very heavy in that direction.

Question. After the line was broken by the enemy, did General McCook leave the field by his own inclination, or was he driven off the field of battle by the enemy?

Answer. I think he was driven from the field by the enemy, unless he wished to be killed.

Question. Did or did not General McCook meet men of every division of the army, and did they or not report their divisions driven from their lines by the enemy?

Answer. Being with the general, I met stragglers not only from his own corps, but from both the others. General Wood's division, General Brannan's, General Baird's, and General Van Cleve's. Men represented themselves as belonging to those divisions, and represented that many of their divisions were cut to pieces.

Question. Did you see Lieut. Col. Lyne Starling, and what report did he make to General McCook?

Answer. I think that Lieut. Col. Lyne Starling, assistant adjutant-general and chief of General Crittenden's staff, rode up to General McCook, and it was understood——

(Here there was an interruption by the Court and the question was withdrawn.)

By the COURT:

Question. Were you or any other staff officer of General McCook sent to look for General Rosecrans?

Answer. Not that I know; I was not.

Question. You have stated that General McCook inquired of a staff officer of General Rosecrans where he was. What answer did he give?

Answer. That the general had gone to Chattanooga.

The Court adjourned to meet at 10 a. m. on the 2d instant.

THIRD DAY.

LOUISVILLE, *February* 2, 1864.

The Court met pursuant to adjournment.

Present, Major-Generals Hunter and Cadwalader, Brigadier-General Wadsworth, and Colonel Schriver, recorder, and Major-General McCook.

The proceedings of the second day were read and approved.

Capt. FRANK J. JONES, aide-de-camp to Major-General McCook (act of July 17, 1862), being duly sworn, says to questions

By the COURT:

Question. Were you with General McCook's command on 20th September?

Answer. Yes.

Question. At what time did the command break?

Answer. It was about 12 o'clock in the morning.

Question. At what time did General McCook meet General Morton and the guide of General Rosecrans?

Answer. I do not know particularly at what time; it was during the excitement of rallying the troops that General McCook was separated from his command.

Question. Were you or any other staff officer sent to look for General Rosecrans?

Answer. I was not, and I do not know of any other officers being sent.

Question. At what time did you reach Chattanooga with General McCook?

Answer. About 4.30 to 5 o'clock. I judge merely by the time elapsing between our arrival and nightfall.

Question. Did you see General Rosecrans immediately?

Answer. No, I did not; because I did not accompany General McCook to General Rosecrans' house.

Question. Did General McCook see him immediately?

Answer. I presume he did. I saw several of his personal staff officers in the town. I went to the adjutant-general's office.

Question. When did General McCook learn when and where his troops had been rallied, after he arrived in Chattanooga?

Answer. I can't say, but it is my impression that he learned on the way to Chattanooga that General Davis had rallied his command, and joined it to the Tenth Ohio.

Question. After you arrived at Chattanooga, were you or any other staff officer sent out to learn what had become of General McCook's command?

Answer. I was not; and I do not know of any one that was. After arriving at Chattanooga, General McCook went to General Rosecrans' headquarters.

By General McCook:

Question. Did you meet or see Captain Sheridan, of General Sheridan's staff, in rear of the battle-field?

Answer. Yes; but I do not remember the time or place.

Question. What instructions did General McCook give him?

Answer. I cannot say; I did not hear.

Question. What report did Captain Sheridan make to General McCook?

Answer. I did not hear him.

Capt. BEVERLY D. WILLIAMS, aide-de-camp to General McCook, being duly sworn, says to questions

By the COURT:

Question. Were you with General McCook's command on the 20th September?

Answer. I was.

Question. What time did the command break?

Answer. It was between 11 and 11.10 o'clock that the troops of General Davis, under General McCook, gave way. I fix the time thus definitely because an order was received from General Rosecrans by General McCook, dated 10.30, at about five minutes before 11. I examined my watch to this effect. This order directed General McCook to move General Sheridan's troops to the left of the line of battle, and send him to the support of General Thomas. General McCook directed me to deliver this order to General Sheridan, who was endeavoring to bring up his troops, which I did, and then returned with General Lytle, who was trying to reach the left of the line of battle, when we discovered that the troops of General Davis were falling back, and then General McCook ordered him to the support of General Davis. He also ordered General [Colonel] Laiboldt, of General Sheridan's division, to take the right of the enemy ; but in consequence of the falling back of General Davis' troops, he was unable to do so.

Question. At what time did General McCook meet General Morton and the guide of General Rosecrans ?

Answer. I think it was half past 11 o'clock.

Question. Were you or any other staff officer sent to look for General Rosecrans ?

Answer. Not to my knowledge. I was not.

Question. At what time did you reach Chattanooga with General McCook ?

Answer. Between 4 and 5 o'clock, I think.

Question. Did you see General Rosecrans immediately ?

Answer. We rode to the headquarters of General Wagner, where General Rosecrans was.

Question. Did General McCook see him immediately ?

Answer. He did.

Question. When did General McCook learn when and where his troops had been rallied, after he arrived at Chattanooga ?

Answer. General McCook, after his arrival in Chattanooga, remained at the headquarters of General Rosecrans, and asked for orders, saying that he was ready to take the field, and in the early part of the night some dispatches came to General Rosecrans, informing him that the troops of Generals Sheridan and Davis had reached Rossville, and General Rosecrans directed General McCook to go and take command of them, which he did. It was about 12 o'clock when he left.

Question. After you arrived at Chattanooga, were you or any other staff officers sent out to learn what had become of General McCook's command ?

Answer. Not to my knowledge.

By Major-General McCook :

Question. Did you proceed from the battle-field direct to Chattanooga ?

Answer. We did not. General McCook remained in the rear of the line and endeavored to rally the troops, for an hour to an hour and a half after the line was broken, before he left the field, and until there was a lull in the firing on the extreme left. He said he should like to reach General Thomas if he could get there, but the firing prevented him from doing so. Both the guide and General Morton said the firing was from the enemy, and that they were between him and General Thomas' command.

Question. What orders did General McCook give on leaving the battle-field ?

Answer. Just before he left the field, he rode up to General Davis, and directed him to rally his men, and to go in the direction of Rossville, as the impression was that the enemy were on the road to Rossville.

Question. Did or did not General McCook meet Captain Sheridan, of General Sheridan's staff, in rear of the field?

Answer. He did, about a mile in rear of the line, and he met the escort of General Rosecrans with the general's flag. He gave some orders to be conveyed to General Sheridan, but I was not present and did not hear them.

Question. How many brigades of Davis' division were present at the battle of Chickamauga?

Answer. Two.

Question. Was not General Davis' small command the only troops under my command, in line, when the assault was made by the enemy?

Answer. Yes; from 1,300 to 1,400 men.

By the COURT:

Question. Was General Sheridan's force in reserve?

Answer. General Sheridan was on the right of the line of battle, coming up to support General Thomas.

Question. What was General Sheridan's numerical strength?

Answer. Four thousand three hundred men; three brigades.

Question. Was any field return sent in on the 20th?

Answer. I do not think there was.

Question. What proportion of General McCook's command was detached from his corps at the time of the assault on Sunday morning?

Answer. General Johnson's Second Division and one brigade of General Davis'.

By General McCOOK:

Question. Was not General Sheridan's division also detached to go to General Thomas?

Answer. It had been ordered to report to General Thomas, and was marching to do so when the assault took place.

Question. Were they not ordered to go to General Thomas with the utmost dispatch, without exhausting the men?

Answer. They were, and were doing so at the double-quick.

Question. Were there any troops on General Davis' left when the assault was made?

Answer. General Wood was marching out of the line of battle, and General Davis, by the left flank, into the line on the right of General Brannan, when the assault took place.

Question. Had not General Davis but one of three things to do: Submit to capture, utter annihilation, or take to flight to save his command?

Answer. No doubt of that, in my opinion.

The Court adjourned to meet at 10 o'clock on 3d of February.

FOURTH DAY.

FEBRUARY 3, 1864.

No proceedings in this case to-day.

FIFTH DAY.

February 4, 1864.

The Court met pursuant to adjournment.

Present, Major-Generals Hunter and Cadwalader, Brigadier-General Wadsworth, and Colonel Schriver, recorder, and Major-General McCook.

The proceedings of third day were read and approved.

The investigation in General McCook's case was proceeded with.

The report of the battle of Chickamauga, as printed [in] the New York Tribune newspaper of the 5th January, was ordered to be read by the recorder, which was done.

Maj. Gen. W. S. Rosecrans, U. S. Volunteers, being duly sworn, says to questions

By the Court :

Question. Were you in command of the United States forces in the battle of Chickamauga on the 19th and 20th of September last ?

Answer. I was.

Question. Please state the positions of the respective corps of your command, and the orders which were given by you to their commanding officers on 20th September, so far as would affect Major-General McCook.

Answer. The order for General McCook for the 20th was to maintain his picket line where it was on the 19th, and to form his command on the right of the line of General Thomas, allowing his picket to remain until driven in. About daylight on the morning of 20th, the general reported to me, then on my way to inspect the lines, stating in general the position of his troops. I told him I thought General Davis' division should be brought down from the hillside, where it was formed in line of battle, moved farther toward our left and placed in close column by division, doubled on the center so as to be ready to move, pointing out a place in the valley which appeared eligible for the division. The general urged the exposure of that position, and I left the exact place to be chosen by him at his discretion. The next order which I remember, was written at my dictation by General Garfield from General Thomas' headquarters at 6.30 a. m., informing General McCook that General Negley was to come over to Thomas' left, and directed him to fill Negley's place in the line. On my return from an inspection of the line, I met General McCook again, and having conversed with him about the state of our front, remarked that I did not very well like our position on the right, pointing out some of its defects, and at his request, accompanied him to General Sheridan's headquarters, on the hill west of Widow Glenn's house, where we further conversed about the value of that position. I mentioned to General McCook during this conversation and subsequently when General Davis had formed his troops east of the Dry Valley road, in line of battle, that whatever might be the value of Sheridan's position, it was still more important that we should keep our line closed to the left, observing in reply to the objection that we might thereby lose the road, that even the loss of the Dry Valley road would be nothing in comparison with the importance of keeping a compact center. There were several orders sent to General McCook during the morning, the hours of which and the substance of which I cannot fully give from memory. I remember that General McCook was advised of the fact that Crittenden had executed the order for relieving General Negley's troops on the line of battle-; that he was directed to send General Davis to close a gap in that line found to the left of Sheridan's and on right of Wood's division ; that he had orders to put Sheridan's entire division in readiness for prompt movement to support Thomas ; and that he was to report to me for further orders. This was given about 11.30 o'clock. I had taken my position in the rear of the left of a portion of the line occupied by General McCook's troops, and one-half mile west from my designated headquarters for the purpose of seeing all the dispositions of the troops on our right executed, or at least so far advanced as to be certain that they would be completed. I occupied this position when Davis' line was broken, and as I was about to move from it to see General Sheridan's division brought to bear, I met General McCook, who reported to me that he had just ordered in Laiboldt's brigade to meet the enemy, which he thought would soon set the matter to rights. I told him I would go to see the other two brigades. I gave him no special orders. I saw him but once after that on the battle-field, when I think he was going toward where Lytle's brigade was advancing ; that was shortly after 1 o'clock. The last order I gave from that point was twenty minutes after 1, but not addressed to General McCook. The next time I saw him he arrived at Chattanooga, and reported to me at Wagner's headquarters. I should think about 4.30 or 5 p. m. I directed him to wait a short time until I should hear General Garfield's report from the extreme front, informing him that we held the field ; that Granger had gone up from Rossville ; that portion of his and Crittenden's corps were reported near Rossville, and that the arrival of a further report from General Garfield would enable me to give more definite instructions, both to him and General Crittenden. On the arrival of that report from General Garfield, I read it to him or stated its substance, and directed him to go out to Rossville and assume the command of his corps ; that we would occupy a position near there, which General Thomas had been directed to select. This was given to General McCook, I should think, about 9.30 p. m.

Question. What was General McCook's command, at 12 m., on the 20th September, 1863 ?

Answer. It consisted of Sheridan's division, three brigades ; Davis' division, two brigades ; and the cavalry had only orders to communicate with him, and close on his right. The senior officers of the cavalry were told that they must take orders from him, though attend to their own business. Each brigade had a battery of artillery.

Question. What is the distance from the field where General McCook's command broke to Rossville, and from Rossville to Chattanooga ?

Answer. The first distance is about 6 miles, and the second 5.

Question. Did the conduct of General McCook, in leaving his command at such a distance, meet with your approval ?

Answer. It did not strike me favorably, but knowing nothing of the circumstances, it did not elicit any expressions of disapprobation. I thought it might have been possible to have done something toward gathering the rallied troops, but having no sufficient data, did not tell General McCook that I thought so.

By General McCOOK :

Question. Was General McCook responsible for the breaking of Davis' line of battle ; was it not mainly caused by the moving of troops on his left ?

Answer. I think the immediate cause was the removal of Wood's division from its place in line, which was done under an order to close instead of opening the line, and while the enemy was advancing in force on his front. It was done with great precipitation, as General Wood has stated in an official letter, at a doublequick, thus giving General McCook no time to close his troops properly and fill the vacant space.

Question. Did any neglect to obey orders on the part of General McCook, or failure on his part to perform his whole duty with the means at his disposal, lead to the disaster on the 20th ?

Answer. I think that there was a want of vigor and close supervision of his line at its loft; that had the troops been held with the view to make his connection with the remaining portion of the line strong and firm, it would have greatly increased our security at that point; but I do not think General McCook disobeyed or failed to obey orders on that day; nor that to him alone is to be attributed the disaster of that day. I consider the defects just mentioned only to have played their part in weakening us for the conflict at the point where the enemy broke through.

Question. When you had learned the reasons for General McCook's presence in Chattanooga, did you censure his conduct ?

Answer. I expressed no censure to him so far as I remember, because I was not sufficiently advised to conclude myself, much less to express to him the opinion that he could have done this or that. I regretted that he had not remained at Rossville, but do not remember that I have ever, until now, expressed that regret.

Question. After the withdrawal of General McCook's troops to re-enforce General Thomas, was it possible for him to have maintained his position against the enemy's attacking forces ?

Answer. It is impossible to say whether with his five brigades he could have maintained a front commensurate with that strength on the right, of what is called in the reports "Thomas' line," but the intention was with General McCook's corps to hold the extension of that line, which in the reports is called "Thomas'," and that General Crittenden should, with what was left of his corps, act as a reserve to support either General McCook or any other portion of the line. It was not expected that General McCook should cover any particular portion of ground, unless he found he could do so, and at the same time maintain his connection with General Thomas. The information on which the orders for 20th were predicated, was that the position of Widow Glenn's house would be amply within the limits of our strength to cover, and keep Crittenden's troops wholly in reserve; but I am satisfied that the distance from that position to the right of Brannan was greater than we at that time supposed, and that the line was, therefore, attenuated. It was an apprehension that this might be the case which led me to bring down Davis' division from the left side of Dry Valley in the morning, as stated in my direct examination. We were fighting very superior numbers, which from several independent sources of information we believed to have been about one and a half to one.

Question. Did not General Sheridan report that he captured prisoners from five rebel divisions that attacked at that point ?

Answer. I do not remember such a report, but I do remember to have heard General Sheridan express the opinion that we were very greatly outnumbered at the point where his division went into the fight on Sunday.

Question. Was or was not Lytle's brigade moving at the double-quick to the left to support General Thomas, agreeably to your orders, when you saw General McCook going toward that brigade ?

Answer. General McCook had been ordered to hold Sheridan's division in readiness to move to Thomas' assistance when, or previous to the time, the left of Davis' line broke. When I saw General McCook, General Lytle's brigade was moving in as I supposed to check the enemy's advance, consequent on the yielding of General Davis' division.

Question. After you sent General McCook the order for Sheridan to be held in readiness to move to Thomas' support, did you or not send me an order for Sheridan's troops to go to Thomas at once ?

Answer. I do not remember positively whether the order was dispatched to him or not, but there was a time when it was believed that the movement of Sheridan toward Thomas ought to begin before the break took place, and I think that the order was dispatched. I remember only that the order was known not to have been executed at the time the break took place, for it was expected this division would be available to throw in on the enemy's flank, as he advanced through the breach in the line.

Question. How long was it from the time you sent the last written order to General McCook until the time you last saw him on the battle-field ?

Answer. I cannot tell. I should think an hour and a half; it may have been longer or shorter.

Question. When you gave General McCook his order to go to Rossville, did you also order him to gather together any troops that he met and take them to Rossville ?

Answer. I do not remember distinctly what or the particulars of his orders. I think it probable such directions may have been given to him, from the fact that it was believed quite a number of stragglers were on the road who might as well be taken forward.

The Court adjourned till 10 o'clock on the 5th instant.

SIXTH DAY.

LOUISVILLE, *February* 5, 1864.

The Court met pursuant to adjournment.

Present, Major-Generals Hunter and Cadwalader, Brigadier-General Wadsworth, and Colonel Schriver, recorder, and Major-General McCook, U. S. Volunteers.

The proceedings of the fifth day were read.

General Rosecrans stated to the Court that he desired to correct his testimony as follows:

The order which was given to General McCook about Sheridan's division, which I could not distinctly remember yesterday, I now call to mind distinctly. It was thus : I directed General Garfield to notify General McCook to hold Sheridan's division in complete readiness, but before he had written that order, a messenger arrived from General Thomas, saying he would need additional support, and General Garfield wrote the order for him to move the division as soon as possible to General Thomas' support, sending two brigades which were supposed to be free, and a third to follow when the line was sufficiently closed. I deemed the wording of the order too precipitate for the events, but unwilling to have it rewritten, I directed General McCook to report to me in person, presuming he would arrive before the troops would move, intending to give him specific directions what to do with them, expecting that events would develop what points would most need them, and expecting, as did actually happen, that General Thomas could maintain his line. I supposed I should be able to leave General McCook on the right with his command intact and solid. General McCook did come over, as I suppose in obedience to that order, and met me probably 100 yards from the stand at which the order was written, where he reported to me the sending in of Laiboldt's brigade, as stated in my testimony yesterday. In my testimony yesterday, I gave it as my impression the next time I saw him he was going in the direction of Lytle's advancing column. I now think, upon further reflection, that he passed me in the Dry Valley, going southwestwardly toward the top of the hill, after Lytle's column had been driven back. I was then proceeding toward the center to join General Thomas, and knew he, General McCook, was engaged among the broken columns of his own troops, as I had no doubt, with the intention of rallying them.

The Court adjourned to meet at 10 o'clock on 6th February.

SEVENTH DAY.

FEBRUARY 6, 1864.

The Court met pursuant to adjournment.

Present, Major-Generals Hunter and Cadwalader, Brigadier-General Wadsworth, and Colonel Schriver, recorder, and Major-General McCook.

The proceedings of the sixth day were read and approved.

Brig. Gen. T. J. WOOD, U. S. Volunteers, being duly sworn, says to questions

By the COURT :

Question. Can you state any material facts bearing upon the conduct of General McCook on the 19th and 20th September, at the battle of Chickamauga ?

Answer. I saw General McCook but once on the 19th, which was at Gordon's Mills, on the Chickamauga, where my division was lying, about 1 p. m. My division was not then engaged. Later in the day, at 3 p. m., I received an order from General Crittenden to move my division to where the battle was then going on, to take part in the action. I sent a staff officer to report this movement at department headquarters, and who met General McCook and told him that I was about moving. General McCook's troops were higher up the creek, and he said to my staff officer he would move some of his troops lower down. I did not, of course, remain to see this was done, as my orders were peremptory, and as I was not then engaged at all. I saw no more nor heard of General McCook that day. My best recollection is I saw General McCook early in the a. m. of the 20th, near what is called the Dry Valley road, but I only saw him for a few moments then, and nothing of interest occurred. Later in the day, about 10.45 a. m., after my division had occupied the position vacated by General Negley's division, General McCook came to where I was, immediately in rear of my division. At that time my division was not at all engaged, and I had dismounted from my horse. General McCook dismounted and entered into conversation with me about the battle. So far as sounds indicated it, there was no fighting from my position to the extreme right of the line. I explained to General McCook I had been ordered to occupy that position, and to rest my left against General Brannan's right, whose division was the next on my left. General McCook informed me that General Davis' division of his corps was closed up on my right. While this conversation was going on I received an order directly from General Rosecrans to close up on General Reynolds as fast as possible and support him. As there was a division between mine and General Reynolds' (Brannan's), and as the firing in that direction indicated that a severe action was going on, I remarked to General McCook I should move my division at once to the support of General Reynolds, and that this movement would necessarily vacate the position I was then in. He replied that he would move Davis' division toward the left, or up, so as to cover the interval which would be vacated by the movement of my division. I at once dispatched my staff officers to the brigade commanders to commence the movement. General McCook immediately mounted his horse and rode briskly to the right, as I understood from him, to move up Davis' division. I went on with my own movement, and saw nothing more of General McCook during the 20th September.

By General MCCOOK:

Question. From what you saw of Major-General McCook on the 20th September, do you or do you not think he was using every exertion to get his troops in proper position?

Answer. So far as I saw him, I certainly observed no want of activity or energy on his part to get his troops into position.

Question. Were General McCook's troops posted in proper position on the right of the main line of battle, and so as to hold the Dry Valley road, early in the morning?

Answer. I saw none of General McCook's troops after daylight Sunday morning, and, therefore, am not able to make any statement as to how they were posted after daylight. Before daylight, when my division was moving to take position on the slopes of Mission Ridge to form a part of the reserve for the coming day, according to the orders we then had, I passed a portion of General Davis' division (of General McCook's corps), which was moving, and appeared to be going into position in such a way as to command the Dry Valley road toward the south. As it was in the night, I could not see distinctly the position of things.

Maj. G. P. THRUSTON, assistant adjutant-general, acting judge-advocate, Department of the Cumberland, duly sworn, says to questions

By the COURT:

Question. What was the position of Major-General McCook's command on Sunday, the 20th September, at the battle of Chickamauga?

Answer. At daybreak on that day it was posted on the extreme right of the line of battle, with only one brigade in line of battle, two brigades of Sheridan's division to the right and rear of that one brigade. On the left of these three brigades in reserve was General Davis' division of two brigades. About 7 a. m. an order was received from General Rosecrans to relieve General Negley, who was in position in front and left of General McCook's troops. General McCook with Sheridan immediately rode to General Negley's position to carry into execution this order. The order from General Rosecrans was dated 6.30 a. m., requiring him to relieve General Negley if practicable. On reaching the position General Negley had occupied he found two brigades of General Wood's division in position there, General Negley's division already relieved. On riding to the right of General Wood's line, he found considerable interval between General Wood's division and General Sheridan's troops. He then ordered General Sheridan to bring forward a brigade of his division and place it to the right and rear of General Wood's position, to fill the gap between Wood and Sheridan.   On returning from General Wood's position he met General Davis' division immediately behind General Wood, advancing.   He asked General Davis who ordered him there.   General Davis said General Rosecrans, or words to that effect.   He then told General Davis to place his division on the right of General Wood, as there was still an interval between that point and the advance brigade of Sheridan brought forward to support Wood.   General Davis' division was placed in position—one brigade in line of battle, one brigade in reserve.   The distance from the right of General Davis' position to the advance brigade of Sheridan's division was about 300 yards to right and rear.   The distance from the right of General Sheridan's advanced brigade to the remaining two brigades of General Sheridan's division in position was one-fourth mile to right and rear.   To the right of General Davis' position and in front of General Sheridan's position were two regiments of dismounted troops of Colonel Wilder's brigade, who were placed there by General McCook's order, to observe and protect the right flank.   The remainder of Colonel Wilder's brigade, with an additional regiment of dismounted troops, was in position to the right and rear of General Sheridan's position upon a commanding eminence.   Very soon after General McCook had placed General Davis in position he received an order from General Rosecrans to hold his troops in readiness to withdraw them to the support of General Thomas, who was heavily pressed; that the entire right must be withdrawn, if necessary, to secure the left.   Orders were dispatched to division commanders to give them this information and order.   Within a few minutes from the time this order was received, another order was received from General Rosecrans, directing him to send two brigades immediately of Sheridan's division, as rapidly as the men could march without exhausting themselves, to the support of General Thomas.   I was dispatched to carry this order.   I ran my horse to General Sheridan's position at the Widow Glenn's, and gave him the order to take his two right brigades.   I watched them file by the Widow Glenn's to the left, down the Dry Valley road toward General Thomas, Generals Sheridan and Lytle at their head.   This took place at 11 o'clock.

Question. How long did it take you to ride from Widow Glenn's house to General Thomas' headquarters ?

Answer. From the last time I was at the Widow Glenn's until I reached General Thomas' headquarters was three hours.   The distance from the Widow Glenn's to General Thomas' position, by the nearest route a person could have rode with safety at 2 or 3 o'clock on Sunday p. m., was about 5 or 6 miles.   The distance was supposed to have been greater, but by actual observation I was enabled to reach that point by riding about that distance.

By General McCook :

Question. How far from the house of Widow Glenn was the brigade of General Lytle placed, and was or not General Rosecrans' headquarters at the house, and he present when they took their position ?

Answer. The Widow Glenn's house was immediately on the line of battle upon which General Lytle's command was placed.   The house was General Rosecrans' headquarters during the afternoon and night of the 19th.   He occupied it till the morning of the 20th.   General Rosecrans saw General Lytle's troops in position there.

Question. Was not General McCook by his orders directed to hold the position at Widow Glenn's house ; and if so, were his troops placed properly to do so, and also to hold the Dry Valley road ?

Answer. His order from General Rosecrans required him to hold the position in which the Widow Glenn's house was located.   It would have required a force twice the size of General McCook's command on that morning to have taken possession of that position and of the Dry Valley road there by an attack in front.

Question. Was not Major-General McCook active and energetic, on the morning of the 20th of September, in getting his troops into position agreeably to orders received from the general commanding ?

Answer. He remained at Widow Glenn's house during the night of 19th.   He left the house in person long before daylight to place his troops in position.   He remained on horseback most of the morning, apparently active in examining his position and placing his troops, until I left him. He visited every part of the line of battle on the right in person.

Question. What hour was the line broken?

Answer. The line was assaulted, as far as I could judge from personal observation and from the noise of battle, at 11 a. m. on 20th. I saw the enemy attack the position at Widow Glenn's at few minutes past 11, by my time. I am not able to say from personal observation when the right of the line of battle gave way. I observed that our troops appeared, from the firing, to be falling back shortly after 11 o'clock.

By the COURT:

Question. Had the troops of General McCook thrown up any breastworks or other defensive works?

Answer. The troops of General Sheridan's division at the Widow Glenn's house had erected very strong breastworks and barricades. The troops of General Davis' division were placed in position behind breastworks already erected. The remaining troops had not been in position long enough to have erected breastworks before they were attacked.

The Court was ordered cleared, with the exception of General McCook and staff.

The Court was opened, and adjourned to meet again at 10 o'clock on the 8th instant.

EIGHTH DAY.

FEBRUARY 8, 1864.

The Court met pursuant to adjournment.

Present, Major-Generals Hunter and Cadwalader, Brigadier-General Wadsworth, and Colonel Schriver, recorder, and Major-General McCook.

Col. J. P. SANDERSON, Thirteenth U. S. Infantry, being duly sworn, says to questions

By the COURT:

Question. Were you at the battle of Chickamauga, and in what capacity?

Answer. I was; in the capacity of aide-de-camp to the commanding general.

Question. Do you know any material facts bearing on the conduct of General McCook on 19th and 20th September, either favorable or unfavorable?

Answer. I suppose to answer that question my only way is to relate what I know of General McCook on that occasion. I saw General McCook on the morning of the 20th, where his corps was posted—I cannot fix the time, but early in the morning, perhaps 8 or 9 o'clock—in company with General Rosecrans and a number of his staff officers. After leaving him there, I have no recollection of having seen him again until after a breach in our lines was made by the enemy. At that time General Rosecrans and his staff were in rear of our lines several hundred yards, I suppose, a little to the left of where the breach took place. Just then the command was given to the staff to mount and fall back to the base of the ridge, several hundred yards, I suppose. The staff and escort fell back accordingly, but while going there I noticed General Rosecrans turning to the left into the ravine and passing over toward the point (place) where General McCook's corps had been posted in the morning, and thus General Rosecrans became separated from the escort and staff. A momentary consultation took place between some of the officers as to whether we should pass over the ravine toward General McCook's headquarters or pass up the ridge and endeavor to reach General Thomas' headquarters, and it was determined to proceed toward Thomas', when, about that time, General McCook and his staff approached us and followed us on the ridge in the direction of Rossville. After passing some distance—I took no note of the time; I should think it was 12 to 1 o'clock—we came to a road in which there were a number of ammunition wagons, horses unhitched, and a number of prisoners. Some of the staff officers halted there, organized a guard to take charge of the prisoners, and marched them to Chattanooga, and some took charge of the ammunition wagons. At that time my attention was drawn to those things as they happened. General McCook passed on to the left, and I did not see him again during the day.

Question. Was General Morton and the guide, McDonald, with you on that occasion?

Answer. General Morton I remember coming up the hill to us just about the time that I first saw General McCook. He fell behind us, or waited and joined General McCook. That is all I remember of General Morton. I next halted about a mile west of Rossville; rallied stragglers; it is difficult to say to what corps they belonged, but to the best of my knowledge they belonged to General McCook's.

Question. Was there any difficulty in going from where you were to General Thomas' headquarters by a *détour* to the left?

Answer. You could go there, as events proved, but, of course, there were difficulties, such as going under fire.

There being no other witnesses in attendance, the Court adjourned till 10 o'clock on 9th instant.

NINTH DAY.

FEBRUARY 9, 1864.

The Court met pursuant to adjournment.
Present, Major-Generals Hunter and Cadwalader, Brigadier-General Wadsworth, and Colonel Schriver, recorder, and Major-General McCook.

LYNE STARLING, late assistant adjutant-general of volunteers, being duly sworn, says to questions

By General McCOOK:

Question. Did you see General McCook on the 20th September at the battle of Chickamauga? If so, state what time, what was said, and what was he doing. State all you know about General McCook's movements at the battle of Chickamauga and until he reached Chattanooga.

Answer. After General Crittenden had sent me to reorganize the scattered troops, and I was in some doubts whether I should go to General Thomas or to Chattanooga, I started through the hills to Rossville—no road—and fell in with General McCook. He asked me where General Crittenden was. I told him I was not sure, but believed he had gone to Chattanooga. I added that he was very cool and a man of sense, and said that it was there a man of sense should go under the circumstances. General McCook expressed a great desire to get to General Thomas, but doubted the possibility of doing it. About this time several officers rode up and one of them, a physician, and General McCook rode to them; they were acquaintances. I left him and went on toward Rossville. At a hill over which a road passed through a gap I found a captain of cavalry had placed a guard across the road and was collecting stragglers, and assisted him until General McCook again came up. He placed Colonel Wiles, General Rosecrans' provost-marshal, in command of the stragglers there when he came up, and rode into Chattanooga. He had a guide with him who deceived me, and I think General McCook, who took us into the Chattanooga Valley, some 10 miles from Chattanooga. We went in that way to Chattanooga, where we arrived, I think, something later than 4 o'clock. I will add we expected to go to Chattanooga by Rossville, or very near it, and thought we were doing so until we struck this valley. The country was rough and hilly, being the Mission Ridge and its spurs.

JOSEPH C. HILL, late captain of Fifth Kentucky Cavalry, duly sworn, says to questions

By General McCOOK:

Question. Did you see General McCook at the battle of Chickamauga, after the line of battle had been broken, the morning of the 20th instant, and what was he doing?

Answer. About 10 o'clock on the 20th, just after the line had been broken, I saw General McCook doing everything in his power to rally the broken troops on a range of hills, just in rear of the line of battle. I remained with him nearly an hour, when I determined to find General Rosecrans, supposing he had gone to General Thomas' headquarters, and started in that direction about 500 yards, and narrowly escaped capture. I found that it was impossible to get to General Thomas' headquarters. Later in the day (3 p. m.) I found he might be reached by way of Rossville, but it was impossible at that time by any other route. I had no means of fixing accurately the time the line broke, but I know when I saw General McCook was after the line had broken.

Question. When did you next see General McCook, and what orders were then given to him?

Answer. At just sunset on 20th, in Chattanooga, at General Wagner's headquarters. I heard General Rosecrans order General McCook to lie down and rest, for, said General Rosecrans, "I am nearly worn out and want some one with me to take command, if necessary to assist me." What called for that order was the fact that I had just reported that General Thomas was all right; had stood his ground, and driven the enemy from the front.

Question. Was not that the first information that General Rosecrans had of General Thomas' condition and position?

Answer. It was.

By the COURT:

Question. Were you in the United States service on the 19th and 20th September, and what duty were you performing during the events you have related?

Answer. I was, and was at General Rosecrans' headquarters in obedience to an order received from him, and during the 19th and 20th was acting as a member of his staff, not by any particular order, but was sent with dispatches and orders by him.

The Court was cleared.

The Court was opened, and it adjourned to meet at 10 a. m. on 10th instant.

TENTH DAY.

FEBRUARY 10, 1864.

The Court met pursuant to adjournment.

Present, Major-Generals Hunter and Cadwalader, Brigadier-General Wadsworth, and Colonel Schriver, recorder, and Major-General McCook.

The proceedings of the ninth day were read and approved.

The Court adjourned to meet at 10 o'clock on 11th instant.

ELEVENTH DAY.

FEBRUARY 11, 1864.

There were no proceedings in this case to-day.

February 12, 1864.

The Court met pursuant to adjournment.

Present, Major-Generals Hunter and Cadwalader, Brigadier-General Wadsworth, and Colonel Schriver, recorder, and Major-General McCook.

Col. J. T. Wilder, Seventeenth Indiana, being duly sworn, says to questions

By General McCook:

Question. Did you see General McCook on the morning of the 20th September?

Answer. I did.

Question. Did not General McCook display zeal, energy, and ability in posting his troops on the morning of September 20, 1863?

Answer. He did.

Question. With what force did the enemy attack General McCook's troops on the morning of September 20, 1863?

Answer. I do not know the exact number. The force I saw consisted of five lines. My command broke their line, exposing their flank to my view, and thus enabled me to see how many lines he had.

By the Court:

Question. What was your command, and to what duty were you assigned on the morning of 20th?

Answer. My command consisted of a brigade of five regiments of mounted infantry, constituting First Brigade, Fourth Division, Fourteenth Army Corps (General Thomas'), and I was ordered by General Rosecrans to report to General McCook, who would assign me to my position, which he did in person.

By General McCook:

Question. Did you receive orders from General McCook that General Sheridan was going to move to the left to support General Thomas, and that you must keep well closed up to the left as he moved, and did you do so?

Answer. I did, and moved to the left to close up on General Sheridan, about one-fourth mile distant. Before I could reach him, although moving at double-quick, his line was driven back by an overpowering rebel force.

By the Court:

Question. What orders did you receive from General McCook after Sheridan was driven back?

Answer. None, as the rebels were between him and me.

Question. Did you receive any further orders from him that day?

Answer. I did not.

The Court adjourned to meet at 10 o'clock on the 13th instant.

February 13, 1864.

The Court met pursuant to adjournment.

Present, Major-Generals Hunter and Cadwalader, Brigadier-General Wadsworth, and Colonel Schriver, recorder, and Major-General McCook.

The proceedings of the twelfth day were read and approved.

Capt. J. ST. C. MORTON, U. S. Corps of Engineers, duly sworn, says to questions

By General McCOOK:

Question. What was your rank and position and duty on 20th September, 1863, during the battle of Chickamauga?

Answer. My rank was brigadier-general of volunteers; was chief engineer of Army of Cumberland, and served in that capacity on the staff of General Rosecrans during the first part of the engagement. Having become separated from General Rosecrans, I reported to General McCook, requesting him to place me temporarily on his staff.

Question. What time in the morning did you last see General McCook before the battle commenced, and was General Rosecrans present, and what did he say about General McCook's position?

Answer. At about 9.30 a. m. General Rosecrans was present. This interview took place on a hill a little in rear of the right of the line. Major-General McCook had posted two brigades and battery there. Major-General Rosecrans made several observations in approval of the position. This was at 9.30 o'clock.

Question. Were you constantly with General Rosecrans from that time until you were wounded, and General Rosecrans left you, after the lines were broken and our troops driven back?

Answer. I was either close alongside of him or within sight of him, and was not separated more than 200 yards from him.

Question. What time were the lines broken?

Answer. Having had no watch on the field, I can only give my judgment in this particular, and in regard to other times to which I may testify. It must have been 11.30 a. m.

Question. What time did you join General McCook, and where was it?

Answer. It must have been between 12 and 1 o'clock, and in the woods in rear of the point where our line had been pierced.

Question. What was the nature of the country and ground around about when you reported to General McCook?

Answer. The ground was hilly and wooded.

Question. Did you inform General McCook, after you examined your maps, and looking at the heavy clouds of dust which were rising on the left and the occasional sounds of artillery, that you believed the whole army was in retreat for Chattanooga?

Answer. I made repeated examinations of my map that day, using a prismatic compass to identify locality of clouds and dust and sound of firing. I made such a remark to Major-General McCook, at a point in Chattanooga Valley road from which a heavy column of dust could be seen moving northward on what I supposed to be the Rossville road.

Question. What was General McCook's conduct on 20th September at the battle of Chickamauga?

Answer. General McCook appeared to be perfectly composed, and appeared to be deeply sensible of the reverse the army sustained. His disposition of the troops under his command was, in my opinion, eminently judicious.

The Court was cleared.
The Court was opened, and adjourned to meet at 10 o'clock on the 15th instant.

FOURTEENTH DAY.

FEBRUARY 15, 1864.

The Court met pursuant to adjournment.

Present, Major-Generals Hunter and Cadwalader, Brigadier-General Wadsworth, and Colonel Schriver, recorder, and Major-General McCook.

The proceedings of the thirteenth day were read and approved.

Brig. Gen. J. C. DAVIS, U. S. Volunteers, being duly sworn, says to questions

By General McCOOK:

Question. Were you in the battle of Chickamauga? In what capacity, and of what rank?

Answer. I was, as division commander and brigadier-general of volunteers, in General McCook's corps.

Question. By whom was your position assigned you at early dawn on the morning of 20th September? Were there natural or artificial defenses?

Answer. My position was assigned by Major-General McCook, commanding the corps. There were natural defenses; no artificial ones.

Question. Was your position seen by General Rosecrans, and was it remarked on by him? If so, what did he say?

Answer. It was frequently seen by his riding along it. He made no remarks whatever concerning it. My right was immediately in rear of his headquarters, where he had them from 12 o'clock on the 19th. The position commanded the Dry Valley road, being on a wooded ridge running parallel with the Dry Valley road, my line being from 100 to 150 yards in rear of the road formed on the summit of the hill. I considered myself in reserve, General Lytle's brigade, of Sheridan's division, being immediately in front of me.

Question. After you were removed from this position, how were you ordered to close your line, and by whom?

Answer. I was ordered to move to the left and close on Crittenden's right. In the morning, when we were put in position, General Wood's division formed General Crittenden's right, as I understood from conversation held with General Wood that morning. I immediately commenced moving by my left flank, and on reaching the position where I supposed General Wood's right rested, I found the troops on my left moving to the front. Upon inquiry I ascertained it was the right of General Van Cleve's division. My instructions being to close on Crittenden's right, I conformed to General Van Cleve's movements and took position on a ridge in an open field south, or to the front of the Dry Valley road. My troops got into position very quickly. General Van Cleve's troops were delayed on account of defiles. While General Van Cleve's troops were getting into position, I sent my adjutant-general, Captain Morrison, to either General Rosecrans or McCook to see if we were in the right position, and, if not, to ascertain where it should be. He returned immediately with an order from General Rosecrans to move to the front and form on General Wood's division, which was then in the woods in our front. The order came direct from General Rosecrans, who was only 150 yards from me, and I could see him.

Question. Had General McCook's troops been allowed to remain where he posted them in the morning, could we not have fought with success on Sunday, and why do you think so?

Answer. I have no doubt about my ability to have held my position against any force that could assault it. I think so because of the natural strength of the position, and of the reliability of the troops I commanded; and I will add that the troops on other parts of the field on the same ridge and similarly wooded, did hold theirs. I moved to the front in compliance with General Rosecrans' order, crossed the open fields, riding in front of my line. I met General McCook in the woods, who asked me some questions, and how I came there, &c., or words to that effect. I told him my instructions. He then rode to the front with me, and pointed out to me my position. This position was on General Wood's right, forming on Colonel Buell's brigade of that division behind some rude breastworks, rails, chunks, &c., piled up. While superintending the movements of my troops to their position Colonel Buell rode up to me and informed me he had orders to move to the left; that the other brigades of his division were leaving, and informed me of his convictions of the close proximity of the enemy to our front, and of his fears of his being attacked as he withdrew his troops. I immediately ordered up my reserve brigade, and as this brigade was getting into position with two or three regiments on the liné, the attack commenced on my right. The regiments not in line pushed forward into line and entered into the engagement, which at that time was becoming very severe. I received the order for the movement from this position early in the morning, at 10.45. I should think the attack was made at 11.15. I think it was half an hour I was getting to the front. The effect of the removal of General Wood's division left a large space unoccupied, through which the enemy advanced in large numbers, turning my flank unopposed on that side.

Question. What was the strength of your command on 20th September, and by what numbers were you assailed?

Answer. It was between 1,300 and 1,400 men, having lost in the vicinity of 1,000 men killed and wounded on 19th, and one of my brigades being then in the vicinity of Crawfish Spring, not on the battle-field, reduced my command to 1,400, in round numbers. I had my rolls called on the night of 19th, and that was about the number that answered to their names. I am satisfied I was assailed by not less than three to one. It was a continuous line of battle nearly surrounding me; there were troops in the woods from which I saw them coming as I was falling back. I have visited the battle-field since frequently, and, judging from the length of the enemy's rifle-pits, the enemy might have outnumbered my force five to one.

Question. How soon after the line of battle was broken did you see General McCook; how was he engaged; what was his demeanor; did you express any opinion to him; if so, what was it?

Answer. I saw General McCook as I fell back on the ridge in the open fields, about or over a quarter mile in rear of our line when attacked. He seemed surrounded by his staff, engaged in rallying the troops. His demeanor was that of a general officer trying to rally his troops under desperate circumstances, under the enemy's fire. I do not think I expressed any opinion to General McCook at that point, but fifteen to thirty minutes after, I saw him on the ridge of the woods north of the Dry Valley road, near the position General Wood occupied in the morning, and spoke to him (McCook). I cannot remember the language used. He was giving me advice about rallying the men, and also expressed fear of the enemy's cavalry getting around in our rear. I expressed an opinion it was impossible to rally troops under such fire (alluding to the fire we had just got from under), and advised to move them as rapidly as possible to the rear, so as to reform the lines. I saw General McCook quarter to half a mile still farther to the rear. I think General McCook came up to me and we had another conversation. I was engaged in completing the removal of my artillery and ammunition trains (also General Reynolds' ammunition train) into the road, and deploying General Reynolds' ammunition guard and my own provost guard which was guarding my ammunition train. General McCook gave me implied instructions to continue to fall back and form my troops, and spoke of the necessity of getting these trains to the rear. I do not think Rossville was mentioned. We were falling back toward Rossville near the Dry Valley road. At the time we were speaking, we were near the Dry Valley road which leads to Rossville, though I did not know it at the time. The country was entirely unknown to me, and I presume it was to most of us, as we were driven on to a new part of the field.

Question. After the line was broken, was it possible for General McCook to have passed to the left to General Thomas' position? Did you contemplate sending artillery to General Thomas, and why did you abandon the intention?

Answer. I think it impossible. I contemplated moving in General Thomas' direction with my artillery, to put it in position, and I abandoned it from the fact that the enemy's advanced skirmishers drove us, compelling us to fall back. A want of knowledge of the country also influenced me in falling back in the direction I did, it being a plain road.

Question. Did you at that time believe that the left was going to the rear on Rossville or Chattanooga, and when did you first change that opinion?

Answer. I believed the left were being driven back, but had no opinion as to where it was going other than that it was driven back. I changed my opinion that the left was driven back when Colonel Thruston reported to me at McFarland's farm that General Thomas was still holding his position. This was, as near as I can remember, between 2 and 3 p.m.

Question. Did not General McCook do everything that a general officer could do to rally the broken troops, and was he in any way responsible for the repulse on the right?

Answer. I think, from what I saw, that he did everything a general officer could do. I do not think he was responsible for the repulse of our troops on the right.

Question. Did or did not General McCook display vigor, energy, and zeal in posting his troops on the morning of the 20th September?

Answer. Yes, as far as I observed, and I judge as a division commander, and from the orders received from him, and his general manner whenever and wherever I saw him.

Question. Did you lose any artillery or any wagons during the battle of Chickamauga?

Answer. No; nor ammunition. Nothing but men.

Question. During the battle what was the condition of your commissariat, and quantity of ammunition on hand?

Answer. I had a large supply of ammunition after the battle. I issued considerable amounts to other commanders. After issuing a few thousand rations to the wounded at Crawfish Spring, I had eleven days' full supply of rations in my train. I had eighteen days' deducting my killed, wounded, and missing.

Question. How far is it from the Widow Glenn's to Chattanooga by Rossville?

Answer. Nine miles, I would call it. I have traveled it several times.

By the COURT:

Question. When and where did you rally your command after it was broken on the morning of the 20th, and where did you take it?

Answer. At a farm known as McFarland's on the Dry Valley road, between 1 and 2 o'clock, and I marched it back by the Dry Valley road, and commenced to form it near General Gordon Granger's right, when I received an order from General Garfield, chief of staff, to return to Rossville with it, being informed at the same time that the whole army was falling back to that point. This was between sunset and dark, and I arrived at Rossville between 9 and 10 o'clock.

By General McCOOK:

Question. Was there anything like a panic among the troops of General McCook's corps after they commenced falling back?

Answer. I did not consider the conduct of the troops indicated the least panic. Their conduct was that of troops being overwhelmed by great numbers.

Question. What troops were detached from General McCook's corps on 19th September, 1863, and by whose order?

Answer. During the night of 18th I received orders to follow Johnson's division, of McCook's corps, which was following Thomas' corps in the general movement of the army to the left. I did so, and on my way passed General McCook, who informed me he had been ordered to remain there and take command of that part of the field, and directed me to move on in the direction of the Widow Glenn's and report for orders to General Rosecrans or Thomas, whomever I could find first. I found General Rosecrans at the Widow Glenn's house, and reported accordingly. I received orders during the day after that from General Rosecrans and reported to him until after night, when General McCook assumed command, at what hour I cannot say—the fore part of the night.

The Court adjourned to meet at 10 o'clock in the council chamber, corner of Jefferson and Sixth streets, on the 16th instant.

FIFTEENTH DAY.

FEBRUARY 16, 1864.

The Court met pursuant to adjournment.

Present, Major-Generals Hunter and Cadwalader, Brigadier-General Wadsworth, and Colonel Schriver, recorder, and Major-General McCook.

The proceedings of the fourteenth day were read and approved.

Lieut. Col. A. C. DUCAT, assistant inspector-general, Department of the Cumberland, being duly sworn, says to questions

By General McCOOK:

Question. Did you see General McCook on the 19th September? What was he doing and what was his demeanor?

Answer. I saw General McCook during the forenoon, and, I think, as late as 2 p. m. His demeanor was becoming a general officer, making disposition of troops when not engaged. He was energetic in pushing troops to the left during the forenoon on the march. I was not acquainted with his orders. He seemed zealous and energetic.

Maj. G. P. THRUSTON, recalled, says to questions

By General McCOOK:

Question. What was your rank, and in what capacity were you acting at the battle of Chickamauga?

Answer. My rank was lieutenant-colonel, assistant adjutant-general, Twentieth Army Corps, and chief of Major-General McCook's staff.

Question. Who had charge of the orders received by General McCook on the 19th of September? Can you produce them, identify them? Can you produce true copies?

Answer. I generally took charge of all orders received by General McCook, filed them, and noted dates of receipt. Here are the original orders.

(Witness produced six pieces, certified copies of which he is to furnish to the Court, marked A in appendix.)

Question. Were all these orders obeyed?

Answer. The orders of the 19th were obeyed, as far as I was capable of judging. I was with General McCook the entire day and feel certain they were explicitly obeyed.

Question. Have you charge of the orders to General McCook on 20th; will you produce them, identify them, and can you furnish true copies?

Answer. I have charge of the orders received on 20th. I here produce them (four pieces), and true copies can be furnished to the Court.

Marked A in appendix.

The order dated 11.45 a. m. should be dated 11.45 p. m. when it was received. General Garfield afterward corrected and explained the date. It was received from General Rosecrans in person, in my presence at midnight on Saturday night.

Question. Did you leave for General Thomas before or after the advance of General Granger's troops, and did you go to the front or rear of his troops?

Answer. General Granger's troops had engaged the enemy before or about the time I passed to General Thomas' headquarters. I do not think I would have been able to reach General Thomas by the route I took, if General Granger had not opened the way. I believe I was the first person who reached General Thomas from the right of the army after the line was broken.

Question. At what hour did you return to the place where you met General Davis at McFarland's farm?

Answer. About 4 p. m. General Thomas states in his official report that I reported to him at 4 p. m.

Here the Court, at the request of General McCook, directed to be inserted in the record an order which was received by General Crittenden from General Garfield, chief of General Rosecrans' staff, and which was put in as evidence by General Crittenden on the fourteenth day. It is as follows:

> HEADQUARTERS DEPARTMENT OF THE CUMBERLAND,
> *Widow Glenn's House, September* 19, 1863—11.20 p. m.
> [Understood to be addressed to]
> General CRITTENDEN:
> GENERAL: The general commanding directs me to inform you that General McCook has been ordered to hold this gap to-morrow, covering the Dry Valley road, his right resting near this place, his left connecting with General Thomas' right.
> Very respectfully, your obedient servant,
>
> J. A. GARFIELD,
> *Brigadier-General, Chief of Staff.*

Question. What was the difference in the times at which orders dated 10.10 a. m. and 10.30 a. m. on 20th September were received by General McCook?

Answer. They were received almost simultaneously; the difference in time could not have been more than six minutes, the staff officers carrying these orders to General McCook's troops following each other almost immediately.

Witness here desired to correct his testimony given on the seventh day.

In my first examination I stated that the order to relieve General Negley was received about 7 a. m. on 20th. Subsequent reflection has led me to believe I was mistaken as to this date. The fog had risen and cleared, and I believe the hour was later, but the precise time I do not feel willing to attempt to state.

Question. What portion of General McCook's troops fought with General Thomas on the 19th September?

Answer. The largest division of General McCook's, General Johnson's, reported to General Thomas early on that day, and remained with him during the entire actions on 19th and 20th. General Davis' division, consisting of two brigades, was sent to the left, by order of General Rosecrans, later in the day. Afterward General Sheridan's entire command was sent to the front and left, and General McCook remained in command of the cavalry only, which had not yet reported to him. These dispositions were made by order of General Rosecrans.

By the COURT:

Question. Did General McCook, so far as you know, give any orders to the cavalry on his right after his own line broke on 20th?

Answer. He did; to close up to the left and fill up the gap made by the withdrawal of General Sheridan. I assisted in person in placing the cavalry in position on the right (Wilder's brigade). I then proceeded to the commanding officer of the nearest cavalry division, and gave him an order in General McCook's name to close to the left, and endeavor to support our right. I sent this order in General Mc-

Cook's name to General Mitchell (commanding the whole cavalry), by a staff officer. General Rosecrans had given General McCook permission to order the cavalry. General Mitchell replied twice that General Rosecrans had ordered him not to leave Crawfish Spring. There was a gap of a mile between the cavalry and Wilder's brigade (mounted infantry, which was immediately on our right). General Rosecrans told General Mitchell subsequently, in my presence, that he should have obeyed General McCook's order, and closed in to the left; that this was in accordance with the general understanding.

Capt. I. C. McElfatrick, Thirtieth Indiana Volunteer Infantry, being duly sworn, says to questions

By General McCook :

Question. What was your rank and in what capacity were you acting at the battle of Chickamauga ?

Answer. Captain and topographical engineer of Twentieth Army Corps.

Question. Where was General McCook at the moment the attack was made on 20th ; what orders did he give ; where did he go ?

Answer. He was just in rear of the position General Davis occupied, perhaps half a mile north of the Widow Glenn's. He ordered Colonel Laiboldt, who was in position there, to move forward in support of General Davis. General McCook remained there until all the troops fell back, and he went with them.

Question. Were you with General McCook at the time he last met General Davis ; do you recollect the instructions he gave him ?

Answer. I was. My recollection is that he instructed him to fall back in the direction of Rossville.

Question. After leaving General Davis, in what direction did General McCook proceed, and with what object ?

Answer. He move ¹ thence in a southwesterly direction, where he expected to find General Sheridan and his troops.

Question. Were you with him when you met Captain Sheridan, of General Sheridan's staff, and did you hear the conversation between them ? What instructions, if any, were given by General McCook ?

Answer. I was ; but being some distance off, I did not hear the conversation.

Question. Did Generals Rosecrans and McCook meet after the attack was made on Davis' line ?

Answer. General Rosecrans passed down the Dry Valley road, but did not stop but a very short time, perhaps half a minute. I think General McCook did not speak to him at all.

Question. At this point of time, what was the condition of Laiboldt's brigade, of Sheridan's division ?

Answer. Laiboldt's brigade had been driven back nearly a quarter of a mile.

Question. Was anything said by General McCook as to reaching General Thomas' position ? Did you make any attempt to go to the left ? Why did you return ?

Answer. I heard him express desire repeatedly to get to General Thomas. I attempted to go to the left myself, but I found the troops on our left in greater confusion than in our immediate front, and it was impossible to go there.

Question. What was General McCook's demeanor on the field during the dispositions preliminary to the attack, and during the attack, and after it ?

Answer. General McCook was zealous and energetic in posting his troops in the morning. During the attack and after the lines were broken, he was cool and collected, and did everything that was possible in rallying his troops.

By the Court :

Question. Did General McCook, so far as you know, give any orders to the cavalry on his right after his line broke on the 20th?

Answer. I do not know.

The Court adjourned to meet at 10 o'clock on the 17th instant.

SIXTEENTH DAY.

FEBRUARY 17, 1864.

The Court met pursuant to adjournment.

Present, Major-Generals Hunter and Cadwalader, Brigadier-General Wadsworth, and Colonel Schriver, recorder, and Major-General McCook.

The proceedings of the fifteenth day were read and approved.

At the request of General McCook, and to prevent the witness, who is now absent, from being recalled, the Court directed the following testimony, given in the case of General Crittenden by Capt. Richard Lodor, Fourth U. S. Artillery, who was lieutenant-colonel and assistant inspector-general of Twenty-first Army Corps in the battle of Chickamauga, to be inserted in this record :

"Question. Did you attempt on Sunday to go to General Thomas, and with what success?

"Answer. I did, and tried hard for three hours to get to General Thomas from the position General Crittenden occupied when he left to find General Rosecrans, and ascertained the only way to get from that position without being captured was by passing back toward Chattanooga. * * * I believe it to have been impossible for any one to pass from the position General Crittenden occupied near the batteries to our lines in the front. I am an artillery officer, and have been serving in that corps nearly eight years."

Captain McElfatrick, recalled, says to questions

By General McCook :

Question. Had not General Rosecrans, by orders, detained General McCook at Chattanooga on the evening of September 20, could not General McCook have reached Rossville before his rallied troops arrived there?

Answer. Yes.

Question. At what point did General Morton take his observation and examine his maps?

Answer. A short distance south of the Dry Valley road, not over a mile in rear of the line of battle.

Capt. ALEXANDER C. McCLURG, Eighty-eighth Illinois Volunteer Infantry, duly sworn, says to questions

By General McCook :

Question. What was your rank and position at the battle of Chickamauga?

Answer. Captain, and detailed to act as assistant adjutant-general of the Twentieth Army Corps, commanded by General McCook.

Question. Did or did not General McCook display energy and zeal in posting his troops on the morning of 20th September?

Answer. He did; a great deal of energy, especially in the early part of the morning, in fixing the position of the right of the line in such position that it would command the Dry Valley road. That seemed to be his particular anxiety.

Question. Did not General McCook frequently express a desire to reach General Thomas after the line was broken ?

Answer. He did. When we were following the guide he kept bearing toward the left. Several times the general expressed the opinion we were going too far to the left ; two or three times he rode to the right himself, stopped, and listened to the artillery firing then going on : said that was certainly General Thomas' guns, and that we should keep more to the right, and not in the direction the guide was taking us. The guide argued the direction he was taking was the only feasible one out of that position across the ridge. I remember myself at that time being so convinced we were going too far to the left, that I asked if the guide was reliable, and whether he would not bring us up in the enemy's lines. I did not express that opinion to General McCook, however.

Question. Did not General McCook do all in his power to rally the broken troops ?

Answer. He did all that one man individually could do by his own efforts ; and also had all his staff and escort, and even the clerks who were with us, to try to rally them.

Question. What was General McCook's demeanor before, during, and after the battle ?

Answer. In the early part of the morning he was calm and confident, and was engaged energetically in posting the troops. Later, and shortly before the attack took place, he seemed very anxious, and several times while watching the dust rising in the woods opposite, said he was satisfied that General Rosecrans was mistaken, and that a very formidable attack would be made there ; that the troops left there were not sufficient to hold the line. He repeated that with a great deal of anxiety in his manner, just after receiving the order to send two brigades of Sheridan's division to the left. Just as the attack was made, I was not with the general. Just after the lines were broken I rejoined him, and was with him for some time under a heavy fire, while he was doing all in his power to rally troops.

Question. Had not General Rosecrans, by orders, detained General McCook at Chattanooga in the evening of the 20th, could not General McCook have reached Rossville before his rallied troops arrived there ?

Answer. Yes.

The Court was closed.

The Court was opened, and adjourned till 10 o'clock on the 18th February.

SEVENTEENTH DAY.

FEBRUARY 18, 1864.

The Court met pursuant to adjournment.

Present, Major-Generals Hunter and Cadwalader, Brigadier-General Wadsworth, and Colonel Schriver, recorder, and Major-General McCook.

The proceedings of the sixteenth day were read and approved.

The Court was cleared.

The Court was opened, and adjourned to meet at 10 o'clock on the 19th instant.

EIGHTEENTH DAY.

FEBRUARY 19, 1864.

The Court met pursuant to adjournment.

Present, Major-Generals Hunter and Cadwalader, Brigadier-General Wadsworth, and Colonel Schriver, recorder, and Major-General McCook.

General McCook being asked if he had any other witnesses, said that Captain Sheridan had been summoned many days ago and had failed to appear. He expressed a willingness, however, to introduce a witness who could give substantially what he desired to prove by Captain Sheridan, and accordingly, by permission of the Court,

Capt. B. D. WILLIAMS, aide-de-camp to General McCook, was recalled, and says to questions

By General McCOOK:

Question. What officer of General McCook's personal staff had charge of obtaining information in regard to roads and country?

Answer. I was the officer, and had that subject specially under my charge.

Question. Had General McCook ever been on the ground over which his troops fought, until Sunday morning, September 20?

Answer. Not to my knowledge. If he had, I think I should have known it.

Question. When General McCook last left General Davis, in what direction did he go, and for what object?

Answer. He went to the right of the main line toward Crawfish Spring. The guide, Mr. McDonald, informed him he would have to go in that direction to strike the road which came from Crawfish Spring, leading in the direction of Chickamauga Creek. The general expressed his desire to find General Sheridan's division of his corps, which had been driven back in the direction of Crawfish Spring.

Question. Did he meet an officer of General Sheridan's staff; if so, whom, and what inquiries were made in regard to General Sheridan?

Answer. About 1½ miles from the point where he left General Davis, and after traveling through the woods without any roads, he met Captain Sheridan, brother of General Sheridan, and aide-de-camp to him, and inquired of him if he knew where General Sheridan was. Captain Sheridan informed him, pointing in the direction of Crawfish Spring, that he was about 1½ miles from there, and sending the wagons to the rear. He, Captain Sheridan, was near the house of Mr. Vidito.

Question. Did you hear what directions General McCook gave Captain Sheridan, or did General McCook inform you what directions he had given to be taken to General Sheridan?

Answer. I did not hear the directions General McCook gave to Captain Sheridan as they rode up the hill together, I being in rear a short distance. General McCook informed me that he had told Captain Sheridan to direct his brother, General Sheridan, to bring his troops in the direction of Rossville and Chattanooga; also to send in all the wounded able to be transported, from Crawfish Spring, where one of our hospitals was ; also to send all the wagons to Chattanooga as he, General McCook, was going in that direction.

Question. Was there any firing in the front or any pursuit by the enemy when General McCook left that part of the field?

Answer. General McCook left the field after the firing had ceased, except an occasional cannon shot away to the left, and said he could do no further good there, after he had given the directions I have stated.

Question. At what point did General McCook ascertain that he was nearer Chattanooga than Rossville?

Answer. He proceeded from the house of Mr. Vidito until he reached the forks of the road, one going to Chattanooga, the other to Rossville, where he met some troops. He inquired whose troops they were, and was informed they were under the command of General Spears. He inquired where General Spears was, and was told he was a short distance off. He rode up to him and had conversation. General Spears informed him General Rosecrans had sent him out from Chattanooga to go to Rossville, to render what assistance he could to the army. We were then 1½ to 2 miles from Chattanooga and about 4 miles from Rossville. General McCook remarked he would gallop into Chattanooga, see General Rosecrans, and get orders from him and return to Rossville by the time his troops could get to that neighborhood. I think General Spears' command was part of the Reserve Corps which was at Chattanooga during the battle.

General McCook here stated he had no other evidence to offer, and that he would be ready to submit a statement to the Court at 6 p. m. to-day.

The Court was closed.

The Court was opened, and adjourned to meet at 6 p. m. to-day.

GALT HOUSE, *February* 19—6 p. m.

The Court met pursuant to adjournment.

Present, Major-Generals Hunter and Cadwalader, Brigadier-General Wadsworth, and Colonel Schriver, recorder, and Major-General McCook.

The proceedings of the morning session were read and approved.

General McCook then read a statement, marked B in appendix.

The Court was cleared.

The Court was opened, and adjourned to meet at 10 a. m. on the 20th instant.

NINETEENTH DAY.

FEBRUARY 20, 1864.

The Court met pursuant to adjournment.

Present, Major-Generals Hunter and Cadwalader, Brigadier-General Wadsworth, and Colonel Schriver, recorder, and Major-General McCook.

The Court was closed.

The Court was opened, and adjourned to meet at the Galt House at 8 this p. m.

FEBRUARY 20, 1864—8 p. m.

The Court met pursuant to adjournment.

Present, Major-Generals Hunter and Cadwalader, Brigadier-General Wadsworth, and Colonel Schriver, recorder.

No proceedings in this case.

The Court was closed.

The Court adjourned till 10 o'clock on the 22d instant, having been previously opened.

TWENTIETH DAY.

FEBRUARY 22, 1864.

The Court met pursuant to adjournment.

No proceedings in this case.

The Court was closed.

The Court was opened, and adjourned to meet at 6 p. m. this day.

6 p. m.

The Court met at 9.30 p. m.

No proceedings in this case.

The Court was closed.

The Court was opened, and adjourned to meet at 10 o'clock on the 23d February.

FEBRUARY 23, 1864.

The Court met pursuant to adjournment.

Present, Major-Generals Hunter and Cadwalader, Brigadier-General Wadsworth, and Colonel Schriver, recorder.

The Court was cleared.

After the reading of the testimony, the Court came to the following

FINDING AND OPINION IN MAJOR-GENERAL M'COOK'S CASE.

It appears from the investigation that Major-General McCook commanded the Twentieth Army Corps, composed of Sheridan's, Johnson's, and Davis' divisions.

His command on the 19th September, 1863 (the first day of the battle of Chickamauga), consisted of Sheridan's and Davis' divisions and of Negley's temporarily, and occupied the right of the line, Johnson's having been detached to Thomas' command.

The evidence shows that General McCook did his whole duty faithfully on that day, with activity and intelligence.

Early on the 20th September, General McCook had under his command the divisions of Sheridan and Davis (the latter only 1,300 to 1,400 strong), and Wilder's brigade; and the senior officers of the cavalry were told they must take orders from him, though attend to their own business.

The posting of these troops was not satisfactory to the commanding general, who, in person, directed several changes between 8 and 10.30 a. m. During these changes, involving a flank movement of the whole right to the left, the enemy made a fierce attack, taking advantage of a break in the line, caused by the precipitate and inopportune withdrawal of his division by Brig. Gen. T. J. Wood, passing through the interval and routing the whole right and center up to Brannan's position.

The Court deem it unnecessary to express an opinion as to the relative merits of the position taken by General McCook and that subsequently ordered to be taken by the commanding general; but it is apparent from the testimony that General McCook was not responsible for the delay in forming the new line on that occasion.

It further appears that General McCook not only had impressed on him the vital importance of keeping well closed to the left, and of maintaining a compact center, but he was also ordered to hold the Dry Valley road. This caused the line to be attenuated, as stated in the testimony of the commanding general, who says that its length was greater than he thought it was when assumed. It is shown, too, that the cavalry did not obey General McCook's orders.

The above facts, and the additional one that the small force at General McCook's disposal was inadequate to defend, against greatly superior numbers, the long line hastily taken, under instructions, relieve General McCook entirely from the responsibility for the reverse which ensued.

It is fully established that General McCook did everything he could to rally and hold his troops after the line was broken, giving the necessary orders, &c., to his subordinates.

The Court are of opinion, however, that in leaving the field to go to Chattanooga, General McCook committed a mistake, but his gallant conduct in the engagement forbids the idea that he was influenced by considerations of personal safety.   Bearing in mind that the commanding general having previously gone to Chattanooga, it was natural for General McCook to infer that all the discomfited troops were expected to rally there, as well as to presume that a conference with the commanding general on that important subject was both desirable and necessary, the Court cannot regard this act of General McCook as other than an error of judgment.

D. HUNTER,
Major-General, President.
ED. SCHRIVER,
Inspector-General, Recorder.

There being no further business, the Court adjourned *sine die.*

D. HUNTER,
Major-General, President.
ED. SCHRIVER,
Inspector-General, Recorder.

ADJUTANT-GENERAL'S OFFICE, *April* 9, 1864.

The record and opinions in the foregoing case have been submitted to the President of the United States.   He is of opinion that no further action is required, and the Court of Inquiry is dissolved.

By order of the Secretary of War:

E. D. TOWNSEND,
Assistant Adjutant-General.

APPENDIX.

A.

COPIES OF WRITTEN ORDERS RECEIVED BY MAJOR-GENERAL M'COOK FROM MAJOR-GENERAL ROSECRANS, ON THE 19TH AND 20TH OF SEPTEMBER, 1863.

HEADQUARTERS DEPARTMENT OF THE CUMBERLAND,
Crawfish Spring, September 19, 1863—12.15 a. m.
(Received September 19, 3.25 a. m.)
Major-General McCOOK,
Commanding Twentieth Army Corps:

The general commanding directs me to acknowledge the receipt of your 8 p. m. dispatch, and to say so soon as General Thomas' command is out of the way, you will close up to this place.

Very respectfully, your obedient servant,

FRANK S. BOND,
Major, and Aide-de-Camp.

—

HEADQUARTERS DEPARTMENT OF THE CUMBERLAND,
Crawfish Spring, September 19, 1863—10 a. m.
Major-General McCOOK:

From present indications the general commanding thinks you had better make your dispositions to relieve General Negley and hold the right.   He sends you this that you need not get too far from water.

Very respectfully, your obedient servant,

J. A. GARFIELD,
Brigadier-General, and Chief of Staff.

HEADQUARTERS DEPARTMENT OF THE CUMBERLAND,
Widow Glenn's, September 19, 1863—1 p. m.
Major-General McCook,
Commanding Twentieth Army Corps:
General Thomas is heavily engaged, and Palmer and Johnson
have been ordered up to support him. All goes well thus far. A
considerable cavalry force of the enemy has got in behind us and
are threatening some of our trains.
The general commanding directs you to hurry Mitchell's cavalry
in upon our right, and send a detachment to look out for our rear.
Very respectfully, your obedient servant,
J. A. GARFIELD,
Brigadier-General, and Chief of Staff.

—

HEADQUARTERS DEPARTMENT OF THE CUMBERLAND,
Widow Glenn's, September 19. (Received 1.25 p. m.)
General McCook:
Your dispatch of 1 p. m. received ; your dispositions approved.
As battle advances prepare to send Negley up here at once, or, if he
cannot get ready, send Sheridan. Send urgent order to Mitchell to
come down this way, and to send a portion of his force down Chat-
tanooga Valley, and with the balance close down on you. Two bri-
gades of Van Cleve are up supporting Palmer, who has not yet be-
come engaged.
By order W. S. Rosecrans :
FRANK S. BOND,
Major, and Aide-de-Camp.

—

HEADQUARTERS DEPARTMENT OF THE CUMBERLAND,
Crawfish Spring, September 19, 1863—10.15 a. m.
Major-General McCook,
Commanding Twentieth Army Corps:
The enemy is still attempting to turn our left and secure the Ross-
ville and Ringgold road. The demonstration on the right is a feint.
The general commanding directs you to send one division of your
corps to Widow Eliza Glenn's, and send forward to report its march
to General Thomas, with orders to close up to General Thomas, if
he shall so direct. The division will receive orders from General
Thomas. General McCook will take command of the right and the
cavalry, and hold himself in readiness to support either flank.
J. A. GARFIELD,
Brigadier-General, Chief of Staff.

—

HEADQUARTERS DEPARTMENT OF THE CUMBERLAND,
Glenn's House, September 19, 1863—12.40 p. m.
Major-General McCook,
Twentieth Army Corps:
GENERAL : The general commanding desires to know how affairs
progress on your front. General Thomas has been engaged, and re-
ports everything favorable. Preserve your signal stations, com-

municate with Summerville [Summertown], and let anything be reported which occurs. Re-enforcements have gone to General Thomas, and he is again engaged.

Very respectfully, &c.,

WILLIAM McMICHAEL,
Major, and Assistant Adjutant-General.

HEADQUARTERS DEPARTMENT OF THE CUMBERLAND,
Widow Glenn's, September 19, 1863—1.45 p. m.

Major-General McCook,
Commanding Twentieth Army Corps:

Your dispatch of 1.30 is received. The general commanding directs you to move Generals Negley and Sheridan this way. Send a brigade to relieve Crittenden, and hold Gordon's Mills. Perhaps Sheridan may be spared to move up that way and be ready for emergencies. Send the forces that you are to spare to General Thomas at once.

Very respectfully,

J. A. GARFIELD,
Brigadier-General, Chief of Staff.

HEADQUARTERS DEPARTMENT OF THE CUMBERLAND,
Widow Glenn's, September 19, 1863—2.40 p. m.

Major-General McCook,
Commanding Twentieth Army Corps:

The tide of battle sweeps to the right. The general commanding thinks you can now move the two brigades of Sheridan to this place. Leave the one brigade posted at Gordon's Mills, to be used there or this way, as circumstances may require. If the right is secure, come forward and direct your forces now fighting.

Very respectfully,

J. A. GARFIELD,
Brigadier-General, Chief of Staff.

HEADQUARTERS DEPARTMENT OF THF CUMBERLAND,
Widow Glenn's, Sept. 19, 1863—11.45 a. m. [11.45 p. m.*]

Major-General McCook,
Commanding Twentieth Army Corps:

The general commanding directs you, as soon as practicable after the receipt of this order, to post your command so as to form the right of the new battle front, and hold this place.

Leave your outposts and grand guards where they now are, till they are driven in by the enemy, when they will fall back on the main body of your command, contesting the ground inch by inch.

Very respectfully,

J. A. GARFIELD,
Brigadier-General, Chief of Staff.

---

* See Thruston's evidence, p. 954.

HEADQUARTERS DEPARTMENT OF THE CUMBERLAND,
McDonald's, September 20, 1863—6.35 a. m.

Major-General McCOOK,
Commanding Twentieth Army Corps:

General Negley's division has been ordered to General Thomas' left. The general commanding directs you to fill the space left vacant by his removal, if practicable. The enemy appears to be moving toward our left.

Very respectfully, your obedient servant,

J. A. GARFIELD,
Brigadier-General, Chief of Staff.

—

HEADQUARTERS DEPARTMENT OF THE CUMBERLAND,
In the Field, September 20, 1863—10.10 a. m.

Major-General McCOOK,
Commanding Twentieth Army Corps:

General Thomas is being heavily pressed on the left. The general commanding directs you to make immediate dispositions to withdraw the right, so as to spare as much force as possible to re-enforce Thomas. The left must be held at all hazards, even if the right is drawn wholly back to the present left. Select a good position back this way, and be ready to start re-enforcements to Thomas at a moment's warning.

J. A. GARFIELD,
Brigadier-General, Chief of Staff.

—

HEADQUARTERS DEPARTMENT OF THE CUMBERLAND,
In the Field, September 20, 1863—10.30 a. m.

Major-General McCOOK,
Commanding Twentieth Army Corps:

The general commanding directs you to send two brigades [of] General Sheridan's division at once, and with all dispatch, to support General Thomas, and send the third brigade as soon as the lines can be drawn in sufficiently. March them as rapidly as you can without exhausting the men. Report in person to these headquarters as soon as your orders are given in regard to Sheridan's movement. Have you any news from Colonel Post?

J. A. GARFIELD,
Brigadier-General, Chief of Staff.

B.

LOUISVILLE, KY.,
February 18, 1864.

On the 28th of September last, an order was issued consolidating with another the Twentieth Army Corps, which it had been my highest honor to command. The order was announced to the army on the 8th of October. I was relieved from command, and have been ever since awaiting the pleasure of the President for the investigation which has just closed.

Conscious that my troops had been subjected to unjust reproach, and that my reputation as their commander and as a soldier had been reviled, I was glad to have this opportunity for vindication—the only means open to me—for on every principle binding the soldier, silence was imposed upon me, when the same order which relieved me from command directed me to await a Court of Inquiry upon my conduct.

I am conscious, too, that the testimony which has been introduced, while it may enable the court to respond to the questions which are vital to myself, has fallen far short of enabling it to report fully upon the battle of Chickamauga, and whatever you may think of the conduct of its commander, surely you must conclude that it was a hurried and a hard sentence which blotted out of existence the Twentieth Army Corps, while others not nearly so large, nor so sorely smitten in battle, have been allowed to retain their organization and recruit their ranks.

The Court will bear me witness that, except where absolutely necessary for a proper understanding of my own conduct, I have abstained from any questions as to the conduct of others, and the same rule shall govern me in the remarks I make upon the testimony.

Indeed, if it were not a departure from the custom in such cases, I feel that I might refrain from this, and submit my cause without a word. If the Court shall be as impartial in judgment as it has been patient and fair in the hearing, I shall be well content.

On the 17th of September, 1863, the Twentieth Army Corps, wearied by its marches over mountain roads toward Rome, Ga., returned and effected its junction with General Thomas by the Winston's Gap, which the latter advised to be the only practicable road. It went into camp at Pond Spring, 7 miles from the slopes of Mission Ridge, at Widow Glenn's house, and only 15 miles from Chattanooga, the objective point of the recent army movements.

It remained there all the day of the 18th, waiting to close up "when General Thomas is out of the way." His troops marched that night, and before daylight the Twentieth Corps started, Johnson's division leading, and when it reached headquarters it was immediately ordered to Thomas.

Davis followed, and received the same order to report to Thomas. Johnson's and Davis' divisions and one brigade of Sheridan's were heavily engaged on the 19th; Davis losing one brigade commander killed, Sheridan 1 wounded.

But I need not delay the court with any *résumé* of the operations of the 19th. My field orders are before the court, and it is enough to say they were obeyed. "I was with General McCook the entire day, and I feel certain they were explicitly obeyed." (Major Thruston's re-examination.)

At dark on the 19th, I went to the council at Widow Glenn's house. At midnight the orders were resolved upon, and I left to rouse my troops and move them to their position for the struggle of the 20th.

Before daylight I reported at Glenn's house that they were moving.

The positions selected were seen by General Morton, the chief of engineers, who testifies that they were "eminently judicious." General Davis testifies he "is confident they could have been held against any attack in front."

General Rosecrans "made several observations in approval of the position." (Morton's testimony.)

Now, admitting the general-in-chief debated some of the positions with me; that he suggested a change in one place; that he answered my objections to his suggestions, and gave replies to the reasons urged for the positions chosen, it is enough to say that he rode the lines; that he saw the positions; it was his to order, it was mine to obey. Nor is it quite accurate to say that "General McCook was not expected to cover any particular portion of the ground, unless he could do so and at the same time maintain his connection with General Thomas." The order to General Crittenden most clearly indicates what McCook was expected to do; nay, commanded to do.

HEADQUARTERS DEPARTMENT OF THE CUMBERLAND,
Widow Glenn's House, September 19, 1863—11.20 p. m.*

GENERAL : The general commanding directs me to inform you that General Mc-Cook has been ordered to hold this gap to-morrow, covering the Dry Valley road, his right resting near this place, his left connecting with General Thomas' right.

The general places your corps in reserve to-morrow, and directs you to post it on the eastern slope of Missionary Ridge, to support McCook or Thomas. Leave the grand guards from your command out, with instructions to hold their ground until driven in, then to retire slowly, contesting the ground stubbornly.

Very respectfully, your obedient servant,

J. A. GARFIELD,
Brigadier General, and Chief of Staff.

But whatever may have been the merits or demerits of the position selected, it is idle to discuss them, for they were not proved by battle, but were changed in respects most vital to their security. Let us inquire how the plan of battle changed.

My proper command was the Twentieth Corps, consisting of Johnson's, Sheridan's, and Davis' divisions, and to these were added all the cavalry—a formidable force, truly; with it the right should have been made secure; and for the employment of this force, by all men who have not carefully studied the battle, I am held responsible. How much I had actually present to engage will be shown in a little while.

General Thomas had his own four divisions, and to strengthen him Johnson's, of McCook's, by far his strongest, and Palmer, of Crittenden's, the strongest of that corps, had been sent the day before, and fought upon his left throughout the day. Crittenden's remaining divisions were to be in reserve, "and ready to support either Thomas or McCook."

I had in line two brigades of Sheridan's, with Laiboldt's brigade in reserve, to support that line, and two brigades of Davis to the left and rear of Sheridan; the other brigade of Davis had been left to hold Stevens' Gap and support the cavalry when the army advanced from Pond Spring.

Colonel Wilder's brigade of mounted infantry extended Sheridan's right, but the rest of the cavalry was not available, the general commanding it, from a misconception of General Rosecrans' orders, having declined to obey the orders given by me.

After daylight the unmistakable tokens of battle manifested themselves on the left; the calls for assistance begin, and the commands to re-enforce follow promptly. Just as the fog begins to lift, Negley is ordered out of line and moves to the left. The reserve is at once

---

*See same dispatch, p. 69, where the hour is given as 10.20 p. m. The language of the two dispatches also differs in some respects.

called upon, and General Crittenden sends in Wood's division to supply the place left vacant. All is yet quiet upon the right, the demands of the left are pressing, and General Van Cleve is ordered to march to Thomas, and afterward Wood's division leaves the line and takes the same direction.

Whether this order was correctly construed or not it is unnecessary to discuss; the consequences to General McCook's troops are the same; the front of a division is suddenly withdrawn from the line, without any information to him except that given by General Wood on an accidental meeting at the moment the movement commenced. "It was done at the double-quick, thus giving General McCook no time to close his troops properly and fill the vacant space." (General Rosecrans' testimony.) There was not only no time to fill the space, but I had no troops to fill it with, unless a small brigade could cover a division interval. "Just as I had formed on General Wood's right I was told by Colonel Buell that he was leaving for the left, and that the other brigades had already moved." (General Davis' testimony.)

At 10 o'clock the attack had not begun upon the right, but, the left being heavily pressed a few moments later, the resolution was taken that everything must be hazarded for the position on the left, and, the reserve having been employed, the right is called upon. At ten minutes after 10 o'clock this order was given:

HEADQUARTERS DEPARTMENT OF THE CUMBERLAND,
In the Field, September 20, 1863—10.10 a. m.
Major-General McCook,
    Commanding Twentieth Army Corps

General Thomas is being heavily pressed on the left. The general commanding directs you to [make] immediate dispositions to withdraw the right, so as to spare as much force as possible to re-enforce Thomas. The left must be held at all hazards—even if the right is drawn wholly back to the present left. Select a good position back this way, and be ready to send [start*] re-enforcements to Thomas at a moment's warning.

J. A. GARFIELD,
Brigadier-General, and Chief of Staff.

At thirty minutes after 10 the order for preparation is followed by the command of execution.

HEADQUARTERS DEPARTMENT OF THE CUMBERLAND,
In the Field, September 20, 1863—10.30 a. m.
Major-General McCook,
    Commanding Twentieth Army Corps:

The general commanding directs you to send two brigades of General Sheridan's division at once, and with all dispatch, to support General Thomas, and send the third brigade as soon as the lines can be drawn in sufficiently. March them as rapidly as you can without exhausting the men. Report in person* to these headquarters as soon as your orders are given in regard to Sheridan's movement. Have you any news from Colonel Post?

J. A. GARFIELD,
Brigadier-General, and Chief of Staff.

At a few minutes before 11 these orders were received, almost simultaneously, "not six minutes' interval," and the fate of the right was sealed.

Well might the general, who was "calm and confident at his lines in the morning," become "anxious when he saw the dust rising

*See p. 70.

through the woods to his front," at the moment when he receives an order to break his line and move his troops by the flank. The attack on the right came at thirty minutes after 11 o'clock, not later, if any reliance is to be placed as to time on the battle-field upon the testimony of soldiers engaged. There seems to be on this point the concurrence of all witnesses.

Where are the troops who occupied the ground in the morning ? Negley was gone ; Wood, who filled his place, had followed him; and Van Cleve was also marching.

The two brigades of Sheridan which were in line on the right are now taken out in obedience to this order, and are marching through the dense woods close in rear of the line of battle toward that same left which is swallowing the army. What is there to resist the coming attack ? Two weak brigades of Davis, the remnant of the bloody fight of yesterday, 1,300 strong, and the brigade of Laiboldt, less in number than Davis' two. What is their position ? Davis had the brigade in line which joined Wood, and behind breastworks, and the other he is just bringing into line as Wood's troops leave it, "two regiments being on it and the others closing to it." (General Davis' testimony.)

Laiboldt, who had been held as a reserve for Sheridan, is now ordered to support General Davis' right. Wilder's mounted infantry is in line, but the cavalry has not reported. So the reserve of the army is gone, and my own weak reserves, my only reliance for a second line, have to be put on the first. An interval of two brigades separates Wilder from Laiboldt, and a division interval separates Davis from the nearest troops on his left.

Through these intervals the enemy's columns come against our little line ; theirs is displayed, overreaching either flank three to one at least, says General Davis, and Colonel Wilder says the attack was made five lines deep. Could the result be for a moment in doubt, and for what part of it is General McCook responsible ? What dispositions could he have made which he omitted ? What skill in the officer, what courage of the troops could have availed ? Troops marching by the flank in the presence of an enemy, covered by a line which is less than the intervals it exposes, must owe their safety to the forbearance of the foe. I do not state these matters in criticism of my military superior, but they are plain, incontrovertible facts, necessary for my vindication. Indeed, although the movement would have uncovered the Dry Valley road, I quite agree with the commanding general's conclusions as indicated in the preparatory order dated 10.10 a. m., "that the left must be held at all hazards, even if the right is drawn back to the present left." But it was too late, there was no opportunity to look for positions, for by the time the dispositions to send the troops were made the enemy was advancing to the attack.

I have not another word as to the battle.

But the Court is required to investigate my conduct in leaving the field as well as in the battle.

I will not before a Court of soldiers answer the imputation, if it be implied, that any considerations of personal safety influenced my conduct. May I not without boasting say that I have faced death on too many fields, and in the presence of too many thousands of men, to require at this day any vindication of my composure or hardihood in action. It would be enough that the firing had terminated upon the right, and that all pursuit had ceased, to leave the question simply one of judgment and duty, under the circumstances by which I was surrounded. My troops had been driven back and scattered, the ground was singularly unfavorable for rallying them, a commanding officer could do little more in that forest and thicket than any other general officer. I remained until I gave orders to my troops and for the safety of the artillery and transportation. I knew that Generals Sheridan and Davis were in safety and with their men, and competent to take charge of them.

The point to be saved or lost was the position at Chattanooga. To that point the general commanding had gone. He had been not far to the left of my lines when they gave way, and as he passed by on the Dry Valley road saw me "among the broken columns trying to rally the troops." I had an order which I believed to be in force, requiring me to report to him in person in the field. As General Rosecrans, in the correction of his testimony, says he supposes I had complied with that part of the order ; that we had met and I informed him I would send in Laiboldt's brigade to set matters to rights, I desire to call the attention of the Court to the terms of the order and the circumstances which preceded and followed it.

It was given after an order dispatched a few minutes before, which required me to look out for a new position farther to the left ; that the exigencies of the day might be so pressing as to require the removal of all the troops from the right, involving consultation and the development of a new plan. Surely it was not to report that I had obeyed him and repeated his order to Sheridan, for that was the duty of a staff officer to perform, for which a general officer would not be taken away from his troops. And at an interview, after such pressing and important orders, nothing took place between us but a reference by myself to one of my brigades.

General Rosecrans' recollection has not served him correctly ; he must have the impression from some previous interview between us.

At the time Laiboldt went in, the testimony shows I was behind his brigade, went forward with it, and was driven back when his troops were repulsed.

Besides, if the situation was so extreme on the left, when the right was intact, as to require a personal interview, surely it was not lessened when the right was broken, and the troops marching to support the left were driven by the enemy.

If there could be a time when an interview between a general and his lieutenant was necessary, that time was then.

If I had troops which I had thought I could have reorganized in time and taken to the left, I concede that when I did not find him upon the field, it would have been my duty to have marched where the cannon yet sounded. Upon the information communicated to me by staff officers whom I met upon the field, and whose testimony is before the court, I determined to go to Chattanooga, but through Rossville, or close to it, that I might get information from General Thomas, and ascertain the situation of the place in the direction of which I had ordered my troops to move, and where I supposed the troops of Thomas would move back. I had no acquaintance with the country or the roads, neither myself nor any of my staff having ever been in Chattanooga, or nearer it than the battle-field. I was compelled to rely upon the guide of General Rosecrans, who assured me there was no other route we could take, and that the one we took led us toward Rossville. I expected to go by Rossville, or near enough to learn the situation of affairs there, until I met the troops of General Spears, and found I was nearer Chattanooga than Rossville, and that General Rosecrans was still at the former place.

And I submit to the Court, that without any order from him at all, if there was to be a to-morrow to that day, it was my duty to see General Rosecrans and know his plans, and see the country nearer Chattanooga, where I had no doubt the army must fall back.

That this, too, was the superior duty for me, if the troops I left behind were in competent hands. By the route I took no body of soldiers was found until I met those of General Spears within 2 miles of Chattanooga, marching to Rossville. I did not, after immediately reporting to General Rosecrans, return to Rossville, on which my troops had been directed to march, because the general ordered me to remain with him until he should receive further information, when he would determine his course and give me orders.

When I left the field it would have been easy to follow impulse, and, notwithstanding the reports I had received, endeavor to reach the left. It was the stronger with me, as one of my own divisions was there, but the path of duty under my conception of my orders, or in the absence of any orders, was the same, and I felt compelled to follow it.

Respectfully submitted.

A. McD. McCOOK,
Major-General of Volunteers.

No. 233.

Record of the Crittenden Court of Inquiry.

RECORD OF THE PROCEEDINGS OF A COURT OF INQUIRY INSTITUTED BY THE FOLLOWING ORDER:

SPECIAL ORDERS, } WAR DEPT., ADJT. GENERAL'S OFFICE,
   No. 13.   }   *Washington, January 9, 1864.*

*   *   *   *   *   *   *

20. By direction of the President of the United States, a Court of Inquiry is hereby appointed to meet at Nashville, Tenn., on the 15th instant, or as soon thereafter as practicable, to investigate the conduct of Maj. Gens. A. McD. McCook, T. L. Crittenden, and James S. Negley, U. S. Volunteers, at the battle of Chickamauga, and in leaving the field, and also to give their opinion upon the facts which may be developed. The Court will adjourn from place to place, as may be deemed necessary to procure the testimony of witnesses, without taking them away from their appropriate duties, and will sit without regard to hours.

Detail for the Court: Maj. Gen. David Hunter, U. S. Volunteers; Maj. Gen. George Cadwalader, U. S. Volunteers; Brig. Gen. J. S. Wadsworth, U. S. Volunteers; Col. Edmund Schriver, inspector-general, recorder.

*   *   *   *   *   *   *

By order of the Secretary of War:

E. D. TOWNSEND,
Assistant Adjutant-General.

FIRST DAY.

NASHVILLE, *January* 29, 1864.

The Court met, pursuant to the above order, at 10 a. m., in the Saint Cloud Hotel.

Present, Maj. Gen. David Hunter, U. S. Volunteers; Maj. Gen. George Cadwalader, Brig. Gen. J. S. Wadsworth, U. S. Volunteers; Col. Edmund Schriver, inspector-general, recorder.

Maj. Gen. T. L. Crittenden, U. S. Volunteers, whose conduct is ordered to be investigated, was also present.

The order appointing the Court was then read. Major-General Crittenden being asked if he had any objections to the officers named in the detail, and replying in the negative, the members and recorder were sworn in his presence.

The Court then proceeded with the investigation, and directed the recorder to make the following communication to Maj. Gen. George H. Thomas:

NASHVILLE, *January* 29, 1864.

Major-General THOMAS,
    Commanding Department of the Cumberland, Chattanooga:

The Court of Inquiry instituted by Special Orders, No. 13, War Department, for the investigation of "the conduct of Major-Generals McCook, Crittenden, and Negley, U. S. Volunteers, at the battle of Chickamauga, and in leaving the field," desire you to send to me at the Galt House in Louisville, as soon as possible, certified copies of all reports which may be in your possession, bearing on the conduct of those officers on the occasion referred to; and also the best map you have of the battlefield and the surrounding country. It is most desirable to have these reports and the map sent by an officer capable of explaining to the Court the position of the troops engaged.

The Court wish you also to send any officers of your command who may have knowledge of the matter to be investigated, to report to the Court in Louisville, the names of whom you are desired to communicate to me. Please acknowledge this.

    ED. SCHRIVER,
    Inspector-General, Recorder.

On being questioned by the Court whether any papers or communications touching the matters to be investigated had been furnished, the recorder stated as follows:

Only one communication, that of General W. S. Rosecrans to the adjutant-general of the Army, dated October 14, 1863, relative to Major-General Negley. That he addressed to the Adjutant-General of the Army the following communications:

LOUISVILLE, *January* 27, 1864.

The ADJUTANT-GENERAL OF THE ARMY:

GENERAL: I have the honor to acquaint you that General Hunter has arrived here, and that the officers detailed for the Court instituted by Special Orders, No. 13, to investigate the conduct of Major-Generals McCook, Crittenden, and Negley, will repair to Nashville to-morrow. At an informal meeting had, it was seen that no papers respecting the conduct of those officers have yet been furnished to the Court, and I was, therefore, directed to request that any reports or communications on the subject, which may be on file in the War Department, as well as the names and address of any persons who are known to be acquainted with the transactions ordered to be investigated, be sent to me at this place, whither the Court will return for the purpose of receiving the testimony of Major-General Rosecrans, on 1st of February.

    Very respectfully, &c.,

    ED. SCHRIVER,
    Inspector-General, Recorder.

NASHVILLE, *January* 29, 1864.

The ADJUTANT-GENERAL OF THE ARMY:

GENERAL : In my communication of the 27th instant, written by order of the Court of Inquiry instituted by Special Orders, No. 13, of 1864, I asked for all reports on file in the War Department bearing on the conduct of Major-Generals McCook, Crittenden, and Negley, at the battle of Chickamauga. I am now directed to ask particularly for the following:

Certified copies of the official reports of the battle of Chickamauga, made by Brigadier-Generals Wood, Brannan, and Davis, and Colonel Harker (Wood's division) ; also the supplementary report and papers appended, which Major-General Negley forwarded October 9, 1863, at the request of and through Major-General Rosecrans ; the same being required by Major-General Negley in his letter of 22d January. Please send them to the Galt House, Louisville.

Very respectfully, &c.,

ED. SCHRIVER,
Inspector-General, Recorder.

The Court here desired Major-General Crittenden to furnish the recorder, from time to time, as far as possible, a list of the witnesses whose evidence he may wish to submit to the Court.

A recess of half an hour was taken, and subsequently an adjournment till 7 p. m. was ordered.

7 p. m.

The Court met pursuant to adjournment.

Present, Major-Generals Hunter and Cadwalader, Brigadier-General Wadsworth and Colonel Schriver, recorder, and Major-General Crittenden.

Capt. THOMAS C. WILLIAMS, Nineteenth U. S. Infantry, aide-de-camp to General Rousseau, being duly sworn, says to questions

By the COURT:

Question. Please state what you know about the conduct of General Crittenden at the battle of Chickamauga and the position of his troops.

Answer. I did not see General Crittenden at the battle of Chickamauga. Two of his divisions reported to General Thomas on Saturday or Sunday ; my impression is on Saturday. They behaved with great gallantry, and were among the last to leave the field on Sunday night.

Question. Do you know under whose orders those divisions reported to General Thomas ?

Answer. About 2 to 3 p. m., on Sunday, General Garfield (General Rosecrans' chief of staff) and Colonel Thruston (chief of General McCook's staff) reported to General Thomas, but I do not know under whose orders the divisions reported.

Question. How many divisions were in General Crittenden's corps?

Answer. I think there were three.

Question. When General Garfield and Colonel Thruston reported to General Thomas, was it with the two divisions alluded to ?

Answer. No; the two divisions were there before.

Question. Do you know where the remaining division of General Crittenden's command was at the time General Garfield and Colonel Thruston reported ?

Answer. I do not.

By General CRITTENDEN :

Question. Do you know the names of the commanders of the divisions that reported to General Thomas ?

Answer. General Wood and General Palmer.

Question. Do you know whether there were three brigades in either of those divisions?

Answer. I do not.

Question. Do you know whether any portion of the remaining division belonging to General Crittenden's corps fought with General Thomas on Sunday, 20th September?

Answer. I do not know. I will state that a considerable number of stragglers of General Davis' division were reformed in rear of the right of the line, among whom were some men belonging to General Crittenden's corps.

Question. Do you know to whose corps General Davis belonged?

Answer. I believe he belonged to General McCook's corps.

The Court adjourned to meet at 11 o'clock on the 1st February, at Louisville, Ky.

SECOND DAY.

LOUISVILLE, *February* 1, 1864.

The Court met, pursuant to adjournment, in the supreme court room.

Present, Major-Generals Hunter and Cadwalader, Brigadier-General Wadsworth, and Colonel Schriver, recorder, and Major-General Crittenden.

The proceedings of the first day were read and approved.

The Court adjourned to meet at 10 o'clock on 2d February.

THIRD DAY.

LOUISVILLE, *February* 2, 1864.

The Court met, pursuant to adjournment, in the supreme court room.

Present, Major-Generals Hunter and Cadwalader, Brigadier-General Wadsworth, and Colonel Schriver, recorder, and Major-General Crittenden.

Maj. LOUIS M. BUFORD, aide-de-camp to Major-General Crittenden (act of July 17, 1862), being duly sworn, says to questions

By the COURT:

Question. Where were the troops of General Crittenden's command posted on Sunday morning, 20th September, and where was General Crittenden at that time?

Answer. They were posted in the reserve, General Wood on the right of the line and General Van Cleve on the left in the rear. General Palmer was detached with General Thomas. We were on the slope of Missionary Ridge, General Crittenden with his command.

Question. At what time did the command break after it was attacked?

Answer. I do not know.

Question. What efforts were made by General Crittenden to rally the troops, and where did he go?

Answer. He was with the batteries on a hill, and sent me off to rally the men, and I did not see him again until I got near Rossville.

Question. Where did you go, and what did you do in the meantime ?

Answer. I went to the left of the rear about a quarter of a mile, picked up some mounted men, and tried to rally the men.   When I saw that I could not rally them I started to return to the general, and on my way back I met an orderly, who told me that the enemy were at the general's.   I then met some of General Rosecrans' officers, and went with them to Rossville.

Question. When did General Crittenden go to Chattanooga, and what did he do when he got there ?

Answer. I do not know at what time he left the field ; he reached Chattanooga about 4 p. m., and went immediately to General Rosecrans' headquarters.

Question. Did you reach Chattanooga before General Crittenden did ?

Answer. No ; I joined him near Rossville, and rode in with him.

Question. When did you see General Crittenden again, and where did he go, and what did he do ?

Answer. I saw him again that evening, but I have forgotten at what time. About midnight he went out on the road near Rossville to report to General Thomas.

Question. How soon after General Crittenden arrived at General Rosecrans' headquarters in Chattanooga did you see him, General Crittenden ?

Answer. I rode to General Rosecrans' headquarters, where I left him.   I do not know how soon after that he left.   I left word with an orderly to be told when the general did leave.   I do not know whether he rode out after that or not.

Question. Do you mean to say that you did not see him until you went out with him to Rossville near midnight ?

Answer. No ; the exact time I do not remember.

Question. Was it before or after dark?

Answer. I do not remember the time.

Question. Where was he at the time?

Answer. I think at General Rosecrans' headquarters.

Question. Were you at General Rosecrans' headquarters after dark?

Answer. Yes ; but at what time I do not remember.

Question. Did General Crittenden send you or any staff officer out to see what had become of his command before he went out to Rossville?

Answer. Captain Knox was sent out toward Rossville, but for what purpose I do not know.

By General CRITTENDEN :

Question. What troops of General Crittenden's were broken on 20th?

Answer. Van Cleve's two brigades.   I am not positive about the rest.

Question. Were these all driven from the field?

Answer. I do not know, as I did not see them after that.

Question. Do you know how they were broken?

Answer. By the troops in front running over them as they fell back.

Question. Were they in motion at the time, and where were they going?

Answer. They were ordered to support General Thomas on the left, and were making the movement.

Question. Were there any other troops of General Crittenden's command subject to his orders at this time?

Answer. I do not think there was.

Question. Were the troops of General Crittenden's command in reserve when broken?

Answer. No.

Capt. George G. Knox, aide-de-camp to General Crittenden (act 17th July, 1862), being duly sworn, says to questions

By the Court :

Question. What was General Crittenden's command on the morning of 20th September?

Answer. A part of the Twenty-first Corps, the First Division of General Wood, and the Third Division of General Van Cleve.

Question. Where was it posted?

Answer. In the reserve in the rear of the line of battle.

Question. At what time did they retreat?

Answer. About 12 o'clock.

Question. Where was General Crittenden as this time?

Answer. He was close to the line of battle until he saw that it was broken and in confusion, and then he went to a hill where some batteries were (in the rear), and staid there till they left and all stragglers had passed, and that no regular line was formed.

Question. Where did he go then?

Answer. He then went to the left of the rear about half a mile to another hill, and rallied some troops there, which he put under the command of a commissioned officer, and started back, stopping frequently to give instructions to the different officers who had rallied men.

Question. What order did he give to officers who had rallied troops?

Answer. I did not hear them.

Question. Where did he go then?

Answer. He stopped at Rossville, and then went on to Chattanooga.

Question. At what time did he arrive at Chattanooga?

Answer. About 4 o'clock, I should think.

Question. Where did he go then, and what did he do till he went out to Rossville.

Answer. He went to General Rosecrans' headquarters and remained about 15 or 20 minutes, when I was ordered to see what men were rallied and where, and to report to him.

Question. At what hour were you sent out to Rossville?

Answer. About 15 minutes after I arrived ; about 15 minutes after four.

By General Crittenden :

Question. At the time Van Cleve's two brigades were broken, were the troops on the right broken?

Answer. I saw stragglers, but could not tell whether the line was broken or not. It is my opinion that it was.

The Court adjourned to meet at 10 o'clock on 3d February.

FOURTH DAY.

LOUISVILLE, *February* 3, 1864.

The Court met pursuant to adjournment.

Present, Major-Generals Hunter and Cadwalader, Brigadier-General Wadsworth, and Colonel Schriver, recorder, and Major-General Crittenden.

The proceedings of third day were read and approved.

Capt. JOHN J. McCOOK, aide-de-camp (act of 17th July, 1862) to Major-General Crittenden, being duly sworn, says to questions

By the COURT :

Question. What was General Crittenden's command and where was he posted ?

Answer. Two divisions ; five brigades. He was posted in reserve, on the east slope of Missionary Ridge, half a mile north of the Widow Glenn's house, a little west of north, three-quarters of a mile in the rear of the line of battle, the divisions being commanded by Brigadier-Generals Wood and Van Cleve.

Question. What troops were in front of it ?

Answer. As near as I can say, in rear of General Brannan's and General Reynolds'.

Question. When did General Crittenden's command break ?

Answer. There was only a part of the two brigades broken, and that I believe was General Van Cleve's division. They broke about 12.30 o'clock.

Question. What became of the other brigades ?

Answer. General Wood's two brigades remained together, and were moved to the left of the army and joined to one of General Van Cleve's.

Question. By whose orders ?

Answer. General Wood was moved by direct order of General Rosecrans, and General Van Cleve was under orders when he broke.

Question. Did this leave General Crittenden only in command of the two broken brigades of General Van Cleve ?

Answer. At that time there was not a soldier under his command when Van Cleve broke. They had been ordered to report to General Thomas.

Question. What did General Crittenden do after this and where did he go ?

Answer. General Crittenden was then in the rear of the line, about 200 yards from it. When General Van Cleve was moved to the left, General Crittenden's attention was called to the batteries on the hill in his rear. Upon looking at the line of battle it was in great confusion, and before he had time to move in any direction the enemy's skirmishers were between him and the troops. He then rode toward the batteries. While going up the hill we noticed General Van Cleve's brigade moving to the left, as ordered by General Rosecrans, in double column closed *en masse.* Soon after this, men came pouring from the line in General Van Cleve's front, also caissons from a battery were driven through his ranks at great speed, seriously injuring several men, and almost at the same time the enemy advanced upon him and attacked before he had time to recover the organization of his troops from the disorder. General Crittenden remained at the batteries for some time, sending officers to the right and left to get information of the condition of affairs. They soon returned, and reported having been fired upon. The general was about to start to find some organized body of troops to support the batteries, when he was called back by some of the artillery officers, asking where they should go in case they were driven from their position. He expected to find support, so he told them they must not be driven, and before he left the batteries a good many of the horses and some of the men had been killed, the enemy being so near upon them. When General

Crittenden first came to this position the fire of the batteries was held, not being certain as to what troops the ones advancing over the open ground in front of the position were, as they carried a blue flag with a gold star, the battle-flag of the regular brigade of our army; but when they were out from the woods, seeing their uniforms, all the guns were opened on them, and kept firing till the enemy were nearly on the guns at the left of the battery. General Crittenden then rode down into the valley toward Mission Ridge to see if he could find or hear of General Rosecrans, General McCook, General Sheridan, or General Davis, or their troops, to find support for these batteries. We soon heard the noise of the batteries moving rapidly away, and were told by Captain Elwood, of Colonel Buell's staff, that the enemy were now at the guns and their skirmishers advancing rapidly. When on the ridge west of the road General Crittenden, with his staff, made every effort to rally the men that were straggling around. About 100 had been got together, when a shell passed over our heads to the rear, when the officers could hardly keep the men already rallied together. Major Mendenhall, General Crittenden's chief of artillery, informed him that the enemy had turned the guns on the hill we had shortly left, and were firing on the transportation, artillery, &c., moving down the Dry Valley road. General Crittenden then determined to go to Rossville or Chattanooga. When about a mile from this point he met Colonel Parkhurst, Ninth Michigan, with a portion of his own and the Tenth Ohio Infantry, as a train guard. He had his men formed across the road, and had stopped enough to form another small regiment. He informed General Crittenden that General Rosecrans had gone to Chattanooga, and then offered the command of the troops with him to General Crittenden. The general told him to retain command; let all transportation, artillery, &c. pass to the rear, and then follow with his command. Soon after this he met Captains Burt and Drouillard, of General Rosecrans' staff, who also said that General Rosecrans was in Chattanooga. He then rode until about a mile from Rossville. He, with Captain Oldershaw, assistant adjutant-general, went to the side of the road to listen if he could still hear firing from the left of the army. He then rode to Rossville, where he found some other members of General Rosecrans' staff, who went with him to Chattanooga, going by the Point Lookout road. He arrived at Chattanooga at 3.30 or 4 p. m.; went direct to General Rosecrans' headquarters, reported condition of affairs, and remained there for more than an hour, until after General McCook had arrived. General Rosecrans told General Crittenden that he must take rest, and be ready to return to the front. At about dusk he went to his own headquarters. After talking and giving directions to Captain Oldershaw, he made arrangements to return to Rossville. At 11.30 he and his staff rode to General Rosecrans' headquarters, where he remained until nearly 2 o'clock on the morning of the 21st, when he received orders from General Rosecrans to go to Rossville, to get together his two divisions, and report to General Thomas. At 2 o'clock he started with General McCook and General Rousseau by direct State road for Rossville.

By General CRITTENDEN :

Question. Was it possible for General Crittenden to go to General Thomas except by Rossville?

Answer. It was not in any way, as the enemy's skirmishers, as he looked from the battery, were in front, right, and left, and he would have to pass through them to reach General Thomas.

Question. About what time did General Crittenden reach Rossville? State, if you know, why the general did not take the direct route to Chattanooga from Rossville.

Answer. I think he reached Rossville about 3 o'clock. His reason for not going by the direct road, as I heard him say, was because it was filled with transportation moving from the field to Chattanooga, and he thought it would be the quickest and best to go by Point Lookout.

Question. While at Rossville, did General Crittenden send officers of his in search of some one who could give information as to the condition of General Thomas' command?

Answer. I think, am not quite certain, that Lieutenant-Colonel Starling rode to General Thomas for information.

The Court adjourned to meet at 10 o'clock on February 4.

FIFTH DAY.

LOUISVILLE, *February* 4, 1864.

The Court met pursuant to adjournment.

Present, Major-Generals Hunter and Cadwalader, Brigadier-General Wadsworth, and Colonel Schriver, recorder, and Major-General Crittenden.

The proceedings of the fourth day were read and approved.

General W. S. ROSECRANS, U. S. Volunteers, being duly sworn, says to questions

By the COURT:

Question. What was General Crittenden's command on the morning of the 20th September, 1863 ?

Answer. It consisted of T. J. Wood's division, two brigades, one being in Chattanooga, and General Van Cleve's division, three brigades ; each brigade had a battery. Palmer's division had been detached during the conflict of 19th and held in position on the line between two of Thomas' divisions. This line, which we had established by fighting, and which covered the main road to Chattanooga, was so important to maintain that neither the division of Palmer, belonging to Crittenden's corps, nor Johnson's, belonging to McCook's corps, could have been so changed as to give the corps commanders their troops in a body. This line is called for convenience "Thomas' line," although it is properly the main part of the line of the whole army.

Question. Were any of these troops transferred to other duty which relieved General Crittenden from the responsibility of command previous to 12 m. of that day ?

Answer. In the first place, General Wood's division was ordered to relieve that of Negley before or about 8 o'clock, in consequence of the non-arrival of General McCook's troops, which in an order from General Thomas' headquarters, written by General Garfield, chief of staff, at 6.30 had been designated for that purpose. On my return from General Thomas' headquarters, finding General Negley about to withdraw his two brigades from the line, I went to him in person and ordered him by no means to do it until they were relieved, informing him that General McCook had orders to relieve him, and that the orders he had received were merely to prevent delay, by the possibility of his orders from General Thomas not reaching him in time. At the same time I dispatched Capt. R. S. Thoms, aide-de-camp to General Crittenden, with an order to relieve General Negley. Captain Thoms met General Wood before he saw General Crittenden, and deeming the case urgent, gave him the orders informing him that he should report the fact of his having done so to General Crittenden. These troops went into line about 9.30. General Crittenden sent one of Van Cleve's brigades to strengthen Wood, and directed Van Cleve, with his two remaining brigades, to move eastwardly. These two brigades, after some changes of position, he was directed to send on urgent call to relieve General Thomas, and as he dispatched the order he said to me, "General, as this is the last of my command, I presume I had better go with it." I said, "Certainly, and take them, general, where you see that smoke and hear that heavy firing, and do what you can there." This point was between the position where Palmer was in the main line, and where Wood was on the right, so as to leave General Crittenden with, in fact, but two brigades of his entire corps under his immediate supervision. This last movement was before or about 12 m.

Question. Were these two brigades broken before the order was executed ?

Answer. I have no doubt they were. I followed them with my eye until the rear of the columns could just be seen between me and the woods, where it seemed to halt. I watched with some anxiety the appearance of the field at that point for some time, when a member of my staff said to me, "Our men are giving away yonder." I said it was impossible, because we had there Van Cleve with two brigades and Brannan with two spare brigades, as I had already ascertained General Thomas had countermanded his order calling him to the left; but the noise of battle increased at that point, and I saw the troops giving way. It was the rear of Van Cleve's column which I saw. I saw no enemy at that point. General Van Cleve in his official report says: " Two batteries belonging to Brannan's command, he believes, ran through his column at that point, cutting off three regiments which remained during the battle of 20th, while the other five fell back and rallied near Rossville."

Question. Did the conduct of General Crittenden in coming into Chattanooga meet your approval ?

Answer. It did not meet my disapproval. I only thought that possibly he might have rendered some assistance in rallying the troops ; but had no sufficient evidence that he could have done so, to warrant me in censuring him.

By General CRITTENDEN:

Question. In your official report you say on my return from an examination of the ground in rear of our left center, I found, to my surprise, that General Van Cleve was posted in line of battle on a high ridge, much too far to the rear to give immediate support to the main line of battle. Did or did not General Van Cleve take this position while General Crittenden was talking with you in plain view?

Answer. My recollections of that are that on my return from toward the left I passed to a battery at the edge of a narrow strip of woods in front of a line of infantry, posted on a hill in the open fields ; that I gave directions to the battery to employ their idle time in cutting passage ways through this wood, and then rode up to the infantry just mentioned, and ascertained they were part of Van Cleve's troops; that General Van Cleve came to me and stated he was just coming up there and was posting them. I told him that was not the place ; he ought to be at a point in advance and in close column by division, doubled on the center so as to be ready for a movement. I then moved toward the right, when General Crittenden and staff in a peach orchard, perhaps 300 yards from the place ; called his attention to General Van Cleve's position, and that at that time some of Van Cleve's troops in column were moving up, and that at my suggestion General Crittenden gave him the orders to form in close column by division, in the direction indicated, reiterating them for fear General Van Cleve would not understand them fully. It may be proper to add that General Crittenden stated to me at that time that General Van Cleve had moved in obedience to his orders, to go eastward from the position which he had occupied during the night, which orders General Crittenden had given on my suggestion as I passed him early in the morning, that it would be better to move his whole force farther toward the left. I think Van Cleve was about 150 or 200 yards farther back than the place where I wanted him to be.

Question. What portion of General Crittenden's corps were driven to or near Rossville?

Answer. About five regiments.

Question. Did any of the corps which fought the battle of Chickamauga, have in proportion to its strength more men engaged throughout the battle, and did any behave better?

Answer. I think the Twenty-first (Crittenden's) had as large a proportion of its strength in the fight, and that they sustained themselves as well, all the circumstances considered, as any other corps. It lost a larger percentage of killed and wounded, if my memory serves me, and a smaller percentage of prisoners.

Question. Was it possible for the general commanding at Chickamauga to send staff officers familiar with the ground, who could show corps commanders the positions they should take, and did he do so?

Answer. The battle was fought mostly on wooded ground, entirely unknown to us; and notwithstanding corps and division commanders had orders to connect their headquarters immediately with those of their superiors, and the commanding general's escort and a battalion of cavalry were employed as couriers, communication with the corps headquarters with those of the subordinate commanders was very imperfect, and much had to be left to the discretion of commanders of troops.

Question. From what you know of his position and occupation, did General Crittenden ever have an opportunity to see General Thomas' line ?

Answer. His opportunity consisted only of the brief interval between daylight a. m. of 20th and the time when the battle began. The battle reached the position occupied first in the a. m. by General Wood in full force near 11 o'clock, but there was skirmishing on that line at 8 in the morning.

Question. Was it foggy on the morning of the 20th ?

Answer. It was foggy and smoky until after 8 o'clock.

The Court adjourned to meet at 10 o'clock on the 6th of February.

SEVENTH DAY.

LOUISVILLE, *February* 6, 1864.

The Court met pursuant to adjournment.

Present, Major-Generals Hunter and Cadwalader, Brigadier-General Wadsworth, and Colonel Schriver, recorder, and Major-General Crittenden.

Brig. Gen. T. J. WOOD, U. S. Volunteers, being duly sworn, says to questions

By the COURT:

Question. Were you under General Crittenden's command in the battle of Chickamauga; and, if so, in what capacity? Did you see General Crittenden during the battle, and how did he conduct himself as a soldier and a general?

Answer. I was; as commander of First Division, of Twenty-first Army Corps. I saw General Crittenden during the p. m. of the 19th several times. We were together at one time for one-half hour, perhaps even longer. I saw him between midnight and daylight Sunday morning, 20th, and received some orders and instructions from him at that time. I saw him again shortly after daylight of same day, and at various intervals during the morning of 20th up to 9 to 9.30 o'clock. During these intervals, till I last saw him, I received some orders and instructions from him. He conducted himself during the whole of the time that I saw him properly, both as a soldier and general officer, in my judgment and opinion.

The Court adjourned to meet at 10 o'clock on the 8th instant.

EIGHTH DAY.

FEBRUARY 8, 1864.

The Court met pursuant to adjournment.

Present, Major-Generals Hunter and Cadwalader, Brigadier-General Wadsworth, and Colonel Schriver, recorder, and Major-General Crittenden.

Col. J. P. SANDERSON, Thirteenth U. S. Infantry, being duly sworn, says to questions

By the COURT:

Question. Were you at the battle of Chickamauga; and, if so, do you know any material facts which bear on the conduct of General Crittenden on 19th and 20th September ?

Answer. I was. I have no personal knowledge of General Crittenden in that battle.

Question. Did you see General Crittenden in the latter part of the day, Sunday, 20th September?

Answer. I did not.

There being no more witnesses in attendance, the Court adjourned to meet at 10 o'clock on the 9th instant.

NINTH DAY.

FEBRUARY 9, 1864.

The Court met pursuant to adjournment.

Present, Major-Generals Hunter and Cadwalader, Brigadier-General Wadsworth, and Colonel Schriver, recorder, and Major-General Crittenden.

LYNE STARLING, late assistant adjutant-general of volunteers, and chief of staff of Twenty-first Army Corps, being duly sworn, says to question

By General CRITTENDEN:

Question. Were you in the battle of Chickamauga, and in what capacity? State what you know of the conduct of General Crittenden in that battle.

Answer. I was in the battle as chief of staff of Twenty-first Army Corps. On Saturday morning, 19th, very early—before daylight—General Crittenden's command was placed in the road from La Fayette to Rossville, from Gordon's Mills extending toward Rossville, with instructions to hold that point at all hazards, while the corps of General Thomas and McCook passed by the Dry Valley road to the rear of his command, and got into position across the Rossville road to his rear. We were in that position for some time before there was any firing, but after a time the firing became very heavy to our left and rear; so much so that General Crittenden was convinced that the battle had commenced with General Thomas, and that he was being closely pressed. General Crittenden ordered General Palmer to go with his division rapidly to the assistance of General Thomas to take the enemy in flank and attack vigorously, and immediately sent word to Generals Thomas and Rosecrans that he had given the order to General Palmer. I thought the movement an exceedingly judicious one, as it afterward proved to be. We got, a few days after, a rebel paper from Atlanta, which stated that that attack of Palmer's was so well timed and made with so much vigor as to entirely disconcert the enemy's movements and prevent their resuming the offensive on that day. But for that attack, made when it was, the enemy would have doubled up Thomas' column and defeated us at once. The paper was handed to General Rosecrans and sent to the War Department, as I understood. This was done without orders from General Rosecrans, and not in conformity to the orders General Crittenden had; but General Rosecrans approved it, and complimented General Crittenden, saying he had but anticipated his orders. After that, the battle becoming general, General Crittenden sent Colonel Lodor, of his staff, to General Rosecrans, for permission to send General Van Cleve's division into the fight, also, which I thought a very judicious movement again. It was evident, from the firing, that the enemy were crossing the Chickamauga River higher up than the first forces had crossed, and that General Palmer was in danger of being outflanked. To support him and prevent his being flanked was the object of General Van Cleve's going in. After a time General Crittenden sent me to General Rosecrans for permission to put in General Wood's division. General Rosecrans readily consented, and told him to take them all in. Major Mendenhall was sent by General Crittenden to order General Wood to bring up his division. A few moments after he sent me also to suggest to General Wood that he might make a very advantageous attack on the enemy's flank as he came to the battle-ground, as at that time General Van Cleve was driving the enemy rapidly in a direction parallel to the road by which General Wood was to come, but told me to make him understand distinctly it was only a suggestion, not an order, leaving him to judge of the propriety of it. When I rode back again to General Crittenden I found he had gone up to General Rosecrans, and just as I got to General Crittenden's headquarters General Davis rode up and expressed great anxiety to see General Crittenden, as he, General Davis, had gone into the fight just about the same point that Van Cleve had gone in, and was being much pressed by the enemy. He said he wished very much he had a brigade, as it would save him. I told him I would immediately bring him one, and brought Colonel Harker, of General Wood's division. I took my position in the road to wait for General Wood, to show him where to take his last brigade. Just before General Wood, who was coming at the head of Buell's brigade, got to my position he called out in a very loud voice : " Why is there no staff officer to show me what position to take? There is no staff officer to show me where to go." I called to him: "General Wood, you are mistaken ; I am here for that purpose. General Davis' forces are already engaged. He knows their position and can best direct you." General Davis was right by me, rode up, and they consulted together, and placed Buell's command in position. But just as Generals Wood and Davis were consulting I saw General Crittenden with his staff near General Wood, and between General Wood and the head of Buell's column, and I called to General Wood: " Here is General Crittenden in person; you had better confer with him." I am thus particular in this narrative, because General Wood says in his official report, notwithstanding all this, that there was no staff officer at that point to show him where to put in his troops. Now, it is proper to state that we were under fire, very near a battery of General Davis', which was firing rapidly, and it is possible General Wood did not hear, though I spoke very loud. In a short time afterward, after Buell's command became engaged, Carlin's brigade, of General Davis' command, who were in front of Buell's, broke over Buell, and the whole were pressed back across the field, through which there was a ravine, at which General Crittenden attempted to rally the men, directing them to form in the gully. He made great efforts to accomplish this, and was more exposed than I have ever seen a general officer in my experience. The firing was so heavy, that I spoke to him and told him we had better form them in the woods on the other side of the field, as the firing was so very heavy that it was impossible to form the men there. He immediately assented to this, and told me to go there and rally them, but rode very leisurely to the same point. We did rally them there; got some two or three batteries into position and drove the enemy back, and our troops recrossed the field and occupied the ground on the other side from which they had been driven. Colonel Buell stated to me (and I think it is in his official report also) that, in collecting his wounded that night, he took over 100 out of that gully or ravine, which shows the excessive severity of the fire. It is proper to state that we had all been excessively exhausted from want of sleep and continuous marching. That night (19th), about midnight, I was ordered 'to join General Crittenden, to join him in arranging our troops in reserve. We did not find General Van Cleve until daylight, although we hunted for him diligently, and consequently did not get him into position until about daylight. At this time General Crittenden's troops were posted as follows:

General Palmer had been detached to the assistance of General Thomas the day before, as I have stated. General Wood, with two brigades, one having been left in Chattanooga as a guard there under General Wagner. General Van Cleve, with three brigades, was placed in reserve at the foot of Mission Ridge, by the Dry Valley road. We were then on the right of the rear of General Thomas' extreme right. General Rosecrans ordered General Wood's division to take the place of General Negley's division, which had been ordered to General Thomas' left. Barnes' brigade, of Van Cleve's division, went with General Wood, by order of General Crittenden. This was early in the morning ; I do not recollect the precise time. General Van Cleve's command was ordered farther to the left, so as to bring it just in rear of General Wood's new position—General Negley's old position. General Van Cleve halted upon a rising ground just to the rear of the open ground, and just to the rear of some four or five batteries which were placed in position. Orders had been sent back not to bring these batteries forward, as the wood was so thick they could not be used, and General Crittenden had directed Major Mendenhall, chief of artillery, to place them in this commanding position. From this position General Rosecrans afterward ordered General Van Cleve to be thrown farther forward and to the left. The troops were in this position when General Rosecrans came up, and General Crittenden and he were together with their staffs. General Rosecrans ordered me, in the presence of General Crittenden, to go to General Wood and order him to close to the left on Reynolds and support him. There was no firing, and no evident need of support for any one, and I hesitated, not understanding the object of the order, when General Garfield, General Rosecrans' chief of staff, called out to me that the object of the order was that General Wood should occupy the vacancy made by the removal of Brannan's division, Brannan having been ordered to General Thomas' left. I gave the orders to General Wood, told him the object of it, and he stated General Brannan was in position, and that there was no vacancy between him and Reynolds. I told him then there is no order, for that was the object of it. I then rode immediately to General Rosecrans, told him what General Wood had said, and added that General Wood had a nice little breastwork in his front and ought not to be moved, as the enemy were in the very act of attacking him, and had driven in his pickets while I was there. Just then General Crittenden started to go to General Van Cleve's command, remarking to General Rosecrans that as that was all which was left of his command he had better go to them. General Rosecrans said, "Yes, and take them where that firing is," or words to that effect, pointing in the direction of General Palmer's command to our left. We immediately rode to General Van Cleve's command, and General Crittenden gave him the order to move in conformity to General Rosecrans' orders, and his troops were in motion, when an officer came from General Thomas asking urgently for further assistance. General Crittenden referred him to General Rosecrans, who was just in sight. The officer in a very short time returned with an order from General Rosecrans to send Van Cleve's division to the assistance of Thomas as rapidly as possible without too much exhausting the men. Just at that time I rode to General Wood to see his exact position. I found him not more than 100 yards in front of General Crittenden's position. General McCook was with General Wood. I mentioned it to General Crittenden, and he said he would like to see him, and I brought General McCook to him, stating to General McCook at the time that General Crittenden was not more than 100 yards to the rear of him. This was just about the time General Van Cleve received his final order to go to General Thomas' left, and I am thus particular in mentioning these facts, which do not appear to bear particularly on General Crittenden's conduct, for a special purpose. General Rosecrans, in his official report, states that great delay intervened between his giving the order for General Wood's division to occupy Negley's position and the execution of it, and that in consequence of that delay unfortunate results took place later in the day. General Wood was in position by 9.30 o'clock, so Generals Rosecrans and Wood state, and that this final order was given to General Van Cleve about 12 m., so that General Negley had two and one-half hours to get to Thomas' left, and General Wood was in position two and one-half hours before the attack was made. General Wood also states in his official report that it is proper he should state that he did not see the corps commander from about 9 o'clock on Sunday morning, but he had positive evidence from my remark that General Crittenden was about 100 yards from him just in his rear at 12 m., and he understood it, for he sent an officer to General Crittenden to inform him he had just received an order direct from General Rosecrans to close to the left and support Reynolds, and was executing the movement. In a very short time after this, and before I thought General McCook had time to get to his command, although it was near, we discovered that Van Cleve's troops were in confusion, and I called General Crittenden's attention to the fact that General McCook's troops were also broken and retreating, and the firing began to be pretty severe where we were, bullets flying around pretty thickly, when General Crittenden called to the staff, and said we will go to the batteries and will yet drive those fellows back and hold them in check, or something like that. We went immediately to them; found there was not an infantry man to support them. We scattered and made great effort to find some support for them. In the meantime the enemy came through the interval Wood left by his movement, but we opened upon them with the artillery and very soon drove them back. Still the enemy's sharpshooters kept up an incessant fire upon us, and killed a number of the men and artillery horses. Just at that time Lieutenant Cushing, commanding a battery of the Fourth U. S. Artillery, came forward and asked General Crittenden which way he should retire. He replied: "You are not to retire at all, but hold your position." A short time afterward Cushing came to General Crittenden and told him the enemy had got to our rear and was firing upon us. General Crittenden told him it was impossible, but started back to a rising ground in rear of the artillery to examine. Just as General Crittenden started I rode to the front of the artillery and took a careful survey of the field, to see where the firing came from. I found there were no troops in line, and that there were merely skirmishers. About 100 yards to the rear General Crittenden met General Van Cleve bringing about 75 men to try and support the artillery. He ordered them to go forward promptly, and just at that time Major Mendenhall rode up and said the batteries had been taken; that it was too late. We then went right across the Dry Valley road, on a hill just back of it, where we saw a few troops, and attempted to rally them to retake the batteries. We could not succeed, and after remaining more than half an hour and until all stragglers had ceased to pass, when General Crittenden remarked: "I believe I have done all I can. Can any of you make a suggestion?" addressing himself to his staff around him. General Crittenden had previously remarked in conversation with us that he had no doubt, or he thought that Generals McCook and Rosecrans were both either killed or taken prisoners, from the position we last saw them in and the position of the enemy near them. I thought the same, from the fact of none of their troops passing down the road to Rossville, which ran at the foot of the hill in which we were. I answered that if General Crittenden regarded public opinion or newspaper reports, he had better try to go to General Thomas, where the firing was still kept up. He interrupted me and said: "You know I care for nothing of that kind. My whole object is to do my duty as an officer." I then told him I thought there could be no doubt, if Generals McCook and Rosecrans were killed or taken, his proper position was in Chattanooga, to reorganize the scattered troops for further operations. Without expressing any opinion that I understood, he ordered me to go and organize the scattered troops that were there on the hill; to place them under a captain he designated; to tell him to collect all stragglers possible as he went in, and constitute his command for a guard for a number of wagons that were passing over the hill to Chattanooga. In this way I became separated from General Crittenden, and did not meet him again until I met him in Chattanooga.

I went in with General McCook, with whom I had fallen in about 4 p. m. Our transportation and servants had been sent in when the battle commenced, and had arranged headquarters. I understood General Crittenden was at General Rosecrans' headquarters, and found him lying down, but in conversation with his adjutant-general, Captain Oldershaw; told him I had had headquarters arranged, and advised him to go there and take some rest while he was waiting for orders. He did so. About 9 p. m. he sent me to General Rosecrans' headquarters to ascertain if any important information had been received. I remained there until 10.30, then returned, found him asleep, but did not disturb him, as there was no information of any importance. At 12 midnight we had orders to repair to General Rosecrans' headquarters, and go with General McCook to the front. We went, but it was some time before we received orders, and got to Rossville at about daylight and reported to General Thomas.

The Court was cleared.

The Court was opened, and adjourned to meet at 10 o'clock on the 10th instant.

TENTH DAY.

FEBRUARY 10, 1864.

The Court met pursuant to adjournment.

Present, Major-Generals Hunter and Cadwalader, Brigadier-General Wadsworth, and Colonel Schriver, recorder, and Major-General Crittenden.

Maj. LYNE STARLING, late assistant adjutant-general of volunteers, states that there are some omissions in his evidence yesterday which he will supply.

General Palmer's division consisted of about 5,000 men, and comprised almost half of General Crittenden's whole force in the field, which was only about 11,000; that the two brigades of General Van Cleve had been very much cut up the day before (19th) and really contained less than 2,000, considerably less on 20th; that when, by the firing of the batteries alluded to, the enemy's troops which were approaching were driven back, the batteries formed the only force that was opposed to the enemy between them and the junction of the roads I have called Dry Valley and Rossville, in the rear of General Thomas' command, and that that junction was less than a mile from the enemy's troops at that time. Although some of the batteries were taken by not being allowed to retire, I consider the fact of the enemy having been driven back by the battery as one of very great importance, and probably prevented very serious disaster to our army.

Some days after the battle of Chickamauga, and just after we received notice that General Crittenden was removed from the command of his corps, I was present with Generals Rosecrans, Garfield, Crittenden, Gordon Granger, and King, and a number of other officers. General Crittenden said he would rather his conduct in the battle of Chickamauga should be investigated than any other event of his military career; that in previous battles it had only been necessary for him to hold positions assigned him, but that in this one he had ordered movements, had acted on his judgment, and had, as he thought, shown some capacity as a general. General Rosecrans immediately spoke with great emphasis, "General Crittenden, it gives me great pleasure to declare that every act of yours in the battle of Chickamauga met my cordial approbation. Every act was but an anticipation of my orders, every movement was well timed, and every lick told."

General Garfield then interposed and said, "General Crittenden acted more frequently without orders, and upon his own responsibility, than any other officer, yet every movement was exactly right and every act approved." I took down the conversation at the time, and I think I have repeated it almost word for word, though I have not a memorandum.

By General CRITTENDEN:

Question. You say we scattered when we went to the batteries. Did or did not General Crittenden direct his staff to scatter and remain himself with the batteries?

Answer. Yes; we did nothing except by his orders.

The Court adjourned to meet at 10 o'clock on 11th instant.

ELEVENTH DAY.

FEBRUARY 11, 1864.

The Court met pursuant to adjournment.

Present, Major-Generals Hunter and Cadwalader, Brigadier-General Wadsworth, and Colonel Schriver, recorder, and Major-General Crittenden.

The proceedings of the tenth day were read and approved.

The Court adjourned to meet at 10 o'clock on the 12th instant.

TWELFTH DAY.

FEBRUARY 12, 1864.

The Court met pursuant to adjournment.

Present, Major-Generals Hunter and Cadwalader, Brigadier-General Wadsworth, and Colonel Schriver, recorder, and Major-General Crittenden.

J. D. BARKER, late captain of First Ohio Cavalry, being duly sworn, says to questions

By General CRITTENDEN:

Question. Did you ride on 20th September from Rossville to General Thomas' line?

Answer. I rode from a mile south of Rossville to General Thomas' line.

Question. What was the distance?

Answer. The route I took was about 7 miles; direct route would have been about 5. I don't think it was much farther from Rossville.

By the COURT:

Question. How do you know you were a mile from Rossville when you started?

Answer. I had been from this point to Rossville three times on the morning of the 19th.

Col. J. T. WILDER, Seventeenth Indiana, being duly sworn, says to questions

By General CRITTENDEN:

Question. Did you see General Crittenden at the battle of Chickamauga? State where, and anything you saw him do showing either negligence or attention to duty.

Answer. I saw him on the 19th. He was very actively engaged disposing troops to meet the rebels, and exhibiting a good deal of anxiety that my men should be properly posted, although not belonging to his command. On the afternoon of the 19th, when General Davis' command was driven back, I saw General Crittenden in person with some of his staff, in a very exposed position, rallying Davis' men. At one time I thought he would certainly be killed or captured, being in an open field between the two lines at the right of my line. One of my regiments went forward and to the right, to relieve him. That is all I saw of him in the battle.

Question. Did one of General Crittenden's staff officers, on the night of 20th, come to you for information in reference to any of his scattered troops?

Answer. Captain Knox, of General Crittenden's staff, came to me in the Chattanooga Valley, about midnight on night of 20th, inquiring what troops I had rallied, and if any belonging to his command. I answered him I had about 2,000, I believed, from every part of the army, and that I sent them to Chattanooga.

Capt. P. P. OLDERSHAW, late assistant adjutant-general, Twenty-first Army Corps, duly sworn, says to questions

By General CRITTENDEN:

Question. Were you in the battle of Chickamauga, and in what capacity?

Answer. I was; acting as assistant adjutant-general Twenty-first Army Corps, commanded by Maj. Gen. T. L. Crittenden.

Question. Did General Crittenden send General Palmer to General Thomas' support early on 19th, and on his own responsibility?

Answer. He sent General Palmer, commanding his largest division, at 11 a. m. on 19th, hearing at that time very heavy firing to his front and left, and supposing that General Thomas was heavily pressed. This he did on his own responsibility, reporting the fact to General Rosecrans, who afterward confirmed the movement by letter, and subsequently by words, thanking him for it.

Question. Did General Crittenden afterward, while waiting for permission to send General Van Cleve to support General Palmer, anticipate the permission and order Van Cleve to move up with two brigades?

Answer. So soon as General Palmer had moved up to the left he was very shortly heavily engaged. It proved so by General Crittenden's chief of artillery, Major Mendenhall (who was dispatched by General Crittenden to know General Palmer's necessities), returning, not having been able to communicate with General Palmer, having ridden into the rebel ranks, though pursuing the same course taken by General Palmer. General Crittenden then at once wrote to General Rosecrans, asking permission to bring up General Van Cleve and his two brigades to the support of General Palmer, and in the interim sent an order to General Van Cleve to move up to the position General Crittenden was then occupying. General Van Cleve arrived nearly at the same moment as the staff officer returning from General Rosecrans, with permission to move up General Van Cleve.

Question. Did General Crittenden, as soon as Van Cleve had moved to Palmer's support, apply for permission to bring up General Wood with his command, and did not General Wood arrive at a very critical moment?

Answer. Soon after General Van Cleve had moved up to the left he also became heavily engaged, and General Crittenden at once dispatched Colonel Starling, chief of staff, to General Rosecrans for permission to move up General Wood. At the same time General Crittenden dispatched Major Mendenhall to General Wood to notify him that his other two divisions were heavily engaged; that General Van Cleve had been moved up from his left; that he must look well to his left, and that he had sent a request to department headquarters that his (Wood's) division might also be moved up. Colonel Starling returned with instructions to move up General Wood and to take entire command of his (General Crittenden's) corps. General Crittenden at once dispatched a staff officer ordering General Wood to move up, and at the same moment rode himself to department headquarters, then distant about three-fourths of a mile. He returned two or three minutes after the arrival of General Wood, who arrived at a moment when General Davis was heavily pressed, and who had a moment before been to me and asked for a brigade to sustain him. Colonel Starling offered a brigade, and rode off and moved up Colonel Harker's brigade, of Wood's division.

Question. Were not General Wood's troops engaged almost from the moment of their arrival on the field, and were they not continuously in conflict with the enemy until night ?

Answer. They were. When they arrived the enemy was plainly in sight in a line of woods. Davis' battery was firing at these troops across an open field, and General Wood had scarcely his last regiment in position before the enemy came out from woods, driving General Wood's brigade last arriving back.

Question. When General Crittenden was ordered to take command of his corps, was he not cut off from communication with Palmer and Van Cleve ?

Answer. He was. Generals Palmer and Van Cleve had been moved up to the assistance of General Thomas before the arrival of Davis' and Sheridan's divisions of McCook's corps. The latter two divisions were formed, I think, on the immediate right of Van Cleve, and a good deal to the right of Palmer, thus severing the component parts of the Twenty-first Army Corps.

Question. Were not all the divisions of General Crittenden's command severely engaged on the 19th ?

Answer. They were. His entire First Division, however, was not present, one brigade of it having been left at Chattanooga.

Question. What was General Crittenden's command on the 20th ? State how it happened that General Crittenden's command was broken on the 20th, and the circumstances under which he left the field.

Answer. It consisted of General Wood's division, two brigades, and General Van Cleve's three brigades, less one regiment left at Whiteside's. These two divisions were put in reserve on the eastern slope of Mission Ridge, by order of General Rosecrans, at midnight 19th, 20th. About 9 a. m. 20th, General Crittenden, having ridden to his two divisions, established his own temporary headquarters near them. General Rosecrans sent for him to ride the lines with him. I did not accompany him, but about 10 a. m., hearing some cannonading on the left, I rode to the front ; found General Crittenden and General Rosecrans in company. General Van Cleve's division in an advanced position near the crest of the hill, and General Wood's division had been moved out of sight when I had arrived. General Rosecrans then instructed General Crittenden to move Van Cleve's division forward, in the direction of some smoke which we all saw rising in the front and little to our left. General Crittenden remarked to General Rosecrans, "As this is the last of my command, I shall accompany it," and did so. While moving in the direction indicated, a staff officer from General Thomas spoke to General Crittenden asking for General Rosecrans, and stating that General Thomas was heavily pressed on his left. General Crittenden soon after received orders from General Rosecrans to move General Van Cleve with his two brigades to General Thomas' left, or to occupy any gap or interval he might find in the lines. From the direction of the firing, General Crittenden and myself both thought it was General Thomas' right that was being pressed, and dispatched me to General Rosecrans to convey the impression, and also to state that the movement of Van Cleve, as ordered, was going on. As I rode to General Rosecrans, I met General Thomas' staff officer returning, and questioned him as to its being the left or right at which General Thomas needed support. He then stated it was his right and not his left, and I so reported to General Rosecrans. I reported the same to General Crittenden on my return, with the additional information that General Rosecrans had ordered General Wood to leave his position and move to Thomas' assistance as soon as he was relieved by General McCook. Van Cleve was to continue with his movement, which he was making by the left oblique. Van Cleve had scarcely got well into the woods before stragglers were seen breaking through his ranks. General Crittenden and his staff were about 100 yards to his rear. The stragglers increased rapidly, and General Crittenden, fearing a disaster, rode rapidly to the crest of the hill on which most of his batteries were stationed, and in plain view of the line of woods out of which the troops were breaking. For some time he hesitated opening these batteries ; afterward, after a large number of troops had passed from the woods into the open field, he ordered the artillery to open fire upon the troops then on the line of the woods. These batteries were unprotected by any infantry, and the general and staff staid there perhaps three-quarters of an hour, when Lieutenant Cushing, commanding Company M [H], Fourth U. S. Artillery, stated a shot had just passed by him from his rear, and believing that the enemy had got entirely to our rear, his guns were faced to the rear. They soon after resumed their former position, and commenced firing rapidly on the enemy, then advancing rapidly up the hill. About a quarter of a hour later the general and staff left the batteries, giving their commanders instructions which I did not hear. At this time the enemy were not only in our immediate front, but also in our left and right, pursuing our troops, who were escaping round the base of the hill, up the valleys. General Crittenden, then, had no alternative but to ride straight to the rear or be killed or captured, as Major Mendenhall, who remained a few moments later at the batteries, soon overtook General Crittenden with the information that the enemy were in the batteries and turning them on us. Crossing the Dry Valley road, we ascended another ridge, on which some troops of the Eighteenth Regulars had been rallied (at least, I was informed they belonged to that regiment). Here General Crittenden halted awhile in hopes of receiving orders or hearing from General Rosecrans. Shortly afterward he rode on further and met Colonel Parkhurst, commanding the provost-guard of the Fourteenth Army Corps, which was in line of battle, increased by other stragglers they had rallied. Colonel Parkhurst tendered the command to General Crittenden, which he declined, stating that he (Parkhurst) was doing very well, and finally gave him instructions to rally and hold all the men he could until the wagons, &c., had passed by, when he was to follow on with his command as a rear guard. General Crittenden was very anxious as to the safety of Generals Rosecrans, McCook, Sheridan, and Davis, all [of] whom he believed to have been to his right at the time of the breaking of the center of the line, and asked Colonel Parkhurst for information concerning them. He had none, except that he believed that General Rosecrans had left for Rossville or Chattanooga. He could gain no information whatever on the road, which was filled with wagons, guns, and men, all marching in orderly disorder, without confusion or noise, and on arriving near Rossville, he met Colonels Ducat, Goddard, Taylor (quartermaster),who, as I understood, stated General Rosecrans had gone to Chattanooga. On arriving at Rossville the general detached me to pass through the troops across the road to ascertain about General Gordon Granger's position, supposing his headquarters were there. I could find nothing of his quarters or learn anything of his movements, and I continued to Chattanooga, where I arrived at 4.15 p. m., not having overtaken General Crittenden.

Question. Did General Crittenden send officers to ascertain whether there were any general officers or troops still on the field, and if any could be found ?

Answer. He did, several times, and from several positions, after the breaking of the lines, but he gained no information from any one until his arrival near Rossville, where he was informed General Rosecrans had gone to Chattanooga.

Question. Did General Crittenden stop at Rossville and endeavor there to get information from General Thomas ?

Answer. He stopped a little while, conversing with several of General Rosecrans' staff officers. Having detached me to hunt up General Gordon Granger's headquarters or troops, I cannot tell what inquiries he made about General Thomas' troops, or how long General Crittenden staid at Rossville.

Question. Did you ride to one side with General Crittenden to see if the battle was still going on ?

Answer. I did.

Question. What did you hear ?

Answer. I heard an occasional cannon shot, which sounded to me in the direction of the Chickamauga Creek, which enters the Tennessee River 8 miles above Chattanooga. There was nothing to be heard there of a general engagement.

The Court adjourned to meet at 10 o'clock on the 13th instant.

THIRTEENTH DAY.

FEBRUARY 13, 1864.

The Court met pursuant to adjournment.

Present, Major-Generals Hunter and Cadwalader, Brigadier-General Wadsworth, and Colonel Schriver, recorder, and Major-General Crittenden.

The proceedings of the twelfth day were read and approved.

Captain OLDERSHAW was permitted to make the following correction and addition to his testimony of the 12th:

In my evidence yesterday I stated that the instructions of General Van Cleve on the morning of the 20th, to "occupy any gap or interval he might find in the lines" while passing to General Thomas' left, were given him as coming from General Rosecrans. I now desire to state that these instructions originated with General Crittenden.

I also desire to state the name of the quartermaster referred to at Rossville was Hodges, and not Taylor.

I wish to add that on the ride from the battle-field to Rossville, on the 20th, that General Crittenden, whom I accompanied, received and could gain no information of the condition or position of General Thomas and his command. Also that no escort accompanied General Crittenden on his ride from the battle-field to Chattanooga, General Crittenden having ordered it to remain in the rear early in the morning, and it did not rejoin the staff until after dark that day.

By General CRITTENDEN:

Question. Did you hear the instructions to General Van Cleve to find an interval and occupy it, and are you sure that the order was not to find an interval and pass through it to attack the enemy?

Answer. I heard the instructions, but am not certain that they were to the effect to find an interval and pass through it, but to occupy any interval and fight the enemy where found.

The Court was cleared.

The Court was opened, and adjourned to meet at 10 o'clock on 15th instant.

FOURTEENTH DAY.

FEBRUARY 15, 1864.

The Court met pursuant to adjournment.

Present, Major-Generals Hunter and Cadwalader, Brigadier-General Wadsworth, and Colonel Schriver, recorder, and Major-General Crittenden.

The proceedings of the thirteenth day were read and approved.

Capt. P. P. OLDERSHAW, recalled, says to questions

By General CRITTENDEN:

Question. State if these are the original orders (nine pieces), which are now delivered into the custody of the Court, received by General Crittenden at the battle of Chickamauga; and state, also, if the book presented contains a transcript of the orders and dispatches issued by General Crittenden.

Answer. These are the original orders (see appendix, marked A), and the book contains true copies of all orders and dispatches issued and sent by General Crittenden during that battle.

Question. State, if you know, what supplies General Crittenden's commissary turned over to the Army of the Cumberland when it withdrew to Chattanooga.

Answer. From the time General Crittenden first occupied Chattanooga up to the battle of Chickamauga nearly his entire transportation was engaged hauling supplies from Bridgeport to Chattanooga. After the battle, on General Rosecrans' order to turn over supplies to other corps, the commissary of General Crittenden's corps turned over between 80,000 and 90,000 rations. My impression is it was 90,000.

Capt. RICHARD LODOR, Fourth U. S. Artillery, being duly sworn, says to question

By General CRITTENDEN:

Question. ₁Were you in the battle of Chickamauga, and in what position?

Answer. I was lieutenant-colonel, and assistant inspector-general of Twenty-first Army Corps.

Question. State what you know as inspector-general of the Twenty-first Army Corps, commanded by General Crittenden, [of] the condition of said corps as to discipline, arms, accouterments, ammunition, clothing, and subsistence.

Answer. I know intimately the condition of the corps at the time, and that it was well supplied and equipped with everything pertaining to the commissary, quartermaster, and ordnance departments. I do not believe that a single gun or round of ammunition was wanting to complete the equipment. I think the entire corps was in as perfect order as any company could be. I know this from personal inspection, and from daily reports which were required of me at that time. The discipline was excellent, and had been improving every day.

Question. State, if you know, what supplies General Crittenden's commissary turned over to the Army of the Cumberland when it withdrew to Chattanooga.

Answer. I only know what the commissary said himself, that he did turn over a quantity of supplies. I know we had on hand more than was wanted for present use by the Twenty-first Army Corps.

Question. How long were you with General Crittenden at the batteries on the 20th September, and how long did these batteries keep back the enemy and how much did the batteries suffer?

Answer. I was not with General Crittenden more than fifteen minutes after he got to the batteries, but was near him, trying to rally the troops with General Van Cleve. My recollection is the batteries held the enemy in check some time, I cannot say how long; perhaps half an hour. The batteries suffered a good deal for the commanding position they occupied, and held it till the last moment. It was with great difficulty that the guns could be got away. The enemy, it seemed to me, came in all directions, and some were among the batteries.

Question. Was there any other position the batteries could have taken from which they could have repulsed the enemy and been less exposed themselves?

Answer. No; I should think it was the best position that I had seen the batteries placed in during the two days' fight, and it was almost impossible to move the batteries farther to the front, even had there been time to do so. When General Van Cleve moved to the front on the 20th the batteries which belonged to the two brigades of his division had to cut roads in order to pass through the woods to the position referred to in General Crittenden's question. I am an artillery officer, and have been serving in that corps nearly eight years.

Question. Did you attempt on Sunday to go to General Thomas, and with what success?

Answer. I did, and tried hard for three hours to get to General Thomas from the position General Crittenden occupied when he left to find General Rosecrans, and ascertained the only way to get from that position without being captured was by passing back toward Chattanooga. I did not arrive in Chattanooga till some time after dark. In going to Chattanooga I started about 4 p. m., and found the officers picking up men, forming them into squads, and found very little confusion considering the circumstances. I believe it to have been impossible for any one to pass from the position General Crittenden occupied near the batteries to our lines in the front.

Question. State what you know of the order to General Van Cleve to attack the enemy on Sunday morning?

Answer. General Rosecrans, in General Crittenden's presence, ordered me to ride rapidly to General Van Cleve, and tell him to form his command in double column, move toward the front in the direction of a certain tree pointed out to me, pass to the first interval he could find near there, but not deploy until near the enemy, and then to do it with great rapidity. General Crittenden repeated the order to me. I gave it to General Van Cleve, rode back and reported to Generals Crittenden and Rosecrans. Shortly after the brigade started I joined General Crittenden, and found him near General Van Cleve's new position.

Lieut. H. C. CUSHING, Fourth U. S. Artillery, duly sworn, says to questions

By General CRITTENDEN :

Question. Were you with your battery on the 20th September, when the disaster occurred on our right and center; how long did the batteries remain in this position holding back the enemy, and what were the casualties in these batteries?

Answer. Yes ; the batteries remained there not quite three-quarters of an hour, and the loss in my own battery was 8 horses killed and wounded ; 1 man killed and 4 wounded ; that is all I can remember. There may have been more. I do not know the losses in the other batteries, but I know they were quite heavy. Captain Stevens, of the Pennsylvania battery, was killed, and 1 or 2 officers were wounded.

The Court adjourned to meet at 10 o'clock on 16th instant in the council room on corner of Jefferson and Sixth streets.

FIFTEENTH DAY.

FEBRUARY 16, 1864.

The Court met pursuant to adjournment.

Present, Major-Generals Hunter and Cadwalader, Brigadier-General Wadsworth, and Colonel Schriver, recorder, and Major-General Crittenden.

The proceedings of the fourteenth day were read and approved.

On the application of General Crittenden, the following testimony of Capt. R. S. Thoms, aide-de-camp to General Rosecrans, given in General Negley's case on the sixth day, to avoid recalling the witness, who is at a distant station, was ordered to be inserted in General Crittenden's record :

"Question. Did or did you not convey an order from General Rosecrans early on the morning of the 20th for General Wood to relieve General Negley?

"Answer. Yes ; I was directed by General Rosecrans to order General Crittenden to relieve General Negley by Wood's division. I found General Wood's division marching into the position which General Negley's reserve brigade had occupied. General Wood was not with them when I first arrived at the division. I told Colonel Harker, who commanded a brigade, that the division was to relieve Negley's, and asked him where Crittenden or Wood was. He told me the direction Wood was. I went to him, and gave him the order, and told him I would tell General Crittenden what I had done. The next time I was sent to Wood directly, to tell him to relieve General Negley at once. He said he did not know the exact position of Negley's troops. I pointed out Major Lowrie, and told him he was an officer of General Negley's staff, who could show him where they were. I told him I had just passed Captain Johnson on the hill, another staff officer of General Negley's, who could also point out the position of Negley. He sent an aide after each officer."

The Court adjourned to meet at 10 o'clock on the 17th February.

SIXTEENTH DAY.

FEBRUARY 17, 1864.

The Court met pursuant to adjournment.

Present, Major-Generals Hunter and Cadwalader, Brigadier-General Wadsworth, and Colonel Schriver, recorder, and Major-General Crittenden.

The proceedings of the fifteenth day were read and approved.

The Court was closed.

The Court was opened, and adjourned to meet at 10 o'clock on 18th February.

SEVENTEENTH DAY.

FEBRUARY 18, 1864.

The Court met pursuant to adjournment.

Present, Major-Generals Hunter and Cadwalader, Brigadier-General Wadsworth, and Colonel Schriver, recorder, and Major-General Crittenden.

Brig. Gen. H. P. VAN CLEVE, U. S. Volunteers, being duly sworn, says to questions

By General CRITTENDEN:

Question. Were you in the battle of Chickamauga, and what was your command?

Answer. I was, and commanded the Third Division, Twenty-first Army Corps, commanded by Maj. Gen. T. L. Crittenden.

Question. Were you, on the morning of the 19th September, 1863, ordered up from Gordon's or Lee's Mills and sent into the fight to support General Palmer?

Answer. I was ordered on that morning by General Crittenden to move forward with two of my brigades to the support of General Palmer.

Question. Did you, or not, become engaged in a severe fight very soon after passing General Crittenden, and do you, or not, think your support was necessary to General Palmer?

Answer. I passed General Crittenden on my road to General Palmer; he was in advance with his staff. His chief of staff, Colonel Starling, told me the exact point at which he wished me to go in, and I became engaged in a severe fight with the enemy, I think in ten minutes after I left him. The support was necessary to General Palmer, as I saved his division, which would have been surrounded by the enemy had I not got there just at the time I did. The ground I passed over was soon after occupied by the enemy, and I was cut off from General Crittenden.

Question. What were your casualties on the 19th? and what in the battle? State also the strength of your command.

Answer. The strength of the two brigades was, I think, 2,000 men; the force I went in with not over that number. I lost in killed and wounded on 19th not less than 300 men, and in the battle 650 killed and wounded and 265 missing. Many of the missing were wounded and taken prisoner. In the numbers 650 and 265 are included the casualties of Barnes' brigade, which fought with General Wood.

Question. When you were ordered into the fight on the 20th, were you not ordered to move toward a smoke which was pointed out, and to attack the enemy?

Answer. I was.

63 R R—VOL XXX PT, I

Question. When your command was broken, under what order were you moving?

Answer. Under an order from General Rosecrans to support General Thomas; to move rapidly, but not to harass my men. I gave the order to double-quick myself, but the men were not to be wearied. My impression is, the order was brought by Major Mendenhall.

Question. Do you remember that after the battle General Crittenden sent to you for that order?

Answer. Yes.

Question. Do you remember that General Crittenden said that the original order had been sent to you to avoid any delay in copying it?

Answer. Yes.

Question. After your command was broken, did you rally all the men you could, and bring them to the support of the batteries, and how many men did you bring?

Answer. I did, and brought a small number, 50 to 100 men.

Question. After the batteries were driven, did you retire at once by the Dry Valley road, and did the enemy pursue on that road?

Answer. I retired by that road, but noticed no pursuit. There was no pursuit, I am confident.

Question. After your command was broken, did you see or hear of any organized troops on the field, or any general officer, except your brigade commander, General Sam. Beatty, and your corps commander, General Crittenden?

Answer. I did not see any general officers except Generals Crittenden and Sam. Beatty. As soon as my command was broken I hastened to rally my men, but being busily engaged in trying to save the batteries, I did not notice whether there were any organized troops.

Question. Before leaving the field did you not look to see if there were any organized troops on the field?

Answer. I did not leave the field until nearly cut off by the enemy, and my mind was not called to the subject of organized troops. I came near being captured.

By the COURT:

Question. Where did you again rally your troops that day, and get them together?

Answer. On what I think is called the Dry Valley road between Rossville and the battle-field.

Question. What did you do with your command after you rallied them?

Answer. My command lay there until midnight; it was about sundown when the rallying was accomplished. After midnight we moved to Chattanooga.

By General CRITTENDEN:

Question. When you rode back to Rossville, did you find any of your men on the road?

Answer. I did not find any in a body.

Question. Did you send word to General Crittenden during the night that you were under orders from department headquarters?

Answer. I sent word about daybreak in the morning, I think, that I was under orders from department headquarters.

Question. How large a force of organized men do you think you saw anywhere on the road as you went to Rossville?

Answer. I saw, probably a mile and a half from the battle-field, some men drawn across the road ; the officer in command I did not know. Colonel Ducat was there, and I supposed they had been rallied by him. I assisted him a long time there in rallying and stationing them, to prevent our men from falling back, or to resist an attack of the enemy. There may have been there some 500 men. It is difficult for me to recollect now. I know that I would rather have had a good regiment than those I saw there.

The Court was cleared.

The Court was opened, and adjourned to meet at 10 o'clock on 19th instant.

EIGHTEENTH DAY.

FEBRUARY 19, 186-.

The Court met pursuant to adjournment.

Present, Major-Generals Hunter and Cadwalader, Brigadier-General Wadsworth, and Colonel Schriver, recorder, and Major-General Crittenden.

The proceedings of the seventeenth day were read and approved.

The Court was cleared.

The Court was opened, and adjourned to meet at 6 p. m. this day.

GALT HOUSE, *February* 19—6 p. m.

The Court met pursuant to adjournment.

Present, Major-Generals Hunter and Cadwalader, Brigadier-General Wadsworth, and Colonel Schriver, recorder.

No proceedings in this case.

The Court was closed.

The Court was opened, and adjourned to meet at 10 o'clock on the 20th instant.

NINETEENTH DAY.

FEBRUARY 20, 1864.

The Court met pursuant to adjournment.

Present, Major-Generals Hunter and Cadwalader, Brigadier-General Wadsworth, and Colonel Schriver, recorder.

No proceedings in this case.

The Court was closed.

The Court was opened, and adjourned to meet at 8 p. m. this day.

GALT HOUSE—8 p m.

The Court met pursuant to adjournment.

Present, Major-Generals Hunter and Cadwalader, Brigadier-General Wadsworth, and Colonel Schriver, recorder, and Major-General Crittenden.

Major-General Crittenden then read the statement marked B in the Appendix.

The Court was closed.

The Court was opened, and adjourned to meet at 10 o'clock on the 22d instant.

TWENTIETH DAY.

FEBRUARY 22, 1864.

The Court met pursuant to adjournment.
There were no proceedings in this case.
The Court was closed.
The Court was opened, and adjourned till 6 p. m. this day.

6 p. m.

The Court met at 9.30 p. m.
The witness expected not having arrived, no proceedings in this case.
The Court was closed.
The Court was opened, and adjourned to meet at 10 o'clock on the 23d February.

TWENTY-FIRST DAY.

FEBRUARY 23, 1864.

The Court met pursuant to adjournment.
Present, Major-Generals Hunter and Cadwalader, Brigadier-General Wadsworth, and Colonel Schriver, recorder.
The Court was cleared.
After the reading of the testimony, the Court came to the following

FINDING AND OPINION IN MAJOR-GENERAL CRITTENDEN'S CASE.

General Crittenden commanded the Twenty-first Army Corps, composed of Palmer's, Wood's, and Van Cleve's divisions.
On the 19th September, 1863 (the first day of the battle of Chickamauga), his command consisted of those divisions, except Wagner's brigade, which garrisoned Chattanooga.
The evidence adduced respecting General Crittenden's operations on that day, not only shows no cause for censure, but, on the contrary, that his whole conduct was most creditable; for, by his watchfulness and prompt and judicious support of troops engaged, serious consequences to our army were prevented, and the enemy's plans for the day disconcerted.
Early on the morning of the 20th, General Crittenden's command consisted of Wood's and Van Cleve's divisions. But as about 8 a. m. Wood's division was detached to take post in Thomas' line, General Crittenden is not responsible for its subsequent conduct. Van Cleve's division was shortly after ordered to the left, and General Crittenden was to accompany it. As it was moving the attack took place, and the troops were broken and scattered by our retreating artillery and infantry, as well as by the furious attack of the enemy.
For the disaster which ensued he is in no way responsible. Changes were ordered to be made in the line. The break which occurred while the troops were moving by flank from the right to the left to conform to these changes, was taken advantage of by the enemy, and disaster and rout ensued. It is amply proven that General Crittenden did everything he could, by example and personal exertion, to rally and hold his troops, and to prevent the evils resulting from such a condition of affairs, but without avail.

Believing that by his presence on the field nothing more could be effected, he left for Rossville, where he learned little else than that the commanding general had gone to Chattanooga. He repaired thither, where one of his brigades was stationed.

In the opinion of the Court, General Crittenden is not censurable for this act.

D. HUNTER,
Major-General, President.
ED. SCHRIVER,
Inspector-General, Recorder.

There being no further business before the Court, it adjourned *sine die.*

D. HUNTER,
Major-General, President.
ED. SCHRIVER,
Inspector-General, Recorder.

ADJUTANT-GENERAL'S OFFICE,
April 9, 1864.

The record and opinions in the foregoing case have been submitted to the President of the United States. He is of opinion that no further action is required, and the Court of Inquiry is dissolved.

By order of the Secretary of War:

E. D. TOWNSEND,
Assistant Adjutant-General.

APPENDIX.

A.

HEADQUARTERS FOURTEENTH ARMY CORPS,
Near McDaniel's (McDonald's) House,
September 15 [19], 1863—10.45. (Received 11.20 a. m.)
Major-General CRITTENDEN :

If another division can be spared, it would be well to send it up without any delay.

By command of Major-General Thomas:

J. P. WILLARD,
Captain, and Aide-de-Camp.

—

[Received Hdqrs. 21st Corps, Sept. 19, 1863—11.19 a. m.]

Headquarters general commanding has moved to the Widow Glenn's.

—

SEPTEMBER 19, 1863—11.10 a. m.
[Received 12 m. at Gordon's Mills.]
Major-General CRITTENDEN,
Twenty-first Army Corps :

The general commanding directs you to order Minty to go to Chattanooga with all practicable speed. Let him come by Widow Glenn's, and report for orders.

C. GODDARD,
Assistant Adjutant-General.

HEADQUARTERS DEPARTMENT OF THE CUMBERLAND,
Crawfish Spring, September 19, 1863—8.10 a. m.
[Received 8.50 a. m.]
Major-General CRITTENDEN, *Comdg. Twenty-first Army Corps:*
Your dispatch of 7.40 this a. m. is received. Col. Dan. McCook's
brigade was at Reed's Bridge early this morning and captured a few
prisoners from the rear of a retreating column. The general com-
manding is anxious to know what are the developments on the left.
We hear artillery at Gordon's Mills and a few dropping shots on
Negley's front.
Very respectfully, your obedient servant,
J. A. GARFIELD,
Brigadier-General, Chief of Staff.

—

HDQRS. DEPARTMENT OF THE CUMBERLAND,
Widow Glenn's House, September 19, 1863—11.20 p. m.
[Received September 20, 12.15 a. m.]
[General CRITTENDEN :]
GENERAL : The general commanding directs me to inform you that
General McCook has been ordered to hold this gap to-morrow, cover-
ing the Dry Valley road, his right resting near this place ; his left
connecting with General Thomas' right. The general places your
corps in reserve to-morrow and directs you to post it on the eastern
slope of Missionary Ridge to support McCook or Thomas. Leave
the grand guards from your command out with instructions to hold
their ground until driven in, and then to retire slowly contesting the
ground stubbornly.
Very respectfully, your obedient servant,
J. A. GARFIELD,
Brigadier-General, Chief of Staff.

—

HEADQUARTERS DEPARTMENT OF THE CUMBERLAND,
September 19, 1863—1.45 p. m. [Received 2 p. m.]
General CRITTENDEN :
Colonel Starling was here just now. I have ordered McCook to
relieve you. You will proceed at once to take command of your
corps. Make your dispositions as best you can ; cheer them up ; see
that their ammunition is right. Sheridan will come in if necessary
on your right, leaving a nominal force to cover our rear. Take care
of your right.
By order General Rosecrans:
C. GODDARD,
Assistant Adjutant-General.

—

HDQRS. DEPARTMENT OF THE CUMBERLAND,
Widow Glenn's, September 19, 1863—3.45 p. m.
(Received 4.35 p. m.)
Major-General CRITTENDEN, *Comdg. Twenty-first Army Corps:*
General Davis is being heavily pressed, or was when the messen-
ger left. Assist him, if you can, by a movement of some of your
command.
Very respectfully, your obedient servant,
J. A. GARFIELD,
Brigadier-General, Chief of Staff.

Hdqrs. Department of the Cumberland,
Widow Glenn's, September 19, 1863—12.20 p. m.
([Received] 1.25 p. m.)

Major-General Crittenden,
   Commanding Twenty-first Army Corps:

Your dispatch of 11.30 received. The sending of Palmer is approved. From present appearances General Thomas will move *en échelon,* his left advanced, threatening the enemy's right. Understanding this will aid your movement and enable you to conform to this state of affairs.

By order of General Rosecrans :

FRANK S. BOND,
Major, and Aide-de-Camp.

—

Hdqrs. Department, *September* 19, 1863.
[Received] (3.10 p. m.)

Major-General Crittenden,
   Commanding, &c. :

Dispatch from General Thomas of 3 p. m., just received, says:

We are driving the rebels in the center handsomely, so General Johnson's aide reports to me. My First Division was considerably cut up, but we have taken many prisoners. I am in hopes we will drive them across the Chickamauga to-night.

Sent by order General Rosecrans :

FRANK S. BOND,
Major, and Aide-de-Camp.

B.

REVIEW OF THE EVIDENCE IN THE CASE OF GENERAL CRITTENDEN.

It appears from the testimony in this case that General Crittenden was ordered by the general commanding the army to hold a position covering the road from La Fayette to Chattanooga (see p. 29*); that General Crittenden's corps numbered 11,000 effective men (see Colonel Starling's evidence, p. 39).

It is proven by the concurrent testimony of all the witnesses that as early as 11 o'clock on Saturday morning, September 19, 1863, and as soon as the sound of musketry demonstrated that a severe battle was raging on our left, General Crittenden sent General Palmer with his division to General Thomas' support; that General Palmer, with his division, numbering about 5,000 men, nearly half of General Crittenden's corps, did fight his way to General Thomas, and remained with him until ordered to withdraw on the evening of the 20th September, when the whole army was withdrawn to Rossville. It is also proven that General Crittenden sent General Palmer's division on his own responsibility, thus undertaking to hold an important position with 6,000 men, instead of 11,000. It is proven, without any conflicting testimony, that General Crittenden, becoming uneasy for General Palmer's rear and flank, asked for permission further to weaken his command by sending General Van Cleve to support General Palmer, and, anticipating the permission, ordered General Van Cleve up; that the arrival of General Van Cleve's com-

*All page references in this " Review " are to original Record of Proceedings.

mand (two brigades), Van Cleve having been ordered by General Crittenden to leave one brigade with General Wood, and the arrival of the permission to send this division, as requested, were simultaneous, and that Van Cleve marched immediately to Palmer's support, and was in a few minutes hotly engaged. (See General Van Cleve's testimony.)

It is also proven beyond doubt that General Crittenden, as soon as Van Cleve became engaged, applied to General Rosecrans for permission to bring up General Wood's command; that he obtained this permission, and immediately brought up General Wood; that General Wood became engaged at the moment of his arrival at General Crittenden's position, and so severely engaged that one of his brigades, commanded by Colonel Buell, lost in a very brief conflict 100 men killed and wounded. (See p. 38.)

It is clear from the whole evidence, as well as from the official report of the commander-in-chief, that the achievements of the Twenty-first Army Corps and the orders of its commander on the 19th afford no subject for censure. That the arrival of Palmer and afterward of Van Cleve upon the left was opportune is shown not only by all the testimony, but by the rebel papers, which say that the vigorous attack of those divisions disconcerted all their plans and prevented their resuming the offensive on that day. (See p. 29.)

A failure to anticipate orders on that day it is obvious would in all probability have resulted in a great disaster.

It is clearly proven that in proportion to its strength the corps of General Crittenden furnished as many men who fought throughout the battle as any other corps; that the officers and men behaved as well as any, and that the corps lost as many killed and wounded and fewer missing than any other corps. (See General Rosecrans' evidence, p. 24.)

The testimony shows that General Crittenden's command was placed in reserve on the night of the 19th September; that his command was then composed of the two divisions commanded by Generals Van Cleve and Wood, General Rosecrans having notified General Crittenden that General Palmer would get his orders from General Thomas.

It is clear from the evidence that General Crittenden, on the 20th, was the last general officer to leave the field, and then only when there was no organized body of troops upon the field.

In the absence of charges he is at a loss to know to what points to direct explanations. Only three occur to him which could suggest themselves to any military man, and upon these he has some hesitation in commenting before a military court, explained as they are by the orders produced before this Court and by the testimony of so many officers of intelligence, including General Rosecrans.

1. In the report of General Rosecrans he speaks of the delay in relieving General Negley's command with the command of General Wood. This could not have been intended as a censure upon General Crittenden, for it is shown by General Rosecrans' evidence that his order was given directly to General Wood, and the fact afterward reported to General Crittenden. (See General Rosecrans' evidence, p. 20, and also Captain Thoms', aide-de-camp, p. 60.)

He will add, however, that the commanding general is mistaken in supposing if there was any delay in General Wood relieving General Negley in the line of battle that it was the cause of serious consequences later in the day, because General Wood did relieve General

Negley, and did afterward reach General Thomas' line with the three brigades under his command, and fought with General Thomas until the army was withdrawn. (See General Rosecrans', Colonel Starling's, &c., evidence.)

2. In the report of General Rosecrans he speaks of the posting of General Van Cleve's command too far to the rear. This was not designed to censure General Crittenden, for by General Rosecrans' testimony it clearly appears that Van Cleve's troops were not in this position, but marching toward it, when the general commanding gave in person the order that Van Cleve should go on to a position which was 150 yards farther in advance. (See p. 23.)

At the time of this order General Van Cleve was marching eastwardly, and if there was any misjudgment as to the position he was directed to assume, it had no influence, for the reason, that before reaching the position, and when marching toward it, the general-in-chief directed that his march should be continued from 150 yards to 200 yards beyond, and he thus assumed the position approved by the general commanding without any delay.

The general commanding thus by his testimony corrects his official report, in which he says "he was surprised on his return to find General Van Cleve posted too far to the rear," for, by his own testimony, General Van Cleve was not in the objectionable position, but moving toward it, when he was ordered to move beyond it from 150 to 200 yards to the front.

3. The terms of the order convening this Court, direct special inquiry as to General Crittenden's conduct in leaving the field. His command, on the morning of the 20th, consisted of General Wood's and General Van Cleve's divisions, comprising together five brigades.

By an order from General Rosecrans, delivered directly to General Wood, he was ordered to relieve General Negley, who was posted in the main line of battle.

General Crittenden was ordered to send General Van Cleve with his division, consisting of two brigades, amounting to less than 2,000 men, in the direction of a cloud of smoke which the general commanding pointed to, and which was to the front, and to reach which by any direct route it would have been necessary to pass through our line of battle, as was evident when we approached it.

The order was to reach that point and attack the enemy. General Crittenden gave the order, and remarked as this was the last of his command he should go with it, and rode on to Van Cleve.

Before this order could be executed, an order came to General Crittenden to move General Van Cleve with the utmost dispatch, not exhausting his men, to the support of General Thomas. This order was sent to General Van Cleve, who was at the time moving to the left, looking for an opening through which he could pass to execute the first order "to attack the enemy."

It was sent with instructions to execute the order, and to take the first place in General Thomas' line where there was any fighting to do. It is obvious that General Rosecrans, in his testimony, has confounded these two orders, and only remembers them as one. (See Oldershaw's testimony, p. —, and Van Cleve's, p. —.)

Shortly before the last movement of General Van Cleve, a message reached General Crittenden that the woods were too thick to use artillery, and he therefore directed Major Mendenhall, his chief of artillery, to place the batteries on the crest of a hill a few hundred yards to the rear. This last order was given when he expected to go to the front and attack the enemy. When the order was changed, and Van Cleve directed to move to General Thomas' support, General Crittenden paused to make some other disposition of his artillery.

In a few moments, and while General Van Cleve was moving rapidly to the left in column doubled on the center, our lines in his front were suddenly attacked and driven back upon his men; two batteries ran furiously through his column, wounding several of his men, and throwing his command into great confusion.

Our broken lines were followed closely by the enemy, who, taking instant advantage of the confusion thus caused, drove five regiments of his (Van Cleve's) command entirely from the field. The remaining three regiments, being at the head of his column, were not thrown into confusion, but made their way to General Thomas' line, where they fought until the army was withdrawn.

General Crittenden at this time was from 100 yards to 300 yards in the rear of Van Cleve's column. The various witnesses differ in their estimate of the distance, and following their statements it is stated as not less than 100 nor more than 300 yards, and instantly the enemy's skirmishers were between him and Van Cleve.

It is shown by the evidence that at this time all our troops on the right of General Crittenden had been broken and driven from the field, the enemy pursuing them. General Crittenden was thus inclosed on three sides by the enemy, who were in plain view on the right and on the left, and who were firing briskly upon himself and his few remaining staff officers from the front. He called to his staff and said: "We will go to the batteries and yet drive those fellows back, or at least hold them in check." (See p. 36.)

The testimony of every witness examined as to what transpired at this time shows that General Crittenden remained with these batteries more than half an hour. For a few moments he hesitated to open their fire, because the troops in front showed a flag similar to the battle-flag of one of our own brigades (see pp. 15, 16, and 37), but the fire was opened, and drove back a body of the enemy who were endeavoring to carry the position. The batteries were wholly without support, until General Van Cleve came up with from 50 to 100 men, all that he could rally from his broken command or from any troops to be found on the field. This support was wholly insufficient, but the batteries still maintained their position and continued their fire until the enemy's skirmishers were among the guns.

The enemy, although driven back and foiled for so long a time in their efforts to carry this position by approaching from the front, still persisted in their efforts to capture these unsupported batteries, and ultimately succeeded in driving us from the position and in capturing some of the guns. This position covered and was but a few hundred yards from the road by which our straggling and wounded men, guns, and wagons were retiring toward Chattanooga.

During all this time General Crittenden's staff were searching in all directions for support for the batteries, and none could be found upon the field except the few rallied and brought up by General Van Cleve, as above mentioned.

Thus, driven from this position, General Crittenden, as is shown by several witnesses—Lodor, Starling, Oldershaw, and McCook— recrossed the Dry Valley road and stopped on the next ridge a few hundred yards distant, where he found a few stragglers, with whom he held that position for nearly half an hour and until the enemy turned our own guns upon us, thus giving the scattered and retreating troops, guns, and wagons upward of an hour in which to with-draw without molestation from the enemy,

There seemed nothing more to be done, except to give general di-rections to the few troops which were found on the road to move quietly along toward Chattanooga, which was done.

It has been shown that General Crittenden's entire corps was well supplied with everything pertaining to the commissary, quarter-master's, and ordnance departments; that not a single gun or round of ammunition was wanting to complete its equipment; that the entire corps was in as perfect order as any company could be. (See inspector-general's evidence, p. 55.)

That the batteries were posted in the best possible position. (In-spector-general, p. 57.)

That his corps maintained the reputation they had won at Shiloh and Stone's River, losing as many in killed and wounded and fewer missing than any other corps; that under orders on the 19th to hold the La Fayette road at all hazards, he detached first 5,000 of his men under General Palmer to support the heavily pressed left, and was immediately cut off from communication with this division.

That he ordered up Van Cleve with 2,000 men to open the way and support Palmer, and was very soon cut off from all communica-tion with him.

That he applied for and obtained permission to bring up General Wood with the remainder of his corps to the conflict; that these troops became engaged at the moment of their arrival, and were under his own eye in constant engagement with the enemy until night.

That on Sunday he was cut off from all communication or com-mand, except the unsupported batteries with which he held the enemy in check, as is abundantly explained.

I have thus furnished to the Court a memorandum of the leading points in the evidence which seemed to me pertinent to this inquiry, and have purposely abstained from argument or comment. If my conduct in this momentous battle, stated fairly as it has been by so many intelligent and reliable witnesses, yet requires further expla-nation it deserves to be condemned. The regret which I feel at hav-ing been relieved from the command of the Twenty-first Army Corps, whose discipline and equipment and *esprit de corps* I had so long and anxiously labored to elevate to a high standard, is some-what relieved by this investigation, which puts upon the record of the country in a permanent form the fact, which does not distinctly ap-pear in the official reports, that they are entitled to as much honor for standing between the overwhelming numbers of the rebels and Chattanooga as the corps of General Thomas or any corps of the army. I have throughout this investigation carefully abstained from asking any questions as to the opinions of witnesses, desiring only to elicit the facts within their knowledge. The reasons why I have asked no questions as to my own personal bearing upon the field will readily occur to a soldier.

When our own guns were turned upon us, as above explained, I directed one of my staff to place the few rallied stragglers under an officer, whom I designated, with instructions for them to act as a rear guard, and then with my few remaining staff officers rode slowly to Rossville.

I had ordered my escort early in the day to remain in the rear, and they also had been driven off and did not rejoin me until night. (See

p. 52.)   No information of General Thomas could be gathered upon the road.   I expected to find General Granger at Rossville, but could hear nothing of him or of General Thomas' condition.   I rode aside to listen for the sound of battle; nothing but an occasional gun could be heard.

I had left a brigade under Brigadier-General Wagner to garrison Chattanooga; these were my only remaining troops that I could reach, and I rode on to that place and immediately reported to General Rosecrans.   Received orders during the night to report to General Thomas at Rossville, to which place the army had been withdrawn.

It has been a source of regret to me that the exigencies of the battle did not permit my corps to fight in a body, but I at the time concurred, and still concur, in the opinion of the general commanding the army, "that the left should be supported if it took the entire corps of McCook and Crittenden."   The great body of the whole army was thrown to General Thomas, and saved Chattanooga.   The so-called disasters upon the right and center were but trifles in comparison.

It is probably superfluous to add that when I rode to Chattanooga I could not know that General Thomas was in the field; that I could not have reached his position, if he still maintained it, before night-fall, and that by going to Chattanooga I could get information and orders and join General Thomas during the night if required.   All subsequent information, as well as all the evidence in this inquiry, has confirmed the correctness of my judgment in this view of my duty.

Very respectfully, your obedient servant,

T. L. CRITTENDEN,
Major-General, U. S. Volunteers.

Col. E. Schriver,
Recorder.

No. 234.

Record of the Negley Court of Inquiry.

RECORD OF THE PROCEEDINGS OF A COURT OF INQUIRY INSTITUTED
BY THE FOLLOWING ORDER:

Special Orders, } War Dept., Adjt. General's Office,
No. 13.   }   *Washington, January 9,* 1864.

*   *   *   *   *   *   *

20. By direction of the President of the United States a Court of Inquiry is hereby appointed to meet at Nashville, Tenn., on the 15th instant, or as soon thereafter as practicable, to investigate the conduct of Maj. Gens. A. McD. McCook, T. L. Crittenden, and James S. Negley, U. S. Volunteers, at the battle of Chickamauga and in leaving the field, and also to give their opinion upon the facts which may be developed.   The Court will adjourn from place to place, as may be deemed necessary to procure the testimony of witnesses, without taking them away from their appropriate duties, and will sit without regard to hours.

Detail for the Court: Maj. Gen. David Hunter, U. S. Volunteers;

Maj. Gen. George Cadwalader, U. S. Volunteers; Brig. Gen. J. S. Wadsworth, U. S. Volunteers; Col. Edmund Schriver, inspector-general, recorder.

*   *   *   *   *   *   *

By order of the Secretary of War:

E. D. TOWNSEND,
Assistant Adjutant-General.

FIRST DAY.

NASHVILLE, *January* 29, 1864.

The Court met pursuant to the above order at 10 a. m. in the Saint Cloud Hotel.

Present, Maj. Gen. David Hunter, U. S. Volunteers; Maj. Gen. George Cadwalader, U. S. Volunteers; Brig. Gen. J. S. Wadsworth, U. S. Volunteers; Col. Edmund Schriver, inspector-general, recorder.

Maj. Gen. James S. Negley, U. S. Volunteers, whose conduct is ordered to be investigated, was also present.

The order appointing the Court was then read. Major-General Negley being asked if he objected to any of the officers named in the detail, and replying in the negative, the members and recorder were sworn in his presence.

The Court then proceeded with the investigation and directed the recorder to make the following communication to Maj. Gen. George H. Thomas:

NASHVILLE, *January* 29, 1864.

Major-General THOMAS,
    Commanding Department of the Cumberland, Chattanooga:

The Court of Inquiry instituted by Special Orders, No. 13, War Department, for the investigation of "the conduct of Major-Generals McCook, Crittenden, and Negley, U. S. Volunteers, at the battle of Chickamauga and in leaving the field," desire you to send to me at the Galt House, in Louisville, as soon as possible, certified copies of all the reports which may be in your possession bearing on the conduct of those officers on the occasion referred to, and also the best map you have of the battle-field and the surrounding country. It is most desirable to have these reports and the map sent by an officer capable of explaining to the court the position of the troops engaged. The Court wishes you also to send any officers of your command who may have knowledge of the matter to be investigated to report to the Court in Louisville, the names of whom you are desired to communicate to me. Please acknowledge this.

ED. SCHRIVER,
Inspector-General, Recorder.

On being questioned by the Court whether any papers or communications touching the matter to be investigated had been furnished, the recorder stated as follows:

Only one communication, that of General W. S. Rosecrans to the Adjutant-General of the Army, dated October 14, 1863, respecting Major-General Negley, which was read, as follows:

HEADQUARTERS DEPARTMENT OF THE CUMBERLAND,
    Chattanooga, Tenn., October 14, 1863.

Brig. Gen. LORENZO THOMAS,
    Adjutant-General, U. S. Army, Washington, D. C.:

GENERAL: Herewith I transmit a special report by Major-General Negley, with accompanying documents, explanatory of the reasons why he left his position in the field of Chickamauga on the 20th so early in the day without orders, and without being driven off, while the troops in front and to the left of their position held their ground.

The general has always been an active, energetic, and efficient commander, and displayed very good judgment in an affair at Widow Davis' house, in front of Stevens' Gap, where he was attacked by a superior force of the enemy and successfully extricated his train and command from a perilous position.   But an impression that he left the field on Sunday without orders or necessity having made its way through the army, and statements having appeared in the official reports of general officers appearing to support the impression, I gave General Negley leave to submit this special report on the subject.   From a careful perusal of that and the accompanying papers it seems that he acted according to his best judgment under the circumstances of the case.

But, satisfied that his usefulness in this army is lost, at least until these facts can be developed by a Court of Inquiry, I have given him a leave of absence for thirty days, and advised him, after this report goes in, to ask for a Court of Inquiry.

Very respectfully, your obedient servant,

W. S. ROSECRANS,
Major-General, Commanding.

That he addressed to the Adjutant-General of the Army the following communications :

LOUISVILLE, *January* 27, 1864.

The ADJUTANT-GENERAL OF THE ARMY:

GENERAL : I have the honor to acquaint you that General Hunter has arrived here, and that the officers detailed for the Court instituted by Special Orders, No. 13, to investigate the conduct of Major-Generals McCook, Crittenden, and Negley, will repair to Nashville to-morow.   At an informal meeting had, it was seen that no papers respecting the conduct of those officers have yet been furnished to the Court, and I was therefore directed to request that any reports or communications on the subject which may be on file in the War Department, as well as the names and address of any persons who are known to be acquainted with the transactions ordered to be investigated, be sent to me at this place, whither the Court will return for the purpose of receiving the testimony of General Rosecrans on 1st February.

Very respectfully, &c.,

ED. SCHRIVER,
Inspector-General, Recorder.

NASHVILLE, *January* 29, 1864.

The ADJUTANT-GENERAL OF THE ARMY:

GENERAL : In my communication of the 27th instant, written by order of the Court of Inquiry instituted by Special Orders, No. 13, of 1864, I asked for all reports on file in the War Department bearing on the conduct of Major-Generals McCook, Crittenden, and Negley at the battle of Chickamauga.   I am now directed to ask particularly for the following :

Certified copies of the official reports of the battle of Chickamauga made by Brigadier-Generals Wood, Brannan, and Davis, and Colonel Harker (Wood's division); also the supplementary report and papers appended, which Major-General Negley forwarded October 9, 1863, at the request of and through Major-General Rosecrans, the same being required by Major-General Negley in his letter of 22d January. Please send them to the Galt House, Louisville.

Very respectfully, &c.,

ED. SCHRIVER,
Inspector-General, Recorder.

The Court here desired General Negley to furnish the recorder from time to time, as far as possible, a list of the witnesses whose evidence he may wish to submit to the Court.

A recess of half an hour was taken, and subsequently an adjournment till 7 p. m. was ordered.

7 p. m.

The Court met pursuant to adjournment.

Present, Major-Generals Hunter and Cadwalader, Brigadier-General Wadsworth, and Colonel Schriver, recorder, and Major-General Negley.

Capt. THOMAS C. WILLIAMS, Nineteenth U. S. Infantry, aide-de-camp to General Rousseau, being duly sworn, says to questions

By the COURT:

Question. Please state what you know about the conduct of General Negley at the battle of Chickamauga and the position of his troops.

Answer. There was one brigade of General Negley's division, commanded by General John Beatty, which reported to General Thomas on Sunday morning, 20th September. I was ordered by General Thomas to endeavor to arrest some stragglers on Sunday morning, and had collected about 350 and formed them in line in the neighborhood of 11 o'clock. I saw General Negley with a battery of artillery; went to him, and reported I had these stragglers, by order of General Thomas, formed at the point where I had collected them. He placed the battery in position and directed me to retain the men there to support it. The battery played on the enemy for a considerable time, and was then withdrawn under orders from General Negley, and I sent the stragglers under their officers to report to their proper regiments.

Question. Do you know where the infantry regiments of General Negley's division were at that time?

Answer. General Beatty's brigade was posted on the left of General Baird's division.

Question. To whose corps did General Negley belong?

Answer. Major-General Thomas', Fourteenth Corps.

By General NEGLEY:

Question. At what hour did General Beatty's brigade report to General Thomas?

Answer. I think it was in the neighborhood of 9 o'clock Sunday morning. I cannot be positive.

Question. Was General Beatty directed to report to General Baird?

Answer. I do not know.

Question. Do you know the words of the order given by General Thomas which posted General Beatty's brigade on the left of General Baird's division?

Answer. I do not.

Question. Do you know whether General Beatty's brigade was posted on the left of General Baird's division?

Answer. I do not know that it was posted.

Question. Did you see the brigade posted on the left of General Baird's division?

Answer. General Beatty's brigade was posted in a position at a point where the left of the regular brigade of General Baird had been driven in. General Beatty's troops had been thrown across the Rossville road. Whether the right of General Beatty connected on the left of General Baird I do not know, as there was considerable confusion.

Question. Did you see Colonel Stanley with or without any portion of his brigade?

Answer. I do not remember seeing Colonel Stanley.

Question. Did you see any portion of his brigade?

Answer. Not that I remember.

Question. Will you describe, briefly, the character of that locality, and whether there were thick woods and broken ridges?

Answer. The woods were very thick; small cedars and undergrowth at that point.

Question. How far distant from where General Beatty's brigade was posted was the point where you collected the stragglers and where General Negley posted the battery of artillery?

Answer. As near as I am able to judge under the circumstances, as the contest was very fierce at that time, I should think it was about from a quarter to half a mile.

Question. Were the enemy approaching in heavy force in front of the line where the battery was posted?

Answer. They were.

Question. Were you able to see whether the opening of the battery checked the advance in that direction?

Answer. Whether it was the battery, I am unable to say. The enemy were held there, and the point occupied by the battery was held until the moment of retreat, about 5 o'clock on Sunday evening. The battery had been withdrawn, as the firing of the enemy ceased in front of that point, about 1 o'clock.

Question. Who commanded the battery General Negley posted there?

Answer. I believe it was Lieutenant Smith, of the Fourth Regular Artillery, if my memory serves me correctly.

Question. Did you see any other artillery of General Negley's command at that point or in rear of it?

Answer. There were several batteries posted on the right of that line, but under whose command they were I do not know.

Question. Was the ground broken and covered with dense woods in rear of where the battery was posted, toward Crawfish Spring?

Answer. It was.

Question. Did you see General Negley at any other portion of the day on 20th?

Answer. I do not remember seeing General Negley at any other portion of that day.

Question. Can you state at what hour the enemy broke through the right and center of the line of the main army?

Answer. I cannot state the exact hour.

Question. When the enemy drove back the troops on the right of General Thomas' position, was the movement sudden and in heavy force?

Answer. As near as I am able to judge, it was. It was driven about a mile in about three-quarters of an hour.

Question. Did you see General Wood's division, and where was it posted?

Answer. I did. The right of General Wood's division rested near the point where the battery had been posted by General Negley.

Question. How far was that position from General Rosecrans' headquarters during Saturday night?

Answer. I did not know where General Rosecrans' headquarters were on Saturday night.

Question. Was General Negley's deportment, when you saw him, cool and collected?

Answer. Perfectly so.

By the COURT :

Question. Did you see anything in the conduct of General Negley on that day objectionable in any respect either in relation to the position to which he gave his own personal attention or otherwise ?

Answer. Nothing ; on the contrary, I remember the circumstance of trying to raise the spirits of the troops as General Negley rode up, calling for three cheers, which they responded to very lustily, and his presence cheered and encouraged them, in my opinion.

The Court adjourned to meet at 11 o'clock on the 1st February, in Louisville, Ky.

SECOND DAY.

LOUISVILLE, *February* 1, 1864.

The Court met, pursuant to adjournment, in the supreme court room.

Present, Major-Generals Hunter and Cadwalader, Brigadier-General Wadsworth, and Colonel Schriver, recorder, and Major-General Negley.

The proceedings of the first day were read and approved.

The Court adjourned to meet at 10 o'clock on the 2d February.

THIRD DAY.

FEBRUARY 2, 1864.

No proceedings in this case to-day.

FOURTH DAY.

FEBRUARY 3, 1864.

The Court met pursuant to adjournment.

Present, Major-Generals Hunter and Cadwalader, Brigadier-General Wadsworth, and Colonel Schriver, recorder, and Major-General Negley.

Lieut. WILLIAM H. H. MOODY, aide-de-camp to General Negley, being duly sworn, says to questions

By the COURT:

Question. What was Major-General Negley's command on the 18th, 19th, and 20th September last, and how was it posted or disposed of?

Answer. The command originally consisted of ten regiments, all but two of which were quite small; the other two perhaps had 100 more each. At 3 o'clock on 18th I carried an order to the brigade commanders to march immediately in the following order: Second, Third, and First. At 5 p. m. we arrived at headquarters of General Hazen, commanding a brigade of General Palmer's division, whose division we were ordered to relieve. General Hazen, not having received orders to this effect, was not willing for General Negley's division to occupy his line. The division (General Negley's) was halted. General Negley started for department headquarters to investigate cause of delay. Having occasion to report to General Negley, I met our First Brigade (General Beatty in command) moving down the Culp's Mill road, preparatory to relieving Colonel Gross' brigade, of Palmer's division. At 9 a. m. I went in search of General Negley. Went down the Culp's Mill road, learned from Colonel Gross that he had not received orders to be relieved. The division at this time was lying along the road in a state of suspense, when an order was received to encamp the division in mass near Spear's house, about the center of the division as it lay at that time. At midnight an order was received to relieve General Palmer. Our Third Brigade was ordered back to relieve General Hazen, distant about 1½ miles. At this time the road was almost effectually blocked up by the troops of General Palmer, his transportation, &c., so it was very difficult to make any progress in getting to our position. Upon returning to General Negley's headquarters, about 1 a. m., I was relieved from duty until 3 a. m. At 1.30 Colonel Ducat, General Rosecrans' staff, stopped at our headquarters, and, in conversation with General Negley, made inquiries relative to the line. General Negley remarked, "Tell General Rosecrans I have great fears for the weakness of the line, it being much attenuated and the men being much harassed by continuous marching." Shortly after an aide of General Thomas came to headquarters with an order from General Thomas for General Negley to report at his headquarters. General Negley, whose health being much impaired, had retired, but on learning the exigencies of the case, prepared immediately to go there. I came on duty at 3 a. m., September 19, carried an order to Colonel Sirwell, commanding Third Brigade, then the right of our division line and the right of the whole army, as I understood it. I found that he had just gotten into position; in fact, had some dispositions yet to make. At 8 a. m. I, in connection with other staff officers, accompanied General Negley around a portion of the line. He gave instructions to Colonel Sirwell to strengthen his position by temporary works, composed of rails, &c.; he also gave orders for a road to be constructed by which artillery and re-enforcements could pass from the Second to First Brigade. At half past 8 or 9 artillery firing was heard immediately in front of our First Brigade, commanded by General Beatty. Upon learning the facts, it was ascertained the enemy had opened on General Beatty with his infantry and two batteries of artillery. General Beatty found it necessary to send for re-enforcements, which consisted of a regiment of infantry and section of artillery; all that could be spared, on account of the length of the line we were protecting. At 3 p. m. General McCook's corps had all passed our position, going to the left. A heavy cloud of dust, as if produced by cavalry, was seen in immediate front of our position. General Negley sent me with this information to General McCook, under whose command he was, and whose headquarters were at least 1 mile distant to the left. General McCook informed me that he had sent written instructions to General Negley for him to move from his position and support him. I was given, by General McCook, directions where the three brigades would be posted, and conveyed the information to General Negley. The division was immediately moved to the left, except the First Brigade, which halted to receive ammunition, having been engaged all morning. I remained back with this brigade and brought it forward to our supposed position, but other orders having been received, the division had been moved to the support of General Thomas. I found the division, when I came up with this brigade, in position to the left of General Rosecrans' headquarters (which I think was the Widow Glenn's house). I met General Negley, and with him went to General Rosecrans' headquarters, he (Negley) informing General Rosecrans that a gap existed in the line, through which the enemy were coming. General Rosecrans instructed him to close that gap and drive the enemy. His division then moved to the left of the La Fayette and Rossville road to an eminence overlooking the country occupied by the enemy, distant from this point not more [than] one-quarter mile. Two brigades were immediately ordered forward, accompanied by one half battery of artillery, the remainder of the artillery being placed in position upon this eminence, supported by our reserve brigade (First). Upon advancing we found a heavy skirmish line of the enemy, and, upon driving it, came upon a heavy force of the enemy in an open field, just beyond the woods, through which we had driven them. It was now dark. General Negley gave me orders to have the brigades halted, open communication between the right and left, fall back to the edge of the woods, and hold the position during the night of Saturday. We did not connect upon either right or left with any other troops until midnight, when our left joined the right of General Brannan's, of General Thomas' corps. I came on duty 3 a. m., September 20, went to the picket line, ascertained from the colonel commanding that, between the hours of 1 and 2, chopping and rumbling of artillery could be distinctly heard, as if troops and artillery were being moved to our right. I reported this to General Negley, was sent by him to department headquarters, reported the same to the chief of staff, was by him ordered to convey the same to General Thomas, but not knowing the location of said headquarters, I asked information, and was unable to learn from any staff officer the location or direction, until I found Capt. Hunter Brooke had sent an orderly the night before to General Thomas' headquarters. I was compelled to wait until this man could be brought, which was after daylight, before I could start for General Thomas' headquarters. I received no special instructions in return. Not being on duty for the next two hours, I cannot state what orders were received. On Sunday, September 20, before 9 o'clock, the command consisted of the same as that of the day previous, ten regiments, three full batteries. At 8 o'clock I was sent to General McCook with this message from General Negley: "Troops having been withdrawn from the left, my reserve having been ordered away and the enemy reported massing heavily on my front, I am left with a very slender line, and ask re-enforcements." General Rosecrans, standing near General McCook when I delivered this message, asked me to repeat it. After doing so, he ordered me to go to General Crittenden and tell him to make General Negley's line strong and good. General Rosecrans also asked : "Has General Wood reported to General Negley?" or words to that effect. I answered, "I know nothing of General Wood." I conveyed the order to General Crittenden about 8.30 or 8.45 a. m., found Generals Crittenden and Wood in conversation and received from General Crittenden the remark that he understood my order. Upon returning to General Negley's headquarters at 9 a. m., I saw the brigade of Colonel Buell, of General Wood's division, moving up upon the ridge which we occupied with our artillery with his skirmishers deployed, moving in a leisurely manner, although then one-quarter to one-half mile in rear of our line. General Negley sent me with instructions to the Third Brigade that General Wood would relieve our division, and that as soon as relieved, the brigade was to move in close column closed *en masse* to the left by a road running parallel with his line of battle. I remained at the headquarters of the division for one hour, as also the remainder of the staff, during this time. General Negley conducted the movements of the division in person. Ten a. m. the staff received an order to report immediately to the general at the Brannan Hospital, on the La Fayette and Rossville road. At this time the fire of the enemy was terrific upon our left, and soon commenced on our immediate front. Gun-carriages, ambulances, and other *débris* of battle came rushing past our position from our left and front. General Negley now ordered our Second Brigade to the left. Our First Brigade had been ordered off as early as 8.30 o'clock to the left (General Thomas' support) ; our Third Brigade had not yet been relieved. General Negley gave me an order to conduct the artillery across the open field to our left, to a point where it would be effective. Upon attempting to report to General Negley, then in our front, I met Major Lowrie, assistant adjutant-general of division, who gave me an order to conduct the Third Brigade after the artillery to a ridge upon the left of the field. The brigade was moved to the left at double-quick. I learned that General Negley had received an order through Captain Gaw, engineer of General Thomas' staff, to take command of a number of batteries, or portion of batteries, then collected on this ridge. This movement of the two batteries to this position and the brigade was preparatory to General Negley's taking command of this artillery. He immediately placed his batteries in position ; the brigade consisted of three regiments and four companies of another, the remaining six of this regiment having been detailed to guard our division train. The firing upon our front and right was continuous and terrific ; stragglers were flocking past our position in great numbers from the command immediately in our front (General Brannan's) and upon our right. The enemy were driving our troops in the front. Bridges' battery of our First Brigade, which was in the front and in rear of General Brannan, lost two guns by capture and 1 lieutenant killed. Two pieces of the battery came back to our position on the ridge near General Negley's headquarters, and were by him placed in position ready for action. One section of Fourth Artillery, commanded by a lieutenant, was also placed in position upon the right of Bridges'; Schultz's battery of our Second Brigade was placed in position on the brow of the hill still farther to the right. The enemy having driven our forces upon the right and front, and could be seen pressing forward, the batteries were opened upon them. There were sixteen effective pieces of artillery, besides fragments of six batteries, not effective, because of want of men and *matériel;* heavy firing upon our left, stragglers coming back in greatest confusion. An officer reported (I don't know who) that the enemy were throwing heavy masses upon the left. At the same time, with glasses, the enemy could be seen crowding through a corn-field to the left oblique from our position in heavy columns, as we judged from the dust and glasses. This was between 11 and 12 o'clock. General Negley immediately put his brigade, which had been acting as support heretofore (Colonel Sirwell's), around the left base of the ridge. They immediately strengthened their position with rail breastworks. The batteries were at the time playing on the enemy in front and diagonally to the right. The number of stragglers or disorganized troops passing our position, and the confusion existing among our ammunition wagons, and the continuous roar of the artillery and musketry, indicated that the right and center were being driven. General Negley, seeing his position, and the exposed condition of his artillery, dispatched Captain Hough and myself to General Rosecrans to explain his position and ask re-enforcements. We took different routes. I was compelled by the presence of the enemy to make a circuit in rear of the ridges, supposing that General Rosecrans was on the right. When about one-half mile from our position I came upon the ridge facing the enemy. Upon the top of the ridge I met General Rosecrans' staff and escort, endeavoring to stop the stragglers, who were coming back in great confusion and in great numbers. I saw General Rosecrans, as near as I can judge, at noon on Sunday, immediately in front about 500 yards, alone. The yell of the enemy could be heard to the right and front and very close. I reported to General Rosecrans, and with him rode a short distance to the rear, at the same time delivering my message. His answer was: "It is too late; I cannot help him." I immediately attempted to return, but finding the enemy in possession of the route, was compelled to make a *détour* and struck the Chattanooga road and came round in rear of the ridges; rode forward with all haste to General Negley's position. I found his staff engaged, as also his escort, in stopping stragglers and collecting them. Meeting Captain Hough, I inquired if the general still occupied the same position, and was much surprised to learn that he did. Upon reporting to the general, I found him, accompanied by an orderly, to the left of the ridge upon a wooded knoll, directing the fire of a battery of Parrott guns, which was then playing upon the enemy to our right. I gave him General Rosecrans' answer. Finding the enemy pressing forward, and their infantry firing upon our position, General Negley withdrew the Third Brigade from the base of the hill, a regiment of which had previously been sent to the assistance of General Brannan; placed it in position in line of battle facing to the right. Also placed Marshall's battery in position to resist the onset of the enemy. General Negley was joined on the left, on the top of the ridge, by a regiment of stragglers that had been collected; the enemy having trained a battery up one of the gorges leading to the top of the ridge, threw some shells, which burst immediately over this regiment, and they vanished. Several staff officers now reported to General Negley, having been cut off from their generals. One officer (Lieutenant Elkin, of General Baird's staff) said to General Negley: "Colonel Parkhurst, with his provost guard of Fourteenth Army Corps, is stationed at the Chattanooga road, stopping the disorganized troops, and forming a new line." General Negley remarked, "To save the army from rout, a new line would have to be formed." The army having given way on the right, our right and left being threatened, endangering the artillery, General Negley gave the command to retire. This was about 3 p. m., as well as I can judge. Captain Schultz's battery was all this time playing on the enemy and exhausted the ammunition in their limbers. He was withdrawn and barely escaped capture. The artillery was moved off with the Third Brigade as a rear guard. I was directed to turn back some caissons that had started down the Dry Valley road and direct them to the Chattanooga road, where a new line would be formed. Upon reaching the road, I found it full of troops, and the battle-flags were those of Twentieth Corps (General McCook's). The road lay between the hills, and was nothing more than a gorge, and it was with great difficulty that a horseman could proceed. About 1½ or 2 miles from our last position I came into an open field, in which were collected a great number of troops, mostly from Twentieth Corps, judging from battle-flags. I met General Negley engaged in putting troops in position, assisted by General Davis, of General McCook's corps. Shortly after General Sheridan (Twentieth Corps) appeared with his command to all appearances intact. This was about 4 to 4.30 o'clock. After consultation, General Negley started back to report in person to General Thomas, the staff reporting to General Davis, to assist in placing troops in position. General Negley, not having been able to join General Thomas since the enemy's cavalry intervened, returned and took command, ordering the artillery and infantry to proceed to Rossville, at which point we arrived about sundown. Troops were put into position, General Sheridan marched by the La Fayette and Rossville road to General Thomas, General Negley placing a guard across the road leading to Chattanooga, stopping all stragglers, and placing them in position by detachments, at the same time ordering me to Chattanooga to obtain provisions for the troops there assembled, which was accomplished by 2 a. m. on 21st, General Negley in the meantime having received orders from General Rosecrans to hold his position, send disorganized troops to Chattanooga, and hold the gaps at all hazards.

By the COURT :

Question. By whose order was General Negley placed under the orders of General McCook ?

Answer. General Rosecrans'; 10.15 a. m. on 19th.

Question. Where did General Negley subsequently go and what did he do ?

Answer. General Negley did not leave Rossville till Monday night, having remained there under orders from General Rosecrans.

Question. Did General Negley receive any other order in the meantime ?

Answer. He received orders from General Thomas, which came on Monday. I left Rossville at 7 on Saturday and returned at 2 next morning.

By General NEGLEY :

Question. When you returned from General Rosecrans, was or was not the enemy then pressing to the rear and close to the right of the position occupied by General Negley's artillery ?

Answer. He was, as I was compelled to make a *détour* to avoid the fire on returning from General Rosecrans' headquarters.

Question. Was or was not Schultz's battery left in its exposed position, firing canister upon the enemy, to hold him in check until the other scattered artillery and troops could be retired or organized ?

Answer. It was.

Question. Did or did not General Negley dispose of his artillery and what infantry he had so as to check the enemy on Sunday morning as they advanced on the line, either to his right or left ?

Answer. He did ; he changed position as necessity required.

Question. When you returned on Sunday at noon from General Rosecrans with his reply to General Negley, did or did not the movements of the enemy, as you then saw them, threaten the immediate capture of General Negley's command, and did not General Negley hold his position as long as prudent?

Answer. The enemy did assume this threatening position, and, in my opinion, he held it as long as prudent.

Question. When General Negley started back to report to General Thomas, was or was he not informed then for the first time that General Thomas was still holding his ground?

Answer. Yes.

Question. What was the military deportment of General Negley during the battle of Chickamauga?

Answer. Cool, deliberate, and comprehensive.

The Court adjourned to meet at 10 o'clock on the 4th instant.

FIFTH DAY.

LOUISVILLE, *February* 4, 1864.

No proceedings in this case to-day.

SIXTH DAY.

LOUISVILLE, *February* 5, 1864.

The Court met pursuant to adjournment.

Present, Major-Generals Hunter and Cadwalader, Brigadier-General Wadsworth, and Colonel Schriver, recorder, and General Negley, U. S. Volunteers.

Maj. Gen. W. S. ROSECRANS, U. S. Volunteers, being duly sworn, says to questions

By the COURT:

Question. Please state what the command of Major-General Negley consisted of on the 20th September, and how it was posted.

Answer. It consisted of three brigades and three batteries. Two of these brigades were in line of battle, into which they had fought themselves the previous evening, closing the fight after dark. The Third Brigade was in reserve. I may add he held this position until relieved by Wood's division. He sent his reserve brigade, upon my verbal orders given to him in person, in advance of his other two which were not relieved until one and a half hours at least after orders for it had been given. When these were relieved I saw the column passing through the field in rear of Reynolds' position toward the left. General Negley was ordered to report his command to General Thomas. I saw nothing more of him. It was as late as 10 o'clock when I met his column just spoken of in the fields in rear of Brannan's division.

Question. What position did General Negley's troops occupy after he was relieved by General Wood?

Answer. I only know from the official reports that the reserve brigade spoken of went to the extreme left and fought with Baird; that Sirwell's brigade was on a wooded eminence in rear of Brannan's division, from which a part of it retired taking care of some artillery, probably about 2 o'clock—1 and 2 o'clock. I do not remember where Stanley's brigade was from the official reports.

Question. What was the conduct of Major-General Negley on the 19th and 20th September, so far as you had an opportunity of observing it?

Answer. On the 19th General Negley behaved as a division commander should while covering the line of the Chickamauga above Crawfish Spring; arrived in obedience to orders at the Widow Glenn's about 4.30 p. m. on 19th; carried his division into action, driving back the rebels from a gap, through which they had followed Van Cleve's troops, very handsomely. On 20th a. m. I found him as vigilant as any other division commander, and thought his behavior very good, except that when he was about to withdraw his troops from before the line I spoke a little sharply, that he should think of doing it before he was relieved. He sent me word from Rossville late in p. m., where he appeared to have been very active in organizing the stragglers; but I knew nothing further than what appeared from these reports of himself and staff officers who saw him there.

By General NEGLEY:

Question. Was or was not the following order issued by your direction?

HEADQUARTERS DEPARTMENT OF THE CUMBERLAND,
McDonald's House, September 20, 1863—6.30 a. m.
Major-General NEGLEY,
Commanding Second Division, Fourteenth Army Corps:

The general commanding directs you to report with your command to General Thomas at once. You are to be posted on his extreme left. Send a staff officer to show General McCook your present position, who is directed to occupy it. Move with dispatch, gathering all your stragglers.

Very respectfully, your obedient servant,

J. A. GARFIELD,
Brigadier-General, and Chief of Staff.

Answer. I have no doubt this order was sent, as I directed General Garfield, after having given the orders to General McCook to relieve General Negley, as a precaution to notify General Negley of the fact to whom General Thomas was about to dispatch an order in pursuance of the determination we had come to of having him as a reserve to support the left.

Question. Do you or do you not recollect receiving information from staff officers from Generals Thomas and Negley several hours after issuing the order for General Wood to relieve General Negley that he (General Negley) had not been relieved?

Answer. I remember distinctly the delay in relieving him, and that it was a matter of the utmost solicitude, and that it excited my surprise, and, I may add, something stronger, to find the relief had been so long delayed, when I met General Negley's two last brigades in the field.

Question. Was or was not the failure of General Wood to relieve General Negley on the morning of the 20th, as ordered, the reason for separating General Negley's division to send support to General Thomas on the left?

Answer. General McCook was to have relieved him, and on my return from the left, when I found he had not done so, I sent word to General Crittenden that such was the fact, and that, promptitude being necessary, he would form his troops, which were nearer, immediately relieve General Negley, and directed General Negley, as the case was urgent, to send his reserve brigade immediately, and to follow it with the other brigades as soon as relieved. The aide whom I sent to General Crittenden met General Wood and gave him the order at once, pointing out to him Major Lowrie, assistant adjutant-general of General Negley's division, and telling him, he (Major Lowrie) would show him where the brigades were which he was to relieve. This must have been as early as 8 a. m.

Question. Did or did not General Wood at the most critical period of the battle on the 20th, and when the enemy confronted his line in force, misinterpret an order, and with great precipitation leave his position, and thus opened the line for the enemy to advance through in unbroken columns and overwhelm the right and center of the army?

Answer. General Wood did leave his place in line of battle, misinterpreting an order, the evident intention of which was to have an opening in the line closed and carry his division in the rear of one on his left, and the enemy did take advantage of that opening and came through it, knocking off at once the left of Davis' division, which was moving to close in, and the right of Brannan's, which was slightly refused, and this position never was recovered, but was the cause of the severance of six or seven brigades on our right from the rest of the army.

Question. When General Negley sent Captain Hough and Lieutenant Moody to you for support on the 20th at noon, was it possible for you to send General Negley any re-enforcements?

Answer. It was not practicable.

Question. After General Negley reported to you from Rossville, on the evening of the 20th, did or did not General Negley use great diligence, prudence, and forethought in organizing the scattered troops, providing them with provisions and ammunition, and making preparations to hold Rossville?

Answer. I have answered that substantially in my direct examination.

Question. Did you or did you not send the following dispatch from Chattanooga to Major-General Negley at Rossville?

SEPTEMBER 20—7 p. m.
(By telegraph from Chattanooga.)

General NEGLEY:

Dry Valley road ought to be covered until it is so that enemy cannot come down if we wish to retire, or the troops are of sufficient vigor and elasticity to go up and attack their right. Every available man should be mustered.

W. S. ROSECRANS,
Major-General.

Answer. A dispatch to that effect was sent; the original telegram before me is the same as given in the question.

Question. Did or did not the re-organization of the scattered forces at Rossville, providing them with food and ammunition, on the evening and night of the 20th, by General Negley, contribute largely toward the successful resistance made against the enemy's advance on Monday and the subsequent safe withdrawal of the army to Chattanooga?

Answer. I have no doubt that it was of great use.

Question. Did or did not General Wood frequently visit your headquarters and criticise the official conduct at the battle of Chickamauga of officers who were his seniors in rank in terms forbidden by the rules of the service ?

Answer. I remember to have heard him speak in very severe terms of General Negley's conduct, but it would not be proper to say that the manner was such as to deserve to be taken official notice of, inasmuch as the conversation was brought on by some one questioning the current reports which he afterward made himself responsible for in his official report. It is not improbable that this may have occurred more than once, but I have no distinct recollection of its having occurred except as I have stated.

Question. Did or did not General Wood, when at your headquarters immediately after the battle of Chickamauga, exhibit great bitterness and prejudice toward General Negley, and did he not threaten to publish matters in his official report which would damage General Negley's reputation?

Answer. He did on the occasion alluded to, and possibly more than once, use very bitter language, and declare that he would put it in his official report, and that any one could tell General Negley he was responsible for it.

General NEGLEY to the Court. I would respectfully inform the Court that General Wood has alluded to my official conduct at the battle of Chickamauga in unfavorable terms. As General Wood was my junior in rank, was not dependent upon me for orders or assistance, and belonged with his division to another corps, the real motive for this gratuitous imputation is, I respectfully suggest, a proper and necessary question for the Court to determine.

Question. Did or did you not address a letter to Adjutant-General Thomas in reference to General Wood's conduct at the battle of Chickamauga and his unofficial explanation of the same. If so, what was the purport of your letter ?

Answer. I did address a letter to the Adjutant-General of the Army, dated January 12 [13*], 1864, in reference to a letter which General Wood had written and sent directly to the headquarters of the Army, commenting on the paragraph in my report which refers to his leaving his position, a copy of which letter I can have handed, and which will express, better than I can from memory, the purport thereof.

(The Court here asked that the letter be furnished.)

CINCINNATI, *January* 12 [13], 1864.

Brig. Gen. LORENZO THOMAS,
    Adjutant-General, Washington, D. C.:

GENERAL : The report of the General-in-Chief shows that a letter from one of my division commanders at the battle of Chickamauga, commenting on the report of his commanding general has been received at the War Department, and subsequently published by its authority.

The General-in-Chief refers to that letter as a rival authority to my own, and as raising doubts upon the accuracy of a part of my report.

The letter dated October 23 [21] ultimo, four days after I left the command, is based on a quotation from my official report, to which evidently the writer was not at that time entitled, and which therefore, *prima facie*, was surreptitiously obtained.

It has been received and publicly used as a document disparaging my report, without having been referred to me or passing through my hands, as required by military courtesy and Army Regulations.

The War Department is therefore respectfully requested, as an act of justice, to cause the above and following observations to be filed and published as an appendix to my official report of the battle of Chickamauga.

(Note in reference to Brig. Gen. Thomas J. Wood's letter, dated October 23, 1863.)

*See p. 102.

Brig. Gen. Thomas J. Wood writes and sends to the War Department a clandestine letter to show, contrary to the inference drawn in my report, that he did right, under an order "to close up on General Reynolds as fast as possible and support him," in taking his division out of the line of battle in the rear of Brannan's division to a reserve position in rear of Reynolds.

My report, dealing with facts and avoiding personal censure, shows that General Reynolds sent me word by Captain Kellogg, aide-de-camp to General Thomas, that there were no troops on his immediate right, and that he wanted support there. That, supposing Brannan's division had been called away, I told an aide to write General Wood "to close up on Reynolds as fast as possible and support him." He wrote as follows:

"Brig. Gen. T. J. WOOD,
　　"*Commanding Division, &c.*:

"The general commanding directs that you close up on Reynolds as fast as possible and support him.
　　"Respectfully, &c.,
　　　　　　　　　　　　　　　　　　"FRANK S. BOND,
　　　　　　　　　　　　　　　　　　"*Major and Aide-de-Camp.*

Now, with this order in his hand:
First. When General Wood found there was no interval to close, because Brannan's troops had not left, his plain duty as a division commander was to have reported that fact to the commanding general, who was not more than 600 yards from him, and to ask for further orders. His failure to do so was a grave military mistake, showing want of military discretion.

Second. When about to move, notwithstanding this his duty, on being informed, as he was by one of his brigade commanders, that his skirmishers were engaged and the enemy in line of battle opposite his position, General Wood was renewedly bound to have reported the facts and taken orders before leaving his position at such a critical time. But instead of doing so, he precipitately withdrew his troops from the line and let the enemy through, in the face of an order, the wording of which shows that no such operation as the opening, but, on the contrary, the closing of a gap was intended.

Third. This conduct of General Wood, treated in my report with all the reserve consistent with the truth of history, contrasts most unfavorably with that of General Brannan, commanding the division next on his left, who, a little earlier in the day, when he received an order to leave his position and support the left, finding his skirmishers engaged, reported the fact to General Thomas, desiring to know if, under such circumstances, he should execute the order. He was told, "No, stay where you are."

Fourth. It also contrasts with General Wood's own conduct and correspondence only a few days previously, when he protested against a reprimand of his corps commander for not occupying a position at Wauhatchie, lecturing his senior on the impropriety of what he termed "blind obedience to orders," and in upwards of 50 pages of manuscript trying to prove his conduct consistent with that sound discretion which a division commander ought to exercise in removing his troops from the danger threatened by the too literal execution of orders. The material difference of circumstances in the two cases, as appears from his own writings, being that the "discretion" he exercises at Wauhatchie and the "blind obedience" he pleads at Chickamauga, both have the effect of getting his troops out of danger.

As the best of generals are liable to mistakes, I should have been content to leave those of General Wood to the simple, historical statement of them, presuming he regretted them far more deeply than even myself, and, so feeling, I called attention to his military virtues, vigilance, discipline, providence of his commissariat, and care of his transportation, but his mean and unsoldierly defense of error shows him wrong both in head and heart.

Respectfully, your obedient servant,
　　　　　　　　　　　　　　　　　W. S. ROSECRANS,
　　　　　　　　　　　　　　　　　　Major-General.

Question. Was not one regiment belonging to one of General Negley's brigades (the Sixty-ninth Ohio Volunteer Infantry) at Chattanooga guarding a train on the 20th?

Answer. I do not know.

Capt. J. P. Drouillard, additional aide-de-camp on General Rosecrans' staff, duly sworn, says to questions

By General Negley :

Question. State, if you please, whether or not you visited the position occupied by General Negley's command on Saturday morning, the 19th, near Crawfish Spring, and whether there was not so much confusion among the troops moving to the left and the roads so obstructed by trains and artillery that it was impossible for General Negley to get his command into position until daylight.

Answer. I did visit his position. I found the road full of troops moving to the left, a narrow road, and was blocked up with infantry, artillery, and ammunition wagons. This was some time after midnight—I think about 2 o'clock—and it was quite daylight before it was practicable for him to move.

Question. Did or did you not send the following dispatch to General Negley, by directions of General Rosecrans ?

September, 1863.
(By telegraph from Chattanooga.)

To Commanding Officer :

The general commanding ᴠesires you to report to him by telegraph all the reliable information you receive.

J. P. DROUILLARD,
Captain, Aide-de-Camp.

Answer. I remember sending this telegram to General Negley, at Rossville, on Sunday night, 20th, from Chattanooga.

Question. Did or did you not send the following dispatch to General Negley, by directions of General Rosecrans ?

September, 1863.
(By telegraph from Chattanooga, 9.15.)

Major-General Negley :

The general commanding directs that all the spare artillery which cannot be used to advantage be sent to this place at once.

J. P. DROUILLARD,
Captain, Aide-de-Camp.

Answer. I did send this telegram on Sunday night from Chattanooga, by direction of the general commanding.

Question. Did or did you not hear Brigadier-General Wood, at department headquarters, criticise the official conduct of Major-General Negley at the battle of Chickamauga in language disrespectful and contrary to the rules of the service ? Can you repeat his remarks ?

Answer. I did hear General Wood speak of General Negley's conduct in very violent and threatening terms, saying that he was a damned poltroon ; exactly in what connection this remark was made I do not know.

Capt. R. S. Thoms, aide-de-camp to General Rosecrans, duly sworn, says to questions

By General Negley :

Question. Did or did you not convey an order from General Rosecrans, early on the morning of the 20th, for General Wood to relieve General Negley ?

Answer. Yes ; I was directed by General Rosecrans to order General Crittenden to relieve General Negley by Wood's division. I found General Wood's division marching into the position which General Negley's reserve brigade had occupied.

General Wood was not with them when I first arrived at the division. I told Colonel Harker, who commanded a brigade, that the division was to relieve Negley's, and asked him where Crittenden or Wood was. He told me the direction Wood was. I went to him and gave him the order, and told him I would tell General Crittenden what I had done. The next time I was sent to Wood directly to tell him to relieve Negley at once. He said he did not know the exact position of Negley's troops. I pointed out Major Lowrie and told him he was an officer of Negley's staff, who could show him where they were. I told him I had just passed Captain Johnson on the hill, another staff officer of General Negley's, who could also point out the position of Negley. He sent an aide after each officer.

Question. Did or did you not return to General Wood sometime after giving the order to relieve General Negley to hasten his execution of the order?

Answer. I have answered this question already. I have said that I went twice.

Question. Was or was not General Wood's delay in executing the order to relieve General Negley the reason for detaching a portion of General Negley's command, and did not General Negley send one of his brigades to General Thomas' support during the interval which occurred between the hours you carried orders to General Wood to relieve General Negley?

Answer. General Negley's reserve brigade was sent at once on the order being issued. The other two brigades were not sent till relieved.

Maj. F. S. BOND, aide-de-camp to General Rosecrans, being duly sworn, says to questions

By General NEGLEY :

Question. Did you send General Negley the following dispatch :

SEPTEMBER 20, 1863.
(By telegraph from Chattanooga, 11.10 p. m.)

Major-General NEGLEY :

The general commanding directs that you make the necessary dispositions to hold the gap, sending in all stragglers, wounded, and sick men. Keep your command clear and free from everything that will impair its fighting condition, sending everything to the rear to-night.

FRANK S. BOND,
Major, Aide-de-Camp.

Answer. I have no doubt that I did.

The Court adjourned to meet at 10 o'clock on 6th February.

SEVENTH DAY.

LOUISVILLE, *February* 6, 1864.

The Court met pursuant to adjournment.

Present, Major-Generals Hunter and Cadwalader, Brigadier-General Wadsworth, and Colonel Schriver, recorder, and Major-General Negley.

Brig. Gen. T. J. WOOD, U. S. Volunteers, being duly sworn, says to questions

By the COURT :

Question. Can you state any material facts bearing upon the conduct of General Negley on the 19th and 20th September last, at the battle of Chickamauga?

Answer. I did not see General Negley, or any part of his command, on the 19th September, and therefore can make no statement about his conduct on that day. In moving my division to close upon and support General Reynolds on 20th, I saw some troops on one of the spurs of Mission Ridge, some distance in rear of the line of battle; they seemed to be nearly in rear of the center of it; the body appeared to me to be about a brigade; this is a matter of opinion. I was at the time trying to find General Reynolds and learn from him how I should bring my division into action to support him. In my inquiries for this purpose, I was informed that the troops which I saw on the spur, as I said above, were part of General Negley's command. I met General Thomas before finding General Reynolds, and communicated to him the order I had received from General Rosecrans. He replied to me General Reynolds did not need support, but if I had anything to spare to send it to General Baird's support on the extreme left. I showed him the order from General Rosecrans, and asked him if he would take the responsibility of changing it. He replied he would, and I asked him for a staff officer to conduct me to General Baird's assistance. I immediately dispatched one brigade with this staff officer, who was to conduct it to General Baird. This was the nearest brigade to where I met General Thomas. I then went to where the other two brigades were, intending to conduct them myself. When I reached their position I found they had already been attacked. I immediately changed the position of the brigades so as to form a crotchet with the original line of battle, facing my troops toward the south. The enemy advanced in very heavy force and we soon became very severely engaged. This I should think was perhaps 12 m.; may be a few minutes before. As it was very evident the enemy's force was very superior to the two brigades then with me, I looked to the rear of my then position and toward the position of the troops, as already described, with a view of obtaining their assistance in repelling this serious attack, as it was evident that the object of the attack was to get in rear of our main line of battle. I could not see any troops there, and they appeared to have been withdrawn. The position I was then in was an open one in the valley, and not at all favorable for a small force to repel the attack of a larger one. For the purpose of securing stronger ground I retired my command to the spur which I have already described as having been occupied as above. When I reached that position I found no troops there.

(The following was here ordered to be put on the record :)

General NEGLEY to the Court. The Court having, in accordance with the spirit of their orders, determined to exclude irrelevant testimony, I respectfully object to the admission upon the record of all statements made by the witness upon hearsay or other than what he knows from personal observation.

The Court directed the witness to confine himself strictly to the question and what he knows of his own personal knowledge.

Question. Who told you that the troops on a spur of the mountain were General Negley's?

Answer. I was so informed by a staff officer to whom I put the question, but do not know his name. He appeared to have come from the direction of the troops.

Question. Was that point at any time occupied by the enemy?

Answer. No.

F. H. GROSS, surgeon, U. S. Volunteers, medical director of Fourteenth Army Corps, duly sworn, says to questions

By General NEGLEY :

Question. Did or did you not at the field headquarters of General Thomas on the morning of the 20th hear General Thomas send orders to General Negley? If so, what were the orders and reply?

Answer. I did, on the morning of the 20th, at the field headquarters of General Thomas, hear him give orders repeatedly to staff officers to go to General Negley and direct that he be brought over to the left. I remember that Captain Willard, aide-de-camp to General Thomas, returning to General Thomas and stating : "General Negley has not been relieved, sir." General Thomas again sent one of his staff officers to General Rosecrans, I do not remember which one, to inform him that he was very anxious to have General Negley posted on his left. I think this was at or before 8 a. m.

Question. Did or did you not subsequently see a portion of General Negley's command, in addition to the First Brigade (Beatty's), marching to General Thomas' assistance?

Answer. I did some time subsequently to the above orders and reports, in going a short distance to the rear to General Thomas' headquarters, see Colonel Stoughton, Eleventh Michigan (of Stanley's brigade, Negley's division), moving with some troops. I recognized them to be Negley's troops from the fact of hearing Colonel Stoughton giving them orders. They were moving, as it appeared, toward the left. I do not know how far they went, as I very soon went toward the right of the line. I was in company at the time of Captain Gaw, topographical engineer, of General Thomas' staff. I remarked to him, "Here are some of Negley's troops now."

Question. Did or did you not see General Negley at any time during the afternoon of the 20th; and if so, what was General Negley's conduct at that time?

Answer. I remember seeing him p. m. of 20th; the exact locality I am unable to give, but think it was in rear of the line. He appeared to be actively engaged in reorganizing a mass of scattered troops. I do not remember seeing him again until the evening at Rossville, after dark, when the troops were withdrawing.

Question. Did or did you not hear Captain Gaw mention having conveyed instructions to General Negley concerning the posting of the artillery?

Answer. I remember hearing Captain Gaw state, in a conversation at Chattanooga, that he had conveyed an order to General Negley during the battle of Chickamauga in relation to the posting of artillery.

Question. Was or was not General Negley's health previous and during the battle in a very critical condition, and would he not have been honorably justifiable in asking to be relieved from duty?

Answer. General Negley was quite ill during our stay at McLemore's Cove, and up to the time we left, which was on the 17th or 18th September. He sent for me to see him professionally. He was under the professional treatment of myself and the medical director of his division. After the battle of Chickamauga, and after our arrival at Chattanooga, I learned his illness had continued and had become more aggravated. He sent for me in great haste at Chattanooga. I found him affected with inflammation of the bowels. I recommended him to retire from camp life as soon as he should be able to travel. A surgeon's certificate of disability was approved at my office a day or two subsequently, on which to base an application for a leave of absence.

The Court adjourned to meet on the 8th instant at 10 o'clock.

EIGHTH DAY.

FEBRUARY 8, 1864.

The Court met pursuant to adjournment.
Present, Major-Generals Hunter and Cadwalader; Brigadier-General Wadsworth, and Colonel Schriver, recorder, and Major-General Negley.

Col. J. P. SANDERSON, Thirteenth U. S. Infantry, being duly sworn, says to questions

By the COURT:

Question. Were you at the battle of Chickamauga, and do you know any material facts which bear on the conduct of General Negley on the 19th and 20th September?

Answer. I was, but I have no personal knowledge of his conduct which bears on this inquiry.

By General NEGLEY:

Question. When you were engaged in examining the official reports of the battle of Chickamauga at General Rosecrans' headquarters, did you or did you not hear General Wood express bitter feelings toward General Negley, and exhibit much anxiety to influence the opinion of General Rosecrans unfavorable toward General Negley?

Answer. I heard General Wood repeatedly give accounts of what he regarded the short-comings of General Negley. What his motives were, of course, I could not testify to. He exhibited a good deal of feeling and indignation, and the conversation impressed me with the conviction of his desire to have General Negley called to account.

There being no further witnesses in attendance, the Court adjourned to meet at 10 o'clock on 9th instant.

NINTH DAY.

FEBRUARY 9, 1864.

The Court met pursuant to adjournment.

Present, Major-Generals Hunter and Cadwalader, Brigadier-General Wadsworth, and Colonel Schriver, recorder, and Major-General Negley.

JOSEPH C. HILL, late captain of Fifth Kentucky Cavalry, being duly sworn, says to questions

By General NEGLEY:

Question. When the line was broken on the 20th, did or did you not make several unsuccessful attempts to reach General Thomas? If so, state briefly where you went, and what you know from personal observation about the conduct of General Negley?

Answer. I did make two unsuccessful attempts to reach General Thomas. The last time I did so was in connection with General Negley, from McFarland's house, I think about 2 p. m., meeting the enemy not more than 500 yards from that point. Returning from my first unsuccessful attempt, I struck the Dry Valley road, which was completely choked up by the *débris* of battle, wagons, &c., and in absence of any other orders, deemed it my duty to see what the trouble was, why it did not move on, &c. I went along the road for 2 or 3 miles; at any rate to the McFarland house, the first point along the Dry Valley road from the battle-field to that point, where a successful defense of the train might be made, and, in connection with four others of General Rosecrans' staff, commenced rallying the troops there. We had succeeded in rallying 1,500 or 2,000 men. General Davis had taken command when General Negley came through a gorge on the Dry Valley road, and asked why the train did not move on. I answered him that we were straightening it out then. General Negley made some remark that it was all right, or satisfactory. He said he had a few troops just in rear who would come up and assist us, and as soon as the train had moved by that point, General Negley ordered his troops into position there. General Davis being in command before General Negley came up. General Negley said, "I will report to General Thomas, inform him of the position here, and tell him that we can assist him." I then accompanied General Negley in his unsuccessful attempt to reach General Thomas' headquarters. After we had returned to McFarland's house, at about 3.30 or 4 p. m., General Negley took command of the force there and tried to organize it. Directly after, fifteen minutes after, perhaps, General Sheridan came to that point, at the head of some 2,500 men, whom he said he had rallied, I think. The only organized regiments there, were two of General Negley's and one of General Sheridan's. General Negley then proposed, with an augmented force, to cut our way through to General Thomas. At the same time General Sheridan wished to move back to Rossville and form the command there. General Negley proposed a consultation, at which I was present, and it was there determined to divide the command, part moving to Rossville and so on to General Thomas' left, the other part to move back by the Dry Valley road to General Thomas' right. This plan had been matured when the first information was received through Colonel Thruston, of General McCook's staff, that General Thomas had stood his ground. The plan was not materially changed, but they determined to organize more fully. I was then ordered to Rossville to report to General Rosecrans, who was supposed to be there. We there learned he had gone to Chattanooga, and I dispatched word to General Negley to that effect.   At the same time I sent him a dispatch that I intercepted from Colonel Minty to General Rosecrans, stating that Forrest was in force on General Thomas' left and rear, on the road from Rossville to Ringgold.   I rode to Chattanooga, and when I reported this fact to General Rosecrans, he said: "All right; could not be better."

Question. From your knowledge of the broken, rugged, and densely-wooded character of the ground which skirted Dry Valley road, was it practicable to form a judicious line of battle or organize the scattered troops between the battle-field and McFarland's house?

Answer. I know it was not, as I was looking myself for a place to defend the train.

Question. Do you or not believe that the assembling and organization of the troops at McFarland's house intimidated the enemy from a further advance on the Dry Valley road toward Rossville, and thereby saved the artillery and trains which choked up the road?

Answer. I do, and know from the fact of having encountered the enemy not more than 500 yards from McFarland's.   By getting on the hills which overhang the valley, the enemy could see the large body of troops there.   We had between 8,000 and 12,000 troops there; I think 10,000, and six or eight pieces of artillery in position covering the Dry Valley road.

Question. Was or was it not possible to provide the troops with water and provisions nearer to the battle-field than Rossville, and were not the troops suffering for both of these necessaries, and greatly exhausted?

Answer. It was not.   The troops were suffering for the want of them, and pretty well worn out from two days' fighting.

Question. What was General Negley's deportment during the time you were with him on 20th?

Answer. He was perfectly cool, and comprehended the extent of the disaster, and did all in his power to meet it and counteract it.   When that council was called he rode into the yard, gave up his horse to the orderly, and treated the matter of personal danger in the most indifferent manner, and I saw nothing in all my intercourse with him during the day which would lead any one to doubt his coolness or courage.

By the COURT:

Question. Were you in the United States service on the 19th and 20th September, and what duty were you performing during the events you have related?

Answer. I was; and was at General Rosecrans' headquarters, in obedience to an order received from him, and during the 19th and 20th was acting as a member of his staff, not by any particular order, but was sent with dispatches and orders by him.

The Court was cleared.

The Court was opened, and adjourned to meet at 10 o'clock on 10th instant.

TENTH DAY.

FEBRUARY 10, 1864.

The Court met pursuant to adjournment.

Present, Major-Generals Hunter and Cadwalader, Brigadier-General Wadsworth, and Colonel Schriver, recorder, and Major-General Negley.

Capt. Joseph C. Hill, (late) Fifth Kentucky Cavalry, desires to amend his testimony of the 9th instant, as follows :

My second attempt to reach General Thomas was between 3 and 3.30 rather than 2, which occurred to me in giving the rest of my testimony.

Capt. G. M. L. Johnson, Second Indiana Cavalry, General Rousseau's staff, acting assistant inspector-general, being duly sworn, says to questions

By General Negley :

Question. Did or did not General Negley receive a peremptory order on the morning of the 20th September from General Thomas to move his (General Negley's) two brigades to the left without delay, and did not General Negley send you in haste to inform General McCook, who he thought was near at hand, or General Rosecrans, that such was his order, and that his present position in the line should be looked to ?

Answer. He did. I did not succeed in finding General McCook, but returned to General Negley, and found him in conversation with General Rosecrans, and, on remarking I had not succeeded in finding General McCook, he replied, it was all right, he had seen General Rosecrans, who was just leaving at the time.

Question. At the time General Negley moved his two brigades to the left, did it not become necessary, and were you not directed by General Negley, to move his ammunition directly to the rear on the ridge, to prevent the train being destroyed by the enemy's shells, which were then falling fast ?

Answer. Yes. I was directed to move the ammunition train in rear of the First Brigade, which had moved toward the left some time before. After moving trains some distance, and in the meantime the other two brigades were being prepared to move to the left, I received an order from General Negley to turn the train toward the ridge in the rear of the line to prevent it from being destroyed by the shells, which order I executed. I was assistant inspector-general at the time.

Question. After General Negley had posted the scattered artillery on the ridge did he not receive information that the enemy were passing in heavy force to the rear via the Rossville and La Fayette road ? Did not General Negley immediately proceed to the threatened point with some artillery and infantry, and open fire on the enemy, checking his farther advance in that direction ?

Answer. He received information of the enemy moving to the left and rear of his position, and then moved artillery in position and shelled them at long range, which prevented them from appearing closer in force.

Question. After General Negley had checked the enemy's advance toward the left, was he not informed that the enemy were advancing upon the position where he had posted the remainder of the artillery, and did he not immediately direct you to gather up all the stragglers and mounted orderlies and post them as vedettes to watch that part of the line, while he (General Negley) started promptly toward the threatened point ?

Answer. He did. That point of the line means the left and rear, as I understood it, he then going toward the right. The line was then formed in the shape of a sickle, refusing the right.

Question. After you had complied with General Negley's order to post vedettes, did or did you not attempt to join General Negley on the right, and were you prevented by the presence of the enemy ?

Answer. I did, and was prevented. This was about 12 m.

Question. Was or was not the ridge where General Negley posted the scattered artillery where General Steedman's division met the enemy in force on the evening of the 20th ?

Answer. General Steedman's division met the enemy on the ridge to the right and rear slightly, on which General Negley had posted some artillery.

Question. Did or did not the First and Second Brigades and one regiment (the Twenty-first Ohio Volunteers) of the Third Brigade of Negley's division remain with General Thomas, rendering effective services and sustaining heavy loss?

Answer. The Second Brigade remained intact, and there was no organization of the First Brigade, though there were scattered troops of it. Also the Twenty-first Ohio, of the Third Brigade, intact. They did remain and perform effective service. The First Brigade was disorganized by an attack on the extreme left, I infer, by a superior force, and fell back in confusion to the point on the ridge then held by General Negley, and where I left him.

Question. When you were with General Negley what was his deportment ?

Answer. His deportment was that of a cool and deliberate general under those circumstances.

Question. While you were with General Negley, did or did you not observe any organized bodies of infantry other than the Third Brigade under General Negley's command ?

Answer. I did not at that time.

By the COURT :

Question. At what hour was General Negley relieved from his position in line on the morning of the 20th ?

Answer. Between 10 and 11 o'clock, by General Wood, after much delay in getting into position.

Question. What were his orders at that time?

Answer. To proceed to the left to support General Thomas.

Question. Did he move to the left directly ?

Answer. He sent one brigade, not in position but in reserve, in advance, and as soon as relieved moved the other two brigades.

Question. Did they move to the left or rear ?

Answer. To the left; a short distance to the rear of the left of the line.

Question. Did they proceed to report to General Thomas ?

Answer. The Second and Third Brigades did not report as brigades to General Thomas. I do not know whether General Negley reported himself or not.

Question. What became of General Negley ?

Answer. He moved to the left at the head of the Second Brigade, and I afterward found General Negley, when I reported with the Third Brigade, on the ridge.

Question. Was there any insurmountable obstacle in moving to the left along the rear of General Thomas' line ?

Answer. We were not interfered with, except by shells and scattering balls. There was no direct fire on us.

Question Then why did not General Negley execute his orders and report with his command to General Thomas ?

Answer. I cannot state. He may have done so.

Question. Did you hear General Negley give any reason why he did not move the Second Brigade according to orders, to the support of General Thomas?

Answer. No.

Question. Do you know of any obstacle which would have prevented General Negley from executing the order which he received to report with his command to General Thomas at this time and from the position now referred to?

Answer. The Second Brigade had been engaged when I came up with the Third, and General Negley's artillery was shelling toward the left and rear of General Thomas' position, stragglers and disorganized troops coming back. The obstacle might be explained in this way: He had charge of a large amount of artillery, five or six batteries (parts of), and the evidence of the enemy being in that position and driving our forces back, and that he had but three regiments to protect this large amount of artillery. I know no other.

Question. Were you engaged with musketry after you came up with the Third Brigade, and had the Second Brigade been engaged with musketry?

Answer. The Second Brigade was, and one regiment of the Third Brigade also; the Second Brigade had been engaged with musketry and executed a charge, driving the enemy and taking prisoners.

Question. At what time did General Negley leave this point?

Answer. About 12 o'clock.

Question. Was he compelled to leave?

Answer. I was not present when he left.

Question. Where did he go?

Answer. Toward the right; where I cannot say, because in attempting to follow him I met skirmishers of the enemy and turned back.

Question. Supposing that General Negley's orders were to report with his command to General Thomas, would the engagement of the enemy to which you refer have prevented him from doing so?

Answer. Not that alone, but in connection with the care of artillery and force of infantry at his disposal for its protection it would have been sufficient cause.

By General NEGLEY:

Question. Do you or do you not know whether General Negley received an order from General Thomas to take charge of the scattered artillery and post it on the ridge in the rear of the center of the line of battle?

Answer. I know that General Negley received such an order, having been told by the officer, Captain Gaw, of General Thomas' staff, who delivered it.

Question. When you attempted to join General Negley at the position where he posted the artillery on the right did not the presence of the enemy prevent you?

Answer. It did.

Question. When you attempted to join General Negley on the right do you or do you not know how many regiments of infantry General Negley had under his command?

Answer. General Negley took away with him two regiments and four companies of Third Brigade and disorganized portions of the First Brigade.

Question. Did or did you not see the Second Brigade (Negley's division) in action near General Thomas on the afternoon of the 20th after you failed to rejoin General Negley?

Answer. I did.

Question. Was or was not the driving back of the right and center of the army the cause of cutting off the position occupied by the artillery under General Negley's command from the left?

Answer. In my opinion it was.

Lieut. W. W. BARKER, Fifth Tennessee Cavalry, being duly sworn, says to questions

By General NEGLEY:

Question. How were you serving on the 19th and 20th September?

Answer. As acting commissary of subsistence, Second Division, Fourteenth Army Corps (General Negley's).

Question. Did or did you not bring provisions from Chattanooga to Rossville on the night of the 20th and issue them to all the troops, as far as the supplies would reach, and were there any provisions but those ordered by General Negley brought to Rossville?

Answer. I brought, by order of General Negley, 13 wagons from Chattanooga to Rossville loaded with subsistence stores—principally bread and meat—5 of which were issued to General Negley's immediate command (Second Division, Fourteenth Army Corps). Seven were issued, or about 2,500 rations, under direction of Capt. J. L. Orr, commissary of subsistence of First Brigade, Second Division, to the detachments of troops assembled at that point.

Question. Were or were not the troops at Rossville on the night of the 20th suffering for food?

Answer. They were.

Question. Did or did not General Negley subsequently have to assume the personal responsibility of issuing the provisions indiscriminately to the suffering troops at Rossville to relieve you from liability?

Answer. He did; by directions of Brigadier-General Taylor, commissary-general of subsistence.

The Court adjourned to meet at 10 o'clock on the 11th instant.

ELEVENTH DAY.

FEBRUARY 11, 1864.

The Court met pursuant to adjournment.

Present, Major-Generals Hunter and Cadwalader, Brigadier-General Wadsworth, and Colonel Schriver, recorder, and Major-General Negley.

The proceedings of the tenth day were read and approved.

The recorder submitted the Adjutant-General's letter of the 5th instant, transmitting reports of the battle of Chickamauga by Brigadier-Generals Wood, Brannan, and Davis, and Colonel Harker.

There being no witnesses in attendance, the Court adjourned till 10 o'clock on 12th instant.

TWELFTH DAY.

FEBRUARY 12, 1864.

The Court met pursuant to adjournment.

Present, Major-Generals Hunter and Cadwalader, Brigadier-General Wadsworth, and Colonel Schriver, recorder, and Major-General Negley.

J. D. BARKER, being duly sworn, says.

I was captain of the First Ohio Cavalry, commanding the escort at General Thomas' headquarters, and acting aide-de-camp on 19th and 20th September.

Answers to questions

By General NEGLEY:

Question. Will you state briefly what you know about the conduct of General Negley, and the movements of his troops at the battle of Chickamauga, on 20th September ?

Answer. I saw General Negley on the morning of 20th, between 10 and 12 o'clock, and had been frequently from General Thomas to General Rosecrans, and was on my fourth trip to General Rosecrans, with a request from General Thomas to General Rosecrans for General Negley's division. I saw General Negley's adjutant-general, General Negley being then at the front, who stated he had already sent one brigade, the other two not having yet been relieved. I then rode back to General Thomas, and he again sent me to General Rosecrans, with a request for more re-enforcements for his left, which was being hotly pressed. General Rosecrans replied General Negley's division was relieved and ordered to General Thomas, and I told him what Major Lowrie had stated to me. General Rosecrans seemed to discredit my report about General Negley's division, and seemed very positive that it had been already relieved and was on its way there, and said he would forward troops as fast as possible. I then rode to General Thomas again, and he immediately ordered me to return to General Rosecrans with the same request, and also to see General Negley and designate the position which he wished the two remaining brigades to occupy, which was the crest of hills a little in rear, to protect any flank movement. In returning to General Rosecrans, I met two brigades of General Negley's division at a double-quick, moving in the direction General Thomas desired them to go. A little farther on I met General Negley, near some artillery on a hill in rear of where General Brannan's division had been posted in reserve on the morning and nearly in rear of where General Reynolds was then posted, and delivered the order to him in reference to the disposition of his troops. General Negley replied to me, his troops were already moving in conformity to the order of General Thomas. He was busily engaged in reorganizing some artillery which he said he was ordered to care for. This was between 10 and 12 o'clock. He had no one with him, except, I think, 1 mounted orderly. He seemed very composed and busily engaged. I then rode to General Rosecrans with a request from General Thomas for more troops, and returned to General Thomas, and he ordered me to return to General Rosecrans again, saying he was very hotly pressed, and he must have more troops or his left would be turned. As I returned and entered the open field, below where I had seen General Negley, and as I emerged from the wood, I was halted and addressed by some one in the woods, "Stop, you damned son of a bitch." I immediately supposed it was the enemy; spurred my horse and rode in the direction of the artillery in the position where I had left the artillery only a few moments before. Almost at the same instant that I halted and turned they fired on me. I turned and saw the enemy at the edge of the woods. The fire seemed to come from a line of skirmishers all along the edge of the woods, and continued hotly until I passed up between the guns, which were firing very fast, and were hotly engaged. Just as I passed the guns, my horse was shot through the neck. I saw General Negley a little to the right of the battery I passed through; paid no attention to what he was doing, though I saw him ride about the artillery. At that time there were no troops to support the batteries. I then immediately passed down under the hill and there met some one of General Negley's staff, and inquired of him if General Negley had got out, about whom I was alarmed, thinking he was captured. The enemy seemed to be moving to the front (in the shape of a sickle, the handle toward Rossville), and trying to encircle the position that was occupied by that artillery and where I saw General Negley. I did not see General Negley after that time. I endeavored to join General Thomas by going toward Rossville and making over the hill toward the position where I left General Thomas, and I soon met the enemy's skirmishers firing very hotly into the valley whence the troops were moving out and creating a great deal of confusion, and in a very few moments the enemy had guns in position very near the place where I had last seen General Negley. After passing I saw they had a battery in position in the valley, which was raking the position General Negley occupied, and in a very few moments they had guns in position which I just passed over and were firing into the valley.

Question. Did or did not the artillery extend along the ridge a considerable distance toward the Dry Valley road, and do you think t was possible for the artillery and trains to have been saved by moving in any other direction than the one they took?

Answer. It did; and I think no portion of the artillery could have been got out, except by moving in the direction it took.

Question. Was there not a large number of ambulances filled with wounded, stopped on the Dry Valley road and woods by the confusion, and if General Negley had not secured their speedy withdrawal, would they not have been captured by the enemy?

Answer. Yes; but I do not know that General Negley was instrumental in withdrawing them.

Question. Did or did you not make a number of attempts to rejoin General Thomas, and were you not finally obliged to follow in the route taken by General Granger's forces, and were you not then fired upon by the enemy?

Answer. Yes; this occurred entirely in the rear.

Question. At any time during the battle of 20th, did you see General Wood or any of his command occupy the position where you saw General Negley with the artillery?

Answer. No.

Question. Can you state how far it was from where you met General Wood in the afternoon to the position you last saw General Negley with his artillery?

Answer. It was not less than 1 mile nor over 1½ miles.

Question. When you returned to General Thomas, in the afternoon of the 20th, did or did you not see General T. J. Wood at a comfortable distance in the rear of the line, without any of his command near him, and entirely ignorant of what had transpired on the right of the general line of battle?

Answer. I did.

Question. Was or was not the ridge held by General Negley in the morning, and the ridges in his rear occupied by the enemy in heavy force during the day, and was it not in that position where General Granger's forces met and fought the enemy?

Answer. Yes. The ridge on which General Negley was. I cannot say about the ridges in rear.

By the COURT:

Question. You have stated that two brigades of General Negley's were not relieved at 10 o'clock on 20th. How do you know as to the time thus stated?

Answer. I do not know the exact time. I only judge from the time at which the battle opened in the morning. I did not look at my watch. I did not make the statement suggested in the question.

Question. State, as nearly as you can, the time when General Negley's two brigades were relieved; when you saw him on the ridge with the artillery, and when he left the ridge?

Answer. The first I saw of the brigades was between 10 and 12 o'clock; then I met them going into the position designated by General Thomas. This was a few moments before I saw General Negley on the ridge with the artillery. I do not know when he left the ridge.

Question. At what time was it that the enemy occupied the ridge upon which General Negley was?

Answer. I don't think it could have been later than 12 o'clock.

Capt. FREDERICK SCHULTZ, First Ohio Artillery, being duly sworn, says to questions

By General NEGLEY:

Question. Was or was not the ridge where General Negley placed the artillery on the morning of 20th the best position to use the artillery to advantage?

Answer. Yes.

Question. Was or was not the ground to the rear and to the left of the artillery very rough and covered thickly with small trees?

nswer. It was.

Question. Was or was not the infantry support General Negley had with him too weak for so much artillery?

Answer. It was too weak.

Question. Did you not ride with General Negley under a heavy fire to get a good position in front for your battery when the enemy made their charge on the right and center of the line?

Answer. I did.

Question. Did not the artillery, ambulances, ammunition wagons, and stragglers rush through General Negley's command and make confusion?

Answer. They did.

Question. Was not General Negley very active in trying to keep the artillery together and put it in good position?

Answer. He was. He did so.

Question. Did you not stay in the position where General Negley placed you until you had exhausted your ammunition and lost a number of horses, and until General Negley sent an orderly to tell you to come back quickly, or your battery would be captured?

Answer. Yes.

Question. When General Negley fell back was not the artillery much scattered through the woods, and was not some of the pieces hauled off by hand?

Answer. Yes.

Question. When the enemy got possession of the ridge, was it not impossible for General Negley to save the artillery and trains by going to the left?

Answer. It was impossible.

Question. After your battery was ordered back by General Negley, did not General Negley try to form a line on the next ridge in rear?

Answer. He did.

Question. When you retreated back was not the enemy very close and getting to your rear?

Answer. He was.

By the COURT :

Question. What made it impossible for General Negley to move his command to the left from the ridge?

Answer. The ground was rough and much obstructed by brush.

Question. Do you know what time General Negley retired from this position?

Answer. It was nearly 2 o'clock.

The Court adjourned to meet at 10 o'clock on the 13th instant.

THIRTEENTH DAY.

FEBRUARY 13, 1864.

The Court met pursuant to adjournment.

Present, Major-Generals Hunter and Cadwalader, Brigadier-General Wadsworth, and Colonel Schriver, recorder, and Major-General Negley.

The proceedings of the twelfth day were read and approved.

Capt. J. ST. CLAIR MORTON, U. S. Engineers, being duly sworn, says to questions

By General NEGLEY :

Question. Please state your rank and duty during the battle of Chickamauga?

Answer. My rank was brigadier-general of volunteers. I served as chief engineer of the Army of the Cumberland, on the staff of Major-General Rosecrans, until I was separated from him ; subsequently on the staff of Major-General McCook.

Question. Please describe the configuration of the ground where General Negley posted the artillery on the morning of 20th September ; state, also, whether a view of the line of battle from any point was not very limited and obscure owing to the irregular and rugged formation of the ridges and the dense growth of heavy foliaged trees.

Answer. The ground was hilly and wooded. The view was greatly obstructed by the foliage. I cannot answer precisely where the artillery was posted.

Capt. THOMAS A. ELKIN, Fifth Kentucky Cavalry, aide-de-camp to General Rousseau, being duly sworn, says to questions

By General NEGLEY :

Question. Please state your rank and position on 19th and 20th September at the battle of Chickamauga.

Answer. I was first lieutenant, Nineteenth Kentucky Volunteers, and aide-de-camp to Brigadier-General Baird, commanding First Division, Fourteenth Army Corps.

Question. Were you not sent toward the right of the line by General Baird for ammunition, and were you not cut off from the left by the charge of the enemy on the ridge?

Answer. General Baird sent me to General Thomas to state he was nearly out of ammunition. General Thomas had no staff officers with him, and directed me to go toward the right of the line, find the ammunition, and return with such as General Baird wished. I started back with 4 wagons loaded, not all together, however. The first 2 wagons I did not see anything more of, and I suppose they were captured by the enemy. I came on soon after with 2 more, and found the enemy had broken our line and entirely separated me from the division of General Baird. I do not know the time of day, but I should think it was three hours after the engagement commenced in the morning, or about 12 to 1 o'clock.

Question. Was or was not the enemy hotly pressing the retreating troops and creating great disorder at the time you came up to General Negley, and was not General Negley using great exertions to restore order?

Answer. When I came as near General Baird's division as I could get I found our troops in great disorder, broken up entirely, and the enemy, I could see, was in close pursuit. Then I rode to the top of the hill opposite where the line was broken, and directly in rear of that point, and just as I got there met a staff officer, Lieutenant Morris, with whom I consulted as to what was best to do, when I saw General Negley trying to rally some troops and reported to him for duty, telling him I was cut off from General Baird. He thanked me and said as most of his staff were separated from him, he could use me.

Question. Did or did you not then report to General Negley for duty and were directed to assist in rallying disorganized troops and scattered artillery?

Answer. Yes.

Question. From what you know of the locality, was not the route taken by General Negley the only open and practicable one for him to secure the safe withdrawal of the artillery?

Answer. I do not know much of the country, but think it was. I went to the battle-field that evening, but by a different route from that by which I came and from Rossville.

Question. What was General Negley's deportment on 20th, while you were with him?

Answer. He seemed perfectly cool and quiet, and was doing all he could to rally the troops; and succeeded in getting a good many together. He sent word by me to General Thomas that he had got together 5,000 or 6,000 from different corps.

By the COURT:

Question. What time did General Negley withdraw his artillery from the position referred to?

Answer. I do not know the time. The artillery was moving about the same time when I reported to him. I should think 12 or 1 o'clock.

Capt. ALFRED L. HOUGH, Nineteenth U. S. Infantry, assistant commissary of musters, Department of the Cumberland, duly sworn, says to questions

By General NEGLEY:

Question. Please state your rank and duty at the battle of Chickamauga.

Answer. Captain Nineteenth U. S. Infantry, assistant commissary of musters, Fourteenth Army Corps, and acting aide-de-camp to General Negley.

Question. Did or did you not personally observe great delay in General Wood's troops relieving General Negley's division on the morning of the 20th September?

Answer. Very great delay. Seeing General Negley's anxiety, without orders, I rode to the rear several times to see if the troops were coming up. Finally I saw a brigade moving from the rear. I rode to them and asked what they were and where they were going? The commanding officer told me it was Colonel Buell's brigade, of General Wood's division, and were going to take position on the hill immediately in front of them, which was the position originally occupied by General Negley's reserve brigade, and which had gone to the left to General Thomas. I asked him if he was not going to relieve General Negley, who was one-quarter or one-third of a mile to the front. He answered, that he had orders to take this position (top of the hill), and took it.

Question. At the time General Negley's two brigades were marching to the left, were they not exposed to a warm fire from the enemy, and was there not heavy firing along the whole line at that time?

Answer. Very heavy firing along the line while they were passing in rear of it, going through and over General Negley's column.

Question. While General Negley was posting the artillery, did he not state to you that he had received an order to do so, and did not Captain Gaw subsequently admit in your presence that he had conveyed such an order to General Negley?

Answer. Yes.

Question. Was or was not General Negley's entire division sent to the left, as ordered, and did not General Negley, with the Third Brigade and some artillery, check the enemy's advance on the extreme left?

Answer. Yes.

Question. When the enemy attacked the position occupied by the artillery under General Negley's charge, did he not send you to General Rosecrans to inform him of the situation and to say that he (General Negley) could not hold the position unless re-enforced, and what was General Rosecrans' reply?

Answer. He did send me, and I went, saw General Rosecrans, and he replied, "I have just sent him word that I could not help it."

Question. When you were returning from General Rosecrans, did or did you not meet the enemy on the ridge you had just passed over, and were they (they enemy) not passing to the right and rear of General Negley's position?

Answer. I attempted to return by the route I went. After riding a short distance, I thought the enemy was between General Negley and myself. I made a slight *détour* to the rear, and again attempted a straight course to General Negley, and riding some distance, received a fire from between me and our former line of battle. I then proceeded cautiously and found the enemy in force on the right of General Negley, where I had passed over, and was compelled to make a large *détour* to the rear to get to him, which I did.

Question. When you returned from General Rosecrans, did or did you not see the artillery, ammunition wagons, and ambulances rushing to the rear, and large numbers of disorganized troops trying to get out of range of the enemy's fire?

Answer. I did.

Question. When you reached General Negley, did you not find him still on the same ridge where you had left him, trying to rally troops, and did he not send you to try and find suitable ground for posting the artillery more to the rear?

Answer. Yes.

Question. Was or was it not to support the artillery and to try to hold the position that General Negley ordered the withdrawal of a portion of the Third Brigade from the left, which at that time was not engaged?

Answer. Yes.

Question. Did you see any organized troops with General Negley on the ridge other than a portion of the Third Brigade of his division?

Answer. No organized troops.

Question. From your personal observation, do you believe it was practicable for General Negley to have withdrawn his artillery in any other direction than the one he took?

Answer. In my opinion it was not.

Question. After arriving at the mouth of the gap in the rear, did not General Negley direct you to report to General Davis to assist in organizing the troops, while he (General Negley) would try and find General Thomas?

Answer. He did.

Question. After arriving at Rossville, did not General Negley send you to Chattanooga to report the condition of affairs to General Rosecrans? If so, what was his reply?

Answer. Not immediately, but about midnight. General Rosecrans directed me to tell General Negley to send to Chattanooga all wounded and disorganized troops, and with the organized troops hold the gaps; that General Thomas would soon join him, and that Generals McCook and Crittenden would also go out there.

Question. Did or did not General Negley, during the battle on 20th, express much dissatisfaction in having his division separated from his command?

Answer. Very frequently.

Question. What was General Negley's deportment during the battle of Chickamauga?

Answer. Cool and self-possessed. In the morning before being relieved, he showed signs of vexation and annoyance.

Question. Was not the Sixty-ninth Ohio Volunteers, of General Negley's division, at Chattanooga, guarding trains during the battle on the 19th and 20th September?

Answer. Yes.

By the COURT:

Question. At what hour were General Negley's troops in line relieved by General Wood's troops?

Answer. I have no idea of time on that day, and cannot state the hour, as I had no watch.

The Court was cleared.

The Court was opened, and adjourned till 10 o'clock on the 15th instant.

FOURTEENTH DAY.

FEBRUARY 15, 1864.

The Court met pursuant to adjournment.

Present, Major-Generals Hunter and Cadwalader, Brigadier-General Wadsworth, and Colonel Schriver, recorder, and Major-General Negley.

The proceedings of the thirteenth day were read and approved.

Lieut. N. D. INGRAHAM, One hundredth Illinois Infantry, being duly sworn, says to questions

By General NEGLEY:

Question. Were you in the battle of Chickamauga? If so, what was your rank and position at that time?

Answer. I was; ranked as first lieutenant and had the position of topographical engineer, Second Division (General Negley's), Fourteenth Army Corps.

Question. State briefly whether General Negley gave you any special instructions on the morning of 20th September, relative to his ammunition train, and the procuring of information for him concerning the topography of the country, and the movement of both armies?

Answer. Early on the morning of 20th, General Negley ordered me to order my brigade engineers to report in person at his headquarters. He stated to us that that day would be the hottest seen by our army; that he must be kept thoroughly posted in regard to the topography of the country, the position of our lines and the rebel lines. He directed Captain Le Fevre, topographical engineer of the Second Brigade, to attend to the local topography, and to me he gave charge of the ammunition and ambulance trains, stating he held me responsible for the safety of the trains, as well as for ammunition when wanted for the troops. We were ordered to report to him at least every half hour, in person, if possible. The two engineers were killed early on the morning of the 20th, and I parked the ammunition train about one-fourth mile to the rear of General Negley's command, and reported the position by an orderly to General Negley. I also advised the ordnance officer in case our division moved to the left, where he could place the train in safety. I then proceeded to examine the ground in rear of our position. On my return, in probably an hour, I found the train removed, and was informed by my orderly it had passed to the left on the ridge. I started to report to General Negley in person, and was told by one of Colonel Wilder's staff officers it was impossible to reach General Negley, as the rebel cavalry were between him and me. I then went to our ammunition train and found the enemy shelling it. I moved it 1½ miles to the rear, across the hill, without roads. In consequence of the shelling, we lost 1 wagon. I parked the train on a cross-road leading from Crawfish Spring and Chattanooga Valley road to the Rossville road. I then sent an orderly to report to General Negley, and went in another direction myself, and found it impossible to reach on account of rebel cavalry. Our train was ordered by General McCook to move to Chattanooga. We remained half an hour, and were then notified by a colonel of cavalry commanding a brigade that he was to cover the retreat of the train to Chattanooga. We then started, being in the rear of the ammunition trains, and arrived in Chattanooga about 3 o'clock in the morning, shortly after which we received orders from General Negley to take the train immediately to Rossville, which was done.

By the Court:

Question. Why did you neglect to obey the order of General Mc-Cook for half an hour to move with the train for Chattanooga?

Answer. I was not in charge of the ammunition. The order was not given to me but to Captain Hayden (ordnance officer of division), whom I heard say that he should wait for orders from General Negley.

The Court adjourned to meet at 10 o'clock on the 16th, at the council chamber, corner of Jefferson and Sixth streets.

FIFTEENTH DAY.

FEBRUARY 16, 1864.

The Court met pursuant to adjournment.

Present, Major-Generals Hunter and Cadwalader, Brigadier-General Wadsworth, and Colonel Schriver, recorder, and Major-General Negley.

The proceedings of the fourteenth day were read and approved.

Lieut. Col. ARTHUR C. DUCAT, assistant inspector-general, U. S. Volunteers, being duly sworn, says to questions

By General NEGLEY:

Question. What was your rank and duty during the battle of Chickamauga?

Answer. Lieutenant-colonel Twelfth Illinois Infantry, assigned by War Department as assistant inspector-general Department of the Cumberland.

Question. Were you present at the consultation of general officers at McFarland's house on the afternoon of the 20th September? If so, what was the decision of the council?

Answer. I was present. We had a consultation at G. McFarland's house. It consisted of Major-Generals Negley and Sheridan, Brigadier-General Davis, myself, and some other staff officers. I was consulted as a member of General Rosecrans' staff. It was thought best for General Davis to remain in Dry Valley, with a command from the troops rallied; that General Sheridan should push cut on the La Fayette road and try and touch General Thomas' left. General Negley should march to Rossville and support either column. It was understood that the object of General Davis' remaining on Dry Valley was to cover the retreat of our trains and artillery not yet passed, and hold the enemy from getting into Rossville, which was the key to our right. I proceeded with General Sheridan to the left and very close to the enemy's lines. A few minutes anterior to this consultation, I knew nothing of the condition of General Thomas' command. I inferred that he yet held his ground, from the fact of his having sent for General Negley, who started to join General Thomas, and reported he could not do so on account of the enemy's cavalry. This message to General Negley was the first intimation I had of the condition of General Thomas' command. I inferred from it that he still held his ground.

Question. What was General Negley's deportment while you were with him on Sunday, 20th September?

Answer. I saw very little of General Negley, except in the Dry Valley, when the troops were being rallied. His deportment was becoming a general officer, under such circumstances.

Question. Will you please state, if you know, what was the state of discipline and military administration in the division commanded by General Negley?

Answer. Good, for troops in campaign.

Maj. JAMES A. LOWRIE, assistant adjutant-general of volunteers, says to questions

By General NEGLEY:

Question. Were you in the battle of Chickamauga? If so, in what capacity?

Answer. I was an assistant adjutant-general on General Negley's staff.

Question. Did or did you not overtake General Negley on the morning of the 20th, as he was leading the Second Brigade of his division to the left, and see Captain Gaw with General Negley, and did not General Negley state to you that he had just received orders from General Thomas to take charge of the artillery and post it on the ridge, which was the one you saw Captain Gaw point toward with his sword?

Answer. Yes.

Question. Did or did not Captain Gaw subsequently state to you that he had delivered an order to General Negley to take charge of and post the artillery on the morning of the 20th?

Answer. He did.

Question. Can you state how many batteries or number of guns were under General Negley's charge?

Answer. There were eight batteries, including three of his own division. I think each battery had six guns.

Question. Was or was not much of the artillery in a disabled condition, having been in action?

Answer. All the batteries but two seemed to have been in action and suffered from loss of horses or men.

Question. Was or was not the artillery in charge of General Negley without infantry support, and when his position was attacked in front, did he (General Negley) not order up a portion of the Third Brigade from the extreme left to support the artillery?

Answer. There was no infantry support at all when he first took the batteries on the ridge ; his Third Brigade subsequently reported to him on the ridge, as I understood, by his order, but I did not hear it given.

Question. Did or did not the artillery under charge of General Negley extend to a considerable distance to the right along the ridge, and was not the ground to the left and rear very much broken and covered with a dense growth of trees?

Answer. Yes.

Question. When the enemy broke through the center of the line of battle, did not large numbers of the retreating troops and artillery pass through General Negley's line, creating confusion?

Answer. It did.

Question. Can you state what was the effective strength of the two regiments and four companies of the Third Brigade under command of General Negley at the time he withdrew from the ridge?

Answer. I think 700 effective men would cover the whole number.

Question. Did you see any other organized troops under command of General Negley than those of the Third Brigade just mentioned?

Answer. No others.

Question. From your personal knowledge of all the circumstances which controlled the conduct of General Negley at the battle of Chickamauga, do you or do you not think General Negley used good judgment, self-possession, skill, and energy in protecting the best interests of the service, regardless of his own personal welfare?

Answer. I don't think he could have acted otherwise than he did.

Question. Did or did you not hear General Negley on the 20th September frequently say that he deeply regretted the causes which separated him from his division, and leaving him on the field of battle without a suitable command, but responsible for a large amount of useless artillery?

Answer. I did.

By the COURT :

Question. What time was General Negley relieved when in line of battle on the morning of the 20th?

Answer. His First Brigade was sent to the left about 8 o'clock ; the Second relieved by General Wood, at about 9.30 ; the Third reached the ridge after General Negley had posted the artillery there. We were looking at our watches at those times.

Question. At what hour did you leave the hill where the artillery was posted?

Answer. I think it was about 2 p. m., but I cannot be positive about that time.

Question. Did you accompany the command to the Dry Valley road?

Answer. I did not start with it, but overtook it in the Dry Valley road.

Question. What organized troops did you meet on the way to the Dry Valley road, or at that point?

Answer. I met none, until we came out into the first open field. There was a large body of troops collected together there; some of them apparently organized, most of them being organized into regiments and companies. I don't know to what command they belonged, except the two regiments and part of a third belonging to the Third Brigade of General Negley's division, commanded by Colonel Sirwell.

Question. Did you meet there, or on your way to Rossville, any troops of General Brannan's division?

Answer. Not that I know.

The Court adjourned to meet at 10 o'clock on 17th instant.

SIXTEENTH DAY.

FEBRUARY 17, 1864.

The Court met pursuant to adjournment.

Present, Major-Generals Hunter and Cadwalader, Brigadier-General Wadsworth, and Colonel Schriver, recorder, and Major-General Negley.

The proceedings of the fifteenth day were read and approved.

At the request of General Negley, and to prevent the recall of the witnesses already discharged, the Court ordered the following evidence, given in the case of General Crittenden by Capt. Richard Lodor, Fourth U. S. Artillery, who was lieutenant-colonel, and assistant inspector-general of Twenty-first Army Corps in the battle of Chickamauga, to be inserted in this record:

"Question. Did you attempt on Sunday to go to General Thomas, and with what success?

"Answer. I did, and tried hard for three hours to get to General Thomas from the position General Crittenden occupied when he left to find General Rosecrans, and ascertained the only way to get from that position without being captured was by passing back toward Chattanooga. * * * I believe it to have been impossible for any one to pass from the position General Crittenden occupied, near the batteries, to our lines in the front. * * * I am an artillery officer, and have been serving in that corps nearly eight years."

Also the testimony of Capt. J. St. C. Morton, U. S. Engineers, given in General McCook's case, as follows:

"Question. Did you inform General McCook after you examined your maps and looking at the heavy clouds of dust which were rising on the left, and the occasional sounds of artillery, that you believed the whole army was in retreat for Chattanooga?

"Answer. I made repeated examinations of my map that day, using a prismatic compass to identify locality of clouds of dust and sound of firing. I made such a remark to Major-General McCook at a point in Chattanooga Valley road from which a heavy column of dust could be seen moving northward, in what I judged to be the Rossville road."

The Court was closed.

The Court was opened, and adjourned to meet at 10 o'clock on the 18th instant.

SEVENTEENTH DAY.

FEBRUARY 18, 1864.

The Court met pursuant to adjournment.
Present, Major-Generals Hunter and Cadwalader, Brigadier-General Wadsworth, and Colonel Schriver, recorder, and Major-General Negley.
The proceedings of the sixteenth day were read and approved.

Brig. Gen. H. P. VAN CLEVE, U. S. Volunteers, being duly sworn, says to question

By General NEGLEY :

Question. While passing on the road from the battle-field to Rossville on the 20th, did you see any organized troops? If so, how many?

Answer. I think not over 500. Colonel Ducat was there, and I supposed they had been rallied by him.

The Court was cleared.
The Court was opened, and adjourned to meet at 10 o'clock on 19th instant.

EIGHTEENTH DAY.

FEBRUARY 19, 1864.

The Court met pursuant to adjournment.
Present, Major-Generals Hunter and Cadwalader, Brigadier-General Wadsworth, and Colonel Schriver, recorder.
The proceedings of the eighteenth [seventeenth] day were read and approved.
The Court was closed.
The Court was opened, and adjourned to meet at 6 p. m. this day.

GALT HOUSE—6 p. m.

The Court met pursuant to adjournment.
Present, Major-Generals Hunter and Cadwalader, Brigadier-General Wadsworth, and Colonel Schriver, recorder.
No proceedings in this case.
The Court was closed.
The Court was opened, and adjourned to meet at 10 o'clock on the 20th instant.

NINETEENTH DAY.

FEBRUARY 20, 1864.

The Court met pursuant to adjournment.
Present, Major-Generals Hunter and Cadwalader, Brigadier-General Wadsworth, and Colonel Schriver, recorder, and Major-General Negley.
No proceedings in this case.
The Court was closed.
The Court was opened, and adjourned to meet at 8 p. m. this day.

8 p. m.

The Court met pursuant to adjournment.
Present, Major-Generals Hunter and Cadwalader, Brigadier-General Wadsworth, and Colonel Schriver. recorder.

No proceedings in this case.

The Court was closed.

The Court was opened, and adjourned to meet at 10 o'clock on 22d instant.

TWENTIETH DAY.

FEBRUARY 22, 1864.

The Court met pursuant to adjournment.

Present, Major-Generals Hunter and Cadwalader, Brigadier-General Wadsworth, and Colonel Schriver, recorder, and Major-General Negley.

On account of the absence of a witness, this case could not be proceeded with, and the Court adjourned to meet at 6 p. m. this day.

GALT HOUSE—6 p. m.

The Court met this evening, but not till half past 9 o'clock, because of the non-arrival of the witness expected.

Present, Major-Generals Hunter and Cadwalader, Brigadier-General Wadsworth, and Colonel Schriver, recorder, and Major-General Negley.

Brig. Gen. J. M. BRANNAN, U. S. Volunteers, being duly sworn, says to questions

By the COURT:

Question. What was your rank and command in the battle of Chickamauga, on the 19th and 20th September, 1863?

Answer. I was brigadier-general of volunteers, and commanded the Third Division of the Fourteenth Army Corps, Army of the Cumberland.

Question. What was the position of your division on the 20th?

Answer. Two brigades of my division were placed in the line of battle, between the hours of 10 p. m. of the 19th and 3 a. m. of the 20th, between the troops of Major-General Negley on my right and Major-General Reynolds on my left, the Third Brigade being in reserve.

Question. At what time was the position of General Negley's command changed?

Answer. I think it was beween 8 and 9 a. m. on the 20th. I understood his command was to move to the extreme left of the line of battle. The battle commenced before the movement was made.

Question. How did you understand that General Negley was to move to the left?

Answer. I understood from General Rosecrans, who came by where I was and he told me so, and gave me orders as to the disposition of my reserve brigade.

Question. What became of Negley's command?

Answer. After the action commenced, and before he moved, I observed the enemy massed on my right. I sent a staff officer to General Rosecrans, to inform him that if General Negley was removed before other troops came in, the line of battle would be broken. He returned word that General Negley would not be moved till General Wood got into position. When General Negley moved and where he went is more than I can tell you, as the country was very thickly wooded.

Question. Do you know anything affecting the conduct of General Negley on the 19th and 20th September in the battle of Chickamauga?

Answer. I don't know anything about General Negley on the 19th September, 1863, but on the 20th, after the line of battle was broken, which I think was about

11.30 a. m., my right was thrown back, and, with other troops that were in rear of my line of battle, I reformed them on a ridge, which brought my line nearly perpendicular to the original line of battle in the morning. The line was broken on the right of my division, which disorganized the troops on my extreme right. After I had taken this position on the ridge I was attacked very furiously by the enemy, which lasted for over an hour, and they were repulsed. I think it was about this time that General Negley came up the ridge in rear of my line at the head of a column of troops, and I turned to him and said, "General Negley, I am very happy to see you with troops, as I am very hardly pressed and want assistance." He said, "Certainly, I'll do all I can." I then requested him to place his command on my right, which was on another ridge, with a small ravine between us. I think he told me he had four regiments, when I requested him to let me have one to complete my line, which he did. He then moved off with the other portion of his command, as I supposed, to take position on my right. Almost immediately after he had gone—it could not have been more than fifteen minutes—the enemy made another assault on my line, which continued for three-quarters of an hour at least, and they were again repulsed. During the action I was riding up and down in rear of the line of battle, and I heard no firing beyond my extreme right. After the assault ceased I sent a staff officer (one of my aides-de-camp, Lieutenant Webb) on the adjoining ridge, where I supposed General Negley was, to ascertain if there were any of our troops there. He rode over to the other ridge and half a mile beyond, and reported that there was no one there. The commander of my First Brigade, Colonel Connell, reported to me that night in Rossville, when I inquired of him why he was not with me after the line was broken, he having only a portion of his brigade with him, that he moved, under the orders of Major-General Negley, to the rear on the road to Chattanooga, and so states in his official report. I did not see anything of General Negley again until I met him at Rossville some time in the night at 10 or 11 o'clock. The position which I asked General Negley to take I looked upon as so important, to protect the right and prevent our whole army from being turned, that I supposed, of course, he had done so. It was the same position which General Gordon Granger took in the evening and repulsed the enemy finally. I found Colonel Stoughton, who commanded a brigade of General Negley's division, on my left, connecting with Colonel Harker, of General Wood's division. Brig. Gen. John Beatty, of General Negley's division, was also there, and remained there until the troops retreated with my division, which was the rear guard of the army. Colonel Connell was on the extreme right of my line when it was broken, and the portion of troops that he was with fell back to the ridge, which was almost parallel to the original line of battle of the morning. He was moving to join me by the left flank when he was taken off by General Negley; so he reported to me. The country was so thickly covered with underbrush, that it was impossible to see more than 50 or 100 yards from the position that I occupied that afternoon.

Question. Did the regiment given you by General Negley remain with you?

Answer. Yes; a portion of them were captured after dusk, during the last assault on my right. If General Granger had not come up at the time he did, I could not have held my position fifteen minutes longer, having been entirely out of ammunition.

Question. What was General Wood's position at the time you formed your second line perpendicular to your first line?

Answer. He was on the left of the line which I held.

Major LOWRIE, assistant adjutant-general, recalled, says to questions

By General NEGLEY:

Question. Did you at any time during the period General Negley held the ridge see any organized bodies of troops belonging to General Brannan's division?

Answer. I did not.

Question. Do you think it was possible for an organized brigade, regiment, or even company, to have been with General Negley, or under his command, without your seeing them?

Answer. It could not have been without my knowledge.   I was on the ridge till General Negley left.

Question. Did not all the larger squads of stragglers pass through General Negley's line to the rear some time before he withdrew?

Answer. They did.   There were very few troops on the hill or ridge, except his organized regiments, at the time he went away and for some time before it.   Those that were there, were very widely scattered.

Captain HOUGH, recalled, says to questions

By General NEGLEY:

Question. Did you at any time during the period General Negley held the ridge see any organized bodies of troops belonging to General Brannan's division?

Answer. I did not.

Question. Did not all the larger squads of stragglers pass through General Negley's line to the rear some time before he withdrew?

Answer. They did.

Lieutenant MOODY, recalled, says to questions

By General NEGLEY:

Question. Did you at any time during the period General Negley held the ridge see any organized bodies of troops belonging to General Brannan's division?

Answer. I did not.

Question. Did not all the larger squads of stragglers pass through General Negley's line to the rear some time before he withdrew?

Answer. They did.

Question. Was or was not the Twenty-first Ohio the largest regiment in General Negley's division, and was it not armed with a superior revolving rifle, which the regiment had learned the use of with great effectiveness?

Answer. It was.   I know this to have been the regiment left with General Brannan.

Question. How many men did General Negley lose in the battle of Chickamauga in killed, wounded, and prisoners?

Answer. As near as I can recollect, from the official returns from brigade commanders, something over 700.

General Negley here stated he had no more witnesses, but submitted a copy of his official report, and one supplementary to it, of the battle of Chickamauga, which he requested might be made a portion of the record and a part of the statement, which was then laid before the court, marked A in the appendix.   The report is marked B, and the supplementary one marked C.

The Court was then cleared.

The Court was opened, and adjourned to meet at 10 o'clock on the 23d instant.

TWENTY-FIRST DAY.

FEBRUARY 23, 1864.

The Court met pursuant to adjournment.

Present, Major-Generals Hunter and Cadwalader, Brigadier-General Wadsworth, and Colonel Schriver, recorder.

The proceedings of the twentieth day were read and approved. The Court was cleared.

After the reading of the testimony, the Court came to the following

FINDING AND OPINION IN THE CASE OF MAJOR-GENERAL NEGLEY.

No question has anywhere been raised as to the conduct of General Negley on the 19th September, the first day of the battle of Chickamauga. He commanded on that day his entire division, and it appears from the evidence that his conduct was throughout creditable. Early on the second day General Negley was assigned a position in the line on the right of General Brannan, from which he was relieved between 8 and 10 o'clock by Wood's division.

He was then ordered to take a position on the extreme left, but his division having been relieved at a later hour than was expected, his reserve brigade was sent meantime in advance of the others, and became separated from him, taking a place in the line under General Baird. Subsequently another of his brigades was placed in line on the left of General Brannan and under the command of that officer.

A little later in the day, as General Negley was moving to a position on Missionary Ridge, to which he had been ordered by General Thomas, he gave up to General Brannan, on his urgent appeal for support, the largest regiment of his last brigade, retaining for himself only two weak regiments and four companies of another regiment.

The point to which he was directed was in rear of the center of the line. Here he found some artillery; other batteries and parts of batteries joined him, and it appears in evidence that he had at last fifty guns under his care, with only the small infantry support above referred to, namely, two small regiments and four companies of another regiment, in all about 600 or 700 men.

The gap in the line made by the withdrawal of Wood's division, the rout of the entire right, and the unresisted advance of the enemy from that direction, as well as the advance of the enemy from the left of the line, the enemy having outflanked and driven in a portion of the left also, subjected General Negley to such hazard of losing this large park of artillery, as made it expedient, in his judgment, to withdraw it to a point on the Dry Valley road, about 2 or 3 miles from Rossville. It appears in evidence that this movement was executed in good order, and all the artillery saved. Here General Negley met Generals Davis and Sheridan, with portions of their commands and considerable bodies of disorganized troops from various commands. He co-operated with the division commanders above referred to in taking such measures as the exigencies of the occasion seemed to require, and toward evening retired to Rossville.

General Negley exhibited throughout the day (the second of the battle) and the following night great activity and zeal in the discharge of his duties, and the Court do not find in the evidence before them any ground of censure.

The impression which seems to have been entertained by General Brannan that General Negley had ordered one of his brigades to the rear is not sustained by the testimony.

It appears in evidence that Brigadier-General Wood, on one or more occasions at the headquarters of the Army of the Cumberland,

and in the presence of the commander of that army and a portion of his staff, indulged in severe reflections upon the conduct of Major-General Negley, applying to him coarse and offensive epithets. When placed upon the stand before the Court, he failed entirely to substantiate any charge as ground of accusation against him.

The Court deem it their duty to express their marked condemnation of such conduct, leading to vexatious and unprofitable investigations prejudicial to the service.

D. HUNTER,
Major-General, President.
ED. SCHRIVER,
Inspector-General, Recorder.

There being no further business, the Court adjourned *sine die.*

D. HUNTER,
Major-General, President.
ED. SCHRIVER,
Inspector-General, Recorder.

ADJUTANT-GENERAL'S OFFICE, *April* 9, 1864.

The record and opinions in the foregoing case have been submitted to the President of the United States, and he is of opinion that no further action is required, and the Court of Inquiry is dissolved.

By order of the Secretary of War:

E. D. TOWNSEND,
Assistant Adjutant-General.

APPENDIX.

A.

LOUISVILLE, KY., *February* 22, 1864.

Major-General HUNTER,
President of Court of Inquiry:

SIR: At Chattanooga, on the evening of October 6, 1863, at a private interview secured for me by a written request from General Thomas to General Rosecrans, I was informed for the first time that the department commander was dissatisfied with my official conduct on the 20th of September. At the same time General Rosecrans referred to statements made by Brigadier-Generals Brannan and Wood as the reasons for his unfavorable opinions.

In reply to my expressions of pain and surprise that he should entertain such reflections without my knowledge, or opportunity for explanation or a proper defense in answer, he requested me to submit a supplementary report, with the written statements of officers (whose names I had mentioned) who were conversant with the facts. This report occasioned General Rosecrans' letter, dated October 14, 1863,* to the Adjutant-General of the Army, in which he states:

The general (Negley) has always been an active, energetic, and efficient commander, and displayed very good judgment in an affair at Widow Davis' house in front of Stevens' Gap, where he was attacked by a superior force of the enemy, and successfully extricated his train and command from its perilous position.

Also—

From a careful perusal of that (my report) and the accompanying papers, [it seems] that he acted according to his best judgment under the circumstances of the case.

*See p. 333.

But as General Wood, aided by several other general officers, labored assiduously to impair my military reputation, and thus my usefulness in the army, I deemed it imperative, being also influenced by the friendly advice of Generals Rosecrans and Thomas, to apply for a Court of Inquiry as the only admitted and honorable means of vindicating my injured honor. This application was considerately complied with in the order convening this Court.

General Rosecrans also states (in the letter referred to)—

But an impression that he left the field on Sunday, without orders or necessity, having made its way through this army, and statements having appeared in the official reports of general officers appearing to support the impression, &c.

The testimony and papers before the Court show conclusively that Generals Brannan and Wood, officers junior to me in rank, and entirely independent of my command, were the authors of these imputations, and that they used their official reports as the medium for otherwise unauthorized censures, which necessitated this investigation. Official copies or extracts from these official reports were not furnished me until submitted before this Court, February 11, 1864, in compliance with my request of January 22, 1864. Nevertheless, true extracts from these reports appeared from time to time in the public press in direct violation of the following order ·

WAR DEPARTMENT, *October* 4, 1862.

*   *   *   *   *   *   *

II. If any officer shall hereafter, without proper authority, permit the publication of any official letter or report, or allow any such document to pass into the hands of persons not authorized to receive it, his name will be submitted to the President for dismissal. This rule applies to all official letters and reports written by an officer himself.

By order of the Secretary of War:

L. TOWNSEND [THOMAS],
Adjutant-General.

The channels through which these extracts were obtained may be plausibly conjectured by the italicizing and the purpose for which they were used. The evidence further shows that the most violent, zealous, and disrespectful accuser, was General Wood ; yet, as a sworn witness before this Court, he not only failed to establish the statements made in his report, but could not mention a single instance where General Negley had failed to do his duty in the battle of Chickamauga, or which would, in the slightest degree, justify the unwarrantable liberty he arrogated in publishing such insinuations. Whether the motives which inspired Generals Brannan and Wood to disregard the established rules of the army, and of society, intended any advantage to the Government and were prompted by the sentiments of virtue, patriotism, and manly honor, I respectfully leave to the unbiased opinion of the Court and the world.

Why General Brannan should pause in his epic description of military achievement on the field of Chickamauga and become the voluntary censor of my conduct, unqualifiedly stating as fact that which it was impossible for him to know from his own observation, is painfully surprising, exhibiting a dangerous precedent in the form of official reports. The positiveness which characterizes his reference to me demands some attention in these remarks.

General Brannan attaches much importance to a pledge that he says I gave to protect his right and rear. Incredible as this appears to me—as it will seem to every one who comprehends, from a view of the facts elicited by the testimony, that at that moment my own right was being turned and my own position so seriously endangered as to induce pressing messages to General Rosecrans for immediate assistance—while such a pledge might attest to zeal and determination, it would not deter the purposes of the enemy without a proper representation of muskets. He further states that so far from holding his right, I carried off his First Brigade. This is not reconcilable with his previous statement, viz : " With, however, the exception of the First Brigade, which, being much exposed, broke with considerable disorder." As he speaks of having swung back his right flank half a mile to the rear, he is prudently silent as to the distance the First Brigade swung back. I mean no disparagement to the brave men of that brigade and its efficient commander.

It is anomalous, indeed I might properly use a stronger term in saying, that if General Brannan had a brigade unoccupied, why should he ask for and take one of my regiments, reducing my then too small force? On this point there is much concurrent testimony.

Again, he speaks of a portion of General Granger's Reserve Corps " taking up the position which should have been occupied during the day by General Negley's division." This would seem to be a bold reflection upon the commanding general for ordering General Negley's division elsewhere. However, it appears from his and other ports that he was commanding a large portion of Negley's divisi n and that the Twenty-first Ohio Volunteer Infantry, of the same division, covered his retreat, losing three-fourths of its strength. General Brannan commanded in this battle the largest division in the army (the same division once commanded by General Thomas). If with this and "portions of Palmer's and Negley's divisions," they " maintained their ground with obstinacy, evincing great gallantry and devotion in the most trying circumstances until re-enforced," and "nothing can exceed the desperate determination with which the rebels endeavored to gain possession of this point, hurling entire divisions on my (Brannan's) small force," think, for an instant, mind of justice, how long my 700 men would hold at bay those "entire divisions."

General Brannan also refers to his failure to obtain ammunition, "thus necessitating the use of the bayonet as my only means of defense." Perhaps his ammunition was ordered to Chattanooga by higher authority, as was the case with mine ; still, great as was this misfortune, it enabled General Brannan, according to his report, to settle the disputed question, whether the bayonet can successfully cope with the improved fire-arms of the present day.

It would be uncharitable for me to omit allusion to the services of my division in this connection. It is sacredly due these heroic men, who left over 700 of their number on that sanguinary field, that they should not suffer reproach from any fault of mine, or share in the envious calumnies bestowed upon me. To them I owe the honor and dignity of my position, but no disgrace. The bodies of the braves who slumber on the banks of the Chickamauga, as well as their bereaved friends at home, appeal to justice against the base accusation that the " bulk of the division retired intact."

The enemy counts not the battle-begrimed, bullet-torn standards of the Second Division among his trophies, but remembers with grief their splendid discipline and glorious charges.

As to the aspersions made against my personal deportment on the field, I yield to the necessity of referring to this envious charge with delicate hesitation. The evidence has awarded me higher honors in this respect than even egotism would have asked. I confess, however, that my highest purpose has been to guide my actions by reason as well as by valor.

I now proceed to consider briefly the intimation that I left the field early and unnecessarily on Sunday. The direction of much explicit testimony bearing on this point has doubtless arrested the attention of the Court, and relieves me from the necessity of doing more than describing my situation and the circumstances which controlled my judgment and actions. Immediately after receiving and complying with the order directing me to take charge of and post the artillery, which virtually deprived me of my legitimate command, already separated widely by the culpable delay of General Wood, I was reliably informed that the extreme left of General Thomas' line, which was then obliquely to my rear and left some distance, was being driven back. I hastened to the threatened point, taking some artillery and Sirwell's brigade, which was just arriving. I found the enemy in heavy force lapping over the extreme left, pressing it back in a crotchet, which was about to be taken in reverse. I opened on the advancing columns with the artillery from a splendid position, which checked the enemy's farther approach on that point. Information then reached me from the right and front that it was threatened by the enemy, and the artillery I had in position endangered, I immediately gave prudent directions for the protection of the left, and passed quickly to the position I was assigned to by the order per Captain Gaw. On my way I met General Brannan, who urgently requested a regiment. I ordered to his support my largest regiment, armed with revolving (five-chambered) muskets. I found affairs in front assuming an alarming condition. The enemy was pushing heavy columns through a gap made in the vertex of the angle of our line in front, which had been hastily abandoned by General Wood; the remainder of the line toward the left of the angle was swinging back like a gate before the wind. The troops from the right, which rested back against the ridge *en échelon*, were now pressed forward with intrepidity to recover the lost ground, but were taken in the flank and crumbled into flying detachments. My situation was desperate, my effective batteries were fast exhausting their ammunition. I had sent on the first view two aides to General Rosecrans to describe my situation and ask immediate re-enforcements; at the same time ordered up the remainder of the Third Brigade, which was not then engaged. Lieutenant Moody returned through a shower of bullets, expressing surprise at finding me still on the ridge, reported General Rosecrans' reply, "Tell Negley it is too late, I cannot help him," who then turned his horse's head and rode toward Chattanooga. The regiment of stragglers on my left had vanished; those upon my right disappearing in the dense woods, their speed redoubled by the far-reaching shells and the exultant yells of the enemy, whose closely planted batteries and long line of musketry were sweeping the ridge with an appalling fire. Yet the batteries of Schultz, Marshall, and one of Parrott guns, were heroically hurling death into the enemy's ranks, so close that the smoke from the guns of each commingled in the upper air. Contemplate my position, if it be possible to do so here, removed from the scene of action. No human eye could penetrate the dark woods to the left where General Thomas, with the flower of the army, was struggling against the inspirited enemy. To seek succor from that quarter was hopeless. None could be expected from General Brannan, as he had just recently applied for and received assistance from me. Words of dispair came from the right. The enemy was gliding up the ravine to the left and almost seizing the guns in action. All was agonizing doubt and irresistible confusion. It was now, in my judgment, time to retire. To continue an unequal combat could only add more graves to the battle-field and contribute more trophies to the enemy. A proper realization of the situation and a just regard for the lives and the material of war intrusted to my care, urged the speedy withdrawal of the artillery which was moved to the second ridge, at which point a portion of the Third Brigade had just arrived. The ground was unfavorable, a dense forest covered the movements of the enemy, who manifested visible intentions to cut off retreat along the only passable route to the Dry Valley road. The artillery was becoming more scattered each moment, trying to escape the falling shells. It became now the question for me to decide whether I should remain with my isolated command and save it all if possible, or to endeavor to reach the left with my infantry, only leaving the ambulances filled with wounded, the stragglers, and the artillery to inevitable capture. Ignorant of the condition of the troops on my left, who might, for aught I knew, have been at the same time in full retreat on the La Fayette and Rossville road—and the indications and general impression were that such was the fact, and it would have been the case had not the approaching column (unknown to me) of General Granger's corps prevented it—my decision was to remain with my special command until relieved by the same (or higher) authority which had assigned me to it. On reaching McFarland's house—in the first open ground on the natural line of communication with Rossville, determined by a long and narrow defile, which could be held with a small force, aided by the natural advantages, against the enemy who were reported by many to be advancing; it is to be reasonably presumed that a knowledge of the assembling force at McFarland's farm intimidated a further pursuit—I now learned for the first time from a cavalryman that General Thomas was holding the enemy in check on the left, and as it would require time to organize the troops and clear the gap, I turned over the command to General Davis and hastened back to find General Thomas, if possible, and report for orders. Meeting General Sheridan entering the defile from the west side with a considerable body of troops, I suggested the propriety of his moving what I thought was his division to the support of General Thomas. He replied "that it was his intention to proceed to Rossville." I passed on and soon met the enemy, who prevented my farther advance. I then returned to McFarland's, and held a consultation with Generals Sheridan and Davis and officers of the staff of General Rosecrans. It was unanimously agreed that General Davis should remain and hold the gap, General Sheridan to pass through Rossville toward General Thomas' left, while I should proceed to Rossville with the *débris* of the army, organize the scattered troops, and be prepared to support either column. About this time a dispatch arrived from Captain Hill, of General Rosecrans' staff, stating that Forrest's cavalry were on the Ringgold and Rossville road, in General Thomas' rear. In view of this new danger, I marched expeditiously to Rossville and prepared to hold it. This entire movement was only an anticipation of the order received from General Rosecrans, then at Chattanooga, sent by telegraph at 7 p. m. (Copy on the record.)

The grand advantages of this effective organization and disposition of the troops, which would not have halted short of Chattanooga, can scarcely be overestimated, and its importance in a tactical point of view must be apparent to every experienced military mind.

If the two roads converging at Rossville had been relinquished to and had been seized by the enemy it would have in all human probability sealed the fate of General Thomas' command, which was compelled to fall back that night for supplies. The influence this judicious movement exerted over subsequent events may be designated in future history as an accident, but it was one of those military accidents which restored order with equilibrium, and changed the front of a defeated army and unquestionably saved Chattanooga. (See testimony of General Rosecrans and others on this point.) Public opinion (however correctly it is for you to determine) estimates the ability of a general by results. The value and importance of my official action from the moment I was assigned to the command of the artillery (without referring to the "handsome" operations of my command on the 19th until the close of the 21st) is not, while in view of the testimony, liable to controversy.

The safety of fifty pieces of artillery is of itself significant. I beg of you to observe in this connection that I possessed no knowledge of the topography of the country, or the disposition of the troops beyond an imperfect view from the positions I occupied. The only intelligence I possessed as to the extent of the disaster was based on the statements of officers passing to the rear. A strong impression was naturally made on my mind by the significant reply sent to me by General Rosecrans, and the information that he with two of his corps commanders had gone toward Chattanooga.

If the department commander, with a large retinue of staff officers, corps of engineers, and a cavalry escort, failed, as he admits, under the circumstances, to correctly comprehend the situation at noon, was it possible for me to know at 1 p. m. with my very limited facilities and almost enveloped by the enemy?

Military history proves beyond contradiction that no single battle, no matter what may be its magnitude and results, is a fair or positive test of the ability of a general as a commander; also the unmanly fear of public opinion after a disastrous battle betrays many officers, sometimes high in command, to deny their (even unavoidable) mistakes and direct attention to the errors of brother officers or claim honors undeserved, and gather laurels never won, and by a skillful use of the pen exaggerate the simple performance of duty into a great achievement. If I know my purposes of life, I seek no consolation from such unsoldierly pretexts and scorn such means of vindication. As this investigation is confined to one battle, it would be unbecoming in me to offer in evidence the complimentary souvenirs of my previous service—the many assurances of confidence and appreciation won on other fields. Therefore, in contemplation of the voluminous testimony which pays a higher tribute to my fidelity to my country, skill as a commander, energy and fortitude in the performance of duty, than I would permit my own pen to do, I respectfully submit my case with full confidence in the justice and integrity of the Court, with my thanks for the patient courtesy and impartiality which enabled me to place so fully upon its records the facts relating to my official conduct in the battle of Chickamauga.

With considerations of personal respect, yours, very truly,

JAS. S. NEGLEY,
Major-General, U. S. Volunteers.

Extract from the report of Brigadier-General Brannan, commanding Third Division, Fourteenth Corps:

In this manner I succeeded in holding the enemy in check for a considerable time until, finding that the rebels were moving on my right to gain command of the valley, by which the right (McCook) was retreating, I swung back my right flank, and, moving about half a mile to the rear, took up a good position on a commanding ridge, *General Negley (who had a portion of his command intact) having pledged himself to hold my right and rear.*

Finding that this latter point was the key to the position so desired by the enemy, I made every preparation to defend it to the last, my command being somewhat increased by the arrival of portions of Palmer's and Negley's divisions and most opportunely re-enforced by Colonel Van Derveer's brigade, which, *having successfully, though with great loss, held its precarious position in the general line until all in its vicinity had retreated, retired in good order, actually cutting its way through the rebels to regain my division. This gallant brigade was one of the few who maintained their organization perfect through the hard-fought passes of that portion of the field.*

Nothing can exceed the desperate determination with which the rebels endeavored to gain possession of this point, hurling entire divisions on my small force, in their fierce eagerness to obtain a position which would undoubtedly have given them the grand advantage of the day. My troops maintained their ground with obstinacy, evincing great gallantry and devotion in the most trying circumstances, until re-enforced, about 3.30 p. m., by a portion of Granger's Reserve Corps, who took up the position that should have been occupied during the day by Negley's division.

General Negley, so far from holding my right as he had promised, retired with extraordinary deliberation to Rossville, at an early period of the day, taking with him a portion of my division, as will be seen by the report of Colonel Connell, commanding First Brigade, leaving me open to attack from the right as well as from the left and front (from which points the rebels attacked me simultaneously on four several occasions), and my rear so far exposed that my staff officers, sent back for ammunition, were successively cut off and the ammunition, of such vital importance at that time, prevented from reaching me, thus necessitating the use of the bayonet as my only means of defense.

Brigadier-General Wood says, in regard to the same subject, at the conclusion of his report:

Before closing my report, I deem it my duty to bring to the notice of the commanding general certain facts which fell under my observation during the progress of the conflict on the 20th. As I was moving along the valley with my command, to the support of General Reynolds, in conformity with the order of the commanding general, I observed on my left, to the west of me, a force posted high up on the ridge. I inquired what force it was, and was informed it was a part (a brigade, perhaps) of General Negley's division. I was informed that General Negley was with the force in person. I remember distinctly seeing a battery on the hillside with the troops. *At the time it was certainly out of the reach of any fire from the enemy.* This was between 11 and 12 o'clock in the day. A little later in the day, perhaps half or three-quarters of an hour, when I became severely engaged, as already described, with the large hostile force that had pierced our lines and turned Brannan's right, compelling him to fall back, I looked for the force that I had seen posted on the ridge and which, as already remarked, I had been informed was a part of General Negley's division, hoping, if I became severely pressed, it might re-enforce me, for I was resolved to check the enemy, if possible. *But it had entirely disappeared. Whither it had gone, I did not then know, but was informed later in the day it had retired toward Rossville; and this information I believe was correct. By whose order this force retired from the battle-field I do not know, but of one fact I am perfectly convinced, that there was no necessity for its retiring. It is impossible it could have been at all seriously pressed by the enemy at the time. In fact, I think it extremely doubtful whether it was engaged at all.*

Near sundown of the 20th, I met General John Beatty, not far from where I had fought the enemy all the afternoon. He was entirely alone when I met him, and did not seem to have any special command. I at once came to the conclusion that he had not retired from the battle-field when the bulk of the division he is attached to did. At the moment I met him, I was engaged halting some troops that were crossing the valley north and west of my position and who appeared to have straggled away from the point on which General Thomas' command had fought all day. General Beatty desired to know where I wished these troops reformed. I pointed out a position to him and desired him to reform them, which he said he would do. I then rode back to my command. It is proper that I should remark that I did not see the corps commander from about half past 9 a. m., of Sunday, the 20th, to some time after sunrise of the 21st, when I met him at Rossville.

B.

LOUISVILLE, KY., *February* 19, 1864.

GENTLEMEN: I respectfully offer in evidence a copy* (from the original) of my official report of the battle of Chickamauga, to exhibit, as compared with the testimony now before you, the sincerity and truthfulness of my statements made at a time when I had no intimation that any fault was found with my conduct, which in itself should remove even a suspicion that I acted otherwise than with judgment, zeal, energy, and a proper appreciation of my duty and responsibility.

I have the honor to remain, yours, respectfully,

JAS. S. NEGLEY,
Major-General, U. S. Volunteers.

ADDENDA.

GENERAL ORDERS, }   WAR DEPT., ADJT. GENERAL'S OFFICE,
No. 322.   }   *Washington, September* 28, 1863.

*   *   *   *   *   *   *

II. It is also directed that a Court of Inquiry be convened, the detail to be hereafter made, to inquire and report upon the conduct of Major-Generals McCook and Crittenden, in the battles of the 19th and 20th instant. These officers are relieved from duty in the Department of the Cumberland, and will repair to Indianapolis, Ind., reporting their arrival, by letter, to the Adjutant-General of the Army.

By order of the Secretary of War:

E. D. TOWNSEND,
Assistant Adjutant-General.

—

GENERAL ORDERS, }   HDQRS. DEPT. OF THE CUMBERLAND,
No. 228.   }   *Chattanooga, Tenn., October* 9, 1863.

I. The President of the United States has directed that the Twentieth and Twenty-first Army Corps be consolidated, and has assigned Maj. Gen. Gordon Granger to the command of the corps thus formed, which will be hereafter known as the Fourth Army Corps. The organization of the corps will be at once arranged and commanding officers notified.

II. In obedience to orders from the Secretary of War, Maj. Gens. A. McD. McCook and T. L. Crittenden are relieved from duty in this department, and will obey the orders they have received from the War Department. They will be accompanied by their aides-de-camp. The remaining officers of their respective staffs will report at these headquarters for other orders.

By command of Major-General Rosecrans:

C. GODDARD,
Assistant Adjutant-General.

---

* Marked C, and omitted here, it being printed on p. 328 *et seq.*

COURT OF INQUIRY,
Louisville, February 25, 1864.

The ADJUTANT-GENERAL OF THE ARMY:

GENERAL: I have this day sent in three packages by mail, the record of the proceedings of the Court of Inquiry instituted by Special Orders, No. 13, Paragraph 20, of January 9, in the cases of Major-Generals McCook, Crittenden, and Negley, U. S. Volunteers.

The three cases, to save time and avoid the detention of the witnesses (sometimes the same person testifying in all the cases), were conducted simultaneously. This will account for the remark, "No proceedings in this case to-day," found in the records, and also for the small amount of evidence which appears sometimes to have been taken in a day.

Some apology may be due for the appearance of the record sent, and I will mention that as neither a competent stenographer or clerk could be obtained, the mass of the work was performed by myself, and the copying, therefore, was necessarily hurriedly done. Did time permit, I would make a neater and fairer copy, although it is hardly work for an officer of my rank. I desire it to be understood that I was merely recorder of the Court, and that the cases were conducted by the members composing it.

Very respectfully, general, your obedient servant.

ED. SCHRIVER,
Inspector-General, Recorder.

—

JUDGE-ADVOCATE-GENERAL'S OFFICE,
March 3, 1864.

The records of the proceedings of a Court of Inquiry in the cases of Major-Generals Crittenden, Negley, and McCook, are respectfully forwarded for the consideration of the Secretary of War.

In the case of General McCook, they believe that "he did everything he could to rally and hold his troops after the line was broken," and that he was not responsible for the reverse which the army suffered; but they think that in "leaving the field and going to Chattanooga, he committed a mistake." They do not regard this act, however, as any other than "error of judgment."

In the cases of Generals Crittenden and Negley, the Court are of the opinion that those officers are not censurable. The grounds of their opinions are set out in full at the end of the records. If their views are concurred in, no further action seems to be called for.

Respectfully submitted.

J. HOLT,
Judge-Advocate-General.

—

WAR DEPARTMENT,
March 10, 1864.

Brig. Gen. E. R. S. CANBY,
War Department:

GENERAL: I have the honor to return herewith the proceedings in the case of Major-General McCook, submitted to me for examination, with the following remarks:

There were seventeen witnesses examined by the Court, four of them general officers, namely, Major-General Rosecrans, Brigadier-

General Davis, Brigadier-General Wood, and Brigadier-General Morton; the others staff officers, aides to General Rosecrans or General McCook.

The examination seems to have been sufficiently thorough to warrant a final disposition of the case on the finding and opinion expressed.

The Court had before it diagrams of the battle-field and reports which do not appear in the records, but must have aided materially in its judgment.

There is no evidence indicating that General McCook failed to do his whole duty on the 19th of September, the first day of the battle, and there seems no question about his conduct on the second day (20th September) except as to two facts:

First. Did he use all the vigor and celerity in his power to close the interval in the line of battle caused by the precipitate shifting of General Wood's division to the support of General Thomas? and

Second. Did he commit a mistake in going to Chattanooga after he was cut off from General Thomas and before the battle closed?

The Court very properly exonerates him of all responsibility for the charges [changes] in the lines on the right which resulted in his repulse and retreat; but an implied censure is given by the Court, though not directly, of General McCook's conduct in going to Chattanooga to report to General Rosecrans, which, upon a careful examination of the testimony, seems hardly sustained. The Court say "that in leaving the field to go to Chattanooga General McCook committed a mistake," * * * "but that it cannot regard this act of General McCook as other than an error of judgment."

From the following remarks of the Court in the same connection it will be seen that this so-thought "mistake" was not committed without some very good reason amounting almost to a necessity.

The Court say:

Bearing in mind that, the commanding general having previously gone to Chattanooga, it was natural for General McCook to infer that all the discomfited troops were expected to rally there, as well as to presume that a conference with the commanding general on that important subject was both desirable and necessary, the Court cannot regard this act of General McCook's as other than an error of judgment.

As the Court do not censure directly, and the implication is so equivocal, it is not thought necessary to review the evidence bearing upon this point. The evidence is abundant and concurrent, showing that this officer behaved with gallantry on both days of the battle, that he did not quit the field till driven from it by overpowering numbers, and that he did not report to General Rosecrans before the battle closed from consideration of personal safety.

Judging from the apparent impartiality of the examination, there seems to have been no suppression of facts which would warrant a further inquiry into the conduct of this officer on the occasion mentioned.

I have the honor to be, general, your obedient servant,

N. P. CHIPMAN,
Colonel, and Additional Aide-de-Camp.

APPENDIX.

AUGUST 16–SEPTEMBER 22, 1863.—The Chickamauga Campaign.

Report of Lieut. Col. Samuel B. Raymond, Fifty-first Illinois Infantry.

HEADQUARTERS FIFTY-FIRST ILLINOIS INFANTRY,
Chattanooga, September 29, 1863.

CAPTAIN: In accordance with your circular of this date, I beg leave to submit the following report of the operations of my command during the engagements of the 19th and 20th instant:

Saturday, 19*th.*—A night march from the position taken near Lee's Mill brought us within about 6 miles of Crawfish Spring, to which point we moved hurriedly on the morning of the 19th, taking a short rest there to fill canteens. The sound of artillery and musketry to the left told of an engagement there. Canteens filled we marched rapidly to the left, and at about 12 m. took position in an open piece of ground and near the Chickamauga River.

Meantime the engagement increased in fury, and a tremendous roll of musketry seemed approaching the right. During some considerable time occupied in shifting our position the battle increased with still greater fury, when, in obedience to orders, we moved by the right flank still farther to the left through a heavy belt of timber at a double-quick, rapidly nearing the scene of conflict.

Arriving there the brigade was formed in two lines, my command being formed in the second line and on the left of the Forty-second Illinois. Before I had completed the formation of my line the command "Forward" was given, thus compelling my three left companies to complete the formation at a run, and while passing through the timber and underbrush and over a rail fence which had not been torn down. This caused a temporary brokenness in my line, which had to be remedied after reaching the open space beyond, and on reaching which brought us under the enemy's fire. But the sight of the foe seemed to nerve every heart, and with a shout and a dash we charged upon them, driving all before us, until we had passed a skirt of woods on our left.

At this point we received a murderous and enfilading fire from a fresh brigade of the enemy, thrown out for the evident purpose of turning our flank, and for a moment were compelled to fall back below the crest of the rising ground, taking shelter in a small water-course. Here rallying the men, we again charged forward, and gained the fence lining the west side of the woods which skirted the crest of the ridge and maintained our ground in the front, while a battery in our rear drove the enemy advancing from the woods on our left. I was compelled to crowd my left toward the right, as the fire from the battery passed through it, killing and wounding sev-

(1055)

eral. I also directed what remained of the left wing to fire "left-oblique," and in a few moments the enemy were flying from our front in great disorder.

My ranks were too much weakened to attempt to follow them, and I so reported to Colonel Walworth, commanding the second line, now becoming the first, the front line having fallen back. I was directed by him to hold my position at the fence "at all hazards," which we succeeded in doing.

During the heaviest of the engagement a portion of my men assisted in hauling off three guns by hand, which had been captured by the enemy but a short time before. The fiercest of the conflict lasted but a few moments, but during those few moments we lost 14 killed, 75 wounded, and 5 missing. My left wing was almost annihilated, and had but a handful of men left, losing all but 3 officers. The adjutant and sergeant-major were severely wounded, and my own and Major Davis' horse shot from under us. During the night we erected breastworks, and otherwise made preparations for a renewal of the attack on—

Sunday, 20th.—This day was the second anniversary of the organization of the regiment. At daybreak I received orders to retire from my position by the left flank, and moving to the rear formed a new line upon the crest of the Missionary Ridge hills, where we remained in position till near 10 a. m., at which time the engagement opened again on the left. About this time we were moved down to the bottom again and formed along the road and directly in rear of the First Brigade, my regiment being posted on the left of the Forty-second Illinois in the first line.

The battle was now raging fearfully on our left and seemed again approaching the right. Again we changed position to the foot of the ridge hills and facing south, and while resting here a most terrific musketry fire suddenly broke out near the center, which rolled rapidly to the right and was followed by deafening cheers from the enemy.

At this time I received orders to move the regiment by the left flank at a double-quick, and to follow the Twenty-second Illinois, keeping well closed up. To accomplish this my men were put upon the run and were thus moved down into the timber toward the point of action, and while thus moving and before we had time to halt and form we were met by our retreating forces, hotly pursued by an eager foe, who poured into us a deadly fire on front and flank.

We had scarce time to deliver one volley before they were upon us, and notwithstanding the most energetic efforts on the part of myself and officers we had to give way, while the fleeing forces of other divisions and brigades, breaking through us, caused confusion and separation which could not be remedied, but grew worse. All of my officers exerted themselves to the utmost to stop any and all men without reference to any particular regiments. A second and third line was thus formed and likewise repulsed, when, in obedience to orders, we fell back to crest of the Missionary Ridge hills and formed the fourth line, which was not penetrated by the enemy, they seeming to turn their attention to the pressing of the flank and center.

Directly after this I was directed to follow, with all men I could gather up irrespective of organizations, a column which was then moving over the ridge hills and thence to Rossville. Making a temporary halt to gather together the fragments of regiments, brigades, and divisions, we moved with our division round through the gap at Rossville and up to the ground occupied by General Thomas. Waiting here some time we faced about, and moved back to Rossville late at night and overcome with fatigue.

Of my command we had gathered together nearly 150, leaving our loss for this day at over 60 in killed, wounded, and missing, a few of whom came in afterward uninjured. Our actual casualties on Sunday were 4 killed, 18 wounded, and 31 missing, among whom were 2 non-commissioned officers.

During the engagement of this day Lieutenant Cummings, of Company D, assisted by a squad of men representing several other regiments, captured the battle-flag of the Twenty-fourth Alabama Regiment.

On Saturday we engaged the troops of Hood's division, of Longstreet's corps, and on Sunday the troops of Polk's corps, the former of whom gave us full credit for the fierceness, valor, and success of our charge.

It is with feelings of gratified pride I speak of the noble and gallant conduct of the officers and men of my command in the engagements of both days. The small number missing on the first day speaks volumes for their individual bravery and faithfulness. Where all did so well it would be invidious to mention names, and I trust our commanders, of whom we all feel so proud, think well of our service.

The honored dead call forth the silent tears of sorrow and sympathy, and we regret that the overwhelming force of the foe compelled us to leave them without the last sad rites of a soldier's burial. The wounded were carefully removed as far as possible, and have received attention of our own surgeon, who remained behind with assistants, in charge of the hospital at Crawfish Spring.

Accompanying this you will find a complete list* of the casualties during Saturday and Sunday, the 19th and 20th instant, corresponding as near as may be to the report already handed in.

SAM. B. RAYMOND,

Lieut. Col. Fifty-first Illinois Infantry, Commanding.

[Capt. GEORGE LEE,
Asst. Adjt. Gen., Third Division, 20th *Army Corps.*]

Report of Col. Newell Gleason, Eighty-seventh Indiana Infantry.

HDQRS. EIGHTY-SEVENTH INDIANA VOLUNTEERS,
Chattanooga, Tenn., September 26, 1863.

CAPTAIN: In compliance with instructions received from brigade headquarters, I have the honor to submit the following report of the part taken by my command in the engagements of the 19th and 20th instant:

Approaching the field of battle on the morning of the 19th instant, my command, formed in double column closed in mass, marched in rear of the battery, and on taking position for action the battery formed on the crest of a small hill, and my command deployed immediately in its rear and was ordered to lie down. The action commenced furiously and brought us under a heavy fire, several of my command being killed and wounded while in this position.

---

*Embodied in revised statement, p. 175.

In a short time my regiment was ordered to relieve the Thirty-fifth Ohio, which was posted to the right of the battery. Moving forward in double-quick we lay down immediately in rear of the Thirty-fifth Ohio until it passed us to the rear, when my regiment, rising and pouring a terrible volley with deliberate aim into the enemy, moved forward and occupied the position just held by the Thirty-fifth Ohio. We continued the fire with vigor until the enemy was driven from his line in front of us. Skirmishers were thrown out, several prisoners sent to the rear, and our wounded cared for. Orders came to call attention, hold our ground, and lie down. Heavy firing commenced upon a brigade at our right, a part of which precipitately retreated over us; we in the mean time receiving a considerable portion of the fire aimed at them. Holding our fire until they had passed, my regiment, without the least confusion, arose in perfect line and poured a volley into the advancing ranks of the enemy, which brought him to a halt. Rapid firing continued, but the enemy maintained his line for a few moments, when, seeing the Ninth Ohio, posted upon my right, about to charge bayonets, with my command I followed the example, and both regiments, advancing at double-quick, drove the enemy before them and recaptured several pieces of artillery previously lost by the brigade at our right.

Learning that the enemy had passed to my left, I changed direction by throwing my left to the rear and my right forward so as to preserve connection with the Second Minnesota on my left. Receiving orders to move to the hill where I was first formed, I moved by the left flank, taking position on the ground occupied by the battery during the first engagement, the Second Minnesota and one section of the battery being upon my right and the other section of the battery and the Thirty-fifth Ohio on my left. Lying down, we retained our fire until the enemy appeared near the crest of the hill, when my regiment poured into him a galling fire, which was repeated until he retired from our front. After providing for the wounded, the brigade moved to another position. Resting a short time in this position, the brigade moved some 2 miles, where we bivouacked for the night

My loss during this day's engagement was 10 killed, among whom were Captain Holliday, Company K; Lieutenant Martin, Company H, commanding Company G, and Lieutenant Bennett, Company E, and 39 wounded, among whom was Captain Ellis, Company C.

On the morning of the 20th, the brigade being held in reserve, formed in double column in mass in front of the ground occupied during the night, the Ninth Ohio on the right and my regiment on the left forming the first line; and the Second Minnesota covering the Ninth Ohio, and the Thirty-fifth Ohio covering the Eighty-seventh Indiana, formed the second line. About 8.30 a. m. the column moved by the left flank in the direction where heavy firing had for some time been raging. It appearing that the enemy was closely pressing the left of our line, our columns, in the above-mentioned order, were deployed facing to the left.

After halting about fifteen minutes, the brigade moved rapidly through a thick wood by the right flank for some distance, and then to the front in line of battle, in the order just described, making an oblique movement to the right until it arrived near the Chattanooga road, where we changed direction slightly to the left and took position in the edge of the timber, in front of a corn-field, the right of my command resting upon the road, which formed an acute angle with the line of battle toward my left. Just before the completion of this movement the enemy opened a severe fire upon our line. We replied with a heavy volley, and my regiment then lay down to load and continued the fire. Presently discovering that the enemy was approaching my left, charging bayonets, my regiment, obeying my orders, rose to their feet, gave him a volley, which checked his advance, causing his line to waver and fall back. At this instant the Thirty-fifth Ohio passed my line to the front and charged across the field, my regiment following. Having crossed the field into the edge of the woods beyond, driving the enemy before us, the brigade was ordered to lie down, the regiments being formed in the rear of each other in the following order : Ninth Ohio, Thirty-fifth Ohio, Second Minnesota, and Eighty-seventh Indiana. My command soon after was formed on the right of the Second Minnesota. In this position the enemy was met and the several regiments passed each other in retreat, retreating in order and firing as we retired.

After returning to the place where the engagement commenced we gathered up our wounded and carried them off the field, when my command retired to the top of the hill occupied by the balance of the division, where we soon joined the brigade and formed upon the left of the Second Minnesota, maintaining our position, fighting the enemy with vigor and determination until the darkness of night brought the engagement to a close.

My loss during this day's engagement was 30 killed, among whom were Captain Baker, Company B; Captain Hughs, Company D; Adjutant Ryland, Lieutenant Brown, Company C, and Lieutenant Andrew, Company I, and 103 wounded, among whom were Lieutenant Biddle, commanding Company I, Lieutenant Beeber, Company F, and Lieutenant Crosby, Company K. Total loss both days : Commissioned officers killed, 8 ; enlisted men killed, 32 ; commissioned officers wounded, 4 ; enlisted men wounded, 138 ; enlisted men missing, 8 ; total killed, wounded, and missing, 190. I went into the engagement with 22 commissioned officers and 344 enlisted men, showing a proportion in loss of nearly three-fifths.

In the first engagement of the second day my regiment was immediately in front of the Adams brigade, Breckinridge's division, composed of the Thirteenth, Sixteenth, Nineteenth, and Twentieth Louisiana Regiments, which line formed an obtuse angle, the apex resting opposite the left wing of my regiment, a battery being placed at said angle in the rebel lines, exposing my regiment to a terrible cross-fire. General Adams and his adjutant-general were wounded and a major killed in front of my regiment. These facts we learned from Captain Troutman, Company E, who had the rebel adjutant-general carried to the hospital.

During both days' engagement the officers and men of my command behaved in the most gallant manner, giving strict attention to orders and keeping the ranks well closed. Our list of wounded being so large, in our anxiety to have them taken from the field, a few became separated from the regiment who joined us at night at Rossville.

Where all behaved so well and did so much, it is with no disparagement to others to state that the bravery of Captain Baker and Adjutant Ryland, among the killed, was especially noticed. All my officers were at their posts and did their whole duty. I cannot fail to acknowledge the assistance of Major Hammond, who was the only field officer I had present, and Captain Sabin, who first discovered the near approach of the enemy on the left, and rallied his command to their feet. Captains Payne and Long were with us doing their whole duty, though both had been sick for several days. Captain Ellis, who was wounded in the first day's engagement, went from the ambulance into the fight. Captain Troutman led his company with bravery during the whole engagement. Lieutenant Russell exhibited great gallantry and daring, exposing himself constantly. The conduct of Lieutenants Burnham, Company A; O'Blenis, Company D, and Agnew, Company B, the two latter commanding their companies after the fall of their captains, is worthy of special notice. The wounds of Lieutenants Biddle, commanding Company I; Beeber, Company F, and Crosby, Company K, testify that they were at their posts. Those who were killed fell while bravely discharging their duty. The color bearer, Corporal Vandever, and many more enlisted men especially deserve notice, but there are so many of them that the limits of this report will not admit of further mention of names.

I am, captain, very respectfully, your obedient servant,

N. GLEASON,
Colonel Eighty-seventh Indiana Volunteers.

Capt. JOHN R. BEATTY,
Actg. Asst. Adjt. Gen., 3d Brig., 3d Div.. 14th Army Corps.

Report of Maj. Robert M. Kelly, Fourth Kentucky Infantry.

HEADQUARTERS FOURTH KENTUCKY INFANTRY,
Chattanooga, Tenn., September 25, 1863.

LIEUTENANT : In accordance with orders, I have the honor to submit the following report of the part taken by the Fourth Kentucky Infantry Volunteers in the actions of September 19 and 20, after I assumed command :

About 10 o'clock a. m. on Saturday, 19th, being at that time with General Brannan, near the left of the division, I heard that Lieutenant-Colonel Hunt, commanding the regiment, was wounded and compelled to retire from the field. The general, at my request, at once relieved me from duty on his staff, and permitted me to report to the regiment. I found it, about 10.30 o'clock, on the left of the rear line of the brigade, having the Fourteenth Ohio on its right, and supporting Southwick's battery. The regiment up to this time had lost about 50 killed and wounded. I immediately assumed command, relieving Captain Myers, who had succeeded Colonel Hunt a half hour previous. Shortly after that I received orders from Colonel Croxton to move by the right flank, following the Fourteenth Ohio. After moving about 150 yards another order was received to move 400 yards farther to the right, and then, forming line, to move forward to open ground. After advancing a little distance the line was fired into by the enemy's skirmishers. The firing became heavier. The double-quick was ordered, and the regiment, supported by the Fourteenth Ohio on the right and the Seventy-fourth Indiana on the left, moved forward till the line came to a road running nearly parallel with its front. Here we came upon the enemy in strong force, separated from us 100 yards or so, having in his front toward our right some felled timber, and in our front and left open woods, and apparently protected by light works. A very severe fire was here opened upon us, enfilading us from the right and causing heavy loss. The line was thrown into some confusion and began to retire, but slowly, and firing as it retreated. At this time the Thirty-first Ohio, Colonel Lister, advanced to our assistance and, moving through the left of the Fourth Kentucky and the right of the Seventy-fourth Indiana, came under the fire of the enemy, which apparently increased in violence upon their appearance. The Thirty-first gave way, and also began to fall back. The enemy followed closely, firing heavily as he advanced. At this time the regiment was losing severely in killed and wounded. Making several partial stands and keeping the enemy in check, the line fell back about 200 yards, till, coming to a favorable rise in the ground, I succeeded, with the energetic assistance of the officers and many of the non-commissioned officers, in making an effective stand. The rest of the line also halted, and we held the ridge under a severe fire for about half an hour, when the division of General Palmer, advancing on our right, drove the enemy and relieved us. I then fell back to the hollow immediately in rear of the ridge, and after resting nearly half an hour and getting a fresh supply of ammunition moved with the brigade by the left flank and formed in rear of Southwick's battery. After remaining there something over an hour and sending details to bring off the wounded, I received orders to move with the brigade to the right.

During our advance Colonel Chapman, Seventy-fourth Indiana, under whose immediate command the three regiments on the right of the brigade line were acting, had his horse shot under him, and his arm broken by the fall, and the line was moved by independent action of the regimental commanders. Upon getting the order to move to the right I followed in rear of the brigade, moving by the right flank, crossing the Chattanooga road and moving through the woods into an open field beyond, where the brigade was formed in two lines, the Fourth Kentucky Infantry occupying the right of the second line and moving in rear of the Seventy-fourth Indiana. After advancing about a half mile the line was halted, my regiment being along a narrow wagon road and my right resting near a hospital tent of the Seventy-ninth Ohio. I lay there till dark, the Third Brigade and perhaps the First passing us, moving to the right, when, by order of Colonel Croxton, I moved the regiment to the right about half a mile and bivouacked in a field near edge of a wood on a hill-side.

About 4 a. m. the next day I moved with the rest of the brigade to the Chattanooga road, crossing it at Kelly's house, leaving that just on our left, and took position on that, holding the left of the front line, supporting Southwick's battery, and sending out a company to the front as skirmishers. After remaining in that position about an hour was relieved by the Seventy-fourth Indiana, and took position in its rear on the left of the second line. The brigade then moved by the left flank about 300 yards, and joined General Reynolds' right. After lying there long enough for the men to make coffee moved a few hundred yards farther to the right, my left resting on a road, the Tenth Kentucky on my right, and the Seventy-fourth Indiana (which had thrown up a rude breastwork of logs) in front. The front line became engaged about 10 o'clock. I caused my men to lie down for cover, and remained so till, the right being turned, the troops to the right of me began to give way. I called my men up and endeavored to change front to the right, but while in the midst of the movement the line was thrown into confusion and the regiment very much scattered by the retreating troops breaking through it. The men were also called on to assist in moving off some of Southwick's guns, which served further to scatter them.

Having no orders, I continued with the colors and such of my own and other regiments as I could gather to move toward my original right, moving my left toward the breastworks, firing at the same time into the flanking column of the enemy. But 2 or 3 officers were with me at this time, and in the mêlée I had lost my horse. I then moved by the left flank down the breastworks to the left, having with me the colors, about 25 of my own men, and a small number from the other regiments, and in a few hundred yards came to the Nineteenth Indiana Battery, supported by some infantry, and a short distance on found Colonel King's brigade and the Third Brigade of this division. I reported to Colonel Van Derveer, who placed me on the right of the Thirty-fifth Ohio.

While here about 40 of my men, under Captain Tompkins and Lieutenants Roberts and Merrimee, with other men of Second Brigade, under Lieutenant-Colonel Taylor, Tenth Indiana, and Lieutenant-Colonel Baker, Seventy-fourth Indiana, joined me. After an hour's rest moved with Colonel Van Derveer to the right and rear through the woods and a corn-field about one-half mile, forming a junction with the troops holding the hill. I there found Colonel Hays, commanding Second Brigade, with a few hundred men, and was joined by 40 or 50 of my men under their officers. After an hour or two of rest moved up the hill and engaged the enemy, who were endeavoring to carry the ridge. Here the regiment suffered severely. After being in action about an hour and a half the enemy was repulsed. I reformed the regiment in line, and shortly afterward was requested by Colonel Stoughton, commanding brigade in [Negley's] division, to move about 100 yards to the left and fill a gap in his line, which I did. Not seeing Colonel Hays at the moment, I reported the fact to General Brannan. There was no further firing, and a little after dark I received orders to move quietly in rear of the brigade off the hill. I proceeded with the brigade that night to Rossville, remained there till the night of the 21st, and then moved with the division to this point.

I regret to report that 2 valuable officers, Captain Givens, Company K, and Lieut. A. Moores, Company E, wounded on the hill and taken to hospital near by, together with some wounded men and 2 men sent to nurse them, were left to fall into the hands of the enemy.

Where all the officers acquitted themselves well, it would be invidious to make distinctions. Lieutenant Spencer, Company I, was detailed early the first day to take charge of prisoners, and was not further in the action. The gallantry of First Sergeants Murrill, of Company K, and More, of Company A, deserves notice; the first-named continued to rally his men after he was severely wounded. I regret that the mustering orders forbid their promotion. Sergeants Swoope and Patten, Company D; Duke, Company B, and others I want space to name, deserve most honorable mention and promotion. Corporal Barkley, Company I, and McGuire, Company G, color bearers, the first wounded on the 19th, did their duty nobly. The men fought bravely, and even when scattered showed, with a few disgraceful exceptions, a disposition to engage the enemy wherever they could find them. The small number reported missing shows that there could have been little straggling in this regiment, and of those so reported all but very few are known almost certainly to have been left on the field either killed or wounded. I append hereto a report of the killed, wounded, and missing during the action.

I have the honor to be, lieutenant, very respectfully, your obedient servant,

R. M. KELLY,
Major, Commanding Fourth Kentucky Infantry.

Lieut. C. V. RAY,
  Actg. Asst. Adjt. Gen., Second Brigade, Third Division.

Report of Lieut. Col. Archibald Blakeley, Seventy-eighth Pennsylvania Infantry.

HDQRS. SEVENTY-EIGHTH REGT. PA. VOL. INFTY,
Chattanooga, Tenn., October 1, 1863.

CAPTAIN : I have the honor to make the following report of the part taken by the Seventy-eighth Regiment Pennsylvania Volunteer Infantry under my command in the movement and actions from the time of leaving Cave Spring, Ala., September 1, 1863, to the occupation of Chattanooga, September 22, 1863 :

On the evening of September 1, at dark, in obedience to an order from headquarters of the brigade, the regiment, under my command, marched from the encampment at Cave Spring, Ala., down the Crow Creek Valley through Stevenson, across the Tennessee River (at midnight), up the Tennessee Valley to near Bridgeport; then via Moore's Spring ascended the Raccoon range of mountains, and on the evening of the 3d bivouacked on the summit at the side of a stream running through a deep ravine which was found to be impassable.

Company C, of my regiment, under command of Lieut. David R. Brinker, was detailed to bridge the ravine. The work was commenced at 5 o'clock in the evening and in ten hours a bridge 160 feet long and 35 feet high at the highest point was completed, over which the Second (Negley's) Division and others of the Fourteenth Army Corps passed in safety. For the construction of this bridge Lieutenant Brinker and his command were complimented by General Thomas in general orders.

On the morning of the 4th I marched from the summit of the Raccoon Mountain, descending its eastern slope, and debouched into the Lookout Valley at Brown's Spring ; thence up the valley to a mill on Lookout Creek. This mill was filled with wheat, corn, and rye. I halted here and placed Captain Marlin, of A Company, in charge of the mill. We ground out all there was in it ; we scoured the Lookout Valley, and gathered and ground all the grain we could find, turning the product over to the passing army. We also gathered and turned in to the troops all the cattle we could find fit for beef, taking care to leave with each family enough grain and cattle for their support.

When the army had passed we had a squad of 16 men too sick to march, and we had no transportation for them. I therefore detailed Private W. S. Hosack, of G Company, an excellent physician, to take charge of them and remain with them, leaving them tents, supplies, and medicines. We have not heard from them and I suppose they have been captured. Our location at the mill was very unhealthy, and we suffered much from sickness there. We followed and passed the greater part of the army by the time we reached Johnson's Crook. We lay one night in the Crook, and then crossed Lookout Mountain into McLemore's Cove at Stevens' Gap, and rested there the night of the 9th.

On the morning of the 10th, under the belief that the enemy was in full retreat, the Second Division moved forward on the road leading through Dug Gap in the Pigeon Mountain to La Fayette, Ga., the Third Brigade having the advance, my regiment leading the column.

Near Dug Gap, as we approached the Chickamauga, we came upon the enemy posted in considerable force at the gap and on the line of the Chickamauga. Falling into line my regiment pressed forward on the left of the La Fayette road, crossing the Chickamauga to the left of the stone fences, through a field of corn, then through a dense forest, emerging into open fields adjoining the Widow Davis' house, and through these fields to the top of a high knob to the east of her house, dislodging and driving the enemy as we advanced. From this knob I was brought back and given position in the woods adjoining and west of the road running north from the house of the Widow Davis.

I remained in this position until near dark, when I was moved northwestwardly three-fourths of a mile, and assigned a position in the woods, my front to the north. Soon after midnight I was moved an eighth of a mile southwestwardly and posted in a dense undergrowth, my front to the north. This movement of my regiment, as well as that of the whole brigade made at that time, was so quietly executed that our pickets did not know of it until morning.

Early in the forenoon of the 11th a vigorous attack was made on that part of the division fronting east by the enemy then occupying the hills we had held the day before. This attack was evidently made to cover an attack on my front, which was commenced at 10 a. m. by a line of skirmishers, followed by a line of sharpshooters, covering infantry, deployed and massed, at least four regiments. My skirmish line, consisting of 8 non-commissioned officers and 60 men, under command of Lieut. David R. Brinker and Lieut. James H. Anchors, all under command of Maj. A. B. Bonnaffon, held this force in check for four hours, with the exception that about half past 12 the Eleventh Michigan on my left and the Seventy-fourth Ohio on my right were withdrawn, leaving my flanks exposed, when they were swung back to a better position. Major Bonnaffon and Lieutenants Brinker and Anchors and the men under their command deserve honorable mention for the work of this day.

At 2 p. m. General Starkweather relieved me, when I was ordered to fall back to General Negley's headquarters, west of the creek. From General Negley's headquarters I again crossed the Chickamauga at the same place I did the day before, deployed and skirmished through the corn-field, but finding no enemy I was withdrawn and supported Captain Schultz' battery, then in action on the hill on the north side of the road west of the white house. From the latter position I fell back by your order to the foot of Lookout Mountain, where we arrived at dark, the enemy pressing us closely during the movement. I lay at the foot of Lookout Mountain from the evening of the 11th to the morning of the 17th behind rudely constructed breastworks.

On the 17th the march was resumed in a northeasterly direction, and at evening I halted on ground occupied by a portion of General Crittenden's corps, where I remained until the evening of the 18th, and then was moved eastwardly 2 miles and halted until midnight, then countermarched 1 mile and, deploying my regiment as skirmishers, with C and H Companies in reserve, moved south to the north bank of the Chickamauga. I was informed by Captain Johnson of General Negley's staff, that the enemy was in force on the opposite side, and it was apprehended he might attempt to cross to strike the flank of General McCook's corps, then moving into position by my rear on its hard march from Alpine.

On the morning of the 19th, by personal examination, I found that I held about 1 mile of the Chickamauga, including two fords. Both sides of the stream were covered by trees and undergrowth. I felled trees in the fords, Captain Ayres reconnoitered the front, and by keeping up a bold appearance we were unmolested, and when the corps of General McCook had passed we followed him to rejoin the brigade, then north of Crawfish Spring.

In moving north to the brigade we passed a part of the line where the division of General Jefferson C. Davis was engaged in a sanguinary conflict with the enemy. We passed under the rebel fire, while the roar of the battle and the sight of the wounded, bleeding and mangled, I feared might make even the heroes of Stone's River quail. Some were cheerful, others quiet and meditative, but determination was pictured on each brow, which satisfied me that there would be no flinching on the part of the Seventy-eighth Regiment.

We found the brigade in line north of Crawfish Spring, the Twenty-first Ohio well advanced engaging the enemy in the woods at the eastern edge of a large field. I was ordered to cross this field to a position on the left of the Twenty-first Ohio. We attained our position under a raking fire, but found that we could not successfully return the fire as the enemy was concealed in the woods on high ground in our front, and being without sufficient support to charge, I ordered the men to lie down until needed. We lay on our arms under a heavy fire until after dark with little damage, but the Twenty-first Ohio suffered severely.

About dark a terrific musketry engagement took place on our left front. After dark I moved to the right of the brigade and threw out pickets covering my front and uniting with the pickets of the Thirty-seventh Indiana on my left and the pickets of Colonel Wilder's mounted brigade on my right. In this position we lay on our arms the night of the 19th.

On the morning of the 20th, Colonel Wilder's pickets were withdrawn, and I immediately fell southward as far as I could safely go, and found no one to connect with, which fact was at once reported to Colonel Sirwell, commanding the brigade.

Soon after the commencement of the battle of the 20th, I discovered the enemy massing troops in the woods on my right front, and reporting this to brigade commander, two pieces of artillery were sent to my aid and a breastwork of old logs thrown up by my regiment.

About 11 a. m. our whole division moved to the left, leaving this line unoccupied. Our new position was on the foot-hills about 1 mile from the position we held in the morning. As we marched from our first to our second position I saw the enemy break through the line we had held in the morning, and this enabled him to cut off the right wing of our army, which produced the great disaster of the day.

In our formation on the foot-hills, the Thirty-seventh Indiana was on my left and the Twenty-first Ohio on my right. I was moved forward to support Captain Bridges' Chicago Battery, then in action on the crest of a hill near a small house used as a hospital. I deployed my regiment on the brow of the hill in front of and below the battery, the gunners firing over us. We defended the battery for a while, when it ceased firing and moved to the rear without indicating to me what its orders were. Soon after the battery left there was a lull in the battle in our immediate neighborhood, but the firing on the left was heavy, and on our right irregular and passing to our rear.

The position of the battery was an advanced one, and I did not connect with other troops by either flank, and in fact after the battery left I could see no Union troops anywhere except those of my own regiment. I directed Major Bonnaffon to take command until my return, and I rode back to where I had parted company with the Thirty-seventh Indiana and the Twenty-first Ohio. They were gone, and so far as I could see our whole line was gone, and the right— McCook and Crittenden—all broken up.

I returned to the regiment and found the enemy closing in on it. Placing Major Bonnaffon in charge of the skirmishers to protect the movement, we marched to the rear, and the enemy, although in overwhelming numbers, did not follow but a short distance. About 800 to 1,000 paces from our position with the battery, we found General Negley alone. He posted us in a ravine or hollow between two foot-hills running down toward the Chickamauga, with orders to prevent the enemy at all hazards from breaking through a chasm or gap in the hill on the south of the ravine. I massed the regiment in the ravine or hollow in front of the gap, and Major Bonnaffon deployed two companies over the hill covering our front. He soon called for me and I rode forward, and found that our position was concealed from the enemy by underbrush, but from the foot of the hill to the Chickamauga, 100 rods or more, the land was clear, and a column of rebel troops, at least a division, were moving over this field westwardly across our front, evidently unaware of our presence. Major Bonnaffon was anxious to charge them. We might have driven them for the time being, but we would have been ultimately lost as we were without support.

Returning to the regiment I did not know what to do. We knew as yet nothing about the lines or the condition of the battle. We knew that the right was broken and that was all. To follow the sound of the battle on our left would probably lead us in the rear of the rebel army, where superior numbers would destroy us. I was about to go forward again to Major Bonnaffon to consider again the proposition to charge on the troops below us, when I noticed a mounted officer well up on the hill north of us. He approached us cautiously until he recognized us, and then came down rapidly. He was one of General Thomas' staff officers. He asked why we were there, and who put us there. I told him. He communicated the fact of the loss of the right wing. He stated that Thomas had the only line unbroken, and he was fighting away for dear life 1½ miles northeast of us. That the only possible way for us to get in was to strike for he Dry Valley road.   He gave me the direction and ordered me to go, and left to find a way to his chief.   We set out on the line indicated, Major Bonnaffon covering the movement with his skirmishers. The march being difficult and the danger imminent I have no correct data of time or distance, but we found the Dry Valley road, and it, and indeed the valley, was filled with a struggling mass of stragglers, batteries, wagons, ambulances, and troops of all arms, on a stampede for Chattanooga and pressed by the enemy's cavalry.

Dividing my command with Major Bonnaffon, he threw his skirmish line to the rear of the broken column, between it and the enemy, and I moved rapidly down to near Rossville, and placing the regiment across the valley we passed to Chattanooga all ambulances with wounded, all wagons, and many wounded on foot, with the necessary assistance.   We halted all unhurt troops and stragglers.   We halted batteries and parts of batteries and ambulances not carrying wounded.   I was informed that by night-fall we had halted seven batteries and about 5,000 men, which were all reorganized that night and ready for action next morning.   Colonel Sirwell, commanding the brigade, came to us at Rossville an hour later, when I reported to him.

On Monday, the 21st, I occupied six different positions, the last of which was on and across Missionary Ridge on the left of your brigade and uniting with the right of General Beatty's brigade.   I was assigned to this position at 12 m., and directed to take orders from General Beatty.   That portion of the ridge which General Beatty and I held being covered with a dense forest, the general ordered a reconnaissance to the front.   I sent out Captain Ayres for that purpose, who went a mile south along the top of the ridge, carefully noting the topography of the country, location of fields, &c.   For this as well as for the reconnaissance of the 19th, Captain Ayres deserves great credit—for the valuable information obtained and the discretion displayed in obtaining it.

On the night of the 21st I fell back with the general movement of the army to Chattanooga.   In this movement I was placed in command of the brigade, and Major Bonnaffon commanded the regiment until after the formation of the lines for the defense of Chattanooga. During the movements and actions described, the Seventy-eighth Regiment was never for an instant broken.

In the trying scenes at Dug Gap and Chickamauga, and in the retreat on Sunday evening, when batteries, wagons, stragglers, and wounded filled Dry Valley in a pell-mell race for Chattanooga, the Seventy-eighth Regiment moved as calmly and with as much precision as on dress parade.   From Cave Spring to Chattanooga but 1 man left the ranks without leave.   Every order was executed to the letter, and when by the casualties of the day we were left without orders, we did the best we could, but with the help of Major Bonnaffon and Adjutant Torbett it was not hard to steer clear of mistakes.

To you personally and to Colonel Sirwell, commanding the brigade, my thanks are due for the plain, common-sense manner in which your orders were given.

ARCHIBALD BLAKELEY,
Lieut. Col., Comdg. Seventy-eighth Regt. Pa. Vol. Infty.

Capt. Wm. B. Gillespie,
  Asst. Adjt. Gen., Third Brig., Second Div., 14th Army Corps.

Report of Col. Gustave Kammerling, Ninth Ohio Infantry.

CAPTAIN : I have the honor to submit the following report in ref
erence to the part taken by my regiment in the battle of the 19th and
20th instant :

Having been ordered to escort the ammunition train of the Third
Division, the Ninth Regiment Ohio Volunteers did not arrive on the
battle-field before noon on the 19th of September, 1863. Here it took
position under your direction on the left of the Second Minnesota
Volunteers, on a line running obliquely from the extreme left wing
of the Third Brigade. A line of skirmishers was established, but
nothing seen of the enemy. Brisk firing then was heard from our
right and the regiment ordered off to this direction. I passed the
rear of the Second Minnesota, Battery I, Fourth U. S. Artillery, and
the Eighty-seventh Indiana Volunteers, on the right of which latter
regiment I was ordered to take position so as to form the right wing
of the line established by the regiments and battery of the Third
Brigade. Companies A and I were immediately deployed as skirmishers, the enemy vigorously advancing toward our line. As soon
as the latter had arrived and was in full sight on and along the slope
extending in our front I ordered my regiment to charge, which having been done with a good will and with great vigor, the enemy was
driven back down the valley and beyond another crest of hills in our
front, leaving a full battery behind, which they shortly before had
captured from Company H, Fifth Artillery, U. S. Army. Besides
the battery we took a number of prisoners, who gave themselves up.
This charge cost us 63 men—1 officer and 12 enlisted men killed, 3
officers and 47 enlisted men wounded.

A short while thereafter I received Colonel Van Derveer's order
to return as quick as possible to the assistance of the remainder
of our brigade, which was just being hard pressed by the rebels. I
marched the regiment back with all possible haste, but on my arrival
at the place designated found the rebels already whipped and gone.
This was about 3 p. m., and ended our work for the day. The rebels
did not attempt to regain the field.

On the top of a large and commanding hill, about 2 miles distant
from the above-described place, the regiment bivouacked during the
night ; this hill being one of the few open ridges in that neighborhood, entirely naked and not covered with woods or underbrush.

At 8 a. m. on Sunday, the 20th, we left this bivouac in accordance
with orders received from brigade headquarters, the regiment marching in center column. Heavy firing was going on in and around the
thick woods in front of us. For about two hours we were held in
reserve of the fire line, and as such changed position accordingly.
Finally, about 10 o'clock, we advanced into the woods, the enemy
apparently retreating before the fire of the front lines. After a mile's
march a large open corn-field was reached, and here the four regiments
of the Third Brigade took position so as to give the Eighty-seventh
Indiana and Ninth Ohio Volunteers the first and the Second Minnesota and Thirty-fifth Ohio the second line. The Ninth Ohio was
posted on the right of the Eighty-seventh Indiana Volunteers, the
whole having changed direction to the left-oblique. Heavy firing
was continually kept up on our right, and soon shots coming from
the woods which in our front surrounded the corn-field, indicated the
presence of the enemy in said woods. This being intolerable, we advanced, charged the enemy, and gained the woods. The enemy, who

t the same time were pressed by troops of the Twentieth Army
Corps marching up through the woods on our right, gradually re-
reated and were followed up for about half a mile, when the fight
ame to a stand.   But our left flank was unprotected, and therefore
he position was at length untenable for a single regiment.   Soon a
rebel battery opened upon us; immediately thereafter rebel infantry
n our front was seen marching off by the right flank, and so the
danger to get flanked made it necessary to fall back to the former
position in the corn-field.   This was completed not without severe
losses sustained from the enemy's fire, but the latter did not follow up
beyond said woods and left us unmolested in possession of the corn-
field.   Meanwhile this place was shelled from the opposite side too,
and I was ordered by Colonel Van Derveer to march off by the flank
with skirmishers ahead and on a parallel line with the Second Minnesota Regiment, in a direction from east to west.   After having
marched about 1 mile through the woods we reached an open corn-
field, passed across the same, and again entered the woods, which we
found filled with our troops.   Here we were ordered to take position
along the crest of a hill-side, on the right of the Eighty-second Regiment Indiana Volunteers.   The whole Third Division was concentrated on this point.   The enemy in force in our front trying
to take the hill occupied by our troops, and so to cut off our communication with Chattanooga.   A terrible fire was incessantly kept
up by both sides.   Desperate efforts were made by the rebels to gain
our hill and storm our little fence breastworks, which, although
hastily erected in a few moments of pause, gave a good cover to our
soldiers and as such were of an immense advantage and saved many
a soldier's life.   In vain the rebels made charge after charge.   Each
was bravely repulsed, and finally just before dark the enemy abstained
from their attempts and let us alone.   An hour after dark our troops
were quietly and unmolested marching back toward Rossville.

Our total loss sustained on the 20th amounts to the number of 185—
2 officers and 33 enlisted men killed, 5 officers and 145 enlisted men
wounded.   The aggregate loss of killed and wounded on both days
amounts to 248.

All of which is herewith respectfully submitted.

[G. KAMMERLING,
Colonel, Commanding.]

[Capt. J. R. BEATTY,]
  Actg. Asst. Adjt. Gen., 3d Brig., 3d Div., 14th Army Corps.

Report of Lieut. Col. Hiram F. Devol, Thirty-sixth Ohio Infantry.

CHATTANOOGA, September 23, 1863.

GENERAL: I have the honor to submit the following report of the
part taken by the Thirty-sixth Regiment Ohio Volunteer Infantry
in the battle of Chickamauga, from the morning of the 19th to reaching this place, the morning of the 22d instant:

On the morning of the 19th, after a wearisome all-night march,
the regiment was at Crawfish Spring, La Fayette and Chattanooga
road.   Moved immediately forward 3½ miles in direction of Chattanooga with brigade until the Dyer house was reached.   Filed right
into the woods, there being quite heavy firing in that direction.

At 2.30 p. m. that part of the brigade consisting of the Eleventh and Thirty-sixth Ohio and Eighteenth Kentucky changed front ob liquely to the right in the direction of very heavy firing. In a few moments a line of our troops came retreating back and through our line, the enemy in close pursuit, but on seeing our line they took cover behind trees and fallen timber, and opened a disastrous fire on our regiment and line. The Thirty-sixth being exposed suffered most. On the right, the contest being so unequal, Company D, Captain Stanley, was suffering terribly. I sought Col. W. G. Jones, colonel of the regiment, but could not find him. Returning to my position in line, and still seeing the destruction going on, I again sought the colonel ; not finding him or any one else in command, I ordered the line to rise and charge, which was obeyed, with the result that we drove the enemy for a quarter of a mile to and beyond one of their batteries.

At this point an aide from you ordered us back. The battery could not be brought off owing to the entanglement of the woods. Fell back through the gap made in the enemy's line, without opposition. Our loss in regiment had been very great—Colonel Jones mortally wounded, Major Adney wounded. Of the fate of these two officers I knew nothing until our falling back. The regiment retired to west side of La Fayette road, where we lay on arms, with two companies as skirmishers at the front, all night.

Sunday morning, the 20th, moved with brigade about one-fourth of a mile to front and east of road. At once commenced constructing breastworks of old logs and rails that were at hand. About 10 a. m. the enemy advanced to the attack, but were forced to fall back. These charges were repeated several times at intervals until 4 p. m. About 2 p. m. our ammunition was exhausted, almost. I sent for a supply. Captain Barker, of General Thomas' staff, came personally with a supply. Just about 3.30 p. m. the troops on the immediate right of my regiment (I think General Brannan's) were driven back, which left the right of my regiment projected and exposed. I turned Captain Stanley, with his company, D, to the right and rear. He soon had all his sergeants killed and many men. About 5 p. m. our front line was withdrawn about half way to the road.

The firing was still on our right and rear. I heard General Reynolds remark that he thought he would have to surrender. The woods were thick with smoke, shells falling thick among us. Fell in and with brigade marched by the flank back of road. Was halted and fronted by the rear facing north, right resting on road. A charge was immediately ordered and at once struck the enemy's flank, driving him easily. A number of my men were sent in charge of prisoners to a line we seemed to have at our left, where we were ordered to go. But the order not being well understood, many of my regiment with the colors pursued the enemy to and beyond the Kelly house, but just before dark all were assembled in rear of the Kelly house in line with Robinson and Willich. Night coming on marched over into the Dry Valley.

21st, remained all day in line; that night marched into Chattanooga.

Casualties September 19 : Field and staff, Col. W. G. Jones, mortally wounded, died the same day ; Maj. William Adney, seriously wounded. Total killed and wounded : killed, 1 officer, 11 men ; wounded, 3 officers, 62 men ; men missing, wounded in hands of enemy, 14 ; total, 91.

Company C, being on detached duty, guarding train, was not engaged with regiment.

In this fifth great battle in which the regiment has participated it is with pride I assure you that both officers and men bore themselves most gallantly, not a man leaving his post except for good cause, notwithstanding the repeated charges of the enemy up to the point of the bayonet, and when the enemy was not only in front but also in flank and rear. They were there to stay or die. To make individual mention would be to include nearly the entire number.

We sadly lament the death of our colonel, W. G. Jones, a brave and experienced soldier. He is the second colonel the regiment has lost killed in battle.

Respectfully, your obedient servant,

H. F. DEVOL,
Lieutenant-Colonel, Commanding Regiment.

General J. B. TURCHIN,
Comdg. 3d Brig., 4th Division, Fourteenth Army Corps.

ALTERNATE DESIGNATIONS

OF

ORGANIZATIONS MENTIONED IN THIS VOLUME.*

Abbott's (Ephraim P.) **Artillery.** See *Tennessee Troops, Union,* 1st *Battalion, Battery A.*

Abernathy's (James L.) **Infantry.** See *Kansas Troops,* 8th *Regiment.*

Aldrich's (Simeon C.) **Infantry.** See *Indiana Troops,* 44th *Regiment.*

Aleshire's (Charles C.) **Artillery.** See *Ohio Troops,* 18th *Battery.*

Alexander's (John W. S.) **Infantry.** See *Illinois Troops,* 21st *Regiment.*

Anderson's (Nicholas L.) **Infantry.** See *Ohio Troops,* 6th *Regiment.*

Anderson's (William G.) **Cavalry.** See *Indiana Troops,* 4th *Regiment.*

Andrew's (William W.) **Artillery.** See *Indiana Troops,* 21st *Battery.*

Ashby's (H. M.) **Cavalry.** See *Tennessee Troops, Confederate.*

Askew's (Frank) **Infantry.** See *Ohio Troops,* 15th *Regiment.*

Atkins' (Smith D.) **Infantry.** See *Illinois Troops,* 92d *Regiment.*

Aumend's (George W.) **Infantry.** See *Ohio Troops,* 124th *Regiment.*

Austin's (J. E.) **Sharpshooters.** See *Louisiana Troops,* 14th *Battalion.*

Ayres' (Robert) **Infantry.** See *Union Troops, Regulars,* 1st *Battalion,* 19th *Regiment.*

Baker's (Myron) **Infantry.** See *Indiana Troops,* 74th *Regiment.*

Baldwin's (Norman A.) **Artillery.** See *Ohio Troops,* 1st *Regiment, Battery B.*

Banning's (Henry B.) **Infantry.** See *Ohio Troops,* 121st *Regiment.*

Barber's (Gershom M.) **Sharpshooters.** See *Ohio Troops,* 5th *Company.*

Barker's (John D.) **Cavalry.** See *Ohio Troops,* 1st *Regiment.*

Barnes' (Milton) **Infantry.** See *Ohio Troops,* 97th *Regiment.*

Barnett's (Charles M.) **Artillery.** See *Illinois Troops,* 2d *Regiment, Battery I.*

Barrett's (Wallace W.) **Infantry.** See *Illinois Troops,* 44th *Regiment.*

Bartleson's (Frederick A.) **Infantry.** See *Illinois Troops,* 100th *Regiment.*

Bartlett's (Prescott) **Cavalry.** See *Illinois Troops,* 7th *Regiment.*

Batman's (George W. L.) **Cavalry.** See *Kentucky Troops, Union,* 2d *Regiment.*

Baumbach's (Carl von) **Infantry.** See *Wisconsin Troops,* 24th *Regiment.*

Beatty's (William T.) **Infantry.** See *Ohio Troops,* 2d *Regiment.*

Beck's (Arnold) **Infantry.** See *Missouri Troops, Union,* 2d *Regiment.*

Bennett's (John E.) **Infantry.** See *Illinois Troops,* 75th *Regiment.*

Berry's (William W.) **Infantry.** See *Kentucky Troops, Union,* 5th *Regiment.*

Bingham's (George B.) **Infantry.** See *Wisconsin Troops,* 1st *Regiment.*

Bissell's (Josiah W.) **Engineers.** See *Missouri Troops, Union.*

Blake's (John W.) **Infantry.** See *Indiana Troops,* 40th *Regiment.*

Blakeley's (Archibald) **Infantry.** See *Pennsylvania Troops,* 78th *Regiment.*

Boone's (Nevil B.) **Infantry.** See *Indiana Troops,* 81st *Regiment.*

Boynton's (Henry V. N.) **Infantry.** See *Ohio Troops,* 35th *Regiment.*

Bradley's (Cullen) **Artillery.** See *Ohio Troops,* 6th *Battery.*

Bridges' (Lyman) **Artillery.** See *Illinois Troops.*

---

* References, unless otherwise indicated, are to index following.

Briggs' (David A.) **Cavalry.** See *Indiana Troops*, 2d *Regiment.*
Brigham's (Joseph H.) **Infantry.** See *Ohio Troops*, 69th *Regiment.*
Brown's (Patrick J.) **Infantry.** See *Kentucky Troops, Union*, 1st *Regiment.*
Brown's (Samuel C.) **Infantry.** See *Ohio Troops*, 65th *Regiment.*
Brownlow's (James P.) **Cavalry.** See *Tennessee Troops, Union*, 1st *Regiment.*
Buckner's (Allen) **Infantry.** See *Illinois Troops*, 79th *Regiment.*
Buell's (Henry M.) **Cavalry.** See *Illinois Troops*, 9th *Regiment.*
Burnham's (Howard M.) **Artillery.** See *Union Troops, Regulars*, 5th *Regiment, Battery H.*
Burton's (Thomas) **Artillery.** See *Illinois Troops*, 1st *Regiment, Battery M.*
Calloway's (James E.) **Infantry.*** See *Indiana Troops*, 81st *Regiment.*
Calvert's (J. H.) **Artillery.** See *Helena Artillery, post.*
Campbell's (Calvin D.) **Infantry.** See *Indiana Troops*, 6th *Regiment.*
Carey's (Oliver H. P.) **Infantry.** See *Indiana Troops*, 36th *Regiment.*
Carlton's (Caleb H.) **Infantry.** See *Ohio Troops*, 89th *Regiment.*
Carnes' (William W.) **Artillery.** See *Tennessee Troops, Confederate.*
Carroll's (William B.) **Infantry.** See *Indiana Troops*, 10th *Regiment.*
Chadbourne's (Alexander S.) **Infantry.** See *Illinois Troops*, 88th *Regiment.*
Chalmers' (Alexander H.) **Cavalry.** See *Mississippi Troops*, 18th *Battalion.*
Champion's (Thomas E.) **Infantry.** See *Illinois Troops*, 96th *Regiment.*
Chandler's (William P.) **Infantry.** See *Illinois Troops*, 35th *Regiment.*
Chapman's (Charles W.) **Infantry.** See *Indiana Troops*, 74th *Regiment.*
Chase's (Seymour) **Infantry.** See *Michigan Troops*, 21st *Regiment.*
Chess' (William E.) **Artillery.** See *Indiana Troops*, 21st *Battery.*
Chicago Board of Trade Artillery. See *Illinois Troops.*
Church's (Josiah W.) **Artillery.** See *Michigan Troops*, 1st *Regiment, Battery D.*
Clark's (John S.) **Infantry.** See *Kentucky Troops, Union*, 8th *Regiment.*
Clements' (Robert) **Pioneers.** See *Union Troops, Pioneer Brigade*, 3d *Battalion.*
Cobb's (Robert) **Artillery.** See *Kentucky Troops, Confederate.*
Cockerill's (Giles J.) **Artillery.** See *Ohio Troops*, 1st *Regiment, Battery F.*
Conrad's (Joseph) **Infantry.** See *Missouri Troops, Union*, 15th *Regiment.*
Cook's (William R.) **Cavalry.** See *Tennessee Troops, Union*, 2d *Regiment.*
Coolidge's (Sidney) **Infantry.** See *Union Troops, Regulars*, 1st *Battalion*, 16th *Regiment.*
Cooper's (Joseph A.) **Infantry.** See *Tennessee Troops, Union*, 6th *Regiment.*
Cooper's (Wickliffe) **Cavalry.** See *Kentucky Troops, Union*, 4th *Regiment.*
Cosgrove's (Horatio G.) **Infantry.** See *Ohio Troops*, 13th *Regiment.*
Cram's (George H.) **Infantry.** See *Kentucky Troops, Union*, 9th *Regiment.*
Crofton's (Robert E. A.) **Infantry.** See *Union Troops, Regulars*, 1st *Battalion*, 16th *Regiment;* also 1st *Battalion*, 19th *Regiment.***
Cross' (William) **Infantry.** See *Tennessee Troops, Union*, 3d *Regiment.*
Culver's (Joshua B.) **Infantry.** See *Michigan Troops*, 13th *Regiment.*
Cummins' (John E.) **Infantry.** See *Ohio Troops*, 99th *Regiment.*
Cupp's (Valentine) **Cavalry.** See *Ohio Troops*, 1st *Regiment.*
Cushing's (Harry C.) **Artillery.** See *Union Troops, Regulars*, 4th *Regiment, Battery H.*
Dawley's (Richard L.) **Artillery.** See *Minnesota Troops*, 2d *Battery.*
Dawson's (Samuel K.) **Infantry.** See *Union Troops, Regulars*, 1st *Battalion*, 19th *Regiment.*
Devol's (Hiram F.) **Infantry.** See *Ohio Troops*, 36th *Regiment.*
Deweese's (John T.) **Cavalry.** See *Indiana Troops*, 4th *Regiment.*
Dibrell's (George G.) **Cavalry.** See *Tennessee Troops, Confederate.*
Dick's (Jacob C.) **Infantry.** See *Indiana Troops*, 86th *Regiment.*
Dilworth's (Caleb J.) **Infantry.** See *Illinois Troops*, 85th *Regiment.*
Doan's (Thomas) **Infantry.** See *Indiana Troops*, 101st *Regiment.*

---

* Temporarily commanding.

Dod's (Albert B.) **Infantry.** See *Union Troops, Regulars, 1st Battalion, 15th Regiment.*
Douglas' (James P.) **Artillery.** See *Texas Troops.*
Drury's (Lucius H.) **Artillery.** See *Wisconsin Troops, 3d Battery.*
Dufficy's (John P.) **Infantry.** See *Indiana Troops, 35th Regiment.*
Dunlap's (Henry C.) **Infantry.** See *Kentucky Troops, Union, 3d Regiment.*
Dunn's (David M.) **Infantry.** See *Indiana Troops, 29th Regiment.*
Eaton's (Willard G.) **Infantry.** See *Michigan Troops, 13th Regiment.*
Edgarton's (Warren P.) **Artillery.** See *Ohio Troops, 1st Regiment, Battery E.*
Élite Corps Cavalry. * See *W. E. Hill.*
Ely's (John H.) **Infantry.** See *Wisconsin Troops, 10th Regiment.*
Embree's (James T.) **Infantry.** See *Indiana Troops, 58th Regiment.*
Erdelmeyer's (Frank) **Infantry.** See *Indiana Troops, 32d Regiment.*
Ernst's (George) **Infantry.** See *Missouri Troops, Union, 15th Regiment.*
Erwin's (Samuel C.) **Infantry.** See *Ohio Troops, 6th Regiment.*
Espy's (Harvey J.) **Infantry.** See *Indiana Troops, 68th Regiment.*
Estep's (George) **Artillery.** See *Indiana Troops, 8th Battery.*
Estes' (W. N.) **Cavalry.** See *Confederate Troops, Regulars, 3d Regiment.*
Eufaula Artillery. See *Alabama Troops.*
Farnan's (James) **Cavalry.** See *Illinois Troops, 5th Regiment.*
Fearing's (Benjamin D.) **Infantry.** See *Ohio Troops, 92d Regiment.*
Ferguson's (T. B.) **Artillery.** See *South Carolina Troops.*
Fessenden's (Joshua A.) **Artillery.** See *Union Troops, Regulars, 5th Regiment, Battery H.*
Fisher's (Joseph) **Infantry.** See *Ohio Troops, 74th Regiment.*
Flad's (Henry) **Engineers.** See *Josiah W. Bissell's Engineers, ante.*
Flansburg's (David) **Artillery.** See *Indiana Troops, 4th Battery.*
Fowler's (W. H.) **Artillery.** See *Alabama Troops.*
Foy's (James C.) **Infantry.** See *Kentucky Troops, Union, 23d Regiment.*
Frambes' (Granville A.) **Infantry.** See *Ohio Troops, 59th Regiment.*
Funkhouser's (John J.) **Infantry.** See *Illinois Troops, 98th Regiment.*
Gardner's (George Q.) **Artillery.** See *Wisconsin Troops, 5th Battery.*
Garrity's (James) **Artillery.** See *Alabama Troops.*
Gary's (Marco B.) **Artillery.** See *Ohio Troops, 1st Regiment, Battery C.*
George's (James) **Infantry.** See *Minnesota Troops, 2d Regiment.*
Gilmer's (Daniel H.) **Infantry.** See *Illinois Troops, 38th Regiment.*
Gleason's (Newell) **Infantry.** See *Indiana Troops, 87th Regiment.*
Gooding's (Michael) **Infantry.** See *Indiana Troops, 22d Regiment.*
Goodspeed's (Wilbur F.) **Artillery.** See *Ohio Troops, 1st Regiment, Battery A.*
Gratz's (Louis A.) **Cavalry.** See *Kentucky Troops, Union, 6th Regiment.*
Gray's (Horace) **Cavalry.** See *Michigan Troops, 4th Regiment.*
Gray's (Samuel F.) **Infantry.** See *Ohio Troops, 49th Regiment.*
Green's (George) **Infantry.** See *Illinois Troops, 78th Regiment.*
Griffin's (Daniel F.) **Infantry.** See *Indiana Troops, 38th Regiment.*
Grinager's (Mons) **Infantry.** See *Wisconsin Troops, 15th Regiment.*
Grosskopff's (Edward) **Artillery.** See *Ohio Troops, 20th Battery.*
Grosvenor's (Charles H.) **Infantry.** See *Ohio Troops, 18th Regiment.*
Guenther's (Francis L.) **Artillery.** See *Union Troops, Regulars, 5th Regiment, Battery H.*
Hadlock's (Alva R.) **Infantry.** See *Kentucky Troops, Union, 1st Regiment.*
Hall's (Duncan J.) **Infantry.** See *Illinois Troops, 89th Regiment.*
Hambright's (Henry A.) **Infantry.** See *Pennsylvania Troops, 79th Regiment.*
Hamilton's (O. P.) **Cavalry.** See *Tennessee Troops, Confederate.*
Hammond's (Charles M.) **Infantry.** See *Illinois Troops, 100th Regiment.*
Hammond's (David) **Infantry.** See *Kentucky Troops, Union, 1st Regiment.*

---

* Improvised.

Hampson's (James B.) **Infantry.** See *Ohio Troops, 124th Regiment.*
Hapeman's (Douglas) **Infantry.** See *Illinois Troops, 104th Regiment.*
Harmon's (Oscar F.) **Infantry.** See *Illinois Troops, 125th Regiment.*
Harris' (Samuel J.) **Artillery.** See *Indiana Troops, 19th Battery.*
Harris' (William C.) **Infantry.** See *Illinois Troops, 38th Regiment.*
Harrison's (Thomas J.) **Infantry.** See *Indiana Troops, 39th Regiment.*
Hart's (John R.) **Cavalry.** See *Georgia Troops, 6th Regiment.*
Haymond's (Henry) **Infantry.** See *Union Troops, Regulars, 2d Battalion, 18th Regiment.*
Hays' (William H.) **Infantry.** See *Kentucky Troops, Union, 10th Regiment.*
Helena Artillery. See *Arkansas Troops.*
Heltemes' (John B.) **Infantry.** See *Kentucky Troops, Union, 18th Regiment.*
Hescock's (Henry) **Artillery.** See *Missouri Troops, Union, 1st Regiment, Battery G.*
Higgins' (David J.) **Infantry.** See *Ohio Troops, 24th Regiment.*
Hilliard's Legion. See *Alabama Troops.*
Hobart's (Harrison C.) **Infantry.** See *Wisconsin Troops, 21st Regiment.*
Hoblitzell's (William T.) **Cavalry.** See *Kentucky Troops, Union, 5th Regiment.*
Holmes' (James T.) **Infantry.** See *Ohio Troops, 52d Regiment.*
Hornung's (George) **Infantry.** See *Kentucky Troops, Union, 1st Regiment.*
Hottenstein's (John A.) **Infantry.** See *Illinois Troops, 42d Regiment.*
Humphrey's (George) **Infantry.** See *Indiana Troops, 88th Regiment.*
Hunt's (P. Burgess) **Infantry.** See *Kentucky Troops, Union, 4th Regiment.*
Hunter's (Morton C.) **Infantry.** See *Indiana Troops, 82d Regiment.*
Hurd's (Orrin D.) **Infantry.** See *Indiana Troops, 30th Regiment.*
Huston's (John M.) **Infantry.** See *Kentucky Troops, Union, 5th Regiment.*
Hutchins' (Rue P.) **Infantry.** See *Ohio Troops, 94th Regiment.*
Innes' (William P.) **Engineers.** See *Michigan Troops, 1st Regiment.*
Jackson's (William H.) **Cavalry.** See *Tennessee Troops, Confederate.*
Jaquess' (James F.) **Infantry.** See *Illinois Troops, 73d Regiment.*
Johnson's (Ole C.) **Infantry.** See *Wisconsin Troops, 15th Regiment.*
Jones' (David J.) **Infantry.** See *Kentucky Troops, Union, 1st Regiment.*
Jones' (William) **Infantry.** See *Ohio Troops, 40th Regiment.*
Jones' (William G.) **Infantry.** See *Ohio Troops, 36th Regiment.*
Jones' (William T.) **Infantry.** See *Indiana Troops, 17th Regiment.*
Jordan's (Henry) **Infantry.** See *Indiana Troops, 17th Regiment.*
Kammerling's (Gustave) **Infantry.** See *Ohio Troops, 9th Regiment.*
Keeler's (Alonzo M.) **Infantry.** See *Michigan Troops, 22d Regiment.*
Kelly's (Robert M.) **Infantry.** See *Kentucky Troops, Union, 4th Regiment.*
Kilgour's (William M.) **Infantry.** See *Illinois Troops, 75th Regiment.*
King's (David) **Infantry.** See *Ohio Troops, 94th Regiment.*
Kingsbury's (Henry D.) **Infantry.** See *Ohio Troops, 14th Regiment.*
Kirk's (George W.) **Infantry.** See *Ohio Troops, 14th Regiment.*
Kitchell's (Edward) **Infantry.** See *Illinois Troops, 98th Regiment.*
Klein's (Robert) **Cavalry.** See *Indiana Troops, 3d Regiment.*
Knefler's (Frederick) **Infantry.** See *Indiana Troops, 79th Regiment.*
Knight's (Chester K.) **Infantry.** See *Illinois Troops, 21st Regiment.*
Lackey's (Robert S.) **Artillery.** See *Indiana Troops, 19th Battery.*
La Grange's (Oscar H.) **Cavalry.** See *Wisconsin Troops, 1st Regiment.*
Lane's (Philander P.) **Infantry.** See *Ohio Troops, 11th Regiment.*
Langdon's (Bassett) **Infantry.** See *Ohio Troops, 1st Regiment.*
Lawson's (Joseph J.) **Infantry.** See *Pennsylvania Troops, 77th Regiment.*
Le Favour's (Heber) **Infantry.** See *Michigan Troops, 22d Regiment.*
Lennard's (George W.) **Infantry.** See *Indiana Troops, 57th Regiment.*
Lilly's (Eli) **Artillery.** See *Indiana Troops, 18th Battery.*
Lister's (Frederick W.) **Infantry.** See *Ohio Troops, 31st Regiment.*

Livingston's (Cortland) **Artillery.** See *Wisconsin Troops, 3d Battery.*
Loomis' (Cyrus O.) **Artillery.** See *Michigan Troops, 1st Regiment, Battery A.*
Louisville Legion, Infantry. See *Kentucky Troops, Union, 5th Regiment.*
McClain's (Richard W.) **Infantry.** See *Ohio Troops, 51st Regiment.*
McCreery's (William B.) **Infantry.** See *Michigan Troops, 21st Regiment.*
McCulloch's (Robert) **Cavalry.** See *Missouri Troops, Confederate, 2d Regiment.*
McDanald's (Bedan B.) **Infantry.** See *Ohio Troops, 101st Regiment.*
McDonald's (Charles) **Cavalry.** See *Tennessee Troops, Confederate.*
McDowell's (Samuel M.) **Artillery.** See *Pennsylvania Troops, Battery B.*
McGuirk's (John) **Cavalry.** See *Mississippi Troops, 3d Regiment, State.*
McIlvain's (Alexander) **Infantry.** See *Ohio Troops, 64th Regiment.*
McIntire's (William T. B.) **Infantry.** See *Indiana Troops, 42d Regiment.*
McIntyre's (James B.) **Cavalry.** See *Union Troops, Regulars, 4th Regiment.*
McKenzie's (G. W.) **Cavalry.** See *Tennessee Troops, Confederate.*
McLean's (John D.) **Artillery.** See *Wisconsin Troops, 8th Battery.*
McMahan's (Arnold) **Infantry.** See *Ohio Troops, 21st Regiment.*
Magee's (David W.) **Infantry.** See *Illinois Troops, 86th Regiment.*
Marsh's (Jason) **Infantry.** See *Illinois Troops, 74th Regiment.*
Marshall's (Alexander) **Artillery.** See *Ohio Troops, 1st Regiment, Battery G.*
Martin's (John A.) **Infantry.** See *Kansas Troops, 8th Regiment.*
Martin's (Robert) **Artillery.** See *Georgia Troops.*
Mast's (Elhannon M.) **Infantry.** See *Ohio Troops, 93d Regiment.*
Mauff's (August) **Infantry.** See *Illinois Troops, 24th Regiment.*
Maxwell's (Obadiah C.) **Infantry.** See *Ohio Troops, 2d Regiment.*
Mayhew's (James D.) **Infantry.** See *Kentucky Troops, Union, 8th Regiment.*
Messer's (John) **Infantry.** See *Ohio Troops, 101st Regiment.*
Mihalotzy's (Geza) **Infantry.** See *Illinois Troops, 24th Regiment.*
Miles' (Jonathan R.) **Infantry.** See *Illinois Troops, 27th Regiment.*
Miller's (Abram O.) **Infantry.** See *Indiana Troops, 72d Regiment.*
Miller's (Silas) **Infantry.** See *Illinois Troops, 36th Regiment.*
Milward's (Hubbard K.) **Infantry.** See *Kentucky Troops, Union, 18th Regiment.*
Mitchell's (James W.) **Infantry.** See *Kentucky Troops, Union, 1st Regiment.*
Monroe's (James) **Infantry.** See *Illinois Troops, 123d Regiment.*
Moore's (Jesse H.) **Infantry.** See *Illinois Troops, 115th Regiment.*
Moore's (Oscar F.) **Infantry.** See *Ohio Troops, 33d Regiment.*
Mudge's (Melvin) **Infantry.** See *Michigan Troops, 11th Regiment.*
Napier's (Leroy) **Infantry.** See *Georgia Troops, 8th Battalion.*
Naylor's (William A.) **Artillery.** See *Indiana Troops, 10th Battery.*
Nelson's (Isaac C.) **Infantry.** See *Ohio Troops, 89th Regiment.*
Newell's (Nathaniel M.) **Artillery.** See *Ohio Troops, 1st Regiment, Battery D.*
Newman's (T. W.) **Infantry.** See *Tennessee Troops, Confederate, 23d Battalion.*
Nicholas' (Thomas P.) **Cavalry.** See *Kentucky Troops, Union, 2d Regiment.*
Noble's (John W.) **Cavalry.** See *Iowa Troops, 3d Regiment.*
O'Brien's (William) **Infantry.** See *Indiana Troops, 75th Regiment.*
O'Connor's (James H.) **Cavalry.** See *Illinois Troops, 3d Regiment.*
Olson's (Porter C.) **Infantry.** See *Illinois Troops, 36th Regiment.*
Opdycke's (Emerson) **Infantry.** See *Ohio Troops, 125th Regiment.*
Palmer's (William J.) **Cavalry.** See *Pennsylvania Troops, 15th Regiment.*
Parkhurst's (John G.) **Infantry.** See *Michigan Troops, 9th Regiment.*
Patten's (Thomas J.) **Cavalry.** See *Ohio Troops, 1st Regiment.*
Payne's (Oliver H.) **Infantry.** See *Ohio Troops, 124th Regiment.*
Perkins' (George T.) **Infantry.** See *Ohio Troops, 105th Regiment.*
Phelps' (Edward H.) **Infantry.** See *Ohio Troops, 38th Regiment.*
Phillips' (Jesse J.) **Infantry.** See *Illinois Troops, 9th Regiment.*

Pioneer Brigade. See *Union Troops;* also *Patrick O'Connell.*

Powell's (Thomas) Infantry. See *Ohio Troops,* 65th *Regiment.*

Prescott's (Mark H.) Artillery. See *Illinois Troops,* 1st *Regiment, Battery C.*

Presdee's (Joseph B.) Cavalry. See *Indiana Troops,* 2d *Regiment.*

Price's (S. Woodson) Infantry. See *Kentucky Troops, Union,* 21st *Regiment.*

Purdy's (George H.) Cavalry. See *Indiana Troops,* 4th *Regiment.*

Putnam's (Douglas, jr.) Infantry. See *Ohio Troops,* 92d *Regiment.*

Raffen's (Alexander W.) Infantry. See *Illinois Troops,* 19th *Regiment.*

Ray's (Daniel M.) Cavalry. See *Tennessee Troops, Union,* 2d *Regiment.*

Raymond's (Samuel B.) Infantry. See *Illinois Troops,* 51st *Regiment.*

Richards' (William J.) Infantry. See *Indiana Troops,* 81st *Regiment.*

Rippey's (Charles H.) Infantry. See *Ohio Troops,* 90th *Regiment.*

Robertson's (Felix H.) Artillery. See *Alabama Troops.*

Robie's (Oliver P.) Cavalry. See *Ohio Troops,* 4th *Regiment.*

Robinson's (Milton S.) Infantry. See *Indiana Troops,* 75th *Regiment.*

Roby's (Jacob W.) Infantry. See *Wisconsin Troops,* 10th *Regiment.*

Rockingham's (Richard) Infantry. See *Kentucky Troops, Union,* 6th *Regiment.*

Rose's (Thomas E.) Infantry. See *Pennsylvania Troops,* 77th *Regiment.*

Russell's (Francis L. D.) Artillery. See *Union Troops, Regulars,* 4th *Regiment, Battery M.*

Russell's (Roswell M.) Cavalry. See *Pennsylvania Troops,* 9th *Regiment.*

Sanborn's (William) Infantry. See *Michigan Troops,* 22d *Regiment.*

Schueler's (Gustavus) Artillery. See *Missouri Troops, Union,* 1st *Regiment, Battery G.*

Schultz's (Frederick) Artillery. See *Ohio Troops,* 1st *Regiment, Battery M.*

Scott's (William L.) Artillery. See *Tennessee Troops, Confederate.*

Scranton's (Leonidas S.) Cavalry. See *Michigan Troops,* 2d *Regiment.*

Sedgewick's (Thomas D.) Infantry. See *Kentucky Troops, Union,* 2d *Regiment.*

Seibert's (James J.) Cavalry. See *Pennsylvania Troops,* 7th *Regiment.*

Seidel's (Charles B.) Cavalry. See *Ohio Troops,* 3d *Regiment.*

Semple's (Henry C.) Artillery. See *Alabama Troops.*

Shackelford's (George T.) Infantry. See *Kentucky Troops, Union,* 6th *Regiment.*

Shelley's (James T.) Infantry. See *Tennessee Troops, Union,* 5th *Regiment.*

Sherer's (Samuel B.) Cavalry. See *Illinois Troops,* 15th *Regiment.*

Simonson's (Peter) Artillery. See *Indiana Troops,* 5th *Battery.*

Slemons' (W. F.) Cavalry. See *Arkansas Troops,* 2d *Regiment.*

Slocomb's (C. H.) Artillery. See *Washington Artillery, post,* 5th *Battery.*

Smith's (Correll) Pioneers. See *Union Troops, Pioneer Brigade,* 2d *Battalion.*

Smith's (Edmund L.) Infantry. See *Union Troops, Regulars,* 1st *Battalion,* 19th *Regiment.*

Smith's (Frank G.) Artillery. See *Union Troops, Regulars,* 4th *Regiment, Battery I.*

Smith's (George W.) Infantry. See *Union Troops, Regulars,* 1st *Battalion,* 18th *Regiment.*

Smith's (John T.) Infantry. See *Indiana Troops,* 31st *Regiment.*

Smith's (Leonard D.) Infantry. See *Ohio Troops,* 101st *Regiment.*

Smith's (Melancthon) Artillery. See *Mississippi Troops.*

Southwick's (Daniel K.) Artillery. See *Ohio Troops,* 1st *Regiment, Battery C.*

Spencer's (George W.) Artillery. See *Illinois Troops,* 1st *Regiment, Battery M.*

Standart's (William E.) Artillery. See *Ohio Troops,* 1st *Regiment, Battery B.*

Stanford's (Thomas J.) Artillery. See *Mississippi Troops.*

Starnes' (James W.) Cavalry. See *Tennessee Troops, Confederate.*

Stevens' (Alanson J.) Artillery. See *Pennsylvania Troops, Battery B.*

Stewart's (Charles J.) Pioneers. See *Union Troops, Pioneer Brigade,* 1st *Battalion.*

Stocks' (J. G.) Cavalry. See *William H. Jackson's Cavalry, ante.*

Stokes' (James H.) Artillery. See *Chicago Board of Trade Artillery, ante.*

Stokes' (William B.) Cavalry. See *Tennessee Troops, Union,* 5th *Regiment.*

Stoughton's (Dwella M.) **Infantry.** See *Ohio Troops, 21st Regiment.*
Stoughton's (William L.) **Infantry.** See *Michigan Troops, 11th Regiment.*
Stout's (Alexander M.) **Infantry.** See *Kentucky Troops, Union, 17th Regiment.*
Stratton's (Henry G.) **Infantry.** See *Ohio Troops, 19th Regiment.*
Strong's (Hiram) **Infantry.** See *Ohio Troops, 93d Regiment.*
Strong's (Luther M.) **Infantry.** See *Ohio Troops, 49th Regiment.*
Suman's (Isaac C. B.) **Infantry.** See *Indiana Troops, 9th Regiment.*
Sutermeister's (Arnold) **Artillery.** See *Indiana Troops, 11th Battery.*
Swaine's (Peter T.) **Infantry.** See *Ohio Troops, 99th Regiment.*
Swallow's (George R.) **Artillery.** See *Indiana Troops, 7th Battery.*
Swanwick's (Francis) **Infantry.** See *Illinois Troops, 22d Regiment.*
Swett's (Charles) **Artillery.** See *Warren Light Artillery, post.*
Taggart's (Wesford) **Infantry.** See *Illinois Troops, 25th Regiment.*
Taylor's (Marion C.) **Infantry.** See *Kentucky Troops, Union, 15th Regiment.*
Taylor's (Marsh B.) **Infantry.** See *Indiana Troops, 10th Regiment.*
Tennessee (Confederate) **First [Sixth] Cavalry.** See *J. T. Wheeler's Cavalry, post.*
Tennessee (Confederate) **Second Cavalry.** See *H. M. Ashby's Cavalry, ante.*
Tennessee (Confederate) **Fourth Cavalry.** See *James W. Starnes' Cavalry, ante.*
Tennessee (Confederate) **Fourth [Eighteenth] Battalion Cavalry.** See *Charles McDonald's Cavalry, ante.*
Tennessee (Confederate) **Fifth Cavalry.** See *G. W. McKenzie's Cavalry, ante.*
Tennessee (Confederate) **Eighth Cavalry.** See *George G. Dibrell's Cavalry, ante.*
Thomas' (Armstrong J.) **Infantry.** See *Ohio Troops, 98th Regiment.*
Topping's (E. Hibbard) **Infantry.** See *Illinois Troops, 110th Regiment.*
Tripp's (Hagerman) **Infantry.** See *Indiana Troops, 6th Regiment.*
Trusler's (Gilbert) **Infantry.** See *Indiana Troops, 36th Regiment.*
Trusler's (Nelson) **Infantry.** See *Indiana Troops, 84th Regiment.*
Urquhart's (Moses J.) **Infantry.** See *Ohio Troops, 98th Regiment.*
Van Pelt's (George W.) **Artillery.** See *Michigan Troops, 1st Regiment, Battery A.*
Van Tassell's (Oscar) **Infantry.** See *Illinois Troops, 34th Regiment.*
Vantine's (Charles H.) **Infantry.** See *Ohio Troops, 21st Regiment.*
Van Vleck's (Carter) **Infantry.** See *Illinois Troops, 78th Regiment.*
Walker's (Charles H.) **Infantry.** See *Wisconsin Troops, 21st Regiment.*
Wall's (Samuel D.) **Infantry.** See *Illinois Troops, 25th Regiment.*
Walworth's (Nathan H.) **Infantry.** See *Illinois Troops, 42d Regiment.*
Ward's (Durbin) **Infantry.** See *Ohio Troops, 17th Regiment.*
Ward's (William D.) **Infantry.** See *Indiana Troops, 37th Regiment.*
Ward's (William M.) **Infantry.** See *Ohio Troops, 10th Regiment.*
Warner's (Darius B.) **Infantry.** See *Ohio Troops, 113th Regiment.*
Warnock's (James) **Infantry.** See *Ohio Troops, 2d Regiment.*
Warren Light Artillery. See *Mississippi Troops.*
Washington Artillery. See *Louisiana Troops.*
Waters' (David D.) **Artillery.** See *Alabama Troops.*
Waters' (Louis H.) **Infantry.** See *Illinois Troops, 84th Regiment.*
Watkins' (William M.) **Infantry.** See *Tennessee Troops, Confederate, 12th Regiment.*
Welling's (George) **Cavalry.** See *Kentucky Troops, Union, 4th Regiment.*
Wemple's (Mindret) **Cavalry.** See *Illinois Troops, 4th Regiment.*
West's (Theodore S.) **Infantry.** See *Wisconsin Troops, 24th Regiment.*
Wharton's (Gabriel C.) **Infantry.** See *Kentucky Troops, Union, 10th Regiment.*
Wheeler's (J. T.) **Cavalry.** See *Tennessee Troops, Confederate.*
Whitaker's (Richard T.) **Infantry.** See *Kentucky Troops, Union, 6th Regiment.*
Whitbeck's (Horatio N.) **Infantry.** See *Ohio Troops, 65th Regiment.*
White's (B. F., jr.) **Artillery.** See *Tennessee Troops, Confederate.*
Whitehurst's (Willis G.) **Infantry.** See *Illinois Troops, 38th Regiment.*
Whiteley's (R. H.) **Sharpshooters.** See *Georgia Troops, 2d Battalion.*

Wilbur's (Almerick W.) **Artillery.**   See *Michigan Troops, 1st Regiment, Battery A.*
Wiley's (Aquila) **Infantry.**   See *Ohio Troops, 41st Regiment.*
Williams' (William D.) **Infantry.**   See *Illinois Troops, 89th Regiment.*
Williston's (John H.) **Infantry.**   See *Ohio Troops, 41st Regiment.*
Willits' (Henry J.) **Artillery.**   See *Indiana Troops, 4th Battery.*
Winters' (Joshua C.) **Infantry.**   See *Illinois Troops, 59th Regiment.*
Wood's (Charles H.) **Infantry.**   See *Ohio Troops, 51st Regiment.*
Wood's (Gustavus A.) **Infantry.**   See *Indiana Troops, 15th Regiment.*
Woodbury's (Albert) **Artillery.**   See *Minnesota Troops, 2d Battery.*
York's (Billington W.) **Artillery.**   See *Georgia Troops, 9th Battalion, Battery E.*
Young's (William H.) **Infantry.**   See *Ohio Troops, 26th Regiment.*

INDEX.

Brigades, Divisions, Corps, Armies, and improvised organizations are "Mentioned" under name of commanding officer; State and other organizations under their official designation. (See Alternate Designations, pp. 1073–1080.)

---

* Formerly Ketchum's.

† Claimed also for Florida; afterward Dent's Battery.

----

*No circumstantial reports on file.

---

* No circumstantial reports on file.

---

* No circumstantial reports on file.

*No circumstantial reports on file.

* No circumstantial reports on file.

---

*No circumstantial reports on file.

*No circumstantial reports on file.

---

* No circumstantial reports on file.

Page.

Page.

Davis' Cross-Roads (or Davis' House), near Dug Gap, Ga. Skirmish at,
Sept. 11, 1863. See *Chickamauga Campaign, Aug. 16–Sept. 22,*
1863. *Reports of*

Baird, Absalom.	Negley, James S.	Stanley, Timothy R.
Blakeley, Archibald.	Rosecrans, William S.	Thomas, George H.
Dana, Charles A.	Scribner, Benjamin F.	Ward, William D.
Hapeman, Douglas.	Sirwell, William.	

See also *Rosecrans to Thomas*, p. 333. Also Part II.

Davis' Gap, Ala. Skirmish at. See *Will's Creek and Davis', Tap's, and Neal's Gaps, Ala. Skirmishes at, Sept.* 1, 1863.

Davis' House, Ga. Skirmish at. See *Davis' Cross-Roads (or Davis' House), near Dug Gap, Ga. Skirmish at, Sept.* 11, 1863.

1108

*No circumstantial reports on file.

Page.

---

* No record of 56th Florida Infantry.
† No circumstantial reports on file.

* No circumstantial reports on file.

---

*Afterward Howell's Battery.

Page.

Granger, Gordon.

Assignment to command... 1051

Assumes command of 4th Army Corps.. 5

Correspondence with

Minty, Robert H. G.. 113

Neff, Andrew J.. 858

Rosecrans, William S... 66,

69, 74, 112, 113, 116, 124, 125, 132, 134, 136, 139, 140, 163

Russell, William C.. 119–121

Steedman, James B.. 119, 120

Thomas, George H... 127, 135, 139

Wagner, George D... 115, 123

Mentioned.................................... 38, 46, 52, 57, 60, 63, 64, 66–68,

80, 81, 83, 84, 86, 87, 89, 90, 92, 95, 97, 113, 132, 140, 141, 143–145, 147, 151,

169, 170, 177, 179, 183, 184, 187, 192–196, 199, 202, 211, 213, 215, 216, 228, 235,

252, 254, 255, 285, 331, 382, 393, 394, 402, 404, 430, 438, 479–481, 483, 495, 604,

630, 638, 639, 695, 745, 763, 817, 852, 859–862, 864, 876, 878, 879, 883, 884, 922–

925, 941, 853, 955, 960, 985, 989, 1004, 1029, 1041, 1046, 1048, 1050, 1051

Report of Chickamauga Campaign, Aug. 16–Sept. 22, 1863................. 852

Granger, Robert S.

Correspondence with Charles A. Dana...................................... 208

Mentioned... 207, 213, 214, 220

Grant, U. S.

Assignment to command... 5

Assumes command of the Military Division of the Mississippi.............. 5

Co-operation with Rosecrans... 4

Correspondence with

Army Headquarters.. 36, 162

Sherman, William T.. 161

Mentioned.. 6, 12, 18, 35–39, 202, 363, 365

Gratz, Louis A. Mentioned.. 46, 915

Graves, George M. Mentioned............................... 180, 783, 784, 790

Gray, Horace. Mentioned.. 47

Gray, John M. Mentioned... 89, 548

Gray, Roman H. Mentioned... 313, 317

Gray, Samuel F.

Mentioned.................................... 43, 87, 90, 99, 536, 538, 541

Report of Chickamauga Campaign, Aug. 16–Sept. 22, 1863.............. 551

Graysville, Ga. Skirmish near. See *Pea Vine Creek, Ga. Skirmishes at and
near Graysville, Ga., Sept. 10, 1863.*

Green, ——. Mentioned... 878

Green, George.

Mentioned... 46, 869

Report of Chickamauga Campaign, Aug. 16–Sept. 22, 1863................. 870

Green, Shep H. Mentioned... 98, 542

Greenwood, William H. Mentioned....................................... 894

Gregg, John. Mentioned..................................... 229, 230, 431, 436

Grenada, Miss.

Expedition from Memphis, Tenn., to, Aug. 12–23, 1863, with skirmishes at
Craven's Plantation, Miss. (14th), and Grenada, Miss. (17th).

Communications from

Armstrong, W. F... 18

Hurlbut, Stephen A... 18

Mersy, August.. 17, 18

Mizner, John K.. 18

Page.

Grenada, Miss.—Continued.

Expedition from Memphis, Tenn., to, etc.—Continued.

Reports of

Coon, Datus E 19

Hurlbut, Stephen A 11, 12

Mersy, August 13

Mizner, John K 12, 13

Phillips, Jesse J 13, 14

Wallace, Martin R. M 21

Skirmish at, Aug. 17, 1863. See *Grenada, Miss. Expedition from Memphis, Tenn., to, etc., Aug. 12-23, 1863. Reports of*

Coon, Datus E.   Mizner, John K.   Phillips, Jesse J.
Hurlbut, Stephen A.

Griffin, Daniel F.

Mentioned 40, 284-286, 289

Report of Chickamauga Campaign, Aug. 16-Sept. 22, 1863 290

Griffith, James R. Mentioned 873

Griffith, William H. Mentioned 396

Griffiths, David J. Mentioned 89, 225, 495, 582

Griffiths, George W. Mentioned 919

Grimes, Derastus L. Mentioned 25

Grimes, Silas. Mentioned 742

Grinager, Mons. Report of Chickamauga Campaign, Aug. 16-Sept. 22, 1863. 533

Grose, William.

Mentioned 45, 73,
80, 83, 85, 86, 88, 89, 93, 95, 98-100, 123, 125, 176, 213, 254, 336, 341, 347,
358, 367, 460, 602, 606, 613, 616, 709, 710, 712-715, 717-722, 724, 725, 729,
730, 737, 743, 744, 752, 753, 778, 784-787, 789-791, 794, 799-801, 838, 1009

Reports of Chickamauga Campaign, Aug. 16-Sept. 22, 1863 .... 779, 780

Gross, Ferdinand H.

Mentioned 62, 89, 227, 256, 264, 1020

Report of Chickamauga Campaign, Aug. 16-Sept. 22, 1863 258

Testimony of. Negley Court of Inquiry 1020, 1021

Gross, Theodore. Mentioned 524

Grosskopff, Edward.

Mentioned 43, 234, 538, 557

Report of Chickamauga Campaign, Aug. 16-Sept. 22, 1863 562

Grosvenor, Charles H. Mentioned 41, 86, 369, 370, 380, 382

Grosvenor, Edward. Mentioned 483

Grove, George J. Mentioned 96, 574

Grover, James A. Mentioned 94, 585

Grubbs, James S. Mentioned 745

Grund, Philip. Mentioned 829

Guiteau, Benjamin F. Mentioned 25

Gunn, T. M. Mentioned 98, 842

Gunsenhouser, John. Mentioned 91, 180, 824, 828

Gunter's Landing, near Port Deposit, Ala. Skirmish at, Aug. 24, 1863* 27

Gustaveson, C. Mentioned 534

Guthrie, James V. Mentioned 376

Gwynne, Llewellyn. Mentioned 894

Hadlock, Alva R.

Mentioned 44, 87, 723-725, 727, 728, 734, 735, 738, 739, 746, 747, 750

Reports of Chickamauga Campaign, Aug. 16-Sept. 22, 1863 .... 742, 743

* No circumstantial reports on file.

---

*No circumstantial reports on file.

Page.
Hurlbut, Stephen A.
Correspondence with
Army Headquarters... 36, 161
Mizner, John K 18
Veatch, James C... 24
Mentioned..16, 35–37, 105, 130, 155, 162, 199
Reports of expedition from Memphis, Tenn., to Grenada, Miss., Aug. 12–23,
1863, with skirmishes at Craven's Plantation, Miss. (14th), and
Grenada, Miss. (17th) 11, 12
Hurley, John P. Mentioned 91, 569, 570
Hurst, Ed. Mentioned 910
Huston, John M.
Mentioned 43, 90, 91, 96, 99, 101, 536, 565, 566, 569
Report of Chickamauga Campaign, Aug. 16–Sept. 22, 1863 569
Huston, John W. Mentioned... 180, 565, 570
Hutchins, John. Mentioned 563
Hutchins, Rue P.
Mentioned 40, 284, 285
Report of Chickamauga Campaign, Aug. 16–Sept. 22, 1863 297
Hutchinson, M. N. Mentioned 96, 314, 320, 322
Hutchison, Samuel C. Mentioned... 881
Hutsler, W. H. Mentioned 274, 285
Hyde, Benjamin F. Mentioned... 22
Hyland, John C. Mentioned.. 739
Illinois Troops. Mentioned.
Artillery, Light—*Batteries :* **Bridges'**, 41, 172, 234, 237, 238, 329, 330, 335,
337, 342, 343, 351–355, 359, 361, 365–368, 371–376, 1011, 1066; **Chicago
Board of Trade,** 47, 918, 922, 927. *Regiments :* **1st** (*Batteries*), **C**, 44, 175,
234, 237, 239, 596, 599–601; **M**, 46, 178, 235, 853, 858, 859, 867, 870; **2d**
(*Batteries*), **I**, 46, 178, 235, 853, 871, 873, 875–880, 882, 883.
Cavalry—*Regiments :* **3d, 4th,** 21–24; **5th,** 8–10; **6th,** 25; **7th,** 719, 723;
9th, 15, 21–24; **11th,** 14, 16, 19; **15th,** 44, 614.
Infantry—*Regiments :* **9th,** 14, 17–20; **19th,** 41, 172, 327, 376–379, 381, 383, 396,
441 ; **21st,** 42, 173, 499, 502, 515–517, 519–521, 523–525, 562, 662; **22d,** 44, 175,
579, 594–596, 598, 1056; **24th,** 40, 171, 271, 273, 284, 303–308, 376; **25th,** 43,
174, 502, 528, 529, 531, 534 ; **27th,** 44, 175, 579, 594–600; **34th,** 557 ; **35th,** 43,
174, 502, 528–531; **36th,** 43, 175, 580, 583, 587 ; **38th,** 42, 173, 502, 515–517,
521–523, 527; **42d,** 44, 175, 579, 594–598, 600, 662, 1055, 1056; **44th,** 43, 175,
580; **51st,** 44, 175, 490, 579, 580, 594–596, 598, 1055–1057; **59th,** 42, 502, 506,
509–511 ; **73d,** 43, 175, 580; **74th,** 42, 502, 506, 509, 514; **75th,** 42, 502, 506,
509, 511–513; **78th,** 46, 178, 858, 867–870 ; **79th,** 43, 174, 554, 555, 557–559,
561; **84th,** 45, 176, 616, 717, 780–787, 789–793, 797, 798; **85th,** 46, 178, 871–
874, 877, 880; **86th,** 46, 178, 871, 873–878, 880; **88th,** 43, 175, 580, 583, 587;
89th, 43, 174, 538, 540–546, 549, 558, 560; **92d,** 42, 173, 247, 248, 260, 440, 442,
445, 446, 450, 453–457, 459, 461, 467, 628, 629 ; **96th,** 46, 177, 858, 861–863, 865,
866, 868 ; **98th,** 42, 173, 445, 446, 448, 449, 451, 453, 457, 458, 461, 465 ; **100th,**
44, 175, 615, 633, 634, 643, 652, 654–656, 658–663, 667, 668, 672–674, 705 ; **104th,**
41, 172, 352, 368–373, 375, 881 ; **110th,** 45, 680, 718; **115th,** 46, 177, 858, 861–
863, 865 ; **123d,** 42, 173, 445, 447, 450, 451, 453, 459–462, 464, 465; **125th,** 46,
178, 871, 873, 877–880.
Indiana Troops. Mentioned.
Artillery, Light—*Batteries :* **4th,** 40, 171, 234, 237, 238, 273, 280–283, 287,
302–308, 376, 422; **5th,** 43, 174, 234, 237, 239, 301, 563–566, 573, 577, 578;
7th, 45, 177, 235, 238, 239, 440, 614, 616, 622–624, 804, 806–808, 811, 820, 830,

71 R R—VOL XXX, PT I

---

* A mistake; this battery served in the Eastern Army.

† No circumstantial reports on file.

---

* No circumstantial reports on file

Page.

McLain, Peter. Mentioned 781
McLaws, Lafayette. Mentioned 203, 231
McLean, John D. Mentioned 43, 234, 503
McLean, Wesley B. Mentioned 797
McLemoresville, Tenn. Expedition from Paducah, Ky., to, Sept. 20–30, 1863.
        See Part II.
McLoughlin, William. Mentioned 92, 642, 644
McMackin, Warren E. Mentioned 501, 518, 520
McMahan, Arnold.
    Correspondence with
        Brannan, John M... 392
        Negley, James S 390–392
    Mentioned.. 41, 88, 386, 405
    Reports of Chickamauga Campaign, Aug. 16–Sept. 22, 1863 ...... 387, 388
McMichael, William. Mentioned 59, 63, 79, 88
        For correspondence as A. A. G., see *William S. Rosecrans.*
McMinnville, Tenn. Skirmish near, Oct. 4, 1863. See *Chickamauga Campaign,*
        Aug. 16–Sept. 22, 1863. Report of Dana, p. 207. Also Part II.
McMoore, A. Mentioned 513
McMurtry, William H. Mentioned 453, 464
McNair, Evander. Mentioned 216, 229, 231, 871
McNeill, James T. Mentioned.................................... 873
McPherson, James B. Mentioned 152, 162
Magarity, William S. Mentioned......................... 877
Magee, David W.
    Mentioned 46, 873
    Report of Chickamauga Campaign, Aug. 16–Sept. 22, 1863 875
Mahan, M. Mentioned.. 313
Malin, Emery. Mentioned 96, 831
Mallory, William L. Mentioned 92, 582, 928
Maney, George. Mentioned 228, 229, 231
Manigault, Arthur M. Mentioned 228, 230
Mann, Charles B. Mentioned............................... 93, 417
Mansfield, Henry O. Mentioned............................. 881
Maps and Sketches. See *Sketches.*
Margedant, W. C. Mentioned 63, 89
Marker, Peter. Mentioned................................ 180, 764, 771
Marks, S. Mentioned..................................... 259, 262, 263
Marl, George E. Mentioned............................... 454
Marlin, John M. Mentioned 1063
Marquis, David D. Mentioned.......................... 458
Marr, Thomas. Mentioned................................... 100, 557
Marrs, John. Mentioned 317, 318
Marsh, Addison M. Mentioned 880
Marsh, Jason. Mentioned................... 42, 85, 506, 509, 514
Marshall, Alexander.
    Mentioned 41, 234, 338
    Report of Chickamauga Campaign, Aug. 16–Sept. 22, 1863 397
Marshall, George K. Mentioned.................................. 769
Martin, Henry B. Mentioned................................. 734, 752
Martin, John A.
    Mentioned 43, 174, 500, 501, 522, 532
    Report of Chickamauga Campaign, Aug. 16–Sept. 22, 1863 528
Martin, Sloan D. Mentioned 180, 1058

* No circumstantial reports on file.

Page.

---

*No circumstantial reports on file.

---

* No circumstantial reports on file.

*No circumstantial reports on file.

---

* No circumstantial reports on file.

* No circumstantial reports on file.

---

* No circumstantial reports on file.

---

* No circumstantial reports on file.
† Afterward 12th U. S. Colored Infantry.

---

* For composition of the battalions, see p. 171.
† Department of the Cumberland.

*No circumstantial reports on file.

---

* No circumstantial reports on file.

* No circumstantial reports on file.

O